(Continued on back endpapers)

Financial Accounting

An Introduction to Decision Making
Second Edition

Henry Dauderis
Concordia University

Holt, Rinehart and Winston of Canada, Limited
Toronto

Canadian Cataloguing in Publication Data

Dauderis, Henry, 1941–
   Financial accounting

2nd ed.
Includes bibliographical references and index.
ISBN 0-03-922672-7

1. Accounting. I. Title.

HF5635.D38 1990   657'.044   C89-094661-2

Acquisitions Editor: Warren Laws
Developmental Editor: Susan Bindernagel
Publishing Services Manager: Karen Eakin
Managing Editor: Liz Radojkovic
Editorial Assistant: Robert Gordon
Copy Editors: Dennis Bockus, Jennifer Dennison/The Editorial Centre
Cover Design: Michael Landgraff
Typesetting and Assembly: Q Composition Inc.
Printing and Binding: John Deyell Company

Printed in Canada

5 4 3 2 1 90 91 92 93 94

To my father,
Joseph Dauderis

CONTENTS IN BRIEF

Chapter 16, Accounting for Manufacturing Operations, is actually part of the conversion cycle. For pedagogical reasons, however, the topic is discussed at the end of this text.

CONTENTS

PART TWO   THE MARKETING CYCLE   170

Chapter 4   Accounting for Merchandising Operations   172

A.   The Calculation of Gross Profit   173

B.   The Sales and Collection Cycle   174

C.   The Purchase and Payment Cycle   177

PART FIVE   THE INVESTMENT CYCLE   542

Chapter 12   The Investment Cycle   544

PART SIX   DISCLOSURE AND FINANCIAL REPORTING   616

Chapter 14   Financial Statements Analysis   618

Financial Accounting: An Introduction to Decision Making, second edition, is a text designed for use in introductory financial accounting courses. It is intended to give students an understanding of issues that face users of financial statements. Business administration and commerce majors will find that organization of the financial accounting topics around business cycles facilitates their understanding of how accounting relates to the functional aspects of a business. Accounting majors will find themselves better prepared for more specialized courses, such as computer-based information systems, electronic data processing, and auditing. Students majoring in other academic disciplines will become accounting literate by having been exposed to the issues with which accounting, the language of business, is involved.

The Big Picture

Canadian professional accountants are creatures of their environment. This environment includes, but is not limited to, the nature of the economy and the political orientation of the provincial and federal governments. Accountants collect, analyze, evaluate, interpret, and report on the myriad of transactions occurring among individuals, corporations, and institutions in this environment. The challenge to professional and academic accountants, as well as to managers and other readers of financial statements, is to become sufficiently familiar with the concepts of accounting to be able to peer through the fog of numbers in financial statements and to make decisions on the basis of fact, and not of fiction.

The accounting concepts covered in this text have a bearing on real issues in your environment. One of these issues is Canada's rapidly escalating national debt. A large part of Canada's national income is required to service this national debt, a legacy of past governments and, in effect, a mortgage that you and future generations will have to deal with. To put it in perspective, more money is paid in interest on this debt than is collected as personal income tax. This increased national debt, if coupled with classical inflation, could lead to a collapsed economy. Similarly, the current controversy about changing unemployment insurance payments, continuing universal medicare, indexing old age pensions, and augmenting welfare payments could have ramifications on the health of our national finances. The decisions that governments make on these issues, such as lowering or raising taxes and/or changing the method by which they collect monies, could lead to economic and social prosperity or to economic collapse.

Similarly, an accounting entity's reliance on debt can lead to prosperity and growth or to economic failure and bankruptcy. Whichever course of action is undertaken by an entity, the accountant will be faced with the challenge of collecting, analyzing, evaluating, and interpreting the financial events that occur. The user of financial statements can appreciate the nature of an entity's course of action only if he or she is accounting literate. The readings interwoven throughout this text are important in relating this literacy to the big picture. They should be incorporated into an introductory accounting course in accordance with curriculum requirements. Technology is revolutionizing the management process and, in particular, the information-collection and dissemination system that is at the heart of the accounting process. Some of the readings are chosen to make students more aware of the impact of computers on the profession of accounting. Students learning financial accounting should also look beyond the numbers contained in the financial statements and should become aware of the social responsibility of the entity. The social responsibility of the accountant is explored in Conceptual Issue 1-1, contributed by Robert Anderson of the University of Regina.

The Cycles Approach

The organization of chapters into business cycles occuring naturally within an entity relates financial accounting topics to the functional aspects of a business entity. It also leads into other courses that delve further into these business cycles.

Part One, Financial Statements and the Accounting Process, provides an overview of the conceptual foundations that underlie financial accounting. It also illustrates the application of these concepts to the accounting process. Part Two, The Marketing Cycle, focuses on the calculation of gross profit, the sales and collection cycle, and the purchase and payment cycle. Part Three (including Chapter 16, Accounting for Manufacturing Operations) focuses on the conversion cycle. Part Four, The Financing Cycle, examines equity and debt financing, which are critical to the well-being of an entity. Part Five describes the investment cycle and business combinations. Part Six, Disclosure and Financial Accounting, concludes this introduction to financial accounting by covering financial statement analysis and cash flow. An overview of the cycles approach used by this text is provided by the Contents in Brief on page v.

New to This Edition

A wider variety of problem material has been added to this text, ranging from short problems covering single topics to more difficult problems covering many topics. New Discussion Cases and Real Life Examples have also been added.

This edition also recognizes the importance of ethical issues in the decision-making process. The Issues in Ethics readings will stimulate thought about some of the issues business students will face upon graduation and employment. Questions of ethics also arise in many of the discussion cases.

Chapter Seven synthesizes the topics introduced in the first six chapters by relating them to the real financial statements of a Canadian company: Mark's Work Wearhouse. This chapter may provide a convenient opportunity to review the course and to focus on published financial statements. It can also set the stage for the discussion of financing and investing activities, covered in subsequent chapters.

Finally, the procedural material on worksheets and special journals has been moved to appendices at the end of the text. Within many of the chapters, some procedural material, such as closing and reversing entries and present value calculations, has been moved to appendices within chapters. This reorganization should help students to follow the flow of ideas presented in the text.

The Rules of the Game

Professional accountants belong to a self-regulating profession that establishes its own rules. These rules, referred to as generally accepted accounting principles (GAAP), are codified in the *CICA Handbook* and have a quasi-legal status in Canada. Accordingly, as professionals, accountants agree to follow a code of ethical conduct. This conduct, however, must take into account the public interest and the changing environment. Accountants must understand, design, and apply GAAP in a way that protects the public interest and adapts to the current environment. The free trade agreement is one such change in the environment. "Free Trade and Accounting" by Dan Thornton discusses one possible impact of free trade on GAAP.

Lyman MacInnis, FCA, a former president of the CICA, described the situation as follows:

> We are in the middle of an era of tremendous change. The very underpinnings of our economy are changing. We are no longer a manufacturing economy: we are now a service and communications based economy. And those are our products: service and communication. Information travels faster and is disseminated more broadly than ever before in history. And information is primarily what we deal in." (From *Dialogue*, published by the CICA, November 1986, p. 1.)

Text Orientation

The introductory financial accounting course evolves continuously. The last decade saw a debate among accounting faculties about course content and the purpose of an accounting course. In Canada, there was also the desire to reflect on the various segments of Canadian business that financial accounting serves. My intention when writing *Financial Accounting: An Introduction to Decision Making*, second edition, was to satisfy the different needs of instructors and students. One of my goals was to make the text clear, readable, and easy to understand. This approach should allow instructors more class time to concentrate on accounting concepts and their applications. One of the most compelling reasons for writing an original Canadian text instead of adapting a text published in the United States was the different environments of the two countries. A Canadian text permitted me to tailor the material to the needs of Canadian accounting students and instructors. Hence, the Real Life Examples, Issues in Ethics, Conceptual Issues, and Discussion Cases included in the text offer a range of issues viewed through the Canadian experience.

This text is designed to be user friendly. The following are some of its features.

1. Student Orientation

The chapter material is clear and readable. Much attention has been paid to text layout, explanatory notes, figures, and the boxed high-interest examples.

2. Teaching Flexibility

Each chapter contains sub-sections that allow the instructor flexibility in course design. Individual sections can be omitted without compromising continuity. Because of the detailed attention spent on its development the text is easy for students to understand, thus allowing the instructor greater opportunity for introducing more interesting and challenging topics. Furthermore, this text has been divided into sections that allow its sixteen chapters to fit into a comprehensible whole. However, instructors may wish to teach a chapter or chapters out of sequence to emphasize certain topics.

3. Assignment Materials

The assignment material included in the text continues to be the most complete and varied available. Eight types of assignment material are available to instructors at the end of the chapters: Discussion Questions, Discussion Cases, Comprehension Problems, Problems, Alternate Problems, Supplementary Problems, Review Problems, and Decision Problems. These assignment materials require different levels of direction from the instructor. The Assignment Materials sections have been designed to be flexible and to allow instructors to assign the material at the level of their students' analytical abilities.

4. Accelerated Coverage

This text provides maximum flexibility in the first three chapters, thus allowing for accelerated coverage early in the course. Some of the procedural material has been moved to appendices to facilitate this. For example, the use of the worksheet appears as Appendix A to the text.

5. Computer Compatibility

The same terminology and chart of accounts is used throughout the text to allow students to operate in a consistent accounting environment. The general ledger package available with this text uses the same chart of accounts. The manual that accompanies this package will minimize not only problems associated with integrating the computer into an introductory accounting course, but will also encourage its use as a supplement to the introductory accounting course.

6. Real Life Examples

Numerous Real Life Examples are used to emphasize concepts and issues. The Real Life Examples have been boxed to allow instructors to skip over some of them and to facilitate student review. A sample of a Real Life Example that might interest an instructor of accounting follows:

Real Life Example

Drexel exams: No more blue books

Drexel University accounting students are taking their final exam on Apple Computer Inc.'s Macintosh personal computer. In addition, students in Accounting B101 are doing their homework on "Macs." As at many engineering and technical schools, all incoming freshmen are required to buy computers. "It takes more time to assign all the homework and put tests on the Mac, but I think it's worth it," says Professor Henry Dauderis. In the two-hour final exam, students are required to prepare and print out a worksheet, an income statement for a merchandising firm and closing entries. One benefit: less cheating since "it's harder to see something off someone else's monitor," says Dauderis.

Source Computerline: A Quick Read on Trends in Personal Computing, *USA Today*, April 17, 1986.

---

7. Conceptual Issues

The Conceptual Issues in the text allow for greater exploration of the issues not normally covered in introductory texts. The Real Life Examples and the Conceptual Issues will motivate students, and will dissuade them from the view that accounting is only "number crunching."

8. Issues in Ethics

Concern about the environment is reminding people that good business practice is concerned with ethical issues. A new feature in this edition, readings on ethical issues, reminds students to relate their growing knowledge of accounting to the world in which they will be working.

9. Running Glossary

All technical terms are defined in the margin when they are first introduced. This eliminates the tendency that many students have of guess reading. By defining the term where it appears, the students will easily see what the definition is and will not substitute what they think it means.

10. Supplementary Materials

The ancillary package that accompanies *Financial Accounting: An Introduction to Decision Making*, second edition, is among the most complete available. A description follows of the carefully developed student and instructor supplements.

For the Student

Self Study Guide

Prepared by Esther Deutsch of Ryerson Polytechnical Institute, this study guide contains Learning Objectives, Chapter Overviews, True-False Questions, Multiple Choice Questions, and Practice Problems with complete and detailed solutions.

Working Papers

A complete set of working papers is provided in order to minimize the formatting aspects of accounting assignments.

Practice Set

The practice set provides students with an opportunity to apply accounting concepts and procedures to a merchandising entity. *Magnamusic*, by Joe Figueredo of Vanier College, can be solved manually or can be assigned with the use of an IBM-PC computer package — The Freelance Accounting System.

For the Instructor

Solutions Manual

This manual provides suggested solutions to all assignment material from the text. Special care has been taken to provide full and complete solutions with explanations. The solutions were prepared by Vittoria Fortunato of the University of Toronto.

Instructor's Manual

The instructor's manual identifies learning objectives and the key terms introduced in the chapters. The manual includes Lecture Outlines, Lecture Topics, and a summary of the Assignment Material for each chapter. Also included is the material on the computer disks (both the *PC General Ledger Package* and the *Lotus 1-2-3* disks) and the solutions to the *Practice Set* that accompanies the text.

Transparencies

The transparencies of the solutions to all the Problems, Alternate Problems, Supplementary Problems, and Review Problems are available upon adoption of the text.

Publisher's Note to Instructors and Students

This textbook is a key component of your course. If you are the instructor of this course, you undoubtedly considered a number of texts carefully before choosing this as the one that would work best for your students and you. The author and publishers of this book spent considerable time and money to ensure its high quality, and we appreciate your recognition of this effort and accomplishment.

If you are a student, we are confident that this text will help you to meet the objectives of your course. You will also find it helpful after the course is finished as a valuable addition to your personal library.

As well, please do not forget that photocopying copyright work means authors lose royalties that are rightfully theirs. This loss will discourage them from writing another edition of this text or other books; doing so would simply not be worth their time and effort. If this happens we all lose — students, instructors, authors, and publishers.

Since we want to hear what you think about this book, please be sure to send us the stamped reply card at the end of the text. This will help us to continue publishing high-quality books for your course.

ACKNOWLEDGEMENTS

This second edition has been enriched by the comments and suggestions of many colleagues, students, and reviewers. I have retained and continued to evolve many unique features of the first edition and have incorporated many of these new ideas. Especially helpful were the comments, support, and suggestions of the following individuals:

J. Amernic	University of Toronto
R. Bates	University of Guelph
D. Brown	Brock University
P. Davidson	Northern Alberta Institute of Technology
S. Felton	Brock University
D. Ferries	Algonquin College
V. Fortunato	University of Toronto
M. Fizzell	University of Saskatchewan
K. Gheyara	Concordia University
A. Gibbons	Carleton University
M. Glynn	Ryerson Polytechnical Institute
M. Hilton	University of Manitoba
K. Lam	Queen's University
P. Marsh	University of Calgary
S. Martin	John Abbott College
S. Salterio	University of New Brunswick
F. Simyar	Concordia University
H. Steinman	Ryerson Polytechnical Institute
K. Sutley	University of Alberta
L. Thorne	Bishop's University
B. Trenholm	University of New Brunswick

Again, thanks to Esther Deutsch of Ryerson, who prepared the Study Guide; Steve Spector, who prepared the *Lotus 1-2-3* templates; Vittoria Fortunato of the University of Toronto, who prepared some of the solutions and reviewed them all; and Adrian Feigelsohn, who proofread the solutions to the problems. I am also indebted to my colleagues and students for their support and suggestions. David F. MacDonald reviewed and improved many of the assignment materials and made constructive comments in many chapters of the text. Thanks also to Wendy Roscoe, who provided that extra help near the end of the process. I am also particularly grateful to Marion Dingman Hebb for her efforts on my behalf.

Also, special thanks to all my editors, Dave Collinge, Warren Laws, Rachel Campbell, and particularly Susan Bindernagel, who underwent her baptism by fire as the deadline for this text approached! I know that Dave Collinge, who worked both as editor and then as publisher on this edition, will never forget *Financial Accounting: An Introduction to Decision Making*, second edition! Warren Laws joined this project midway and helped to keep it on track and within budget.

I would also like to thank Ron Munro, Vice-President of the Holt, Rinehart and Winston College Division, for always understanding and being supportive; Dave Collinge as publisher; and Louis Tetu, the local sales representative in Montreal. I also appreciate the work contributed to the project by Dennis Bockus and Jennifer Dennison, copy editors; Karen Eakin, Publishing Services Manager; Liz Radojkovic, Managing Editor; and Lynda Sydney, Editorial Assistant at Holt, Rinehart and Winston. They were able to understand the difficulties that are encountered in writing an accounting text and were able to accommodate all of the peculiar demands that an accounting text presented.

Henry Saunders

You are about to begin the study of accounting. This prologue outlines the importance of financial accounting in Canadian business. In Canada, transactions are completed in terms of Canadian dollars. These dollars are the numerical units that accountants have accepted as being the most appropriate method of recording transactions and communicating them to interested parties who use the reported amounts to evaluate business organizations.

The term *accounting process* is applied to the way in which the dollar amount of transactions is transformed into financial statement information for communication purposes. This process consists of three steps, as shown in Figure 1.

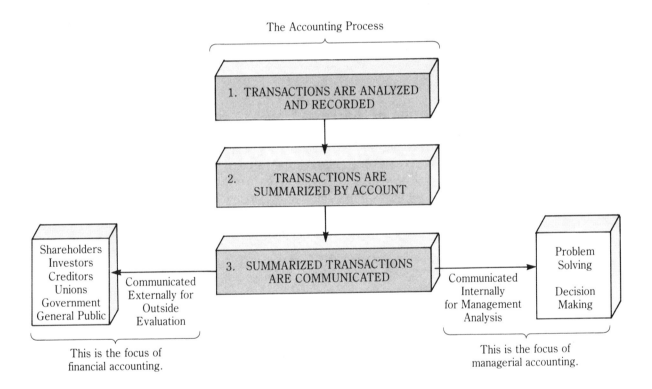

Figure 1   The accounting process and its uses

Step 1:   Transactions Are Analyzed and Recorded

Transactions are first analyzed and then recorded in a manner that has gradually evolved for this purpose. This recording process is often referred to as *bookkeeping*, and those involved in this work are usually called *bookkeepers*. The increased use of computers has greatly reduced the manual work required.

Step 2:   *Transactions Are Summarized*

This step is usually referred to as *classifying accounting information*. Accounting information is accumulated and a total calculated for each related group of transactions at the end of a time period, so that the financial information can be communicated.

Step 3:   *Transactions Are Communicated*

The summarized transactions are communicated through the preparation and distribution of financial statements at regular time intervals. These statements satisfy external reporting requirements and also management's need for information on which to base decisions and problem solving.

Financial and Managerial Accounting

The purpose of financial accounting is to communicate information that has been generated through the accounting process. This information is communicated to external users through the publication of financial statements. Management accounting, on the other hand, is often viewed as the financial planning and controlling process; financial data are communicated internally for analysis and evaluation so that managers can decide future courses of action and reflect on past decisions.

Organization of the Text

Accountants do not work in a vacuum. Regulations, rules of conduct, as well as the day-to-day operations of a company are all part of a complex environment that influences the practice of accounting. This text has been organized to reflect these complexities.

The first three chapters describe the accounting process — how financial data are collected, analyzed, recorded, summarized, and communicated. Describing the process, however, is not always enough. Certain concepts and assumptions underlie this process and give it meaning. The concepts will show you *why* to do something before you get immersed in details of *how* to do it.

The next eleven chapters discuss the major elements of financial statements. You will discover not only how these elements are recorded, but how they are used and how they relate to one another and to the operations of a business.

These remaining chapters are grouped into specific cycles: the Marketing Cycle, the Conversion Cycle, the Financing Cycle, and the Investing Cycle. These groupings reflect natural business cycles so they should make the interrelationships between accounting and other subjects within the business curriculum more clear to you. Finally, chapters fourteen and fifteen discuss the disclosure of financial statements and how to use that information when analyzing a company.

As you read through the chapters of this text, you will gain an appreciation of accounting that will serve you well in your career. Note that the numbers that appear in this and any other accounting text appear to be artificial; indeed, marketing, management, and external economic factors such as inflation directly influence the results generated by accountants. Nevertheless, the contents of this text should bridge this gap and provide you with a true appreciation of the role of financial accounting in the business world.

Financial Statements and the Accounting Process

Accountants must be familiar with the accounting process in order to understand the methods underlying the accumulation of financial information and to direct the efforts of bookkeepers responsible for the recording and summarizing of this information. Familiarity with accounting methods is also required for making sound interpretations of the information communicated in the financial statements and for adjusting recorded information as necessary. The techniques for adjusting financial information to meet the requirements of generally accepted accounting principles are explained and illustrated in Chapter 3.

Financial Statements and the Accounting Model

Accountants communicate financial information to interested users for decision-making purposes. The answers to the following questions are discussed in Chapter 1.

1. What is a financial transaction from the accountant's point of view?
2. In what way do financial transactions constitute one of the boundaries of accounting?
3. What specialized vocabulary is used to condense transactions?
4. How are financial transactions completed in Canada?
5. How do accountants communicate financial information to interested parties?
6. What is the entity concept, and how is it one of the boundaries of accounting?
7. What are the advantages and disadvantages of different forms of business organization?
8. Which accounting report measures profitability? financial position?
9. What information does the statement of cash flow provide?
10. What was Luca Pacioli's role in establishing the accounting model?
11. Accountants view financial transactions as economic events that change components within the accounting equation. What are these components and how do they change?
12. How does the accounting process transform transactions into financial statement data?
13. How do shareholders participate in day-to-day management?
14. What is the distinction between a calendar year-end and a fiscal year-end?
15. What impact does the periodicity concept have on the reporting of financial information?
16. What are the authoritative accounting bodies in Canada? How do they interact in issuing pronouncements relating to accounting?
17. What is the function of the auditor's report in relation to generally accepted accounting principles?

A. Financial Statements

Accounting
The process of recording, classifying, and accumulating financial transactions of an entity; the reporting of these transactions to interested individuals through the preparation of financial statements; the interpretation of these financial statements.

Asset
An economic resource that is expected to bring future benefits to its owners.

Liability
An obligation to pay an economic resource or to provide services or goods in the future.

Transaction
An exchange of assets, obligations, services, or goods.

Financial transaction
The financial aspect of a transaction; expressed in terms of dollars in Canada.

Financial accounting
A method of accounting that focuses on the analysis of financial transactions, in order to provide financial information to interested parties.

Entity
A unit of accountability that exists separately from its owners; the term *legal entity* is used when referring to a corporation, which has a legal existence separate from its owners.

Accounting is often called the language of business. Like any language, **accounting** is used to communicate information, in this case, financial information. Like any language, too, accounting has its own special vocabulary. Two commonly used terms are *assets* and *liabilities*. **Assets** are economic resources that are expected to bring future benefits to their owners. **Liabilities** are obligations to pay an economic resource at some time in the future or to perform a service or provide goods at a later date. (An economic resource is anything that can be bought or sold.)

Assets are continually being exchanged, as are obligations; each exchange is referred to as a **transaction**. Any exchange of an asset for another asset is a transaction. Acceptance of an obligation in return for an asset is also a transaction. Because exchanges usually involve dollar amounts, they are called **financial transactions**. **Financial accounting** is essentially a system for processing and analyzing these transactions and reporting their results.

For example, a financial transaction occurs when the Hudson's Bay Company exchanges a cash asset for land and buildings assets. Or, instead of paying cash, the company may incur a liability in the form of a mortgage. The mortgage is an obligation to pay for an asset at a later date.

The Entity Concept

There are always two or more parties to each transaction. Accountants view each party as a separate financial unit — that is, as a separate entity. An **entity** can be thought of as a unit of accountability that exists separately from other units of accountability and also exists separately from those who own the entity. The accountant for the entity focuses only on the transactions of the business, which he/she translates into accounting information.

1. Business transactions are translated into accounting information.
2. In selecting transactions to be translated into accounting information, the accountant is only interested in those affecting the unit of accountability, or entity.

In Canada, entities seek to use their assets in activities that will not only increase the value of the assets but will also increase the total assets of the entity. For example, the Hudson's Bay Company operates a chain of department stores where assets, in the form of merchandise, are exchanged for customers' assets, usually in the form of cash but sometimes in the form of credit. Similarly, PetroCanada uses its assets in the exploration of oil, so that the oil can be exchanged for other assets of its customers. Both of these entities provide goods in exchange for assets belonging to others. The emphasis in chapters 1 to 3 is on a company that provides a service. In Chapter 4, the focus is on companies providing goods, commonly referred to as merchandising. In Chapter 16, accounting for manufacturing operations is introduced.

Some entities are more successful than other entities in the performance of the activities for which they were formed; accounting information is necessary to measure the progress of each entity and to conform with legal requirements. This information is reported in terms of dollars, and the accounting reports that communicate this information are commonly referred to as *financial statements*. Financial accounting is the process of recording transactions and preparing financial statements for external users, such as creditors and investors.

Objectives of Financial Statements

Financial statements communicate accounting information that is useful to investors and creditors for making decisions and for assessing the stewardship of management.

The information included in financial statements should be designed to present fairly the entity's economic resources (*assets*), obligations (*liabilities*), and owners' claims (*equity*). Changes to these assets, liabilities, and equity, as well as information for evaluation of the entity's performance, should also be included.

Required Financial Statements

Accountants and the users of financial reports have developed standard categories for financial statements. Three of the most widely used financial statements are the *income statement*, the *balance sheet*, and the *statement of cash flow*, which are discussed in the sections that follow. The *statement of retained earnings* is covered in Chapter 4.

The **income statement** communicates the generation of assets (called revenues) and the consumption of assets (called expenses) resulting from the entity's activities. An excess of total revenues over total expenses is called **net income**. An excess of total expenses over total revenues is called a **net loss**.

The **balance sheet** communicates in dollar amounts what the entity owns (assets), what the entity owes to outsiders (liabilities), and the difference between the assets and liabilities, called *equity*. The equity amount represents the balance that belongs to owners of the entity.

As its name suggests, the **statement of cash flow** shows what cash has been received or spent by the entity during a specified time period.

The Income Statement

The income statement can be compared to a movie camera with a counter that continually records transactions of an entity; the counter accumulates these transactions while the camera records them. The income statement, however, is very selective, in that it accumulates only the revenue and expense transactions of the entity. When the camera stops, the counter shows the accumulated total of all these revenue and expense transactions.

In the adjacent income statement of Bluebeard Computer Corporation (BCC), the camera was started on January 1 and was stopped at January 31; the counter shows a net income of $2,000. In this income statement, the expenses of the January time period are deducted from the revenue of the same time period. Identifying expenses and revenues with a time period is referred to as the **accrual method of accounting**.

Income statement
A financial report summarizing the entity's progress during a time period; summarizes revenue earned and expenses incurred, and calculates net income for the period.

Net income
The excess of revenues over expenses during a period of time.

Net loss
The excess of expenses over revenue for a period of time.

Balance sheet
A financial report showing the assets, liabilities, and equities of an entity on a specific date; also referred to as a *statement of financial position* or *a statement of financial condition*.

Statement of cash flow
A statement showing the sources and uses of cash.

Accrual method of accounting
Method of accounting that recognizes revenues when they are earned and expenses when they are incurred; ignores when cash is received or paid in recognizing revenues or expenses; also referred to as *accrual basis of accounting*.

Bluebeard Computer Corporation
Income Statement
For the Month Ended January 31, 19X1

Revenue		
Repair Revenue		$7,000
Expenses		
Rent Expense	$ 600	
Salaries Expense	2,500	
Supplies Used	1,200	
Truck Expense	700	
Total Expenses		5,000
Net Income		$2,000

When the camera begins again in February, the counter continues to accumulate revenue and expense transactions; that is, it adds the February transactions to those of January.

One film is used for each 12-month time period. At the end of the year, December 31, 19X1 in this case, the exposed film is removed and a new film is inserted for the next 12 months. When the new film is inserted, the counter in the camera is automatically reset to zero; in this way only the transactions of the new year are accumulated. The income statement is therefore referred to as a *period-of-time financial statement*.

What Is Revenue?

Revenue represents the generation of assets by an entity in return for services performed or goods sold during that period. It is expressed in terms of dollars. In the case of Bluebeard Computer Corporation, the services performed are computer repairs.

What Are Expenses?

Expenses represent the consumption of an entity's assets. They are the resources belonging to the entity that have been used up or the obligations incurred in the course of earning revenue. The Bluebeard Computer Corporation uses parts, for example, to make repairs; these parts are a resource of the entity used up in performing repairs. These expenses represent the consumption of assets needed to earn the $7,000 revenue.

What Is Net Income?

The difference between revenue and expenses is net income. Net income is a guide for the reader of the income statement as to how profitably the activities of the entity are being conducted; it is a measure of the entity's success. The net income calculation is also used in calculating taxes payable to government, and it is one criterion used to determine the amount of dividends to be paid. (*Dividends* are payments made by a corporation to its owners and are never included in an income statement.) The accumulated net income that has not been paid as dividends is referred to as *retained earnings*.

The Balance Sheet

The balance sheet can be compared to a snapshot camera that produces a picture of the entity at a point in time. In the adjacent balance sheet of Bluebeard Computer Corporation, the snapshot was made on January 31. It shows the corporate assets, liabilities, and equity on that date. A balance sheet can be compiled whenever necessary but is *always* taken at the end of the corporation's business year. The balance sheet is therefore referred to as a *point-in-time financial statement*.

The economic resources owned by the entity are listed as assets on the balance sheet; these assets are individually described and their costs are indicated. Those having a claim against these assets are listed as liabilities and equities. Note that the total amount of assets equals the total claims against those assets. The date of the balance sheet is important because it identifies the date at which the assets owned and the existing claims against the assets are listed.

Revenue
The generation of assets by an entity in return for services performed or goods sold during that period.

Expenses
An outflow of assets or the resources of an entity used up, or obligations incurred during a time period, in the course of earning revenue.

Bluebeard Computer Corporation
Balance Sheet
At January 31, 19X1

Assets			Liabilities		
Cash	$ 4,300		Bank Loan	$ 5,000	
Accounts Receivable	3,000		Accounts Payable	1,000	
Prepaid Insurance	1,200		Unearned Rent	500	
Equipment	3,000		Total Liabilities		$ 6,500
Truck	8,000				
			Equity		
			Common Stock	$11,000	
			Net Income	2,000	13,000
			Total Liabilities and		
Total Assets	$19,500		Equity		$19,500

The term *balance sheet* is widely used in Canada. However, other titles are also used: *statement of financial position* and *statement of financial condition*.

What Is an Asset?

An asset was broadly defined at the beginning of this chapter as an economic resource that will bring future benefits to the entity. Assets include tangible resources, such as equipment, as well as other resources, such as accounts receivable and patents. To be called assets, they must have some future value to the entity in generating revenue. Assets are recorded and shown on the balance sheet at cost because cost is an objective amount resulting from arm's-length bargaining between a buyer and seller. **Accounts receivable**, for example, represent an amount due to be collected for goods sold or services rendered. The recorded asset cost does not necessarily indicate the asset's current value, the cost of replacing the asset, nor the amount for which it could be sold if offered for sale.

Accounts receivable
An asset arising from the sale of goods or services to customers on account; an account receivable originating from a loan made to an officer or employee of the entity is excluded from accounts receivable and must be disclosed separately in the financial statements.

What Is a Liability?

A liability was defined at the beginning of this chapter as an obligation to pay some economic resource in the future or to provide a service or goods at some later date. Until the obligation is paid, creditors (those to whom the entity is obligated) have a claim against the assets of the entity. For example, a bank loan is an obligation to repay cash in the future, both the amount borrowed and the interest. *Accounts payable* are obligations to pay a supplier for goods purchased or services rendered. *Unearned rent* represents an advance payment for a service that BCC will provide in the future.

What Is Equity?

Equity represents the amount of net assets remaining to owners after liabilities have been paid. In the case of Bluebeard Computer Corporation, this equity belongs to shareholders; it is shareholders who own a corporation. Equity is the balance that remains after liabilities are deducted from assets. In BCC's January 31 balance sheet, equity is calculated as $13,000 ($19,500 assets minus $6,500 liabilities).

Equity
The amount of economic resources available to owners of the entity after all obligations have been satisfied; also referred to as *owners' equity* and *net assets*.

What Is Common Stock?

Common stock
The class of shares that is a basic ownership unit in a corporation.

Share certificate
Printed form representing a unit of corporate ownership.

Common stock represents all the common shares that are the ownership interest of shareholders in the net assets (assets minus liabilities) of the corporation. This ownership interest carries the right to vote and to share in dividends. A **share certificate** (sometimes referred to as a stock certificate) represents a unit of ownership in the corporation; it is nothing more than an elaborately printed piece of paper indicating a particular investor's writ of ownership. A typical share certificate is illustrated in Figure 1-1.

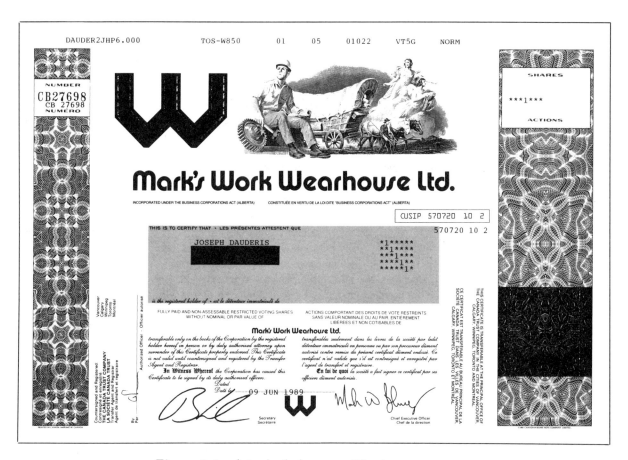

Figure 1-1   A typical share certificate

The Statement of Cash Flow

The third principal financial statement is the statement of cash flow (SCF) — also known as the *statement of changes in financial position*. The SCF is prepared to explain the sources (inflows) and uses (outflows) of cash over a period of time. While the income statement shows a net income or loss, it does not deal with these other important activities of the entity involving cash. The statement of cash flow shown below is a simplified version, intended for illustrative purposes only.

Bluebeard Computer Corporation
Statement of Cash Flow
For the Month Ended January 31, 19X1

Sources of Cash		
Revenue Collected in Cash	$ 4,000	
Issuance of Common Stock	11,000	
Increase in Unearned Rent	500	
Total Sources		$15,500
Uses of Cash		
Expenses Paid in Cash	$ 5,000	
Paid for Truck	3,000	
Paid Prepaid Insurance	1,200	
Payment to Creditors	2,000	
Total Uses		11,200
Increase in Cash		$ 4,300

Since this is the first month of BCC's operations, the difference between the sources and uses of cash is calculated as an increase of $4,300. The corporation had no opening cash balance before the issuance of shares. The president of BCC didn't understand why the corporation's cash balance is $4,300 when the company received $11,000 cash from the issuance of common shares and had a net income of $2,000. He can now see from the statement of cash flow that BCC's business operations resulted in a negative cash flow ($4,000 cash collected as revenue minus $5,000 cash operation expenses equals a cash deficit of $1,000).

This cash flow statement is useful to management when making financial decisions. For example, this statement shows BCC the importance of collecting the $3,000 accounts receivable. If management were planning a major acquisition of new assets, an additional issuance of common shares or a new bank loan might be necessary.

The statement of cash flow is also useful to creditors and to anyone considering making loans to BCC in the future. BCC's bank manager may be concerned not only about collecting the current $5,000 loan, but also about whether to grant a new line of credit to the entity. The statement of cash flow together with a cash budget would be an important factor in this decision. The statement of cash flow provides a historical basis on which to project future cash flow.

Other Business Reports

In addition to the list of financial statements in the preceding section, management may also want to prepare other accounting and business reports. One example of regular reports prepared and forwarded to outside advisors and creditors is discussed in Real Life Example 1-1.

Real Life Example 1-1
The Case for Accountability

One of the joys of owning your own company is that, in a formal sense at least, you're not answerable to anybody. You can make decisions without waiting months for feedback from those higher up on the corporate ladder. You can take actions that feel right to you *when* they feel right to you. No one is badgering you if your numbers come in under your projections.

When Charles Bodenstab purchased Battery & Tire Warehouse Inc., now a $12-million company, five years ago, he had a nagging concern that maybe too little accountability could be a problem. He'd be able to rationalize poor results and discount their implications, and could easily fall into a pattern of denying things, with no fear of repercussions.

To correct this, he established a system that would make him feel — and act — accountable to people outside the company even though they had no formal power over his decisions. Besides creating an outside board of directors, he prepared and sent quarterly financial reports and an annual business plan to each member of the board, the banker, major suppliers with whom he had substantial credit lines, and selected outsiders. The payoffs have been tremendous. Not only have these systems kept Bodenstab on his toes but the feedback they provide has been invaluable.

The board members are people Bodenstab knows he cannot con or manipulate. It's true that they don't own stock and they can't dismiss him for poor performance, but they are people he respects. And they serve his purpose perfectly, which is to have a group of people with whom he can discuss a problem — and then be too embarrassed to show up at the next meeting without having tackled it.

At a meeting last July, for example, Bodenstab acknowledged that a key manager wasn't up to the performance level they were going to need as the company grew. Since he was able to handle the job at the moment, though — and had helped the company throughout the early, messy transition

period — Bodenstab agonized over taking any action. The thought of facing the board at its next meeting without a resolution to the problem, however, was sufficient to force the issue, and make him face what he considered to be a very distasteful task.

Bodenstab uses the quarterly report in much the same way. The format is a summary of financial results for the quarter, compared with both the prior year and with the business plan. In the report he discusses any deviation from earlier expectations and reviews any major events, such as the demise of a major competitor.

The reports buy the company a great deal of credibility and also solicit some good feedback. The chief executive officer of one major supplier, for example, always writes a comprehensive critique, which gives a perspective on the business that is quite different from Bodenstab's.

The annual business plan provides one more way to go on the record, to create another pseudo-accountability. The plan includes a summary of the prior year's results, a business plan for the coming year, and a general discussion of the company. After a report is published, it's hard to ignore events that contradict situations described in it.

Some people think that disclosure of bad news to the bank or major creditors is a mistake, but it can build tremendous credibility and a willingness to work together.

Bodenstab has found that deliberately relinquishing some of the comfort, privacy, and convenience that comes with being the sole owner of a private company is well worth it. It hasn't always been easy, but it has made him tackle issues he'd like to bury, and it has certainly paid off for the company.

Source   Reprinted with permission, *Inc. magazine*, (June 1988) Copyright © (1988) by Goldhirsh Group, Inc., 38 Commercial Wharf, Boston, MA 02110.

B.   Forms of Business Organizations

Proprietorship and Partnership Equity

Proprietorship
An entity owned by one person who has unlimited liability for the obligations of the entity; often referred to as a *sole proprietorship*.

The preceding discussion of equity relates to a corporate form of business organization. A business entity can also be a sole-owner **proprietorship** or a multiple-owner **partnership**. The only significant difference in the balance sheet of a proprietorship or a partnership is in the treatment of equity. A Capital account is used to record owner contributions to the business. Any owner withdrawals, usually called *drawings*, reduce this Capital account; net income earned by the business increases the Capital account. No distinction is made in the balance sheet between owner capital contributions and

Partnership
An entity owned by two or more persons, each of whom has unlimited liability for the obligations of the entity.

net income earned and retained in the business, as does occur with the corporate form of organization. If Bluebeard Computer Corporation were a proprietorship or a partnership instead of a corporation, the equity would appear on the balance sheet as one of the following:

Proprietor's Equity		Partners' Equity	
Bruce Bluebeard, Capital	$13,000	Bruce Bluebeard, Capital	$ 9,000
		Bill Dill, Capital	4,000
		Total	$13,000

A partnership has the advantage over a proprietorship of a greater amount of capital contributed by the several partners and the different abilities that they bring to the management of the business. The primary disadvantage of a partnership is that each owner can be held personally responsible for all the debts of the business.

Neither a proprietorship nor a partnership pays income tax itself to government as does a corporation; rather, the proprietor or partners personally pay income tax on the net income of the business in addition to their other income.

Corporate Organization

Board of directors
Elected representatives of a corporation's shareholders.

Shareholders do not usually participate in the day-to-day management of a business. They participate indirectly through the election of a **board of directors**, although a shareholder may become a member of the board or a corporate officer or both. The board of directors also does not participate in the day-to-day management of the corporation but delegates this responsibility to the officers of the corporation — the president, secretary, treasurer, and vice-presidents. This delegation of responsibility is illustrated in Figure 1-2.

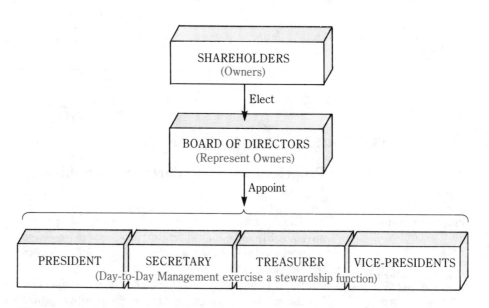

Figure 1-2   Corporate organization

Shareholders usually meet annually to vote for a board of directors — either to re-elect the current directors or to elect new directors. The board of directors meets monthly or quarterly to review the operations of the corporation and to set policies for future operations. Based on the performance of the corporation, the board may decide to distribute some assets, usually in the form of cash, as dividends to shareholders.

C. The Accounting Model

Luca Pacioli
The first person to publish a description of double-entry record keeping, designed to ensure the accuracy of transactions being recorded. His book, *Arithmetic, Geometry and Proportion*, was published in 1494 in Italy.

Double-entry record keeping system
The method of account-ing that recognizes the dual nature of each transaction; used in conjunction with the accounting equation in recording transactions.

Accounting equation
The foundation on which accounting is developed and the basic formula for the balance sheet. It expresses the dollar amounts of assets, liabilities, and equities and can be stated as ASSETS = LIABILITIES + EQUITY.

Total equities
Claims against assets of the entity; consists of creditor claims and owner claims.

Creditors
Individuals or organiza-tions to whom money is owed by an entity. Creditor claims are *primary claims*.

The mechanics used in the accounting process were first published in 1494 by a Franciscan friar living in Italy. In his book *Arithmetic, Geometry and Proportion*, **Luca Pacioli** included a description of a **double-entry record keeping system** designed to ensure the accuracy of transactions being recorded. As early as 1200, a more primitive version of this recording system was in use in Venice, and by Pacioli's time the double-entry system was widely used. Although Pacioli is often given credit for its invention, it is doubtful that he originated the double-entry model, often referred to as the *accounting equation*. It is more likely that he either refined the recording practice of the day or integrated the system into the wider mathematical context of his book.

The **accounting equation** states that the total assets belonging to an entity must always equal the total claims (called **total equities**) against those assets. The equality between assets and equities is shown by an equals sign. The equation is expressed as follows:

$$\text{ASSETS} = \text{TOTAL EQUITIES}$$

The use of the phrase *total equities* in this expression of the accounting equation includes claims of both **creditors** (anyone to whom the business owes money) and owners against the assets of the entity. Total equities is different than *equity*, which refers only to owners' equity; this restricted use of the word is the more widely accepted in accounting literature.

There is another way of expressing the relationship between assets and total equities that is equally correct:

$$\text{ASSETS} = \text{SOURCES OF ASSETS}$$

Since assets have to be received from some source, this form of the equation empha-sizes the contribution of assets by various individuals, including creditors and owners.

Creditors' claims to the assets of the entity (primary claims) equal the amount owed to them. The owners' claims (residual claims) consist of the amount left after the entity has taken into consideration the amounts due to everyone else. The accounting equation is therefore expanded into this form:

ASSETS	=	LIABILITIES	+	EQUITY
(economic resources owned by an entity)		(creditors claims to assets = primary claims)		(owners' claims to assets = residual claims)

This basic accounting model forms the foundation on which accounting is built. In addition to providing this foundation, it also expresses an equality between the assets and the total claims against those assets.

The Accounting Equation Illustrated

The following example illustrates the use of the equation. Assume that a business owns one asset, a truck, which has a purchase price of $8,000, and that $3,000 has been paid at the purchase date, with a $5,000 balance due to the bank (a creditor) remaining. The equation now appears in the following form:

$$\text{ASSETS} = \text{LIABILITIES} + \text{EQUITY}$$
$$\$8,000 = \$5,000 + \$3,000$$

In this situation, the entity owns $8,000 of assets (truck), a creditor (the bank that lent the money) has a primary claim of $5,000, and the owners have residual claims (the balance remaining) of $3,000. It is clear that the *asset* total of $8,000 *equals* the total *equities* side of the equation, $5,000 + $3,000.

Since owners are interested in knowing the amount of their equity in an entity, financial statements are designed to show the amount left for them after all other claims have been recognized. Owners' claims are expressed as the difference between total assets and total liabilities. The accounting equation is often stated in the following manner to emphasize owners' claims:

$$\text{ASSETS} - \text{LIABILITIES} = \text{EQUITY}$$
$$\$8,000 - \$5,000 = \$3,000$$

Net assets
The excess of assets over liabilities: often referred to as *equity*.

Since total assets minus total liabilities also equals net assets, it is obvious that net assets is synonymous with the owners' equity interest in total assets. The $3,000 difference between assets and liabilities can also be referred to as **net assets**.

Financial Structure

Financial structure
The components of an entity's equity, including creditor and shareholder capital; often referred to as the capital structure.

The accounting equation therefore expresses a relationship between assets owned by the entity and the claims against those assets. Although shareholders own a corporation, shareholders alone do not finance the corporation; creditors also finance a part of its activities. Creditors and shareholders together are said to form the **financial structure** of a corporation. What is Bluebeard Computer Corporation's financial structure like?

Accounting Equation			
ASSETS	= LIABILITIES	+	EQUITY
$19,500	= $6,500	+	$13,000

BCC has a low reliance on debt in its financial structure, and therefore creditors have only a small claim against its assets. Analysts and investors are concerned with the financial structure of a corporation; that is, with the proportion of shareholders' claims against the assets of a corporation as compared with creditors' claims. What is the proportion of shareholders' and creditors' claims to the assets of BCC?

This proportion is important because the long-term financial strength of the corporation depends on its financial structure. In any given situation, a corporation is said to be *underfinanced* if it has inadequate equity capital; it is said to be *overfinanced* if shareholder capital is excessive. The proportion of shareholders' to creditors' claims is calculated by dividing shareholders' equity by total liabilities. Here is relevant financial information to calculate this proportion for BCC:

		19X1
Equity	(a)	$13,000
Total Liabilities	(b)	$ 6,500
Equity to Debt	(a ÷ b)	2 : 1

These calculations tell us that Bluebeard has $2 equity for each $1 of liabilities. Shareholders, therefore, are currently financing the bulk of BCC's operations. This fact can be a cause for concern.

> On the one hand, management's reliance on shareholder financing is good. Creditors are usually willing to extend additional financing for business operations when shareholders finance the bulk of a corporation's activities. The entity is spared from the sale of additional shares to finance expansion. On the other hand, management's over-reliance on shareholder financing is poor policy. Interest does not usually have to be paid to short-term creditors (trade accounts payable), and the corporation thereby has the free use of credit for business operations. Shareholders can invest less in a corporation when it has a greater reliance on creditor financing.

The proportion of shareholders' and creditors' claims is a management decision. In the final analysis, a reasonable balance has to be maintained. Although there is no fixed rule for an appropriate proportion, there are ways of designing an optimum balance. The evaluation of an existing financial structure is discussed further in chapters 7 and 14.

D.   Transactions Analysis

Documents
The raw data of the financial transactions of an entity; also referred to as *source documents*. They include bank deposit slips, cancelled cheques, sales invoices, purchase invoices, insurance policies, contracts of the entity, and utility bills.

Accountants view financial transactions as economic events that change components within the accounting equation. These changes are usually measured by reference to **documents**; documents provide objective and verifiable data, so that anyone can make the same measurements using these documents. Documents can be prepared internally or externally. An internally prepared document supporting the purchase of supplies is called a *purchase order*; the supplier's invoice is the externally prepared document supporting the purchase. The financial transactions resulting in changes within the accounting equation are then recorded. The accounting equation can be expanded as follows:

ASSETS					=	LIABILITIES			+	EQUITY	
Cash +	Accounts Receivable +	Prepaid Insurance +	Equipment +	Truck =		Bank Loan +	Accounts Payable +	Unearned Rent +		Common Stock +	Net Income

In the following example of transaction analysis, assets are broken down into five groups:

1. Cash, which includes coins, currency, and bank deposits

2. Accounts receivable, which consists of amounts due from customers for services rendered by Bluebeard Computer Corporation
3. Prepaid insurance, which covers a one-year insurance policy
4. Equipment, which is used for repairing computers
5. A truck, which permits the repairer to conduct business.

Additional assets will be introduced in later chapters.

Liabilities consist of a bank loan and accounts payable, the amounts owed to creditors resulting from obligations incurred by the corporation in exchange for the acquisition of an asset. Unearned Rent represents an advance payment for a service which the company will provide in the future.

Equity is broken down into

1. Common stock, which represents the investments of shareholders in the corporation
2. Net income for the period (the difference between revenue and expenses)
   a. Revenues, which represent the performance of repair services by the corporation in exchange for assets of the customers (asset inflows)
   b. Expenses, which represent an outflow or consumption of assets from the corporation incurred in earning the revenue.

Double-Entry Accounting

Pacioli's double-entry model reflects the dual nature of each transaction: each one affects at least two different items within the equation. If one item within the equation is changed, then another item must also be changed to balance it. In this way, the equality of the equation is maintained. For example, if there is an increase in an asset, then there must be a decrease in another asset or a corresponding change in a liability or equity. This equality is the essence of double-entry record keeping. The equation itself always remains in balance after each transaction.

Canada Business Corporations Act (CBCA)
Law governing the incorporation of federal companies.

The operation of double-entry accounting is illustrated in the following section, which shows eight transactions of Bluebeard Computer Corporation, an entity formed to perform computer repairs for customers and recently incorporated under the **Canada Business Corporations Act** (CBCA).

Note the effect of each transaction on the accounting equation; a change in one item within the equation always results in another change elsewhere within the equation. The equality of the equation is maintained in this way.

Each of these January transactions represents an exchange of something of value in return for something else of value or the incurring of an obligation to be paid in assets at a future date. The following section and Figure 1-3 summarize these transactions, their effects on the accounting equation, and the manner in which they are recorded. These financial transactions of BCC will also be used in Chapter 2 to illustrate the application of a debit-credit shorthand for recording and summarizing transactions. They will be continued in Chapter 3 to illustrate the preparation of adjusting entries. This continuity is designed to facilitate your understanding of the accounting cycle.

Transaction Number	Date	Description of Transaction	ASSETS	=	Effect on the Accounting Equation LIABILITIES	+	EQUITY
1	Jan. 1	*Bluebeard Computer Corporation issued 1000 shares of common stock for $11,000 cash.* This transaction has a dual nature: the asset Cash is increased while the equity Common Stock is also increased. After the transaction is recorded, the equation will appear as follows:	(+)				(+)
		CASH	+ $11,000	=			
		COMMON STOCK					+ $11,000
		Note that both sides of the equation are in balance.					
2	Jan. 2	*The corporation purchased $3,000-worth of equipment on account. This purchase on account represents an obligation for the corporation, to be paid at a later date.* The increase of the asset Equipment is one side of this transaction; the obligation to pay for this asset at a later date is the other side of the transaction. The obligation results in an increase in the liability Accounts Payable. This transaction will affect the equation as follows:	(+)		(+)		
		EQUIPMENT	+ $3,000	=			
		ACCOUNTS PAYABLE			+ $3,000		
		Again, the equation is in balance.					
3	Jan. 3	*The corporation purchased a delivery truck for $8,000, paying $3,000 cash and incurring a bank loan for the balance.* In this transaction, the asset Cash is decreased, while the asset Truck is increased; the liability Bank Loan is also increased. The equation will appear as follows:	(−)(+)		(+)		
		CASH	− $3,000	=			
		TRUCK	+ $8,000				
		BANK LOAN			+ $5,000		
		The equality of the equation is maintained.					
4	Jan. 5	*Bluebeard Computer Corporation paid $1,200 for a comprehensive one-year insurance policy, effective January 1.* Here the asset Prepaid Insurance is increased; Cash is decreased. The equation appears as follows:	(−)(+)				
		PREPAID INSURANCE	+ $1,200	=			
		CASH	− $1,200				
		Since the one-year period will not expire at January 31 when financial statements are prepared, the insurance cost is considered to be an asset at the payment date. Note that this exchange of the Cash asset for the Prepaid Insurance asset does not affect liabilities or equity; nevertheless the equation is in balance.					

Transaction Number	Date	Description of Transaction	ASSETS	=	Effect on the Accounting Equation LIABILITIES	+	EQUITY
5	Jan. 10	*The corporation paid $2,000 on account to the creditor in transaction 2. This payment on account represents a partial payment of the obligation incurred by the corporation when the equipment was purchased.* The asset Cash is decreased as one side of this transaction; the other side of the transaction decreases the obligation Accounts Payable. This transaction has the following impact on the equation:	(−)		(−)		
		ACCOUNTS PAYABLE			− $2,000		
		CASH	− $2,000	=			
		Again, the equality of the equation is maintained.					
6	Jan. 15	*The corporation received $500 as an advance payment of the part-time rental of the corporate truck for three months as follows: $100 for January, $200 for February, $200 for March.* The asset Cash is increased by $500; a liability, Unearned Rent, is also increased since the revenue will not be earned by the end of January.	(+)		(+)		
		CASH	+ $500	=			
		UNEARNED RENT			+ $500		
		This cash receipt is considered to be a payment received in advance of its being earned. The amount would have to be paid back if the truck were not available for some reason.					
7	Jan. 31	*Computer repairs of $7,000 were made for customers during the month as follows: $4,000 worth of repairs were made for cash and $3,000 worth of repairs were made on account; that is, payment will be received at a later date for these repairs.* On one side of this transaction, the Cash and Accounts Receivable assets of the corporation increase; there is also an increase in equity on the other side of the transaction.	(+)(+)				(+)
		CASH	+ $3,000				
		ACCOUNTS RECEIVABLE	+ $4,000	=			
		REPAIR REVENUE					+ $7,000
		Equity is only temporarily increased by this transaction, because the expenses incurred in making these repairs must be deducted so that net income for the month can be calculated. It is the net income that actually increases equity.					

Transaction Number	Date	Description of Transaction	ASSETS	=	Effect on the Accounting Equation LIABILITIES	+	EQUITY
8	Jan. 31	*The corporation paid operating expenses for the month as follows: $600 for rent; $2,500 for salaries; $1,200 for supplies expenses; and $700 for truck expenses (oil, gas, etc.).*	(−)				(−)

The dual nature of this transaction consists of a decrease in the asset Cash on one side of the transaction and, on the other side, the decrease of computer repair revenue recorded in transaction 7.

RENT EXPENSE		− $ 600
SALARIES EXPENSE		− 2,500
SUPPLIES EXPENSE	=	− 1,200
TRUCK EXPENSE		− 700
CASH	− $5,000	

These expenses reduce the assets and equity (net income) in the equation.

As Figure 1-3 illustrates, these various transactions are summarized as financial statements.

Transactions:	Cash	+ Accounts Receivable	+ Prepaid Insurance	+ Equipment	+ Truck	= Bank Loan	+ Accounts Payable	+ Unearned Rent	+ Common Stock	+ Net Income
1. Issued common stock for $11,000 cash	+ $11,000								+ $11,000	
2. Purchased equipment for $3,000 on account (for credit)				+ $3,000			+ $3,000			
3. Purchased truck for $8,000; paid $3,000 cash and incurred a bank loan for the balance	− 3,000				+ $8,000	+ $5,000				
4. Paid $1,200 for a comprehensive one-year insurance policy effective January 1.	− 1,200		+ $1,200							
5. Paid $2,000 on account for credit to the corporation's creditor	− 2,000						− 2,000			
6. Received $500 as an advance payment for the part-time rental of the truck for three months as follows: $100 for January, $200 for February, $200 for March	+ 500							+ $500		
7. Performed repairs for $4,000 cash and $3,000 on account (for credit)	+ 4,000	+ $3,000								+ $7,000
8. Paid operating expenses incurred during the month: Rent $600, Salaries Expense $2,500, Supplies Expense $1,200, Truck Expense $700.										− 600 − 2,500 − 1,200 − 700
Balances	$ 4,300	+ $ 3,000	+ $ 1,200	+ $ 3,000	+ $ 8,000	= $ 5,000	+ $ 1,000	+ $ 500	+ $ 11,000	+ $ 2,000

Used To Prepare the Statement of Cash Flow Illustrated on Page 11

Used To Prepare the Income Statement

Used To Calculate Equity

Used To Prepare the Balance Sheet

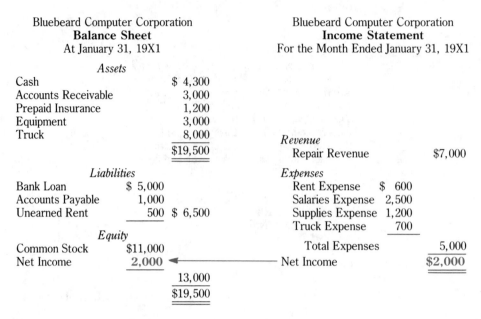

Bluebeard Computer Corporation
Balance Sheet
At January 31, 19X1

Assets

Cash	$ 4,300
Accounts Receivable	3,000
Prepaid Insurance	1,200
Equipment	3,000
Truck	8,000
	$19,500

Liabilities

Bank Loan	$ 5,000	
Accounts Payable	1,000	
Unearned Rent	500	$ 6,500

Equity

Common Stock	$11,000	
Net Income	2,000	
		13,000
		$19,500

Bluebeard Computer Corporation
Income Statement
For the Month Ended January 31, 19X1

Revenue

Repair Revenue	$7,000

Expenses

Rent Expense	$ 600	
Salaries Expense	2,500	
Supplies Expense	1,200	
Truck Expense	700	
Total Expenses		5,000
Net Income		$2,000

Figure 1-3   Transactions worksheet for Bluebeard Computer Corporation for January

Issues in Ethics 1-1

Students Urge Business Schools To Emphasize Ethical Behaviour

Business students are not convinced that ethical behaviour is something a school can teach, but many are not satisfied with the attention it now receives and want their institutions to address business ethics in a more structured way.

Nearly 125 students from leading business schools agreed in a survey that "good ethics is good business." They said business schools should reflect that maxim by requiring every student seeking a degree in business administration to take an ethics course.

"Certainly ethical considerations are already being raised in the classroom, but the school is not raising ethical consciousness," said Max Cohen, a business student at Canada's York University, which has an elective ethics course.

Some students at the 1989 Graduate Business Conference said they were troubled by the public's low respect for business in general, and by the image of M.B.A. graduates as "pond scum" — in the words of one business professor — who flaunt huge starting salaries. Through ethics courses, they said, schools can at least raise ethical awareness before students leave to enter the business world.

"The bottom line is to create this sense of awareness that may not have been there before," said Frederick Stow, Jr., a graduate of the University of Virginia's business school who attended the conference.

The conference brought together students from 25 of the nation's leading business schools and from four institutions in Canada and Europe. It has been held annually since 1983 and is organized by students at a different institution and on a different subject each year.

Some students at the conference said the continuing national debate on ethics might simply be a fad, and they questioned the motives of business schools in adopting ethics

Accounting Time Periods

Financial statements are prepared at regular intervals — usually monthly or quarterly — and at the end of each 12-month period. The timing of these financial statements is determined by the needs of management in running the entity. Financial statements may also be required by outside parties, such as bankers, before the granting of loans to the entity can be considered. It is also customary for corporations listed on stock exchanges to prepare quarterly accounting reports for the use of shareholders, investors, and other interested parties in evaluating the progress of these corporations.

Calendar Year-End

Year-end
The last day of a 12-month period, when annual financial statements are prepared.

Interim financial statement
A financial report prepared for a time period, usually monthly or quarterly, of less than 12 months.

An entity operates on the basis of 12-month time periods. Accounting reports, called the *annual financial statements*, are prepared at the end of each 12-month period, which is known as the **year-end** of the entity. Companies having a year-end that coincides with the calendar year are said to have a December 31 year-end. While financial statements can also be prepared quarterly or monthly (these are commonly referred to as **interim financial statements**), they are always prepared at the calendar year-end, December 31.

---

courses. The subject of ethics is treated as an afterthought, those students said, added to the curriculum in an effort to seek favorable publicity or donations.

The conference survey found students both concerned about ethics and realistic about the business world. While 97 per cent agreed that "good ethics is good business," 71 per cent acknowledged that being ethical in business could hurt them in some instances. About 56 per cent said the business world operates on a separate ethical standard, but only 22 per cent believed that it should. Nearly 70 per cent agreed that the "rhetoric of business ethics exceeds the reality for most companies."

About 65 per cent of the conference participants responded to the survey. Among the survey's other findings:

• Of the students with business experience before attending an M.B.A. school, 60 per cent had witnessed unethical business practices, primarily in the form of bribes, conflicts of interest, price-fixing, and insider trading.
• Nineteen per cent of those surveyed said they would trade stock on inside information, while 26 per cent would pay a $100 bribe to a city inspector to "speed up" procedures.
• Nearly all of those surveyed said an employer should pro-

vide training in the company's ethical standards and on the consequences of violating them.

Students in the survey were often more confident in their own sense of ethics than in the morality of their peers. While 46 per cent said their own ethics were about the same as those of other students at their school, 51 per cent reported their own ethics were higher.

Teaching business ethics is not simply about insider trading and other obvious ethical violations, said Tom Peters, author of *Thriving on Chaos* and co-author of *In Search of Excellence*, who spoke to the conference. Ethics is a "minute-by-minute affair," he said, and involves things as simple as acknowledging customers and employees as human beings.

Business schools emphasize abstract management theories at the expense of the human elements of leadership, such as spirit, trust, grace, warmth, and energy, Mr. Peters said. But it is the "frightful arrogance" and "lack of touch with customers and employees" that give M.B.A. graduates a poor reputation, he said.

Source   Copyright 1989, *The Chronicle of Higher Education*. Reprinted with permission.

Fiscal Year-End

Companies whose year-end does not coincide with the calendar year are said to operate on a **fiscal year**. For example, some corporations have a June 30 fiscal year-end; others choose a year-end that coincides with their natural year. A *natural year* ends when business operations are at a low point. A ski resort will probably have a year ending in late spring or early summer, when its business operations are at their lowest point: for example, April 30. Although interim financial statements can also be prepared quarterly or monthly, annual financial statements are always prepared at the fiscal year-end, in the case of the ski resort, April 30. The relationship of the interim and year-end financial statements is illustrated in Figure 1-4.

The headings of the financial statements shown in this chapter are designed to identify the entity for which the statements are being prepared (Bluebeard Computer Corporation); the name of the statement (income statement or balance sheet); and the date of the statements (January 31, 19X1).

> The *income statement* is dated *For the Month Ended January 31, 19X1* because it is intended to show the performance of the entity over the January time period.
> The *balance sheet* is dated *At January 31, 19X1* because it is designed to show the financial position of the entity at a particular point in time — January 31.

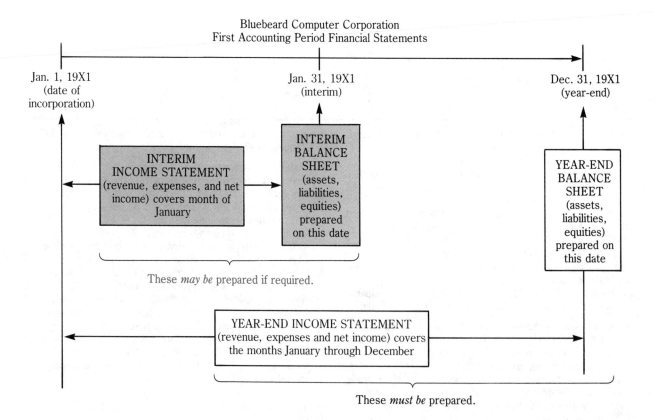

Figure 1-4   The relationship of interim and year-end financial statements

The Time-Period Assumption

Periodicity concept
The preparation and issuance of financial statements on a timely basis; used as a measure of performance and accomplishment for decision-making purposes. Also called the *time-period assumption.*

The time-period assumption requires the preparation of timely and useful financial statements. Underlying this assumption, however, is the concept that the entity's activities can actually be broken into meaningful time periods. Although necessary for financial reporting, this concept — also called the **periodicity concept** — results in accounting measurement problems that require compensation through the use of accrual accounting and the matching concept. As noted earlier, the accrual method of accounting aligns expenses and revenues with a particular time period; under this method, the cost of assets transferred to customers or consumed during the period are considered as expenses; the revenue generated by these expenses is included in the income statement of the same time period. In this way, expenses incurred are matched with revenue generated. The application of these concepts is explained and illustrated further in Chapter 3.

E. The Accounting Profession and the Development of GAAP

You have been introduced, however briefly, to some of the concepts and procedures that underlie the practice of financial accounting. These concepts and procedures — these standards — did not appear suddenly; they are the result of many years of thought, debate, and research.

The considerable time and effort invested in the formulation of these standards ensures that financial accounting information is reported in a fair, objective, and relevant fashion to outside parties who rely upon this information for making business decisions.

Together, the standards that apply to financial accounting are called *generally accepted accounting principles* (GAAP). A number of authoritative accounting organizations concerned with the formulation of GAAP are briefly discussed below.

Accounting Standards Committee (ACSC)
A committee responsible for issuing pronouncements relating to accounting: exposure drafts are used to obtain views on proposed recommendations.

The **Accounting Standards Committee** (ACSC) is responsible for the issuance of pronouncements relating to accounting. Membership in ACSC includes representatives from organizations such as the Canadian Institute of Chartered Accountants (CICA), the Financial Analysts Federation, the Financial Executives Institute of Canada, the Canadian Certified General Accountants' Association, and the Society of Management Accountants. In developing Canadian accounting standards and research, the ACSC uses exposure drafts to obtain the views of members and the business community on proposed recommendations.

CICA Handbook
A codification of research pronouncements and accounting principles published by the CICA; has been given a quasi-legislative weight in Canada.

Pronouncements of the ACSC are published in the **CICA Handbook** and represent standards to be adhered to. The fact that the *CICA Handbook* has received general acceptance in the formulation of accounting principles makes the Canadian experience somewhat different from that in other parts of the world, as has been observed:

In all the world, we are unique, because we have been singled out as the professional body responsible for developing accounting standards for Canadian business by the Canadian Business Corporations Act, some provincial corporations acts, and securities regulations. Such recognition is noteworthy, but the quasi-legislative weight of the *CICA Handbook* must not obscure the fact that the status of our standards must be maintained as it was earned: by treating standard setting as an independent, professional responsibility. The profession

Canadian Institute of Chartered Accountants (CICA)
The national professional accounting association of Chartered Accountants in Canada.

Chartered Accountant (CA)
A professional accountant who has passed the CICA national examination and satisfied all other requirements for admittance.

Canadian Certified General Accountants' Association of Canada (CGAAC)
The national professional accounting association of Certified General Accountants in Canada.

Certified General Accountant (CGA)
A professional accountant who has completed all CGA courses and satisfied all other requirements for admittance.

SMA
The national professional accounting association of Certified Management Accountants in Canada.

CMA
A professional accountant who has passed the FAE national examination and satisfied all other requirements for admittance.

Ordre des comptables agréés du Québec
The provincial association of chartered accountants in Quebec.

FASB
A United States group formed in 1973 to issue research pronouncements and accounting principles; exposure drafts are used to obtain views on proposed recommendations.

developed the handbook as a guide to best practice for its own members, for the protection of its own standards. Implicit in these standards, however, is the basic goal of protecting the public. Developing standards based on a complex professional body of knowledge but directed toward the needs of a wide group of users is a test of professional judgement.[1]

The dominant group of accountants is the **Canadian Institute of Chartered Accountants** (CICA), whose members are **Chartered Accountants** (CAs). An important group of public accountants is the **Certified General Accountants' Association of Canada** (CGAAC). Its members use the designation **Certified General Accountant** (CGA). Although CGAs practise public accounting in certain provinces, many specialize in management, government accounting, and taxation, as do CAs.

The dominant group of management accountants is the **Society of Management Accountants** (SMA), whose members use the designation **Certified Management Accountant** (CMA). The SMA develops managerial accounting education materials and publishes special studies dealing with areas of management accounting.

Each Canadian organization is incorporated under federal legislation and has associations in every province. Everyone who holds membership in a provincial association is automatically a member of the national group, and membership is fully portable between provinces. The first accounting body in North America was formed in Canada in 1880 and was called the Association of Accountants in Montreal (now the **Ordre des comptables agréés du Québec**).

In addition to these bodies, each province has a securities commission or other government body that exercises a considerable amount of control in the securities markets. These provincial commissions have formally defined generally accepted accounting principles for financial disclosure as those pronouncements that are set out in the *CICA Handbook*.

The **Financial Accounting Standards Board** (FASB) is the leading independent non-government body in the United States responsible for the development and issuance of financial accounting standards. A large part of the GAAP in use today was established by the FASB. In addition, it has focused on the development of a conceptual framework of accounting to re-evaluate basic accounting theory. This FASB conceptual framework has been referred to as the constitution for accounting. CAs and other public accountants in Canada are strongly influenced by these and other American accounting pronouncements and research.

The **Securities and Exchange Commission** (SEC) is a government body in the United States that issues pronouncements and regulations forming part of GAAP. Large Canadian public corporations listed on American stock exchanges are affected by these pronouncements and regulations. The SEC mandate focuses on the identification of information that must be disclosed by listed corporations and on the establishment of accounting procedures to be used in making these disclosures. Fortunately, the SEC generally relies on the accounting profession to establish accounting procedures.

The dominant group of accountants in the United States is comprised of **Certified Public Accountants** (CPAs), who are members of the **American Institute of Certified Public Accountants** (AICPA). The AICPA was formerly responsible for the development of GAAP; in 1973 this role was undertaken by the then-newly-created FASB.

SEC
An agency of the U.S. federal government that is influential in the development of accounting principles and reporting practices. It focuses on securities traded on U.S. stock exchanges.

CPA
A professional accountant who has passed the Uniform CPA Examination and satisfied all other professional requirements for admittance.

AICPA
The national professional accounting association of Certified Public Accountants in the United States.

CAAA
An organization in Canada primarily for academic accountants; it is also open to anyone interested in accounting and accounting education.

AAA
An organization in the United States primarily for academics in accounting.

Auditor's report
An opinion of a professional accountant on the financial statements of an entity; states whether the financial statements present fairly the financial position and operating results of the entity and whether these statements have been prepared according to generally accepted accounting principles.

The **Canadian Academic Accounting Association** (CAAA) is an association formed for accountants in academic work but open to anyone interested in accounting and accounting education. The CAAA encourages the improvement of accounting education, sponsors various types of accounting research, and publishes its semi-annual publication *Contemporary Accounting Research*. As well, many Canadians in academic work are also members of the **American Accounting Association** (AAA), whose objectives are similar to those of the CAAA.

The Auditor's Report

When year-end financial statements are published, they are usually accompanied by an **auditor's report**. The auditor's report indicates that the statements have been examined by an independent, professional accountant who is legally permitted to do so and that the statements present fairly the financial position of the entity and the results of its operations for a particular time period. The independent, professional accountant, usually referred to as the *auditor*, also indicates whether the financial statements have been prepared in accordance with generally accepted accounting principles and whether these accounting principles have been used in a consistent way. If there is a violation of GAAP in the financial statements, then the auditor's report is modified so as to alert readers to the violation.

Conceptual Issue 1-1

Social Responsibility

Robert H. Anderson, University of Regina

There is more to a business operation than accounting reports show. As illustrated by Figure 1 (on p. 1), accounting deals with transactions that at present are limited to financial transactions which accountants view as economic events. Thus the accounting model introduced in Figure 1 is limited to what can be objectively measured in dollars. The net income, often referred to as profit, does not show the effect on the corporation of everything it does; it only summarizes the financial transactions. One of the unreported aspects is social responsibility.

Social responsibility is the need for all individuals and institutions, governments, not-for-profit organizations, corporations, and other businesses to assess the effect of decisions and actions taken from those decisions on the entire social system. That most basic and important concept of accounting, the entity concept, no longer applies in its accounting meaning. Social responsibility concerns the total costs and benefits to a larger entity, society, not solely to the accounting entity. Some attempts have been made to develop social responsibility performance measurement systems or social responsibility accounting systems, that is, a systematic assessment of and reporting on those parts of an organization's activities that have a social impact. Very little is done in actual practice.

The interest in and concern about social responsibility has grown from two major forces that are related to each other. The first is an increasing awareness by the public of the power and control that corporations have, which leads to a need for accountability to the public. The second is an increasing decline in the popularity (or increase in the unpopularity) of business. Because the public is generally better educated, questioning, discerning, and informed, the public holds increased social, moral, and economic expectations of corporations; widespread doubts have developed about how responsible business corporations in particular are, resulting mainly from the power and control corporations can exercise.

Research over the past 25 years shows that significantly fewer Canadians view business favourably than was the case in the early 1960s, while many more view business unfavourably over the same period. Part of this decline in business acceptability is a result of media communication of the flaws in business people and their organizations, particularly in relation to the issues of the environment and bribery. Environmental damage that can be directly attributed to a specific firm is an instant news item. A cartoon in the New Yorker expresses the bribery issue well, showing a smiling corporate executive saying, "It looks as if, this year, our kickbacks will exceed our bribes!" This common view of corporations contributes to their declining popularity. Also contributing is the largeness, inflexibility, and conservatism of business institutions, especially in the area of consumer affairs. The matter of a small consumer fighting a huge corporation over a defective product induces distrust of the corporation and cheers for the individual. This lack of acceptability leads to a need for business to be able to explain its role more understandably. For corporations, this does not mean to not consider profits; profit-making remains an important social responsibility. It does mean making profits in a socially acceptable way, that is, in a positive, constructive manner — not by taking advantage of corporate power.

Similar social responsibilities exist for not-for-profit institutions as well as for individuals, and, in particular, professionals. Society expects that anyone privileged with professional status ought to use his/her talents for something more than individual advancement and benefit.

The main arguments for having organizations accept increased social responsibility can be summarized as follows:

• It will serve their interests in the long run by promoting a better public image, providing a better operational environment, and ensuring the long-run viability of business. Corporations exist at the will of society and must produce social benefits if they are to survive. In the past, if a product was salable, it was considered socially acceptable; this is no longer so.

• Corporations are more likely to have the resources — both human and financial — to solve social problems.

• Corporations should seek to balance power with responsibility. The public and government may be more tolerant of concentrated corporate economic power if increased social responsibility goes with it.

• Increased social responsibility will help business to avoid further government intervention and regulation. Social action, either through corporate acceptance or through government intervention, is inevitable. If corporations initiate the action, they'll have more effect in determining what it will be. Also prevention is easier than curing; governments seem to concentrate on curing.

• The public now expects more of business and, as part of the public, so do shareholders. They have diverse ownership and individual interests and thus benefit or suffer from corporate activities in the environment external to the corporation.

• Increased social responsibility may provide hidden profit opportunities for corporations. Sometimes problems turn into profits. For example, pollution-control requirements have already brought profit opportunities to many corporations making the necessary equipment.

There are, however, equally strong arguments against corporations accepting increased social responsibility:

• Corporations should be concerned only with profit maximization, as this is their fundamental purpose. The costs of social involvement could drive marginal firms out of business, in turn, increasing social costs not only through lost jobs but through giving the surviving firms more concentrated powers.

• Corporations already have enough power; social power should not be added, especially with the current lack of accountability. Also, since co-ordinated efforts among numerous corporations are often needed to accomplish social objectives, this co-operation would further increase concentration and power.

• Corporations do not have the required social skills. They are equipped to do only certain jobs well and should concentrate on those jobs. Such is the basis of the North American competitive economic system.

• With a basic need for profit, can corporate managers be relied on to continue to be socially responsible in difficult economic times? Often social costs outweigh social benefits, especially when considered in terms of a single firm; social responsibility programs are likely to be dropped quickly when business drops off.

• Managers are not very good at recognizing public consensus on social concerns and their priorities. If managers are to serve the interests of society as a whole, then ultimately they must be controlled by governments that can determine politically what social priorities exist.

Whether they should or not, corporations have, for the most part, accepted some sort of social responsibility. They already spend money on, or allocate employee time to, social action programs, athletic sponsorship, or community services without expecting any income as a result of these expenditures. Therefore, what is important is to formulate accounting principles for measuring, reporting, and auditing social programs.

Three basic assumptions underly an increased public demand for social responsibility and the increased corporate need for some attempt at measurement and accountability. The first assumption is that management wants socially responsible behaviour. This aim is not always obvious in actions taken, particularly with respect to protection of the environment. However, it is true that corporate management generally supports socially responsible behaviour. The second assumption is that finances limit social investments. That is, corporations do not have unlimited money to spend on socially responsible activities: a sound assumption. The third assumption is that increased social performance requires improved efficiency in order to compensate for the second assumption of scarce resources. That is, some method of measuring the effectiveness of spending on social objectives would help to allocate scarce resources.

A report on the measurement of social responsibility performance can range from a simple, totally subjective report that describes actions taken, to a complex report completely in dollars. The following list illustrates the range of complexity that such reports may take:

• a word summary of activities performed (sometimes called an *inventory*)

• a word summary of objectives and activities and an assessment of the extent to which the activities met the objectives

• a simple statement of costs or outlays on socially responsible activities

• a program management approach (similar to the second type of report, except it includes spendings; it shows the activities and programs, the amount spent on each, and whether the objectives of the activities and programs have been met)

• a cost or outlay statement showing both improvements and detriments (what was done and what is not yet done) and cost estimates for these (this produces what is sometimes called a *socio-economic operating statement*)

• a statement of costs compared to benefits for all activities and programs undertaken (this is the most complex, most complete, and most difficult report to prepare).

The ultimate in reporting on the performance of social responsibility is to produce the last type of report; accountants should be pressing to reach that stage. A major factor in starting the process of social responsibility accounting is to concentrate on a small number of key issues when first reporting on social responsibility performance. Then specific results will be quickly and easily seen.

The reports discussed above have been difficult for accountants to accept for several reasons. First, they lack objectivity; that is, they are not made up of solid, provable figures. Different people could see the results in different ways. Accounting data have always been assessed on their objectivity. A second difficulty is that social responsibility measures are often qualitative, that is, word descriptions; reports may simply be in terms of "good", "better", "worse", "satisfactory". Accountants and people who use accounting reports prefer quantitative measures, that is, in quantities, usually, in dollars. In many cases, then, social responsibility performance measurement would be based on opinions and would be hard to compare. Finally, the shifting nature of social responsibility makes measurement and comparison difficult. Social targets are moving targets. What was not required five years ago becomes expected today and will be legally required five years from now. Is a corporation socially responsible if it meets legal requirements? Or does corporate social action have to be above minimum legal standards? If legal standards increase, does a corporation's social responsibility decrease? These questions are currently unanswerable.

Why should introductory financial accounting students be concerned about the issue of corporate social responsibility? Students need to be aware that published financial statements do not contain all that is necessary to know about a corporation. A naïve belief in the accuracy and usefulness of net profit as the sole measure of corporate success leads to two errors: first the assumption that financial health is adequately measured by reported net income and, second, the discarding of efforts at measuring social responsibility performance merely because they lack precision or objectivity. If the social impacts of a corporation's activities are not included in the formal measurement process, then these impacts are not likely to be considered in a corporation's planning decisions or performance evaluations.

The long-term aim should be a system of social responsibility accounting that records, regularly and routinely, in the same way economic events are reported, the corporation's social impact on products, environment, employees, and the community. This information is necessary both for management's internal use and for its external reporting.

Source   Courtesy of Robert Anderson.

APPENDIX: Detailed Transactions Analysis

Jan. 1   **Transaction 1:   Common Stock Issued for Cash**
Bluebeard Computer Corporation issued 1000 shares of common stock for a total of $11,000 cash.
Analysis: This is the corporation's first transaction. The issuance of common shares results in cash being received by the corporation. The asset Cash is therefore increased by this transaction. The equity Common Stock is also increased by $11,000.
Recording: When the amounts are entered into the accounting equation, the transaction has been recorded according to Pacioli's double-entry system and appears as follows:

ASSETS					=	LIABILITIES			+	EQUITY	
Cash	Accounts Receivable	Prepaid Insurance	Equipment	Truck	=	Bank Loan	Accounts Payable	Unearned Rent	+	Common Stock	Net Income
+$11,000										+$11,000	

Notice that this transaction does not affect the liabilities component of the equation.
Note: In this and following transactions, the plus and minus signs are used to show the direction of change in each item caused by the transaction.

Jan. 2   **Transaction 2:   An Asset Acquired on Account (for Credit)**
Equipment to be received January 30 was purchased for $3,000 on account (for credit). The equipment is said to be purchased on account because it will be paid for at a later date.
Analysis: An asset is acquired and a liability incurred in this transaction. The asset Equipment is acquired here and is therefore recorded as an increase. By the purchase of equipment, a liability is incurred, and is thus recorded as an increase on the other side of the equation.
Recording: When the amounts are entered into the accounting equation, it shows the following balances:

ASSETS					=	LIABILITIES			+	EQUITY	
Cash	Accounts Receivable	Prepaid Insurance	Equipment	Truck	=	Bank Loan	Accounts Payable	Unearned Rent	+	Common Stock	Net Income
			+$3,000				+$3,000				

Jan. 3   **Transaction 3:   An Asset Purchased in Part for Cash and in Part for Credit**
A repairer's truck was purchased for $8,000; BCC paid $3,000 cash and incurred a $5,000 loan for the balance.
Analysis: One asset is exchanged in this transaction; an obligation to pay an asset in the future is also incurred. The asset Truck is acquired by this purchase and is therefore recorded as an increase. The asset Cash is decreased by the purchase of the truck. A liability is incurred in connection with the truck purchase and is recorded as an increase on the other side of the equation.

Recording: When the amounts are entered into the accounting equation, it appears as follows:

ASSETS					=	LIABILITIES			+	EQUITY	
Cash	Accounts Receivable	Prepaid Insurance	Equipment	Truck		Bank Loan	Accounts Payable	Unearned Rent		Common Stock	Net Income
− $3,000	+	+	+	+ $8,000	= + $5,000	+	+	+	+	

Notice that the equation is in balance after the recording of this transaction.

Jan. 5   Transaction 4:   *Asset Exchanged for Another Asset*

Bluebeard Computer Corporation paid $1,200 cash for a comprehensive one-year insurance policy, effective January 1.

Analysis: Since the one-year period will not expire by the time financial statements are prepared at January 31, the insurance cost is considered to be an asset at the payment date. The asset account, Prepaid Insurance, is increased by this transaction. Payment of the insurance results in a decrease in the asset account, Cash.

ASSETS					=	LIABILITIES			+	EQUITY	
Cash	Accounts Receivable	Prepaid Insurance	Equipment	Truck		Bank Loan	Accounts Payable	Unearned Rent		Common Stock	Net Income
− $1,200	+	+ + $1,200	+	+	=	+	+	+	+	+	

Jan. 10   Transaction 5:   *A Liability Paid*

The corporation paid $2,000 on account (for credit) to the creditor in transaction 2.

Analysis: This payment decreases Accounts Payable, a liability, because the $2,000 is due to a creditor of the corporation. The payment of cash also decreases an asset.

Recording: When the amounts are entered into the accounting equation, it shows the following balances:

ASSETS					=	LIABILITIES			+	EQUITY	
Cash	Accounts Receivable	Prepaid Insurance	Equipment	Truck		Bank Loan	Accounts Payable	Unearned Rent		Common Stock	Net Income
− $2,000	+	+	+	+	=	+ − $2,000	+	+	+	+	

Jan. 15   Transaction 6:   *Cash Received in Advance of Its Being Earned*

The corporation signed a contract for the use of its truck on a part-time basis and received an advance payment of $500 for use of the truck as follows: $100 for January, $200 for February, and $200 for March.

Analysis: The revenue relating to this cash receipt will not be earned by the end of the current accounting period. Therefore, it is considered to be a payment received in advance of its being earned. An asset account, Cash, is increased at the time the contract is signed. A liability account, Unearned Rent, is increased by this transaction.

Recording: When the amounts are entered in the equation, it appears as follows:

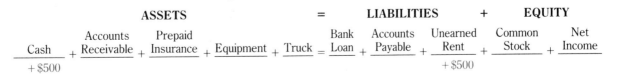

ASSETS					=	LIABILITIES			+	EQUITY	
Cash	Accounts Receivable	Prepaid Insurance	Equipment	Truck		Bank Loan	Accounts Payable	Unearned Rent		Common Stock	Net Income
+ $500	+	+	+	+	=	+	+ + $500	+	+		

Jan. 31   Transaction 7:   Revenue Earned for Cash and on Account (for Credit)

A total of $7,000 worth of computer repairs were made for customers by the corporation during the first month of business activities.

Analysis: An analysis of these revenue-creating activities reveals that the company earned $4,000 from cash customers and also earned $3,000 for repairs made on account. These activities increase two assets: the asset Cash is increased by $4,000 and the asset Accounts Receivable is increased by $3,000. The total revenue earned during the month is $7,000; this transaction increases the net income component of equity.

Recording: When the amounts are entered into the accounting equation, it shows the following balances:

Cash	+	Accounts Receivable	+	Prepaid Insurance	+	Equipment	+	Truck	=	Bank Loan	+	Accounts Payable	+	Unearned Rent	+	Common Stock	+	Net Income
ASSETS									**=**	**LIABILITIES**						**+**		**EQUITY**
+$4,000		+$3,000																+$7,000

Equity is only temporarily increased by this transaction, because the expenses incurred to make these repairs must be deducted from revenue so that net income for the month can be calculated. It is the net income that actually increases equity.

Jan. 31   Transaction 8:   Expenses Paid

BCC paid operating expenses that it incurred during the month to earn the repair revenue described in transaction 7. These expenses consist of rent, $600; salaries expense, $2,500; supplies used, $1,200; and truck expense, $700 (for oil, gas, etc.).

Analysis: These expenses, summarized here as one transaction for illustrative purposes, reduce the assets and the net income component of equity by the $5,000 of expenses.

Recording: When the paid amounts are recorded in the equation, the asset Cash is reduced by $5,000 ($600 + $2,500 + $1,200 + $700) and equity is reduced by the same amount, leaving the accounting equation as follows:

Cash	+	Accounts Receivable	+	Prepaid Insurance	+	Equipment	+	Truck	=	Bank Loan	+	Accounts Payable	+	Unearned Rent	+	Common Stock	+	Net Income
ASSETS									**=**	**LIABILITIES**						**+**		**EQUITY**
−$5,000																		−$ 600
																		− 2,500
																		− 1,200
																		− 700

The above expenses are deducted from repair revenue to determine net income for the month.

⌐ A S S I G N M E N T   M A T E R I A L S ⌐

Discussion Questions

1. Explain, using an example, what is meant by the term *financial transactions*.
2. What is the entity concept of accounting? Why is it important?
3. How does an accountant select business transactions that are translated into accounting information applicable to a particular entity?
4. What are financial statements?
5. What is the purpose of an income statement? a balance sheet? How do they interrelate?
6. Define the terms *revenue* and *expense*, as they are understood by accountants.
7. What is net income? Why is it a useful measure for readers of financial statements?
8. What are assets? Where do they appear in financial statements?
9. What do the terms *liability* and *equity* refer to? In what way can they both be referred to as equity?
10. What is the purpose of a statement of cash flow?
11. Why are financial statements prepared at regular intervals? Who are the users of these statements?
12. What is a year-end? How does the timing of year-end financial statements differ from that of interim financial statements?
13. How does a fiscal year differ from a calendar year?
14. Define the accounting process. What are the three steps in this accounting process?
15. What is the accounting model? How does it work?
16. Why is the accounting equation expanded when financial transactions are recorded? Illustrate, using the example of Bluebeard Computer Corporation.
17. The accounting model is often referred to as a double-entry accounting system. Explain how it works.
18. What is the financial structure of a corporation?
19. What is the importance of the proportion of shareholders' and of creditors' claims against the assets of the entity?
20. Is management's reliance on shareholder financing good or bad for the business? Explain.
21. Name the North American accounting organizations concerned with the formulation of accounting principles.
22. What is the *CICA Handbook*? How does the CICA separate the Canadian experience in formulating accounting principles from that in other parts of the world?
23. What is an auditor's report? What does it indicate?
24. Refer to Conceptual Issue 1-1, "Social Responsibility": how might accountants quantify corporate social responsibility? How subjective would this accounting be? Do you favour rigid guidelines for accountants in the quantifying of social actions, or do you believe accountants should be left to judge each case on its own merits?

Discussion Cases

Discussion Case 1-1:   Soldiers of "Fortune"

Mirror, mirror on the wall, who is the richest of them all?

If you believe *Fortune* magazine's estimate, non-drinking, non-smoking, non-swearing Kenneth C. Irving is the wealthiest person in Canada.

If you prefer *Forbes* magazine's assessment, it's the grim brothers Albert, Paul and Ralph Reichmann.

Maybe it's the Establishment inheritors Charles Bronfman or Ken, His Lordship Thomson; Galen Weston or the Eatons.

Then, perhaps it's Paul Desmarais or Robert Campeau, founders of two do-it-yourself dynasties.

They're all in the billionaire league, and they're all Canadians who have just made this year's rich-richer-richest lists

of the gilt-edged among the blue-chip families. But who are they? What do they own? Why are they worth billions when most of us are in debt?

A new candidate who's thrust his way to the top of the list is Campeau who, after a recent series of up-up-and-away bids for U.S.-based Federated Department Stores, is estimated to control assets worth about $16 billion.

Not bad for a Grade 8 dropout who grew up poor as a French-Canadian kid in English-run Sudbury during the Depression.

He's described as aggressive, loud, irascible; witty, flamboyant — and, above all, brilliant. Now 63, he started work as a trainee-machinist at Inco, eventually working his way into house building.

He built Toronto's Harbour Castle Westin (previously Harbour Castle Hilton), and initiated the city's downtown Scotia Plaza complex.

And he overcame a stonewall team of blue-blood executives to pull off his latest takeover, which includes the world-renowned Bloomingdale's department store.

Paul Desmarais, also from Sudbury and a former business associate, is in the same league as Campeau and also is said to control assets in the $16-billion range.

His money is threaded through financial services, newsprint, publishing and broadcasting and he entertains show-biz personalities and politicians lavishly.

A graduate of the University of Ottawa, he started by rebuilding a near-bankrupt bus company in which his lawyer-father had a minor interest, even doing the maintenance himself.

It grew into the largest inter-city bus service in Eastern Canada, and was later sold.

He took over cash-rich — and appropriately named — Power Corp. in 1968, and has parlayed his holding into an empire.

As the major shareholder in Power, he controls such companies as paper-maker Consolidated Bathurst Ltd., the Great-West Lifeco Inc. insurance company and the Montreal Trust group of financial services companies.

Power also owns Gesca Ltée, which publishes several newspaper in Quebec including *La Presse*.

Kenneth Irving, 88, is a self-made mogul, too. He has turned the family name into a way of life for many people in New Brunswick since he took over his father's lumber business and went on to dominate the province's economy.

Known for extreme privacy to the point of secrecy, this son of a Scottish immigrant has more money than most of the leading names of Canadian finance, yet remains the least known.

His interests have been valued at as much as $8 billion.

Irving, a pilot in the First World War, returned to civilian life and started selling Ford cars in his home town of Buctouche. For him, it seemed logical to market the gasoline that powered them, so he started opening gas stations. Later Kenneth branched out. He built Canada's largest refinery to process his own gasoline, bought ships and trucks to form his own distribution system, then opened shipyards to build his own tankers.

His network of companies grew until Irving owned about a quarter of all New Brunswick's woodlands. (They've planted more than 200 million trees over the years under a reforestation program.)

He added bus, food and retail operations, owns the province's four English-language newspapers, and is New Brunswick's largest employer with 25,000 employees in 300 firms.

The largest of those firms is Irving Oil Ltd. in which Chevron Corp. of San Francisco has a significant holding — although "K.C." controls the company with 51.2 per cent of the stock.

The brothers Reichmann own Olympia and York Developments, the biggest real-estate developer in North America.

They own 8.5 per cent of all the premium office space in Manhattan, have 80 per cent of the Abitibi Price newsprint giant in their bank accounts.

Three-quarters of Canada's 20th largest company — Gulf Canada Resources — is included in the family's assets, together with control of Hiram Walker Resources.

They sweep up real estate at a staggering pace, owning the boardrooms of many a multinational corporation. Their buildings are valued at more than $8 billion.

Orthodox Jews, they're very religious. The 10,000 construction workers who built their Battery Park City in New York were sent home at 2 p.m. every Friday for the Jewish sabbath, and family members won't even press an elevator button on the holy day.

The brothers live modestly and have the reputation of being nice to do business with.

It's been estimated they'd have $5 billion left if they paid off all their property loans.

Lord Ken of Fleet, Roy Thomson's boy, heads a dynasty that's said to be worth $5.5 billion. The family's interests encompass a vast chain of newspapers around the world, North Sea oil reserves and control of Hudson's Bay Co., Simpsons and Zellers.

Shy, scholarly and in his mid-60s, Thomson lives in a 23-room mansion in Toronto's exclusive Rosedale and collects Krieghoff paintings and ivory sculptures. He rarely gives interviews, occasionally goes grocery shopping with his wife and has been spotted checking the prices at some of his Bay outlets.

When considering investments, he's said, "I always ask: Will the business be there in 50 or 100 years?"

The Weston family is acknowledged as having the oldest billion-dollar fortune in Canada.

The Canadian branch, headed by 48-year-old polo-playing Galen, counts the Loblaw supermarket chain as its flagship investment and is worth an estimated $1.2 billion.

And it's all grown from the 106-year-old bread business started in Toronto by George Weston, an 18-year-old baker's apprentice who bought a bread-delivery route and parlayed it into a string of bakeries.

Galen commutes every summer — with his wife and two children — between Toronto and baronial homes in Ireland and England.

From booze to boots, from paint to pain-killers, the Bronfman fortune covers the globe and includes enough real estate to cover 300 football fields.

The leader of the pack in Canada is Charles who, with New York-based brother Edgar, shares control of Seagram, the world's biggest distillers.

They are the sons of Sam Bronfman, who grew rich selling liquor in the United States during prohibition. When he died, in 1971, Sam was the highest-paid business executive in North America. The family is estimated to be worth $2 billion.

Then there are the Eatons, the inheritors of a fortune founded by an Irish merchant whose life-long motto was: "Early to bed, early to rise, never get tight — and advertise."

Today, they run the largest privately owned department store chain in North America with sales of more than $2 billion a year.

They also have interests in Canada's biggest and best shopping malls and control Baton Broadcasting.

The chain is run by four brothers: John, Fredrik, George and Thor. The brothers live like movie stars in a world of corporate jets and swimming pools.

Could you buy them out? It would cost at least $1 billion.

Then there are the also-rans, the common, garden-variety multi-millionaires — such as high-profile publisher Conrad Black.

He's said to have told friends he's worth $190 million. Petty cash.

Source   John Picton, "The Richest of Them All", *The* (Montreal) *Gazette*, April 24, 1988, p.B-8.

For Discussion

1. All of the individuals in this article have had successful business careers. What kind of accounting information is useful to them for making decisions? for evaluating the stewardship of management?
2. Evaluate the advantages of proprietorship, partnership, and corporate forms of organization for these billionaires. Which organizational structure would you recommend? Why?
3. What kind of financial structure would they most likely choose: shareholder financing or creditor financing? Why? What proportion of each type?
4. How can profit-driven companies become more principle-driven?

Discussion Case 1-2:   Rodolph and Marmaduke

Scene: The great hall of that fine old English castle, Dogsberry Towers. The date is 1291. As the curtain rises, that good, simple-minded old knight, Sir Rodolph the Uninspired, is discovered behind a large table littered with bits of paper, slate, and sharp stones (the recording implements of the time), among which the old fellow is shuffling about, pausing from time to time to scratch a figure laboriously, with much licking of pointed stones. Finally, he gives up in exasperation and bangs loudly on the table with a tankard.

RODOLPH: What ho, without there! Fetch me another double mead — standing up.
VOICE WITHOUT: Coming, sire.
[*A servant shuffles in with a tankard.*]
ROD.:   And where is my steward Marmaduke? Is he not yet arrived?
SERVANT: I was on the point of showing him in, sire.
[*He does so. Enter Marmaduke.*]
ROD.:   Dear Marmaduke! I am so glad to see you. Something terrible has happened — you see before you a ruined man.
MARMADUKE: [*Incredulously.*] A ruined man? But, my lord, you are one of the wealthiest men in Christendom.
ROD.:   I was once, but I am sinking fast. I have it all here. [*He fumbles about and finally emerges with a piece of slate.*] Yes, since you made up the last statement of my affairs a few years ago, my wealth has declined. Here, let me see . . . [*reads*] from 812 to 533.
MAR.:   From 812 to 533? But what figures are these?
ROD.:   [*Excitedly.*] Well, they are my own invention. You see, I listed down everything I owned — just as you showed me. But when I was finished, I wanted to see whether I was going ahead or behind. So [*with an expression of delight at his own cunning*] I added all the things up. Last time, I had 812 things; this time 533. It's as simple as that — bankruptcy in a few more years, at this rate.

MAR.:   But you can't do that. That's like adding barrels of ale and goblets of wine.
ROD.:   Well, what's wrong with that? Three barrels and two goblets make five things, right?
MAR.:   [*Effort at control*] I am a member of the guild of stewards, after serving the customary 25-year apprenticeship. May I respectfully suggest that you leave these counting matters to me.
ROD.:   [*Piteously*] But you had taught me to add . . . and I thought you would be so pleased.
MAR.:   [*Relenting.*] Look, my lord. Would you rather have three horses and one rabbit, or one horse and ten rabbits?
ROD.:   Naturally, I would rather have three horses and one rabbit.
MAR.:   Quite right. You see, you would be better off with four animals than with eleven [*his voice gradually rises as he loses his control*] because they are not the same kind of animal! [*He continues more calmly.*] You see, the reason you had so many things at the time of the first count was that you had just bought 500 exotic birds.
ROD.:   They were a passing fancy of my wife's. I can deny her nothing.
MAR.:   Whereas, they are all gone now, my lord.
ROD.:   [*Indulgently.*] She changed her mind, the little dear.
MAR.:   So you see, if you disregard the birds — which you didn't like anyway — you have actually increased your possessions from 312 to 533.
ROD.:   But then, I lost some large items, too. After all, that bastard Guido the Provocative burned down one of my best manor houses.
MAR.:   On the other hand, however, in a reprisal raid you took from him half his holdings.
ROD.:   I counted that. I added in a half for that.
MAR.:   That's just fine: you get half Guido's holdings and you lose 500 birds — so it's a net loss of 499½. As a matter of fact, the guild is very worried about this. There is some nut

—from Edinburgh, of course (wouldn't you know it)—who is going about the kingdom advocating a new idea in which you value everything and add it all up to a big total. Our Conduct and Discipline Committee think they can hang a witchcraft charge on him. This whole idea of his involves the introduction of new mathematical techniques, such as long division. And of course the guild believes that long division is too erratic and too subjective a process to be relied on for accounting. Our Research Committee has got out a pronouncement saying that it has considered the use of long division and has concluded that it is inappropriate at this time.

ROD.: [*Shyly.*] Do you think that your guild members would be interested in my idea of just counting things?

MAR.: I'm afraid not, my lord. At best, they might endorse it as an alternative procedure, which is what they do when they want to go out of their way to be patronizing.

[*Curtain.*]

Source Adapted from Howard Ross, *Financial Statements: A Crusade for Current Values* (Toronto: Pitman, 1969), pp. 30–33.

For Discussion

1. Rodolph, a separate entity, has been counting his assets. Has he also been accounting for them? Why or why not?
2. Valuing assets requires the use of some common denominator so that different kinds of assets can be added together. Is the common denominator in use today better than that used by Rodolph? Why or why not?

Discussion Case 1-3:   Majestic Contractors Limited

PART A

TO OUR SHAREHOLDERS

For the first quarter ended March 31, 1987, the company recorded a profit of $663,000 compared to a loss in 1986 of $394,000. No new contracts were received during this quarter. The profit results primarily from the disposal of surplus assets in North America.

This is a difficult period for pipeline contractors throughout the world as there is over capacity in the industry and margins are depressed due to severe competition. In order to remain viable during this market cycle, we have temporarily discontinued operations in the U.S., sold surplus assets and reduced overhead expenses in Canada.

As a result of our downsizing, the company currently has $18,740,000 ($2.32 per share) of cash in the bank and $20,046,000 ($2.48 per share) of working capital. We continue to actively pursue additional business activities for the company and anticipate major changes in our business activities by year end.

On March 17, 1987 the company announced its intention to purchase up to 403,828 shares (5%) of its common stock through the facilities of the Toronto Stock Exchange. At March 31, 1987 the company had not purchased any shares.

A. J. Cressey
President and
Chief Executive Officer
Majestic Contractors Limited

Edmonton, Alberta
April 22, 1987

MAJESTIC CONTRACTORS LIMITED

Consolidated Statement of Income
For The Three Months Ended March 31, 1987
(with the three months ended March 31, 1986 for comparison)
(unaudited)

	1987	1986
Revenues	$ 46,000	$ 530,000
Expenses:		
Operating	(1,270,000)	1,103,000
General and administrative	594,000	809,000
Other (income) and expenses, net	(411,000)	(335,000)
Total expenses	(1,087,000)	1,577,000
Income (loss) before income taxes	1,133,000	(1,047,000)
Provision for (recovery of) income taxes	470,000	(653,000)
Net income (loss)	$ 663,000	$ (394,000)
Earnings (loss) per share:		
On weighted average number of shares outstanding (1987 — 8,083,706 shares; 1986 — 8,220,154 shares)	8¢	(5¢)

PART B

TO OUR SHAREHOLDERS

Revenues increased significantly in the first six months of 1988 due to increased pipeline construction and the inclusion of 45% of Monenco Limited revenues. Losses incurred were due to an unusually mild winter for pipeline construction in Western Canada and a $562,000 loss in Monenco Limited.

Majestic Pipeliners, our pipeline construction division, was awarded three (3) contracts during the second quarter:
— Replacement of sections of 762 mm gas mainline near Chilliwack, B.C. for Westcoast Energy Inc.
— Two contracts from B.C. Telephone for the installation of Fibre Optic Cables at six river crossings on the Coquihalla River near Hope, B.C.

The company is encouraged by the number of new major pipeline expansion programs planned for next year and expects to be a major participant in this work. Revenues for 1988 will increase significantly over those reported in 1987

and the company expects this division to be profitable in 1988.

Monenco Limited, our 45% owned associate, suffered losses in the first six months due primarily to losses incurred in a non-engineering subsidiary, which has been re-organized, and to the costs of excess lease space. Demand for Monenco's engineering services is expected to increase due to the recent announcement in Canada for major new projects, such as Hibernia and the P.E.I. to New Brunswick Bridge. Monenco is well positioned to participate in these major projects.

A. J. Cressey
President and
Chief Executive Officer

Edmonton, Alberta
August 10, 1988

MAJESTIC CONTRACTORS LIMITED
Consolidated Statement of Income
(unaudited)

	Three Months Ended June 30		Six Months Ended June 30	
	1988	1987	1988	1987
Revenues	$18,820,000	$ 136,000	$36,130,000	$ 182,000
Expenses:				
Operating	18,811,000	(225,000)	36,904,000	(1,495,000)
General and administrative	741,000	878,000	1,191,000	1,472,000
Other (income) and expenses, net	(89,000)	(566,000)	(120,000)	(977,000)
Total expenses	19,463,000	87,000	37,975,000	(1,000,000)
Income (loss) before income taxes	(643,000)	49,000	(1,845,000)	1,182,000
Provision for (recovery of) income taxes	(233,000)	12,000	(668,000)	482,000
Net income (loss)	($ 410,000)	$37,000	($ 1,177,000)	$ 700,000
Earnings (loss) per share: On weighted average number of shares outstanding (1988 — 8,076,454 shares; 1987 — 8,080,110 shares)	($0.06)	$0.01	($0.15)	$0.09

Source Majestic Contractors Limited, *Annual Report*, 1988. Reprinted with permission.

For Discussion

Part A
1. When is Majestic's fiscal year-end?
2. Review its consolidated income statement. How would you summarize the company's recent performance?

3. Net income is determined by deducting expenses from revenue. Why, in 1987, would operating expenses ($1,270,000) *increase* net income?
4. As an investor, what can you conclude from the information presented? What additional information do you require?
5. What are the future prospects for this entity?

Part B

6. From a review of the quarterly information, indicate the progress that Majestic had made up until the six months ended June 30, 1988.
7. Review each revenue and expense from 1986 to 1988. Which items do you believe are common and which unique?

8. Do you feel that the accounting information being communicated is useful? Why or why not?
9. Is the publication of quarterly information useful for investors and creditors?

Comprehension Problems

Comprehension Problem 1-1

The following list covers many of the transactions that can occur in accounting. Notice that each transaction has a dual effect.

Types of Accounting Transactions

	ASSETS	=	LIABILITIES	+	EQUITY
1.	(+)				(+)
2.	(+)		(+)		
3.	(+)(−)				
4.	(−)				(−)
5.	(−)		(−)		
6.			(+)		(−)
7.			(−)		(+)
8.			(+)(−)		
9.					(+)(−)

The dual effect of each transaction illustrated above maintains the equality of the accounting equation.

Required: Study the following transactions and identify, using the accounting equation, the effect of the transaction. Use a (+) to denote an increase and a (−) to denote a decrease. Some of the transactions do not involve accounting.

A = L + E

Example:

(+)   (+)   Issued common shares for cash

_____ 1. Purchased a truck for cash
_____ 2. Incurred a bank loan as payment for equipment
_____ 3. Made a deposit for electricity service
_____ 4. Paid rent expense
_____ 5. Signed a new union contract that provides for increased wages
_____ 6. Hired a messenger service to deliver letters during a mail strike and wrote a letter of complaint to the prime minister about the strike
_____ 7. Received a collect telegram from the prime minister; paid the messenger
_____ 8. Billed customers for services performed
_____ 9. Made a payment on account
_____ 10. Received a payment on account
_____ 11. Collected cash from a customer
_____ 12. Paid for truck expenses (gas, oil, etc.)
_____ 13. Made a monthly payment on the bank loan; this payment included a payment on part of the loan and also an amount of interest expense. (*Hint:* This transaction affects more than two parts of the accounting equation.)

Comprehension Problem 1-2

Refer to the list of accounting transactions in Comprehension Problem 1-1.

Required: Study the following transactions and identify, by number (1 to 9), the type of transaction. Some transactions do not involve accounting.

Example:
<u>   1   </u>   Issued common shares for cash

_____ Paid an account payable
_____ Borrowed money from a bank and issued a note
_____ Collected an account receivable
_____ Collected a commission on a sale made today
_____ Paid for an advertisement in a newspaper
_____ Borrowed cash from the bank
_____ Signed a contract to purchase a computer
_____ Received a bill for supplies used during the month
_____ Received a payment on account
_____ Sent a bill for repairs made today
_____ Sold equipment for cash
_____ Purchased a truck on account
_____ Requested payment of an account receivable that is overdue
_____ Settled a union dispute by increasing vacations from four to six weeks
_____ Recorded the amount due to the landlord as rent
_____ Received the monthly telephone answering service bill

Comprehension Problem 1-3

Required: Calculate the missing amounts for companies A to E.

	A	B	C	D	E
Cash	$3,000	$1,000	?00	$6,000	$2,500
Equipment	8,000	6,000	4,000	7,000	35?C
Accounts Payable	4,000	3,?00	1,500	3,000	4,500
Common Stock	2,000	3,000	3,000	4,000	500
Net Income	?	1,000	500	?00	1,000

Comprehension Problem 1-4

Required: Calculate the net income earned during the year. Assume no common stock has been issued.

	Assets	Liabilities
Balance Jan. 1	$50,000	$40,000
Balance Dec. 31	40,000	20,000

Comprehension Problem 1-5

The following accounts are taken from the records of Jasper Inc. at January 31, 19X1, its first month of operations.

Cash	$13,000
Marketable Securities	20,000
Accounts Receivable	80,000
Note Receivable	2,000
Supplies	2,000
Land	25,000
Building	70,000
Equipment	30,000
Bank Loan	15,000
Accounts Payable	2,000
Mortgage Payable	25,000
Common Stock	?
Net Income	40,000

Required:
1. Calculate the amount of total assets.
2. Calculate the amount of total liabilities.
3. Calculate the amount of common stock.

Comprehension Problem 1-6

Required: Indicate whether each of the following is an asset (A), liability (L), or an equity (E) item.

1. Accounts Payable
2. Accounts Receivable
3. Bank Loan
4. Building
5. Cash
6. Common Stock
7. Loan Payable
8. Office Supplies
9. Prepaid Insurance
10. Temporary Investments

Comprehension Problem 1-7

A junior bookkeeper of Producers Inc. prepared the following financial statements at January 31, 19X1, the end of its first month of operations.

Producers Inc.
Income Statement

Revenue		$3,335
Expenses		
Accounts Payable	$ 300	
Land	1,000	
Miscellaneous Expenses	335	1,635
Retained Earnings		$1,700

Balance Sheet

Assets		Liabilities and Shareholders' Equity	
Cash	$1,000	Rent Expense	$ 300
Repair Supplies	500	Common Stock	3,000
Salaries Expense	1,000	Net Income	1,700
Building	2,500		
	$5,000		$5,000

Required: Prepare revised financial statements in good form.

Comprehension Problem 1-8

Required: From these balances, complete the following income statement and balance sheet.

Accounts Receivable	$ 4,000
Accounts Payable	5,000
Cash	1,000
Common Stock	?
Equipment	8,000
Insurance Expense	1,500
Miscellaneous Expense	2,500
Office Supplies Expense	1,000
Service Revenue	20,000
Wages Expense	9,000

Income Statement

Service Revenue		$
Expenses		
Insurance Expense	$	
Miscellaneous Expense		
Office Supplies Expense		
Wages Expense		
Net Income		$

Balance Sheet

Assets		Liabilities and Shareholders' Equity	
Cash	$	Accounts Payable	$
Accounts Receivable		Common Stock	
Equipment		Retained Earnings	
	$		$

Problems

Problem 1-1

Following are the asset, liability, and equity balances of Hick's Services Corporation at January 31, 19X1, its first month of operations.

ASSETS		=	LIABILITIES		+	EQUITY	
Cash	$1,300		Bank Loan	$8,000		Common Stock	$2,000
Accounts			Accounts			Service Revenue	7,500
Receivable	2,400		Payable	1,000		Advertising Expense	500
Prepaid						Commissions Expense	720
Insurance	550					Insurance Expense	50
Supplies	750					Interest Expense	80
Truck	9,000					Rent Expense	400
						Supplies Expense	100
						Telephone Expense	150
						Wages Expense	2,500

Required:
1. Prepare an interim income statement for the month ending January 31, 19X1 in proper form. Record the expenses in alphabetical order.
2. Prepare an interim balance sheet at January 31, 19X1 in proper form.

Problem 1-2

The following is an alphabetical list of data from the records of Jopling Services Corporation at March 31, 19X1.

Accounts Payable	$9,000		Equipment Rental Expense	$ 500
Accounts Receivable	3,900		Fees Earned	4,500
Advertising Expense	300		Insurance Expense	400
Cash	3,100		Interest Expense	100
Common Stock	2,000		Truck Expense	700
Equipment	5,000		Wages Expense	1,500

Required: Prepare an interim income statement and an interim balance sheet for March 31 in proper form. Record the expenses on the income statement in alphabetical order.

Problem 1-3

The following financial statement was prepared from the records of Densmore Reports Inc. at August 31, 19X1.

Annuity Reports Inc.
Financial Statement
At August 31, 19X1

Cash	$ 400	Accounts Payable	$ 7,800
Accounts Receivable	3,800	Common Stock	3,200
Supplies	100	Service Revenue	6,000
Equipment	8,700		
Advertising Expense	300		
Interest Expense	500		
Maintenance Expense	475		
Supplies Used	125		
Wages Expense	2,600		
	$17,000		$17,000

Required:
1. What kind of statement is this?
2. Using the above data, prepare an interim income statement and balance sheet as discussed in this chapter.

Problem 1-4

The following balances appeared on the transactions worksheet of Naro Tables Inc. on April 1, 19X1.

ASSETS				=	LIABILITY	+	EQUITY	
	Accounts	Prepaid			Accounts		Common	[+ Revenue]
Cash +	Receivable +	Rent +	Supplies =		Payable	+	Stock +	[− Expense]
$1,400	$3,600	$1,000	$350		$2,000		$4,350	

The following transactions occurred during April:
a. Collected $2,000 cash on account
b. Billed $3,000 to customers for tables rented to date
c. Paid the following expenses: advertising, $300; salaries, $2,000; telephone, $100
d. Paid half of the accounts payable
e. Received a $500 bill for April truck expenses
f. Collected $2,500 on account
g. Billed $1,500 to customers for tables rented to date
h. Transferred $500 of prepaid rent to rent expense
i. Counted $200 of supplies still on hand (recorded the amount used as an expense).

Required: Record the opening balances and the above transactions on a transactions worksheet as discussed in this chaper and calculate the total of each column at the end of April. (Use the headings above on your worksheet.)

Problem 1-5

The following transactions occurred in Hoyle Accounting Services Inc. during August 19X1, its first month of operations.

Aug. 1   Issued common shares for $3,000 cash
     1   Borrowed $10,000 cash from the bank
     1   Paid $8,000 for a used truck
     4   Paid $600 for a one-year truck insurance policy effective August 1 (recorded as Prepaid Insurance since it will benefit more than one month)
     5   Collected $2,000 fees from a client for work performed
     7   Billed $5,000 fees to clients for services performed to date
     9   Paid $250 for supplies used to date
    12   Purchased $500 supplies on account (recorded as an asset)
    15   Collected $1,000 of the amount billed August 7
    16   Paid $200 for advertising in *The News* during the first two weeks of August
    20   Paid half of the amount owing for the supplies purchased August 12
    25   Paid the following expenses: rent for August, $350; salaries, $2,150; telephone, $50; truck, $250
    28   Called clients for payment of the balance owing from August 7
    29   Billed $6,000 fees to clients for services performed to date
    31   Transferred the amount of August's truck insurance to Insurance Expense
    31   Counted $100 of supplies still on hand (recorded the amount used as an expense).

Required:
  1. Record the above transactions on a transactions worksheet, as discussed in this chapter, and calculate the total of each column at the end of August. Use the following headings on your worksheet.

ASSETS					=	LIABILITIES		+	EQUITY		
	Accounts	Prepaid				Bank	Accounts		Common		[+ Revenue]
Cash +	Receivable +	Insurance +	Supplies +	Truck =		Loan +	Payable +		Stock +		[− Expense]

  2. Prepare an interim income statement at August 31 in proper form. Identify the revenue earned as Fees Earned. Record the expenses in alphabetical order.

Problem 1-6

The following transactions took place in Casa Renovations Inc., during June 19X1, its first month of operations.

Jun. 1   Issued common stock for $8,000 cash
     1   Purchased $5,000 equipment on account
     2   Collected $600 cash for repairs completed today
     3   Paid $20 for supplies used June 2
     4   Purchased $1,000 supplies on account (recorded as an asset)
     5   Billed customers $2,500 for repairs completed to date
     8   Collected $500 of the amount billed June 5
    10   Paid half of the amount owing for equipment purchased June 1
    15   Sold excess equipment for $1,000 on account (the same amount as the original cost of this equipment)
    18   Paid for the supplies purchased June 4
    20   Received a bill for $100 for electricity used to date (recorded as Utilities Expense)
    22   Paid $600 to the landlord for June and July rent (recorded as Prepaid Rent, since it will benefit more than one month)
    23   Signed a union contract
    25   Collected $1,000 of the amount billed June 5

Jun. 27 ✓ Paid the following expenses: advertising, $150; telephone, $50; truck expense (rental, gas), $1,000; wages, $2,500
      30   Billed $2,000 for repairs completed to date
      30   Transferred the amount for June rent to Rent Expense
      30   Counted $150 of supplies still on hand (recorded the amount used as an expense).

Required:
1. Record the above transactions on a transactions worksheet and calculate the total of each column at the end of June. Use the following headings on your worksheet.

		ASSETS			=	LIABILITY	+		EQUITY	
Cash +	Accounts Receivable +	Prepaid Rent +	Supplies +	Equipment =		Accounts Payable	+	Common Stock +		+ Revenue − Expense

2. Prepare an income statement and a balance sheet for June 30 in proper form. Identify the revenue earned as Repair Revenue. Record the expenses on the income statement in alphabetical order.

Problem 1-7

Weil Boucher Limited had the following balances in its accounting equation at the end of September 30.

ASSETS		=	LIABILITIES		+	EQUITY	
Cash	$14,215		Accounts			Common Stock	?
Accounts			Payable	$ 3,750			
Receivable	11,785		Notes Payable	25,000			
Office Supplies	1,220		Income Tax				
Land	10,000 ? – 1/3		Payable	103			
Building	20,000? – 2/3						
Furniture	8,000						
Equipment	60,000						
Truck	3,210						99,577
	$? 108,430			$28,853			$?

Land and building were acquired at a cost of $30,000. It was determined that one-third of the total cost should be applied to the cost of land. The following transactions were completed during the month of October:

Oct. 2   Paid $110 on account
      3   Collected in full an account receivable of $670
      4   Purchased office supplies for $400 on account
      8   Issued additional common stock for $16,000 cash
    10   Collected $1,000 on account
    11   Purchased equipment for $22,000; made a cash payment of $2,000, the balance to be paid within 30 days
    15   Paid $400 on account
    20   Paid $10,000 in cash in partial settlement of the liability of October 11; issued a note payable for the balance
    31   Collected in full an account receivable of $300.

Required:
1. Calculate the missing figures in the September 30 accounting equation.
2. Record the September 30 balances on a transactions worksheet and record the October transactions. Total the columns. Does the accounting equation balance?

Alternate Problems

Alternate Problem 1-1

The following asset, liability, and equity accounts are taken from the transactions worksheet of Kanaan Services Corporation at December 31, 19X1, its first month of operations.

ASSETS		=	LIABILITIES		+	EQUITY	
Cash	$ 1,000		Accounts Payable	$17,000		Common Stock	$25,000
Accounts Receivable	9,000		Salaries Payable	2,000		Fees Earned	13,600
Prepaid Taxes	2,250					Advertising Expense	1,000
Land	10,000					Insurance Expense	250
Building	25,000					Property Tax Expense	200
Equipment	5,800					Salaries Expense	3,000
						Telephone Expense	100

Required:
1. Prepare an interim income statement for the month ending December 31, 19X1 in proper form. Record the expenses in alphabetical order.
2. Prepare an interim balance sheet for December 31, 19X1 in proper form.

Alternate Problem 1-2

The following is an alphabetical list of data from the records of Managerial Services Inc. at September 30, 19X1.

Accounts Payable	$2,200	Repair Revenue	$6,550
Accounts Receivable	6,000	Rent Expense	400
Advertising Expense	50	Salaries Expense	2,350
Cash	700	Supplies Expense	100
Common Stock	5,000	Telephone Expense	75
Equipment	2,000	Truck Expense	325
Maintenance Expense	250	Wages Expense	1,500

Required: Prepare an interim income statement and an interim balance sheet for September 30 in proper form. Record the expenses on the income statement in alphabetical order.

Alternate Problem 1-3

The following financial statement was prepared from the records of Cann Connections Corporation at November 30, 19X1.

Cann Connections Corporation
Financial Statement
At November 30, 19X1

Cash	$ 750	Bank Loan	$5,000
Accounts Receivable	2,200	Accounts Payable	3,000
Prepaid Insurance	550	Common Stock	1,000
Supplies	300	Repair Revenue	5,000
Equipment	6,000		
Advertising Expense	200		
Commissions Expense	1,500		
Insurance Expense	50		
Rent Expense	450		
Wages Expense	2,000		
	$14,000		$14,000

Required:
1. What kind of financial statement is this?
2. Using the above data, prepare an interim income statement and balance sheet, as discussed in this chapter.

Alternate Problem 1-4

The following amounts appeared on the transactions worksheet of Nhut Tool Rentals Inc. on May 1, 19X1.

Cash	+	Prepaid Insurance	+	Supplies	+	Equipment	+	Truck	=	Accounts Payable	+	Common Stock	+	[+ Revenue − Expense]
$1,600				$400		$3,000		$7,000		$4,000		$8,000		

ASSETS = LIABILITY + EQUITY

The following transactions occurred during May:
a. Collected $5,000 cash for tool rental during the month (Hampstead does not rent tools on account)
b. Paid $500 rent expense
c. Paid $1,500 on account
d. Paid $600 for a one-year insurance policy effective May 1 (recorded as Prepaid Insurance, since it will benefit more than one month)
e. Purchased used truck for $5,000 on account
f. Paid the following expenses: advertising, $300; salaries, $2,500; telephone, $150; truck, $550
g. Transferred the amount of May's insurance to Insurance Expense
h. Estimated $200 of supplies to have been used during May.

Required: Record the above transactions on a transactions worksheet as discussed in this chapter and calculate the total of each column at the end of May. Use the headings above on your worksheet.

Alternate Problem 1-5

Watt Contractors Corp. was incorporated on May 1, 19X1 and had the following transactions during its first month of operations.

May 1   Issued common shares for $5,000 cash
1   Paid $1,500 in advance for three months' rent: May, June, and July (recorded as Prepaid Rent, an asset)
2   Purchased $1,000-worth of supplies on account (recorded as an asset)
3   Billed a customer $1,500 for repairs performed
4   Paid $50 for an advertisement in *The News*
5   Received $250 cash for work completed today
10   Collected the amount billed on May 3
15   Paid $500 on account to a creditor
18   Borrowed $2,000 cash from the bank
20   Signed a major contract for work to be done in June
22   Purchased for cash $3,000-worth of equipment
25   Billed customers $3,500 for work completed to date
27   Paid the following expenses: electricity, $75; telephone, $25; and wages, $2,000
31   Transferred the amount of May's rent from Prepaid Rent to Rent Expense
31   Counted $200-worth of supplies still on hand; the rest had been used during May.

Required:
1. Record the above transactions on a transactions worksheet and calculate the total of each column at the end of May. Use the following headings on your worksheet.

		ASSETS			=	LIABILITY	+		EQUITY	
	Accounts	Prepaid				Bank	Accounts	Common		[+ Revenue]
Cash +	Receivable +	Rent	+ Supplies	+ Equipment =		Loan +	Payable +	Stock	+	[− Expense]

2. Prepare an interim income statement for the month of May. Identify the revenue earned as Repair Revenue. Record the expenses in alphabetical order.

Alternate Problem 1-6

Sasquatch Snow Removal Inc. was incorporated on December 1, 19X1 and had the following transactions during its first month of operations.

Dec. 1   Issued common shares for $6,000 cash
1   Purchased a used truck for $9,000: paid $4,000 cash, balance due January 15
2   Purchased on account a $2,000 snowplough to be attached to the truck (recorded as an increase in the cost of the truck)
3   Billed customers $5,000 for December snow removal (customers will always be billed at the beginning of each month)
5   Purchased on account salt, sand, and gravel for $500 (recorded as supplies)
6   Paid truck expenses of $200
7   Paid $360 for a one-year truck insurance policy effective December 1 (recorded as Prepaid Insurance)
14   Paid $1,500 in wages for two weeks
16   Paid $40 traffic ticket (recorded as Truck Expense)
20   Received a bill for $350-worth of truck expenses
24   Purchased tire chains for $100 on account (recorded as Truck Expense)
24   Collected $3,500 of the amount billed December 3
27   Paid for the purchase made on December 5
28   Collected $400 for snow removal performed today for a new customer
28   Paid $1,500 in wages for two weeks
30   Called customers owing $1,500 billed December 3

Dec. 31 Transferred the amount of December's truck insurance to Insurance Expense

Dec. 31 Counted $100-worth of salt, sand, and gravel still on hand (recorded the amount used as an expense)

Dec. 31 Recorded wages for three days applicable to December in the amount of $450 (enter amount owing in Wages Payable column).

Required:

1. Record the above transactions on a transactions worksheet and calculate the total of each column at the end of December. Use the following headings on your worksheet.

		ASSETS			=	LIABILITY	+		EQUITY		
Cash +	Accounts Receivable +	Prepaid Insurance +	Supplies +	Truck =		Accounts Payable +	Wages Payable +	Common Stock +		[+ Revenue − Expense]	

2. Prepare an income statement and a balance sheet in proper form for December 31. Identify the revenue as Service Revenue. Record the expenses in alphabetical order.

Decision Problems

Decision Problem 1-1

Hick's Services Corporation (described in Problem 1-1) and the Kanaan Services Corporation (described in Alternate Problem 1-1) are involved in similar, competing business activities. You are considering investing some money in one of these two businesses. While the Kanaan Services Corporation is larger, it appears to you that Hick's Services Corporation has more activity during business hours. Both Hick's and Kanaan have provided you with the information that was contained in Problem 1-1 and Alternate Problem 1-1. While you would want more information if you were actually investing in these corporations, base your responses solely on the information provided.

Required:

1. Comment on the financial structure of both Hick's Services Corporation and the Kanaan Services Corporation.
2. Which of the two corporations is more efficient in its business activities?
3. How much of the bank loan must Hick's Services Corporation repay each month in order to pay it back in full but remain solvent? (The payment is due on February 1, 19X1.)
4. What further information would you, as a user of financial information for investment purposes, want to be provided with?

Decision Problem 1-2

Required: Would financial reports provide equally useful information under each of the following conditions?

1. An economic depression, such as the depression in the 1930s
2. Labour negotiations
3. Double-digit inflation
4. Sharply rising real estate values in Toronto
5. A wave of mergers and takeovers.

GAAP and the Accounting Process

Accounting information is prepared and communicated in accordance with accepted practice and pronouncements by authoritative accounting bodies. The answers to the following questions are discussed in Chapter 2:

1. What is the framework of principles that has received general acceptance within the Canadian business community and accounting profession?
2. Has the accounting profession in Canada actually agreed on a definitive list of fundamentals underlying the accounting process?
3. Is the Canadian dollar a stable unit of measure? Is it the most appropriate measure for transactions and for the reporting of accounting information?
4. Financial statements are prepared on the basis of historical cost. Why is historical cost used to measure financial transactions?
5. In what way does accrual accounting match revenue with expenses?
6. When do accountants assume that revenue is earned?
7. What is the impact of conservatism and consistency in situations where a choice is made between equally defensible accounting principles?
8. What qualities is financial information expected to have?
9. How is the balance sheet classified?
10. How are accounts used in the accounting process?
11. What are the meanings of the terms *debit* and *credit*? Should they be associated with "good" and "bad" or "increase" and "decrease"?
12. How does use of debits and credits facilitate and control the accounting process?
13. What is the function of a trial balance? a general journal? a general ledger?
14. What are the sequential steps performed by the accountant in converting economic data into financial information?

A. Generally Accepted Accounting Principles

Generally accepted accounting principles (GAAP)
A set of accounting principles and practices that have become generally accepted and are used by accountants in the preparation of financial statements.

As noted in the previous chapter, financial statements are prepared according to a number of assumptions about the entity and about the environment within which the entity operates and according to a number of accounting practices. A consensus has been arrived at over the years as to how assets, liabilities, and equities should be recorded and communicated. This consensus is necessary because of the wide range of users of financial statements, most of whom are external to the firm; these include shareholders, investors, creditors, customers, unions, governments, and the general public. Within the entity itself, management needs financial statements for decision making and problem solving.

The framework of principles that has received general acceptance within the business community and accounting profession, referred to as **generally accepted accounting principles** (usually shortened to GAAP), are reviewed in detail in the following sections, and for this text's purposes are referred to as assumptions.

Generally Accepted Assumptions

Assumption 1: The Entity

Each entity is seen as an individual unit of accountability separate from the owners of the entity. Separate records are kept for the transactions of each entity; the assets and obligations of each entity are kept separate from the assets and obligations of those who own it. This assumption was introduced in Chapter 1.

As noted earlier, a corporation is a legal entity; although there are a few exceptions concerning personal guarantees and bankruptcy laws, the assets of the corporation cannot be used to pay the obligations of the owners and vice versa. No legal distinction exists, however, between the assets and obligations of a proprietorship and its owner or a partnership and its owners. In these cases, personal assets of the owner(s) may be used to pay the entity's obligations; the assets of the entity may be used to pay personal obligations of the owner(s). Nevertheless, separate records are still maintained for the entity and for its owner(s).

Assumption 2: The Going Concern

Going concern
An entity that should be able to continue to operate for the foreseeable future.

Liquidation values
The valuation of assets at the net realizable value; based on the assumption that the entity will go out of business and will sell its assets.

One of the most fundamental assumptions in financial accounting is the **going concern**, or continuity, concept. It assumes that an entity will continue to operate for an indefinite period of time without being sold or liquidated. If one assumed that a business *could* cease operations in the near future, the entity would have to pay its liabilities immediately and its assets would be undervalued when sold. This situation would not reflect the true status of the entity. The going concern concept provides the rationale for using historical cost (discussed below) as the basis for the measurement of assets since it assumes that assets will be used in the entity rather than sold at market or **liquidation values**.

The going concern assumption also provides the foundation for the periodic accounting reports that measure an entity's performance; such performance reports cannot wait to be made until the end of an entity's life, since it is assumed to be indefinite.

Assumption 3: The Measuring Unit

Accounting transactions are recorded and measured around the world in monetary terms; in Canada, they are recorded in Canadian dollars. By expressing all assets and liabilities in monetary measuring units (money), accountants create a common denominator that allows for uniform and readily understandable accounting information. Imagine a world or country that doesn't use this assumption, where everyone is allowed to choose a different unit of financial measurement. The ensuing attempt to examine and compare accounting information would be chaotic at best.

This assumption also states that the measuring unit is stable; that is, changes to the general purchasing power of the dollar (inflation or deflation) are considered insignificant enough not to warrant adjustments to financial statements.

Assumption 4: Historical Cost

Financial transactions are recorded at historical cost. This cost consists of the economic resources given up or exchanged to acquire other goods and services; it is measured in units of money.

Cost is viewed as a reasonable measure of an acquired asset because it is objectively determined, usually as a result of bargaining at arm's length. This assumption minimizes the possibility of manipulation since each party to the transaction is assumed to be free to act independently.

Financial transactions based on historical cost can be verified by documents, such as invoices, receipts for cash paid or received, cancelled cheques, cash register tapes, and sales tickets. The cost is a matter of record.

During periods of inflation, the cost of a good or service incurred in the past (or the future) will differ from the cost of an identical one incurred in the present. Therefore, it will cost a different amount to replace an asset in the future. For this reason, similar goods may be listed on accounting reports at different values if they were obtained at different costs. It is not in accordance with GAAP to alter recorded cost despite changes in current worth.

Use of historical cost is appropriate when the entity is a going concern. Its use is inappropriate in the case of a bankrupt entity, for which the use of liquidation values is necessary.

Assumption 5: Periodicity

It is assumed that an entity's business activities can be broken into reporting periods so that performance reports (financial statements) can be prepared in a meaningful way; expenses and revenues must be allocated to time periods in such a way that expenses and revenues can be properly matched. Reports can be prepared monthly, quarterly, or for any other useful time period; they must always be prepared annually. The application of this assumption is introduced in Chapter 1 with the preparation of an income statement and a balance sheet.

Assumption 6: Accrual Accounting and Matching

The measurement of net income for an accounting time period requires the matching of expenses incurred and revenue generated during that particular time period. The cost of assets transferred to customers or consumed during the period are considered as expenses; the revenue generated by these expenses is included in the income statement of the same period. Matching is accomplished through use of the accrual method of accounting, which is further illustrated in this chapter; the use of Pacioli's debit and credit methodology to control its accuracy is discussed and illustrated in section B of this chapter. The application of matching to measure net income is developed and illustrated in more detail in Chapter 3 and subsequent chapters.

Assumption 7: Revenue Recognition

Revenue recognition is concerned with establishing the point at which the revenue of the entity is earned. Although revenue has unquestionably been earned by the time the service is completed or the goods are exchanged and cash is collected, accountants generally assume that revenue is earned at an earlier point — after the service has been performed or the goods have been exchanged but before payment has been received. This point in time can be objectively determined, thereby avoiding the need for subjective estimates. In actual practice, it is convenient to recognize revenue at the point when an invoice is prepared and sent to the customer. The application of this assumption is discussed further in Chapter 3.

There are exceptions to this assumption. Revenue can sometimes be recognized before the service has been completed or the goods have been exchanged, for example, in the case of a long-term construction contract where revenue, expenses, and net income can be recognized by a method called *percentage of completion*.

Revenue can sometimes be recognized after the service has been performed or the goods have been exchanged. A typical case involves the use of the installment method, whereby revenue is recognized in proportion to the percentage of accounts receivable collected.

Although these seven assumptions are said to be generally accepted, it is important to note that the accounting profession has yet to agree on a definitive list of the fundamentals underlying the accounting process. This lack of agreement exists because of the nature of these assumptions, which

> are not derivable from physical science or natural law; they are, rather, conventions, related to certain necessarily pragmatic postulates, whose existence and validity derive from public exposure, debate, and acceptance. Generally accepted accounting principles, . . . in short, are not discovered, but declared. Their existence cannot forerun their utterance and acceptance by the profession itself.[1]

Because accounting principles are declared rather than discovered, accounting literature and practice include variations and differences, which result in some lack of precision in financial statements.

Figure 2-1 summarizes the way the seven generally accepted accounting assumptions relate to the accounting process.

ENTITY	FINANCIAL TRANSACTIONS
1. The Entity	3. The Measuring Unit
2. The Going Concern	4. Historical Cost

5. Periodicity
6. Accrual Accounting and Matching
7. Revenue Recognition

INCOME STATEMENT

BALANCE SHEET

Figure 2-1   Interrelationships of generally accepted accounting assumptions

The entity's financial transactions are recorded in accordance with these assumptions; the content of financial statements is influenced by the operating cycle concept, which identifies certain activities that are repeated regularly during the accounting time period. The sequence of activities takes the following form:

1. Operations begin with some cash on hand.
2. This cash is used to make purchases and to pay expenses.
3. Revenue is earned as goods are sold and services are performed. (An account receivable may result.)
4. Cash is collected.

Operating cycle
The cash-to-cash sequence of events for the revenue-producing operations of an entity.

This cash-to-cash sequence is referred to as the **operating cycle**. Chapter 3 discusses the impact of this operating cycle on financial statement disclosure and the identification of revenue with different time periods.

Qualities of Accounting Information

Accounting converts transactions of an entity into financial statement information. The framework of principles involved in the preparation of these statements was discussed in the preceding pages. The subsequent reporting of this financial information is intended to facilitate decision making by its users. Accordingly, it is necessary to understand what qualities this information is expected to have.

Understandability

Financial statements must present information that people with a reasonable knowledge of business activities and accounting can understand. Balance sheets, income statements, and other financial statements have standard formats so that users do not have to decipher the presentation of the material before being able to analyze the information.

Relevance

Investors, creditors, and other users of financial statements find the accounting information presented in those statements relevant if it helps them to make decisions, predict likely outcomes, and later to confirm those outcomes.

Reliability

The information that accountants provide must accurately reflect the actual financial transactions that took place. It must be free from errors, bias, and misrepresentation. Accountants follow practices such as conservatism to ensure that the information they communicate is reliable.

Conservatism

Conservatism represents the accounting profession's preference for prudence when dealing with conditions involving uncertainty and risk. When making a choice between equally defensible alternatives, the accountant chooses the alternative that will produce the least favourable result for the entity. Therefore, when estimating the useful life of Bluebeard's equipment and truck, for example, BCC's accountant should use the lowest estimate if two or more equally defensible estimates are available.

In the past, an extreme application of conservatism required the selection of an alternative that "anticipates no profit and provides for all possible losses". The intent, then, was for financial statements to avoid favourable exaggeration; an understatement of reported net income and balance sheet amounts was intended to protect users making decisions based on this information. Today, the emphasis is on the fair presentation of financial statement information; therefore, the focus is on a choice only between equally defensible alternatives. The choice of an alternative simply to produce the least favourable result is not in accordance with GAAP.

Comparability

The usefulness of financial statements is enhanced by the consistent use of accounting principles chosen from among alternatives. By applying these principles consistently, there is a uniformity in financial information produced by the entity; changes between accounting time periods can then be attributed to operations and not to changes in the selection of accounting principles. Comparability of financial statement information from one time period to another of the same entity and among different entities is thereby enhanced.

Changes in accounting principles are discouraged unless such changes improve financial statement reporting or are required because of changed conditions. Such changes must be disclosed in the financial statements; this disclosure is usually made through notes to the financial statements.

Limitations on the Disclosure of Useful Accounting Information

Financial statements are prepared and distributed at regular accounting time periods so that useful information is available for decision making. Useful information is not always reported. The accountant uses materiality to decide whether particular items of information need be disclosed. The accountant, in addition, makes a cost-benefit judgement, which also limits the disclosure of useful information.

Materiality

Some information may not be sufficiently large in amount or importance to affect the judgement of a reasonably knowledgeable user. For example, the cost of a calculator is not material when compared to the cost of Bluebeard's truck. Although both are theoretically assets until their useful lives expire, the calculator cost would never be shown as an asset in an accounting report; rather, it would be expensed when purchased.

In actual practice, no clear cut distinction can be drawn between material and immaterial amounts. Each case has to be considered on its own merits. As a matter of expediency, policies are usually established within the entity to facilitate consistent recording of certain transactions. Their subsequent disclosure is influenced by materiality.

Cost-Benefit Judgements

Useful information is not always reported if the costs associated with its preparation exceed the expected benefits. For example, the decision to prepare inflation-adjusted financial statements in addition to historical cost financial statements is influenced by cost-benefit considerations. As with materiality, individual, highly subjective judgement is required in the application of the cost-benefit decisions; accountants have developed, and use, consistent guidelines in actual practice to minimize this subjective element.

Conceptual Issue 2-1

Free Trade and Accounting

Daniel B. Thornton, Chartered Accountants'
Professor, University of Calgary

The 1988 free trade agreement between Canada and the United States did little to disrupt the day-to-day activities of professional accountants. Yet, the prospect of freer trade between the two countries caused all producers and consumers of goods and services, including accountants, to think critically about global opportunities and threats to their enterprises. This outline of accounting issues raised by free trade is meant to be evocative rather than conclusive; it is meant to foment debate rather than to provide answers to the issues.

Trade requires communication. Accounting is a language of trade. Business firms use that language in dealing with each other across international borders as well as at home. Investors use it to help decide where to allocate their scarce savings worldwide, in markets for corporate securities — i.e., in capital markets.

The syntax of accounting language is supported by the generally accepted accounting principles (GAAP) promulgated by standard-setting bodies. There are more than 40 such bodies around the world. If international traders and investors do not speak the same language, they must make a choice. Either they must translate from one trader's language to the other, or they must agree on a third language to use as a basis for their transactions. Developing countries often do the latter: they use accounting standards set down by the International Accounting Standards Committee to speak to and attract capital from the developed world.

Canada, on the other hand, has always adhered to its own standards. Though Canadian and U.S. GAAP share many common concepts, there are significant differences in how the standards deal with contingencies, earnings per share, and a host of other computations. Because of these differences, a firm operating in the United States may report a profit, while an identical one operating in Canada reports a loss. Advocates of uniquely Canadian standards have relied on rhetoric rather than logic to justify their position. They claim that Canadian culture differs from that of the United States and that distinctive accounting standards are required to reflect such differences. Can you think of one example of a significant cultural difference between the countries and precisely why it means Canada needs its own standards? Even if you can, do you think it will persist in the wake of closer cooperation between the two trading partners?

Canadian firms that raise capital in the United States willingly file financial statements, based on U.S. GAAP, with the American Securities Exchange Commission (SEC). They simultaneously publish financial statements in Canada using Canadian GAAP. If investors and creditors without easy access to SEC filings must incur the costs of translation in order to make valid comparisons between firms in the United States and Canada, the very existence of different GAAP in the two countries will be a trade barrier. The principal accounting issue raised by free trade, therefore, is whether Canadian standards will be desirable at all in the future.

If accounting standards are regarded as commodities, then they should be subject to the law of comparative advantage, just like other commodities. That is, the country with a comparative advantage in developing accounting standards should take over the standard-setting process for both countries. There can be little doubt that the United States has, by virtue of economies of scale, tremendous advantages over Canada in developing and promulgating accounting standards. Thus, a strong argument can be mounted in support of Canada's adopting the accounting standards of the United States and doing away with its own standard-setting body.

The adoption of U.S. GAAP by Canada would have several benefits besides removing a potential trade barrier. First, Canada would economize on resources used for standard setting. Canadian standard setters are volunteers whose time, now devoted to standard setting, could be productively spent serving their clients and helping them to compete more effectively internationally. Second, the rest of the world would have one less language to learn in trading with Canada and in supplying investment capital to Canada. Finally, there would be savings in educating accounting students. Existing U.S. standards are by far the most highly developed in the world. Unlike most other countries' standards, they are accompanied by reasoned arguments justifying them in preference to alternative possible standards. This makes them comparatively easy to understand, to use, and to teach. Distinctly Canadian textbooks would be unnecessary. Educators could concentrate on fundamental principles of accounting, which are applicable to any country. Educators could then use U.S. GAAP as examples of how the standards are implemented.

Free trade also raises the issue of homogeneity of professional services in the two countries. Comprehensive professional services, including auditing, tax, management advice, and personal financial planning, will be required to foster international trade and investment and the mobility of scarce managerial talent north and south. Users of these services will need to know that the standards of professional conduct and the educational backgrounds and training of accountants are equivalent in the two countries. This, too, argues for common education and training of accountants in Canada and the United States.

It is unlikely that trade between Canada and the United States will ever be completely free. There will always be subtle barriers to international trade, such as health regulations, building codes, and differential tax laws. Accounting, however, should facilitate trade, not impede it. If goods and services flow freely north and south, if technology is exchanged freely across the border, and if other ideas are generally shared between the trading partners, why should Canada continue to insist on parochial accounting standards?

Source   Courtesy of Daniel B. Thornton.

B.   Use of Accounts

The preceding chapter illustrated how accounting converts information from financial transactions into financial statements. In this conversion process, transactions are analyzed, recorded, and summarized. The process we used was a convoluted one, chosen to show how the accounting equation influences the recording of transactions. Can you imagine Canadian Pacific or any other large entity recording its millions of financial transactions during the course of a time period in this manner? In actual practice, even small entities usually use a more efficient and convenient method. The widespread use of computers has revolutionized this record-keeping and calculation process. However, a manual debit-credit methodology that is more efficient than that used in the preceding chapter is introduced in this chapter.

Account
An accounting record designed to classify and accumulate the dollar effect of financial transactions.

Each accounting transaction is recorded in, and accumulated by, an **account**. A separate account is used for each asset, liability, equity, type of revenue, and type of expense. A simplified account, called a **T-account** (because it resembles the letter T), is often used. The term **debit** is used to describe the left side of the account, the term **credit** the right side:

T-account
The form of an account that is used in accounting courses and elsewhere to illustrate the accumulation of financial information.

Debit	*Credit*
(always the left side)	(always the right side)

Debit
The left side of a T-account.

While the terms *debit* and *credit* had a specific meaning in their Latin roots and were used as recently as A.D. 1200, today the accountant uses them to mean "place an amount on the left side of an account" for debit and "place an amount on the right side of an account" for credit. Other than this, these terms have no other meaning in accounting. Students tend to associate "good" and "bad" or "increase" and "decrease" with *credit and debit*, but this is not a valid association and it should be avoided. For convenience, debit is often abbreviated as "Dr." and credit as "Cr."

Credit
The right side of a T-account.

The *type* of account determines whether a debit represents an increase or a decrease in a particular transaction or whether a credit represents an increase or a decrease.

> The pattern of recording increases and decreases is common to accounts representing *assets* and *expenses*.

This guideline can be explained using the graphic T-account.

Debit	*Credit*
(always the left side)	(always the right side)
A debit records an increase in assets and expenses.	A credit records a decrease in assets and expenses.

> The pattern of recording increases and decreases is common to accounts representing *liabilities, equity*, and *revenues*.

This guideline can be explained using the graphic T-account.

Debit (always the left side)	Credit (always the right side)
A debit records a decrease in liabilities, equity, and revenues.	A credit records an increase in liabilities, equity, and revenues.

Students often have difficulty at first with this debit-credit, increase-decrease methodology. The following summary shows how debits and credits are used to record increases and decreases in various types of accounts.

ASSETS EXPENSES	LIABILITIES EQUITY REVENUES
Increases are DEBITED. Decreases are CREDITED.	Increases are CREDITED. Decreases are DEBITED.

As you use this system over time, you'll find that the debit-credit system used in recording transactions becomes second nature. However, the summary given above is repeated on some of the following pages where transactions of Bluebeard Computer Corporation are recorded to help you become familiar with the process. Refer to it as often as you find necessary.

> Accounting converts the transactions of an entity into financial statement information. In this conversion process, transactions are analyzed and recorded, summarized, and subsequently communicated to interested individuals. The equality of debits with credits is used to control the accuracy of this process. The basic accounting model is used not only to organize the transactions but also to communicate financial statement information. Accounting is essentially an art; it is not a science.

Classification of Accounting Entries

The dual nature of accounting transactions was explained and illustrated in the preceding chapter. Transactions were first analyzed to determine the change in each item of the accounting equation as a result of each transaction. Increases and decreases were then recorded in an expanded accounting equation.

Double-entry accounting requires a separate T-account for each account. There will be accounts for Cash, Accounts Receivable, Prepaid Insurance, Equipment, Truck, Bank Loan, Accounts Payable, Unearned Rent, Common Stock, Repair Revenue, Rent Expense, Salaries Expense, Supplies Expense, Truck Expense, and other items. Each transaction of an entity affects more than one of these accounts. In fact, if a transaction affects the left side of one account, it also affects the right side of another account, and vice versa. This duality is always true of all accounting transactions, including the three types of transactions shown in Figure 2-2.

Type of Transaction	AN ASSET		=	A LIABILITY		+	EQUITY	
	Debit (increase)	*Credit* (decrease)		*Debit* (decrease)	*Credit* (increase)		*Debit* (decrease)	*Credit* (increase)
1. An increase in an asset and an increase in equity: For example, the first transaction was to deposit $11,000 in the name of the business.	11,000							11,000
2. An increase in an asset and an increase in a liability: The next transaction was the acquisition of an asset (a truck) for credit.	3,000				3,000			
3. An increase in an asset and a decrease in another asset: This transaction involved the exchange of one asset (money) for another asset (prepaid insurance).	1,200	1,200						

Figure 2-2   Double-entry accounting on T-accounts

Notice that, in each type of transaction affecting the accounts shown, a change on one side of a T-account always results in a change on the other side of an account. This dual feature of the debit-credit mechanism is common to every accounting transaction that is recorded in accounts; it is part of the double-entry model.

Although the evolution of this mechanism is uncertain, a set of rules has gradually developed to record transactions in a manner that results in an equality of debits with credits. These rules are not self-evident truths, but rather a methodology that has become generally accepted. They have to be learned before double-entry record keeping as it is practised today can be mastered.

The Classified Balance Sheet

Classified accounts
Accounts grouped on financial statements by category.

To make financial statement data easier to interpret, similar information is grouped together in categories. In other words, the data are grouped into **classified accounts**. Financial statements that classify data into categories are often referred to as *classified financial statements*.

Classifications vary in arrangement and terminology depending upon the company and the needs of users. The merchandiser's balance sheet, like that of a service entity, is prepared from amounts in the general ledger. The classification of accounts into meaningful categories is designed to facilitate the analysis of balance sheet information. Assets and liabilities are customarily classified as either current or long-term. Listed in the following sections are some of the classified accounts used by BCC.

Current Assets

Current assets Economic resources that are to be converted to cash or consumed during the next year.

Current assets are those resources that the entity expects to convert to cash or to consume during the next year or within the operating cycle of the entity. Included in this category are the following accounts, listed in order of their liquidity:

1. **Cash**, the most liquid asset, comprising Canadian dollars and coins, deposits at banks, cheques, and money orders
2. Temporary Investments, the investment of temporarily idle cash
3. Accounts Receivable that are due to be collected within one year — not as easily converted into cash as temporary investments
4. Notes Receivable, **notes** that are due to be collected within one year — not as easily converted into cash as accounts receivable
5. Merchandise Inventory (covered in Chapter 4) that is expected to be sold within one year — not as easily converted into cash as accounts or notes receivable.

Cash Anything that will be accepted by a bank for a deposit; serves as a unit of account, a medium of exchange, and a store of purchasing power. Includes cash in the bank, cash on hand, and petty cash.

The current asset category also includes accounts whose future benefits are expected to expire in a short period of time. These are not expected to be converted into cash:

Note A written promise to pay a specified amount.

6. Prepaid Expenses that will expire in the next year, usually consisting of advance payments for insurance, rent, and other similar items
7. Supplies that will be used during the next year.

For convenience, all prepaid expense and supplies accounts are grouped together into one amount on the balance sheet as Prepaid Expenses. This grouping is convenient, because the amounts are usually small and their individual disclosure would provide no meaningful information to the reader of financial statements.

Long-Term Assets

Long-term assets Assets that will be useful for more than one year; commonly referred to as *fixed assets* in Canada.

Long-term assets are commonly referred to as *fixed assets* in Canada. (We will use both terms in this text.) These assets will be useful for more than one year. With the exception of Land, however, they do wear out over time. Fixed assets are customarily listed in the inverse order of their liquidity, with Land shown first.

8. Land on which buildings have been constructed, the least liquid asset
9. Buildings used in the business
10. Equipment used in the business
11. Trucks used in the business.

The cost of depreciable assets is allocated to operations over the useful lives of the assets. The recording of depreciation expense is explained in Chapter 3.

Current Liabilities

Current liabilities Obligations that will be paid within one year or within the normal operating cycle, whichever is longer.

Current liabilities are obligations that must be paid within the next 12 months or the operating cycle of the entity. They are listed in order of their due dates, with any bank loans shown first:

1. Bank Loans that are payable on demand or due within the next fiscal year, the most current obligation
2. Accounts Payable, obligations that must be paid within a relatively short period of time
3. Accruals (often small in amount compared with accounts payable), usually grouped with accounts payable and disclosed as Accounts Payable and Accruals

4. The current portion of long-term debt, such as a partial repayment of a mortgage within the next fiscal year, listed in order of due date in relation to other current liabilities
5. Income tax liabilities, which usually follow the Accounts Payable and Accruals amount.

The current liability category also includes accounts that represent the unearned portion of amounts received from customers or obligations to provide goods or services within the next year.

Long-Term Liabilities

Long-term liabilities
Obligations that do not require repayment for one or more years.

Long-term liabilities are obligations that do not require repayment for one or more years, such as non-current loans and mortgages. Reference has been made to the next year in the distinction of assets and liabilities as either current or long term. Where the operating cycle of the entity is longer than one fiscal year — the manufacture and aging of scotch, for example — exceptions to the one-year rule are permitted.

Equity

The shareholders' equity category of the classified balance sheet consists of two major accounts: Common Stock and Retained Earnings. Equity is discussed in Chapter 9.

The following balance sheet illustrates the classification of Bluebeard Computer Corporation's accounts.

Bluebeard Computer Corporation
Balance Sheet
At December 31, 19X3

Assets			*Liabilities*		
CURRENT ASSETS			CURRENT LIABILITIES		
Cash	$ 10,800		Bank Loan — Current	$39,000	
Accounts Receivable	26,000		Accounts Payable	25,000	
Inventory	120,000		Income Tax Payable	15,000	
Prepaid Insurance	1,200				
Total Current Assets		$158,000	Total Current Liabilities		$ 79,000
FIXED ASSETS			LONG-TERM LIABILITIES		
Equipment	$ 13,600		Bank Loan — Long Term		
Accum. Depreciation	1,600		(note 1)		48,500
Total Fixed Assets		12,000			
			Total Liabilities		$127,500
			Shareholders' Equity		
			Common Stock (note 2)	$10,000	
			Retained Earnings	32,500	
			Total Shareholders' Equity		42,500
			Total Liabilities and		
Total Assets		$170,000	Shareholders' Equity		$170,000

Balance Sheet Form

Account form balance sheet
A balance sheet where the liabilities and equities are listed to the right of the assets.

Report form balance sheet
A balance sheet in which the sections for liabilities and equities are listed below those for the assets.

The balance sheet can be presented in either the **account form**, that is, with the liabilities and equities presented to the right of the assets, or in the **report form**, with the liabilities and equities presented below the assets. Both formats are acceptable; the account form seems slightly more popular in published financial statements.

Conceptual Issue 2-2

Prehistoric Accounting

Daniel B. Thornton, Chartered Accountants' Professor, University of Calgary

Most financial accounting students are introduced, however briefly, to a history of accounting. Generally, the point of departure is Luca Pacioli's description of the double-entry record keeping system published in 1494 under the title *Arithmetic, Geometry and Proportion*. Professor Richard Mattessich of the University of British Columbia recently introduced to accounting literature some startling archeological evidence. (Mattessich cites several works by Schmandt-Bessarat, most notably "The Emergence of Recording", *American Anthropologist*, vol. 84, 1984, p. 871-878.)

The evidence indicates that by 3500 BC, accountants in the Fertile Crescent of the Middle East had fully developed the three fundamental accounting concepts of *resources*, *entities*, and *control*. Moreover, they had implemented an ingenious system of double-entry accounting long before they

even knew how to count! This research illuminates accounting's rich intellectual heritage and shows us why accounting has evolved in the way that it has.

By 3500 BC, Sumerian accountants were making kiln-fired "tokens", which represented resources such as cows and wheat. Professor Mattessich interprets each different shape of token as an *account*. Suppose that Smith, a land owner, placed five cows under the care of Jones, a farmer. Jones was viewed as an accounting entity. Five cow-tokens would be deposited in a clay urn, which served as a *balance sheet*. Just before the tokens were dropped into the urn, however, they were pressed on its soft clay surface. This left visible impressions, much like those that rings make on sealing wax. The impressions, along with various other marks indicating the identities of Smith and Jones, are an early example of

C. Transactions Analysis Using Accounts

Every business is involved in the analysis and recording of financial transactions. Accountants use the debit and credit system as a shorthand to keep track efficiently of the thousands of different financial events that occur during a time period.

The use of this debit and credit shorthand can be illustrated in the recording of the January transactions of Bluebeard Computer Corporation that were first examined in section D of Chapter 1. The transactions are analyzed and recorded, then are summarized by account.

The analysis and recording process involves the use of accounting procedures; the focus, however, is on the accounting process and how GAAP are applied in the records of an entity so that useful information is made available for decision making.

Illustrative Problem — The Debit-Credit Mechanism and Use of Accounts

The January transactions for Bluebeard Computer Corporation are used to illustrate the debit-credit mechanism and use of accounts. Where each transaction is discussed, the data are accumulated in the conceptual T-accounts to the right of the text.

disclosure, because anyone observing the impressions on the outside of the urn could plainly see that Jones was operating a farm and that he owed Smith five cows.

The tokens inside the urn represented *assets* under Jones' control — i.e., debits — while the impressions on the outside represented *liabilities* to Smith (or Smith's equity in the business) — i.e., credits. The urns were sealed and placed in a temple, which was guarded by priests. Sealing exacted *control*, because no one could tamper with the information on this prehistoric balance sheet except the priests, who had no incentive to do so.

Professor Mattessich conjectures that the urns also acted as *income statements*. If Smith and Jones agreed in advance that Smith should earn a return on his investment, a sixth impression could be made on the outside of the urn, representing interest. Thus, at the end of the farming season, Jones would owe Smith an extra cow in return for the use of the five during the season.

The concept of a number per se did not exist, however. Indeed, numbers are not needed in simple systems of double-entry accounting. Observers of the urns would merely reason that "there should be a cow in Jones' field for each token in the urn, and each of these cows is owed to Smith." In this way, ancient accountants were able to track *resources* under the *control* of *entities* by matching the tokens, one for one, with resources.

Of course, modern historical cost accounting deals with much more complex transactions. Consequently, historical cost accounting introduces money as a numeraire, or common denominator in financial statements. Note, however, that every dollar on an historical cost balance sheet can (at least in principle) be traced back to an actual transaction of an accounting entity, just as in ancient times every token in an urn could be traced to a transaction. Thus, historical cost accounting serves the same purpose as the urns and tokens: it provides a basis for tracking resources under the control of entities. Any departure from pure historical cost accounting would spoil the analogy between the ancient and the modern systems and would ignore the original rationale for accounting. I believe that this explains why historical cost accounting has remained viable: it performs a function that people, five to ten thousand years ago, recognized as vital to their socioeconomic relationships.

Source Courtesy of Daniel B. Thornton.

Transaction Number	Date	Description of the Transaction	Application of Debit-Credit Methodology	
			Debit	Credit
1	Jan. 1	Issued 1000 shares of common stock for $11,000 cash	Cash	Common Stock
2	2	Purchased $3,000-worth of equipment for credit	Equipment	Accounts Payable
3	3	Purchased a repairer's truck for $8,000; paid $3,000 cash and incurred a $5,000 bank loan for the balance	Truck	Cash, Loan
4	5	Paid $1,200 for a comprehensive one-year insurance policy effective January 1	Prepaid Insurance	Cash
5	10	Paid $2,000 to a creditor in transaction 2	Accounts Payable	Cash
6	15	Received $500 as an advance payment for the rental of the truck for three months: $100 for January, $200 for February, $200 for March	Cash	Unearned Rent
7	31	Made computer repairs amounting to $7,000 for customers during the month as follows: $4,000 of repairs were made for cash, $3,000 of repairs were made for credit	Cash	Repair Revenue
8	31	Paid operating expenses for the month as follows: $600 for rent, $2,500 for salaries, $1,200 for supplies expense, $700 for truck expenses (oil, gas, etc.).	Rent Expense Salaries Expense Supplies Expense Truck Expense	Cash Cash Cash Cash

Note that the expenses in transaction 8 have been summarized as one transaction for illustrative purposes. In actual practice, each expense transaction would be recorded separately when it is incurred.

REFER TO THE FOLLOWING CHART AS YOU ANALYZE EACH TRANSACTION

ASSETS EXPENSES	LIABILITIES EQUITY REVENUES
Increases are DEBITED. Decreases are CREDITED.	Increases are CREDITED. Decreases are DEBITED.

Jan. 1 Transaction 1: Common Stock Issued for Cash

Bluebeard Computer Corporation issued 1000 shares of common stock for a total of $11,000 cash.

Analysis: This is the corporation's first transaction. The issuance of common shares results in cash being received by the corporation. An asset account, Cash, is therefore increased by this transaction.

Debit: An asset is increased by a debit.

    Debit   Cash   11,000

Cash	
Debit	*Credit*
11,000	

An equity account, Common Stock, is also increased by $11,000 from this transaction.

Credit: An equity is increased by a credit.

    Credit   Common Stock   11,000

Common Stock	
Debit	*Credit*
	11,000

Jan. 2 Transaction 2: Asset Acquired on Account (for Credit)

Equipment to be received January 30 was purchased for $3,000 on account (for credit).

Analysis: An asset is acquired and a liability incurred in this transaction. The asset Equipment is acquired here and is therefore recorded as an increase in the Equipment account.

Debit: An asset is increased by a debit.

    Debit   Equipment   3,000

Equipment	
3,000	

By the purchase of equipment, a liability is incurred and is therefore recorded as an increase.

Credit: A liability is increased by a credit.

    Credit   Accounts Payable   3,000

Accounts Payable	
	3,000

Jan. 3 Transaction 3: An Asset Purchased in Part for Cash and in Part for Credit

A truck for the repairer was purchased for $8,000; BBC paid $3,000 cash and incurred a $5,000 bank loan for the balance.

Analysis: One asset is exchanged in this transaction; an obligation to pay an asset in the future is also incurred. An asset Truck is acquired from this purchase and is therefore recorded as an increase in the Truck account.

Debit: An asset is increased by a debit.

    Debit   Truck   8,000

Truck	
8,000	

The asset Cash is decreased by the purchase of the truck.

Credit: An asset is decreased by a credit.

    Credit   Cash   3,000

Cash	
11,000	
	3,000

REFER TO THE FOLLOWING CHART AS YOU ANALYZE EACH TRANSACTION

ASSETS	LIABILITIES
EXPENSES	EQUITY
	REVENUES
Increases are DEBITED.	Increases are CREDITED.
Decreases are CREDITED.	Decreases are DEBITED.

A liability, Bank Loan, is incurred in the acquisition of the asset truck.

Credit: An obligation is increased by a credit.

   Credit Bank Loan   5,000

Bank Loan	
	5,000

Jan. 5 Transaction 4: *Asset Exchanged for Another Asset*

Bluebeard Computer Corporation paid $1,200 cash for a comprehensive one-year insurance policy, effective January 1.

Analysis: Since the one-year period will not expire by the time financial statements are prepared, the insurance cost is considered to be an asset at the payment date. The asset account, Prepaid Insurance, is increased by this transaction.

Debit: A debit records an asset increase.

   Debit Prepaid Insurance 1,200

Prepaid Insurance	
1,200	

Payment of the insurance results in a decrease in the asset account, Cash.

Credit: A credit records an asset decrease.

   Credit Cash   1,200

Cash	
11,000	3,000
	1,200

Jan. 10 Transaction 5: *A Liability Paid*

The corporation paid $2,000 on account (for credit) to a creditor in transaction 2.

Analysis: This payment decreases Accounts Payable, a liability account, because the $2,000 is due to a credit of the corporation.

Debit: A liability is decreased by a debit.

   Debit Accounts Payable 2,000

Accounts Payable	
	3,000
2,000	

The payment also decreases the asset Cash.

Credit: An asset is decreased by a credit.

   Credit Cash   2,000

Cash	
11,000	3,000
	1,200
	2,000

Jan. 15 Transaction 6: *Cash Received in Advance of Its Being Earned*

The corporation signed a contract for the use of its truck on a part-time basis and received an advance payment of $500 for use of the truck as follows: $100 for January, $200 for February, and $200 for March.

Analysis: The revenue relating to this cash receipt will not be earned by the end of the current accounting period. Therefore, it is considered to be a payment received in advance of its being earned. An asset account, Cash, is increased at the time the contract is signed.

Debit: A debit records an asset increase.

   Debit Cash   500

Cash	
11,000	3,000
500	1,200
	2,000

REFER TO THE FOLLOWING CHART AS YOU ANALYZE EACH TRANSACTION

ASSETS EXPENSES	LIABILITIES EQUITY REVENUES
Increases are DEBITED. Decreases are CREDITED.	Increases are CREDITED. Decreases are DEBITED.

A liability account, Unearned Rent, is increased by this transaction.

Credit: A credit records a liability increase.

    Credit   Unearned Rent   500

Unearned Rent

	500

Jan. 31 Transaction 7: *Revenue Results in an Inflow of Assets*

A total of $7,000-worth of computer repairs were made for customers by the corporation during its first month of business activities.

Analysis: An analysis of these revenue-creating activities reveals that the company earned $4,000 from cash customers and also earned $3,000 for repairs made on account. These revenue activities increase two asset accounts: the asset Cash is increased by $4,000 and the asset Accounts Receivable is increased by $3,000.

Debit: Both of these assets are increased by a debit.

    Debit   Cash   4,000
    Debit   Accounts Receivable 3,000

Cash

11,000	3,000
500	1,200
4,000	2,000

Accounts Receivable

3,000	

The total revenue earned during the month is $7,000 and this increases revenue of the corporation.

Credit: An increase of revenue is recorded by a credit.

    Credit   Repair Revenue   7,000

Repair Revenue

	7,000

Jan. 31 Transaction 8: *Expenses Result in an Outflow of Assets*

Operating expenses were incurred and paid during the month to earn the repair revenue described in transaction 7. These expenses consist of rent, $600; salaries expense, $2,500; supplies expense, $1,200; and truck expense, $700 (for oil, gas, etc.).

Analysis: These expenses, summarized here as one transaction for illustrative purposes, are recorded as increases.

Debit: Expenses are increased by a debit.

    Debit   Rent Expense   600
    Debit   Salaries Expense   2,500
    Debit   Supplies Expense   1,200
    Debit   Truck Expense   700

Rent Expense

600	

Salaries Expense

2,500	

Supplies Expense

1,200	

Truck Expense

700	

Note that each expense is recorded in a separate expense account. Each type of expense is always recorded in its own individual T-account. The total payment of these expenses amounts to $5,000 ($600 + $2,500 + $1,200 + $700) and since they have been paid in cash, the Cash account, an asset account, is decreased by $5,000.

Credit: An asset is decreased by a credit.

    Credit   Cash   5,000

Cash

11,000	3,000
500	1,200
4,000	2,000
	5,000

Because the expenses have been summarized here as one transaction for illustrative purposes, the total payment is also summarized. In actual practice, each paid expense would be recorded individually by a debit to the appropriate expense account and a credit to Cash. Since the transactions are summarized here, only one credit of $5,000 is made to Cash.

Trial Balance Preparation

Footing
The totalling of a
column of figures

After the January transactions of the Bluebeard Computer Corporation have been analyzed and recorded, the amounts are transferred to T-accounts in a process called *posting*. At month-end, these T-accounts are totalled in a process called **footing**, as shown in the following diagram. Each account with more than one transaction on the debit or credit side is totalled and the difference between the debit balance and the credit balance is calculated. In the case of the Cash account in the diagram, the balance of $5,000 is called a *debit balance*. In the following T-accounts, the numbers in parenthesis refer to the transaction numbers used in the preceding pages; the date of the transaction generally would be inserted here.

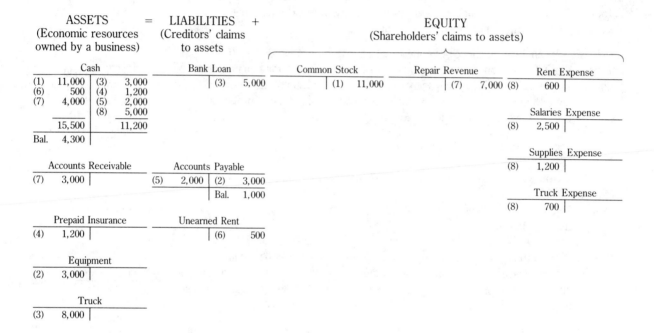

Trial balance
A list of each account
together with its
individual debit or
credit balance; used
to establish the equality
of debits with credits
before the preparation
of financial statements.

A **trial balance** lists and totals all the debit and credit account balances in a two-column schedule. It is prepared after all transactions for the accounting period (January in this case) have been recorded in appropriate accounts. The end of the month is the usual time for trial balance preparation, although it can be prepared any time that the mathematical accuracy of the T-account balances needs to be checked.

The form and content of a trial balance is illustrated below, using the account labels and account balances of Bluebeard Computer Corporation:

Bluebeard Computer Corporation
Trial Balance
January 31, 19X1

	Account Balances	
	Debit	*Credit*
Cash	$ 4,300	
Accounts Receivable	3,000	
Prepaid Insurance	1,200	
Equipment	3,000	
Truck	8,000	
Bank Loan		$ 5,000
Accounts Payable		1,000
Unearned Rent		500
Common Stock		11,000
Repair Revenue		7,000
Rent Expense	600	
Salaries Expense	2,500	
Supplies Expense	1,200	
Truck Expense	700	
	$24,500	$24,500
	Total	Total
	Debits =	Credits

These accounts are used to prepare the Income Statement.

Since a double-entry system has been used in recording the transactions of Bluebeard Computer Corporation, the total of debit account balances must equal the total of credit account balances. The trial balance establishes that this equality actually exists, but it does not ensure that each item has been entered in the proper account. Neither does it ensure that all items that should have been entered have in fact been entered. Both of these errors could occur and the trial balance would still balance. In addition, a transaction may be recorded twice. Nevertheless, a trial balance is prepared before the financial statements are begun.

Preparation of Financial Statements

An interim income statement is a statement to be prepared before the entity's year-end from the Revenue and Expense accounts listed in the trial balance.

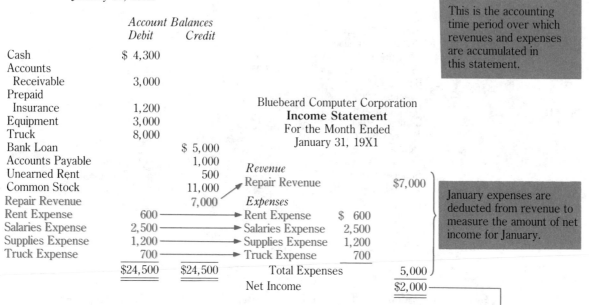

Bluebeard Computer Corporation
Trial Balance
January 31, 19X1

	Account Balances	
	Debit	*Credit*
Cash	$ 4,300	
Accounts Receivable	3,000	
Prepaid Insurance	1,200	
Equipment	3,000	
Truck	8,000	
Bank Loan		$ 5,000
Accounts Payable		1,000
Unearned Rent		500
Common Stock		11,000
Repair Revenue		7,000
Rent Expense	600	
Salaries Expense	2,500	
Supplies Expense	1,200	
Truck Expense	700	
	$24,500	$24,500

> This is the accounting time period over which revenues and expenses are accumulated in this statement.

Bluebeard Computer Corporation
Income Statement
For the Month Ended
January 31, 19X1

Revenue		
Repair Revenue		$7,000
Expenses		
Rent Expense	$ 600	
Salaries Expense	2,500	
Supplies Expense	1,200	
Truck Expense	700	
Total Expenses		5,000
Net Income		$2,000

> January expenses are deducted from revenue to measure the amount of net income for January.

The interim balance sheet is prepared next. The assets, liabilities, and equities belong in the balance sheet.

Bluebeard Computer Corporation
Trial Balance
January 31, 19X1

	Account Balances	
	Debit	*Credit*
Cash	$ 4,300	
Accounts Receivable	3,000	
Prepaid Insurance	1,200	
Equipment	3,000	
Truck	8,000	
Bank Loan		$ 5,000
Accounts Payable		1,000
Unearned Rent		500
Common Stock		11,000
Repair Revenue		7,000
Rent Expense	600	
Salaries Expense	2,500	
Supplies Expense	1,200	
Truck Expense	700	
	$24,500	$24,500

Bluebeard Computer Corporation
Balance Sheet
January 31, 19X1

> This is the date at which this statement reflects assets, liabilities and equity.

Assets		
Cash		$ 4,300
Accounts Receivable		$ 3,000
Prepaid Insurance		1,200
Equipment		3,000
Truck		8,000
Total Assets		$19,500
Liabilities		
Bank Loan	$ 5,000	
Accounts Payable	1,000	
Unearned Rent	500	$ 6,500
Equity		
Common Stock	$11,000	
Net Income	2,000	13,000
Total Liabilities and Equity		$19,500

Note that the actual format of the balance sheet can vary. Two commonly used formats are the *account form* and the *report form*. They are illustrated below so that you can compare them. The same information is conveyed by both formats.

Balance Sheet Formats

Account Form				Report Form	
Assets	$xxx	*Liabilities*	$ xx	*Assets*	$xxx
		Equity	x		
	$xxx		$xxx		$xxx
				Liabilities	$ xx
				Equity	x
					$xxx

Assets appear on the left side, and liabilities and equity appear on the right side when the account form is used.

Assets are presented first, with liability and equity items following when the report form is used.

D. Using Formal Accounting Records

$A = L + E$
$6500 + 11000$ 17500

General journal
A chronological record of an entity's financial transactions; often referred to as a *book of original entry*.

Journalizing
The process of recording a transaction in a journal.

Journal entry
An entry recorded in the general journal with at least one debit and one credit.

General ledger
A book that contains the asset, liability, equity, revenue, and expense accounts of an entity; often referred to as a *book of final entry*.

Posting
The process of transferring amounts from the journal to a ledger account.

The preceding analysis of financial transactions included a debit and credit entry for each transaction as well as the accumulation of dollar amounts in T-accounts. Formal accounting records are kept in a general journal and general ledger.

A **general journal** is a ruled form used to record chronologically the debit and credit analysis of the entity's financial transactions (see Figure 2-3). It is often referred to as a book of original entry. **Journalizing** is the process of recording a financial transaction (called a **journal entry**) in the journal. In addition to a general journal, formal accounting records also include specialized journals.

A **general ledger** is a ruled form used to maintain all the accounts of the entity in one place. **Posting** is the process of transferring amounts from the journal to a ledger account. Because amounts recorded in the journal eventually end up in a ledger account, the general ledger is sometimes referred to as a book of final entry.

Recording Transactions in the General Journal

A general journal provides a complete record of transactions in chronological order in one place. Each transaction is recorded first in the journal. The January transactions of Bluebeard Computer Corporation are recorded in its general journal in Figure 2-3. The journalizing procedure follows a number of steps:

1. The year is recorded at the top and the month is entered on the first line of page 1. This information is repeated only on each new journal page used to record transactions.
2. The date of the first transaction is entered in the second column, on the first line. The day of each transaction is always recorded in this second column.
3. The name of the account to be debited is entered in the description column on the first line. Accounts to be debited are always recorded before accounts to be credited. The amount of the debit is recorded in the debit column. A dash is often used by accountants in place of .00 cents.

The positioning of the debit-credit entry is smilar in some respects to a programming language. This entry instructs:

Post $11,000 to the debit side of the Cash account (increasing cash by $11,000), and

Post $11,000 to the credit side of the Common Stock account (increasing this equity by $11,000).

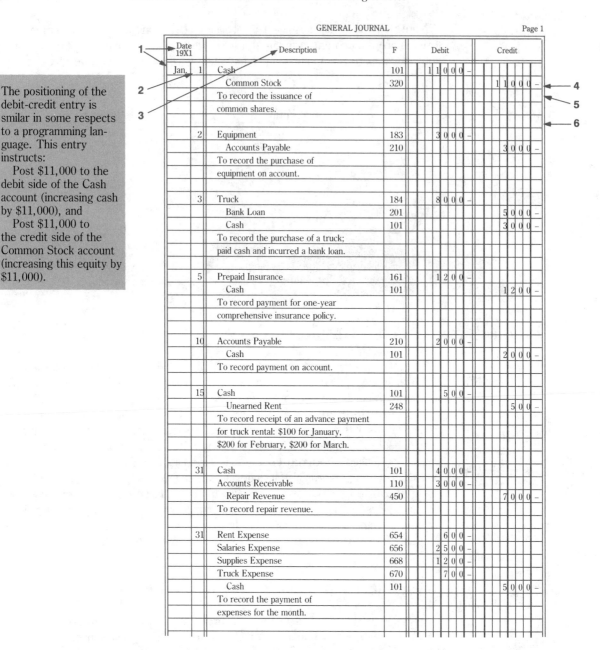

GENERAL JOURNAL   Page 1

Date 19X1		Description	F	Debit	Credit
Jan.	1	Cash	101	1 1 0 0 0 –	
		Common Stock	320		1 1 0 0 0 –
		To record the issuance of			
		common shares.			
	2	Equipment	183	3 0 0 0 –	
		Accounts Payable	210		3 0 0 0 –
		To record the purchase of			
		equipment on account.			
	3	Truck	184	8 0 0 0 –	
		Bank Loan	201		5 0 0 0 –
		Cash	101		3 0 0 0 –
		To record the purchase of a truck;			
		paid cash and incurred a bank loan.			
	5	Prepaid Insurance	161	1 2 0 0 –	
		Cash	101		1 2 0 0 –
		To record payment for one-year			
		comprehensive insurance policy.			
	10	Accounts Payable	210	2 0 0 0 –	
		Cash	101		2 0 0 0 –
		To record payment on account.			
	15	Cash	101	5 0 0 –	
		Unearned Rent	248		5 0 0 –
		To record receipt of an advance payment			
		for truck rental: $100 for January,			
		$200 for February, $200 for March.			
	31	Cash	101	4 0 0 0 –	
		Accounts Receivable	110	3 0 0 0 –	
		Repair Revenue	450		7 0 0 0 –
		To record repair revenue.			
	31	Rent Expense	654	6 0 0 –	
		Salaries Expense	656	2 5 0 0 –	
		Supplies Expense	668	1 2 0 0 –	
		Truck Expense	670	7 0 0 –	
		Cash	101		5 0 0 0 –
		To record the payment of			
		expenses for the month.			

Figure 2-3   General journal transactions for BCC in January

4. The name of the account to be credited is on the second line of the description column and is indented about one-quarter inch into the column. Accounts to be credited are always indented in this way in the journal. The amount of the credit is recorded in the credit column. Again, a dash is used in place of .00 cents.

5. An explanation of the transaction, usually referred to as a journal entry narrative, is entered also in the description column, on the next line. It is not indented.

6. A line is usually skipped after each journal entry to separate individual journal entries and the date of the next entry recorded. It is unnecessary to repeat the month (January here) if it is unchanged from that recorded at the top of the page.

BCC's first two journal entries have one debit and credit. An entry can also have more than one debit or credit, in which case it is referred to as a *compound entry*. The entry of January 3 is an example of a compound entry.

Posting Transactions to the Ledger

Ledger account
An account kept in a book called a ledger.

The **ledger account** is a more formal variation of the T-account and is used by companies with a manual accounting system. Ledger accounts are kept in the general ledger, often a loose-leaf binder. Debits and credits recorded in the general journal are posted to appropriate ledger accounts so that the balance of each account can be found easily at any time. The posting of amounts and recording of other information is illustrated in Figure 2-4, using the first transaction of Bluebeard Computer Corporation.

The journal connects the transaction with the ledger.

The ledger is a device to classify and store transactions.

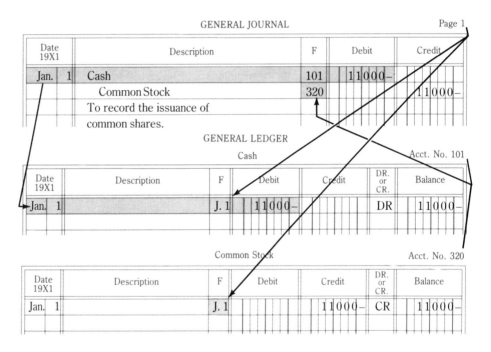

Figure 2-4   A transaction posted in general ledger

1. The date and amount are posted to the appropriate ledger account. Here the debit Cash entry is posted to the Cash ledger account and the credit Common Stock entry to the Common Stock ledger account.
2. The journal page number is recorded in the folio (F) column of each ledger account as a cross reference. In this case, the posting has been made from journal page 1; the reference is recorded as J.1.

3. The appropriate ledger account number is recorded in the folio (F) column of the general journal to indicate the posting has been made to that particular account. Here the debit Cash entry has been posted to Account No. 101 and the credit Common Stock entry to Account No. 320.

Following the posting process, a balance is calculated for each ledger account. A notation is recorded in the Dr./Cr. column of the general ledger indicating whether the balance in the account is a debit or credit. This manual posting is a slow process. Many accounting departments, especially in large companies, use specially designed mechanical equipment where the volume of transactions justifies their use. More recently, computers have replaced most of these posting machines, since the accumulation of debit and credit amounts by account is most efficiently performed by a computer.

In this and subsequent chapters, either the conceptual T-account or the more formal three-column ledger account can be used in completing assignment material. Both types of accounts are used in subsequent chapters, although your instructor may prefer the use of one or the other.

Chart of Accounts

Chart of accounts
A list of account names and numbers used in the general ledger; usually found in the order they are presented on the financial statements.

The ledger accounts used by an entity are always organized using a **chart of accounts**. Typically, accounts are grouped within asset, liability, equity, revenue, and expense classifications; a number is assigned to each account to be used by the entity. Flexibility exists in the chart of accounts through the inclusion of gaps in the numerical sequence, so that other accounts can be added. Here is the chart of accounts for Bluebeard Computer Corporation, which is used in the assignment material and throughout the text. **It is for illustrative purposes only.**

Chart of Accounts

100–199 *Current Assets*	242 Unearned Commissions
100 Petty Cash	244 Unearned Fees
101 Cash	246 Unearned Interest
106 Temporary Investments	247 Unearned Repair Revenue
110 Accounts Receivable	248 Unearned Rent
111 Allowance for Doubtful Accounts	249 Unearned Revenue
116 Interest Receivable	250 Unearned Subscriptions
120 Notes Receivable	260 Income Tax Payable
150 Merchandise Inventory	
160 Prepaid Advertising	*Long-Term Liabilities*
161 Prepaid Insurance	271 Bank Loan — Long-Term
162 Prepaid Rent	272 Bonds Payable — Long-Term
170 Office Supplies	275 Mortgage Payable — Long-Term
171 Repair Supplies	280 Notes Payable — Long-Term
172 Service Supplies	
173 Supplies	

Fixed Assets
180 Land
181 Building
182 Furniture
183 Equipment
184 Trucks
191 Accumulated Depreciation — Building
192 Accumulated Depreciation — Furniture
193 Accumulated Depreciation — Equipment
194 Accumulated Depreciation — Truck

300–399 *Shareholder's Equity*
320 Common Stock
340 Retained Earnings
350 Dividends
360 Income Summary

400–499 *Revenue*
410 Commissions Earned
420 Fees Earned
430 Interest Earned
440 Rent Earned
450 Repair Revenue
460 Revenue (for other types not identified within the revenue category)
470 Service Revenue
480 Subscription Revenue

200–299 *Current Liabilities*
201 Bank Loan — Current
210 Accounts Payable
214 Loans Payable
215 Mortgage Payable — Current
220 Notes Payable — Current
221 Dividends Payable
222 Interest Payable
226 Salaries Payable
231 Property Tax Payable
236 Utilities Payable
237 Wages Payable
240 Unearned Advertising

500–549 *Sales Accounts*
500 Sales
508 Sales Returns and Allowances
509 Sales Discounts

550–599 *Purchases Accounts*
550 Purchases
558 Purchases Returns and Allowances
559 Purchases Discounts
560 Transportation In

600–699 *Expenses*
610 Advertising Expense
613 Bad Debt Expense
615 Commissions Expense
620 Delivery Expense
621 Depreciation Expense — Building
622 Depreciation Expense — Furniture
623 Depreciation Expense — Equipment
624 Depreciation Expense — Truck
630 Equipment Rental Expense
631 Insurance Expense
632 Interest Expense
641 Maintenance Expense
650 Office Supplies Expense
651 Property Tax Expense
652 Miscellaneous General Expense
653 Miscellaneous Selling Expense
654 Rent Expense
655 Repair Supplies Expense
656 Salaries Expense
657 Salespersons' Salaries Expense
668 Supplies Expense
669 Telephone Expense
670 Truck Expense
676 Utilities Expense
677 Wages Expense

700–749 *Other Gains and Revenues*
732 Interest Income

750–799 *Other Losses and Expenses*
760 Loss on Sale of Equipment

800–899 *Other Accounts*
830 Income Tax Expense

A common practice is to have the accounts arranged in a manner that is compatible with the order of their use in financial statements. Although it is not a rigid rule to number accounts in this manner, it does have considerable advantages and is recommended in this text. (List accounts in the above sequence when completing assignment material for this text that requires the preparation of financial statements. The above accounts and account numbers are applicable to all the assignment material in this and the following chapters.)

The Accounting Cycle

In the preceding pages, the January transactions of Bluebeard Computer Corporation were used to demonstrate the sequential steps performed by the accountant in converting economic data into financial information. This conversion was carried out in accordance with the basic double-entry accounting model. These sequential steps can be visually summarized as follows:

Step 1: Transactions are analyzed and recorded.
Journalizing consists of analyzing transactions as they occur, to see how they affect the accounting equation, and then recording the transactions chronologically in the general journal.

Step 2: Transactions are summarized by account.
Posting consists of transferring debits and credits from the general journal to the appropriate ledger accounts.

Step 3: The equality of debits with credits is established to ensure accuracy.
Preparing a trial balance consists of listing account names and balances to prove the equality of total debit balances with total credit balances.

Step 4: The summarized transactions are communicated.
Preparing financial statements at this point consists of using the data listed in the columns of the trial balance to prepare the income statement and the balance sheet.

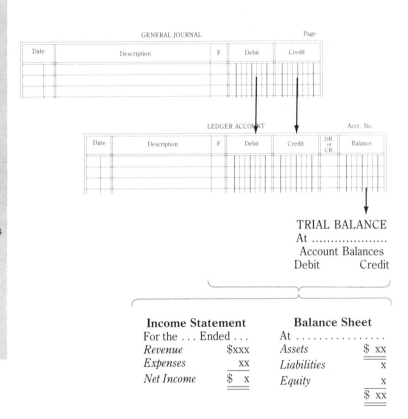

Accounting cycle
The individual steps required to process accounting information during an accounting period.

The sequence just described, beginning with the journalizing of the transactions and ending with the communication of financial information in financial statements, is commonly referred to as the **accounting cycle**. Although the number of steps is expanded somewhat in Chapter 3, the basic sequence is not changed; these additional steps are needed because of the large number of transactions facing the modern corporation and the special accounting procedures needed for the artificial time periods within which financial information is communicated.

A S S I G N M E N T   M A T E R I A L S

Discussion Questions

1. What are generally accepted accounting principles (GAAP)?
2. What is the recognition concept?
3. How does the matching concept attempt to determine accurately the income of a business?
4. What are the qualities that accounting information is expected to have?
5. Why is the use of a transactions worksheet impractical in actual practice?
6. What is an account? How are debits and credits used to record transactions?
7. Students tend to associate "good" and "bad" or "increase" and "decrease" with credits and debits. Is this a valid association? Explain.
8. The pattern of recording increases and decreases is common to asset and expense accounts. Explain, using an example.
9. The pattern of recording increases and decreases is common to liabilities, equity, and revenues. Explain, using an example.
10. Summarize the rules for using debits and credits to record assets, expenses, liabilities, equity, and revenues.
11. Define accounting.
12. Is accounting an art or a science?
13. What categories of assets and liabilities are indicated on a classified balance sheet?
14. What is a trial balance? Why is it prepared?
15. How is a trial balance used to prepare financial statements?
16. A general journal is often called a book of original entry. Why?
17. The positioning of a debit-credit entry in the general journal is similar in some respects to programming methods. Explain, using an example.
18. What is a ledger? Why is it prepared?
19. What is a chart of accounts? What is the advantage of arranging the accounts in a manner that is compatible with the order of their use in financial statements?
20. List the steps in the accounting cycle.
21. Refer to Discussion Case 1-2 in Chapter 1. Accountants refer to GAAP when valuing assets shown on a balance sheet. Identify the accounting principles that relate directly to Sir Rodolph and explain the application of each principle in Sir Rodolph's cases.

Discussion Cases

Discussion Case 2-1:   Massey Combines Corp.

Massey Combines Corp. never had a chance.

It was born in 1985 into a dying industry, $200-million in debt. Competition was cutthroat and potential customers around the world were struggling through their worst financial conditions since the Great Depression.

The company's greatest asset was its famous name, the symbol of Canada around the world for nearly a century. But even that name had been sullied by years of financial problems, endless bailouts and the omnipresent threat of a total collapse.

Many of Massey Combines' competitors have failed since the industry turned sour in 1981, and their names are as famous as that of Massey.

There was International Harvester Co., which brought the industrial revolution to rural America. There was White Farm Equipment Ltd., a partner to Massey in Brantford,

Ont., since the 1880s, and Versatile Corp., Steiger Tractor Inc., Sperry-New Holland and Allis Chalmers Corp.

"The list is as long as your arm," Mr. Porter said. "We suffered through the worst decade in the history of the industry, and the market just kept on getting worse."

When the markets do eventually turn up, Canadian farmers will have no option but to import their most basic equipment from foreign plants owned by foreign manufacturers.

The industry's best year was 1981. Nearly 30,000 combines were sold across North America that year, even though doomsayers were already warning the market would crash.

They were right. In 1982, sales fell by a half and then they fell by half again. By 1987, sales were only 8,700 units, and the Canadian Farm and Industrial Equipment Institute was predicting another drop to 8,470 in 1988.

Declining Combine Sales

Year	U.S.	Canada	Total
1980	15,719	4,115	19,834
1981	24,909	5,043	29,952
1982	13,943	3,541	17,484
1983	12,755	2,922	15,677
1984	10,537	2,721	13,258
1985	7,488	2,838	10,326
1986	7,164	2,818	9,982
1987	7,184	1,517	8,701
1988	6,890	1,580	8,470

The root problem is the much-publicized collapse in the world price of grain. Thousands of North American farmers have gone bankrupt since 1981, and the survivors are in no mood to buy a $150,000 gas-guzzling machine they can manage without.

Faced with such bleak markets, combine manufacturers did all they could to stay alive. They discounted prices by more than half, closed plants and laid off staff.

The Massey group was typical of the industry. It closed every manufacturing plant in North America, dismembered an international empire that operated in more than 100 countries, and retrenched to a handful of plants in Britain, France and Italy.

In the process, staff was cut to 16,500 from 68,000.

Virtually every other company went through similar struggles.

Given such conditions, many in the industry were surprised Massey survived as long as it did.

Certainly, the lenders and governments took a good hard look at the company when they agreed to the restructuring of Massey-Ferguson Ltd. in 1985 and the subsequent creation of the two divisions, Massey Combines Corp. and Varity Corp.

Mr. Porter said the lenders prepared detailed market forecasts that showed "assuming the market didn't get any worse, that Massey was structured in such a way that it would survive and eventually prosper.

"But instead of getting better, the markets got a damn sight worse."

Robert White, president of the Canadian Auto Workers, was more critical of the restructuring agreement. "The way it was restructured, there would have to be a miracle for them to save it, and the miracle never came."

Since the collapse of the company, union officials and former employees have claimed Varity stripped assets, inflated the value of collateral and under-financed the employees' pension plan in order to save itself. The company denies these allegations, and the issue will not be settled until receiver Peat Marwick Ltd. goes through the books in coming weeks.

Peat Marwick is responsible for the future of Massey Combines and it is aware the outlook is bleak.

To start with, Massey has been staggering since its formation in 1985, and the parent was in trouble for many years before that.

The staff tried desperately to keep Massey open until May 8, 1988, when $25-million of pension obligations would be removed. But it couldn't last that long before National Trust Co. and several other lenders pulled the plug.

When it was placed in receivership earlier this month, Gary Colter, receiver for Peat Marwick, estimated Massey's assets at about $200-million, and the liabilities at about $290-million.

The physical assets have some potential, Mr. Porter said. They comprise three modern buildings in Brantford, lots of metal-working machinery, some modern technology and lots of rusting combines.

Given these assets, the receiver has only a handful of alternatives and none of them are particularly promising.

For one, Massey could be sold to another farm equipment company, either in its entirety or in parts.

"Any one of the remaining companies could fill the entire world market from his own plant," Mr. Porter said. "There's still too much overcapacity in the industry."

Source Oliver Bertin, "Famous Name Not Enough To Save Massey", *The Globe and Mail*, Toronto, May 12, 1988, p.B-1.

For Discussion

1. Is Massey still considered an entity? Why or why not?
2. Explain why Massey can no longer be referred to as a going concern, particularly when every entity is assumed to have an unlimited life.
3. Are the cost amounts shown in Massey's financial statements relevant at this point? Why or why not?
4. Is cost (the amount paid by Massey) an appropriate measure to be used by purchasers of Massey's assets? Should purchasers continue to use the cost recorded in Massey's records since the assets are the same and accountants try to be consistent?
5. What does it mean that the accounting firm of Peat Marwick is responsible for the future of Massey?
6. The article states the Peat Marwick estimates Massey's assets at $200 million and its liabilities at about $290 million. On what basis is the $200 million estimate made? Who will absorb the difference of $90 million? What do the shareholders get?
7. When Massey's assets are put up for sale, which method would result in a larger price: sale as a viable entity or sale piece by piece.

Discussion Case 2-2:   Laser International Composites Inc.

The wind has gone out of the sails of a major Canadian boat-building company; Laser International Composites Inc. of Hawkesbury, Ont., is in receivership.

Officials of receiver Peat Marwick spent yesterday with Laser representatives, trying to package the $6-million-a-year business in a way to attract new owners.

The company, which manufactures a one-person sailboat known and raced the world over, is about $2-million in debt, according to Peat Marwick spokesman Richard Harris.

"The company was very highly leveraged," Mr. Harris said.

He added that it is difficult to blame any one factor for the receivership, but noted there are no problems with the company's main product, a 14-foot dinghy that has been in production since 1971. More than 130,000 Lasers have been sold since that time in 72 countries around the world.

A tired-sounding founder, Ian Bruce, said yesterday there is only a small inventory at present at the Hawkesbury plant — about 80 or 90 boats — and that manufacturing has stopped for the time being.

The plant makes boats for the Canadian, U.S. and Caribbean markets. The boats are made under licence in nine countries around the world.

"I have to take my share of the blame for not attracting the right person to the [financing side of the] job," he said.

Mr. Bruce, who acknowledges he is neither an administrator nor a finance man, is an industrial designer with a passion for sailing who formed the company in 1971. He left it but returned in 1983 after it had gone into receivership for the first time.

He said his troubles came to a head last June, when it became clear that the company could not attract new financing in a soft sailboat market. In the past five years, sailboats have dropped to 11 per cent from 68 per cent of the recreational boating market in Canada, Mr. Bruce said.

Private financing arranged for October, 1987, did not come through in the wake of the stock market collapse.

"We were unable to continue under the constraints of the Royal Bank," he said.

One of Laser's main creditors is the Eastern Ontario Development Corp., a provincial government agency that gave Laser a $300,000 loan in 1984.

Six months ago, the company had 100 employees. Only 35 are left, all of whom have been laid off.

Bruce Kirby, who designed Canada 1 and Canada 2 for the America's Cup challenges, designed the Laser and receives royalties for each sale.

The company made a mistake trying to diversify into a bigger cruising boat, the Laser 28, and motor boats, Mr. Kirby said.

"It was too expensive to tool up for and they didn't sell many," he said.

He said he also felt the drag of the Laser 28 and other products forced the company to charge more for the smaller boat than it should have.

"My little boat has financed the foibles of that company," he said.

The Laser sells for about $2,695 in Canada.

Susan Rogers, manager of Fogh Marine Ltd., in Toronto, the biggest Laser dealer in North America, said all her Laser customers will get their boats.

"It's more popular than ever. It's a Visa purchase," she said.

Ms Rogers said she is optimistic about the company because the product is high-quality and the market has not softened for small boats.

Several groups are interested in the company, Mr. Harris said, including some foreign interests.

Laser is not the only big boat-builder to experience difficulties recently.

C&C Yachts Ltd. of Niagara-on-the-Lake, Ont., went into receivership three years ago and was bought for $9-million by Brian Rose.

Mr. Rose relinquished his control of the company last year, according to C&C spokesman Doug Smith. A new numbered company under general manager Robert Stuebing now runs the show.

"I hope we're going to be more than survivors," Mr. Smith said yesterday.

Tanzer Industries Inc. of Dorion, Que., also has gone into receivership.

Source   Vivian Smith, "Receiver Takes Over at Laser; Boatbuilder's Debt Is $2 Million", *The Globe and Mail*, Toronto, February 28, 1989, p.B-4

For Discussion

1. Mr. Bruce, founder of Laser, is quoted as saying that "I have to take my share of the blame for not attracting the right person to the [financing side of the] job." What does this statement mean? How could someone on the financing side have helped avoid the problems that Laser is currently facing?

2. What financing was the company unable to attract? Why couldn't they make do with the financing they had?

3. What role did the Laser 28 play in Laser's current difficulties?

4. Is Laser a going concern at this point?

5. Would you recommend that a friend of yours invest in this business? Why or why not?

Discussion Case 2-3:   Transport Route Canada Inc.

A trucking company that Canadian National Railways sold in 1986 for $29-million had a portfolio of real estate with a value of at least $54-million at the time, a bankruptcy hearing has been told.

The valuation as reported by trustee Deloitte Haskins & Sells Ltd. is much higher than the $34-million cited as the properties' worth by the Conservative government when the sale was questioned in the House of Commons.

Through an order-in-council, Crown-owned Canadian National sold money-losing Transport Route Canada Inc. to three Toronto investors — brothers David and Paul Fingold and Manfred Ruhland. Aside from the real estate, other assets were estimated to be worth $17-million.

The three investors had limited experience in trucking, and within 30 days had set up a second company, Route Canada Real Estate Inc., to hold the land. That move, the trustees in the bankruptcy case said, drained the trucker of its assets and working capital.

"On its 1987 income tax filings, TRCI reported the fair market value at the time of the transfer to be approximately $54-million," said Deloitte Haskins & Sells.

Opposition critics have said that the land — much of it in areas suited for development — has a current market value of about $80-million, and that the investors have mortgaged almost the full amount.

They also say the federal government allowed the buyers to strip the company of assets.

Transport Route was officially deemed bankrupt at the hearing of creditors yesterday, and the trustees said about 4,000 creditors have virtually no chance of being paid. Even the bills for the trustees' services will not be covered.

The bankrupt company has marketable assets valued at $27-million and liabilities estimated conservatively at $84-million.

Union officials representing Transport Route workers told the bankruptcy hearing that many of their members have declared personal bankruptcy and are on welfare because the company had not paid unemployment insurance premiums that were deducted from their pay.

The union representatives also said the pension plans are in jeopardy and that workers have not received vacation or holiday pay.

Union and Opposition spokesmen have attributed the bankruptcy largely to Ottawa's deregulation and privatization policies. They have been badgering Ottawa to hold a public inquiry into the sale of the company and the land transfer.

The RCMP's commercial fraud division is investigating the transactions. The trustees said the RCMP file is still open and indicated that the formal declaration of bankruptcy means they will be able to cooperate more fully with the force.

Mr. Ruhland, who attended the meeting with his lawyer, was asked several questions by creditors and frequently responded by saying he could not remember the facts. But he denied there was a connection between the Transport Route deal and the purchase of Holmes Transport Inc., a trucking company in Framingham, Mass.

Jerrold Gunn, a lawyer for some of the creditors, gave the trustees a copy of a submission that a subsidiary of Transport Route had made to the Interstate Commerce Commission in Washington for approval of the Holmes purchase.

The Commons transport committee had scheduled public hearings into the sale of the trucking division, but the federal election was called before the first meeting.

In reconstructing the financing of Transport Route, the trustees said the three investors borrowed $23-million from the Bank of Montreal and received a mortgage of $6-million from CNR against a property in Lachine, Que. They used the land as collateral.

Before the company was handed over, CNR wrote off about $90-million of debt. It also gave a commitment to pay severance for up to 1,500 of the 2,300 employees transferred with the company. About 500 workers benefited from this, at a cost of $18-million to CNR.

Source Cecil Foster, "Real Estate Value Alone Almost Double the Price CN Got for Trucking Firm", *The Globe and Mail*, Toronto, November 11, 1988, p.A-1, A-2.

For Discussion

1. What is the role of the accounting firm of Deloitte Haskins & Sells at this point?
2. How is the $54 million value of Transport Route Canada calculated? Is it recorded in their books? How do you know?
3. Why would Canadian National Railways sell this entity for $29 million if it had real estate worth at least $54 million? Who approves a sale of this type?
4. As well as the $54 million in real estate, the company had $17 million in other assets. What is the company's value? How much money does it owe? How much will its creditors get?
5. If the land has a value of $80 million, why would the investors have mortgaged the full amount?
6. Was there enough money to pay UIC premiums, vacation pay, etc. to the employees?
7. How was the financing of Transport Route arranged?
8. What role does the $90 million write-off and severence payments of $18 million made by CNR play in this situation?
9. In your own words, write an analysis, using the amounts quoted in the article, of what has occurred in this situation.
10. At what point did this entity cease to be a going concern?

Discussion Case 2-4: One Million Dollars

It may once have been true, as John Jacob Astor III insisted at the turn of the century, that "a man who has a million dollars is as well off as if he were rich." But a million doesn't stretch very far these days: if you have been pondering of late what prompts the ravenous grasping of Wall Street insider traders and other overreaching corporate miscreants, consider that a thin million is just mad money for the rich and famous.

Still, for most of us, a million is surely better than a kick in the head. With your humble million, you can still get:

- three seats on the Toronto Stock Exchange
- four Rolls-Royce Corniche convertibles
- a 27-unit, four-story "income property" (apartment building) on the outskirts of Halifax
- the deposit on Rio Vista, a palatial South West Marine Drive estate in Vancouver, including music and billiard rooms; library with wet bar; wine cellar; floodlit tennis court; and Roman gardens
- sponsorship of three theatre productions at the Stratford festival — say, *Othello, Much Ado About Nothing* and *Cabaret* — about 40 performances each. Added bonus: instant entry into high society
- a Penny Magenta postage stamp, issued by British Guyana in 1856

- a 50-foot Hatteras motor yacht with three staterooms, described as a "condo on waves"
- a six-seater, single-engine Piper Malibu with TV, stereo system, all leather interior and customized bar
- a 107-day round-the-world cruise for two in a luxury split-level apartment on the recently refurbished Queen Elizabeth II
- a flawless nine-carat diamond mounted on a gold ring encrusted with three-carat diamond studs; or a pair of one-of-a-kind Piaget watches handmade in Switzerland, with an emerald-and-diamond bracelet for him and an all-diamond bracelet for her
- 81,428,572 Smarties.

Source 'It's Getting Easier To Spend a Million All in One Place", *The Globe and Mail Report on Business Magazine*, November 1987, p.12.

For Discussion

1. How useful is accounting information expressed in dollars?
2. What are the implications of this discussion case on the value of measuring units?

Discussion Case 2-5: Bureau International d'Echange Commercial (BIEC)

The first exchange Jean-Pierre Monette can remember making on the international barter scene was a tractor in return for a boatload of bananas.

"For some reason, that one sticks in my mind," Monette said in an interview recently.

The 1985 exchange between a Canadian company and a Central American country is part of a booming business, said Monette, manager of the Laval-based Bureau International d'Echange Commercial (BIEC).

Exchanges in which cash does not change hands are a growing trend, say BIEC officials, and the deals can be a godsend to companies with cash-flow problems.

BIEC's main function as a barter company is to act as go-between in the trade of goods or services between member companies of the organization, in return for a commission.

Although BIEC is still involved in international barter, also called counter-trade, 85 per cent of its business is transacted within Quebec.

Monette predicted that next year, privately owned BIEC would triple the 1987-88 figure of $300 million in goods and services he says were traded by member companies under its auspices.

The commission it collects ranges from 0.02 per cent to 10 per cent. The higher the value of the deal, the lower the commission it gets.

The organization has created its own unit currency — 1 unit equals $1 — an internal credit-card system and has a

database to match members' needs with supplies.

For example, Monette said a member restaurant can provide meals to a member advertising company in return for magazine or broadcast ads.

This helps many businesses with a cash-flow problem, since they don't need a cash outlay for services, Monette said.

He conceded that the counter-trade system creates a small parallel economy in which transactions are not of the basic monetary-exchange variety, but he said his company is governed by federal tax laws and pays the same taxes as if cash were involved.

But Gilles Bordeleau, a Revenue Canada auditor, said in a telephone interview there is "a little problem of evaluation (of the value of transactions)."

What if, for example, a $60,000 tractor was sold by a company which declared receiving goods worth only $40,000 in exchange?

"There's no special control mechanism," the auditor said.

BIEC has 4,500 members, 80 per cent of which are in Quebec, Monette said.

Bryce Fraser, marketing director of Ski Morin Heights Inc., 70 kilometres north of Montreal in the Laurentians, thinks of BIEC as "a sort of a brokerage in certain respects."

Ski Morin Heights has gotten about $200,000 worth of goods via BIEC, Fraser said, in exchange for such items as rooms, meals, ski-lift tickets and rental equipment.

He has bought everything from gym equipment to cash registers and office furniture from BIEC members.

Source   François Shalom, "Laval Firm Acts as Go-Between in Deals Done through Bartering", *The (Montreal) Gazette*, December 14, 1988, P.E-1.

For Discussion

1. According to generally accepted accounting principles, Canadian business exchanges are measured in Canadian dollars. How do you account for the exchange of a tractor for a boatload of bananas? What measuring unit was used?

2. How does barter facilitate exchanges made by entities experiencing cash flow problems? The entities still don't have cash after the exchange and they have to pay a commission to BIEC.

3. Explain how the BIEC unit replaces the dollar. Is its use in accordance with the fundamental concepts of accounting?

4. Is the exchange of one item for another an arm's length transaction? What about the "little problem of evaluation (of the value of the transactions)"?

5. Is exchanging rooms, meals, ski-lift tickets, and rental equipment during slow periods a windfall for Ski Morin Heights? What is the impact on their earnings?

Discussion Case 2-6:   The Day They Sold Toronto

Two hundred years ago, Wabakinine, head chief of the western Mississauga, and two fellow chiefs reached an agreement with the British. Yes, they would allow settlement around the spot where the canoe route turned north from Lake Ontario toward Lake Simcoe, the place the Iroquois called "Toronto."

The price? A shipment of arms, ammunition, tobacco and, 18 years later, a cash payment of 10 shillings or one-half a British pound, which at today's exchange rate amounts to about one Canadian dollar.

The tract the Mississauga surrendered ran 22½ kilometres along the waterfront from Etobicoke Creek in the west to a point just east of the Don River, extending north for 45 kilometres as far as present-day Aurora. But the "Toronto Purchase" was part of a much larger acquisition. Early in 1787, Lord Dorchester, then British governor-in-chief at Quebec, had instructed Sir John Johnson, his superintendent-general of Indian affairs, to buy more Mississauga land for thousands of Loyalists who had sided with the Crown during the recent American Revolutionary War. Before the refugees could settle, however, Britain had to deal with the local Indians, whom the fur traders had termed Chippewa, Ojibwa or most frequently Mississauga.

After the conquest of Quebec, the British officially recognized that the Great Lakes Indians held title to their hunting grounds. The Royal Proclamation of 1763 prohibited settlers from occupying territory the Indians had not surrendered, and the Crown reserved the right to acquire Indian lands, which had to be purchased with the consent of the respective bands at a general assembly of the Indians concerned.

On Sept. 23, 1787, more than 600 Mississauga assembled at Sir John's council fire. Leading the contingent was Wabakinine, a man "of greater size than common men," as one white settler described him. A loyal British ally, the head chief of the western Mississauga had served in many Revolutionary War expeditions against the Americans, and had encouraged other Mississauga to fight for the Crown.

When approached in 1781 to surrender a strip of land 6½ kilometres wide on the west bank of the Niagara River, he had obliged. With three other chiefs he ceded the tract in return for "three hundred suits of clothing." In 1784 he and nine other "sachems and War Chiefs and Principal Women" had given up the remainder of the Niagara peninsula for goods worth £1,180. When Sir John asked Wabakinine and his followers for more lands, in the Mississauga's own words (recorded two decades later), "we gave them without hesitation."

Why did Wabakinine agree to what, in retrospect, seems a genuine giveaway? The British regarded these land transactions as simple real-estate deals. They gained complete title to the land in return for arms, ammunition and trade goods paid on a once-and-for-all-time basis.

Simply put, Wabakinine and his people wanted British trade goods. The French had given the Great Lakes Indians gifts every year for the use of the land for their forts at Niagara, present-day Kingston and Toronto. Later, the Mississauga had obtained generous supplies for joining British and Loyalist raiding parties in the Revolutionary War. Dependent on these supplies, they were anxious to obtain more.

Furthermore, the Mississauga did not realize what they were getting into. Their whole system of land use differed drastically from that of the British. Among the Mississauga, individual families could use a recognized hunting ground or fishing spot, or maple sugar bush, but once they stopped going there, it reverted to the collective ownership of the band. Their behavior subsequent to the Toronto Purchase suggests that, in line with their communal concept of property, the Mississauga believed they had only granted the British tenant status, the right to use the land, while they retained the right to "encamp and fish where we pleased" throughout the territory.

Another reason for their willingness to cooperate was military weakness. These coastal Indians numbered only 1,000 on the north shore of Lake Ontario, and were separated from their fellow Ojibwa to the north and west by immense distances.

Few in number, reliant on European trade goods and believing they were receiving British goods in perpetuity for the use of their land — without surrendering their hunting and fishing rights — Wabakinine and his people accepted the deal.

Sir John, however, made one important mistake. He acted carelessly in executing and recording the deed. He left it without signatures and without any specification of the area of land surrendered. The treaty was bogus. It did not conform to the Royal Proclamation.

In 1805, the Toronto Purchase had to be reaffirmed because the new provincial capital of York stood on unsur-rendered land.

By then the Mississauga had learned a great deal about the British newcomers. The settlers denied them a right of way across their property. If the Indians camped on farmers' land, the white men shot their dogs. Still, it was too late to resist.

With proper legal counsel, the Indians could have refused the British request to reaffirm the pact, but they still had little understanding of their rights under British law. In 1787, Sir John had given them arms, ammunition and tobacco, adding another 149 barrels of supplies the following year at Toronto. Reminded of these gifts, on Aug. 1, 1805, the Mississauga accepted the token 10 shillings and sealed the Toronto Purchase.

The issue rested until the mid-1820s when an amazing transformation overcame the Mississauga. Rev. Peter Jones, the son of a white surveyor and a Mississauga woman, converted the tribe to Christianity. Known to his people as Sacred Feathers, this extraordinary bilingual and bicultural clergyman could not undo the formal surrender of Toronto or the loss of the other Mississauga lands, but he fought to preserve his people's remaining base at the Credit River, 20 kilometres west of Toronto. Had he succeeded, Toronto today would have an Indian reserve on its western boundary, right in the heart of the aptly named regional municipality of Mississauga.

The Indians became educated, learned English and the meaning of British law. But the pressure of the white settlers was too great, and in 1847 they moved to a new home beside the Iroquois on the Grand River south of Brantford, naming it New Credit. Outnumbered by the white arrivals, the Mississauga and their old foes decided to live together.

From New Credit they kept up their demands for a proper settlement of their land claims. Rev. Jones died in 1856, but the struggle continued. For more than a century the New Credit band has maintained its claim to what is now the Toronto Islands, which it argues were exempted from the Toronto Purchase.

In 1923, the Mississauga in the Ride Lake area were given the opportunity to sign a new treaty for their land east of Toronto and west of the Bay of Quinte, but the 10-shilling bargain in 1805 prevented those at New Credit from taking part in the treaty. The mind boggles at the sum they might have asked.

Source   Donald B. Smith, "The Day They Sold Toronto", *The Globe and Mail*, Toronto, September 22, 1987, p.A-7.

For Discussion

1. In accounting, financial transactions are recorded at cost. What is the cost of the place the Iroquois called "Toronto"? Prepare some numbers to support your answer. Can we consider the agreement between Sir John and Wabakinine as a financial transaction?
2. What was the cost of the 1781 purchase? How much was the amount worth at that time?
3. How did the system of land use differ between the Mississauga and the British? What did the Indians believe they had ceded? What did the British believe they had purchased?
4. Was the land deal an arm's-length transaction despite the military weakness of the Indians?
5. The treaty did not conform to the Royal Proclamation of 1763, which prohibited settlers from occupying territory the Indians had not surrendered. What would an Indian reserve in the heart of the municipality of Mississauga be worth today?
6. How much could have been asked by the New Credit Mississauga in 1923?
7. What is the difference between the 1805 purchase cost and the land's market value at that time? What amount would accountants enter in the records?

Comprehension Problems

Comprehension Problem 2-1

The following T-accounts show the relationship of increases and decreases to debits and credits:

Trans-action	Any Asset		Any Liability		Common Stock		Net Income	
	Debit (increase)	Credit (decrease)	Debit (decrease)	Credit (increase)	Debit (decrease)	Credit (increase)	Debit (decrease)	Credit (increase)
(1)	X					X		
(2)	X			X				
(3)		X						
(4)								
(5)								
(6)								
(7)								
(8)								
(9)								
(10)								
(11)								
(12)								
(13)								

Required: For each of the following transactions, indicate in the chart above with an X with accounts are debited and credited (transaction 1 is done for you):

1. Issued common stock for cash
2. Paid cash for a truck
3. Paid for prepaid rent
4. Borrowed cash from the bank
5. Received a bill for extermination services performed last week
6. Collected cash for services performed today
7. Billed customers for services performed last week
8. Repaid part of the bank loan
9. Made a deposit for electricity service
10. Paid cash for truck expenses
11. Received a bill for repair supplies used during the month
12. Made a payment on account
13. Received a payment on account

Comprehension Problem 2-2

The following lists show selected statement totals for four different firms: A, B, C, and D. In each case, the amount is omitted for one total.

	A	B	C	D
Current Assets	$100	$ 72	$?	$ 20
Fixed Assets	200	130	71	200
Current Liabilities	50	10	5	10
Long-Term Liabilities	75	?	25	61
Common Stock	175	50	100	?
Net Income	?	20	6	10

Required: In each case, compute the missing figure.

Comprehension Problem 2-3

Required: Record the debit and credit for each of the following transactions (transaction 1 is done for you):

	Assets		Liabilities		Equity	
	Debit (increase)	*Credit* (decrease)	*Debit* (decrease)	*Credit* (increase)	*Debit* (decrease)	*Credit* (increase)
1. Purchased a $10,000 truck for credit (on account)	10,000			10,000		
2. Borrowed $5,000 from the bank	5000			5000		
3. Paid $2,000 of the bank loan		2000	2000			
4. Paid $600 in advance for a one-year insurance policy	600	600				
5. Received $500 in advance for next month's rental of office space.	500			500 *cause we owe that service*		

Comprehension Problem 2-4

Required: Record the debit and credit to the appropriate account for each of the following transactions (transaction 1 is done for you):

	Debit	*Credit*
1. Issued common stock for cash	Cash	Common Stock
2. Purchased equipment for credit (on account)		
3. Paid for a one-year insurance policy		
4. Billed a customer for repairs completed today		
5. Paid this month's rent		
6. Collected the amount billed in transaction 4 above		
7. Collected cash for repairs completed today		
8. Paid for the equipment purchased in transaction 2 above		
9. Signed a union contract		
10. Collected cash for repairs to be made next month		
11. Transferred this month's portion of insurance to Insurance Expense.		

Comprehension Problem 2-5

Required: Post the following transactions to the appropriate accounts:
1. Issued common stock for $5,000 cash
2. Paid $900 in advance for three months rent, $300 for each month
3. Billed $1,500 to customers for repairs completed today
4. Purchased $2,000-worth of supplies for credit (on account) (Hint: Debit the asset Supplies)
5. Borrowed $7,500 from the bank
6. Collected $500 for the amount billed in transaction 3
7. Received a $200 bill for electricity used to date (the bill will be paid next month)
8. Repaid $2,500 toward the bank loan in transaction 5
9. Used $800-worth of the supplies purchased in transaction 4
10. Paid $2,000 for the supplies purchased in transaction 4
11. Transferred this month's rent to Expenses.

Cash		Bank Loan		Common Stock		Repair Revenue	
(1) 5,000	(2) 900	(8) 2500	(5) 7500		(1) 5,000		(3) 1500
(5) 7500	(8) 2500						
(6) 500	(10) 2000						

Accounts Receivable		Accounts Payable		Electricity Expense	
(3) 1500	(6) 500	(3) 1500	(4) 2000	(7) 200	
		(10) 2000	(7) 200		

Prepaid Rent		Rent Expense	
(2) 900	(11) 300	(11) 300	

Supplies		Supplies Expense	
(4) 2000	(9) 800	(9) 800	

Comprehension Problem 2-6

Required: Prepare journal entries for each of the following transactions:
1. Issued common stock for $3,000 cash
2. Purchased $2,000-worth of equipment for credit (on account)
3. Paid $400 cash for this month's rent
4. Purchased $4,000-worth of supplies for two months for credit (on account)
5. Billed $2,500 to customers for repairs made to date
6. Paid cash for one-half of the amount owing in transaction 4
7. Collected $500 of the amount billed in transaction 5
8. Sold one-half of the equipment purchased in transaction 2 above for $1,000 in cash.

Comprehension Problem 2-7

Required: The following accounts appear in the ledger of Brooks Sisters Inc. Prepare the journal entries that were posted to these accounts.

Cash		Bank Loan		Rent Expense	
5	3		3	1	
4	2				
1	1				
3					

Accounts Receivable		Accounts Payable		Supplies Expense	
2		1	3	3	
1			3		
			2		

Prepaid Rent		Common Stock		Truck Expense	
2	1		5	2	

Equipment		Revenue	
6	1		6
			1

Comprehension Problem 2-8

The following ledger accounts are taken from the books of Lax Ltd. at the end of its first month of operations, January 31, 19X2.

Cash			
Jan. 1	10,000	Jan. 5	200
11	1,300	9	4,000
		28	450
		30	1,800

Temporary Investments	
Jan. 9	4,000

Accounts Receivable	
Jan. 31	1,600

Common Stock	
	Jan. 1 10,000

Service Revenue	
	Jan. 11 1,300
	31 1,600

Repair Supplies Expense	
Jan. 28 450	

Rental Expense	
Jan. 5 200	

Salaries Expense	
Jan. 30 1,800	

Required:
1. Prepare journal entries for the transactions recorded in these ledger accounts.
2. From the journal entries, prepare a trial balance.
3. Prepare a statement of cash flow at January 31, 19X2.

Comprehension Problem 2-9

The following trial balance was prepared from the books of Pipu Inc. at its year-end, December 31, 19X1. After the company's bookkeeper had left, the office staff were unable to balance the accounts or even to place them in their proper order. Individual account balances, prepared by the bookkeeper prior to leaving Pipu's employ, are correct.

Cash 120,400
Land
Bldg.
A/R
N/R
Supplies

Account Title	Debits	Credits
Cash	$120,400	
Commissions Earned	5,000	
Common Stock		$170,000
Accounts Payable	20,000	
Notes Payable	10,000	
Insurance Expense	100	
Land		8,000
Building		120,000
Rent Expense		1,000
Accounts Receivable		14,000
Notes Receivable		12,000
Supplies	6,000	
Supplies Expense		300
Mortgage Payable		80,000
Salaries Expense		3,000
Telephone Expense	200	
Totals	$161,700	$408,300

Required: Prepare a corrected trial balance showing the accounts in proper order.

Comprehension Problem 2-10

This transactions worksheet is for Lelik Corporation at March 31. Each line represents a transaction during the month.

| | ASSETS | | | | = | LIABILITY | + | EQUITY |
Transaction	Cash +	Accounts Receivable +	Prepaid Rent +	Equip- ment =		Accounts Payable +	Common Stock +	[+ Revenue] [− Expense]
1.	+$5						+$5	
2.	− 3			+ $6		+$3		
3.	− 2		+$2					
4.	+4	+$2						+$6
5.	+1			− 1				
6.						+3		− 3 (supplies)
7.		+1						+1
8.			− 1					− 1 (rent)
9.						+2		− 2 (truck)
10.	− 1					− 1		

Required:
1. Prepare journal entries for the ten transactions.
2. Post the journal entries to T-accounts.
3. From the T-accounts, prepare a trial balance. List expenses in alphabetical order.
4. Calculate the total of each asset, liability, and equity column on the worksheet; prove that the total of assets equals the total of liabilities and equity.
5. What is the relationship of the equality of transactions entered on the worksheet and the equality of debits with credits on the trial balance?

Comprehension Problem 2-11

The following trial balance was prepared from the books of Kaku Corp. at its year-end, December 31, 19X1. The new bookkeeper was unable to balance the accounts or to list them in their proper order. Individual account balances are correct.

Account Title	Account Balances	
	Debit	*Credit*
Accounts Payable	$ 8,550	
Accounts Receivable		$10,000
Building	50,000	
Common Stock	75,000	
Cash	15,500	
Furniture	6,000	
Land		12,000
Temporary Investments		9,600
Mortgage Payable		20,000
Notes Payable	10,350	
Notes Receivable		8,000
Service Supplies	2,800	
Totals	$168,200	$59,600

Required: Prepare a corrected trial balance showing the accounts in proper order.

Comprehension Problem 2-12

The following ledger accounts are taken from the books of Benny and Barry at June 30, 19X1, the end of the first year of operations.

Cash			
June 1	25,000	June 1	500
20	5,000	15	1,000
		23	4,000
		30	1,000
		30	2,000
		30	16,000

Mortage Payable	
June 30	4,000

Temporary Investments	
June 30	2,000

Common Stock	
June 1	25,000

Accounts Receivable	
June 30	3,000

Repair Revenue	
June 20	5,000
30	3,000

Office Supplies			
June 23	4,000	June 30	200

Office Supplies Expense	
June 30	200

Land			Rent Expense		
June 30	5,000		June 1	500	

Building			Salaries Expense		
June 30	15,000		June 15	1,000	
			30	1,000	

Accounts Payable			Telephone Expense		
		June 27 100	June 27	100	

Required:
1. Prepare journal entries to record the June transactions.
2. Prepare a trial balance at June 30.
3. Prepare a statement of cash flow.

Comprehension Problem 2-13

The following trial balance has been prepared from the ledger of Muirhead Voyages Inc.

Muirhead Voyages Inc.
Trial Balance
January 31, 19X1

	Account Balances	
	Debits	*Credits*
Cash	$ 60	
Accounts Receivable	140	
Supplies	10	
Equipment	300	
Bank Loan		$100
Accounts Payable		20
Common Stock		250
Service Revenue		990
Fees Earned		885
Advertising Expense	200	
Salaries Expense	800	
Supplies Expense	20	
Telephone Expense	10	
Utilities Expense	5	
Wages Expense	700	

Required:
1. Calculate the total debits and credits.
2. From the accounts in the trial balance, prepare an interim income statement and an interim classified balance sheet.

Problems

Problem 2-1

Financial statements are prepared according to a number of accounting assumptions (principles) and qualities (conventions), which are listed below:

Assumptions
1. The Entity
2. The Going Concern
3. The Measuring Unit
4. Historical Cost
5. Periodicity
6. Accrual Accounting and Matching
7. Revenue Recognition

Qualities
1. Comparability
2. Reliability
3. Materiality
4. Relevance
5. Understandability

Required: Identify the assumption or quality that would apply in each of the following situations. Be prepared to explain why you have selected a particular assumption or quality.

*Assumption
or
quality*

_____ The BAP Corporation closes its books each December 31 and prepares financial statements for the year.

_____ Caldwell Limited, with total assets of $100,000, records as an expense a $25 stapler with a five-year life.

_____ Steve Goss, an independent consultant, must keep a set of books for his consulting firm and a separate set of books for his personal records.

_____ A machine is recorded at its purchase price of $9,000 and is not revalued at the end of the accounting period to reflect its market value of $10,000.

_____ An asset purchased in 19X1 for $10,000 and an asset purchased in 19X8 for $10,000 are both recorded as $10,000, even though inflation has reduced the purchasing power of the dollar by 50 percent.

Problem 2-2

The following account balances are taken from the records of Pana-Micro Inc. at October 31, 19X1.

Accounts Payable	$9,000	Insurance Expense	$	500
Accounts Receivable	6,000	Repair Revenue		19,000
Advertising Expense	2,200	Supplies Expense		800
Bank Loan	5,000	Telephone Expense		250
Cash	1,000	Truck		9,000
Common Stock	2,000	Truck Expense		1,250
Commissions Expense	4,500	Wages Expense		4,000
Equipment	7,000	Wages Payable		1,500

Required:
1. Prepare a trial balance at October 31.
2. Prepare an interim income statement for October 31 in proper form.
3. Prepare an interim balance sheet at October 31 in proper form.

Problem 2-3

The following ledger accounts were prepared for Sait Tool Rentals Corporation during the first month of operations ending May 31, 19X1. No journal entries were prepared in support of the amounts recorded in the ledger accounts.

Cash		Equipment		Commissions Expense	
5,000	1,000	2,000	800	1,100	
2,000	500				
1,500	300				
1,200	600				
800	400				
	3,500				

		Accounts Payable		Rent Expense	
		600	1,000	400	
			150		
			1,100		

Accounts Receivable		Common Stock		Salaries Expense	
3,000	1,500		5,000	3,500	
2,500	1,200				

Prepaid Advertising		Revenue		Supplies Expense	
500	250		3,000	100	
			2,000		
			2,500		

Supplies		Advertising Expense		Telephone Expense	
300	100	250		150	

Required:
1. Reconstruct the transactions that occurred during the month and prepare journal entries to record these transactions.
2. Calculate the balance in each account and prepare a trial balance at May 31, 19X1.

Problem 2-4

The following trial balance was prepared for Prentice Consultants Corp. at January 31, 19X1, its first month of operations, by a newly hired clerk who has insufficient training.

Prentice Consultants Corp.
Trial Balance
January 31, 19X1

	Account Balances	
	Debits	*Credits*
Accounts Payable	$ 9,000	
Accounts Receivable		$ 8,000
Advertising Expense	150	
Bank Loan		3,625
Cash	2,000	
Common Stock		7,000
Equipment		4,000
Furniture		1,000
Interest Expense	200	
Maintenance Expense		250
Prepaid Advertising	300	
Repair Revenue	9,500	
Rent Expense		400
Salaries Expense		2,600
Salaries Payable		1,500
Supplies Expense	350	
Telephone Expense	125	
Truck	9,000	
Truck Expense		750
Wages Expense		1,500
	$30,625	$30,625

Required:
1. Prepare a corrected trial balance at January 31. List the accounts by the sequence in the chart of accounts in the text and record the amounts in their proper debit-credit positions.
2. How is it possible that the debit-credit totals amount to $30,625 in both trial balances? (Assume that individual amounts are correct.)

Problem 2-5

The following balances appeared in the general ledger of Naro Tables Inc. at April 1, 19X1.

Cash	$1,400	Accounts Payable	$2,000
Accounts Receivable	3,600	Common Stock	4,350
Prepaid Rent	1,000		
Supplies	350		

The following transactions occurred during April:
a. Collected $2,000 cash on account
b. Billed $3,000 to customers for tables rented to date
c. Paid the following expenses: advertising, $300; salaries $2,000; telephone, $100
d. Paid half of the accounts payable
e. Received a $500 bill for April truck expenses
f. Collected $2,500 on account
g. Billed $1,500 to customers for tables rented to date
h. Transferred $500 of prepaid rent to rent expense
i. Counted $200-worth of supplies on hand; recorded the amount used as an expense.

Required:
1. Open Ledger accounts for the following and enter the April 1 balances: Cash, Accounts Receivable, Prepaid Rent, Supplies, Accounts Payable, Common Stock, Revenue, Advertising Expense, Rent Expense, Salaries Expense, Supplies Expense, Telephone Expense, Truck Expense.
2. Prepare journal entries to record the April transactions. Post these entries to the ledger accounts.
3. Prepare a trial balance at April 30.
4. Prepare an interim income statement and interim classified balance sheet at April 30 in proper form.

Problem 2-6

The following transactions occurred in Hoyle Accounting Services Inc. during August 19X1, its first month of operations.

Aug. 1 Issued common shares for $3,000 cash
1 Borrowed $10,000 cash from the bank
1 Paid $8,000 for a used truck
4 Paid $600 for a one-year truck insurance policy effective August 1 (recorded as Prepaid Insurance)
5 Collected $2,000 cash fees from a client for work performed today (recorded as Revenue)
7 Billed $5,000-worth of fees to clients for services performed to date (recorded as Revenue)
9 Paid $250 for supplies used to date
12 Purchased $500-worth of supplies on account (recorded as an asset)
15 Collected $1,000 of the amount billed on August 7
16 Paid $200 for advertising in *The News* during the first two weeks of August
20 Paid half of the amount owing for the supplies purchased on August 12
25 Paid the following expenses: rent for August, $350; salaries, $2,150; telephone, $50; truck, $250
28 Called clients for payment of the balance owing from August 7
29 Billed $6,000-worth of fees to clients for services performed to date (recorded as Revenue)
31 Transferred the amount of August's truck insurance to Insurance Expense
31 Counted $100-worth of supplies still on hand (recorded the amount used as an expense).

Required:
1. Open ledger accounts for the following: Cash, Accounts Receivable, Prepaid Insurance, Supplies, Truck, Bank Loan, Accounts Payable, Common Stock, Revenue, Advertising Expense, Insurance Expense, Rent Expense, Salaries Expense, Supplies Expense, Telephone Expense, Truck Expense.
2. Prepare journal entries to record the August transactions. Post these entries to the ledger accounts.
3. Prepare a trial balance at August 31.
4. Prepare an interim income statement and classified balance sheet at August 31 in proper form.

Problem 2-7

The following transactions took place in Casa Renovations Inc. during June 19X1, its first month of operations.

Jun. 1 Issued common shares for $8,000 cash
      1 Purchased $5,000-worth of equipment on account
      2 Collected $600 cash for repairs completed today
      3 Paid $20 for supplies used on June 2
      4 Purchased $1,000-worth of supplies on account (recorded as an asset)
      5 Billed customers $2,500 for repairs collected to date
      8 Collected $500 of the amount billed on June 5
    10 Paid half of the amount owing for equipment purchased on June 1
    15 Sold on account excess equipment for $1,000 (its original cost)
    18 Paid for the supplies purchased on June 4
    20 Received a $100 bill for electricity used to date (recorded as Utilities Expense)
    22 Paid $600 to the landlord for June and July rent (recorded as Prepaid Rent)
    23 Signed a union contract
    25 Collected $1,000 of the amount billed on June 5
    27 Paid the following expenses: advertising, $150; telephone, $50; truck expense (for rental and gas), $1,000; wages, $2,500
    30 Billed $2,000 for repairs completed to date
    30 Transferred the amount for June's rent to Rent Expense
    30 Counted $150-worth of supplies still on hand (recorded the amount used as an expense).

Required:

1. Open ledger accounts for the following: Cash, Accounts Receivable, Prepaid Rent, Supplies, Equipment, Accounts Payable, Common Stock, Repair Revenue, Advertising Expense, Rent Expense, Supplies Expense, Telephone Expense, Truck Expense, Utilities Expense, Wages Expense.
2. Prepare journal entries to record the August transactions. Post these entries to the ledger accounts.
3. Prepare a trial balance at June 30.
4. Prepare an interim income statement and classified balance sheet at June 30 in proper form.

Problem 2-8

The following balance sheet was prepared by the bookkeeper of Hoffman Limited:

Hoffman Limited
Balance Sheet
As at November 30, 19X1

Assets			Liabilities		
Current Assets			*Current Liabilities*		
Cash	$1,000		Accounts Payable	$5,600	
Accounts Receivable	6,000		Notes Payable (due 19X2)	2,000	
Building	12,000		Notes Payable (due 19X8)	1,000	
Merchandise Inventory	3,000		Total Current Liabilities		$8,600
Total Current Assets		$22,000	*Long-Term Liabilities*		
Fixed Assets			Mortgage Payable		
Temporary Investments	$3,000		(due 19X9)	$8,000	
Equipment	1,500		Salaries Payable	250	
Supplies	100		Total Long-Term Liabilities		8,250
Truck	1,350		Total Liabilities		$16,850
Total Fixed Assets		5,950			
			Equity		
			Common Stock		11,100
Total Assets		$27,950	Total Liabilities and Assets		$27,950

Required:
1. Identify the errors that exist in the balance sheet of Hoffman Limited and list these errors on a sheet of paper, with an explanation of why each is an error.
2. Prepare a corrected interim balance sheet that is also classified.

Problem 2-9

Accounts included in the trial balance of the Karl Kutz Corporation as of November 30 were as follows:

Account Title	Account Balance
Cash	$25,200
Accounts Receivable	12,000
Office Supplies	1,500
Land	?
Building	?
Furniture	9,000
Equipment	75,000
Truck	3,500
Accounts Payable	4,000
Notes Payable	30,000
Common Stock	?

Land and building were acquired at a cost of $36,000. It was determined that one-third of the total cost should be applied to the cost of land.

The following transactions were completed during the month of December:

Dec. 2 Paid $200 of the accounts payable
3 Collected in full an account receivable of $700
4 Purchased equipment for $500
8 Issued additional shares for $20,000 cash
10 Collected $1,500 on account
11 Purchased equipment for $25,000; paid $5,000 cash, the balance to be paid within 30 days
15 Paid $600 of the accounts payable
20 Paid $15,000 cash in partial settlement of the liability of December 11; issued a note payable for the balance
31 Collected in full an account receivable of $400.

Required:
1. Open ledger accounts for the accounts listed above.
2. Journalize the transactions.
3. Enter the balances of November 30 in ledger accounts, post the December entries, and determine the new balances.
4. Prepare a trial balance as at December 31.
5. Prepare an interim classified balance sheet as at December 31.

Alternate Problems

Alternate Problem 2-1

The following account balances are taken from the records of Saunders Repairs Corp. at November 30, 19X1.

Accounts Payable	$5,000	Rent Expense	$ 700
Accounts Receivable	6,000	Repair Revenue	8,350
Advertising Expense	500	Salaries Expense	3,000
Bank Loan	4,500	Salaries Payable	1,000
Cash	2,000	Supplies	500
Common Stock	8,000	Supplies Expense	250
Commissions Expense	1,500	Truck	8,000
Equipment	3,500	Truck Expense	900

Required:
1. Prepare a trial balance at November 30.
2. Prepare an interim income statement for November 30 in proper form.
3. Prepare an interim balance sheet at November 30 in proper form.

Alternate Problem 2-2

The following accounts were prepared for York Garage Inc. during the first month of operations ending July 31, 19X1. No journal entries were prepared in support of the amounts recorded in the ledger accounts.

Cash		Truck	Advertising Expense
3,000	1,000	7,000	100
1,500	400		
1,200	600		
2,000	300		
	1,100		
	3,200		

Accounts Receivable	
2,500	1,200
3,500	2,000

Accounts Payable	
300	6,000
1,100	500
	200
	100

Insurance Expense	
50	

Prepaid Insurance	
600	50

Common Stock	
	3,000

Rent Expense	
400	

Supplies	
500	150

Revenue	
	2,500 ∕
	1,500
	3,500 ✓

Supplies Expense	
150	

Salaries Expense	
3,200	

Truck Expense	
200	

Required:
1. Reconstruct the transactions that occurred during the month and prepare journal entries to record these transactions.
2. Calculate the balance in each account and prepare a trial balance at July 31, 19X1.

Alternate Problem 2-3

The following trial balance was prepared for Rosen Services Corp. at March 31, 19X1, its first month of operations, by a part-time clerk who has insufficient training.

Trial Balance
March 31, 19X1

	Account Balances	
	Debits	*Credits*
Accounts Payable	$ 5,000	
Accounts Receivable		$ 3,000
Bank Loan		3,550
Cash	1,500	
Common Stock	3,000	
Equipment	2,000	
Fees Earned	6,900	
Insurance Expense	50	
Interest Expense		100
Rent Expense		600
Truck		8,000
Utilities Expense		200
Wages Expense		3,000
	$18,450	$18,450

Required:
1. Prepare a correct trial balance at March 31. List the accounts by the sequence in the chart of accounts in the text and record the amounts in their proper debit-credit positions.
2. How is it possible that the debit-credit totals amount to $18,450 in both trial balances? (Assume that individual amounts are correct).

Alternate Problem 2-4

The following balances appeared in the general ledger of Nhut Tool Rentals Inc. on May 1, 19X1.

Cash	$1,600	Accounts Payable	$4,000
Supplies	400	Common Stock	8,000
Equipment	3,000		
Truck	7,000		

The following transactions occurred during May:
a. Collected $5,000 cash for tool rental during the month (Nhut does not rent tools on account)
b. Paid $500 rent expense
c. Paid $1,500 on account
d. Paid $600 for a one-year insurance policy effective May 1
e. Purchased a used truck for $5,000 on account
f. Paid the following expenses: advertising, $300; salaries, $2,500; telephone, $150; truck, $550
g. Transferred the amount of May's insurance to Insurance Expense.
h. Estimated $200 of supplies to have been used during May.

Required:
1. Open ledger accounts for the following and enter the May 1 balances: Cash, Prepaid Insurance, Supplies, Equipment, Truck, Accounts Payable, Common Stock, Revenue, Advertising Expense, Insurance Expense, Rent Expense, Salaries Expense, Supplies Expense, Telephone Expense, Truck Expense.
2. Prepare journal entries to record the May transactions. Post these entries to the ledger accounts.
3. Prepare a trial balance at May 31.
4. Prepare an interim income statement and interim balance sheet at May 31.

Alternate Problem 2-5

Electrical Contractors Corp. was incorporated on May 1, 19X1 and had the following transactions during its first month of operations.

May	1	Issued common shares for $5,000 cash
	1	Paid $1,500 for three months rent in advance: May, June, and July (recorded as Prepaid Rent)
	2	Purchased $1,000-worth of supplies on account (recorded as an asset)
	3	Billed a customer $1,500 for repairs performed
	4	Paid $50 for an advertisement in *The News*
	5	Received $250 cash for work completed today
	10	Collected the amount billed on May 3
	15	Paid $500 on account to a creditor
	18	Borrowed $2,000 cash from the bank
	20	Signed a major contract for work to be done in June
	22	Purchased $3,000-worth of equipment; paid cash
	25	Billed customers $3,500 for work completed to date
	27	Paid the following expenses: electricity, $75; telephone, $25; wages, $2,000
	31	Transferred the amount of May's rent from Prepaid Rent to Rent Expense
	31	Counted $200-worth of supplies still on hand; the rest had been used during May.

Required:
1. Open ledger accounts for the following: Cash, Accounts Receivable, Prepaid Rent, Supplies, Equipment, Bank Loan, Accounts Payable, Common Stock, Repair Revenue, Advertising Expense, Rent Expense, Supplies Expense, Telephone Expense, Utilities Expense, Wages Expense.

2. Prepare journal entries to record the May transactions. Post these transactions to the ledger accounts.
3. Prepare a trial balance at May 31.
4. Prepare an interim income statement and interim classified balance sheet at May 31 in proper form.

Alternate Problem 2-6

Sasquatch Snow Removal Inc. was incorporated on December 1, 19X1 and had the following transactions during its first month of operations.

Dec. 1 Issued common shares for $6,000 cash
1 Purchased a used truck for $9,000: paid $4,000 cash, balance owing until January 15
2 Purchased a $2,000 snow plough on account (recorded as an increase in the cost of the truck)
3 Billed customers $5,000 for December snow removal (Sasquatch's customers are billed at the beginning of each month)
5 Purchased salt, sand, and gravel for $500 on account (recorded as Supplies)
6 Paid truck expenses of $200
7 Paid $360 for a one-year insurance policy effective December 1 (recorded as Prepaid Insurance)
14 Paid $1,500 for two weeks wages
16 Paid $40 traffic ticket (recorded as Truck Expense)
20 Received a bill for $350-worth of truck expenses
24 Purchased tire chains for $100 on account (recorded as Truck Expense)
24 Collected $3,500 from customers billed on December 3
27 Paid for the purchase made on December 5
28 Collected $400 for snow removal performed today for a new customer
28 Paid $1,500 for two weeks wages
30 Called customers owing $1,500 billed on December 3 and not yet paid
31 Transferred the amount of December's truck insurance to Insurance Expense
31 Counted $100-worth of salt, sand, and gravel still on hand (recorded the amount used as an expense)
31 Recorded three days wages applicable to December 29, 30, and 31, to be paid in January.

Required:
1. Open ledger accounts for the following: Cash, Accounts Receivable, Prepaid Insurance, Supplies, Truck, Accounts Payable, Wages Payable, Common Stock, Service Revenue, Insurance Expense, Supplies Expense, Truck Expense, Wages Expense.
2. Prepare journal entries to record the December transactions. Post transactions to the ledger accounts.
3. Prepare a trial balance at December 31.
4. Prepare an income statement and a classified balance sheet at December 31 in proper form.

Alternate Problem 2-7

The following alphabetical list of accounts is taken from the records of the Jensen Company Ltd. at December 31:

Account Title	Account Balances
Accounts Payable	$125
Accounts Receivable	138
Building	400
Cash	250
Common Stock	400
Equipment	140
Land	115
Mortgage Payable (due 19X8)	280
Notes Payable	110
Notes Receivable	18
Prepaid Insurance	12
Retained Earnings	214
Salaries Payable	14
Supplies	70

Required: Prepare a classified balance sheet.

Alternate Problem 2-8

The Booker Corporation has been operating for a period of years. On October 31, the accountant of the company disappeared, taking the records with him. You are hired to reconstruct the accounting records, and with this in mind you make an inventory of all company assets. By checking with banks, counting the materials on hand, investigating the ownership of buildings and equipment, and so on, you develop the following information as of October 31.

Account Title	Account Balances
Land	$15
Equipment	25
Buildings	20
Accounts Receivable	10
Temporary Investments	5
Inventories	14
Cash	56

Statements from creditors and unpaid invoices found in the office indicate that $40 is owed to trade creditors. There is a $10 long-term mortgage (five years) outstanding.

Interviews with the board of directors and a check of the common stock record book indicate that there are 1000 shares of common stock outstanding and that the shareholders have contributed $30 to the corporation. No record is available regarding past retained earnings.

Required: Prepare an interim classified balance sheet at October 31.

Decision Problem

Decision Problem 2-1

Ron McCharles, a second-year business student at the University of Alberta, has had a hard time finding an enjoyable summer job that pays well. He has therefore decided to begin his own business for the summer. He and two high school friends meet and decide to establish a home repair company. Ron will run the business side of the operations while his two friends, Warren MacDonald and Dave Victor, who are enrolled in the technology program at the Northern Alberta Institute of Technology, will do the majority of the home repairs with Ron filling in whenever he can.

A corporation is formed and issues $1,000 of common shares to each student and receives a total of $3,000 cash for these shares on June 1.

The three decide to call their corporation the Mic Mac & Vic Corp. (MMV). MMV agrees to rent a van from Jim Stephens for $200 per month; under this agreement, MMV will be liable for all fuel and repair bills. After this transaction, the corporation is ready to begin business.

The business proved to be successful from the start. Ron, a marketing major, spent most of his time promoting the business, making sales calls, and writing up estimates. Ron devoted little effort toward establishing an accounting system or keeping formal accounting records. He had not particularly liked his first accounting course at the U of A and thought that MMV could do with only a chequebook. So that all transactions would pass through the chequebook, Ron arranged with the local Canadian Tire Store, McBride's Shell Service Station, and Bittners Hardware to pay all bills by cheque.

On August 31, the students had completed their summer's work and were preparing to return to school. All payments from customers had been received and all bills had been paid. The students agreed that Warren's sister, Betty MacDonald, a third-year accounting student at NAIT, would determine the financial position of MMV at August 31.

From the records, Betty discovered that receipts from customers for the summer totalled $35,542. The materials bought for use by MMV amounted to $24,500, with $2,500 of unused material, such as paint, lumber, nails, and electrical fixtures remaining; of these 80 percent could be returned for full credit, while 20 percent had to be expensed. Other expenses incurred were $75 for advertising and $375 for fuel and oil for the van. Luckily, the van did not need any repairs. As well, the students paid themselves $1,500 each on August 1. The Bank balance for MMV on August 31 showed a total of $8,492.22. The unused supplies had not yet been returned for credit.

Required:

1. Prepare two balance sheets: one dated June 1 and one dated August 31.
2. Prepare an income statement for MMV for the three months ended August 31.
3. If each student worked 190 hours per month from June 1 through August 31, how successful have they been?
4. Betty was also asked to make recommendations to Ron, Warren, and Dave since they plan to resume the business next summer. What should Betty suggest to these entrepreneurs?

GAAP and the Operating Cycle

Each business entity has a series of financial transactions that occur continuously during the accounting time period. As noted in Chapter 2, such repeated activities comprise the operating cycle. The following questions are answered in Chapter 3:

1. What is the basic sequence of an operating cycle?
2. How can incomplete cycles exist at the end of an accounting time period?
3. What theoretical problems are involved with revenue recognition? In actual practice, at what point is revenue recognized?
4. How should a payment received before a service is performed be recorded?
5. How should expenses that are made continuously during the operating cycle be recorded?
6. How do financial statements made at the end of an accounting time period accurately reflect expenses, even if these may have been inaccurately stated during the accounting period?
7. How is it possible to manipulate the operating results and financial position of an entity?
8. What is the relationship between accrual accounting and the matching concept?
9. What are three categories of expenses requiring alignment with revenue? How is this accomplished through the recording of adjusting entries?
10. What are mixed balance sheet accounts, income statement accounts, and accruals?

A. The Operating Cycle

Financial transactions that occur continuously during an accounting time period are part of a sequence of activities. In Bluebeard Computer Corporation, this sequence of activities takes the following form:

> 1. Operations begin with some cash on hand.
> 2. This cash is used to purchase supplies and to pay expenses incurred while performing computer repairs.
> 3. Revenue is earned as repair services are performed. (An accounts receivable may result.)
> 4. Cash is collected.

This cash-to-cash sequence of events is commonly referred to as an operating cycle, as described in Chapter 2. This cycle is illustrated in Figure 3-1.

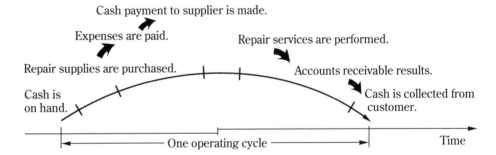

Figure 3-1   One operating cycle

During this operating cycle, financial statements are prepared at specific time intervals. For example, a balance sheet is prepared at December 31, 19X3 and 19X4, and an income statement is prepared for the year ended December 31, 19X4. The timeframe of these statements is illustrated in Figure 3-2. Balance sheets, income statements, and other financial statements, such as cash flow statements, are often prepared monthly and/or quarterly as well as annually.

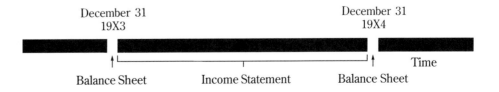

Figure 3-2   Periodic preparation of financial statements

Because they cover specific periods of time, these financial statements are based on some operating cycles that have been completed and others that are still incomplete. The overlapping of these cycles is illustrated in Figure 3-3.

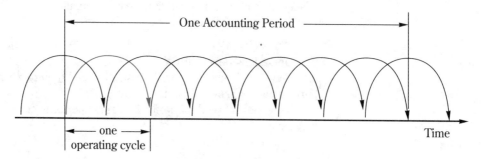

Figure 3-3   Overlapping operating cycles

As some transactions in one cycle are being completed, others are only beginning. For example, while repairs are being completed in one cycle, repair supplies are being purchased for use in another cycle; while expenses are being paid in one cycle, repairs are beginning in another cycle; and, while all this is going on, cash is being collected and being paid out continuously. A similar operating cycle exists for every entity, whether it provides a service, buys and sells merchandise, or manufactures products. Although the cycle of each type of entity may have different components, the basic sequence remains the same.

Under the going-concern assumption, any incomplete cycles that exist at the beginning and end of each operating cycle will be completed during the unlimited life of the entity. Accordingly, the use of historical costs to prepare financial statements is a reliable measure of financial transactions as they are completed, because it is objectively determined and can be verified by reference to documents.

Accountants are obviously concerned with the accurate recording of all these transactions. However, the recording of some transactions causes more theoretical problems than the recording of others. For example, the choice of a point at which revenue can be said to be earned causes numerous problems for accountants; the point at which an asset becomes an expense is not always clear-cut either. Later in this chapter, we examine further some transactions of Bluebeard Computer Corporation in order to focus on two major categories of transactions that cause recording problems for accountants. These two categories are:

1. Transactions involving services performed or goods sold by the business (because of the need to establish *the point at which revenue is earned*).
2. Transactions involving expenses incurred to earn revenues.

Revenue Recognition

Accounting concepts provide guidance as to when an economic activity should be recognized in financial statements. An economic activity is recognized when it meets three criteria:

1. It has an appropriate basis of measurement
2. The amount involved can be reasonably estimated
3. There are probable future economic benefits.

This section discusses these recognition criteria in terms of revenue recognition and expense recognition and explains the need for consistency.

Revenue recognition
Revenue is recognized as having been earned when the service is completed or the goods sold.

Revenue recognition is the process of identifying revenue with a particular time period, and it occurs when the entity acquires the right to receive payment from its customers. However, three possibilities remain:

1. Is revenue earned throughout the accounting cycle, while the service is being completed? If so, how is an estimate accurately made?
2. Is revenue earned only when the service has been completed?
3. Is revenue earned when cash from the service is collected?

Although revenue has certainly been earned by the time the service is completed and the cash is collected, accountants generally assume that revenue is earned at an earlier point — when the service is completed, whether or not payment has been made. This point can be more objectively determined than other subjective estimates. In actual practice, it is convenient to recognize revenue at the point when an invoice is prepared and sent to the customer. On this date, it is assumed that goods have been delivered or services have been rendered. This transaction creates an asset called *accounts receivable*, which is exchanged for the asset cash when payment is received.

In some cases, a deposit or advance payment is obtained before the service is performed. When an advance payment is received, accountants use the following accepted practice to record this type of receipt consistently:

1. The receipt is recorded as a *liability* if the service is not expected to be completed before the end of the current accounting period.
2. The receipt is recorded as a *revenue* if the service is expected to be completed during the current accounting period.

Expense Recognition

Cash payments, referred to as *cost outlays*, are made continuously during the accounting time period and are recorded at cost, that is, at the amount paid. Each cost outlay is recorded either as an *asset*, if it can be used to produce future revenues, or as an *expense*, if it does not have the potential to produce future revenues. The following practice is often used by accountants to record cost outlays consistently:

1. The cost is recorded as an *asset* if it will be incurred in producing revenue in future accounting time periods.
2. The cost is recorded as an *expense* if it will be consumed during the current accounting period.

This interrelationship between assets and expenses is illustrated in Figure 3-4.

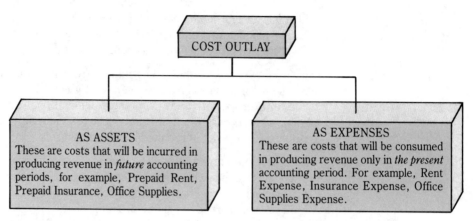

Figure 3-4   The interrelationship of assets and expenses

Theoretically, any cost outlay that has a future value — that is, it will be used in producing revenue in future accounting time periods — should be recorded as an asset. In actual practice, an arbitrary rule is usually adopted to facilitate the need to keep track of assets that expire in the future:

> If the future value of the asset provides benefits during more than the current accounting period, then it is recorded as an *asset*. If the future value of the asset expires during the current accounting period, then it is recorded as an *expense*.

In this way, the financial statements prepared at the end of the time period accurately reflect the status of the cost, although the cost outlay may be inaccurately stated during the accounting period. Thus, while the payment of rent on January 1 is an asset during January, it is properly reflected as an expense at January 31, if it was originally recorded as rent expense on January 1.

Varying practices depend on the accounting policies adopted by the particular entity. Some large entities record all cost outlays of one kind as assets and all cost outlays of another kind as expenses. If this practice is followed during the accounting period, then the expired portion of assets and the unexpired portion of expenses must be accurately reflected in the financial statements at the end of the accounting period. Adjusting journal entries, explained in sections D and E of this chapter, are prepared to record the proper end-of-period status of such items.

The Need for Consistency

An overall concern of the accountant in recording revenues and cost outlays is that the income statement and balance sheet reflect the operating results and financial position of the entity at the end of the period.

One possible manipulation of an entity's operating results and financial position results when different accounting policies and rules are used from one accounting period to another. Although many revenues and expenses can be recorded properly in more than one way, the accounting practice of consistency requires that the same policies and rules be used from one time period to another. In this way, there is uniformity in the financial information recorded and reported in financial statements. Such uniformity means that changes in the operating results and financial position of an entity are caused by its operations and not by changes in accounting policies and rules. Changes in these policies and rules are discouraged unless the change results in improved reporting in financial statements. (Any such change must be noted in the financial statements.)

B. Transactions Analysis Involving Expense and Revenue Recognition

The January and February transactions of Bluebeard Computer Corporation will be used to demonstrate record keeping using the expense and revenue recognition assumptions made by accountants. January transactions 1 to 8 were previously recorded and discussed in chapters 1 and 2; this chapter continues with February transactions 9 to 13. The following summary of these February transactions appears with a guide to which assumption — expense or revenue recognition — is being discussed in each transaction.

**Illustrative Problem —
Expense and Revenue Recognition Analysis**

The analysis and recording of each transaction is described in detail in the following pages. The numbers in parentheses in T-accounts refer to the transaction number. The posted ledger accounts appear to the right of the text.

		Application of Accounting Assumption	
Transaction Number Date	Description of Transaction	Expense Recognition	Revenue Recognition
9. Feb. 5	The corporation purchased on account $900-worth of repair supplies expected to be used during February.	EXPENSE	
10. Feb. 13	The corporation performed $5,000-worth of repairs for a customer who signed a 60-day, 12-percent, interest-bearing note as payment.		REVENUE
11. Feb. 26	The corporation received $2,000 from a customer for repairs that are expected to be done before the end of February.		REVENUE
12. Feb. 28	Additional computer repairs were made for customers during February as follows: $9,395-worth were repairs made for cash, $500-worth were repairs made on account.		REVENUE
13. Feb. 28	Miscellaneous expenses were paid during the month: $600, rent expense; $2,500, salaries; $700, truck; and $300, utilities.	EXPENSE	

REFER TO THE FOLLOWING AS YOU ANALYZE EACH TRANSACTION	
EXPENSE RECOGNITION	REVENUE RECOGNITION
The cost is recorded as an ASSET if it will be used in producing revenue in future accounting time periods.	*The receipt is recorded as a LIABILITY* if the service is not expected to be completed before the end of the current accounting time period.
The cost is recorded as an EXPENSE if it will be used up during the current accounting period.	*The receipt is recorded as a REVENUE* if the service is expected to be completed during the current accounting period.

Transaction 9

The corporation purchased on account $900-worth of supplies expected to be used during February.

Analysis: Since the repair supplies are expected to be used during the current accounting period, the cost of the supplies is considered to be an expense.

Journal Entry: An expense account, Supplies Expense, is increased by this transaction. (An expense is increased by a debit.) A liability account, Accounts Payable, is increased by the transaction. (A liability is increased by a credit.) The journal entry appears as follows:

	Supplies Expense	
(9)	900	

Feb. 5	Supplies Expense	668	900	
	Accounts Payable	210		900
	To record purchase of supplies.			

Accounts Payable		
	(9)	900

Transaction 10

The corporation performed $5,000-worth of repairs for a customer who signed a 60-day, 12-percent, interest-bearing note as payment. The $5,000 principal and interest will be paid at the end of 60 days.

Analysis: These repairs were completed before the end of February; revenue has therefore been earned and must be recorded.

Journal Entry: An asset account is increased by this transaction. (An asset increase is recorded by a debit.) A revenue account, Repair Revenue, is increased by this transaction. (A revenue increase is recorded by a credit.) The journal entry appears as follows:

Notes Receivable	
(10) 5,000	

Feb. 13	Notes Receivable	120	5,000	
	Repair Revenue	450		5,000
	To record payment for repairs by note.			

Repair Revenue	
	(10) 5,000

Transaction 11

The corporation received $2,000 from a customer for repairs that are expected to be done before the end of February.

Analysis: Since the repairs are expected to be done before the current accounting period ends, the $2,000 is recorded as a revenue.

Journal Entry: An asset account, Cash, is increased in this transaction. (An asset is increased by a debit.) A revenue account, Repair Revenue, is also increased by the transaction. (A revenue is increased by a credit.) The journal entry appears as follows:

Cash	
(11) 2,000	

	Repair Revenue
	(11) 2,000

Feb. 26	Cash	101	2,000	
	Repair Revenue	450		2,000
	To record payment for repairs to be made in February.			

Transaction 12

An additional $9,895-worth of computer repairs were made for customers during February; $9,395-worth of repairs were made for cash; $500-worth of these repairs were made on account.

Analysis: These revenue activities affect two asset accounts. The asset accounts, Cash and Accounts Receivable, are increased by the revenue earned during the month. Because three accounts are involved in this transaction, a compound journal entry is necessary.

Journal Entry: The asset accounts, Cash and Accounts Receivable, are increased by this transaction. (Assets are increased by a debit.) A revenue account, Repair Revenue, is increased by this transaction. (A revenue is increased by a credit.) The journal entry appears as follows:

Cash	
(12) 9,395	

Accounts Receivable	
(12) 500	

	Repair Revenue
	(12) 9,895

Feb. 28	Cash	101	9,395	
	Accounts Receivable	110	500	
	Repair Revenue	450		9,895
	To record repairs made during February.			

Transaction 13

Paid expenses incurred during the month to earn the repair revenue consist of Rent Expense for February, $600; Salaries Expense for four weeks in February, $2,500; Truck Expense for gas, oil, etc., $700; and Utility Expense, $300.

Analysis: These expenses, summarized here for demonstration, are applicable to the current accounting period, since their costs have been used up during the month.

Journal Entry: In actual practice, each paid expense would be recorded individually as the payment was made. Each expense is increased in this transaction. (An increase in an expense is recorded by a debit to each expense account.) An asset account, Cash, is decreased by these expenses. (A decrease in an asset is recorded by a credit.) Since the transactions are summarized here, only one credit of $4,100 is made to the Cash account. The journal entry appears as follows:

Rent Expense	
(13) 600	

Salaries Expense	
(13) 2,500	

Truck Expense	
(13) 700	

Utilities Expense	
(13) 300	

	Cash
	(13) 4,100

Feb. 28	Rent Expense	654	600	
	Salaries Expense	656	2,500	
	Truck Expense	670	700	
	Utilities Expense	676	300	
	Cash	101		4,100
	To record miscellaneous expenses paid.			

C.   Accrual Accounting and the Matching Concept

At the beginning of this chapter, the transactions of business entities were shown to comprise a sequence of events, identified as an operating cycle. Each entity's accounting time period consists of a series of such cycles. As the transactions in one operating cycle are completed, other cycles are beginning; still others are in progress. Financial statements are prepared on the basis of data originating with fully completed and partially completed cycles. Accrual accounting, as described in Chapter 1, matches expenses to revenues of a particular time period. The matching of revenues with expenses is the objective; the accrual method of accounting is the basis on which accounts are adjusted to reach the objective. Under this method, the cost of assets transferred to customers or consumed during the period are considered as expenses; these expenses are matched to the revenues generated by these expenses and are included in the income statement of the same period.

Reported net income, therefore, results from the application of accrual accounting and the matching concept. Their relationship within an accounting time period can be illustrated as in Figure 3-5.

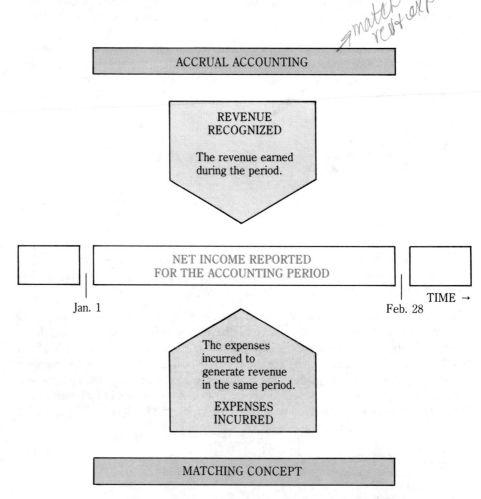

Figure 3-5   **The relationship among accrual accounting, the matching concept, and net income reported for one accounting period**

Since only the cost of assets transferred to customers or consumed during the period are considered as expenses, any expenses relating to other accounting periods are excluded from the calculation of net income for the current time period — except for certain extraordinary items that do not occur regularly and are material in amount; these are discussed in Chapter 4.

For accrual accounting, three different categories of expenses require alignment with revenue. They can be distinguished as follows:

Category 1
The cost of goods (either items sold or services provided) transferred to customers can be easily aligned as expenses incurred in the same period that revenue is generated. For example, at Bluebeard Computer Corporation, the use of parts in repairing computers can be identified with revenue generated by the repairs that required those parts.

Category 2
The cost of assets only partially consumed during the time period is not always easily aligned with revenue generated. For example, Bluebeard's equipment and truck were used to generate revenue in January and February 19X1 but were not fully used up during its first months of operation; that is, they still have some future benefit. Accordingly, the amount used up of the useful "life" of the equipment and the truck must be estimated, and this estimate allocated as an expense incurred in generating the revenue of that time period. The estimate is often not easily calculated in actual practice.

Category 3
The cost of some expenses incurred during the period is also not always identified easily with revenue generated. For example, the president of Bluebeard maintains that part of his salary benefits future time periods; for instance, his time spent soliciting future customers in January and February resulted in no generation of revenue during that time period. His accountant agrees. However, in this and similar cases, his salary is recorded as a 19X1 expense, the time period in which his services as an employee are performed. This practice is in accordance with GAAP because no future benefit can be identified clearly with salary expense; therefore, the salary does not qualify as an asset, the only other way it could have been recorded.

Cash basis of accounting
Cash payments are recorded when they are made, and receipts are recorded when cash is received.

These categories relate to the accrual method of accounting. An alternate method, used primarily by full-time farming and fishing entities, is referred to as the **cash basis of accounting**. Under this method, cash payments and cash receipts are aligned with a particular time period. The excess of cash receipts over cash payments indicates a positive cash flow, and an excess of cash payments over cash receipts represents a negative cash flow. However, cash receipts are seldom the same as revenue earned; customarily, for example, credit is extended to customers, who are permitted to pay at a later date. Similarly, cash payments are seldom the same amount as expenses incurred because of the purchase of services and goods on account. As a result, the cash basis of accounting, while it measures cash flow, fails to provide an accurate measurement of net income; its use, therefore, is not recommended by GAAP. From this introduction, you can see that the matching concept is difficult to achieve in practice; for a further discussion, see Conceptual Issue 3-1.

Conceptual Issue 3-1

The Matching Principle: Why It's So Hard To Achieve in Practice

By Ross Skinner

In an exchange economy, the goal of productive activity is to sell a product or service for more than its cost of production. In accounting, income is the difference between costs (sacrifices) and revenues (benefits). If one visualizes a business in the form of a single venture, income over its entire lifetime will be the difference between cash receipts (excluding capital paid in) and cash disbursements (excluding capital withdrawn or return on capital, such as dividends, paid out). It is natural, therefore, to think of revenue as an inflow of assets — ultimately, cash—in exchange for the product of the enterprise.

This discussion oversimplifies matters. An enterprise may receive cash other than in exchange for product or service or as a capital contribution. For example, if an asset is destroyed by fire, the insurance proceeds would not represent payment for the productive activity of the enterprise. It is still true that over the lifetime of an enterprise the excess of cash receipts over cash disbursements (excluding cash associated with capital transactions) will equal the net gain. But that net gain will consist of (1) the excess of revenues from

productive activity over costs of earning those revenues, together with (2) miscellaneous gains or losses on events or activities that are not part of the main activity of the enterprise.

When speaking of the lifetime of an enterprise from initial cash investment to ultimate cash realization, it is possible to talk solely about movements in cash. Accounting for a period shorter than enterprise lifetime, however, presents a problem. At any given point of time, the enterprise will have delivered product or services for which it has not yet received payment. Conversely, it may have received payment for which it has not yet satisfied its obligation to deliver. It will also have incurred other costs and acquired rights or items that may reasonably be expected to be rewarded by the receipt of cash in a future exchange transaction. Moreover, it may not yet have paid for goods or services it has received. Thus, estimation of income for a period based on transactions is considerably more difficult than determination of income for a completed business lifetime. Such estimation requires that

The Need for Adjusting Entries

At the end of an accounting period, accountants prepare financial statements. First, however, they must change some accounting entries. During the period, assets may partially or completely expire, and the entity may partially or completely earn liabilities. These changes must be recorded with **adjusting entries**.

The purpose of adjustments is to report all asset, liability, and owners' equity amounts fairly and to recognize all revenues and expenses for the period on an accrual basis. These changes are made so that both the balance sheet and the income statement will reflect the correct operating results and financial status at the end of the accounting period.

Adjusting entry
An adjustment made at the end of an operating cycle to update the accounts of an entity; the adjustment is required by the matching concept.

non-capital cash inflows of past, present, and future periods be assigned to periods in which they are "earned". Similarly, non-capital cash outflows of past, present, and future periods must be assigned to the period in which any benefit from them is used up. That is, the goal of income accounting under the transaction-based model is to provide rules for assigning revenues and expenses from operating transactions and gains and losses from peripheral activities to accounting periods.

Because income accounting associates cash flows with time periods, it automatically results in recognizing assets and liabilities. For example, a cash receipt today that is associated with revenue of a future period must be recorded as unearned revenue—a liability to deliver product or service in the future. A cash disbursement today associated with revenue of future periods must be recorded as an asset — an expectation of future benefit. In other words, asset and liability recognition (and changes in assets and liabilities previously recognized) can result from income accounting conventions as well as the conventions governing initial recognition of asset and liabilities.

It is convenient to summarize here the definitions of elements of financial statements provided by the FASB. These definitions make a useful distinction whereby revenues and expenses are described as the outcome of the primary business operations, and gains and losses are described as the result of incidental or peripheral events or activities.
• Assets are probable future economic benefits obtained or controlled by a particular entity as a result of past transactions or events.
• Liabilities are probable future sacrifices of economic benefits arising from present obligations of a particular entity to transfer assets or provide services to other entities in the future as a result of past transactions or events.
• Revenues are inflows or other enhancements of assets of an entity or settlements of its liabilities (or a combination of both) during a period from delivering or producing goods, rendering services, or other activities that constitute the entity's ongoing major or central operations.
• Expenses are outflows or other using up of assets or incurrences of liabilities (or a combination of both) during a period from delivering or producing goods, rendering services, or carrying out other activities that constitute the entity's ongoing major or central operations.
• Gains are increases in equity (net assets) from peripheral or incidental transactions of an entity and from all other transactions and other events and circumstances affecting the entity during a period, except those that result from revenues or from investments by owners.
• Losses are decreases in equity (net assets) from peripheral or incidental transactions of an entity and from all other transactions and other events and circumstances affecting the entity during a period, except those that result from expenses or from distributions to owners.[1]

Source   Courtesy of Ross Skinner.

D.   Adjusting Balance Sheet Accounts

The trial balance of Bluebeard Computer Corporation at February 28 includes cost outlays that have been recorded as *assets* of the corporation. These cost outlays are recorded as assets during an accounting period if they can be used to produce future revenue. At the end of the period, an accounting measurement is required. The amount of the asset that has expired during the period must be calculated and that amount transferred to *expense*. In this way, revenues for the period are matched to expenses incurred to earn that revenue.

The February 28 trial balance of the corporation also includes receipts that have been recorded as *liabilities*. These receipts are recorded as liabilities during an accounting period if they have not been earned when received. At the end of the period, an accounting measurement is also required. The amount of the liability that has been earned during the period must be calculated and the amount transferred to *revenue*. In this way, revenues for the period are matched to expenses incurred to earn that revenue.

Adjusting Asset and Liability Accounts

Mixed accounts
Accounts containing both a balance sheet and income statement portion at the date of adjusting entry preparation.

The asset and liability accounts referred to above are sometimes called **mixed accounts** by accountants. They are given this name because they include both a *balance sheet* portion and an *income statement* portion at the end of the accounting period. The income statement portion must be removed from the account by an adjusting entry.

Illustrative Problem — Adjusting Asset and Liability Accounts

The following balance sheet accounts of Bluebeard Computer Corporation require this kind of adjustment at February 28:

Partial Trial Balance
February 28, 19X1

	Account Balances	
	Debit	*Credit*
a. Prepaid Insurance	$1,200	
b. Unearned Rent		$600

This is a LIABILITY account balance.

These accounts are analyzed and it is determined that adjusting entries for items a and b need to be prepared.

Each of the above accounts is analyzed in the following manner:

Step 1
At the end of the accounting period, determine which portion of the mixed account belongs in the balance sheet and which belongs in the income statement.

Step 2
The portion that does not belong in the asset or liability account must be transferred out. An adjusting entry is made in the general journal and posted to the proper accounts to accomplish this transfer.

(a)

In January, the company paid for a 12-month insurance policy, effective January 1 (transaction 4).

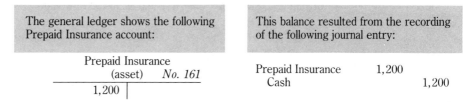

The general ledger shows the following Prepaid Insurance account:	This balance resulted from the recording of the following journal entry:

Prepaid Insurance
(asset)   *No. 161*
1,200 |

Prepaid Insurance   1,200
    Cash   1,200

At February 28, only two months of the policy have expired.

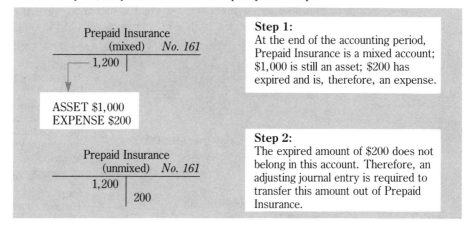

Prepaid Insurance
(mixed)   *No. 161*
1,200 |

ASSET $1,000
EXPENSE $200

Prepaid Insurance
(unmixed)   *No. 161*
1,200 |
         | 200

Step 1:
At the end of the accounting period, Prepaid Insurance is a mixed account; $1,000 is still an asset; $200 has expired and is, therefore, an expense.

Step 2:
The expired amount of $200 does not belong in this account. Therefore, an adjusting journal entry is required to transfer this amount out of Prepaid Insurance.

This is the adjusting entry:

Feb. 28   Insurance Expense   631   200
              Prepaid Insurance   161   200
              To record insurance expense for January
              and February.

This adjusting entry transfers the expired $200 of prepaid insurance to the Insurance Expense account. The balance remaining in the Prepaid Insurance account after the entry is posted ($1,200 − $200) represents the unexpired asset that will benefit future periods.

When the adjusting entry is posted, the expense portion is transferred as follows:

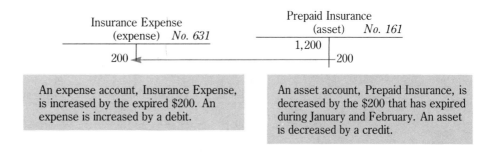

Insurance Expense
(expense)   *No. 631*
200 |

Prepaid Insurance
(asset)   *No. 161*
1,200 |
         | 200

An expense account, Insurance Expense, is increased by the expired $200. An expense is increased by a debit.	An asset account, Prepaid Insurance, is decreased by the $200 that has expired during January and February. An asset is decreased by a credit.

(b)

On January 15, the corporation signed a contract for the use of its truck on a part-time basis and received an advance payment of $500 for use of the truck as follows: $100 for January, $200 for February, and $200 for March.

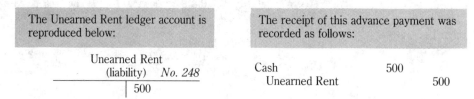

The Unearned Rent ledger account is reproduced below:	The receipt of this advance payment was recorded as follows:

	Unearned Rent			Cash	500	
	(liability) *No. 248*			Unearned Rent		500
	500					

This advance payment was recorded as unearned, since it was received before it was earned. At February 28, however, two months of the rent have been earned.

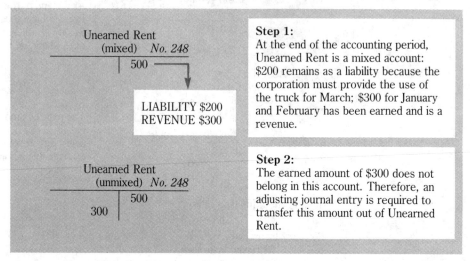

Unearned Rent
(mixed) *No. 248*
| 500

LIABILITY $200
REVENUE $300

Step 1:
At the end of the accounting period, Unearned Rent is a mixed account: $200 remains as a liability because the corporation must provide the use of the truck for March; $300 for January and February has been earned and is a revenue.

Unearned Rent
(unmixed) *No. 248*
| 500
300 |

Step 2:
The earned amount of $300 does not belong in this account. Therefore, an adjusting journal entry is required to transfer this amount out of Unearned Rent.

This is the adjusting entry:

Feb. 28	Unearned Rent	248	300	
	Rent Earned	440		300
	To record rental earned during January and February.			

This adjusting entry transfers the $300 of rent earned to revenue. The balance remaining in Unearned Rent after the entry is posted ($500 − $300) represents the unearned amount that will be earned in future periods.

When the adjusting entry is posted, the revenue element is removed from the mixed account as follows:

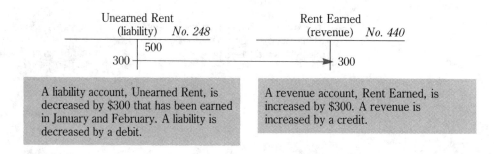

Unearned Rent (liability) *No. 248*		Rent Earned (revenue) *No. 440*
500		
300		300

A liability account, Unearned Rent, is decreased by $300 that has been earned in January and February. A liability is decreased by a debit.	A revenue account, Rent Earned, is increased by $300. A revenue is increased by a credit.

Adjusting Fixed Asset Accounts

Depreciation
The decline in the useful life of a fixed asset.

Depreciation expense
That part of the original cost of a fixed asset allocated to a particular accounting period.

Accumulated depreciation
The total amount of an asset's original cost that has been allocated to expense since the asset was acquired. The account where these expenses are entered is called an *asset valuation account* or *contra-asset account.*

Valuation account
An account that is deducted from another account to modify the recorded amount of that latter account; sometimes called a *contra account.*

Contra account
An account used to accumulate amounts that are related; sometimes called a *valuation account.*

Useful life
An estimate of the time during which an asset will be used by the entity; the term is used in connection with a fixed asset.

Scrap value
The estimated amount for which the asset can be sold at the end of its useful life; also called *salvage value.*

The expired portion was transferred from the asset account in the case of insurance. The expired portion of a fixed asset, however, is handled in a different manner — it is not transferred from the fixed asset account.

1. The expired portion of a fixed asset is called **depreciation**. The periodic expired cost, called **depreciation expense**, requires no periodic cash outlay but, nevertheless, is a continuous expense of operating the business.
2. The amount of depreciation is not transferred from the asset account, since both the original cost and recorded depreciation are relevant pieces of information to readers of financial statements. Therefore, two new accounts are used to record the estimated depreciation.

Adjusting journal entries used to record depreciation take the following form:

Depreciation Expense	XX	
Accumulated Depreciation		XX

The Depreciation Expense account records the amount of estimated expense that belongs to the accounting period under consideration. This account is shown on the income statement as an expense. The amount of **accumulated depreciation** is deducted from the asset on the balance sheet to disclose the net book value of the asset; accordingly, it is referred to as a **valuation account** or **contra account**. The balance in the Accumulated Depreciation account represents the amount of an asset's original cost that has been allocated to expense.

The amount of depreciation is calculated using an estimate of the **useful life** of the asset and its subsequent **scrap value**. The calculation is illustrated in the examples that follow.

Illustrative Problem — Adjusting Fixed Asset Accounts

The following fixed assets of Bluebeard Computer Corporation consist of mixed balances at the end of the accounting period:

Partial Trial Balance
February 28, 19X1

	Account Balances	
	Debit	Credit
c. Equipment	$3,000	
d. Truck	8,000	

cost - salvage value (handwritten annotation)

Each account is analyzed in the following manner:

Step 1
At the end of the accounting period, determine the amount of depreciation expense.

Step 2
The estimated depreciation is *not* transferred from the asset account; rather, an adjusting journal entry is prepared using two new accounts, one of which is a contra-asset account. Note that a contra-fixed asset account *always has a credit balance.*

(c)

BCC owns $3,000-worth of equipment (transaction 2).

The Equipment ledger accounts appears as follows:

Equipment
(asset)   No. 183
3,000 |

This account balance resulted from two journal entries, which are summarized below for illustrative purposes only:

Equipment   3,000
     Cash   3,000

Calculation of Straight-Line Depreciation

$$\frac{Cost - Salvage\ value}{Useful\ life}$$

$$\frac{\$3,000 - \$200}{60} = \$45$$

Straight-line method of depreciation
A method in which equal amounts of depreciation expense are recorded for each time period over the useful life of the asset.

The equipment was recorded as a fixed asset because it has a useful life of 60 months and will have a scrap value of $200. Although this equipment had been purchased in January, it was only received in February. At February 28, one month of the net asset cost has expired. The depreciation expense for the equipment in February is calculated as $45 [($3,000 − 200) ÷ 60 = $45]. This estimate is calculated using the **straight-line method of depreciation**.

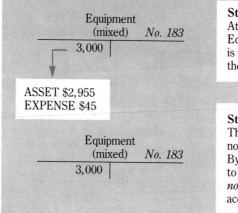

Equipment
(mixed)   No. 183
3,000 |

ASSET $2,955
EXPENSE $45

Step 1:
At the end of the accounting period, Equipment is a mixed account: $2,955 is still an asset; $45 has expired and is, therefore, an expense.

Equipment
(mixed)   No. 183
3,000 |

Step 2:
The expired amount of $45 does not belong in an asset account. By accounting convention with respect to fixed assets, the expired portion is *not* removed from the Equipment account.

The following adjusting journal entry is made:

Feb. 28 Depreciation Expense — Equipment   623   45
              Accumulated Depreciation — Equipment   193   45
         To record depreciation for February.

This adjusting entry records the $45 of depreciation on equipment. The mixed balance remains in the Equipment account.

When the adjusting entry is posted, the accounts appear as follows:

Equipment
(asset)   No. 183
3,000 |

Depreciation Expense
(expense)   No. 623
45 ←

Accumulated Depreciation
(asset
valuation)   No. 193
→ 45

This account remains unchanged.

An expense account, Depreciation Expense, is increased by $45 that has expired. An expense is increased by a debit.

The valuation account, Accumulated Depreciation, is also increased by the $45 that has expired. This valuation account is increased by a credit.

(d)

BCC owns a truck for which it paid $8,000 (transaction 3).

The truck ledger account appears as follows:

The truck purchase journal entry appears as follows:

Truck
(asset)   *No. 184*

8,000 |

Truck	8,000	
Bank Loan		5,000
Cash		3,000

The truck was recorded as a fixed asset because it has a useful life of 60 months; it will have a scrap value of $800. At February 28, two months of the truck cost have expired. Using the straight-line method of depreciation, the depreciation expense is calculated as: ($8,000 − $800) ÷ 60 months × 2 months = $240.

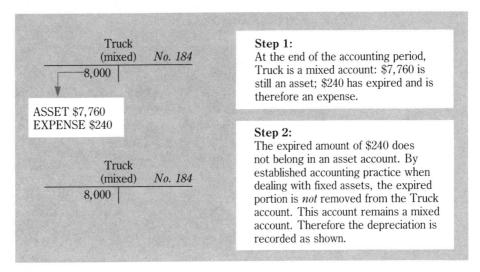

Truck
(mixed)   *No. 184*

8,000 |

ASSET $7,760
EXPENSE $240

Truck
(mixed)   *No. 184*

8,000 |

Step 1:
At the end of the accounting period, Truck is a mixed account: $7,760 is still an asset; $240 has expired and is therefore an expense.

Step 2:
The expired amount of $240 does not belong in an asset account. By established accounting practice when dealing with fixed assets, the expired portion is *not* removed from the Truck account. This account remains a mixed account. Therefore the depreciation is recorded as shown.

The following adjusting journal entry is made:

Feb. 28	Depreciation Expense — Truck	624	240	
	Accumulated Depreciation — Truck	194		240
	To record depreciation for January and February.			

This adjusting entry records the $240 of depreciation on trucks. The mixed balance remains in the Truck account. Depreciation expense is shown on the income statement as an expense. Accumulated depreciation is a valuation account deducted from the cost of the truck on the balance sheet.

When the adjusting entry is posted, the accounts appear as follows:

balance sheet

Truck
(asset)   *No. 184*

8,000 |

Depreciation Expense
(expense)   *No. 624*

240 |

Accumulated Depreciation
(asset valuation)   *No. 194*

| 240

This account remains unchanged.

An expense account, Depreciation Expense, is increased by $240, which has expired. An expense is increased by a debit.

The valuation account, Accumulated Depreciation, is also increased by $240 that has expired. This valuation account is increased by a credit.

E.   Adjusting Income Statement Accounts

The trial balance of Bluebeard Computer Corporation at February 28 includes a receipt that has been recorded as a revenue of the corporation.

> Receipts are recorded as *revenues* during an accounting period if they are expected to be earned during the period. If, in fact, they have not been earned by the end of the period, an accounting measurement is required. The amount of revenue unearned must be calculated and the unearned revenue recognized as a *liability* at the end of the period. In this way, only revenues earned during the period are matched with expenses incurred to earn those revenues.

The trial balance of the corporation also includes a cost outlay that has been recorded as an expense of the corporation.

> Cost outlays are recorded as *expenses* during an accounting period if they are expected to be used up (that is, if they are expected to expire) during the period. If, in fact, they have not been completely consumed by the end of the accounting period, an acccounting measurement is required. The amount of the expense that has not expired must be calculated and the unexpired amount recognized as an *asset* at the end of the period. In this way, revenues for the period are matched with expenses incurred to earn those revenues.

The revenue and expense accounts referred to above are also mixed accounts, since they include both an income statement portion and a balance sheet portion at the end of the period.

Illustrative Problem — Adjusting Income Statement Accounts

The following income statement accounts of Bluebeard Computer Corporation require adjustment at February 28:

Partial Trial Balance
February 28, 19X1

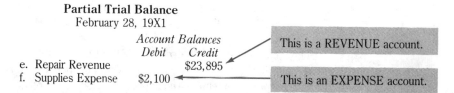

		Account Balances	
		Debit	*Credit*
e.	Repair Revenue		$23,895
f.	Supplies Expense	$2,100	

This is a REVENUE account.

This is an EXPENSE account.

These accounts are analyzed and adjusted as follows:

Step 1
At the end of the accounting period, determine which portion of the mixed account belongs in the balance sheet and which belongs in the income statement.

Step 2
The portion that does not belong in the revenue or expense account must be transferred out. An adjusting entry is made in the general journal and posted to the proper accounts to make this transfer.

(e)

BCC received $2,000 on February 26 for repairs to be made in February (transaction 11). According to its best estimates, the company would begin the repairs in March and hopefully have the work completed by mid-April.

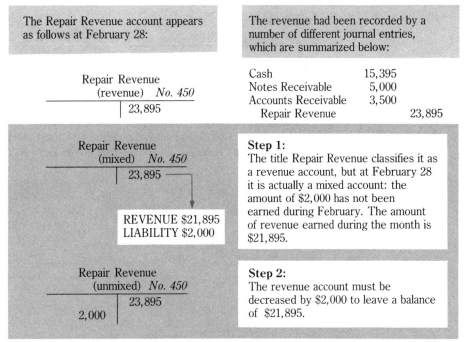

| The Repair Revenue account appears as follows at February 28: | The revenue had been recorded by a number of different journal entries, which are summarized below: |

Repair Revenue
(revenue) *No. 450*
| 23,895

Cash   15,395
Notes Receivable   5,000
Accounts Receivable   3,500
  Repair Revenue   23,895

Repair Revenue
(mixed) *No. 450*
| 23,895

REVENUE $21,895
LIABILITY $2,000

Step 1:
The title Repair Revenue classifies it as a revenue account, but at February 28 it is actually a mixed account: the amount of $2,000 has not been earned during February. The amount of revenue earned during the month is $21,895.

Repair Revenue
(unmixed) *No. 450*
| 23,895
2,000 |

Step 2:
The revenue account must be decreased by $2,000 to leave a balance of $21,895.

This is the adjusting journal entry:

Feb. 28   Repair Revenue   450   2,000
      Unearned Repair Revenue   247   2,000
    To record unearned repair revenue
    at February 28.

The revenue account, Repair Revenue, is decreased by the $2,000 that has not yet been earned. In this way, the mixed revenue account is split into two portions: the unearned amount is transferred to the balance sheet liability account; what remains in the account is the income statement portion.

When this adjusting entry is posted, the unearned portion is transferred from the mixed account as follows:

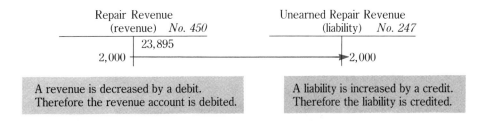

| Repair Revenue (revenue) *No. 450* | Unearned Repair Revenue (liability) *No. 247* |

23,895
2,000 | 2,000

| A revenue is decreased by a debit. Therefore the revenue account is debited. | A liability is increased by a credit. Therefore the liability is credited. |

(f)

BCC purchased $2,100-worth of supplies to be used during January and February (transactions 8 and 9). Since these supplies were expected to be used during that accounting period, their cost was recorded as an expense.

The Supplies Expense account appears as follows at February 28:	This expense had been recorded by a number of different journal entries, which are summarized below:

```
          Supplies Expense
            (expense)  No. 668
          ─────────────────────
             2,100  |
```

```
Supplies Expense        2,100
   Cash                         1,200
   Accounts Payable               900
```

At February 28, a physical count of inventory of supplies showed that $495-worth of supplies were still on hand, indicating that not all the supplies were used during the two months.

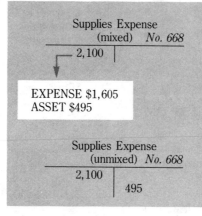

Step 1:
At the end of February, the Supplies Expense account is actually a mixed account: an amount of $495 has not been used during the month. The amount of the expense is actually $1,605.

```
          Supplies Expense
            (mixed)  No. 668
          ─────────────────────
             2,100  |

          ┌──────────────────┐
          │ EXPENSE $1,605   │
          │ ASSET $495       │
          └──────────────────┘

          Supplies Expense
            (unmixed)  No. 668
          ─────────────────────
             2,100  |
                    |   495
```

Step 2:
This expense account has to be decreased by $495. An adjusting journal entry is prepared.

This is the adjusting journal entry:

```
Feb. 28  Supplies                              173    495
            Supplies Expense                   668          495
         To record unused supplies at
         February 28.
```

When this adjusting entry is posted, the unexpired portion is transferred from the mixed account as follows:

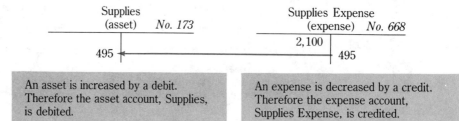

```
          Supplies                        Supplies Expense
          (asset)    No. 173              (expense)  No. 668
       ──────────────────────        ──────────────────────
                                           2,100  |
          495  ◄──────────────────────────────────┤  495
```

An asset is increased by a debit. Therefore the asset account, Supplies, is debited.	An expense is decreased by a credit. Therefore the expense account, Supplies Expense, is credited.

F. Accruals

Accruals
Items that accumulate or increase and are usually recognized to increase during the adjustment phase of the accounting cycle.

Accrued expenses
An increase in expenses during the current accounting period that is due to be paid in a future accounting period.

Accrued revenues
An increase in revenues during the current accounting period that is due to be received in a future accounting period.

Some revenues and expenses increase as time passes and are therefore said to accrue. An **accrual** is an item that increases with the passage of time and is often used by accountants in reference to adjusting entries. Several examples of items that accrue on a day-to-day basis are the following:

Revenues that Accrue	*Expenses that Accrue*
Interest Earned	Interest Expense
Rent Earned	Rent Expense
	Salaries Expense
These revenues are usually recorded when cash is received.	These expenses are usually recorded when cash is paid.

Interest, as an example, accrues (increases) daily but is received or paid only at certain specified times: perhaps monthly, in the case of banks, or at the due date of a note when the principal and interest are paid. No accounting problem is caused by the fact that these items have not been recorded during the accounting period, but accounting principles require that revenues earned and expenses incurred during the period must be matched in the accounts. Accordingly, at the end of the period, an adjusting journal entry is made so that revenues are properly matched with expenses of the same period.

> During the accounting period, regular business transactions are recorded as they occur. At the end of the period, the accountant may find that ledger account balances are incomplete. In the case of revenue and expense items that accrue, some new amounts must be brought into the accounts. The adjusting entries to accomplish this balance are referred to as *accruals*.

Illustrative Problem — Recording Accruals

The following accounts of Bluebeard Computer Corporation require an accrual at February 28:

Income Statement Account	*Balance Sheet Account*
Interest Earned	Interest Receivable
Salaries Expense	Salaries Payable
Interest Expense	Interest Payable
Income Tax Expense	Income Tax Payable

The accounts are discussed and adjusting entries are prepared in the following pages, under headings g, h, i, and j.

Unrecorded Revenues

Unrecorded revenues
Revenues earned during
an accounting period
that are not due to be
collected until the next
period.

Unrecorded revenues consist of revenues that have been earned during the accounting period but that are not due to be collected until sometime in the next period.

(g)

Bluebeard Computer Corporation performed $5,000-worth of repairs for one of its customers, who signed a 60-day, 12-percent, interest-bearing note dated February 13 (transaction 10).

Although interest accrues daily on the $5,000 loan, the interest is actually received only at the maturity date of the note, April 14, when the amount due (principal plus interest) is paid by the customer. At February 28, the end of the accounting period for BCC, interest has been earned for 15 days in February (February 13-28), as shown in Figure 3-6, but this interest earned has not yet been recorded by the company.

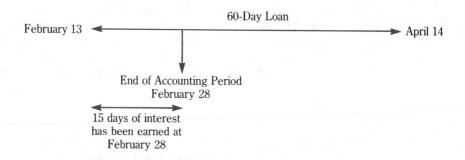

Figure 3-6   Interest earned during an accounting period

The formula for computing interest is shown below:

$$\text{Interest} = \text{Principal} \times \text{Interest rate} \times \frac{\text{Elapsed time in days}}{365}.$$

The interest revenue accrued at February 28 is computed as follows:

$$\text{Interest} = \$5,000 \times 0.12 \times \frac{15}{365} = \$24.66 \text{ (or \$25 rounded for illustrative purposes)}.$$

The principal multiplied by the interest rate equals the total interest for one year ($5,000 × 0.12 = $600); the interest for a year ($600) multiplied by the elapsed fraction of a year (15/365) is the interest revenue for 15 days ($600 × 15/365), or $25. The use of 365 days in the formula, ignoring leap years, is consistent with commercial practice, the primary reason being simplicity of calculation.

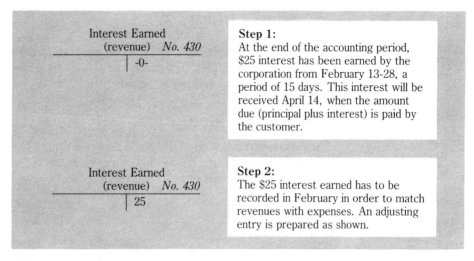

This is the adjusting journal entry:

Feb. 28   Interest Receivable   116   25
                Interest Earned   430   25
                        To record interest accrued at February 28.

This adjusting entry enables BBC to include in income of the period the interest earned, even though the payment has not yet been received. The entry created an accrued receivable — that is, a receivable for an income earned during an accounting period but collectible in another accounting period.

When the adjusting entry is posted, the accounts appear as follows:

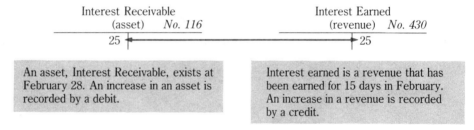

Other adjusting entries for various revenues, which have been earned by the company during the accounting period but have not been received or are not due to be collected until some time in the next period, are recorded in a manner similar to the adjustment for interest earned. The amount earned must be calculated and is recorded in the accounts by the following type of journal entry:

                    Receivable   XX
                        Earned   XX
                            To accrue revenue.

Unrecorded Expenses

Unrecorded expenses are expenses that have been incurred during the accounting period but have not been paid during the accounting period or that are not due to be paid until some time in the next period.

(h)

At February 28, the end of the accounting period for Bluebeard, salary expense had been incurred for three days in February, as shown in Figure 3-6, but this expense had not been recorded.

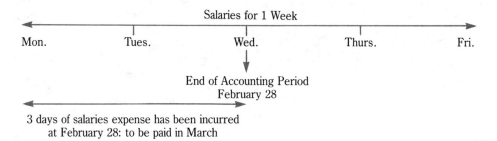

Salaries for 1 Week

Mon.   Tues.   Wed.   Thurs.   Fri.

End of Accounting Period
February 28

3 days of salaries expense has been incurred
at February 28: to be paid in March

Figure 3-6   Salary expense incurred but not paid during one accounting period

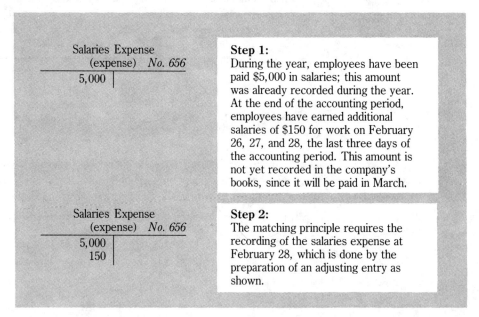

| Salaries Expense (expense) *No. 656* | **Step 1:** During the year, employees have been paid $5,000 in salaries; this amount was already recorded during the year. At the end of the accounting period, employees have earned additional salaries of $150 for work on February 26, 27, and 28, the last three days of the accounting period. This amount is not yet recorded in the company's books, since it will be paid in March. |
| 5,000 | |

Salaries Expense (expense) *No. 656*	**Step 2:** The matching principle requires the recording of the salaries expense at February 28, which is done by the preparation of an adjusting entry as shown.
5,000	
150	

This is the adjusting entry:

Feb. 28	Salaries Expense	656	150	
	Salaries Payable	226		150
	To record salaries accrued at February 28.			

This entry enables the company to include in expense all salaries earned by employees, even though not all salaries have yet been paid. The entry creates an accrued liability — that is, a liability for an expense incurred during one accounting period (February) but payable in another accounting period (March).

When the adjusting entry is posted, the accounts appear as follows:

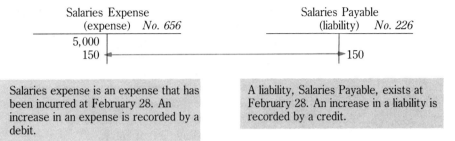

Salaries expense is an expense that has been incurred at February 28. An increase in an expense is recorded by a debit.

A liability, Salaries Payable, exists at February 28. An increase in a liability is recorded by a credit.

(i)

Bluebeard Computer Corporation had incurred a $5,000 bank loan in the purchase of a truck in January. The interest rate was 12-percent per annum. Although interest accrues daily on this bank loan, no interest has yet been paid at the end of the accounting time period.

At February 28, the end of the accounting period for BCC, interest has accrued for 56 days to February 28 (January 3 to February 28), but this interest expense has not yet been recorded by the company.

The interest expense accrued at February 28 is computed as follows:

$$\text{Interest} = \$5{,}000 \times 0.12 \times \frac{56}{365} = \$92.05 \text{ (or \$92 rounded for illustrative purposes)}$$

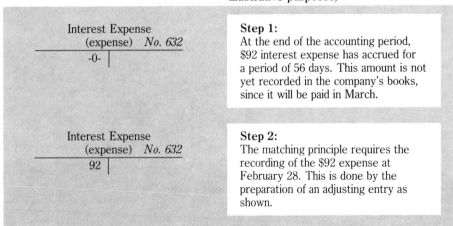

Step 1:
At the end of the accounting period, $92 interest expense has accrued for a period of 56 days. This amount is not yet recorded in the company's books, since it will be paid in March.

Step 2:
The matching principle requires the recording of the $92 expense at February 28. This is done by the preparation of an adjusting entry as shown.

This is the adjusting entry:

Feb. 28 Interest Expense   632   92
              Interest Payable   222   92
              To record interest accrued at February 28.

The entry creates an accrued liability — that is, a liability for an expense incurred during the current accounting period but payable in another accounting period (March).

When the adjusting entry is posted, the accounts appear as follows:

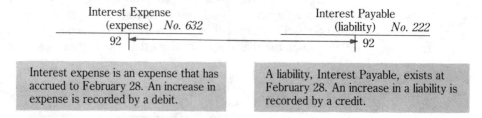

Interest Expense (expense) *No. 632*	Interest Payable (liability) *No. 222*
92	92

| Interest expense is an expense that has accrued to February 28. An increase in expense is recorded by a debit. | A liability, Interest Payable, exists at February 28. An increase in a liability is recorded by a credit. |

Other adjusting entries for expense (such as utilities, telephone, and so on) that have been incurred by the company during the accounting period but that are not due to be paid until the next period are recorded in a manner similar to the adjustment for salaries and interest expenses. The amount of the expense must be calculated and then recorded in the following type of entry:

Date	Expense	XX	
	Expense Payable		XX
	To accrue an expense.		

Recording Taxes

Another adjustment that is required for Bluebeard Computer Corporation involves the recording of $5,994 estimated income taxes due to the government. This payment is necessary because a corporation is taxed as an entity separate from its shareholders.

(j)

Income Tax Expense (expense) *No. 830*	**Step 1:** An estimate of the current period's income tax has not yet been recorded.
-0-	

Income Tax Expense (expense) *No. 830*	**Step 2:** The corporation's estimate of income taxes at February 28 is $5,994. These income taxes are recorded by an adjusting entry as shown.
5,994	

This is the adjusting entry:

Feb. 28	Income Tax Expense	830	5,994	
	Income Tax Payable	260		5,994
	To record estimated income taxes at February 28.			

When the adjusting entry is posted, the accounts appear as follows:

Income Tax Expense	Income Tax Payable
(expense) *No. 830*	(liability) *No. 260*
5,994	5,994

> Income Tax Expense is an expense that has been incurred. An expense is increased by a debit.

> Income Tax Payable is a liability that has accrued at February 28. A liability is increased by a credit.

The above adjusting entry enables the company to show the income taxes applicable to the income earned during the period. However, not all organizations are required to pay income tax; a case in point is not-for-profit organizations.

G.   The Accounting Process — Review of Steps 1–6

In this chapter, six individual steps of the accounting process have been reviewed. The first two steps occur continuously through the time period; the third to sixth steps occur at the end of the accounting period. The seventh step, preparing financial statements, is discussed in section H.

Step 1:   *Transactions Are Analyzed and Recorded in the Journal*
The general journal provides a complete record of a corporation's transactions, listed in chronological order. Because this journal is the first place a transaction is recorded, the general journal is commonly referred to as a *book of original entry*.

GENERAL JOURNAL

19X1				
Feb. 5	Supplies Expense	668	900	
	Accounts Payable	210		900
	To record purchase of supplies.			
13	Notes Receivable	120	5,000	
	Repair Revenue	450		5,000
	To record payment for repairs by note.			
26	Cash	101	2,000	
	Repair Revenue	450		2,000
	To record payment for repairs to be made in February.			
28	Cash	101	9,395	
	Accounts Receivable	110	500	
	Repair Revenue	450		9,895
	To record repairs made during February.			
28	Rent Expense	654	600	
	Salaries Expense	656	2,500	
	Truck Expense	670	700	
	Utilities Expense	676	300	
	Cash	101		4,100
	To record miscellaneous expenses paid.			

Step 2: The Journal Entries Are Posted to Ledger Accounts

When the posting of February transactions has been completed, the ledger accounts are footed and a net debit or credit balance calculated for each account. In the case of the Cash account, for example, a debit balance of $11,695 remains at the end of February. (The ledger accounts for Bluebeard Computer Corporation follow.) The conceptual T-account is used in place of the more formal ledger account, in order to emphasize the relationship between the accounting equation and the accounts that fall under each equation component. Because of space limitations, the January transactions are not repeated here; rather the January 31 balance of each account is carried forward from Chapter 2 (under "Trial Balance Preparation").

ASSETS	=	LIABILITIES	+	EQUITY

ASSETS

Cash   No. 101

Bal.	4,300	(13)	4,100
(11)	2,000		
(12)	9,395		
	15,695		4,100
Bal.	11,595		

Accounts Receivable No. 110

Bal.	3,000	
(12)	500	
Bal.	3,500	

Notes Receivable No. 120

(10)	5,000	

Prepaid Insurance No. 161

Bal.	1,200	

Equipment No. 183

Bal.	3,000	

Truck   No. 184

Bal.	8,000	

LIABILITIES

Bank Loan No. 201

	Bal.	5,000

Accounts Payable   No. 210

	Bal.	1,000
	(9)	900
	Bal.	1,900

Unearned Rent   No. 248

	Bal.	500

EQUITY

Common Stock   No. 320

	Bal.	11,000

Repair Revenue   No. 450

	Bal.	7,000
	(10)	5,000
	(11)	2,000
	(12)	9,895
	Bal.	23,895

Rent Expense   No. 654

Bal.	600	
(13)	600	
Bal.	1,200	

Salaries Expense   No. 656

Bal.	2,500	
(13)	2,500	
Bal.	5,000	

Supplies Expense   No. 668

Bal.	1,200	
(9)	900	
Bal.	2,100	

Truck Expense   No. 670

Bal.	700	
(13)	700	
Bal.	1,400	

Utilities Expense   No. 676

(13)	300	

Note: The highlighted items are the February 28 balances.

Step 3: The Equality of Debits with Credits Is Established by the Trial Balance

The account balances are listed in the trial balance to establish the equality of total debit balances with total credit balances. The following February trial balance is for the Bluebeard Computer Corporation.

Bluebeard Computer Corporation
Trial Balance
February 28, 19X1

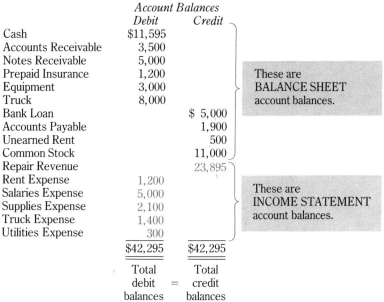

| | *Account Balances* | |
	Debit	*Credit*
Cash	$11,595	
Accounts Receivable	3,500	
Notes Receivable	5,000	
Prepaid Insurance	1,200	
Equipment	3,000	
Truck	8,000	
Bank Loan		$ 5,000
Accounts Payable		1,900
Unearned Rent		500
Common Stock		11,000
Repair Revenue		23,895
Rent Expense	1,200	
Salaries Expense	5,000	
Supplies Expense	2,100	
Truck Expense	1,400	
Utilities Expense	300	
	$42,295	$42,295
	Total debit balances	= Total credit balances

These are
BALANCE SHEET
account balances.

These are
INCOME STATEMENT
account balances.

Step 4: The Account Balances Are Analyzed and Adjusting Entries Prepared

As is the case with the February transactions (recorded in section B of this chapter), the adjusting entries are also recorded in the journal of the Bluebeard Computer Corporation at the end of February.

The caption *Adjusting Entries* is written in the journal on the line following the last regular journal entry of the corporation.

After the adjusting entries have been posted, the mixed elements in the accounts have been eliminated. Account numbers are recorded in the folio column to indicate that the amounts have been posted to the particular account involved.

Step 5: The Adjusting Entries Are Posted to Ledger Accounts

When the February adjusting entries have been posted to the ledger accounts, the ledger accounts are footed and any debit or credit balances are calculated. For example, the Prepaid Insurance account has a debit balance of $1,100 after it has been footed.

Step 6:   An Adjusted Trial Balance Is Prepared To Prove the Equality of Debits and Credits

A trial balance prepared after the posting of adjusting entries to the ledger would contain the accounts and account balances shown below. Note that new accounts have been included as required by the adjusting entries, and that this trial balance is labelled as an **adjusted trial balance** to distinguish it from the *unadjusted* trial balance prepared earlier.

Adjusted trial balance
A listing of accounts and their balances after the posting of adjusting entries to the accounts of the entity.

The purpose of any trial balance is to establish the equality of debits and credits, to ensure the accuracy of the mechanical process of recording transactions and the posting of journal entries to the ledger.

The trial balance, or in this case, the adjusted trial balance, is useful to the accountant in the preparation of financial statements. The accountant could prepare these statements directly from the ledger accounts, but the trial balance or adjusted trial balance is a convenient summary of this information for the preparation of financial statements.

Bluebeard Computer Corporation
Adjusted Trial Balance
February 28, 19X1

	Account Balances Debit	Credit	
Cash	$11,595		
Accounts Receivable	3,500		
Interest Receivable	25		
Notes Receivable	5,000		
Prepaid Insurance	1,000		
Supplies	495		
Equipment	3,000		
Truck	8,000		
Accumulated Depreciation — Equipment		$ 45	These accounts are used to prepare the balance sheet.
Accumulated Depreciation — Truck		240	
Bank Loan		5,000	
Accounts Payable		1,900	
Interest Payable		92	
Salaries Payable		150	
Unearned Repair Revenue		2,000	
Unearned Rent		200	
Income Tax Payable		5,994	
Common Stock		11,000	
Interest Earned		25	
Repair Revenue		21,895	
Rent Earned		300	
Depreciation Expense — Equipment	45		These accounts are used to prepare the income statement.
Depreciation Expense — Truck	240		
Insurance Expense	200		
Interest Expense	92		
Rent Expense	1,200		
Salaries Expense	5,150		
Supplies Expense	1,605		
Truck Expense	1,400		
Utilities Expense	300		
Income Tax Expense	5,994		
	$48,841	$48,841	

H. Preparation of Financial Statements

The data listed in the adjusted trial balance can be used to prepare the entity's financial statements. This step is the seventh in the accounting process.

Income Statement Preparation

The income statement is the first statement to be prepared from the amounts listed in the adjusted trial balance. Notice that all revenue and expense amounts are repeated in the formal statement and that a net income amount is calculated. Since a corporation pays income tax on its income, the income statement includes the estimated amount of income tax payable. The income statement preparation process is illustrated in Figure 3-7 and the balance sheet preparation process is illustrated in Figure 3-8.

Bluebeard Computer Corporation
Adjusted Trial Balance
February 28, 19X1

	Account Balances	
	Debit	*Credit*
Cash	$11,595	
Accounts Receivable	3,500	
Interest Receivable	25	
Notes Receivable	5,000	
Prepaid Insurance	1,000	
Supplies	495	
Equipment	3,000	
Truck	8,000	
Accumulated Depreciation — Equipment		$ 45
Accumulated Depreciation — Truck		240
Bank Loan		5,000
Accounts Payable		1,900
Interest Payable		92
Salaries Payable		150
Unearned Repair Revenue		2,000
Unearned Rent		200
Income Tax Payable		5,994
Common Stock		11,000
Interest Earned		25
Repair Revenue		21,895
Rent Earned		300
Depreciation Expense — Equipment	45	
Depreciation Expense — Truck	240	
Insurance Expense	200	
Interest Expense	92	
Rent Expense	1,200	
Salaries Expense	5,150	
Supplies Expense	1,605	
Truck Expense	1,400	
Utilies Expense	300	
Income Tax Expense	5,994	
	$48,841	$48,841

Bluebeard Computer Corporation
Income Statement
For the Two Months Ended
February 28, 19X1

Revenue			
Interest Earned	$ 25		
Repair Revenue	21,895		
Rent Earned	300		
		$22,220	
Expenses			
Depreciation Expense — Equipment	45		
Depreciation Expense — Truck	240		
Insurance Expense	200		
Interest Expense	92		
Rent Expense	1,200		
Salaries Expense	5,150		
Supplies Expense	1,605		
Truck Expense	1,400		
Utilities Expense	300		
Total Expenses		10,232	
Income before Income Tax		$11,988	
Income Tax		5,994	
Net Income for the Period		$ 5,994	

Figure 3-7   The preparation of the income statement

Balance Sheet Preparation

The balance sheet is prepared from the asset, liability, and equity accounts. Note that the Net Income amount is carried forward from the income statement on the previous page. The balance sheet preparation process is illustrated in Figure 3-8.

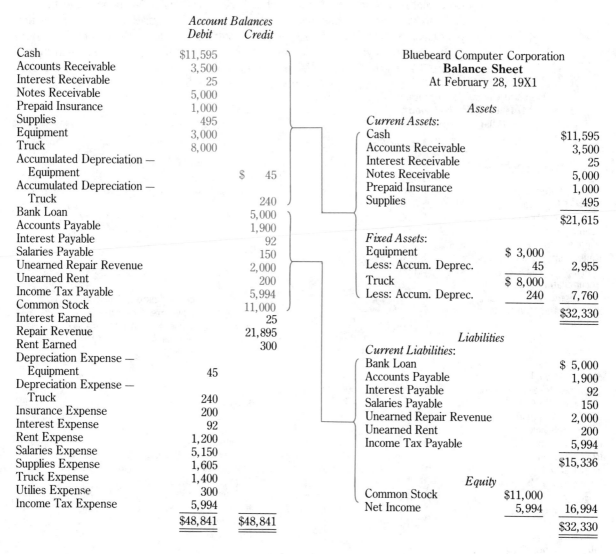

Bluebeard Computer Corporation
Adjusted Trial Balance
February 28, 19X1

	Debit	Credit
Cash	$11,595	
Accounts Receivable	3,500	
Interest Receivable	25	
Notes Receivable	5,000	
Prepaid Insurance	1,000	
Supplies	495	
Equipment	3,000	
Truck	8,000	
Accumulated Depreciation — Equipment		$ 45
Accumulated Depreciation — Truck		240
Bank Loan		5,000
Accounts Payable		1,900
Interest Payable		92
Salaries Payable		150
Unearned Repair Revenue		2,000
Unearned Rent		200
Income Tax Payable		5,994
Common Stock		11,000
Interest Earned		25
Repair Revenue		21,895
Rent Earned		300
Depreciation Expense — Equipment	45	
Depreciation Expense — Truck	240	
Insurance Expense	200	
Interest Expense	92	
Rent Expense	1,200	
Salaries Expense	5,150	
Supplies Expense	1,605	
Truck Expense	1,400	
Utilies Expense	300	
Income Tax Expense	5,994	
	$48,841	$48,841

Bluebeard Computer Corporation
Balance Sheet
At February 28, 19X1

Assets

Current Assets:
Cash		$11,595
Accounts Receivable		3,500
Interest Receivable		25
Notes Receivable		5,000
Prepaid Insurance		1,000
Supplies		495
		$21,615

Fixed Assets:
Equipment	$ 3,000	
Less: Accum. Deprec.	45	2,955
Truck	$ 8,000	
Less: Accum. Deprec.	240	7,760
		$32,330

Liabilities

Current Liabilities:
Bank Loan	$ 5,000
Accounts Payable	1,900
Interest Payable	92
Salaries Payable	150
Unearned Repair Revenue	2,000
Unearned Rent	200
Income Tax Payable	5,994
	$15,336

Equity
Common Stock	$11,000	
Net Income	5,994	16,994
		$32,330

Figure 3-8   The preparation of the balance sheet

I. Closing the Books

Closing entries
The entries that reduce revenue and expense balances to zero in preparation for the next fiscal year.

Temporary accounts
Accounts that accumulate data for a fiscal year and are closed at the end of the fiscal year; also called *nominal accounts*. All revenue and expense accounts are temporary accounts.

Permanent accounts
Accounts that have a continuing balance from one fiscal year to another; also called *real accounts*. All balance sheet accounts are permanent accounts.

Income Summary
A temporary account used to accumulate all revenue and expense balances at the end of the fiscal year. This account summarizes the net income (or loss) for the period and is closed to the Retained Earnings account.

At the end of a fiscal year, following the recording of all entries that belong to that operating period, the revenue and expense accounts have accumulated all the amounts affecting the business; these *revenue* and *expense accounts* must now be reduced to zero balances, so that they can begin to accumulate the amounts that belong to a new fiscal year. It is customary in business record-keeping that the books be closed at the end of every fiscal year. **Closing entries** are made to transfer the revenue and expense balances from the **temporary accounts**. **Permanent accounts** are those that have a continuing balance from one fiscal year to the next. The different types of temporary and permanent accounts are listed below.

At the end of the fiscal year, these accounts must be closed; that is, they must have a zero balance when the new fiscal year begins.

Temporary Accounts	Permanent Accounts
Revenue Accounts	Asset Accounts
Expense Accounts	Liability Accounts
	Common Stock Account
	Retained Earnings Account

The Closing Procedure

An intermediate summary account, called **Income Summary**, is used to close the revenue and expense accounts. The balances in these accounts are transferred to the Income Summary account. The accounts of the Bluebeard Computer Corporation at February 28 are used in Figure 3-9 to illustrate the closing procedure. (*Note*: the Bluebeard Computer Corporation is used for illustration only. Closing entries are normally prepared at the end of the fiscal year.)

Entry 1: Closing the Revenue Accounts
The revenue accounts are closed in one compound closing journal entry to the Income Summary account. (All revenue accounts with credit balances are debited to bring them to zero. Their balances are transferred to the Income Summary account.)

Entry 2: Closing the Expense Accounts
The expense accounts are closed in one compound closing journal entry to the Income Summary account. (All expense accounts with debit balance are credited to bring them to zero. Their balances are transferred to the Income Summary account.)

Entry 3: Closing the Income Summary Account
The Income Summary account is next closed to the Retained Earnings account.

The caption *Closing Entries* is written in the general journal on the line following the last adjusting entry. Unlike regular transaction entries, which require analysis and judgement, the closing process is purely mechanical and involves only the shifting and summarizing of amounts already recorded in the worksheet.

The balance in the Income Summary account is transferred to Retained Earnings because the net income (or net loss) belongs to the shareholders. The closing entries for Bluebeard Computer Corporation are shown in Figure 3-9.

GENERAL JOURNAL

Date 19X1		Description	F	Debit	Credit
		Closing Entries			
Feb.	28	Repair Revenue		2 1 8 9 5 –	
		Rent Earned		3 0 0 –	
		Interest Earned		2 5 –	
		Income Summary			2 2 2 2 0 –
		To close revenue account balances			
		Income Summary		1 6 2 2 6 –	
		Depreciation Expense — Equipment			4 5 –
		Depreciation Expense — Trucks			2 4 0 –
		Insurance Expense			2 0 0 –
		Interest Expense			9 2 –
		Rent Expense			1 2 0 0 –
		Salaries Expense			5 1 5 0 –
		Supplies Expense			1 6 0 5 –
		Truck Expense			1 4 0 0 –
		Utilities Expense			3 0 0 –
		Income Tax Expense			5 9 9 4 –
		To close expense account balances			
		Income Summary		5 9 9 4 –	
		Retained Earnings			5 9 9 4 –
		To close Income Summary			
		account balance			

Figure 3-9   Closing entries

Posting the Closing Entries to the Ledger

As entries 1 and 2 are posted to the ledger, the balances in all revenue and expense accounts are transferred to the Income Summary account. The transfer of these balances is shown in Figure 3-10. Notice that a zero balance remains in each revenue and expense account after the closing entries are posted.

2. Closing Expense Accounts   1. Closing Revenue Accounts

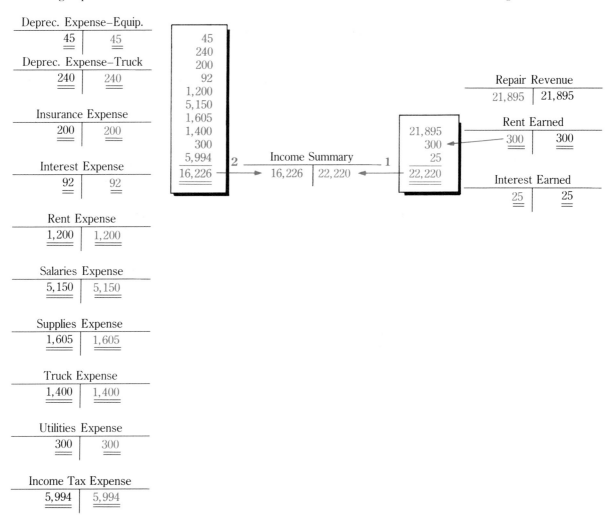

Figure 3-10   Closing revenue and expense accounts

Closing Revenue and Expense Accounts

Following the closing of the revenue and expense accounts to the Income Summary account, the balance in the Income Summary account is equal to the net income of $5,988.

Closing the Income Summary Account

The Income Summary account is now closed to Retained Earnings, as shown in Figure 3-11.

Figure 3-11   Closing the Income Summary account

The Post-closing Trial Balance

A **post-closing trial balance** is prepared immediately following the posting of closing entries and before the posting of transactions for the next accounting time period. The purpose of its preparation is to ensure that the debits and credits in the general ledger are equal and that all revenue and expense accounts have in fact been closed. Here is the post-closing trial balance of Bluebeard Computer Corporation.

Bluebeard Computer Corporation
Post-Closing Trial Balance
At February 28, 19X1

	Account Balances	
	Debit	Credit
Cash	$11,595	
Accounts Receivable	3,500	
Interest Receivable	25	
Notes Receivable	5,000	
Prepaid Insurance	1,000	
Supplies	495	
Equipment	3,000	
Truck	8,000	
Accumulated Depreciation — Equipment		$ 45
Accumulated Depreciation — Truck		240
Bank Loan		5,000
Accounts Payable		1,900
Interest Payable		92
Salaries Payable		150
Unearned Repair Revenue		2,000
Unearned Rent		200
Income Tax Payable		5,994
Common Stock		11,000
Retained Earnings		5,994
	$32,615	$32,615

Note that only balance sheet accounts still have a balance that is carried forward to the next accounting time period. All revenue and expense accounts begin the new time period with a zero balance, so that they can be used to accumulate amounts belonging to that new time period. Accordingly, the accounting model, A = L + E, is not only the model for the balance sheet but is also the model for the post-closing trial balance.

The Sequence of Steps in the Accounting Process

The periodicity, or time period, concept was introduced and its application explained in the preceding chapters; it assumes that an entity's business activities can be broken into meaningful accounting time periods, for which financial statements are prepared. Certain accounting measurement problems result from the periodicity concept; accrual accounting and application of the matching of revenues with expenses were illustrated in section F.

The accounting process is the way in which the dollar amount of transactions during the accounting time period is transformed into financial statement information. A sequence of steps is followed by the accountant during the time period; as noted in Chapter 2, these steps are collectively referred to as the accounting cycle. This sequence of steps is shown in its relation to the accounting time period of Bluebeard Computer Corporation in Figure 3-12.

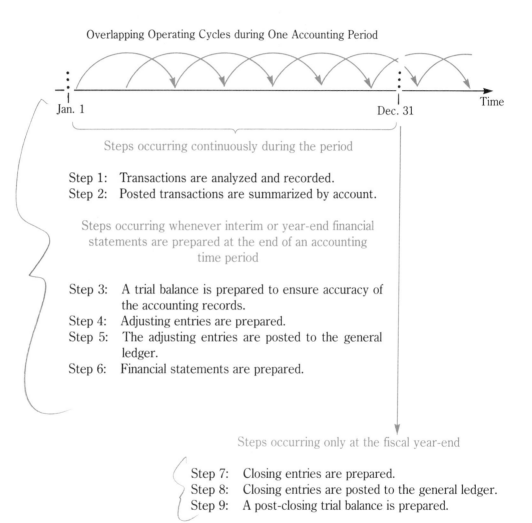

Overlapping Operating Cycles during One Accounting Period

Jan. 1   Dec. 31   Time

Steps occurring continuously during the period

Step 1: Transactions are analyzed and recorded.
Step 2: Posted transactions are summarized by account.

Steps occurring whenever interim or year-end financial statements are prepared at the end of an accounting time period

Step 3: A trial balance is prepared to ensure accuracy of the accounting records.
Step 4: Adjusting entries are prepared.
Step 5: The adjusting entries are posted to the general ledger.
Step 6: Financial statements are prepared.

Steps occurring only at the fiscal year-end

Step 7: Closing entries are prepared.
Step 8: Closing entries are posted to the general ledger.
Step 9: A post-closing trial balance is prepared.

Figure 3-12   Sequence of steps through an accounting period

APPENDIX: Reversing Entries

During the 19X1 accounting period, regular business transactions of Bluebeard Computer Corporation were recorded as they occurred. At the end of the period, BCC's accountant found it necessary to prepare adjusting journal entries so that expenses incurred would be matched to the revenue generated during the same accounting period. Adjusting entries were prepared for mixed balance sheet accounts, mixed income statement accounts, and accruals. The preparation of these entries was discussed in Chapter 3.

Reversing entries are prepared at the beginning of the next accounting time period — March 1, 19X1, in this case — to reverse accrual adjusting entries made at February 28, 19X1 for Bluebeard Computer Corporation.

The use of reversing entries promotes the efficient operation of the accounting function, particularly in large corporations where numerous routine transactions are recorded.

Accrual Adjustments

At the end of the accounting period, the accountant of Bluebeard Computer Corporation had found that some ledger accounts were incomplete because some revenues and expenses accrue. No accounting problem is caused by the absence of these items during the accounting period; the matching concept requires, however, that they be recorded when financial statements are prepared. The following BCC accounts required an accrual adjustment at February 28:

Income Statement Accounts	Balance Sheet Accounts
Interest Earned	Interest Receivable
Salaries Expense	Salaries Payable
Interest Expense	Interest Payable
Income Tax Expense	Income Tax Payable

These are the accounts that are reversed. (In practice, however, reversing entries for accruals are optional.)

When no reversing entry is prepared, the following procedure, using BCC's adjusting entry (h) as an example, can be followed. Three days of salary amounting to $150 was incurred in February but was payable at the end of the week — which was in March 19X1. The accountant recorded an accrual at February 28, so that revenues would match expenses incurred during the same period.

February Accrual Entry		March Payment of Salary		
Salaries Expense	150	Salaries Expense	100	
Salaries Payable	150	Salaries Payable	150	
		Cash		250

Here, the recording of the March salary payment was not recorded in the normal way; the accountant had to recall the previously recorded February accrual entry. Since additional analysis of this transaction is needed, this is an inefficient recording practice.

Note that the amount of expense applicable to March is only $100, the salary for the two days of the first week of March. In effect, the original February credit to Salaries Payable is reduced to a zero balance in recording the March payment.

Preparation of Reversing Entries for Accruals

Reversing entries are prepared at the beginning of a new fiscal year or whenever financial statements are prepared; they reverse an accrual recorded in the immediately preceding period. To demonstrate, take once more the salary accrual prepared as adjusting entry (h) as an example.

February Accrual Entry			March Reversing Entry			March Payment of Salary		
Salaries Expense	150		Salaries Payable	150		Salaries Expense	250	
Salaries Payable		150	Salaries Expense		150	Cash		250

The recording of the March salary payment was made in the normal way; it was not necessary for the accountant to recall the previously recorded February accrual entry. Therefore, the reversing entry is a more efficient accounting practice.

Note that, when the reversing and salary payment entries are posted to ledger accounts, the amount of expense applicable to March is only $100, the salary for two days of March. This is the same amount that resulted in the preceding example, where a reversing entry was not prepared, although the March entry was different.

	Salaries Expense		Salaries Payable	
				150
Bal. (March 1, 19X1)	-0-			
Reversing entry		150	150	
			150	150
Payment of salary	250			
Salary expense	100			

The use of a reversing entry therefore results in the same salary expense figure in the next accounting period under both methods.

The non-use of reversing entries depends on accountants having to recall previously recorded adjusting entries. Using reversing entries permits accountants to record subsequent payments in the normal way, thereby minimizing errors.

Other reversing entries applicable to accruals of Bluebeard Computer Corporation recorded in February are next prepared for adjusting entries g, i, and j.

February Adjusting Entry			March Reversing Entry			March Cash Payment or Cash Receipt		
(g) Interest Receivable	25		Interest Earned	25		Cash	100	
Interest Earned		25	Interest Receivable		25	Interest Earned		100
(i) Interest Expense	92		Interest Payable	92		Interest Expense	99	
Interest Payable		92	Interest Expense		92	Cash		99
(j) Income Tax Expense	5,994		Income Tax Payable	5,994		Income Tax Expense	5,994	
Income Tax Payable		5,994	Income Tax Expense		5,994	Cash		5,994

The use of this simple rule may be useful in the preparation of reversing entries for accruals: *reverse any previous accounting's adjusting entry* (February for Bluebeard) *that follows with a cash payment or cash receipt the next period* (March for Bluebeard). Notice that all the reversing entries in the examples here resulted in a debit or a credit to Cash in the subsequent accounting period.

A S S I G N M E N T   M A T E R I A L S

Discussion Questions

1. Explain the sequence of financial transactions that occur continuously during an accounting time period. What is this sequence of activities called?
2. Do you have to wait until the operating cycle is complete before you can measure income by the accrual basis of accounting?
3. What is the relationship of the matching concept to accrual accounting? Are revenues matched to expenses, or are expenses matched to revenues? Does it matter one way or the other?
4. What is the impact of the going concern concept on accrual accounting?
5. Identify three different categories of expenses.
6. What are adjusting entries and why are they required?
7. Why are asset accounts adjusted? How are they adjusted?
8. How are fixed asset accounts adjusted? Is the procedure similar to the adjustment of other asset accounts?
9. What is a contra account and why is it used?
10. How are liability (unearned revenue) accounts adjusted?
11. Explain the term *accruals*. Give examples of items that accrue.
12. Why is an adjusted trial balance prepared?
13. How is the trial balance used to prepare financial statements?
14. List the steps in the accounting cycle.
15. Which steps in the accounting cycle occur continuously throughout the accounting period?
16. Which steps in the accounting cycle occur only at the end of the accounting period? Explain how they differ from the other steps.
17. How does the adjustment of revenue and expenses differ from the adjustment of asset and liability accounts? Give several examples.
18. Customarily, in business record-keeping, income statement accounts accumulate amounts for a time period not exceeding one year. Why is this custom necessary?
19. Identify which accounts are temporary and which are permanent.
20. What are the entries used to close the books at the fiscal year-end?
21. What is the Income Summary account, and why is one used?
22. Why is a post-closing trial balance prepared?
23. Why are reversing entries prepared when revenue and expense accounts are adjusted?
24. Are reversing entries prepared when asset and liabilities are adjusted? Why or why not?
25. Are accrual adjustments reversed?

Discussion Cases

Discussion Case 3-1:   Roberto Vascon

Roberto Vascon is a one-man Brazilian leather factory. Since coming to New York three years ago from Rio de Janeiro, he has been selling his distinctive pocketbook designs. He cuts and hand-stitches 70 to 80 leather bags a week, and sells them exclusively at . . . the Columbus Avenue Flea Market.

Their modest venue notwithstanding, his evening bags in square, half-moon and triangular styles make a fashion splash in snakeskin, eel, suede, embossed calfskin and patent leather. The flea market, at 76th Street and Columbus Avenue, is open Sundays 10 A.M. to 5 P.M.

"And nearly every woman comes back," he said. "They're waiting for me when I open up the following Sunday morning." Many customers snap up more than one bag, which at $25 to $50 apiece are affordable.

"I have an American Express machine now," the 26-year-old designer said. "So it makes it really easy." When you're hot, you're hot.

Source Woody Hochswerger, "Leather Wizardry", *The New York Times*, November 13, 1988, p. B-6.

For Discussion

1. What is the length of Mr. Vascon's operating cycle?
2. Calculate how much revenue Mr. Vascon makes every week.
3. How much would you estimate he pays for materials?
4. Comment on his selling and advertising costs.
5. Prepare a weekly income statement for Mr. Vascon's project. (How often should you prepare financial statements? And for whom?)

Discussion Case 3-2:   The Government's Accounting

Revenue Minister Michel Gratton yesterday defended the destruction of more than 91,000 tax-refund cheques last spring to keep the Quebec government within its financial targets.

Auditor General Rhéal Chatelain said in his annual report Tuesday that the cheques, worth more than $31 million, were ordered destroyed last March by the Finance Department to keep Quebec's 1985-86 deficit from rising above $3.15 billion.

The cheques were reissued and dated after April 1 so the $31 million could be included in the 1986–87 fiscal year.

The operation cost "less than $100,000," Gratton said.

"It's a lot of money, obviously, but a lot less money than would have resulted if the financial statements had read otherwise," he told reporters.

He said it is "common practice" to include tax refunds under the next fiscal year to keep the deficit down.

But Gratton denied the auditor general's statement that his department's officials destroyed the cheques.

And Daniel Johnson, acting finance minister, dodged the issue, saying that although the Finance Department ordered the disposal of the cheques, "who physically destroys the cheques is neither here nor there."

Johnson said that "in order to reach financial objectives, the cheques should not have been issued before March 31 (the end of the fiscal year)."

He said delaying the issuing of tax-refund cheques is a common procedure in government that "always occurs."

Source   *Canadian Press*, "Holding up tax cheques 'common,' Gratton says", November 27, 1986.

For Discussion

1. Is the revenue minister moving receipts and disbursements from one period to another? Is this ethical?
2. The operation cost less than $100,000. Gratton is quoted as saying, "It's a lot of money, obviously, but a lot less money than would have resulted if the financial statements had read otherwise." What does he mean?

Discussion Case 3-3:   Ford Motor Company

On May 28, 1972, Richard Grimshaw, then 13, was offered a lift in a new Ford Pinto by a friend of his family, Mrs. Lily Gray. They were heading for the southern California desert resort of Barstow on Interstate Route 15 when Gray's Pinto stalled because of a faulty carburetor and was hit from behind by another car.

The Pinto's gas tank, located only 7 in. (18 cm) behind the rear bumper was ruptured by the impact. Fumes from the gas that escaped mixed with air in the passenger compartment, a spark ignited the mixture and the Pinto was enveloped in flames.

Lily Gray was so badly burned that she died in hospital two days later. Richard suffered 90 percent burns; he lost four fingers. Miraculously, he survived. After 52 operations he has now a new nose and ear, but his face will always be a mass of twisted scar tissue and there are more operations to come.

He has also been awarded $128 million in damages, the highest-ever personal injury award. The award was made after a jury heard how Ford had calculated the cost of building greater safety into its cars against the probable amount the company would save in protecting car owners from death or injury by burning.

Based on the probability of 180 burn deaths in a year, and 180 severe burn injuries, Ford came up with a "unit cost" of $200,000 per death, $67,000 per injury and $700 per vehicle, for a total of $49.5 million.

The cost of altering cars and light trucks to conform with safety standards then being proposed by the United States Congress to prevent gas tanks exploding after an accident was put at $137 million. Ford's engineers concluded that such changes would not be "cost effective".

Richard's legal team had access to valuable background material before the case began. The hazards presented by

---

BENEFITS:
Savings — 180 burn deaths, 180 serious injuries, 2100 burned vehicles
Unit Cost — $200,000 per death, $67,000 per injury, $700 per vehicle
Total — 180 × $200,000 + 180 × $67,000 + 2100 × $700 = *$49.5 million*

COSTS:
Sales — 11 million cars, 1.5 million light trucks
Unit Cost — $11 per car, $11 per truck
Total Cost — 11,000,000 × $11 + 1,500,000 × $11 = *$137 million*

These are the confidential calculations that convinced a southern California jury that Ford Motor Company had knowingly sold cars with a potentially lethal design fault. The formula illustrated is taken from a 1972 Ford memo.

the design and positioning of the Pinto's gas tank had been investigated by several independent organizations since the model went into production in August 1970.

A study in 1973 by the University of Miami's accident analysis unit, examining four years of car crashes, had singled out the Pinto for comment. Under the heading "Gas Tank Integrity/Protection (Ford Pinto)", the Miami unit observed: "In each case the gas tank was buckled and gas spewed out. In each case, the interior of the vehicle was totally gutted by the ensuing fire. It is our opinion that three such conflagrations (all experienced by one rental agency in a six-month period) demonstrates a clear and present safety hazard to all Pinto owners."

Shortly before Richard's case began, Dr. Leslie Ball — former safety chief for the NASA manned space program and founder of the International Society of Reliability Engineers — had publicly asserted that "the release to production of the Pinto was the most reprehensible decision in the history of American engineering".

Ball was particularly scathing about the design and location of the Pinto's gas tank. There were, he said, a large number of European and Japanese cars in the same price and weight range as the Pinto which were more safely designed. Most used a "saddle style" gas tank placed above the car's back axle, out of the line of direct impact. The basic patent on the saddle-tank, Ball noted, was owned by Ford.

And the greatest damage to Ford's case was done by its own analysis of the price of building greater safety into Ford cars against the expected benefit derived from saving Ford owners from death or injury by burning.

Some common measure was required to make the comparison.

The memo noted: "the measure typically chosen is dollars". Ford's calculations of the value of a human life were based on a 1972 study by the National Highway Traffic Safety Administration (NHTSA) which sought to establish the cash cost of death in a car crash by breaking down and valuing ten separate components.

"Future productivity losses" were so much, medical costs so much, insurance administration and legal expenses so much. There was even a figure — $10,000 — for "Victim's pain and suffering" though the NHTSA steadfastly refused to say how it had been arrived at.

The overall "societal cost" came to $200,000. Ford also allowed a figure of $67,000 for non-fatal burn injuries.

From official statistics, Ford extracted the figure of 180 deaths per year from burns in rollover accidents.

Where some experts disagree with Ford is in its further estimate that numbers emerging alive from such accidents, but suffering severe burns, would also be 180 a year. Some authoritative studies have put this figure 10 times higher at 1,800 a year.

Based on the benefits of saving 180 lives and preventing another 180 people from being burned, with an allowance for the cost of damaged cars, Ford put the total benefits of a design change at slightly less than $50 million. That was set against the costs — $11-worth of modifications per Ford vehicle sold — of $137 million.

That, Ford's engineers observed, was almost three times greater than the benefits, "even using a number of highly favourable benefit assumptions". They could not envisage any developments which "could make compliance with the rollover requirement cost effective".

On the heels of that chilling memo, the Santa Anna jury heard something of the background to Ford's decision to place the Pinto's gas tank in such an exposed position.

First, Richard Grimshaw's lawyers produced their star: "defector" Harley F. Copp, a senior design engineer with Ford for 20 years, retired at the time of the trial.

Against a stream of objections from Ford's team of lawyers, Copp demonstrated with blackboard, wall chart, and models to the evident discomfort of his former employers (helped by occasional indulgence from the bench: "I will allow hearsay" the judge declared at one point, "provided it is reliable hearsay").

Copp had worked on Ford's successful Capri range in which the gas tank rode, saddle-style, above the back axle; he was certain that this was the safest design (Ford had, in fact, considered using the Capri design on the Pinto).

What could a designer like him do, Richard's lawyers asked, if "corporate management" specified the location of the gas tank? "Follow corporate policy," Copp replied.

Had Ford's top management, in fact, issued a design directive for the Pinto's tank? "Behind the rear axle, beneath the floor." Could Copp estimate how much extra it would have cost to place the Pinto's tank above the axle? "About $9 more per car."

Copp's testimony was reinforced by more memos from Ford's confidential files, demonstrating, Richard's lawyers argued, how Ford had disregarded danger signals in its rush to get the Pinto onto the lucrative United States small car market. (The company's share of this market had been declining at an alarming rate in the face of competition from European and Japanese models.)

Shortly after Pinto's production began, several Capris with saddle-style tanks came through crash tests with flying colours; next day, Capris with modified tanks placed, like the Pinto's, behind the rear axle were crash-tested and leaked gas in every case.

Like every company in the ferociously competitive small-car market, Ford was exceedingly price conscious.

A Ford U.S. engineer told the American magazine *Mother Jones* that the Pinto was rigidly governed by "the limits of 2000" — it was not to weigh more than 2000 lb. (907 kg) and not to cost more than $2,000. (The magazine, named after the formidable Mary Harris Jones, self-styled "hell-raiser", was the first to publish some of the Ford documents used in Richard Grimshaw's case.)

A $25 increase in production costs could price a compact out of its market; so could a marginal reduction in sales features, such as the size of the trunk. "Do you realize that, if we put a Capri-type tank in the Pinto, you could only get one set of golf clubs in there?" another Ford engineer told the magazine.

It took the jury in Richard Grimshaw's case one minute to reject Ford's argument that the speed at which Gray's Pinto had been hit — from 50 to 65 mph — was the chief cause of the tragedy rather than any deficiency in the design of its gas tank. (The jury concluded that the speed at impact was 35 mph at the most.)

Punitive damages verdicts in California have, in the past, invariably come unstuck in subsequent courts of appeal, and Ford said two weeks ago that it would continue to fight against ''this unreasonable and unwarranted award''.

Ford's position is that every Pinto it manufactured had met or surpassed the government safety standards applicable at the time, and Pintos produced since September 1976 meet the revised rear-impact standards introduced since Richard was involved in his accident.

Source Philip Jacobson and John Barnes, *The Sunday Times*, London, February 1978. © Times Newspapers Limited 1978.

For Discussion

Management is concerned with planning and controlling to meet the goals of the entity. Based on this case:

1. What appear to be the goals and objectives of this business entity?
2. Identify the planning activities that took place, as revealed at the trial.
3. Recalculate the savings that would result if the number of serious burns were 1800 rather than 180. How does this compare with the $137 million total cost amount?
4. Identify the controlling activities of the entity that took place, as revealed in the article.
5. Did management achieve the goals and objectives of this entity?
6. What ethical issues are involved in this situation? Refer to "Issues in Ethics 1-1: Students Urge Business Schools To Emphasize Ethical Behaviour" (p. 22) in preparing your reply.

Discussion Case 3-4:   Montreal Artist Rues Day Taxman Brought His Slippers

At 8:30 on a Monday morning, 53-year-old Montreal sculptor Yves Trudeau looked out his window and saw The Taxman pacing back and forth in front of his house.

Nervous ("I thought I could be arrested"), yet confident that he had nothing to hide, Trudeau opened the door.

The taxman came in, hung up his coat, put on his bedroom slippers, and stayed.

He came again each day, for three weeks.

He said he had the power of the RCMP (though in truth he doesn't) Trudeau recalls, demanded to see the house from roof to cellar, and sat down at the dining room table. He scoured through receipts, cancelled cheques, everything, all the while sitting in the middle of the house in his bedroom slippers.

"I couldn't stand it," says Trudeau. "Every half hour he would ask my wife a question. She panicked." Finally, Trudeau called his accountant with an ultimatum: "Take him out of my house or I'll kill him."

In the end, the sculptor of 30 years had to cough up $6,000 in back taxes.

Trudeau is one of the hundreds of artists across Canada who say that Revenue Canada is persecuting them.

When Toni Onley in Vancouver threatened to torch $1 million-worth of his works in October, that's exactly what he was trying to tell the country.

These artists claim that, although the Income Tax Act has never had a section dealing specifically with them, things had gone along merrily for years, with them paying taxes according to the way that law was applied in *practice*.

Suddenly, the artists say, Revenue Canada changed its interpretation of the same laws, reprogrammed its trusty computers, and began demanding thousands of dollars in back taxes that the artists almost always don't have. Now, the computer tells the taxman, if an artist isn't making a profit on his art, he/she is merely a "hobbyist", not an artist at all. So he can't deduct the cost of his materials.

On the other hand, says the computer, if they *are* making a profit, they are to be treated exactly the same way as a businessperson manufacturing widgets. That means, for one thing that, until a piece of work is sold, an artist cannot write off the cost of producing it.

Under these rules, artist Emily Carr, who didn't make a profit with her work, would have been considered a hobbyist by Revenue Canada. . . .

What makes it complex is, that, until recently, artists were informally allowed a dual status that, they say, worked. They used to be able to hold another job to support their art and at the same time be considered self-employed so they could deduct the costs of supplies, travel, instruments, whatever.

Now artists feel they are the victims of a streamlined computer program that turns a blind eye to the precarious life of Canada's artists. The facts show that an artist almost always needs a second job to survive. In 1982, the average income of a self-employed professional writer was approximately $6,100; a visual artist $2,100; a professional actor $9,100. The poverty line for a single person living in cities of more than 500,000 in Canada was $8,970 that year. The average annual income of self-employed artists fell from $4,835 in 1974 to $4,352 in 1980.

Miserable facts

With these miserable facts to live with, artists feel that Revenue Canada threatens to cut off the country's creative juices, which, ironically, many other departments in Ottawa have done much to encourage.

No one, with the possible exception of Revenue Canada, can say exactly how many artists consider themselves to be victims of the tax department. But Jane Condon, national director of an Ottawa group called Canadian Artists' Representation which claims to speak for 800 visual artists, says: "Based on our experience, the number who have contacted this office directly would indicate that hundreds of visual artists have been affected."

Condon says it is particularly hard to know how many artists have been harassed by the tax department because: "Nobody really wants to talk about money — how much they make and how much they pay in taxes except in a very general sense. So getting people to talk about it is not easy.

In fact, most of the artists who eventually went public thought they were isolated cases until Onley captured media attention last October. Onley decided to burn his paintings because a tax officer suggested that by destroying "inventory" (like any other manufacturer), the artist could write off the expenses he incurred in producing them.

Communications Minister Francis Fox telegraphed Onley and asked him to wait while Fox presented "the concern of Canada's artists to the minister of national revenue".

The tax department is giving some writers a hard time, too. Dale Thomson, McGill University political science professor, former vice-principal, and author of political biographies was nabbed by Revenue Canada who, he says, treated him in a "crude, callous and indifferent" way.

Source   Brenda Zosky Proulx, "The Day the Taxman Brought his Slippers", *The* (Montreal) *Gazette*, January 7, 1984, pp. A-1, A-4.

For Discussion

1. Should an artist who is making a profit be treated differently from one who is not? Why or why not?
2. Accrual accounting aligns expenses with revenues of a time period. Under this method, the cost of assets transferred to customers or used up during the period are considered as expenses; these expenses are matched with the revenue generated by these expenses and are included in the income statement of the same time period. How does accrual accounting apply in the position of the tax collector that, "until a piece of work is sold, artists cannot write off the cost of production"?
3. How does the destruction of "inventory" justify the writing off of the expenses incurred in producing paintings? Is the cash method or the accrual method more appropriate for artists? Why or why not?

Discussion Case 3-5:   Privatize Revenue Canada

Though not a betting man, I would be willing to chance a small wager — say, my tax refund — that there is one simple and obvious way of reforming the tax system, a way that would be agreeable to business, welcome to taxpayers and pleasing to Conservatives, a way that Finance Minister Michael Wilson probably hasn't even considered. Privatize it. Sell off Revenue Canada, and entrust tax collection to the private sector.

Anyone with the benefit of a classical education can tell you that was how the ancient Romans did it. It worked like this. In the first century BC, Roman citizens living in Italy didn't pay much tax, serving in the military instead. Provincial residents, meanwhile, were taxed — sometimes a property tax, sometimes a tax on produce or harvests, sometimes a flat rate per person. The government set the tax rates, and every year auctioned off to the highest bidder the right to collect them. The actual collection was done by private companies in competition (and sometimes in cahoots) with each other. Shares in them were traded publicly. You could buy into a tax company and, in a bizarre anticipation of Social Credit, the more tax that was wrung out of the taxpayers, the better a dividend you got.

In theory, a profit margin of half a per cent was built into the contract price. In reality, you bid as high as you dared to land the contract and then stung the taxpayers for every cent you could get, since everything over the contract price was gravy.

In the provinces, where you were not dealing with Roman citizens, this meant that claims for a refund were often settled by the tax inspector arriving on the doorstep accompanied not by his accountants and auditors, but by half a dozen goons from the Roman army barracks down the road. In this healthy demonstration of the spirit of free enterprise, an amicable settlement would be reached right speedily.

As with all private ventures, there was, of course, a risk. To avoid the trap of overbidding, you had to have some idea of how much blood really could be squeezed from the stone. Most companies accordingly ran a kind of private intelligence service, with agents reporting on how the harvest was shaping up, and other potential plums for the picking, in another bizarre anticipation, this time of industrial espionage.

But man is fallible, and sometimes an incautiously high bid led to a situation distressingly reminiscent of Dome Petroleum, de Havilland Aircraft, Maislin trucking and other familiar names on the Canadian economic scene. In 59 BC, the Roman government found itself faced with an appeal from the tax-collecting companies operating in the province of Asia. They had committed themselves to what they now saw was a grossly optimistic contract and, if held to it, they were staring bankruptcy in the face. Speakers urged that the law was the law and a contract was a contract, but students of political economy won't be surprised to learn the companies were bailed out by remission of one-third of the debt.

The tax companies were big business, and investing in the industry was a good way to get rich quick, though not perhaps quite on a moral level with some of the older and more respected Roman traditions, such as bribery, extortion and the sale of political influence. What the ordinary taxpayer thought of it all is perhaps summed up in one word. The Latin term for the tax companies and their representatives was *publicani*. All it really means is "public servants," but it normally appears in the New Testament as "publicans" (and it's not necessary to read very far to find what kind of reputation they enjoyed among their friends and neighbors).

That, however, surely cannot be enough to stop consideration of this system as a modest proposal for tax reform in Canada. Taxpayers, who are going to be skinned anyway, may seek solace in the adage about joining them if you can't lick them, and would surely welcome the principle that the bigger the bite, the bigger the dividend cheque. Business could not but hail the opening of a profitable field for commercial expansion, with the creation of jobs for Canadians. The provinces could scarcely withhold approval if the companies were organized on a provincial basis, such as Albertax, or Taxbec.

At the federal level, this offers Canada a chance to get in on the ground floor of a new industry. If we can get in first and keep the lead, we may see the Internal Revenue Service being taken over by Cantax (USA) Inc. No doubt Brian Mulroney would take some pleasure in asking U.S. free-trade negotiators, "Should not everything be on the bargaining table?"

Source A. Trevor Hodge, Carlton University, "Sell Revenue Canada and Collect as the Romans Did".

For Discussion

1. Would you be in favour of selling Revenue Canada as suggested? Why or why not?
2. Do you think more income taxes would be collected if Revenue Canada were privatized? Where would the extra tax come from?
3. What is your general reaction to the way Roman taxes were collected?
4. What kind of accounting records would Revenue Canada keep if it were privatized? What kind of financial statements would it prepare?

Comprehension Problems

Comprehension Problem 3-1

The following are account balances of Sirois Limited:

Account Title	Amount in Trial Balance	Balance after Adjustment
Interest Receivable	$ -0-	$110
Prepaid Insurance	1,800	600
Interest Payable	-0-	90
Salaries Payable	-0-	450
Unearned Rent	700	200

Required:
1. Enter the unadjusted balance for each account in the following T-accounts: Interest Receivable, Prepaid Insurance, Insurance Expense, Interest Payable, Interest Expense, Salaries Payable, Salaries Expense, Unearned Rent, and Rent Earned.
2. Enter the adusted balance in the appropriate T-account.
3. Reconstruct the adjusting entry that must have been recorded for each account and prepare these adjusting entries.

Note: For general journal entries throughout solutions for this chapter, do not include explanation lines.

Note: Complete solutions requiring reversing entries only if that appendix was studied in your course.

Comprehension Problem 3-2

The following ledger accounts are taken from the books of the Lupton Corporation at the end of its fiscal year, December 31, 19X6:

Cash	
750	50
950	150
90	50
	24
	20
	70

Accounts Receivable	
228	90

Prepaid Insurance	
24	2

Office Supplies	
50	25

Repair Revenue	
	950
	228

Depreciation Expense	
2	

Insurance Expense	
2	

Repair Supplies	
145	80

Furniture	
150	

Accumulated Depreciation	
	2

Accounts Payable	
70	145

Common Stock	
	400

Retained Earnings	
	350

Office Supplies Expense	
25	

Rent Expense	
50	

Repair Supplies Expense	
80	

Telephone Expense	
20	

Required:
1. Indicate the amounts that represent adjustments made at December 31.
2. Prepare the adjusting entries made at December 31.

Comprehension Problem 3-3

The trial balance of Whyte Corporation, before and after the posting of adjusting entries, follows.

	Trial Balance		Adjustments		Adjusted Trial Balance	
	Dr.	Cr.	Dr.	Cr.	Dr.	Cr.
Cash	$ 4,000				$ 4,000	
Accounts Receivable	5,000				5,000	
Prepaid Insurance	3,600				3,300	
Prepaid Rent	1,000				500	
Truck	6,000				6,000	
Accumulated Depreciation						$ 1,500
Accounts Payable		$ 7,000				7,400
Salaries Payable						1,000
Unearned Rent		1,200				600
Common Stock		2,700				2,700
Revenue		25,000				25,000
Rent Earned						600
Advertising Expense	700				700	
Commissions Expense	2,000				2,000	
Depreciation Expense					1,500	
Insurance Expense					300	
Interest Expense	100				500	
Rent Expense	5,500				6,000	
Salaries Expense	8,000				9,000	
Totals	$35,900	$35,900			$38,800	$38,800

Required:
1. Indicate the debit or credit difference between the trial balance and the adjusted trial balance.
2. Prepare the adjusting entries that had been recorded in a general journal.

Comprehension Problem 3-4

The preparation of adjusting entries requires a debit entry to one account and a credit entry to another account.

A	B
a. Insurance Expense	1. Commissions Earned
b. Rent Earned	2. Supplies Expense
c. Prepaid Rent	3. Salaries Expense
d. Interest Payable	4. Unearned Fees
e. Interest Receivable	5. Accumulated Depreciation
f. Fees Earned	6. Rent Expense
g. Supplies	7. Prepaid Insurance
h. Unearned Commissions	8. Interest Earned
i. Salaries Payable	9. Interest Expense
j. Depreciation Expense	10. Unearned Rent

Required: Match each account in column A with the appropriate account in column B.

Comprehension Problem 3-5

The following data are taken from an unadjusted trial balance at December 31, 19X2:

Prepaid Rent	$ 600
Office Supplies	700
Income Tax Payable	0
Unearned Commissions	1,500
Salaries Expense	5,000

Additional Information:

a. The prepaid rent consisted of a payment for three months rent — December 19X2, January 19X3, February 19X3.
b. Office supplies on hand at December 31, 19X2 amounted to $300.
c. The estimated income tax for 19X2 is $5,000.
d. All but $500 in the Unearned Commissions account has been earned in 19X2.
e. Salaries for the last three days of December amounting to $300 have not yet been recorded.

Required:
1. Prepare all necessary adjusting entries.
2. Indicate the financial impact on the income statement and balance sheet of failure to record adjusting entries.

Comprehension Problem 3-6

The following are ledger accounts extracted from the records of Zoom Inc. at December 31, 19X2, its year-end:

Prepaid Advertising	
1,000	500

Supplies	
750	400

Accumulated Depreciation — Equipment	
	1,500
	250

Accounts Payable	
10,000	15,000
	200
	100
	400
	800

Salaries Payable	
	700

Unearned Subscriptions	
5,000	10,000

Subscription Revenue	
	5,000

Advertising Expense	
500	

Commissions Expense	
800	

Depreciation Expense — Equipment	
250	

Maintenance Expense	
200	

Salaries Expense	
9,500	
700	

Supplies Expense	
2,500	
400	

Telephone Expense	
100	

Utilities Expense	
400	

Required: Prepare the adjusting entries that were posted.

Comprehension Problem 3-7

An extract from the worksheet of Max Corp. at June 30, 19X5 is reproduced below:

Account	Amount in Trial Balance	Amount in Adjusted Trial Balance
Office Supplies	$ 190	$ 55
Accumulated Depreciation	0	400
Prepaid Insurance	850	610
Interest Payable	0	100
Unearned Rent	1000	500

Required: Prepare the journal entries that would have been recorded.

Comprehension Problem 3-8

The following unadjusted accounts are extracted from the ledger of A Corp. at December 31, 19X1:

Truck		Depreciation Expense		Accumulated Depreciation	
10,000		1,300			1,300

Additional Information: The truck was purchased January 1, 19X1; it has an estimated life of 4 years and a scrap value of $2,000.

Required: Prepare the adjusting entry at December 31, 19X1.

Comprehension Problem 3-9

The following unadjusted accounts are taken from the records of B Corp. at December 31, 19X1:

Bank Loan		Interest Expense		Interest Payable	
	12,000	1,100			100

Additional Information: The bank loan bears interest of 10 per cent, paid monthly. The business makes no other payments that bear interest charges.

Required: Prepare the adjusting entry at December 31, 19X1.

Comprehension Problem 3-10

The following ledger accounts and additional information are taken from the records of Cristhop Corp. at the end of its fiscal year, December 31, 19X1.

Cash		Supplies		Advertising Expense	
Bal. 900		Bal. 700		Bal. 200	

Accounts Receivable		Common Stock		Salaries Expense	
Bal. 2,000			Bal. 3,800	Bal. 4,500	

Prepaid Insurance		Revenue		Telephone Expense	
Bal. 1,200			Bal. 7,750	Bal. 250	

Additional information:
a. The prepaid insurance is for a one-year policy, effective July 1, 19X1.
b. A physical count indicated that $500-worth of supplies are still on hand.
c. A $50 December telephone bill has not yet been received or recorded.

Required:
1. Record all necessary adjusting entries for the general journal.
2. Post the adjusting entries to the necessary ledger accounts.
3. Prepare all closing entries.
4. Post the closing entries to the applicable ledger accounts. Balance and rule each account closed.
5. Prepare the necessary reversing entries.
6. Post the reversing entries to the applicable ledger accounts.

Problems

Problem 3-1

Zanibbi Contractors Corp. was incorporated on December 1, 19X1 and had the following transactions during December:

Part A

Dec.	1	Issued common shares for $5,000 cash
	1	Paid $1,200 for three months rent: December, January, and February
	1	Purchased a used truck for $10,000 on account
	1	Purchased on account $1,000-worth of supplies, which are expected to be used during the month (recorded as expense)
	3	Paid $1,800 for a one-year truck insurance policy, effective December 1
	5	Billed customers $4,500 for work completed to date
	6	Collected $800 for work completed today
	14	Paid the following expenses: advertising, $350; interest, $100; telephone, $75; truck, $425; wages, $2,500
	14	Collected $2,000 of the amount billed December 5
	20	Billed customers $6,500 for work completed to date
	23	Signed a $9,000 contract for work to be performed in January
	28	Paid the following expenses: advertising, $200; interest, $150; truck, $375; wages, $2,500
	29	Collected a $2,000 advance on work to be done in January (the policy of the corporation is to record such advances as revenue at the time they are received)
	31	Received a bill for $100 for electricity used during the month (recorded as utilities expense).

Required:

1. Open ledger accounts for the following: Cash, Accounts Receivable, Prepaid Insurance, Prepaid Rent, Truck, Accounts Payable, Common Stock, Revenue, Advertising Expense, Interest Expense, Supplies Expense, Telephone Expense, Truck Expense, Utilities Expense, Wages Expense.
2. Prepare journal entries to record the December transactions. Post the entries to the ledger accounts.

Part B

At December 31, the following information is made available for the preparation of any required adjusting entries.

a. One month of the Prepaid Insurance has expired.
b. The December portion of the December 1 rent payment has expired.
c. A physical count indicates that $350-worth of supplies are still on hand.
d. The amount collected on December 29 is unearned at December 31.
e. Three days of wages for December 29, 30, and 31 are unpaid; the unpaid amount of $1,500 will be included in the first Friday wages payment in January.
f. The truck has an estimated useful life of 4 years with an estimated salvage value of $880.

Required:

3. Open additional ledger accounts for the following: Supplies, Accumulated Depreciation, Wages Payable, Unearned Revenue, Depreciation Expense, Insurance Expense, Rent Expense.
4. Prepare all necessary adjusting entries. Post the entries to the ledger accounts.
5. Prepare a trial balance at December 31.

Problem 3-2

Part A

The following transactions are from the records of Laflair Services Corp. during the month of January 19X1. The company started operations with $15,000 cash and $15,000-worth of common shares.

a. Purchased a truck for $15,000 cash
b. Collected three months advertising revenue amounting to $12,000 (recorded as revenue)
c. Paid $600 for a one-year insurance policy, effective January 1
d. Received two months of interest amounting to $150 (recorded as a revenue)
e. Purchased $500-worth of supplies on account (recorded as an expense)
f. Received three months of commissions amounting to $900 (recorded as revenue)
g. Invested $5,000 temporarily idle cash in a term deposit (debited Temporary Investments)
h. Paid $5,000 for equipment
i. Received $900 for a three-month sublet of some office space
j. Paid $3,000-worth of wages during the month.

Required:

1. Open ledger accounts for the following: Cash, Temporary Investments, Prepaid Insurance, Equipment, Truck, Accounts Payable, Unearned Advertising, Unearned Commissions, Unearned Rent, Supplies Expense, Wages Expense, Common Stock.
2. Prepare journal entries to record the January transactions. Post the entries to the ledger accounts.

Part B

At the end of the month, the following information is made available for the preparation of any required adjusting entries.

k. The truck purchased in transaction a on January 1 has a useful life of five years and an estimated salvage value of $1,500.
l. One-third of the advertising has been earned.
m. The January portion of the insurance policy has expired.
n. Half of the two months of interest has been earned.
o. A physical count indicates $200-worth of supplies are still on hand.
p. The January component of the commissions has been earned.
q. An amount of $50 interest is accrued on the term deposit; this amount will be included with the interest payment to be received at the end of February.
r. The equipment, purchased in transaction h on January 1, is expected to have a useful life of four years and an estimated salvage value of $200.
s. One-third of the three-month sublet has been earned.
t. Three days of wages amounting to $150 remain unpaid; the amount will be included in the first Friday payment in February.

Required:
3. Open additional ledger accounts for the following: Supplies, Accumulated Depreciation — Equipment, Accumulated Depreciation — Truck, Wages Payable, Depreciation Expense — Equipment, Depreciation Expense — Truck, Insurance Expense, Interest Receivable, Unearned Interest, Unearned Rent, Unearned Commissions, Unearned Revenue, and Supplies.
4. Prepare all necessary adjusting entries. Post the entries to the ledger accounts.
5. Prepare a trial balance at January 31.

Problem 3-3

The following unrelated accounts are extracted from the records of Figueredo Corp. at December 31, its fiscal year-end.

		Balance	
		Unadjusted	*Adjusted*
a.	Prepaid Rent	$ 300	$ 600
b.	Wages Payable	500	700
c.	Income Tax Payable	-0-	1,000
d.	Unearned Commissions	2,000	3,000
e.	Unearned Revenue	25,000	20,000
f.	Advertising Expense	5,000	3,500
g.	Depreciation Expense — Equipment	-0-	500
h.	Supplies Expense	850	625
i.	Truck Expense	4,000	4,500

Required: For each of the above unrelated accounts, prepare the adjusting entry that was probably made.

Problem 3-4

The trial balance of Hitchcock Films Corp. includes the following account balances at December 31, 19X1, its fiscal year-end. No adjustments have yet been recorded.

	Debit	Credit
Prepaid Rent	$ 1,500	
Equipment	2,500	
Unearned Advertising		1,000
Insurance Expense	900	
Supplies Expense	600	
Telephone Expense	825	
Wages Expense	15,000	

The following information is available:

a. A physical count of supplies indicates that $300-worth of supplies have not yet been used at December 31.
b. A $75 telephone bill has not yet been received or recorded.
c. One day of wages amounting to $125 remains unpaid and unrecorded at December 31; the amount will be included with the first Friday payment in January.
d. The equipment was purchased December 1; it is expected to last 2 years and its estimated salvage value is $100. No depreciation has yet been recorded.
e. The prepaid rent is for December 19X1 and for January and February 19X2.
f. Half of the advertising has been earned at December 31.
g. The $900 amount in Insurance Expense is for a one-year policy, effective July 1, 19X1.

Required: Prepare all necessary adjusting entries.

Problem 3-5

The trial balance of Stellar Services Inc. includes the following account balances at December 31, its fiscal year-end. No adjustments have yet been recorded.

Temporary Investments	$10,000
Prepaid Insurance	600
Supplies	500
Bank Loan	5,000
Subscription Revenue	9,000
Salaries Payable	500
Rent Expense	3,900
Truck Expense	4,000

The following information is available:

a. The Temporary Investment balance represents an investment of temporarily idle cash in interest-bearing investments; an amount of accrued interest amounting to $250 has not yet been recorded.
b. The $600 prepaid insurance is for a one-year policy, effective September 1.
c. A physical count indicates that $300-worth of supplies are still on hand.
d. Interest on the bank loan is paid on the fifteenth day of each month; the unrecorded interest for the last 15 days of December amounts to $25.
e. The Subscription Revenue is for 6-month subscriptions to the corporation's *Investment Trends* report; the subscriptions began December 1.
f. Three days of salary amounting to $300 remain unpaid at December 31, in addition to the previous week's salaries, which have not yet been paid.
g. The monthly rent amounts to $300.
h. A bill for December truck expenses has not yet been received; an amount of $400 is estimated as owing.

Required: Prepare all necessary adjusting entries.

Problem 3-6

The following accounts are taken from the records of Harrison Forbes Inc. at the end of its first 12 months of operations, December 31, 19X1.

In addition to the balances in each set of accounts, additional data are provided for adjustment purposes if applicable. Treat each set of accounts independently of the others.

a.

Truck		Depreciation Expense — Truck		Accumulated Depreciation — Truck	
7,000		600			600

Additional information: The truck was purchased July 1 and has a useful life of 4 years and an estimated salvage value of $1,000.

b.

Unearned Rent		Rent Earned	
	-0-		6,000

Additional information: The monthly rental revenue is $500. A part of Harrison's office was sublet during the entire 12 months at $500 per month.

c.

Supplies		Supplies Expense	
		1,250	

Additional information: A physical inventory indicated $300-worth of supplies to be still on hand.

d.

Prepaid Rent		Rent Expense	
1,200		4,400	

Additional information: The monthly rent is $400.

e.

Wages Expense		Wages Payable	
6,000			500

Additional information: In addition to these balances, unrecorded wages at December 31 amount to $250.

f.

Bank Loan		Interest Expense		Interest Payable	
	8,000	600			100

Additional information: The bank loan bears interest at 10 percent. The money was borrowed on January 1, 19X1.

g.

Utilities Expense		Utilities Payable	
1,200			200

Additional information: The December bill has not yet been received or any accrual made; the amount owing at December 31 is estimated at $150.

h.

Prepaid Insurance		Insurance Expense	
600		600	

Additional information: A $1,200 one-year insurance policy had been purchased effective April 1, 19X1; there is no other insurance policy in effect.

i.

Unearned Rent		Rent Earned	
	900		300

Additional information: The Unearned Rent balance is applicable to the months of November and December 19X1 and to January 19X2.

j.

Unearned Revenue		Revenue	
	-0-		25,200

Additional information: An amount of $2,000 has not been earned at December 31.

Required: Prepare all necessary adjusting entries.

Problem 3-7

The following trial balance has been taken from the records of Davey Penciles Inc. at the end of its first year of operations, December 31, 19X1:

Cash	$ 3,300	
Accounts Receivable	4,000	
Prepaid Insurance	1,200	
Supplies	500	
Truck	8,500	
Accounts Payable		$ 5,000
Unearned Rent		2,400
Common Stock		6,000
Revenue		16,600
Advertising Expense	200	
Commissions Expense	1,000	
Interest Expense	400	
Rent Expense	3,600	
Salaries Expense	7,000	
Telephone Expense	300	
	$30,000	$30,000

The following additional data are available:
a. Prepaid insurance at December 31 amounts to $600.
b. A physical count indicates that $300-worth of supplies are still on hand at December 31.
c. The truck was purchased on July 1 and has a useful life of 4 years with an estimated salvage value of $500.
d. One day of salaries for December 31 is unpaid; the unpaid amount of $200 will be included in the first Friday payment in January.
e. The unearned rent represents six months rental of some warehouse space, effective October 1.
f. A $100 bill for December telephone charges has not yet been received or recorded (record in Accounts Payable).

Required:
1. Prepare all necessary adjusting entries.
2. Prepare an adjusted trial balance.
3. Prepare all necessary reversing entries.

Alternate Problems

Alternate Problem 3-1

Multi-Publishers Corp. was incorporated at June 1, 19X1 and had the following transactions during its first month of operations.

Part A

Jun. 1 Issued common shares for $10,000 cash
     1 Purchased equipment for $6,500 on account
     2 Purchased on account $750-worth of supplies, which are expected to last 3 months (recorded as an asset)
     3 Paid 2 months of newspaper advertising for $500
    ⌐5 Collected $12,000 of three-month subscriptions to its *PC REVIEW* magazine, effective June 1
    14 Paid the following expenses: telephone, $350; rent for June, $500; salaries, $3,000
   ⌐16 Collected $5,000 from advertisers for the June edition of *PC REVIEW* magazine
    18 Paid half of the equipment purchased June 1
    20 Paid $2,000 for supplies used
    28 Paid the following expenses: telephone, $250; salaries, $3,000
    30 Received a $200 bill for electricity used during the month (recorded as a utilities expense).

Required:
  1. Open ledger accounts for the following: Cash, Prepaid Advertising, Supplies, Equipment, Accounts Payable, Unearned Subscriptions, Common Stock, Advertising Revenue, Advertising Expense, Rent Expense, Revenue, Salaries Expense, Telephone Expense, Utilities Expense, Supplies Used.
  2. Prepare journal entries to record the June transactions. Post the entries to the ledger accounts.

Part B

At June 30, the following information is made available for the preparation of any required adjusting entries.
  a. The June portion of advertising paid on June 3 has expired.
  b. One month of the subscriptions collected June 5 has been earned.
  c. A physical count indicates that $100-worth of supplies are still on hand.
  d. A 5 percent commission is owed on the June portion of the subscriptions collected June 5.
  e. Two days of salary for June 29 and 30 are unpaid; the unpaid amount will be included in the first Friday salary payment in July. The salary for each day during the week amounts to $300.
  f. The equipment purchased on June 1 has an estimated useful life of 5 years and is estimated to have a salvage value of $500.

Required:
  3. Open additional ledger accounts for the following: Accumulated Depreciation, Salaries Payable, Unearned Subscriptions, Advertising Expense, Commissions Expense, Depreciation Expense, Subscription Revenue, Supplies Expense.
  4. Prepare all necessary adjusting entries. Post the entries to the ledger accounts.
  5. Prepare a trial balance at June 30.

Alternate Problem 3-2

Aberle Productions Inc. began operations January 1, 19X1 with $50,000 cash and $50,000-worth of common shares.

Part A

The following are from the transactions of Breen Productions Inc. during January 19X1.
a. Paid salaries of $15,000 during the month
b. Purchased on account $750-worth of supplies (recorded as an asset)
c. Paid $8,000 for equipment
d. Invested $10,000 temporarily idle cash in a term deposit (debited Temporary Investments)
e. Paid $1,200 for a one-year insurance policy, effective January 1 (recorded as an asset)
f. Collected $6,000-worth of one-year subscriptions, beginning January 1 (recorded as unearned revenue)
g. Paid $1,500 for three months of rent (recorded as an asset)
h. Collected $600 for a two-month sublet of part of the company's warehouse, effective January 1 (recorded as unearned revenue)
i. Paid $7,000 for a used truck.

Required:
1. Open ledger accounts for the following: Cash, Temporary Investments, Prepaid Insurance, Prepaid Rent, Supplies, Equipment, Truck, Accounts Payable, Unearned Rent, Unearned Subscriptions, Salaries Expense, Common Stock.
2. Prepare journal entries to record the January transactions. Post the entries to the ledger accounts.

Part B

At the end of the month, the following information is made available for the preparation of any required adjusting entries.
j. Two days of salary amounting to $1,000 remain unpaid; the amount will be included in the first Friday salary payment in February.
k. A physical count of supplies indicates that $250-worth are still on hand.
l. The equipment, purchased in transaction c on January 1, has useful life of 3 years and an estimated salvage value of $800.
m. An amount of $100 interest is accrued on the term deposit; this amount will be included with the interest payment of February 28.
n. One month of the insurance policy has expired.
o. The January portion of the subscriptions has been earned.
p. The January portion of the rent payment has expired.
q. Half of the sublet has been earned.
r. The truck, purchased in transaction i on January 1, has a useful life of 4 years and an estimated salvage value of $1,000.

Required:
3. Open additional ledger accounts for the following: Interest Receivable, Salaries Payable, Accumulated Depreciation — Equipment, Accumulated Depreciation — Truck, Interest Earned, Rent Earned, Subscription Revenue, Depreciation Expense — Equipment, Depreciation Expense — Truck, Insurance Expense, Rent Expense, Supplies Expense.
4. Prepare all necessary adjusting entries. Post the entries to the ledger accounts.
5. Prepare a trial balance at January 31.

Alternate Problem 3-3

The following unrelated accounts are from the records of Bockus Inc. at December 31, its fiscal year-end.

		Balance	
		Unadjusted	Adjusted
a.	Prepaid Insurance	$ 500	$ 300
b.	Supplies	850	400
c.	Accumulated Depreciation — Truck	-0-	1,200
d.	Salaries Payable	2,500	2,600
e.	Unearned Fees	5,000	1,000
f.	Income Tax Payable	-0-	3,500
g.	Revenue	50,000	45,000
h.	Commissions Expense	4,000	5,500
i.	Interest Expense	800	850

Required: For each of these unrelated accounts, prepare the adjusting entry that was probably recorded.

Alternate Problem 3-4

The trial balance of Streep Productions Corp. includes the following account balances at December 31, 19X1, its fiscal year-end. No adjustments have been recorded.

	Debit	*Credit*
Prepaid Insurance	$ 1,800	
Truck	19,000	
Unearned Commissions		$ 9,000
Rent Earned		-0-
Advertising Expense	5,000	
Salaries Expense	25,000	
Supplies Expense	900	

The following information is available:

a. A physical count indicates that $200-worth of supplies have not yet been used at December 31.
b. The prepaid insurance consists of a one-year policy, effective October 1.
c. The truck was purchased on July 1; it is expected to have a useful life of 6 years and its estimated salvage value is $1,000. No depreciation has been recorded during the year.
d. The unearned commissions at December 31 actually amount to $7,500.
e. Two days of salary amounting to $200 remain unpaid at December 31; the amounts will be included with the first Friday's payment in January.
f. A rent payment has not yet been received for a sublet of part of a warehouse for 2 weeks during December. Payment of the $300 has been promised for the first week in January.
g. A $300 bill for December advertising has not yet been received or recorded.

Required: Prepare all necessary adjusting entries.

Alternate Problem 3-5

The trial balance of Giancarlo Corp. includes the following account balances at December 31, 19X1, its fiscal year-end. No adjustments have yet been recorded.

Temporary Investments	$15,000
Prepaid Rent	1,200
Bank Loan	7,500
Unearned Subscriptions	9,000
Insurance Expense	2,400
Salaries Expense	75,000
Supplies Expense	600
Utilities Expense	-0-
Supplies	-0-

The following information is available:
a. Accrued interest on the temporary investment amounts to $40 at December 31.
b. The prepaid rent is for the months of November and December 19X1 and January 19X2.
c. Accrued interest on the bank loan amounts to $40 at December 31.
d. One-third of the subscriptions remain unearned at December 31.
e. Insurance expense includes the cost of a one-year insurance policy, effective January 1, 19X1, and the cost of a one-year renewal, effective January 1, 19X2. The premium cost for each year is $1,200.
f. Two days of salary have not yet been accrued at December 31; the usual salary for a five-day week is $2,500.
g. A physical count indicates that $100-worth of supplies are still on hand at December 31.
h. A $200 bill for electricity has not yet been received or recorded for December.

Required: Prepare all necessary adjusting entries.

Alternate Problem 3-6

The following accounts are taken from the records of Brouard Ltd. at the end of its first twelve months of operations, December 31, 19X1. In addition to the balances in each set of accounts, additional data are provided for adjustment purposes, if applicable. Treat each set of accounts independently.

a.

Prepaid Rent		Rent Expense	
-0-		5,200	

Additional information: The monthly rent is $400.

b.

Bank Loan		Interest Expense		Interest Payable	
	10,000	850			-0-

Additional information: Unpaid interest on the bank loan amounts to $150.

c.

Supplies		Supplies Expense	
-0-		800	

Additional information: Supplies still on hand amount to $300.

d.

Salaries Expense		Salaries Payable	
5,000			-0-

Additional information: Salaries owing at December 31 amount to $1,000.

e.

Prepaid Advertising		Advertising Expense	
800		3,000	

Additional information: Prepaid Advertising at December 31 amounts to $1,200.

f.

Equipment		Depreciation Expense — Equipment		Accumulated Depreciation — Equipment	
7,000		500			500

Additional information: The equipment was purchased on July 1 and has a useful life of 5 years with an estimated salvage value of $1,000.

g.

Unearned Rent		Rent Earned	
	-0-		10,000

Additional information: Unearned Revenue at December 31 amounts to $2,500.

h.

Prepaid Insurance		Insurance Expense	
100		500	

Additional information: The monthly insurance amounts to $50; $600 was paid for a 1-year policy effective January 1, 19X1.

i.

Utilities Expense		Utilities Payable	
875			-0-

Additional information: The December bill has not yet been received; the amount owing has been estimated at $225.

Required: Prepare all necessary adjusting entries.

Alternate Problem 3-7

The bookkeeper for Dutoit Movers Corp. prepared the following trial balance at the end of its first year of operations, December 31, 19X1:

Cash	$ 1,500	
Accounts Receivable	7,000	
Prepaid Rent	1,200	
Supplies	100	
Equipment	3,500	
Accounts Payable		$ 6,000
Unearned Commissions		3,000
Common Stock		1,000
Revenue		20,000
Advertising Expense	850	
Commissions Expense	3,600	
Interest Expense	550	
Rent Expense	4,400	
Supplies Expense	700	
Wages Expense	6,600	
	$30,000	$30,000

The following additional data are available:
a. Prepaid rent represents rent for the months of December 19X1 and January and February 19X2.
b. A physical count indicates that $200-worth of supplies are on hand at December 31.
c. The equipment was purchased on July 1 and has a useful life of 3 years with an estimated salvage value of $500.
d. Wages for December 30 and 31 are unpaid; the unpaid amount of $300 will be included in the first Friday payment in January.
e. Revenue includes $2,500 received for work to be started in January 19X2.
f. Unrecorded interest expense amounts to $150.

Required:
1. Prepare all necessary adjusting entries.
2. Prepare an adjusted trial balance.
3. Prepare all reversing entries.

Review Problem

Review Problem 3-1

The general ledger of Robinson Limited showed the following balances at the end of its first 12-month time period:

Robinson Limited
Trial Balance
At August 31, 19X3

	Debits	Credits
Cash	$ 12,000	
Accounts Receivable — Advertisers	2,500	
Accounts Receivable — Subscribers	1,100	
Prepaid Insurance	-0-	
Supplies	2,500	
Land	15,000	
Building	60,000	
Equipment	20,000	
Furniture	3,000	
Accumulated Depreciation — Building		-0-
Accumulated Depreciation — Equipment		-0-
Accumulated Depreciation — Furniture		-0-
Accounts Payable		$ 2,600
Notes Payable		1,800
Unearned Advertising		1,200
Unearned Subscriptions		800
Salaries Payable		-0-
Interest Payable		-0-
Mortgage Payable		47,600
Common Stock		52,100
Retained Earnings		-0-
Income Summary	-0-	-0-
Advertising Revenue		37,900
Subscriptions Revenue		32,700
Advertising Expense	4,300	
Depreciation Expense — Building	-0-	
Depreciation Expense — Equipment	-0-	
Depreciation Expense — Furniture	-0-	
Interest Expense	2,365	
Insurance Expense	1,800	
Salaries Expense	33,475	
Supplies Expense	15,800	
Utilities Expense	2,860	
Totals	$176,700	$176,700

At the end of August, the following additional information is available:

a. The company's insurance coverage is provided by a single comprehensive 12-month policy that began on March 1, 19X3.

b. Supplies on hand total $2,850.

c. The building has an estimated useful life of 50 years.

d. The equipment has an estimated useful life of 11 years and an estimated salvage value of $2,400.

e. The furniture has an estimated useful life of 11 years and an estimated salvage value of $300. (*Round your answer to the nearest dollar.*)

f. Interest of $9 on the note payable for the month of August will be paid on September 1, when the regular $50 payment is made.

g. Unearned advertising as of August 31 is determined to be $450.

h. Unearned subscriptions as of August 31 are determined to be $2,800.
i. Salaries that have been earned by employees but are not due to be paid to them until the next payday (in September) amount to $325.
j. Interest of $199 on the mortgage payable for the month of August will be paid on September 1, when the regular $300 payment is made.

Required:
1. Set up T-accounts and record their balances.
2. Prepare and post the adjusting and closing journal entries.
3. From the T-accounts, prepare a post-closing trial balance.
4. Prepare an income statement and a balance sheet.
5. Prepare all necessary reversing entries. NOT RESPONSABLE FOR YET (?)

Decision Problems

Decision Problem 3-1

John Rook has decided to create a limited edition chess set of the Battle of the Plains of Abraham, which he will sell to chess lovers and history buffs for $400 a set. He plans to commemorate other national battles for future sets. Rook offers the following guarantee with each set sold: if the purchaser is not satisfied with the set for any reason at the end of three years, the set may be returned for a full refund. Moreover, the returned sets will be destroyed to enhance the value of the other limited edition sets. Each set costs Rook a total of $200 to produce and ship. He estimates that about 50 percent of the sets sold will be returned at the end of 3 years. Assume that Moss's entire stock of the first limited edition set of 10,000 units is sold in 19X1.

Required:
1. Determine the amount of income that John Rook will recognize in each of the years 19X1, 19X2, and 19X3.
2. Determine the amount of cash that John Rook will receive and pay each year and the total cash effect over the 3-year period. Assume that 50 percent of the sets sold are returned at the end of 3 years.
3. Based on your answer to question 2, is it sensible for John Rook to offer future sets at the same selling price and with the same refund guarantee if his costs stay the same? Explain.

Decision Problem 3-2

Net income over a period is determined in accordance with the matching concept. It is based on the cash flows arising from the operations of the entity (non-capital cash flow), not on owners' investments, withdrawals, and dividends. In Conceptual Issue 3-1, Ross Skinner states, "Estimation of income for a period based on transactions is considerably more difficult than determination of income for a completed business lifetime. Such estimation requires that non-capital cash inflows of past, present, and future periods be assigned to periods in which they are 'earned'. Similarly, non-capital cash outflows of past, present, and future periods must be assigned to the period in which any benefit from them is used up."

Required: Indicate how each of the following transactions should be accounted for according to the matching concept. Provide reasons for your answer.

1. An advertising expenditure of $100,000 is made this period. The company's advertising agency estimates that three-fourths of the expected increase in sales will take place this period but that there will be a delayed effect and one-fourth of the increase in sales attributable to the advertising outlay will occur next period.
2. The company sustained a fire loss this period (in excess of insurance proceeds) of $180,000.
3. Research outlays amounting to $80,000 this period are believed to be patentable and will increase revenues in the future.
4. A machine is purchased for $10,000 that is expected to have a 10-year life. Each period is expected to benefit equally from the machine's output. In the first period the machine operated according to expectations. However, in the second period, because of a recession, the machine was idle.

5. At the end of a period, salaries and wages for services performed were unpaid in the amount of $25,000.
6. The company is faced with a pending lawsuit. The company's attorneys refuse to predict the outcome of the case but indicate the damages could conceivably be as high as $400,000.
7. At the end of the period, accounts receivable from sales to customers amounted to $190,000. Based on past experience it is estimated that $6,000 of this amount will have to be written off as bad debts.

8. Estimated pension expense for employees applicable to this period is $95,000. The pensions will only be payable to workers still employed by the company at the time of their retirement.
9. The bill for property taxes will not be received until the beginning of next period. However, it is expected that the property tax will amount to $30,000, of which three-fourths applies to this period.
10. A fire insurance premium is paid on the first day of this period. The premium covers three periods.

The Marketing Cycle

Part Two focuses on the marketing cycle. Chapter 4 covers the recording of the transactions of sales and collections (the sales and collection cycle) and of purchases and payments (the purchase and payment cycle). The relationship of gross profit to sales is explained. As well, the chapter discusses inventory and its recognition in the entity's financial statements.

Chapter 5 continues the discussion of the purchase and payment cycle. The calculation of inventory cost and the relative advantages and disadvantages of each cost assumption are described and contrasted.

The sales and collection cycle is further discussed in Chapter 6. Sales on account involve the extension of credit; unfortunately, not every acount receivable is collectible. Accountants apply the matching concept to align bad debt expenses with revenues of the same accounting period. The use of accrual accounting to make this alignment and the methods of calculating bad debt expense are discussed and illustrated.

Chapter 6 also discusses internal control systems, which are designed to ensure the accurate recording of accounting information and the safeguarding of the entity's assets. A good system of internal control minimizes bad debt losses and protects cash.

Accounting for Merchandising Operations

The accounting for a merchandiser differs from that required for a service business for decision-making purposes. Classified financial statements of merchandising operations facilitate short-term solvency analyses and analyses of operational efficiency.

1. In what way is the matching principle emphasized in the income statement prepared for a merchandising firm?
2. What is the usefulness of the gross profit calculation?
3. What is the sequence of events in the sales and collection cycle?
4. What accounts are used to modify sales revenue?
5. What is the sequence of events in the purchase and payment cycle?
6. How is the cost of goods sold calculated?
7. What is the periodic inventory system, and how does it differ from the perpetual inventory system?
8. How is ending inventory recorded in the accounts under the periodic inventory system?
9. What internal control features are incorporated in the perpetual inventory system?
10. How do closing entries for a merchandiser differ from those prepared for a service business?
11. What are the advantages of classified financial statements?
12. What is the purpose of the statement of retained earnings?
13. What is the distinction between selling expenses and general and administrative expenses?
14. What is short-term solvency analysis, and why is it important?
15. How can the efficiency with which an entity uses its assets be established?

A. The Calculation of Gross Profit

Merchandising
The activity of buying and selling goods that are already made.

Gross profit
The excess of the sales price over the net cost of the goods sold, also referred to as *gross margin*.

The income statement for a merchandising firm differs from that prepared for entities providing a service. The differences result from the fact that **merchandising** involves the purchase and subsequent resale of goods; matching the cost of the goods sold with the sales revenue generated from this sale is emphasized in the income statement. An income statement for a merchandising entity discloses this matching of cost with revenue in a different manner from that used by a service business; it shows the calculation of a **gross profit**, the excess of sales revenue over the cost of goods sold. A simple gross profit analysis was made for management of Bluebeard Computer Corporation when they were evaluating the start of their merchandising operations. The data involved the purchase for resale (rather than for internal use by BCC) of a portable computer for $2,000. They decided to sell the computer for $3,000. A gross profit calculation was prepared as follows:

Partial Income Statement

Sales	(a)	$3,000
Cost of Goods Sold		2,000
Gross Profit	(b)	$1,000
Gross Profit (%)	(b) ÷ (a)	33⅓%

Cost of goods sold
Accounting term used to describe the cost of merchandise sold during an accounting period.

The $1,000 gross profit is essentially a subtotal calculation, which is usually shown separately in the income statement. This calculation is particularly useful in establishing the spread between the **cost of goods sold** (a computer, which cost BCC $2,000 in this case) and revenue from its sale (the selling price of $3,000).

In the BCC example, the spread, which amounts to $1,000, is the gross profit. The word "gross" is used by accountants to indicate that other expenses incurred in running the business must still be deducted from this amount before net income for the accounting period is established. In other words, the gross profit of $1,000 represents the amount of sales revenue that remains to pay operating expenses, interest expense, and income tax.

Gross profit percentage
Gross profit divided by sales price times 100.

A **gross profit percentage** can be calculated to express the relationship of gross profit to sales. The sale of the portable computer that cost $2,000 results in a 33⅓ percent gross profit. Users of financial statements are interested in establishing this percentage in order to evaluate the performance of this entity with other entities in the same industry; they also want to know whether the percentage is increasing or decreasing from one accounting time period to another. For decision-making purposes, it is important to identify the reasons causing a change. Of necessity, the change in a gross profit percentage must be attributable to a change in either the sales price or the cost, or possibly a combination of both.

The impact of prices on profits is discussed in Real Life Example 4-1 on page 176.

B.   The Sales and Collection Cycle

Sales
An account used to
accumulate revenue
transactions wherein
merchandise is sold to
others.

A retail or wholesale merchandising entity accumulates revenue in a **Sales** account. Sales of merchandise on account result in an accounts receivable; the subsequent collection of cash completes the sales and collection cycle, which is sometimes identified as the revenue cycle. The distinct transactions making up this cycle are influenced by marketing techniques that are designed to increase sales. For example, a customer may be permitted to return merchandise if it is not satisfactory; an allowance may be given if the merchandise is damaged or differs cosmetically from that ordered. Collection techniques also affect the transactions in this cycle; discounts may be permitted for prompt payment. These techniques are monitored by management through the creation of special general ledger accounts designed for a merchandising or a manufacturing business for sales returns and allowances or for sales discounts.

The sequence of events in the sales and collection cycle is illustrated in Figure 4-1.

Sales

Revenue resulting from the sale of merchandise is recorded in a Sales (revenue) account. An account receivable results when the sale is made on account. The sale of Bluebeard's portable computer for $3,000 on account is recorded as follows:

Accounts Receivable	3,000	
Sales		3,000

The Sales account is a revenue account, similar to the Repair Revenue account used when BCC had not begun merchandising operations; the normal balance of the Sales account is a credit balance. It is commonly referred to as gross sales because it excludes amounts resulting from sales returns and allowances or from sales discounts. Only sales of merchandise purchased for resale are recorded in this account. The disposal of other corporate assets, such as equipment or a truck, are not credited to the Sales account; rather, the cost of these assets is removed from the appropriate asset account with a gain or loss being recognized.

Other accounts involved in keeping track of the revenue-generating activities of a merchandising firm are contra accounts. They are contra accounts because they are

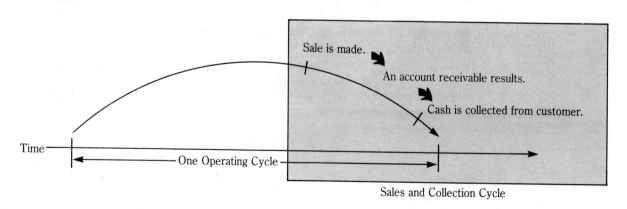

Figure 4-1   The sales and collection cycle

deducted from Sales; in this way a net sales amount is calculated for a particular accounting time period. As noted in the introduction, these additional accounts are identified as Sales Returns and Allowances, and Sales Discounts.

Sales Returns and Allowances

Sales Returns and Allowances
A contra account to Sales; goods returned by customers or price adjustments allowed to customers are recorded in this account.

It is not unusual for merchandise to be returned to the retailer by the customer. It may be the wrong model, it may be defective, or it may have been damaged in shipment; a reduction in the sales price may result. The amount of merchandise returns and allowances given on merchandise is accumulated in a **Sales Returns and Allowances** contra account. A $100 allowance for damage to a BCC computer during shipment to a customer is recorded by the following entry:

Sales Returns and Allowances	100	
Accounts Receivable		100

A separate account is used to accumulate the amount of sales returns and allowances for purposes of control. A large balance in this account is a signal to management of a potential problem that requires study and resolution.

The Sales Returns and Allowances account is a Sales contra account and is deducted from the Sales balance when preparing an income statement. In this way, the reported sales revenue is reduced by the amount of returns and allowances. Accounts Receivable is credited (assuming the original sale was made on account), since the amount owing from the customer is reduced.

Sales Discounts

Sales Discounts
A contra account to Sales; cash discounts taken by customers if payment is made within a certain discount period are recorded in this account.

Another Sales contra account, **Sales Discounts**, accumulates sales discounts. These may apply to a sale made on account, if the customer pays within a time period that is specified on the sales invoice. For example, the sales terms may require payment within 30 days. However, a discount is often permitted if payment is made earlier. The exact terms are stated on the sales invoice of Bluebeard Computer Corporation as "2/10, n30". This short form means that the amount owed must be paid within 30 days; however, if the customer chooses to pay within 10 days, a 2 percent discount may be deducted by the customer from the amount owed.

Consider the sale on account of BCC's $3,000 personal computer (less the $100 return for damage), with the above terms. Payment within 10 days entitles the customer to a $58 discount, calculated as follows: ($3,000 − $100 allowance) = $2,900 × 0.02 = $58. Note that the discount percentage is applied directly to the selling price involved. BCC receives $2,842 cash ($2,900 − $58) and prepares the following entry, if payment is made within the discount period.

Cash	2,842	
Sales Discounts	58	
Accounts Receivable		2,900

The Sales Discounts account is also a Sales contra account and is deducted from the Sales balance when preparing an income statement. In this way, the reported sales revenue is reduced by the amount of the discount; in effect, sales discounts are considered as a reduction of the selling price.

If Bluebeard had sold a computer and subsequently allowed a $100 allowance and $58 discount, these amounts would be deducted from sales in the calculation of net sales as follows:

Sales			$3,000
Less:	Sales Returns and Allowances	$100	
	Sales Discounts	58	158
	Net Sales		$2,842

Because they are usually immaterial in amount, the amounts of the Sales Returns and Allowances and Sales Discounts contra accounts are often omitted on income statements of merchandisers; their disclosure consists simply of the net Sales amount.

Real Life Example 4-1
Pricing for Profit

In every business I've ever seen, there's always some manager who wants to cut prices. If business is good, the reasoning goes, a lower price will help to capture an even greater share of the market. And if business is bad, cutting prices will help avoid disaster.

Well, that's nonsense. In my experience, at least, most companies don't charge enough for their products. When business is good, you need cash to fuel growth, cash that could be generated by high margins. When business is bad, cutting prices often makes matters worse. You have to increase sales *significantly* to recover the dollars lost by the cuts.

Let me try to convince you of the folly of charging too little. Suppose that you sell 100 fishing lures a month at $1 each. They cost 55¢ each, giving you a gross profit of $45 and a gross profit margin of 45%. If you cut your prices by 15% and your unit volume stayed the same, your sales would drop to $85 and your gross profits to $30. But if you want to maintain your original $45 gross profit after the price cut, you'll have to increase your monthly sales by 50%. Here's the formula I used to come up with that figure, with GPM representing gross profit margin:

$$\frac{GPM\ \%}{GPM\% \pm \text{price change }\%} - 1 = \text{unit vol. \% change}$$

In the example, for ease of calculation, I changed the percentages to decimals.

$$\frac{.45}{(.45 - .15)} - 1 = .50$$

In other words, with the cut in price, you'd need to sell 150 units instead of the 100 per month you are currently selling.

A price hike might make more sense. If, instead of lowering the price of the fishing lures, you raised it by 15%, and your unit volume stayed the same, your sales would go up to $115 and your gross profits to $60. To figure out how much your sales would have to fall off before your gross profit in dollars would drop below the original $45, use the same formula, but this time add, rather than subtract, the price-change percentage:

$$\frac{.45}{(.45 + .15)} - 1 = -.25$$

The price increase would *improve* your gross profit in dollars from the original $45, even with a sales drop, so long as gross sales don't fall below 75 units a month.

Despite what seems to me to be the obvious benefits of price increases, I've seen many companies continue to underprice their products — particularly companies in financial trouble. Here are some of the reasons why:

Laziness

When prices are low, salespeople don't have to sell; they need only take orders. And marketers find nearly any marketing campaign is a satisfactory one. You sacrifice margins, of course, along with many potential opportunities.

Fear

Managers fear that higher prices won't stick, that customers won't like them anymore, that salespeople will leave. But the fact is, you won't know the effect of a price increase until you try it.

C. The Purchase and Payment Cycle

A merchandising entity usually makes its purchases of items for resale on account; the subsequent payment of cash completes the purchase and payment cycle, which forms part of a broader revenue expenditure cycle that encompasses selling, general and administrative, and other expenses. The distinct transactions of the purchase and payment cycle are the focus of this section. For example, purchasing activities include the occasional return to a supplier of merchandise; often an allowance is given by a supplier for damaged merchandise. These transactions result in the reduction of the amount due to the supplier. If the amount has already been paid, then an asset, an Accounts Receivable, results. Purchase activities involve the payment of transportation associated with the purchase. Payment activities also include the availability of discounts for prompt payment. These activities are monitored by management through the

---

The idea is to charge what the market will bear. The most effective way to do this is to bump prices up a little, then bump them again and again, until you meet true sales resistance. Then back off.

Markup pricing

Many businesses set prices as a markup of costs, a practice that virtually guarantees trouble. If your costs are higher than the competition's, you price yourself out of the marketplace. If your costs are lower, you leave money on the table.

Incorrect cost information

While product costs shouldn't limit what you charge for your product, they do limit the least you can charge, and they influence the urgency with which you should probe for the larger amount. Incorrect costs can make pricing analysis worthless.

Inattention

With so much else going on, managers often ignore pricing. The most careful attention that I've ever seen given to pricing was by the president of a fast-growing chain of restaurants. During the late 1970s, when inflation was high, his staff checked prices and costs every week. If margins dropped to a certain level, the president immediately repriced and reprinted his menus. At times he reprinted menus every six weeks or so.

Full product lines

Many small manufacturing companies are convinced they must offer customers a full product line. But the financial reality is that you may lack the resources and the sales volume to develop, price, and sell the additional products profitably.

If you need a full product line, there are other approaches, such as forming a strategic alliance with other firms also looking to fill out your lines.

Inappropriate objectives

Marketing theorists talk a lot about pricing objectives. Is your objective to maximize current profits? To penetrate new markets? To capture market share? To discourage entrants? To build traffic in a retail store? Or something else? Your pricing policies, they tell us, can be a very effective device to achieve these and other objectives.

Unfortunately, if your company is like most I've seen, you have a hard enough time generating current profits. Trying to achieve the other objectives through general price cuts usually requires more cash, more market knowledge, and more ability to forecast the future than you can muster. This is not to say, however, that if you have a Cadillac product you must ignore the Chevrolet marketplace. It does say that you should protect your Cadillac margins by selling Chevys in the Chevrolet marketplace.

When sales are slower than you would like, it takes knowledge and creativity to turn the situation around without sacrificing margins. Perhaps the positioning of the product needs to be changed or new segments found. Perhaps the product needs to be changed or redefined.

Sometimes, of course, when nothing else seems to work, a price cut may be the only way to increase sales. But sharp entrepreneurs will look to price cuts as a last resort, not as the first point of attack.

Source   Reprinted with permission, *Inc. magazine*, (April, 1987). Copyright © (1987) by Goldhirsh Group, Inc., 38 Commercial Wharf, Boston, MA 02110.

special general ledger accounts for purchases returns and allowances, purchases discounts, and transportation in. The sequences of events in the purchase and payment cycle is illustrated in Figure 4-2.

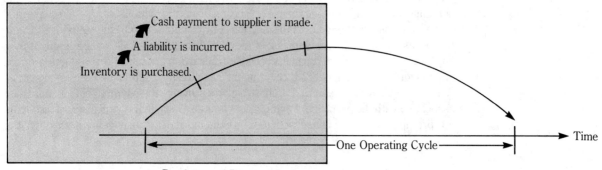

Purchase and Payment Cycle

Figure 4-2   The purchase and payment cycle

F.O.B. shipping pt = purchaser pays.

It is important to note that, in actual practice, the cash payment may follow the collection of cash resulting from sale of the item; the actual sequence of cash payments and cash collections is influenced by the length of time between delivery from a supplier and sale to a customer. Purchases, the calculation of the cost of goods sold, and the accounting for inventory are discussed in the following sections.

Purchases

Purchases
Expense accounts used to accumulate the purchase cost of merchandise held for resale.

The cost of merchandise from suppliers is recorded in the **Purchases** account when the periodic inventory method is used. An account payable results when the purchase is made on account. When BCC purchases a portable computer from its supplier on account, the transaction is recorded as follows:

Purchases	2,000	
Accounts Payable		2,000

Only the purchase of merchandise for resale is recorded in the Purchases account; the Purchases account has a debit balance. Purchases of supplies to be used in the business or purchases of other assets are recorded in other more appropriate accounts, as was discussed in preceding chapters.

Establishing Cost of Goods Sold

Merchandise inventory
Goods held for resale by a retailer or a wholesaler.

In order to establish the cost of goods sold in an accounting period, the number of items for sale must be controlled. An important difference between a merchandising firm and a service business relates to the existence of **merchandise inventory**, in this case, any merchandise for sale held by the entity between delivery from the supplier and sale to a customer. It is not unusual to have merchandise on hand at the end of an accounting time period; such merchandise is called *ending inventory*. For example, assume that Bluebeard Computer Corporation made the following purchases and sales during a particular time period:

Purchases	5 portable computers at $2,000 each
Less: Sales	− 3 portable computers at $3,000 each
Ending Inventory	2 portable computers at $2,000 each

The gross profit calculation for that time period would be as follows:

Gross Profit Calculation

	Units	*Dollars*
Sales (net)	3	$9,000
Cost of Goods Sold:		
Cost of Purchases	5	$10,000
Less: Ending Inventory	− 2	4,000
Total Cost of Goods Sold	3	6,000
Gross Profit		$3,000

The format used for this calculation is patterned after the income statement. The units included here are not actually indicated on an income statement; they are shown to demonstrate that sales of 3 units are matched with the purchase cost of 3 units in the calculation of gross profit. The remaining 2 units comprise ending inventory.

In this example, the cost of ending inventory is deducted from the cost of the 5 units purchased; in this way, the cost of the 3 units sold is matched with the sales revenue generated from their sale. An understanding of the deduction methodology used in the calculation of cost of goods sold can be facilitated by the following comparison:

Conventional Method		*Income Statement Method*	
Units Purchased	5	Units Purchased	5
Less: Units Sold	3	*Less:* Ending Inventory	2
Equals: Ending Inventory	2	*Equals:* Units Sold	3

The gross profit amount is a subtotal calculation on the income statement; its disclosure is designed to facilitate evaluation of an entity's operations during a particular time period. Its disclosure is not required, but is often made. The gross profit may not be disclosed for any number of reasons; one often cited is marketing strategy: management often doesn't want competitors to have this information.

Opening Inventory

The ending inventory of one accounting time period becomes the opening inventory of the next accounting time period. Assume that Bluebeard Computer Corporation had the following transactions in the next accounting time period:

Opening Inventory	2 portable computers at $2,000 each
Purchases	6 portable computers at $2,000 each
Sales	5 portable computers at $3,000 each

The gross profit calculation disclosed on the interim income statement of both accounting periods appears below. Note that the ending inventory in Period 1 becomes the opening inventory of Period 2.

	Period 1		Period 2	
	Units	Dollars	Units	Dollars
Sales (net)	3	$9,000	5	$15,000
Cost of Goods Sold:				
Opening Inventory	0		2	$
Cost of Purchases	5	$10,000	6	12,000
Goods Available	5		8	$16,000
Less: Ending Inventory	−2		−3	6,000
Total Cost of Goods Sold	3	6,000	5	10,000
Gross Profit		$3,000		$ 5,000

Again, although units are not actually included in an income statement, they are shown here to emphasize the matching of costs with revenues. In Period 2, 8 portable computers are available for sale; 3 are not sold and are indicated as ending inventory. The cost of the 5 portable computers sold is matched with the revenue generated from the sale of these 5 portable computers.

Students usually find it difficult to follow the income statement calculation of cost of goods sold. This calculation can be further illustrated as follows:

$$
\begin{aligned}
& \text{Opening Inventory} \\
+\ & \underline{\text{Cost of Purchases}} \\
=\ & \text{Cost of Goods Available for Sale} \\
-\ & \underline{\text{Ending Inventory}} \\
=\ & \text{Cost of Goods Sold.}
\end{aligned}
$$

This discussion has focused on purchases and inventory in the calculation of cost of goods sold. There are, however, several other accounts also used in merchandising operations.

There are two contra accounts deducted from purchases in the calculation of net purchases. These accounts are
1. Purchase Returns and Allowance
2. Purchases Discounts.
There is also an account that is included in the cost of purchases for the accounting time period. This account is
3. Transportation In.

These additional accounts are necessary in merchandising operations to accumulate amounts for activities related to the purchase of merchandise for resale. These accounts provide additional information for decision-making purposes.

Purchases Returns and Allowances

Assume that one computer sent to Bluebeard by a supplier is slightly damaged. When purchased merchandise is not satisfactory, it may be returned to the supplier, or an allowance that reduces the purchase amount may be received from the supplier. The

Purchases Returns and Allowances
A contra account to Purchases; goods returned to suppliers or price adjustments allowed by suppliers are recorded in this account.

amount of purchases return or allowance is accumulated in a separate **Purchases Returns and Allowances** account. If the account has not yet been paid, a $100 allowance for BCC would be recorded by the following entry:

Accounts Payable	100	
Purchases Returns and Allowances		100

Accounts Payable is debited, as the item was supplied on account and has not yet been paid for.

A separate account is used to accumulate purchases returns and allowances for purposes of control. A large balance signals management that a particular supplier or group of suppliers may require attention. For instance, investors in the stock of Verbatim — a Sunnyvale, California manufacturer of floppy disks — were recently startled to learn that one of the company's largest customers had returned some $2 to $3 million-worth of disks. Industry sources report that the Verbatim customer in question was IBM and that the disks were rejected because Verbatim had changed the design of the disk jacket so that its corners were more pointed than on the disks previously supplied by the manufacturer.[1]

The Purchases Returns and Allowances account is a Purchases contra account and is deducted from the amount of Purchases when preparing an income statement. In this way, the reported purchase cost is reduced by the amount of returns and allowances.

Purchases Discounts

Purchases Discounts
A contra account to Purchases; cash discounts taken if payment is made within a certain discount period.

Another Purchases contra account, **Purchases Discounts**, accumulates purchases discounts. These may apply to purchases made on account, if payment is made within a time period specified in the supplier's invoice. For example, the terms on the $2,000 invoice for one portable computer received by Bluebeard indicates "1/15, n45". This shorthand means that the $2,000 must be paid within 45 days; however, if payment is made within 15 days, a 1 percent discount can be taken.

Consider the slightly damaged computer received by BCC. If the 1/15, n45 terms apply to its purchase and the accounting policy of the company is to take advantage of such discounts, Bluebeard will make the payment within 15 days. The supplier's terms entitle Bluebeard to deduct $19 calculated as follows: ($2,000 − $100) = $1,900 × 0.01 = $19. Therefore, an $1,881 cash payment is made to the supplier and is recorded as follows:

Accounts Payable	1,900	
Purchases Discounts		19
Cash		1,881

The Purchases Discounts account, a Purchases contra account, is deducted from the amount of Purchases in the income statement. In this way, the cost of purchases is reduced by the discounts taken.

Transportation In

Fob shipping point
A term indicating that title to shipped goods passes when the goods leave the shipping point so the purchaser pays for shipping.

The purchase invoice for merchandise usually indicates who will pay for the cost of transporting it. The term *fob* (meaning "free on board") is commonly used: **fob shipping point** means the purchaser pays, and **fob destination** means the supplier pays.

Assuming that Bluebeard's supplier sells on the basis of fob shipping point, the transportation cost is the responsibility of Bluebeard and its cash payment would be recorded as follows:

Transportation In	125	
Cash		125

Fob destination
A term indicating that title to shipped goods passes when the goods reach their destination so the supplier pays for shipping.

The **Transportation In** account is added to the cost of Net Purchases in the income statement. In this way, the reported cost of purchases is increased by the amount for transportation.

An alternative way of accounting for transportation could have been used in this case. Although Bluebeard is responsible for the costs involved, the shipment could have been *freight prepaid* by the supplier. In this case, the supplier would have paid the transportation and BCC would have to reimburse the supplier. Of course, no discount for prompt payment would apply in this situation.

Transportation In
Expense account used to accumulate freight charges on merchandise purchased for resale; these charges are added to the purchase cost of this merchandise.

Alternatively, if Bluebeard purchased from a supplier whose terms were fob destination and the shipment had been sent *freight collect*, then BCC would deduct the transportation charges owed to that supplier.

The composition of the **cost of purchases** made during the accounting period is therefore calculated as Purchases less Purchases Returns and Allowances and Purchases Discounts plus Transportation In. The cost of BCC's purchased computer is as follows:

Cost of purchases
Purchases less purchases returns and allowances and purchases discounts, plus transportation in; also referred to as *cost of goods purchased*.

Purchases		$2,000
Less: Purchases Returns and Allowances	$100	
Purchases Discounts	19	119
Net purchases		$1,881
Add: Transportation In		125
Total Cost of Goods Purchased		$2,006

The cost of goods purchased can also be indicated as Cost of Purchases on the income statement.

Inventory

The Perpetual Inventory System

Perpetual inventory system
A method of inventory valuation in which purchases and sales are recorded as they occur and a continuous balance of inventory on hand is calculated in terms of units and often in terms of cost. The cost of goods sold is determined for each sale and is recorded. A physical count at the end of the period is used to verify the quantities that should be on hand.

Under the **perpetual inventory system**, a continuous balance of inventory on hand is calculated in terms of units and, often, in terms of cost. As a purchase is received, the quantity received is added to the quantity recorded as being on hand. When inventory is sold, the sold units are deducted and a new balance of inventory on hand is calculated. Inventory on hand at the end of the accounting period is counted to verify the quantities actually on hand. One cause of fluctuations in the gross profit percentage can be inventory losses through theft and errors; management control over inventory, if this is the case, needs to be strengthened.

The perpetual inventory system, therefore, incorporates an important internal control feature. Losses resulting from theft and error can easily be determined when the actual quantity counted is compared with the quantities that ought to be on hand. This advantage is reduced, however, by the time and expense required for continuously updating the inventory records. Computerization makes this record-keeping easier and less expensive, particularly when the inventory system is tied into the sales system, so that inventory is updated whenever a sale is recorded. The actual procedures involved in a perpetual inventory system and the impact of inventory errors on the income statement are further discussed in Chapter 5.

The Periodic Inventory Method

Periodic inventory method
A method whereby a record of the opening inventory and purchases during the period is kept. Ending inventory is calculated by physically counting the goods on hand and assigning a cost to these goods; all goods not on hand at the end of the period are assumed to have been sold.

Accounting for purchases, as described here, is in accordance with an inventory control system called the **periodic inventory method**. Merchandise purchased for resale is recorded into a Purchases account; whenever financial statements are prepared, a physical count is made to determine the amount of inventory on hand. The amount of goods sold during the accounting period is calculated at the time these financial statements are prepared, as discussed earlier. Therefore, the change in inventory between the beginning and end of an accounting time period is recorded only periodically, usually at year-end. The interrelationship of inventory disclosed in the income statement and balance sheet can be illustrated as follows:

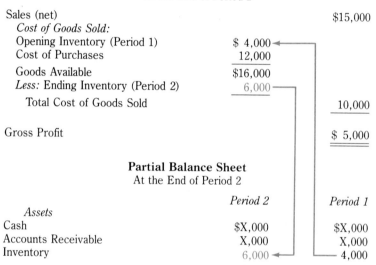

Partial Income Statement
At the End of Period 2

Sales (net)		$15,000
Cost of Goods Sold:		
Opening Inventory (Period 1)	$ 4,000	
Cost of Purchases	12,000	
Goods Available	$16,000	
Less: Ending Inventory (Period 2)	6,000	
Total Cost of Goods Sold		10,000
Gross Profit		$ 5,000

Partial Balance Sheet
At the End of Period 2

	Period 2	*Period 1*
Assets		
Cash	$X,000	$X,000
Accounts Receivable	X,000	X,000
Inventory	6,000	4,000

A physical count of inventory requires careful planning and accurate inventory-taking procedures. For instance, pre-numbered inventory tags can be attached to all inventory items; quantities are recorded on these tags; the numerical sequence of the completed tags is subsequently checked to ensure that all counted quantities are accounted for.

The periodic inventory system is most useful where many different or low value items are kept in stock and where maintaining detailed records would be expensive.

Purchase and Payment: Related Recording

Debit and Credit Memos

Debit or credit memo
A document issued to alter an amount between seller and purchaser.

The return of merchandise, the granting of an allowance, or the discovery of an invoicing error are among the reasons for the preparation of a document referred to as a **debit** or **credit memo**. The accounting for such memos involves a different account when dealing with sales, as opposed to purchases. The Accounts Receivable account is debited or credited when a sales-related memo is issued; a purchase-related memo involves Accounts Payable. A debit or credit memo can be issued by either the seller or the purchaser.

Seller-Issued Memos

• A debit memo issued by a seller results in a debit to the customer's Accounts Receivable account. The increase in the amount due from the customer could be, for instance, the result of a calculation error in an original invoice that undercharged the customer.

• A credit memo issued by a seller results in a credit to the customer's Accounts Receivable account. This decrease in the receivable may be, for instance, the result of an allowance for damaged goods granted to the customer.

Purchaser-Issued Memos

• A debit memo issued by a purchaser results in a debit to the supplier's Accounts Payable account. This decrease in the amount owed to the supplier may be, for instance, a result of a pricing error in an original invoice that overcharged the purchaser.

• A credit memo issued by a purchaser credits the supplier's Accounts Payable account. This credit memo increases the amount owed the supplier.

Trade Discounts

Trade discount
A percentage or dollar amount used to calculate the actual sales or purchase price of merchandise.

The preceding discussion of sales and purchases involved use of an established dollar amount for price. In actual practice, these amounts are often determined through use of a suggested list price in conjunction with a catalogue indicating the merchandise offered. **Trade discounts** from the suggested list price are used to calculate prices for different categories of buyers and for different quantities. For example, a 30 percent discount may be offered to colleges and universities, and a different discount percentage to retailers. Trade discounts can be in terms of a percentage or dollar amount deducted from the suggested list price.

A Bluebeard software package with a suggested list price of $250 less a 20 percent discount would be priced at $200 = ($250 × 20% trade discount).

The sale to a BCC customer of this software would be recorded as follows:

Accounts Receivable	200	
Sales		200

The purchase by BCC from a supplier of this software would be recorded as follows:

Purchases	200	
Accounts Payable		200

The amount of the trade discount, $50 in this case, is not recorded in the books and should not be confused with cash discounts offered for prompt payment; the recording of cash discounts for both sales and purchases was discussed previously.

Issues in Ethics 4-1

Executives Must Add Ethics to Their Schooling

Ethical behavior in business is more important today than ever before, yet ethics is one of the most perplexing issues business leaders have to face. It has always been an important issue and it will probably become one of the primary challenges confronting managers in the years to come.

Corporations have always been purveyors of values, and now the changes in individual and social values are having an impact on the workplace, and the role of business is shifting. Business must fully meet its obligations to its customers, employees and shareholders and to society in general.

Responsible decision makers need to ask some penetrating questions:

- Is it fair?
- Is it the truth?
- Is there a mutual benefit?
- Will I feel right about this decision?

Questions like these must be asked as decisions are made. The benefits include better employee relations, more open and honest communications, more satisfied and loyal customers, and a company that is respected in its community.

The benefits are real in terms of profitability and corporate growth — good business ethics make good business sense.

Fortunately, most business people act responsibly. Unfortunately, some don't and their actions have given business a bad name.

Their rationalization was that they wanted to implement a solution that served their short-term corporate purposes. This was usually at the long-term expense of their employees and/or community.

Stories abound about businesses that seem to have operated in a vacuum, devoid of responsible behavior.

The oil companies, for example, have been reputed to dump harmful acids into the oceans. The forest products companies have been cited for stripping the forests, failing to replant enough trees and then, when processing the timber, pumping PCBs into the lakes and streams.

The notorious example of Hooker Chemical Co., which poured toxic pollutants into the Love Canal in upstate New York, created a furor. The company's actions to improve its bottom line at any cost made Attila the Hun look good by comparison.

The rationalization of the management of such companies, which may have been acceptable at one time, was that jobs were being created and local communities were being developed.

Consequently, some companies took advantage of the lack of government regulations — regulations which ordinarily would safeguard the common good. They sought the cheapest solution and abdicated their responsibility to their local community and the environment.

Partly because no accountant could mathematically determine the environmental costs, management failed to evaluate the full cost of its production decisions, such as the effect of acid rain on lakes and forests.

Progress was the excuse; it was all that mattered. The shareholders' gain became the general public's pain and society's loss.

Unfortunately, some companies still conduct their businesses in the same way, apparently oblivious to the reality that the environment is fragile and that they have a social responsibility.

Public outcries discourage such actions, for the cost is too high. It is now clearly a travesty of justice when flagrant violations of the environment are allowed to continue when we have the technology to clean things up.

This type of behavior may have been considered acceptable at one time — it was done in pursuit of progress — but this argument is now inappropriate.

Additional examples pose more difficult problems, such as replacing labor investment with capital investment.

While technology is being touted as the salvation of the fledgling company, the tradeoff is jobs. Investing in machines, instead of people, presents a dilemma. The company may benefit, but what becomes of the person who has been loyal and has served the company and is now dislocated, unemployable or untrainable?

What is a responsible corporate policy for dealing with those who are displaced because of technology? Should the company take care of its people or should it manage people as a resource to be used and disposed of?

And what about smoking in the workplace? What is a company's responsibility to protect the rights of non-smokers who want to breathe clean air?

Cigaret smoke is a proven carcinogen and the detrimental effects of secondhand smoke are well documented, so why do many companies, indeed even some hospitals, resist implementing a "no smoking" policy?

Corporate managers are under greater pressure to question their ethics and to instill a strong sense of ethics and values in their people. Business leaders have training in areas such as marketing, production management and labor relations, but they are not generally schooled in ethics.

The corporation, which is just a combination of people, is a social organization with an economic purpose. It is molded by the decisions of the manager. Today, that means decisions have not only a local but also a national and international impact.

For the manager of the present and the future, training must include ethics so that the corporation and the individuals in it act responsibly in the local, national and international community.

Source Andrew Campbell, "Executives Must Add Ethics to Their Schooling", *The Globe and Mail*, Toronto, January 24, 1988, p. B-4.

D.   Closing Entries

The recording of adjusting entries and subsequent preparation of closing entries, as illustrated in Chapter 3, also applies to merchandisers. At the end of a fiscal year, the revenue and expense accounts are reduced to zero balances, so that they can begin to accumulate amounts for the new fiscal year. Closing entries are prepared to close these income statement accounts; dividend accounts are also closed at the end of the corporate year.

The closing process for merchandisers includes new Sales and Purchases accounts, as well as their contra accounts. The closing procedure remains the same as for service entities; all accounts listed in the income statement columns are transferred to the Income Summary account. This includes the debit balance relating to opening inventory and the credit balance relating to the ending inventory.

Under the periodic inventory system, the opening inventory is removed, and ending inventory recorded, as part of the closing process. The following T-account illustrates how this occurs.

		Merchandise Inventory *No. 150*	
Jan. 1	Opening bal.	80,000	
	Less: Opening inventory (closing entry posted)		80,000
	Bal.	-0-	
	Add: Ending inventory	120,000	
Dec. 31	Ending bal.	120,000	

The closing entries prepared for Bluebeard Computer Corporation at December 31, 19X3 are shown in Figure 4-3. Note the inclusion of the Merchandise Inventory opening and ending balances.

Entry 1
The revenue accounts are closed in one compound closing journal entry to the Income Summary account. (All revenue accounts with credit balances are debited to bring them to zero. Their balances are transferred to the Income Summary account.)

Entry 2
The expense accounts are closed in one compound closing journal entry to the Income Summary account. (All expense accounts with debit balances are credited to bring them to zero. Their balances are transferred to the Income Summary account.)

Entry 3
The Income Summary account is next closed to the Retained Earnings account.

Entry 4
The dividend account is closed directly to the Retained Earnings account. Since Dividends is not an expense account, it is not closed to Income Summary; rather, it is closed directly to Retained Earnings, because dividends are a distribution of earnings made by the corporation to its owners, the shareholders.

GENERAL JOURNAL

Date 19X1		Description	F	Debit	Credit
		Closing Entries			
Dec.	31	Merchandise Inventory (ending)	150	120000 –	
		Sales	500	308500 –	
		Purchases Returns	558	12600 –	
		Purchases Discounts	559	2400 –	
		Income Summary	360		443500 –
		To record ending inventory and			
		to close income statement			
		accounts with a credit balance.			
	31	Income Summary	360	428500 –	
		Merchandise Inventory (opening)	150		80000 –
		Sales Returns and Allowances	508		6000 –
		Sales Discounts	509		2500 –
		Purchases	550		240000 –
		Transportation In	560		15000 –
		Advertising Expense	610		10000 –
		Commissions Expense	615		15000 –
		Delivery Expense	620		6000 –
		Depreciation Expense-Equipment	623		1600 –
		Insurance Expense	631		1200 –
		Interest Expense	632		10000 –
		Rent Expense	654		3600 –
		Salaries Expense	656		20000 –
		Telephone Expense	669		1080 –
		Utilities Expense	676		1520 –
		Income Tax Expense	830		15000 –
		To record opening inventory and			
		to close income statement			
		accounts with a debit balance.			
	31	Income Summary	360	15000 –	
		Retained Earnings	340		15000 –
		To close Income Summary account.			
	31	Retained Earnings	340	4250 –	
		Dividends	350		4250 –
		To close Dividend account.			

Figure 4-3   Closing entries

E.   Classified Financial Statements

Accountants are concerned with the application of GAAP to the recording of financial transactions; the impact of GAAP on the accounting process has been the focus of preceding chapters. This section focuses on the preparation of financial statements, that is, the disclosure in financial statements of financial information recorded in the company's books. The issues involved include financial statement preparation and classification (the way accounts are grouped). Look at Chapter 2 to review the classification of balance sheets.

The Classified Income Statement

In Chapter 1, income statements were classified into revenue and expense accounts. In actual practice, the income statement of a merchandising firm is usually further classified, with revenues and expenses broken into categories and subtotals provided for each classification. This classification highlights interrelationships of important amounts by making the information readily available.

The importance of the gross profit subtotal was previously discussed; it represents the amount of sales revenue that remains to pay expenses necessary to operate the business (operating expenses) and financing expenses, such as interest expense and the amount paid to the entity's silent partner, the government, as income tax expense. The balance is the bottom line — the net income amount. Net income represents the return on shareholders' investment and the amount available for dividends to shareholders. For bankers, the net income represents the ability of the entity to expand its operations through debt financing and its ability to support increased interest charges that result from increased debt. For labour unions, the entity's net income is an indication of what they perceive as a basis for increased salary demands in labour negotiations.

Operating expenses
Expenses incurred in the operation of the business, except items classified as *other expenses* or as *income tax expense*.

The adjacent classified income statement of Bluebeard Computer Corporation for the year ended December 31, 19X3 also includes the classification of **operating expenses** into two categories: selling expenses and general and administrative expenses.

Selling expenses — those incurred to sell the merchandise — are classified as part of operating expenses. General and administrative expenses are those incurred to administer the merchandising operations. While most operating expenses are easily distinguished as one or the other category, some require allocation; for example, rent expense may include both the sales area and the office. Sometimes, classification is made on the basis of expediency, particularly if the amounts involved are not material; insurance expense, which covers both the sales area and office space, has not been allocated by Bluebeard.

Interest expense is classified separately because of the impact that financing the entity's activities through debt has on the bottom line calculation of net income.

The 19X3 year-end income statement illustrates all the major classifications required for Bluebeard. Other entities may require further classifications indicating other subtotals to highlight important interrelationships relevant to specific aspects of their operations.

In actual practice, the financial statements would indicate not only the 19X3 data, but the comparative data for the preceding year, 19X2 in this case. These are then referred to as comparative financial statements; comparative amounts would be provided in each of the financial statements prepared.

Often a condensed income statement is reproduced in published annual reports. One such condensed statement could be designed as shown on page 190.

Bluebeard Computer Corporation
Income Statement
For the Year Ended December 31, 19X3

Sales			$308,500
Less: Sales Returns and Allowances		$ 6,000	
Sales Discounts		2,500	8,500
Net Sales			$300,000
Cost of Goods Sold:			
Opening Inventory (Jan. 1)		$ 80,000	
Purchases	$240,000		
Less: Purchases Returns and Allowances	$12,600		
Purchases Discounts	2,400	15,000	
Net Purchases		$225,000	
Add: Transportation In		15,000	
Cost of Goods Purchased		240,000	
Cost of Goods Available		$320,000	
Ending Inventory (Dec. 31)		120,000	
Total Cost of Goods Sold			200,000
Gross Profit			$100,000
Operating Expenses:			
Selling Expenses:			
Advertising Expense	$ 10,000		
Commissions Expense	15,000		
Delivery Expense	6,000		
Total Selling Expenses		$ 31,000	
General and Administrative Expenses:			
Depreciation — Equipment	$ 1,600		
Insurance Expense	1,200		
Rent Expense	3,600		
Salaries Expense	20,000		
Telephone Expense	1,080		
Utilities Expense	1,520		
Total General and Administrative Expenses		29,000	
Total Operating Expenses			60,000
Income from Operations			$ 40,000
Financing Costs:			
Interest Expense			10,000
Income (before income tax)			$ 30,000
Income Tax			15,000
Net Income for the Year			$ 15,000

Bluebeard Computer Corporation
Income Statement
For the Year Ended December 31, 19X3

Net Sales		$300,000
Costs and Expenses:		
Cost of Goods Sold	$200,000	
Selling, General and Administrative	58,400	
Depreciation	1,600	260,000
Income from Operations		$ 40,000
Financing Costs:		
Interest Expense		10,000
Income (before income tax)		$ 30,000
Income Tax		15,000
Net Income for the Year		$ 15,000

Note that, for disclosure purposes, in accordance with GAAP, the depreciation has been shown separately from the amount of general and administrative expenses. The total amount still agrees with the selling and general and administrative expenses reported on the preceding classified income statement.

Notes to Financial Statements

Following its financial statements, a corporation discloses what accounting policies it has followed in their preparation. These policies are summarized to facilitate the review and analysis of the financial statements. The matters covered could include revenue recognition, valuation of inventories, the accounting treatment of fixed asset expenditures, the accounting for income taxes, and other issues significant to the business. Any changes in accounting policy from previous years must be noted.

In addition to a discussion of accounting policies, information that helps users of financial statements to understand individual items are indicated through disclosures in notes. These notes may explain extraordinary items or prior-period adjustments, if any, details about income tax matters, transactions with related companies, commitments entered into by the company, and events subsequent to the data of the financial statements that are important and may affect the reader's interpretation.

Schedules

Additional disclosure may be made through schedules that disclose inventory calculations and details of operating expenses. Additional schedules may be attached to the financial statements to disclose the effects of inflation or information required by securities exchanges or regulatory agencies.

The Statement of Retained Earnings

Statement of retained earnings
A statement showing the changes that have occurred in retained earnings during a particular time period.

Retained earnings
Net income that is not paid out as dividends; net income that is reinvested in the entity for expansion and growth of the entity.

Dividend
A distribution to corporate shareholders; can consist of cash, property of the corporation, or shares of stock.

The net income (or loss) for the period, as well as dividends for the accounting time period, are reported in the **statement of retained earnings**. This statement is a link between the income statement and balance sheet. **Retained earnings** represent the earnings of the entity that have not been distributed to shareholders as dividends.

Since its inception in 19X1 until the beginning of 19X3, Bluebeard Computer Corporation has retained $21,750. It earned $15,000 in 19X3 and paid $4,250 cash dividends to shareholders during the year. A **dividend** results in the reduction of retained earnings, which consists of net income earned in the current or prior periods. The asset Cash is decreased by the payment, and the shareholders' equity item, Retained Earnings, is also decreased. During 19X3, BCC declared and paid a $4,250 dividend authorized by its board of directors. This payment was recorded by the following entry:

Dividends	4,250	
Cash		4,250

The pattern of recording dividend payments is similar to that used for assets and expenses. Debits record an increase in assets, expenses, and dividends.

The 19X3 ending amount of earnings retained in the business amounts to $32,500 ($21,750 + $15,000 − $4,250). This amount of retained earnings is represented by assets held by the corporation; these assets are available not only for use in the future expansion of the business but also to absorb any losses that may occur. If a net loss had occurred in 19X3, the amount of loss would have been deducted from the opening Retained Earnings balance of $21,750.

The adjacent statement of retained earnings is for Bluebeard Computer Corporation for the year ended December 31, 19X3. Note that the Dividends balance is deducted on the statement.

Bluebeard Computer Corporation
Statement of Retained Earnings
For the Year Ended December 31, 19X3

Balance (Jan. 1)	$21,750
Add: Net Income for the Year	15,000
Total	$36,750
Less: Dividends	4,250
Balance (Dec. 31)	$32,500

The net income for the year is taken from the income statement illustrated in an earlier section. This statement discloses the changes during the year to the Retained Earnings account reported in the balance sheet at December 31, 19X3.

Prior-Period Adjustments

Prior-period adjustments
Gains and losses that are applicable to the net income reported in prior years; disclosed in the statement of retained earnings.

An additional category of amounts, referred to as **prior-period adjustments**, are also reported in the statement of retained earnings. This category relates to gains or losses that constitute changes in the net income reported in the prior year. They are excluded from the current year's income statement; they are disclosed in the statement of retained earnings because the net income (or loss) of the prior year is included in the opening Retained Earnings balance.

The recording of adjustments to net income reported in prior periods is restricted by the *CICA Handbook*, section 3600, and is meant to appear infrequently in actual practice. Prior-period adjustments are recorded in the case of non-recurring items, consisting of adjustments or settlements of income taxes and settlements of claims resulting from litigation, for example. Items are prior-period adjustments only if they have all of the following four characteristics:

- if they are specifically identified with and directly related to the business activities of particular prior periods
- if they are not attributable to economic events, including obsolescence, occurring subsequent to the date of the financial statements for such prior periods
- if they depend primarily on decisions or determinations by persons other than management or owners
- if they could not be reasonably estimated prior to such decisions or determinations.

The more complex aspects of the treatment of prior-period adjustments are the subject matter of intermediate accounting courses.

don't have to know F + G

F. Evaluation of the Entity

Solvency
The ability to pay current liabilities as they become due.

Accountants, analysts, and investors often talk about the solvency of a company. What does this mean? The term **solvency**, when applied to a company, refers to its ability to pay current liabilities as they become due. Why is it important to know whether a company is solvent? If a company is insolvent, then it is unable to pay its creditors, who have provided goods and services on account. The implications of being insolvent are

1. Current Liabilities
   Creditors can refuse to provide any further goods or services on account.
   Creditors can sue for payment.
   Creditors can put the company into bankruptcy.
2. Long-Term Liabilities
   Creditors can refuse to lend additional cash.
   Creditors can demand repayment of their long-term debts under some circumstances.
3. Shareholders' Equity
   Shareholders risk the loss of their investment if the corporation is placed into bankruptcy.

At the present time, Bluebeard Computer Corporation is a solvent corporation. What is the structure of BCC's creditor financing? An analysis of the company's balance sheet reveals the following liabilities:

	19X3
Current Liabilities	$79,000
Long-Term Liabilities	48,500

This information indicates that the company's management relies on both short-term and long-term creditor financing. If the bank decides not to continue lending money to BCC, its ability to pay its other liabilities as they become due may be compromised. Management needs to be able to analyze its short-term solvency.

Short-Term Solvency Analysis

Ratio
The quotient resulting when one number is divided by another.

Ratios are one way of evaluating any company's solvency. Two commonly used methods of **ratio analysis** are introduced and explained below. More will be introduced in the next section of this chapter. Others will be discussed in Chapter 14.

Ratio analysis
Analysis of inter-relationships of different financial statement items as a method of financial statement evaluation.

Short-Term Solvency Analysis	*Indicates*
1. The Current Ratio	How many current asset dollars exist to pay current liabilities. This ratio is only a crude measure of solvency.
2. The Acid-Test Ratio	Whether the company is able to meet the immediate demands of creditors. This ratio is a more severe measure of solvency. Inventory and prepaid items are excluded from the calculation.

The Current Ratio

Current ratio
Current assets divided by current liabilities; indicates how many asset dollars are available to pay current liabilities. This is a *crude* measure of solvency; also called the *working capital ratio*.

An overall analysis of solvency is made by a ratio labelled the **current ratio**. Is the firm able to repay short-term creditors? The current ratio answers this question by expressing a relationship between current assets and current liabilities — current assets are divided by current liabilities. These are the relevant BCC financial data required to calculate this ratio:

		19X3
Current Assets	(a)	$158,000
Current Liabilities	(b)	$ 79,000
Current Ratio	(a ÷ b)	2 : 1

The results of this calculation are an indication of how many current asset dollars exist to pay current liabilities. $2 of current assets exist in 19X3 to pay each $1 of current liabilities. Is $2 adequate? Unfortunately, there is no one current ratio that indicates whether an amount is adequate. There are three possibilities in any given situation; these are given in Figure 4-4.

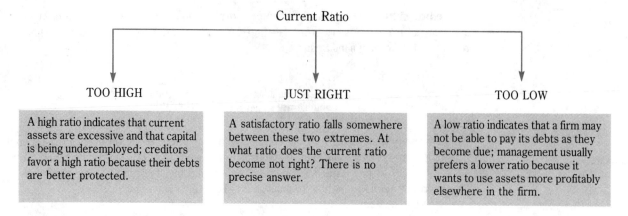

Figure 4-4   Current ratio analysis

In the past, a current ratio of two-to-one (2 : 1) was considered necessary. For example, if there were $2 of current assets to pay each $1 of current liabilities, an entity's management would have thought these current assets could shrink considerably and the firm would still be able to pay its debts. By this guide, the current ratio of Bluebeard Computer Corporation would be acceptable.

Today, however, analysts generally agree that no one ratio is sufficient for all businesses and that other factors — such as the composition of current assets, the credit terms extended to customers, or the credit terms extended by suppliers — must also be considered to arrive at an acceptable ratio.

Dun and Bradstreet, as well as various trade publications, provides a range of current ratios that may be applicable to companies in a particular industry at one point in time. It is noteworthy that the adequacy of a current ratio depends on other developments within a company and, while a particular ratio may be satisfactory one year, it may not be adequate the next year.

Composition of Specific Items in Current Assets

In the following example, each company has a 2 : 1 ratio. Is each company equally able to repay its short-term creditors?

	A Corp.	B Corp.
CURRENT ASSETS		
Cash	$ 1	$10
Accounts Receivable	2	20
Inventory	37	10
Total Current Assets	$40	$40
Current Liabilities	$20	$20
Current Ratio	2 : 1	2 : 1

Each company has equal dollar amounts of current assets and current liabilities, but their debt-paying abilities are not equal. Company A must first sell some inventory and collect the resulting accounts receivable, or it can immediately sell its inventory as a single lot for cash, probably for less than its cost. This type of shrinkage is provided for in the 2 : 1 current ratio. The current ratio is, therefore, only a rough indicator of how able a firm is to pay its debts as they become due. The criticism of this ratio is that it doesn't consider the components of current assets in analyzing the solvency of a firm.

The Acid-Test Ratio

Acid-test ratio
Quick current assets divided by current liabilities; indicates the ability of the entity to meet the immediate demands of creditors. This is a more severe measure of solvency than the current ratio; also called the *quick* ratio.

A more severe test of solvency is provided by the so-called **acid-test ratio**, which is often called the *quick ratio*. It provides an indication of instant solvency — the ability to meet the immediate demands of creditors. To calculate this ratio, current assets have to be broken down into quick and non-quick current assets:

Quick Current Assets:

Cash
Temporary Investments
Accounts Receivable — Trade

These current assets are considered to be readily convertible into cash.

Non-quick Current Assets:

Inventory
Prepaid Items

Cash could not be obtained immediately from these current assets.

Quick current assets
Assets that can be converted into cash in a short period of time, including cash, marketable securities, accounts receivable — trade, and excluding inventory and prepaid items.

Inventory and prepaid items are not usually convertible into cash in a short period of time. They are therefore excluded from **quick current assets** in the calculation of this ratio. The acid-test ratio is calculated by dividing the total of quick current assets by current liabilities. These are the relevant BCC financial data used to calculate the acid-test ratio:

		19X3
Quick Current Assets	(a)	$36,800
Current Liabilities	(b)	79,000
Acid-Test Ratio	(a ÷ b)	0.47 (rounded)

This ratio indicates how many quick asset dollars (cash, temporary investments, and trade accounts receivable) exist to pay each $1 of current liabilities. As can be seen, there are $0.47 of quick assets in the Bluebeard Computer Corporation to pay each $1 of current liabilities.

What Is an Adequate Acid-Test Ratio?

Analysts generally consider that a one-to-one (1 : 1) acid-test ratio is adequate to ensure that a firm is able to pay its current obligations. However, this is a fairly arbitrary guideline and is not necessarily reliable in all situations. A lower ratio than 1 : 1 can often be found in successful companies.

A company tries to keep a reasonable balance in its current assets among cash, receivables, and inventory. Unfortunately, there is no one indicator of what this balance really is. The balance is acceptable when debts are being paid. The "end of the rope" comes when current liabilities are not being paid; in such a case, a reasonable balance does not exist.

What Is the Relationship between the Current Ratio and the Acid-Test Ratio?

When taken together, these ratios give the financial statement reader a better understanding of the inventory implications for a company. While the current ratio may be favourable, the acid-test ratio may be such that it alerts the reader to the non-quick current assets of the company.

G.   Analysis of Operations Efficiency

Each entity uses its assets as resources to earn net income. However, some entities do so more successfully than others. How can the efficiency with which a company is using its assets be established?

An evaluation of an entity's operations efficiency can be established through the calculation and study of relevant ratios. Of particular interest is the current status of the entity, the record of the entity over a number of years, and a comparison of the entity's financial performance with that of others in the same industry and in other industries.

The net income earned is the starting point for this ratio analysis. The efficient use of assets can be measured by expressing net income as a return on assets, on shareholders' equity, on sales, and on each share. An additional measurement used in the stock market to evaluate the selling price of shares relates the selling price to the share's earnings.

Analysis of Operations Efficiency:	*Indicates:*
1. Return on Total Assets	How efficiently a company uses its assets as resources to earn net income.
2. Return on Shareholders' Equity	The adequacy of net income as a return on shareholders' equity.
3. Return on Sales	The percentage of sales revenue earned by the business after payment of creditor interest and government income tax.
4. Return on Each Share	The amount of net income that has been carried for each share of common stock.
5. Price-Earnings Ratio	The reasonableness of market price in relation to per share earnings.

The relationship of the first three of these ratios to the balance sheet and income statement of an entity is shown in Figure 4-5.

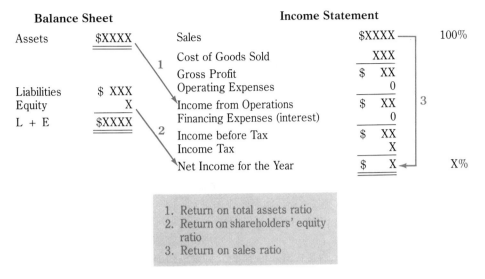

Figure 4-5   Relationship of three ratios to financial statements

Return on Total Assets Ratio

Return on total assets ratio
Income from operations is divided by average total assets. This ratio indicates how efficiently a company uses its assets as resources to earn net income.

An efficient use of assets should result in a higher return on these assets; a less efficient use should result in a lower return. The **return on total assets ratio** is designed to measure the efficiency with which assets are used. The ratio is calculated as follows:

$$\frac{\text{Income from Operations}}{\text{Average Total Assets}}$$

Attention is focused on net income from operations, which is the amount earned by the entity from the use of its assets. Expenses not applicable to operations of the entity, such as interest (expenses to finance the entity) and income taxes (expenses on income due to the government) are excluded. Average total assets are used in the calculation because the amount of assets used varies during the year.

Return on Shareholders' Equity Ratio

The assets of an entity are financed by both creditors and shareholders. In return for their share of financing, creditors are paid interest. Shareholders have claim to whatever remains after interest is paid to creditors and income taxes are paid to the government. This **return on shareholders' equity ratio** is calculated as follows:

Return on shareholders' equity ratio
Net income for the year is divided by average shareholders' equity. This ratio indicates the adequacy of net income as a return on shareholders' equity.

$$\frac{\text{Net Income for the Year}}{\text{Average Shareholders' Equity}}$$

Net income after interest and income taxes is used in this calculation because only the balance remains to shareholders. Average equity is used because the amount of equity can vary during the year.

Return on Sales Ratio

Return on sales ratio
Net income for the year is divided by net sales. This ratio indicates the percentage of sales revenue left in the business after payment of expenses, creditor interest, and government income taxes.

The efficiency, of *productivity*, of each sales dollar is established through the calculation of the **return on sales ratio**. This percentage of sales revenue retained by the entity — after payment of creditor interest expenses and government income taxes — is an index of performance that can be used to compare this entity with others in the same industry, or in other industries. The percentage return on sales is calculated as follows:

$$\frac{\text{Net Income for the Year}}{\text{Sales}}$$

Earnings per Share

The return to shareholders discussed earlier indicates the return on assets financed by shareholders. This return to shareholders can also be expressed on a per-share basis. That is, the amount of net income can be divided by the number of common shares outstanding in order to establish how much net income has been earned for each share of stock. This return per share is calculated as follows:

$$\frac{\text{Net Income for the Year}}{\text{Number of Common Shares Outstanding}}$$

Earnings per share
A dollar amount calculated by dividing income available to common shareholders by the number of common shares outstanding.

This expression of net income as a per-share amount is widely quoted in financial circles and, as noted, is called **earnings per share (EPS)**. Earnings per share is of particular interest to investors because of its importance in influencing share market values. For this reason, in actual practice, EPS must be disclosed on the income statement or in a note to the statements.

Price-to-Earnings Ratio

Price-to-earnings ratio
The market price per share is divided by earnings per share. This ratio indicates the reasonableness of market price in relation to earnings per share.

The **price-to-earnings ratio** is calculated by dividing the market value of a share by earnings per share:

$$\frac{\text{Market Price per Share}}{\text{Earnings per Share}}$$

This ratio indicates the reasonableness of market price in relation to earnings per share.

ASSIGNMENT MATERIALS

Discussion Questions

1. How does the income statement prepared for a merchandising firm differ from that prepared for a service business?
2. What relationship does a gross profit calculation express? Explain, using an example.
3. How does the gross profit appear on an income statement? Could its calculation be omitted from the income statement?
4. Is the gross profit always disclosed on the income statement? Why or why not?
5. Contrast and explain the sales and collection cycle and the purchase and payment cycle.
6. What contra accounts are used for Sales and Purchases? What are their functions?
7. How is cost of purchases calculated?
8. List the components of the cost of goods sold calculation.
9. Contrast the differences between the periodic inventory method and the perpetual inventory system.
10. Explain how ending inventory is recorded in the accounts of a merchandiser using a periodic inventory system.
11. Why is interest expense classified separately on the income.
12. What are prior-period adjustments?
13. What are the implications of a firm being insolvent?
14. What are financial ratios, and why are they calculated?
15. Distinguish between the current ratio and the acid-test ratio.
16. Is any one current ratio or acid-test ratio adequate for all businesses? Why or why not?
17. What ratios are relevant for an evaluation of an entity's operations efficiency?

Discussion Cases

Discussion Case 4-1: Pricing for Profit

The following questions relate to Real Life Example 4-1.

For Discussion

1. Do you agree with the comment that "When business is bad, cutting prices makes matters worse"? Why or why not?
2. The author writes, "You have to increase sales significantly to recover the dollars lost by the cuts." If you don't reduce prices to meet competition, won't you be worse off than if you did cut prices?
3. A price hike would produce more profit if unit sales volume stayed the same. Is it ethical to increase prices to make more profit? Assume that the product is a drug that limits the spread of cancer.
4. The author claims that many companies, particularly those in financial trouble, continue to underprice their products. Would knowing whether a company is underpricing its products be useful for investors? Where would this information be available?

Discussion Case 4-2:   The Price Is Right

We can estimate what it would cost to produce a typical small PC [personal computer] software package in the customary vinyl folder: about $5 a copy, exclusive of overhead and the mental effort expended to create the software itself.

Now let's look at what you can sell your product for. If you don't know the practices of distribution and mark-ups—and most of us really don't—then you may be in for some shocks.

For the moment, we'll ignore the official list price of your product and what it ought to be. We'll come back to that subject later. Instead, let's consider everything in terms of a percentage of the list price as is the custom in discussions of distribution and pricing.

Slicing Up the Pie

If we're lucky enough to sell our software to the end-user at 100 percent of the list price, that's all gravy for us. Unfortunately, we can't get it very much of the time. If we want to sell as many copies of our programs as possible and make as much money as possible, we have to get retailers, distributors, discounters, and others involved and give each a slice of the pie. As it turns out, they expect a bigger slice than most people imagine.

It's customary for a retail store to buy its goods at roughly 60 percent of the list price. It sounds as though they're getting 40 percent of your customer's dollar, but retailers have rent, salespeople to pay, and lots of overhead costs. Retailers don't bank much of their 40 percent cut.

The same holds true, by the way, of the mail-order discounters. Discounters save overhead and pass it on to the end-user. They typically sell at about 70 to 75 percent of the list price and cover their costs and profit on a margin of 10 to 15 percent, instead of the retailer's 40 percent.

If you're lucky enough to be selling directly to retailers and not being buried alive in the process, then you're doing very nicely to be getting up to 60 percent of the list price of your programs. There is a good reason, though, why software distributors exist. Distributors act as buffers between software producers and computer retail stores. A retail store can turn to a distributor for one-stop shopping instead of ordering from dozens of suppliers and trying to keep track of who ships quickly and reliably and who takes frightfully long to send the goods. From the point of view of a retailer, the distributor smooths out the uneven response time from software producers. Budding software producers like us get a lot from distributors as well: one source of orders instead of a flood of phone calls from many stores, a sales force that knows all those computer stores, and an accounting department that knows how to pay its bills.

Distributors get their own slice of pie. Retailers buy from the distributors at about 60 percent of list, and the distributors expect to buy from us at no more than 40 percent of list. Often they will require a price as low as 35 or even 30 percent.

The Publisher's Piece

If you end up selling your product for about 35 percent of the list price, you make a lot less profit than you might have expected. Let's suppose that you've created a game or some other piece of software that can't sell for a high ticket price. Typical game prices are $30, $35, $40 tops. Let's slice up the pie on a $30 product.

The customer pays 100 percent, $30. The retailer pockets 40 percent, $12, to cover costs and profit, passing on $18 to the distributor, who pockets 25 percent or $7.50. You get your 35 percent, some $10.50. But unlike everyone else, you've got the actual production cost, which we ball-park at $5, so your gross profit is a mere $5.50. For you, though, that's just a gross—out of it you have to cover your overhead, including any advertising you might be doing. Whatever is left is your profit as software author and software publisher —not sudden riches in anyone's book.

We've been assuming all along that you're both author and publisher of your own software. What if you don't plan on wearing both hats? Perhaps you've written something and you'd just as soon let someone else have the hassles of publishing it.

Although any kind of deal can be struck, the software publishing business has settled down to some stable standards that closely match the customs of the book publishing business. An often-quoted figure is a royalty to the author of 15 percent of the publisher's gross. That's not, as many people assume, 15 percent of the list price. In the case of software publishing, it's typically 15 percent of 35 percent of the list—or a net royalty of about 5 percent of list. For our hypothetical $30 software package, the royalty would be about $1.50 on each copy. That's far from a fat slice of the pie, but the author is relieved of all the business of making and selling and is responsible just for creating (which the business world never considered an important activity anyway).

It should be clear now why so much software is priced in the hundreds of dollars. It takes lots of investment in teams of programmers and in advertising to get big, serious software onto the streets. While a kitchen table software house might be able to thrive on a gross profit of $5 or $10, Ashton-Tate, MicroPro, and Peachtree can't. If a software publisher needs $100 gross profit to pay those hungry programmers, then his/her product is going to have a list price in the $300 to $400 range.

Source   Peter Norton, "Make Sure the Price Is Right", *P.C. Magazine*, June 26, 1984.

For Discussion

1. Prepare an income statement using the numbers in this article, assuming that
   a. You are both author and publisher of your own software
   b. You are the author of the software but someone else is publishing it.
   Which alternative is preferable? Why?
2. How many copies would have to be sold for you to be financially compensated for your efforts?
3. Who makes the largest share of the profits from selling the software?
4. Suggest an alternative way to sell software. How would it work?

Discussion Case 4-3:   The Crown Victoria

Its design is two decades old, it guzzles gas and it handles like a small ocean liner.

One day it will be in a museum, but not yet. Not when farmers love it, cops love it, retirees love it.

Not when the Ford LTD Crown Victoria is selling so well that the 3,800 workers who build it in St. Thomas, Ont., have been on overtime for four years.

Ford's befuddled executives still regard the mild-mannered antique-mobile as a supercar and keep postponing the execution date because people just won't stop buying it. "That car was supposed to be dead 10 years ago," said Ottawa auto analyst Jim Dancey. "But there's too much demand to kill it."

The LTD's popularity is one reason why Ford Canada recently reported a doubling of profits. "You have to believe the profit margin on the LTD is unbelievable," said New York analyst Philip Fricke.

For the St. Thomas plant — which is operating at 120 per cent capacity and is one of the world's most profitable — the LTD is an investment that keeps paying dividends. While Ford and North America's other automakers took lessons from the Japanese, spending billions of dollars on robots and computer-run assembly plants, the St. Thomas plant, with its capital costs amortized many times over, has simply plodded along, making huge wads of money.

To company executives, the lesson of St. Thomas is that one does not always have to spend billions to make billions. "Some of the modernistic ways don't run so well," said plant manager Robert Kurtz.

Indeed, the St. Thomas plant is like an automotive time warp. Instead of rows of synchronous robots and new-age auto workers in white lab coats, the 21-kilometre assembly line is manned by thousands of blue-collar workers. Their job is tedious, manual, dirty — and well-paying. The average pay, including overtime, for a 48-hour week: $857.35.

The LTD and its sister model, the Mercury Grand Marquis, were built at plants in Oakville, Ont., and St. Louis until the tooling and production were consolidated at St. Thomas in 1983. New plants can easily cost $1 billion, but by using an existing plant and old equipment, St. Thomas cost Ford less than $100 million.

Ford did invest another $100 million in St. Thomas, upgrading quality-control equipment. That step helped enable the car to win Ford's highest-quality designation last year. But Ford designers have also avoided changing its appearance too much, for fear of losing loyal buyers.

But design isn't the only factor in the LTD's success. "There is still a need for that kind of vehicle," explains Fricke. "And the availability of big cars has been reduced." The LTD's list price — at $22,000 — is also below that of other big cars.

How long the LTD relic will remain relevant is unclear. With more than half the buyers of the LTD Crown Victoria–Mercury Grand Marquis older than 60, Ford officials are unsure of whether the model will benefit from the aging population — or whether the traditional buyers are a dying breed.

Paul Caron, Ford's manager of sales planning and analysis, said the car will likely remain a strong seller if the economy turns sour — because retirees' income tends to remain fixed through various economic cycles. Another 20 per cent of the vehicles sell to fleet owners, mostly police forces; most of the remaining buyers are farmers.

Source   Adam Corelli, "Aging LTD Model Keeps Workers on Overtime", *The* (Montreal) *Gazette*, March 10, 1989, p. E-3.

For Discussion

1. How can the popularity of the Crown Victoria result in a doubling of profits when it continues to sell at around $20,000?
2. Apparently, the costs of the tooling and production have been "amortized" many times over. If we assume that amortized here means depreciated, how can these costs be amortized more than once (100%)?
3. Ford gave the Crown Victoria its highest-quality designation last year. Is this one reason for the car's success? Why is it so successful?

Discussion Case 4-4:   Computerized Shopping

You're in a clothing store.

You pick up a sweater and try it on. Definitely you! You insert the tag on the garment in the scanner on the side of the rack, put your credit (or debit) card in the slot below; watch the adjacent screen for the amount of your purchase and validate it by keying in your PIN (personal identification number).

While you wait for the message that your purchase is authorized, the screen tantalizes you with discount offers on a matching shirt or pants and news of other items currently on sale. The authorization completed, the scanner deacti-

vates the security tag on your sweater, the screen displays your "frequent shopper" credits and you bag your sweater and leave.

Does the prospect of this appeal? To some it will; to others, not. But it's just another retailing step in the tradition of self-serve gas pumps and automated teller machines. The focus is on the convenience and flexibility of self-service, and personal service is provided only where it can provide extra value to the customer.

Or how would you like to do your shopping from home? No, not just the kind of home shopping club you can see on television today, but a service where, using your touchtone phone, you can let your fingers do the walking through an "electronic mall." You can go to the store you want, browse (in full motion video) through the items, make your purchase (or not) and move to another store. The goods you buy will be delivered to your home.

Farfetched? Not at all. Just such a home shopping service is being piloted by Bell Canada in Quebec. Alex provides a computer terminal that will enable home shopping, among other things. In France, a similar service called Minitel has a large base of customers.

The electronic mall in your future will also offer you completely electronic services ranging from travel and theatre reservations to banking and insurance transactions.

At a recent conference on Future Strategies for Point of Sale, many speakers' definitions of "point of sale" included the words "payment" and "electronic" — an obvious reference to the increasing role that credit, and now debit, cards play in the way we shop.

Debit cards, which will allow your purchase to be directly charged against your bank account, are already used in many countries. There have been several pilot programs in Canada, the most recent a major test by the Royal Bank of Canada with stores in the London area.

The principal objection voiced against debit cards is that they don't offer the credit card's "free float." (The "float" means a user doesn't pay interest until the due date, and no interest at all if the monthly balance is paid in full.)

However, research shows that very few of us are really adept at taking full advantage of this feature.

Beyond debit cards, we are seeing the emergence of the "smart card," a piece of plastic with a microchip providing a variety of functions from holding security information or personal health records to "storing" value. The value-loaded smart card is already in use for phone calls or for other small payments.

The future value of smart cards at point of sale will be in providing the customer with additional services. For example, the card could keep track of all your purchases and monitor them against a preset budget or provide you with a statement itemized by category of expenditure.

From the retailer's point of view, in the case of that sweater sale, when the scanner read the purchase information from the coded item tag, it was only awaiting payment authorization to deactivate the security chip on the garment tag; record the sale by amount, item, color and size; create a record of the discounts offered and whether you had accepted them; log that information against your generic customer profile (socio-economic group, area of residence, and so on); update your personal purchasing history; update the inventory figure and, if necessary, re-order; and update the store's cash flow position and projects for the month.

Your reaction to discounts or other sale information might also determine for a store that shelf space can be used more profitably.

In other words, the retailer, the distributor and the manufacturer can all learn much more about you and your wants from the information captured at the point of sale. This can mean better inventory control, better product design and better use of existing floor or shelf space.

But while there are real benefits, there are some clear problems for the retail industry.

Competition, particularly for electronically delivered services, will intensify with the increasing globalization of trade. Home shopping allows manufacturers to become retailers simply by arranging delivery from warehouse to customer. Canada already has an extremely high per capita square footage of retail space. Yet the drive to open more retail space continues. If home shopping and other electronic services start to displace a significant number of our traditional purchases, there could be a lot of empty real estate.

Source   Andrew Lamb, "Want To Shop until Your Computer Drops?", *The Globe and Mail*, Toronto, March 13, 1989, p. C-1.

For Discussion

1. In the scenario discussed above, how will merchandising operations maintain their records? How will they record the sales invoice and the payment? Will the buyer be required to sign something as proof that he or she made a purchase?
2. How do you feel about a computer keeping track of your purchasing history? Could a business use this information to sell you more merchandise? Explain.
3. Explain how this system would provide better inventory control.

Discussion Case 4-5:   Shildan Knitting Mills Ltd.

Officials in the department of national revenue have wrapped up their inquiry into the biggest income-tax evasion scheme ever uncovered in Canada, after two years of digging by investigators who, at the peak, numbered 150 persons.

The racket involved 347 companies and unreported incomes of $56.8 million. Both figures are records, according to a source in the department. So are the number of investigators and the money that will be recovered.

The fraud involved the selling of false invoices and became known as the Shildan affair after a small Montreal knitter, Shildan Knitting Mills Ltd., one of the linchpins.

Under the scheme no merchandise changed hands. When the vendor was paid he/she retained a commission, usually from 6 percent to 10 percent of the invoice value, and remitted the balance to the owner or owners of the buying company.

According to the scheme, a vendor operating a limited company would make out a normal invoice for $10,000 to a buyer, which issues a cheque for the full amount but never receives any merchandise. The vendor would then cash the cheque, keep $1,000 commission, and give the $9,000 balance to the buyer.

Principals of both companies in this fictitious example would thus be able to divert cash from their companies into their own pockets. For the buyer there is a further advantage: $10,000 marked on the false invoice is an expense that reduces the company's taxable income.

The fraud came to light when a Shildan employee quarrelled with Shildan's president over his severance pay. Early in 1976 the employee tipped off the Toronto Dominion Bank, from which the president had a loan of $1.33 million, as well as several federal agencies. The tale sounded so unlikely that it was originally scorned. However, in the face of growing rumors the Toronto Dominion sent its agents to investigate Shildan in May 1976 and on July 8 the knitter was declared bankrupt. The deficiency was $1.5 million.

At a bankruptcy hearing, the president admitted Shildan had sold phony invoices worth $18 million from August 1974, when it was incorporated, through May 1976. The company netted from $300,000 to $400,000 in commissions on the transactions. Shildan's president also admitted he had begun selling false invoices in 1969.

He testified that three dummy companies had been set up to handle the accommodation invoices, as they are called by the revenue department.

Source Alan D. Gray, "Income Tax Probe Uncovered 347 Evaders and $56 Million", *The* (Montreal) *Gazette*, July 7, 1978, p. 31.

For Discussion

1. Prepare journal entries to record the following:
   a. The sale of a false invoice by Shildan of $1,000
   b. The purchase of this $1,000
   c. The payment for the purchase made in question b
   d. Collection of the amount by Shildan.
2. How would these amounts appear in the income statements of
   a. Shildan
   b. The purchaser.
3. Explain how money could be diverted by principals from their companies into their own pockets. Use the journal entries in question 1 to explain the process.
4. What kind of gross profit did Shildan have?
5. Would the 6 to 10 percent be recorded as a cash discount? as a trade discount? as something else?

Discussion Case 4-6:   Computers Take Care of the Nuts and Bolts

The nuts and bolts of industry are still, for the most part, nuts and bolts.

And purchasing those nuts and bolts — or bearings, or fasteners or batteries or any number of other high-volume, low-cost items — can be a nightmare of order processing and record keeping.

But wherever there is a business problem there is a business opportunity, and in this case a new Toronto company thinks it is a $65-million opportunity to bring low-cost, high-volume buyers and sellers together by computer.

"I wanted to cut down on the labor-intensive, paper-intensive purchasing process and to speed it up," said Ken Bishop, vice-president and general manager of Novatron Purchasing Services Inc., a subsidiary of Halifax-based Novatron Information Corp.

A decade ago, Mr. Bishop was working at Ontario Hydro, marvelling at how little industry had advanced when it came to buying large amounts of low-value items.

"You think of everybody being in the computer age, of things roaring along technologically, and we were putting in purchasing orders that weren't really all that advanced from the industrial revolution," he recalled.

While working at Ontario Hydro a decade ago, Bishop found that trying to integrate Hydro's mainframe computer into the purchasing process was "horrifyingly expensive." When the personal computer came on to the scene in the early 1980s it was just the tool he was seeking.

In 1984, Mr. Bishop began developing the predecessor to Supplyline, a system to update and automate purchasing.

What he developed has since saved Hydro millions of dollars.

"It has saved us a pile of money, quite a few millions of dollars in the cost of the materials and the cost of processing multitudes of small requirements," said Dennis Irwin, who was Mr. Bishop's boss at Hydro.

The problem, Mr. Bishop explained, is that when a requisition goes to a generating station, "it goes to the bottom of the pile and bubbles up. Lots of errors can happen as it works its way through piles of purchasing orders. And it's slow, from seven to 28 days from sending the requisition to the time it gets to the main computer."

The major objective of Supplyline is to have the whole process handled by computers.

"It reduces the price we pay for goods," Mr. Bishop said. "When you've got a lot of paper in front of you and your boss is pushing you as a buyer to get his paper off the desk, you hand out the orders to the first guy who comes along, you don't get competition on it and the prices go up and up."

Mr. Bishop said that before he retired from Hydro in May, some of the prices it paid had come down 85 per cent, and on average they had come down 21 per cent.

That translates to about a $1.5-million saving in 1987 alone for Hydro. Over five years, it is estimated Hydro saved $7.6-million using the electronic marketplace system developed by Mr. Bishop for less than $145,000.

Mr. Bishop expects Supplyline will offer its customers similar savings, so for access to the system Novatron will charge an average commission of 8 per cent a transaction, with a 10 per cent cap. For that price, the users get access to the databases and the computer programs necessary to use them.

Supplyline works through a system of standing offers.

At Hydro they requested quotes from vendors on all items processed, creating a database of standing offers on all kinds of off-the-shelf items. All the vendors are aware that they are competing on each item.

The requisition is fed into the computer. It finds the best standing offer, creates a requisition form and, through electronic mail, sends the order to the vendor.

Supplyline has a few features the Hydro system does not have. It can be used to track the delivery performance of individual vendors, it will penalize vendors for unauthorized substitutions and it can negotiate high-volume rebates.

The system is also being linked in a test to point-of-sale terminals through an agreement with Transact Data Services Inc.

A dentist could buy instruments or latex gloves, a welder could order supplies, and they could do it from home at night.

Mr. Bishop is projecting a $10-million market for Supplyline in its first year and a $65-million market within five years.

Source   Geoffrey Rowan, "In Purchasing, Computers Take Care of the Nuts and Bolts", *The Globe and Mail*, Toronto, November 22, 1988, p. B-8.

For Discussion

1. Why is the perpetual inventory system not used when inventory consists of high-volume, low-cost items?
2. If a perpetual system is not used, then how does the purchaser know when to order? Consider the case of Ontario Hydro as an example.
3. It used to take from 7 to 28 days for a purchase requisition to result in the preparation of a purchase order. If the purchasing department had a previously negotiated purchase price, couldn't the purchase requisition be used as a purchase order? Wouldn't this procedure have expedited the purchasing process?
4. If using the computer reduces costs by 21 percent and results in a savings of $1.5 million for Ontario Hydro, what conclusions can you draw about the purchasing process prior to the use of computers?
5. If Ontario Hydro saved $7.6 million over five years, didn't someone lose $7.6 million? Who? What is the impact on those who lose?
6. How could some of the prices paid by Ontario Hydro come down 85 percent?
7. Are the discounts from list prices discussed in the article cash discounts? Explain.

Comprehension Problems

Comprehension Problem 4-1

Sierra Ltd. uses the periodic inventory method. Its transactions during June 19X5 are as follows:

June 3   Sierra sold $1,500-worth of merchandise for credit to Pierrefonds Inc. for terms 2/10, net 30.
     8   Pierrefonds returned $800-worth of defective merchandise purchased June 3.
    13   Sierra received payment from Pierrefonds for the balance owed.

Required: Prepare journal entries to record the above transactions.

Comprehension Problem 4-2

Centre Corp. uses the periodic method of inventory. Its transactions during July 19X4 are as follows:

July 6   Purchased $600-worth of merchandise on account (for credit) from St. Luc Inc. for terms 1/10, net 30
     9   Returned $200-worth of defective merchandise
    15   Paid the amount owing to St. Luc.

Required: Prepare journal entries to record the above transactions.

Comprehension Problem 4-3

The following data pertain to Max Co. Inc.

Ending Inventory	$ 440
Opening Inventory	375
Purchases	2,930
Purchase Discounts	5
Purchase Returns	20
Transportation In	105

Required: Calculate the cost of goods sold. You are not required to prepare an income statement.

Comprehension Problem 4-4

Required: Calculate the missing amounts for each of the following four companies.

	A	B	C	D
Opening Inventory	$?	$ 184	$ 112	$ 750
Purchases	1,415	? 344	840	5,860
Transportation In	25	6	15	? 10
Cost of Goods Available	1,940	534	? 967	6,620
Ending Inventory	340	200	135	? 880
Cost of Goods Sold	?	? 324	? 832	5,740

Comprehension Problem 4-5

Required: Calculate the missing amounts for each of the following four companies.

	A	B	C	D
Opening Inventory	$ 155	$ 400	$?	$ 100
Purchases	973	?	3,500	200
Purchase Returns	16	80	200	?
Transportation In	2	3	100	8
Cost of Goods Available	?	536	3,400	303
Ending Inventory	179	?	?	80
Cost of Goods Sold	?	448	3,200	?

Comprehension Problem 4-6

The following information is taken from the records of Byrd Corp. at June 30, 19X3:

Advertising Expense	$ 1,500
Commissions Expense	4,000
Delivery Expense	500
Depreciation Expense — Equipment	500
Ending Inventory	10,000
Insurance Expense	1,000
Opening Inventory	6,000
Purchases	35,000
Purchase Returns	2,000
Rent Expense	2,500
Salaries Expense	5,000
Sales (gross)	72,000
Sales Returns	2,000
Transportation In	1,000

Required: Calculate the following lines. You are not required to prepare an income statement.
1. Cost of Goods Available for Sale
2. Gross Profit
3. Net Income

Comprehension Problem 4-7

Required: Calculate the missing amounts.

	A	B	C
Sales	$10,000	$?	$?
Cost of Goods Sold	?	20,000	3,000
Gross Profit	3,000	?	6,000
Expenses	1,000	6,000	2,000
Net Income	?	4,000	?

Comprehension Problem 4-8

The following balances are taken from the records of D-Liver Corp. at December 31, 19X2, its first year-end:

Transportation In	$ 500
Delivery Expense	1,200
Sales	25,000
Purchases	20,000
Sales Returns	2,000
Purchase Returns	1,000
Sales Discounts	400
Purchase Discounts	300
Interest Expense	4,000

The inventory at December 31, 19X2 amounts to $7,900.

Required:
1. Calculate the gross profit. (You are not required to prepare a partial income statement.)
2. What is the percentage of gross profit to net sales?
3. Is D-Liver using a periodic or perpetual inventory system? How can you tell?

Comprehension Problem 4-9

The following information is taken from the records of four different entities:

	Sales	Opening Inventory	Purchases	Cost of Goods Available for Sale	Ending Inventory	Cost of Goods Sold	Gross Profit
1.	$300	?	240	320	?	?	100
2.	$150	40	?	?	60	100	?
3.	$?	40	?	260	60	200	100
4.	$ 90	12	63	?	15	60	?

Required: Calculate the missing amounts.

Comprehension Problem 4-10

The following information is taken from the records of three different entities:

	1	2	3
Opening Inventory	$ 3	$?	$ 6
Ending Inventory	?	7	8
Sales	52	34	51
Cost of Goods Sold	35	22	32
Sales Discounts	2	1	?
Gross Profit	?	?	17
Cost of Goods Purchased	36	23	?

Required: Calculate the missing amounts.

Comprehension Problem 4-11

Sherbrooke Inc. uses the periodic inventory system. It had the following transactions:

May 5   Sherbrooke sold $4,000-worth of merchandise on account to Kirkland Centres Ltd. for terms 2/10, net 30.

7   Kirkland Centres returned $500-worth of merchandise; Sherbrooke issued a credit memo.

15   Sherbrooke received the amount due from Kirkland Centres Ltd.

Required: Prepare journal entries to record the above transactions
1. In the records of Sherbrooke Inc.
2. In the records of Kirkland Centres Ltd.

Comprehension Problem 4-12

CKU Emporium had the following transactions:

Oct. 8 Purchased $2,800-worth of merchandise on account from St Luc Wholesalers Corp. for terms 1/10, net 30

    12 Received a credit memo from St Luc Wholesalers Corp. for $800-worth of defective merchandise included in the October 8 purchase and subsequently returned to St Luc.

Additional Information: St Luc uses the periodic inventory system.

Required:
1. Prepare journal entries in the records of CKU, assuming that they paid the amount due on
   a. October 8
   b. October 25.
2. Prepare journal entries in the records of St Luc Wholesalers Corp., assuming that they received payment on
   a. October 18
   b. October 25.

Problems

Problem 4-1

The following data pertain to Conestogo Hardware Inc. for the year ended December 31, 19X9:

Salespersons' Salaries Expense	$ 16,400
Salaries Expense (office)	6,200
Sales	157,500
Transportation In	2,200
Rent Expense (selling space)	9,600
Rent Expense (office space)	1,200
Rent Payable	800
Sales Discounts	1,500
Depreciation Expense — Equipment (office)	320
Delivery Expense	2,700
Purchases	97,300
Sales Returns and Allowances	1,300
Merchandise Inventory (Jan. 1)	15,500
Advertising Expense	1,800
Insurance Expense	130
Merchandise Inventory (Dec. 31)	17,900
Purchases Discounts	1,100
Supplies Expense (store)	850
Purchases Returns and Allowances	550
Office Supplies Expense	250
Depreciation Expense — Equipment (store)	1,550
Dividends Payable	2,500

Required: Prepare a classified income statement.

Problem 4-2

The following information is extracted from the general ledger of Maritimes Limited at December 31, 19X4:

Merchandise Inventory	$ 184,000	$ 200,000
Sales		781,600
Sales Returns and Allowances	16,400	
Sales Discounts	16,480	
Purchases	364,000	
Purchases Returns and Allowances		15,200
Purchases Discounts		4,800
Transportation In	6,560	
Salespersons' Salaries Expense	88,000	
Advertising Expense	15,600	
Delivery Expense	69,200	
Miscellaneous Selling Expense	15,000	
Salaries Expense (office)	80,000	
Property Tax Expense	13,500	
Miscellaneous General Expense	32,440	
Supplies Expense	9,060	
Interest Earned		840
Insurance Expense	11,160	
Depreciation Expense	22,080	
Interest Expense	2,112	
Income Tax Expense	18,530	
Totals	$ 964,122	$1,002,440
Net Income for the Year	38,318	
	$1,002,440	$1,002,440

Required:
1. Prepare an income statement in proper form (record Miscellaneous General Expense and Depreciation Expense as General and Administrative Expense).
2. Prepare all necessary closing journal entries.

Problem 4-3

The income statement of Stan and Ollie Limited is presented below:

Income Statement
For the Year Ended December 31, 19X8

	($000)	
Sales		$2,500
Cost of Goods Sold		
Opening Inventory (Jan. 1)	$ 500	
Purchases	1,415	
Transportation In	25	
Cost of Goods Available	$1,940	
Ending Inventory (Dec. 31)	340	
Total Cost of Goods Sold		1,600
Gross Profit		$ 900
OPERATING EXPENSES		
Selling Expenses		
Advertising Expense	$ 40	
Miscellaneous Selling Expense	75	
Total Selling Expenses	$ 115	
General and Administrative Expenses:		
Depreciation Expense	$ 28	
Insurance Expense	6	
Miscellaneous General Expense	86	
Rent Expense	48	
Utilities Expense	50	
Wages Expense	385	
Total General and Administrative Expenses	603	
Total Operating Expenses		718
Income from Operations		$ 182
Financing Costs		
Interest Expense	$ 161	
Other Revenue		
Interest Earned	$ 80	
Rent Earned	70	150	11
Income (before income tax)		$ 171
Income Tax		35
Net Income for the Year		$ 136

Required: Prepare closing journal entries at December 31, 19X8.

Problem 4-4

Kawartha Corp. was incorporated on July 2, 19X2 to operate a merchandising business. All its sales on account are made according to the following terms: 2/10, n/30. Its transactions during July 19X2 are as follows:

Jul. 2   Issued common shares for $5,000 cash to George Hill, the incorporator and sole shareholder of the corporation

2   Purchased $3,500 merchandise on account from Westmount Pencils Ltd. for terms 2/10, n/30

2   Sold $2,000-worth of merchandise on account to Hampstead Tool Rentals Inc.

3   Paid Concordia Rentals Corp. $500 for July rent

5   Paid Westwood Furniture Ltd. $1,000 for equipment

8   Collected $200 for a cash sale made today to Byron Peel

8   Purchased $2,000 merchandise on account from MacDonald Distributors Inc. for terms 2/15, n/30

9   Received the amount due from Hamstead Tool Rentals Inc. for the July 2 sale (less discount)

10   Paid Westmount Pencils Ltd. for the July 2 purchase (less discount)

10   Purchased $200-worth of merchandise on account from Peel Products Inc. for terms n/30

15   Sold $2,000-worth of merchandise on account to Condor Products Corp.

15   Purchased $1,500-worth of merchandise on account from Draper Door Inc. for terms 2/10, n/30

15   Received a credit note memo from MacDonald Distributors Inc. for $100-worth of defective merchandise included in the July 8 purchase

16   Condor Products Corp. returned $200-worth of merchandise: issued a credit memo

20   Sold $3,500-worth of merchandise on account to Pine Promotions Ltd.

20   Paid MacDonald Distributors Inc. for half the purchase made July 8 (less credit note, less discount on payment)

24   Received half the amount due from Condor Products Corp. in partial payment for the July 15 sale (less discount on payment)

24   Paid Draper Doors Ltd. for the purchase made July 15 (less discount)

26   Sold $600 merchandise on account to Daytona Sales Ltd.

26   Purchased $800-worth of merchandise on account from Gold & Silver Co. for terms 2/10, n/30

31   Paid Real-Quick Transport Co. $350 for transportation to our warehouse during the month (all purchases are fob shipping point).

Required: Prepare journal entries to record the July transactions.

Problem 4-5

Redox Sales Corp. was incorporated on May 1, 19X1 to operate a merchandising business. All its sales on account are made according to the following terms: 2/10, net 30. Its transactions during May 19X1 are as follows:

May 1   Issued common shares for $2,000 cash to Harry Jones, the incorporator and sole shareholder of the corporation

1   Received $10,000 from the Second Canadian Bank as a demand bank loan

1   Paid Cadillac Corp. $1,500 for 3 months rent in advance — May, June, and July (recorded as an asset)

1   Paid Avanti Equipment Ltd. $5,000 for equipment

1   Purchased $2,000-worth of merchandise on account from St Luc Wholesalers Ltd. for terms 2/10, n/30

1   Sold $2,500-worth of merchandise on account to Montreal West Distributors

May 2 Purchased $1,800-worth of merchandise on account from Rosedale Products Ltd. for terms n/30

2 Sold $2,000-worth of merchandise on account to Terrebonne Sales Inc.

3 Collected $500 for a cash sale made today to Irwin Peabody

5 Paid All Province Insurance Inc. $1,200 for a 1-year insurance policy, effective May 1 (recorded as an asset)

5 Sold $1,000-worth of merchandise on account to Brock Stores Corporation

6 Terrebonne Sales Inc. returned $500-worth of merchandise: issued a credit memo

8 Received a credit memo from St Luc Wholesalers Ltd. for $300-worth of defective merchandise included in the May 1 purchase and returned subsequently to St Luc

8 Purchased $2,800-worth of merchandise on account from Elmhurst Novelties Ltd. for terms 2/15, n/30

9 Received the amount due from Montreal West Distributors from the May 1 sale (less discount)

9 Paid St Luc Wholesalers Corp. for the May 1 purchase (less discount)

10 Sold $400-worth of merchandise on account to Western Warehouse

11 Received the amount due from Terrebonne Sales Inc. (less the May 6 credit memo and discount)

13 Paid Express Corporation $100 for transportation in

15 Purchased $1,500-worth of merchandise on account from Hudson Distributors Inc. for terms 2/10, n/30

15 Sold $1,500-worth of merchandise on account to Roxboro Outlets Inc.

15 Paid $500 in commissions to Harry Jones, *re*: sales invoices nos. 1, 2, and 3

19 Paid Rosedale Products Inc. for the May 2 purchase

19 Purchased $1,200-worth of merchandise on account from Mid-Island Stores Corp. for terms 1/10, n/30

22 Purchased $600-worth of merchandise on account from Quick Sales Co. for terms n/30

22 Paid to Elmhurst Novelties Inc. for the May 8 purchase (less discount)

24 Paid to Express Corporation $150 for transportation in

25 Sold $900-worth of merchandise on account to Kirkland Centres Ltd.

26 Received the amount due from Brock Stores Corporation

27 Paid $200 to Yale Deliveries Ltd. for deliveries made to customers

28 Collected $300 for a cash sale made today to Joe Montclair

28 Made a $200 cash purchase from Ballantyne Sales Inc. today; issued cheque #11 (debited purchases)

28 Sold $900-worth of merchandise on account to Lachine Wharf Corp.

29 Purchased $100-worth of merchandise on account from Sidekicks Inc.

29 Paid Speedy Ltd. $300 for deliveries (debited account 620)

29 Paid Impetus Advertising Agency $400 for advertising materials used during May

29 Paid Hydro-Bec $100 for electricity

29 Paid Harry Jones $350 commission, *re*: sales invoices nos. 4, 5, 6, and 7

30 Collected $1,000 on account from Roxboro Outlets Inc.

31 Paid Mid-Island Stores Corp. $700 on account

31 Paid Harry Jones $100 for dividends declared today.

Required: Prepare journal entries to record the May transactions.

Problem 4-6

The following accounts and account balances are taken from the records of Fraser Enterprises Ltd. at December 31, 19X6, its fiscal year-end.

Account Title	Dr.	Cr.
Cash	2,000	
Accounts Receivable	8,000	
Merchandise Inventory	19,000	
Prepaid Insurance	1,000	
Land	5,000	
Buildings	25,000	
Equipment	20,000	
Accum. Deprec. — Buildings		1,000
Accum. Deprec. — Equipment		4,000
Bank Loan (due 19X7)		5,000
Accounts Payable		7,000
Income Tax Payable		3,000
Mortgage Payable (due 19X9)		50,000
Common Stock		3,000
Retained Earnings		2,000
Dividends	1,000	
Totals	81,000	75,000
Net Income		6,000
Totals	81,000	81,000

Required:
1. Using the above information, prepare a classified balance sheet.
2. Make the following calculations:
   a. The proportion of shareholders to creditors claims on the assets of Fraser
   b. The current ratio
   c. The acid-test ratio.
3. Assume that you are the loan officer of the bank where Fraser has applied for a 120-day loan of $10,000. Would you grant the loan? Why or why not?
4. If the loan were granted, calculate the current ratio and acid-test ratio immediately following the receipt of the loan on January 2, 19X7.

Problem 4-7

The following closing entries were prepared for Heli Products Inc. at December 31, 19X3, the end of its fiscal year. (The journal entry narratives have been omitted.)

Dec. 31		Merchandise Inventory	6,000	
		Sales	31,000	
		Purchases Returns	575	
		Purchases Discounts	225	
		Income Summary		37,800
	31	Income Summary	32,800	
		Merchandise Inventory		4,000
		Sales Returns		690
		Sales Discounts		310
		Purchases		22,500
		Transportation In		300
		Operating Expenses		5,000

31	Income Summary	5,000	
	Retained Earnings		5,000
31	Retained Earnings	1,000	
	Dividends		1,000

Required:
1. Post and rule the above Merchandise Inventory (with a January 1 balance of $4,000) and Income Summary accounts to T-accounts.
2. Using the data in the preceding closing entries, prepare a classified income statement.

Problem 4-8

The following trial balance has been extracted from the records of Rose Jewellery Inc. at December 31, 19X5, its fiscal year-end. The balances for Merchandise Inventory and Retained Earnings have not changed during the year.

	Account Balances	
	Dr.	Cr.
Cash	$ 750	
Accounts Receivable	12,000	
Merchandise Inventory	6,000	
Prepaid Rent	-0-	
Office Supplies	-0-	
Equipment — Office	4,400	
Accumulated Depreciation		-0-
Bank Loan		$ 5,000
Accounts Payable		12,540
Income Tax Payable		2,400
Common Stock		2,000
Retained Earnings		1,500
Dividends	900	
Sales		50,000
Sales Returns	1,500	
Sales Discounts	500	
Purchases	35,000	
Purchases Returns		1,700
Purchases Discounts		300
Transportation In	1,000	
Advertising Expense	1,700	
Commissions Expense	4,800	
Delivery Expense	650	
Depreciation Expense	-0-	
Insurance Expense	350	
Interest Expense	600	
Office Supplies Expense	350	
Rent Expense	1,950	
Telephone Expense	300	
Utilities Expense	290	
Income Tax Expense	2,400	
Totals	$75,440	$75,440

Required:
1. Prepare adjusting entries for the following:
   a. $1000 of the accounts receivable not yet recorded have just been received.
   b. A physical count of supplies indicates that $100-worth are still on hand.
   c. No depreciation has yet been recorded on the office equipment. An amount of $400 is estimated applicable to 19X5.

   d. The December telephone bill has not yet been received. An amount of $60 is estimated as owing. Record as Accounts Payable.

   e. A physical count of inventory indicates that $8,000-worth of merchandise is still on hand at December 31, 19X5.

2. Prepare the following financial statements in good form:

   a. Classified income statement (the advertising, commissions, and delivery expenses are considered as selling expenses)

   b. Statement of retained earnings

   c. Classified balance sheet.

3. Prepare all necessary closing entries.

4. Make calculations to answer the following questions:

   a. What is the proportion of shareholder to creditor claims on the assets of the corporation?

   b. What is the current ratio?

   c. What is the acid-test ratio?

5. Assume that you are the loan officer of a bank to which the corporation has applied for an additional 3-month $10,000 bank loan. Would you grant the loan? Why or why not?

6. If the loan were granted on January 2, 19X6, calculate the working capital, current ratio, and acid-test ratio immediately following receipt of the loan.

Problem 4-9

The assets, liabilities, and equity of Andrew's Corporation at December 31, 19X5 are as follows:

Cash	$ 5,600
Accounts Receivable	15,200
Notes Receivable	3,000
Merchandise Inventory	5,600
Prepaid Insurance	400
Supplies	200
Land	5,000
Building	13,000
Equipment	3,500
Accounts Payable	10,000
Notes Payable	7,500
Mortgage Payable — Long-Term	8,000
Common Stock	10,000
Retained Earnings	16,000

Required:

1. Prepare a classified balance sheet.

2. Make the following calculations:

   a. What is the proportion of shareholder and creditor claims to the assets of the corporation?

   b. What is the structure of the corporation's creditor financing?

   c. What is the current ratio?

   d. What is the acid-test ratio?

3. Are you able to make any evaluation of the corporation on the basis of the above calculations? Discuss.

Alternate Problems

Alternate Problem 4-1

The following information relates to the Interprovincial Colossus Corporation for the current year.

a. Merchandise inventory on hand January 1 is $100,000.
b. During the year, the company purchased merchandise on account for $200,000 for terms 2/10, n/30. Half of the purchases were paid within the discount period.
c. The company paid $8,000 in freight charges on merchandise purchased.
d. Damaged merchandise with an invoice price of $4,000 was returned to the supplier. A cash refund for the returned amount less discount was received. This merchandise was part of the purchase in transâction b that had been paid within the discount period.
e. An allowance of $2,750 was granted customers because merchandise was not satisfactory. Cheques were issued to the several customers.
f. The ending inventory was $80,000 at cost.

Required:
1. Prepare journal entries where necessary for each of the transactions. (Omit explanation lines and assume the company uses periodic inventory method.)
2. Prepare the necessary closing entries based on the above information.
3. What was the cost of goods sold? (December 31 is year-end.)

Alternate Problem 4-2

Northern Corporation supplies you with the following information applicable to the current year. The year-end is December 31.

Transportation In	$ 3,000
Delivery Expense	2,000
Sales	100,000
Merchandise Inventory (Jan. 1)	12,000
Merchandise Inventory (Dec. 31)	15,000
Purchases	70,000
Office Supplies Expense	7,000
Purchases Discounts	4,000
Purchases Returns and Allowances	6,000
Sales Returns and Allowances	10,000
Supplies	5,000

Required:
1. Prepare in proper form a partial income statement including sales, cost of goods sold, and gross profit.
2. Prepare all closing entries required for the above data.

Alternate Problem 4-3

Sim Co. Products Inc. was incorporated on April 1, 19X1 to operate a merchandising business. All its sales on account are made according to the following terms: 2/10, n30. Its transactions during April 19X1 are as follows:

Apr. 1   Issued common shares for $3,000 cash to Rosco Simcoe, the incorporator and sole shareholder of the corporation

1   Purchased $4,000-worth of merchandise on account from Beaconsfield Wholesalers Inc. for terms 2/10, n/30

1   Sold $3,000-worth of merchandise on account to Ahuntic Products Corp.

2   Collected $500 for a cash sale made today to George Kirkland

2   Purchased $750 merchandise on account from Dorval Wholesalers Ltd. for terms n/30

2   Sold $1,200-worth of merchandise on account to Chambly Stores Inc.

5   Received half the amount due from Ahuntic Products Corp. for the April 1 purchase (less discount on payment)

8   Received the amount due from Chambly Stores Inc. for the April 2 purchase (less discount)

9   Paid Beaconsfield Wholesalers Inc. for the April 1 purchase (less discount on payment)

10   Purchased $2,000-worth of merchandise on account from Carlton Distributors Inc. for terms 2/15, n/30

11   Sold $500-worth of merchandise on account to Presidential Sales Inc.

12   Presidential Sales Inc. returned $100-worth of merchandise; issued a credit memo

15   Received a credit memo from Dorval Wholesalers Ltd. for $150-worth of defective merchandise included in the April 2 purchase and subsequently returned

15   Purchased $1,500-worth of merchandise on account from Atwater Distributors Inc. for terms 2/10, n/30

19   Purchased $1,250-worth of merchandise on account from Kildare Sales Ltd. for terms n/30

20   Sold $2,000-worth of merchandise on account to Salaberry Corp.

20   Received the amount due from Presidential Sales Inc. for the April 11 purchase (less return and less discount)

22   Paid Carlton Distributors Inc. for the April 10 purchase (less discount on payment)

24   Paid Atwater Distributors Inc. for the April 15 purchase (less discount on payment)

27   Sold $800-worth of merchandise on account to Bishop Emporium Corp.

30   Paid Rapid Delivery Inc. $200 for deliveries made to customers during the month (debited account 620)

30   Paid Truck Forwarders Ltd. $500 for transportation to the warehouse during the month. (All purchases are fob shipping point.)

Required: Prepare journal entries to record the April transactions.

Alternate Problem 4-4

Bould Wholesalers Inc. was incorporated on March 1 to operate a merchandising business. All its sales on account are made according to the following terms: 2/10, n/30.

Mar. 1 Issued common shares for $410,000 cash to Michael Strong, the incorporator and sole shareholder of the corporation

1 Paid Brunswick Fixtures Inc. $4,000 for equipment

1 Purchased $2,100-worth of merchandise on account from Mid-Island Stores Corp. for terms 2/10, n/30

2 Sold $2,000-worth of merchandise on account to Kirkland Centres Ltd.

2 Collected $300 for a cash sale made today to Irving Clayton

3 Purchased $500-worth of merchandise on account from Quick Sales Co. for terms 1/10, n/30

4 Sold $2,500-worth of merchandise on account to Western Warehouse

4 Kirkland Centres Ltd. returned $200-worth of merchandise: issued a credit memo

5 Purchased $1,400-worth of merchandise on account from St Luc Wholesalers Corp. on account for terms n/30

6 Received a credit memo from Mid-Island Stores Corp. for $100-worth of defective merchandise included in the March 1 purchase and subsequently returned to Mid-Island

6 Sold $1,500-worth of merchandise on account to Lachine Wharf Corp.

7 Purchased $600-worth of merchandise on account from Brock Stores Corporation for terms 2/15, n/30

8 Received the amount due from Kirkland Centres Ltd. (less credit memo, less discount)

10 Paid Quick Sales Co. for the March 3 purchase (less discount)

11 Received $7,500 from the Royal Canadian Bank as a demand bank loan

12 Paid Fairview Realty Corp. $1,000 for 2 months rent, March and April (recorded as an asset)

12 Sold $700-worth of merchandise on account to Hudson Distributors Inc.

13 Received the amount due from Western Warehouse (less discount)

15 Paid Michael Strong $350 for commissions earned to date

15 Paid Mid-Island Stores Corporation $1,000 on account

15 Purchased $1,000-worth of merchandise on account from Rosedale Products Ltd. for terms 2/15, n/30

18 Paid Brock Stores Corporation for half of the March 7 purchase (less discount on payment)

19 Collected $100 for a cash sale made today to Al Trudeau

20 Purchased $1,200-worth of merchandise on account from Sheraton Centres Inc. for terms n/30

20 Paid $400 for a cash purchase from Roslyn Distributors Inc. (debited purchases)

20 Sold $600-worth of merchandise on account to Sidekicks Inc.

21 Paid St Luc Wholesalers Corp. $700 on account

22 Received $500 on account from Lachine Wharf Inc.

23 Paid All City Insurance Ltd. $2,400 for a 1-year insurance policy, effective March 1 (recorded as an asset)

24 Paid $300 for a cash purchase from C.K.U. Emporium (debited purchases)

25 Sold $1,400-worth of merchandise on account to Elmhurst Novelties Inc.

26 Purchased $700-worth of merchandise on account from Grand Markets Ltd. for terms 2/10, n/30

30 Paid D-Liver Corp. $500 for deliveries (debited account 620)

30 Paid Michael Strong $400 for commissions earned to date

30 Paid Bell-Bec $75 for the monthly telephone bill

30 Paid Johnson Visuals Ltd. $250 for advertising materials used during the month

31 Paid Michael Strong $200 for dividends declared today.

Required: Prepare journal entries to record the March transactions.

Alternate Problem 4-5

The following journal closing entries were prepared for Shelley Services Ltd. at December 31, 19X7, its fiscal year-end. (The journal entry narratives have been omitted.)

Dec. 31	Merchandise Inventory	7,000	
	Sales	34,000	
	Purchases Returns	1,760	
	Purchases Discounts	240	
	Income Summary		43,000
31	Income Summary	40,000	
	Merchandise Inventory		6,000
	Sales Returns		660
	Sales Discounts		340
	Purchases		24,000
	Transportation In		1,000
	Operating Expenses		8,000
31	Income Summary	3,000	
	Retained Earnings		3,000
31	Retained Earnings	750	
	Dividends		750

Required: Calculate the gross profit, using the form of a classified income statement.

Alternate Problem 4-6

Product Promotions Corp. had the following accounts and account balances at December 31, 19X6, its fiscal year-end:

	Dr.	Cr.
Merchandising Inventory	$ 3,000	$ 4,000
Sales		52,000
Sales Returns	1,480	
Sales Discounts	520	
Purchases	37,000	
Purchases Returns		1,130
Purchases Discounts		370
Transportation In	500	
Advertising Expense	1,250	
Insurance Expense	600	
Rent Expense	1,800	
Salary Expense	6,350	
Income Tax Expense	2,500	
Totals	$55,000	$57,500
Net Income	2,500	
Totals	$57,500	$57,500

Required: Prepare the classified income statement.

Alternate Problem 4-7

The following trial balance has been extracted from the records of Van der Aa Merchants Inc. at December 31, 19X2, its fiscal year-end. The balances for Merchandise Inventory and Retained Earnings have not changed during the year.

	Account Balances	
	Dr.	*Cr.*
Cash	$ 1,500	
Accounts Receivable	5,000	
Merchandise Inventory	5,000	
Prepaid Insurance	1,300	
Prepaid Rent	600	
Equipment — Office	12,500	
Accumulated Depreciation		-0-
Bank Loan		$ 10,000
Accounts Payable		8,350
Income Tax Payable		3,600
Common Stock		3,000
Retained Earnings		2,000
Dividends Payable	600	
Sales		75,000
Sales Returns	2,250	
Sales Discounts	750	
Purchases	60,000	
Purchases Returns and Allowances		9,400
Purchases Discounts		600
Transportation In	2,000	
Advertising Expense	1,800	
Commissions Expense	7,200	
Delivery Expense	1,600	
Depreciation Expense	-0-	
Insurance Expense	1,100	
Interest Expense	1,200	
Rent Expense	3,300	
Telephone Expense	550	
Utilities Expense	100	
Income Tax Expense	3,600	
Totals	$111,950	$111,950

Required:
1. Prepare adjusting entries for the following:
   a. The balance in Prepaid Rent consists of rent for the months of December 19X2 and January 19X3.
   b. Interest on the bank loan applicable to the month of December amounts to $100. This amount has not yet been recorded. Record as Interest Payable.
   c. No depreciation has yet been recorded on the office equipment. An amount of $500 is estimated applicable to 19X2.
   d. The December telephone bill has not yet been received. An amount of $50 is estimated as owing. Record as Accounts Payable.
   e. The balance in Prepaid Insurance includes an amount applicable to December 19X2 and the twelve months of 19X3.
   f. A physical count of inventory indicates that $10,000-worth of merchandise is on hand at December 31, 19X2.
2. Prepare the following financial statements in proper form:
   a. Classified income statement (the advertising, commission, and delivery expenses are considered as selling expenses)
   b. Statement of retained earnings
   c. Classified balance sheet.
3. Prepare all necessary journal closing entries.

4. Make calculations to answer the following questions:
   a. What is the proportion of shareholder to creditor claims on the assets of the corporation?
   b. What is the current ratio?
   c. What is the acid-test ratio?
5. Assume that you are the loan officer of a bank to which the corporation has applied for an additional 6-month $5,000 bank loan. Would you grant the loan? Why or why not?
6. If the loan were granted on January 2, 19X3, calculate the working capital, current ratio, and acid-test ratio immediately following receipt of the loan.

Alternate Problem 4-8

Sharp Inc. operated a hat shop, but had not kept careful records of its business. The following data were secured from various memoranda and records found in the office.

An analysis of canceled cheques revealed the following cash expenditures: expenses, $4,800; accounts payable, $9,200. A total of $3,600 in dividends had been paid during the year. All cash receipts were deposited in the bank. A list of assets and liabilities that was developed follows:

	19X5	
	January 1	*December 31*
Cash	$ 1,200	$ 900
Accounts Receivable	1,000	1,500
Inventories	3,900	4,600
Prepaid Expenses	100	60
Equipment (net)	4,200	3,800
	$10,400	$10,860
Accounts Payable	1,100	1,300
Common Stock	1,000	1,000
Retained Earnings	$ 8,300	$ 8,560

Required:
1. Calculate total expenses for the year.
2. Calculate net income for the year.
3. Calculate total purchases for the year.
4. Calculate total sales for the year.

(You are not required to prepare an income statement to answer this question.)

Review Problems

Review Problem 4-1

The following information is made available to you for Keaton Inc. The year-end of the company is April 30.

Keaton Inc.
Balance Sheet
At April 30, 19X1

Assets			*Liabilities*	
CURRENT ASSETS			Accounts Payable	$ 10
Cash		$ 20	Unearned Revenue	15
Accounts Receivable		30	Total Liabilities	$ 25
Inventory of Merchandise		25		
Prepaid Insurance		16	*Shareholders' Equity*	
Total Current Assets		$ 91	Common Stock	10
FIXED ASSETS			Retained Earnings	146
Equipment (purchased Feb. 1, 19X1)	$96			
Accum. Deprec. — Equipment	6	90	Total Equities	$181
Total Assets		$181		$181

May Transactions:

May 2	Sales on Account	$100
May 6	Purchases on Account	55
May 8	Collection of Accounts Receivable	95
May 12	Payment of Accounts Payable	40
May 15	Dividends	20
May 16	Sales Returns and Allowances	2
May 23	Purchases Returns and Allowances	1
May 27	Payment of Wages During May	10
May 27	Payment of Other Expenses	8

Data for adjustment:
a. Accrued unpaid wages on May 31 amounted to $1.
b. A 1-year insurance policy was purchased on January 1, 19X1.
c. Equipment has an estimated service life of 4 years.
d. The necessary deliveries were made to all customers who had paid in advance. All unearned revenue was earned in May.
e. A physical count of inventory was made on May 31, 19X1, and its cost was determined to be $20.

Required:
1. Journalize the May transactions.
2. Post to appropriate general ledger accounts.
3. Prepare in proper form the balance sheet and the income statement at May 31.
4. Journalize the adjusting entries.
5. Post the adjusting entries.
6. Prepare a trial balance from the adjusted ledger accounts.

Review Problem 4-2

Nu-Vogue Hat Shop maintained incomplete records. After investigation, you uncovered the following assets and liabilities:

Assets

	19X6	
	January 1	December 31
Cash	$ 2,680	$ 2,060
Accounts Receivable	13,400	13,660
Merchandise Inventory	6,200	7,600
Equipment (net of depreciation)	10,400	11,200
Prepaid Insurance	240	120
	$32,920	$34,640

Liabilities

	January 1	December 31
Accounts Payable	$ 2,000	$ 4,400
Bank Loan		6,000
Accrued Selling Liabilities	180	100
	$ 2,180	$10,500
Common Stock	1,600	4,000
Retained Earnings	29,140	20,140
	$32,920	$34,640

An analysis of cash inflow and outflow showed:

Collections from Customers	$17,940
Proceeds of Bank Loan	6,000
Additional Common Stock Issued	2,400
Payment to Creditors	12,200
Payment of Expenses (selling)	9,000
Returned Sale Items	700
Dividends	3,000
Interest on Bank Loan	60
Purchase of Equipment	2,000

Required:

1. Compute the net income (or loss) by analyzing the changes in retained earnings.
2. Prepare an income statement in proper form.

Decision Problems

Decision Problem 4-1

Allan Dwyer owns a store that sells musical instruments. After operating the store for one year, he prepared the following income statement as of December 31, 19X1:

Statement of Profit
For the Year Ended December 31, 19X1

Cash collected from customers and deposited in the bank	$35,000
Expenses paid by cheque	32,000
Profit	$ 3,000

Mr. Dwyer has hired you as an accountant and financial consultant. In one of your first conversations with him, he says, "This business is fantastic. I never expected to make a profit until the second or third year of operations, but not once during the past year did we ever overdraw our chequing account."

The items listed below come to your attention during the first few weeks on the job:
a. On December 31, 19X1, customers owed $2,500 from the sale of instruments on credit.
b. Mr. Dwyer has not paid rent since September 30, 19X1. Monthly rental for the retail space is $1,000.
c. Mr. Dwyer financed the business with a $10,000, 5-year loan from his father. The terms of the agreement call for a lump-sum payment of $12,500 on December 31, 19X5 (principal, $10,000; interest, $2,500).

Required:
1. Based on Allan Dwyer's statements and actions, how do you think he defines the term *profit*?
2. Did Mr. Dwyer violate generally accepted accounting principles in preparing his statement of profit? Explain.
3. Prepare an income statement in proper form for the year ended December 31, 19X1.

Decision Problem 4-2

The selected financial information presented below has been derived from the financial statements of four firms. Each of the firms belongs to one of the following industries: (1) data processing software and services, (2) telephone utility, (3) airline, and (4) broadcast entertainment.

	Firm A	*Firm B*	*Firm C*	*Firm D*
Percentage of total assets in:				
Cash and temporary investments	21%	5%	7%	38%
Receivables	8	23	18	12
Inventories	–	12	2	3
Other current assets	2	3	22	7
Total current assets	31%	43%	49%	60%
Property, plant, and equipment (net)	62	55	24	28
Other noncurrent assets	7	2	27	12
Total assets	100%	100%	100%	100%
Percentage relative to total sales:				
Net income	.5%	4%	6%	9%
Cost of goods sold	–	33	1	2
Depreciation, amortization, and depletion	3	8	2	9
Total assets	110	132	120	88

Required:
1. Which of the firms would be expected to have relatively large investments in receivables? in inventories? in property, plant, and equipment? in other noncurrent assets?
2. Which firms would have relatively large percentages of sales represented by cost of goods sold? by depreciation, amortization, and depletion?
3. Which firm appears to be using its assets most effectively? least effectively?
4. Based on your answers to questions 1 through 3 and on your own observations, attempt to identify the industry to which each firm belongs.

Decision Problem 4-3

Joe Campbell, a friend of your father's, is considering investing in one of two construction corporations. Both began operations on January 1, 1985 and have been in operation for two years. Campbell shows you the following information on each corporation and asks you for your opinion on the financial health of each.

Glionna Construction Corporation

Sales Payment Received 1985	$1,622,500
Expenses 1985	2,427,400
Accounts Receivable (Dec. 31, 1985)	1,947,600
Sales Payment Received 1986	947,400
Expenses 1986	1,747,400
Accounts Receivable (Dec. 31, 1986)	3,427,400

Montreal Builders Ltd.

Sales Payment Received 1985	$1,240,000
Expense 1985	977,200
Accounts Receivable (Dec. 31, 1985)	142,500
Sales Payment Received 1986	1,625,500
Expenses 1986	1,222,000
Accounts Receivable (Dec. 31, 1986)	247,000

Campbell also tells you that all of Glionna Construction's accounts receivable are for the construction of a new post office building in Pictou on June 1. If Glionna does not complete the building on time, there will be a five-percent penalty levied on the amount that remains to be paid. All construction is ahead of schedule, though, and no problems are anticipated.

Montreal Builders Ltd., Campbell tells you, builds for the residential market and does renovations to existing houses. Currently, it has six projects in progress. As he is leaving, Campbell gives you two final pieces of information: Glionna expects expenses for the first six months of 1987 to be $750,000 and is bidding on another post office construction project it is likely to get. Campbell says that the manager of Montreal Builders is complaining about some of its customers being late in paying their bills.

Required:

1. From the information provided, what can you tell Joe Campbell?
2. What can you deduce about the credit practices of each company?
3. Should Campbell be worried about the large amount of accounts receivable for Glionna Construction Ltd.?
4. Discuss the matching principle as it relates to these two entities.
5. What other information should Campbell consider before investing?

Inventory

Inventory is usually a major financial statement amount. Matching cost of goods sold with revenue and inventory valuation in the balance sheet is particularly important.

1. In what way can the actual flow of goods differ from the flow of costs?
2. What compromises are made by accountants when calculating the cost of inventory?
3. What impact does the practice of consistency have on changing from one cost flow assumption to another?
4. How is the laid-down cost of goods calculated?
5. What meaning is attributed by accountants to the word *market* when calculating inventory at the lower of cost and market?
6. What impact does the use of different cost flow assumptions have on financial statements?
7. What is the relationship between the cost of ending inventory and the resulting net income?
8. How is current cost information recommended to be disclosed on financial statements?
9. What is the distinction between a trading gain and a holding gain?
10. What different methods can be used to calculate inventory?

A.   Continuation of the Purchase and Payment Cycle — Inventory

Transactions in the purchase and payment cycle were introduced and discussed in Chapter 4. In this cycle, merchandise is purchased for subsequent resale to customers. This section continues the discussion of how merchandise inventory that remains on hand at the end of an accounting period is treated in financial statements.

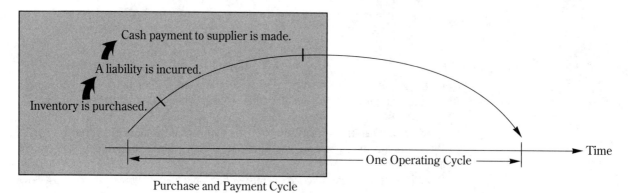

Purchase and Payment Cycle

Figure 5-1   The purchase and payment cycle

Impact of Inventory Errors

There are two problems in determining inventory. The first problem, described in Chapter 4, involves calculating the quantity of inventory on hand at the end of an accounting period. Usually, this is not a difficult problem to solve. The second problem involves assigning the most appropriate cost to this quantity of inventory. Choosing the most appropriate cost *can* be difficult. Furthermore, an error in calculating either the quantity or the cost of ending inventory will misstate reported profit for two time periods.

The following comparative income statements illustrate the effect of an error in ending inventory one year and its impact the following year. A constant amount of sales, purchases, and inventory is assumed in order to highlight the impact of a $1,000 ending inventory understatement in 19X6 and the resulting $1,000 opening inventory understatement in 19X7.

| | 19X6 Ending Inventory | | 19X7 Opening Inventory | |
	Correct	Under-*Stated*	Under-*Stated*	*Correct*
Sales	$30,000	$30,000	$30,000	$30,000
Cost of Goods Sold:				
Opening Inventory	$ 2,000	$ 2,000	$ 1,000	$ 2,000
Purchases	20,000	20,000	20,000	20,000
Cost of Goods Available	$22,000	$22,000	$21,000	$22,000
Ending Inventory	2,000	1,000	2,000	2,000
Total Cost of Goods Sold	$20,000	$21,000	$19,000	$20,000
Gross Profit	$10,000	$ 9,000	$11,000	$10,000

These figures are
both wrong.

As can be seen, income is misstated in both 19X6 and 19X7, because the ending inventory of 19X6 is the opening inventory of 19X7. The opposite occurs when inventory is overstated. The effect of inventory errors on both ending and opening inventory can be summarized as follows:

1. Error in ending inventory (19X6 example):
   If *ending* inventory is understated (stated at $1,000 instead of $2,000), income will also be understated ($9,000 instead of $10,000). Conversely, if ending inventory is overstated, then income will also be overstated.
2. Error in opening inventory (19X7 example):
   If *opening* inventory is understated (estimated at $1,000 instead of $2,000), income will be overstated ($11,000 instead of $10,000). Conversely, if opening inventory is overstated, then income will be understated.

It is also interesting to note that an error in ending inventory is offset in the next year because one year's ending inventory is the next year's opening inventory. This process can be illustrated by comparing profits for 19X6 and 19X7. The total of both years' gross profit is the same.

	Correct Inventory	*Understated Inventory*
Gross Profit for 19X6	$10,000	$ 9,000
Gross Profit for 19X7	10,000	11,000
Total	$20,000	$20,000

Estimating the Cost of Ending Inventory

The calculation of ending inventory estimates will help to ensure that the inventory amount is reasonable. In fact, an estimate of ending inventory is often used for the preparation of monthly or quarterly financial statements because it is expensive and time-consuming to do a **physical inventory** more than once a year. Two methods of estimating inventory are the gross profit method and the retail inventory method, both of which are discussed in section E.

Physical inventory
A counting and valuation of merchandise inventory.

B.   Calculation of Inventory Cost

The cost of ending inventory can be determined in several different ways. Each method may result in a different dollar amount of inventory. Consider the following: five gadgets are purchased for resale on different dates during a period of rising prices.

1st purchase:	1 gadget at $1
2nd purchase:	1 gadget at $2
3rd purchase:	1 gadget at $3
4th purchase:	1 gadget at $4
5th purchase:	1 gadget at $5

At the end of the accounting period, four of these gadgets have already been sold and only one gadget remains in ending inventory. What is the cost of the one remaining gadget in ending inventory? Is it $1, $2, $3, $4, or $5?

According to generally accepted accounting principles, as recommended in the *CICA Handbook* (section 3030.09), the inventory cost should be the one that "results in the fairest matching of costs against revenues", with due regard to its usefulness as a measure of balance sheet inventory cost. Which gadget cost results in the fairest matching? Why aren't costs fairly matched against revenues when any one of the gadget costs is used for the whole inventory? Or are they? Which cost is the most useful measure of the balance sheet cost? How are inventories normally costed? How would cost be assigned to the gadget in inventory in actual practice? If a method is chosen that measures net income best, what effect is there on the amount then shown on the balance sheet as inventory cost?

These are some of the questions that must be dealt with when considering ending inventory costs. The different methods used to calculate inventory cost are discussed in this section.

Specific Identification

Specific identification costing
A method of inventory costing in which goods are specifically identified with their purchase costs; an assumption on the flow of costs is not necessary when this method is used.

Flow of goods
The sequence in which purchased goods are sold; includes FIFO, LIFO, and average sequences.

Under the **specific identification costing** method, each inventory item is identified with its purchase cost. This method is most practical when inventory consists of relatively few, expensive items, particularly when individual units can be checked with serial numbers, as in the case of motor vehicles. Its usefulness is limited when inventory consists of a large number of inexpensive items purchased at various times during the period at different prices; in this case, calculating specific identification costs is not cost effective. Consequently, a method of assigning costs to inventory items based on an assumed **flow of goods** is usually adopted. Whatever method is chosen, the method must be followed consistently so as to match costs with revenues.

There is another feature of specific identification that is objectionable to accountants. There is the possibility of *profit enhancement opportunities* being available to management: when inventory purchase costs are increasing for identical units, management can show a larger net income by "selecting" for sale units that cost less; similarly, net income can be reduced if management "selects" for sale units that cost more.

The Actual Flow of Goods

FIFO (first in, first out)
Either an actual flow or an assumed flow can be used in relation to the flow of goods or costs or both; the first goods purchased are assumed to be the first goods sold.

LIFO (last in, first out)
Either an actual flow or an assumed flow can be used in relation to the flow of goods or costs or both; the last goods purchased are assumed to be the first goods sold.

Assigning the cost to inventory is easy under the specific identification method because the cost of each item sold is known. Inventory costing would be even easier if the price of goods did not change; in this case, the same cost would always apply and it would not be necessary to key the cost of each item separately — it would be the same for each one.

Prices of goods *do* change. Therefore, costs have to be assigned to closing inventory according to a flow of goods. What are the different flows of goods that accountants have identified? There are three possible ways to analyze the flow of goods: they are known as **first in, first out (FIFO)**; **last in, first out (LIFO)**; and the **average** method. The actual flow of goods depends on the conditions that exist in a particular company.

Average
Either *weighted* or
moving average; an
average is calculated by
dividing an amount by a
quantity.

The FIFO Assumption

Assume that a company purchases and sells eggs. Their perishable nature requires a flow of goods that ensures that the first eggs on hand are sold first; the eggs acquired next are next to be sold; and so on. This is a FIFO flow of goods. This flow can be thought of as a "conveyor belt" flow of goods. As each lot of eggs is purchased, it is placed on the "conveyor belt", as shown in Figure 5-2, for sale.

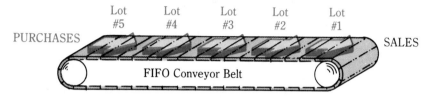

Figure 5-2   The FIFO flow of goods

Lot No. 1 is sold first. It is the first in; therefore it is the first out. Lot No. 2 is the next lot to be sold, and so on. A flow of costs that assumes that the first goods on hand (Lot No. 1) are the first to be sold is obviously the best method of calculating inventory cost in this situation. In addition to the egg example, a FIFO flow of goods is desirable where drugs, photo films, and other time-dated items make up inventory; a FIFO flow of costs is the most suitable accounting assumption in these situations.

The LIFO Assumption

Assume that a company purchases and sells coal. As coal is purchased, it is dumped on each preceding purchase, with the result that a pyramid of coal is formed, as illustrated in Figure 5-3.

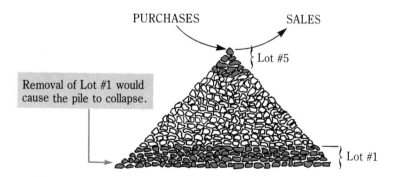

Figure 5-3   The LIFO flow of goods

As can be seen, coal at the top of the pile is the first to be sold. If an attempt were made to remove coal at the bottom, a dangerous landslide of coal could result. Therefore, the last purchased (at the top) is sold first, and the physical flow of goods is called a LIFO flow. A flow of costs that assumes that the last goods purchased (coal at the top of the pile) are the first to be sold is obviously the best method of calculating inventory cost in this type of situation.

The Average Assumption

In actual practice, an average may be used in both the egg and coal business, since goods purchased on different dates are mixed in common storage facilities and specific identification of each inventory item is impractical. Further, such costs as shipping and handling may not be readily assignable to specific items. The average method does not assume any particular flow of goods but is a reasonable compromise.

One of the problems in dealing with inventory was earlier identified as the need to calculate the quantities of goods in closing inventory. The calculating itself is not particularly difficult. But once the quantity of goods has been determined, an assumption must be made:

1. These goods have resulted from a FIFO flow of goods during the accounting period, or
2. These goods have resulted from a LIFO flow of goods during the accounting period, or
3. These goods are mixed at the end of the period and an average assumption is the most reasonable compromise.

The Actual Flow of Costs

Flow of costs
The sequence in which costs are assigned to merchandise sold and remaining in inventory; includes FIFO, LIFO, and average cost sequences.

Once the flow of goods has been recognized, the **flow of costs** can be determined and costs can easily be assigned to closing inventory. The calculation of inventory cost under each of the three methods follows. The purchase of five gadgets is used to illustrate the calculation of the ending inventory under the three flow-of-goods assumptions.

FIFO Cost

FIFO assumes that the first units on hand are the first to be sold, the units acquired next are the next to be sold, and so on. The calculation of inventory cost should correspond to this flow. For example, the FIFO cost of one gadget remaining in ending inventory (four gadgets have been sold) would be $5, calculated as follows.

1st purchase:	1 gadget at $1	(1st to be sold)
2nd purchase:	1 gadget at $2	(2nd to be sold)
3rd purchase:	1 gadget at $3	(3rd to be sold)
4th purchase:	1 gadget at $4	(4th to be sold)
5th purchase:	1 gadget at $5	(ending inventory is the cost of this purchase).

Thus, the first four gadgets purchased are the first four gadgets sold; the cost of the one remaining gadget in closing inventory is the cost of the fifth gadget purchased.

FIFO is a popular method in actual practice because, in most merchandising entities, it coincides with the actual flow of goods and is not susceptible to the type of manipulation by management possible under the specific identification method.

LIFO Cost

LIFO assumes that the last unit purchased is the first to be sold, and the calculation of inventory cost has to correspond to this flow. The LIFO cost of one gadget remaining in ending inventory (four gadgets have been sold) would be $1, calculated as follows:

1st purchase:	1 gadget at $1	(ending inventory is the cost of this purchase)
2nd purchase:	1 gadget at $2	(4th to be sold)
3rd purchase:	1 gadget at $3	(3rd to be sold)
4th purchase:	1 gadget at $4	(2nd to be sold)
5th purchase:	1 gadget at $5	(1st to be sold).

Thus the last four gadgets purchased are the first four gadgets to be sold; the cost of the one remaining gadget in closing inventory is the cost of the first gadget purchased.

As long as the ending inventory quantity is maintained or increased, the first costs are not related to the cost of gadgets sold and, therefore, do not appear on the income statement. However, if the ending inventory quantity is sold, then first costs *are* included in the income statement.

Average Cost

Weighted average
The average cost of inventory items under a periodic inventory system.

Since the average cost method does not assume any particular flow, the cost of each gadget sold is simply a computed average cost of all gadgets purchased. The calculation of this average depends on whether a *periodic* (**weighted average**) or *perpetual* (moving average) inventory system is in use. (The moving average costing procedure is discussed further in section D.)

> Assuming a periodic inventory system, the average cost (called weighted average) of a gadget would be $3 ($1 + $2 + $3 + $4 + $5 = $15 ÷ 5 units = $3 per unit). Note that the ending inventory cost is computed by dividing the total cost of units available for sale ($15) by the quantity of units available for sale (5 units).

The average cost assumption is popular in actual practice because it is easy to calculate. It is also particularly well suited to situations in which inventory is mixed in common storage facilities, for example, oil. In such cases, average cost is representative of all costs incurred in filling the oil storage tanks. The average cost amount calculated usually falls between the costs calculated by FIFO and LIFO and is a compromise between these two methods.

The calculation of inventory cost under each of the three methods is summarized below:

1st purchase:	1 gadget at $ 1	Under LIFO, inventory is given the cost of $1.
2nd purchase:	1 gadget at $ 2	
3rd purchase:	1 gadget at $ 3	Under FIFO, inventory is given the cost of $5.
4th purchase:	1 gadget at $ 4	
5th purchase:	1 gadget at $ 5	

$15 ÷ 5 units purchased = $3.

Under the average cost assumption, all unit costs are added together and the total divided by the number of units available for sale to calculate a $3 average cost per unit purchased.

Inventory Costing Practice in Canada

Studies of financial statements prepared by the CICA indicate that FIFO costing is the most frequently used method to calculate cost. While the LIFO costing method is not permitted for Canadian income tax purposes, Canadian companies may use this method for inventory costing provided they use a method acceptable to Canadian tax authorities for income tax purposes.

The recommendation in the *CICA Handbook* is that the cost flow method that results in the fairest matching of costs with revenues be used in calculating cost.

The Importance of Consistency

Although use of the most suitable cost flow assumption is encouraged by GAAP, emphasis is also placed on the consistent use of the assumption selected. The accountant's practice of consistency does not prevent a change from a cost flow assumption that is no longer suitable. Rather, it is designed to facilitate meaningful year-to-year comparisons of operating results and balance sheet valuation. Accordingly, where the cost flow assumption has changed, the *CICA Handbook* (section 3030.13) recommends that the effect of the change on net income should be disclosed in notes to the financial statements.

Accounting Compromises

Accountants make a number of compromises between what is conceptually correct and what is done in practice when calculating the cost of inventory. One of these involves the use of an assumed flow of costs that differs from the actual flow of goods. Another involves what is referred to as *laid-down cost,* discussed later.

Mismatched Flow of Costs with Flow of Goods

The previous paragraphs focused on the different ways that goods can flow through an entity. Inventory costs should be calculated on the FIFO basis where there is a FIFO flow of goods and on the LIFO basis where there is a LIFO flow of goods; an average method should be used when an average is the most reasonable assumption that can be made about the flow of goods.

In actual practice, however, the flow of costs assumed by management in calculating the cost of ending inventory may not be the same as the actual movement of goods.

- A FIFO cost flow can be assumed where a LIFO flow of goods actually exists, or
- A LIFO cost flow can be assumed where a FIFO flow of goods actually exists, or
- Any other combination of one cost flow with a different flow of goods may be used.

This mismatching of the actual flow of costs with the movement of goods can result in a substantial miscalculation of net income or represent, in some cases, profit enhancement opportunities.

> The use of an assumed flow of costs that differs from the actual flow of goods is permitted by generally accepted accounting principles.

Laid-Down Cost

The discussion in this chapter so far emphasizes the calculation of inventory cost. For a wholesale or retail business, inventory is generally understood to mean *goods owned and available for sale to customers*; it is recommended in the *CICA Handbook* (section 3030.05) that this cost be the **laid-down cost**. This laid-down cost includes the invoice price of the goods (less purchase discounts) plus transportation in, insurance while in transit, and any other expenditure made by the purchaser to get the merchandise to the place of business.

The cost of merchandise available for sale is usually considered as the laid-down cost. In the following partial income statement (based on the one in section D of Chapter 4), which amount is the laid-down cost?

Laid-down cost (of inventory)
Includes every cost incurred by the purchaser to get the merchandise to his or her place of business.

All merchandise a company has for sale during the accounting period is sometimes called a *pool of costs*.

This is the laid-down cost.

Cost of Goods Sold:			
Opening Inventory			$ 80,000
Purchases		$240,000	
Less: Purchases Returns and			
Allowances	$12,600		
Purchases Discounts	2,400	15,000	
Net Purchases		$225,000	
Transportation In		15,000	
Cost of Goods Purchased			240,000
Cost of Goods Available			$320,000
Ending Inventory (Dec. 31)			120,000
Total Cost of Goods Sold			$200,000

The pool of goods available for sale is divided into two categories at the end of an accounting period.

If transportation in and other such costs are insignificant in relation to the invoice price of the merchandise, a proportionate amount of these costs should theoretically be added to the cost of ending inventory. In actual practice, these costs are often significant and are hence considered as expenses of the accounting period in which they were incurred and are not allocated to ending inventory. Similarly, purchase discounts are not usually deducted from inventory.

The exclusion of these items from ending inventory is also in accordance with the practice of conservatism subscribed to by accountants. Although these laid-down costs are usually omitted for convenience from the calculation of ending inventory, their exclusion is justified by materiality and cost-benefit considerations, as well as conservatism. Conservatism permits the misstatement of an item if the end result is less favourable in its impact on net income and/or asset valuation. It is interesting to note that the accountant's view of conservatism was considered peculiar by Professor Henry Rand Hatfield, an eminent accountant, who wrote:

> The accountant transcends the conservatism of the proverb "Don't count your chickens before they are hatched", saying "Here are a lot of chickens already safely hatched but, for the love of Mike, use discretion and don't count them all, for perhaps some will die".[1]

It is noteworthy that Hatfield's observation was made 15 years ago; not all accounting policies today emphasize this extreme conservatism.

Lower of Cost and Market

As discussed, historical cost is the generally accepted method used for inventory costing. The use of replacement cost is also in accordance with GAAP when the replacement cost of an inventory item in the market place decreases, for whatever reason, in relation to the cost of that item recorded in the books of the company.

The term **market** in this context means the cost of replacing the goods; the CICA has observed that

> in view of the lack of precision in meaning, it is desirable that the term "market" not be used in describing the basis of valuation. A term more descriptive of the method of determining market, such as replacement cost, net realizable value, or net realizable value less normal profit margin, would be preferable (section 3030.11).

Market
The cost of replacing an asset on the open market.

LOCAM (lower of cost and market)
A method of inventory valuation that calculates inventory cost at *cost* or *market*, whichever is lower; the term is also used in relation to temporary investments.

LOCAM, as applied on a unit-by-unit basis and on a group inventory basis, is illustrated below:

	Total Cost	Total Market	Unit Basis	Group Basis
Item X	$1,250	$1,200 →	$1,200	
Item Y	1,400	1,500	1,400	
Total	$2,650	$2,700		$2,650
Ending Inventory (LOCAM)			$2,600	$2,650

Depending on which calculation you use, the valuation of ending inventory will be either $2,600 or $2,650. Under the unit basis, the lower of cost and market is selected for each item, while, under the group basis LOCAM, which is total cost of $2,650 in this example, an increase in Item Y is offset by a decrease in Item X. However, both methods, as well as sub-totals of different categories, are acceptable in the calculation of LOCAM. These calculations will not be affected by the method you use to establish your inventory cost.

The use of LOCAM is usually supported with an assumption that retail selling prices are expected to decline as inventory purchase cost declines. This assumption, however, is not always correct; and if declines in sales price do occur, they are not always proportional to the decline in inventory purchase cost, that is, "market". The accountant's practice of conservatism is therefore invoked to justify use of LOCAM, although balance sheet valuation of inventory and measurement of net income is initially adversely affected. The business community seems to demand conservatism on the part of accountants.

This approach was adopted in the days when conservatism was a dominant consideration for asset valuation. What it means is that, when the goods in inventory can be replaced for an amount that is less than their assumed cost, the inventory should be costed at this lower amount. A more accurate matching of costs and revenues in the next accounting period also results from this recognition of the lower cost of ending inventory, if sales prices are falling.

LOCAM is most useful when inventory costs are decreased because of obsolescence or damage.

C.   Impact of Different Inventory Cost Assumptions

The application of different cost flow assumptions was illustrated in section B. If the cost of purchases did not increase during the period, then each method would allocate similar amounts to cost of goods sold and ending inventory. A problem arises, however, when purchase cost fluctuates during the accounting period. Typically, in a period of rapid inflation, cost increases can be significant. The resulting impact on the income statement and balance sheet are described next.

Impact on the Income Statement

When purchase costs are increasing or decreasing, each cost flow method results in a different amount of ending inventory, cost of goods sold amount, and net income.

An example can be drawn from an analysis made for management of Bluebeard Computer Corporation. Three different cost flows were considered: FIFO, LIFO, and weighted average (average cost). Use was made of the data from section B concerning the purchase costs increase from $1 to $5 during the period; the result was a total purchase cost of $15 ($1 + $2 + $3 + $4 + $5). These increases reflected the period of rapidly rising purchase costs, which had occurred recently. Assume now that sales prices were also rising and that 4 gadgets had been sold for a total of $20 ($2 + $4 + $6 + $8). Assume also that expenses remain constant at $6.

Note that the differences in net income are not caused by differences in the physical flow of goods; rather, they result from assumptions made about the flow of costs.

	FIFO Cost Flow		LIFO Cost Flow		Weighted Average Cost Flow	
Sales		$20		$20		$20
Cost of Goods Sold:						
Purchases	$15		$15		$15	
Less: Ending Inventory	5		1		3	
Total Cost of Goods Sold		10		14		12
Gross Profit		$10		$ 6		$ 8
Operating Expenses		6		6		6
Net Income		$ 4		$ -0-		$ 2

As can be seen, the impact of different cost flow assumptions is dramatic. FIFO maximizes income when purchase costs are rising and may result in a distorted net income amount. LIFO minimizes net income when purchase costs are rising and results in a more accurate matching of current revenue with current costs; it also tends to approximate inflation-adjusted accounting. Unfortunately, it also results in an unrealistic amount of inventory reported on the balance sheet. The weighted average method results in a net income figure between those for FIFO and LIFO.

> The choice of a particular inventory costing assumption can result in substantially different amounts of net income when purchase costs are fluctuating (and inventory turns over quickly).

In view of the impact that different cost flow assumptions can have on the financial statements, GAAP requires that the cost flow assumption used by an entity be disclosed in its financial statements.

A relationship between the cost of an ending inventory and the resulting net income is also apparent from the analysis. The FIFO method, with a larger ending inventory value ($5), also has the largest net income ($4). The LIFO method, with a smaller ending inventory value ($1), also has the lowest net income ($0). Therefore, we can conclude that if ending inventory is higher or increases, net income also is higher or increases; if ending inventory is lower or decreases, net income also is lower or decreases.

If ending inventory cost increases ⬆ net income will increase. ⬆ income taxes will increase. ⬆

If ending inventory cost decreases ⬇ net income will decrease. ⬇ income taxes will decrease. ⬇

The ability to predict this relationship between net income and changes in the cost of ending inventory is important for business decisions.

1. If the objective of management is to increase reported net income, then the inventory method that gives the highest ending inventory should be adopted.
2. If the objective of management is to minimize income taxes, then the inventory cost method that results in the lowest ending inventory should be adopted.

The Canadian federal and provincial governments, aware of the implications of this choice and the popularity it would have with businesses wishing to reduce income taxes, must have considered the advisability of permitting the use of LIFO inventory costing for income tax purposes. This consideration probably did not take long.

Although the use of LIFO is permitted for income tax purposes in the United States, it is not permitted for income tax reporting in Canada. This policy does not mean that LIFO costing cannot be used in business. It simply means that this method cannot be used in the calculation of income taxes. Therefore, a business using LIFO costing in its records has to recalculate LIFO inventory cost to FIFO, average, or another acceptable method for income tax purposes.

During a period of falling prices, FIFO results in the lowest ending inventory cost; LIFO would produce the opposite results.

Phantom Profits

The comparison of the effects of FIFO and LIFO costing methods on net income (discussed above) show that a larger net income results when FIFO costing is used during a period of increasing prices provided the number of units sold is less than the number purchased during the period. In the Bluebeard Computer Corporation example, the net income on sales was $4 using FIFO and actually nil using LIFO. That is, FIFO showed profits of $4 more than LIFO.

	FIFO	LIFO
Net Income	$4	$-0-

Phantom profits
(from inventory)
A term used to describe the extra profits reported under the FIFO method of assigning costs to inventory, as compared with the LIFO method, during a period of rising prices (costs).

Such profits are sometimes referred to as **phantom profits**. The word *phantom* implies that these profits are an illusion.

Why are the extra profits under FIFO an illusion? Under FIFO, earlier costs are included in cost of goods sold. In the income statement these *earlier* costs are matched with *current* sales prices, with the result that there is no real profit under LIFO and a phantom profit of $4 under FIFO.

Under LIFO, the most recent costs are included in cost of goods sold. In the income statement these *more recent* costs are matched with *current* sales prices, and a closer matching of costs with revenue is achieved. Therefore LIFO costing, it is claimed, is more realistic with respect to the measurement of income.

In actual practice, a good matching occurs under LIFO only when purchases and sales occur frequently and in approximately the same quantity.

Real Life Example 5-1

Surprise!

During the first year of running my own company, I thought we were doing really great. Then, at year end, I was shocked by a write-down of $66,000 in inventory that offset about a quarter of our pretax profits. I felt like I'd been kicked in the stomach. My illusion of having established control was shattered. Was it theft? Were our systems that screwed up? What was going on?

That was when I learned about accounting systems. In order to balance perfectly, they drive all sorts of errors into a misstatement of inventory throughout the year. Then, when you do your annual physical inventory and compare it with the books, you discover a discrepancy, usually a shortfall. For example, if you understate your costs when computing gross margins, it will show up on the books as more dollars of inventory than you actually have. If you understate product adjustment costs or scrap, that's another contribution to the shortfall. If a product is shipped and somehow not invoiced, same result. If a product is short-shipped by the vendor and not caught, more shortages. The list goes on and on. And until all the accounting and procedural causes for inventory shrinkage are cleared up, your month-to-month operating statements will be misleading.

I'd like to say it was easy, but at Battery & Tire Warehouse Inc., it took us four years before we straightened out our system completely. And it's a grungy job. There are dozens of places to look for slipups, and only a methodical plugging away at the possibilities will bring you any answers. In the end, we resorted to doing a physical inventory every month, and then comparing the physical counts with the books to see what progress we'd made in our internal controls. By comparing each stockkeeping unit, we also were able to reassure ourselves that our problem was not any major organized theft — the unit count differences were pluses and minuses in a fairly random pattern typical of minor paperwork errors.

Our monthly operating statements now are reasonably clean and show what is actually happening. And personally, I have a much stronger feeling of control. That's why I've been surprised to learn over the past few years that many small and midsize companies experience year-end book-to-physical inventory shrinkage, but do little to attack it directly.

Some companies mask the year-end shrinkage problem by offsetting the loss with year-end windfalls, such as vendor rebates or FIFO (first in, first out) inflationary gains. We could have done that last year, for example, when our vendors raised their prices, which made our inventory worth $56,000 more. But what's the point of playing with numbers on the books? Such actions are useless if you're interested in getting the information you need to run your company. So we set up windfall gains as separate accounts and formally recognize shrinkage on its own.

A similarly useless game played by some managers is to build into their system automatic gains under the guise of conservatism. Back when I was in the *Fortune* 500 world, I was admonishing a division general manager for less than sterling profit results as the year was drawing to a close. His comment was, "Don't worry; we'll hit plan since we'll have a major year-end inventory pickup." I asked how he could be so sure. "Oh, we always have a major gain since we are conservative in our manufacturing costs and scrap rates." After being pulled down from the ceiling I asked, dumbfounded, "How the hell do we know what our inventory shortfall should be? Maybe we're experiencing major problems and we'll have no way to tell. What have we done to scrap controls?"

Don't get me wrong — I think a certain amount of inventory shrinkage is inevitable. In our business as a $12-million distributor, we reserve $2,000 per month for shrinkage. This 0.2% covers miscellaneous breakage, some minor pilferage, mispulled product, and so on. The key point, though, is that we set up the reserve as a bona fide item on our books, so it can be compared with the actual shrinkage. To my mind, there are enough nasty surprises in running a business without adding inventory shrinkage to the list.

Source Reprinted with permission, *Inc. magazine*, (Sept. 1988). Copyright © (1988) by Goldhirsch Group, Inc., 38 Commercial Wharf, Boston, MA 02110.

Impact on the Balance Sheet

Despite its advantages in matching inventory costs with revenue in the income statement, a major disadvantage of LIFO costing is its understatement of the inventory figure that appears on the balance sheet. This disadvantage in turn limits the significance and usefulness of this financial statement.

The gadget data used in the preceding discussions are repeated here to compare the inventory values that appear on the balance sheet as an asset, under each of the three cost assumptions:

	FIFO	*LIFO*	*Weighted Average*
Ending Inventory	$5	$1	$3

As is obvious, LIFO provides an unrealistic ending inventory value. If this comparison of ending inventory under the three cost assumptions is representative of what occurs in actual practice — which it tends to be when prices are rising — care has to be exercised by the reader of financial statements in interpreting the amounts reported in the financial statements.

> Full disclosure of the inventory costing assumption used in the financial statements is essential, because inventory is often the largest single item in the current assets section of the balance sheet.

The differences between the cost flow assumptions and their impacts on the income statement and balance sheet are compared in the adjacent table.

Comparison of Cost Flow Assumptions

	FIFO	*LIFO*	*WEIGHTED AVERAGE*	*SPECIFIC IDENTIFICATION*
Physical flow vs cost flow	The flow of goods approximates the flow of costs in most cases.	The flow of goods does not approximate the flow of costs in most cases.		The flow of goods is the same as the flow of costs since costs are identified with specific goods.

INCOME STATEMENT:

	FIFO	*LIFO*	*WEIGHTED AVERAGE*	*SPECIFIC IDENTIFICATION*
Matching of expenses with revenues	The earlier costs in opening inventory and earlier purchases are matched with current revenues.	Emphasizes the matching of the most current costs with current revenues.	An average cost for the period is matched with revenues.	The actual cost of each item sold is matched with the revenue resulting from the sale.
Net income determination	Maximizes income when prices are rising because the earlier (and lower) costs are included in cost of goods sold.	Minimizes net income when prices are rising and sales are greater than purchases because more current, and therefore higher, costs are included in cost of goods sold.	When prices are rising, results in a net income figure that is less than the FIFO calculation but more than the LIFO calculation.	When prices are rising (or falling), the user can arrange to sell identical higher-cost or lower-cost items.
	Therefore FIFO can result in a distorted net income figure.	Therefore LIFO results in a more accurate net income figure.	Therefore weighted average results in a net income figure that is between FIFO and LIFO.	Therefore specific identification can be more susceptible to net income manipulation.

BALANCE SHEET:

	FIFO	*LIFO*	*WEIGHTED AVERAGE*	*SPECIFIC IDENTIFICATION*
Inventory valuation	Approximates replacement cost (particularly when inventory turnover is rapid) since ending inventory consists of most current costs.	Consists of the earliest costs, which may not approximate current replacement cost.	Consists of average cost, which is more current than that calculated under LIFO but which does not approximate replacement cost as well as that occurring under FIFO.	The actual cost of each item in inventory is included in inventory.
	Therefore FIFO results in a more current balance sheet inventory figure.	Therefore LIFO can result in a distorted balance sheet inventory figure.		

D. Inventory Systems

There are four different methods that can be used to calculate inventory. Two of these methods are based on *calculations* made by the company: the periodic inventory method and the perpetual inventory method. Two are based on *estimates* made by the company: the gross profit method and the retail inventory method. They are shown in Figure 5-4.

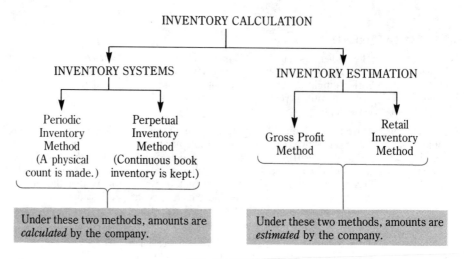

Figure 5-4   Methods for calculating inventory

These four different quantity calculation methods are discussed in the remaining part of this chapter.

Perpetual Inventory System

The perpetual inventory system, as discussed in Chapter 4, requires a continuous balance of inventory on hand to be calculated in terms of units and often also in terms of cost. The use of this system requires maintaining a subsidiary inventory record; an example of a subsidiary accounts receivable record is illustrated in Appendix B. An example of a subsidiary inventory record with recorded purchases and sales in terms of units is illustrated in Figure 5-5

	Purchased		Sold		Balance		
	Quantity	*Unit Cost*	*Quantity*	*Unit Cost*	*Quantity*	*Unit Cost*	*Total Cost*
Purchase #1	1				1		
Sale #1			1		0		
Purchase #2	1				1		
Purchase #3	1				2		
Sale #2			1		1		
Purchase #4	1				2		
Sale #3			1		1		
Purchase #5	1				2		
Sale #4			1		1		

Figure 5-5   Inventory record card

As each purchase is received, the quantity received and the balance on hand are recorded in the appropriate columns. When inventory is sold, units sold are recorded in the units sold column; a new balance on hand is also calculated and recorded. Thus, a change in inventory quantity is recorded each time a purchase or sale is made. The inventory at the end of the accounting period is one unit in Figure 5-5. This is a *book* inventory. A *physical* inventory is made periodically to verify the quantities that are actually on hand.

Note the availability of columns for cost calculations. As purchases and sales are made, costs are assigned to the goods using whatever cost flow assumption is in use.

Periodic Inventory System

Under the periodic inventory system, as discussed in Chapter 4, the inventory is determined by a physical count. Therefore, the change in inventory is recorded only periodically, usually at the end of each year. A physical count requires careful planning and inventory-taking procedures: numbered inventory tags are attached to all inventory items; quantities counted are recorded on these tags; and the numerical sequence of the completed tags is subsequently checked to ensure that quantities are accounted for. The inventory descriptions and quantities are next transferred to inventory summary sheets, which also have blank columns for the entry of costs and the calculation of total costs.

Chartered accountants and other independent auditors make test counts during a physical count to satisfy themselves that inventory quantities to be used to calculate total inventory cost are correct. Following the physical count, costs are assigned to the units in inventory. As discussed, specific identification, FIFO, LIFO, or average (weighted) costing can be used.

Illustrative Problem — FIFO Costing under the Perpetual System

In Figure 5-6, the purchases and sales from Figure 5-5 are repeated, incorporating unit costs.

	Purchased		Sold		Balance		
	Quantity	Unit Cost	Quantity	Unit Cost	Quantity	Unit Cost	Total Cost
Purchase #1	1	1			1	× 1	= 1
Sale #1			1	1	0	× 0	0
Purchase #2	1	2			1	× 2	2
Purchase #3	1	3			2	1 × 2, 1 × 3	5
Sale #2			1	2	1	× 3	3
Purchase #4	1	4			2	1 × 3, 1 × 4	7
Sale #3			1	3	1	× 4	4
Purchase #5	1	5			2	1 × 4, 1 × 5	9
Sale #4			1	4	1	× 5	= 5

Figure 5-6 Inventory record card using FIFO costing

Under FIFO, the earliest purchase costs are assigned to sales. Note that the cost of ending inventory under the perpetual system is the same as the calculation for FIFO under the periodic inventory system. When FIFO is used as the cost flow assumption, the calculation of ending inventory under the perpetual and periodic system will always be the same. (This correlation is not the case for LIFO or weighted average costing.)

Illustrative Problem — LIFO Costing under the Perpetual System

The example in Figure 5-5 is repeated in Figure 5-7, using the LIFO cost flow assumption.

Under LIFO, the cost of ending inventory is assumed to consist of the first unit purchased and not sold. In the case of Purchase #1, only one unit was on hand at the time of the sale. Therefore, the cost of $1 left the system when Sale #1 was made. The first unit purchased and still on hand is Purchase #2 for $2.

	Purchased		Sold		Balance		
	Quantity	Unit Cost	Quantity	Unit Cost	Quantity	Unit Cost	Total Cost
Purchase #1	1	1			1	× 1	= 1
Sale #1			1	1	0	0	0
Purchase #2	1	2			1	2	2
Purchase #3	1	3			2	1 × 2 } 1 × 3	5
Sale #2			1	3	1	× 2	2
Purchase #4	1	4			2	1 × 2 } 1 × 4	6
Sale #3			1	4	1	× 2	2
Purchase #5	1	5			2	1 × 2 } 1 × 5	7
Sale #4			1	5	1	× 2	= 2

Figure 5-7   Inventory record card using LIFO costing

The ending inventory cost under LIFO with the perpetual inventory system differs from that calculated under LIFO with the periodic system as follows:

	LIFO Periodic	LIFO Perpetual
Ending Inventory	$1	$2

The difference in amounts calculated is attributable to the fact that, under LIFO/perpetual, the most recent cost immediately prior to a sale leaves the system when the sale is actually made. Under LIFO/periodic, the calculation is made at year-end; therefore, the most recent cost at that date leaves the system. In periods of rising prices, LIFO/perpetual usually produces a higher ending inventory amount than LIFO/periodic.

Illustrative Problem — Moving Average Costing under the Perpetual System

Moving average
The average cost of an inventory item under the perpetual inventory system.

The calculation of ending inventory under **moving average** costing is illustrated in Figure 5-8, using the same data as before.

	Purchased		Sold		Balance		
	Quantity	Unit Cost	Quantity	Unit Cost	Quantity	Unit Cost	Total Cost
Purchase #1	1	1			1	× 1	= 1
Sale #1			1	1	0	0	0
Purchase #2	1	2			1	2	2
Purchase #3	1	3			2	× 2.50	5
Sale #2			1	2.50	1	× 2.50	2.50
Purchase #4	1	4			2	× 3.25	6.50
Sale #3			1	3.25	1	× 3.25	3.25
Purchase #5	1	5			2	× 4.125	8.25
Sale #4			1	4.125	1	× 4.125	= 4.125

Figure 5-8   Inventory record card using moving average costing

The moving average is calculated as follows:

$$1 \times \$2.00 = \$2.00$$
$$1 \times \$3.00 = \$3.00$$
$$\underline{2} \qquad \underline{\$5.00}$$

Average = $2.50

$$1 \times \$2.50 = \$2.50$$
$$1 \times \$4.00 = \$4.00$$
$$\underline{2} \qquad \underline{\$6.50}$$

Average = $3.25

$$1 \times \$3.25 = \$3.25$$
$$1 \times \$5.00 = \$5.00$$
$$\underline{2} \qquad \underline{\$8.25}$$

Average = $4.125

Under moving average, a weighted average is calculated each time a purchase is made. Accordingly, a weighted average is calculated after purchases #3, #4, and #5. The ending inventory cost is $4.125 under moving average costing; under weighted average costing, ending inventory amounts to $3. In periods of rising prices, moving average usually produces a higher ending inventory than weighted average.

Inventory Systems Compared

The results produced by each of the cost flow assumptions under both periodic and perpetual systems are compared; these results also assume that prices are rising.

	FIFO		LIFO		Average	
	Periodic	Perpetual	Periodic	Perpetual	Periodic	Perpetual
Ending Inventory	$5	$5	$1	$2	$3	$4.125

Ending inventory is always the same under both systems. FIFO always produces the highest ending inventory amount (and therefore income) when prices are rising because ending inventory consists of the most recent costs.

Ending inventory usually differs under both systems; LIFO/periodic usually produces a lower amount when prices are rising because ending inventory is calculated at the end of the period under periodic; under perpetual, the inventory balance is calculated after each sale. LIFO always produces the lowest ending inventory amount (and therefore income).

Ending inventory usually differs under both systems; periodic/weighted average usually produces a lower amount than perpetual/ moving average when prices are rising. Under periodic, one average cost is calculated for the whole period; under perpetual, an average is calculated following each purchase. An average method produces an ending inventory amount that is between the amounts for FIFO and LIFO.

The amount of difference between LIFO costs calculated on either the periodic or the perpetual system and between FIFO costs calculated on either system will correspond to the magnitude of the change in prices during the period and to the rapidity of inventory turnover.

When prices are falling, the results produced under the different cost flow assumptions are reversed. LIFO produces the highest ending inventory, and FIFO the lowest. The average method produces an amount between those under LIFO and FIFO.

Under the periodic inventory method, the quantity of the ending inventory is determined by a complete physical count; the quantity in inventory is not readily available during the accounting period. When a perpetual inventory method is used, a continuous book inventory is kept for each type of item in inventory. The quantity in inventory is readily available at any time under this method.

The perpetual inventory incorporates an internal control feature that is lost under the periodic inventory method. Losses resulting from theft and error can easily be determined when the actual quantity of goods on hand is compared with the quantities shown in the inventory records as being on hand. This advantage is offset, however, by the time and expense required to update the inventory records continuously, particularly where there are thousands of different items of various sizes in stock. Computerization makes this record-keeping easier and less expensive, particularly when the inventory accounting system is tied in to the sales system in such a way that inventory is updated whenever a sale is recorded.

The perpetual inventory system also requires that the cost of inventory sold — which is an expense — be recorded periodically, so that a dollar amount of inventory is accurately shown in the general ledger.

The journal entries required under the FIFO/perpetual and FIFO/periodic systems differ for Purchase #1 and Sale #2, as illustrated below. Under the perpetual system, purchases are debited to the asset account Merchandise Inventory. Under the perpetual system, when a sale is made, the cost of inventory is recorded as an expense.

Periodic Inventory			*Perpetual Inventory*		
Purchases	1		Merchandise Inventory	1	
Accounts Payable		1	Accounts Payable		1
To record Purchase #1.			To record Purchase #1.		
Accounts Receivable	2		Accounts Receivable	2	
Sales		2	Sales		2
To record Sale #1.			To record Sale #1.		
			Cost of Goods Sold	1	
			Merchandise Inventory		1
(No Entry Required)			To record the cost of Sale #1.		

E. Estimating Inventory Cost

The periodic and perpetual inventory systems have the following procedure in common: both begin with quantities of items that are either listed on cards (perpetual) or counted during a physical count (periodic), and costs are assigned to the counted units; a total dollar amount of inventory is subsequently calculated. By this means, individual inventory items are summed to get an inventory total amount.

The next two inventory systems to be discussed differ from these two in that they do not begin with inventory quantities that are then used to arrive at an inventory dollar amount. Rather, these methods calculate only the total dollar amount of inventory and do not consider quantities. How is this possible? By *estimating* the inventory dollar amount, using financial data of the firm. There are two reasons why estimating inventory is useful:

Reason 1:   Useful for the Preparation of Interim Financial Statements

Estimating the inventory amount offers a means of determining a company's inventory at frequent intervals, thereby avoiding the cost and inconvenience of taking a physical count each time monthly or periodic statements are being prepared.

Reason 2:   Useful for Inventory Control

A physical inventory count determines the quantity of items on hand. When costs are assigned to these items and these individual costs are added, a total inventory amount is calculated. Is this dollar amount correct? Should it be larger? How can one tell if the physical count is accurate? An estimate of what the inventory amount should be is one answer. The two methods used to estimate the inventory dollar amount are the *gross profit method* and the *retail inventory method*.

Both methods are based on a calculation of the gross profit percentage in the income statement. The following partial income statement reviews how to calculate the gross profit percentage calculation. For more information, refer back to Chapter 4, section A.

Sales		$15,000	100%	
Cost of Goods Sold:				
Opening Inventory	$ 4,000			
Net Purchases	12,000			
Cost of Goods Available	$16,000			
Estimated Ending Inventory	6,000			The gross profit
Total Cost of Goods Sold		10,000	66⅔%	in this case is
Gross Profit		$ 5,000	33⅓%	33⅓%.

Here, the gross profit is $5,000. This amount results when the cost of the goods sold ($10,000) is deducted from net sales ($15,000). As calculated, the gross profit is 33⅓ percent of net sales.

The word *gross* is used by accountants in this case to indicate that the operating expenses necessary to run the business must still be deducted before (net) profit can be calculated. As is shown, the gross profit is 33⅓ percent of the net sales ($15,000 × 33⅓% = $5,000).

> The calculation of the gross profit percentage is the first step in making an estimate of the ending inventory amount.

Ending inventory estimation also requires an understanding of the relationship of ending inventory with cost of goods sold. As can be seen in the following comparative examples, certain data has been removed from the preceding partial income statement:

Cost of Goods Sold:			Cost of Goods Sold:	
Opening Inventory	$ 4,000		Opening Inventory	$ 4,000
Net Purchases	12,000		Net Purchases	12,000
Cost of Goods Available	$16,000		Cost of Goods Available	$16,000
Estimated Ending Inventory	?		Estimated Ending Inventory	6,000
Total Cost of Goods Sold	$10,000		Total Cost of Goods sold	?

How much of the $16,000-worth of goods that the company had available to sell is still not sold at December 31 (that is, how much is in ending inventory)? How do you calculate the dollar amount of this inventory?		How much of the $16,000-worth of goods that were available to be sold have been sold? And how do you calculate the dollar amount of this inventory at December 31?	
It had	$16,000	It had	$16,000
It sold	10,000	It still has	6,000
∴ It still has	$6,000	∴ It must have sold	$10,000

The following questions are posed in the above examples: What is the amount of cost of goods sold at December 31? What is the amount of ending inventory at December 31? What should now be obvious is that once one of these two questions is answered, the answer to the other question can be easily calculated. The cost of goods sold and ending inventory are two sides of the same coin. Knowing this relationship will make it easier to understand how estimating inventory works in the gross profit and retail inventory method.

Gross Profit Method

Gross profit method A method of estimating the amount of inventory without taking a physical count. This method can be used to verify the reasonableness of the actual inventory calculated, but it is not usually acceptable for calculating the amount of inventory to be reported in financial statements.

The **gross profit method** assumes that the *rate* (percentage) of gross profit on sales remains approximately the same from year to year. Therefore, if this rate (percentage) can be calculated, the dollar amount of inventory can be estimated easily. Assume that, during the previous two years, Bluebeard Computer Corporation has averaged a gross profit rate of 40 percent, as shown below.

	Prior Years			This Year	
	1	*2*	*Totals*		
Sales	$400	$600	$1,000	$2,000	
Cost of Goods Sold	200	400	600	?	
Gross Profit	$200	$200	$ 400	? ←	Calculated as $800.
Gross Profit (%)	50%	33⅓%	40%	40% assumed	

In this case, with the assumption made by the gross profit method, the gross profit rate for Year 3 is 40 percent, and the gross profit is calculated at $800 ($2,000 sales × 40% gross profit). Therefore, cost of goods sold must be the difference between $2,000 and $800; that is, $1,200. The income statement for Year 3 now can be completed.

	Prior Years			This Year
	1	*2*	*Totals*	
Sales	$400	$600	$1,000	$2,000
Cost of Goods Sold	200	400	600	1,200
Gross Profit	$200	$200	$ 400	$ 800
Gross Profit (%)	50%	33⅓%	40%	40%

These amounts are calculated based on the assumed GP rate.

← 40% assumed

Using these figures, the partial income statement for Year 3 appears as follows, after the inclusion of the opening inventory and purchases amounts:

Sales		$2,000
Cost of Goods Sold:		
Opening Inventory	$ 200	
Net Purchases	1,100	
Cost of Goods Available	$1,300	
Estimated Ending Inventory	?	
Total Cost of Goods Sold		1,200
Gross Profit		$ 800

This information is always given to students for problem solving. In actual practice, if necessary, these amounts can also be reconstructed from company and other records.

How much is the ending inventory at December 31? It must be $100, the difference between the goods the company had available to sell ($1,300) and the amount it actually sold ($1,200).

The gross profit method of estimating inventory is particularly useful in situations where goods have been stolen or destroyed by fire; in these cases it is obviously impossible to make a physical inventory count.

Retail Inventory Method

Retail inventory method
A method of estimating the amount of inventory without taking a physical count; converts retail value of inventory to cost.

Under the **retail inventory method**, both the cost and selling prices of goods purchased (called *retail* prices) are recorded and are available at the time of inventory estimation. This method is particularly useful for costing retail inventory without going to invoices to identify the cost of different items.

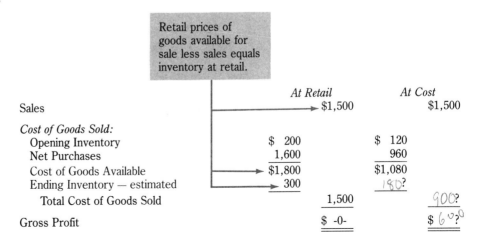

Retail prices of goods available for sale less sales equals inventory at retail.

	At Retail	At Cost
Sales	$1,500	$1,500
Cost of Goods Sold:		
Opening Inventory	$ 200	$ 120
Net Purchases	1,600	960
Cost of Goods Available	$1,800	$1,080
Ending Inventory — estimated	300	180?
Total Cost of Goods Sold	1,500	900?
Gross Profit	$ -0-	$ 600?

As can be seen, the ending inventory at retail is easily calculated by deducting sales during the period ($1,500) from the goods available for sale priced at retail ($1,800). How much is the ending inventory at retail for this company?

It sold	$1,500	(using retail sales prices)
It had available	1,800	(using retail cost of goods available prices)
∴ It must still have	$ 300	(this is the ending inventory at retail prices)

How much is the ending inventory at cost? Ending inventory at retail is converted to cost by applying the cost percentage to the $300 ending inventory at retail prices. First, the *cost percentage* is calculated:

	Cost	Retail
Opening Inventory	$ 120	$ 200
Net Purchases	960	1,600
Goods Available for Sale	$1,080	$1,800

The *cost percentage* is the ratio of cost of goods available to the retail price of those goods.

Cost Percentage (Ratio of Cost to Retail)
$$= \frac{\$1,080}{\$1,800} = 60\%.$$

Then the cost percentage is used to convert the $300 ending inventory at retail prices:

The retail inventory of $300 is converted to cost inventory of $180 using the cost percentage.

Ending Inventory at Retail = $300
Estimated Ending Inventory at Cost (60% of $300) = $180

The retail inventory method of estimating ending inventory is commonly used by department stores, where inventory is taken at the selling price. It is easy to calculate and produces a relatively accurate cost of ending inventory, provided that no change in the cost percentage has occurred during the current period. This method results in an average cost of ending inventory, because the cost percentage is an average and therefore makes no assumption that goods are sold in any particular order.

Certain terms such as *mark-ups* and *mark-downs* have become associated with the retail inventory method but are more appropriately dealt with in a more advanced accounting course. For purposes of this text, mark-ups and mark-downs are ignored in the calculation of the cost percentage.

Inventory Estimation Systems Compared

Both the gross profit method and the retail inventory method are based on calculation of the gross profit rate. The gross profit method uses past experience as a basis; the retail inventory method uses current experience, which is more reliable and therefore preferable.

APPENDIX: The Current Cost Model

Current cost
Replacement value.

The *CICA Handbook* recommends that certain current cost information relating to both the income statement and the balance sheet be disclosed as supplementary information to financial statements based on historical cost. In the case of inventories, cost of goods sold should be measured on a **current cost** basis, using costs that were current at the date of sale (section 4510.38), as distinct from the date on which the inventory was acquired. The balance sheet inventory valuation should also be measured on a current cost basis, using current costs at the balance sheet date (section 4510.42).

The use of current costs in record-keeping, or the incorporation of current costs into the body of financial statements, is not included among the *CICA Handbook* recommendations. Availability of current cost supplementary information is seen as adequate for the financial statement reader to assess the impact of changing prices on the entity's need to set aside funds for inventory replacement and thereby maintain its level of **operating capability**. The objective of the current cost model is the maintenance of operating capability; this capability at the end of the accounting period must be the same as at the beginning of the period before income was earned.

Operating capability
The ability to operate at the same level at year-end as existed at the beginning of the year.

Impact on the Income Statement

The cost flow analysis made for management at Bluebeard Computer Corporation is further developed to consider the impact of current costs. Following the recommendation in the *CICA Handbook*, the current cost to replace each of the 4 units at the time of each sale was used; the total current cost of these 4 units amounted to $18. With this additional datum, income measurement using the FIFO and LIFO cost flow assumptions was compared with that resulting when current costs were used. BCC's executives are astounded with the results.

	Measurement of Income		
	FIFO Cost Flow	*LIFO Cost Flow*	*Current Cost Model*
Sales	$20	$20	$20
Cost of Goods Sold:			
Purchases	$15	$15	
Ending Inventory	5	1	
Total Cost of Goods Sold	10	14	18
Gross Profit	$10	$ 6	$ 2
Operating expenses	6	6	6
Net Income (Loss)	$ 4	$-0-	$(4)

This further analysis indicates that using FIFO not only produces a phantom profit of $4 but also that the current cost calculation indicates BCC would be losing its ability to operate at the same level in the future; that is, its operating capability would be reduced. Eventually, it might even be unable to replace inventory without increased borrowing. Even worse, the $4 net income under FIFO might be considered by shareholders to be available for the payment of dividends. Employees might also feel justified in asking for increased remuneration and bonuses, while government would, regardless, continue to collect income taxes on these phantom profits.

It is true that the LIFO cost flow assumption produces a more realistic measurement of income than FIFO. However, only the current cost model indicates that BCC is losing its operating capacity and might be unable to replace inventory without increased borrowing.

Impact on the Balance Sheet

The impact of balance sheet inventory valuation for Bluebeard was also calculated. Following the recommendation in the *CICA Handbook,* the current cost to replace ending inventory at the balance sheet date was calculated; the current cost of the 1 unit in ending inventory at the balance sheet date was $7. With this additional datum, a comparison of balance sheet inventory valuation yielded the following:

	FIFO Cost Flow	*LIFO Cost Flow*	*Current Cost Model*
Ending Inventory	$5	$1	$7

The management at BCC are aware that the LIFO cost flow assumption generally produces an unrealistic ending inventory amount when prices are rising. They are surprised that FIFO, which is generally supposed to approximate replacement cost, could still be so short of the mark in their case. The current cost model calculation of ending inventory reinforces further the fact that BCC will lose its operating capability if it continues to operate at the same level in the future.

Income Measurement and Asset Valuation

The choice between a cost flow assumption and the use of current cost involves the continuing controversy between the importance of income measurement and of asset valuation. If prices were stable, this controversy would not exist: each cost flow assumption and the current cost model would produce approximately the same result. A problem arises, however, because prices fluctuate.

Income Measurement

When prices are rising, FIFO can result in a distorted net income figure because earliest — usually lower — costs are matched with current — usually higher — sales prices. LIFO, on the other hand, results in a more accurate net income calculation because more current — and usually higher — costs are matched with these same current — and usually higher — sales prices.

The use of current costs at the date of sale, as is recommended in the *CICA Handbook,* would appear to satisfy best the *CICA Handbook* recommendation that "the method selected for determining cost should be one which results in the fairest matching of costs against revenues regardless of whether or not the method corresponds to the physical flow of goods" (section 3030.09). On the surface, it would appear that no fairer matching than current cost with current revenue would be possible.

Asset Valuation

When prices are rising, FIFO results in a more current — and usually higher — balance sheet inventory figure, while LIFO can result in a less current — usually lower — balance sheet amount, because the earliest cost may not even approximate current replacement value.

Again, the use of current cost at the balance sheet date in this case — to value ending inventory, as is recommended in the *CICA Handbook* — results in the most current balance sheet inventory cost amount. In this way, problems associated with cost flow assumptions are avoided.

The Matching Concept in Perspective

As explained earlier, the emphasis of the current cost model is its concern with the maintenance of the entity's operating capability, which should be the same at the end of an accounting period as it was at the beginning.

A dilemma for the accounting profession centres on the historical cost concept. It is retained for financial statement purposes because historical costs are objectively determined — even though the measure used, the stable dollar concept, is invalid in periods of rapid inflation. Although current cost data are more relevant, the objection to their incorporation into the body of financial statements is that their determination of current costs is generally a subjective process, based in some cases on management's estimates and assumptions. One wonders if the choice is in reality between being approximately right or precisely wrong.

Although current cost data are more relevant, their use in record-keeping, as well as their incorporation into financial statements, is not included among the *CICA Handbook* recommendations. As noted, the availability of current cost supplementary information is assumed to be adequate for the financial statements reader. A review of published supplementary information leads one to question the validity of this assumption.

A Word of Caution

In addition to the recommendations for the measurement of cost of goods sold and ending inventory using current costs, there are also certain other effects associated with changing prices. These relate to the impact of financing or other adjustments that may alleviate, at least in part, the loss of operating capability during the year.

A more complete treatment of these topics is usually the subject matter of advanced accounting courses and is not attempted here. Caution must also be exercised in generalizing to other situations the impact of price changes on Bluebeard Computer Corporation. Different circumstances can be expected to yield different results.

The current cost model is in an experimental state at the present time and is under constant evaluation. No general concensus has yet emerged concerning the usefulness of the information generated; it is expected, however, to provide useful insights into the operations of each entity using the model.

ASSIGNMENT MATERIALS

Discussion Questions

1. Explain the importance of maintaining inventory levels for (a) management, (b) accountants, (c) investors, and creditors.
2. What is meant by the laid-down cost of inventory?
3. How does a flow of goods differ from a flow of costs? Do generally accepted accounting principles require that the flow of costs be similar to the movement of goods? Explain.
4. What factors are considered in costing inventory? Which of these factors is most difficult to determine? Why?
5. Under the LIFO cost flow assumption, do ending inventories consist of the earliest or most recent costs? Does the cost of goods sold include the earliest or most recent costs?
6. In recent years, the cost of goods has been increasing because of inflation. What problems for financial reporting have resulted?
7. In a period of rising prices, which method of inventory valuation will result in the highest net income figure? the highest ending inventory amount?
8. Assume that you are paid a year-end bonus according to the amount of net income earned during the year. When prices are rising, would you prefer to value inventories on a FIFO or a LIFO basis? Explain, using an example to support your answer. Would your choice be the same if prices were falling?
9. Why is consistency in inventory valuation necessary? Does the application of the consistency principle preclude a change from LIFO to FIFO? Explain.
10. The ending inventory of CBCA Inc. is overstated by $5,000 at December 31, 19X4. What is the effect on 19X4 net income? What is the effect on 19X5 net income assuming that no other inventory errors have occurred during 19X5?
11. How does the use of current costs eliminate the need for any cost flow assumption?
12. What is the primary reason for the use of the LOCAM method of inventory valuation? What does the term *market* mean? What is recommended in the *CICA Handbook* regarding use of this term?
13. When inventory is valued at LOCAM, what does *cost* refer to?
14. What is the generally accepted method used for inventory valuation?
15. When can inventory be valued at less than cost?
16. When should ending inventory be shown at cost, even though cost is higher than replacement cost?
17. What are the objections to LOCAM? Evaluate these objections.
18. LOCAM assumes that retail prices will decline when inventory cost declines. Is this realistic? Why or why not?
19. A book inventory is required under the perpetual inventory system. What is the difference between a book inventory and a physical inventory?
20. What internal control feature of the perpetual inventory method is lost under the periodic inventory method? Would you recommend that a hardware store use the perpetual inventory method? Why or why not?
21. What procedure do the periodic and perpetual inventory systems both have in common?
22. Discuss the methods available to cost inventory under each of the periodic and perpetual inventory systems.
23. Why is estimating inventory useful?
24. Contrast the journal entries required under the periodic and perpetual inventory systems.
25. Do the gross profit and retail inventory methods use inventory quantities to calculate the dollar amount of inventory?
26. How does the calculation of ending inventory differ in the gross profit method and the retail inventory method? Use an example to illustrate.
27. When is the use of the gross profit method particularly useful?
28. Does the retail inventory method assume any particular movement of inventory? What cost flow is calculated under this method?

Discussion Cases

Discussion Case 5-1:   Surprise!

Read Real Life Example 5-1 on page 239, and discuss the following questions.

For Discussion

1. Is Battery & Tire Warehouse using a periodic or perpetual inventory system? How can you tell?
2. Comment on the comparison of a physical inventory with a book inventory.
3. How can understating costs "show up on the books as more dollars of inventory than you actually have"?
4. Explain how ending inventory errors in 19X1 affect 19X1 and 19X2 income. What is the effect if there are also other errors in the ending inventory of 19X2?
5. How could an increase in vendors' prices make the inventory of Battery & Tire Warehouse worth $56,000 more? Which inventory cost method is the entity using? Explain, using an example.
6. What is the meaning of the following comment: "So we set up windfall gains as separate accounts and formally recognize shrinkage on its own"?
7. The author writes, "A similarly useless game played by some managers is to build into their systems automatic gains under the guise of conservatism"? What does he mean?
8. Could the situation described in Real Life Example 5-1 lead management in other entities to make bad decisions? Explain.

Discussion Case 5-2:   Postech's Squirrel

Don Gray learned the hard way that for a restaurant to be successful it must be well managed, which means tight inventory controls and minimal waste.

In 1983 he ran his Vancouver eatery into the ground after barely 18 months but now he's back in a business he knows a little better, running one of the handful of computer companies that cater to the restaurant industry.

"I had a successful computer company (before the restaurant), and I thought I could run anything," Mr. Gray said in an interview in the Toronto offices of Postech Corp., which makes the Squirrel point-of-sale system for restaurants.

Postech's Squirrel is a touch-screen computer that simultaneously sends food orders to the kitchen, drink orders to the bar and guest cheques to a printer. As well, it stores inventory data for transfer to accounting and tracks employee productivity.

"I had to learn the hard way, but as a result I learned a lot about controls and where the money can leak out the back door in a restaurant."

The primary margin-killer, restaurant owners say, is waste.

"Nobody's doing anything overtly wrong," Mr. Gray said. "It's not like there's theft, it's just mismanagement."

Everyone notices when their favorite restaurant raises its prices but few patrons — and few owners — are aware of the impact the increased cost of ingredients has on the profit margins of specific menu offerings.

Likewise, a generous kitchen staff doling over-size orders can wreak havoc on inventory control.

"Or you find your hot-selling item is the one you're making a small margin on while the items you make most of your money on don't sell very much, so your mix of product is wrong," Mr. Gray said.

Point-of-sale products such as Squirrel, or the Electronic Service Pad made by Remanco Systems Inc., have harnessed microchip technology to streamline restaurant order-taking, making waiters and waitresses more efficient by cutting the number of trips to the kitchen and bar in half, and ensuring that everything ordered is rung into the cash register.

The result is improved inventory control, better customer service and increased profit margins, said Sharon Horn of Remanco.

Source   Geoffrey Rowan, "Restaurants Keep Control with Computer Tracking", *The Globe and Mail*, Toronto, August 2, 1988, p. B-6.

For Discussion

1. List the inventory controls required in a restaurant. How can money "leak out the back door"?
2. How can a computer be used to increase efficiency? Describe the management features of a point-of-sale product such as the Squirrel.

Discussion Case 5-3:   Just-in-Time

Although just-in-time systems were once used exclusively by large manufacturers, a wide range of non-manufacturing companies are beginning to use such systems successfully to increase their competitiveness and extend their geographic reach. Just-in-time techniques applied to retailing and services offer benefits for small and large companies as dramatic as those they offer manufacturing.

The computer service industry is subject to intense competition. Smaller companies must find ways to market their parts and services over larger geographic areas and provide sufficient speed of delivery to increase their market share. To accomplish this R.T.K. Computer Services Inc. is using a just-in-time system for their national computer replacement parts business.

Rather than duplicate critical parts inventories in a dozen locations around the country in order to have them close to the consumers, the just-in-time approach used by R.T.K. was to position the parts inventory at the hub of a premium overnight transportation carrier. In this way, high-speed transportation can be used to send parts to customers wherever they are needed on a timed delivery or as-needed basis.

In practice, R.T.K. provides an innovative variation of the old replacement parts warehouse supply model. Customers register the specification of their microcomputers with the company and if there is a problem with their equipment that requires major repair, the piece is replaced rather than repaired. Using Airborne Express, R.T.K. ships a replacement component to the customer. This strategy has enabled R.T.K. to expand its reach without laying out the heavy investment needed to maintain separate warehouses around the country.

I have also observed just-in-time techniques working well with a number of small and large retailing companies. Merchandisers for years have recognized that one way to reduce costs is to delay delivery to the latest possible moment. The Kroger Company, a nationwide grocery, drug and convenience store chain, gives grades to its suppliers based upon the timing of delivery. If goods are sent in too soon, they increase the space needed to store inventory, slow the turnover and create the probability that the goods will have to be paid for before they are resold. Kroger's grading system allows the company to track accurately all their suppliers and know which are the most reliable and fastest.

Chain retailers typically have central distribution centers to supply their stores, but an increasing trend among merchants is to use just-in-time systems to bypass the distribution center for at least a portion of the merchandise. That portion is then shipped directly from manufacturers or distributors to the stores. Following such a strategy requires precise control of transportation, in order to delay delivery to the last minute. This allows new merchandise to be placed on the retailers' shelves, not stored in non-revenue-producing warehouse and storage areas.

Auto Shack Inc. provides an excellent example of how a medium-sized retail merchant can profitably use just-in-time techniques. Auto Shack operates 386 automobile parts stores in 15 states from Arizona to the Atlantic. The company's marketing and competitiveness plan emphasizes three goals: to offer merchandise at a discount price; to have top-level quality either through private branded merchandise or leading names in auto parts, and to provide service that will always save the sale by keeping the customer from going to a competitor. Yet a typical Auto Shack store cannot carry all 29,000 parts maintained throughout the system.

One separate division of Auto Shack known as Express Parts maintains a computerized warehouse in Memphis that holds all 29,000 parts and has direct telecommunications links to each retail store. If a customer stops at an Auto Shack store and cannot find the part wanted, the store management immediately contacts the Express Parts group in Memphis. Express Parts then looks at three just-in-time solutions.

The first is to see if another Auto Shack store that has the part in stock is reasonably close to the customer. If not, a second option is to ship the product from the Express Parts warehouse by overnight air transportation, with a promise that the part will be available the following day. A third option is to ship the part overnight directly from the vendor.

Using a national air delivery system, Auto Shack can offer this delivery service seven days a week, including holidays. Anything from an automobile engine to a set of spark plugs can be shipped immediately. From Auto Shack's perspective, the cost of air shipment is secondary. The prime goal is to save the sale. This service policy has been one of the prime factors behind the rapid growth of Auto Shack as a chain retailer of automobile parts.

Just in time cannot always be applied in the United States in the same way as in other countries because of its size. Unlike Japan, American retailers do not have all their branch stores within a few miles of a central distribution center, to facilitate a traditional just-in-time approach relying on inexpensive truck and van transportation. Instead, many just-in-time applications in the United States must use premium air transportation. The goal is to improve service — which is increasingly the most important element in any company's competitive strategy.

Source   Kenneth B. Ackerman, "Just-in-Time, Right for Retail". Copyright © 1988 by *The New York Times Company*. Reprinted by permission.

For Discussion

1. What exactly are just-in-time systems?
2. Is replacing a part less expensive than repairing it? Doesn't the cost of air freight offset any savings in inventory costs? How does just-in-time reduce the cost of inventory?
3. Evaluate the Kroger Company's system of giving grades to its suppliers based on the timing of delivery. How does this system fit into this chapter's discussion of inventory?

4. Do you agree that placing merchandise on retailers' shelves is preferable to using non-revenue-producing warehouse and storage areas? What if you run out of stock? What would be the impact of quantity discounts on this type of purchasing?

5. Which of the just-in-time solutions used by Express Parts is preferable to the customer? to Auto Shack? Explain.

Comprehension Problems

Comprehension Problem 5-1   (CGA adapted)

Listed below are four common accounting errors. Using the format shown, indicate the effect, if any, of each of the errors on the company's statements for the items shown. The company uses a periodic inventory method.

	19X2 Statements				19X3 Statements			
Errors:	*Open. Invent.*	*End. Invent.*	*19X2 Total Assets*	*19X2 Net Income*	*Open Invent.*	*End. Invent.*	*19X3 Total Assets*	*19X3 Net Income*
1. Goods bought in 19X2 were included in December 31 inventory, but purchases and liability were not recorded until early 19X3.	-0-							
2. Goods bought in 19X3 were included in December 31, 19X2 inventory, and purchases were recorded in 19X2.	-0-							
3. Goods were bought in 19X2 and purchases were recorded in that year; however, the goods were not included in the December 31 inventory as they should have been.	-0-							
4. Goods bought in 19X2 were excluded from December 31 inventory, and purchases were recorded early in 19X3.	-0-							

Required: Use a + (plus sign) to denote that an item is too high as a result of the error, a − (minus sign) to denote that it is too low, and a 0 (zero) to indicate no effect. The answer for the 19X2 opening inventory is indicated.

Note: Answer problems regarding the current cost model only if the Appendix was studied in your course.

Comprehension Problem 5-2

The records of Gaber Corporation show the following information for 19X4. Sales during the period were $276,000. Opening inventory amounted to $26,000 at cost and $80,000 at retail. Purchases were $200,000 at retail and $90,000 at cost. The company paid $4,000 for transportation in.

Required: Choose the best answer for each of the following:
1. Gross profit at retail was
   a. $157,720   c. -0-
   b. $153,720   d. None of the above.
2. The ending inventory at retail was
   a. -0-   c. $1,720
   b. $4,000   d. $9,333.
3. The cost percentage would be calculated as follows:
   a. $\dfrac{280,000}{120,000}$ b. $\dfrac{120,000}{280,000}$ c. $\dfrac{116,000}{280,000}$ d. $\dfrac{280,000}{116,000}$.
4. The ending inventory at cost was
   a. $1,720   c. $4,000
   b. $9,333   d. -0-.
5. The gross profit at cost was
   a. $157,720   c. $153,770
   b. -0-   d. None of the above.
6. The following are all characteristics of the retail method except
   a. Results in an average cost of ending inventory
   b. Assumes goods are sold in a particular order
   c. Is commonly used by department stores.

Comprehension Problem 5-3

The following transactions took place in AB Limited in 19X4.

Opening Inventory	2000 units @ $0.50
Purchases	1000 units @ $2.00
	500 units @ $1.00
	1000 units @ $2.50
Sales	2000 units

Required:
1. Ending inventory under LIFO/periodic would be:
   a. $3,000   c. $2,660
   b. $5,000   d. $2,000.
2. Ending inventory under FIFO/periodic would be:
   a. $3,333   c. $5,000
   b. $2,660   d. none of these.
3. Ending inventory under weighted average would be:
   a. $5,000   c. $3,000
   b. $3,333   d. none of these.
4. Cost of goods sold under LIFO/periodic would be:
   a. $2,660   c. $3,000
   b. $4,000   d. none of these.
5. Cost of goods sold under FIFO/periodic would be:
   a. $4,000   c. $2,660
   b. $1,000   d. none of these.
6. Cost of goods sold under weighted average would be:
   a. $2,667   c. $3,100
   b. $1,000   d. none of these.

Comprehension Problem 5-4

Lemon Inc. sells golf balls. The following data are available regarding transactions relating to Brand X during the month of January:

	(a)	(b)	(c)	(d)	(e)	(f)	(g)	(h)	(i)
Jan. 1 bal.							100	(j)	100
7 (k)	20	1.10	(l)				100	1.00	
							20	1.10	(n)
14 Purchase	200	(m)	300				100		
							20		
							200	(o)	422
19 Sale				100					
22 Purchase	(p)	1.00	120						
23 (q)				220					
29 Sale				10					

Required:

1. Complete the schedule.
2. If Dunn were to use a LIFO/perpetual inventory system, what would the ending inventory amount to?
   a. $113.10   c. $135.50
   b. $111.00   d. $110.00
3. If a FIFO/perpetual inventory system were used, what would be the value of the ending inventory?
   a. $110.00   c. $133.10
   b. $111.10   d. $135.50
4. If a weighted average system of inventory were used, what would be the cost of Brand X golf balls available for sale at the end of January?
   a. $110.00   c. $133.10
   b. $111.00   d. $135.50
5. Which method would yield an inventory of $133.10?
   a. LIFO/perpetual   c. Weighted average
   b. FIFO/perpetual   d. Moving average
6. Under which of the following methods is the ending inventory lowest?
   a. LIFO/perpetual   c. Moving average
   b. FIFO/perpetual   d. Weighted average
7. If Dunn wishes to show the highest net income, which method of inventory evaluation should it choose?
   a. LIFO/perpetual   c. Weighted average
   b. FIFO/perpetual   d. Moving average
8. Under which method would the cost of goods sold be lowest?
   a. Weighted average   c. LIFO/perpetual
   b. FIFO/perpetual

Comprehension Problem 5-5

The following transactions took place during January 19X7 in Lappe Inc.; the company sold 200 units during this month.

	Units	Unit Cost
Opening Inventory	100	$1
Purchase #1	10	1
Purchase #2	20	2
Purchase #3	30	3
Purchase #4	40	4
Purchase #5	50	5

Required: Calculate the cost of goods on hand, cost of goods sold, and ending inventory by completing the schedule for each of

1. FIFO/periodic   2. LIFO/periodic.

	Goods on Hand			–	Goods Sold			=	Ending Inventory		
	Units	Unit Cost	Total Cost		Units	Unit Cost	Total Cost		Units	Unit Cost	Total Cost
Inventory (Jan. 1)	100	× $1	= $100		100	100					
Purchase #1	10 × $1		= $10		10	10	400				
Purchase #2	20 × $2		= $40		20	40					
Purchase #3	30 × $3		= $90		30	90					
Purchase #4	40 × $4		= $160		40	160			50	250	250
Purchase #5	50 × $5		= $250								

Comprehension Problem 5-6

Required: Choose the method of inventory valuation that corresponds to each of the statements that follow:

1. FIFO   2. LIFO   3. Weighted Average.

_____ Matches actual flows of goods with actual flow of costs in most cases
_____ Matches new costs with new sales prices
_____ Matches old costs with new sales prices
_____ Results in phantom profits in a period of rising prices
_____ Results in the lowest net income in periods of falling prices
_____ Best matches current costs with current revenues
_____ Does not assume any particular flow of goods
_____ Results in the same inventory valuation, regardless of whether a periodic or perpetual inventory system is used
_____ Best suited for situations in which inventory consists of perishable goods
_____ Not accepted for income tax purposes in Canada
_____ Emphasizes income determination
_____ Emphasizes balance sheet valuation
_____ Values inventory at approximate replacement cost
_____ Results in lower income in a period of deflation
_____ Results in higher income in a period of deflation

Comprehension Problem 5-7

Partial income statements of Rosedale Products Inc. are reproduced below:

	19X7		19X8		19X9	
Sales		$30,000		$40,000		$50,000
Cost of Goods Sold:						
Opening Inventory	-0-		$ 5,000		$12,000	
Purchases	25,000		30,000		28,000	
Cost of Goods Available	$25,000		$35,000		$40,000	
Ending Inventory	5,000		12,000		15,000	
Total Cost of Goods Sold		$20,000		$24,000		$25,000
Gross Profit		$10,000		$16,000		$25,000

Required:
1. Calculate the impact of the two errors listed below on the gross profit calculated for the three years:
   a. The 19X7 ending inventory was understated by $2,000.
   b. The 19X9 ending inventory was overstated by $5,000.
2. What is the impact of these errors on total assets as listed on the balance sheet?

Comprehension Problem 5-8

The following information is taken from the records of Westmount Distributors Inc. The company uses the periodic inventory system.

		Quantity	Unit Cost
May 1	Opening Inventory	100	$1
6	Purchase #1	200	1
12	Purchase #2	125	2
19	Purchase #3	350	2
29	Purchase #4	150	3

On May 31, 200 units remain unsold.

Required:
1. Calculate the cost of ending inventory under each of the following costing methods:
   a. FIFO　　b. LIFO　　c. Weighted average.
2. Which costing method would you choose in the circumstances?
3. Complete the following partial income statements using FIFO and LIFO costing methods.

	FIFO		LIFO	
Sales		$1,500		$1,500
Cost of Goods Sold:				
Opening Inventory	$100		$100	
Purchases	1,600		1,600	
Cost of Goods Available	$1,700		$1,700	
Ending Inventory	550		200	
Total Cost of Goods Sold		1,150		1,500
Gross Profit		$350		$0

4. Compare the usefulness of FIFO and LIFO costing during a period of rising prices.
5. Calculate the amount of phantom profits, if any. Are these profits really phantom?
6. What is the preferable costing method in terms of balance sheet valuation? Why?

Comprehension Problem 5-9

Rosedale Products Ltd. have the following items in inventory at year-end:

Item	Quantity	(FIFO) Cost	Market
X	2	$50	$60
Y	3	150	75
Z	4	25	20

Required: Calculate the cost of ending inventory using LOCAM on
1. A unit-by-unit basis
2. A group inventory basis.

Comprehension Problem 5-10

All City Insurance Ltd. has received a fire-loss claim of $45,000 from Bell-Bec Corp. A fire destroyed Bell-Bec's inventory on May 25, 19X1. Bell-Bec has an average gross profit of 33⅓ percent. You have obtained the following information:

Inventory, May 1, 19X1	$ 80,000
Purchases, May 1-May 25	150,000
Sales, May 1-May 25	300,000

Required:
1. Calculate the estimated amount of inventory lost in the fire.
2. How reasonable is Bell-Bec's claim?

Comprehension Problem 5-11

Mid-Island Corp. is in the process of preparing its financial statements as at May 31, 19X3. As its accountant, you are asked to estimate the ending inventory at May 31. You have obtained the following information:

	Cost	Retail
Opening Inventory	$10,000	$ 20,000
Net Purchases	90,000	180,000
Sales		150,000

Required: Estimate the amount of inventory at May 31.

Comprehension Problem 5-12

Elmhurst Novelties Inc. had the following transactions:

July 6 Elmhurst Novelties purchased from Western Warehouse 200 cases of novelties at $25 per case on account for terms 2/15, net 30.

9 Elmhurst Novelties sold cases of novelties to Lachine Wharf Corp. for $50 per case on account for terms 2/10, net 30.

13 Lachine Wharf Corp. returned 10 cases of defective novelties; Elmhurst Novelties issued a credit note.

15 Elmhurst Novelties returned 10 cases of defective novelties to Western Warehouse and received a credit memo.

16 Elmhurst Novelties paid in full the amount owing to Western Warehouse (less return, less discount).

Required: Prepare journal entries to record the above transactions in the records of Elmhurst, assuming:
1. Elmhurst uses the periodic inventory system
2. Elmhurst uses the perpetual inventory system.

Comprehension Problem 5-13

On March 15, 19X3, Quick Sales Co. purchased $5,000-worth of merchandise for cash.

Required: Assuming that Quick Sales uses the periodic inventory system, calculate the cost of goods sold in each of the following circumstances:
1. Opening inventory, -0-; ending inventory, $2,000
2. Opening inventory, $3,000; ending inventory, $4,000
3. Opening inventory, $1,000; ending inventory, $1,500
4. Opening inventory, $2,000; ending inventory, -0-.

Problems

Problem 5-1

The following purchases were made during 19X8 at Xie Corporation. The opening inventory consisted of 50 units at $1 each.

		Units	Unit Cost
Apr.	15	200	$2
May.	25	200	$3
Jun.	7	200	$4
Oct.	15	200	$5

Required:
1. Calculate the number of units for opening inventory, purchases, and goods available for sale. Also calculate cost of goods available for sale at December 31, 19X8, under each of FIFO/periodic, LIFO/periodic, and weighted average flows of goods.
2. If there are 200 units on hand at December 31, 19X8, calculate the cost of this inventory under each of FIFO/periodic, LIFO/periodic, and weighted average flows of goods.
3. Calculate the number of units for goods available for sale, ending inventory, and goods sold. Calculate also the cost of goods sold under each of FIFO/periodic, LIFO/periodic, and weighted average flows of goods.
4. The president of Xie Corporation has asked you to consider the implications of using a weighted average cost flow method when in fact a LIFO flow of goods exists in the company. He is concerned that reported income does not reflect the real income of the firm. Prepare some calculations comparing the effect on income of
   a. Using a weighted average cost flow method when there is LIFO flow of goods
   b. Using a FIFO cost flow method when there is a LIFO flow of goods
   c. Using a LIFO cost flow method when there is a LIFO flow of goods.
   What method of cost flow would you recommend in this case? Why?

Problem 5-2

The following data are taken from the records of Vezina Inc. for the month of January 19X8.

	Purchases			Sales	
	Units	*Unit Cost*		*Units*	*Unit Price*
Opening Inventory	25	$5			
Purchase #1	15	4	Sale #1	30	$6
Purchase #2	10	3	Sale #2	20	4
Purchase #3	35	2	Sale #3	50	2
Purchase #4	40	1			

Required:
1. Calculate the amount of inventory at the end of January assuming that inventory is costed using FIFO/periodic.
2. How would the ending inventory differ if it was costed using LIFO/periodic?
3. Calculate the amount of gross profit under each of the above costing methods. Which method matches inventory costs more closely with revenues? Why?
4. Assume that the LIFO costing method was permitted in Canada for income tax purposes and that the income tax was calculated at 50 percent of net income. Would more income tax be payable under the FIFO or LIFO method? Explain why.

Problem 5-3

SR Corporation sells three products. The inventory valuation of these products is shown below for years 19X3 and 19X4.

	19X3			19X4		
	Cost	*Market*	*Unit Basis (LOCAM)*	*Cost*	*Market*	*Unit Basis (LOCAM)*
Product X	$14,000	$15,000	?	$15,000	$16,000	?
Product Y	12,500	12,000	?	12,000	11,500	?
Product Z	11,000	11,500	?	10,500	10,000	?
Total	?	?	?	?	?	?

The partial comparative income statements for the two years follow:

	19X3		19X4	
Sales		$240,000		$280,000
Cost of Goods Sold:				
Opening Inventory	$ 20,000		$?	
Purchases	240,000		260,000	
Cost of Goods Available	$?		$?	
Ending Inventory	?		?	
Total Cost of Goods Sold		?		?
Gross Profit		$?		$?

Required:
1. If SR values its inventory using LOCAM/unit basis, complete the 19X3 and 19X4 cost, market, and LOCAM calculations and the partial income statements for 19X3 and 19X4.
2. Complete the partial income statements, assuming SR uses LOCAM/group basis to value its inventory.
3. Complete the partial income statements, as if the inventory were valued at cost.

4. Which two methods of inventory valuation would yield the same gross profit for 19X3 and 19X4?
   a. Cost and LOCAM/unit basis
   b. Cost and LOCAM/group basis
   c. Cost basis.
5. Which two methods yield the maximum reported profit?

Problem 5-4

The Northern Company Limited made the following purchases during the year:

Jan. 7	8000 units @ $12.00 = $ 96,000	Jul. 04	16000 units @ $12.60 = $201,600
Mar. 30	9000 units @ $12.40 = $111,600	Sep. 02	6000 units @ $12.80 = $ 76,800
May 10	12000 units @ $12.00 = $144,000	Dec. 14	7000 units @ $12.70 = $ 88,900.

Closing inventory at December 31 amounted to 15 000 units. Selling price during the year was stable at $16 per unit. Opening inventory at January 1 amounted to 4000 units at $11.90 per unit.

Required:
1. Prepare a schedule of inventory as at December 31, under both a FIFO/periodic and LIFO/periodic system.
2. Prepare an income statement showing sales, cost of goods sold, and gross profit on both a FIFO and LIFO basis, using the above data.
3. Which method of inventory valuation matches revenues more closely with costs in this company under current conditions? Why?
4. The company is concerned about the continually increasing cost of its purchases. In January of the next year the cost price of each unit was $13. You are asked to explain the concept of phantom profits to the president. What will you say?

Problem 5-5

The comptroller of Cambridge Products Ltd. has asked your help in forecasting the effect of rising and falling prices on income when FIFO and LIFO costing are used. The following inventory data are made available:

Opening Inventory	100 units at $10 = $1,000
Purchases	500 units at $12 = $6,000
Ending Inventory	250 units.

Partially completed income statements are presented:

	Rising Prices		Falling Prices	
	FIFO	LIFO	FIFO	LIFO
Sales	$5,000	$5,000	$5,000	$5,000
Cost of Goods Sold:				
Opening Inventory	$1,000	$?3000	$?	$?
Purchases	6,000		?	?
Cost of Goods Available	$7,000	$?	$?	$?
Ending Inventory	3,000	?	?	?
Total Cost of Goods Sold		4,000	?	?	?
Gross Profit	$1,000	$?	$?	$?

The statement for FIFO rising prices has been completed. The ending inventory is calculated as follows for FIFO — 250 units at $12 = $3,000.

Required:
1. Complete the statement for LIFO rising prices using the data provided. (Note that you have to recalculate the ending inventory cost.)
2. Complete the statement for FIFO falling prices by assuming that purchases were made at $8 per unit. (Note that this changes cost of purchases and ending inventory cost.)
3. Complete the statement for LIFO falling prices by assuming that purchases were made at $8 per unit. (Note that this changes cost of purchases and ending inventory cost.)
4. Assume that LIFO costing was permitted in Canada for income tax purposes and that income tax was 50 percent of income. Which costing method would be most advantageous from the company's point of view when prices are rising? when prices are falling?

Problem 5-6

Weintrop Products Corp. sells gadgets. During the month of January 19X3, the number of gadgets purchased and sold is shown below:

			Purchases			Sales			Balance		
			Units	Unit Cost	Total Cost	Units	Unit Cost	Total Cost	Units	Unit Cost	Total Cost
Jan.	1	Balance	100	$1							
	3	Purchase	100	1							
	8	Purchase	200	2							
	10	Sale				200	$3				
	15	Purchase	300	3							
	20	Sale				500	5				
	27	Purchase	400	1							

Required:
1. Calculate the cost of the month-end inventory under each of the following costing assumptions:
   a. FIFO/perpetual   b. LIFO/perpetual   c. Moving average.
2. Prepare the journal entries required under the perpetual inventory method for the LIFO costing method.
3. Prepare the journal entries required under the periodic inventory method for the LIFO costing method.
4. Why are different journal entries prepared under each method?

Problem 5-7

The Kamloops Retail Company Ltd. has consistently averaged 39 percent gross profit. The company's inventories, which are on a periodic basis, were recently destroyed by fire. The following data are available:

Sales	$305
Purchases	175
Opening Inventory	25
Sales Returns	5
Purchases Returns	5
Delivery Expense	8
Transportation In	3
Repairs to Delivery Truck	3
Selling Commissions	6
Administrative Expense	3

Required:
1. Calculate the estimated ending inventory.
2. Prepare journal entries (with explanation lines) to record
   a. The destruction of the inventory by fire
   b. The recovery of $30 from the insurance company.
3. Why did the insurance recovery exceed the inventory cost?

 # Problem 5-8

The president of Royer Corporation is concerned that the year-end inventory amounting to $5,000 at cost is less than expected. Although a physical count was made and the costing was accurately calculated using FIFO, the president asks you to estimate the year-end inventory using the following data:

	At Retail	At Cost
Sales for the Year	$160,000	
Sales Returns	10,000	
Purchases for the Year	164,000	$80,000
Purchases Returns	4,000	2,000
Transportation In		1,000
Opening Inventory	20,000	11,000

Required:
1. Calculate the estimated ending inventory at retail.
2. Calculate the cost percentage (ratio of cost to retail).
3. Calculate the estimated ending inventory at cost.
4. Calculate the amount of inventory lost during the year.
5. Assuming that the current replacement cost of the inventory is covered by insurance, calculate the amount paid by the insurer if
   a. The current replacement cost is 25 percent greater than the inventory FIFO cost,
   b. The insurer pays 80 percent of the current replacement cost.
6. Prepare the journal entry to record the amount recovered from the insurer.

Problem 5-9

Ajax Corporation uses LIFO in costing the inventory. During the first three years of operation, the year-end inventory, computed by different methods for comparative purposes, was as follows:

	Closing Inventory		
	19X4	19X5	19X6
LIFO	$360	$400	$320
FIFO	300	320	280
Weighted Average Cost	340	420	300

Required: Calculate net income under each method, showing calculations. Results under LIFO method are

	Net Income		
	19X4	19X5	19X6
LIFO	$80	$140	$60
FIFO			
Weighted Average Cost			

Problem 5-10

The year-end inventory of Vernon Inc. consisted of the following groups of items, priced at cost and at market:

Item	Cost	Market
A	$60	$63
B	40	40
C	80	78
D	50	42

Required: What inventory amount should be used in the financial statements? Why?

Alternate Problems

Alternate Problem 5-1

The following transactions took place during January 19X6 at Sanda Corp. The opening inventory consisted of 100 units at a total sales price of $100.

			Units	Total Cost
Jan.	5	Purchase #1	100	$ 100
	9	Purchase #2	200	400
	16	Purchase #3	300	900
	26	Purchase #4	400	1,600

Units sold during the month were as follows:

			Units	Total Sales Price
Jan.	10	Sale #1	200	$ 600
	17	Sale #2	500	1,500

Required:
1. Calculate the cost of ending inventory and the cost of goods sold under each of
   a. FIFO/periodic
   b. LIFO/periodic
   c. Weighted average
   d. Specific identification (assume that the 700 units sold were identified as being made from the 100 units in opening inventory, the 200 units purchased on January 9, and the 400 units purchased January 26).
2. The accountant of Kelly Corp. is concerned that the LIFO cost flow method used by the company does not represent the FIFO flow of goods that exists in this company. What are the implications of mismatching cost flow and the flow of goods? Make some calculations to support your answer.

Alternate Problem 5-2

The Seok Company Ltd. is considering the use of different methods of calculating its ending inventory. The following data are applicable to its December operations:

	Purchases			Sales	
Dec.	4	1000 units @ $2.50	Dec.	5	600 units
	11	800 units @ $2.60		12	500 units
	23	1600 units @ $2.30		17	500 units
	29	900 units @ $2.40		27	400 units
				31	600 units

Required:
1. Calculate the amount of ending inventory under each of
   a. FIFO/periodic   b. LIFO/periodic   c. Weighted average /periodic.
2. Which method presents the most appropriate balance sheet valuation of inventory? Explain, using appropriate amounts to support your answer.
3. Which method results in the most realistic income statement? Why?

Alternate Problem 5-3

Carchrae Corporation began operating on January 2, 19X1. The following table shows the valuation of its inventory, using four different inventory valuation methods:

	LIFO	FIFO	Market	LOCAM
Dec. 31, 19X1	$ 9,200	$10,000	$ 9,600	$ 8,900
Dec. 31, 19X2	9,100	9,000	8,800	8,500
Dec. 31, 19X3	10,300	11,000	12,000	10,900

Required:
1. Which inventory method shows the highest net income for 19X1?
   a. LIFO   c. Market
   b. FIFO   d. LOCAM
2. Which inventory method shows the highest net income for 19X2?
   a. LIFO   c. Market
   b. FIFO   d. LOCAM
3. For 19X3, how much higher or lower would net income be if FIFO valuation were used instead of LOCAM?
   a. $100 lower   e. $1,000 higher
   b. $100 higher   f. $1,000 lower
   c. $400 higher   g. $1,400 higher
   d. $400 lower   h $1,400 lower
4. Which inventory method shows the lowest net income for the three years combined?
   a. LIFO   c. Market
   b. FIFO   d. LOCAM
5. On the basis of the data in this problem, the movement of inventory prices was
   a. Up in 19X1 and down in 19X3
   b. Up in both 19X1 and 19X3
   c. Down in 19X1 and up in 19X3
   d. Down in both 19X1 and 19X3.

Alternate Problem 5-4

The Single Product Company Ltd. had the following inventory transactions for the month of December:

Nov. 30	Inventory of	20 units @ $4.60
Dec. 8	Purchased	80 units @ $5.00
15	Purchased	40 units @ $5.30
22	Purchased	60 units @ $5.60
31	Purchased	40 units @ $5.50

By December 31, 190 of the units had been sold by Single.

Required:
1. Calculate the cost of the ending inventory using each of
   a. FIFO/periodic   b. LIFO/periodic   c. Weighted average.
2. The prices of the company's purchases have been increasing during the month and the controller is concerned about the possible existence of phantom profits under the FIFO method of costing inventory. If the sales price of each unit was $7 during December, prepare calculations necessary to isolate the existence of phantom profits.

Alternate Problem 5-5

The following transactions took place in the month of May at Crown Corporation. The opening inventory consisted of 50 units at $10. On May 2, the company purchased 60 units at $12. On May 10, it sold 10 units. On May 22, it purchased an additional 100 units at $15. On May 24, 150 units were sold.

Required:
1. Calculate the cost of goods sold for each of LIFO/perpetual, FIFO/perpetual, and moving average inventory methods.
2. Calculate the cost of goods sold under each of LIFO/periodic, FIFO/periodic, and weighted average inventory methods.

Alternate Problem 5-6

Pan Products Inc. sells television sets. The following information relates to January 19X7 purchases and sales of Brand X 20-inch [50 cm] colour television sets:

| | | | Purchases | | | Sales | | | Balance | |
			Units	Unit Cost	Total Cost	Units	Unit Cost	Total Cost	Units	Unit Cost	Total Cost
Jan.	1	Balance							6	$400	
	2	Sale				1	$600				
	3	Purchase	2	450							
	7	Sale				2	700				
	10	Sale				1	650				
	15	Purchase	3	500							
	20	Sale				4	750				
	25	Purchase	1	500							
	29	Sale				1	800				

Required:
Calculate the cost of the month-end inventory under each of
   a. FIFO/perpetual   b. LIFO/perpetual   c. Moving average.

Alternate Problem 5-7

The Kenilworth Mall housed the premises of the Handy Hardware Company Ltd. On the morning of November 1, fire gutted the hardware store and some of the other tenant shops. Handy Hardware had been a popular location for homeowners and had, as a result, consistently earned a gross profit on net sales of 40 percent over the year. Appropriate data to date were as follows:

Sales	$1,220
Purchases	700
Purchases Returns	20
Sales Returns	16
Delivery Expense	30
Transportation In	12
Administrative Expense	8
Opening Inventory (Jan. 1)	100
Advertising Expense	20
Salaries	85
Sales Discounts	4

Required:
1. Calculate the estimated closing inventory.
2. Prepare the entries required to show the claim set up by Handy Hardware and the collection of a settlement in full of $60.
3. Did the insurance settlement exceed the inventory cost? Why?

Alternate Problem 5-8

College Men's Shop Corp. takes a year-end physical inventory at marked selling prices and reduces the total to a cost basis for year-end statement purposes. University also uses the retail method to estimate the amount of inventory that should be on hand at year-end. By comparison of the two totals, it is able to determine inventory shortages resulting from theft. The following information at the end of December is available:

	At Retail	At Cost
Sales	$234,680	
Sales Returns	3,740	
Opening Inventory	36,200	$ 24,420
Purchases	239,800	166,770
Purchases Returns	3,900	2,830
Inventory Count (Dec. 31)	40,900	

Required:
1. Use the retail method to estimate the year-end inventory at cost.
2. Use the retail method to reduce the shop's year-end physical inventory to a cost basis.
3. Prepare a schedule showing the inventory shortage at cost and at retail.

Alternate Problem 5-9

The beginning inventory, purchases, and sales of an item by St. Clair Corporation for the month of July were as follows:

July 1   Inventory on hand consisted of 100 units at $3.15 each
     12   Sold 50 units
     15   Purchased 40 units at $3.00 each
     17   Purchased 60 units at $2.70 each
     19   Sold 30 units
     26   Purchased 50 units at $3.45 each
     29   Sold 40 units.

Required: What was the value of the units on hand on July 31 under the following methods:
1. Perpetual inventory, moving average
2. Periodic inventory, weighted average.

Alternate Problem 5-10

The inventory of the Kaufman Upholstering Corp. on December 31 consisted of the following items:

		Unit	
	Quantity	Cost	Market
Frames			
Type F-1	110	$14.25	$15.50
Type F-12	75	26.00	22.50
Type F-15	60	21.50	21.00
Springs (sets)			
Type S-1	760	7.28	8.50
Type S-12	625	10.50	11.50
Type S-15	340	8.60	6.00

Required:
1. Calculate the ending inventory at the lower of cost and market, applied
   (a) to each item, (b) to each category, and (c) to the entire inventory.
2. What is the effect of each application of LOCAM on the gross profit in the current year? in the following year?

Supplementary Problems

Supplementary Problem 5-1

The following transactions took place during January 19X9 at Collins Inc. The opening inventory consisted of 100 units of Brand X at $10 per unit. The following purchases were made during the month:

		Units	Unit Cost
Jan.	3	200	$10
	11	400	9
	19	500	8
	24	600	7
	30	200	6

During the month, 1700 units were sold for $12 each.

Required:
1. Calculate the cost of ending inventory and cost of goods sold under each of FIFO/periodic, LIFO/periodic, and weighted average.
2. Calculate the gross profit under each of the above methods.
3. Under what circumstances will the cost of inventory under the LIFO assumption result in a lower net income than the FIFO assumption? in a higher net income than the FIFO assumption?

Supplementary Problem 5-2

The following partial income statements have been prepared for Cockburn Video Inc.:

	19X2		19X3		19X4	
Sales		$3,000		$7,000		$10,000
Cost of Goods Sold:						
Opening Inventory	$1,000		$ 4,000		$ 8,000	
Purchases	5,000		9,000		11,000	
Goods Available for Sale	$6,000		$13,000		$19,000	
Ending Inventory	4,000		8,000		12,000	
Total Cost of Goods Sold		2,000		5,000		7,000
Gross Profit		$1,000		$2,000		$ 3,000

Subsequent to the preparation of these income statements, two inventory errors were found: (a) the 19X2 ending inventory was overstated by $1,000 and (b) the 19X3 ending inventory was understated by $1,000.

Required:
1. Prepare corrected income statements for the three years, using the comparative format above.
2. What is your explanation for the difference in the 19X3 gross profit?
3. Is the balance of retained earnings at the end of 19X4 affected by the errors?

Supplementary Problem 5-3

Chesley Corporation prepares monthly financial statements; it made a physical inventory count in January and February but intends to use the gross profit method of estimating inventory in March and April. Partial income statements appear below:

	January		February		March		April	
Sales		$40,000		$60,000		$50,000		$75,000
Cost of Goods Sold:								
Opening Inventory	$?		$?		$?		$?	
Purchases	50,000		30,000		20,000		40,000	
Goods Available for Sale	$ 60,000		$ 70,000		$ 50,000		$ 60,000	
Ending Inventory	?		?		?		?	
Total Cost of Goods Sold		20,000		40,000		?		?
Gross Profit		$?		$?		$?		$?

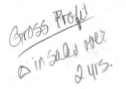

Required:

1. Calculate the gross profit percentage to be used in estimating March and April ending inventories.
2. Using the percentage calculated in question 1, complete the partial income statements for March and April.
3. A physical count was made at April 30 and the inventory was accurately costed at $10,000. The controller, sceptical of estimates, attributes the differences to the gross profit percentage used to estimate ending inventory. Under what circumstances would you agree? disagree?

Supplementary Problem 5-4

The following transactions took place during January 19X7 at Jeno Corp.

Jan.	1	Opening Inventory	200	$1
	10	Purchase #1	200	2
	15	Sale #1	200	
	20	Purchase #2	300	3
	25	Sale #2	400	
	30	Purchase #3	300	3

Required:

1. Calculate ending inventory and cost of goods sold under each of
   a. FIFO/perpetual   b. LIFO/perpetual.
2. Calculate the cost of the January 15 and 25 sales using the moving average assumption.
3. How much would the cost of the January 15 and 25 sales amount to under the weighted average assumption? Why does this cost differ from that calculated in question 2?
4. Which inventory cost assumption would you choose
   a. To reflect the probable flow of goods
   b. To report the lowest net income for the month?

Supplementary Problem 5-5

Part A

The accountant of Loyola Inc. is concerned about the inventory in its bookstore. A physical count at May 31, 19X8 showed that $10,000 inventory (at cost) was on hand. The following information for the year then ended is available.

	At Retail	At Cost
Sales for the Year	$62,500	
Sales Returns	2,500	
Opening Inventory	14,000	$10,000
Purchases for the Year	55,000	39,000
Purchases Returns	3,000	2,000
Transportation In		1,000

Required:
1. Calculate the estimated ending inventory at retail.
2. Calculate the cost percentage (ratio of cost to retail).
3. Calculate the May 31, 19X8 estimated ending inventory at cost.
4. Why is the inventory calculated in question 3 different from the physical count at May 31?

Part B

The comptroller of Sir George Corp. is calculating the amount of inventory lost during the year ended May 31, 19X8. A physical count was not made at May 31 due to circumstances beyond his control. The following information for the year then ended is available from the general ledger.

Sales for the Year	$50,000
Sales Returns	5,000
Opening Inventory	6,000
Purchases for the Year	35,000
Purchases Returns	3,000
Purchases Discounts	2,000
Transportation In	1,500
Delivery Expense	1,000
Depreciation Expense — Truck	400
Insurance Expense	100

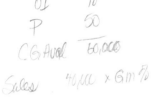

The following are partial income statements of Sir George Corp. for years 19X5 to 19X7 (amounts are in thousands of dollars):

	19X5	19X6	19X7	Totals
Sales	$20	$30	$40	$ 90
Cost of Goods Sold	10	20	30	60
Gross Profit	$10	$10	$10	$ 30

Required: Using the gross profit method, calculate the May 31, 19X8 estimated ending inventory at cost.

Supplementary Problem 5-6

The following data are taken from the records of the Pearson Promotions Ltd.:

Opening Inventory		Transportation In	$ 500
At retail	$ 7,000	Purchases Returns	
At cost	5,000	At retail	2,000
Purchases		At cost	1,500
At retail	25,000	Sales	22,000
At cost	16,000	Sales Returns	1,000

1. Calculate the estimated ending inventory at cost, using the retail inventory method.
   a. Calculate the ending inventory at retail.
   b. Calculate the cost percentage (ratio of cost to retail).
   c. Calculate the ending inventory at cost.
2. Calculate the ending inventory at cost, using the gross profit method. A gross profit rate of 35 percent is considered reasonable in the circumstances.
3. Explain why the ending inventory would be different under the two methods.

Decision Problems

Decision Problem 5-1

The records of the Redgrave Trading Corporation show the following data about item A. The balance on January 1 was 200 units at $10 per unit. The selling price was $15 per unit throughout the year.

| | | Purchases | |
| | | Purchase Price | Sales |
	Units	per Unit	Units
Jan. 12	100	$11	
Feb. 1			200
Apr. 16	200	$12	
May 1			100
Jul. 15	100	$14	
Nov. 10			100
Dec. 5	200	$17	
	600		400

Required:

1. Calculate the cost of the ending inventory under the FIFO method when a perpetual inventory system is followed.
2. Calculate the cost of the ending inventory under the LIFO method when perpetual inventory records are maintained. Prepare a perpetual inventory card.
3. The company has experienced a period of rapidly rising prices for its purchases during the year. If selling price has remained fairly constant during this period because of heavy competition in the marketplace, what effect will result from the use of FIFO, as compared to LIFO, on
   a. The income statement
   b. The balance sheet.
4. Assume that the sale of February 1 was on credit to customer B, that perpetual inventory records were maintained, and the LIFO method was used. Prepare the required journal entry or entries to record the sale and the cost of the goods sold February 1.

Decision Problem 5-2

The president's assistant of TSOE Limited asks you to come to a board of directors meeting to explain some accounting problems to the members of the board. The questions will be concerned with the problems of inventories. As the comptroller of the firm, you are fully aware that the corporation has used the lower of FIFO cost and market value in accounting for the inventory. At the board meeting, the following questions are raised. How would you answer them?

1. What is the objective of determining the cost of the inventory and cost of goods sold in accordance with the principles of the LIFO method?
2. Are there some accounting assumptions or conventions that are responsible for the development of this method?
3. What effect would the adoption of this method have on the financial statements?

Decision Problem 5-3

Consider the controversy that exists as to whether LIFO, FIFO, average, or some other cost is most appropriate in measuring income for a period and asset position at the end of a period.

Required:
1. Discuss the extent to which this controversy is (or is not) solved by switching to some form of current value accounting. For simplicity, assume the replacement cost version of current value.
2. Illustrate your analysis, using the following data. Use a perpetual inventory system to demonstrate that there is no arbitrary choice in measuring cost of goods sold and inventory position.

Inventory of Laser Class Sailboats

	In	*Out*	*Balance*
19X1			
Jan. 31	Bought 5 @ $1,000		5 @ $ ___
May 30	Bought 10 @ $1,200		15 @ $ ___
July	Sold	12 @ $ ___	3 @ $ ___
Nov. 30	Bought 2 @ $1,300		5 @ $ ___
19X2			
Jan. 31	Bought 4 @ $1,300		9 @ $ ___
May 30	Bought 10 @ $1,400		19 @ $ ___
July	Sold	15 @ $ ___	4 @ $ ___

Decision Problem 5-4

Iliuk Inc. reported net income (loss) for the years 19X7, 19X8, and 19X9 as follows:

19X7	$290.7 million
19X8	$ 88.7 million
19X9	$ (7.6) million

In the company's annual report for 19X9, the following statement appeared in a footnote:

Inventories are stated at lower of cost or market for the period January 1, 19X7, through December 31, 19X8. Last-in, first-out (LIFO) method of inventory valuation had been used for approximately 60 percent of consolidated inventory. Cost of the remaining 40 percent of inventories was determined using first-in, first-out (FIFO) or average-cost methods. Effective January 1, 19X9, FIFO method of inventory valuation has been adopted for inventories previously valued using LIFO method. This results in a more uniform valuation method throughout the corporation and makes financial statements with respect to inventory valuation comparable with those of the other manufacturers. As a result of adopting FIFO in 19X9, net loss reported is less than it would have been by approximately $20.0 million or $.40 a share. Inventory amounts at December 31, 19X9 are stated higher by $150 million than they would have been had LIFO been continued.

Required:
1. Why do you think Iliuk made the change in its inventory costing method in 19X8 and not previously?
2. Do you believe the market regarded this change as cosmetic or that the price of Iliuk's shares was affected?

Cash and Receivables

The collection of cash completes the sales and collection cycle. Management is responsible for the design of an effective system of internal control to safeguard the cash asset. Sales on account involve the extension of credit; the amount of uncollectible accounts must be estimated in order to match expenses with revenues.

1. How is the estimation of uncollectible accounts receivable part of the matching concept?
2. How are uncollectible accounts disclosed on financial statements?
3. What are the different methods used for calculating estimates for uncollectible accounts receivable?
4. How is an ageing of accounts receivable used in estimating uncollectible accounts?
5. How are credit balances in accounts receivable classified on the balance sheet?
6. How does the preparation of a bank reconciliation facilitate control over cash?
7. What is the imprest petty cash system and how is it used to control this fund?
8. What constitutes a good system of internal cash control?

Allowance for Doubtful Accts
Bad debt expence

A. Completion of the Sales and Collection Cycle — Accounts Receivable

This chapter completes the sales and collection cycle introduced in Chapter 4 and reviewed in Figure 6-1. In this cycle, the entity makes sales and records accounts receivable if the sale is made on account (for credit); the collection of cash completes the cycle. This section discusses issues related to accounts receivable and their collection.

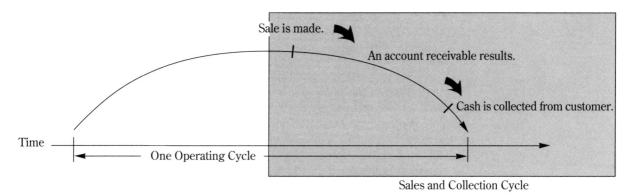

Figure 6-1   Sales and collection cycle

Uncollected Accounts Receivable

Unfortunately, not all receivables are collected; uncollected receivables result in the cycle being completed not with cash but with a bad debt. This section discusses the accounting treatment required when cash is not collected.

Uncollectible accounts result from the extension of credit to an entity's customers. The expectation of increased profits resulting from increased sales is a strong motivation to extend credit to customers. Also, competition may make the extension of credit a necessary business practice.

A risk inherent in the sales and collection cycle, therefore, includes the possibility that some accounts receivable will not be collected. The existence of a good internal control system is designed to minimize bad debt losses. One such control is to permit sales on account only to credit-worthy customers; however, at some point, the decision of who is credit-worthy involves a trade-off between increasing this entity's sales and profit or risking an increase in competitors' sales and potential profit. Even so, each entity realizes that a certain percentage of all credit sales will never be collected and some may be collected long after the sale was made.

Classification of Allowance for Doubtful Accounts

Accountants applying the matching concept to this cycle must match expenses of a particular time period to revenues of the same time period. The accrual method of accounting is used as the vehicle in making the matching of bad debt expense with

Allowance for Doubtful Accounts
A contra asset (valuation) account, showing the estimated amount of accounts receivable that may not be collected.

revenue. For this alignment, use is made of an **Allowance for Doubtful Accounts** account to estimate potential uncollectibles; this account is a contra account to Accounts Receivable and is disclosed on the balance sheet as follows:

Partial Balance Sheet
At December 31, 19X4

Current Assets:		
Cash		$ 5,000
Temporary Investments		10,000
Accounts Receivable	$25,000	
Less: Allowance for Doubtful Accounts	1,400	23,600
Inventory		50,000
Prepaid Expenses		3,450
Total Current Assets		$92,050

As can be seen in the preceding balance sheet, the contra Allowance for Doubtful Accounts account reduces Accounts Receivable to the amount that is expected to be collected. Because the estimated uncollectible amount is usually immaterial, it is not disclosed on the balance sheet; instead only the net amount collectible is shown. Where the estimated uncollectible amount is significant, this information can be disclosed in the statement or in a footnote attached to the financial statements.

Classification of Bad Debt Expense

Bad debt expense is usually classified in the income statement as a general and administrative expense since — for internal control purposes — the sales department should not authorize credit. This arrangement avoids a possible conflict between the approval of credit and the primary objective of a sales department, increasing the sales, particularly when sales bonuses are calculated on sales volume or remuneration includes a commission component. At year-end, the Bad Debt Expense account is closed to the Income Summary.

Estimating Uncollectible Accounts Receivable

An allowance account is used to match bad debt expense with revenue to assist management in estimating the amount of uncollectible accounts receivable. Once the estimate of uncollectible accounts is made, a journal entry is prepared with a debit to Bad Debt Expense and a credit to Allowance for Doubtful Accounts. Two different methods can be used to calculate the estimated amount; both follow the matching concept. One method focuses on the income statement, while the other focuses on the balance sheet.

Income Statement Method:	*Balance Sheet Method:*
This method assumes that a certain percentage of sales on account made during the accounting time period will result in bad debts. In order to match all expenses with sales revenue, an estimate of bad debts is made at the end of the accounting period on the basis of bad debts experienced in prior years (or expected this year) in relation to credit sales.	This method assumes that a certain amount of accounts receivable will never be collected. In order to establish the amount that is expected to be collected (often called the *realizable value of the receivables*), an estimated uncollectible amount is calculated using an ageing schedule. In this way, the net collectible amount can be reported on the balance sheet.
This estimated bad debt expense is calculated independent of any current balance in the Allowance for Doubtful Accounts account.	The estimated bad debt expense is the difference between the current allowance balance and the amount required at the end of the accounting period.

The Income Statement Method

Under this method, estimated bad debt expense is calculated by applying an estimated loss percentage to net sales for the accounting time period involved. The percentage used can be calculated using actual losses experienced in prior years:

Year	Net Sales	Accounts Written Off	Loss Percentage
19X1	$150,000		
19X2	200,000		
19X3	250,000		
	$600,000	$3,000	0.005 = 0.5%

The average loss over these years is ½ of 1%. If management anticipates that similar losses may be applicable to 19X4, the estimated bad debt expense is calculated as follows: 19X4 sales $300,000 × .005 = $1,500 estimated uncollectible accounts receivable. Under this income statement method, the $1,500 is recorded as the estimated uncollectible accounts receivable by the following entry:

Dec. 31	Bad Debt Expense	1,500	
	Allowance for Doubtful Acounts		1,500

When posted to the allowance account, the new account balance becomes $1,750.

The balance remaining in the account is $250.	The estimated balance of $1,500 is added to the existing balance.

Allowance for Doubtful Accounts		Allowance for Doubtful Accounts	
	Bal. 250		Bal. 250
			1,500
			1,750

Note that this method calculates the estimated uncollectible amount for the current year; it also matches bad debt expense with revenue. The emphasis of the income statement method is therefore on matching expenses with revenues; the remaining balance in the allowance account does not influence the amount of bad debt expense for the accounting period.

The Balance Sheet Method

Ageing of accounts receivable
The detailed analysis of trade accounts receivable, by time elapsed since the creation of the receivable.

The estimated bad debt expense can also be calculated by first ageing the accounts receivable. The **ageing of accounts receivable** is illustrated in the following schedule. In the schedule, each account is classified as either not yet due or past due. The number of days is indicated at the top of each column.

Analysis of Accounts Receivable by Age
December 31, 19X4

Customer	Total	Not Yet Due	1–30	31–60	61–90	Over 90
Bendix Inc.	$ 1,000					$1,000
Devco Marketing Inc.	6,000	$ 1,000	$3,000	$2,000		
Horngren Corp.	4,000	2,000	1,000	–	$1,000	
Perry Co. Ltd.	5,000	3,000	1,000	–	1,000	
Others	9,000	4,000	–	–	5,000	
Totals	$25,000	$10,000	$5,000	$2,000	$7,000	$1,000

Each account balance is listed and extended to the appropriate not-yet-due or past-due columns. An estimated loss percentage is then applied to each total, thereby calculating the estimated uncollectible amount as follows:

Calculation of Uncollectible Amount
December 31, 19X4

	Accounts Receivable	Estimated Loss Percentage	Uncollectible Amount
Not yet due	$10,000	1%	100
Past due:			
1–30 days	5,000	3%	150
31–60 days	2,000	5%	100
61–90 days	7,000	10%	700
Over 90 days	1,000	40%	400
Totals	$25,000		$1,450

The estimated loss percentage can be calculated on the basis of prior experience with past due accounts — they usually become less collectible the longer they remain uncollected. The above calculation indicates that $1,450 is estimated as uncollectible at December 31, 19X4.

Under the balance sheet method estimated bad debt expense consists of the difference between the current Allowance for Doubtful Accounts balance ($250) and the estimated uncollectible amount ($1,450) required at year-end.

The balance remaining in the account is $250.	The estimated uncollectible amount is $1,450.	An amount of $1,200 must be recorded to bring the account to $1,450.

Allowance for Doubtful Accounts		Allowance for Doubtful Accounts		Allowance for Doubtful Accounts	
	Bal. 250		Bal. 250		Bal. 250
			___		1,200
			1,450		1,450

> Under the balance sheet method, therefore, the calculation of the bad debts expense amount of $1,200 in this case is dependent on whatever balance remains at the end of the accounting time period.

The amount is recorded by the following journal entry:

Dec. 31	Bad Debt Expense	1,200	
	Allowance for Doubtful Accounts		1,200

This entry records the amount required to bring the balance in the allowance account to the $1,450 estimated uncollectible amount; it thereby applies the matching concept to the sales and collection cycle in a different manner from that used in the income statement method. Although both methods match expenses with revenues, one result may differ from the other.

Writing Off Bad Debts

Once the estimated uncollectibles are in place, accounts receivable that are not collected in the subsequent year are written off to the allowance account. The example provided here is based on the uncollectible amount calculated by the balance sheet method. Assume that the account of Bendix Inc. becomes uncollectible by Bluebeard as a result of the bankruptcy of Bendix. The uncollectible account receivable is removed by this entry:

Apr. 1	Allowance for Doubtful Accounts	1,000	
	Accounts Receivable		1,000
	To write off uncollectible account		
	from Bendix Inc.		

Note that the write-off is made to the contra allowance account, which is debited. In this way, both the Allowance for Doubtful Accounts and Accounts Receivable accounts are reduced.

Accounts Receivable		Allowance for Doubtful Accounts	
Bal. 25,000			Bal. 1,450
	1,000	1,000	

The $1,000 write-off reduces both Accounts Receivable and the allowance account. The balance remaining in the allowance account represents the estimated amount of other accounts receivable that may also become uncollectible. Note that the use of an allowance account for the write-off of an uncollectible account does not affect the net Accounts Receivable amount.

	Before Write-Off	Following Write-Off
Accounts Receivable	$25,000	$24,000
Less: Allowance for Doubtful Accounts	1,450	450
Net Accounts Receivable	$23,550	$23,550

Note also that the Bad Debt Expense balance is not affected by the Bendix account receivable write-off. The Bad Debt Expense account was debited to record the estimated bad debt expense and was closed to Income Summary at year-end.

The amount estimated as an allowance for doubtful accounts seldom agrees with the amount that actually proved uncollectible. A credit balance remains in the allowance account if fewer bad debts occur during the year than are estimated. There is a debit balance in the allowance account if more bad debts occur during the year than are estimated. Subsequently an adjusting entry is prepared to set up the uncollectible balance that is estimated at year-end.

Collection of Amounts Previously Written Off

When Bendix Inc. went bankrupt, its debt to Bluebeard Computer Corporation was written off in anticipation that there would be no recovery of the amount owed. Later, an announcement was made that 25 percent of amounts owed by Bendix would in fact be paid by the trustee handling the bankruptcy. This new information requires the reinstatement of the amount *expected* to be collected by BCC — $250 in this case. This transaction is recorded by this journal entry:

Accounts Receivable	250	
Allowance for Doubtful Accounts		250

This entry reverses part of the amount previously written off and sets up the amount collected as a receivable. As a result, both accounts are increased:

Accounts Receivable		Allowance for Doubtful Accounts	
Bal. 25,000	1,000	1,000	Bal. 1,450
250			250

Since Bendix Inc. is a bankrupt entity (a gone concern), its credit-worthiness is no longer an issue. It may occur, however, that the previously written off amount of an entity is reinstated and further sales contemplated. The reinstatement of the accounts receivable when full payment is anticipated has an effect on that customer's future credit-worthiness. Therefore, Bluebeard records recoveries on each customer's subsidiary ledger account as a credit reference. (Subsidiary accounts are discussed in Appendix B at the end of the book.)

The actual collection of the reinstated amount is recorded by a second journal entry:

Cash	250	
Accounts Receivable		250

The collection is thereby recorded in the normal manner.

Credit Balances in Accounts Receivable

Accounts receivable subsidiary account balances usually have a debit balance because amounts are receivable from customers. Occasionally a credit balance occurs in some accounts as a result of double payment, merchandise being returned, or an allowance granted. Theoretically, the total amount of credit balances should be classified on the balance sheet as a liability, since the individual amounts are actually owing to the customers involved. In actual practice, the net amount is usually shown as part of the Accounts Receivable total on the balance sheet, unless the credits would materially misrepresent the amount reported.

Instalment Accounts Receivable

The sale of merchandise on account was discussed under the assumption that a single payment would be made. In actual practice, payments often consist of periodic payments, usually on a monthly basis; these are referred to as *instalment accounts receivable*. Department stores, such as Eaton's and the Bay, often have instalment accounts receivable. Because payment is made over a period of time under the instalment method, it requires special rules in order to be recognized as revenue from sales. Often a portion of revenue is recorded as earned only as the payments are received; however, there are many possible variations. The accounting for instalment sales is usually dealt with in more advanced accounting courses.

B.   Cash Collections and Payments

The widespread use of banks for the deposit of cash, collection of negotiable instruments (such as notes receivable), and the payment of cheques not only facilitates cash transactions between entities, but also provides a safeguard for each entity's cash assets. The use of bank reconciliation is one method of controlling cash. The preparation of a bank reconciliation is discussed in the following section.

Book Reconciling Items

Collections are often made by a bank on behalf of its customers; these collections are frequently recorded in the entity's books only after receipt of the bank statement.

Bank service charges for cheques paid and other services provided are deducted from the customer's bank account; these reductions of cash are also customarily recorded in the entity's books following receipt of the bank statement.

Cheques returned to the bank because there were not sufficient funds to cover them cannot be credited to the customer. These NSF cheques appear on the bank statement as a reduction of cash. (Such amounts must be re-demanded by the entity.) In addition, cheques received by the entity and deposited in its account may be returned by the cheque-maker's bank, because they are stale-dated, unsigned, illegible, or show the wrong account number. These dishonoured cheques must be deducted from the balance of Cash appearing in the entity's books.

Book recording errors can occur. They usually surface when the bank statement arrives and the bank reconciliation is prepared; the result may be either an increase or a decrease of the Cash balance.

Bank Reconciling Items

Cheques are recorded by the entity as a reduction of Cash at the date of their preparation; in actual fact, the cost is not paid until the cheque is cleared by the bank. Cheques that are recorded in the entity's books as cash disbursements but are not yet paid out of the entity's bank account are referred to as *outstanding cheques*. When the entity's bookkeeper requests that a cheque be certified, the bank deducts the amount of the cheque from the entity's bank balance and deposits it in a special account of the bank. When the certified cheque comes to the bank, it is deducted from this special account and not from the entity's bank balance. Cash receipts are recorded as an increase of cash when they are received; however, the bank records an increase in cash only when it actually receives the deposit. Certified cheques are *not* outstanding cheques because the money has already been deducted from the depositor's balance. There is usually a time interval between the recording of cash in the books and the receipt of a deposit by the bank. Outstanding deposits consist of amounts that are not yet recorded by the bank.

Bank errors sometimes occur. These errors may increase or decrease the bank cash balance; the bank is responsible for the correction of these errors.

Bluebeard Computer Corporation banks at the Second Chartered Bank. The entity's bank account is carried as a liability in the records of the bank, since the amount is owed to BCC. Accordingly, credit memos included with the bank statement are for items that have also increased the bank balance. Debit memos included with the bank statement are for items that have also decreased the bank balance. These credit and debit memos must be taken into consideration when BCC prepares its bank reconciliations.

This involvement of banks as intermediaries between entities has accounting implications. Usually, the cash balance in the accounting records of a particular entity differs from the bank cash balance of that entity at any time period. The differences are usually attributable to the fact that, at the given time period, cash transactions recorded in the accounting records have not yet been recorded by the bank and, conversely, cash transactions recorded by the bank have not yet been recorded in the entity's accounting records.

The Bank Reconciliation

Bank reconciliation
A comparison of the items shown on the bank statement with entries made in the records of the entity. A schedule called a bank reconciliation is prepared to explain the differences and to reconcile the amounts of cash shown by the bank and the entity's books.

Control over cash requires an accounting for the different book and bank cash balances; this accounting is accomplished through the preparation of a schedule frequently referred to as a **bank reconciliation**. The cash balance reported in the accounting records and bank are established at a particular time, usually month-end. The balance of cash according to the entity's books appears in the general ledger Cash account; the cash according to the bank is reported in a bank statement. The bank reconciliation process calculates an adjusted book cash balance and adjusted bank cash balance. These adjusted amounts must agree.

The following are reconciling items usually appearing in the bank reconciliation; they are discussed in detail in later sections of this chapter:

Book Reconciling Items:	*Bank Reconciling Items:*
1. Collection of negotiable instruments	1. Outstanding deposits
2. NSF cheques	2. Outstanding cheques
3. Bank charges	3. Bank errors.
4. Book errors.	

The preparation of a bank reconciliation alone does not always represent sufficient internal control over cash, as is illustrated in Real Life Example 6-1.

Illustrative Problem — Bank Reconciliation

Assume that a bank reconciliation is prepared by Bluebeard Computer Corporation at April 30. At this date, the general ledger Cash account shows a balance of $21,929 and includes the cash receipts and disbursements shown in Figure 6-2.

	Cash							Acct. No. 101	
Date 19X1	Description	F	Debit	Credit	DR. or CR.	Balance			
Mar. 31	Balance				DR	20673			
Apr. 30	April cash receipts	CR	9482		DR	30155			
30	April cash payments	CP		8226	DR	21929			

Figure 6-2   Bluebeard's Cash account at April 30

Extracts from BCC's accounting records are reproduced with the bank statement for April in Figure 6-3. Note the outstanding cheques from the preceding month.

PER COMPANY BOOKS

Outstanding Cheques
at March 31:

Cheque No.	Amount
580	$4,051✓
599	196✓
600	7✓

March 31 outstanding cheques compared with cheques cashed to see if still outstanding at April 30.

Cash Disbursements
for the Month of April:

Cheque No.	Amount
601	$ 24✓
602	1,720✓
603	230✓
604	200✓
605	2,220✓
606	287
607	1,364
608	100
609	40
610	1,520
611	124✓
612	397✓

Cash disbursements compared with cheques cashed to locate outstanding cheques.

Cash Receipts for
the Month of April:

Date	Amount
April 5	$1,570✓
10	390✓
23	5,000✓
28	1,522✓
30	1,000

Cash receipts compared with deposits to locate outstanding deposits.

PER BANK RECORDS

The Bank Statement
It is customary for banks to send depositors a monthly statement together with the cancelled cheques and notices of bank charges and credits. The statement shows the activities for the month; it should list:
1. Beginning balance
2. Deposits received and credits to the account
3. Cheques paid and other charges to the account
4. Ending balance.

The bank statement for the month of April was as follows:

Second Chartered Bank
Statement of Account
with Bluebeard Computer Corporation

Cheques			Deposits	Date	Balance
				April 1	24,927
4,051✓				2	20,876
196✓	24✓	230✓	1,570✓	6	21,996
200✓			390✓	11	22,186
124✓	397✓	7✓		16	21,658
2,220✓	180	NSF		21	19,258
1,720✓	31		5,000✓	26	22,507
6 SC			1,522✓	29	24,023

CC — Certified Cheque   DM — Debit Memo
NSF — Not Sufficient Funds CM — Credit Memo
SC — Service Charge   OD — Overdraft

Figure 6-3   The relationship of company and bank records

The bank reconciliation underscores the reciprocal relationship between the bank's records and the depositor's. For each entry in the depositor's books, there should be a counterpart in the bank's books.

In the Books:	*In the Bank:*
1. All cash receipts are recorded by a debit to Cash.	1. When the bank receives the cash, it credits the depositor's account.
2. All cash disbursements are recorded by a credit to Cash.	2. When the bank pays the cheque, it debits the depositor's account.

The five steps in reconciling the cash per books (Figures 6-2 and 6-3) with cash per bank (Figure 6-3) are as follows.

Step 1

The cheques paid by the bank in April are matched. Any cancelled cheques returned with the bank statement are compared with cheques recorded as cash disbursements.

The bank reconciliation from the preceding month is inspected for the existence of any outstanding cheques at March 30.

In the Books:	*In the Bank:*
These cheques were recorded in March; therefore, the Cash balance per books is correctly stated.	These outstanding March cheques may or may not have been paid by the bank in April. If some of the cheques have not yet been paid by the bank in April, the bank balance is overstated at April 30 by the amount of these cheques.

In fact, the March outstanding cheques were paid by the bank in April; no adjustment is therefore required in the April 30 bank reconciliation — the cash balance per books and per bank are correctly stated in relation to these March outstanding cheques.

The returned cancelled cheques are compared with the cheques recorded in the April cash disbursements journal. This comparison indicates that the following cheques are outstanding because they have not yet been paid by the bank.

Cheque No.	Amount
606	$ 287
607	1,364
608	100
609	40
610	1,520

In the Books:	*In the Bank:*
These cheques were recorded in April; therefore, the Cash balance per books is correctly stated.	These outstanding cheques were not paid by the bank in April; therefore, the bank balance is overstated at April 30.

In reconciling the cash balance per books and per bank, the outstanding cheques must be deducted from the bank account's cash balance.

Step 2
Debit memos made by the bank must be examined.

In the Books:	*In the Bank:*
If these debit memos have not yet been recorded in April, then the Cash balance per books is overstated at April 30.	The bank has already made deductions from the cash balance per bank when these debit memos were recorded.

In reconciling the cash balance per books and per bank, these debit memos must be deducted from the Cash balance per books, if they were not recorded.

An examination of the April 30 bank statement shows that the bank had deducted the NSF cheque of John Donne for $180.

In the Books:	*In the Bank:*
The cheque of John Donne had originally been recorded as a cash receipt (a payment on account). During April, no entry was made regarding this returned cheque; therefore, the Cash balance per books is overstated at April 30.	The cheque of John Donne was originally deposited in the bank. However, John Donne's bank did not pay this cheque because of insufficient funds in Donne's account. The cheque was returned to BCC's bank and was then deducted from the company's cash balance.

In reconciling the cash balance per books and bank, this returned cheque must be deducted from the Cash balance per books. (A notice must be sent to Donne to request payment again, preferably by certified cheque.)

An examination of the April 30 bank statement also shows that the bank had deducted a service charge of $6 during April.

In the Books:	*In the Bank:*
This service charge was not deducted from the Cash balance per books during April; therefore, the Cash balance per books is overstated at April 30.	This service charge has already been deducted from the cash balance per bank.

In reconciling the cash balance per books and bank, this service charge must be deducted from the Cash balance per books.

Step 3

Deposit in transit
Deposit made too late to appear on the current bank statement.

The deposits shown on the bank statement are compared with the amounts recorded in the cash receipts journal. This comparison indicates that the April 30 cash receipt amounting to $1,000 is not included as a deposit in the bank statement. This amount is an outstanding deposit, or a **deposit in transit**.

Cash Receipts for the Month of April:

Date	Amount
Apr. 5	$1,570✓
10	390✓
23	5,000✓
28	1,522✓
30	1,000

The bank statement for the month of April was as follows:

Second Chartered Bank
Statement of Account
with Bluebeard Computer Corporation

Cheques			Deposits	Date	Balance
				Apr. 1	24,927
4,051✓				2	20,876
196✓	24✓	230✓	1,570✓	6	21,996
200✓			390✓	11	22,186
124✓	397✓	7✓		16	21,658
2,220✓	180 NSF			21	19,258
1,720✓	31		5,000✓	26	22,507
6 SC			1,522✓	29	24,023

In the Books:	*In the Bank:*
The April cash receipts have been recorded in the books during April.	The April cash receipts have been deposited in the bank during April; however, the April 30 deposit was not recorded by the bank in April. Therefore, the cash balance per bank is understated at April 30.

In reconciling the cash balance per books and per bank, the outstanding deposit must be added to the cash balance per bank.

Step 4
The March bank reconciliation is inspected for outstanding deposits at March 31.

In the Books:	*In the Bank:*
The cash receipts of March had been recorded in the books during March.	Any outstanding deposits at March 31 should have been recorded by the bank in April. If any March deposit is outstanding at April 30, an investigation should be made.

In reconciling the cash balance per books and per bank, any March outstanding deposit should be investigated. In fact, there were no deposits in transit at March 31.

Step 5
Any errors in the books or in the bank account that become apparent during the reconciliation process must be taken into consideration.

In the Books:	In the Bank:
Any error recorded in the books requires a correction in the Cash balance per books.	Any error recorded in the bank statement requires a correction in the cash balance per bank.

In reconciling the cash balance per books and per bank, any book error must be added or subtracted from the Cash balance per books; any bank error must be added or subtracted from the cash balance per bank.

An examination of the April 30 bank statement shows that the bank had deducted, in error, a cheque from Lou Board for $31. The bank indicated it would make a correction in May's bank statement.

In the Books:	In the Bank:
This cheque of Lou Board does not belong to Bluebeard and does not require any change on the books.	This cheque of Lou Board should not have been deducted from the account of Bluebeard; therefore, the cash balance per bank is understated at April 30.

In reconciling the cash balance per books and per bank, this bank error must be added to the cash balance per bank.

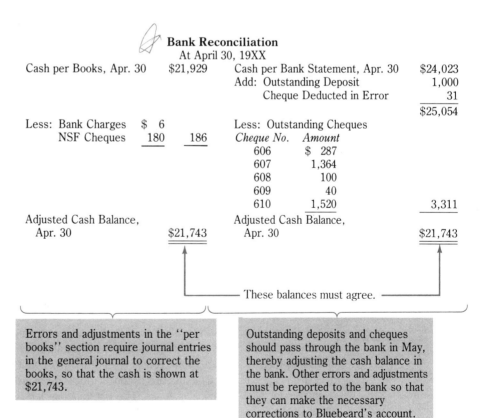

Bank Reconciliation
At April 30, 19XX

Cash per Books, Apr. 30	$21,929	Cash per Bank Statement, Apr. 30		$24,023
		Add: Outstanding Deposit		1,000
		Cheque Deducted in Error		31
				$25,054
Less: Bank Charges	$ 6	Less: Outstanding Cheques		
NSF Cheques	180	186	*Cheque No.*	*Amount*	
		606	$ 287	
		607	1,364	
		608	100	
		609	40	
		610	1,520	3,311
Adjusted Cash Balance, Apr. 30	$21,743	Adjusted Cash Balance, Apr. 30		$21,743

These balances must agree.

Errors and adjustments in the "per books" section require journal entries in the general journal to correct the books, so that the cash is shown at $21,743.	Outstanding deposits and cheques should pass through the bank in May, thereby adjusting the cash balance in the bank. Other errors and adjustments must be reported to the bank so that they can make the necessary corrections to Bluebeard's account.

A bank reconciliation is prepared after the above five steps have been completed; as shown below, it accounts for the difference between the cash per books ($21,929) and the cash per bank ($24,023) and calculates adjusted cash balances at April 30. The adjusted Cash balance in the books of BCC is the reported amount of cash in its interim balance sheet. The adjusted balance represents the actual cash that belongs to BCC, the amount that can still be withdrawn from the bank. The adjusted cash balance that appears in the books of Bluebeard is illustrated in the general ledger account in Figure 6-4.

Cash   Acct. No. 101

Date 19X1		Description	F	Debit	Credit	DR. or CR.	Balance
Mar.	31	Balance				DR	2 0 6 7 3 –
Apr.	30	April cash receipts	CR	9 4 8 2 –		DR	3 0 1 5 5 –
	30	April cash payments	CP		8 2 2 6 –	DR	2 1 9 2 9 –
	30	Bank charge expense	JI		6 –	DR	2 1 9 2 3 –
	30	NSF cheque	JI		1 8 0 –	DR	2 1 7 4 3 –

> This is the adjusted cash balance shown in the bank reconciliation.

Figure 6-4   Updated Cash account in the general ledger

Updating the Accounting Records

The preparation of the bank reconciliation must be followed by an updating of the accounting records. [As a general rule, every reconciling item used in the calculation of an adjusted cash balance per books requires the preparation of an adjusting journal entry to update the accounting records.] A reconciling item added to the book Cash balance requires a debit to Cash and a deduction from the bank cash balance requires a credit to Cash. The following journal adjusting entries are prepared at April 30.

Apr. 30	Bank Charges Expense	6	
	Cash		6
	To record bank service charge for April.		
30	Accounts Receivable — NSF cheque	180	
	Cash		180
	To record amount due from John Donne.		

Note that these adjusting entries include all book reconciling items. The general ledger cash account is then brought up to date, as illustrated in Figure 6-4.

Note that the balance in the general ledger Cash account is the same as the adjusted cash balance calculated on the bank reconciliation. Bluebeard doesn't make any adjusting entries for bank reconciling items. The outstanding deposit and outstanding cheques will probably be paid by the bank in May. Adjustments for bank errors are made by the bank.

Petty Cash Transactions

not on

Petty cash fund
A small amount of money kept on hand in order to pay small cash disbursements. The fund saves the time and expense involved in writing cheques.

Imprest petty cash system
The reimbursement of petty cash equal to the amounts disbursed.

The payment of small bills by cheque is not only inconvenient but also costly. The payment of postage due on some incoming mail, for example, might be less than the bank charge to process payment of a cheque. It is therefore useful to have a relatively small amount of cash on hand to pay small disbursements; this cash is usually referred to as a **petty cash fund**. There are different ways of handling such petty cash transactions; the imprest system is discussed in the following sections. Under this **imprest petty cash system**, a fixed petty cash fund is maintained, being increased or decreased in amount according to needs.

Establishing the Petty Cash Fund

Under the imprest system, a regular cheque is prepared in the amount of the petty cash fund; this cheque can be payable either to the Petty Cash account or to the custodian of the fund. If the fund is found subsequently to be too small, it can be increased; it can be decreased if changed circumstances result in its being too large. It is only in these cases that the Petty Cash general ledger account is affected.

Establishing the Fund		Increasing the Fund		Decreasing the Fund	
Petty Cash	200	Petty Cash	100	Cash	50
Cash	200	Cash	100	Petty Cash	50

The amount of the fund is established by this entry.	The additional debit increases the fund to $300.	The credit of $50 decreases the fund to $250.

The above transactions affect the size of the petty cash fund; they do not involve the record of disbursements paid out of the fund.

Reimbursing the Petty Cash Fund

Payments are made out of the fund as required; payments should be supported by a petty cash voucher signed by the recipient of the payments, in addition to any supporting documents, such as a taxi receipt. When the amount of cash has been reduced to a pre-determined level, say $10 or $20, then the petty cash fund is reimbursed for the total amount of payments made. A regular cheque is prepared in the total amount of all these payments and is made payable to Petty Cash or to the custodian, as the practice may be.

The cheque is recorded in the cash disbursements journal with the appropriate expense accounts debited. For example, the following compound journal entry would record the following payments: delivery charges totalling $35, light bulbs and other building maintenance items totalling $14, miscellaneous general expenses totalling $31 (including a $30 amount for postage and a $1 shortage in the petty cash fund), and miscellaneous office supplies amounting to $45. Because there is no specific postage account in BCC's ledger (as noted on its chart of accounts), the $30 postage payment is recorded as Miscellaneous General Expense.

Delivery Expense	35	
Maintenance Expense	14	
Miscellaneous General Expense	31	
Office Supplies Expense	45	
Cash		125
To replenish the petty cash fund.		

The shortage in a fund is usually recorded in a miscellaneous account. The petty cash vouchers and supporting documents should be cancelled at the time of reimbursement in order to prevent their reuse for duplicate reimbursements. The vouchers and shortage (or excess, as sometimes occurs) should be approved by a responsible employee.

Responsibility for the fund should be delegated to only one person, who should be held accountable for its contents. At any given time, the petty cash amount should consist of cash and supporting vouchers, all totalling the Petty Cash Fund amount.

C.   The Importance of Internal Control

Internal control
The system used to ensure accurate record keeping and the timely preparation of financial statements, in order to safeguard the assets of the entity and to promote efficiency.

The accounting process transforms the dollar amounts of transactions into financial statement information for communication purposes. The steps involved in and the generally accepted accounting principles applied to this accounting process have been discussed. The way transactions are processed in an accounting system was illustrated in the preceding chapter. Internal controls must be applied to the accounting system to ensure that transactions processing results in reliable records and that assets of the entity are protected. **Internal control** is defined as

the plan of organization and all the co-ordinate systems established by management of an enterprise to assist in achieving management's objective of ensuring, as far as practical, the orderly and efficient conduct of its business, including the safeguarding of assets, the reliability of accounting records, and the timely preparation of financial information (*CICA Handbook*).

Although not formally a part of financial accounting, internal control is useful in understanding the accounting process. Real Life Example 6-1 describes the disastrous consequences resulting from a breakdown in internal control.

Real Life Example 6-1
Secretary Takes Home $39,000 a Week

A petite blonde secretary, who rode to work in a limousine while her employer took the subway, was arrested yesterday and charged with stealing $384,451 from the boss's chequing account.

During last summer, the indictment said, Jeanne Jantzen, 26, was cashing cheques at the rate of $39,000 a week.

District Attorney Frank Hogan said the boss, real estate man Paul Yanowicz, did not notice for two years and four months because Miss Jantzen, who had the authority to sign cheques, kept the accounts balanced. Then, Hogan said, an accountant mentioned to Yanowicz that, while his chequing accounts balanced, he seemed to be taking a lot of money out of the business account and putting it in his personal one.

Yanowicz replied, Hogan said, that he took only $250 at a time to which the accountant pointed out that the accounts showed he took $7,250 at a time.

Assistant District Attorney Leonard Newman, chief of the frauds bureau, said Miss Jantzen and another employee had joint authority to sign cheques. When Yanowicz asked for $250, he said, Miss Jantzen would get the other employee to sign for the requested amount then take the business account cheque, raise the amount by $7,000, sign it herself and deposit this in Yanowicz's personal account. Then, Newman said, Miss Jantzen would draft a $250 cheque on the personal account, go through the signing process again, raise this cheque to $7,250, cash it, give Yanowicz $250 and keep $7,000 for herself.

Source   Associated Press, *The Montreal Star*, November 24, 1971, p. 19.

One part of a good system of internal controls is the accounting system, which must be designed to produce timely, accurate records. The chart of accounts is an important control; it describes what type of transaction should be recorded in each account. For example, assets are classified and recorded in asset accounts, and expenses are classified and recorded in expense accounts. In addition, financial statements, prepared according to generally accepted accounting principles, are useful not only to external users in evaluating the progress of the entity, but also to management making decisions. The design of accounting records and documents is an important aspect of control. Financial information is entered and summarized in records and transmitted by documents. A good system of internal control requires that these records and documents be prepared at the time a transaction takes place or as soon as possible afterward, since they become less credible and the possibility of error increases with the passage of time. The documents should also be consecutively pre-numbered, to provide a control for missing documents.

Another aspect of internal control is the use of a procedures manual that sets out the procedures necessary for proper record-keeping. Employees must be trained in the application of control procedures; they must also be competent to carry out their responsibilities. Incompetent or dishonest employees can make even the best control procedures ineffective.

Management is responsible for the installation and operation of internal controls. This responsibility is often acknowledged in published annual reports, as in the example shown in Figure 6-5. Failure to provide an adequate division of duties can have serious consequences to the entity's wealth, as illustrated in Real Life Example 6-2.

MANAGEMENT'S RESPONSIBILITY FOR FINANCIAL STATEMENTS

The accompanying consolidated financial statements of the Company were prepared by management in accordance with accounting principles generally accepted in Canada applied on a consistent basis and conform on an historical cost basis in all material respects with International Accounting Standards. The significant accounting policies, which management believes are appropriate for the Company, are described in note 1 to the financial statements. The financial information contained elsewhere in this Annual Report is consistent with that in the financial statements.

Management is responsible for the integrity and objectivity of the financial statements. Estimates are necessary in the preparation of these statements and, based on careful judgments, have been properly reflected. Management has established systems of internal control which are designed to provide reasonable assurance that assets are safeguarded from loss or unauthorized use and to produce reliable accounting records for the preparation of financial information.

The board of directors is responsible for ensuring that management fulfills its responsibilities for financial reporting and internal control. The audit committee of the board of directors is responsible for reviewing the annual consolidated financial statements and reporting thereon to the board, making recommendations to the board with respect to the appointment and remuneration of the Company's auditors and reviewing the scope of the audit.

Management recognizes its responsibility for conducting the Company's affairs in compliance with established financial standards and applicable laws and maintains proper standards of conduct for its activities.

M.A. Blumes
Executive Vice President and Chief Financial Officer

Figure 6-5 Statement of responsibility of Mark's Work Wearhouse management, from its annual report

Real Life Example 6-2
To Catch a Thief

Few things are more discouraging to a company owner than discovering that somebody you've trusted has had his hand in the till. There are limitless opportunities in most small companies for people to steal. Often there are few procedures and controls in place — and for a reason. If you wanted to work in a big-corporation bureaucracy, you probably wouldn't have started your own company in the first place. Still, having no controls can be very costly. The fact is, embezzlers are drawn to a few weak spots that many small companies share. By concentrating on these, you can go a long way toward finding and preventing embezzlement in your company.

When managers are tempted to steal, there's often a shadowy accomplice: a messy set of books. I know of a controller in a manufacturing company, for example, who actually had the accounting records randomly stacked in two-foot-high piles around his office. He was the only person who could even hope to find anything there. One day when the president of the company was looking for something in one of the stacks, he came upon some suspicious-looking records quite by accident. When the dust settled, it turned out that the controller had given himself $40,000 worth of raises and bonuses over the course of the year.

Not infrequently — and often appropriately — "clean books" as a business goal become subordinate to more urgent concerns. But your books document the financial transactions of the business, and that includes criminal transactions. And, as with any criminal, the embezzler minimizes the chances of being caught if he or she destroys or hides the evidence, which is exactly what sloppy bookkeeping can accomplish.

Most embezzlers want to, and do, work alone. Someone, for example, who is completely responsible for every step of the weekly payroll can easily add imaginary employees to the payroll, increase wages, and tinker with payroll deductions for employee benefits and taxes. Payroll, accounts payable, accounts receivable, inventory, and investment portfolios are all wonderful targets for embezzlers. It follows, then, that if you segregate duties in some key areas so that what one employee is doing, another is checking, you'll probably keep temptation at bay — it's unlikely that a potential thief could successfully enlist another employee as an accomplice. So, as a general rule, try to separate the bookkeeping for an asset or event from the physical custody of the asset or management of the event.

You'll reduce your chances of hiring an embezzler if you closely check the backgrounds of candidates for accounting and managerial positions. In my experience, someone who has embezzled once is likely to be a repeat offender. And why not? Embezzlers are rarely prosecuted — company owners are usually too embarrassed to press charges. Some say you'll never turn up something as dirty as embezzlement with reference and background checks, but I don't buy that. Usually a lot of people know about the problem when it's being investigated — and when the embezzler is forced to leave a company. I'm thinking of the owner of a closely held research-and-development company who, in the process of dealing with an embezzler, discussed the problem with his law and accounting firms, corporate officers and directors, the bank, the investment bankers, and the investors. Plus everyone in the embezzler's department knew why she had been fired.

If you follow these suggestions, it won't be easy for someone to pull a simple scam in your company. But to keep a check on exceptionally clever thieves, there's one more step you should take. Require your employees to take long enough vacations so that somebody else has to take over their responsibilities. Many of the embezzlement schemes are so fragile they require a lot of day-to-day maintenance, and they'll fall apart without it. A common example is "lapping" — whoever handles accounts receivables skims cash off the incoming collections, and uses other collections to cover for it, in essence robbing Peter to pay for Paul.

There's another reason to require employees to take vacations. You may well notice some changes occurring in your cash flow, say, or maybe a cost line item will suddenly drop. The most extreme story I've heard along these lines was about the assistant manager of a barely profitable concessions business who had worked for years without a vacation or break. Then, sadly, he had a heart attack and was out for months. Profits quadrupled. Predictably, the owner took a more than casual interest in the change. He discovered that the assistant manager had several tricks for increasing his own income at the expense of the business: taking a little money out of the cash register, selling some of his own inventory instead of the owner's, and buying supplies from vendors who understood that his palms needed a little grease. The plan was simple, and it was successful for years: a little here, a little there, and never so much from any one place that somebody would notice. Until he was forced to take time off.

Source   Stephen Nelson, "To Catch a Thief", *Inc. Magazine*, January 1988, p. 89-90.

Conceptual Issue 6-1

The Cost of Control

by James Gaston, Price Waterhouse

If there is one activity modern business considers exempt from cost controls, it's controls themselves.

Most managers wouldn't dream of expanding production or embarking on an advertising campaign without demanding cost estimates to justify such expenditures. Yet, they never stop to question the cost or necessity of the staggering number of controls designed to ensure the accuracy of financial and operational data; the reasonableness of assumptions used as a basis for budgets and cash flow projections; the safety of assets; and employee compliance with company policies.

Doubts about the need for all these controls are usually dispelled by controllers or auditors, who raise the spectre of disastrous losses the company might suffer if an error were to occur or remain undetected.

While such a danger may indeed exist, its size, the likelihood it will happen, and its potential impact should all be weighed against the amount of money being spent to prevent it.

An expenditure of $3,000 is justified if it prevents a loss of $10,000 or more. But if the loss isn't likely to exceed $1,000, then controls of that magnitude make no more sense than an expensive insurance policy on a car that can be sold only for scrap.

To minimize the cost of controls without exposing their business to unjustifiable risks, managers should answer the following questions:

What potential errors need to be controlled? Many businesses have elaborate controls without being quite sure what it is they're trying to prevent. As a first step, compile an inventory of risks and their possible consequences.

Which controls deserve the highest priority? Once you've identified the risks, categorize them as (1) totally unacceptable, (2) controllable, providing the cost does not outweigh the losses you're trying to prevent, and (3) acceptable, therefore requiring no further action.

If you start by developing controls for unacceptable risks, you may achieve other controls as a bonus.

Let's say that supplying customers with parts quickly and efficiently is the cornerstone of your business. If you can control your perpetual inventory records well enough, you will probably get as a by-product the financial information needed to make the right production and purchasing decisions.

Risks

What are the odds that expensive errors will occur? The less likely the risk, the less money you'll need to spend to prevent it.

If you've dealt with most of your suppliers for years — and they're reliable — the arithmetic on their purchase invoices isn't likely to be wrong. While you may want to keep checking prices, there's probably no need to have your staff check every addition and multiplication — unless unusual circumstances come to your attention.

How important are the errors being found? Ask your employees who perform control activities to keep track of the dollar savings they achieve. How much money did you save last year by having them check prices on all purchase invoices, or by cross-checking all the freight bills with shipping records? How much did you spend to achieve these savings? The answers may surprise you.

Can you recoup the cost of an error after it has occurred? Most control systems combine preventive features with detective ones, so errors slipping through the preventive screen will later be caught.

If you're satisfied an error can be corrected once it's found, consider reducing the amount of money you spend preventing it from occurring in the first place.

Spend less time checking and reviewing sales tax exemption certificates, for example, if you are reasonably sure your customers will reimburse you should Revenue Canada challenge the exemptions.

Are you a victim of the "all or nothing" syndrome? Applying the sme controls to all your transactions, regardless of their nature or size, wastes time and money. In the case of purchase invoices, for instance, check all invoices over a certain dollar value, as well as those from new suppliers.

Sampling

With the rest, statistical sampling will provide all the information you need to project the dollar value of undetected errors. Using that calculation, then decide whether it is worthwhile to check individually all invoices for small purchases.

Can you mechanize your control procedures? Because computers can perform control activities faster and more accurately than humans, all businesses, regardless of size, should consider computerizing. For example, computer systems can check a series of documents for missing numbers, or match receiving report quantities with purchase invoices.

Should you contract out your controls? Outside agencies will verify your costs either on a fee basis, or for a percentage of the money saved. In addition to routine applications, such as purchase invoices and inventory, some agencies check advertising, freight or sales tax costs.

Of course, periodically review the fees you pay to ensure your staff couldn't perform the same duties at a lower cost.

Source   James Gaston, ''How to check if your control systems are worth the cost'', *The Financial Post*, March 24, 1984, p. 18.

A S S I G N M E N T   M A T E R I A L S

Discussion Questions

1. How does use of an Allowance for Doubtful Accounts account match expense with revenue?
2. How is bad debt expense classified in the income statement?
3. How does the income statement method calculate the estimated amount of uncollectible accounts?
4. What is an ageing schedule for bad debts, and how is it used in calculating the estimated amount of uncollectible accounts?
5. How are credit balances in accounts receivable reported on the financial statements?
6. How does the preparation of a bank reconciliation strengthen the internal control of cash?
7. What different reconciling items appear in a bank reconciliation?
8. What are the steps in preparing a bank reconciliation?
9. What is an NSF cheque?
10. What is a deposit in transit?
11. What is an imprest petty cash system?
12. What is the difference between establishing and replenishing the petty cash fund?
13. What is an entity's internal control?

Discussion Cases

Discussion Case 6-1:   Cash on the Balance Sheet

The following is a letter to a professional accounting journal. It discusses the question of whether the cash balance in the books or the cash balance in the bank is the right cash balance to be shown on the balance sheet.

SIR — Traditionally, accountants show in balance sheets against the above heading the balance as shown in the firm's cashbook. This figure is often at variance with the balance shown in the books of the firm's bankers owing usually to unpresented cheques and lodgements not credited.

It is submitted that, in the context of showing "a true and fair view", cash at bank (and bank overdraft) should be the unadjusted but, nevertheless, reconciled bank balance according to the firm's bankers.

While cheques are unpresented, there is always the possibility that they may be stopped or held over. It would seem, therefore, that the only accurate balance is that as shown in the bank statement.

I should be interested in your readers' views on this subject.
Yours faithfully,
DATESEC

Source   Letter to the editor, *The Accountant*, August 28, 1965, p. 280.

For Discussion

Use the bank reconciliation in section B of this chapter to discuss this case.
1. Usually there is a difference between the balance of cash shown in the books of an entity and the balance of cash shown by the bank statement. Accountants reconcile these different amounts when they prepare a bank reconciliation. Which is the correct balance of cash at the end of a time period — the balance per books or the balance per bank? Why?
2. If the cash balance per bank were used as the amount reported in the balance sheet, how would the following items be handled?
   a. Outstanding cheques   b. Outstanding deposits
3. Using the bank reconciliation in this chapter, prepare a bank reconciliation in accordance with the view that the cash balance shown in the bank statement is the proper cash balance to be reported in the balance sheet. (Note that the cash balance per books and the cash balance per bank would still be reconciled. Only the reconciling items used would change.)

Discussion Case 6-2:   Juliano's Family Restaurant

At most restaurants, you get what you pay for, but at Juliano's Family Restaurant, it's the other way around. With no prices on the menu, customers are asked to pay what their palates — and conscience — tell them.

Whatever the inspiration, the results have been stupendous. Never mind the marketing textbooks and their pricing strategies; for Juliano's, having no prices has led to an increase of 25 percent to an average of $6,000 per month. Patronage has also soared at the 48-seat eatery. Thus far, most customers are "coming pretty close to the prices I had," Juliano says. Only two diners have left without leaving anything.

When looking for a place to open a restaurant in 1983, Juliano found three places he could afford, but the two best spots could not be secured. By default, Juliano decided to take a former waterbed shop, which he leases for $800 a month. He spent $20,000 for used kitchen equipment, furniture and minor repairs. "When we opened in December, we had $400," he said.

When Juliano decided to remove his prices, "We didn't have anything to lose." He alerted two local newspapers, which promptly dispatched two reporters to the scene. Subsequent stories attracted the Associated Press and a National TV network with the story of the restaurant with no prices racing across the country.

Lest you think that this might go too far, Juliano drew the line when he recently hired two employees. He is leaving the salaries to his discretion.

Source   Adapted from " 'Price-less' menu brings Juliano's customers", *Restaurant News*, by Marilyn Alva, April 22, 1985 and "We can Name Lots of Restaurants That Wouldn't Dare Attempt This", by Terrence Roth, *Wall Street Journal*, Feb. 21, 1985, p. 35e.

For Discussion

1. If we think in terms of the sales and collection cycle, what part of the cycle is uncertain for this restaurant?
2. How should Juliano's accounts record sales revenue: collected or uncollected?
3. If payment is not received from some clients, how can the expense of the meal be matched with non-existent revenue?

Discussion Case 6-3:   Panama City

In cash-starved Panama, Horacio Icaza has added one of mankind's oldest forms of trade to his business skills. He barters.

Mr. Icaza, whose company Casa del Medico is the nation's largest medical equipment supplier, recently worked out a deal with the Government-owned water and power companies.

He pooled some of his employees' water and electric bills, then told the utilities he would erase a similar amount from the debts they owed his company for laboratory equipment.

They agreed, and debts on both sides of the ledger were wiped out — without any money changing hands.

Panama, suffering from sweeping U.S. economic sanctions and the nearly two-month closing of its once formidable banking centre, now has become a barter economy.

"It stops people from starving to death, but it doesn't get the economy moving," said a Western European diplomat, who spoke on condition of anonymity.

"Panamanians have surpassed by much the traditional banking ability and capability of Swiss bankers," said former banker Luis Moreno. "We have been able to do banking outside of banks."

Panama's economic crisis was caused by the controversy surrounding General Manuel Antonio Noriega, the nation's military leader and the power behind the civilian Government. Gen. Noriega is under federal indictment in the United States on drug trafficking and money-laundering charges.

In a bid to oust him, Washington has cut off military and economic aid to Panama, frozen its assets in the United States and prohibited U.S. companies and individuals from making payments to the Government.

The sanctions, combined with the closing of the banking system and a two-week general strike in March, have virtually paralyzed the economy.

The U.S. dollar, the national currency, has become scarce. Its place has been partially filled by cheques issued in small amounts by the Government to pay its employees and social security recipients.

With those cheques, Panamanians can buy groceries at supermarkets or clothing at department stores. They also can send the cheques back to the Government to pay taxes or utility fees they owe the state-run water, electric and telephone companies.

The cheques, say businessmen, have become a quasi-currency.

Late one afternoon, the Rodriguez family kept a close tab on the price-tags of the meat, chicken, cheese, bread, juice, fish, milk and eggs piled into a shopping basket at the Rey supermarket on Via Espana.

They planned to fill the basket with food totalling $100 (U.S.), the amount of a social security cheque the elder Rodriguez had received from the Government. The Rey chain accepts Government cheques but gives no change on any unused portion.

Down the street, Blanca Robles, who teaches English and art, used a $50 paycheque from the Government to buy clothing at a department store, which had sharply reduced the prices on much of its merchandise.

With the cheques, businesses can turn around and pay taxes, duties or other fees owed the Government, all without dipping into scarce cash.

Some of the savvy dealers approach people waiting to pay their utility bills, offering to swap a Government cheque for their cash.

Still others offer to give Government employees and retired people cash for their cheques, but at a discounted rate. A $100 cheque, for example, can bring $80 or so.

Some corporate cheques also have become a form of currency.

Supermarkets have made arrangements to accept cheques issued by their suppliers. The suppliers pay their employees in small-denomination cheques, which can be used to buy food or other necessities.

In a complicated arrangement, the supermarkets then return the cheques to the suppliers in payment against their accounts, businessmen said.

Source Associated Press, Sally Jacobsen, "Cash is checked, now cheques are cash", *The Globe and Mail*, Toronto, April 26, 1988, p. B-8.

For Discussion

1. Explain in more detail how Panamanians are able to do banking outside of banks.
2. Prepare journal entries to record the following:
   a. Casa del Medico sold $5,000-worth of equipment to public utilities.
   b. Its employees received $3,000-worth of bills for water and electricity.
   c. Casa del Medico exchanged the $3,000-worth of utility bills for part of the debt owed by the utility companies to Casa del Medico.
3. How did the employees fare under this arrangement?
4. What are the implications for internal control of the use of cheques as a quasi-currency? How could you handle change from large cheques?

Discussion Case 6-4:   Mark's Work Wearhouse Ltd.

Read Figure 6-5 on p. 295, and discuss the following questions.

For Discussion

1. What are management's financial statements based on?

2. What are management's responsibilities for financial statements?
3. What are the board of directors' responsibilities?

Comprehension Problems

Comprehension Problem 6-1

Minks Co. Ltd. had the following transactions during 19X3, 19X4, and 19X5. Minks began operations on January 1, 19X3.

Required: Prepare journal entries to record the following transactions:

19X3	Dec. 31	Estimated uncollectible accounts as $5,000 (2% of sales)
19X4	Apr. 15	Wrote off the balance of N. Poloski, $700
	Aug. 8	Wrote off $3,000-worth of miscellaneous customer accounts as uncollectible
	Dec. 31	Estimated uncollectible accounts as $4,000 (1½% of sales)
19X5	Mar. 6	Recovered $200 from N. Poloski, whose account was written off in 19X4; no further recoveries are expected
	Sept. 4	Wrote off as uncollectible $4,000-worth of miscellaneous customer accounts
	Dec. 31	Estimated uncollectible accounts as $4,500 (1½% of sales).

Comprehension Problem 6-2

Brown Inc. had the following unadjusted account balances at December 31, 19X3, its year-end.

	Account Balances	
	Debit	*Credit*
Accounts Receivable	$125,000	
Allowance for Doubtful Accounts		$ 3,000
Sales		750,000

Brown estimates its uncollectible accounts as five percent of its December 31 Accounts Receivable balance.

Required:
1. Calculate the amount of estimated uncollectible accounts that will appear on Brown's balance sheet at December 31, 19X3.
2. Calculate the amount of bad debt expense that will appear on Brown's income statement at December 31, 19X3.
3. Prepare a partial balance sheet at December 31, 19X3 showing Accounts Receivable, Allowance for Doubtful Accounts, and the Net Accounts Receivable.

Comprehension Problem 6-3

The following information is taken from the records of Hilroy Corp. at its December 31 year-end:

	19X5	*19X6*
Accounts Written Off		
During 19X5	$2,400	
During 19X6		$1,000
Recovery of Accounts Written Off		
Recovered in 19X6		300
Allowance for Doubtful Accounts		
(adjusted balance)		
At December 31, 19X4	8,000	
At December 31, 19X5	9,000	

Hilroy had always estimated its uncollectible accounts at two percent of sales. However, because of large discrepancies between the estimated and actual amounts, Hilroy decided to estimate its December 31, 19X6 uncollectible accounts by preparing an ageing of its accounts receivable. An amount of $10,000 was considered uncollectible at December 31, 19X6.

Required:
1. Calculate the amount of bad debt expense for 19X5.
2. Calculate the amount of bad debt expense for 19X6.

Comprehension Problem 6-4

Lisa Ltd. had the following unadjusted account balances at December 31, 19X5:

Accounts Receivable	$150,000
Allowance for Doubtful Accounts	3,000
Sales	750,000

Required:
1. Assume that Lisa Ltd. estimated its uncollectible accounts at December 31, 19X5 to be two percent of Sales.
   a. Prepare the appropriate adjusting entry to record the estimated uncollectible accounts at December 31, 19X5.
   b. Calculate the balance in the Allowance for Doubtful Accounts account after posting the adjusting entry.
2. Assume that Lisa Ltd. estimated its uncollectible accounts at December 31, 19X5 to be ten percent of the Accounts Receivable balance.
   a. Prepare the appropriate adjusting entry to record the estimated uncollectible accounts at December 31, 19X5.
   b. Calculate the balance in the Allowance for Doubtful Accounts account after posting the adjusting entry.
3. Why is there a difference in the calculated estimates of doubtful accounts in questions 1 and 2?

Comprehension Problem 6-5

Lawf Inc. has the following unadjusted account balances at December 31, 19X4:

	Account Balances	
	Debit	Credit
Accounts Receivable	$50,000	
Allowance for Doubtful Accounts	1,000	
Sales		$200,000

Required:
1. Assume Lawf estimates that two percent of its sales will not be collected.
   a. What amount of bad debt expense will be reported on Lawf's income statement at December 31, 19X4?
   b. What amount of allowance for doubtful accounts will be reported on Lawf's balance sheet at December 31, 19X4?
2. Assume Lawf estimates that five percent of accounts receivable will not be collected.
   a. What amount of bad debt expense will be reported on Lawf's income statement at December 31, 19X4?
   b. What amount of allowance for doubtful accounts will be reported on Lawf's balance sheet at December 31, 19X4?
3. Which calculation is preferable to Lawf: that made in question 1 or in question 2? Why?

Comprehension Problem 6-6

The following information belongs to Fox Corp. at December 31, 19X2, its year-end:

Cash per books	$5,000
Cash per bank statement	7,000
Bank service charges not yet recorded in books	25
Note collected by bank not yet recorded in books	1,325

Amount of note	$1,300
Amount of interest	25
	$1,325

FAX Inc. cheque deducted by bank in error	200
Certified cheque outstanding	300
December cheques not yet paid by bank in December	1,600

#631	$ 354
#642	746
#660	200
#661	300
	$1,600

December 31 deposit recorded by the bank January 3	700

Required: Prepare a bank reconciliation and all the related journal entries at December 31, 19X2.

Comprehension Problem 6-7

The Cash account balance of Victor Ltd. was $2,501 at March 31, 19X4. On this same date, the bank statement had a balance of $1,500. There were also a number of other differences:

a. A deposit of $1,000 made on March 30, 19X4 was not yet recorded by the bank on the March 31 statement.
b. A customer's cheque amounting to $700 and deposited on March 15 was returned NSF with the bank statement. The bookkeeper was surprised, since she had not been aware of the NSF cheque.
c. Cheque #4302 for office supplies, correctly made out for $125, was recorded in the books as $152.
d. A memo listing $20-worth of service charges for March was included with the bank statement.
e. A cancelled cheque for $250 belonging to Actor Corp. and charged by the bank to Victor Ltd. was included with the cancelled cheques returned by the bank.
f. There were $622-worth of outstanding cheques at March 31.
g. The bank collected a note receivable for $300 on March 31. They charged Victor Ltd. $30 in interest and $10 in service charges.

Required: Prepare a bank reconciliation, and record all necessary adjusting entries at March 31, 19X4.

Comprehension Problem 6-8

The following transactions were made by Hedges Corp. in March 19X3.

Mar. 1 Established a petty cash fund of $200
     12 Reimbursed the fund for the following:

Postage	$ 10
Office supplies	50
Taxi charges	35
Meals (selling expenses)	25
	$120

     18 Increased the fund by an additional $200
     25 Reimbursed the fund for the following:

Office supplies	$ 75
Taxi charges	30
	$105

     28 Reduced the amount of the fund to $350.

Required: Prepare journal entries to record these transactions.

Problems

Problem 6-1

The reconciliation of the cash balance per bank statement with the cash balance per general ledger usually results in one of five types of adjustments. These are
a. Additions to the reported general ledger cash balance
b. Deductions from the reported general ledger cash balance
c. Additions to the reported cash balance per the bank statement
d. Deductions from the reported cash balance per the bank statement
e. Information that has no effect on the current reconciliation.

Required:
1. Using the above letters a to e from the list, indicate the appropriate adjustment for each of the following items that apply to XYZ Ltd. for December:

_____ The company has received a $3,000 loan from the bank, which was not recorded in the books of the company.
_____ A $250 cheque, certified on December 27, was not returned with the bank statement.
_____ Cheques amounting to $4,290, shown as outstanding on the November reconciliation, still have not been returned by the bank.
_____ A $1,000 collection of a note receivable made by the bank has not been previously reported to XYZ.
_____ The bank has erroneously charged XYZ with an $1,100 cheque, which should have been charged to XXZ Ltd.
_____ A $350 cheque made out by ABC Company and deposited by XYZ has been returned by the bank marked NSF; this is the first knowledge XYZ has of this action.
_____ A cheque which has been deposited in the bank, for $840 by KLM Ltd., a customer, was erroneously recorded by the bookkeeper as $730.
_____ A $600 bank deposit of December 31 does not appear on the statement.
_____ Bank service charges amounting to $75 were reported to XYZ.
_____ The company declared a $1,500 cash dividend to shareholders on December 15.

2. Prepare a bank reconciliation using the data given above. On December 31, the Cash account of XYZ Ltd. showed a balance of $84,293. The bank statement showed a balance of $90,568.
3. Prepare journal entries required to adjust the Cash account of XYZ Ltd. to the reconciled balance.

Problem 6-2

The following balances appear in the unadjusted trial balance of Juneau Inc. at its year-end, December 31, 19X3.

	Account Balances	
	Debit	*Credit*
Accounts Receivable	$100,000	
Allowance for Uncollectible Accounts		$ 5,000
Sales (all on credit)		600,000

Juneau uses the balance sheet method of calculating its Allowance for Doubtful Accounts account. At December 31, 19X3, it estimates that three percent of accounts receivable would not be collected.

Juneau had the following transactions during 19X4:
a. Accounts receivable worth $9,000 were written off.
b. Credit sales amounted to $800,000.
c. Collections of accounts receivable amounted to $700,000.
d. Juneau collected $2,000 in 19X4 that was previously written off in 19X3. This amount is not included in the collection of accounts receivable described in c.
e. At year-end, Juneau estimated that the amount of doubtful accounts at December 31, 19X4 was $10,000.

Required:
1. Prepare all journal entries required for 19X3 and 19X4.
2. If Juneau had used the income statement method of estimating uncollectible accounts, calculate the balance in the Allowance for Doubtful Accounts account at December 31, 19X3 and 19X4. Assume that Juneau estimated doubtful accounts to be one percent of sales for both years.

Problem 6-3

The following balances are taken from the unadjusted trial balance of Pagnudo Inc. at its year-end, December 31, 19X4.

	Account Balances	
	Debit	*Credit*
Accounts Receivable	$150,000	
Allowance for Doubtful Accounts		$ 1,500
Sales	500,000	
Sales Returns and Allowances		50,000

An ageing of accounts receivable at December 31, 19X4 reveals the following information:

	Accounts Receivable	*Estimated Loss Percentage*
Not yet due	$ 50,000	2%
Past due:		
1–30 days	27,000	4%
31–60 days	40,000	5%
61–90 days	30,000	10%
Over 90 days	3,000	50%
Total	$150,000	

The balance for R. Wills of $1,000 is over 90 days past due. It is included in the ageing of accounts receivable chart and has not yet been written off.

Part A: 19X4

Required: Prepare journal entries to record:
1. The write-off of R. Wills' account of $1,000 on December 31, 19X4
2. The appropriate adjusting entry to set up the required balance in the Allowance for Doubtful Accounts account at December 31, 19X4. (*Hint:* Remember that R. Wills' account has been written off.)

Part B: 19X5

The following transactions were made in 19X5.
a. Sales on account were $700,000.
b. Collections of accounts receivable amounted to $599,000.
c. Juneau wrote off $10,000-worth of accounts receivable.
d. An ageing of accounts receivable at December 31, 19X5 revealed the following information:

	Accounts Receivable	Estimated Loss Percentage	
Not yet due	$170,000	2%	3400
Past due:			
1–30 days	35,000	3%	1050
31–60 days	-0-	4%	0
61–90 days	27,000	25%	6750
Over 90 days	8,000	50%	4000
Total	$240,000		$15 200

Required: Prepare the appropriate adjusting entry to set up the required Allowance for Doubtful Accounts account balance at December 31, 19X5.

Problem 6-4

– 700,000 credit sales

Norkis Inc. made $1,000,000 in sales during 19X2. Thirty percent of these were cash sales. During the year, $25,000-worth of accounts receivable were written off as being uncollectible. In addition, $15,000-worth of the accounts that were written off in 19X1 were unexpectedly collected. At its year-end, December 31, 19X2, Norkis had $250,000-worth of accounts receivable. The balance in the Allowance for Doubtful Accounts account was $15,000 credit at December 31, 19X1.

	Accounts Receivable
Not yet due	$100,000
Past due:	
1–30 days	50,000
31–60 days	25,000
61–90 days	60,000
Over 90 days	15,000
Total	$250,000

AFDA 25,000
  AIR 25000
AIR 15000
  AFDA 15000
Cash 15000
  AIR 15000

Required:
1. Prepare journal entries to record the following 19X2 transactions:
    a. The write-off of $25,000
    b. The recovery of $15,000.
2. Next, recalculate the balance in the Allowance for Doubtful Accounts account at December 31, 19X2.

3. Prepare the adjusting entry required at December 31, 19X2 for each of the following scenarios:
   a. On the basis of experience, the estimated uncollectible accounts at December 31, 19X2 is three percent of credit sales.
   b. On the basis of experience, the estimated uncollectible accounts at December 31, 19X2 is estimated at five percent of accounts receivable.
   c. On the basis of experience, the estimated uncollectible accounts at December 31, 19X2 is calculated as follows:

	Estimated Loss Percentage	
Not yet due	2%	2000
Past due:		
1–30 days	4%	2000
31–60 days	5%	1250
61–90 days	10%	6000
Over 90 days	50%	

Problem 6-5

The General Co. Ltd. has, since inception, estimated its bad debts at 1 percent of net credit sales. During 19X5, General decided to calculate the required balance for the allowance account at year-end, December 31, by ageing its accounts receivable. The review suggested a required balance of $7,200. The following data, which already have been recorded in the company's books, are also available:

	19X4	19X5
Accounts Written Off		
On March 14, 19X4 (Brown)	$600	
On March 30, 19X5 (Smith)		$300
Recoveries of Accounts Written Off		
On June 5, 19X5 (Brown)		400

The Allowance for Doubtful Accounts account reported the following balances: January 1, 19X4 — $1,500 and January 1, 19X5 — $3,900.

Required: Prepare journal entries to record
1. The amount of bad debt expense for the year 19X4
2. The bad debt expense on December 31, 19X5
3. The collection from Brown on June 5, 19X5.

DON'T KNOW JOE!

CR. Balance of 10,000
+ credit of 15
25

1,250
35,000

Problem 6-6

At December 31, 19X3, the Wawa Lumber Company Ltd. balance sheet had a balance of $1,268,800 in trade accounts receivable. In addition, a contra account showed an Allowance for Doubtful Accounts balance of $32,400. Credit sales for 19X4 were $8,540,000, with collections of the receivables amounting to $8,262,560, including $15,600 that Wawa had written off as uncollectible in December 19X3 from Superior Lumber Ltd. During 19X4, Wawa wrote off $33,660 as uncollectible.

On November 1, 19X4, a customer with a $720,000 balance in accounts receivable sent $200,000 in cash (included in the cash collections) and a 12-percent per annum 6 months note for the balance. The account was considered to be collectible.

At December 31, 19X4, Wawa's year-end, the balance in trade accounts receivable included $200,580 of past due accounts, which management estimated would result in a 10 percent loss, based on past experience. In addition, it was management's policy to set up an allowance on current accounts receivable equal to 2 percent of the balance outstanding.

Required:
1. Prepare general journal entries for all 19X4 transactions relating to notes and accounts receivable.
2. Prepare all adjusting entries at December 31, 19X4. (Include explanations, showing calculations.) (*Hint:* accrue interest at December 31, 19X4.)
3. Show the amount that should appear in the 19X4 income statement as Bad Debt Expense.
4. What is the total for the Allowance for Doubtful Accounts account?

Problem 6-7

The balance of the Accounts Receivable account of Ramseur Ltd. at December 31 was $74,460. Included in this balance are the credit balances of two customers, amounting to $3,200 and $1,800.

Required:
1. What amount for Accounts Receivable would be shown under current assets?
2. How would the credit balances in the customers' accounts be disclosed?

Problem 6-8

The accounts receivable ledger of Sydney Corporation shows the following data on December 31 of the current year. (The general ledger showed a $200 credit balance in Allowance for Doubtful Accounts before adjustment.)

Name of Customer	Invoice Date	Amount
Fairmont Fruit Pickers Reg'd.	May 2	$ 600.00
Glenville Brothers Ltd.	August 15	335.50
Keyser Fruitees Inc.	October 2	719.85
	December 8	275.00
Shepherd Fruit Inc.	March 3	445.00
Bethany Fruit Company	November 11	822.50
Morgantown Produce Corp.	November 20	250.00
	September 4	465.75
	July 10	922.00
Others	December 5	20,000.00
Terms of Sale are n/30		

Required:
1. Prepare an age analysis of accounts receivable.
2. Compute the estimated loss based on the following fixed rates:

	Estimated Percent Uncollectible
Not yet due	0.5%
Past due:	
1–30 days	1%
31–60 days	3%
61–90 days	10%
91–120 days	25%
121–365 days	50%

3. Record the bad debt expense.

Problem 6-9

MacDonald Corp. had the following transactions relating to uncollectible accounts during 19X4:

Feb. 15 Wrote off F. Harrahan's account of $200 as uncollectible

Apr. 30 Collected from George Mulroney $100 that had been written off in 19X3

June 26 Received $300 from P. Martin (Martin's previous balance was $700); no further payments are expected and the balance was written off

Sept. 7 Wrote off H. Mann's account of $350

Dec. 31 Analyzed accounts receivable, revealing the following:
    a. Accounts to be written off:

Sue Bellingham	$300
P. Parizeau	400
T. Simyar	100

    b. Ageing of accounts receivable:

	Accounts Receivable	*Estimated Loss Percentage*
Not yet due	$20,000	2%
Past due:		
1–30 days	12,000	4%
31–60 days	5,000	5%
61–90 days	3,000	10%
Over 90 days	10,000	50%
Total	$50,000	

Required:
1. Assuming that there was a credit balance of $1,735 in the Allowance for Doubtful Accounts account at December 31, 19X3, prepare the entry to write off the uncollectible accounts at December 31, 19X4.
2. Prepare the appropriate adjusting entry to set up the required balance in the Allowance for Doubtful Accounts account at December 31, 19X4.

Problem 6-10

Paper Book Shop Ltd. effectively controls its cash by depositing receipts on a daily basis and making all disbursements by cheque. After all the posting for the month of November was completed, the cash balance in the general ledger was $4,209. The statement received from the Bank of Nova Scotia showed the balance to be $4,440. The following data are available for the purpose of reconciling these balances:

a. Cash receipts for November 30 amounting to $611 have been placed in the night depository and do not appear on the bank statement.

b. Bank memos previously not available to Paper Book are included with the bank statement. A debit memo for an NSF cheque, originally received as payment for an account receivable of $130, is included. A debit memo for bank charges of $6 is also included. A credit memo advises Paper Book Shop Ltd. that $494 has been deposited to the account, ($500 less a bank charge of $6). This represents the net proceeds of a collection the bank had made on behalf of Paper Book Shop Ltd. on a $500 note.

c. Cheques written during November but not included with the vouchers are no. 1154, $32; no. 1192, $54; no. 1193, $83; no. 1194, $109.

d. Cheque no. 1042 is returned with the bank statement. The cheque was made for $494, the correct amount owing for office expense. The cheque was recorded in the books as $548.

e. Cheques outstanding at the end of October included cheques no. 1014 for $152 and no. 1016 for $179. Cheque no. 1016 was paid in the bank statement; cheque no. 1014 was not.

Required:

1. Prepare a bank reconciliation at November 30.
2. Prepare the necessary adjusting journal entries required to make the Cash account agree with the bank reconciliation adjusted cash balance at November 30.

Alternate Problems

Alternate Problem 6-1

The following balances appear in the unadjusted trial balance of Rudis Corp. at its year-end, December 31, 19X2:

	Account Balances	
	Debit	*Credit*
Accounts Receivable	$200,000	
Allowance for Uncollectible Accounts		$ 10,000
Sales (70% on credit)		1,200,000

Rudis uses the balance sheet method of calculating its allowance for doubtful accounts. At December 31, 19X2, it estimated that three percent of accounts receivable would not be collected.

Rudis had the following transactions during 19X3:
a. It wrote off $18,000-worth of accounts receivable.
b. Credit sales amounted to $1,600,000.
c. Collections of accounts receivable amounted to $1,400,000.
d. Rudis collected $4,000 that was previously written off in 19X2. This amount is not included in the collections described in transaction c.
e. At year-end, it was estimated that the amount of doubtful accounts at December 31, 19X3 was $10,000.

Required:
1. Prepare all journal entries required for 19X2 and 19X3.
2. If Rudis had used the income statement method of estimating uncollectible accounts, calculate the balance in the Allowance for Doubtful Accounts account at December 31, 19X2 and 19X3. Assume that Rudis estimates doubtful accounts to be one percent of sales for both years.

Alternate Problem 6-2

The following is information for the Vancouver Company Ltd.:
a. Balance per the bank statement dated December 31 is $25,430.
b. Balance of the Cash account on the company books at December 31 is $11,040.
c. A cheque for $840 that had been deposited in the bank was erroneously recorded by the bookkeeper as $930.
d. A cheque for $2,100, deposited on December 21, is returned by the bank marked NSF; no entry has been made on the company records to reflect the returned cheque.
e. Among the cancelled cheques is one for $345 given in payment of an account payable; the bookkeeper had recorded the cheque at $480 in the company records.
f. Bank service charges for December amount to $50.
g. The bank erroneously charged the Vancouver Company account for a $10,000 cheque of the Victoria Company; the cheque was found among the cancelled cheques returned with the bank statement.
h. The bank had collected a $15,000 note plus accrued interest amounting to $75; $15,075 was credited to Vancouver's account; a collection fee of $10 was debited to Vancouver Company's account.
i. The bank deposit made December 3 for $1,570 does not appear on the bank statement.
j. Outstanding cheques at December 31 were no. 197, $4,000, and no. 199, $9,000.

Required:
1. Prepare a bank reconciliation statement at December 31.
2. Prepare the necessary adjusting journal entries to make the Cash account agree with the bank reconciliation adjusted cash balance at December 31.

Alternate Problem 6-3

Helena Inc. had the following transactions relating to uncollectible accounts during 19X3:

Jan.   22   Wrote off J. Anvari's account of $400 as uncollectible
Mar.   6   Collected from John Fisher $200 that had been written off in 19X2
July   4   Received $600 from J. Valdez (Valdez's previous balance was $1,400); no further payments are expected and the balance was written off
Sept. 7   Wrote off R. Lam's account for $700
Dec. 31   Analyzed accounts receivable, revealing the following:
        a. Accounts to be written off:
           Sean Levesque $600
           Rene Ohara   800
           Cher Archibald   200
        b. Ageing of accounts receivable:

	Accounts Receivable	Estimated Loss Percentage
Not yet due	$ 40,000	2%
Past due:		
1–30 days	24,000	4%
31–60 days	10,000	5%
61–90 days	6,000	10%
Over 90 days past due	20,000	50%
Total	$100,000	

Required:
1. Assuming that there was a credit balance of $3,000 in the Allowance for Doubtful Accounts account at December 31, 19X2, prepare the entry to write off the uncollectible accounts at December 31, 19X3.
2. Prepare the appropriate adjusting entry to set up the required balance in the Allowance for Doubtful Accounts account at December 31, 19X3.

Alternate Problem 6-4

Part A: 19X5

The following balances are taken from the unadjusted trial balance of McKenzie Corp. at its year-end, December 31, 19X5:

	Account Balances	
	Debit	*Credit*
Accounts Receivable	$ 300,000	
Allowance for Doubtful Accounts		$ 3,000
Sales	1,000,000	
Sales Returns and Allowances		100,000

An ageing of accounts receivable at December 31, 19X5 reveals the following information:

	Accounts Receivable	*Estimated Loss Percentage*	
Not yet due	$100,000	2%	2000
Past due:			
1–30 days	54,000	3%	1620
31–60 days	80,000	4%	3,200
61–90 days	60,000	25%	15000
Over 90 days	6,000	50%	3000
Total	$300,000		24820

The balance for V. Barbieri of $2,000 is over 90 days past due. It is included in the ageing of accounts receivable chart and has not yet been written off.

Required: Prepare journal entries to record
 1. The write-off of V. Barbieri's account on December 31, 19X5
 2. The appropriate adjusting entry to set up the required balance in the Allowance for Doubtful Accounts account at December 31, 19X5. (*Hint:* Remember that V. Barbieri's account has been written off.)

Part B: 19X6

The following 19X6 transactions were made in 19X6:
 a. Sales on account were $1,400,000.
 b. Collections of accounts receivable amounted to $1,198,000.
 c. McKenzie wrote off $20,000-worth of accounts receivable.
 d. An ageing of accounts receivable at December 31, 19X6 revealed the following information:

	Accounts Receivable	*Estimated Loss Percentage*	
Not yet due	$340,000	2%	6800
Past due:			
1–30 days	70,000	3%	
31–60 days	-0-	4%	
61–90 days	54,000	25%	
Over 90 days	16,000	50%	
Total	$480,000		

30400 . -24820 / 5580

Required: Prepare the appropriate adjusting entry to set up the required Allowance for Doubtful Accounts account balance at December 31, 19X6.

Alternate Problem 6-5

Tilbury Carpet Centre Ltd. reports to its shareholders the following balances on its December 31, 19X2 year-end report:

Accounts Receivable	$104,400	
Less: Allowance for Doubtful Accounts	(2,000)	$102,400

The following occurred in January 19X3:
a. Accounts of $1,200 were written off as uncollectible.
b. An account for $300 previously written off was collected.
c. A customer's note for $250 was written off against the allowance account.
d. An analysis of the aged accounts receivable indicated a need for an allowance of $3,500 to cover the possibility of uncollectible accounts.

Required: Reconstruct the journal entries to record the above items.

Alternate Problem 6-6

On January 1, the Accounts Receivable account balance of Carlton Iron Works Inc. was $265 and an Allowance for Doubtful Accounts was $7. The firm's credit sales during the year were $2,105 and cash collections from customers amounted to $2,025. Among these collections was the recovery in full of a $3 receivable from James Walburn, a customer whose account had been written off as uncollectible in the previous year. During the current year it was necessary to write off as uncollectible customers' accounts totalling $8.

At December 31, the accounts receivable included $40 of past-due accounts. After careful study of all past-due accounts, the management estimated that the probable loss contained therein was 20 percent and that, in addition, 2 percent of the current accounts receivable might prove uncollectible.

Required:
1. Calculate the balance of the Accounts Receivable account at December 31.
2. Prepare the necessary adjusting entry for the bad debts at December 31.
3. What amount should appear in this year's income statement as Bad Debt Expense?
4. Show the balance sheet presentation of accounts receivable at December 31.

Alternate Problem 6-7

The Accounts Receivable controlling account of the Warm Springs Corporation shows a balance of $370,500 on June 30. A summary of the analysis of accounts receivable by age shows accounts outstanding from the date of the invoice as follows:

	Accounts Receivable
Not yet due	$300,000
Past due:	
1–30 days	25,000
31–60 days	30,000
61–150 days	12,500
Over 151 days	3,000
Total	$370,500

On June 30, Allowance for Doubtful Accounts has a debit balance of $310 before adjustments. The adjustment of the Allowance account is to be based on the following schedule of percentages estimated uncollectible:

	Estimated Loss Percentage
Not yet due	0.5%
Past due:	
1–30 days	4%
31–60 days	5%
61–150 days	15%
Over 151 days	40%

Required: Prepare the necessary adjusting entry.

Alternate Problem 6-8

Kingsman Miniatures Corporation had credit sales of $610,000 for the year, accounts receivable of $60,500, and a credit balance of $250 in the Allowance for Doubtful Accounts account at the end of the year.

Required:

1. Record the bad debt expense for the year, using each of the following methods for the estimate:
   a. The allowance for doubtful accounts is to be increased to 4 percent of accounts receivable.
   b. Bad debt expense is estimated to be 0.45 percent of charge sales.
   c. The allowance for doubtful accounts is to be increased to $3,700, as indicated by an ageing schedule.
2. Which method would you choose and why?

Alternate Problem 6-9

The preparation of the bank reconciliation is an important function of the accountant at Long Life Ltd. Normally, five types of adjustments are used:
a. Additions to the reported general ledger cash balance
b. Deductions from the reported general ledger cash balance
c. Additions to the reported cash balance per the bank statement
d. Deductions from the reported cash balance per the bank statement
e. Information that has no effect on the current bank reconciliation.

Required:
1. Using the letters a to e from the list, indicate the appropriate adjustments for each of the following pieces of information derived from Long Life Ltd.'s January bank statement.

_____ A bank collection of $2,000 was not previously reported to Long Life.

_____ A certified cheque amounting to $500 and dated January 15 was not returned with the January bank statement.

_____ The January 31 $1,000 deposit arrived too late at the bank to be included in the January statement.

_____ The $225 cheque of Phantom Truckers was returned with the voucher, marked NSF; the Long Life people were surprised.

_____ A cheque received for $540 was deposited by the accounts receivable clerk as $450.

_____ A debit memo for $13 for service charges was received with the bank statement.

_____ A $10,000 loan received from the bank was included in the bank statement only.

_____ A $150 December cheque was still not paid by the bank.

_____ The bank credited Long Life with a $2,000 deposit that should have been credited to Long Life Insurance.

2. Prepare a bank reconciliation using the data given above. On January 31, the Cash account of Long Life Ltd. showed a balance of $24,848. The bank statement showed a balance of $37,850.

Alternate Problem 6-10

The following items relate to the activities of Eastern Company Ltd.:
a. At June 30, the Cash account shows a balance of $1,200.
b. The June bank statement shows a balance of $64.
c. Of four cheques not returned by the bank in May, one still has not been returned in June: cheque no. 208 in the amount of $80.
d. Eastern deposited cash received on June 29 (in the amount of $1,000) and June 30 (in the amount of $200) in the night depository on June 29 and 30, a Saturday and Sunday, respectively; these deposits do not appear on the bank statement.
e. On checking the cheques returned with the bank statement, Eastern found the following: cheque no. 214, properly made out for $45, was coded as a debit to Office Expense and a credit to Cash for $54; a cheque of Western Company in the amount of $200 was incorrectly processed through Eastern's bank account by the bank.
f. Bank service charges for the month totalled $5.
g. Cheque no. 261 for $180 written in June was not returned with the cancelled cheques.

Required:
1. Prepare a bank reconciliation at June 30.
2. Prepare the necessary adjusting journal entries to make the Cash account agree with the bank reconciliation adjusted cash balance at June 30.

Alternate Problem 6-11

Baltas Corp. had $2,000,000 in sales during 19X3. Thirty percent of these were cash sales. During the year, $50,000-worth of accounts receivable were written off as being uncollectible. In addition, $30,000 of the accounts that were written off in 19X2 were unexpectedly collected. Accounts receivable at the year-end of Baltas, December 31, 19X3 amounted to $500,000. The balance in the Allowance for Doubtful Accounts account was $30,000 credit at December 31, 19X2.

	Accounts Receivable
Not yet due	$200,000
Past due:	
1–30 days	100,000
31–60 days	50,000
61–90 days	120,000
Over 90 days	30,000
Total	$500,000

Required:

1. Prepare journal entries to record the following 19X2 transactions:
   a. The write-off of $50,000
   b. The recovery of $30,000.
2. Next, recalculate the balance in the Allowance for Doubtful Accounts account at December 31, 19X3.
3. Prepare an adjusting entry required at December 31, 19X3 for each of the following scenarios:
   a. On the basis of experience, the uncollectible accounts at December 31, 19X2 is estimated at four percent of credit sales.
   b. On the basis of experience, the uncollectible accounts at December 31, 19X3 is estimated at six percent of accounts receivable.
   c. On the basis of experience, the estimated uncollectible accounts at December 31, 19X3 is calculated as follows:

	Estimated Loss Percentage
Not yet due	1%
Past due:	
1–30 days	3%
31–60 days	4%
61–90 days	5%
Over 90 days	30%

Decision Problems

Decision Problem 6-1

You have been given the following bank reconciliation of AB Ltd. at November 30 and asked to review the value of outstanding cheques at November 30 and of cheques written from December 1 to 15.

You obtained a bank statement and cancelled cheques from the bank on December 15. Cheques issued from December 1–15 per the books were worth $11,241. Cheques returned by the bank on December 15 amounted to $29,219. Of the cheques outstanding at November 30, $4,800-worth were not returned by the bank with the December 15 statement, and,

of those issued per the books in December, $3,600 were not returned.

Required:

1. Using the information relating to cheques, compare the cheques returned by the bank on December 15 with the cheques outstanding on November 30 and issued in December.
2. Suggest at least three possible explanations for any discrepancies that exist.

Bank Reconciliation
at November 30

Cash per Books	$12,817	Cash per Bank	$15,267
		Add: Outstanding Deposits	18,928
			$34,195
		Less: Outstanding Cheques	(21,378)
		Adjusted Cash Balance	$12,817

Decision Problem 6-2

The internal control procedures for cash transactions in the Algonquin Corporation were not adequate. James Shifty, the cashier-bookkeeper, handled cash receipts, made small disbursements from the cash receipts, maintained accounting records, and prepared the monthly reconciliations of the bank account. At November 30, the bank statement showed a balance of $17,500. The outstanding cheques were as follows:

Cheque No.	Amount
7062	$268.55
7183	170.00
7284	261.45
8621	175.19
8623	341.00
8632	172.80

There was also an outstanding deposit of $3,347.20 at November 30.

The cash balance as shown on the company records was $20,258.31, which included some cash on hand. The bank statement for November included $200 arising from the collection of a note left with the bank; the company's books did not include an entry to record this collection.

Recognizing the weakness existing in internal control over cash transactions, Shifty removed the cash on hand and then prepared the following reconciliation in an attempt to conceal his theft.

Bank Reconciliation

Cash per Books	$20,258.31	Cash per Bank	$17,500.00
		Add: Outstanding Deposit	3,347.30
			$20,847.30
		Less: Outstanding Cheques	

Cheque No.	Amount
8621	$175.19
8623	341.00
8632	172.80

	(588.99)
Adjusted Cash Balance	$20,258.31

Required:

1. Calculate the amount of cash taken by Shifty.
2. Explain how Shifty attempted to conceal his theft of cash.

Financial Statement Disclosure

Chapters 1 through 6 discuss and illustrate the steps in the accounting cycle. They also discuss the concepts, assumptions, and procedures that provide a framework for financial accounting as a whole.

Chapter 7 consolidates what you have learned in previous chapters by relating the material to a real life example: the 1989 annual report of Mark's Work Wearhouse. The chapters you have already studied told you the rules of the game; this chapter will give you a better understanding of how the game is played.

Following the annual report is a series of questions, each keyed to the chapter where the material is covered. These questions should help you apply the theoretical concepts you have learned to the actual practice of accounting.

A.   Financial Statement Disclosure

The objective of financial statements is to communicate information (*CICA Handbook*, section 1000). This objective focuses on the needs of financial statement *users*, including the entity's management, investors, and creditors. Accounting information should make it easier for management to allocate resources and for shareholders to evaluate management. A related objective of financial statements is the fair presentation of the entity's economic resources, obligations, and equity. As well, financial statements should fairly present the economic performance of the entity.

Fulfilling these objectives is difficult. Accountants must make a number of subjective decisions about how to apply generally accepted accounting principles (GAAP). For example, they must decide how to measure wealth and how to apply recognition criteria. They must also make practical cost-benefit decisions about how much information it would be useful to disclose. Some of these various decisions are discussed in the following section.

Making Accounting Measurements

Economists often define wealth as an increase or decrease in the entity's ability to purchase goods and services. Accountants use a more specific measurement — they consider only increases and decreases resulting from actual transactions. If a transaction has not taken place, they do not record a change in wealth.

The accountant's measurement of wealth is limited by the fundamental accounting concepts introduced and discussed in Chapter 2: historical cost, the measuring unit, the entity, and the going concern. Accountants expect the entity to continue operating in the foreseeable future. They record only those transactions that can be measured in dollars. They assume the dollar is a stable measuring unit; except in supplemental disclosures, increases and decreases in market value and the purchasing power of the dollar are left unrecorded.

Economists do recognize changes in market value. For example, if an entity purchased land for $100,000 that subsequently increased in value to $125,000, they would recognize a $25,000 increase in wealth. Accountants, however, would not. Until the entity actually disposes of the asset, they would continue to value the land at its $100,000 purchase cost. This practice is based on the application of the historical cost concept, which is a part of GAAP.

Economic wealth is also affected by changes in the purchasing power of the dollar. For example, if the entity has a $50,000 cash asset at the beginning of a time period and purchasing power drops by 10 percent, the entity has lost wealth since the same $50,000 can only purchase $45,000-worth of goods and services. Conversely, the entity gains wealth if purchasing power increases by 10 percent. In this case, the same $50,000 can purchase $55,000 worth of goods and services. However, accountants do not record any changes because of the GAAP assumption that the dollar is a stable unit of measure.

Accountants must also consider the impact of recognition criteria. At what point in time will they record an item in the financial statements? Based on GAAP, accountants recognize an item when it has an appropriate basis for measurement and the transaction involves probable future benefits. At this time, accountants can make a reasonable estimate of the amount involved.

Real Life Example 7-1 reviews the application of GAAP to the financial statements of Calgroup Graphics Corp. Ltd. For more information on the application of GAAP, refer to Chapter 2.

Real Life Example 7-1
Holders Watch Equity Evaporate

Films worth $15-million when Price Waterhouse audited Calgroup Graphics Corp. Ltd. in 1985 should have been valued at $32, the company's new auditor says.

Price Waterhouse failed to prepare Calgroup's financial statements for the year ended March 31, 1985, in accordance with generally accepted accounting principles, chartered accountant firm Collins Barrow said in new statements presented yesterday to the Ontario Securities Commission.

After tabling 24 pages of new financial statements and more than 30 pages of material for a shareholders' meeting, OSC chairman Stanley Beck said trading could resume on Monday, Dec. 8.

"This brings to a conclusion a rather long and unhappy event," he said, but shareholders "now have an accurate idea of the worth and value of the corporation."

Financial statements showing "full true and accurate information" are "the absolute rock on which securities regulation is based," he added.

Calgroup is listed on the Alberta Stock Exchange. It last traded at $4.60. But at that time, its most recent audited statements — prepared by Price Waterhouse — showed film assets valued at $15 million.

The assets were put into Calgroup — then Gowganda Resources Inc. — in the form of a movie company in return for a control block of 10 million shares.

In the course of the OSC hearing, Price Waterhouse first withdrew its original audit, then substituted a new audit, and then resigned. Collins Barrow was subsequently appointed auditor.

In the new audit, the films are valued at $32, or $1 each, for fiscal 1985. In notes to the audit, Collins Barrow said: "The previously issued financial statements were not in accordance with generally accepted accounting principles" as films were carried at ascribed values, while other assets were carried at book value.

The purchase of the film company should have been accounted for as a reverse takeover, but wasn't, and "certain transactions were not appropriately recorded . . . because of misclassification or omission," Collins Barrow said.

Commissioner Alfred Holland asked if the re-evaluation of the films was based on the fact that their cost to the selling party had been "negligible or nominal." A Calgroup lawyer replied, "that's my understanding," but also pointed to Collins Barrow's difficulty in assessing the value.

As a result of the re-evaluation, shareholders' equity of about $17.9-million in the Price audit shrunk to $2.4-million, and subsequently fell to $1.7-million in fiscal 1986, ended March 31.

Assets of $18-million — mostly the films — have been revalued at $3-million. More than half of the assets, or $1.6-million, are loans to directors, officers, employees and a related company.

During the summer of 1985, shortly after Calgroup moved its listing to Alberta from the Toronto Stock Exchange and the price began a rapid move to $7.50 a share, the company lent $1,275,350 to officers and employees so they could buy shares.

Four directors bought 700,000 shares between April 2 and July 31, through previously granted options. The shares were bought for $3.2-million less than the market value at the time of purchase.

None of the borrowers "has alternative financial resources to repay their loans," Collins Barrow said in the financial statements.

The statements show a loss of $1.7-million in fiscal 1986 on revenue of $115,282. The costs include $665,718 paid to directors and officers, and $363,951 "directly related to attempting to resolve financial reporting issues to the OSC's satisfaction," the statements said.

Three of Calgroup's senior officers and directors have contracts totalling $600,000 a year until 1990.

But Collins Barrow points out the company may not last that long. Calgroup has not been able to finance its movie and computer businesses, and there has not been enough cash coming in "to satisfy its obligations and meet its liabilities as they become due."

While Calgroup is still optimistic about the profit potential in movies, the OSC's Mr. Groia expressed satisfaction that the financial statements show "the contingent nature of the film investment."

Film profits depend on Calgroup being able to raise money, which it has not so far been able to do. Negotiations with financial institutions are continuing.

At the shareholders' meeting Dec. 22, owners will be asked to confirm the film company takeover. The controlling shareholders will not vote. If the takeover is not confirmed, it will be undone.

Shareholders will also be asked to approve changes to a share escrow agreement.

The Ontario Institute of Chartered Accountants is looking into the original audit.

Source Dan Westell, "Calgroup Films Worth $32: New Auditor", *The Globe and Mail*, Toronto, November 29, 1988, p. B-1.

Qualities of Accounting Information

Accountants do not always report information that would be useful. Of necessity, they make cost-benefit judgements, using materiality to decide whether particular items of information should be disclosed.

If the costs associated with its preparation is too high or if it is not sufficiently large in amount or importance, financial information will not be disclosed. For example, Mark's Work Wearhouse does not disclose the effects of inflation on its financial statements. Neither does it list small office equipment as assets.

Accountants must also make decisions based on the qualities of accounting information: understandability, relevance, reliability, conservatism, and comparability. For example, you can see that the financial statements of Mark's Work Wearhouse are consistent — they use the same accounting practices in 1987 to 1989 and in their forecasts for 1990. This consistency enables users to compare results from different accounting periods more easily. For more information on the qualities of accounting information, refer to Chapter 2.

Real Life Example 7-2

Financial Statements Miss the Boat

Take note, Imperial Oil, Alcan and Maritime Tel: A quarter of your shareholders think your annual reports are almost useless.

Almost as many would be happier if you scrapped the reports and used the money saved to pay higher dividends or invest in the business.

The rest seem remarkably content with the information they are getting in the annual reports of each company, according to the results of a survey carried out by a professor of administration at the University of Regina.

Robert Anderson sent questionnaires to 3,000 randomly chosen shareholders — of Imperial Oil Ltd. of Toronto, Alcan Aluminium Ltd. of Montreal and Maritime Telegraph and Telephone Co. Ltd. of Halifax.

The 1,000 responses he got offer a fascinating glimpse of the kind of things shareholders want to know about their companies and of the shareholders themselves.

Almost 25 per cent agreed with a statement that because "annual reports are so difficult to understand and read, they are of no substantial help to me." An even 20 per cent agreed that there is no need for them to study or analyze the annual reports because their stockbrokers and financial analysts have already done the job for them.

The survey, carried out on behalf of the Society of Management Accountants, was designed to offer company accountants some guidelines for what Mr. Anderson calls the "non-audited content of annual reports," the information that companies are not required to report, but often do.

Mr. Anderson was reluctant to talk in detail about what conclusions he draws from the survey because his full study will not be complete until later this year. He sent the survey results as a thank you for their help to all of the respondents, one of whom provided a copy to The Globe and Mail.

The object of the study is "to tell the people who prepare the reports what shareholders want and what they don't want," he said.

What they don't want, among other things, are the names of the companies' auditors, lawyers and bankers or — to Mr. Anderson's surprise — information on corporate efforts to be socially responsible.

Almost 30 per cent of the respondents said such items are "not useful" in making investment decisions. "The interest from management is higher" on social issues, Mr. Anderson said.

Another surprise for Mr. Anderson was shareholders' lack of interest in being told who bears the responsibility for the annual report and for the accounting policies of the companies; only a fifth of the respondents said they would find such information useful.

Mr. Anderson asked the shareholders to assess the useful-

B.   Classified Financial Statements

Because users of financial statements have no access to the accounting records of the entity, it is important that financial statements be organized in a manner that is easy to understand. Thus, financial data are grouped into useful categories on classified financial statements. For more information on classified financial statements, refer back to chapters 2 and 4.

The Classified Income Statement

Figure 7-1 shows the classified income statement of Mark's Work Wearhouse. It includes amounts for discontinued operations and an extraordinary item. It is interesting to note that although footnote 10 in the annual report of Mark's Work Wearhouse identifies the nature of the discontinued operations and the extraordinary item, it makes no mention of income tax. According to GAAP, these items should be net of applicable tax; that is, the tax implications should be listed with the extraordinary item.

ness of 37 types of information in addition to the financial statements that can appear in annual reports by grading each on a scale of one (not useful) to five (very useful.)

If those who straddled the fence with a safe three reply are eliminated, the survey results indicate that only three kinds of information really grab the attention of stockholders: anything about the future, extra financial background and details on who controls the companies.

Future-oriented data are a clear preference. By a ratio of more than four to one, respondents asked for more discussion by management of the outlook for sales and profits.

By a ratio of five to two, they wanted more information on their companies' plans for capital spending, financing and research and development. By the same ratio they would like to see more comparative financial highlights, especially if these are bolstered by graphs and charts.

Although just over half found the names of the companies' auditors, lawyers and bankers not useful, 56 per cent would like to see a report on who owns or controls the company.

When Mr. Anderson asked shareholders if there was any other information they would like to see, most came up dry. The biggest clamor — if it can be called that — was for details on how much remuneration goes to the officers and directors of the companies.

A mere 27 respondents, fewer than 3 per cent, asked for those numbers. More than that, 33 people, asked for reports that were smaller, briefer, less elaborate, less glossy and less frequent.

Only 52 per cent of those surveyed spend more than 10 minutes reading the financial statements in their annual reports, while 46 per cent devote more than 10 minutes to other parts. "That's as good as or better than other studies have shown in the United States, Britain and Australia," Mr. Anderson said.

About 40 per cent said they read thoroughly core financial information such as the income statement, balance sheet and funds flow statement.

As a group, shareholders in the three companies are older, better educated and much more active than the average person who owns shares.

A survey by the Toronto Stock Exchange last year found that almost a third of all shareholders are over 45. Mr. Anderson's survey indicates that 85 per cent of the Imperial Oil, Alcan and Maritime Tel shareholders are over 50.

University graduates account for a third of all shareholders, according to the TSE survey, but 56 per cent of the shareholders of the three companies chosen by Mr. Anderson. Stocks played a more important role in the investment activities of Mr. Anderson's group than they did for the TSE's broader sample.

About 45 per cent of Mr. Anderson's sample reported that stocks accounted for more than half of their invested dollars, excluding their homes; in the TSE group, only 7 per cent had more than 40 per cent of their personal assets in stocks.

Almost half of those surveyed by Mr. Anderson had more than $100,000 each invested in common stocks.

Source Bruce Little, "Forget Kudos, Give Us Future and Bucks: Shareholders", *The Globe and Mail*, Toronto, July 6, 1987, p. B-9.

Mark's Work Wearhouse Ltd.
Consolidated Income Statement
(Adapted from the Consolidated Statement of Earnings)

	53 weeks ended Jan. 31, 1987	52 weeks ended Jan. 30, 1988	52 weeks ended Jan. 28, 1989
Sales	$159,054	$175,918	$194,514
Cost of Goods Sold	108,102	116,636	131,913
Gross Profit	50,952	59,282	62,601
Operating Expenses	45,902	55,625	58,836
Income (before income tax)	5,050	3,657	3,765
Income Tax	2,584	2,003	1,610
Income from Continuing Operations	2,466	1,654	2,155
Loss in Discontinued Operations	(853)	(93)	—
Income before Extraordinary Item	1,613	1,561	2,155
Extraordinary Item	(638)	—	—
Net Income for the Year	$975	$1,561	$2,155
Earnings per Share			
From Continuing Operations	25¢	17¢	22¢
Before Extraordinary Item	16¢	16¢	22¢
Net income for the Year	10¢	16¢	22¢

Figure 7-1   Mark's Work Wearhouse income statement

The comparative amounts for three years is useful in evaluating the entity's progress. Note how the earnings per share differ between 1987, 1988, and 1989. These earnings-per-share calculations are made on the basis of three different definitions of income.

Extraordinary Items

Extraordinary items
Material gains and losses that do not occur regularly, do not arise from normal business operations, and do not depend primarily on decisions or determinations by management or owners; they are classified separately on the income statement, net of related income tax.

Extraordinary items require special income statement classification. These items have the following characteristics:

1. They are not expected to occur frequently over the next several years.
2. They are not typical of the normal business activities of the enterprise.
3. They do not depend primarily on decisions or determinations made by management or owners.

Examples of extraordinary items are provided in section 3480 of the *CICA Handbook*. They include expropriation of property by government or other regulatory bodies, as well as the effects of earthquakes, floods, and similar events.

Because extraordinary items, by definition, do not arise from normal operations, their separate classification on the income statement facilitates the evaluation of the entity's normal business activities. Therefore, extraordinary gains and losses are classified separately on the income statement, net of income tax. Note that the amount of tax applicable to the extraordinary item is separate from the income tax on Income from Continuing Operations. The amount of tax applicable to the income from the extraordinary item must be calculated, and the "after tax" income is added to the net Income before Extraordinary Items.

The Classified Balance Sheet

Figure 7-2 shows the classified balance sheet of Mark's Work Wearhouse. The Liabilities and Shareholders' Equity sections identify how much capital to purchase assets was provided by creditors and how much by owners. The two major accounts under Shareholders' Equity are Common Stock (assets provided directly by shareholders) and Retained Earnings (assets resulting from successful operations). Shareholders' equity is discussed in greater detail in Chapter 9.

Mark's Work Wearhouse
Consolidated Balance Sheet
At January 28, 1989

	January 31, 1987	*January 30, 1988*	*January 28, 1989*
		(thousands)	
Assets			
Current Assets:			
Cash	$ 4,334	$ 1,905	$ 9,116
Accounts receivable	3,036	4,202	6,712
Inventories (Note 2)	28,334	37,447	28,454
Prepaid expenses and deposits	1,391	1,169	1,410
	37,095	44,723	45,692
Investment in Discontinued Operations	976	—	—
Investment and Other Assets (Note 3)	1,289	1,066	889
Fixed Assets (Note 4)	9,598	15,480	19,657
Deferred Income Taxes (DR.)	1,485	1,380	1,571
Intangible Assets (Note 5) GOODWILL ETC.	1,654	1,348	1,089
	$52,097	$63,997	$68,898
Liabilities			
Current Liabilities:			
New vehicle financing (Note 6)	$ 3,528	$ 3,775	$ 3,794
Accounts payable and accrued liabilities	20,461	27,580	24,745
Income taxes payable	1,212	1,625	3,813
Current portion of long-term debt	1,254	1,415	1,781
	26,455	34,395	34,133
Long-Term Debt (Note 7)	7,419	9,803	12,811
Shareholders' Equity			
Capital Stock (Note 8)	14,543	14,558	14,558
Retained Earnings	3,680	5,241	7,396
	18,223	19,799	21,954
	$52,097	$63,997	$68,898

Figure 7-2   Consolidated balance sheet for Mark's Work Wearhouse

The balance sheet of Mark's Work Wearhouse includes some interesting long-term assets. Investment in Discontinued Operations involved a long-term commitment of cash to a particular business segment in 1987. Deferred Income Taxes represents an asset that will be used in the following year. Intangible Assets refers to goodwill and an option to purchase land.

Discontinued Operations

Business segment
A segment of an entity
whose activities, assets,
and results of operations
are distinguishable from
those of other segments.

**Discontinued
operations**
A business segment
that has been sold,
abandoned, shut down,
or otherwise disposed of.

Most publicly listed corporations consist of a number of different **business segments**. For example, an entity may include segments in Canada and in the United States. Unprofitable segments may be closed down or sold; they are then referred to as **discontinued operations**. Any gains or losses realized from these discontinued operations must be included in the income statement and must be shown separately from continuing operations. This practice is in accordance with GAAP. Each gain or loss resulting from discontinued operations must be net of income tax. That is, the amount of income tax applicable to the discontinued operation is separated from total income tax expense. This separate amount is then included within the discontinued operation information to calculate an amount that is referred to as being *net of income tax*.

The Statement of Cash Flow

Together with the income statement, statement of retained earnings, and balance sheet, the statement of cash flow is a primary financial statement. Cash flow refers to the amount of cash received and paid by the entity. The actual amounts received and paid are recorded in the general ledger Cash account. The balance of cash in the general ledger represents the net balance of this inflow and outflow of cash.

Figure 7-3 shows Mark's Work Wearhouse's statement of cash flow. It classifies cash flow into operations, financing activities, and investing activities. Operations represents cash inflow less cash outflow. Financing activities show the changes in the liabilities and equity side of the balance sheet. Investing activities show the changes in long-term assets. Chapter 15 discusses the statement of cash flow in more detail.

Mark's Work Wearhouse Ltd.
Consolidated Statement of Cash Flow

	53 weeks ended January 31, 1987	52 weeks ended January 30, 1988	52 weeks ended January 28, 1989
	(thousands)		
Cash generated (deployed)			
Operations			
Cash receipts	$157,854	$173,977	$191,153
Payments for inventories and operating expenses	(152,827)	(170,255)	(179,670)
Interest on long-term debt	(466)	(709)	(1,204)
Income taxes	—	(1,485)	387
	4,561	1,528	10,666
Financing			
Proceeds of long-term debt	5,253	3,735	5,741
Retirement of long-term debt	(3,928)	(1,482)	(3,084)
Vehicle leasing, net	369	(66)	15
Issuance of capital	(21)	15	—
	1,673	2,202	2,672
Investing			
Purchase of fixed assets — retail	(4,607)	(4,261)	(1,442)
— automotive	(127)	(2,347)	(4,728)
Investment and other assets	(349)	57	43
Proceeds on disposition of net assets of discontinued operations	—	392	—
Discontinued operations	870	—	—
	(4,213)	(6,159)	(6,127)
Net cash generated (deployed)	2,021	(2,429)	7,211
Cash, at beginning of year	2,313	4,334	1,905
Cash, at end of year	$ 4,334	$ 1,905	$ 9,116

Figure 7-3 **Consolidated statement of cash flow for Mark's Work Wearhouse**

Using Classified Financial Statements

Classified financial statements and other information included in the annual report are useful for analyzing an entity's activities. For example, the reader of financial statements can tell whether an entity is solvent and what its financial structure is (whether it is over- or underfinanced). Some types of financial analysis are described in chapters 4 and 14, including

1. Current ratio
2. Return on total assets ratio
3. Return on shareholders' equity ratio
4. Return on sales ratio
5. Earnings per share
6. Price-to-earnings ratio.

C.   The Annual Report of Mark's Work Wearhouse Ltd.

This section reproduces the entire annual report of Mark's Work Wearhouse. Mark's Work Wearhouse Ltd. has been chosen for a number of reasons: it was founded by a successful and colourful entrepreneur; readers can relate to its business activities because it is visible throughout Canada; and it raises a number of interesting issues. Most importantly, Mark's Work Wearhouse has made a concerted effort to design an effective and attractive annual report as the basis for communicating financial information to investors, creditors, and other readers.

Following the annual report, a number of questions, grouped by chapter, apply the concepts reviewed in this text to the real-life situation of Mark's Work Wearhouse.

The report to shareholders (p. 333) provides useful background to the financial statements. Read this report and answer the following questions:

1. What is the mission of Mark's Work Wearhouse?
2. What are the company's financial objectives?

When reading the annual report, keep in mind the necessity for a business to reconcile its social conscience with its profit-making objectives.

Real Life Example 7-3

Blumes Determined To Put the Bloom Back in Results

The founder of a company that sold $136-million worth of clothing and shoes last year wore a golf shirt, khaki pants and tennis shoes to meet the shareholders in the company cafeteria.

Mark Blumes, president of Mark's Work Wearhouse Ltd., limped around the annual meeting, while directors kidded him about not being able to walk after having run about 11 kilometres in the morning.

But once Mr. Blumes got down to business, it was obvious that more than just his knee was causing him pain. There was no more Mr. Casual.

"We are substantially outperforming our competition, but we are not doing as well as we would like to do or want to do," he said.

Calgary-based Mark's Work Wearhouse, which Mr. Blumes founded 11 years ago, sells casual and work clothing in 106 stores across Canada (16 were opened last year) and owns three car dealerships in Calgary. It had an operating profit of $1.6-million for the year ended Jan. 31, down more than $800,000 from the year before.

The car dealerships, which include two that sell BMWs, lost $172,000.

Mr. Blumes insisted that his company, known for innovative advertising campaigns such as promoting blue jeans in Russian during the Winter Olympics, is still succeeding by avoiding the discount gimmicks that major department stores use.

"Last week, they (a major department store) had something like scratch and sniff (cards) and then it's a third off these items or 10 per cent off those. . . . We just aren't going to play in that arena."

The Mark's name has been built on selling durable work and sports clothes.

"We're a product-driven organization," Mr. Blumes said in an interview. "The typical retailer chases pink shirts one year and the next year he sells yellow shirts. We try to make a better pink shirt."

The company did start selling more trendy clothes through Wind River Outfitting Co. outlets, one each in Calgary and Toronto, last year.

The two stores were part of a wave of new merchandising and distribution ideas at Mark's over the past two years.

Mr. Blumes said the new ideas were useful, but he warned the 1,600 employees that it's time to make money from the innovations before embarking on new ventures.

"I don't think operating in the retail industry is going to be as much fun as we had hoped it would be," he told shareholders.

"The clothing business generally is pretty tough. There is no clear direction in ladies' fashion, and this has been one of the worst springs I can remember in that area."

In the interview, he said Olympic advertising attracted international publicity and increased Calgary sales to record levels.

But the Olympics also hurt automobile sales, said executive vice-president Moe Blumes, who is Mark Blumes' brother. Sales of luxury cars in Calgary have been in a slump since the October stock market crash.

"The BMW business has been a struggle. We had a disastrous February because, during the Olympics, BMW purchases were hardly a priority."

Mark Blumes said the company has introduced individual performance contracts for staff, which cover such things as sales results to the number of customer comment cards filled out that mention a specific employee.

The company pays such close attention to staff performance that it even breaks down sales for each dollar of salary paid: $20.99 for the retail operation and $10.39 for the car dealerships.

The Blumes brothers are determined to improve the financial performance to produce a return on shareholders' equity of 20 per cent from the fiscal 1988 level of 8 per cent.

"I think over the next couple of years we are going to be focusing on improving our earnings . . . making our ideas work," Mark Blumes said.

Source Kevin Cox, "Olympics Put Mark's Work in Rough Patch", *The Globe and Mail*, Toronto, January 13, 1988, p. B-1.

Mark's Work Wearhouse
Annual Report
January 28, 1989

Reprinted with permission.

Highlights

(all dollar amounts in thousands)	52 weeks ended January 26, 1985	52 weeks ended January 25, 1986	53 weeks ended January 31, 1987	52 weeks ended January 30, 1988	52 weeks ended January 28, 1989	Forecast* 52 weeks ending January 27, 1990 Conservative	Optimistic
Sales							
Retail (corporate stores)	$ 92,581	$104,576	$116,843	$136,083	$152,779	$ 161,524	$163,640
Automotive	34,659	42,689	42,211	39,835	41,735	47,858	50,925
	$127,240	$147,265	$159,054	$175,918	$194,514	$ 209,382	$ 214,565
Number of stores							
Retail – corporate	80	85	92	106	105	101	100
– franchise	–	3	10	18	30	44	47
	80	88	102	124	135	145	147
Automotive	3	3	3	3	3	3	3
Earnings (loss) from continuing operations							
Retail	$ 521	$ 1,847	$ 2,192	$ 1,826	$ 2,423	$ 2,521	$ 3,075
Automotive	371	619	282	(172)	(268)	(200)	(54)
	$ 892	$ 2,466	$ 2,474	$ 1,654	$ 2,155	$ 2,321	$ 3,021
Earnings per share from continuing operations	9¢	24¢	25¢	17¢	22¢	23¢	30¢
Net earnings	$ 1,001	$ 3,145	$ 975	$ 1,561	$ 2,155	$ 2,321	$ 3,021
Net earnings per share	10¢	32¢	10¢	16¢	22¢	23¢	30¢
Weighted average number of shares outstanding ('000)	9,895	9,947	9,968	9,968	9,971	9,971	9,971
Shareholders' equity at end of period	$ 14,083	$ 17,269	$ 18,223	$ 19,799	$ 21,954	$ 24,275	$ 24,975
Return on average equity	7%	20 %	5%	8 %	10%	10%	13%

* The reader is cautioned that the forecasts are based upon management's judgment and on assumptions, some or all of which may prove incorrect. Accordingly, actual results achieved during the forecast period will inevitably vary from those forecast and any variation may be material.

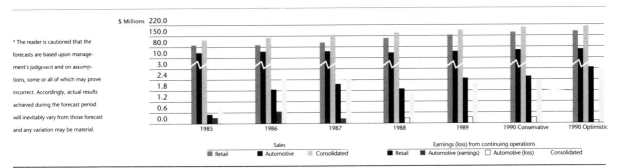

Executive Summary

Mark's Work Wearhouse Ltd.

Annual Report, January 28, 1989

This summary is intended to allow a brief overview of the Company's progress. A comprehensive review of the Company's operations and complete financial information is provided in the balance of the annual report.

Capital Stock

The issued shares of Mark's Work Wearhouse Ltd. as at January 28, 1989 consisted of 877,000 Class A Shares and 9,094,306 Restricted Voting Shares. The Restricted Voting Shares are listed on The Toronto Stock Exchange.

The Class A Shares and Restricted Voting Shares rank equally as to dividends and upon any liquidation or dissolution of the Company. The voting rights attached to the Restricted Voting Shares are limited in that the holders thereof are entitled to elect three members of the board of directors while M.W. and M.A. Blumes (the holders of the Class A Shares and the Company's two senior executives) are entitled to determine the size of the board and to elect the remaining members thereof. The holders of the Class A Shares have provided undertakings that they will not tender any Class A Shares upon any offer made for such shares unless a tender offer at the same price per share on substantially similar terms is made to holders of Restricted Voting Shares.

Market Value By Quarter

The Toronto Stock Exchange Merchandising Index (+1000)

Book value per share

Volume of shares traded (thousands)

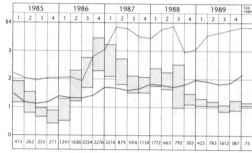

Quarterly Financial Information ('000)

(all information from continuing operations)		1st Quarter	2nd Quarter	3rd Quarter	4th Quarter	Total
Fiscal 1989						
Retail	Sales	$ 28,216	$ 28,213	$ 39,304	$ 57,046	$152,779
	Earnings (loss) before income tax	(1,556)	(1,939)	1,522	6,129	4,156
Automotive	Sales	8,461	11,689	11,270	10,315	41,735
	Earnings (loss) before income tax	(158)	19	(35)	(217)	(391)
Fiscal 1988						
Retail	Sales	23,877	24,266	35,937	52,003	136,083
	Earnings (loss) before income tax	(427)	(782)	1,007	4,088	3,886
Automotive	Sales	8,219	10,790	10,861	9,965	39,835
	Earnings (loss) before income tax	(240)	(90)	96	5	(229)
Fiscal 1987						
Retail	Sales	20,989	22,231	28,234	45,389	116,843
	Earnings (loss) before income tax	(704)	(436)	1,397	4,155	4,412
Automotive	Sales	9,456	11,929	11,203	9,623	42,211
	Earnings (loss) before income tax	316	185	250	(113)	638

Report to Shareholders

We are pleased to report earnings per share of 22¢. After a very disappointing first half, we responded with several initiatives in fundamental elements of our business. These resulted in a very gratifying improvement in second half performance. Perhaps even more important than the results for the year are the significant improvements in several key areas of our operations including product manager training, inventory turnover and a sharpened focus on profitability.

Our Company's investor relations budget is, and will continue to be, totally dedicated to the preparation of thorough, complete and descriptive analyses in our annual and quarterly reports. The Financial Post has recognized our effort by awarding us 'Annual Report Awards' in four of the last five years. The absence of employee and product pictures in this report does not reflect a weakening of that resolve; rather, our tone in this report and its relatively inexpensive production is reflective of our commitment to profitability.

Our mission as a Company is to emerge as a mature and stable enterprise, reputed nationwide:
- for being the most customer sensitive, customer responsive, 'Customer Driven' specialty retail organization in Canada;
- for having created a 'People Oriented' work environment where people have the greatest possible freedom to carry out their responsibilities, to own what they do, to have fun and to earn fair financial rewards; and
- for providing a worthwhile financial return to investors through the successes that flow from being 'Customer Driven' and 'People Oriented'.

The result (not the objective) of dedicating ourselves to meeting the first two elements of our mission will be attainment of the third. Our story is not going to be a parable about the dangers of putting short term flash above long term strategy.

We are driven to serve customers well with better and better value in our products. Consistent dedication to product development, while problematic, was, in relative terms, easy to achieve. Replenishing our stores efficiently and encouraging the levels of service to customers that we wanted was and is a much more difficult task. By establishing and committing ourselves to the second element of our mission, we have seen better and friendlier service in our stores and a growing awareness of both of the necessary disciplines and freedoms. All of our people have careers in retail in support of which we offer training and incentive programs unparalleled in our industry. The result of dedication to our customers and personnel, as reflected in the positive performance for the year just completed, will be enhanced customer loyalty in a growing business, offering steadily improving returns to shareholders.

In defining a worthwhile financial return we have established the following financial objectives:
- to attain contribution margins in retail operations from 20% to 22% and to attain absorption in automotive operations greater than 90%;
- to achieve at least a break even in each retail store in the spring season and to eliminate loss months in automotive operations;
- to maintain rent and interest on long-term debt coverage of 1.75 to 2 times; and
- to earn a 20% annual return on average shareholders' equity.

We must and do, for each of the regional and dealership operations, temper our progress towards these financial objectives through the implementation of tactical strategies responsive to our customers, our personnel and our longer term success. Each of our regional executives and general managers understand and accept their responsibility for the first two of the financial objectives. Budgets, freedom levels and incentives are negotiated in relation to their progress in attaining what have been elusive targets. Yet each of our managers must strive continually to serve customers better, to develop personnel and to seize strategic opportunities in his or her particular market. For example, by sacrificing store expansion and expenditures to enhance market penetration we could move our Toronto operations into the high range of our financial objectives. It is in our longer term interest to pursue growth opportunities. While we will offer greater and greater latitude to managers operating their businesses within the desired ranges, prudence dictates that, through the next two years, we must sacrifice short term gains for longer term rewards. Thus, we will not expand our corporate store base (other than marginally) but rather, will continue to make the necessary investment in improving existing operations.

Our priorities in retail operations have a people orientation. We have seen the improvement possible by harnessing well motivated and better and better trained individuals to serve our customers. We will continue to stress the use of individual performance agreements, the tackling and passing of yet another of our diploma programs (we have two courses in development to add to our three course College of Retailing) and will, selectively, add experienced re-

tailers from other organizations to compliment our internal promotion mentality.

We have been in the automotive business for five years. The initial years were very satisfactory from an earnings point of view, yet, through the travails of the past two years, we have come to understand our linkage to these operations. We have people committed to be the most customer sensitive, responsive automotive professionals in Canada. Past year performance reflects very satisfactory progress at what was our problem dealership, T & T Honda. Unhappily, for reasons detailed elsewhere in this report, our BMW dealership had a disastrous year. We believe that an attractive return on our investment in the BMW dealership is possible, even probable. Yet, in this and in our other automotive operations, success will require the effective collaboration of our franchisors with our hard-working automotive professionals. Our forecast reflects our belief that the highly competitive automotive market place is going to forestall what will be a progressively improving result in these operations.

Hopefully, the data and descriptions provided throughout our Annual Report will help you, our shareholders, develop the confidence and conviction that we have in our products, our service and our people.

Human Resources

Our Mission

To create a 'People Oriented' work environment where people have the greatest possible freedom to carry out their responsibilities, to own what they do, to have fun and to earn fair financial rewards.

The Attitude We Seek

We learn, we confirm our learning, and then we teach; EACH AND EVERYONE OF US. We want to be the place where people come to learn the retail business in the 1990's.

What It Means

We conquer the myriad of tasks by mobilizing everyone in the ownership of the products, the stores, and the dealerships. We all learn and perform specific, small tasks. We repeat those tasks to allow the confirmation of that learning (and so that the Company gets a payback) and then we teach what we have learned.

The Delivery (our "College of Retailing")

First and foremost – all who know must teach.

Second – we supply task directed diploma courses in merchandising which define and characterize our way of carrying on business.

Third – we offer formalized training utilizing manuals, videos and other training aids.

Fourth – we promote an attitude of excellence.

The Pace

Our people are the most important of our assets. We will equip them as well as we can for the challenges ahead.

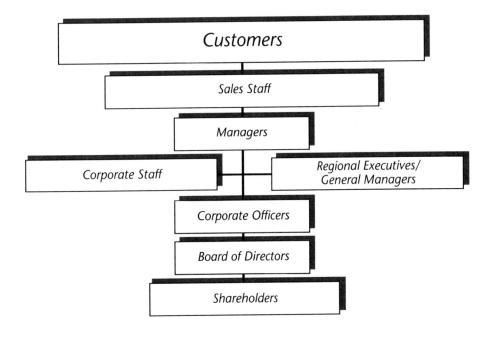

Forecast

Earnings per Restricted Voting share and Class A share for the 52 weeks ending January 27, 1990 are forecast to be in the range of 23¢ to 30¢ per share.

Company at the time of preparation, may prove to be incorrect. The actual results achieved during the forecast period will inevitably vary from the forecast results and any variations may be material.

The Company completed its forecast on April 3, 1989. Quarterly reports issued by the Company to its shareholders during the forecast year will contain either a statement that there are no significant changes to be made to the forecast or an updated earnings per share forecast accompanied by explanations of significant changes.

Sales and pre-tax earnings projected and attained in each of the last three fiscal years and the fiscal 1990 forecast are depicted graphically on page 24.

Retail

For the 1990 fiscal year we present our 'optimistic' and 'conservative' forecasts reflecting sales, contribution margin, fixed costs and pre-tax earnings. These present the most likely set of conditions and the Company's most likely course of action, within

1990 Forecasts – Key Assumptions

	January 28,1989 Achieved	January 27, 1990 Conservative	Optimistic
Retail			
Sales per square foot	$ 251	$ 265	$ 269
Gross profit (%)	36.9	37.3	37.5
Inventory Turnover	2.8	3.4	3.4
Contribution Margin (%)	18.8	18.9	19.1
Interest Rate (%)	10.6	13.7	13.7
Automotive			
New units sold	1,181	1,237	1,297
Used units sold	1,042	1,127	1,217
Gross profit (%)	14.9	14.6	14.6
Interest Rate (%)	10.9	13.7	13.7
Absorption (%)	71.5	69.0	69.4

The forecast presented represents, in management's opinion and based upon management's judgment, the most likely set of conditions and the Company's most likely course of action. The reader is cautioned that some assumptions used in the preparation of our forecast, although considered reasonable by the

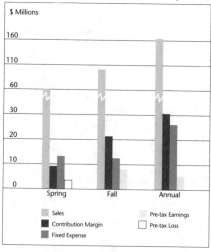

Retail - Optimistic

both the controllable criteria of merchandise assortment, price, quality and customer service, and factors outside of our control, such as economic conditions, weather and competition.

We intend to improve performance of existing corporate stores through improved inventory turnover and to add up to 17 franchise stores. Modest sales growth of 5.7% at the conservative forecast level and 7.1% at the optimistic forecast level has been forecast. Gross margins are expected to improve only slightly as we will maintain our everyday low price strategy.

Capital expenditures for store refurbishment, new store construction, distribution and office facilities and computer system equipment are forecast at $4,200,000. This includes $700,000 (of an approximate $3,000,000 planned) for merchandising systems over the next three years. The capital expenditure forecast includes, as a contingency, provision for the construction of five new stores, although none are included in the profit and loss forecast.

Automotive

We present 'optimistic' and 'conservative' forecasts for automotive operations. These represent, in management's opinion and based upon management's judgment, the most likely set of conditions and the Company's most likely course of action, and have been developed mindful of our perception of the local economy, the increased occupancy costs in the two dealerships located at the Calgary Auto Centre, the 1988 turnaround and further expected improvement in 1989 in our T & T Honda store, the profit reversal in our BMW operation, and the potential of a continued slide of the Canadian dollar against the Japanese Yen and the Deutsch Mark.

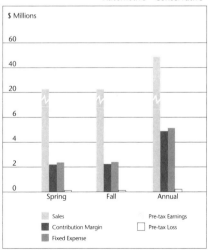

Retail - Conservative

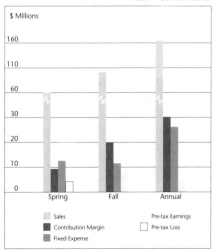

Automotive - Conservative

Discussion and Analysis of Financial Results

Consolidated Results

Net earnings improved to 22¢ per share from 17¢ per share from continuing operations recorded in fiscal 1988. Retail operations rebounded from a disappointing spring season to record net earnings of $2,423,000. Automotive results deteriorated from a loss of $172,000 in the prior year to a loss of $268,000 in the current year.

Working capital has improved to $11,559,000 from $10,328,000 at January 30, 1988. This is reflective of a very strong retail fourth quarter. However, the objective by which we plan our commitments, rent and interest on long-term debt coverage, has deteriorated in the current year to 1.4 times coverage. This is considerably short of our objective and reflects the poor automotive result, increased automotive commitments resulting from the move of two dealerships to the Auto Centre and retail results at the low end of our forecast.

Cash flow from operations improved from $1,528,000 in the prior year to $10,666,000 in the current year. Much of this improvement was due to the reduction of retail inventory levels. While cash flow utilized to purchase fixed assets in the retail operations was significantly reduced, the Company made major property acquisitions in the automotive operation ($4,418,000, financed in part by first mortgages of $2,886,000).

Retail Operations

Retail sales grew by 12.3% over the prior year (5.6% when calculated on a same store basis) while gross margins decreased by 2.0% to 36.9% in the current year. The effect was the generation of $3,424,000 in additional gross margin.

Personnel, advertising and other variable expenses declined from 20.1% of sales in fiscal 1988 to 17.2% of sales in the current year, the result of reduced advertising expenditures and increased royalties from franchise stores. Sales per dollar of selling salaries slipped from $20.99 in fiscal 1988 to $20.52 in the current year as a result of efforts to improve the quality of our product managers. Increased salary costs are expected to be more than offset by downstream sales gains. Occupancy costs increased by $3,067,000 to $14,597,000 in the current year, primarily due to operating 16 stores opened in fiscal 1988 throughout the full year.

Significant efforts were made to better manage inventories through the fall season and resulted in year end inventories (at retail) declining by $15,485,000 to $36,422,000. While the lower inventory level had a negative impact on sales in December and January, it leaves us in a position to improve inventory turnover through the upcoming year.

Consolidated Capital Expenditures

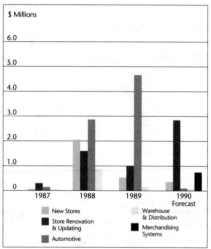

Automotive Operations

While automotive sales improved by 4.8% over the prior year, cost of sales increased significantly and resulted in a decrease in gross margin of $105,000. Personnel, advertising and other variable expenses were $133,000 less than the prior year, the result of aggressive cost cutting and efforts to match compensation more closely with profit performance. Interest on new vehicle financing and operating loans reflects an $82,000 increase, the result of higher inventory levels due to increased vehicle costs and cash flow shortfalls. The remainder of the increase in expenses is due to the higher overheads resulting from the relocation of two dealerships.

POST MORTEM ON PRIOR YEAR'S FORECAST
Retail

Retail sales of $152,779,000 fell short of the conservative forecast of $161,419,000. The shortfall was due to a poor retail economy in the spring, weak sales in Saskatchewan and slower than expected market recognition for new stores in Quebec, Winnipeg and Ontario.

Declining gross margin was due to a highly competetive retail environment resulting in a .5% reduction in initial margin and a .7% increase in markdowns. Shrinkage increased by .5%.

Sales shortfalls and declining margins resulted in a $5,813,000 shortfall in gross margin from that conservatively forecast. Personnel, advertising and other variable expense reductions mitigated the shortfall to $2,042,000 at the contribution margin line. Fixed costs less than those forecast further reduced the shortfall to $391,000 in pre-tax earnings from the $4,547,000 conservative forecast.

Automotive

Automotive sales fell $6,159,000 short of those conservatively forecast. Supply of new Hondas and the fragmentation of the Calgary marketplace with the fourth Honda franchise introduced in 1987 were problematic. The decrease in new car unit sales at T&T BMW is reflective of our franchisor's marketing bias away from its entry level products.

While gross margin rates of 14.9% exceeded the conservative forecast by 1%, the sales shortfall resulted in a gross margin of $468,000 less than the conservative forecast. This was mitigated by fixed expenses $282,000 below those conservatively forecast, of which $218,000 was due to the timing of the purchase of the Calgary Auto Centre facilities.

Financial Objectives

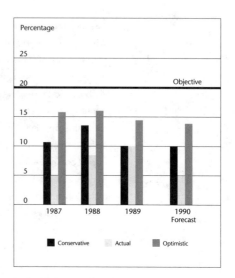

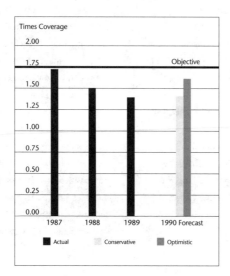

Objective: To maintain rent and interest on long-term debt coverage in the range of 1.75 to 2 times.

Objective: To earn a 20% return on average shareholders equity.

Objective: To achieve at least a break even in each retail store in the spring season.

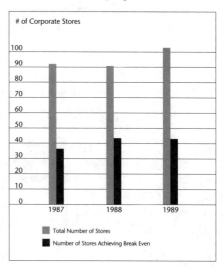

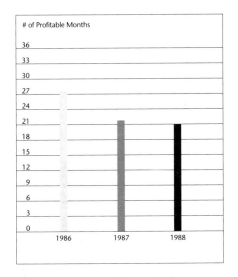

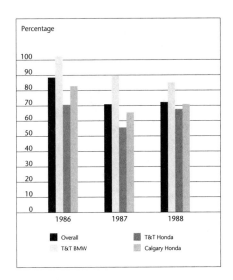

Objective: To eliminate loss months in automotive operations.

Objective: To attain absorption in automotive operations greater than 90%.

Objective: To attain contribution margins in retail operations from 20% to 22%.

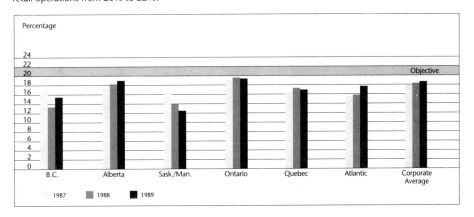

Comparison of Actual Results to Prior Forecast

Earnings per Share

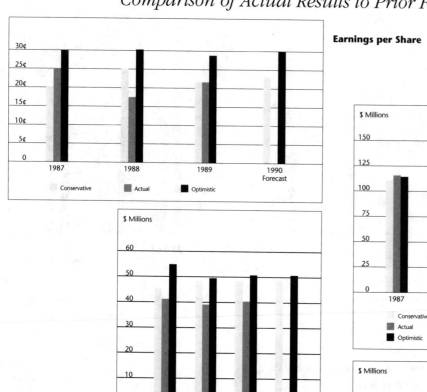

Retail - Sales

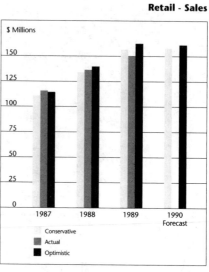

Automotive - Sales

Automotive - Pre-tax Earnings

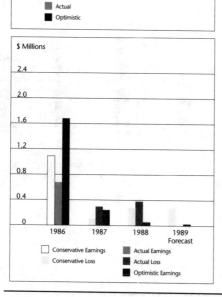

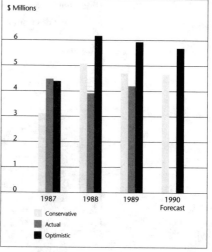

Retail - Pre-tax Earnings

Management's Responsibility for Financial Statements

The accompanying consolidated financial statements of the Company were prepared by management in accordance with accounting principles generally accepted in Canada applied on a consistent basis and conform on an historical cost basis in all material respects with International Accounting Standards. The significant accounting policies, which management believes are appropriate for the Company, are described in note 1 to the financial statements. The financial information contained elsewhere in this Annual Report is consistent with that in the financial statements.

Management is responsible for the integrity and objectivity of the financial statements. Estimates are necessary in the preparation of these statements and, based on careful judgments, have been properly reflected. Management has established systems of internal control which are designed to provide reasonable assurance that assets are safeguarded from loss or unauthorized use and to produce reli-

able accounting records for the preparation of financial information.

The board of directors is responsible for ensuring that management fulfills its responsibilities for financial reporting and internal control. The audit committee of the board of directors is responsible for reviewing the annual consolidated financial statements and reporting thereon to the board, making recommendations to the board with respect to the appointment and remuneration of the Company's auditors and reviewing the scope of the audit.

Management recognizes its responsibility for conducting the Company's affairs in compliance with established financial standards and applicable laws and maintains proper standards of conduct for its activities.

M. A. Blumes
Executive Vice President and Chief Financial Officer

Auditors' Report

To the Shareholders of Mark's Work Wearhouse Ltd. – We have examined the consolidated balance sheet of Mark's Work Wearhouse Ltd. as at January 28, 1989, January 30, 1988 and January 31, 1987 and the consolidated statements of earnings, retained earnings and cash flow for each of the years in the three year period ended January 28, 1989. Our examination was made in accordance with generally accepted auditing standards, and accordingly included such tests and other procedures as we considered necessary in the circumstances.

In our opinion, these consolidated financial statements present fairly the financial position of the company as at January 28, 1989, January 30, 1988 and January 31, 1987 and the results of its operations and the changes in its financial position for each of the years in the three year period ended January 28, 1989 in accordance with generally accepted accounting principles applied on a consistent basis.

Calgary, Alberta
March 31, 1989   Chartered Accountants

Consolidated Balance Sheet

	January 31, 1987	January 30, 1988	January 28, 1989
Assets			
		(thousands)	
Current Assets:			
Cash	$ 4,334	$ 1,905	$ 9,116
Accounts receivable	3,036	4,202	6,712
Inventories (Note 2)	28,334	37,447	28,454
Prepaid expenses and deposits	1,391	1,169	1,410
	37,095	44,723	45,692
Investment in Discontinued Operations	976	–	–
Investment and Other Assets (Note 3)	1,289	1,066	889
Fixed Assets	9,598	15,480	19,657
Deferred Income Taxes	1,485	1,380	1,571
Intangible Assets (Note 5)	1,654	1,348	1,089
	$52,097	$63,997	$68,898
Liabilities			
Current Liabilities:			
New vehicle financing (Note 6)	$ 3,528	$ 3,775	$ 3,794
Accounts payable and accrued liabilities	20,461	27,580	24,745
Income taxes payable	1,212	1,625	3,813
Current portion of long-term debt	1,254	1,415	1,781
	26,455	34,395	34,133
Long-Term Debt (Note 7)	7,419	9,803	12,811
Shareholder's Equity			
Capital Stock (Note 8)	14,543	14,558	14,558
Retained Earnings	3,680	5,241	7,396
	18,223	19,799	21,954
	$52,097	$63,997	$68,898

[handwritten annotations: "MINIMUM DISCLOSURE", "QUARTERLY BUSINESS REPORT", "? LOSES A WEEK"]

Consolidated Statement of Earnings

	53 weeks ended January 31, 1987	52 weeks ended January 30, 1988	52 weeks ended January 28, 1989
	(thousands)		
Sales	$159,054	$175,918	$194,514
Cost of sales	108,102	116,636	131,913
	50,952	59,282	62,601
Expenses			
Personnel, advertising and other variable expenses	23,525	28,935	27,809
Interest on operating loans	1,095	1,352	1,814
Occupancy	10,575	12,295	15,015
Administration and other expenses	8,318	10,307	10,086
Interest on long-term debt	650	744	1,222
Depreciation and amortization	1,739	1,992	2,890
	45,902	55,625	58,836
Earnings before income taxes	5,050	3,657	3,765
Income taxes (Note 9)			
Current	1,212	1,733	1,825
Deferred (recovery)	1,372	270	(215)
	2,584	2,003	1,610
Earnings from continuing operations	2,466	1,654	2,155
Loss in discontinued operations (Note 10)	(853)	(93)	–
Earnings before extraordinary item	1,613	1,561	2,155
Extraordinary item (Note 10)	(638)	–	–
Net Earnings	$ 975	$ 1,561	$ 2,155
Earnings per Restricted Voting and Class A share			
From continuing operations	25¢	17¢	22¢
Before extraordinary item	16¢	16¢	22¢
Net earnings	10¢	16¢	22¢

Consolidated Statement of Retained Earnings

	53 weeks ended January 31, 1987	52 weeks ended January 30, 1988	52 weeks ended January 28, 1989
	(thousands)		
Retained earnings, at beginning of year	$ 2,705	$ 3,680	$ 5,241
Net earnings	975	1,561	2,155
Retained earnings, at end of year	$ 3,680	$ 5,241	$ 7,396

Consolidated Statement of Cash Flow

	53 weeks ended January 31, 1987	52 weeks ended January 30, 1988	52 weeks ended January 28, 1989
	(thousands)		
Cash generated (deployed)			
Operations			
Cash receipts	$157,854	$173,977	$191,153
Payments for inventories and operating expenses	(152,827)	(170,255)	(179,670)
Interest on long-term debt	(466)	(709)	(1,204)
Income taxes	–	(1,485)	387
	4,561	1,528	10,666
Financing			
Proceeds of long-term debt	5,253	3,735	5,741
Retirement of long-term debt	(3,928)	(1,482)	(3,084)
Vehicle leasing, net	369	(66)	15
Issuance of capital	(21)	15	–
	1,673	2,202	2,672
Investing			
Purchase of fixed assets – retail	(4,607)	(4,261)	(1,442)
– automotive	(127)	(2,347)	(4,728)
Investment and other assets	(349)	57	43
Proceeds on disposition of net assets of discontinued operations	–	392	–
Discontinued operations	870	–	–
	(4,213)	(6,159)	(6,127)
Net cash generated (deployed)	2,021	(2,429)	7,211
Cash, at beginning of year	2,313	4,334	1,905
Cash, at end of year	$ 4,334	$ 1,905	$ 9,116

Notes to Consolidated Financial Statements

JANUARY 28, 1989   (Dollar amounts in tables in thousands)

1. SIGNIFICANT ACCOUNTING POLICIES

These financial statements are prepared by management on an historical cost basis in accordance with accounting principles generally accepted in Canada and conform on an historical cost basis in all material respects with International Accounting Standards.

(a) Basis of Presentation – The consolidated financial statements include the accounts of the Company and its subsidiaries. The accounts of Pro-Formance Automotive Ltd. ('Pro-Formance'), in which the Company holds 100% of the shares outstanding, are consolidated on a one month delay basis for its fiscal year ended December 31.

The Company accounts for its common share investment in J.D.A. Software Services Ltd. ('JDA') on the equity basis. Pursuant to a reorganization of JDA effective December 15, 1987, the Company increased its investment in JDA from 22% to 50%. The Company's share of earnings is included as a reduction of administration and other expenses.

(b) Inventories – Retail inventories are accounted for by the retail method and accordingly are carried at the lower of estimated cost and anticipated selling price less an expected gross margin. Automotive inventories are valued at the lower of cost, being specific cost for automotive vehicles and list price less normal gross margin for parts, and net realizable value.

(c) Deferred Charges – System development costs related to a merchandising information project have been deferred and are amortized on a straight line basis over 5 years.

(d) Fixed Assets – Depreciation is designed to amortize fixed assets on a straight line basis over their estimated useful lives at the following annual rates:

Buildings	4%-5%
Leasehold improvements	Term of the Lease
Furniture, fixtures and equipment	20%

Lease vehicles are depreciated on a straight line basis over the term of the lease at a rate sufficient to write down the cost of each unit to its estimated residual value.

(e) Intangible Assets – Goodwill is amortized on a straight line basis over 10 years.

(f) Franchise Fees and Royalties – Initial franchise fees are recorded as income when the cash has been received and the store has been opened. Costs related to the sale of a franchise are expensed as incurred. Continuing royalties which are based on sales of the franchise are recorded as a reduction of personnel, advertising and other variable expenses.

(g) Store Opening Expenses – Costs incurred in connection with the opening of a new store are charged against earnings in the year in which the store commences operations.

(h) Earnings Per Share – Basic earnings per share are calculated using the weighted average number of Restricted Voting and Class A shares outstanding during the year. Exercise of outstanding options would not be dilutive.

2. INVENTORIES

	1987	1988	1989
Retail	$ 22,618	$ 31,221	$ 22,362
Automotive	5,716	6,226	6,092
	$ 28,334	$ 37,447	$ 28,454

3. INVESTMENT AND OTHER ASSETS

	1987	1988	1989
Investment in J.D.A. Software Services Ltd.	$ 144	$ 169	$ 216
Deferred system development costs, net of accumulated amortization	666	500	319
Employee relocation loans	479	397	354
	$ 1,289	$ 1,066	$ 889

4. FIXED ASSETS

	1987	1988	1989	
	Net Book Value	Net Book Value	Cost	Net Book Value
Land	$ 505	$ 1,626	$ 2,399	$ 2,399
Buildings	2,583	4,181	7,698	7,119
Lease vehicles	1,988	2,334	3,931	2,964
Leasehold improvements	1,646	2,062	6,502	2,292
Furniture, fixtures and equipment	2,876	5,277	11,928	4,883
	$ 9,598	$ 15,480	$ 32,458	$ 19,657
Retail	$ 6,387	$ 9,278	$ 19,305	8,427
Automotive	3,211	6,202	13,153	11,230
	$ 9,598	$ 15,480	$ 32,458	$ 19,657

Depreciation on lease vehicles in the amount of $606,000 (1988 – $527,000; 1987 – $432,000) has been charged to cost of sales.

5. INTANGIBLE ASSETS

	1987	1988	1989
Goodwill, net of accumulated amortization	$ 1,154	$ 1,348	$ 1,089
Land option, at cost	500	–	–
	$ 1,654	$ 1,348	$ 1,089

6. CREDIT FACILITIES

The Company has credit facilities as follows:

Type		Amount	Interest Rate
Retail	– Operating	$ 17,000	prime + 1/2%
Automotive	– Operating	$ 1,250	prime + 1/2%
	– New vehicle financing	$ 4,700	prime + 5/8%

Credit Facilities continued

The retail operating line of credit is limited to the lesser of (i) $17,000,000, (ii) 55% of inventories and (iii) the aggregate of 60% of inventories and 50% of accounts receivable, as defined, less retail bank term loans outstanding.

The automotive operating line of credit is limited to the lesser of (i) $1,250,000 and (ii) the sum of 75% of accounts receivable, 50% of parts inventories at cost and 60% of used vehicle inventories at the lower of cost and market value. A further $1,000,000 new vehicle financing facility is available at the same interest rate for two three-month periods during the year.

Security provided includes a first fixed and floating charge debenture on the assets of the Company together with a registered general assignment of book debts and assignment of inventories.

7. LONG-TERM DEBT

a) Balances outstanding

	1987	1988	1989	
	Amount Outstanding	Amount Outstanding	Amount Outstanding	Due Within One Year
Retail				
First mortgages – 10-1/4% to 10-3/4%, amortized over periods from 20 to 30 years, due 1993 to 1997	$ 2,344	$ 2,134	$ 2,099	$ 19
Bank term loans – prime plus 1% to prime plus 1–1/4%, secured as per Note 6, evidenced by a demand note	3,144	4,090	4,073	1,229
	5,488	6,224	6,172	1,248
Automotive				
First mortgages, prime plus 1%, with an option to fix interest rate, repayable over 15 years	–	–	2,774	192
First mortgage – 10%, amortized over 25 years, due March 1993	–	1,935	1,918	21
First mortgage – 12-1/4%, amortized over 25 years, due December 1990	194	192	190	2
Vehicle lease – prime plus 1-1/4% to 1-1/2%	1,784	2,076	2,793	–
Bank term loans – prime plus 1-1/4%, secured as per Note 6, evidenced by a demand note	1,207	791	745	318
	3,185	4,994	8,420	533
Total	8,673	11,218	14,592	$ 1,781
Less amount due within one year	1,254	1,415	1,781	
	$ 7,419	$ 9,803	$ 12,811	

(b) Vehicle Lease – The vehicle lease loan is secured by and will be repaid out of future lease rentals derived from lease vehicles included in fixed assets. The principal repayment schedule (Note 7(c)) includes amounts related to repayment of the vehicle lease loan.

(c) Principal Repayments – The aggregate repayments of principal required to meet long-term debt obligations in each of the next five years and thereafter are as follows:

1990	$2,982	1992	$ 1,857	1994	$ 366
1991	$2,349	1993	$ 1,359	Thereafter	$ 5,679

8. CAPITAL STOCK

The authorized capital stock of the Company is divided into 8,000,000 First Preferred Shares of no par value; 877,000 Class A Shares of no par value; and 50,000,000 Restricted Voting Shares of no par value.

The Class A Shares and Restricted Voting Shares rank equally as to dividends and upon any liquidation, dissolution or winding up of the Company. The voting rights attached to the Restricted Voting Shares are limited in that the holders thereof are entitled to elect three members of the board while the holders of Class A Shares are entitled to determine the size of the board and to elect the remaining members thereof. Class A Shares are convertible into Restricted Voting Shares on a one for one basis.

The Class A Shares shall have these rights so long as either M.W. Blumes or M.A. Blumes is an officer and director of the Company and the Restricted Voting and Class A Shares controlled by either or both of them aggregate more than 650,000 shares and more than 5% of the total number of outstanding Restricted Voting and Class A Shares.

M.W. Blumes and M.A. Blumes have provided undertakings that they will not directly nor indirectly vote any Restricted Voting Shares resulting from the conversion of Class A Shares, nor will they tender any Class A Shares upon any offer made for such shares unless a tender offer on substantially similar terms is made to holders of Restricted Voting Shares.

The issued capital stock of the Company is as follows:

	1987	1988	1989
877,000 Class A Shares	$ 2	$ 2	$ 2
9,094,306 Restricted Voting Shares (1987 – 9,082,806)	14,541	14,556	14,556
	$14,543	$14,558	$14,558

11,500 Restricted Voting Shares were issued during 1988 pursuant to the exercise of employee stock options. 11,287 Restricted Voting Shares were cancelled during 1987 in settlement of an employee loan balance.

Options to purchase Restricted Voting Shares granted to employees and outstanding as at January 28, 1989 are as follows:

Number of Restricted Voting Shares	Exercise Price	Expiry Date
32,000	$2.92	Dec., 1990
495,000	$1.15	June, 1992

9. INCOME TAXES

The provision for income taxes varies from the amount computed by applying the combined federal and provincial income tax rates of approximately 48.7% (1988 – 51.0%; 1987 – 50.1%) for the year as follows:

	1987		1988		1989	
Federal and provincial income taxes	50.1%	$2,534	51.0%	$1,866	48.7%	$1,834
Increase (decrease) resulting from:						
Amortization of Intangible assets	2.1%	107	3.5%	127	3.3%	124
Tax rate changes	–	–	–	–	(9.0%)	(340)
Inventory allowance	(1.0%)	(43)	–	–	–	–
Other	(0.1%)	(14)	0.3%	10	(0.2%)	(8)
Provision for income taxes	51.1%	$2,584	54.8%	$2,003	42.8%	$1,610

At January 28, 1989 the Company had net capital loss carryforwards in the aggregate amount of $1,138,000 available to reduce future years' taxable capital gains, the benefit of which has not been recorded in these financial statements.

10. DISCONTINUED OPERATIONS AND EXTRAORDINARY ITEM

		1987	1988	1989
Discontinued Operations				
Revenue	– U.S. retail	$ 10,001	$ –	$ –
	– Automotive	$ 18,338	$ 2,221	$ –
Net earnings (loss)	– U.S. retail	$ (879)	$ –	$ –
	– Automotive	26	(93)	–
		$ (853)	$ (93)	$ –
Extraordinary Item				
Loss on closure of U.S. retail operation		$ (638)	$ –	$ –

11. LEASE AND PROPERTY COMMITMENTS

The Company has entered into operating lease agreements terminating at various dates to 2008. The minimum annual rentals, excluding tenant operating costs, under these agreements are as follows:

1990	$ 8,552	1993	$ 4,526
1991	8,006	1994	2,535
1992	6,282	In aggregate thereafter	9,851

In addition to minimum annual rentals, contingent rentals may be paid under certain store leases on the basis of sales in excess of stipulated amounts.

12. SUBSEQUENT EVENT

Subsequent to January 28, 1989 the Company disposed of land and buildings with a net book value of $901,000 for net proceeds of $1,429,000.

13. SEGMENT INFORMATION

The Company's operations are in two industry segments, both in Canada.

(a) Retail operations at January 28, 1989 were conducted through 105 corporate stores and 30 franchise stores (from which the Company derives royalty revenue) which provide a complete range of workwear, casual wear and related apparel.

(b) Automotive operations include three new car dealerships (two Honda and one BMW) and an autobody operation.

		1987	1988	1989
Sales	– Retail	$116,843	$136,083	$152,779
	– Automotive	42,211	39,835	41,735
		$159,054	$175,918	$194,514
Earnings (loss) before income taxes	– Retail	$ 4,412	$ 3,886	$ 4,156
	– Automotive	638	(229)	(391)
		$ 5,050	$ 3,657	$ 3,765
Retail stores at year end	– Corporate	92	106	105
	– Franchise	10	18	30
		102	124	135
Identifiable assets	– Retail	$ 38,196	$ 49,076	$ 48,889
	– Automotive	10,762	12,193	17,349
		48,958	61,269	66,238
Deferred income taxes		1,485	1,380	1,571
Intangible assets		1,654	1,348	1,089
Total assets		$ 52,097	$ 63,997	$ 68,898

14. SELECTED QUARTERLY FINANCIAL INFORMATION FOR CONTINUING OPERATIONS (Unaudited)

Fifty-two weeks ended January 28, 1989

		First	Second	Third	Fourth
Sales	– Retail	$28,216	$28,213	$39,304	$57,046
	– Automotive	8,461	11,689	11,270	10,315
		$36,677	$39,902	$50,574	$67,361
Gross margin percentage	– Retail	38.5%	34.5%	37.4%	36.9%
	– Automotive	16.2%	15.0%	14.9%	13.8%
Earnings (loss) before income taxes	– Retail	$ (1,556)	$ (1,939)	$ 1,522	$ 6,129
	– Automotive	(158)	19	(35)	(217)
		$ (1,714)	$ (1,920)	$ 1,487	$ 5,912
Earnings (loss) per share		(9)¢	(11)¢	7¢	35¢
Retail Stores at end of quarter		106	106	106	105

Fifty-two weeks ended January 30, 1988

		First	Second	Third	Fourth
Sales	– Retail	$23,877	$24,266	$35,937	$52,003
	– Automotive	8,219	10,790	10,861	9,965
		$32,096	$35,056	$46,798	$61,968
Gross margin percentage	– Retail	37.9%	38.8%	40.3%	38.5%
	– Automotive	16.9%	15.4%	16.0%	15.4%
Earnings (loss) before income taxes	– Retail	$ (427)	$ (782)	$ 1,007	$ 4,088
	– Automotive	(240)	(90)	96	5
		$ (667)	$ (872)	$ 1,103	$ 4,093
Earnings (loss) per share		(3)¢	(6)¢	5¢	20¢
Retail Stores at end of quarter		91	95	105	106

Fifty-three weeks ended January 31, 1987

		First	Second	Third	Fourth
Sales	– Retail	$20,989	$22,231	$28,234	$45,389
	– Automotive	9,456	11,929	11,203	9,623
		$30,445	$34,160	$39,437	$55,012
Gross margin percentage	– Retail	36.4%	37.7%	38.4%	36.6%
	– Automotive	20.8%	16.7%	17.0%	17.2%
Earnings (loss) before income taxes	– Retail	$ (704)	$ (436)	$ 1,397	$ 4,155
	– Automotive	316	185	250	(113)
		$ (388)	$ (251)	$ 1,647	$ 4,042
Earnings (loss) per share before extraordinary item		(3)¢	(8)¢	6¢	21¢
Retail Stores at end of quarter		89	89	90	92

A S S I G N M E N T   M A T E R I A L S

Discussion Questions

Chapter 1:   Financial Statements and the Accounting Model

1. Identify the economic resources of Mark's Work Wearhouse.
2. Mark's Work Wearhouse is a separate legal entity. Are T & T Honda and T & T BMW separate legal entities? How do these business segments fit in?
3. Who are the auditors? Specifically what does their report tell you?
4. Which categories of financial statements are included in the annual report? What do they purport to report? (Note that the statement of retained earnings is discussed in Chapter 4.)
5. What classifications are found in the income statement? in the balance sheet?
6. What are the objectives of the financial statements used by Mark's Work Wearhouse? How are these objectives expressed in the report? *-RETAINED EARNINGS NOTES TO FIN. STATEMENTS*
7. How would the equity of Mark's Work Wearhouse appear if the company were
   a. A proprietorship?
   b. A partnership?
8. From the balance sheet at January 31, 1989, extract the appropriate amounts to complete the following accounting equations:
   a. ASSETS = LIABILITIES + EQUITY
   b. ASSETS − LIABILITIES = EQUITY
9. If ASSETS − LIABILITIES = NET ASSETS, how much is net assets? Is net assets synonymous with equity?

10. Comment on the financial structure of Mark's Work Wearhouse. Does the company have a high reliance or a low reliance on debt?
11. What is the proportion of shareholders' and creditors' claims to the assets of Mark's Work Wearhouse? Is the company overfinanced or underfinanced?
12. Comment on leverage (the proportion of debt) as it relates to Mark's Work Wearhouse.
13. Financial transactions are usually backed up by documents such as receipts and cancelled cheques. What documents do you think Mark's Work Wearhouse uses?
14. What types of assets are reported by Mark's Work Wearhouse? What types of liabilities?
15. What were the major sources and uses of cash? Is the cash balance increasing or decreasing?
16. What is the company's year-end? Why did the year consist of 53 weeks in 1987 (refer to the financial statements)?
17. The periodicity concept assumes that the entity's activities can be broken into meaningful time periods. Review the quarterly financial information. What becomes apparent when you compare different quarters within one year and the same quarter between different years? Can the business activities of Mark's Work Wearhouse be accurately broken into quarters?

Chapter 2:   GAAP and the Accounting Process

18. Accounting for financial transactions makes it possible to measure the progress of the entity. How do generally accepted accounting principles affect this measurement?
19. Does the auditor's report indicate whether Mark's Work Wearhouse has been consistent in the application of GAAP?
20. How large do you think Mark's Work Wearhouse's chart of accounts is? How does using many different accounts

facilitate the interpretation of financial data?
21. What formal accounting records do you think Mark's Work Wearhouse uses?
22. From reading the annual report, can you tell whether the company has made any cost-benefit judgements about including disclosures? Do they take materiality into account?

Chapter 3:   GAAP and the Operating Cycle

23. What kind of recognition criteria do you think Mark's Work Wearhouse uses?

24. At what point is revenue recognized in Mark's Work Wearhouse? What would the journal entry be if the company received $10,000 in advance of its being earned?

25. Does Mark's Work Wearhouse use the cash basis of accounting or the accrual basis? How can you tell?

26. What kind of assumptions are made by Mark's Work Wearhouse over what period of time as an asset wears out?

27. Should the salary of Mark Blumes be recorded as an asset since his salary brings benefits to the company in future accounting periods? Why or why not?

28. What do the accountants at Mark's Work Wearhouse measure when they prepare periodic accounting reports? Consider the following categories:
    a. Adjusting asset accounts
    b. Adjusting fixed asset accounts
    c. Adjusting liability accounts
    d. Unrecorded accruals.
    Indicate several examples in each category. Use the financial statements for ideas.

29. What sequence of steps is followed in preparing the following reports?
    a. Quarterly accounting reports
    b. Fiscal year-end accounting reports

30. What are reversing entries and why would the accountants at Mark's Work Wearhouse consider using them? (If you were not assigned the material in the Appendix: Reversing Entries, omit this question.)

Chapter 4:   Accounting for Merchandising Operations

31. How much is the gross profit of Mark's Work Wearhouse for 1989? Calculate the gross profit percentage for 1987, 1988, and 1989. Is it increasing or decreasing? What are the implications of this change?

32. What steps does the sales and collection cycle include at Mark's Work Wearhouse? What accounts are used?

33. What is included in Mark's Work Wearhouse's purchase and payment cycle? What accounts does this cycle involve?

34. What components are involved in the calculation of the cost of goods sold? What is the opening inventory for the year ended January 28, 1989? What is the closing inventory? What is the net cost of purchases for the year?

35. Is a periodic or a perpetual inventory system used by Mark's Work Wearhouse? How can you tell?

36. How does Mark's Work Wearhouse make it easier to compare information from one time period to another?

37. Mark's Work Wearhouse calculates earnings per share in three different ways:
    a. From continuing operations
    b. Before extraordinary items
    c. From net earnings.
    Comment on the differences in the EPS calculated by each method. Which method provides the most meaningful results?

38. What are prior-period adjustments? Are any reported in the financial statements of Mark's Work Wearhouse? What sort of items would qualify as prior-period adjustments?

Chapter 5:   Inventory

39. Refer to point 1(b) in Notes to Consolidated Financial Statements in the annual report. What method does the company use to account for inventory? Explain how inventory cost is calculated.

40. If the ending inventory of Mark's Work Wearhouse at January 30, 1988 were understated by $1 million, what would be the impact on the following financial statements?
    a. The 1988 income statement
    b. The 1988 balance sheet
    c. The 1989 income statement
    d. The 1989 balance sheet

41. What is the most appropriate cost flow method for a merchandiser to use? Is Mark's Work Wearhouse using this method? What might be the impact on the following financial statements of using a different method?
    a. The income statement
    b. The balance sheet

42. Do you think that Mark's Work Wearhouse has some phantom profits? Explain using calculations.

43. Does the LOCAM method play a role at Mark's Work Wearhouse? How would it work?

Chapter 6:   Cash and Receivables

44. According to the balance sheet, accounts receivable are $6,712,000, with no indication of bad debts. Doesn't Mark's Work Wearhouse have any bad debts? Why aren't they indicated?

45. Cash is handled at many locations. What kind of cash controls should Mark's Work Wearhouse use?

46. Mark's Work Wearhouse has 105 stores. How might the company do its bank reconciliations?

47. Should some of Mark's Work Wearhouse's cash be put into short-term investments? Isn't the company losing interest on their $9,116,000 cash?

48. What are management's responsibilities for the financial statements? Do the financial statements belong to management? to the board of directors? to the auditors?

Chapter 7:   Financial Statement Disclosure

49. How does the accountant's measurement of wealth differ from that of the economist? According to the accountant's measurement, what is the amount of wealth created by Mark's Work Wearhouse during the year ended January 28, 1989? How could you calculate the amount according to the economist's measurement? Which is a more precise calculation?

50. According to Real Life Example 7-3, Mark Blumes tells employees that it's time to make money. From your reading of the annual report, how has he played the game of financial performance? Consider
    a. Return on total assets
    b. Return on shareholders' equity
    c. Return on sales.

51. What categories are presented in the classified income statement of Mark's Work Wearhouse? Would additional categories be useful? If so, which ones?

52. What are the advantages of using a classified balance sheet? What categories does Bluebeard Computer Corporation use that Mark's Work Wearhouse does not? Which set of categories is preferable?

53. What disclosure is provided about discontinued operations reported on the income statements from 1987 to 1989? Exactly what was discontinued and why? Was there a positive impact on net income after the discontinuation?

54. What characteristics must an extraordinary item have? Give examples of extraordinary items.

55. Refer to Real Life Example 7-2. Given a choice between social responsibility and profits, what are shareholders likely to ask for?

The Conversion Cycle

Part 3 focuses on the conversion of an entity's resources acquired through expenditures. Conversion refers not only to the resale of assets but also to their use and consumption. Inventory and fixed assets are included in this category; their use or consumption in manufacturing operations usually represents a substantial amount of the entity's resources.

Fixed assets are often used in the operations of an entity. A truck, for example, can be used for deliveries, a building for storage of unsold inventory. Chapter 8 deals with establishing the cost of long-term assets and their depreciation over their estimated useful lives; it also includes a comparison of depreciation allocation assumptions.

In a manufacturing entity, inventory — often called raw materials — is transformed through production into finished goods ready for sale. An intermediate inventory production stage is referred to as work in process. Finished goods and work-in-process cost normally include material, labour, and overhead components. Fixed assets, as used in manufacturing operations, form part of the overhead cost. Chapter 16, which discusses the accounting required for manufacturing operations, is part of the conversion cycle, although it appears later in the text for pedagogical reasons.

Fixed Assets

Fixed assets are used in the normal operating activities of the business and are expected to provide benefits for a period in excess of one year. Depreciation is calculated to allocate a part of fixed asset cost over its useful life.

1. What is the distinction between capital expenditures and revenue expenditures?
2. How do generally accepted accounting principles prescribe what amount should be capitalized?
3. How should a corporation record the cost of an asset it has constructed?
4. What is the distinction between a betterment and an extraordinary repair?
5. What is the primary objective of recording periodic depreciation?
6. What different methods can be used in the calculation of depreciation?
7. What is the maximum amount of depreciation on fixed assets that is permissible for income tax purposes?
8. Is the value of services rendered by a fixed asset in the first year of its life the same as in its last year?
9. What is the impact on fixed assets of the changing purchasing power of the dollar through inflation?
10. How does current cost accounting provide for the maintenance of operating capacity?

A. Establishing Cost of Fixed Assets

At the time of its acquisition, a long-term asset can be thought of as a bundle of services that will be used up over a period of years. Each year, as a part of this bundle of services is used up, a part of its cost is written off. Eventually the asset is all used up and is no longer useful. At this point, the asset is disposed of. This life cycle of a fixed asset is illustrated in Figure 8-1.

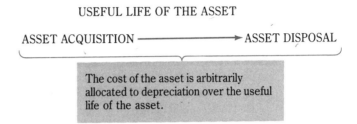

USEFUL LIFE OF THE ASSET

ASSET ACQUISITION ⎯⎯⎯⎯⎯⎯⎯⎯→ ASSET DISPOSAL

The cost of the asset is arbitrarily allocated to depreciation over the useful life of the asset.

Figure 8-1   Life cycle of a fixed asset

Capital Expenditures

Capital expenditures
Asset costs plus costs to prepare the asset for use.

(to) Capitalize
To record an expenditure as an asset, rather than as an expense; often referred to as a *capital expenditure*.

Capital expenditures consist of the asset cost less any applicable cash discounts, plus any additional costs involved in preparing the asset for use. Assume that equipment is purchased for a net price of $20,000, transportation costs $500, installation requiring special wiring costs $1,000, construction of a cement foundation costs $2,500, and test runs to debug the equipment cost $2,000. The total cost of the asset, then, is $26,000. In addition to the purchase price or invoice cost of the asset acquired, the costs to prepare the asset for use are also **capitalized**. The various costs that may be incurred in the course of acquiring and preparing the asset for use are listed below.

Capital Expenditures

	Land	*Building*	*Equipment*
Cost To Acquire the Asset	Purchase price Commission to real estate agent Legal fees	Purchase price Commission to real estate agent Legal fees	Invoice cost Transportation Insurance (during transportation)
Costs To Prepare Asset for Use	Costs of draining, clearing, and landscaping Assessments for streets and sewage system	Repair and remodelling costs before use Payments to tenants for premature termination of lease	Assembly Installation (including wages paid to company employees) Special floor foundations or supports Wiring Inspection Test run costs

There are well-established principles for determining what amounts should be included in the cost of the asset in most situations.

> Generally accepted accounting principles require that all costs benefitting future accounting periods in which the asset will be used be included in the cost of the asset.

The preceding types of cost are clear examples of expenditures made in the course of acquiring the asset and preparing it for use. However, other expenditures are often more difficult to allocate. These are discussed next.

Land

In addition to the costs listed in the preceding schedule, the cost of land will be increased by the cost of removing any useless structures found on the land. This cost is reduced by the proceeds, if any, obtained from the sale of the scrap. Assume that the total cost of land is $100,000 before an additional $15,000 cost to raze an old building: $1,000 is expected to be received for salvaged materials. The cost of the land is $114,000.

Total Cost of Land		$100,000
Razing Costs for Building	$15,000	
Less: Salvage Proceeds	1,000	14,000
		$114,000

Frequently, land and useful buildings are purchased for a lump sum. If the buildings will be used for business purposes, the purchase price must be apportioned between the land and buildings, because buildings are subject to depreciation. Land does not usually depreciate, since its utility for building or for other purposes does not diminish. The purchase price is usually allocated to the acquired assets on the basis of their market values. Assume that a lump sum of $150,000 is paid for land and buildings. This cost can be allocated as follows:

	Market Value	*Percent of Total Market Value*	*Cost Allocation*
Land	$ 50,000	25%	$ 37,500 ($150,000 × 25%)
Building	150,000	75%	112,500 ($150,000 × 75%)
Total	$200,000	100%	$150,000

The allocation can also be made on some other basis; it may be based on municipal assessed values or on estimates made by a professional appraiser.

As stated earlier, land does not normally depreciate. An exception to this rule occurs where non-renewable mineral deposits or oil are to be removed from the land during future accounting periods. In such cases, the mineral deposit component of the land is subject to depletion, and is deducted from the asset account as the non-renewable resource is removed from the land. Further discussion of this topic is in section F of this chapter.

Building and Equipment

When an asset is purchased, its cost includes the net purchase price plus all costs to prepare the asset for use. In some cases, a business may construct its own building or equipment. In the case of a building, for example, cost includes all pertinent expenditures, including costs for excavation, building permits, insurance and property taxes during construction, engineering fees, the cost of labour incurred by having company employees supervise and work on the construction of the building, and the cost of any interest incurred to finance the construction during the construction period.

The cost of an asset constructed by the company is never recorded at the amount that it would have cost to have someone else construct the same building or piece of equipment. Accounting principles do not permit the recording of an unrealized profit — from construction of an asset at less than purchase cost, in this case.

In some cases, one asset is exchanged for another asset. Assume that a piece of land acquired several years ago at a cost of $25,000 is exchanged for a piece of equipment owned by another company. At the time of the exchange, the **fair market value (FMV)** of the land is $50,000 and the FMV of the equipment is $60,000. What is the cost of the equipment?

Fair market value (FMV)
The price or cost of an asset negotiated between two parties dealing at arm's length.

The rule followed by most accountants in this type of situation requires that the cost of the asset acquired (equipment) be the FMV of the asset given up (land, FMV $50,000); if the FMV of the land cannot be established or is not clear, then the FMV of the asset acquired (equipment, FMV $60,000) is used.

Real Life Example 8-1

Buy or Lease?

Should You Buy or Lease Space?

There is no best, least expensive, route to acquiring business space. Each company must decide from among a broad spectrum of financial and non-financial options and considerations.

Without denying the importance of non-financial and even emotional factors, however, you should explore your financial options on their own merits. One of the biggest decisions any company can make is whether to lease or buy.

Both owning and leasing have benefits and drawbacks. A company's existing circumstances, projected position, and goals can turn some of the intrinsic benefits of one into drawbacks, and vice versa.

Buying Takes Capital

To buy space usually takes a lot of initial capital as well as borrowing ability. The purchase uses funds that you could invest in other areas, within or outside the company.

The major advantage of buying include tax benefits, depreciation's contribution to cash flow, the possibility of appreciation in value, and of course the warm feeling that comes from owning something of value.

But the property investment is only as liquid as the real estate marketplace, on which also depends the owner's future freedom to move or to rent out excess space. While ownership gives a company control over the management and use of the space, it also imposes responsibilities and requires attention that the company might more productively give to its primary business.

Leasing: Pay As You Go

Leasing does not require a major capital outlay. Leasing preserves the company's existing capital and borrowing power for other investments, but lease payments aren't likely to appreciate in value.

You can often negotiate favourable settlements or terms if you must move out of or change leased space early. You may even be able to negotiate some tax benefits. But these benefits will rarely match those of ownership.

Though a tenant usually exercises less control over leased space than owned space, degrees of control are negotiable in leases. The tenant also does not have to be concerned with building management. That's the property owner's responsibility.

The decision to lease or buy may rest on your choice of location. It is harder to buy a prime location than to rent one.

Assessing Future Costs Today

To evaluate and compare the financial elements of the buying or leasing option, you must assign a value to each element of a lease and to each element of the cost of buying. To make the comparison's outcome comprehensible, if inexact, you must measure the value in today's dollars. Be aware, though, that no amount of forecasting can produce a precise dollar comparison that will remain valid for 15 or 20 years. Inflation and interest rates are only two of the many variables that one cannot accurately foresee. The future is risk by another name.

Net present value (NPV), however, is a useful tool for analyzing future costs in today's dollars. NPV should be viewed as an index, rather than a dollar figure. It represents the present value of future payments discounted at the opportunity rate, i.e., the projected loss from not investing the same money elsewhere.

Source   Marita Thomas, ''Facilities Planning, Evaluation and Acquisition for Smaller Corporations'', *Inc. Magazine*, September 1984, p. 111.

One exception to this rule occurs when one asset is traded in for a similar asset — an old piece of equipment for a new piece of equipment, for example. This topic is treated in section C of this chapter.

Capital and Revenue Expenditures

Expenditure
A cash disbursement to obtain an asset, goods, or services.

Any cash disbursement is referred to as an **expenditure**. All expenditures made to purchase an asset and for its preparation for use are capitalized. When these expenditures are debited to an asset account, they are said to be capitalized and are referred to as capital expenditures. An expenditure of this kind produces an asset. Some expenditures occur during the asset's life, rather than at the time the asset is acquired.

> Generally accepted accounting principles require expenditures to be capitalized when they will benefit more than one accounting period, when they are significant in amount, and when they can be measured with reasonably objective evidence.

Betterment
A change to an asset that increases its efficiency.

For capital expenditures, a distinction is often made between a betterment and an extraordinary repair. A **betterment** results in a change to the asset that increases its efficiency; the estimated useful life of the asset does not change. For example, if a tape drive in a personal computer is replaced by a disk drive, the cost of the betterment is added to the existing asset cost and is depreciated over the existing asset's useful life. The cost of the replaced part and accumulated depreciation attributable to it are removed from the accounts.

Extraordinary repair
A change to an asset that increases its estimated useful life.

An **extraordinary repair** results in a change of the estimated useful life of the asset. The cost is debited to accumulated depreciation rather than to asset cost, since it is viewed as reducing the previously recorded depreciation. The resulting net asset cost is then depreciated over the asset's remaining useful life. The accounting procedures in establishing the revised depreciation charges are discussed later in this chapter.

Revenue expenditure
An expenditure recorded as an expense to be matched with the current period's revenue; often thought of as routine maintenance expenses, as opposed to a capital expenditure that is recorded as an asset.

Not all asset-related expenditures incurred after the purchase of an asset are capitalized. Other expenditures, called **revenue expenditures**, result in an addition to an expense account. Examples of these expenditures include the cost of replacing parts of an asset (e.g., in the case of a truck, new tires, new muffler, new battery), continuing expenditures for maintaining the asset in good working order (e.g., oil changes, antifreeze, transmission fluid changes), and costs of renewing structural parts of an asset (e.g., repairs of collision damage, repair or replacement of rusted parts).

> An expenditure made to maintain an asset in satisfactory working order is a *revenue expenditure* of the accounting period in which the expenditure was made.

Although some revenue expenditures will benefit more than one accounting period, they do not increase the serviceability of the asset beyond its original useful life and therefore are treated as normal maintenance costs.

Three criteria should be considered when establishing a policy to distinguish between capital and revenue expenditures incurred after the purchase and installation of an asset.

Asset-Related Expenditures Following Purchase of the Asset

Criterion	*Capital Expenditure*	*Revenue Expenditure*
1. Life of the Part	Will benefit two or more accounting periods.	Will benefit the current accounting period.
2. Expenditure for Repairs	Will prolong the useful life of the asset beyond the original estimate; make it more valuable or more adaptable.	Will not prolong the useful life of the asset beyond the original estimate; doesn't make it more valuable or more adaptable.
3. Materiality of the Expenditure	Dollar amount of expenditure is large, is not made often, and will benefit two or more accounting periods.	Dollar amount of expenditure is small, is made relatively often, and does not materially affect net income.

The concept of *materiality* enters into the distinction between capital and revenue expenditures. As a matter of expediency, an expenditure of $200 that has all the characteristics of a capital expenditure would probably be expensed rather than capitalized in an entity such as General Motors, because the effort to capitalize and depreciate the item is so much greater than the benefits to be derived. Policies are established by many companies to resolve the problem of distinguishing between capital and revenue expenditures. For example, all capital expenditures in excess of $1,000 are capitalized; all capital expenditures under $1,000 are expensed.

B. The Nature of Depreciation

It is unfortunate but true that the new sportscar you would like to purchase or are thinking of purchasing will wear out — probably in five to seven years. The engine will begin to break down; the five on the floor will become two-and-a-half; the imitation leather seats will tear; within five years, depending on where you live, the car will rust through. Meantime (probably within two years), the price of gas will have increased to such an extent that you will not be able to afford the car's 3 km/L (9 mi./gal.), and you will be forced to purchase a mini-bike — a case of technological obsolescence in action.

Tangible assets
Assets of a physical and relatively permanent nature, acquired for use in the regular operations of an entity; for example, land, building, equipment, and trucks.

Unfortunately, **tangible assets** come to the end of their usefulness, whether from physical deterioration (cars, lawn mowers) or obsolescence caused by such factors as technology (monaural record players) or the enactment of prohibitory laws (selling cigarettes to minors). A classic description of the nature of depreciation was given by Professor Henry Rand Hatfield, an eminent accountant, when he wrote:

> All machinery is on an irresistible march to the junk heap, and its progress, while it may be delayed, cannot be prevented by repairs.[1]

Useful life
(of an asset) An estimate of the time over which an asset will benefit the operations of an entity.

The role of depreciation is to recognize this limited **useful life** and to allocate the cost of the asset over its useful life; that is, over the accounting periods expected to receive benefits from its use.

Assume that a machine acquired for $20,000 will have an estimated useful life of 5 years, after which time it will be scrapped for $2,000. The company has purchased for $20,000 a 5-year bundle of services, part of which will be used up each year, as shown in Figure 8-2.

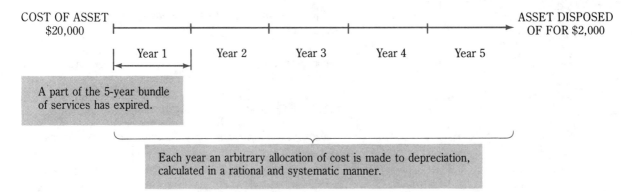

Figure 8-2   Allocation of cost over the useful life of an asset

Depreciation
The expiration of a fixed asset's usefulness; the process of allocating the cost of a fixed asset to each accounting period that will benefit from its use. The amount recorded during an accounting period depends on an estimate of (1) the asset's useful life; (2) the asset's scrap value; and (3) the method of depreciation used.

Depletion
Physical exhaustion of a natural resource; the process of allocating the cost of a natural resource to each accounting period receiving benefits. The exhaustion of part of the natural resource results in an allocation of cost to expense.

Amortization
The process of allocating the cost of an asset to each accounting period receiving benefits; usually used in the case of intangible assets.

Each year, part of the bundle of services of the asset is allocated to expense. The problem is: how do you measure the benefits that flow from an asset? Without this information (and it is difficult to obtain in practice) how do accountants rationally allocate the cost of an asset to a particular accounting period? The answer is that they can't! In actual practice, an estimate is made.

Assets included within the non-current asset category for fixed assets are
1. Depreciable tangible assets, such as buildings and equipment; **depreciation** is the term used to describe the allocation of a tangible asset's cost to expense over its useful life
2. Depreciable natural resource assets, such as oil and coal; **depletion** is the term used to describe the allocation of a natural resource's cost to expense over its useful life
3. Depreciable intangible assets, such as patents and goodwill; **amortization** is the term used to describe the allocation of an asset's cost to expense over its useful life
4. Other assets, such as investment assets and non-production assets.

Fixed Asset Cost Allocation Methods

Income determination is a primary objective of the depreciation process.

According to generally accepted accounting principles, a firm should adopt the method of allocating the cost of an asset to depreciation expense that produces the most appropriate matching of depreciation costs with revenues earned.

The most frequently used methods to allocate asset cost over its estimated useful life are
- Usage methods
- Time-based methods : Straight-line method
                               : Declining balance method.

Usage Methods

Usage methods of calculating depreciation are useful when wear and tear is the major cause of depreciation and when the amount of asset use may vary from period to period. Depreciation is calculated on the basis of an equal amount charged for each unit produced, each hour worked, each kilometre driven, each tonne hauled. Assume that a machine costing $20,000 has a **salvage value** of $2,000 and is expected to have an estimated productive life of 10 000 units. If 1500 units were processed during the current period, the depreciation expense for the period would be $2,700.

$$\frac{\text{Cost} - \text{Salvage value}}{\substack{\text{Number of units of}\\\text{estimated productive life}}} = \substack{\text{Depreciation}\\\text{per unit}} \times \substack{\text{Number of units}\\\text{produced}} = \substack{\text{Depreciation expense}\\\text{for the period}}$$

or, using the figures given:

$$\frac{\$20,000 - \$2,000}{10\ 000\ \text{units}} = \$1.80 \times 1500\ \text{units} = \$2,700\ \text{depreciation expense.}$$

Usage methods assume that the asset will contribute to the earning of revenues in relation to the amount of use during the accounting period. Therefore, the depreciation expense under this method records the decline in the capacity of the asset during the period.

Time-Based, Straight-Line Method

The straight-line method — introduced briefly in Chapter 3 — ignores asset usage and assumes that the asset will contribute to the earning of revenues equally during each period; that is, each period will receive services of equal value. Therefore, equal amounts of depreciation are recorded during each year of its useful life.

The straight-line method is, therefore, appropriate for an asset that makes an equal contribution to operations during each year of its productive life. It is not appropriate when the asset does not contribute uniformly to operations during each year of its life.

> Under the straight-line method, depreciation expense for each accounting period remains the same dollar amount during the useful life of the asset.

The straight-line method can be calculated as follows:

$$\frac{\text{Cost} - \text{Salvage value}}{\text{Estimated useful life}} = \text{Depreciation expense.}$$

Assume that the same $20,000 machine used earlier, with an estimated service life of 5 years and an estimated net salvage value of $2,000, is depreciated on the straight-line method. The annual depreciation charge is:

$$\frac{\$20,000 - \$2,000}{5} = \$3,600.$$

Figure 8-3 illustrates the arbitrary method of allocating costs in the straight-line method.

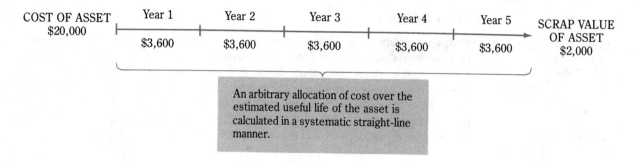

Figure 8-3   Allocation of cost using the straight-line method

The straight-line method considers depreciation as a function of time and its main advantage is its simplicity of calculation. Since it is usually difficult to judge what the pattern of an asset's use will be, this method is the one that is least likely to be subject to bias.

Time-Based, Declining Balance Method

Declining balance method
(of depreciation)
Depreciation is calculated on the assumption that during the useful life of an asset, each period receives unequal benefits from the use of the asset; a constant rate is applied to the remaining carrying value of each period.

The **declining balance method** of allocating fixed asset costs assumes that the asset will contribute more to the earning of revenues in the earlier stages of its useful life than in the later stages. Accordingly, more depreciation is recorded in earlier years with the depreciation expense gradually decreasing each year. Because more depreciation is calculated initially, it is often referred to as an *accelerated depreciation method.*

The declining balance method is most appropriate where assets experience high technological obsolescence in the early part of their useful lives (for example, computers) or where the value of the service rendered is not the same in the first year when the asset (for example, a machine) is new and efficient, as in the last year when it is nearly broken down.

> Under the declining balance method, depreciation expense becomes smaller each year during the useful life of the asset.

Note, however, that some accountants consider that the amount of maintenance required in later years of the asset's life may equal the difference between the lower depreciation amount calculated under the declining-balance method and the amount that would result under the straight-line method. Accordingly, the total of depreciation and maintenance expense may result in virtually equal amounts of expense during future years.

Net book value
(of an asset)
Cost less accumulated depreciation.

Under the declining balance method, a constant rate is applied to the balance of the **net book value**, also called the *net carrying value* (cost less accumulated depreciation). This rate is calculated in actual practice by a somewhat involved mathematical formula, designed to measure best the amount of depreciation to be recorded for each accounting period. The method of calculating such a rate is complex and accordingly is left for coverage in a quantitative methods course. For our purposes, a rate can be calculated at double the straight-line rate (double declining balance), at one-and-one-half times the straight-line rate (150 percent declining balance), or in any other manner appropriate in the circumstances.

For example, the $20,000 machine has an estimated useful life of 5 years. The straight-line rate is 20 percent calculated by dividing 100 percent by 5 years (100% ÷ 5 = 20%). In order to calculate the declining balance rate, this straight-line rate of 20 percent is doubled to obtain the *double-declining balance rate* (20% × 2 = 40%); it is multiplied by one-and-one-half times to obtain a 150 percent declining balance rate (20% × 1½ = 30%).

For income tax purposes, the rate cannot exceed the maximum allowed by official government regulations. It is important to note that declining balance rate is applied to the net book value, that is the carrying value, of the asset before any deduction for salvage value. However, the asset is not depreciated below its salvage value. In other words, in the example used, depreciation expense would not be recorded once the net book value is $2,000, since the asset has an estimated salvage value of $2,000 and, therefore, will not depreciate below this amount. A 40 percent depreciation rate — double the straight-line rate of 20 percent — applied to the carrying value remaining at the end of each year gives the following results for the 5 years. (Note that salvage value is ignored in the amount being depreciated.)

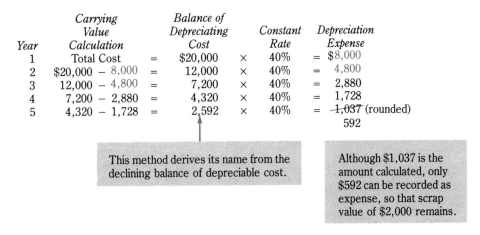

Figure 8-4 illustrates the arbitrary method of allocating costs in the declining balance method.

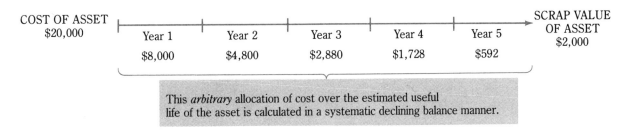

Figure 8-4   Allocation of costs using the declining balance method

Capital cost allowance
An income tax term meaning depreciation. It results from the use of a declining balance method of depreciation permitted by the Income Tax Act.

For income tax purposes, depreciation is referred to as **capital cost allowance**. Depreciable assets are grouped into classes and can be depreciated at any rate up to a maximum allowed by official regulations. For example, automobiles and trucks may be depreciated at a maximum rate of 30 percent, calculated on the balance at year-end. Equipment may be depreciated at a maximum rate of 20 percent. Each class of assets is treated separately and is subject to a specific maximum depreciation rate. This system minimizes disputes between the taxpayer and the income tax authorities.

Actual Practice versus GAAP

The most important part of the cost allocation process is the recognition of the portion of the asset services that have expired. In actual practice, there is considerable evidence that the value of services rendered by an asset in the first year of its life is not the same as in its last year. An apartment building, for example, commands greater rent and occupancy when it is new than when it is older. Similarly, a lathe produces fewer rejects in its initial year than in its later years. This phenomenon has resulted in a belief among many accountants that depreciation of assets should be recorded so that a larger amount of depreciation is allotted to earlier years and a smaller amount to the later years. The depreciation pattern can therefore be illustrated as a curve, as shown in Figure 8-5.

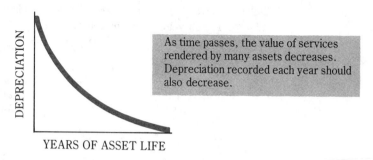

As time passes, the value of services rendered by many assets decreases. Depreciation recorded each year should also decrease.

Figure 8-5   The depreciation curve

This diagram reflects the belief that the efficiency of an asset is greater during its initial years and less during its later years. The accounting problem becomes one of allocating the expired part of the asset cost to a particular accounting period. This allocation is essentially arbitrary.

The declining balance method using income tax depreciation rates is popular because it is acceptable for income tax purposes. Many firms have adopted this method for book purposes in order to reduce the inconvenience of maintaining two different calculations of depreciation — one for book purposes and another for income tax purposes.

> Use of a declining balance method with depreciation rates permitted by the income tax authorities is in accordance with generally accepted accounting principles if the cost allocation pattern conforms with the pattern of services rendered by the asset. In this case, net income will properly show the earning power of the company.

Unfortunately, some firms use the income tax declining balance method for accounting purposes even when its use does not produce the most appropriate matching of fixed asset costs with revenues. This practice is, in fact, a stretching of principles, but it is accepted by accountants. The fact that the estimate of the useful life of fixed assets and the allocation of depreciation are arbitrary tends to justify this departure from generally accepted accounting principles.

One adverse result of using the income tax method of depreciation is the possibility that a distorted net income figure will be produced. This figure might mislead investors who are attempting to evaluate the entity's performance and to compare its performance with that of another entity using a different depreciation method.

C. Depreciation Allocation Assumptions Compared

Cost Allocation Methods Compared

As discussed, the role of depreciation is to allocate to expense the cost of limited-life fixed assets over their estimated useful lives. A problem arises, however, with predicting the useful life of an asset. The approaches to this problem taken by the different cost allocation methods are various.

Approach 1:   Usage Method of Cost Allocation

This method attempts to relate the amount of cost allocated as an expense to the actual physical use of the asset. A unit cost is computed by dividing depreciable cost (cost less salvage value) by the expected output: for example, total units to be produced, total tonnes to be hauled, total hours to be worked. The amount of depreciation expense for any accounting period is found by multiplying the calculated unit cost by the number of units produced or used during that period. Depreciation, therefore, depends on the amount that the asset is used. The validity of this method depends on the accuracy of the estimate made of total units to be produced, total tonnes to be hauled, or total hours to be worked. Unfortunately, estimates are subject to considerable error.

Time-Based Methods of Cost Allocation

Two other methods are widely used in actual practice to allocate the cost of limited life assets. Both ignore the actual amount an asset is used during the accounting period, and each makes an assumption about how cost should be allocated over the useful life of the asset.

Approach 2:   Straight-Line Method

This method assumes that each period receives services of equal value from the asset. Therefore, equal amounts of cost are allocated as depreciation expense to each period.

Approach 3:   Declining Balance Method and Capital Cost Allowance

This method assumes that the asset will contribute more to the earning of revenues in the earlier years of useful life than in later stages. Therefore, larger amounts are allocated as depreciation expense to earlier periods and smaller amounts to later periods.

A comparison of the straight-line method and declining balance method is made in Figure 8-6 over five years, using each method.

As illustrated in Figure 8-6, the declining balance method records a larger amount of depreciation in Years 1 and 2 and a progressively smaller amount in Years 3, 4, and 5. However, both methods allocate the total $18,000 depreciable cost of the asset expense over the 5-year period. This periodic allocation of cost is often graphed to show the dollars of depreciation each year.

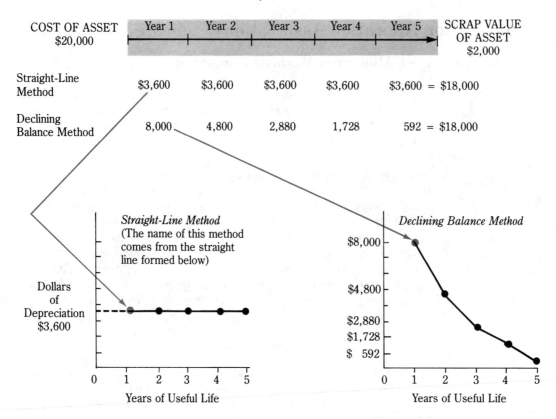

Figure 8-6   Comparison of straight-line and declining balance methods

Matching Fixed Asset Costs with Revenues

Generally accepted accounting principles require the entity to choose the method of allocating cost that best matches expired fixed asset costs with revenues. Therefore, the matching concept, as applied to fixed asset cost allocation, stresses the calculation of net income and not the balance sheet valuation of the asset.

The effect of the straight-line and declining balance methods on a net income is illustrated below. Which is the most appropriate method of allocating costs?

COST OF ASSET IS $20,000	Year 1	Year 2	Year 3	Year 4	Year 5	SCRAP VALUE OF ASSET IS $2,000
Straight-line method		$3,600	$3,600	$3,600	$3,600	$3,600
Declining balance method		8,000	4,800	2,880	1,728	592
Reduction in net income, using declining balance method		$4,400	$1,200			
Increase in net income, using declining balance method				$ 720	$1,872	$3,008

In actual practice, it is very difficult to predict accurately such issues as estimated useful life and scrap value. These and other issues, such as the value of service rendered by an asset during different years, complicate the identification of the most appropriate method of allocating fixed asset costs.

Use of the declining balance method for income tax purposes decreases net income and, therefore, results in less income taxes during Years 1 and 2; it increases net income and, therefore, results in more income taxes during Years 3, 4, and 5. Thus, there is delayed payment of income taxes when this method is used. If income taxes are assumed to be 50 percent, then this firm will delay payment of income taxes amounting to $2,800.

$$
\begin{array}{lll}
\text{Year 1} & \$4,400 \times 50\% & = \$2,200 \\
\text{Year 2} & \$1,200 \times 50\% & = \$\ \ 600 \\
& \text{Total Taxes Delayed} & \underline{\underline{\$2,800}}
\end{array}
$$

These delayed income taxes in Years 1 and 2 are usually seen as an interest-free loan to the taxpayer. In actual practice, as business operations expand, more fixed assets are acquired and, in some cases, continue the delay of income taxes almost indefinitely. A problem arises, however, when capital expenditures are reduced; at that point the income taxes must be paid.

Phantom Profits

One problem affecting depreciation that accountants have been unable to solve is the changing purchasing power of the dollar through inflation and the resulting effect on net income.

> In matching depreciation costs with revenues in the income statement, revenues are stated in dollars that have this year's purchasing power, while depreciation costs are stated in terms of old dollars, that is, dollars that had a different purchasing power.

Assume that a machine was acquired 10 years ago at a cost of $100,000; the identical machine would cost $200,000 today. During this 10-year period, the selling prices of the firm have also increased proportionately. In recording current sales revenue and matching these with 10-year-old costs, the firm shows a larger net income than it would if there were no inflation. The reported net income includes two different components: the normal income from operations and an income from comparing old costs with current revenues — a holding gain. As noted in Chapter 5, this holding gain is referred to as phantom profits. Recall that income taxes are calculated on the total net income, which includes these phantom profits; therefore, income tax, in real dollars, is paid on phantom profits.

D. Depreciation and Financial Statements

Fixed Assets on the Balance Sheet

The objective of the depreciation process is that the appropriate allocation of cost be matched with revenues for net income determination. The resulting balance sheet valuation of fixed assets is a secondary consideration. What are the implications of this emphasis?

- Depreciation allocation methods are all based on estimates, and estimates are subject to error. Accordingly, the undepreciated cost and the net book value shown on the balance sheet will not be the market value anyway. Therefore, why should we be particularly concerned about the balance sheet value of fixed assets?
- Depreciation for a time period varies considerably, depending on the allocation method used. Accordingly, the undepreciated cost shown on the balance sheet of a firm can also vary considerably. Using amounts calculated earlier in this chapter, equipment would appear on the balance sheet at the end of Year 1 as follows:

	Under Straight-Line Method	Under Declining Balance Method
Fixed Assets:		
Equipment	$20,000	$20,000
Less: Accumulated Depreciation	3,600	8,000
Net Book Value	$16,400	$12,000

- Historical cost is the commonly used basis for recording and depreciating fixed assets; its popularity is based on the fact that it is an objectively determined amount.
- Some readers misunderstand the significance of the undepreciated cost shown on the balance sheet. They assume that it represents the cost to replace the asset at the end of its useful life or that it represents the net replacement value of the asset. However, because of inflation, the expenditure needed to replace the asset will probably exceed the original cost paid $20,000) by a substantial amount. Replacement of the asset represents a financing problem and depends on the entity's cash flow and financial position.

Trends in Reporting Fixed Asset Depreciation

Disclosure requirements for fixed assets are stated in the *CICA Handbook*. The CICA suggests that fixed asset cost and accumulated depreciation be disclosed on the balance sheet, or in a note, and that the accumulated depreciation should be deducted from fixed assets, which preferably should be disclosed by major category (sections 3060.02 and 3060.03).

Studies of balance sheets prepared by leading corporations show that there is increasing support for the segregation of fixed assets but not for the segregation of accumulated depreciation.

The income statement should also disclose the amount of depreciation and the methods and rates used in its calculation, according to the CICA. Where the amount of depreciation is significant, separate amounts for each type of fixed asset should be disclosed.

Partial Year Depreciation

Assets may be both purchased and sold during that accounting year. Should depreciation be calculated for a whole year in such a case? The answer depends on individual circumstances and corporate accounting policy. A number of practices can be chosen. One is to record half a year's depreciation regardless of when an asset purchase or sale occurs during the year. Another alternative is to calculate partial depreciation from the month of asset purchase or sale. In the case of an asset purchased June 7, for example, depreciation for seven months would be recorded if the corporate fiscal year coincided with the calendar year. If the asset purchase had been made June 17, then only six months depreciation would be recorded. The general rule to be followed in this case is the recording of depreciation from the month of acquisition (June) if the asset was purchased during the first half of the month (June 7); depreciation would be calculated from the next month (July) if the asset purchase was made during the second half of the month (June 17). (For problem-solving purposes in this text, it is recommended that this practice be used.)

The annual calculation of straight-line depreciation for the $20,000 machine with an estimated useful life of 5 years and an estimated salvage value of $2,000 can be contrasted with partial year depreciation.

Purchase Jan. 1	*Purchase Jun. 7*	*Purchase Jun. 17*
The depreciation is allocated among five years as follows: ($20,000 − $2,000) ÷ 5 years = $3,600 per year.	The depreciation is allocated as follows: $3,600 per year × 7/12 months = $2,100.	The depreciation is allocated as follows: $3,600 per year × 6/12 months = $1,800.

Depreciation Expense	3,600		Depreciation Expense	2,100		Depreciation Expense	1,800	
Accumulated Depreciation		3,600	Accumulated Depreciation		2,100	Accumulated Depreciation		1,800

This example shows the recording of partial depreciation when an asset is purchased. Partial depreciation must also be recorded when asset disposal occurs.

Group Depreciation

The preceding examples discussed the calculation of depreciation for individual assets. In actual practice, depreciation is usually calculated on a group basis, particularly when the assets are similar. In this situation, a **group rate** is used; an average useful life is calculated and applied to the total asset cost. A group rate can also be calculated when there is a mixture of dissimilar assets. In this case, the rate is referred to as a **composite rate**.

The calculation of group rates can be complex and is beyond the subject matter of this chapter. Advanced accountancy courses examine not only the methodology used to establish group rates but also the ramification of having assets replaced before the expiration of their estimated useful lives.

Group rate
Depreciation calculated on a group of homogeneous fixed assets taken as a whole, as opposed to calculating depreciation on individual assets.

Composite rate
Depreciation calculated on a group of non-homogeneous (heterogeneous) assets taken as a whole, as opposed to calculating depreciation on individual assets.

Revision of Depreciation Charges

The useful life of an asset is estimated at the time an asset is acquired and, as is the case with any estimate, it is subject to considerable error.

Equipment		Accumulated Depreciation	
20,000		Year 1 3,600	
		Year 2 3,600	

Total accumulated depreciation is $7,200.

This machine that cost $20,000 had been estimated to have a useful life of 5 years and a scrap value of $2,000. At the end of the first 2 years, it was discovered that the asset would have a useful life of 10 years, but that scrap value would amount to only $1,000. At the end of 2 years, the remaining undepreciated cost of the asset was $12,800 (cost of $20,000 − $7,200 accumulated depreciation to date). In fact, the proper accumulated depreciation should be $3,800.

	Revised Estimates	Original Estimates
Equipment Cost	$20,000	$20,000
Less: Revised Scrap Value	1,000	2,000
Amount To Be Depreciated	$19,000	$18,000
Estimated Useful Life	10 years	5 years
Annual Depreciation	$ 1,900	$ 3,600
Accumulated Depreciation for Two Years	$ 3,800	$ 7,200

An excessive amount of depreciation has been recorded in Years 1 and 2.

What is the proper accounting procedure for this situation? The accepted procedure in Canada is to leave unchanged the depreciation recorded to date and to revise the annual depreciation to be recorded over the remaining estimated life of 8 years. This method is easy to apply. The amount of depreciation to be recorded in each of the remaining years is calculated as follows:

Actual Book Value ($20,000 − 7,200)	$12,800
Actual Scrap Value	1,000
Undepreciated Amount over Remaining 8 Years	$11,800
Depreciation for Each of the Next 8 Years Is $11,800 ÷ 8 Years =	$ 1,475

Accordingly, $1,475 would be recorded as the depreciation expense in the current year and in each of the next 7 years. Obviously there is a substantial difference between $1,475 and $3,600 recorded in each of the 2 preceding years; however, the overcharge of depreciation in Years 1 and 2 is offset by an undercharge of depreciation in the remaining 8 years. (If accurate information had been available at the outset, each year would have had a depreciation expense of $1,900.)

E. Disposal of Fixed Assets

The disposal of a fixed asset requires the elimination from the balance sheet of both its cost and accumulated depreciation. As discussed, partial depreciation must be recorded when an asset disposal occurs. The sale, or abandonment, and trade-in of assets are discussed next.

Sale or Abandonment of Fixed Assets

When an asset has reached the end of its useful life it can be either sold or abandoned. In either case, the asset cost and accumulated depreciation are removed from the records, after depreciation expense has been recorded in the books up to the date of disposal.

Recall the calculation of straight-line depreciation for the $20,000 machine with an estimated useful life of 5 years and an estimated salvage value of $2,000. Assume that the general ledger accounts of the equipment and its related accumulated depreciation amount contain the following entries:

Equipment		Accumulated Depreciation	
Year 1 20,000			Year 1 3,600
			Year 2 3,600
			Year 3 3,600
			Year 4 3,600
			Year 5 3,600

When a fully depreciated asset is abandoned, or simply thrown away, the asset is written off. If there are any proceeds from a sale of the asset, a gain or loss may be recognized.

Assume that the same machine is sold at the end of Year 5, when accumulated depreciation amounted to $18,000. Book value at this date was $2,000 ($20,000 cost — $18,000 accumulated depreciation). Three different situations are possible.

EITHER ① or ③

Sale at Book Value		*Sale above Book Value*		*Sale below Book Value*	

Sale at Book Value
The asset is sold for $2,000. The journal entry to record the sale is:

Cash	2,000	
Accumulated Depreciation	18,000	
Equipment		20,000

→ NO GAIN OT LOSS
→ PROCEEDS = NET BOOK VALUE

Sale above Book Value
The asset is sold for $3,000. The journal entry to record the sale is:

Cash	3,000	
Accumulated Depreciation	18,000	
Gain on Disposal		1,000
Equipment		20,000

Sale below Book Value
The asset is sold for $1,000. The journal entry to record the sale is:

Cash	1,000	
Accumulated Depreciation	18,000	
Loss on Disposal	1,000	
Equipment		20,000

LOSS ON I/S ACCOUNT

In each of these cases, the cash proceeds must be recorded (by a debit) and the cost and accumulated depreciation must be removed from the accounts. At this point the debits of the journal entry must equal the credits. A credit difference represents a gain on disposal; a debit difference represents a loss on disposal.

Disposal Involving Trade-In

Trade-in
The exchange of one asset for another.

Trade-in allowance
The amount allocated to an asset being exchanged for another asset; often the trade-in allowance is not realistic.

It is a common practice to exchange a used asset as a **trade-in** when a new asset is acquired. Usually a **trade-in allowance** is applied to the sales price of the new asset, and the purchaser pays the difference. If the trade-in allowance approximates the fair market value of the used asset on the open market, the new asset is recorded at its list price. If the trade-in allowance is not realistic — as is usually the case, particularly in the case of motor vehicles — the new asset is recorded at its cash market price.

$$\text{Cost of New Asset} = \text{Cash Paid} + \text{Fair Market of Asset Traded in.}$$

If there is a difference between this calculated fair market value of the asset traded in and the book value of the asset traded-in, then a gain or loss results.

Assume that the same machine that cost $20,000 and has an accumulated depreciation of $18,000 at the end of Year 5 is traded in for a new machine with a list price of $25,000. A trade-in allowance of $2,000 is given on the old machine, which has a fair market value of $1,000. In this case, the cost of the asset is calculated as follows:

Cash paid + Fair Market Value of Asset Traded in = Cost of New Asset
= $24,000

$23,000 + $ 1,000

List Price:	$25,000
Trade-in:	2,000
Cash Paid:	$23,000

The journal entry to record the purchase of the new machine and trade-in of the old follows:

Equipment (new)	24,000	Debits = $42,000
Accumulated Depreciation	-18,000	
Loss on Disposal of Equipment	1,000	
Equipment (old)	20,000	Credits = $43,000
Cash	23,000	

A debit difference means a loss of $1,000.

In this entry, the cost of the new machine ($24,000) is entered into the accounts, the accumulated depreciation and cost of the old machine is removed from the accounts, and the amount of cash paid is recorded. At this point the total debits equal $42,000 ($24,000 + $18,000) and total credits equal $43,000 ($20,000 + $23,000), with debit shortage of $1,000 ($42,000 debits versus $43,000 credits). The debit difference of $1,000 represents a loss on disposal.

F.   Depletion of Natural Resources

Natural resources include timberlands, mines, oil wells, and natural gas deposits. They are recorded in asset accounts at cost. These natural resources are sometimes referred to as *wasting assets* because the resource in most cases is not renewable and, once extracted, the asset value is reduced. This expiration of the asset is recorded in the books as depletion. (Natural resources deplete, while non-natural assets depreciate.) The journal entry usually takes the following form:

Depletion Expense	xxx	
Accumulated Depletion — Mine		xxx

Theoretically, the depletion becomes a part of the inventory cost, which includes labour and other costs of extracting the ore (overhead). Therefore, depletion is a part of the cost of goods sold on the income statement. In the balance sheet, Accumulated Depletion — Mine is deducted from the cost of the mine resource:

Property:

Gold Mine	$xx,xxx	
Less: Accumulated Depletion	xxx	$xx,xxx

The periodic depletion charge is usually calculated on a usage basis called *units of production*. A depletion cost per unit is multiplied by the number of units extracted in order to calculate the periodic depletion expense. For example, a mine having an estimated 100 000 tonnes of nickel would have a cost of $3 per tonne if its cost less salvage value amounted to $300,000 ($350,000 cost − $50,000 salvage value). If 20 000 tonnes are extracted during the year, the depletion would amount to $60,000.

$$\frac{\$350,000 \text{ cost} - \$50,000 \text{ salvage value}}{100\ 000 \text{ tonnes}} = \$3 \text{ per tonne} \times 20\ 000 \text{ tonnes}$$
$$= \$60,000$$

The depletion for the year would be recorded in the general journal this way:

Depletion Expense	60,000	
Accumulated Depletion — Mine		60,000

In the example, the output of the mine was measured in tonnes. Usually the marketing unit is used as the unit of production in calculating depletion expense — *board metres* or (*feet*) of lumber, *tonnes* of ore, *barrels* of oil, and *cubic metres* (or *feet*) of natural gas.

APPENDIX 1:   The Current Cost Model

The *CICA Handbook* (section 4510.42) recommends that current cost fixed asset data be disclosed as supplementary information to historical cost based financial statements. The balance sheet fixed asset valuation should use current costs at the balance sheet date.

Impact on the Balance Sheet

This calculation of fixed asset current cost can be illustrated from an analysis made for management of Bluebeard Computer Corporation. Two different years were considered. Fixed assets were assumed to cost $20,000, and had an estimated useful life of 5 years and a salvage value of $2,000; a straight-line method of depreciation was used. It was further calculated that year-end fixed asset current cost was $28,000 in Year 1.

Asset Valuation

	Under Historical Cost December 31, Year 1	*Under Current Cost* December 31, Year 1
Balance Sheet		
Fixed Assets	$20,000	$28,000
Less: Accumulated Depreciation	3,600 (18%)	5,040 (18)%
Carrying Value	$16,400	$22,960

> In Year 1, accumulated depreciation amounts to 18% of fixed asset cost. Under the historical cost assumption, depreciation expense amounts to $3,600 per year. Note that the calculation of depreciation expense is different under the current cost model.

> In Year 1, the 18% is used to calculate accumulated depreciation ($28,000 × 18% = $5,040). Under the current cost model, depreciation expense can amount to $5,040.

As can be seen, fixed asset current costs result in entirely different cost, accumulated depreciation, and carrying value amounts. A more complete discussion of current cost accounting is beyond the scope of this chapter; it is usually the subject matter of more advanced accounting courses.

A number of different measurement techniques have been suggested to calculate the current cost of fixed assets. These include the use of price indices and appraisals; engineering estimates of the impact of technological change and other factors can also be considered. Because the calculation of these current costs is in an experiential stage, further refinements to current techniques are expected as experience in their calculation and use develops. The same estimated useful life and straight-line depreciation method is used as in the historical cost calculation presented here.

Calculation of current costs is essentially a subjective process; here it is based on management's estimates and assumptions regarding matters such as replacement costs, and impacts of technology.

Impact on the Income Statement

The analysis prepared in Chapter 5 for management of Bluebeard Computer Corporation showed the impact of current cost calculations on net income when inventory purchase costs are increasing. This analysis is developed in this chapter to consider the impact of current cost on depreciation expense. The same sales, cost of goods sold, and gross profit data were used for this new analysis.

With the additional straight-line depreciation data, a comparison of net income was prepared under the historical cost assumption the current cost model. The BCC executives were stunned by the results.

	Historical Cost	*Current Cost*
Sales	$20,000	$20,000
Cost of Goods Sold	10,000	18,000
Gross Profit	$10,000	$ 2,000
Operating Expenses:		
Depreciation	$ 3,600	$ 5,040
Other Expenses	2,400	2,400
	$ 6,000	$ 7,440
Operating Income (loss)	$ 4,000	($ 5,440)
Income Tax (50%)	2,000	2,000
Net Income (loss)	$ 2,000	($ 7,440)

The *CICA Handbook* (section 4510.38) recommends that current costs information relating to depreciation expense and its impact on the reported net income figure be disclosed as supplementary information to financial statements based on historical cost.

This further analysis clearly shows a wider spread between the phantom profit, produced under the historical cost assumption, and the increased loss under the current cost model. Bluebeard's executives had been told that, under current cost accounting, depreciation expense is viewed as the part of the asset that has been used during the year. On the basis of the above net income (loss) calculations, it is apparent that the company would be unable to replace its fixed assets without additional borrowing; it is losing its ability to operate at the same level in the future.

Even worse, income tax estimated at 50 percent and calculated at $2,000 would be paid on the historical cost calculation of operating income while, in fact, there was an operating loss under the current cost model. The payment of income tax on these phantom profits is not at all satisfactory.

The current cost model indicates that Bluebeard is losing its operating capacity and will eventually be unable to replace its fixed assets without increased borrowing.

The Historical Cost Dilemma

As explained, the emphasis of the current cost model is its concern with the maintenance of the entity's operating capability, which should be as great at the end of the accounting period as it was at the beginning.

A dilemma for the accounting profession centres on the historical cost concept. As noted earlier, it is retained for financial statement purposes because historical costs are objectively determined — even though the measure used, the stable dollar concept, is invalid during periods of rapid inflation. Although current cost figures are more relevant, their incorporation into the body of financial statements is questioned because the determination of current costs is generally a subjective process, based, in some cases, on management's estimates and assumptions.

Although current costs seem more relevant, their use in record-keeping or incorporation into the body of financial statements is not included among the *CICA Handbook* recommendations. As explained before, the availability of current cost supplementary information is assumed to be adequate for financial statement readers to assess the impact of changing prices or the entity's ability to maintain its level of operating capability. A review of published supplementary information leads some experts to question the validity of this assumption.

A Word of Caution

In addition to the recommendations for the measurement of depreciation expense and fixed assets using current costs, there are also certain other effects associated with changing prices. These relate to the impact of financing and other adjustments that may alleviate, at least in part, the loss of operating capability. There is also the use of recoverable amounts in certain cases which, in effect, is an exception to the use of current costs.

A more complete treatment of these topics is usually the subject matter of advanced accounting courses. Caution must also be exercised in generalizing to other situations the impact of price changes on Bluebeard Computer Corporation. Different circumstances can be expected to yield different results.

The current cost model is in an experimental stage at the present time and is being evaluated. No general concensus has emerged concerning the usefulness of the information generated; however, it is expected to provide useful insights into the operations of each entity using the model.

APPENDIX 2:   Intangible Assets

Intangible assets
Non-physical assets, such as patents, copyrights, trademarks, and goodwill.

Fixed assets are referred to as tangible assets because they have physical substance. Another major category of assets do not have physical substance; these are referred to as intangible assets. The *CICA Handbook* (section 3080.01) recommends that the major categories of **intangible assets**, such as goodwill, franchises, patent rights, copyrights, and trademarks, should be shown separately. Other assets — for example, accounts receivable, pre-paid expenses, and investments — although they do not have a physical substance as such, are reported under other asset classifications in the balance sheet. They are never called intangible assets.

Intangible assets, as discussed in this section, are sometimes referred to as "soft assets" because of the uncertainty associated with their estimated useful lives. This uncertainty makes allocating their cost over the accounting periods that will be benefitted difficult. Where an intangible asset is acquired other than through payment of cash or its equivalent, the *CICA Handbook* recommends that the basis of valuation should be fully disclosed (section 3080.02). The *Handbook* further recommends that the amount of amortization for the current period and the basis of amortization should also be disclosed (section 3080.04).

Intangible assets share two additional characteristics: they are all long-term assets and, as detailed later, they all bestow certain legal rights.

Patents

Patent
A 20-year exclusive right to produce and sell an invention granted by the federal government to the first inventor to file a patent application.

Patents are intangible assets that affect how the entity produces its products. A **patent** is granted by the federal government and gives the holder an exclusive legal privilege to produce and sell a product for a period of 20 years from the date the patent application is filed. When two or more applications for the same invention are pending at the same time, the patent is granted to the applicant who filed first, even if there is a dispute about who created the invention first. This is in accordance with international practice regarding patent laws. The useful life of the patent may be less than 20 years because of changes in technology or in the marketplace. On the other hand, modifications to the original product can result in a new patent being granted, in effect extending the original 20-year life of the original patent. Patents can be purchased or sold.

Patents are recorded at cost. If purchased from an inventor, the patent's cost is easily identified; if developed internally, the patent's cost includes all expenditures incurred in the development of the patent, with the exception of those expenditures classified as research and non-deferable development costs. The detailed coverage of the distinction between expenditures to be classified as either patent or research and development costs is the subject matter of advanced accounting courses. In addition to the capitalization of the legal and registration costs associated with the patent, the costs of any successful patent infringement lawsuits would be included in the Patent account.

Because of changes in technology and in the marketplace, a conservative estimate is usually made for a patent's useful life. A straight-line method of amortization is usually used and is recorded directly to the asset account.

Patent Amortization Expense	XXX	
Patent		XXX

Copyrights

Copyright
The exclusive right granted by the federal government to publish a literary or artistic work; exists for the lifetime of the author and an additional fifty years after his/her death.

A **copyright** is another intangible asset that confers on the holder an exclusive legal privilege; in this case, the federal government grants control over a published or artistic work for the life of the artist and 50 years afterward. This control extends to the reproduction, sale, or other use of the copyrighted material.

While the cost to obtain a copyright is minimal, the purchase of a copyrighted work can be substantial. Purchased copyrights are recorded at cost; this cost is amortized over the estimated useful life of the copyright, which is often less than its legal life. As is the case with patents, the costs of any successful copyright infringement lawsuits or out-of-court settlements are added to the cost of the assets and amortized over its remaining useful life.

Trademarks

Trademark
A legal right granted by the federal government to use a symbol or a word to identify a company or one of its products or services.

A **trademark** is a symbol or a word used by a company to identify itself or one of its products in the marketplace. Symbols are often logos printed on company stationery or displayed at company offices, on vehicles, or in advertising. Well-known word examples are Coke and CN. The right to use a trademark can be protected by registering it with the registrar of trademarks. Normally a trademark does not diminish in value through the passage of time or usage but is affected by its success or lack of success. Trademarks are usually carried at cost and not amortized. Two unusual issues involving trademarks are discussed in Real Life Example 8-2.

Franchises

Franchise
A legal right to render a service or to produce a good.

A **franchise** is a legal right granted by an entity or a government to sell particular products or to provide certain services in a given territory using a specific trademark or trade name. In return for the franchise, the franchisor often pays a fee that constitutes his/her franchise cost. McDonald's is one example of a franchised fast-food chain. The right to manufacture and sell Coke is another example.

Another example of a franchise is one granted by government for the provision of certain services within a given geographical location: for example, television stations

Real Life Example 8-2

Trademarks

An example of a trademark that was once widely used by RCA, discontinued in 1968, and is once again being used, follows.

Remember Nipper? He first appeared in 1901 on the first RCA gramophone ad — "His Master's Voice". Now RCA has gone to the dog again — he has been collared as the logo for all new RCA audio and video products.

But wait, that's not the tail-end of the story. Nipper was a real fox terrier pooch born near Bristol, England, in 1884, and he really did look into a gramophone that way. He was captured on canvas by Francis Barraud, the brother of Nipper's real master, who died. Times were ruff, so Barraud sold the painting and rights to RCA for £100. Nipper died in 1895, but his bonefied replicas live on. However, reproducing him will not come as cheap. It's estimated that the logo, along with the ad campaigns, will put the bite on RCA for some $8 million a year — and that's nothing to shake a stick at.

In some cases, a trademark is not issued, as in the following case.

No doubt much to entertainer Johnny Carson's relief, the phrase "Here's Johnny" is not an acceptable trademark for portable toilets.

A "john" might be a portable toilet or "a client of a lady of negotiable virtue", a Federal Court of Canada ruling said yesterday. But "Here's Johnny" is just too readily associated with Johnny Carson and the Tonight Show to be allowed as a trademark for portable toilets, Mr. Justice Patrick Mahoney said.

Carson had appealed a decision by the registrar of trademarks to allow William Reynolds of St. Catharines to use the trademark for his business of renting portable outhouses.

The judge hinged his decision on a section of the Trade Marks Act that says no one shall adopt a trademark that may falsely suggest a connection with any living individual. He accepted as evidence a random survey in which people surveyed where handed a card bearing the words "Here's Johnny" and were asked, "What does this mean to you?". Of those surveyed, 63 percent mentioned Carson or the Johnny Carson Show. While it was clear a significant number of people connected the phrase with Carson, there was no connection between Reynolds or the talk-show host, Judge Mahoney said.

authorized by the Canadian Radio-television and Telecommunications Commission, telephone services authorized in a particular province, or garbage collection authorized within a given community.

As in the case of patents and copyrights, the cost of a franchise should be amortized over its useful life. In addition to the payment of a franchise fee, which is capitalized, a franchise agreement usually requires annual payments. These payments, when incurred, are considered as an operating expense.

Secret Processes

Secret processes are not normally subject to amortization because they are assumed to have an unlimited life. Real Life Example 8-3 illustrates how important a secret process can be to a corporation. If the process will benefit the business as long as it is a going concern, then the cost of the process should not be amortized.

Research and Development Costs

Research and development activities are distinguished as follows in the *CICA Handbook*, section 3450.02:

Research is planned investigation undertaken with the hope of gaining new scientific or technical knowledge and understanding. Such investigation may or may not be directed towards a specific practical aim or application. In this case, it is recommended that the research costs be expensed during the period in which they are incurred.

Development is the translation of research findings or other knowledge into a plan or design for new or substantially improved materials, products, processes, systems

Real Life Example 8-3
Coca-Cola Releases Secret Data

For years people have speculated about the secret formula of Coca-Cola and the "natural flavor" ingredients it contains.

The formula has been locked in a bank vault, and only a few company executives can see it.

This week the curtain of secrecy rose, if only slightly, as Coca-Cola Co. officials acknowledged what had been long suspected.

The world's best-selling soft drink once contained cocaine and is still flavored with a non-narcotic extract from the coca, the plant from which cocaine is derived.

Details of how Coca-Cola obtains the coca and how it is processed emerged from interviews with U.S. Government officials and scientists involved in drug research programs.

They identified the Illinois-based Stepan Co. as the importer and processor of the coca used in Coke.

After Stepan officials acknowledged their ties to Coca-Cola, the soft drink giant broke its silence.

In a telephone interview from Coca-Cola's Atlanta headquarters, Randy Donaldson, a company spokesman, said, "Ingredients from the coca leaf are used, but there is no cocaine in it and it is all tightly overseen by regulatory authorities."

A beverage industry analyst said, "this is old hat to people in the industry, but might come as a surprise to others. But it also makes sense: when you have a good product you change it as little as possible."

The first batch of Coca-Cola was brewed in 1886 by John Styth Pemberton, a pharmacist, who described the product as a "brain tonic and intellectual beverage."

The original recipe included coca with cocaine, but the narcotic was removed just after the turn of the century, according to company spokesmen.

Cans and bottles of Coca-Cola list only "natural flavors,"

in addition to water, high-fructose corn syrup and/or sucrose, caramel color, phosphoric acid and caffeine.

A Stepan laboratory in Maywood, N.J., is the United States' only legal commercial importer of coca leaves, which it obtains mainly from Peru and, to a lesser extent, Bolivia.

Besides producing the coca flavoring agent for Coca-Cola, Stepan extracts cocaine from the coca leaves, which it sells to Mallinckrodt Inc., a St. Louis pharmaceutical manufacturer that is the only company in the United States licenced to purify the product for medicinal use.

Some coca cultivation is still permitted in Peru, where coca leaves have been both chewed and brewed into teas for centuries.

Mr. Donaldson declined to discuss whether the Reagan Administration's planned attempt to reduce South American coca growing could have an impact on the company and the formula used to make its soft drink.

Around the turn of the century, the Coca-Cola Co. actually publicized the unusual ingredients in its soft drink.

An advertisement that ran in Scientific American magazine in 1906 showed pictures of Peruvian peasants chewing narcotic coca leaves, a practice still common in that country, and of Africans gathering cola nuts, which are also used as a stimulant.

Coca-Cola, the ad said, "is the perfectly balanced combination of these valuable tonics in the form of a healthful drink."

The ad also quoted the Spanish conquistador Francisco Pizarro as saying that the use of coca enabled both Indians and foreigners in the high Andes "to endure without distress physical trials which are otherwise unendurable."

or services prior to the commencement of commercial production or use. These expenses should also be written off as incurred unless they meet certain circumstances set out in Section 3450.21 in which case they should be capitalized and amortized over future periods.

Because of the difficulty in meeting all the criteria set out in the *CICA Handbook*, most research and development expenses tend to be written off as incurred. The detailed coverage of research and development expenditures is the subject matter of more advanced accounting courses.

Goodwill

Goodwill is an example of an intangible asset that may or may not appear in an entity's books. This apparent inconsistency results because there may have been no purchased cost of goodwill and, under GAAP, it cannot be recorded as an asset, even though the

Goodwill
The value attached to the ability of an entity to make superior earnings as compared with other entities in the same industry; this value is usually not recognized in the financial statements of the entity, unless the entity is purchased; when purchased, it is recorded at acquisition cost and amortized over its remaining useful and legal life.

Organization costs
Fees for incorporation, including lawyers and other costs incurred to establish the business; such costs are an intangible asset, not an equity item.

entity may have superior earning power, better business locations, particularly effective management, or a secret process that set it apart from its competitors. **Goodwill** is seen as a composite of all these and other factors that individually cannot be valued.

Goodwill is recorded only when it is purchased; it usually arises in a business consolidation and is calculated as the difference between the purchase cost of an interest in another entity and the acquiring company's interest in its net assets. The detailed coverage of goodwill is further discussed in Chapter 13. The *CICA Handbook* (section 1580.58) recommends that the amount of goodwill should be amortized over its useful life using a straight-line amortization method; the period should not exceed 40 years.

Organization Costs

Expenditures made to incorporate or to establish the entity are referred to as **organization costs**. These costs are usually seen as having a benefit over the life of the entity and, therefore, are considered as an asset. (This issue is discussed further in Chapter 9.) In actual practice, the amount involved is small in relation to total assets; it is usually written off. The *CICA Handbook* recommends that when organization costs are amortized, the amortization be disclosed.

A S S I G N M E N T   M A T E R I A L S

Discussion Questions

1. The cost of an asset is said to be capitalized. What does this mean?
2. How does a capital expenditure differ from a revenue expenditure? Assume that you have purchased a mini-computer for business use; illustrate, using examples, capital and revenue expenditures associated with the computer.
3. CBCA Inc. has purchased land and buildings for a lump sum. What does this mean? What is the acceptable manner of accounting for a lump sum purchase?
4. When one fixed asset is exchanged for another, how is the cost of the newly acquired asset determined?
5. Contrast the accounting for a betterment and an extraordinary repair. Give an example of each.
6. How does the concept of materiality affect the distinction between a capital and a revenue expenditure?
7. Fixed assets are often thought of as a bundle of services to be used over a period of years. The value of these services in the first year of the useful life of such assets, it is claimed, is not the same as in later years. Using a car as an example, indicate whether you agree or disagree.
8. Distinguish among depreciation, depletion, and amortization. Give an example of each.
9. Assume that you have recently purchased a new sports car. Is a usage or a time-based method preferable in recording depreciation? Why?
10. Why is salvage value ignored when depreciation is calculated according to the declining balance method but not the straight-line method? Is this inconsistent? Why or why not?
11. What is the derivation for the declining balance method of depreciation? the straight-line method?
12. How is the double-declining balance rate of depreciation calculated for an asset that is expected to have a five-year useful life?
13. What is capital cost allowance? Why is it a useful method of depreciation calculation?
14. The use of the capital cost allowance method, it is claimed, sometimes involves a stretching of accounting principles. Explain how this might occur. What are the disadvantages of this method?
15. When referring to fixed asset cost allocation, do generally accepted accounting principles stress balance sheet valuation or net income calculation? Explain.

16. a. The payment of income tax is often delayed through the use of capital cost allowance. Does this delay constitute an interest-free loan? If so, when will this loan be repaid?
    b. What are phantom profits in relation to fixed assets, and where do they come from?
17. a. Why don't accountants use the replacement cost of an asset when calculating periodic depreciation?
    b. Your friend is concerned that the calculation of depreciation relies too much on the use of estimates that are usually erroneous. Your friend believes that accountants should be precise. Do you agree that accountants are imprecise in the use of estimates for depreciation? Why or why not?
18. What is the commonly used basis for the recording and depreciating of fixed assets? What other methods could be used?
19. What is the proper accounting procedure to be followed in Canada when the previously estimated useful life of an asset is found to be erroneous? Why is more accurate information unavailable when fixed assets are initially acquired?
20. What is a trade-in? Explain whether one is or is not the same as the sale of an asset.
21. Why is the trade-in allowance, particularly in the case of a car, usually unrealistic? Why would a dealer give more trade-in allowance on a used car than it is worth?
22. What are wasting assets? Give some examples. Explain why all assets aren't wasting.
23. Why is a declining balance method unrealistic for natural resources? What method is permitted for income tax purposes in Canada?
24. What is a patent? Does a patent's useful life usually correspond to its legal life? Why or why not? Support your answer with an example.
25. How does a copyright differ from a trademark? Give an example of each.
26. Why are secret processes not usually subject to amortization? Explain whether or not this practice is inconsistent with generally accepted accounting principles.
27. What is recommended in the *CICA Handbook* for intangible asset valuation and disclosure?
28. What is goodwill? Why is an entity's goodwill usually not recorded in its books?

Discussion Cases

Discussion Case 8-1:   J. R.'s Ranch

In the 1950s, Quaker Oats promoted its cereals with an unusual offer: the purchaser of a box of Quaker Oats was entitled to an inch-square [6.5 cm^2] piece of land in the Yukon. Now the same gimmick is being used to popularize not cereal but a serial. According to an advertisement in the *National Enquirer*, $25 will purchase a square foot [0.1 m^2] of land in J. R.'s South Fork Ranch, the place where the television show *Dallas* was filmed.

"South Fork Ranch is mine," said J. R. Duncan, owner of 8,712,000 square feet [246 700 m^2] of Texas soil, who was christened Joseph Rand Duncan, giving him the same initials as the popular *Dallas* character, J. R. Ewing. "By coincidence," said Duncan, "I have not been shot."

"We have actual deeds we send out with the documents to transfer the land to the new buyer," Duncan said, contrasting his land sale with the Quaker Oats giveaway, in which the individual deeds weren't formally registered.

Duncan said he was selling grazing land in the southeastern section of the ranch. Those who buy the land will have only limited rights to it. Although Duncan has built a separate entrance for the new ranch partners, there will be no picnic tables or kiddie rides. In fact, Duncan said he still intended to have his cattle graze the land. Duncan has also arranged to pay property taxes so the city clerk will not have to send thousands of assessment bills around the world.

As part of the deal for shooting on the ranch, Lorimar Productions, the makers of *Dallas*, have granted Duncan exclusive world-wide marketing rights for products carrying the South Fork name. Besides the obligatory T-shirts, belt buckles, and hatbands, Duncan has licensed the company to sell South Fork dirt and another gentleman to sell pieces of the fence.

"He's going to pay me to tear down my fence and cut it up in little pieces for wall plaques and desk weights," Duncan said. "And then he is going to build me a new fence. I'll tell you, I'm open to new ideas."

Source   Copyright © 1980 by The New York Times Company. Reprinted with permission.

For Discussion

1. Would you pay $25 for a square foot of J. R.'s South Fork Ranch? Consider the following in your answer:
   a. Your use of this land
   b. Novelty value among your friends
   c. Possible increase in value in the future as a collector's item
   d. Other similar implications, including future land taxes applied to you if there were a default on tax payment.
2. How much would Duncan receive for the land if all 8,712,000 square feet were sold? How would this compare to the probable current market value of this land?
3. If South Fork dirt is sold, would a part of the proceeds constitute a sale of land, depletion expense recovered, or something else? How would Duncan account for this transaction? Prepare a few journal entries to illustrate your solution to this question.
4. a. Is the original fence generally considered by accountants as part of the cost of the land, a land improvement, equipment, or something else?
   b. If this land is sold as indicated in this article, what is the proper journal entry to record the sale?
   c. If a new fence is going to be built on J.R.'s ranch by the purchaser of the old fence at no charge to Duncan, what is the proper journal entry, if any, to record the new fence? Discuss and illustrate with appropriate journal entries, if applicable.
   d. Explain, using your knowledge of accounting theory, why the new fence would not be recorded, if you support this view.
5. What is your estimate of Duncan's probable success in
   a. Selling a square foot of J.R.'s ranch
   b. Selling South Fork dirt
   c. Selling wall plaques and desk weights made from the fence on South Fork.

Discussion Case 8-2: Canada's Secret Computer Centre

The building looks like one of those nondescript factories that dot the west end of Mississauga, near Toronto, where that industrial playground fades off into its drowsy suburbs. Nothing is manufactured there and, despite the building's size (60,000 square feet or 5575 m²), hardly anyone ever enters or leaves through its imposing shock-sensored doors.

This is the headquarters of Combac Management Corp., one of the more esoteric offshoots of our computer age. Except for its president, a bearded former Winnipegger of Icelandic origin named Gunnar Helgason, and his secretaries, the building is deliberately kept empty — empty, that is, but for the banks of silent sentinels in its lower level. This is a "computer back-up centre", quietly financed by three dozen of Canada's big-ticket corporations. Except for a similar arrangement in Philadelphia, it is the largest facility of its kind in the free world.

It has yet to be used, but its very existence — which has been kept secret because of potential security risks — indicates how dependent Canadian companies have become on their electronic software and hardware. "It's not a published statistic," Helgason told me in an exclusive interview, "but all it would take for the chartered banks to lose financial control of their operations would be 36 hours with their computers down. The Bank of Montreal, for example, is one of the largest private users of computer power in the world today. As the capacities of these computers get larger and faster, the dependency of business people on these machines is growing exponentially. If a computer goes down, it can bring a company to its knees."

It's to provide for such emergencies, whatever their cause, that Helgason created his enterprise. "It's a place where company executives temporarily deprived of their own computer can almost immediately get back to business. We even have a war room for them with audio-visual facilities from which the president and his senior people can operate."

The Mississauga location was chosen because it is near Toronto International Airport, so that the facility is readily available to firms across Canada. Helgason refuses to list his clients, all of whom have insisted on a confidentiality clause in their contracts. The building bristles with closed-circuit television sets, and every window has its own shatter-guard system which will go off at the sound of a scratch. Fire detection and prevention includes not only the standard sprinkler system but heat, smoke and ionization detectors which can report a blaze in its incipient stages. Any fire will trigger clouds of Halon gas — an inert substance (kept in tanks in the building's basement) that deprives fire of oxygen. A 900-circuit telephone switchboard has been installed, and there is a large (eerily vacant) cafeteria, as well as an infirmary for medical emergencies. As many as half a dozen companies can be accommodated at any one time. "In an atomic war, of course," Helgason admits, "all bets are off. Countries and economies can be crippled by attacking just their computer systems. Any intelligent insurrection would pick data centres as prime targets.

"Computers can also be hit during thunderstorms; if an installation's lightning arresters and surge protectors should fail, a bolt out of the sky can zap high voltage into a computer's front end, rendering it useless. Every Canadian company of any size now depends on at least one data centre, and without a back-up facility like this their hands would be tied in the event of any emergency. But it's just too expensive for each company to operate its own back-up system."

Space is allocated for future application of laser, fibre optics and satellite communication facilities. Helgason refuses to discuss the operational details of any of his clients but he has been briefed on the critical time path of each of their decision-making processes and knows how long any company could survive without computer access. "One of our users," he says, "has recently finished a cost analysis of not being able to use their data centre. They have a total of 200 applications running on their computers, and *one* of those applications alone would cost the company $12 million a month if they weren't able to process."

The facility is owned by a limited company named Combac, with 61 partners, many of them major Canadian investors who estimate that it would cost about $10 million to duplicate the Mississauga computer centre. Its heart is a specially acclimatized area with a mammoth IBM-compatible installation (a V-8 Amdahl) and a tape library capable of holding 25,000 reels of tape. (The computer is now being upgraded to a larger model.)

Helgason loosely classifies himself as a financial consultant. He was invited to leave the University of Manitoba after two years of science courses for playing cards once too often in the students' union. He then became a chartered accountant, worked for Manitoba Hydro, Ducks Unlimited, Coopers & Lybrand and Thorne Riddell. He has packaged tax shelters, sold MURBS and now has interests in half a dozen Journey's End Motels, as well as doing the syndication packaging for Golden Griddle restaurants, and dealing in Florida real estate. His most interesting venture (with a partner, Frank Dwyer) is Manu-Comp Systems, which sells computer software to doctors and dentists. He is also a partner in New Age Softwear Ltd., which has developed a new computer language that will allow machines to communicate with one another. (That's referred to in the trade as "a fourth-generation system interface".)

At 38, Helgason claims he really doesn't "work" any more. "I've retired," he says. "That's the way I look at it."

He spends most of his time in that big empty building in Mississauga, planning for a day that may never come — when he could be running the decision-making centre of industrial Canada.

Source Peter C. Newman, "Canada's Secret Computer Centre", *Maclean's*, September 19, 1983.

For Discussion

Tangible assets come to the end of their useful lives; depreciation is recorded in recognition of the assets' useful life. How should depreciation be recorded for Combac's computers? What issues would you consider in your decision?

Discussion Case 8-3:   Bionics

Artificial knees. Artificial hips. Artificial blood. Artificial ears. Artificial arteries. Artificial hearts. Such are the wondrous products of the ultimate business: the replication of the human body. Substitutive medicine — replacing real parts with fake ones — has blossomed into one of the most important trends in health care and has, in turn, spawned a fast-growing community of manufacturers that try to replace the irreplaceable.

More than a million people have artificial parts implanted inside them every year. Individuals in excruciating pain from arthritis now walk more peacefully with artificial hips. Victims of atherosclerosis, a form of hardening of the arteries, have had their circulation bettered by vascular grafts. Cataract patients see because of intraocular lenses. Years in the future, anything may be possible, since the consuming belief of medical researchers is that everything in the body will ultimately be duplicated by parts flowing out of a factory.

Ear — *$8,000–12,000*
Lens Implant — *$300*
Wrist — *$280–295*
Heart — *$50,000–80,000*
Heart Valve — *$2,000*
Knee — *$1,500–2,000*
Finger Joint — *$99*
Leg or Arm — *$1,000–3,000*
Ankle — *$700*
Blood Vessel — *$300*
Toe Joint — *$92–99*
Shoulder and Knee Ligament — *$200–500*
Shoulder — *$900*
Elbow — *$1,200*
Hip — *$1,000–2,000*

Design proliferation characterizes the industry. Need a knee? Choose from hundreds. A lens? Hundreds to pick from. Differences are usually too subtle for the eye to detect. Ask about how perfectly the fake parts work, and the answers from executives are like this: "There is no ideal heart valve" or "There are over 300 designs for the knee and we haven't found the perfect solution yet."

An artificial part in place, patients may be liberated from pain, but they are often foolhardy, expecting it to be as good as new.

Talking about artificial joints, Frank Lewis, director of engineering at Richards, says: "How long one lasts depends on the surgeon's skill, the type of implant, and the patient. The most important are the patients. What do they do after they get the prosthesis? Do they go jogging? Do they go mountain climbing? These people are out of pain for the first time, so they tend to abuse the new joints. I think the *Six Million Dollar Man* on television didn't help any. You would think the artificial joint would be stronger because it's metal rather than bone. But the bone reheals itself. The metal just wears down. And you can't do maintenance. You can't get in there and give it a shot of grease."

For all its promise, the artificial body parts business is laden with risks. There is a rising tide of transplants of living organs. What's more researchers might strike it big with a miracle drug that will tame one of the horrid diseases that cause patients to seek new parts. A Pfizer official commented: "If our pharmaceutical division comes up with a drug that cures arthritis, then I guess we send our prothesis division down the tubes."

The list of products runs on and on, until the bionic human is nearly complete.

Need some bones? Calcitek, a division of Intermedics, makes a fake bone mineral fashioned out of hydroxylapatite. "When you implant any form of this synthetic bone mineral, it fools the bone into believing it is real bone," explains Dr. Michael Jarcho, the company's president. "So the actual living bone grows and attaches itself to the substance." Though currently restricted to dental applications, the substance is expected to spread to orthopaedic applications and be used as a bone graft substitute.

Need blood? Green Cross, a Japanese drug company, has Fluosol, an artificial blood. Still years away from distribution, Fluosol is not without drawbacks, for instance carrying no white cells to combat infections. But in emergency situations it could be a life-saver.

Musing about the hunt for new and better products as the clatter from the Howmedia parts factory reverberated in the background, Dave Fitzgerald said, "You gotta wonder sometimes if maybe we live too long. But, as long as people get older this market gets bigger. As you get older, your parts wear down. That's what it really comes down to. This whole business is the wearing down of parts. As long as they wear out, we'll put in new ones."

Source *The New York Times,* November 20, 1983, p. 1-F.

For Discussion

1. In accounting terms, would you view the purchase of an artificial joint as a capital expenditure or as a revenue expenditure? Why?
2. Comment on the accounting issues involved in the sale of transplant organs.
3. In Canada, people donate blood voluntarily to Red Cross reserves; in the United States, people are paid for giving blood. Comment on accounting issues for the Red Cross that differ between the two countries, regarding blood collection.

Discussion Case 8-4: Air Canada's "Newest" Aircraft

Air Canada's newest aircraft, unveiled yesterday, is also one of its oldest — a sign of tough economic times.

They used to be called DC-8s in the 1960s, but with a facelift and four new CFM-56 engines, they are now known as DC-8 Super 73s.

Six are being refurbished for cargo service in a $147-million program, mainly because it would cost more than twice as much to replace them with new aircraft.

Without the new engines, they, like hundreds of DC-8s and Boeing 707s, would be grounded by tough aircraft noise-abatement rules that take effect in 1986.

Air Canada is one of only four companies in the world doing the re-engining itself and hopes to get outside contracts for similar jobs. It would like the Canadian Forces to re-engine its four 707s, or even better, buy some of Air Canada's surplus DC-8s — it has 19 to sell — and have the airline do the work.

"This is an expertise we paid to acquire and we hope to use it to our advantage," said Pierre Jeanniot, the airline's executive vice-president.

The work was to be performed by Cammacorp of California, but was reclaimed by Air Canada during the recession, allowing the recall of 65 laid-off mechanics.

Source Canadian Press, "A DC-8 by any other name . . .", *The* (Montreal) *Gazette*, November 8, 1983, p. D-1.

For Discussion

1. Recall the claim that tangible assets are on an "irresistible march to the junk heap". How does the re-emergence of the DC-8 square with this claim?
2. What would be the appropriate cost allocation method?

Comprehension Problems

Comprehension Problem 8-1

Barbieri Corporation purchased a new laser printer to be used in its business. The printer, which was chosen from a number of alternatives, had a purchase price of $4,000, but Barbieri was able to purchase it for $3,250. The company expects it to have a useful life of approximately 5 years, after which time it will have a scrap value of $250. Barbieri is paying the delivery costs of $100, set-up and debugging costs of $300, and the costs of purchasing an appropriate table for $50. There was sales tax of 10 percent on the purchase price of the printer but not on the other costs.

Required:
1. Calculate the total cost of the laser printer.
2. Barbieri asks you whether the straight-line or double-declining balance method of depreciation would be most appropriate for the printer. Make some calculations to support your answer, and compare the amounts you calculated.
3. Calculate the first year's depreciation, assuming the printer was purchased on January 2, 19X1 and the company's fiscal year ends December 31.

Comprehension Problem 8-2

Vic Holdings Inc. purchased a property including land and a building for $300,000. The market value of the land was $100,000 and the building, $300,000.

Required: Using these appraisals, prepare a journal entry to record the purchase.

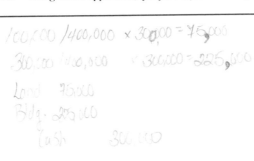

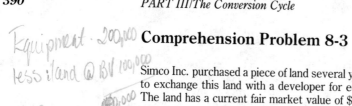

Comprehension Problem 8-3

Simco Inc. purchased a piece of land several years ago for $100,000. Now, the company is going to exchange this land with a developer for equipment having a fair market value of $240,000. The land has a current fair market value of $200,000.

Required:　Prepare the journal entry on the books of
1. Simco
2. The developer.

Comprehension Problem 8-4

Computer Pros Inc. purchased an AT-compatible computer on January 1, 19X1. They estimated that it had a useful life of 3 years. In 19X2, Computer Pros made the following changes to the computer:

Mar. 1　Added a 150 meg hard disk at a cost of $1,000
Apr. 1　Added a new processing board for $2,000, which extended the life of the computer another 3 years.

Required:
1. Prepare a journal entry to record each of the above expenditures.
2. Discuss why the two transactions are treated differently in the accounting records.

Comprehension Problem 8-5

Leopold Inc. purchased a factory machine on January 1, 19X1 for $110,000. The machine is expected to have a useful life of 10 years with a scrap value of $10,000.

Required:　Compute the depreciation for 19X1 and 19X2 using
1. The straight-line method
2. The double-declining balance method.

Comprehension Problem 8-6

Refer to the information in Comprehension Problem 8-5. At January 1, 19X3, Leopold revised its estimate of the machine's useful life from 10 to 6 years with no scrap value.

Required:　Calculate the depreciation for 19X3 using
1. The straight-line method
2. The double-declining balance method.

Comprehension Problem 8-7

Refer to the information in Comprehension Problem 8-6. Leopold disposed of the machine at January 1, 19X4.

Required: Using the straight-line method of depreciation, make the necessary calculations, assuming
  1. The equipment was sold for $60,000
  2. The equipment was sold for $85,000
  3. The equipment was sold for $50,000.

Comprehension Problem 8-8

Refer to the information in Comprehension Problem 8-6. Leopold traded in the machine on an improved model. (The best of the new models was $150,000.) The company got a trade-in allowance of $100,000 on the old machine. The fair market value of the old machine was $95,000.

Required: Prepare the journal entry to record the trade-in on the equipment at January 1, 19X4 (include all depreciation to January 1, 19X4). Assume the straight-line method of depreciation is used.

Comprehension Problem 8-9

Tonka Corp. purchased a new car on January 1, 19X1 for $25,000. The estimated life of the car was 5 years or 500 000 km, at which time the car would have a fair market value of $2,000.

Required: Calculate the depreciation for 19X1 and 19X2 using
  1. The straight-line method
  2. Usage method (kms)
  3. Double-declining balance method.

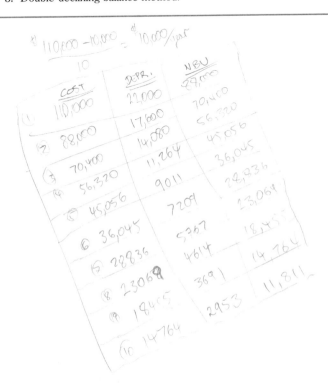

Comprehension Problem 8-10

Accountants distinguish between capital and revenue expenditures when referring to cash disbursements made for asset-related reasons. The debit entry for such expenditures can be made to any one of the following accounts:

Balance Sheet Accounts
a. Land
b. Buildings
c. Equipment
d. Trucks
e. Automobiles
f. Accumulated Depreciation

Income Statement Accounts
g. A revenue account   h. An expense account.

Required: For each transaction, indicate the account to be debited.

Example:
___b___ Architect fees to design building

___h___ Battery purchased for truck
___c___ Cash discount received on payment for equipment
___a___ Commission paid to real estate agent to purchase land
___c___ Cost of equipment test runs
___b___ Cost to remodel building
___b___ Cost to replace manual elevator with automatic elevator
___a___ Cost of sewage system
___c___ Equipment assembly expenditure
___c___ Expenditures for debugging of equipment
___e___ Installation of air-conditioner in automobile
___b___ Insurance paid during construction of building
___a___ Legal fees associated with court case to defend title to land purchased
___h___ Oil change for truck
___a___ Payment for landscaping
___a___ Proceeds received on demolition of useless building on land purchased
___a___ Expenditures for removal of useless structures
___h___ Repair made to building after moving in
___h___ Repair of collision damage to truck
___h___ Repair of torn imitation leather seats in automobile
___h___ Replacement of rusted fender on automobile
___h___ Replacement of transmission on automobile
___c___ Special floor foundations for installation of equipment
___h___ Tires purchased for truck
___c___ Transportation expenditures to bring equipment to plant.

Note: Answer problems regarding intangible assets or current costs only if the Appendixes were studied in your course.

Comprehension Problem 8-11

Atlantic Limited purchased a $30,000 depreciable asset with a 5-year life expectancy and no salvage value. Two alternative methods of depreciating this asset are presented below.

Year	Depreciation Method A	Method B
1	$6,000	$12,000
2	6,000	7,200
3	?	?

Required:

1. Identify the method of depreciation and compute the depreciation expense for the third year under each depreciation method.
2. The comptroller of Atlantic considers the difference in annual depreciation to be nothing more than a change in the estimate of depreciation required; she proposes to use Method B for Years 1 and 2 and Method A for Years 3, 4, and 5. In this way, she can deduct the maximum depreciation each year over the life of the asset. Is her proposal acceptable? Why or why not?
3. What factors should be considered in choosing a method of depreciation?

Comprehension Problem 8-12

The Alberta Corporation purchased three milling machines on January 1, 19X3 and immediately placed them in service. The following information relates to this purchase:

	Machine 1	Machine 2	Machine 3
Cost	$7,500	$7,500	$7,500
Salvage Value	-0-	1,200	300
Useful Life	5 Years	6 Years	8 Years

The company uses the straight-line method of depreciation. Five years after the purchase, Machine 1 was sold for $500. Management elected to re-evaluate the estimated useful life and the salvage value estimates of the remaining machines. They came to the conclusion that Machine 2 had a remaining useful life of 2 years as of January 1, 19X8; salvage value remained unchanged. Machine 3 had a remaining useful life of 5 years but, likely, no salvage value.

Required: Prepare journal entries required during 19X8

1. To record the sale on January 1, 19X8
2. To record the revised depreciation expense for Machine 2 at December 31, 19X8
3. To record the revised depreciation expense for Machine 3 at December 31, 19X8.

Comprehension Problem 8-13

The following equipment and accumulated depreciation accounts appear in the general ledger of the Big Corporation at December 31, 19X6.

Equipment   No. 183

Date 19X6		Description	F	Debit	Credit	DR. or CR.	Balance
Jan.	1	Machine #1		5 0 0 0		DR	5 0 0 0
Jan.	1	Machine #2		1 0 0 0 0		DR	1 5 0 0 0

Accumulated Depreciation — Equipment   No. 193

Date 19X6		Description	F	Debit	Credit	DR. or CR.	Balance
Dec.	31	Depreciation 19X6			1 5 0 0	CR	1 5 0 0

At the time of purchase, the equipment was expected to have a useful life of 10 years with no salvage value at the end of that time. A straight-line method of depreciation was used by the company in 19X6. On January 1, 19X7, it was discovered that the equipment would in fact last only 4 more years.

Required:
1. Calculate the depreciation required in 19X7, using the new facts concerning the revised useful life of the equipment.
2. Prepare the entry to record depreciation in 19X7 in the general ledger.
3. Post the accumulated depreciation part of the entry in 2, above, to the ledger and calculate the new balance in the account.
4. When you consider the substantial difference between the depreciation amounts in 19X6 and 19X7, what is your impression of the validity of the information conveyed to the reader of Big Corporation's balance sheet in 19X6 as compared with 19X7? How much should the depreciation amount have been in each year if the actual 5-year useful life of the equipment had been known in 19X6?

Comprehension Problem 8-14

Brinks Limited purchased a truck on January 1, 19X4. The following details are made available:

Cost	Useful Life	Salvage Value	Depreciation Method
$10,500	5 years	$500	Capital Cost Allowance (30% declining balance)

In 19X5, the company paid $3,500 for gas and oil, a tune-up, new tires, and a battery. On January 1, 19X5, the company also paid $4,000 to install a lift on the back of the truck (consider this addition as a betterment). The year-end of the company is December 31.

Required:
1. Prepare journal entries to record
   a. The purchase of the truck
   b. Depreciation for 19X4
   c. The 19X5 expenditures relating to the truck
   d. Depreciation for 19X5.
2. Do you think that using the income tax capital cost allowance method of calculating depreciation involves a "stretching" of accounting principles in this case? Why or why not?

Comprehension Problem 8-15

A truck was purchased by Jennifer's Transport Inc. on June 30, 19X3.

Cost	Useful Life	Salvage Value	Depreciation Method
$13,500	6 years	$1,500	Capital Cost Allowance (30% declining balance)

Required:
1. Calculate the depreciation for 19X3 and 19X4.
2. Using the information calculated in question 1, prepare journal entries if the truck is sold January 2, 19X5 for cash for
   a. $6,615   b. $7,615   c. $5,615.
3. Do you think that using the income tax capital cost allowance method of calculating depreciation involves a "stretching" of accounting principles in this case? Why or why not?
4. Assume that the old truck was traded in for a new truck instead of being sold; prepare the journal entry to record the trade-in on January 2, 19X5. The list price of the new truck is $15,000. The old truck had a fair market value of $5,000. Jennifer's Transport Inc. traded in the old truck and paid an additional $7,500 cash in acquiring the new truck.

Problems

Problem 8-1 (SMA adapted)

The following items relate to the acquisition of a new machine by the Burlington Group Inc. On the right-hand side is a number of possible accounting treatments; on the left-hand side is a number of independent accounting situations:

Situation

_____ Invoice price of new machine, net of the cash discount offered

_____ Cash discount on the above, which has not yet been taken

_____ Anticipated first year's savings in operating costs from use of new machine

_____ Two-year service contract on operations of new machine paid in full

_____ Cost of materials used while testing new machine

_____ Cost of installing sound insulation in wall near machine so that nearby office employees will not be disturbed by it

_____ Cost of removing machine that new machine replaces.

Accounting Treatment

(1) Debit Machinery account

(2) Debit an expense account for the current period

(3) Debit an asset other than the machine and amortize the asset separately from the machine

(4) Credit Machinery account

(5) Use an accounting treatment other than the above; explain what account would be appropriate.

Required: Indicate the appropriate accounting treatment for each situation. Record any assumptions that you think might be necessary for any given situation.

Problem 8-2

Mirth Amusement Park Ltd. acquired a new amusement ride, on which it took a July 1 delivery. The following details apply to the purchase:

Cost per supplier's invoice	$20,000
(The invoice provided a 1% cash discount if paid within 30 days. Paid for above item on July 15.)	
Payment on July 4 to Howe Construction Ltd. for cement base for new ride	4,000
Transportation paid on purchase, July 5	520
Insurance paid on ride July 5 — 3-year term	90
Installation costs, July 6	188
Alterations to new ride	900
(This was covered up to 25% by the vendor under terms of its guarantee. Bill received and paid July 5.)	

Required:

1. Prepare journal entries to record the activities of Mirth Amusement Park in acquiring its new ride.
2. Calculate the carrying value of the asset after accounting for the above.

Problem 8-3

Corin Corporation purchased a piece of machinery at the beginning of 19X5. The following information is made available.

Cost	Useful Life	Salvage Value	Depreciation Method
$90,000 installed	9000 units	-0-	usage

Output during 19X5 and 19X6 was 2000 and 3000 units, respectively.

Required:
1. Calculate the depreciation expense for 19X5 and 19X6.
2. What is the balance of accumulated depreciation at the end of 19X6?
3. What is the net amount of the machinery shown on the balance sheet at the end of 19X6?
4. Prepare a partial comparative balance sheet for Corin Corporation at the end of 19X6.

Problem 8-4

Petersen Corp. purchased a business microcomputer on January 1, 19X3. The company year-end is December 31. The following information is made available.

Cost	Useful Life	Salvage Value	Depreciation Method
$5,000	4 years	$1,000	(to be discussed)

Required:
1. Calculate the depreciation expense for a 4-year period under each of these depreciation methods; straight-line, double-declining balance (calculate the rate), and capital cost allowance (30%).

	Depreciation Expense		
YEAR	STRAIGHT-LINE	DOUBLE-DECLINING BALANCE	CAPITAL COST ALLOWANCE
1	$1000	$2500	$1,500.00
2	1000	1250	1,050.00
3	1000	250	735.00
4	1000	-0-	514.50
TOTAL	$4000	$4000	$3,799.50

30% OF 5000

2. Since computers are subject to rapid changes in technology, the president asks you to explain what impact potential changes may have on the microcomputer's useful life. What factors should you cover in your explanation?
3. Which method of depreciation would you recommend in this case? Why?

Problem 8-5

Shelenz Trucks Inc. purchased a delivery van on January 1, 19X3. The following information is available.

Cost	Useful Life	Salvage Value	Depreciation Method
$11,000	4 Years (consisting of 75 000 km)	$2,000	(to be discussed)

The truck covered 20 000 km in 19X3.

Required:
1. Calculate the depreciation for 19X3 under each of the following methods:
   - a. Usage
   - b. Straight-line
   - c. Single-declining balance
   - d. Double-declining balance
   - e. Capital cost allowance (30%).
2. Compare the depreciation expense, accumulated depreciation, and net book value for 19X3 for each of these methods:
   - a. Usage
   - b. Straight-line
   - c. Single-declining balance
   - d. Double-declining balance
   - e. Capital cost allowance.
3. Which of these methods can be used for income tax purposes? Why?
4. Which method would result in the lowest income taxes paid in 19X3? Calculate the income tax saving in 19X3 if the income tax rate is 50 percent. (*Hint*: The maximum allowable depreciation for income tax purposes cannot exceed the amount calculated using the CCA method.)
5. Which method results in the lowest income taxes paid in 19X6? Show details to support your answer. (Assume that the income tax rate is 50 percent.)
6. Is it fair to try to save on income taxes in 19X3?

Problem 8-6

The Collinge Co. Ltd. purchased a machine on January 1, 19X6 for $23,000. Transportation charges paid by Collinge amounted to $600 and another $1,400 cost was incurred for installation. The estimated salvage value of the machine is $1,000.

Required:
1. Calculate the depreciable cost of the machine.
2. In journal entry form, record the depreciation each year of the expected life of the machine under
   - a. Straight-line method (estimated life 3 years)
   - b. Declining balance method (at 40% rate).
3. On January 1, 19X7, Collinge changed the life estimate on the machine from a total of 3 to a total of 5 years. Salvage value remains at an estimated $1,000. You are required to calculate the depreciation that should be recorded in 19X7 and each year thereafter. The company used the straight-line method.

Problem 8-7

On January 1, 19X1, Savard Inc. purchased a machine for $30,000. The engineers had established a life duration for that machine of 20 years. The scrap value is estimated to be 10 percent of the original cost. On January 1, 19X8, experts were hired to review the expected life and scrap value of the machine. Here are the findings:

New Estimated Life   15 years
New Estimated Scrap Value $6,000

Depreciation has not yet been recorded in 19X8. Assume that the straight-line method of depreciation is used.

Required:
1. Calculate the book value of the machine at December 31, 19X7.
2. Calculate the undepreciated cost of the machine at January 1, 19X8, assuming that the straight-line method of depreciation is used.
3. Calculate the amount of depreciation expense to be recorded at December 31, 19X8, and prepare the necessary journal entry.
4. If the current replacement value of the machine is $51,000, comment on the existence of phantom profits in this company. Make some calculations to support your answer.

Problem 8-8 (SMA adapted)

Part A

Rosen Manufacturing Inc. started business on May 1, 19X4. It commenced operations by signing a 20-year lease for a factory building. The year-end of the company is December 31. On May 5, 19X4, the company purchased equipment for $130,000. The equipment had an estimated useful life of 4 years, or a production of 100 000 units, with a salvage value of $10,000. The equipment over 3 years produced the following numbers of units: 19X4 — 12 000; 19X5 — 30 000; and 19X6 — 20 000.

On January 4, 19X7, the company traded in all the original equipment on new equipment. The company traded in its old equipment and paid cash ($140,000) to receive delivery of the new equipment. The company had used the units-of-output (usage) method of calculating the depreciation on the manufacturing equipment. The fair market value of the original equipment was $60,000 at the date of the trade.

Part B

On January 5, 19X5, Rosen Manufacturing Inc. was able to buy a nearby warehouse for the storage of its finished product. The cost included land, $50,000; building, $300,000. The company signed a 10-year mortgage for $320,000 and paid the balance in cash. The building had a useful life of 50 years with no salvage value. On June 28, 19X9, the warehouse was totally destroyed by fire. Owing to a strike by the company employees at the time, the warehouse was empty and the company received $270,000 from the insurance company as settlement in full for the building. The building was depreciated on a straight-line basis.

Required: Prepare journal entries to record the transactions on the following dates:
1. May 5, 19X4 (part A)   3. January 5, 19X5 (part B)
2. January 4, 19X7 (part A)   4. June 28, 19X9 (part B).

Problem 8-9

A bank manager, a friend of yours, discusses with you the matter of goodwill, which appears so often in financial statements. She mentions that she does not think that such an account should appear in the financial statements, particularly since the rules for evaluation and presentation vary from one company to another.

Required:
1. What is goodwill? Name some factors or situations that justify recording it.
2. Give the essential condition(s) that would justify showing goodwill in the financial statements.

Alternate Problems

Alternate Problem 8-1

Lebas Corp. operates a plant building adjacent to its office building. The plant building is old and requires continuous maintenance and repairs. On the first day of the current fiscal period, the Plant Building account shows a $250,000 balance and the Accumulated Depreciation account shows a $150,000 balance. During the year, the following expenditures relating to the plant building were incurred:

a. Continuing, frequent, and low-cost repairs	$26,000
b. Overhaul of the plumbing system (old costs not known)	17,000
c. New storage shed attached to the plant building (estimated life, 10 years)	48,000
d. Replaced an old shingle roof with a new tile roof (cost of the old shingle roof was $30,000)	60,000
e. Unusual infrequent repairs	10,000

Required:
1. Prepare journal entries to record each of items a to e.
2. Explain your treatment of each item.

Alternate Problem 8-2

Gibbins Limited purchased the following equipment on January 1, 19X2.

Cost	Useful Life	Salvage Value	Depreciation Method
$6,000	5 Years	$300	(to be discussed)

Required:
1. Calculate the total depreciation for the 5-year period 19X2–19X6, under each of these depreciation methods: straight-line and double-declining balance.
2. Both methods of calculating depreciation are used in actual practice. List the advantages of
   a. The straight-line method
   b. The double-declining balance method.

Alternate Problem 8-3

Skinner Inc., a speculative mining organization, purchased a machine on April 1, 19X4. The following information is made available.

Cost	Useful Life	Salvage Value	Depreciation Method
$40,000	3 years (consisting of 100 000 tonnes)	$4,000	(to be discussed)

The machine has an estimated life in production output of 100 000 tonnes. Actual output was: Year 1 — 40 000 tonnes; Year 2 — 20 000 tonnes; Year 3 — 10 000 tonnes. The year-end of the company is March 31.

Required:
1. Calculate the depreciation expense and the net book value at year-end for the 3-year period under each of these depreciation methods: straight-line, double-declining balance, capital cost allowance (20%), and usage.
2. Assume that the machine is no longer useful at the end of 3 years and must be sold. Although depreciation has been recorded based on machine usage as calculated in 1, above, the president believes that it could have been used to process an additional 30 000 tonnes. He fears that an excessive amount of depreciation has been charged against income during the 3 years and that the company has issued incorrect financial statements. Do you agree? Why or why not?

Alternate Problem 8-4

Kelly Inc. purchased its first piece of equipment on January 1, 19X6. The following information pertains to this machine:

	Cost	Useful Life	Salvage Value	Depreciation Method
	$11,000	5 Years	$1,000	(to be discussed)

As the chief accountant for the company, you are faced with making a choice of a depreciation method to be used.

Required:
1. Calculate the straight-line and double-declining balance method depreciation for 19X6, 19X7, and 19X8.
2. Using the format provided, complete comparative partial income statements and balance sheets at December 31 for both the straight-line and declining balance methods of depreciation.

Partial Income Statement	19X6	19X7	19X8
Net Income before Depreciation and Income Taxes	$30,000	$25,000	$35,000
Depreciation Expense	?	?	?
Income from Operations	$?	$?	$?
Income Taxes (50%)	$?	$?	$?
Net Income for the Year	$?	$?	$?
Partial Balance Sheet			
Equipment	$?	$?	$?
Less:			
Accumulated Depreciation	?	?	?
Net Book Value	$?	$?	$?

3. Which depreciation method should be used for deferral of income taxes? Explain.

Alternate Problem 8-5

The Pyle Carpet Centre purchased a cutting machine at the beginning of 19X4 for $46,000. Pyle paid additional charges of $1,200 and $2,800 for freight and installation, respectively. Salvage value was estimated at $2,000.

Required:
1. Calculate the depreciable cost of the machine.
2. In journal form, record the depreciation for each year, using
   a. Straight-line method (with a life estimate of 3 years)
   b. Declining balance method (at 40% rate — depreciate for only 3 years).
3. On January 19X5, Pyle revised the life estimate on the machine from a total of 3 years to a total of 5 years. Estimated salvage remained at $2,000. Calculate the depreciation that should be recorded in 19X5 and each year thereafter. Use the straight-line method of depreciation.

Alternate Problem 8-6

On the first business day of the new year 19X1, Thesberg Truckers Ltd. purchased for cash a new truck from its local dealer. The truck was a heavy-duty type, and records indicated it should have a 10-year life span but no salvage value. The vehicle cost $12,000. During the first week of January, 19X5, the truck was repaired and rebuilt. The total cost was $3,200, of which $2,400 was for additions (considered as a betterment) and $800 for ordinary repair. The former increased the efficiency of the truck, but no change was contemplated in life expectancy or salvage value. On April 1, 19X6, the truck was completely wrecked. Gamma Insurance Co. settled the claim for $4,000.

Required: Prepare journal entries for
1. Purchase of the truck
2. Depreciation of the truck (straight-line method)
3. 19X5 transaction involving rebuilding

4. 19X5 depreciation
5. 19X6.

Alternate Problem 8-7

The following account appears in the general ledger of the Tiessen Corp. at December 31, 19X4.

Equipment   No. 183

Date 19X4		Description	F	Debit	Credit	DR. or CR.	Balance
Jan.	1	Machine #1		6400		DR	6400

Accumulated Depreciation — Equipment   No. 193

Date 19X4		Description	F	Debit	Credit	DR. or CR.	Balance
Dec.	31	Depreciation for 19X4			1000	CR	1000
19X5							
Dec.	31	Depreciation for 19X5			1000	CR	2000

Machine No. 1 was estimated to have a useful life of 6 years, with an estimated salvage value of $400. On January 1, 19X6, Machine No. 1 was traded in for Machine No. 2. The list price of Machine No. 2 was $8,000 and the S. Hudas Corp. received a trade-in allowance of $4,500.

Machine No. 2 is estimated to have a useful life of 8 years, with an estimated salvage value of $1,000. The fair market value of machine No. 1 was $4,000 at the date of the trade-in.

Required:
1. Prepare a journal entry to record the trade-in of Machine No. 1 for Machine No. 2.
2. Post the appropriate parts of the entry prepared in 1, above, to the general ledger accounts, and calculate the new balance in each account.
3. The installation cost of Machine No. 2 amounted to $500 and was recorded in the Maintenance Expense account when paid. Prepare a correcting entry at December 31, 19X6.
4. Prepare the entry to record the depreciation for 19X6. (The correcting entry required in 3, above, has already been made.) Post the appropriate part of this entry to the Accumulated Depreciation account, and calculate the new balance in that account.

Alternate Problem 8-8

In accounting, certain intangible assets are subject to the process of amortization, whereas others are not. Listed below are three intangibles that an accountant might encounter:
a. Trademarks
b. Patents
c. Goodwill.

Required: Explain the accounting treatment you would suggest for each, incorporating in your answer reasons for the suggested treatment.

Supplementary Problems

Supplementary Problem 8-1

Four machines were purchased by Lelik Co. Ltd. during 19X4 and 19X5. Machine A was finally placed in use at the end of August 19X4. The cost was $26,400, the estimated life 8 years, and the estimated salvage value $2,400. Depreciation was to be on a straight-line basis. The company year-end is December 31.

Machine B was ready for use October 1, 19X4. Depreciation was to be on a units of production basis. The cost was $23,600, with a 5-year life expectancy and an estimated salvage value of $3,600. Estimated production over the 5 years would be 50 000 units. In 19X4, 3000 units were produced, 11 500 in 19X5 and 12 000 during 19X6. Machines C and D were purchased for $34,200 in April 19X5 and were in production on July 1 of that year. The following additional information about Machines C and D is available:

Machine	Appraised Value	Salvage Value	Estimated Life	Installation Cost	Depreciation Method
C	$16,000	$1,000	6 Years	$ 500	Straight-line
D	20,000	1,600	10 Years	1,000	Declining balance

Required:
1. For each of the 4 machines, calculate the total amount to be charged to depreciation and the depreciation for 19X4, 19X5, and 19X6. Assume that double the straight-line rate was used for the declining balance depreciation.
2. Prepare journal entries to record payment and to record installation for Machines C and D. Installation costs were paid on the date they were placed in service.
3. Prepare a compound journal entry to record the 19X6 depreciation on the four machines.

Supplementary Problem 8-2 (SMA adapted)

The comparative statements for Reliable Enterprises Corporation are as follows:

Income Statements

	19X4	19X3
Sales	$600,000	$540,000
Cost of Goods Sold	360,000	324,000
Gross Profit	$240,000	$216,000
Operating Expenses	150,000	140,000
Net Income	$ 90,000	$ 76,000

Statement of Retained Earnings

	19X4	19X3
Balance (Jan. 1)	$256,000	$200,000
Add: Net income	90,000	76,000
	$346,000	$276,000
Less: Dividends	30,000	20,000
Balance (Dec. 31)	$316,000	$256,000

In 19X4, Reliable decided to switch its depreciation method from the declining balance to the straight-line method. The differences in the two methods are

	19X4	19X3
Declining balance	$58,000	$65,000
Straight-line	40,000	40,000
Difference	$18,000	$25,000

The income statement for 19X4 includes $58,000 in depreciation expense. Also, it was discovered that there was an overstatement of $20,000 in the 19X3 ending inventory balance. Reliable uses a periodic inventory system. 19X4 ending inventory is correct.

Required: Correct the financial statements.

Supplementary Problem 8-3

Corporations X and Y are identical in almost every respect. Both began business during the first days of January, 19X6, with equipment costing $40,000, and having a 10-year life with no salvage value. Neither X nor Y added to equipment during 19X6. At year-end, Corporation X decided to depreciate its equipment using the declining balance method at double the straight-line rate, while company Y chose straight-line depreciation. On December 31, before depreciation was recorded, the ledgers included the following items:

	Company X	Company Y
Sales	$75,000	$75,000
Salaries Expense	7,000	7,000
Rental Expense	2,500	2,500
Other Expenses	300	300

During 19X6, both purchased merchandise as follows:

Jan. 6	400 units @ $12.50/unit
Mar. 13	1200 units @ $12.00/unit
Jun. 28	800 units @ $13.50/unit
Oct. 10	800 units @ $14.00/unit
Dec. 20	400 units @ $15.00/unit

Corporation X priced its 440 units of ending inventory on a LIFO basis, while Corporation Y used FIFO for its 440-unit ending inventory.

Required: Prepare an income statement for X and for Y, showing the results for 19X6. Show your calculations of the inventory as a note to the statement.

Supplementary Problem 8-4

On January 1, 19X2, Doyle Construction Corporation purchased for $120,000 cash a new excavating machine for use in its business. The new machine was expected to have a useful life of 10 years with no salvage value. On January 2, 19X5, a device was added to the machine, increasing its output by 10 percent. The cost was $5,600 cash. This addition brought no change to either life expectancy or salvage value. The machine was overhauled (considered as an extraordinary repair) during the first week of January 19X9 for $36,000. The salvage value still remained the same, but the life expectancy was increased by 3 years.

Required: Prepare journal entries to record
1. The original purchase
2. Depreciation for 19X2 (straight-line; the year-end is December 31)
3. The addition to the equipment
4. The depreciation for 19X5
5. The overhauling of the equipment
6. The depreciation for 19X9.

Supplementary Problem 8-5

On January 1, 19X1, Eastern Construction Limited purchased new heavy-duty equipment and placed it in service. The cost to the company was $60,000 cash. The equipment was expected to have no salvage value after a life expectancy of 10 years. On January 1, 19X4, a device was added to the equipment that increased its output by approximately 20 percent. The cost was $2,800. This addition brought no change to either life expectancy or salvage value.

The equipment was overhauled (considered as an extraordinary repair) during the first week of January 19X8, for $18,000 cash. The salvage value still remained the same, but the life expectancy increased by 3 years. On July 1, 19X9, the equipment was a total loss following a fire. The insurance company arranged for settlement and paid the company $20,000.

Required:
1. Prepare journal entries to record
    a. Depreciation for 19X1 (straight-line; year-end is December 31)
    b. The addition to the Equipment account after the January 2 addition
    c. The depreciation for 19X3, 19X4, 19X5, 19X6, and 19X7
    d. The overhauling of the equipment in January 19X8
    e. The depreciation for 19X8
    f. The fire loss and settlement on July 1, 19X9.
2. Post the appropriate part of these entries to the ledger accounts, Equipment and Accumulated Depreciation — Equipment, and calculate the balance in each account.

Supplementary Problem 8-6

The Norwich Manufacturing Co. Ltd., which uses the straight-line method of depreciation, purchased three pieces of equipment (Machine A, Machine B, and Machine C) on the first day of business in January 19X3. Details of the acquisition are as follows:

	Machine A	Machine B	Machine C
Original Cost	$30,000	$30,000	$30,000
Estimated Salvage	-0-	4,800	1,200
Life Expectancy	5 Years	6 Years	8 Years

During the first week of business in 19X8, Machine A was sold for $2,000. This encouraged management to re-examine the useful life expectancy and the expected salvage value of Machines B and C. Management decided that Machine B had a remaining life of 2 years as of January 2, 19X8, and that the salvage expectation was about right. Machine C, on the other hand, had a remaining life of 5 years and, likely, there would be no scrap value.

Required: Prepare journal entries required in 19X8 to record
  1. Sale of Machine A
  2. Depreciation on Machines B and C as at December 31, 19X8.

Supplementary Problem 8-7

The Acland Corp. applied for and received in 19X6 a patent on a new manufacturing process for aluminum tubing. Research costs amounting to $40,000 were incurred in 19X6, and $30,000 of research costs were incurred in 19X5. The following expenses were also incurred:

	19X6	19X5
Cost of drawings	$1,000	$2,000
Legal fees	500	3,000
Patent application	200	—
Cost of testing	2,500	500
Fees paid to an engineer	2,000	3,000
Estimated salary for time spent on project:		
President	5,000	2,000
Treasurer	2,000	7,000

Required:
  1. On the basis of the above information, calculate the cost of the patent at the end of 19X5 and 19X6.
  2. Give the balance sheet presentation of the patent at the end of 19X5 and 19X6. (Assume that the patent was not used in 19X5 nor in 19X6.)
  3. What is the legal life of this patent?

Decision Problems

Decision Problem 8-1

Lakeshore Construction Company Ltd. purchased a farm from J.B. Smith. Lakeshore and Smith completed the transaction under the following terms: a cheque from Lakeshore to Smith for $140,000; mortgage on property assumed by Lakeshore, $100,000. Legal, accounting, and brokerage fees amounted to $20,000.

It was Lakeshore's intention to build homes on the property after sub-dividing. Crops on the farm were sold for $6,000; a house, to be moved by the buyer, was sold for $1,600; barns were razed at a cost of $6,000, while salvaged lumber was sold for $4,400. The property was cleared and levelled at a cost of $10,000.

The necessary property was turned over to the township for roads, schools, churches, and playgrounds. Riverside still expected to secure a total of 500 lots from the remaining land.

Required: Prepare a schedule showing the cost to Lakeshore of the 500 lots.

Decision Problem 8-2

Goulet Ltd. commenced construction of a new plant on July 1, 19X1. All construction activities were completed by March 31, 19X2, after which time the plant went into operation. Total cost incurred during the construction period included

	(000s)
Cost of Land (includes the cost of an old building on it)	$ 55
Engineering Fees:	
Analysis of the sub-soil	$ 8
Construction supervision	50
Analysis of the electrical system	30
Planning of a new production process (required in order to use new equipment that will be installed in the new building)	45
	$ 133
Subcontractor's Charges:	
Demolition of the old building	$ 3
Wages and material (excluding landscaping)	531
Landscaping	4
	$ 538
Charges Included in the Company's Operating Accounts:	
Wages of employees on construction site	$ 460
Construction materials	1,267
Taxes and interest (payable in advance, for the entire year commencing July 1, 19X1)	18
	$1,745

The company is to receive a government grant of $200,000 for having selected a recommended site as the actual location of the new plant.

Required: As comptroller of Goulet Ltd., determine which of the above costs should properly be included in the cost of the new plant accounts. Briefly explain why you would include or exclude each cost item.

Decision Problem 8-3

The Zin Corp. manufactures light fixtures for the wholesale trade. A major piece of machinery is a drill press that cost $220,000 on January 1, Year 1. This press is being depreciated, using the declining balance method of depreciation; it has an estimated $20,000 scrap value and an estimated useful life of 4 years. As of January 1, Year 3, the company will change its depreciation method to straight-line. Management thinks that this method will provide a better matching of revenues and expenses. The company has a December 31 year-end.

Required:
1. Prepare a schedule of depreciation for Years 1, 2, 3, and 4, using the declining balance method and the straight-line method. Calculate the difference for each year between the methods. (The declining balance rate is calculated at 50 percent.)
2. The comptroller of Zin notes that the estimate of yearly depreciation using the declining balance method will differ from the estimate of depreciation using the straight-line method. She considers the change to be nothing more than a change in the estimate of depreciation required. Do you agree that this change from declining balance to straight-line method is really a change in the estimate of depreciation required? Why or why not?

Decision Problem 8-4

Meagher Mines Ltd., incorporated March 31, 19X1, had an asset, land, bearing recoverable ore deposits, estimated by geologists to contain 800 000 tonnes. The cost of this land was $450,000, and it was estimated to be worth $50,000 after extraction of the ore. During this year, mine improvements totalled $17,500. Various buildings and sheds were constructed at a cost of $22,500. During the year, 35 000 tonnes were mined. Of this tonnage, 6500 tonnes were on hand unsold on March 31, 19X2, the balance having been sold for cash at $4.50 per tonne. Expenses incurred and paid during the year, exclusive of depletion and depreciation, were as follows:

Mining	$84,000
Delivery	9,250
Administration	8,800

It is believed that buildings and sheds will be useful over the life of the mine only; therefore, depreciation should be recognized in terms of mine output.

Required: Prepare an income statement for the year ended March 31, 19X2.

Decision Problem 8-5

Z Ltd. was incorporated on January 1, 19X3 and on that date purchased these assets:

Land	$100,000
Buildings	150,000
Equipment	75,000
Trucks and automobiles	30,000

On December 14, 19X3, the president of Z Ltd. asks you for advice in selecting a realistic depreciation policy for the company. The president informs you that the subject has been discussed with the manager and the bookkeeper and that the following views have been expressed:

President — No depreciation should be provided for land and buildings, because the inherent increase in land values will more than compensate for any physical deterioration of the buildings. Equipment, trucks, and automobiles should be written off in the year of purchase in order to ensure that they will be purchased only in years when there are sufficient profits to absorb the costs of such fixed assets.

Manager — No depreciation should be provided for land, because land is not used to earn profits. Buildings and equipment should be written off over the estimated useful life of the assets — 40 years for buildings and 10 years for equipment. Trucks and automobiles should be written off over a period of 3 years, since the company intends to trade them in for new ones every 3 years.

Bookkeeper — No depreciation should be provided for land, because few companies ever depreciate land and, therefore, any write-offs would not conform to generally accepted accounting principles. All other fixed asset costs should be written off by the declining balance method, calculated on the following annual rates:

Buildings	8%
Equipment	25%
Trucks and automobiles	35%

Required: What is your advice to the president of Z Ltd. as to the most acceptable depreciation policy for the company? Explain your comments on the validity of each of the views expressed by the president, the manager, and the bookkeeper.

Decision Problem 8-6

The Caitlin Corp. reported a net income of $150,000 for the year. The president of the corporation noted that the beginning and ending inventories were $600,000 and $750,000, respectively, although the physical quantities on hand were relatively stable. She also noted that deductions for depreciation averaged 10 percent on plant and equipment costing $1,350,000, although the current dollar value of the assets is estimated at $1,800,000. The president suggests that the reported net income is erroneous.

Required: Do you agree with the president? Explain, using calculations to support your answer.

Decision Problem 8-7

Court Inc. has acquired depreciable fixed assets totalling $100,000.

Required:
1. Using a 10-year life and no salvage value, calculate which of the following methods of depreciation results in the lowest income for the first three years:
   a. Straight-line
   b. Double-declining balance.
2. Why would Court Inc. want to delay the payment of income taxes? (Assume that there is no salvage value for the assets and that Court Inc. is subject to an income tax rate of 50 percent.)

Decision Problem 8-8

On January 1, Year 1, Jen Co. purchased a machine for $175,000. It was estimated that the machine would have a useful life of 10 years and no salvage value.

When the machine was purchased, it was charged to expense in error. The company uses straight-line depreciation for such assets.

At the end of Year 10, it was found that the machine would most likely last another 10 years. The books have not been closed for Year 10.

Required:
1. Assume that the books are closed and that the error was discovered at the end of Year 5. Prepare a journal entry to record depreciation expense for Year 6.
2. The realization that the machine would last another ten years requires appropriate accounting action. If this is considered a change in estimate, what is the appropriate action to be taken in this case? Explain. Do not prepare a journal entry.

The Financing Cycle

Equity and debt comprise the financing cycle of the entity. Equity financing includes capital contributions by owners and earnings made and retained by the entity. Debt financing includes money "borrowed" by issuing bonds for long-term financing.

Chapter 9 discusses how corporations issue different types of shares to obtain capital and how these transactions are recorded. Share transactions and other transactions involving shareholders' equity must be disclosed in the balance sheet.

Chapter 10 discusses matters related to the declaration and payment of dividends. Both creditors and shareholders are interested in the amount of assets that can be distributed as dividends. Retained earnings of the entity can be either restricted (unavailable for distribution as dividends) or unrestricted.

Chapter 11 deals with accounting for an entity's efforts to obtain long-term debt in order to finance operations. Bond issues are an important source of debt financing. The proportion of debt to equity varies from one entity to another. There are many factors influencing management's choice between the issue of equity and debt. The advantages and disadvantages must be weighed according to the risk involved.

Equity Financing

Corporations finance their operations through issues of share capital. The financial statement reader is interested in shareholders' equity information to answer such questions as:

1. What different classes of shares does the corporation have available to interested investors?
2. How much is the corporation's stated capital?
3. What are the different rights of shareholders in the corporation?
4. What dividends are preferred shareholders entitled to if dividends are declared by the corporation?
5. How much are the claims of preferred shareholders in the event of liquidation?
6. What is the status of corporate shares at year-end?
7. What is the maximum amount of dividends that could be declared by the corporation?
8. Have any assets of the corporation been revalued?
9. Are there any unusual components of shareholders' equity?
10. What is the book value of common shares?

This chapter will enable you to answer these questions about shareholders' equity. It will also answer the following questions about partnerships.

11. How do the characteristics of a partnership differ from those of a corporation?
12. What unique accounting characteristics are required for a partnership?

A. The Corporate Structure

Share capital
A generic classification for all shares, both common and preferred; also referred to as *capital stock*.

The accounting equation expresses a relationship between assets owned by a corporation and the claims against those assets by creditors and shareholders. The accounting for assets and their financial statement disclosure was discussed in preceding chapters. The accounting for shareholders' equity is covered in this chapter. Corporate accounting for equity focuses on the distinction between the two main sources of shareholders' equity: **share capital** and retained earnings.

These two basic components are discussed in detail in order to explain the main features of corporate accounting and the guidelines used by accountants for shareholders' equity disclosure. Their relationship to the accounting equation is shown in Figure 9-1.

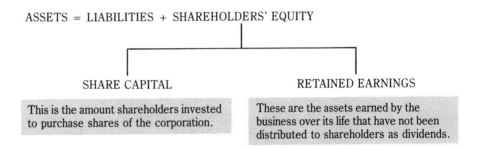

Figure 9-1   Share capital and retained earnings

Corporate Characteristics

The distinguishing characteristics of the corporation are that it is created by law, it has an unlimited life, it has limited liability, it can acquire capital easily, and it pays income tax on earnings.

Creation by Law

Canada Business Corporations Act (CBCA)
Statute regulating federally incorporated companies.

In Canada, an entity can become a corporation under either federal or provincial law. Each province has a corporations act that regulates the formation of corporations. Federal incorporation is made under the **Canada Business Corporations Act** (CBCA). One difficulty in gathering information about a corporation is that federal and provincial laws differ, making it hard to determine the rights and obligations of any one corporation or shareholder. The corporation is also subject to these government regulations:

1. It must file reports with the government.
2. It cannot distribute profits arbitrarily but must treat all shares of the same class alike.
3. It is subject to special taxes and fees.

Nevertheless, a corporation's advantages far outweigh its disadvantages.

Unlimited Life

A corporation has an existence separate from that of its owners. Individual shareholders may die, but the corporate entity continues. The life of a corporation comes to an end only when it is dissolved, becomes bankrupt, or has its charter revoked. In general, it has many of the rights and responsibilities that an individual citizen has. It can own property, for instance; it can sue and be sued.

Limited Liability

The corporation's owners are liable only for the amount that they have invested in the corporation. If the corporation fails, its assets are used to pay creditors. If insufficient assets exist to pay all debts, there is no further liability on the part of shareholders. For the protection of creditors, the limited liability of a corporation must be disclosed in its name. The words *Limited, Incorporated,* or *Corporation* (or the abbreviations Ltd., Inc., or Corp.) must be used as the last word of the name of a company incorporated federally or provincially. An exception is Quebec, where only the French terms *Limitée* or *Incorporée* (or the abbreviations Ltée or Inc.) and the French version of the entity's name must be used, regardless of where the company was incorporated.

Ease of Acquiring Capital

A corporation is a multiple-ownership organization and *shares* are the ownership units. The issue of shares allows many individuals to participate in the financing of a corporation. Both small and large investors are able to participate because of the ease with which ownership can be transferred — shares are simply purchased or sold.

There are many different types of shares. Differences exist with regard to voting rights, dividend rights, liquidation rights, and other preferential features. The rights of each shareholder depend on the class or type of shares held, and the amount of ownership by each shareholder depends on the number of shares he/she holds in relation to total shares outstanding. Through the issue of shares on stock markets like the Toronto Stock Exchange, large amounts of capital can be raised.

Income Taxes on Earnings

That corporations should pay income tax is understandable. However, individual shareholders are taxed on dividends on which the corporation already pays tax. The federal government allows shareholders a dividend tax credit to minimize the effect of this double taxation. Large corporations are taxed at one of two rates, depending on the amount of taxable income. This form of taxation is more advantageous than the escalating rates applied to individual taxpayers, which increase as earnings increase.

Rights of Shareholders

Ownership of a share certificate carries with it certain rights. These rights are printed on the certificate itself if they differ between classes of shares. (Figure 1-1 in Chapter 1 is a typical share certificate.) Each share in a class must be treated like every other share in that class with respect to whatever rights and privileges attach to it.

The rights and privileges usually attached to common shares are

1. The right to participate in the management of the corporation by voting at shareholders' meetings (this participation includes voting to elect a board of directors; each share corresponds to one vote)
2. The right to participate in dividends when they are declared by the corporation's board of directors
3. The right to participate in a distribution of assets on liquidation of the corporation
4. The right to appoint auditors.

These rights attach to each common share unless otherwise restricted in the *articles of incorporation* or *letters patent*. In some cases, these rights are restricted in other classes of shares. The articles of incorporation may also grant the shareholders the **preemptive right** to maintain their proportionate interests in the corporation if additional shares are issued. However, the corporation is permitted to ask its shareholders to waive that right.

Preemptive right
The right of shareholders to maintain their proportionate ownership of the corporation.

Shareholders of a corporation formed under the Canada Business Corporations Act also have additional rights if they are entitled to vote at an annual meeting. Such shareholders — except in very small corporations — can submit a proposal to raise any matter at an annual meeting and have this proposal circulated to other shareholders at the corporation's expense. If the corporation intends to make fundamental changes in its business, shareholders may require the corporation to buy their shares at their fair value. In addition, shareholders can apply to the courts for an appropriate remedy if they find themselves oppressed or find their interests unfairly disregarded by the corporation.

Board of Directors

Shareholders usually meet annually to vote for a board of directors — either to re-elect the current directors or to vote in new directors. Individual directors do not participate in daily management. The board of directors meets monthly or quarterly to review the operations of the corporation and to set policies for future operations. Based on the performance of the corporation, the board may decide to distribute some assets as a dividend to shareholders. It may also decide that some percentage of the net assets of the corporation legally available for dividends should be made unavailable for dividends; in this case, a restriction on the distribution of assets is created. Such restrictions are discussed in Chapter 10.

Corporate Terminology

Students sometimes have difficulty with the specialized meaning of terms required for corporate accounting, especially such terms as *value*; it has different meanings for non-accountants and accountants.

The Meaning of "Value"

Value
The amount at which an item appears in the general ledger. Value can be cost value, LOCAM, net realized value, no par-value, or book value.

The word **value**, in accounting terminology, usually refers to an amount that appears in the general ledger accounts of a business or in its financial statements. The word *value* does not express what an item is actually "worth" if offered for sale on the market. Study the following examples.

> 1. *Assets are normally recorded at cost.*
> Value here refers to the cost of assets, not to their worth; cost is the way the value of assets is determined.
>
> 2. *Inventories are sometimes recorded at the lower of cost and market (LOCAM).*
> The value of inventories is the amount calculated under the LOCAM rules. LOCAM does not intend to convey what this inventory is worth if resold; rather, it is a method by which a dollar amount of inventory is determined.

The word *value* is used by accountants to quantify assets and liabilities in monetary terms; it is also used in relation to share capital. *Value* has a precise meaning when used to describe the shares issued by a corporation.

Market Value

Market value of a share is the price at which a share is trading on the stock market. In one manner of speaking, this amount *can* be considered to represent what shares are worth.

Book Value

Book value of a share is the amount determined by dividing shareholders' equity by the number of shares outstanding. If 1000 common shares are outstanding and shareholders' equity totals $50,000, each of the 1000 shares has a book value of $50. Book value *does not* connote the worth of shares.

Three different classes of terms can be identified. These are shown in Figure 9-2 and are discussed later in this section.

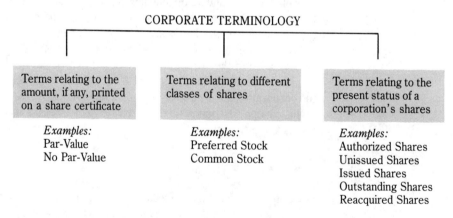

Figure 9-2   **Corporate accounting terminology**

Share Values

The word *value*, for corporate accountants, takes on a precise meaning indicated by its preceding adjective. For example, *market* indicates the precise meaning of *value* in market value. In each of the above examples, *value* only refers to an amount: a market amount in one case and a book amount in the other. Printed on a corporation's shares, the word *value* is explained by the adjectives *par* and *no par*.

Par-Value

Par-value is a per share amount specified in a corporation's charter. It is a monetary amount printed on each share of the corporation, and it bears no relationship to the market value or book value of the share. The issuance of par-value shares is prohibited under the Canada Business Corporations Act and their accounting is omitted from this text. Only in some provincial jurisdictions is the issue of par-value shares still permitted; the issue of these shares is authorized at the time these companies are incorporated.

No Par-Value

No par-value is the term used in situations where no amount is specified for shares in a corporation's charter. The amount received from the issuance of a share is considered as the minimum amount that has to be paid to the issuing corporation by the original purchaser of a share.

Under the CBCA and some provincial jurisdictions, only the issue of no par-value shares is permitted in companies incorporated under their legislation. This restriction is imposed in the belief that par-values are arbitrary and can be misleading to the unsophisticated investor; also, their use can result in unnecessary accounting complications. Some provinces permit the issue of both par-value and no par-value shares; the issue of such shares is authorized at the time these companies are incorporated in these provincial jurisdictions.

Classes of Shares

All corporations issue common stock. Some corporations, in order to appeal to as large a group of investors as possible, also issue **preferred stock**. Different classes of shares permit different risks to be assumed by different classes of shareholders in the same company.

Of the two groups of investors, common shareholders normally accept a larger element of risk that the corporation will be successful. In return for this risk-taking, they expect that they will receive dividends and/or an increase in the market value of their shares. To accomplish these goals, common shareholders usually exercise voting control of the corporation.

Preferred shareholders typically assume less risk than common shareholders. They are also entitled to a limited amount of dividends and are given little or no real influence in the control of the corporation. Sometimes a corporation may issue only common stock but will divide it into classes to represent different voting rights or dividend privileges. Such shares are usually identified as *class A* and *class B* stock, as opposed to common and preferred. In this case, only one of these classes represents the basic ownership interest in the corporation. The particular features of both common and preferred shares and the rights they confer on their owners are indicated in the corporation's articles of incorporation. Although these may vary somewhat, certain typical features of this ownership can be stated.

Rights of Common Shareholders:

1. They have the right to vote on matters requiring owner approval. This right includes the election of the board of directors, who appoint the officers of the corporation, declare dividends, etc.

2. They are entitled to dividends only after preferred shareholder claims have been satisfied. Common shareholders, however, have the potential for receiving substantial dividends if the corporation is successful.

3. They receive the balance of assets, if any, after all other claims have been satisfied. Usually, no such balance exists if the corporation becomes bankrupt.

Rights of Preferred Shareholders:

1. They do not normally have the right to vote for the board of directors, and, therefore, do not have a voice in the control of the corporation. (One exception sometimes occurs when there is a default on dividends by the corporation, in which case they may have the right to vote for directors.)

2. They are entitled to the receipt of dividends before any payments are made to common shareholders. Preferred shareholders, therefore, have more assurance of receiving dividends, although there is usually a limit on the amount of these dividends.

3. In the event of the corporation's dissolution, preferred shareholders usually have a preferred claim on the assets of the corporation. This claim on assets cannot, however, exceed the stated value of the shares issued.

Status of Shares

Authorized shares
The designated number of shares of share capital that a corporation may issue.

At the time of incorporation under the Canada Business Corporations Act (CBCA) and in some provincial jurisdictions, a company indicates in its articles of incorporation the permitted issue of either an unlimited number of shares or a designated number of shares. If a designated number of shares, usually referred to as **authorized shares**, is indicated in the articles of incorporation, then the amount of authorized shares can be shown in the accounts and in the shareholders' equity section of the balance sheet as follows:

Recording in the Accounts:

GENERAL JOURNAL

19X1
Apr. 1   Memorandum
         Authorized under the CBCA to issue 10 000 common
         shares of no-par-value.

GENERAL LEDGER
Common Stock   *No. 320*

19X1
Apr. 1 Authorized to issue 10 000 common shares, no par-value.

Balance Sheet Presentation:

Shareholders' Equity

Common Stock, No Par-Value
   Authorized — 10 000 Common Shares

The number of authorized shares may be changed by amending the articles of incorporation.

Some provinces limit the number of authorized shares a corporation can issue. In the examples used in this text and in the problem assignments, it is assumed that the charters of all the corporations limit the number of shares that can be issued, unless otherwise indicated.

The shares of a corporation can have a different status at different points in time. They can be either **unissued** or **issued**, issued and **outstanding**, or issued and in the treasury. The meaning of these terms is summarized in Figure 9-3.

Unissued shares
The shares of share capital that a corporation is authorized to issue but has not yet issued.

Issued shares
The cumulative total number of authorized shares that has been issued in the name of shareholders; issued stock may or may not actually be in the hands of shareholders.

Outstanding shares
Authorized shares that have been issued and are actually in the hands of shareholders.

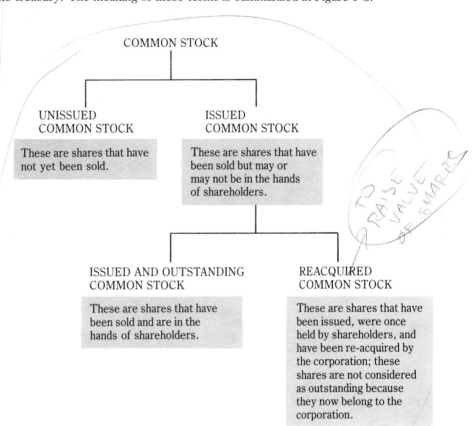

Figure 9-3   Status of common stock

Students are sometimes confused by these different classifications. Take sufficient time to understand the distinctions before continuing with this chapter.

Real Life Example 9-1

Why Common Shares Are Special

There is nothing ordinary about the common share.

In fact, a common share is quite special. Without it, for example, there would be no need for stock markets.

Simply put, a common share entitles its holder to a share of the ownership of the company that issued it.

If a company issues 1,000 common shares and you buy 100, you own 10 per cent of that company.

A company sells its shares — or goes public, in the jargon of the investment industry — because it needs money.

In return for investment, it gives an ownership stake in the company to the shareholders who, in theory, are entitled to share in its profits and to vote on major decisions about how the firm should be managed.

The stock market exists so that shareholders can trade their shares in an orderly, efficient manner.

Whether you buy your shares directly from the company or on the secondary market of the stock exchange, you get the same thing — a piece of paper that represents your share of the ownership of the company.

Most people buy shares because they want to share in the profits of the company, which are paid out in the form of dividends.

Dividends are the portion of the company's profit that management decides to pass on to the company's owners.

Since most companies don't make more than, say, a 10-percent return on their capital — or shareholders' investment — investors can generally expect something considerably less than that percentage in dividends.

The company's management will decide how much of its profits it wants to retain to keep the business growing and how much it wants to pay out to its shareholders to reward them for the use of their money.

Generally — and you probably won't be too surprised at this — management prefers to hang on to as much of the profits as possible. But management is under pressure on various fronts to keep the dividends coming.

First of all, there's the threat that shareholders could change management if they aren't satisfied.

Second, most companies regularly issue new common shares and if they want to attract new shareholders they must have a competitive dividend-payment record.

And, finally, a company that hoards its profits and therefore depresses its share prices becomes vulnerable to takeovers.

Corporate raiders of the last decade have made staggering fortunes by taking over companies that have not paid out enough to shareholders.

There is a second and perhaps even better known way that shareholders make money on their investments — by having the shares appreciate in value.

If, for example, you buy a share for $10 and a few months later it's selling on the stock market for $12, you've made a quick 20-percent return on your investment. That's far better than the four or five per cent you might collect annually in dividends.

Although common shares generally come with fewer conditions than preferred shares, there are certain features that prospective investors will want to keep in mind.

Because a common share symbolizes ownership of a company, it seems reasonable to expect the principle of one-share-one-vote.

But in recent years, partly because of the threat of hostile takeovers, many companies have issued what are called subordinate voting or non-voting common shares which limit investors' say in company activities.

These shares are usually similar to the company's other common shares in every way except that they do not carry a vote. Because of that, they generally trade for slightly less than the basic common share.

One other feature that some common shares carry is the ability to pay dividends in stock rather than in cash. For example, instead of paying $1 a share in dividends, a company might offer a stock dividend at a rate of one new share for every 25 shares already held.

This is a particularly attractive feature for some investors because they can gradually increase their stock holdings without having to pay brokerage commissions.

There's one last point to keep in mind.

Although common shares are not the most complex of investments, it is wise to remember that not all common shares are created equal. Check the terms of any common share before you buy. For instance, does it entitle you to a vote and under what conditions does it pay dividends?

Source "Why Common Shares Are Special", *The* (Montreal) *Gazette*, July 6, 1987, p. C-9. Reprinted by permission of The Canadian Press.

B. Share Capital Transactions

Share capital refers to all of a corporation's preferred and common stock. (Share capital is also called *capital stock*.) The recording of share capital transactions is influenced by the legislation of the jurisdiction under which the company is incorporated. The provisions of the Canada Business Corporations Act (CBCA) are used to illustrate the recording of stock transactions and to explain the various applications of the provisions.

Incorporation under the CBCA

**Stated value
(stated capital)**
The amount received from the sale of shares; a term used in the CBCA to refer to the amount of capital that cannot be paid to shareholders as a dividend.

The term **stated value** is used in the CBCA to indicate a restriction on the return of share capital to shareholders; it consists of the amount recorded as share capital in the books of the corporation, as shown in Figure 9-4. Shareholders' investment in a corporation is often seen as a margin of safety for creditors, because the limited liability feature of corporations restricts claims against the corporation to corporate assets.

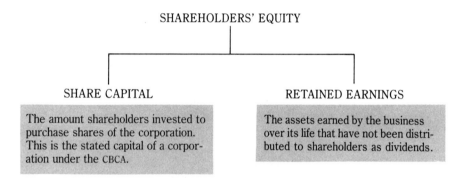

Figure 9-4   Sub-classes of shareholders' equity

A legal limit on shareholder withdrawals of share capital assures creditors that corporate losses, should they occur, will be absorbed from the capital contributed by shareholders up to the amount of the corporation's stated capital; any remaining loss will be absorbed by creditors.

Recording Share Transactions

As explained, some jurisdictions only permit the issue of no par-value shares. The accounting for no par-value stock is discussed next.

Assume that the following three transactions took place at the New Canada Corporation, which has an authorized capital consisting of an unlimited number of no par-value common shares.

Transaction 1
New Canada sells 1000 shares for $10,000 cash. The journal entry to record this transaction reads:

Cash	10,000	
Common Stock		10,000

Transaction 2

A further 2500 shares are issued for land and buildings that have a fair market value of $35,000 and $50,000, respectively. The journal entry to record this transaction reads:

Land	35,000	
Buildings	50,000	
Common Stock		85,000

Transaction 3

Next, 500 shares are issued to the organizers of the corporation in payment for their services, valued at $5,000. (These are organization costs, discussed in Chapter 8.) The journal entry to record this transaction reads:

Organization Costs	5,000	
Common Stock		5,000

The shareholders' equity section of the New Canada Corporation balance sheet shows the following items after these three transactions:

Shareholders' Equity

Common Stock, No Par-Value
    Authorized — An Unlimited Number of Shares
    Issued and Outstanding — 4000 Common Shares $100,000

The amount of stated capital in this example is $100,000; this amount is not available for the payment of dividends.

Transaction 4

Reacquired shares Issued and outstanding shares that have been repurchased by the corporation; also referred to as *treasury shares*.

The CBCA permits a corporation to reacquire some of its shares, provided that the purchase does not cause insolvency. The Act requires the **reacquired shares** to be restored to the status of authorized but unissued stock and also requires the appropriate stated capital account to be reduced by the payment.

    Assume that 1000 shares are repurchased. The use of an average per-share amount is recommended in the *CICA Handbook* (section 3240.18) in accounting for reacquired shares. The calculation for the reacquisition of New Canada's shares is made from the balances immediately preceding the reacquisition.

$$\frac{\text{Stated Capital Balance}}{\text{Number of Shares Issued}} = \frac{\$100,000}{4000} = \$25 \text{ average per share.}$$

The weighted average cost of 1000 shares, therefore, is $25,000 (1000 shares × $25 average per share).

    As can be seen, this weighted average amount is identical to the amount paid by the corporation. In actual practice, the payment is either in excess of or below the weighted average.

    The journal entry for the 1000 shares, which are repurchased for $25,000, reads

Common Stock	25,000	
Cash		25,000

The reacquired shares are restored to the status of authorized but unissued stock.

The shareholders' equity section of the balance sheet now appears as follows:

Shareholders' Equity
Common Stock, No Par-Value
    Authorized — An Unlimited Number of Shares
    Issued and Outstanding — 3000 Common Shares $75,000

As permitted by the CBCA, the reacquired 1000 shares are removed from the issued shares, and the stated capital amount, common stock, is reduced by $25,000.

Transaction 5
At a later date, 10 000 shares are issued for $150,000. The journal entry reads

    Cash   150,000
            Common Stock   150,000

The shareholders' equity section of the balance sheet for the New Canada Corporation now shows the following entries:

Shareholders' Equity
Common Stock, No Par-Value
    Authorized — An Unlimited Number of Shares
    Issued and Outstanding — 13 000 Common Shares $225,000

The amount of stated capital amounts to $225,000 following transaction 5; this amount is not available for the payment of dividends.

Reacquired Shares

Companies incorporated in some provinces and under the CBCA are permitted to reacquire some of their own shares. However, unlike the requirements of the CBCA, provincial requirements legislate that these reacquired shares can be either cancelled or reissued. If all the reacquired shares are not cancelled and have not been reissued, they are called **treasury stock**. The cost of treasury stock is deducted from the total shareholders' equity on the balance sheet. They are *never* shown as an asset on the balance sheet.

Treasury stock
Reacquired shares that have not been cancelled or reissued.

Stock Splits

The corporation may find its shares selling at a high price on the stock market, thereby putting them beyond the reach of many investors. To solve this problem, management may opt for a **stock split** to increase the marketability of a corporation's shares; the corporation issues, for example, three new shares to replace each old share. The old outstanding share certificates are *called in* and three new certificates are issued as replacements for each old share. The number of outstanding shares has now been tripled and the market price of each share tends to decrease to one-third of its former market price. This increase in shares and the change in market price is illustrated on the following page, using the data of the New Canada Corporation.

Stock split
An action taken by a corporation to increase the number of shares outstanding; involves the exchange of originally issued shares for a larger number of new shares: a stock split reduces the per-share market value of the stock.

	Number of Shares Outstanding	Total Common Stock on Balance Sheet	Market Price per Share (Assumed)
Before Stock Split	13 000	$225,000	$75
After Stock Split (3 for 1)	39 000	225,000	25

This information appears in the financial statements of the corporation.	This information is available from the Toronto Stock Exchange.

As can be seen, the number of outstanding shares triples and the market price of each share decreases proportionately. The shareholders' equity section of the New Canada Corporation would be shown on the balance sheet as follows:

Before Split:
Shareholders' Equity
Common Stock, No Par-Value
  Authorized — An Unlimited Number
    of Shares
  Issued and Outstanding —
  13 000 Shares $225,000

After Split:
Shareholders' Equity
Common Stock, No Par-Value
  Authorized — An Unlimited Number
    of Shares
  Issued and Outstanding —
  39 000 Shares $225,000

Notice that the amount of shareholders' equity has not changed. The only change is the increase in issued and outstanding shares from 13 000 to 39 000. Since there is no change in the $225,000 of shareholders' equity, no debit-credit entry is required to record the stock split. A memorandum should be recorded, however, indicating the new number of shares outstanding.

Common Stock   Acct. No. 320

Date 19X1	Description	F	Debit	Credit	DR. or CR.	Balance
	Memorandum					
	The outstanding shares were					
	increased from 13 000 to 39 000					
	by a 3-for-1 stock split.					

Remember that the purpose of a stock split is to increase the marketability of a share and, thereby, to permit more investors to own shares of the corporation. The advantage to the corporation is the potentially wider ownership base.

Sometimes, management decides to effect a **reverse stock split**; in this case, the old shares are called in and fewer new shares are issued. This action may be taken when management considers that the market price of the stock is too low. A contraction of the number of shares outstanding increases the market price.

Reverse stock split An action taken by a corporation to decrease the number of shares outstanding; involves the exchange of originally issued shares for a smaller number of new shares; a reverse stock split increases the per-share market value of the stock.

Stock Subscriptions

The discussion of share capital transactions assumed that full payment was received and that shares were issued at once. However, these exchanges happen only in the case of small or closely held corporations. In actual practice, shares can be sold through a **stock subscription**, with payment being made later. The subscriber signs an agreement to buy a certain number of shares and to make certain specified payments.

Share certificates are issued only when full payment for the subscribed share is made. The shares are considered to be issued and outstanding only when the shares are in the name of the subscriber. In fact, legally, the subscriber is not considered to be a shareholder.

No entry is made in the books of the corporation at the time an agreement is made with the subscriber; the first entry occurs when cash is received from the subscriber. A debit is made to Cash and a credit is made to a liability account; the use of a liability account indicates that no shares are issued to the subscriber as payments for shares are received by the corporation. Assume that New Carlisle Corporation, a corporation incorporated under the CBCA, accepts subscriptions for 1000 common shares at a total subscription price of $1,500 to be paid in two instalments of $750 each. At this point, a memorandum entry similar to the following can be prepared.

Stock subscription An agreement to purchase share capital from a corporation with payment to be made at a later date; subscribed stock becomes issued but is not outstanding until fully paid for and given to shareholders.

Common Stock — Acct. No. 320

Date 19X1	Description	F	Debit	Credit	DR. or CR.	Balance
	Memorandum					
	Accepted subscriptions for					
	1000 common shares at a total					
	subscription price of $1,500.					

The acceptance of the subscription is not recorded in the accounts and no amount should appear in the shareholders' equity section of the balance sheet, since the subscriber is not considered to be a shareholder.

When the first instalment of $750 is received, it is recorded as follows:

Cash 750
  Payments for Stock Subscriptions 750
Received first instalment on common shares subscribed.

A liability account is credited, because the $750 is not considered to be payment for shares.

The journal entry to record collection of the second instalment is

Cash 750
  Payments for Stock Subscriptions 750
Received second instalment on common shares subscribed.

The shares have now been paid for in full, and the common shares can be issued to the subscriber. The following journal entry records the issue of the shares:

Payments for Stock Subscriptions	1,500	
Common Stock		1,500

The subscriber has now acquired the full status of a shareholder, and only after he/she actually receives the shares are the shares referred to as issued and outstanding.

A balance sheet prepared at this time shows the increase in issued and outstanding shares from 10 000 shares to 11 000 shares.

New Carlisle Corporation
Partial Balance Sheet
At December 31, 19X1
Shareholders' Equity

SHARE CAPITAL:	
Preferred Stock, No Par-Value	
Authorized, Issued and Outstanding — 500 Shares	$ 500
Common Stock, No Par-Value	
Authorized — 15 000 Shares	
Issued and Outstanding — 11 000 Shares	6,500
	$7,000

C. Other Components of Shareholders' Equity

The emphasis in corporate accounting is on the distinctions among various sources of shareholders' equity. The accounting for share capital was illustrated in the earlier sections of this chapter. Discussed below are two additional categories classified separately in shareholders' equity: donated capital and appraisal increase.

Donated Capital

The earlier discussion of share capital described the contribution of capital to a corporation by shareholders through the purchase of shares. Shareholders can also donate assets to the corporation. These donations are viewed as additional contributions of capital. Land donated to the corporation by a shareholder would be recorded as follows:

Land	50,000	
Donated Capital — Land		50,000

Donated capital
A contribution of capital to a corporation by parties other than shareholders.

This **donated capital** is classified as a part of contributed surplus in shareholders' equity on the balance sheet. Other assets given to a corporation by shareholder donation are recorded in the accounts and classified in a similar manner.

Capital can also be contributed to a corporation by parties other than shareholders. For example, land or cash is sometimes given by a municipality or province to a corporation as an inducement to locate a plant within its boundaries. The asset received belongs to the corporation once contractual agreements have been fulfilled. Under

GAAP, such assets are not considered as contributions of capital to the corporation. Rather, they are viewed as income items; the accounting for these contributions is beyond the scope of this text and is covered in depth in more advanced accounting courses.

Appraisal Increase

Appraisal increase
The increase that results when corporate assets are revalued upward.

An **appraisal increase** occurs when corporate assets — usually land and buildings — are revalued upward to reflect current market values. The usefulness of historical cost is limited when there is a continuing increase in price levels. A wide disparity develops between original cost and market (or replacement) values.

The recording of an appraisal increase, however, violates generally accepted accounting principles, which require that assets be recorded at cost; they also require that only revenues realized by a market transaction be shown in the financial statements. Although recording an appraisal is permitted when a corporate reorganization occurs, these appraisal increases are rarely recorded in other circumstances, since any appraisal increase would be taxed. The journal entry to record the appraised difference between cost and market increases assets by a debit and credits the Appraisal Increase account.

Assume that a corporation's land, which had been recorded at $100,000 cost in the accounts, was appraised at $250,000. The increase in value to $250,000 would be recorded as follows:

Land — Appreciation in Value	150,000	
Appraisal Increase		150,000

Following this entry, the Land account continues to show its original cost of $100,000, and the new account, Land — Appreciation in Value, shows the $150,000 increase.

The official CICA position is that long-term asset values should not be revalued upward in normal circumstances. However, where an appraisal has been recorded,

1. Future depreciation charges should be based on the appraised amount.
2. The appraisal increase credit must be left indefinitely in the financial statements and must be transferred to Retained Earnings in amounts not exceeding the increase in depreciation charges or the realization of the increase through a sale of the asset.

The appraisal increase results in a larger shareholders' equity amount, and this increase comes neither from capital contributions of shareholders nor from corporate earnings. Therefore, the appraisal amount of $100,000 should be classified in the financial statements separately from contributed surplus or retained earnings. Usually it is shown as the last item in the shareholders' equity section.

D. Book Value

Book value
The amount of net assets represented by one share of stock. When referring to common stock, book value represents the amount not claimed by creditors and preferred shareholders; when referring to preferred stock, book value represents the amount that preferred shareholders would receive if the corporation were liquidated.

The **book value** of a share is the amount determined by dividing shareholders' equity by the number of shares outstanding:

$$\frac{\text{Shareholders' Equity}}{\text{Number of Shares Outstanding}} = \text{Book Value.}$$

This calculation is easy when only one class of shares exists in the corporation. Some complications occur, however, when two or more classes of shares are outstanding. If both preferred and common shares are outstanding, the shareholders' equity must be divided between both classes of shares. Preferred shares are allocated the amount that they would receive if the corporation were liquidated. The common shares receive the balance, if any remains.

Liquidation Value of Preferred Shares

Cumulative dividend
An undeclared dividend that accumulates and has to be paid in the future before any dividends can be paid on common shares.

The liquidation value of a preferred share is always printed on the share certificate. Some preferred shares are entitled to dividends that are in arrears. This involves a **cumulative dividend** feature that is attached to some preferred shares.

For the problems in Chapter 9, it is assumed that no cumulative dividend feature exists. Therefore, the liquidation value of the preferred shares is that indicated in the problem narrative.

Calculation of the Book Value of Shares

The calculation of the book value of preferred and common shares can be illustrated by using the following shareholders' equity data:

Shareholders' Equity

Preferred Stock, No Par-Value	
Authorized — 5000 Shares	
Issued and Outstanding — 1000 Shares	$ 10,000
Common Stock, No Par-Value	
Authorized — 200 000 Shares	
Issued and Outstanding — 60 000 Shares	20,000
Retained Earnings	105,000
Total Shareholders' Equity	$135,000

Note: There are $5,000-worth of dividends in arrears on the preferred shares. The liquidation value of preferred shares is $10,000.

Book value is calculated as follows:

Preferred Shares		*Common Shares*	
Dividends in Arrears	$ 5,000	Total Shareholders' Equity	$135,000
Liquidation Value	10,000	*Less:* Preferred Claims	15,000
Total	$15,000	Balance	$120 000
Shares Outstanding	1000	Shares Outstanding	60 000
Book Value per Share	$15	Book Value per Share	$ 2

A change in book value from one period of time to another may be significant in some circumstances, since it indicates a change in dollar equity per share. Comparison of book value with market value gives an insight into investors' evaluations of the corporation.

Some shares regularly sell for less than their book value on the Toronto Stock Exchange. This does not necessarily mean they are a bargain investment. The market price of a share is related to such factors as the company's earnings, dividend record, future potential to generate earnings, and so on. A higher book value than market price of a share may be interpreted as investor judgement that a corporation's shares are a poor investment.

APPENDIX: Accounting for Partnerships and Proprietorships

Partnership
An unincorporated form of business organization in which the entity is owned by two or more persons.

A **partnership** combines the abilities and capital of any number of individuals who together own and operate a business. Although a partnership is a business entity, it is not a legal entity as is a corporation; that is, a partnership has a limited life. Partnerships also have a number of unique characteristics; therefore, accounting for partners' equity differs from accounting for shareholders' equity. Whereas other chapters in this part focus on accounting for equity in the corporate form of business organization, this appendix discusses the accounting treatment of partnership equity.

Characteristics that influence equity accounting for a partnership include limited life, unlimited liability, mutual agency, co-ownership of assets, and sharing of profits and losses.

Advantages of a Partnership

A partnership has several advantages over other forms of business organizations. It can be easily formed through provincial registration, without the legal process and costs involved in incorporation. A partnership is less subject to government supervision; there are fewer government regulations and less paper work regarding partnerships than corporations. Because a partnership is not a legal entity, it is not subject to corporate income tax; individual partners file personal income tax returns, which include their allocation of partnership profits. Since a partnership includes at least two, and often more, individuals, it has access to more capital and expertise than does a proprietorship.

Disadvantages of a Partnership

A partner has to answer to other partners for his/her actions and has mutual agency and unlimited liability. Therefore, individual partners are legally liable for the financial debt arising from actions of other partners. (Recall that corporations are legally liable for their own actions and have limited liability.) A partnership is dissolved on the death or withdrawal of a partner, although the business may continue with new partners. This arrangement is more cumbersome than the selling of shares in a corporation. Also, a corporation usually has access to a larger amount of capital, since it appeals to more investors, particularly those who want to make a good investment but do not want to get involved with running the business. In addition, corporate tax rates can be more favourable than personal tax rates; moreover, dividends received by a corporate shareholder are taxed more favourably than the earnings of business income.

Capital and Drawings Accounts

Capital account
A permanent account used to record the capital, investment and withdrawals of each partner and his/her allocation of the profits and losses of the partnership; the Drawings account of each partner is closed to his/her Capital account at the end of each fiscal year.

Business transactions for a partnership are recorded in the same manner as those for a corporation. The only significant accounting difference between a partnership or a proprietorship and corporation is in the treatment of owners' equity. A **Capital** account is used to record owner contributions to a partnership or a proprietorship. Partner or owner withdrawals, called drawings, reduce the Capital account(s). Individual Capital accounts and **Drawings accounts** are maintained for each partner. The Drawings account balance is closed to each partner's Capital account at the end of the accounting time period.

Partnership Accounting

Partner investments in a partnership are recorded into a Capital account. Each partner has an individual account that is credited with capital contributions to the partnership. The following entry records a $5,000 cash investment by partner **A**.

Cash	5,000	
A, Capital		5,000
To record investment by **A**.		

Drawings account
A temporary account used to record the withdrawal of cash or assets by a partner during the fiscal year; this account is closed to the partner's Capital account at the end of the fiscal year.

If non-cash assets are contributed, then the appropriate asset account is debited.

Partner withdrawals of assets from the partnership are recorded in each partner's Drawings account. If partner **A** withdraws $1,000 cash, for example, the following entry is recorded:

A, Drawings	1,000	
Cash		1,000
To record drawings by **A**.		

At year-end, each partner's Drawings account is closed to his/her Capital account. The following closing entry would close partner **A**'s Drawings account, assuming no further drawings have been made.

A, Capital	1,000		The Drawings account
A, Drawings		1,000	is closed directly to the
To close **A**'s Drawings account.			Capital account of each
			partner.

Proprietorship Accounting

Proprietorship
An unincorporated form of business organization, in which the entity is owned by one person.

A **proprietorship** business is owned by one individual who usually also manages the operation. The proprietorship is a business entity that is handled as a separate entity from its owner, although it is not a legal entity, as is a corporation. Proprietor investments in the business are recorded in a Capital account in the same way as in a partnership. Proprietor withdrawals from the business are also recorded as drawings; the Drawings account balance is closed to the Capital account at year-end.

Division of Partnership Profits and Losses

Partnership profits and losses are divided equally among partners if no profit and loss sharing ratio is indicated in the partnership agreement. Otherwise, the ratio specified in the agreement is used; this ratio can be fixed, such as 3 : 2 or ⅔ to ⅓, for example. Profits and losses may also be shared according to a formula specified in the agreement. This formula usually considers three factors: a return to each partner for the amount of his/her capital invested in the partnership, a payment to each partner for services rendered, and a further division of any remaining profit (or resulting loss) in the profit and loss sharing ratio. Although a partnership agreement may not include separate calculations for each of these factors, the ratio should be calculated after considering their impact on each partner's remuneration.

Division Using a Fixed Ratio

The division of profits and losses according to a fixed ratio is appropriate when each partner makes an equal contribution to the business. Ideally, each partner would have an equal amount of capital invested in the partnership and would devote an equal amount of time and effort in the business. However, usually the amount of capital differs, and time and effort devoted to the business is unequal. The initial calculation of a fixed ratio inclusion in the partnership agreement would consider the weight of these factors.

Assuming that **A** and **B** share profits in the ratio of 3 : 2, a $15,000 profit would be divided and recorded by the following entry.

Income Summary	15,000	
A, Capital (3/5 × 15,000)		9,000
B, Capital (2/5 × 15,000)		6,000
To record division of partnership profits.		

Division Using Capital Balances

An alternative method of allocating partnership profits and losses uses partners' Capital balances. This method is most suitable where large amounts are invested by partners and where profits are mainly attributable to these invested amounts. Use of this method must be specified in the partnership agreement; otherwise, profits and losses are divided equally among partners.

Assuming that use of Capital balances are indicated in the **A** and **B** partnership agreement and that these balances amount to $10,000 for each partner, the $15,000 profit would be divided equally in this case (by coincidence). It is recorded as follows:

Income Summary	15,000	
A, Capital		7,500
B, Capital		7,500
To record division of partnership profits.		

Note that the partnership agreement should indicate whether the opening, ending, or average Capital balances are to be used in dividing profits and losses. Each balance would result in a different amount calculated unless the capital invested in the partnership by each partner did not change during the year. The use of opening or ending Capital balances, however, may not be an equitable method in many circumstances.

Salaries to partners
A mechanism used for dividing a portion of the income of the partnership among partners. Such a division recognizes the value of services rendered by each partner; this is not the same as a salary expense.

Interest on partners' Capital balances
A mechanism used for dividing a portion of the income of the partnership among partners having different capital investments.

Division Using Salary and Interest Allocations

Since the time and effort devoted by individual partners to the business is often unequal and the amount of Capital balance varies among partners, another allocation method can be chosen. Profits and losses can be divided using an allocation through **salaries to partners** and **interest on partners' Capital balances** in accordance with individual contributions. Any remaining profits and losses can be divided through the profit and loss sharing ratio. The salary and interest allocations are not deducted as expenses on the income statement; *salary* and *interest* used here refer only to individual factors used in dividing profits and losses among partners.

Before beginning their partnership, **A** and **B** recognize that **A** deserved more salary compensation because of his technical skills and the fact that he had been earning more than **B**. Accordingly, the following salary allocations were specified in their partnership agreement: $7,000 to **A** and $5,000 to **B**. The agreement also indicated that 12 percent interest should be allocated to their Capital balances and that any remaining profit and loss should be shared in the ratio of 3 : 2.

The following calculation shows how a $15,000 profit is divided according to these provisions of the **A** and **B** partnership agreement. Remember that these salary and interest amounts have not been paid to partners; rather they are a calculation for allocating partnership net income to partners.

	A	**B**	*Total*
Amount of Profit To Be Allocated to Partners			$15,000
Interest Allocation:			
A: $10,000 × 12%	$1,200		
B: $10,000 × 12%		$1,200	2,400
Balance			$12,600
Salary Allocation	7,000	5,000	12,000
Balance			$ 600
Balance Allocated in Profit and Loss Sharing Ratio:			
A: $600 × 3/5	360		
B: $600 × 2/5		240	600
Balance			-0-
Allocated to Partners	$8,560	$6,440	

The following entry records this profit allocation between **A** and **B**:

Income Summary	15,000	
A, Capital		8,560
B, Capital		6,440

These calculations illustrate the allocation of partnership net income using a combination of interest and salary elements, with any remaining balance being allocated to partners according to their profit and loss sharing ratio. Alternatively, the partnership agreement may only provide for allocation of salary, with the remaining balance being allocated according to the profit and loss sharing ratio. In actual practice, the agreement may also provide periodic drawings to individual partners equal to their salary allocation; the Drawings account is closed to each partner's capital account at year-end.

Partnership Financial Statements

Partnership and proprietorship financial statements are similar. The income statement of a partnership might include this allocation of income to individual partners:

A and B
Income Statement
For the Year Ended December 31, 19X4

Sales	$150,000
Cost of Sales	

Net Income for the Year	$ 15,000

Net Income Allocation:

A	$8,560	
B	6,440	$ 15,000

Statement of partners' capital
A statement required in partnership accounting, summarizing the changes that occurred in partners' capital during the period.

A **statement of partners' capital** replaces the statement of retained earnings. It shows partner contributions to the business, changes in capital resulting from net income (or loss) allocations, and drawings representing withdrawals during the period. The partners' capital statement for **A** and **B** would appear as follows:

A and B
Statement of Partners' Capital
For the Year Ended December 31, 19X3

	A	B	Total
Capital Balance (Jan. 1)	$ 5,000	$ 5,000	$10,000
Add: Investments during 19X3	5,000	5,000	10,000
Net Income for the Year	8,560	6,440	15,000
	$18,560	$16,440	$35,000
Less: Drawings	7,000	5,000	12,000
Capital Balance (Dec. 31)	$11,560	$11,440	$23,000

It is assumed in this statement of partners' capital that each partner made additional $5,000 investments during the year and that net income is divided using salary and interest allocations.

The balance sheet of a partnership shows the Capital balance of each partner if there are only a few partners. Otherwise, only a total Capital amount is indicated, with details appearing in the statement of partners' capital. Note that no distinction is made between owner capital contributions and net income earned and retained in the business, as occurs in corporate financial statements. The owners' equity of **A** and **B** may appear as follows on the balance sheet:

Partners' Equity

A, Capital	$11,560
B, Capital	11,440
Total Equity	$23,000

A S S I G N M E N T   M A T E R I A L S

Discussion Questions

1. What are some advantages and disadvantages of the corporate form of organization?
2. What is meant by the limited liability feature of corporations? How does it influence creditors?
3. In what way is there double taxation for a corporation? Are there tax advantages with a corporate form of organization?
4. What rights are attached to common shares? Where are these rights indicated?
5. What are the typical features of incorporation?
6. What is a board of directors and whom does it represent? Are the directors involved in the daily management of the entity?
7. Corporate accounting involves the use of specialized terminology. Explain:
   a. The different terms relating to the amount, if any, printed on a share certificate
   b. The different classes of shares
   c. The different terms relating to the current status of a corporation's shares.
8. The word *value* has a specific meaning for accountants. What exactly does it mean? Give examples of different uses.
9. Distinguish between par-value stock and no par-value stock. What does the CBCA require?
10. In what way is stock "preferred"? In which way is it similar to common stock? Different from common stock?
11. Distinguish among authorized, unissued, issued, and outstanding shares.
12. Describe the accounting treatment of reacquired shares as required in the CBCA. Can these shares be resold? Explain.
13. Why do corporations sometimes opt for a stock split? What is a reverse stock split?

14. Assume a 2-for-1 stock split occurs. Explain
    a. The effect on each share split
    b. The effect on the total amount of issued and outstanding shares.
15. Define *donated capital*. How does it differ from share capital? Where is donated capital classified in the balance sheet?
16. What is the justification for the creation of an appraisal increase? Is it in accordance with generally accepted accounting principles? Why or why not?
17. Identify the major components of the shareholders' equity section of a balance sheet. Why are these components distinguished?
18. What does the book value of shares represent? How is it calculated?
19. A corporate entity has both preferred and common classes of shares. How is the book value of common shares calculated in this case? What is meant by the liquidating value of preferred shares?
20. Does the book value change from year to year? Of what value is its calculation to the reader of financial statements?
21. The market price of a share is less than its book value; is it a bargain? Why or why not?
22. How does accounting for a partnership differ from that for a corporation?
23. How are partnership profits and losses divided among partners?
24. Why are salary and interest allocations included in the division of profits and losses?
25. How are partners' Capital balances disclosed in the balance sheet?

Discussion Cases

Discussion Case 9-1:   Alcan Aluminum Ltd.

Alcan Aluminium Ltd. spent $256-million in 1988 to buy back its own shares, the company said yesterday.

The Montreal-based aluminum producer bought 6.9 million common shares during 1988, about 2.3 million of them between Oct. 27 and Dec. 31, 1988. The company bought the stock under normal course issuer bids, the first having come into effect Oct. 27, 1987. The second bid kicked in the same day and expires next Oct. 27.

The average purchase price for the last two months of 1988 was $34.48 a share, but the year's average was not available. The stock is trading at $41.

Alcan's move received high marks from analysts who said the stock buyback increased shareholder values. "It's the biggest equity financing Alcan has ever done," said Terence Ortslan, metals analyst for Deacon Morgan McEwen Easson Ltd.

Not only will Alcan save about $10-million on dividend payments, but the buyback sends a signal to corporate raiders that management will support the stock price, making a takeover of the widely held company an expensive proposition.

Source   Harvey Enchin, "Alcan Pays $256 Million for Stock Buy-back", *The Globe and Mail*, Toronto, January 12, 1989, p. B-3.

For Discussion

1. Under the CBCA, what procedure does a corporation follow when reacquiring its own shares?
2. Assuming that the repurchase price was $34 per share, calculate the amount Alcan "saved" by reacquiring its shares.
3. Alcan will save about $10 million in dividends a year. If it had to borrow the $256 million to buy back its shares, how much interest would it have to pay? Would this repurchase make sense?

Discussion Case 9-2:   Stock Options

Before consultant Barrie Sprawson invests in a company, he checks to see if its own senior managers have done so.

"If I am going to take a risk, I like to see them take one too," says the managing principal of Sibson & Co., compensation specialists.

Hey wait a minute, retorts the new president of a troubled company. He came to his job to offer his management expertise. He isn't sure he will be able to save the company. Why should he invest his own money as well as his talent?

Those are two sides of an argument that seems to have been going on since Adam Smith. In 1766 he wrote in The Wealth of Nations about directors who were managing other people's money: " . . . it cannot well be expected that they should watch over it with the same anxious vigilance with which the partners in a private co-partnery frequently watch over their own."

Basically it comes down to whether firms perform differently when management has a substantial equity stake.

Today the issue comes up when men like J. Howard Macdonald are brought in to run troubled Dome Petroleum Ltd. without owning a single share. Or when it is noticed that Varity Corp. chairman Victor Rice only owns outright 703 shares of his company, although according to the circular for the 1988 annual meeting he has 800,000 options. Options, of course, do not put their holders at risk because nothing says they have to be exercised.

Opinions remain divided on the share-ownership issue. Ken Hugessen, a compensation specialist with William M. Mercer Ltd., takes vigorous exception to senior executives who don't. If they have low ownership in a company, they can get off track in their priorities and do things that won't add shareholder value, he says.

"They don't have quite the burning desire every day to add value to the company. If you own a lot of shares, there is this constant testing of priorities and of how you are spending your time."

A vivid example of this philosophy is Hees International Bancorp Inc., the Toronto merchant bank at the heart of Edward and Peter Bronfman's empire. The managing partners are reportedly paid salaries averaging only about $60,000 a year and make most of their money by owning shares.

Arthur Earle, a retired businessman and academic with wide board experience himself, represents the other side of the argument. He does not think officer-directors, or any directors for that matter, should have to have shares in a company. And he says most boards with which he is familiar do not require it.

"Directors in a Canadian company are there by law to manage the company. You (an investor) should buy or not buy shares according to your judgment at how competent they are at doing that," says Dr. Earle, the former deputy chairman and managing director of the British appliance company Hoover Ltd., a subsidiary of Hoover Co. of North Canton, Ohio.

"I quite understand the view of people (like Mr. Sprawson and Mr. Hugessen)," he says. "Ideally it is good to have senior managers and directors in that position. But there are many negatives to it and on balance they are stronger."

It is not always easy for a director to dispose of shares

when he wants to, he says, and people often draw erroneous conclusions when he does. "Many, for precisely that reason, prefer not to be shareholders."

(The Ontario Securities Act considers company directors insiders and says they must not buy or sell securities of a company when they know of "a material fact or material change" regarding the company that has not generally been disclosed.)

In a 1985 survey of executive pay and performance done by Sibson in the United States, 41 per cent of directors responding said they thought stock ownership by top executives is a personal investment decision and that the company should set no goals for the amount executives should own.

Although considerable amounts of academic and other research have been done *around* this field, little seems to have looked specifically at how stock ownership affects the behavior of company officers.

It would make sense for executives to behave differently when they own a substantial stake, says University of Saskatchewan professor Richard Long, who has done research on employee share ownership. "In general people work best for themselves." But he says he is not sure there is enough evidence to prove anything about low share ownership.

Michael Jensen, now of Harvard University and William Meckling, the former dean of management at the University of Rochester, wrote a 1976 article considered seminal in the field: as a manager's share of equity decreases, so does the cost to him of decisions which are not optimal to other shareholders, they say.

On the other hand, several researchers argue, a manager has all of his "human capital" tied up in the company he works for and his talents will be worth less on the outside market if he is not seen to be doing a good job.

If you have your money invested in the same company you work for, that's a lot of eggs in one basket, says Ross Archibald, a professor at the University of Western Ontario School of Business Administration.

As well, there is the problem that behavior of the company's stock may have very little to do with how well it is managed. "In a boom time even the turkeys go up," Dr. Archibald notes.

But the bulk of the academic literature on this subject consists of mathematical model-building; it is a very difficult thing to test in real life situations because there are so many variables.

The Toronto Stock Exchange did a 1987 study of employee share ownership in Canadian corporations and concluded that companies with share purchase plans "dramatically outperform" their TSE-listed competitors that do not have such plans. Measures tested included profitability, productivity and debt-equity levels.

The good performance was particularly marked when more than 20 per cent of staff held shares, says author Nancy Nightingale, now a vice-president of Central Capital Management Inc. But the study did not look specifically at share ownership by company officers.

Just how much share ownership is necessary to put managers at risk in the way Mr. Sprawson likes to see? "I wouldn't want to see management walk away without feeling penalized," he says, and suggests a figure at least equal to annual salary. Mr. Hugessen says his rule of thumb would be shares worth five to 10 times base salary.

Source   Margot Gibb-Clark, "Managers' Stake in Firm Can Be a Valuable Asset", *The Globe and Mail*, Toronto, August 13, 1988, p. B-1, B-4.

For Discussion

1. Is holding stock options adequate to motivate company officers to make decisions that benefit shareholders?
2. If the entity fails, does that mean management and the officers didn't try hard to save it?
3. What kind of motivation — burning desire — do the managing partners of Hees International Bancorp Inc. have that adds value to the company?
4. What are the negatives about directors owning shares referred to by Arthur Earle? How does the Ontario Securities Act affect directors who own shares in the company?
5. "In general people work best for themselves." What percentage of ownership in a corporation would make people feel they're working for themselves?
6. Do you think Adam Smith was correct in his observation quoted in this case?
7. If managers are focused on adding to shareholder value, particularly when they have large ownership in a company themselves, are they more or less likely to have difficulties reconciling profits and ethics?

Discussion Case 9-3:   CP Stock Split

Canadian Pacific Ltd. of Montreal, one of Canada's most widely held companies, is planning a three-for-one split of ordinary shares and preferred shares, its first split since 1971 and only its third since 1930.

The news is a "pleasant surprise" for the company's thousands of shareholders, one Toronto analyst said. At the end of 1984, CP LTD. had about 47 000 shareholders.

Shareholders will be asked at the annual meeting May 1 to approve the split on the 3-for-1 basis. Previous splits were 5 for 1 in 1971 and 4 for 1 in 1930.

The company also reported profit for the year ended December 31, 1984, rose to $5.21 a share from $1.98 a year earlier. The analyst said the 1984 figure was generally higher than expected and about 30 cents a share above his estimate. Total 1984 profit rose to $375 million from $143 million in 1983.

The shares, which have swung widely in the 14 years since the last split, have risen sharply this year from $50 at the end of 1984. The price was as low as $24.87 in 1982.

The shares have often been promoted by analysts as offering investors "a piece of Canada" because of the company's widespread interests. It is involved, directly and through subsidiaries, in rail, truck, telecommunications, airline, hotel and shipping enterprises. A subsidiary, Canadian Pacific Enterprises Ltd. of Calgary, has natural resource and manufacturing interests.

CP LTD. said it plans to redeem, "as soon as practicable," all 7.25 per cent cumulative redeemable series A preferred shares outstanding at $10 a share, plus accrued and unpaid dividends to the date of redemption.

The number of shareholders in CP LTD. is among the half-dozen highest in Canada, analysts said. Others include Bell Canada Enterprises Inc. of Montreal, with the largest number, Imperial Oil Ltd. of Toronto and British Columbia Resources Investment Corp. of Vancouver.

Source   George Linton, "Rare CP Ltd. stock split surprises shareholders", *The Gazette*, February 13, 1985, p. B-12.

For Discussion

1. Equity is unchanged by a stock split. Why would CP investors view this split as a "pleasant surprise"?
2. "The CP LTD. stock split is like taking a twenty-dollar bill to the bank and getting two tens in return." Comment on this statement.

Discussion Case 9-4:   A Reverse Stock Split

Askin Service Corp. and Motor Oil Refinery Holding Co. of Chicago have reached an agreement in principle for the combination of the two companies.

Askin, which has been reducing its retail operations and has announced a plan to enter the energy field, would issue 10 520 298 common shares and warrants to purchase another 450 000 in the transaction, which would result in a transfer of control to the Chicago firm.

Askin currently has 818 922 shares outstanding and warrants to buy 400 000 additional shares.

Askin said the companies are considering a possible reverse split to reduce the shares outstanding of the combined company. The transaction is subject to the approval of a definite contract by the boards of Askin and Motor Oil Refinery and the shareholders of Askin.

For Discussion

1. The company is reported to be considering a reverse stock split. What are the implications of this decision for the market price of shares, the number of shareholders and the shareholder base, and the number of shares outstanding?
2. A student friend, a major in hotel administration, is having difficulty understanding the idea of a stock split. Someone has suggested using, instead of shares, a banana to be split. How is it comparable and how is it not comparable?
3. Prepare a short example of a reverse stock split, using a banana split to get the idea across.

Discussion Case 9-5:   Conversion of Debt to Equity in Massey-Ferguson Ltd.

Massey had tried to raise $700 million to pay off some of its $2.6 billion in debts. Besides the government-guaranteed issue of $200 million in shares, Massey received $150 million from the Canadian Imperial Bank of Commerce, partly in fresh equity and partly through the conversion of debt to equity.

The company also asked its 250 lenders to forgive $350 million in interest on loans in exchange for equity in the company.

For Discussion

1. If creditors agreed to accept shares in the corporation in place of the interest owing, what would be the journal entry on the books of
   a. Massey-Ferguson Ltd.?   b. The creditors?
2. Is the interest and debt forgiven by the issue of shares, or do the shares pay the interest? Explain.

Discussion Case 9-6:   Book Value

I often see references to "book value" in relation to a company or stock. Since I have some accounting knowledge, I know that book value in most cases is fictitious and irrelevant. It gets even more unrealistic when acquisitions of various sorts are added at the original acquisition cost, with no allowance for the present value of a dollar. Is there any situation where this yardstick has a value?
R. G. Graham,
Armstrong, B.C.

According to generally accepted accounting principles, a company's assets are valued at their acquisition cost and not their current market price. This may be fictitious, but it's the traditional way of doing things. Explains Ira Katzin, director of research at Merit Investment Corp.: "If you valued everything at current prices, you would have massive fluctuations in values on company balance sheets."

In actual practice, there may be little relationship between a company's book value and market value. But book value is still a useful measurement, says John McKimm, an analyst with Prudential-Bache Securities Canada Ltd. Because it's not a true reflection of current assets, it gives investors an idea of the minimum value of a company. Most stocks sell well above book value, so if a stock is trading at book value, the price has more or less bottomed out.

Book value also helps to analyze companies in regulated industries such as pipelines, telephones, electricity and natural gas. Since regulators usually decide how much equity a company can have on its balance sheet and how much of a return on equity it can make, the issue for investors is how many times book value they want to pay. "The price you're willing to pay is a function of what you are allowed to earn," Mr. McKimm says.

Source   Ellen Roseman, "Portfolio: Does Book Value Help in Assessing Stocks?", *The Globe and Mail*, Toronto, February 7, 1989, p. B-18.

For Discussion

1. Do you agree with the way GAAP handle the valuation of assets? What are some of its advantages? its disadvantages?
2. Why do GAAP include unrealized gains in their definition of wealth?

Comprehension Problems

Comprehension Problem 9-1

Bindernagel Cosmos Corp. was incorporated under the CBCA on January 1, 19X1 to prepare horoscopes for business people.

Required: Prepare journal entries to record the following transactions:
1. Received a charter authorizing the issuance of an unlimited number of common shares
2. Issued for cash 10 000 shares at $1 each
3. Issued for cash 1000 shares at $3 each
4. Reacquired 500 shares for $500.

Comprehension Problem 9-2

A tract of land has been given to a corporation by a major shareholder.

Required:
1. Prepare the journal entry to record the transaction.
2. Where would the transaction be classified in the balance sheet?

Comprehension Problem 9-3

The following information is extracted from the shareholders' equity section of the balance sheet of George Inc. at December 31, 19X5:

Preferred Stock	
Issued and Outstanding — 5000 shares	$ 20,000
Common Stock, No Par-Value	
Issued and Outstanding — 20 000 shares	40,000
Retained Earnings	150,000
Total Shareholders' Equity	$210,000

Additional information:
a. There are $2,000-worth of dividends in arrears on the preferred stock.
b. The liquidation value of the preferred stock is $25,000.

Required: Calculate the book value of preferred and common shares.

Comprehension Problem 9-4

The shareholders' equity section of Rittberger Corporation's balance sheet at December 31, 19X3 is given below.

Shareholders' Equity

SHARE CAPITAL:	
Preferred Stock, No Par-Value	
Authorized — 100 shares	
Issued and Outstanding — 64 Shares	$3,456
Common Stock, No Par-Value	
Authorized — 2000 Shares	
Issued and Outstanding — 800 Shares	1,680
Total Share Capital	$5,136
Retained Earnings	600
Total Shareholders' Equity	$5,736

Required:
1. What is the average price received for each issued preferred share?
2. What is the average price received for each issued common share?
3. What is the total stated capital of the company?

Comprehension Problem 9-5

The ledger accounts of Chivers Corp. have the following amounts recorded during December:

Cash		Land		Building	
₁30,000	₂5,000	10,000	4,000	12,000	
₌15,000	8,000			8,000	
7,000	6,000				
4,000					
14,000					

Preferred Stock, No Par-Value		Common Stock, No Par-Value	
6,000	₃15,000	₂5,000	₁30,000
	14,000		22,000
			7,000

Required: Reconstruct the transactions that occurred during December and prepare the journal entries to record these transactions.

Comprehension Problem 9-6

The classification of assets, liabilities, and equities that appear on the balance sheet of Ostell Inc. follows:

Balance Sheet Accounts

Assets	*Liabilities and Equities*
a. Current Assets	d. Current Liabilitiese
b. Fixed Assets	e. Long-Term Liabilities
c. Intangibles	f. Preferred Stock
	g. Common Stock
	h. Retained Earnings
	i. Appraisal Increase

Required: Using this classification, indicate where each of the following accounts would be presented or disclosed on the balance sheet.

_____ Allowance for Doubtful Accounts
_____ Authorized Preferred Shares
_____ Donated Capital
_____ Appraisal Increase
_____ Common Shares Authorized
_____ Accumulated Depreciation
_____ Prepaid Insurance
_____ Salaries Payable
_____ Land — Appraisal Increase

Comprehension Problem 9-7

The following captions are sub-totals appearing in the shareholders' equity section of the balance sheet for Tyme Corporation:

a. Total Share Capital
b. Total Retained Earnings
c. Total Surplus.

Required: For each event listed below, indicate, in the format provided, whether each sub-total is increased (↑) or decreased (↓). Indicate with an X if there is no change to a particular sub-total. Consider each event to be unrelated to the others, unless otherwise indicated.

	a	b	c
Example:			
Issued no-par value common stock	↑	x	x
Split 2 for 1 the common stock of the corporation			
Created an allowance for doubtful accounts			
Recorded an appraisal increase in an asset of the corporation			
Recorded a net income for the year from operations			
Recorded a net loss for the year from operations			

Comprehension Problem 9-8

The shareholders' equity section of Bonn Manufacturing Limited's balance sheet at December 31, 19X6 is shown below.

Shareholders' Equity

SHARE CAPITAL:

Preferred Stock, No Par-Value	
Authorized — 500 shares	
Issued and Outstanding — 300 Shares	$300
Common Stock, No Par-Value	
Authorized — 100 Shares	
Issued and Outstanding — 20 Shares	500
Total Share Capital	$800
Retained Earnings	192
Total Shareholders' Equity	$992

Required:

1. Calculate the book value per share of
   a. The preferred shares
   b. The common shares (no dividends are in arrears at December 31).
2. Assume that the common stock was split 2 for 1 on January 2, 19X7 and that there was no change in any other account at that time. Calculate the new book value of common shares immediately following the stock split.

Comprehension Problem 9-9

Zeff Inc. received a charter that authorized it to issue 100 shares of common stock. The following transactions were completed during 19X6:

Jan.   5   Sold and issued 30 shares of common stock for a total of $150 cash
      12   Exchanged 50 shares of common stock for assets listed at their fair market values: Machinery — $100; Building — $100; Land — $50
      30   Received subscriptions on 10 shares of common stock at $6 each; downpayments amounting to 20 percent accompanied the subscription contracts
Feb. 28   Received payment of the balance due on the subscriptions of Jan. 30; the stock was then issued
Dec. 31   Closed the net income of $41 to retained earnings.

Required:
1. Prepare journal entries for the 19X6 transactions, assuming that Zeff was incorporated under the CBCA.
2. Assuming that Zeff was incorporated under the CBCA, prepare the shareholders' equity section of the balance sheet at
   a. January 31   b. February 28   c. December 31.

Comprehension Problem 9-10

You are given the following data for the partnership of S. Himmel and R. Rennie.

S. Himmel and R. Rennie
Trial Balance
December 31, 19X4

Cash	$ 41,000	
Accounts Receivable	68,400	
Inventory (Jan. 1, 19X4)	22,500	
Accounts Payable		$ 45,800
S. Himmel, Capital		30,000
S. Himmel, Drawings	7,000	
R. Rennie, Capital		20,000
R. Rennie, Drawings	5,000	
Sales		322,000
Purchases	168,000	
Purchases Returns and Allowances		3,000
Rent Expense	36,000	
Advertising Expense	27,200	
Delivery Expense	9,600	
Office Expense	12,800	
Other Store Expense	23,300	
	$420,800	$420,800

Inventory at December 31, 19X4 amounted to $27,000. Each partner had added $10,000 capital during the year; the opening credit balance in each Capital account had been Himmel $20,000 and Rennie $10,000. The partners share profits and losses equally.

Required:
1. Prepare closing entries at year-end, omitting explanation lines.
2. Prepare an income statement for the year.
3. Prepare a statement of partners' capital for the year.

Himmel and Rennie
Statement of Partners' Capital
For the Year Ended December 31, 19X4

	Himmel	*Rennie*	*Total*
Capital Balance (Jan. 1)	$	$	$
Add: Investments during 19X4			
Net Income for the Year			
	$	$	$
Less: Drawings			
Capital Balance (Dec. 31)	$	$	$

Problems

Problem 9-1

Mawani Inc. was incorporated on June 1 and was authorized under its provincial charter to issue the following shares — 20 000, 5% preferred shares of no par-value and 10 000, common shares of no par-value.

Required:
1. Prepare journal entries to record the following June transactions:
   a. Issued 3000 preferred shares for $6 cash each
   b. Issued 5000 preferred shares for $5 cash each
   c. Issued 2000 common shares for $2 cash each
   d. Issued 1000 common shares for $1 cash each
   e. Issued 500 common shares for land valued at $1,500.
2. Prepare the shareholders' equity section of the balance sheet at June 30.
3. On July 15, the common stock was split 2 for 1. Assuming no other transactions occurred since June 30, prepare the shareholders' equity section on July 15 following the stock split.

Problem 9-2

Following is the shareholders' equity section of Bindy's Book Mart Inc. shown before and after a stock split on April 15.

Before Split		**After Split**	
Shareholders' Equity		*Shareholders' Equity*	
Common Stock, No Par-Value		Common Stock, No Par-Value	
Authorized — 5000 Shares		Authorized — ? Shares 26,000	
Issued and Outstanding —		Issued and Outstanding —	
1000 Shares	$100,000	5000 Shares	$?

On April 15, the company decided to increase the marketability of its shares by opting for a 5 for 1 stock split.

Required:

1. Complete the shareholders' equity section of the balance sheet after the split.
2. Joe Carlos, the president, asks you to record a memorandum indicating the new number of shares. Record the appropriate journal memorandum.
3. How would a reverse stock split of 1 for 2 on April 15 affect the common stock? Record your answer using this schedule form.

	Number of Shares Outstanding	Total Common Stock on Balance Sheet	Market Price per Share
Before Stock Split	1000	$100,000	$200
After Stock Split			

4. On the basis of the information given in the shareholders' equity section (before split), would a stock split or reverse stock split be most appropriate? Explain.

Problem 9-3

The trial balance of Dwyer Limited at December 31, 19X2 included the items listed below:

Mortgage Payable	$10,000
Common Stock, No Par-Value, 500 Shares	
Authorized and Issued	10,000
Allowance for Doubtful Accounts	40
Accumulated Depreciation	1,200
Retained Earnings	3,140
Preferred Stock, No Par-Value	
1000 Shares Authorized and Issued	1,020
Capital Arising from Donation of Plant Site	750
Income Tax Payable	400

Required: Prepare the shareholder's equity section of the balance sheet in proper form.

Problem 9-4

The following is the shareholders' equity section of the balance sheet of Boritz Foods Limited at December 31, 19X5.

Shareholders' Equity

SHARE CAPITAL:
Common Stock, No Par-Value
Authorized — 500 shares
Issued and Outstanding — 300 Shares $3,070

Retained Earnings   500
Total Shareholders' Equity $3,570

Required:
1. What is the book value per common share?
2. On December 31, the Boritz common shares traded at a high of $24. What is the explanation of this price, related to your answer to question 1, above?

Problem 9-5

On January 1, 19X3, ABC partnership had capital balances of $60,000, $100,000, and $20,000 for **A**, **B**, and **C** respectively. In 19X3, the partnership reported net income of $40,000. None of the partners withdrew any assets in 19X3. The partnership agreed to share profits and losses as follows:

a. A monthly salary allowance of $2,000, $2,500, and $4,000 to **A**, **B**, and **C** respectively
b. An annual interest allowance of 10 percent to each partner based on his/her Capital balance at the beginning of the year
c. Any remaining balance to be shared in a 5 : 3 : 2 ratio (**A** : **B** : **C**).

Required:
1. Using the form shown in the appendix in this chapter, prepare a schedule to allocate the 19X3 net income to partners.
2. Assume all the income statement accounts for 19X3 have been closed to the Income Summary account. Prepare the entry to record the division of the 19X3 net income.

	A	B	C	Total
Amount of Profit To Be Allocated to Partners				$
Interest Allocation:				
A:$ x %	$			
B:$ x %		$		
C:$ x %			$	
Balance				$
Salary Allocation				
Balance				$
Balance Allocated in Profit and Loss Sharing Ratio:				
A:$ x	$			
B:$ x		$		
C:$ x			$	
Balance				-0-
Allocated to Partners	$	$	$	

Problem 9-6

X and **Y** have decided to establish a partnership in a local mall. They are evaluating two plans for a profit and loss sharing agreement:

Plan A **X** to receive a salary of $15,000 per year, the balance to be divided in their Capital balance ratios of $50,000 for **X** and $100,000 for **Y**.
Plan B **X** to receive a salary of $1,000 per month, 8 percent per year interest each on their investments and the balance equally.

Required: Calculate the division under each plan in the following schedule, assuming: (a) a profit of $60,000 per year, and (b) a loss of $30,000 per year.

Profit and Loss Sharing Plan	Division with Profit of $60,000		Division with Loss of $30,000	
	X	Y	X	Y
Plan A:				
Salary				
Balance				
Plan B:				
Salary				
Interest				
Balance				

Alternate Problems

Alternate Problem 9-1

Hunter Corporation was incorporated on May 1, 19X3. The following transactions occurred during the month:

May 1 Issued 1000 preferred shares for $3 cash each
2 Issued 2000 common shares for $5 cash each
5 Issued 1500 common shares for $2 cash each
10 Issued 1000 preferred shares for $1 cash each
15 Issued 3000 preferred shares for $2 cash each
21 Issued 5000 common shares for $3 cash each.

Assume that Waterhouse was incorporated under the CBCA and was authorized to issue an unlimited number of preferred shares of no par-value and common shares of no par-value.

Required:
1. Prepare journal entries to record the May transactions.
2. Prepare the shareholders' equity section of the balance sheet at May 31, 19X3.

SHARE CAPITAL:
Pref. stock   12,500
Comm. Stock   50,000
TOT. SH.CAP.   62,500
SURPLUS:
CONTR. SURPLUS   1200
APPRAISAL INCREASE-LAND   2000
R/E   5700   8900
TOTAL S/E   71,400

Alternate Problem 9-2

Irvine Software Inc. was incorporated under the CBCA on April 15, 19X4 to design instruction software for colleges and universities. The following transactions occurred during April:

Apr. 15 Received a corporate charter authorizing the issue of an unlimited number of no par-value common shares
16 Issued 5000 common shares for $10,000 cash $10,000   5000
20 Issued 10 000 common shares for land to be used for the construction of a building; the shares were selling for $3 each on this date $30,000   10000
25 Issued 1000 common shares for $4 cash each $4000   1000
30 Reacquired 1000 common shares for $2,750.

Required:
1. Prepare journal entries to record the April transactions.
2. Prepare the shareholders' equity section of the balance sheet at April 30.
3. Assume that on May 25 the stock was split 2 for 1. How would the stock split affect the common stock? Record your answer using the following schedule form.

	Number of Shares Outstanding	*Total Common Stock on Balance Sheet*	*Market Price per Share*
Before Stock Split	15,000	41250	$6
After Stock Split	30,000	41250	U3

Alternate Problem 9-3

SW

The trial balance of Raith Limited at December 31, 19X6 includes the following items:

SURPLUS

R/E Retained Earnings	$ 5,700	R/E
OTHER Allowance for Doubtful Accounts	7,500 FROM A/R ON B/S	
SHARE CAPITAL Common Stock, No Par-Value, 10 000 Shares Authorized and Issued	50,000	SHARE CAPITAL
OTHER Dividends Payable	1,000 CUR.LIAB	62,300
OTHER Mortgage Payable	35,000 LT.LIAB	SHARE CAPITAL
SHARE Preferred Stock, No Par-Value 100 Shares Authorized and Issued	12,500	
CONTRIBU Capital from Land Donation	1,200 CONTRIBUTED	3,200
CONTRIBU Appraisal Increase — Land	2,000 CONTRIBUTED	
Income Tax Payable	500	

Required: Prepare in proper form the shareholders' equity section of the balance sheet as at December 31.

Alternate Problem 9-4

Partners **A** and **B** are subject to the following agreement for the sharing of profits/losses:
a. Annual salaries are allowed — $12,000 to **A**, $14,000 to **B**.
b. Interest at 10 percent is allowed on original capital contributions of $100,000 from **A**, and $70,000 from **B**.
c. Any remainder is to be split in the ratio of 3 : 2.

Required: How much net income must be earned by the partnership for **A** to be allocated a total of $47,000? (Use the form from section B of the chapter.)

Alternate Problem 9-5

Opper and Parker have decided to open a business partnership. Opper is familiar with the business and is expected to spend a good deal of time running it. Parker, on the other hand, will be the "financial" person of the partnership. They have the ramifications of changes in the net income under discussion. The following plans for sharing profits and losses are being considered:

Plan A   Salary with balance equally: Opper's salary $10,000 per year, Parker's nil.
Plan B   Salary, interest on investment and balance equally: Opper $10 000 salary, Parker nil, both to receive 10 percent per year on beginning investment. Beginning investments: Opper $50,000, Parker $200,000.

Required: Calculate the division under each plan assuming: (a) a profit of $150,000, and (b) a loss of $25,000.

Dividend Decisions

The amount of a corporation's retained earnings is an important input for management decisions regarding dividend declaration. Dividends reduce retained earnings.

1. What part of retained earnings is actually available for paying dividends?
2. Why would a corporation choose not to declare dividends?
3. At what point does a dividend become a legal liability of the corporation?
4. How are declared dividends disclosed?
5. Which shares of the corporation have a preference to dividends?
6. Do undeclared dividends in any of the corporation's shares accumulate?
7. Which features are included with certain classes of shares to make them more attractive to investors?
8. Does a stock dividend have any effect on the investor's portfolio?
9. Does a stock dividend change the investor's percentage of corporate ownership?
10. How does the corporation record a stock dividend?

A.   Internal Financing

Retained earnings represent the assets earned by a business over its life that have not been distributed as dividends to shareholders. Rather, these assets have been reinvested; that is, they have been ploughed back into the business to finance its operations.

Deficit
A debit balance in the Retained Earnings account of a corporation.

The Retained Earnings account normally has a credit balance. If the Retained Earnings account has a debit balance, the corporation has incurred a **deficit**; that is, its expenses have exceeded revenues, or excessive dividends have been paid. The result of a deficit is that no assets of the corporation can be used for the payment of dividends.

Restrictions on Retained Earnings

Restricted retained earnings
The assets of a corporation represented by an amount of retained earnings that is not available for dividends.

Unrestricted retained earnings
An amount of retained earnings representing assets of the corporation that are available for dividends, also known as *free retained earnings*.

The assets represented by retained earnings can be either **restricted** or **unrestricted** for dividend distributions. Study Figure 10-1 to better understand the concept of restricted and unrestricted retained earnings.

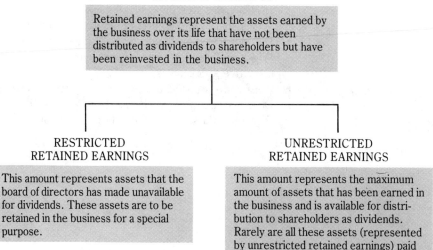

Figure 10-1   Restricted and unrestricted retained earnings

Assume that a corporation has $120,000 of retained earnings at the balance sheet date. The board of directors passes a resolution to restrict $70,000 for a plant expansion. The balance remains unrestricted for dividend purposes, although the directors have not yet decided whether to pay dividends this year. The $70,000 restricted amount remains a part of retained earnings; the full cycle of the restriction for plant expansion is shown in Figure 10-2.

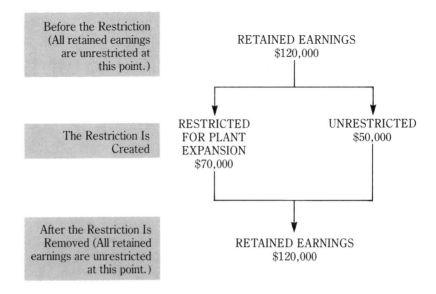

Figure 10-2   Restriction for plant expansion: creation and removal

As can be seen, the creation of a restriction on retained earnings divides the $120,000 amount into a restricted component of $70,000 and an unrestricted component of $50,000. The latter amount is sometimes called *free retained earnings*.

Students sometimes do not understand why the unrestricted retained earnings of $50,000 cannot be paid out as dividends. Unrestricted retained earnings are an equity and not an asset; only assets can be paid out as dividends. The $50,000 equity amount is represented by assets in the company, but these assets consist of receivables, inventory, and fixed assets. Retained earnings amounts may not necessarily be matched with cash asset amounts. It is possible — but rare — that a fixed asset dividend could be issued. To understand this relationship of assets and dividends better, study the following examples.

Cash dividends are possible.		Cash dividends are not possible. (Only a fixed asset dividend is possible but this is highly improbable.)	
Assets		*Assets*	
Cash	$150,000	Fixed Assets	$150,000
Equity		*Equity*	
Common Stock	$ 30,000	Common Stock	$ 30,000
Retained Earnings	120,000	Retained Earnings	120,000
	$150,000		$150,000

When cash is not available to pay dividends, dividends cannot be paid. Even when cash is available, dividends may still not be paid. The growth of a corporation is dependent to some extent on the retention of earnings within the corporation, their investment in corporate assets, and their use for working capital and other purposes.

Recording a Restriction on Retained Earnings

The creation of special restrictions on retained earnings is made by the board of directors to indicate management's intention to use assets for a particular purpose; such assets are unavailable for dividends. These restrictions do not in any way alter the total amount of retained earnings or the total amount of shareholders' equity.

The journal entry to record the creation of the above $70,000 restriction for plant expansion reads:

Retained Earnings	70,000	
Retained Earnings — Restricted		
for Plant Expansion		70,000

This restriction does not reduce the total retained earnings but rather records a portion of these earnings in an account specifically designated to indicate its purpose — plant expansion. The restricted amount is still part of retained earnings; it is classified as retained earnings in the shareholders' equity section of the balance sheet.

It is important to understand that recording a restriction for plant expansion does not set up some kind of cash fund for the expansion. The restriction is an equity account; it is represented by corporate assets, but these assets may be fixed assets, accounts receivable, or some other assets.

Removing a Restriction on Retained Earnings

When the special restriction account has served its purpose and the requirement for which it was set up no longer exists, the amount in the restriction account is returned to the Retained Earnings account from which it was created. The entry setting up the restriction is reversed. The entry to return the restricted amount for plant expansion to Retained Earnings is

Retained Earnings — Restriction for		
Plant Expansion	70,000	
Retained Earnings		70,000

Note that any restriction is created *within* the Retained Earnings account. The construction of the plant is recorded in the normal manner. Assume that the plant expansion is paid for in cash. The construction and payment is recorded in the journal as follows.

Plant	70,000	
Cash		70,000

This journal entry records the actual plant expenditure. It also shows that restricted retained earnings are *not* used to pay for the plant. The expenditure is paid with the asset cash. The restriction account is reversed when the plant has been built, because dividends are no longer restricted by the need for a plant expansion. *Dividends are now restricted by the lower amount of corporate cash* that is available to pay them.

Importance of Disclosing Restrictions

Are restrictions of retained earnings the best means for indicating and explaining management's intentions? Probably not! Most financial statement readers are not sufficiently familiar with accounting terminology to appreciate the nature of retained earnings restrictions. In addition, the use of the word *restriction* (or *appropriation,* as is used in some cases) is misleading. Nothing tangible has been restricted or appropriated as such. Rather, the restriction only indicates management's intention to use

$70,000 of corporate assets for plant expansion at some time in the future. A note to the financial statements and an explanation of management's intentions in the president's letter to shareholders are probably more meaningful to the average investor. The reference to a note and the note itself can take the following form:

Retained Earnings (*Note 1*) $120,000

Notes to Financial Statements
Note 1:   The board of directors has established a $70,000 restriction on retained earnings for a plant expansion. The assets represented by this amount are therefore not available for dividend purposes. The plant expansion is discussed further in the president's letter to shareholders.

The use of notes has become more popular in recent years. Note disclosure and balance sheet disclosure of the actual restriction in the shareholders' equity section are equally acceptable alternatives.

B.   Dividends

Both creditors and shareholders are interested in the amount of assets that can be distributed as dividends. Stated capital and restricted retained earnings represent assets that are not available for distribution as dividends. These categories are intended to protect creditors because they prevent shareholders from withdrawing assets as dividends to the point where assets become insufficient to pay creditors; they are also intended to ensure the continued operation of the business.

Real Life Example 10-1
Shares Tumble

Luckless owners of Financial Trustco Capital Ltd. preferred stock saw the market value of their shares fall another 25 cents to $1.35 each yesterday as the Toronto holding company announced it will pay no dividends until further notice.

The preferred shares, theoretically an investment for people seeking reliable dividend cheques, traded for as much as $10 apiece in January. The last quarterly cheque went out in September.

In a written statement, Financial Trustco said it is thinking about restructuring its debts, including more than $100-million (U.S.) in so-called junk bonds, high-yield speculative securities issued in the United States.

Meetings of bondholders have been scheduled for later this month, the statement said. The company's chairman, Edmund Clark, did not return phone calls.

Financial Trustco's common stock dividend likewise was suspended. The common shares, which also hit $10 early in the year, closed at 80 cents, unchanged from Thursday.

Financial Trustco, controlled by Toronto businessman Gerald Pencer, has sold its flagship operation, Financial Trust Co., and its stake in stockbroker Walwyn Inc. in the past two months. At the same time, credit rating agencies have been ringing louder and louder alarm bells.

In New York, Standard & Poor's Corp. reduced its rating on Financial Trustco's junk bonds in October by eight notches — from double-B minus to a subterranean single-C.

In Montreal, Canadian Bond Rating Service Ltd. cut its rating on the preferred stock in September by five notches — from P-3 (low) to the lowest rating of all, P-5.

On Oct. 21, CBRS suspended the rating entirely, "which means effectively you could expect them to cut the dividend," said Robert Ulicki, a credit analyst at the agency.

Mr. Ulicki said CBRS calculated that Financial Trustco needs about $25-million a year to pay bond interest and preferred share dividends and won't have the money unless it sells more assets or goes deeper into debt.

The company lost another source of cash when its major remaining subsidiary, Morgan Financial Corp., stopped paying dividends last month, he noted.

In better days, Financial Trustco's preferred stock promised a fixed dividend of $1.02 a year, or 25.6 cents a share every three months. The dividend is cumulative, meaning the company is obliged to catch up later if it skips a payment. No dividends are to be paid on the common stock when the preferred share dividend is in arrears.

Source John Saunders, "Shares Tumble after Trust Firm Halts Dividend", *The Globe and Mail*, November 11, 1988, p. B-7.

Dividend Policy

Sometimes a board of directors may choose not to declare any dividend. There may be financial conditions in the corporation that make the payment impractical or impossible, even though the corporation has unrestricted retained earnings.

Consideration 1:   There May Not Be Adequate Cash

Corporations regularly reinvest their earnings in assets in order to make more profits. Growth occurs in this way and reliance on creditor financing can be minimized.

Consideration 2:   Policy of the Corporation May Preclude Dividend Payments

Some corporations pay no dividends. They reinvest their earnings in the business. Shareholders benefit through increased earnings, which are translated into increased market prices for the corporation's shares. The pressure from shareholders for the corporation to provide dividends is reduced in this way. This type of dividend policy is often found in growth-oriented corporations.

Consideration 3:   No Legal Requirement that Dividends Have To Be Paid

The board of directors may decide that no dividends should be paid. If shareholders are dissatisfied, they can elect a new board or, failing that, sell their shares.

Consideration 4:   Dividends May Be Issued in Shares of the Corporation Rather than in Cash

Stock dividends may be issued to conserve cash or to increase the number of shares to be traded on the stock market. Stock dividends are discussed in section C of this chapter.

Dividend Declaration

Dividends can be paid only if they have been officially declared by the board of directors. The board must pass a formal resolution authorizing the dividend payment. Notices of the dividend are then published. It is noteworthy that once a dividend declaration has been made public, the dividend cannot be rescinded. At this point, the dividend becomes a liability and must be paid. An example of a dividend notice is shown in Figure 10-3.

Bluebeard Computer Corporation
Dividend Notice
On May 25, 19X1 the Board of Directors of Bluebeard Computer Corporation declared a semi-annual dividend of $0.50 per share on common shares. The dividend will be paid on June 26, 19X1 to shareholders of record on June 7, 19X1.

By Order of the Board
[signed]
Lee Bluebeard
Secretary

May 25, 19X1

Figure 10-3   A typical dividend notice

Three different and important dates are associated with the dividend. Usually dividends are declared on one date, the **date of dividend declaration**; they are payable to shareholders on a second date, the **date of record**; and the dividend itself is actually paid on a third date, the **date of payment**.

Date of Dividend Declaration

The dividend declaration provides an official notice of the dividend. It specifies the amount of the dividend and which shareholders will receive the dividend. The liability for the dividend is recorded in the books of the corporation at its declaration date. Shareholders become creditors of the corporation until the dividend is paid.

Date of Record

Shareholders who own the shares on the date of record will receive the dividend even if they have sold the share before the dividend is actually paid. This date is usually a week or two after the date of declaration. This fact is important for corporations whose shares are actively traded on the stock market. Investors whose names appear in the shareholders' ledger on the date of record will receive the dividend. Shares sold on the stock market after the date of record are sold *ex-dividend*, that is, without any right to the dividend.

Date of Payment

The dividend is actually paid on this date to investors whose names appear in the shareholders' ledger on the date of record. This date is several weeks after the date of record, in order to allow share transfers to be recorded to the date of record and dividend cheques to be prepared.

Accounting for Dividends

Dividends are usually paid as **cash dividends**. They can also be paid in other assets of the corporation, or in shares of the corporation itself. (The latter case is discussed in section C.) When dividends are declared in assets other than cash, they are usually referred to as **property dividends**. Property dividends usually create problems in dividing the property pro-rata (in proportion) so that it can be distributed to shareholders in proportion to the number of shares they own. Usually, inventory of the corporation and temporary investments are the first assets to be considered for property dividends. The journal entries for cash dividends and property dividends take the following form:

Cash Dividends

At the declaration date
Dividends xx
  Dividends Payable xx

At the payment date
Dividends Payable xx
  Cash xx

Property Dividends

At the declaration date
Dividends xx
  Dividends Payable xx

At the payment date
Dividends Payable xx
  Inventory xx
  Investments xx

Shareholder Preference to Dividends

Preferred shareholders are usually entitled to dividends before any dividends are distributed to common shareholders. They may also have other dividend preferences, depending on what rights have been attached to preferred shares at the date of incorporation. Two additional preferences can be
• The accumulation of undeclared dividends from one year to the next — referred to as *cumulative dividends*, as compared with *non-cumulative dividends*, which do not accumulate
• The participation of preferred stock with common stock in dividend distributions beyond the usual preferred dividends — referred to as a *participating* feature of preferred stock as compared with a *non-participating* feature.
The relationships among these dividend preferences are shown in Figure 10-4.

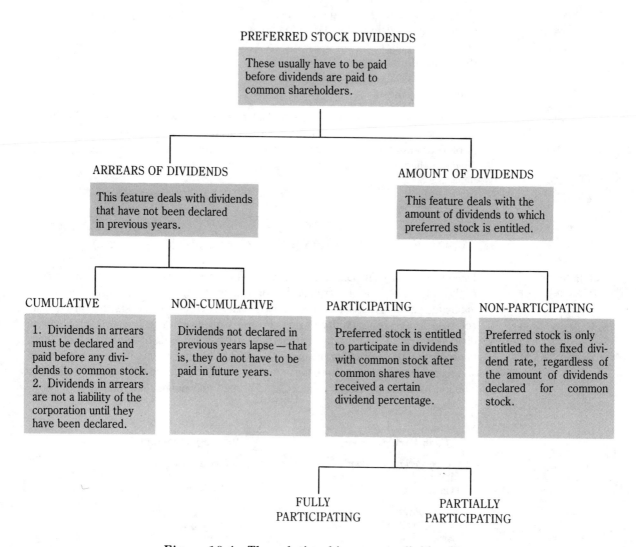

Figure 10-4   The relationships among dividend types

Cumulative Dividend Preferences

Cumulative preferred stock
Stock on which undeclared dividends accumulate and have to be paid in the future before any dividends can be paid on common shares.

The **cumulative** preference means that an unpaid dividend accumulates from year to year and is payable from future earnings if a dividend declaration is made by the entity. These accumulated dividends must be paid before any dividends are paid on common stock. The unpaid dividends are usually referred to as *dividends in arrears*. Dividends in arrears are not recorded as a liability on the balance sheet of the company unless and until they have been declared by the board of directors. Disclosure of dividends in arrears must, however, be made in a note in the financial statements.

Preferred Shares with a Cumulative Preference

Assume that George Williams Inc. declared dividends totalling $92,000 when the shareholders' equity section of its balance sheet contained the following classes of shares:

Preferred stock, No Par-Value, $8 Dividends,
Cumulative
    Authorized — 3000 Shares
    Issued and Outstanding — 2000 Shares $200,000
Common Stock, No Par-Value
    Authorized — 35 000 Shares
    Issued and Outstanding — 30 000 Shares $300,000
                                    $500,000

A note to the balance sheet indicates that there were two years of preferred dividends in arrears. How much of the $92,000 cash dividend is paid to each class of shares? The preferred shares are entitled to $16,000 dividends per year (2000 shares × $8) whenever dividends are declared. Because these shares have a cumulative preference, they are also entitled to dividends in arrears.

Shareholder Preference to Dividends		**Dividend Distribution**		
		To Preferred	*To Common*	*Balance*
	Total Dividend Declared			$92,000
1st Preference:	Arrears ($16,000 × 2 Years)	$32,000	–	60,000
2nd Preference:	Current Year — Preferred	16,000	–	44,000
	Balance to Common	–	$44,000	-0-
	Total	$48,000	$44,000	

Non-cumulative preferred stock
Stock on which a dividend, if not declared in a given year, will not accumulate to be received at a later date.

The cumulative preference has resulted in the payment to preferred shareholders of dividends unpaid in the previous two years; this amounts to $32,000. For the current year, preferred shareholders receive only $16,000, compared with $44,000 paid to common shareholders. The normally cautious preferred shareholder is usually content with a smaller share of the profits as long as there is a reasonably certain return. The cumulative feature ensures that, if any dividends are declared by the corporation, the preferred shareholder will be paid.

If a preferred stock is **non-cumulative**, a dividend not declared by the board of directors in any one year is lost forever.

Participating Dividend Preferences

Participating preferred stock
Stock entitled to participate in dividends with common stock after common stock have received a certain dividend percentage.

Non-participating preferred stock
Stock not entitled to participate in additional dividends after receiving the specified dividend percentage to which they are entitled.

A **participating** feature is sometimes added to preferred stock to make it more attractive to shareholders. This feature permits, under certain circumstances, the shareholders' participation in the earnings of the entity in excess of the stipulated rate. The extent of this participation can be limited or unlimited. **Non-participating** preferred stocks do not receive a share of additional dividends.

Investments in shares of a corporation carry with them an element of risk that the investment may be lost if the corporation is unsuccessful. Different classes of shares with different features are therefore used to appeal to investors with differing willingness to take risks. In the case of George Williams Inc., the preferred shareholders have less risk than the common shareholders. However, while cumulative features occur, participating features are rarely found.

C. Stock Dividends

Stock dividend
A dividend paid in shares of the corporation instead of in cash.

A **stock dividend** is a dividend payable to shareholders in shares of the declaring corporation; these shares are given in place of a cash dividend. In this way, the declaring corporation is able to reinvest its earnings in the business and reduce the need to finance its activities through borrowing.

Assume that the Sherbrooke Corporation declares a 10 percent, common stock dividend to common shareholders. At the time of this declaration, the shareholders' equity of the corporation consists of the following:

Shareholders' Equity

Common Stock, No Par-Value		
Authorized — 20 000 Shares		
Issued and Outstanding — 5000 Shares	$ 25,000	
Retained Earnings	100,000	$125,000

At the date of dividend declaration, the common shares of the corporation were trading on the Toronto Stock Exchange at $4.

In this case, the stock dividend is expressed as a percentage of the outstanding common stock. The stock dividend amounts to 500 shares (5000 outstanding shares × 10%). This means that an investor owning 1000 shares receives 100 new shares when the dividend is issued.

Is There Any Dollar Effect on the Investor's Portfolio?

Theoretically, the market value of the common shares should fall somewhat to compensate for the increased number of shares. For example, the market price of the share would, theoretically, decrease as shown on the facing page.

	Before *Stock Dividend*	*After* *Stock Dividend* (*Theoretically*)
Market Price of Common Share	$4	A New, Lower Market Value
Total Market Value of Shares		
1000 Shares × $4	$4,000	
1100 Shares × New Market Price		$4,000

Theoretically, the total market value of the common shareholding would remain the same, at $4,000. In reality, the market price rarely decreases proportionately to the percent of the stock dividend. Usually, if the stock dividend is not large in relation to the total of outstanding shares, no change in the market value of the shares occurs.

A distinction is usually made between a small stock dividend (of approximately 20 percent of outstanding shares), which does not tend to affect the market price of that stock, and large stock dividends, which result in a proportionate decrease in the stock's market value. An extreme example of a 100 percent stock dividend would tend to reduce by half the market value of that stock. In this case, the total market value of the investor's portfolio remains the same. However, since the market price of the stock is materially reduced, a large stock dividend — one in excess of 20 to 25 percent — is usually regarded as a stock split. There is no agreement in the accounting profession regarding the recording of a large dividend; further discussions are usually dealt with in advanced accounting courses. What is important at this level is to be aware that there is a difference between the accounting for what is regarded as a stock dividend and for a stock split. A stock dividend results in the transfer (capitalization) of retained earnings to share capital. No such transfer occurs when there is a stock split.

The CICA has not recommended any particular handling of stock dividends. In accordance with generally accepted accounting principles, the fair market value of stock dividends is transferred to share capital from retained earnings, since the CBCA requires that shares be issued at their fair market value.

For example, since the market value of shares rarely changes when a stock dividend is small, an investor in shares of the Sherbrooke Corporation would see the market value of his/her shares as follows:

	Market Value of Investor Shares	
	Before Stock Dividend	*After Stock Dividend*
Common Shares — 1000 × $4	$4,000	
Common Shares — 1100 × $4		$4,400

That is, the investor sees his/her total market value of common shares increase by $400. No journal entry is made by the investor on receipt of a stock dividend, since there is no dividend income. The investor simply increases the number of shares owned in the corporation and, of course, has 100 additional share certificates. The investor's total cost of shares in Sherbrooke Corporation remains the same as was originally paid for the 1000 shares.

	Investment in Sherbrooke Corporation			
	Before Stock Dividend		*After Stock Dividend*	
	Cost	Shares Owned	Cost	Shares Owned
	$5,000	1000 shares	$5,000	1100 shares
Cost per Share				
$5,000 ÷ 1000 Shares	$5			
$5,000 ÷ 1100 Shares			$4.55 (approx.)	

As can be seen in these calculations, the $5,000 cost of this investor's shares is allocated over 1000 shares before the stock dividend and over 1100 shares after the stock dividend. The cost of the shares continues to be $5,000 in total.

Is There Any Change in the Investor's Percentage of Corporate Ownership?

Since a stock dividend is issued to all shareholders, each shareholder has a larger number of shares after the stock dividend, but his/her ownership percentage of the company and his/her dollar equity in the company remains the same, as illustrated in the following example.

Assume that there are 5 shareholders in Sherbrooke Corporation, each of whom owns 1000 shares before the stock dividend. Each of these shareholders receives a 10 percent stock dividend, that is, 100 new shares.

Conceptual Issue 10-1

The Fine Line between Dividends and Stock Splits

by Alfred L. Kahl and William F. Rentz, University of Ottawa

If a firm wants to reduce the price of its stock, should a stock split or a stock dividend be used? Stock splits are generally used after a sharp price run-up, when a large price reduction is sought. Stock dividends are frequently used on a regular annual basis to keep the stock price more or less constrained. For example, if a firm's earnings and dividends are growing at about 10 percent per year, the price would tend to go up at about that same rate and it would soon be outside the desired trading range. A 10 percent annual stock dividend would maintain the stock price within the optimal trading range.

Although the economic effects of stock splits and dividends are virtually identical, accountants treat them somewhat differently. On a 2-for-1 split, the shares outstanding are doubled and the stock's par value (if any) is halved. This treatment is shown in the adjacent table, section 2, for Carson Computer Corporation, using a pro forma 19X7 balance sheet. With a stock dividend, the par value is not reduced, but an accounting entry is made transferring capital from retained earnings to common stock and to paid-in capital. The transfer from retained earnings is calculated as follows:

$$\text{Dollars transferred from retained earnings} = \left(\begin{array}{c}\text{Number} \\ \text{of shares} \\ \text{outstanding}\end{array}\right)\left(\begin{array}{c}\text{Percentage} \\ \text{of the stock} \\ \text{dividend}\end{array}\right)\left(\begin{array}{c}\text{Market} \\ \text{price of} \\ \text{the stock}\end{array}\right)$$

For example, if Carson, selling at $60, declared a 20-percent stock dividend, the transfer would be

Dollars transferred = (50 million)(0.2)($60) = $600,000,000.

As shown in section 3, of this $600 million transfer, $10 million is recorded in common stock and $590 million in additional paid-in capital. Retained earnings are reduced to $1.25 billion.

Price Effects

Several empirical studies have examined the effects of stock splits and stock dividends on stock prices. The findings of the Barker study[1] are presented next. When stock dividends were associated with a cash dividend increase, the value of the company's stock six months after the ex-dividend date had risen by 8 percent. On the other hand, where stock dividends were not accompanied by cash dividend increases, stock values fell by 12 percent, which approximated the percentage of the average stock dividend.

Price Effects of Stock Dividends
Price at Selected Dates

	Six Months prior to Ex-Dividend Date	At Ex-Dividend Date	Six Months after Ex-Dividend Date
Cash dividend increase	100%	109%	108%
No cash dividend increase	100%	99%	88%

Corporate Ownership

	Before Stock Dividend		After Stock Dividend	
Shareholders	Shares	Percent	Shares	Percent
A	1000	20%	1100	20%
B	1000	20%	1100	20%
C	1000	20%	1100	20%
D	1000	20%	1100	20%
E	1000	20%	1100	20%
	5000	100%	5500	100%

Each shareholder has received 100 new shares but his/her ownership percentage of the company remains 20 percent. Each shareholder holds more shares but the *percentage of ownership remains the same, as do the net assets of the company.*

Carson Computer Corporation Shareholders' Equity Accounts, Pro Forma, 19X7/12/31

1. Before a stock split or a stock dividend:

Common stock (60 million shares authorized, 50 million outstanding, $1 par)	$ 50,000,000
Additional paid-in capital	100,000,000
Retained earnings	1,850,000,000
Total common shareholders' equity	$2,000,000,000

2. After a 2-for-1 stock split:

Common stock (120 million shares authorized, 100 million outstanding, $0.50 par)	$ 50,000,000
Additional paid-in capital	100,000,000
Retained earnings	1,850,000,000
Total common shareholders' equity	$2,000,000,000

3. After a 20 percent stock dividend:

Common stock (60 million shares authorized, 60 million outstanding, $1 par)[a]	$ 60,000,000
Additional paid-in capital[b]	690,000,000
Retained earnings[b]	1,250,000,000
Total common shareholders' equity	$2,000,000,000

[a]Shares outstanding are increased by 20 percent, from 50 million to 60 million.
[b]A transfer equal to the market value of the new shares is made from retained earnings to additional paid-in capital and common stock: Transfer = (50 million shares)(0.2)($60) = $600 million.

These data seem to suggest that stock dividends are seen for what they are — simply additional pieces of paper — and that they do not represent true income. When stock dividends are accompanied by higher earnings and cash dividends, investors bid up the value of the stock. However, when stock dividends are not accompanied by increases in earnings and cash dividends, the dilution of earnings and dividends per share causes the price of the stock to drop by about the same percentage as the stock dividend. The fundamental determinants of price are the underlying earnings and dividends per share.

Assuming that each of the 5 investors had originally paid the same amount to the corporation for his/her shares, their corporate ownership in dollars before and after the stock dividend appears as follows:

Corporate Ownership

	Before Stock Dividend		After Stock Dividend	
Shareholders	Shares	Dollar Equity	Shares	Dollar Equity
A	1000	$ 25,000	1100	$ 25,000
B	1000	25,000	1100	25,000
C	1000	25,000	1100	25,000
D	1000	25,000	1100	25,000
E	1000	25,000	1100	25,000
	5000	$125,000	5500	$125,000

Since each shareholder owns 20 percent of the company, the share of shareholders' equity owned by each is $25,000 ($125,000 total equity × 20%). No assets are received by the corporation when the additional shares are issued as a stock dividend, and therefore *the total equity remains unchanged* at $125,000.

Accounting for Stock Dividends

The market price of the shares is used to record a stock dividend. This market price is usually the closing market price per share on the day preceding the declaration of the stock dividend. If the shares are not traded on the stock exchange, then a fair market value can be sought from expert appraisers. The recording of a stock dividend requires a transfer from Retained Earnings to Common Stock. This transfer is illustrated in Figure 10-5.

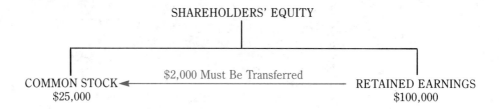

SHAREHOLDERS' EQUITY

COMMON STOCK ← $2,000 Must Be Transferred ← RETAINED EARNINGS
$25,000 $100,000

Figure 10-5   Transfer from Retained Earnings to Common Stock

Since the stock is recorded at market value, the amount of transfer from Retained Earnings to Common Stock is $2,000 (500 stock dividend shares × $4 market value). The $2,000 transfer to Common Stock means that this amount becomes a part of stated capital and the assets represented by the $2,000 are no longer available for the payment of future cash dividends. After the transfer has been recorded, shareholders' equity appears as shown in Figure 10-6.

This transfer reduces Retained Earnings and increases Common Stock by the same $2,000 amount. Total shareholders' equity, however, remains unchanged. This result of the stock dividend differs from the distribution of a cash dividend, which reduces both Retained Earnings and Cash and results in a *lower* total shareholders' equity after the cash dividend distribution.

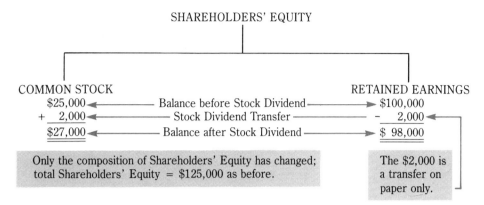

Figure 10-6 **Shareholders' equity after dividend transfer**

The transfer of retained earnings to a share capital account, Common Stock, is often referred to by accountants as a **capitalization of retained earnings**. The share capital of the corporation has been increased, even though no new assets have been acquired. Two journal entries at different dates are required to record the stock dividend. The original dividend declaration would be recorded as follows:

Capitalization of retained earnings
The transfer of an amount from Retained Earnings to a share capital account as in the case of a stock dividend.

Stock Dividends	2,000	
Stock Dividend To Be Issued		2,000
To record the declaration of a		
10% common stock dividend.		

When a stock dividend is declared, the debit could be made to Stock Dividends rather than Retained Earnings. At the year-end of the corporation, this Stock Dividend account would be closed to Retained Earnings in the same way a Cash Dividend account is closed. The closing entry for a stock dividend would be

Retained Earnings	2,000	
Stock Dividends		2,000
To close the Stock Dividends account.		

No assets are required for a stock dividend and therefore an equity account is credited. The entry is comparable to the entry required for a cash dividend that reduces Retained Earnings and credits a cash-payable account. If a balance sheet is prepared at this point, a declared cash dividend is shown as a current liability. In the case of a stock dividend, the Stock Dividends To Be Issued account is not a liability of Sherbrooke Corporation, because there is no liability incurred by a corporation declaring and issuing shares as a dividend. If financial statements are prepared between the declaration and payment of stock dividends, the Stock Dividends To Be Issued account is shown as an addition to share capital.

Shareholders' Equity

Share Capital:		
Common Stock, No Par-Value		
Authorized — 20 000 Shares		
Issued and Outstanding — 5000 Shares	$25,000	
To Be Issued as a Stock Dividend — 500 Shares	2,000	$ 27,000
Retained Earnings		98,000
		$125,000

Dividends, as noted, are usually declared on one date, payable to shareholders of record on a second date, and actually paid on a third date. In the case of the stock dividend made by Sherbrooke Corporation, the dividend was declared on December 15, payable to common shareholders of record on December 20, 19X1. The stock dividends were issued January 10, 19X2. The journal entry to record the stock dividend issue is shown below:

```
19X2
Jan. 10   Stock Dividends To Be Issued              2,000
              Common Stock                                    2,000
          To record the issue of
          the stock dividend declared
          December 15, 19X1.
```

Is the Stock Dividend Income to the Shareholders Receiving It?

No, a stock dividend is simply a distribution of shares to shareholders. The shareholders' percentage ownership of the corporation remains the same; the amount of shareholders' equity is unchanged.

Each shareholder has more shares after a stock dividend. However, no assets of the corporation have been issued to shareholders. Therefore, there is no income involved.

Some shareholders may perceive a stock dividend as income, but technically it is not. Theoretically, the market value of common shares should fall somewhat to compensate for the increased number of shares outstanding. In reality, it rarely decreases proportionately to the percent of the stock dividend, if at all. Therefore, an increase in the market value of a shareholder's investment occurs. Study the following example, in which an investor owns 100 shares, to understand how this increase occurs.

Shareholder Investment

	Before Stock Dividend			After Stock Dividend		
	Shares Owned	Cost	Market	Shares Owned	Cost	Market
Investment in Shares	100	$120		110	$120	
Cost per Share						
$120 ÷ 100 Shares		$1.20				
$120 ÷ 110 Shares					$1.09 approx.	
Market Price per Share			$5			$5
Market Value of Shares						
$5 × 100 Shares			$500			
$5 × 110 Shares						$550

In this example, with the assumption of no fall in market price of the common shares, this investor is $50 ahead ($550 − $500) after the stock dividend. This is a gain as far as investors are concerned, although no gain has been realized by them. However, a gain may be realized when these additional shares are sold; any such gain (or loss) would be reflected in the entry recording the sale.

Stock Dividend or Stock Split?

Stock dividends under 20 percent are considered to be stock dividends rather than stock splits under guidelines issued by the American Institute of Certified Public Accountants. Since no contradictory CICA guidelines exist, accountants are usually influenced by the 20 percent recommendation. Therefore, this 10 percent common stock dividend is to be recorded as a stock dividend. The stock dividend is calculated as follows:

$$\begin{array}{ccc} \text{Common Shares} \\ \text{Outstanding} \end{array} \times \begin{array}{c} \text{10\% Common Stock} \\ \text{Dividend} \end{array} = \text{Stock Dividend}$$

$$250 \text{ Shares} \times 10\% = 25 \text{ Shares.}$$

The fair market value of the stock dividend is calculated as follows:

$$\begin{array}{c} \text{Common Stock} \\ \text{Dividend} \end{array} \times \begin{array}{c} \text{Fair Market Price} \\ \text{per Share} \end{array} = \text{Value of Dividend}$$

$$25 \text{ Shares} \times \$5 = \$125.$$

The amount of the stock dividend is therefore calculated at $125.

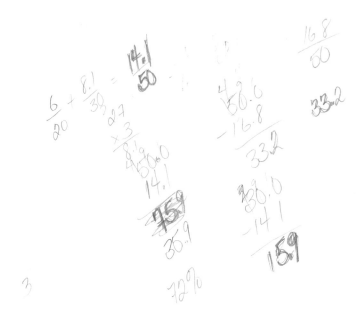

ASSIGNMENT MATERIALS

Discussion Questions

1. In what way have retained earnings been ploughed back into an entity?
2. What is the difference between restricted and unrestricted retained earnings? Why would some retained earnings be restricted? Prepare the journal entry used to make a restriction.
3. Are restrictions of retained earnings the best method for indicating and explaining management's intentions? Explain.
4. When making a decision involving the declaration of dividends, what are some of the main considerations used by a board of directors?
5. Even if a corporation is making a substantial net income each year, why might it not pay any dividends?
6. Distinguish among the date of dividend declaration, the date of record, and the date of payment.
7. Is a corporation legally required to declare a dividend? At what point do dividends become a liability of the corporation?
8. What is the difference in accounting between cash dividends and property dividends? Give a sample journal entry for each.
9. Explain the different dividend preferences that may be attached to preferred shares. Why would preferred shares have these preferences over common shares? Does it mean that purchasing preferred shares is better than purchasing common shares?
10. What are dividends in arrears? Are they a liability of the corporation?
11. Distinguish between a stock dividend and a cash dividend. Which is preferable from a shareholder's point of view? Why?
12. How does a stock dividend differ from a stock split?
13. Is there any dollar effect on an investor's portfolio when a stock dividend is declared and paid? Why or why not?
14. Does a stock dividend change an investor's percentage of corporate ownership? Explain, using an example.
15. What does a capitalization of retained earnings refer to when it is made in relation to the declaration and payment of a stock dividend?
16. How is a stock dividend recorded at the date of declaration? at the date of payment?
17. What should the investor in an entity look for: dividends or stock price? Discuss.

Discussion Cases

Discussion Case 10-1:   Poison Pills

A majority of Inco Ltd. shareholders have approved the company's controversial recapitalization plan in a vote that is expected to have far-reaching implications for how Canadian companies defend themselves during takeovers.

The Toronto-based nickel producer's strategy includes a shareholder rights plan, or so called "poison pill" takeover defence tactic, and a special $1.05-billion (U.S.) dividend. Payment of the $10 a share dividend, which will be made Jan. 9 to holders of record on Dec. 22, was contingent upon approval of the poison pill.

At a special meeting of more than 400 Inco shareholders yesterday, 72 per cent or 53.5 million of those shares voted favored the recapitalization. A surprising 28 per cent rejected the proposal. Inco has 105 million shares outstanding.

The vote followed a rare display of shareholder resistance to a proposal backed by company management. Historically, Canadian managers of public companies have been assured of widespread shareholder support for their plans, but Inco executives encountered much opposition because its poison pill is the first of its kind in Canada.

Ultimately, observers said, the plan was approved because of the lucrative special dividend. "This isn't a vote in favor of poison pills, it's a vote for a $10 dividend," said William Allen, president of Toronto stockbroker Allenvest Group Ltd., which represented several opponents to Inco's recapitalization.

A poison pill is designed to make hostile takeovers prohibitively expensive. The tactic has been widely used by U.S. companies to force unfriendly buyers to negotiate with directors of a target company. Detractors of the plan argue that it reduces shareholders to spectators because they no longer have the right to sell their shares to any acquirer.

"The result was very satisfactory," a visibly relieved Donald Phillips, chairman and chief executive officer, said after the meeting. "It was the first one in Canada, clearly we had a large selling job to do."

Inco's positive vote is expected to pave the way for other widely held Canadian companies to adopt similar measures. Inco's plan has prompted a lawsuit from one of its largest shareholders, pension fund manager Caisse de Dépôt et Placement du Québec. But legal and investment authorities said a number of companies have stalled their own plans for poison pills to await the outcome of Inco's vote.

If other companies embrace poison pills, shareholders can expect more protracted and complex takeover battles. Poison pills are attractive to managers because the strategy gives them more time to woo other buyers or propose alternative recapitalizations. Takeover raiders and shareholders often contest such plans, which promise a greater burden for securities regulators and the courts.

Inco's vote followed a two-hour meeting in which shareholders, executives of other companies and even a Greenpeace representative criticized the recapitalization. Previous shareholder threats of amendments to alter Inco's plan did not materialize, and the meeting was largely filled with supporters of the plan.

Those companies that follow in Inco's footsteps are expected to adopt varying types of poison pills. For example, Pegasus Gold Inc. of Vancouver unveiled a plan that allows shareholders to vote on hostile takeovers after certain conditions are met. The Ontario Securities Commission is expected to reach a decision on Pegasus's plan next week.

Despite shareholder approval of Inco's poison pill, the caisse intends to pursue its lawsuit. "Our lawyers are of the opinion that the plan is illegal. Even the votes of shareholders won't change the fact that it is illegal," Mr. Scraire said. Inco has said the lawsuit could take years to resolve because it will likely be fought in several courts.

One of the contentious aspects of Inco's recapitalization was the linking of the poison pill vote with the special dividend vote. Allenvest's Mr. Allen said he is concerned that other companies may also promise large dividends to "induce shareholders to approve poison pills."

Source Jacquie McNish, "Inco Majority Opts for Poison Pill", *The Globe and Mail*, Toronto, December 10, 1988, p. B-4.

For Discussion

1. What is a poison pill? How does it work? Why is it attractive to management?
2. What implications will this case have for how Canadian companies defend themselves during takeovers?
3. Prepare the journal entry to record the dividend declaration and payment. It will be paid January 9 to holders of record on December 22. What does this mean?
4. What are some of the reasons 28 percent of shareholders rejected a proposal that would have paid them a $10 (U.S.) dividend?
5. Was the vote really in favour of a $10 dividend or in favour of a poison pill?
6. Are any ethical issues involved in the decision to accept a poison pill?

Discussion Case 10-2:   Falconbridge Ltd.

Record high nickel prices caused Falconbridge Ltd. of Toronto to generate cash of $536 million in 1988, compared with $81.5 million a year earlier, the company's annual report says.

That cash-generating ability is vital to the company, which has a lot of uses for the money, including repayment of debt and continued development of its ore reserves.

The debt was mainly the result of Falconbridge paying $949 million last year to buy out the share position of its largest shareholder at the time, Placer Dome Inc. of Vancouver, and paying a special dividend of $4.75 a share to all its shareholders.

And William James, Falconbridge chairman, continues to push to develop the company's ore reserves — when he is not looking over his shoulder at a possible hostile takeover bid by Noranda Inc. of Toronto. Noranda would like to add Falconbridge's Kidd Creek mine near Timmins, Ont., to its own reserve base. Noranda owns 19.9 per cent of Falconbridge and intends to buy more.

To finance the dividend and $536-million share acquisition from Placer Dome, Falconbridge used $291 million of cash on hand and borrowed $658 million. It repaid $404 million of the debt, and $145 million in debentures were converted to common shares, meaning long-term debt increased by only $72 million to $816 million at Dec. 31, 1988.

The ratio of debt to equity was 41:59 at Dec. 31, 1988, compared with 33:67 at Dec. 31, 1987.

Falconbridge is accelerating the expansion of its base metal business. It spent $165 million on development work and capital expenditures during 1988, up from $118 million in 1987. It has budgeted $233 million for 1989 on its integrated nickel operations. About $97 million will be spent at the Sudbury operations, $85 million at Kidd Creek and $24 million on its Norwegian refinery.

The Strathcona mine's new high-grade deep copper and nickel zones near Sudbury are expected to be operating at full capacity during 1989 and 1990.

Falconbridge is also spending $44 million on the Craig mine, which will account for a substantial portion of the Sudbury nickel production beyond the year 2000. The ore reserves at the Craig mine are estimated at 15 million tonnes of 2 per cent nickel.

At Kidd Creek, studies are under way to consider a $46-million development of the No. 3 mine below the 1,400-metre level. The company estimates there are three million tonnes of reserves above 1,584 metres.

Falconbridge has also budgeted to spend $57 million during 1989 on mineral exploration in the Timmins and Sudbury areas. During 1988, it spent $38 million, compared with $25 million in 1987.

Among the larger projects is a $44 million shaft and underground development on the Lindsley property near Sudbury, which is expected to be complete by 1992. Four potentially mineable small zones of nickel and copper have been discovered.

Falconbridge had a profit before extraordinary items of $341 million or $4.57 a share in 1988, compared with $29.7 million or 42 cents a year earlier. Revenue was $2.1 billion, compared with $1.3 billion.

Source   Allan Robinson, "Falconbridge Cash Generation Boosted by Record Nickel Prices", *The Globe and Mail*, March 17, 1989, p. B-8.

For Discussion

1. Does the decision to acquire $536 million-worth of shares from Placer Dome and to pay a $4.75 dividend to shareholders make sense? Why or why not?
2. Evaluate the ratio of debt to equity in Falconbridge
   a. before the share reacquisition and dividend payment
   b. after the share reacquisition and dividend payment.
3. Falconbridge used $291 million in cash on hand and borrowed $658 million. It repaid $404 million of the debt, and converted $145 million in debentures to common shares. Prepare the journal entries to record these transactions.
4. Would it be wiser for Falconbridge to invest its earnings in its base metal business rather than to reacquire shares?
5. Compare Falconbridge's profit before extraordinary items of $4.57 per share in 1988 to $0.42 per share in 1987. What questions would you ask to obtain more information about Falconbridge's profitability?

Discussion Case 10-3:   Bank of Montreal

The Bank of Montreal plans to provide shareholders with various options for enlarging their holdings.

Under the plan, shareholders could receive dividends in three ways: as a cash dividend as at present; as a cash dividend that would be reinvested automatically in the bank's common shares at a discount of 5 percent from the average market price over a determined period; and as a stock dividend.

In addition, common shareholders would be entitled to purchase shares directly from the bank at the average market price, subject to a limitation of $5,000 a shareholder a quarter.

The plan is subject to regulatory approval and the waiver of pre-emptive rights by shareholders, which will be voted upon at the annual meeting January 19.

For Discussion

1. What are the advantages and disadvantages of each of the following three different forms of dividends proposed by the Bank of Montreal:
   a. Cash dividends?
   b. Reinvested cash dividends?
   c. Stock dividends?
2. Which form of dividend would you prefer? Why?
3. Bank of Montreal shareholders apparently have a pre-emptive right. What does this mean?
4. a. What effect on shareholder percentage ownership would result under each of the three dividend forms?
   b. What would be the amount of shareholders' equity?
   c. What amount of assets would remain in the bank after the dividend?

Discussion Case 10-4:   Canada Development Corporation

Canada Development Corp. says holders of the company's class B preferred shares registered at the close of business on February 27 will receive one bonus common share for each class B preferred share held.

As a result, an additional 1 380 000 common shares will be in the hands of 13 400 shareholders, increasing by 60 per cent the number of CDC common shares on the stock market.

A CDC spokesperson said the move would decrease the federal government's share in the company's voting stock to 48.7 percent from 49.9 percent.

When issued in 1975, each class B preferred share carried the right to receive 2 bonus common shares. The first of these was distributed in the fall of 1979, one year ahead of schedule. This second distribution comes more than four years earlier than the originally scheduled date of October 1, 1985.

H. Anthony Hampson, president, said the decision to issue the second bonus common share was based on the board's desire to increase the number of shares available for trading.

Hampson said early distribution of the bonus shares should not be taken as an indication of any change with respect to dividend policy on common shares, and the company plans to continue to invest earnings in profitable, high-growth industries.

"The board continues to believe that the best return on shareholders' equity can be attained by this policy of expanding the corporation's investments in strong companies oriented to the future," Hampson said.

The company said other conditions of the class B preferred shares have not changed as a result of the decision. This includes the dividend rate and the right to convert each class B preferred share into 10 common shares at any time at the holder's option.

For Discussion

1. Is this second bonus share a stock split or a stock dividend? Refer to the guideline issued by the AICPA in this chapter.
2. What journal entry, if any, would be made on the books of the CDC?
3. Would the market price of the preferred or common shares be affected by this bonus share distribution? Explain.

Discussion Case 10-5:   International Harvester Co.

Massey-Ferguson Ltd., you're not alone.

Chicago-based International Harvester Co. is also plagued by a staggering debt load, climbing interest rates, weak markets and high-cost plants. But officials of International Harvester expect to muddle through the beginning of 1981. The chairman and chief executive of the beleaguered farm-equipment maker, Archie McCardell, even says he expects the company's setback to be brief.

The market penetration of the 150-year-old company reached new highs in trucks and farm equipment in recent months, he said in a recent interview, and the company rebounded vigorously between April, when a six-month strike ended, and the current lull. McCardell expects the company to benefit also from a record number of new and updated products that would hit the market next year.

But most important, according to company executives, is that cost-cutting measures and operating efficiencies are finally beginning to show their effects. These changes, they said, will reduce annual operating costs by U.S. $400 million from the level of three years ago.

The strike settlement, McCardell said, gave the company work rules and labour costs that are now comparable to those of Harvester's competition. Several operations have been sold, phased out or cut back, ending losses of more than $25 million annually. Strict new inventory-control guidelines were adopted after the company learned during the strike that it could get by on less inventory. As a result, Harvester says, working capital requirements were $800 million less in 1980 than they would have been under previous practices.

The distance Harvester still has to go, however, was highlighted early this month, when Harvester directors decided to reduce the quarterly dividend to shareholders by more than 50 percent to $0.30 a share. The move upset many investors, who had held the stock for its traditionally generous dividends.

Three days before the board meeting, McCardell ignored his own prediction that the company, which lost $397.3 million in the year ended October 31, would suffer a loss in the first quarter. He said that the dividend cash requirements were inconsequential. "It's only $80 million a year," McCardell said.

McCardell, who was wooed from the presidency of the Xerox Corp. to Harvester three years ago, was awarded a controversial $1.7-million bonus a few months ago on the strength of 1979 earnings of $369.6 million on record revenues of $8.4 billion. This fiscal year, sales plunged to $6.3 billion under the impact of a six-month-long strike and a faltering economy.

With the mounting possibility of a severe cash crunch facing the company early next year, an event that could require putting more of the company's assets on the auction block, Harvester directors agreed to cut the dividend.

That was the latest of a series of austerity measures and strategy changes for the company. This fall Harvester cancelled a $100-million preferred stock issue and chopped $150 million from next year's capital and research budgets, the cornerstones of McCardell's revival strategy.

McCardell conceded that "over the years we had lost a lot of our operating flexibility", a condition for which he blamed union work rules. "We were undercapitalized and couldn't borrow, so we had a lot of old plants and equipment," he continued, a condition for which he blamed the dividend policy and high wages rates. "And we were not as wise as we could have been in our use of working capital."

The company's staggering debt load of $2.2 billion, about a quarter of which is tied to movements in the prime rate, is expected to help push the company into the red in the first quarter. High interest rates will also depress Harvester's sales volume. McCardell said, however, that he expected interest rates to peak sometime in January, which would relieve the credit pressures later in the year.

In addition to weak markets and climbing interest expenses, International Harvester is saddled with high-cost plants. In addition, the company makes nearly all its products for mature markets with slow growth rates. Its common stock is selling at less than 50 percent of book value.

For Discussion

1. If the strike settlement gave the company labour costs that are comparable to those of Harvester's competition, it appears that its labour costs had been lower than those of competitors in the past. Therefore, labour costs would necessarily be a larger expense to the company in the future. In view of "weak markets and climbing interest rates, high cost plants, mature markets with slow growth rates", would you tend to agree with McCardell's belief that the company's set-back will be brief? Why, or why not? (In your decision, consider market penetration of trucks and farm equipment and the introduction of new products to be introduced during the following year. Also do not ignore the $150 million chopped from the capital and research budget.)

2. Why do you think Harvester cancelled a $100-million preferred stock issue? Consider its undercapitalization and difficulty in borrowing at the time of the article in evaluating the implications of this cancellation.

3. The common stock was reported to be selling at less than 50 percent of book value. Why was this so? Consider in your answer the fact that the company had old plant and equipment that should be considerably depreciated in the books of the company, leaving a low net book value of these assets. Is the stock of a company with such a lower market price a "real bargain"?

4. Evaluate the stewardship of this company. Consider in your evaluation:
   a. The company learned during the strike that it could get by on less inventory.
   b. The company has a number of old buildings and much old equipment.
   c. The company has traditionally declared generous dividends.
   Include the role of both the board of directors and management in your evaluation.

5. Dividends were only $80 million a year in this company. Yet many investors had held the stock for its "traditionally generous dividends." There seems to be a contradiction here. What is it? Couldn't the company issue stock dividends? Why or why not?

6. Is the payment of the "traditionally generous dividends" part of the company's misfortune? Why or why not?

7. The name of Harvester does not contain any word indicating limited liability of shareholders. Does this mean that shareholders may be responsible for claims of creditors?

Harvester Losses Mount

International Harvester Co., struggling to emerge from a financial crisis, yesterday reported a net loss of $534 million for its first quarter ended January 31.

The loss was attributed primarily to a $479-million write-off of assets in its money-losing farm equipment division, which it sold to Tenneco Inc. during the period. (All figures are in U.S. funds.)

Chicago-based Harvester said that its continuing operations, consisting of its medium-and heavy-duty truck and diesel engine businesses, earned $42 million during the quarter. Those same operations reported a loss of $5 million during the first quarter of fiscal 1984.

Harvester, which announced in November that it would sell its farm-equipment operations to Houston-based Tenneco for $430 million in cash and stock, said yesterday the actual price at the close of the sale on January 31 came to $488 million, including $301 million in cash and $187 million in Tenneco preferred stock.

But that price was still far below the value at which the division had been carried on Harvester's books. As a result, Harvester was forced to write off the difference, including the value of its big Farmall tractor plant in Rock Island, Ill., which was not purchased by Tenneco and is being closed.

Harvester also said that its farm-equipment division suffered a $97-million operating loss for the quarter before it was turned over to Tenneco.

Source "Harvester losses mount", *The* (Montreal) *Gazette*, February 23, 1985, p. C-8.

For Discussion

8. As a shareholder, how would you evaluate the performance of Harvester and its future potential?

Comprehension Problems

Comprehension Problem 10-1

Pagnuelo Inc. has 100 000 common shares outstanding on January 1, 19X1. On May 25, 19X1, the board of directors declared a semi-annual dividend of $1 per share. The dividend will be paid on June 26, 19X1 to shareholders of record on June 7, 19X1.

Required: Prepare journal entries for
1. The declaration of the dividend
2. The payment of the dividend.

Comprehension Problem 10-2

Maxwell Inc. has 1000 cumulative preferred shares outstanding on which the $500 dividends have not been paid last year. The corporation also has 5000 common shares outstanding. Maxwell declared a $1,500 dividend to be paid in the current year.

Required: Calculate the amount of dividends received by
1. The preferred shareholders
2. The common shareholders.

Comprehension Problem 10-3

The shareholders' equity section of Royal Corporation's balance sheet at December 31, 19X3 is reproduced below.

Shareholders' Equity

Common Stock	
Authorized 10 000 shares	
Issued 5000 shares	$ 20,000
Retained Earnings	100,000
	$120,000

On January 15, 19X4, Royal Corporation declared a 10 percent common stock dividend to holders of common shares. At this date, the common shares of the corporation were trading on the Toronto Stock Exchange at $10 each.

Required: Prepare the journal entries to record these transactions.

Comprehension Problem 10-4

Lux Corporation has 10 000 common shares outstanding at January 1, 19X3 with a book value of $100,000. On April 1, Lux declared and paid a 10 percent stock dividend. The market value of Lux's shares on April 1 was $15. On June 1, Lux declared and paid a $2 dividend per share.

Required: Prepare journal entries for the above transactions.

Comprehension Problem 10-5

The following note appeared on the balance sheet of Fidelity Data Limited:

As of December 31, 19X2, dividends on the cumulative
preferred shares were in arrears for 3 years to the extent of
$15 per share and amounted in total to $15,000.

Required:
1. Does the amount of the arrears appear as a liability on the December 31, 19X2 balance sheet? Explain your answer.
2. Is Fidelity Data Limited necessarily in a deficit position? (A deficit position occurs when there is a debit balance in the Retained Earnings account.) Explain your answer.
3. The comptroller of Fidelity Data projects net income after taxes for the 19X3 fiscal year of $35,000. When the company last paid dividends, the directors allocated 50 percent of current year's net income after taxes for dividends. If dividends on preferred shares are resumed at the end of 19X3 and the established policy of 50 percent is continued, how much will be available for dividends to the common shareholders if the profit projection is realized?

Comprehension Problem 10-6

The following 19X1 information was taken from the shareholders' equity section of the balance sheet of Carstairs Inc.:

Common Stock, No Par-Value	
Issued and Outstanding — 10 000 shares	$ 10,000
Donated Land	25,000
Appraisal Increase — Building	20,000
Restriction — Plant Addition	100,000
Restriction — Contingencies	50,000
Retained Earnings — Jan. 1	75,000
Revenues (total for 19X1)	2,500,000
Expenses (total for 19X1)	2,000,000
Dividends Declared	25,000

Required: Prepare the shareholders' equity section of Carstairs' balance sheet.

Problems

Problem 10-1

Required: Using the format shown, indicate the effect in terms of assets, liabilities, and shareholders' equity of the items given. For no change indicate 0; for increase, +; and for a decrease, −.

	Assets	Liabilities	Shareholders' Equity
1. Declaration of a stock dividend	0	0	0
2. Declaration of a cash dividend	0	+	−
3. Issue of new shares in place of old shares associated with a stock split	0	0	0
4. Distribution of stock dividend in item 1	0	0	0
5. Payment of cash dividend in item 2	−	−	0

Problem 10-2 (SMA adapted)

Mulroney Enterprises Ltd. was incorporated February 20, 19X4 with the following authorized share capital: (a) preferred shares, no par-value, redeemable, non-participating, 2000 shares authorized; (b) 50 000 common shares, no par-value. The following transactions occurred during the first two years of operation:

19X5
Jan. 3   Issued the following shares for cash: 1000 preferred shares for $103 per share and 10 000 common shares for $11 per share

Dec. 20   Declared a regular cash dividend of $9 on the outstanding preferred shares payable January 6, 19X6 and a 5 percent stock dividend on the outstanding common shares to be distributed January 12, 19X6 (current market value of the common shares is $15 per share).

19X6
Mar. 1   The company announced a stock split of all common shares on the basis of four new common shares for each outstanding share; the new shares are to be issued March 31, 19X6 (current market value of the common stock is $18)

Dec. 20   Declared a cash dividend of $0.10 payable on January 6, 19X7 to the common shareholders of record January 2, 19X7; also declared the regular dividend on the preferred shares.

Other information:
a. Net income for the year ended December 31, 19X5: $32,000
b. Net income for the year ended December 31, 19X6: $45,000.
(Record the closing entry for each year.)

Required:
1. Prepare journal entries to record the 19X5 and 19X6 transactions.
2. Prepare the shareholders' equity section of the balance sheet at December 31, 19X6 in proper form.

Problem 10-3 (CGA adapted)

The shareholders' equity section of the balance sheet of Boyle Services Inc. at December 31, 19X7 appears below.

Shareholders' Equity

SHARE CAPITAL:	
Preferred Stock, No Par-Value	
Cumulative Non-participating	
Issued and Outstanding — 40 Shares	$ 400
Common Stock, No Par-Value	
Issued and Outstanding — 2000 Shares	2,000
Total Share Capital	$2,400
Retained Earnings	900
Total Shareholders' Equity	$3,300

The following transactions occurred during 19X8:

Feb. 15 Declared the regular $0.60 per share semi-annual dividend on its preferred stock and a $0.05 per-share dividend on the common stock to holders of record March 5, payable April 1

Apr. 1 Paid the dividends declared February 15

May 1 Declared a 10 percent stock dividend to common shareholders of record May 15 to be issued June 15, 19X6 (the common stock closed at a price of $2 on this date on the Toronto Stock Exchange; this price was designated by the board as the fair market value)

Jun. 15 Paid the dividends declared May 1

Aug. 15 Declared the regular semi-annual dividend on preferred stock and a dividend of $0.05 on the common stock to holders of record August 31, payable October 1

Oct. 1 Paid the dividends declared August 15

Dec. 15 Declared a 10 percent stock dividend to common shareholders of record December 20 to be issued on January 15, 19X9 (the common stock closed at a price of $3 on this date on the Toronto Stock Exchange; this price was designated by the board of directors as the fair market value)

Dec. 31 Net income for the year ended December 31, 19X8 was $1,400 (record the closing entry).

Required:
1. Prepare journal entries to record the 19X8 transactions.
2. Prepare the shareholders' equity section of the balance sheet at December 31, 19X8 in proper form.

Problem 10-4

At December 31, 19X3, the shareholders' equity section of the balance sheet for the Walkerville Automobile Corporation totalled $2,207,000. Following are the balances of various accounts at that date.

			('000s)	
Preferred Stock	Issued	50 shares	$500
Common Stock	Issued	50 shares	750
Restriction for Plant Extension			150
Retained Earnings—Unrestricted			600

Following are the transactions that occurred during the year 19X4.

Mar. 20   The regular semi-annual preferred dividend of $0.40 per share was declared payable April 1.
Apr. 1   Payment of previously declared dividend was made.
Jun. 15   The regular semi-annual common dividend of $0.40 per share was declared payable July 10.
Jul. 10   Payment of the previously declared dividend was made.
Sep. 20   Regular semi-annual preferred dividend of $0.40 per share was declared payable October 1.
Oct. 1   Payment of previously declared dividend was made.
Nov. 15   The board of directors met today and appropriated an additional $50 for the restriction for plant extension and $25 restriction for contingencies relating to an impending court case.
Dec. 15   The regular semi-annual common dividend of $0.40 per share was declared payable January 10. In addition, a 10 percent stock dividend was declared on the common shares outstanding to shareholders of record December 20, the stock to be issued January 20. The market price of the stock was $20, which the directors consider to be the fair value.

Required:
1. Prepare journal entries for the 19X4 transactions.
2. Prepare the shareholders' equity section of the balance sheet at December 31, 19X4, assuming profit for the year amounted to $165,000.

Problem 10-5

The shareholder's equity section of the balance sheet of Kwaschen Limited, as at December 31, 19X1, shows the following amounts:

Shareholders' Equity

SHARE CAPITAL:		
Preferred Stock, $8, No Par-Value		
Authorized — 1000 shares		
Issued and Outstanding — 150 Shares	$15,000	
Common Stock, No Par-Value		
Authorized — 10 000 Shares		
Issued and Outstanding — 4800 Shares	24,000	
Total Share Capital		$39,000
Retained Earnings		
Restricted for Plant Expansion	$12,000	
Unrestricted	28,000	
Total Retained Earnings		40,000
Total Shareholders' Equity		$79,000

Kwaschen Limited is incorporated under the CBCA. The following transactions occurred during 19X2:

a. Reacquired 400 shares of common stock at $10 each
b. Split the common stock 2 for 1
c. Issued for $3 cash each, an additional 200 shares of common stock
d. The board authorized a further addition of $5,000 to the retained earnings restricted for plant expansion
e. Transferred net income of $19,500 from Income Summary to Retained Earnings.

Required:
1. Prepare journal entries for the 19X2 transactions.
2. Prepare the shareholders' equity section of the balance sheet at December 31, 19X2.

Alternate Problems

Alternate Problem 10-1

Required: Using the format shown, indicate the effects in terms of assets and shareholders' equity of the items below. For no change indicate 0; for increase, +; for decrease, −.

	Assets	*Shareholders' Equity*
1. Declaration of a cash dividend		
2. Declaration of a stock dividend		
3. Payment of the cash dividend in item 1		
4. Distribution of stock dividend in item 2		
5. Issue of new shares in place of old shares in connection with a stock split.		

Alternate Problem 10-2 (SMA adapted)

Neanderthal Company Ltd., a progressive company in the glue business, has the following capital:

100 000 class A, cumulative, non-participating, $10 preferred shares, $10,000,000. These shares have a preference as to dividends over all other shares.

50 000 class B non-cumulative, non-participating $5 preferred shares, $5,000,000. These shares participate equally with common shares after common dividend of $3.

450 000 common shares no par-value, $45,000,000.

The company distributes 75 percent of net income earned each year. However, the company pays dividends on both classes of preferred shares up to the point at which further payment would place the company in a deficit position. (A deficit position occurs when there is a debit balance in Retained Earnings.) All dividends are declared at the end of the fiscal year and are payable on January 15 of the following year. The balance of the Retained Earnings January 1, 19X4 and net income each year is shown in the schedule.

Required: Calculate the amount of dividends declared each year to complete the schedule.

Neanderthal Company Ltd.
Schedule of Distribution of Dividends
For the Years Ended December 31, 19X4 to 19X7

	19X4	*19X5*	*19X6*	*19X7*
Balance (Jan. 1)	$1,200,000	$?	$?	$?
Add: Income (Loss)	4,000,000	(1,000,000)	(2,000,000)	7,000,000
Balance Available for Distribution	$5,200,000	$?	$?	$?
Dividends:				
Class A Pref.				
Class B Pref.				
Participation				
Common				
Participation				
Total Dividends				
Balance (Dec. 31)				

Alternate Problem 10-3 (SMA adapted)

On January 1, 19X3, the Kildonan Corporation Ltd. began operations. It had authorization to issue 20 000 no par-value common shares and 10 000 no par-value, cumulative, redeemable preferred shares. The dividend on preferred shares is $1 per year. The company issued 4000 no par-value common shares for $120,000 on January 1, 19X3. The Retained Earnings balance on December 31, 19X3 was $145,000. During 19X4 the following transactions occurred:

Feb. 15	Issued 1000 preferred shares at $8 each
Mar. 1	Acquired a parcel of land adjacent to the present building, having an appraised market value of $40,000 in exchange for 1500 common shares
Jun. 1	Declared a $5 cash dividend on outstanding common shares and the annual cash dividend on outstanding preferred shares payable July 1, 19X4
Dec. 1	Declared a 10 percent common stock dividend to common shareholders (the market value of common stock on this day was $35 per share; the dividend was payable on December 20, 19X4)
31	Net income for the year was $98,000 (record the closing entry).

Required:

1. Prepare journal entries to record the 19X4 transactions.
2. Prepare the statement of retained earnings at December 31, 19X4 in proper form.
3. Prepare the shareholders' equity section of the balance sheet at December 31, 19X4 in proper form.

Alternate Problem 10-4

On December 31, 19X4, the shareholders' equity section of the Fingal Company Limited balance sheet was as follows:

Shareholders' Equity

SHARE CAPITAL:
  Preferred Stock, Cumulative and Non-participating, No Par-Value —
  Authorized 5000 Shares $20,000
      Issued and Outstanding — 200 Shares
  Common Stock, No Par-Value Authorized — 2000 Shares
      Issued and Outstanding — 100 Shares   1,000
            Total Share Capital $21,000

Retained Earnings   5,450
      Total Shareholders' Equity $26,450

During 19X5, Fingal engaged in the following transactions:

Mar. 15   Declared the regular semi-annual $3 per-share dividend on the preferred stock and $0.50 per-share dividend on the common stock
Apr. 30   Paid the dividends previously declared
Sep. 15   Declared the regular semi-annual $3 per-share dividend on the preferred stock and a $0.50 per-share dividend on the common shares
Oct. 30   Paid the dividends previously declared
Dec. 15   Declared a 10 percent common stock dividend distributable on January 15 to shareholders of record January 10, 19X6. (The common shares were trading and closed on the Toronto Stock Exchange December 15 at $18 per share; this amount was approved by the board for the dividend.)

Required: Prepare journal entries to record the 19X5 transactions.

Alternate Problem 10-5

The shareholders' equity section of the Plain Machine Company Limited balance sheet at December 31, 19X3 appears below.

SHARE CAPITAL:
  Preferred Stock, $6, No Par-Value,
  Liquidation Value $101
      Authorized — 10 Shares
      Issued and Outstanding — 8 Shares $ 848
  Common Stock, No Par-Value
      Authorized — 200 shares
      Issued and Outstanding — 80 Shares   860
            Total Share Capital $1,708

Retained Earnings
  Restricted for Plant Expansion $ 200
  Unrestricted   900
            Total Retained Earnings   1,100
            Total Shareholders' Equity $2,808

Required:
1. Why do you think the directors established a restriction for plant expansion on retained earnings?
2. Assume that the plant expansion was completed by June 30, 19X4 and that the new facilities were all paid for. What entry would be made to the restriction?

Supplementary Problems

Supplementary Problem 10-1

Sharp Furniture Limited pays dividends on the issued and outstanding preferred and common shares twice a year. In December, 19X2, the directors declared the $1.25 semi-annual dividend on preferred shares and $0.60 per share on the common. The dividends are to be paid January 31, 19X3. The shareholders' equity at December 31, 19X2 consisted of the following:

Preferred Shares, $2.50
  Issued and Outstanding 5000 Shares
Common Shares — No Par-Value,
  Issued and Outstanding 30 000 Shares
Retained Earnings $560,000.

In 19X3 the following transactions affecting the company's shares took place.

Jan. 31   Paid the dividends declared in December, 19X2
Mar. 31   Sold 10 000 common shares at $30 per share
Jun. 28   Declared the regular semi-annual dividend on preferred shares and a dividend of $0.60 per share on common shares
Jul. 31   Paid the dividends declared in June
Sep. 21   Declared a 10 percent stock dividend on outstanding common shares to be issued October 31 to the shareholders of record October 12; market price of $31 to be used
Oct. 31   Issued the stock dividend declared in September
Dec. 28   Declared the regular semi-annual preferred share dividend and a cash dividend of $0.50 per share on common shares outstanding.

Required:
1. Prepare journal entries to record the 19X3 transactions.
2. If Sharp Furniture had a net profit of $100,000 in 19X3, what is the balance of Retained Earnings after closing the books on December 31, 19X3?

Supplementary Problem 10-2

Axworthy Productions Ltd. had the following shareholders' equity at January 1, 19X7:

Common stock	
1000 shares outstanding	$11,000
Retained earnings	9,000
Total shareholders' equity	$20,000

Part A

The following transactions occurred during the year:

Jun.　1　Declared a cash dividend of $1 per share to common shareholders of record June 15, payable June 30

　　30　Paid the dividend declared June 1

Dec.　1　Declared a 10 percent stock dividend to common shareholders of record December 15 to be issued January 1, 19X8; the fair market value was designated by the board at $20 per share

　　31　Net income for the year amounted to $5,000 (record the closing entry.)

Required:
1. Prepare journal entries to record the 19X7 transactions.
2. Compute the book value per share at January 1, 19X7.
3. Prepare the shareholders' equity section of the balance sheet at December 31, 19X7 in proper form.
4. Compute the book value per share at December 31, 19X7.
5. Prepare the shareholders' equity section of the balance sheet at January 1, 19X8 immediately following the issue of the stock dividend.
6. Compute the book value per share at January 1, 19X8 immediately following the issue of the stock dividend.

Part B

The following transactions occurred during 19X8:

Feb. 15　Declared a cash dividend of $1 per share to common shareholders of record March 1, payable March 15

Mar. 15　Paid the dividend declared February 15

Jun. 30　Split the common stock on the basis of 2 new common shares for each outstanding share; the market value of each share was designated by the board at $40 per share at the date of the split (the new shares are to be issued July 23)

Jul. 23　Issued the new common shares

Dec. 31　Net income for the year amounted to $8,000 (record the closing entry).

Required:
7. Prepare journal entries to record the 19X8 transactions.
8. Prepare the shareholders' equity section of the balance sheet at December 31, 19X8 in proper form.
9. Compute the book value per share at December 31, 19X8.
10. What are the advantages of a stock split to shareholders?

Supplementary Problem 10-3 (SMA adapted)

The shareholders' equity section of Waterloo Computers Inc. balance sheet at January 1, 19X6, is as follows:

Shareholders' Equity

Common Stock, No Par-Value	
Authorized — An Unlimited Number of Shares	
Issued and Outstanding — 400 000 Common Shares	$3,600,000
Retained Earnings	4,800,000
Total Shareholders' Equity	$8,400,000

On April 15, a 5 percent stock dividend was declared, payable June 1 to shareholders of record on May 15. On July 1, a 2-for-1 stock split was announced. Net income for the year was $2,400,000. The fair market price of Waterloo's shares were as follows:

Apr. 15	$12	Jun. 1	$15	
May 15	14	Jul. 1	8	

Required:
1. What was the issue price per share of the shares outstanding January 1, 19X6, assuming they were all issued at one time?
2. How much was the dollar change in retained earnings as a result of the stock dividend? Explain.
3. How much was the dollar change in shareholders' equity as a result of the stock dividend? Explain.
4. How much was the dollar change in shareholders' equity as a result of the stock split? Explain.
5. Prepare the shareholders' equity section of the balance sheet at December 31, 19X6 in proper form.
6. If Mary Munroe, a shareholder, owned 20 common shares at January 1, 19X6, what was the dollar amount of her equity in Waterloo at April 14, immediately before the declaration of the stock dividend at June 1? immediately after the stock dividend had been paid?
7. How did the declaration of a stock split on July 1 affect Mary Munroe?
8. What are the advantages and disadvantages of a stock dividend
   a. to Waterloo Computers Inc.?   b. to Mary Munroe?
9. What are the advantages and disadvantages of a stock split
   a. to Waterloo Computers Inc.?   b. to Mary Munroe?

Supplementary Problem 10-4

The shareholders' equity section of Guild Company Ltd.'s balance sheet shows the following:

Common Stock, No Par-Value, Issued 15 000 Shares	$270,000
Retained Earnings	90,000
Total	$360,000

Required: What is the cumulative effect on shareholders' equity of each of the following events, occurring in sequence:
1. The declaration of a 5 percent stock dividend on shares with a market value of $18
2. The distribution of the dividend
3. The acquisition of 200 shares of the company's own stock for $18 a share
4. The issuance of these shares for $20 a share
5. The declaration of a cash dividend of $1 per share
6. The payment of the dividend.

Supplementary Problem 10-5

The annual report of Williams Canada Ltd. states in a note to its financial statements, "The terms of certain note agreements restrict the payment of cash dividends on common stock. The amount of retained earnings not so restricted on December 31 was approximately $122,000."

Required:
1. Of what usefulness is the statement regarding the amount of restricted retained earnings? the amount not restricted?
2. The cash dividend distributions were $14,908; net income for the year was $84,010. Do the shareholders have the right to dividends up to $14,908? up to $122,000?
3. Total shareholders' equity at December 31 was $860,703. Does this indicate what the shareholders would receive in the event of liquidation? in the event of sale? Explain.

Supplementary Problem 10-6

Part A

Pike Corp. is incorporated under the CBCA and is authorized to issue an unlimited number of shares of $0.30 preferred stock and 30 000 common shares. Pike earned $40,000 during 19X7. The following shareholders' equity sections are for 19X6 and 19X7.

At December 31, 19X6			At December 31, 19X7		
Shareholders' Equity			*Shareholders' Equity*		
SHARE CAPITAL:			SHARE CAPITAL:		
Common Stock, No Par-Value			Common Stock, No Par-Value		
Authorized — 30 000 Shares			Authorized — 30 000 Shares		
Issued and Outstanding — 1000 Shares	$10,000		Issued and Outstanding — 5000 Shares	$10,000	
Retained Earnings	25,000		Retained Earnings	50,000	
Total Shareholders' Equity	$35,000		Total Shareholders' Equity	$60,000	

Required:
1. Explain what changes occurred in shareholders' equity during 19X7.

Part B

During 19X8, Pike had the following equity account transactions:
a. Issued 6000 preferred shares to a contractor and also paid him $30,000 for the construction of a building valued at $66,000
b. Issued 5000 common shares for $5,000 cash; used the proceeds to pay for new equipment
c. Established the following restrictions during the year:

Restriction for Plant Expansion	$15,000
Restriction for Lawsuit	8,000

d. Calculated net income after income tax (and after all other transactions) for the year at $30,000 (make the closing entry).

Required:
2. Prepare journal entries to record the 19X8 transactions.
3. Prepare the shareholders' equity section of Pike's balance sheet at December 31, 19X8.

Part C

During 19X9, Pike had the following equity account transactions:
a. Acquired for $11,000 cash, and cancelled, 1000 preferred shares
b. Settled the lawsuit for $5,000; the $8,000 restriction was returned to retained earnings
c. Paid a $3,000 cash dividend
d. Net income for the year after income tax and after all other transactions was $40,000 (make the closing entry)
e. Split the common stock 2 for 1.

Required:
4. Prepare journal entries to record the 19X9 transactions.
5. Prepare the shareholders' equity section of Pike's balance sheet at December 31, 19X9.

Decision Problems

Decision Problem 10-1

The Wayne-Kett Plastics Company Limited was incorporated in June 19X2. Preferred shares were issued in January, 19X4 for $100 per share and carried a $6 per share cumulative dividend up to January 1, 19X7. The last audited balance sheet showed the following accounts (summarized):

Balance Sheet
At June 30, 19X7

Cash	$ 22,000
Other Current Assets*	152,000
Temporary Investments	60,000
Fixed Assets	620,000
Intangible Assets	30,000
Other Assets	16,000
	$900,000
Current Liabilities	$ 76,000
Long-Term Loans	120,000
Preferred Shares (1000 shares), No Par-Value	100,000
Common Shares (30 000 Shares), No Par-Value	300,000
Retained Earnings	304,000
	$900,000

*Accounts Receivable $72,000
 Merchandise Inventory $80,000

The board of directors had not declared a dividend since incorporation; instead, the profits were used to expand the company. The board is planning to declare a year-end dividend (December, 19X7).

Required:
1. If the required dividend on the preferred and $0.50 per share on the common shares was to be paid in December, what amount would be required? Prepare the necessary journal entry (entries) for the declaration of such dividends.
2. If the dividends are paid in 19X7 as proposed in 1, above, the company expects to implement the following policy: retain 50 percent of net income for expansion and pay 50 percent in dividends. Determine the necessary 19X8 net income to implement the policy if a $1 per share dividend is to be paid on the common shares.

Decision Problem 10-2

Toward the end of the current year, the board of directors of the London Corporation Ltd. is presented with the following shareholders' equity section of the balance sheet.

Shareholders' Equity

SHARE CAPITAL:
Common Stock, No Par-Value
    Authorized — 5000 Shares
    Issued and Outstanding — 1500 Shares $48,000

Retained Earnings   24,000
    Total Shareholders' Equity $72,000

London Corporation Ltd. has paid dividends of $3.60 per share in each of the last five years. After careful consideration of the company's cash needs, the board of directors declared a stock dividend of 300 shares of common stock. Shortly after the stock dividend had been distributed and before the end of the year, the company declared a cash dividend of $3 per share.

James Brown owned 360 shares of London Corporation common stock, which he acquired several years ago. The market price of this stock when the stock dividend was declared was $60 per share.

Required: Answer the following questions, showing calculations.

1. What is Brown's share (in dollars) of the net assets of London Corporation Ltd. before the stock dividend action? What is his share after the stock dividend action? Explain why there is (or is not) any change as a result of the stock dividend.

2. What are the probable reasons why the market value of Brown's stock differs from the amount of net assets per share shown on the books?

3. Compare (with comment) the amount of cash dividends that Brown receives this year with dividends received in previous years.

4. On the day the common stock went ex-dividend (with respect to the stock dividend), its quoted market value fell from $60 to $50 per share. Did this represent a loss to Brown? Explain.

5. If the London Corporation Ltd. had announced that it would continue its regular cash dividend of $3.60 per share on the increased number of shares outstanding after the stock dividend, would you expect the market value of the common stock to react in any way different from the change described in 4, above? Why?

Debt Financing

A corporation often incurs debt in order to finance its operations. Bond issue is an important source of long-term capital.

1. What are bonds, and what rights are attached to bond certificates?
2. What are the impacts of different financing methods on the earnings per share of common shareholders?
3. What are the advantages of debt financing for common shareholders? the disadvantages?
4. What types of bonds are available to satisfy various borrowing situations and investor preferences?
5. Why would investors pay a premium for a corporate bond? a discount?
6. How are bonds and related premiums or discounts disclosed on the balance sheet?
7. What accounting procedures are used by accountants to handle bonds?
8. How is the amortization of bond premiums recorded in the books? of bond discounts?
9. What is the effective interest method of amortization, and how does it differ from the straight-line method?
10. What is the purpose of a bond sinking fund?

A.   The Decision To Issue Bonds

Bond
A debt security requiring the payment of a sum of money at some date in the future, together with periodic interest payments during the life of the bond.

Bond indenture
A legal document specifying the terms with which the issuing corporation will comply.

Trustee
An intermediary between a corporation issuing bonds and the bond-holders.

Corporations acquire long-term capital through the issue of shares and bonds. In Chapter 9, the acquisition of capital from share capital issues is discussed. This chapter discusses the acquisition of capital — that is, the financing of the corporation — through issues of bonds.

A **bond** is a debt security that requires a future payment of money, as well as periodic interest payments during its life. A contract called a **bond indenture** is prepared between the corporation and the future bondholders. It specifies the terms with which the corporation will comply. One of these terms may be a restriction on further borrowing by the corporation. A **trustee** is appointed to be an intermediary between the corporation and the bondholder.

Rights of Bondholders

Ownership of a bond certificate carries with it certain rights. These rights are printed on the actual certificate and vary among bond issues. The various characteristics applicable to bond issues are the subject of more advanced courses in finance and are not treated here. It is appropriate to point out, however, that individual bondholders always acquire two rights.

1. It is the right of the bondholder to receive the face value of the bond at a specified date in the future, referred to as the *maturity date*; and
2. It is the right of the bondholder to receive periodic interest payments, usually semi-annually, at a specified percent of the bond's face value.

Bond Authorization

Every corporation is legally required to follow a well-defined sequence in authorizing a bond issue. The bond issue is presented to the board of directors by management and must be approved by shareholders. Legal requirements must be complied with and disclosure is required in the financial statements of the corporation.

Shareholder approval is an important step because bondholders are creditors with a prior claim on the assets of the corporation if liquidation occurs. Further dividend distributions may be restricted during the life of the bonds, for which shareholder acceptance is necessary. These restrictions are usually reported to the reader of financial statements through note disclosure.

Recording the Bond Authorization

Assuming that Bluebeard Computer Corporation decides to issue bonds amounting to $30 million to finance its expansion, the amount of authorized bonds, their interest rate, and their maturity date can be shown in the accounts as follows:

General Journal
Memorandum

19X1

Jan. 1   Authorized to issue $30,000,000 of 12%
3-year bonds due January 1, 19X4.

General Ledger
Bonds Payable
(Due January 1, 19X4)

19X1

Jan. 1   Authorized to issue $30,000,000 of 12%
3-year bonds, dated January 1. 19X1

> Different general ledger accounts are opened for each type of bond approved. The caption used for the bonds payable should generally indicate the type of bonds involved in the issue.

Bond Issues in the Financial Statements

Each bond issue is disclosed separately in the financial statements because each issue may have different characteristics. The descriptive information disclosed to readers of financial statements includes the interest rate and maturity date of the bond issue. Also disclosed in a note are any restrictions imposed on the corporation's activities in the bond indenture and the assets pledged, if any.

The Bond Financing Decision

Cash Required in the Immediate and the Foreseeable Future

Most bond issues are sold in their entirety when market conditions are favourable. However, more bonds can be authorized in a particular bond issue than will be immediately issued (sold). Authorized bonds, like authorized share capital, can be issued whenever cash is required. They do not have to be issued immediately.

Important Terms of the Bonds

The interest rate of the bonds, their maturity date, and other important provisions — such as convertibility into share capital and restrictions on future dividend distributions of the corporation — are also considered. The success of a bond issue often depends on the proper combination of these and other similar features.

Assets of the Corporation To Be Pledged

The pledging of mortgageable assets is an important consideration for bondholders because it safeguards their investments. It is important to the corporation because the pledging of all these assets may restrict future borrowings. The total amount of authorized bonds is usually a fraction of the mortgageable assets, for example, 50 percent. The difference is the margin of safety to bondholders, since it permits the proceeds from the sale of these assets to shrink substantially but still permit reimbursement of bondholders should the need arise.

Other Methods of Raising Cash

Various methods of raising cash, such as issues of common or preferred stock, are also reviewed by management as alternatives to issuing bonds. There are many factors influencing management in its choice between the issue of bonds and the issue of share capital. One of the most important considerations is the potential effect of each of these financing methods on the present owners of the corporation, that is, the common shareholders. How would their earnings per share be affected?

Consider the example of Bluebeard Computer Corporation, which has 100 000 common shares outstanding, is a growth company, and is profitable. BCC requires $30 million in cash to finance its seventh new plant, complete with new equipment. Management is currently reviewing three financing options:

1. Issue 12-percent bonds, due in three years
2. Issue 300 000 preferred shares (dividend $8 per share)
3. Issue an additional 200 000 shares of common stock.

Erecting a new plant and placing it in operation should result in a net income of $6 million before interest financing expenses, if any, and income taxes (assumed to be 50 percent of net income and calculated after the deduction of interest expenses from net income).

Management has prepared the following analysis to compare and evaluate each financing option. Study the details of this schedule and consider which plan is most attractive to the common shareholders.

	Plan 1: Issue Bonds	Plan 2: Issue Preferred Shares	Plan 3: Issue Common Shares
Net Income before Interest and Income Taxes	$6,000,000	$6,000,000	$6,000,000
Less:			
Bond Interest Expense	3,600,000	-0-	-0-
Earnings before Taxes	$2,400,000	$6,000,000	$6,000,000
Less:			
Income Tax at 50 percent	1,200,000	3,000,000	3,000,000
	$1,200,000	$3,000,000	$3,000,000
Less:			
Preferred Dividends (300 000 × $8 per share)	-0-	2,400,000	-0-
Net Available to Common Shareholders	$1,200,000	$ 600,000	$3,000,000
Number of Common Shares Outstanding	100,000	100,000	300,000
Earnings per Share on Each Common Stock	$12	$6	$10

On study, it becomes clear that Plan 1, the issue of bonds, has several advantages for existing common shareholders.

Advantage 1:   Earnings per Share

If the additional long-term financing were acquired through the issue of bonds (Plan 1), the corporate earnings per share (EPS) on each common share would be $12. This EPS is greater than the EPS earned through financing with either preferred or additional common shares. On this basis alone, the issue of bonds is more financially attractive to existing common shareholders. However, there are other notable advantages to long-term financing with bonds.

Advantage 2: Control of the Corporation

Bondholders have no vote in the corporation. If common shares were issued there might be a loss of management control by existing shareholders because corporate ownership would be distributed over a larger number of shareholders. In the BCC case, outstanding common shares would increase from 100 000 to 300 000 shares.

Advantage 3: Income Tax Expenses

Interest financing expenses are deductible for income tax purposes. Dividend payments are distributions of retained earnings and are not deducted from net income and are not deductible for tax purposes. With a 50 percent income tax rate, the after-tax interest expense to the corporation is only 6 percent ($12\% \times 50\%$). By contrast, dividends to preferred shareholders would not be tax deductible.

Advantage 4: The Impact of Inflation

The corporation would receive $30 million with today's purchasing power. If the purchasing power of the dollar declines in three years, the $30 million borrowed would be repaid in dollars with a considerably lower purchasing power; an unrecognized gain thereby would accrue to the common shareholders.

Bond Financing Disadvantages

There are also some disadvantages in long-term financing with bonds that must be carefully reviewed by management and the board of directors. The most serious disadvantage is the possibility that the corporation might earn less than $6 million before interest expense and income taxes. The bond interest expense is a fixed amount. If net income were to fall below the $3,600,000 annual interest expense, one of the other plans might become more advantageous.

Another disadvantage is the fact that bonds have to be repaid at maturity, whether or not the corporation is financially able to do so, while shares do not have to be repaid. However, the company might issue a new series of bonds to replace the old ones, effectively postponing the payment.

Since the securities market and corporate net earnings remain uncertain, there is no mathematical formula to dictate what form of financing is appropriate for a given situation. The financing decision requires sound judgement, based on past experiences and projected future needs.

Real Life Example 11-1
The Financial Planning Formula

I've talked to any number of business owners over the years who felt buried under a mountain of debt. But none of them say whether they were making or losing money on the cash they borrowed, or precisely how their debt would have to change for it to reach a manageable level.

Fortunately, a simple but little-known formula shows how leverage, interest rates, and operating performance all affect a company's financial results. I use it to quickly combine planned operating performance with a planned debt structure to assess total financial performance.

Let's suppose that in a weak moment you agree to loan $100,000 to Leach, your brother-in-law, who has promised to pay you 60% interest. (What kind of business is Leach in? Don't ask.) And further suppose that because you have only $10,000, you make up the difference by borrowing $90,000 from the mob at a 40% interest rate.

At the end of the first year, Leach pays you $60,000 interest, as promised. After you pay the mob $36,000 your pretax earnings equal $24,000. Before taxes, therefore, you earn a return on equity (ROE) of 240% ($24,000 divided by $10,000). After taxes of 30%, your earnings come to $16,800, for an ROE of 168%.

The financial-planning formula in figure 1 shows that your ROE is equal to the sum of two rates (B) and (C) that is reduced by taxes (A). The rate labeled B is the ratio of your earnings before interest and taxes (EBIT) on assets (EOA). This is the return you earn on the fraction of your business financed with equity. In other words, if your company were debt free, this ratio would equal your total ROE before taxes. Suppose, for example, that you gave Leach $100,000 that you withdrew from savings. With no interest of your own to pay, your earnings before taxes would be $60,000 and your equity would be $100,000, yielding a 60% ROE before taxes, compared with the 240% (before taxes) in the illustration.

The rate labeled C shows your total pre-tax return on the fraction of your business financed with debt. This rate is the product of two calculations. One is the difference between the EOA and the interest rate, which I call the debtor's margin. This is the difference between what you earn on every dollar borrowed and what you pay. The other calculation is your debt divided by your equity. The higher this debt-to-equity ratio, the more it magnifies your debtor's margin when you calculate your ROE.

In the example, therefore, you're earning a debtor's margin of 20%, which the debt-to-equity ratio of 9 magnifies into a return of 180% of equity. Adding the 60% return on your own $10,000 gives you a before-tax ROE of 240%, and an aftertax ROE of 168% (figure 1, year one).

In the second year, Leach can pay you only 40% interest. When you plug these results into the formula you get an ROE of 28% (figure 1, year two).

Because Leach has paid you the same interest rate that you're paying the mob, you break even on every dollar you've borrowed — your debtor's martin equals zero. Your only profits come from the $4,000 return on your own $10,000. After taxes, you're left with a measly ROE of 28% or $2,800.

In the third year, Leach brings even worse news: he can pay only 10% interest. The magic of leverage turns your negative debtor's margin of 30% into a negative return of 270% on equity. With the positive return of 10% on your own investment, your ROE becomes a negative 260% before taxes and a negative 182% after taxes (figure 1, year three). So Leach has paid you $10,000; two guys from the mob are at your door to collect their $36,000; and you don't have the cash to pay them.

How to calculate your own ratios

When you apply the financial-planning formula to your own financial statements, you probably will discover at least two practical concerns. First, unlike the example, your own company has several sources of debt so you should calculate the financial benefit separately for each type of debt (figure 3).

The other problem is that you aren't sure what your EBIT is going to be. Or it may be that you've borrowed a lot of

Figure 1
Financial Planning Formula

$$\text{ROE} = \underbrace{(1 - \text{Tax Rate})}_{A} \times \left(\underbrace{\text{EOA}}_{B} + \underbrace{\frac{\text{Debt}}{\text{Equity}} \times (\text{EOA} - \text{Interest Rate})}_{C} \right)$$

YEAR ONE

$$\text{ROE} = (1 - 30\%) \times \left(60\% + \frac{\$90,000}{\$10,000} \times (60\% - 40\%) \right) = \textbf{168\%}$$

YEAR TWO

$$\text{ROE} = (1 - 30\%) \times \left(40\% + \frac{\$90,000}{\$10,000} \times (40\% - 40\%) \right) = \textbf{28\%}$$

YEAR THREE

$$\text{ROE} = (1 - 30\%) \times \left(10\% + \frac{\$90,000}{\$10,000} \times (10\% - 40\%) \right) = \textbf{-182\%}$$

Figure 2
Financial Benefit from the Use of Debt

$$\frac{\text{Debt}}{\text{Equity}} \times (\text{EOA} - \text{Interest Rate})$$

$$\frac{350,000}{\$150,000} \times (9\% - 4.57\%) = \textbf{10.33\%}$$

Figure 3
Financial Benefit by Type of Debt

Accounts payable:

$$\frac{\$200,000}{\$150,000} \times (9\% - 0\%) = \textbf{12.00\%}$$

Long-term debt:

$$\frac{\$100,000}{\$150,000} \times (9\% - 10\%) = \textbf{-0.67\%}$$

Short-term debt:

$$\frac{\$50,000}{\$150,000} \times (9\% - 12\%) = \textbf{-1.00\%}$$

The financial-planning formula, though little known, is a powerful tool.

money recently, which throws all your ratios off. What, then, are the correct values to use in the financial-planning formula?

During the year, I generally calculate the EOA by dividing the EBIT over the most recent 12 months (the "rolling EBIT") by the total assets on the current balance sheet. I also use the current or the average debt-to-equity ratio, and the stated interest rates for debt.

How to use the ratios in your company

• Pay attention to your EOA, your ratio of EBIT on assets — it's a critical measure of business performance. If your EOA is comfortably above your interest rate, you're making money on borrowed cash.

• Leverage multiplies good and bad performance. Raising your debt-to-equity ratio shifts your financial performance into a higher gear, which causes your business to move forward or backward more rapidly.

• Because your EOA rises in good times and falls in bad times, and because leverage magnifies the effect of these swings on your ROE, be sure your financial structure allows your company to hang on for the bad times.

• When you evaluate your ROE, balance your returns against your risks. For example, in the second year of Leach's loan I referred to a "measly" ROE of 28%, although many managers would be delighted with that return. But considering the huge risks this enterprise bears, that 28% return signaled failure.

• Watch your cash flow. Whatever your plans may tell you about an impressive return on equity, you won't survive unless you can pay lenders and vendors on time, and still have cash for payroll.

Source Reprinted with permission, *Inc. magazine* (December, 1988). Copyright © 1988 by Goldhirsh Group Inc., 38 Commercial Wharf, Boston, MA 02110.

B. Bond Characteristics and Terminology

Students sometimes encounter difficulty with the new terminology involved in accounting for bonds. Three main types of bond terminology can be identified. These are shown in Figure 11-1 and are discussed next.

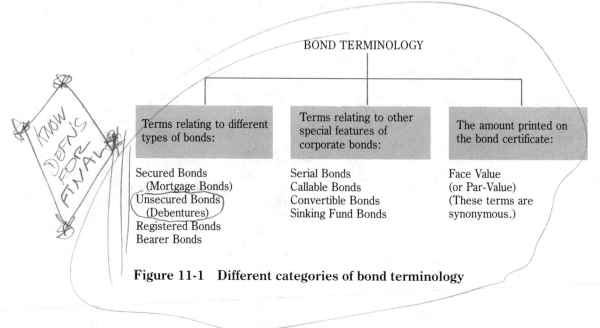

BOND TERMINOLOGY

Terms relating to different types of bonds:	Terms relating to other special features of corporate bonds:	The amount printed on the bond certificate:
Secured Bonds (Mortgage Bonds) Unsecured Bonds (Debentures) Registered Bonds Bearer Bonds	Serial Bonds Callable Bonds Convertible Bonds Sinking Fund Bonds	Face Value (or Par-Value) (These terms are synonymous.)

Figure 11-1   Different categories of bond terminology

Classification of Bonds

Each corporation issuing bonds has unique financing needs and attempts to satisfy various borrowing situations and investor preferences. Many types of bonds have been created to meet these varying needs. Some of the common types are described here.

Bonds Can Be Secured or Unsecured

Secured bonds
A bond issue backed by mortgageable assets of the corporation; also referred to as *mortgage bonds*.

Secured bonds are backed by mortgageable assets of the corporation. These mortgageable assets are pledged as security for the bonds, and these secured bonds are consequently referred to as *mortgage bonds.*

Unsecured bondholders are ordinary creditors of the corporation and **unsecured bonds** are secured only by the future financial success of the corporation. Such bonds are commonly referred to as *debentures*. These debenture bonds usually command a higher interest rate because of the added risk for investors.

Unsecured bonds
A bond issue backed by the future financial success of the corporation; also referred to as *debentures*.

Bonds Can Be Registered or Bearer Bonds

Registered bonds require the name and address of the owner to be recorded by the corporation or its trustee.

The title to bearer bonds passes on delivery of the bonds. Payment of interest is made when the bearer clips coupons attached to the bond and presents them to the bank.

Special Features of Bonds

Special features can be attached to bonds in order to make them more attractive to investors, as discussed next.

Varying Maturity Dates

Serial bond
A bond issue with a special feature whereby parts of the bond issue mature on one date and other parts mature on other dates.

When **serial bonds** are issued, the bonds have differing **maturity dates**, as indicated on the bond contract. Investors are able to choose bonds with a term that agrees with their investment plans. For example, in a $30 million serial bond issue, $10 million-worth of the bonds may mature each year for three years.

Maturity date
The date specified for repayment.

The issue of bonds with a **call provision** permits the issuing corporation to redeem, or call, the bonds before their maturity date. The bond indenture usually indicates the price at which bonds are callable. Borrowers are thereby protected in the event that market interest rates decline below the bond contract interest rate. In such an event, the higher interest rate bonds can be called to be replaced by bonds bearing a lower interest rate.

Call provision
A bond feature that permits the early redemption of the bond at a specified price, usually above face value.

Conversion Privilege

Bonds with a conversion privilege are called **convertible bonds**; they allow the bondholder to exchange his/her bonds for a specified amount of the corporation's share capital. This feature permits the bondholder to enjoy the security of being a creditor, while having the option of becoming a shareholder if the corporation is successful.

Convertible bond
A bond that may be exchanged for common stock under certain specified conditions.

Sinking Fund Requirement

The corporation is required to deposit funds at regular intervals, usually with a trustee, when **sinking fund** bonds are issued. This feature ensures the availability of adequate cash for the redemption of the bonds at maturity.

Sinking fund
A special fund into which assets are transferred in order to pay bonds at their maturity date; the fund is called "sinking" because the transferred assets are tied up or "sunk", and cannot be used for any purpose other than the redemption of the bonds.

Restriction of Dividends

The corporation issuing bonds is required to restrict its retained earnings, thereby limiting the amount of dividends that can be paid from assets represented by retained earnings. The creation of such a restriction is discussed in Chapter 10.

Investors look at the interest rates of bonds, but in the final analysis, a bond is only as good as the quality of the assets, if any, that are pledged as its security. The other provisions in a bond contract are of limited or no value if the issuing corporation is in financial difficulties. A corporation in such difficulties may not be able to sell its bonds, regardless of the attractive provisions attached to them.

Face Value

Face value (of bonds)
The amount to be paid at the maturity date of a bond, which is printed on a bond certificate; also referred to as *par-value* of the bond.

Each bond has an amount printed on the face of the bond certificate. This is called the **face value** of the bond; it is also commonly referred to as the *par-value* of the bond. When the cash received is the same as a bond's face value, the bond is said to be issued *at par*. A common face value of bonds is $1,000, although bonds of other denominations exist. A sale of a $1,000 bond for $1,000 is referred to as a sale at its par-value. A $1,000 bond is sold at a **premium** when it is sold for more than its face value. If the bond is sold for less than $1,000, then the bond has been sold at a **discount**.

Premium
The excess of the amount received by the issuer over the face value of the bond; usually results when the bond interest rate is higher than the market interest rate.

Discount
The excess of the face value of a bond over the amount received by the issuer; usually results when the bond interest rate is lower than the market interest rate.

Market interest rate
The percentage per time period paid on the open market for the use of money.

With a face value of $1,000, a $30 million bond issue can be divided into 30 000 bonds. This number permits a large number of individuals and institutions to participate in corporate financing. As pointed out earlier, the opportunity to raise large amounts of capital is one of the important advantages of the corporate form of organization.

Interest paid to bondholders is *always* calculated on the face value of the bond — the contract amount — regardless of whether the bonds are issued at par, at a premium, or at a discount. For example, a $1,000 bond with a contract interest rate of 12 percent pays the following total annual interest:

$$\$1,000 \times 12\% = \$120 \text{ annual interest.}$$

This interest is usually paid semi-annually, that is, $60 every six months.

Why would investors pay a premium for a corporate bond? Why would a corporation sell its bonds at a discount? The answer to these questions lies in the relationship between the bond contract interest rate and the prevailing **market interest rate**. Figure 11-2 illustrates the relationship between the bond contract interest rate and the prevailing market interest rate.

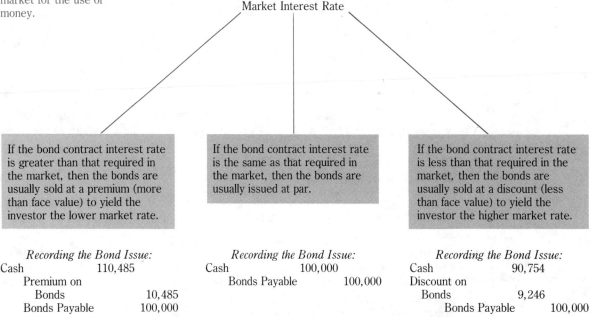

Figure 11-2   **Relationship between bond contract interest rate and market interest rate**

The Price of a Bond

The actual selling price of a bond is related to the future cash flows associated with the bond:

1. A single amount, the face value, to be paid at maturity
2. Semi-annual interest payments to be paid during the life of the bond.

These future cash flows are a *future value*; that is, they include an interest component. This interest component can be removed through a *present value* calculation. The selling price of a bond is this present value of all future cash flows resulting from that bond. (For a further discussion of present value, see Appendix 1 of this chapter.) Consider Bluebeard's issue of 12-percent, $100,000-face value, three-year bonds. In this example, interest is payable semi-annually each June 30 and December 31 for three years.

1. The $100,000 single amount is to be paid at the end of three years; this is the face value of the bonds. It is a future value, because it will not be redeemed for that full amount until 3 years have passed.
2. The $6,000 semi-annual interest payments are to be paid to bondholders for 6 periods during the 3-year bond life ($100,000 face value bonds × 12% annual interest = $12,000 interest per year; the amount paid every semi-annual period is calculated at $6,000). The individual payments are referred to as an annuity. The $6,000 also constitutes a future value. The selling price of the bonds will be a *discounted* amount calculated from the bond's future value.

The use of mathematical tables facilitates the discounting of future cash flows into present value dollars. The prevailing market rate of interest, recalculated into period rates (half the yearly rate, in this example), is used in the calculations that follow. The present value tables are reproduced in Appendix 1.

Calculating Present Value

In the following three scenarios, present-value calculations are used to establish the issue price of the bonds. This issue price is usually stated as a percentage of face value. An issue at 100 means 100 percent of face value; an issue at 110 means 110 percent of face value; and an issue at 90 means 90 percent of face value. Regardless of the issue price, interest is always paid as a percentage of face value.

Scenario 1: The Bond Contract Interest Rate (12%) Is the Same as the Market Interest Rate (12%)

In this case, the bonds are sold at face value. An investor is willing to pay face value because the present value of the future cash flow is $100,000.

1. The $100,000 bond face value is due at the end of six periods.
   The present value of this cash flow is calculated as
   $100,000 × 0.704961 (Table A in Appendix 1) $ 70,496 (rounded)
2. The semi-annual $6,000 interest is to be received for six periods in total. The present value of this cash flow is calculated as
   $6,000 × 4.917324 (Table B in Appendix 1)   29,504 (rounded)

Total present value of these bonds is $100,000

When the bond contract interest rate is the same as the market interest rate, the present value of all cash flows is the same as the bond's face value, other things — such as risk or inflation — being equal.

In actual practice, however, the market interest rate is seldom the same as the bond contract interest rate; also some other factor (risk or inflation) often creates an impact. Scenarios 2 and 3 deal with this situation.

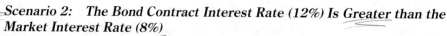

Scenario 2: The Bond Contract Interest Rate (12%) Is Greater than the Market Interest Rate (8%)

Here the bonds are sold at a premium. An investor is willing to pay more than face value because the present value of the future cash flow amounts to $110,485.

1. The $100,000 bond face value is due at the end of six periods. The present value of this cash flow is calculated as
$100,000 × 0.790315 (Table A in Appendix 1) $ 79,032 (rounded)

2. The semi-annual $6,000 interest is to be received for six periods in total. The present value of this cash flow is calculated as $6,000 × 5.242137 (Table B in Appendix 1) 31,453 (rounded)

Total present value of these bonds is $110,485

Therefore, when the bond contract interest rate is greater than the market interest rate, the present value of all cash flows is greater than the face value of the bonds, other things being equal. This excess amount, calculated as $10,485 in this example, is considered to be a premium.

Scenario 3: The Bond Contract Interest Rate (12%) Is Less than the Market Interest Rate (16%)

In this case, the bonds are sold at a discount. An investor will pay less than face value because the present value of future cash flow amounts to only $90,754.

1. The $100,000 bond face value is due at the end of six periods. The present value of this cash flow is calculated as
$100,000 × 0.630170 (Table A in Appendix 1) $ 63,017

2. The semi-annual $6,000 interest is to be received for six periods in total. The present value of this cash flow is calculated as
$6,000 × 4.622880 (Table B in Appendix 1) 27,737 (rounded)

Total present value of these bonds is $90,754

Therefore, when the bond contract interest rate is less than the market interest rate, the present value of all cash flows is less than the face value of the bonds, other things being equal. This difference, calculated as $9,246 ($100,000 − $90,754) in this example, is considered to be a discount.

C.　The Bond Accounting Process

Bond accounting often appears complex to students. They may be daunted by the interplay of different variables, such as the issue of bonds between interest dates, interest dates that do not coincide with the year-end of the corporation, and the calculation of bond premiums or discounts.

Interest on a Bond

Interest begins to accumulate from the previous interest payment date of the bond and is usually paid semi-annually, regardless of when the bond is actually sold. As noted earlier, interest paid to bondholders is *always* calculated on the face value of the bond, regardless of whether the bonds are issued at par, at a premium, or at a discount. For example, a $100,000 bond issue with an interest rate of 12 percent pays the following total annual interest:

$$\$100,000 \times 12\% = \$12,000 \text{ annual interest.}$$

This interest is usually paid semi-annually, that is, $6,000 every six months. Individual bondholders would receive $6,000 each semi-annually.

In this text, it is recommended that bond premium and discount be amortized each time bond interest expense is recorded. The recording of amortization emphasizes that it is an adjustment of bond interest expense. The interest payments for the first year of BCC's $100,000 bond issue, together with the appropriate amortization entry, are recorded below.

Payment of Interest				*Amortization of Premium*				*Amortization of Discount*		
Jun. 30	Bond Interest Expense	6,000		Bond Premium	1,747.50			Bond Interest Expense	1,541	
	Cash		6,000	Bond Interest Expense		1,747.50		Bond Discount		1,541
	To record semi-annual bond interest.			To record amortization of bond premium.				To record amortization of bond discount.		
Dec. 31	Bond Interest Expense	6,000		Bond Premium	1,747.50			Bond Interest Expense	1,541	
	Cash		6,000	Bond Interest Expense		1,747.50		Bond Discount		1,541
	To record semi-annual bond interest.			To record amortization of bond premium.				To record amortization of bond discount.		

Similar entries are made each June 30 and December 31 until the bonds are retired in three years. The bond interest is entered in a separate Bond Interest Expense account, because it is usually a large amount. In this example, the interest payment date, December 31, is also the corporation's year-end. Therefore, no adjustment for interest expense is required at year-end. When the interest payment date does not coincide with the year-end, an adjusting journal entry is required at December 31 for the interest owing and any amortization required at that date. The credit part of the entry is made to Bond Interest Payable. At maturity, the bonds are retired by the payment of cash to bondholders.

19X4			
Jan. 1	Bonds Payable	100,000	
	Cash		100,000
	To record retirement of bonds.		

Remember that, before the bonds are retired, the final interest payment and applicable amortization has to be recorded.

Amortization

Amortization is essentially an adjusting entry for bonds sold at a discount or at a premium. This occurs in order to conform to the matching principle of GAAP. If a bond is sold at a discount, accrued interest expense will exceed interest payments. An amount is transferred from bond discount to interest expense. On the other hand, if a bond is sold at a premium, accrued interest expense will be less than interest payments. This principle will become more clear as you work through the calculations presented in this section.

The amortization is made over the remaining life of the bonds from the date of sale. If the bonds are sold on January 1, the amortization at June 30 is calculated as follows:

Amortization of a Premium:			*Amortization of a Discount:*	
Premium is	$10,485.00 (a)		Discount is	$9,246.00 (a)
Number of 6 month interest periods	6 (b)		Number of 6 month interest periods	6 (b)
Calculation:			*Calculation:*	
(a ÷ b)			(a ÷ b)	
($10,485 ÷ 6) =	$1,747.50		($9,246 ÷ 6) =	$1,541.00

Premium Amortization Adjusting Entry:			*Discount Amortization Adjusting Entry:*	
Bond Premium	X		Bond Interest Expense	X
Bond Interest Expense	X		Bond Discount	X

Amortization of premium reduces bond interest expense.

Amortization of discount increases bond interest expense.

Note that the amortization of the premium requires a debit to Bond Premium in order to decrease the $10,485.00 premium balance. The credit is made to Bond Interest Expense and thereby reduces the $6,000 interest expense recorded.

The credit required to amortize Bond Discount results in a debit to Bond Interest Expense. The amortization represents, therefore, an additional interest expense over the 12 percent interest rate.

These ledger accounts illustrate this reduction.

These ledger accounts illustrate this increase.

Premium on Bonds		Bond Interest Expense		Discount on Bonds		Bond Interest Expense	
	10,485.00	6,000.00	→1,747.50	9,246.00		6,000.00	
1,747.50◄		6,000.00			1,541.00◄	→1,541.00	
1,747.50◄			→1,747.50		1,541.00◄	6,000.00	
3,495.00	10,485.00	12,000.00	3,495.00	9,246.00	3,082.00	→1,541.00	
	6,990.00	8,505.00		6,164.00		15,082.00	

The premium is reduced each interest period by amortization.

Amortization of a bond premium results in a decrease of bond interest expense.

The discount is reduced each interest period by amortization.

Amortization of a bond discount results in an increase of bond interest expense.

Amortizing Premiums and Discounts Using the Straight-Line Method

Where a bond premium or discount results from a bond issue, the amount of the premium or discount can be amortized in equal amounts over the life of the bond remaining from its date of sale, as shown in Figure 11-3. This method is in accordance with the straight-line method of recording of amortization. An alternative, more accurate method of amortization is discussed in Appendix 2 of this chapter.

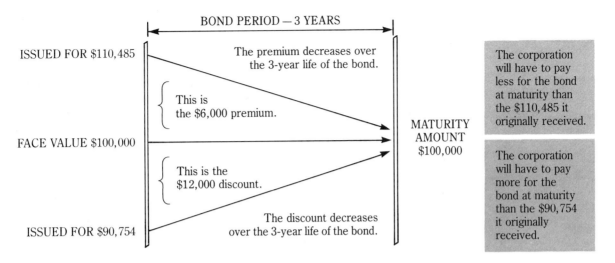

Figure 11-3   Straight-line amortization of bond premium or discount over the life of the bond issue

What Is the Impact of Premium Amortization on Interest Expense?

It is sound accounting practice to allocate part of the premium to each semi-annual interest payment period. The effect of amortizing the premium of each interest payment date during the three years is shown in Figure 11-4. Study the effect of premium amortization (column D) on interest expense (column B).

Issue of $100,000 Bonds Payable for $110,485
Amortization Table

		A	B	C	D	E
						(A − D)
		Jan. 1	(C − D)	Actual	(C − B)	Dec. 31
	Six-	Bond	Periodic	Cash	Periodic	Bond
	Month	Carrying	Interest	Interest	Premium	Carrying
Year	Period	Value	Expense	Paid	Amortization	Value
1	1	$110,485.00	$ 4,252.50	$ 6,000.00	$ 1,747.50	$108,737.50
	2	108,737.50	4,252.50	6,000.00	1,747.50	106,990.00
2	3	106,999.00	4,252.50	6,000.00	1,747.50	105,242.50
	4	105,242.50	4,252.50	6,000.00	1,747.50	103,495.00
3	5	103,495.00	4,252.50	6,000.00	1,747.50	101,747.50
	6	101,747.50	4,252.50	6,000.00	1,747.50	100,000.00
			$25,515.00	$36,000.00	$10,485.00	

The interest expense of the corporation has been reduced by the premium amortization.

Figure 11-4   Effect of straight-line amortization of bond premium at each interest payment date

The total interest expense over the life of the bonds (column C) consists of $36,000 of interest less the $10,485 amortization of the premium (the total of column D). The $10,485 premium received when the bond was sold represents a reduction of the corporation's bond interest expense during each year of the bond's life. Interest actually paid to bondholders is $36,000. The interest expense to BCC is $25,515. This difference of $10,485 results from the favourable bond interest rate in relation to the prevailing market interest rate. In other words, receiving $110,485 on January 1, 19X1 is to the corporation's benefit as it only has to repay $100,000 on January 1, 19X4. This benefit is reflected in a reduced net annual interest expense during the life of the bonds.

Therefore, accountants record the decrease in bond interest expense as an amortization of the premium. The interest expense of $8,505 is therefore lower than the 12 percent bond interest expense of $12,000. Accordingly, whenever a corporation sells a bond for more than its face value, the corporation's total cost of borrowing is decreased.

What Is the Impact of Discount Amortization on Interest Expense?

The discount is amortized through the straight-line method by equal periodic debits to Bond Interest Expense over the three-year life of the bonds. This amortization is recorded every time Bond Interest Expense is entered in the books. The effect of amortizing the discount at each interest payment date during the three years is shown in Figure 11-5. Study the effect of discount amortization on interest expense.

Issue of $100,000 Bonds Payable for $90,754
Amortization Table

Year	Six-Month Period	A Jan. 1 Bond Carrying Value	B (C + D) Periodic Interest Expense	C Actual Cash Interest Paid	D (B − C) Periodic Discount Amortization	E (A − D) Dec. 31 Bond Carrying Value
1	1	$90,754	$ 7,541	$ 6,000	$1,541	$ 92,295
	2	92,295	7,541	6,000	1,541	93,836
2	3	93,836	7,541	6,000	1,541	95,377
	4	95,377	7,541	6,000	1,541	96,918
3	5	96,918	7,541	6,000	1,541	98,459
	6	98,459	7,541	6,000	1,541	100,000
			$45,246	$36,000	$9,246	

The interest expense of the corporation has been increased by the discount amortization.

Figure 11-5   Effect of straight-line amortization of bond discount at each interest payment date

The total interest expense over the life of BCC's bonds consists of $36,000 interest plus the $9,246 amortization of discount. The discount on the bond issue represents an increase of the corporation's bond interest expense during each year of the bond's life. Interest actually paid to bondholders is $36,000. However, the interest expense to the corporation is actually $45,246. The additional $9,246 compensates investors for the unfavourable bond interest rate in relation to the prevailing market interest rate. In other words, receiving only $90,754 on January 1, 19X1 is an additional cost to the corporation since it must repay $100,000 on January 1, 19X4. This cost is reflected in the increased net annual interest expense during the life of the bonds.

Therefore, in the case of bonds issued at a discount, the interest rate consists of the 12 percent bond rate plus the amortized bond discount. It is therefore higher than the bond interest rate. Thus, whenever a corporation sells a bond for less than its face value, its total cost of borrowing is increased because of discount amortization.

Bond Redemption

The redemption, or retirement, of bonds at their maturity date requires a cash payment to bondholders; the cash payment is the face value of the bonds. The accounting entry for the retirement of BCC's bonds on January 1, 19X4 follows.

19X4			
Jan. 1	Bonds Payable	100,000	
	Cash		100,000

A bond issue can also be retired in whole, or in part, before its maturity date. There are several different possibilities:
1. The bonds can be repurchased on the open market if the purchase is financially advantageous to the issuer.
2. A call provision is sometimes included in a bond indenture permitting early redemption at a specified price, usually higher than face value. The issuer may decide to exercise this call provision if it is financially advantageous.
3. The bondholder may be able to exercise a conversion privilege if one was provided for in the bond indenture; in this case, the bonds can be converted into no par-value shares at the option of the bondholder. The conversion date can be an interest payment date if specified as such in the bond indenture, in order to simplify the accounting required in a conversion.

Whenever bonds are retired before the maturity date, the amount payable to bondholders is the face amount of the bonds or the amount required by a call provision. Any unamortized premium or discount must be removed from the accounts. The accounting required for BCC's January 1, 19X1 issue of $100,000 face value 12 percent bonds has been illustrated. Suppose that $50,000 face value bonds are redeemed at 102 on December 31, 19X1, when the account balances are as follows:

19X1	Bonds Payable		Premium on Bonds	
Jan. 1		100,000		10,485
Jun. 30			1,747.50	
Dec. 31			1,747.50	
			3,495.00	10,485
				6,990

Real Life Example 11-2

LBOs, Junk Bonds, and Poison Pills

A few small words with big implications, some of which are gigantic, describing corporate business deals have been added to our vocabulary in recent years: leveraged buyouts (LBOs), junk bonds and poison pills.

In a leveraged buyout, the buyer (think of this party as the hunter) borrows money to purchase a company, then pays off the debt by doing one or all of the following:

- Diverting the company's revenue.
- Cutting its operating costs.
- Selling off part of it.
- Having it issue junk bonds.

Often, the management of the company taken over (the hunted) will resist such outside interference by devising ingenious defences known as poison pills to at least discourage, if not thwart, such unfriendly, unwelcome and, hence, hostile takeovers.

Buying and selling companies is part and parcel of capitalism — always has been. So what's new about it? Plenty.

For starters, look at the hunter's tactics in paying off the newly created debt: they don't include plans to increase profits by increasing revenues but by lowering operating costs. Second, that increase thus achieved will accrue mostly to the holders of the newly created debt — that is, to the junk bondholders — rather than to the owners of the outstanding shares.

Two fundamental questions among many concerning LBOs beg to be asked: Why is it happening and what are the future implications to corporations, investors and the economy? Bear with me, I will answer those questions, but first, let's look at some of the nitty-gritty details and hear from some of the key players.

According to takeover experts, buyers invest about 10% of the purchase price, and use the proceeds from asset sales and cash flow to pay off their transaction debt. It's been estimated that $25 billion is stockpiled in the hands of leveraged buyout firms, that could, without much trouble, finance up to $250 billion worth of takeovers.

A few of the more spectacular recent LBOs are RJR Nabisco (more than $20 billion), originated by management and now contested by a professional LBO firm and Proctor and Gamble; a proposal by Philip Morris to take over Kraft for $11.5 billion; and the recently completed takeover of Allied Stores ($6.5 billion) by Canada's Campeau Corporation.

John Phelan, chairman of the New York Stock Exchange, is "greatly concerned" that the current wave of billion-dollar company buyouts has unleashed a flood of new debt that poses risks to corporate America. And Alan Greenspan, chairman of the Federal Reserve Board, echoes his concern in terms of how, in a recession, these loans will affect banks and corporations.

That those are not idle worries is illustrated by Revco, the 2,000-store American drug chain that declared bankruptcy

---

Since $50,000 of the bonds are redeemed, only half of the $6,990 premium balance ($3,495) is applicable to the redeemed bonds.

The retirement by repurchase or by conversion would be recorded as follows:

Retirement by Repurchase:				*Retirement by Conversion:*		
Bonds Payable	50,000			Bonds Payable	50,000	
Premium on Bonds	3,495			Premium on Bonds	3,495	
Gain on Bond Retirement		2,495		Common Stock		53,495
Cash		51,000				

In this case, retirement results in a gain; under different circumstances, a loss may result.

In this case, the amount of common stock is usually calculated as the carrying value of the bonds redeemed. No gain or loss is recorded.

in July 1988, only 19 months after going private in a $1.3 billion leveraged buyout. The bankruptcy was largely attributed to its huge debt load.

In contrast, David Ruder, chairman of the Securities and Exchange Commission, says he sees no problem with the current US wave of leveraged buyouts. Even if some companies fail, others, he says, may be able to carry a higher debt load due to streamlining and cost cutting.

The typical interest yield on junk bonds is 14%. A junk bond is offered to the public by the successful buyer of an LBO with a view to recouping some of the original investment. The company taken over pays the interest out of its original cash flow, which is augmented by cost reductions resulting from plant or store closings, staff attrition and asset sales. (In the recent movie "Wall Street," a $75 million surplus in the employee pension fund was almost bagged by the star hunter of the movie and of Wall Street.)

At the time of writing, Robert Campeau had to twice restructure his junk bond offering, and ended up paying 16% interest on two of his three offerings. That the bonds still sold at 16% shows that investors will buy "junk" even at higher risks.

Many economists believe it will take a recession that reduces corporate profits, combined with higher interest rates, to sort out the boys from the men. Until then, the jury is still out on the hunters, the hunted and the junk buyer.

In Canada, LBOs are still relatively scarce, but that hasn't stopped Inco, a Canadian incorporated company (approximately 50% American owned) from introducing Canada's first sugar-coated poison pill. The poison part is the stipulation that shareholders will be allowed to buy Inco shares at 50% of the market price, provided an outsider accumulates more than one-fifth of the shares. The sugar part is a special dividend of $10 (US) per share.

The "protection" from outsiders reminds me of feudal lords defending their castles from invaders and plunderers. To snuff out any further attraction, the company intends to finance the special dividend by borrowing $500 million (US) from banks, $265 million (US) in subordinated debentures and, surprise, $500 million (US) from cash flow. So what's really happening? The textbook theory that corporations grow and reward risk-taking shareholders is obsolete for large, mature companies, though it's still valid for vibrant small and medium-sized ones. For the largest, money is made by dismantling and restructuring, and the beneficiaries are financial rather than corporate entrepreneurs. LBOs increase corporate and investor risk and decrease shareholder profit. Furthermore, the economy as a whole is more vulnerable in a recession if large corporations go under due to their inability to meet debt obligations rather than their ability to produce efficiently.

Taken together the LBO, junk bond, poison-pill scene is a sad commentary on the state of corporate management in a capitalist society. Management is supposed to maximize profits for shareholders by running the corporation efficiently, and that includes the fair treatment of its employees. Instead, we see corporations "streamlined" in order to pay usurious interest to junk bond holders. Even worse, management defends inefficient enterprises with poison pills rather than healthy policies. This is no way to treat a shareholder, or a capitalist society, unless it just doesn't matter to anyone any more.

Source   Reprinted with permission, from the December 1988 issue of *CA Magazine*, published by the Canadian Institute of Chartered Accountants, Toronto, Canada.

The BCC retirement occurred on an interest payment date, December 31, 19X1; interest and premium amortization were already recorded. If the retirement had occurred between interest payment dates, then accrued interest also would be paid to the bondholders and amortization would be recorded in the issuer's books.

In addition to retirement by repurchase or conversion of bonds, it is also possible for an existing bond issue to be replaced by a new issue, usually at a lower interest rate; this is referred to as **refunding**. Outstanding bonds can also be repurchased by assets accumulated in a bond sinking fund.

Refunding
The replacing of one bond issue by a new bond issue.

Balance Sheet Presentation

Bonds payable are classified as long-term liabilities for disclosure on the balance sheet.

LONG-TERM LIABILITIES:
Bonds Payable
    Authorized — $30,000,000, 12%, Due 19X4
    Issued — $100,000

When the bonds become payable within one year from the balance sheet date, then they are classified on the balance sheet as a current liability (*CICA Handbook*, section 3210.03).

The balance of unamortized discount can be classified as a deferred charge on the assets' side of the balance sheet (*CICA Handbook*, section 3070.02). The balance of unamortized premium can be shown as a deferred credit on the liabilities side of the balance sheet. The amount amortized during the year should also be disclosed on the financial statements.

	Assets			*Liabilities*	
Deferred Charge			Deferred Credit		
Discount on Bonds	$9,246		Premium on Bonds	$10,485	

An acceptable alternative method advocated in the United States results in the balance of unamortized premium being added to the bonds payable balance; unamortized discount is deducted from the balance of bonds payable. This method of balance sheet disclosure is illustrated below.

LONG-TERM LIABILITIES:
  Bonds Payable
    Authorized — $30,000,000,
    12%, Due 19X4
    Issued — $100,000
    Less: Discount on Bonds ($9,246)
        $ 90,754

LONG-TERM LIABILITIES:
  Bonds Payable
    Authorized — $30,000,000,
    12%, Due 19X4
    Issued — $100,000
    Add: Premium on Bonds $10,485
        $110,485

Operation of a Bond Sinking Fund

The fund set up to retire bonds is called a sinking fund because the assets in the fund are tied up or "sunk". The assets in the sinking fund cannot be used for any purpose other than the redemption of the bonds at maturity, or before maturity, if permitted in the bond indenture.

There are three phases in the operation of a bond sinking fund:
1. The contributions to the fund
2. The earnings of the assets in the fund
3. The use of assets in the funds to retire bonds payable.

Each of these phases is discussed in this section, using the data of Bluebeard Computer Corporation. Assume that its bonds contain a sinking fund feature. Bonds amounting to $100,000 are issued on the authorization date, January 1, 19X1, and are due in three years. The bond indenture requires an annual contribution to the sinking fund at the end of each of the three years to provide for the retirement of the bonds at maturity. Assets in the sinking fund are guaranteed by the trustee to earn 10 percent annually.

The required annual contributions to the sinking fund, together with anticipated compound interest on the amount deposited, are assumed to equal the $100,000 needed

Annuity
A series of equal periodic deposits made at equal time intervals; in the case of a bond sinking fund, these deposits are made to a trustee.

to retire the bonds at the end of three years. If equal amounts, each called an **annuity**, are to be deposited with the trustee and the fund is to earn 10 percent compounded annually, the annual deposit required can be calculated using an annuity table.

The following schedule accumulates the equal annual contributions and the 10 percent annual revenue earned by the assets in the sinking fund.

	Annual Contributions	10% Annual Revenue	Annual Total	Fund Balance
Dec. 31				
19X1	$30,211	-0-	$30,211	$ 30,211
19X2	30,211	(10% × $30,211 =) $3,021	33,232	63,443
19X3	30,211	(10% × $63,433 =) $6,346*	36,557	100,000

*Increased to adjust the fund balance to $100,000.

The annual contributions to the fund and earnings of the assets in the fund are recorded, using 19X2 amounts from this schedule.

LONG-TERM INVESTMENT

B/S

Recording Annual Contribution:

Bond Sinking Fund	30,211	
Cash		30,211

The annual contribution is invested by the trustee.

I/S

Recording Earnings of the Fund:

Bond Sinking Fund	3,021	
Sinking Fund Revenue		3,021

The earnings remain in the fund but are recorded in the books of the corporation.

The bond sinking fund is reported on the balance sheet as a long-term investment. The bond sinking fund revenue is reported on the income statement as "Other Income".

When Bluebeard management receives notice from its trustee that the bonds have been retired on January 1, 19X4, the following entry is made to remove the bond liability from BCC's books.

19X4			
Jan. 1	Bonds Payable	100,000	
	Bonds Sinking Fund		100,000
	To record the retirement of bonds by the trustee.		

This entry eliminates both the Bonds Payable and Bond Sinking Fund accounts.

In this example, the trustee guaranteed a 10 percent return on investments in the sinking fund and an assumption has been made that only 10 percent was earned by the fund. In actual practice, it is possible that a balance of cash may still remain in the fund. The trustee returns any such balance to the corporation, which records the receipt of cash as follows:

19X4			
Jan. 1	Cash	XX	
	Bond Sinking Fund		XX
	To record receipt of balance in sinking fund.		

Sale of Bonds between Interest Dates

Not all bonds are issued on the date when interest begins to accumulate on the bond. For example, consider the sale of an additional $50,000-worth of BCC bonds on April 1, 19X1. Interest began to accumulate on January 1 and, regardless of the date on which the bond was issued, a six-month interest payment is made to the bondholder on June 30. This payment is owing to the bondholder even though the bond has been held for only three months, from April 1 to June 30. This $50,000-worth of bonds is said to be sold at *par plus accrued interest*. The bonds could also have been sold at a premium or a discount and accrued interest. See Figure 11-6.

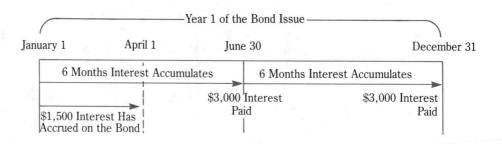

Figure 11-6 Accrued interest on bond issue

Accrued Interest on a Bond

Interest begins to accumulate from the previous interest payment date of the bond and is usually paid semi-annually, regardless of when the bond is actually sold. If the bond is sold between interest dates, the purchaser pays the accrued interest at the date of purchase.

In this case, $1,500 of interest has accrued on the bond from January 1 to April 1. When the bond is sold between interest dates specified in the bond indenture, it is accepted practice for the purchaser to pay accrued interest at the date of purchase, April 1. This amount, $1,500, is returned to the investor by the corporation at the next interest date, which in this case is June 30.

Assuming reversing entries are not used, the corporation records the receipt of the accrued interest as a liability, because this amount is owing to the bondholders:

A liability account is created for the accrued interest, because this amount is owing to the bondholder.

Recording the Bond Issue:

Cash	51,500	
Bond Interest Payable		1,500
Bond Payable		50,000

The investor pays the issue price of the bonds plus accrued interest.

Payment of Interest:

Bond Interest Expense	1,500	
Bond Interest Payable	1,500	
Cash		3,000

The interest payment returns the accrued interest to the bondholder (previously recorded as a liability) plus the interest earned since he/she purchased the bond.

The regular semi-annual interest payment is made on June 30. For this example, the above interest calculation applies only to the $50,000 bonds issued on April 1 and excludes interest on the bonds sold January 1.

In bond transactions, the investor pays the issue price of the bonds plus an amount for accrued interest. In turn, the first interest payment is for one full interest period — six months — thereby returning to the purchaser the accrued interest paid plus the interest earned from the date of purchase to the next interest payment date.

Amortizing Premiums and Discounts

If the sale made on April 1 had been made at a premium or a discount, the amortization at June 30 would be calculated as follows:

Amortization of a Premium:		*Amortization of a Discount:*	
Premium is	$10,485 (a)	Discount is	$9,246 (a)
Months left are	33 (b)	Months left are	33 (b)
Months amortized	3 (c)	Months amortized	3 (c)

Calculation: *Calculation:*
(a ÷ b) × c   (a ÷ b) × c
($10,485 ÷ 33) × 3 = $953.18 (approx.)   ($9,246 ÷ 33) × 3 = $840.54 (approx.)

It is necessary to calculate the number of months remaining in the life of the bonds at the date bonds are sold.

If the bond has interest payment dates that do not coincide with the year-end of the issuing corporation, an adjusting journal entry is required at year-end to record interest owing at that date:

Adjusting Entry:		*Payment of Interest after Year-End:*	
Bond Interest Expense X		Bond Interest Expense X	
Bond Interest Payable	X	Bond Interest Payable X	
		Cash	XX

> The bondholder receives six months of interest on the payment date. Part of the interest was recorded as an expense in the prior period; part is recorded in the current period. This entry assumes that the corporation does not use reversing entries for accruals.

APPENDIX 1:   Present Value Calculations

A distinction between future value and present value is useful to illustrate that interest is the time value of money. If you borrow $1 today for one year at 10 percent interest, its future value in one year is $1.10. The increase of 10 cents results from the interest on $1 for the year. Conversely, if you are to pay $1.10 one year from today, the present value is $1, since the present value calculation excludes interest to be earned in the future. The exclusion of applicable interest in calculating present value is referred to as *discounting*.

The future value of $1.10 is applicable to the first year. If the $1.10 amount at the end of the first year is borrowed for an additional year at 10 percent interest, its future value would be $1.21 ($1.10 + $0.11 interest). In this case, interest is earned on both the original $1 and on the 10 cents interest earned during the first year. This increase provides an example of *compound interest*: interest can be earned on interest.

If the future value of today's $1 at 10 percent interest compounded annually amounts to $1.21 at the end of 2 years, the present value of $1.21 to be paid in 2 years, discounted at 10 percent is $1. That is, the present value of $1.21 excludes interest of 21 cents.

This illustration demonstrates the two different components that exist in every future cash flow: the dollar amount involved, and the time value implications.

Future Cash Flows

Any cash amount to be received in the future can be discounted in a similar manner to calculate its present value, that is, the amount that excludes the interest on money.

Two tables, applicable to this calculation, are Table A: the present value of a single future amount, and Table B: the present value of an annuity.

Present Value of a Single Future Amount

The present value of a single future amount — $100,000 in this case — can be calculated using Table A. Since there are six semi-annual interest payments during the three years, six periods are used in calculating the present value of the $100,000.

Table A   Present Value of 1

$$P = \frac{1}{(1 + i)^n}$$

	4%	6%	8%	10%	12%	14%	16%
1	.961538	.943396	.925926	.909091	.892857	.877193	.862069
2	.924556	.889996	.857339	.826446	.797194	.769468	.743163
3	.888996	.839619	.793832	.751315	.711780	.674972	.640658
4	.854804	.792094	.735030	.683013	.635518	.592030	.552291
5	.821927	.747258	.680583	.620921	.567427	.519369	.476113
6	.790315	.704961	.630170	.564474	.506631	.455587	.410442
7	.759918	.665057	.583490	.513158	.452349	.399637	.353830
8	.730690	.627412	.540269	.466507	.403883	.350559	.305025
9	.702587	.591898	.500249	.424098	.360610	.307508	.262953
10	.675564	.558395	.463193	.385543	.321973	.269744	.226684
11	.649581	.526788	.428883	.350494	.287476	.236617	.195417
12	.624597	.496969	.397114	.318631	.256675	.207559	.168463
13	.600574	.468839	.367698	.289664	.229174	.182069	.145227
14	.577475	.442301	.340461	.263331	.204620	.159710	.125195
15	.555265	.417265	.315242	.239392	.182696	.140096	.107927
16	.533908	.393646	.291890	.217629	.163122	.122892	.093041
17	.513373	.371364	.270269	.197845	.145644	.107800	.080207
18	.493628	.350344	.250249	.179859	.130040	.094561	.069144
19	.474642	.330513	.231712	.163508	.116107	.082948	.059607
20	.456387	.311805	.214548	.148644	.103667	.072762	.051385

Calculation 1:   The Market Interest Rate Is 12 Percent (per Annum)
Since semi-annual interest payments are made, the 6-month rate is half the annual rate. Therefore, the compounding rate is 6 percent (12% × ½) in this case; there are 6 periods in this 3-year bond.

According to Table A, the present value of $1 compounded at 6 percent for 6 periods is 0.704961. The present value of the bonds is therefore calculated as follows: $100,000 × 0.704961 = $70,496 (rounded).

Calculation 2:   The Market Interest Rate Is 8 Percent (per Annum)
Again since semi-annual interest payments are made, the 6-month rate is half the annual rate. Therefore, the compounding rate this time is 4 percent (8% × ½); there are 6 periods in this 3-year bond.

According to Table A, the present value of $1 compounded at 4 percent for 6 periods is 0.790315. The present value of the bonds is therefore calculated as follows: $100,000 × 0.790315 = $79,032 (rounded).

Calculation 3:   The Market Interest Rate Is 16 Percent (per Annum)
For these semi-annual interest payments, the 6-month rate is 8 percent (16% × ½); there are 6 periods in this 3-year bond.

According to Table A, the present value of $1 compounded at 8 percent for 6 periods is 0.630170. The present value of the bonds is therefore calculated as follows: $100,000 × 0.630170 × $63,017.

Present Value of Multiple Future Amounts

The present value of multiple future amounts (each referred to as an annuity) — in this instance, $6,000 semi-annually for 6 periods — can be calculated using Table B. Since BCC's payments are made semi-annually, the rate used is half the prevailing market rate of interest.

Table B   Present Value of an Annuity of 1

$$P = \left[\frac{1 - \dfrac{1}{(1 + i)^n}}{i} \right]$$

	4%	6%	8%	10%	12%	14%	16%
1	.961538	.943396	.925926	.909091	.892857	.877193	.862069
2	1.886095	1.833393	1.783265	1.735537	1.690051	1.646661	1.605232
3	2.775091	2.673012	2.577097	2.486852	2.401831	2.321632	2.245890
4	3.629895	3.465106	3.312127	3.169865	3.037349	2.913712	2.798181
5	4.451822	4.212364	3.992710	3.790787	3.604776	3.433081	3.274294
6	5.242137	4.917324	4.622880	4.355261	4.111407	3.888668	3.684736
7	6.002055	5.582381	5.206370	4.868419	4.563757	4.288305	4.038565
8	6.732745	6.209794	5.746639	5.334926	4.967640	4.638864	4.343591
9	7.435332	6.801692	6.246888	5.759024	5.328250	4.946372	4.606544
10	8.110896	7.360087	6.710081	6.144567	5.650223	5.216116	4.833227
11	8.760477	7.886875	7.138964	6.495061	5.937699	5.452733	5.028644
12	9.385074	8.383844	7.536078	6.813692	6.194374	5.660292	5.197107
13	9.985648	8.852683	7.903776	7.103356	6.423548	5.842362	5.342334
14	10.563123	9.294984	8.244237	7.366687	6.628168	6.002072	5.467529
15	11.118387	9.712249	8.559479	7.606080	6.810864	6.142168	5.575456
16	11.652296	10.105895	8.851369	7.823709	6.963986	6.265060	5.668497
17	12.165669	10.477260	9.121638	8.021553	6.119630	6.372859	5.748704
18	12.659297	10.827603	9.371887	8.201412	7.249670	6.467420	5.817848
19	13.133939	11.158116	9.603599	8.364920	7.365777	6.550369	5.877455
20	13.590326	11.469921	9.818147	8.513564	7.469444	6.623131	5.928841

Calculation 1:   The Market Interest Rate Is 12 Percent (per Annum)
According to Table B, the present value of an annuity of $1 compounded at 6 percent (12% × ½) for 6 periods is 4.917324. The present value of an annuity of $6,000 is therefore calculated as follows: $6,000 × 4.917324 = $29,504 (rounded).

Calculation 2:   The Market Interest Rate Is 8 Percent (per Annum)
Again using Table B, the present value of an annuity of $1 compounded at 4 percent (8% × ½) for 6 periods is 5.242137. The present value of an annuity of $6,000 is therefore calculated as follows: $6,000 × 5.242137 = $31,453 (rounded).

Calculation 3:   The Market Interest Rate Is 16 Percent (per Annum)
The present value of an annuity of $1 compounded at 8 percent (16% × ½) for 6 periods is 4.622880 according to Table B. The present value of an annuity of $6,000 is therefore calculated as follows: $6,000 × 4.622880 = $27,737 (rounded).

APPENDIX 2:   The Effective Interest Method of Amortization

A bond premium or discount is amortized over the bond life remaining from the date of the bond's issue. The straight-line method, as discussed in the last section, allocates an equal amount of amortization to each semi-annual interest period. The simplicity of this method makes it appropriate as an introduction to the bond accounting process.

A more theoretically acceptable method has been advocated by some accountants; it uses the market rate of interest and is commonly referred to as the *effective interest method*. Under this method, the amount of amortization calculated differs from one period to another. The calculation is facilitated through the preparation of an amortization table.

Essentially, an amortization table calculates the interest expense on the carrying value of the bond; in this calculation, use is made of the market rate of interest at the date of the bond issue. The difference between the market rate of interest and actual bond contract interest paid is the amortization applicable to the current period.

Note that, for this method, interest rates are usually expressed in annual rates. When semi-annual interest payments are made, the interest is compounded semi-annually; therefore, the period rate is half the annual rate, since six months is half a year.

For this discussion of the effective interest method, assume that Bluebeard Computer Corporation uses this method of amortization for the issue of its bonds on January 1, 19X1.

Calculating Interest Expense and Premium Amortization

The following amortization table is prepared for the BCC issue of $100,000 face value bonds at a premium for $110,485. The calculation begins with the $110,485 issue amount in period 1 (January 1 to June 30, 19X1); this amount is referred to as the bond carrying value. The objective of this amortization method is to reduce this carrying value to the face value of $100,000 over the life of the bonds; the decrease is shown in column E of the table.

In this case, the market interest rate of 8 percent, commonly referred to as the effective rate, is expressed as an annual rate. Because BCC makes semi-annual interest payments, the 6-month rate is 4 percent (half of the 8 percent annual rate), which is the rate used in column B each semi-annual period. For convenience, all column B calculations are rounded to the nearest dollar.

The calculation in column D provides the premium amortization amount for each period. In period 1, for example, the difference between the $4,419 market rate interest expense (column B) and the $6,000 actual bond contract interest paid (column C) calculates the premium amortization at $1,581 (column B − column C).

Columns E and A show the decreasing carrying value of the bonds during their three-year life; these are the amounts actually used, it is claimed, in financing the entity. Accordingly, the market interest method calculates interest expense at a constant 4 percent of the bond financing in effect each period. In this way, interest expense (column B) decreases each period as less bond financing is used. From a theoretical point of view, it is preferable to show a financing interest expense that decreases (column B) as the amount of financing decreases (column A).

Issue of $100,000 Bonds Payable for $110,485
Amortization Table
Using Market Interest Rate of 8%

Year	Period	A *Jan. 1* *Bond* *Carrying* *Value*	B ([½ of 8% = 4%] × A) *Using 8% Market Rate* *To Calculate* *Six-Month Interest* *Expense*	C *Actual* *Cash* *Interest* *Paid*	D (B − C) *Periodic* *Premium* *Amortization*	E (A − D) *Dec. 31* *Bond* *Carrying* *Value*
19X1	1	$110,485	(4% × $110,485 =) $4,419	$6,000	$1,581	$108,904
	2	108,904	(4% × 108,904 =) 4,356	6,000	1,644	107,260
19X2	3	$107,260	(4% × $107,260 =) $4,290	$6,000	$1,710	$105,550
	4	105,550	(4% × 105,550 =) 4,222	6,000	1,778	103,772
19X3	5	$103,772	(4% × $103,772 =) $4,151	$6,000	$1,849	$101,923
	6	101,923	(4% × 101,923 =) 4,077	6,000	1,923	100,000

> Note the use of a constant interest rate under this method.

> This amount is the interest expense for each 6-month period.

> This amount is the amortization for each 6-month period.

Recording Interest Payments and Premium Amortization

Journal entries to record interest payments and amortization of the premium are made every June 30 and December 31 in the same manner as for straight-line amortization (shown in section C). The actual interest paid to bondholders amounts to $6,000 each semi-annual period; the amount of premium amortization for each period is taken from column D of the amortization table. These are the entries for period 1.

	Payment of Interest:				*Amortization of Premium:*		
Jun. 30	Bond Interest Expense	6,000			Bond Premium	1,581	
	Cash		6,000		Bond Interest Expense		1,581
	To record semi-annual bond interest.				To record amortization of bond premium.		

The entries for each remaining period are similar; only the amounts used for premium amortization differ, as shown in column D of the amortization table. After the posting of the June 30 entries, the following balances result:

Balance Sheet Accounts

Bonds Payable		Premium on Bonds	
	100,000		10,485
		1,581	
			8,904

> The bond carrying value is $108,904 ($100,000 + $8,904) at June 30; this is the amount that appears in column E of the amortization table.

Income Statement Account

Bond Interest Expense

6,000	
	1,581
4,419	

This amount is the balance that was calculated in column B of the amortization table.

Calculating Interest Expense and Discount Amortization

The following amortization table is prepared for the BCC issue of $100,000 face value bonds at a discount for $90,754. The calculation begins with the $90,754 carrying value in column A. The amortization objective is to increase this carrying value to the face value of $100,000 over the 3-year life of the bond; this increase appears in column E.

The annual market interest rate in this case is 16 percent. Half this rate — 8 percent — is used in the column B calculations, since interest payments are made semi-annually. For convenience, all column B calculations are rounded to the nearest dollar. The calculation in column D provides the amortization amount. In period 1, for example, the difference between the $7,260 market rate interest expense (column B) and the $6,000 actual bond contract interest paid (column C) calculates the discount amortization at $1,260 (column B − column C).

Issue of $100,000 Bonds Payable for $90,754
Amortization Table
Using Market Interest Rate of 16%

Year	Period	**A** Jan. 1 Bond Carrying Value	**B** ([½ of 16% = 8%] × **A**) Using 8% Market Rate To Calculate Six-Month Interest Expense	**C** Actual Cash Interest Paid	**D** (**B** − **C**) Periodic Discount Amortization	**E** (**A** + **D**) Dec. 31 Bond Carrying Value
19X1	1	$90,754	(8% × $90,754 =) $7,260	$6,000	$1,260	$ 92,014
	2	92,014	(8% × 92,014 =) 7,361	6,000	1,361	93,375
19X2	3	$93,375	(8% × $93,375 =) $7,470	$6,000	$1,470	$ 94,845
	4	94,845	(8% × 94,845 =) 7,588	6,000	1,588	96,433
19X3	5	$96,433	(8% × $96,433 =) $7,715	$6,000	$1,715	$ 98,148
	6	98,148	(8% × 98,148) =) 7,852	6,000	1,852	100,000

Note the use of a constant interest rate under this method.

This amount is the interest expense for each 6-month period.

This amount is the amortization for each 6-month period.

Columns E and A show the increasing carrying value of the bonds during their 3-year life; these are the actual amounts used, it is claimed, in financing the entity. Accordingly, the market interest method calculates interest expense at a constant 8 percent of each period's balance of bond financing. In this way, interest expense (column B) increases each period as financing increases. From a theoretical point of view, it is preferable to show a financing interest expense that increases (column B) as the amount of financing increases (column A).

Recording Interest Payments and Discount Amortization

Journal entries to record interest payments and amortization are made each June 30 and December 31 in the same manner as for the straight-line method (shown in section C). The actual interest paid to bondholders amounts to $6,000 each semi-annual period; the amount of discount amortization is taken directly from column D of the amortization table. These are the entries for period 1.

Payment of Interest			*Amortization of Discount*		
Jun. 30 Bond Interest Expense	6,000		Bond Interest Expense	1,260	
Cash		6,000	Bond Discount		1,260
To record semi-annual bond interest.			To record amortization of bond discount.		

The entries for each remaining period are similar; only the amounts used for discount amortization differ, as shown in column D of the amortization table. After the posting of the June 30 entries, the following balances result:

Balance Sheet Accounts			Income Statement Account
Bonds Payable	Discount on Bonds		Bond Interest Expense
100,000	9,246	1,260	6,000
	7,986		1,260
			7,260

The bond carrying value is $92,014 ($100,000 − $7,986) at June 30; this is the amount in column E of the amortization table.

This amount is the balance that was calculated in column B of the amortization table.

Comparison of the Effective Interest Method with the Straight-Line Method

A comparison of the two amortization methods can be made using the data applicable to the issue of BCC's bonds at a discount; $100,000 face value bonds are issued for $90,754, resulting in a discount of $9,246 ($100,000 − $90,754). Under the straight-line method, this $9,246 discount is amortized in equal amounts over the 3-year life of the bonds. The discount is calculated for 6-month periods, because amortization is recorded at the time that semi-annual interest payments are made. The straight-line method amortization is calculated as follows:

Discount:	$9,246 (a)
Number of 6 month periods remaining:	6 (b)
Calculation: (a ÷ b) ($9,246 ÷ 6) =	$1,541

As explained in section C of this chapter, amortization of a discount increases interest expense. Therefore, the $1,541 is added to the $6,000 interest payment to calculate the $7,541 interest expense applicable to each 6-month period.

Under the effective interest method, the $9,246 discount amortization is calculated in column D of amortization table. The relevant details are shown next to compare with the appropriate calculations under the straight-line method. For convenience, all percentage calculations are rounded.

		Effective Interest Method			Straight-Line Method		
			Interest			*Interest*	
		Carrying	*(Expense)*	*(B ÷ A)*	*Carrying*	*(Expense)*	
Year	*Period*	*Value (A)*	*Amount (B)*	*%*	*Value*	*Amount*	*%*
19X1	1	$90,754	$ 7,260	8	$90,754	$ 7,541	8.3
	2	92,014	7,361	8	92,295	7,541	8.2
19X2	3	93,375	7,470	8	93,836	7,541	8
	4	94,845	7,588	8	95,377	7,541	7.9
19X3	5	96,433	7,715	8	96,918	7,541	7.8
	6	98,148	7,852	8	98,459	7,541	7.7
		$45,246			$45,246		

Under this method the financing percentage is constant.

Under this method the financing percentage varies.

As can be seen, there is a constant financing expense of 8 percent each 6-month period (16 percent per annum) under the effective interest method. The financing rate varies from period to period under the straight-line method. Theoretically, accounting purists insist that a correct financing charge is calculated only under the effective interest method. However, others argue that, from a practical point of view, there is no material difference in the amounts calculated and the additional accuracy obtained using the market interest is not worth the effort involved. Note that the total interest expense of $45,246 for the 3-year period is the same under both methods. The straight-line method is widely used because of its simplicity. Using either of these methods is in accordance with Canadian GAAP.

This comparison involved the issue of bonds at a discount. A similar comparison for bonds issued at a premium would indicate a similar difference in the calculation of a periodic financing charge. Under the straight-line method, however, the percentage of financing charge would increase in the case of a premium, rather than decrease as here.

Accrual of Bond Interest at Year-End

In these examples, interest is paid at June 30 and December 31; here, the year-end coincided with the December 31 payment. When these two dates do not coincide, it is necessary to accrue interest at year-end and to record an appropriate amount of amortization. These adjustments are made to comply with the principle of the matching concept, which requires that all expenses be matched with revenues for that same year. The adjusting entry accruing interest requires a credit to Bond Interest Payable.

Assume that the fiscal year-end is September 30, but that interest on bonds is still paid June 30 and December 31. In this case, three months of interest has to be accrued (July, August, and September); amortization must also be recorded for three months. The amount of interest would be $3,000 ($100,000 $\times$ 12% $\times$ ¼); the amount of amortization, assuming the effective interest method is used, would be half of the appropriate semi-annual periodic amortization recorded in column D of the amortization table.

A S S I G N M E N T   M A T E R I A L S

Discussion Questions

1. What is a bond? a bond indenture? Why is a trustee usually necessary?
2. A bondholder has certain rights. List and explain these rights.
3. What is the significance of shareholder approval before an issue of bonds?
4. How are different bond issues reported in the financial statements of a corporation?
5. Three different categories of bond terminology are identified in this chapter. Identify these categories and list the major types falling within each category.
6. Why would investors pay a premium for a corporate bond? Why would a corporation issue its bonds at a discount? Explain, using the relationship between the bond contract interest rate and the prevailing market interest rate.
7. What method of balance sheet classification of bond premium or bond discount is in accordance with Canadian GAAP?
8. How is the actual price of a bond determined? Give an example.
9. If the bond contract interest rate is greater than that required in the market, what is the effect on the selling price of the bond? Why?
10. What are the different methods used in amortizing premiums and discounts? Explain.
11. How is the interest paid to bondholders calculated? How does this practice affect the sale of bonds between interest dates?
12. How is the amortization of bond premium recorded in the books? the amortization of bond discount?
13. Explain what a bond sinking fund is. What are the three phases in its operation?
14. What are the different possibilities in the redemption of bonds before their maturity?
15. If a bond is sold between interest dates, what is the accepted practice for handling accrued interest?
16. From a theoretical point of view, why is the effective interest method of amortization more acceptable than the straight-line method? Evaluate the usefulness of the effective interest method from a practical point of view. effective interest method from a practical point of view.
17. Explain how the amortization under the effective interest method is calculated. Use an example.
18. How does the calculation of a periodic financing charge differ from the market interest method to the straight-line method?
19. Distinguish between future value and present value. What is the time value of money? Why is it important?
20. Why is it necessary to discount future cash flows when calculating the present value of a bond? Explain, using the different cash flows that are associated with bonds.
21. How does the use of mathematical tables facilitate the calculation of present values?
22. Contrast the calculation of present value when (a) the market interest rate is greater than the bond contract interest rate, and (b) when the market interest rate is less than the bond contract interest rate.

Discussion Cases

Discussion Case 11-1:   Inco Ltd.

The proposed $1.05-billion (U.S.) dividend payout by Inco Ltd. does not sit well with debt watchers.

Bond rating agencies reacted quickly and negatively to the nickel giant's plans to launch a controversial takeover defence, which includes the dividend payments to shareholders.

One influential New York agency cut Inco's ranking immediately and another is considering similar action. The two Canadian bond raters have cancelled plans to upgrade the company's debt.

"There are a wide range of implications to this transaction, with virtually all of them being negative," Dominion Bond Rating Service Ltd. of Toronto said in a report.

In light of a surge in cash flow and profit stemming from sharply higher nickel prices, DBRS was set to raise Inco's rating — to single-A (low) from triple-B (low) — until the mining giant announced the special dividend as part of a recapitalization designed to fend off unwanted acquisitors.

The rating increase would have made Inco debentures more attractive to a wider range of institutional investors, many of which shy away from debt ranked below the single-A level.

Standard & Poor's Corp. of New York cut its closely watched rating to triple-B minus from triple-B, while Moody's Investors Service Inc. put the company under review for a possible downgrade. Moody's rates Inco BAA1, equivalent to triple-B plus.

"We upgraded them twice in the past year with the understanding Inco would pursue a conservative financial policy, retaining a substantial cushion of cash," said Scott Sprinzen, a rating officer with Standard & Poor's.

A lower rating generally increases the cost of raising money in the debt markets. But Inco's standing remains higher than it was a year ago, when S&P, for example, pegged its debt at double-B plus.

DBRS is keeping Inco's rating where it is, with the warning that the company is severely weakening its balance sheet and limiting future expansion at a time when the cyclical trend is likely to be downward.

Canadian Bond Rating Service Ltd. also expressed dismay over the Inco move and has similarly shelved plans to improve the company's debt rating. The agency ranks Inco B double-plus, equivalent to triple-B.

Inco's recapitalization, announced Monday, will be financed partly from available cash, but also from bank or commercial paper borrowings. The company also intends to float a $265-million debenture, with the coupon rate tied to nickel prices.

When the plan, which is subject to shareholder approval, is completed, Inco's debt will double to $1.5-billion.

As a result, DBRS said, debt will shoot up to more than 60 per cent of capitalization. "The maximum prudent level of debt in the capital structure for a cyclical company such as Inco is 40 per cent."

The company's net interest costs will increase $100-million to $105-million annually, the rating agency said.

While equity investors would certainly benefit, bondholders will be exposed to greater financial risks as a result of the higher debt load.

"This action has washed away the long-awaited recovery and financial flexibility of the company, which it strived to achieve during the past five years," CBRS said.

Nevertheless, the agency said it would maintain Inco's existing rating because strong cash flow stemming from the higher nickel prices and good demand will enable the company to reduce long-term debt in the next six to nine months.

"We feel they can bring their capital structure back into order," said Zaheer Khan, resources analyst with CBRS.

Source   Brian Milner, "Bond Rating Agencies Anxious over Inco Payout", *The Globe and Mail*, Toronto, October 8, 1988, p. B-1, B-5.

For Discussion

1. If the recapitalization plan is approved, Inco's debt will double to more than 60 percent of capitalization. Does Inco warrant a downgrade in its credit rating? Why is the Dominion Bond Rating Service particularly concerned?

2. Having a lower rating generally increases a company's cost of raising money through bonds. How can you, as an investor, know whether Inco is severely weakening its financial position and limiting its future expansion? Is a secure financial position especially important when the cyclical trend is likely to be downward?

3. Financed with available cash, banks or commercial paper borrowings, and a $265 million debenture, what are the advantages of having the bond coupon rate tied to nickel prices?

4. "While equity investors would certainly benefit, bondholders will be exposed to greater financial risks as a result of the higher debt load." Whose interests should Inco represent when proceeding with the recapitalization? Why?

Discussion Case 11-2:   Joe Robbie Stadium

When Super Bowl XXIII kicked off yesterday at Joe Robbie Stadium, it marked the moment a gambler finally hit the big one.

Joe Robbie, who had put everything he owned — including the Miami Dolphins — in hock to build his dream, finally had the last laugh on the politicians.

The plush stadium that carries his name was financed entirely by private money, particularly by season-ticket holders and luxury-box owners. The money they advanced, plus the collateral of the Dolphins, enabled Robbie to receive loans and bonds to make up the $115-million cost of the stadium.

But the procedure leading to building the 75,000-seat facility wasn't that simple. Robbie had to battle local politicians for 11 years before the project was finished in August, 1987.

When Robbie announced in March, 1984 that he planned to build a stadium 16 miles northwest of downtown Miami, local politicians had a good laugh. Especially when he said it would be financed privately.

Robbie began the venture after years of fruitless attempts to convince the city to repair the ramshackle Orange Bowl near downtown Miami. When former Miami mayor Maurice Ferre told Robbie he should build his own stadium if he wanted one so much, the plans began.

An added incentive was the fact National Football League owners told Robbie there would never be another Super Bowl in Miami as long as the Orange Bowl was the only stadium. Yesterday's game was the first in Miami in 10 years.

Robbie began marketing executive suites and club seats at the stadium in July, 1984. On Dec. 31, 1985, he secured the rest of his financing through loans and bonds, using the

$12-million he raised on 10-year leases for the suites and club seats as security along with his football team.

The skyboxes were sold for prices from $29,000 to $65,000 a season on a 10-year lease, depending on the size of the box. Club seats — much like those sold at Toronto's Sky Dome — were priced from $600 to $2,000 a season.

Construction of the stadium began on July 22, 1985 and was completed two years later.

The stadium was originally to be called Dolphin Stadium, but Robbie's children had it renamed for their father.

"We have seen our father lay everything he owns and everything he has accomplished on the line to build the stadium, putting himself in a real bind," said Tim Robbie, a vice-president of the Dolphins. "If he had flunked the marketing test or the private-financing test, the project would have been Joe Robbie's Folly. So why not Joe Robbie Stadium?"

The elder Robbie's next dream is a major-league baseball franchise for his stadium by 1992. The venue can be converted to accommodate 50,000 fans for baseball.

Source David Shoalts, "Joe Robbie's Gamble of a Lifetime Paid Off with Super Bowl Jackpot", *The Globe and Mail*, Toronto, January 27, 1989, p. A-17.

For Discussion

1. Explain how Joe Robbie financed the stadium.
2. Why did local politicians laugh when Robbie said the stadium would be financed privately?
3. Evaluate the marketing system used by Robbie to finance the stadium.

Discussion Case 11-3:   Jasmine Technologies Inc.

Like many an entrepreneur before him, Dennis Chang was long on chutzpah and short on cash. After bouncing around the computer industry for eight years, he had a business plan modeled after IBM's and Apple Computer's. But he had no savings, no investors, and no willing lenders.

He still doesn't. Yet for the fiscal year ended last September, his San Francisco company, Jasmine Technologies Inc., logged sales of more than $35 million on its disk drives and other Macintosh-compatible components. Chang, 40, financed this astonishing growth with some of the most reluctant lenders around: his suppliers.

Supplier financing is often messy and precarious. It had one serious advantage for Chang, however; it was his only option.

Everyone knows the official textbook rule on such backdoor finance. It says: Put off paying your suppliers as long as possible — period. That's fine if you already have suppliers. But if like Chang you barely have a product, much less a track record, it simply doesn't apply. The trick was to get not only his raw materials, but his office equipment, advertising — his entire business — on credit.

Fortunately, Chang didn't know the first thing about official finance. "Everything I was doing was intuitive, seat of the pants," he recalls — thus the birth of Finesse Finance.

Chang's first lesson was about the power of the personal guarantee. With no other means of selling or distributing its Macintosh-clone peripherals, Jasmine was relying on an advertisement in *Macworld* magazine to educate Macintosh users, to promote its product, and to produce prepaid orders. Trouble was, *Macworld* insisted that Chang pay for his ads. But he couldn't; he had to get them on credit.

All it took was conversation — a couple of months of it. Chang was on the phone almost every day with San Francisco account executive Penny Rigby and the magazine's credit department. They discussed Chang's education, previous jobs, personal finances, business plan, marketing strategy. In the end, he consented to personally guarantee a credit line of about $30,000, an obligation he could meet only by selling his house.

By the end of those months of talking, Rigby and the credit people were emotionally committed to him. Chang's guarantee gave the magazine's bean counters a security blanket — so they could do what they already wanted to do, which was to back Chang. Lesson one: The power of the personal guarantee lies mostly in what you do before you give it.

Now, Chang was really rolling. Or so he thought, until he tried to find a leasing company that would agree to rent him some telephones, typewriters, copiers, and computers. It didn't take long before the solution hit him: he'd simply "recycle" his personal guarantee. All the money he had was $40,000 of equity in his house. Guaranteeing $12,000 to $15,000 in payments to a leasing company couldn't make him any more vulnerable. What's more, he soon discovered, few ever asked how many other credit lines he had personally guaranteed. And therein lay the second lesson: The first guarantee devalues all subsequent guarantees, but your suppliers don't know that.

For some people, Chang learned, getting paid wasn't nearly as important as growth, or, say, bucking the status quo. These were the suppliers who were motivated by the same thing that drove him, his soul mates in ambition. He spent hours with such small companies describing his vision of Jasmine's future. "I sold them on the value of our growth," Chang says.

Chang got two of his most important vendor relationships by being a good Samaritan to one that stumbled. Chang offered to buy a huge batch of excess inventory of platters from a grateful disk supplier. The disk maker also introduced Chang to Arrow Electronics Inc., where Chang bumped into the invisible credit limit.

"Arrow initially gave us a $50,000 credit line," remembers Chang. "We were growing 30% a month, so we exceeded it." Nothing happened. Jasmine paid Arrow's bills, then it again exceeded the credit limit. Again nothing happened. Eureka! "I finally realized that we didn't really have a credit limit. I started ordering product like crazy."

It wasn't long before Chang faced a new problem with his vendors. It was no longer a matter of persuading them to be his suppliers — it was that little matter of how to pay them. In the beginning, he had made certain all bills were paid on time. But now Jasmine's growth was chewing up cash. Chang looked at his suppliers and saw a few dozen small, relatively unimportant ones and a handful of crucial ones. Rather than spend all his money on the important suppliers, he devised a kind of reverse triangle: he'd pay the small bills right away and drag out the big ones. He figured that if they shut him off, the small vendors could hurt him just about as much as the big ones. And besides, he could afford to pay the little bills. And the big vendors? Well, they would get plenty of Dennis Chang's private currency — personal attention.

He talked to them every day. He returned their phone calls immediately. He took their families out to breakfast or lunch. If he managed to scrape together part of the money Jasmine owed, he personally hand-delivered the check. In short, he paid them with evidence of his intense commitment. When the cash crisis was over, he found, those suppliers felt like partners in his success.

Despite that success, it's clear that supplier financing is no substitute for more conventional forms of capital. With no outside equity in the company, Jasmine's heavy reliance on suppliers' credit makes it look terribly overleveraged. That, in turn, makes the company unappealing to banks and other lenders. Lack of both equity and borrowing capacity means it has no cushion against a temporary drop in sales, such as it suffered early last year.

There is an upside, though. It worked. It worked well enough that Jasmine is no longer a seed company or a start-up — it's up and running hard. And that makes a world of difference to potential investors. Chang says he's constantly being approached by venture capitalists, investment bankers, and other investors, but he's not letting them turn his head. As usual, he has a plan: "The longer we hold them off, the less we have to give away of our company," he explains.

This could be the start of chapter two of Finesse Finance — but that's another story.

Source   Reprinted with permission, *Inc. magazine*, February 1989. Copyright © 1989 by Goldhirsh Group, Inc., 38 Commercial Wharf, Boston, MA 02110.

For Discussion

1. What exactly is supplier financing? Explain how it works. Why is supplier financing messy and precarious?
2. How could Chang finance $35 million in sales without savings, investors, or willing lenders? Are there any ethical issues involved in this situation?
3. Chang's personal guarantee "gave the magazine's bean counters a security blanket." Who are the bean counters?
4. How many times did Chang recycle his personal guarantee? Could any entrepreneur have used this technique? How? Exactly how does "Finesse Finance" work?
5. Explain Chang's invisible credit line with Arrow.
6. Discuss Chang's "private currency."
7. Explain in what way Jasmine is overleveraged.

Comprehension Problems

Comprehension Problem 11-1

Required: Complete the following by responding either *premium* or *discount*.
1. If the market rate of interest is 15 percent and the bond interest rate is 10 percent, the bonds will sell at a ___discount___.
2. If a bond's interest rate is 10 percent and the market rate of interest is 8 percent, the bonds will sell at a ___premium___.
3. In computing the carrying value of a bond, unamortized ___discount___ is subtracted from the face value of the bond.
4. In computing the carrying value of a bond, unamortized ___premium___ is added to the face value of the bond.
5. If a bond sells at a ___premium___, an amount in excess of the face value of the bond is received on the date of issuance.
6. If a bond sells at a ___discount___, an amount less than the face value of the bond is received on the date of issuance.

Note: Answer problems regarding present value calculations and the effective interest method of amortization only if the appendices were studied in your course.

Comprehension Problem 11-2

On January 1, 19X1, the date of bond authorization, Sarasota Inc. issued a 3-year, 12-percent bond with a face value of $100,000 at 94. Semi-annual interest is payable on June 30 and December 1.

Required:
1. Prepare journal entries to record the following transactions:
   a. The issuance of the bonds
   b. The interest payment on June 30, 19X1
   c. The authorization of the discount on June 30, 19X1 (use the straight-line method of amortization).
2. Calculate the amount of interest paid in cash during 19X1 and the amount of interest expense that will appear in the 19X1 income statement.
3. Prepare a partial balance sheet at December 31, 19X1 showing how the bonds payable and the discount on the bonds should be shown on the balance sheet.
4. Prepare the journal entry to record the retirement of the bonds on December 31, 19X3.
5. Prepare the journal entry on January 1, 19X2 when the bonds were called at 102.

Comprehension Problem 11-3

On January 1, 19X3, the date of bond authorization, Hawker Corp. issued 3-year, 12-percent bonds with a face value of $200,000 at 112. Semi-annual interest is payable on June 30 and December 31.

Required:
1. Prepare the journal entries to record the following transactions:
   a. The issuance of the bonds
   b. The interest payment on June 30, 19X3
   c. The authorization of the premium on June 30, 19X3 (use the straight-line method of amortization).
2. Calculate the amount of interest paid in cash during 19X3 and the amount of interest expense that will appear in the 19X3 income statement. Why are these amounts different?
3. Prepare a partial balance sheet at December 31, 19X3 showing how the bonds payable and the premium on bonds should be shown on the balance sheet.
4. Prepare the journal entry on January 1, 19X5 when the bonds were called at 106.

Comprehension Problem 11-4

On January 1, 19X4, the date of bond authorization, Hawley Inc. issued 3-year, 12-percent bonds. Semi-annual interest is payable on June 30 and December 31. Hawley uses the straight-line method of amortization. The following journal entry records the first payment of interest:

	19X4		
June 30	Bonds Interest Expense	17,000	
	Cash		16,500
	Discount on Books		500

Required: Reconstruct the journal entry made to record the issuance of bonds on January 1, 19X4.

Comprehension Problem 11-5

Bryan Inc. issued 3-year, 12-percent bonds on January 1, 19X6, the date of bond authorization. Semi-annual interest is payable on June 30 and December 31. Bryan uses the straight-line method of amortization. The following journal entry records the payment of interest on December 31, 19X6:

	19X6		
Dec. 31	Bonds Interest Expense	17,900	
	Premium on Bonds	100	
	Cash		18,000

Required: Reconstruct the entry made to record the issuance of bonds on January 1, 19X6.

Comprehension Problem 11-6

Bilodeau Corporation, a profitable growth company with 200 000 shares of common stock outstanding, is in need of approximately $40 million in new funds to finance required expansion. Currently, there are no other securities outstanding. Management has three options open:
a. Sell $40 million-worth of 12-percent bonds at face value
b. Sell preferred stock: 400 000 shares at $100 per share
c. Sell another 200 000 shares of common stock at $200 per share.
Operating income (before interest and income tax) on completion of the expansion is expected to average $12 million per annum; the income tax rate is 50 percent.

Required:
1. Prepare a schedule (using the form from section A) to calculate the earnings per common share. Beginning with the amount for earnings before interest and income tax, calculate the earnings per share of common for $12 million-worth of each of bonds, preferred shares, and common shares.

	Bonds	Preferred Shares	Common Shares
Income before Interest and Tax	$12,000,000	$12,000,000	$12,000,000
Deduct Bond Interest	4,800,000	0	0
Income before Tax	7,200,000	12,000,000	12,000,000
Tax at 50%	3,600,000	6,000,000	6,000,000
Balance	3,600,000	6,000,000	6,000,000
Preferred Dividends	0	4,000,000	
Net Available to Common (a)	3,600,000	2,000,000	6,000,000
Common Shares Outstanding	200,000	200,000	400,000
Earnings per Common Share (a) ÷ (b)	$18	$10	$15

2. Which financing option is most advantageous to the common shareholders?
3. What are the advantages of issuing shares rather than bonds? of issuing bonds rather than shares?

① $40,000,000 × 12% = $4,800,000

② 400,000 × $100 × 10% = $4,000,000
            ↑
          DIDN'T
          GIVE

Comprehension Problem 11-7

Kim Corporation was authorized to issue $500,000 face value bonds. The corporation issued $100,000-worth of face value bonds on January 1, 19X1.

Date of Authorization	Term	Bond Contract Interest Rate	Interest Payment Dates
January 1, 19X1	3 years	12%	Semi-annually on June 30 and December 31

Required: Answer the questions for each of the following cases.
Case A: The bonds were issued at face value and purchased at par.
Case B: The bonds were issued for $112,000 and purchased at a premium.
Case C: The bonds were issued for $88,000 and purchased at a discount.

1. How much cash does Kim receive for the bonds?
2. How much annual interest must the corporation pay? On what face value amount do they pay?
3. Prepare the journal entry to record the sale of the bonds.
4. Record the entries applicable to interest and straight-line amortization for June 30, 19X1 and for December 31, 19X1.

Comprehension Problem 11-8

Hwan Distributors Ltd. was authorized to issue $500,000-worth of face value bonds. On January 1, 19X1, the corporation issued $200,000-worth of face value bonds for $210,152. On this date, the market rate of interest was 10 percent.

Date of Authorization	Term	Bond Contract Interest Rate	Interest Payment Dates
January 1, 19X1	3 years	12%	Semi-annually on June 30 and December 31

Required:
1. Calculate the amount of interest paid every interest payment date.
2. Prepare an amortization table like the one in Appendix 2. (The carrying value at January 1, 19X1 is $210,152 and periodic interest is $10,507.) For convenience round all column B calculations to the nearest dollar. Use the effective interest method of amortization.

Issuance of $200,000 Bonds Payable for $210,152
Amortization Table
Using Market Interest Rate of 10%

Year	Period	A Jan. 1 Bond Carrying Value	B ([½ of 10% = 5%] × A) Using 10% Market Rate To Calculate Six-Month Interest Expense	C Actual Cash Interest Paid	D (B–C) Periodic Premium Amortization	E (A–D) Dec. 31 Bond Carrying Value
1	1	$210,152	(5% × $210,152 =)$10,507			
	2		(5% × =)			
2	3		(5% × =)			
	4		(5% × =)			
3	5		(5% × =)			
	6		(5% × =)			

3. Calculate the financing percentage under the effective interest method of amortization for each six-month period. (Use the format in section D.) For convenience round all percentage calculations to the nearest percent.)

Year	Period	A *Jan. 1 Bond Carrying Value*	B ([½ of 10% = 5%] × A) *Using 10% Market Rate To Calculate Six-Month Interest Expense*	(B ÷ A) *Financing %*
1	1	$210,152	(5% × $210,152 =)$10,507	
	2		(5% × =)	
				_____ %
2	3		(5% × =)	
	4		(5% × =)	
				_____ %
3	5		(5% × =)	
	6		(5% × =)	
				_____ %

4. Comment on the financing percentage that results in each period. Do you think that this financing percentage should remain constant from period to period? Why or why not?

Comprehension Problem 11-9

The following diagram shows how the carrying value of bonds payable changes over time for bonds issued at a premium, at par, and at a discount.

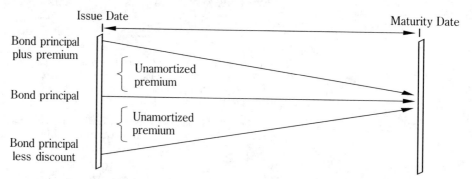

Required:
1. Explain the change in carrying value of the bonds, in terms of the difference between the periodic interest expense and the periodic interest payments to investors.
2. Explain why the slopes of the lines for unamortized premiums and discounts become *steeper* as the maturity date of the bonds approaches.

Problems

Problem 11-1

The board of directors of Oligopoly Inc. has approved management's recommendation to expand the production facilities. The firm currently manufactures only heavy machinery, but plans are being developed for diversifying the corporation's activities through the production of smaller and more versatile equipment. The directors have concluded that attention should be devoted to observing the expected effect on earnings per common share in selection of a financing method. They are considering the following financing methods:

a. Sell $2 million-worth of 12-percent bonds at face value
b. Sell $8 dividend per share preferred stock: 20 000 shares at $100 a share (no other preferred shares are outstanding)
c. Sell another 50 000 shares of common stock at $400 a share (currently 40 000 common shares are outstanding).

Operating income (before interest and income tax) is expected to average $1,000,000 per annum following the expansion; the income tax rate is expected to be 50 percent.

Required:
1. Calculate the earnings per common share for each alternative: 12-percent bonds, preferred shares, and common shares.
2. Which financing method best meets the board of directors' criteria?
3. What factors should the board of directors consider, in addition to earnings per share?

Problem 11-2

Part A

Radzichowsky Corporation was authorized to issue $300,000-worth of face value bonds. On January 1, 19X1, the corporation issued $150,000-worth of face value bonds for $147,000.

Date of Authorization	Term	Bond Contract Interest Rate	Interest Payment Dates
January 1, 19X1	3 years	12%	Semi-annually on June 30 and December 31

Required:
1. Calculate
   a. The amount of interest paid every interest payment date
   b. The amount of amortization to be recorded at each interest payment date (use the straight-line method of amortization).
2. Prepare a schedule, like the one in Figure 11-5, to show the effect of discount amortization at each interest payment date. Note that amortization is recorded each time interest expense is recorded.
3. Prepare the journal entries to record the interest and amortization at June 30, 19X1.
4. Prepare a partial balance sheet showing the bond liability and the bond discount as a deferred charge on the following dates:
   a. December 31, 19X1 (note that the bonds are a long-term liability on this date, since they will not be redeemed in 19X2)
   b. December 31, 19X2 (note that the bonds are a current liability on this date, since they will be redeemed on Jan. 1, 19X4).

Part B

The bond indenture contained a sinking fund provision requiring equal annual contributions that are transferred to a trustee who guarantees a 10 percent annual return. Annual contributions were to be made on December 31, 19X1, 19X2, and 19X3. The amount of the contributions and the 10 percent revenue in the sinking fund are calculated below.

December 31	Annual Contribution	10% Annual Revenue	Annual Total	Fund Balance
19X1	$45,317	-0-	$45,317	$ 45,317
19X2	45,317	(10% × $45,317 =)$4,532	49,849	95,166
19X3	45,317	(10% × $95,166 =)$9,517	54,834	150,000

Required: Prepare journal entries to record
5. The annual contribution in each of the three years
6. The 10 percent annual revenue in each of the three years
7. The redemption of the bonds at maturity.

Problem 11-3

The Ace Manufacturing Company Limited has made arrangements to sell bonds with a face value of $8,000,000 to Chatham Insurance Corporation to help finance a multi-million dollar expansion to Ace. The following data are available to you:

19X1
Jun. 1   Ace received authorization for an issue of $8,000,000 3-year 12-percent bonds dated June 1, 19X1. The interest is to be paid semi-annually June 1 and December 1 of each year.
       1   Issued for cash $4,000,000 face value of the bonds for $4,142,800.

19X2
Jun. 1   Issued another $4,000,000 face value of the bonds for 97.76 plus accrued interest.

The year-end of Ace is December 31.

Required: Prepare the journal entries necessary to record the following:
1. The issue of the bonds on June 1, 19X1
2. The payment of bond interest expense on December 1, 19X1
3. The accrual of bond interest expense and recording of amortization on December 31, 19X1
4. The payment of bond interest expense on June 1, 19X2
5. The issue of bonds on June 1, 19X2
6. The interest payment on and the retirement of the bonds at maturity.

Problem 11-4

On the date of bond authorization, Wensley Corporation issued $100,000-worth of face value bonds.

Date of Authorization	Term	Bond Contract Interest Rate	Interest Payment Dates
January 1, 19X1	3 Years	12%	Semi-annually on June 30 and December 31

Required: Consider these three cases. Case A: the bonds are issued at face value. Case B: the bonds are issued for $103,000. Case C: the bonds are issued for $94,000. For each of them

1. Calculate
   a. The amount of interest paid every interest payment date
   b. The amount of amortization to be recorded at each interest payment date, if applicable (Use the straight-line method of amortization.)
2. Prepare journal entries to record
   a. The issue of bonds on January 1, 19X1
   b. The payment of interest on June 30, 19X1
   c. The amortization on June 30, 19X1
   d. The payment of interest on December 31, 19X1
   e. The amortization on December 31, 19X1
   f. The payment of interest on December 31, 19X3
   g. The amortization on December 31, 19X3
   h. The redemption of the bonds at maturity, January 1, 19X4.
3. Calculate the amount of interest expense shown in the income statement at December 31, 19X1. Is this amount the same as cash interest paid by Wensley? Why or why not?
4. On December 31, 19X2, the corporation exercised a call feature included in the bond indenture and retired the $50,000-worth of face value bonds issued January 1, 19X1. The bonds were called at 102. Prepare the December 31, 19X2 journal entry to record the exercise of the call option.

Problem 11-5

Mink Products Inc., which uses straight-line amortization calculation, was authorized to issue $1,000,000 face value bonds. On January 1, 19X1, Mink issued $300,000-worth of face value bonds for $272,263.

Date of Authorization	Term	Bond Contract Interest Rate	Interest Payment Dates
January 1, 19X1	3 Years	12%	Semi-annually on June 30 and December 31

Required:
1. Calculate
   a. The amount of interest paid every interest payment date
   b. The amount of amortization to be recorded at each interest payment date (use the straight-line method).
2. Prepare an amortization table like the one in section C. (Note that amortization is recorded each time interest expense is recorded.)
3. Calculate the financing percentage under the straight-line method of amortization for each six-month period. (For convenience round all percentage calculations to one decimal place.)
4. Comment on the financing percentage that results in each period. Do you think that this financing percentage should vary from period to period? Why or why not?

Problem 11-6

Selected accounts from three trial balances of the Cameron Corporation are presented below:

	Adjusted 12/31/X1	Adjusted 12/31/X2	Unadjusted 12/31/X3
Debits			
Bond Interest Expense	$ 7,100	$ 42,600	$ 31,950
Credits			
Bond Interest Payable	11,250	11,250	-0-
9% Bonds Payable — Issued 11/1/X1	500,000	500,000	500,000
Premium on Bonds	23,400	21,000	19,200

The data from the adjusted trial balances are correct. The bonds were issued between interest payment dates and straight-line amortization is used: amortization is recorded each time the bond interest expense is recorded.

Required:
1. Compute the following:
   a. original issue price as of November 1, 19X1
   b. maturity date
   c. semi-annual interest payment dates.
2. Reconstruct the journal entry to record the issuance of the bonds on November 1, 19X1.
3. Prepare any required adjusting entries as of December 31, 19X3.

Problem 11-7

Art's Autos Inc. was authorized to issue $500,000-worth of face value bonds.

Date of Authorization	Term	Bond Contract Interest Rate	Interest Payment Dates
January 1, 19X3	5 Years	12%	Semi-annually on June 30 and December 31

The following transactions occurred during 19X3:

Jan. 31   Issued $500,000-worth of face value bonds
Jun. 30   Paid the semi-annual interest on the issued bonds and made a straight-line entry to record amortization
Dec. 31   Paid the semi-annual interest on the issued bonds and made an entry to record amortization.

Required: Answer the questions for each of these cases.
Case A: the bonds were issued at a price to yield 12 percent.
Case B: the bonds were issued at a price to yield the market rate of interest (18%).
Case C: the bonds were issued at a price to yield the market rate of interest (8%).

1. Calculate
   a. The amount of each semi-annual interest payment on the issued bonds
   b. The issue price of the bonds, consisting of the present value of the bond face value and the present value of the 10 semi-annual interest payments to be made during the 5-year period (for convenience, round all calculations to the nearest dollar)
   c. The amount of amortization applicable to each interest payment date (use the straight-line method of amortization; for convenience, round all calculations to the nearest dollar).
2. Prepare journal entries to record the 19X3 transactions.

Problem 11-8

A 3-year $1,000,000, 10 percent bond issue was authorized for Murphy Corporation on April 1, 19X1. Interest is payable on March 31 and September 30. The year-end of the Corporation is December 31.

Required: Consider the following independent cases:
1. The Murphy Corporation issued the bonds to the Prost Investment Company on April 1, 19X1 at 97. Prepare the journal entries required on April 1, 19X1, September 30, 19X1, and December 31, 19X1. Assume straight-line amortization.
2. The bonds are issued at 106 on April 1, 19X1. Prepare the journal entries to record the sale of the bonds on April 1, 19X1 and entries required on September 30, 19X1 and December 31, 19X1.
3. Due to unfavourable market conditions, the bonds are not issued until October 1, 19X2 at 103 plus accrued interest. Prepare the journal entries on October 1, 19X2 and December 31, 19X2 (year-end). Assume straight-line amortization.

Problem 11-9

Snopes Products Inc., which uses effective interest amortization calculation, was authorized to issue $1,000,000-worth of face value bonds. On January 1, 19X1, Snopes issued $300,000-worth of face value bonds for $272,263. On this date, the market rate of interest was 16 percent.

Date of Authorization	Term	Bond Contract Interest Rate	Interest Payment Dates
January 1, 19X1	3 Years	12%	Semi-annually on June 30 and December 31

Required:
1. Calculate the amount of interest paid every interest payment date.
2. Prepare an amortization table. (The carrying value at January 1, 19X1 is $272,263 and periodic interest is $21,781.) For convenience, round all column B calculations to the nearest dollar. Use the effective interest method of amortization.
3. Calculate the financing percentage under the effective interest method of amortization for each six-month period. For convenience round all percentage calculations to the nearest percent.
4. Comment on the financing percentage that results in each period. Do you think that this financing percentage should remain constant from period to period? Why or why not?

Problem 11-10

Woudstra Corp. was authorized to issue $1,000,000-worth of face value bonds. The corporation has issued $100,000-worth of face value bonds on the date of bond authorization for $107,721. The market rate of interest on the issue date was 10 percent.

Date of Authorization	Term	Bond Contract Interest Rate	Interest Payment Dates
January 1, 19X4	5 Years	12%	Semi-annually on June 30 and December 31

Required: Consider these cases.
Case A: Woudstra uses the straight-line method of amortization.
Case B: Woudstra uses the effective interest method of amortization.

Prepare an amortization table to calculate the amount of amortization applicable to the first three six-month periods. For each of the cases

1. Calculate
   a. The amount of interest paid on $100,000-worth of face value bonds every interest payment date
   b. The amount of amortization to be recorded at each interest payment date; for convenience, round all calculations to the nearest dollar.
2. a. Prepare a schedule comparing the financing charge for the first year under both effective interest and straight-line methods. For convenience, round all percent calculations to one decimal place.
   b. Comment on the financing percentage that results under each amortization method. Which method is most appropriate? Why?
3. Prepare journal entries to record
   a. The issue of the bonds
   b. The payment of interest and amortization applicable at June 30, 19X4
   c. The payment of interest and amortization applicable at December 31, 19X4
   d. The redemption of the bonds at maturity, January 1, 19X6.

Alternate Problems

Alternate Problem 11-1

The financing structure of Dune Corp. is currently as follows:

Current Liabilities	$200,000
Bond Payable	-0-
Preferred Stock — $8, 1000 shares outstanding	100,000
Common Stock — 50 000 shares	500,000
Retained Earnings	300,000

Management is considering a plant expansion costing $1,000,000. Several different factors have been considered in a selection of a financing method; the effect of alternative financing methods on earnings per common share remains to be analyzed. The following financing methods are being considered:
a.   Sell $1 million-worth of 12-percent bonds at face value
b.   Sell another 10,000 common shares at $100 per share.
Dome is a profitable growth company and operating income (before interest and tax) is expected to average $200,000 per annum; the income tax rate is 50 percent.

Required:
1. Prepare a schedule to compare the effect on earnings per common share of each of the financing options.
2. Based on earnings per common share, which method is financially advantageous to common shareholders?
3. What other factors should be considered before a final decision is made?

Alternate Problem 11-2

Russel's Rugs Corp. was authorized to issue $500,000-worth of face value bonds. The corporation issued $250,000-worth of face value bonds on January 1, 19X4.

Date of Authorization	Term	Bond Contract Interest Rate	Interest Payment Dates
January 1, 19X4	3 Years	12%	Semi-annually on June 30 and December 31

Required: Answer the questions for each of these cases.
Case A: the bonds are issued at face value.
Case B: the bonds are issued for $256,000.
Case C: the bonds are issued for $242,800.

1. Calculate
   a. The amount of interest paid on the issued bonds every interest payment date
   b. The amount of amortization, if any, applicable to each interest payment date (use the straight-line method of amortization).
2. Prepare journal entries to record
   a. The issue of the bonds
   b. The payment of interest and recording of amortization, if any, on June 30, 19X4
   c. The payment of interest and recording of amortization, if any, on December 31, 19X4.
3. Calculate the amount of interest expense shown in the income statement at December 31, 19X4. Is this amount the same as cash paid by Russel's in 19X4? Why or why not?
4. On December 31, 19X4, the corporation exercised a call feature included in the bond indenture and retired the $250,000-worth of face value bonds issued January 1, 19X4. The bonds were called at 103. Prepare the December 31 journal entry to record the exercise of the call option.

Alternate Problem 11-3

Cathy's Copper Products Inc. was authorized to issue $1,000,000-worth of face value bonds.

Date of Authorization	Term	Bond Contract Interest Rate	Interest Payment Dates
January 1, 19X7	3 Years	12%	Semi-annually on June 30 and December 31

The following transactions occurred during 19X7.

Jan. 1 Issued $100,000-worth of face value bonds
Jun. 30 Paid the semi-annual interest on the issued bonds and made an entry to record straight-line amortization
Dec. 31 Paid the semi-annual interest on the issued bonds and made an entry to record amortization.

Required: Answer the questions for each of these cases.
Case A: the bonds were issued at a price to yield 12 percent.
Case B: the bonds were issued at a price to yield the market rate of interest (16%).
Case C: the bonds were issued to yield the market rate of interest (10%).

1. Calculate
   a. The amount of each semi-annual interest payment on the issued bonds
   b. The issue price of the bonds, consisting of the present value of the bond face value and the present value of the 6 semi-annual interest payments to be made during the 3-year period (for convenience, round all calculations to the nearest dollar)
   c. The amount of amortization applicable to each interest payment date (use the straight-line method of amortization; for convenience, round all calculations to the nearest dollar).
2. Prepare journal entries to record the 19X7 transactions.

Alternate Problem 11-4

The HAB Company Limited arranged to sell two million dollars of its bonds to the XYZ Insurance Corporation to finance a substantial increase in capacity. The following data are available:

19X1

Jul. 2 HAB received authorization for an issue of 2 million 10-year, 12 percent bonds dated this date. Interest is payable semi-annually: January 2 and July 2.
(HAB closes its books December 31 of each year.)

Aug. 1 HAB issued for cash $1,000,000 face value of the bonds for $1,045,700 plus accrued interest.

19X2

Mar. 1 HAB issued the remaining $1,000,000 face value of the bonds for 97.76 plus accrued interest. The new price reflects the change that took place during the period in interest rates.

Jul. 2 HAB recorded the necessary entry related to the bond issue.

Required:
1. Record all necessary entries for the period July 2, 19X1 to July 2, 19X2 inclusive, including December 31, 19X1, the year-end of the company.
2. Calculate the balance of the Bond Premium account at December 31, 19X1.
3. Prepare the long-term liability section of HAB's balance sheet for December 31, 19X1.
4. If the market interest rate is 18 percent at December 31, 19X1, what would be the effect on the market value of HAB's bonds?
5. How much cash interest was paid to bondholders in 19X2? Is this more or less than the bond interest expense appearing on the income statement at December 31 of 19X2? Explain, showing calculations to support your answer.

Alternate Problem 11-5

On January 2, 19X1, Hamilton Company Ltd. issued $2,000,000 face value 3-year 12 percent first mortgage bonds at 97. Interest on the bonds is payable semi-annually on June 30 and December 31. Hamilton's year-end is December 31.

Required:
1. Prepare all journal entries necessary on the following dates:
   a. January 2, 19X1
   b. June 30, 19X1
   c. December 31, 19X1
   d. January 2, 19X4.
2. Calculate the amount of interest paid in cash in 19X1.
3. Calculate the true interest expense for 19X1.
4. What is the balance of the Discount on Bonds account at December 31, 19X1?
5. If the purchasing power of the dollar declines 15 percent in each of the 3 years, would you consider these bonds a good investment?

Alternate Problem 11-6

Part A

Plumbum Inc. was authorized to issue $500,000-worth of face value bonds. On January 1, 19X1, the corporation issued $200,000-worth of face value bonds for $212,000.

Date of Authorization	Term	Bond Contract Interest Rate	Interest Payment Dates
January 1, 19X1	3 Years	12%	Semi-annually on June 30 and December 31

Required:
1. Calculate
   a. The amount of interest paid every interest payment date
   b. The amount of amortization to be recorded at each interest payment date (use the straight-line method of amortization).
2. Prepare a schedule like the one in Figure 11-4 to show the effect of premium amortization at each interest payment date. (Note that amortization is recorded each time interest expense is recorded.)
3. Prepare the journal entries to record the interest and amortization at June 30, 19X1.
4. Prepare a partial balance sheet, showing the bond liability, and the bond premium as a deferred credit, on the following dates:
   a. December 31, 19X1 (note that the bonds are a long-term liability on this date, since they will not be redeemed in 19X2)
   b. December 31, 19X2 (note that the bonds are a current liability on this date, since they will be redeemed on January 1, 19X4).

Part B

The bond indenture contained a sinking fund provision requiring equal annual contributions that are transferred to a trustee who guarantees a 10 percent annual return. Annual contributions are made on December 31, 19X1, 19X2, and 19X3. The amount of the contributions and the 10 percent revenue in the sinking fund are calculated in the following schedule.

December 31	Annual Contribution	10% Annual Revenue	Annual Total	Fund Balance
19X1	$60,423	-0-	$60,423	$ 60,423
19X2	60,423	(10% × $ 60,423 =) $ 6,042	66,465	126,888
19X3	60,423	(10% × 126,888 =) $12,689	73,112	200,000

Required: Prepare journal entries to record
5. The annual contribution in each of the three years
6. The 10 percent annual revenue in each of the three years
7. The redemption of the bonds at maturity.

Alternate Problem 11-7

On the date of authorization, January 1, 19X1, the Pittsboro Corporation issued 4-year sinking fund bonds with a face value of $800,000 at 100. The sinking fund indenture requires an annual contribution at the end of each of the 4 years to provide for the retirement of the bonds at maturity. As an added protection, the terms of the bond indenture require that retained earnings be restricted in an annual amount equal to the total addition to the sinking fund. The Pittsboro Corporation is to make a deposit to the Bank of Nova Scotia, which has been named trustee of the sinking fund, of amounts that when added to the sinking fund earnings will total $200,000 each year. The Bank of Nova Scotia guaranteed the Pittsboro Corporation a return of 8 percent annually. The bank will credit the Sinking Fund account with this return each December 31.

Required:
1. Record the issuance of the sinking fund bonds.
2. Give all the entries for the four years to record the deposits to the sinking fund and the related restrictions on retained earnings.
3. Record the retirement of the sinking fund bonds by the trustee on the maturity date and the removal of the retained earnings restriction.

Alternate Problem 11-8

Selected accounts from the trial balances of Norkis Corp. are presented below:

	Adjusted		Unadjusted
	12/31/X1	*12/31/X2*	*12/31/X3*
Debits			
Bond Interest Expense	$ 10,650	$ 63,900	$ 47,925
Credits			
Bond Interest Payable	16,875	16,875	-0-
9% Bonds Payable — Issued 11/1/X1	750,000	750,000	750,000
Discount on Bonds	35,100	31,500	28,800

The data from the adjusted trial balances are correct. The bonds were issued between interest payment dates. Straight-line amortization is used.

Required:
1. Compute the following:
   a. original issue price as of November 1, 19X1
   b. maturity date
   c. semi-annual interest payment dates.
2. Reconstruct the journal entry to record the issuance of the bonds on November 1, 19X1.
3. Prepare any required adjusting entries as of December 31, 19X3. Assume that straight-line amortization is recorded each time bond interest expense is recorded.

Alternate Problem 11-9

Savard Distributors Ltd. was authorized to issue $500,000-worth of face value bonds. On January 1, 19X1, the corporation issued $200,000-worth of face value bonds for $210,152.

Date of Authorization	*Term*	*Bond Contract Interest Rate*	*Interest Payment Dates*
January 1, 19X1	3 Years	12%	Semi-annually on June 30 and December 31

Required:
1. Calculate
   a. The amount of interest paid every interest payment date
   b. The amount of amortization to be recorded at each interest payment date (use the straight-line method of amortization).
2. Prepare an amortization table. (Note that amortization is recorded each time interest expense is recorded.)
3. Calculate the financing percentage under the straight-line method of amortization for each six-month period. For convenience round all percentage calculations to one decimal place.
4. Comment on the financing percentage that results in each period. Do you think that this financing percentage should vary from period to period? Why or why not?

Alternate Problem 11-10

Ross Ltd., which uses effective interest amortization calculation, was authorized to issue $500,000-worth of face value bonds. On January 1, 19X1, Ross issued $200,000-worth of face value bonds for $210,152. On this date, the market rate of interest was 16 percent.

Date of Authorization	*Term*	*Bond Contract Interest Rate*	*Interest Payment Dates*
January 1, 19X1	3 Years	12%	Semi-annually on June 30 and December 31

Required:
1. Calculate the amount of interest paid every interest payment date.
2. Prepare an amortization table. (The carrying value at January 1, 19X1 is $210,152 and periodic interest is $16,812.) For convenience, round all column B calculations to the nearest dollar. Use the effective interest method of amortization.
3. Calculate the financing percentage under the effective interest method of amortization for each six-month period. For convenience round all percentage calculations to the nearest percent.
4. Comment on the financing percentage that results in each period. Do you think that this financing percentage should remain constant from period to period? Why or why not?

Alternate Problem 11-11

Khom Inc. was authorized to issue $250,000-worth of face value bonds. These bonds were issued on the authorization date for $216,449. The market rate of interest on the issue date was 16 percent.

Date of Authorization January 1, 19X1	Term 5 Years	Bond Contract Interest Rate 12%	Interest Payment Dates Semi-annually on June 30 and December 31

Required: Answer the questions for these cases.
Case A: Khom Inc. uses the straight-line method of amortization.
Case B: Khom Inc. uses the effective interest method of amortization.
Prepare an amortization table to calculate the amount of amortization applicable to the first two six-month periods. For each of the cases

1. Calculate
   a. The amount of interest paid on the $250,000-worth of face value bonds every interest payment date
   b. The amount of amortization to be recorded at each interest payment date (for convenience round all calculations to the nearest dollar).
2. a. Prepare a schedule to compare the financing charge for the first year under both effective interest and straight-line methods. (For convenience, round all percent calculations to one decimal place.)
   b. Comment on the financing percentage that results under each amortization method. Which method is most appropriate? Why?
3. Prepare the journal entries to record
   a. The issue of the bonds
   b. The payment of interest and amortization applicable at June 30, 19X1
   c. The payment of interest and amortization applicable at December 31, 19X4
   d. The redemption of the bonds at maturity, January 1, 19X6.

Supplementary Problems

Supplementary Problem 11-1

Eni Corporation was authorized to issue $150,000-worth of face value bonds. On January 1, 19X1, the corporation issued $100,000-worth of face value bonds to finance the construction of a new plant. The bonds were issued for $100,000.

Date of Authorization January 1, 19X1	Term 3 Years	Bond Contract Interest Rate 12%	Interest Payment Dates Semi-annually on June 30 and December 31

Required:
1. Calculate the amount of interest paid every six months.
2. Prepare journal entries to record
   a. The issue of the bonds on January 1, 19X1
   b. The payment of interest on June 30, 19X1
   c. The payment of interest on December 31, 19X1.

An additional $50,000-worth of face value bonds were issued January 1, 19X2. These bonds were issued for $48,000.

    3. Calculate the following:
       a. The amount of interest paid on the $150,000-worth of face value of bonds every interest payment date
       b. The amount of amortization to be recorded at each interest payment date (use the straight-line method of amortization).
    4. Prepare journal entries to record
       a. The issue of the bonds on January 1, 19X2
       b. The payment of interest on June 30, 19X2 on bonds with a face value of $150,000
       c. The amortization of bond discount on June 30, 19X2
       d. The payment of interest on December 31, 19X2
       e. The amortization of bond discount on December 31, 19X2.
    5. Prepare a partial balance sheet at December 31, 19X2 to show the bond liability and the bond discount as a deferred charge. (Note that the bonds are to be redeemed on January 1, 19X4.)
    6. Prepare a journal entry to record the redemption of the bonds at maturity, January 1, 19X4.

Supplementary Problem 11-2

Grandma's Kitchen Inc. was authorized to issue $800,000-worth of face value bonds. The corporation issued bonds of $200,000 face value for $207,200.

Date of Authorization	Term	Bond Contract Interest Rate	Interest Payment Dates
January 1, 19X7	3 Years	12%	Semi-annually on June 30 and December 31

Required: Answer the questions for each of these cases.
Case A: the bonds are issued on January 1, 19X7.
Case B: the bonds are issued on April 1, 19X7. (Note that the issue price includes accrued interest.)
Case C: the bonds are issued on July 1, 19X7.

    1. Calculate
       a. The amount of interest paid on the issued bonds every interest payment date
       b. The amount of amortization, if any, applicable to each month remaining in the life of the bonds subsequent to the issue date (calculate separately the amortization to be recorded at each interest payment date; use the straight-line method of amortization).
    2. Prepare journal entries to record
       a. The issue of the bonds
       b. The payment of interest and recording of amortization, if any, on June 30, 19X7
       c. The payment of interest and recording of amortization, if any, on December 31, 19X7.
    3. Calculate the amount of interest expense shown in the income statement at December 31, 19X7. Is this amount the same as cash paid as interest in 19X7? Why or why not?

Supplementary Problem 11-3

The following information appears in the published balance sheet of Eykelbosh Corporation at December 31, 19X3, its fiscal year-end.

Deferred Charges:	
Discount on Bonds Payable	$ 4,000
Long-Term Liabilities:	
Bond Payable	500,000

The corporation was authorized to issued $500,000-worth of face value bonds to finance the construction of a new solar cell assembly plant. The bonds were issued on their authorization date. The corporation uses the straight-line method of amortization.

Date of Authorization	*Term*	*Bond Contract Interest Rate*	*Interest Payment Dates*
January 1, 19X3	3 Years	12%	Semi-annually on June 30 and December 31

Required:
1. Calculate
   a. The proceeds from the bond issue on January 1, 19X3
   b. The amount of cash interest paid in 19X3
   c. The amount of amortization recorded during 19X3
   d. The total amount of amortization to be recorded during the life of the bonds
   e. The amount of interest expense appearing in the 19X3 income statement.
2. Prepare journal entries to record
   a. The issue of the bonds on January 1, 19X3
   b. The payment of interest and recording of bond discount amortization on June 30, 19X3
   c. The payment of interest and recording of bond discount amortization on December 31, 19X3.

On January 1, 19X4, some bondholders exercised a conversion feature contained in the bond indenture; $100,000-worth of face value bonds were converted into the corporation's common shares.

3. Prepare a journal entry to record the conversion.

Supplementary Problem 11-4

Lloyd's Software House Inc. was authorized to issue $400,000-worth of face value bonds. On April 1, 19X5, the corporation issued bonds of $100,000 face value in order to purchase the rights to a word processing software package.

Date of Authorization	*Term*	*Bond Contract Interest Rate*	*Interest Payment Dates*
January 1, 19X5	3 Years	12%	Semi-annually on June 30 and December 31

Required: Consider these cases. Case A: the bonds are issued for $100,000, an amount which includes the accrued interest. Case B: the bonds are issued for $106,600, an amount which includes the accrued interest. Case C: the bonds are issued for $96,700, an amount which includes the accrued interest. For each of the cases

1. Calculate
    a. The amount of interest paid on $100,000 face value bonds every interest payment date
    b. The amount of accrued interest on the bonds issued April 1, 19X5
    c. The amount of amortization applicable to each month remaining in the life of the bonds, subsequent to the issue date; calculate separately the actual amount of amortization to be recorded at each interest payment date, using the straight-line method of amortization.
2. Prepare journal entries to record
    a. The issue of bonds on April 1, 19X5 (including accrued interest)
    b. The payment of interest on June 30, 19X5
    c. The amortization on June 30, 19X5
    d. The payment of interest on December 31, 19X5
    e. The amortization on December 31, 19X5
    f. The redemption of the bonds at maturity, January 1, 19X8.
3. Calculate the amount of interest expense shown in the income statement at December 31, 19X5.
4. Prepare a partial balance sheet at December 31, 19X5, to show the bond liability and bond premium or discount, if applicable.

Supplementary Problem 11-5

Fertuck Ltd. was authorized to issue $800,000-worth of face value bonds. On the date of authorization, the corporation issued bonds of $200,000 (face value) at a price to yield the market 18 percent rate of interest.

Date of Authorization	Term	Bond Contract Interest Rate	Interest Payment Dates
January 1, 19X2	3 Years	12%	Semi-annually on June 30 and December 31

Required:

1. Calculate
    a. The amount of each semi-annual interest payment on the issued bonds
    b. The issue price of the bonds, consisting of the present value of the bond face value and the present value of the 6 semi-annual interest payments to be made during the 3-year period (for convenience, round all calculations to the nearest dollar)
    c. The amount of amortization applicable to each 19X2 interest payment date; prepare, using the effective interest method of amortization, an amortization table for the 3-year period (for convenience, round all calculations to the nearest dollar).
2. Prepare journal entries to record the 19X3 transactions.
3. a. Compare the financing percentage for 19X3 under both effective interest and straight-line methods. (For convenience, round all percent calculations to one decimal place.)
    b. Comment on the financing percentage that results under each amortization method. Which method is most appropriate? Why?

The Investment Cycle

Part 5 deals with the investment activities of an entity. These activities may be either an investment of temporarily idle cash or may involve the acquisition of a long-term position in another entity to exercise a degree of control over the other entities.

The investment cycle views equity and debt from the viewpoint of the purchaser — the investor who transfers capital to a corporation. The relative risk of investing in bonds and shares is reviewed and differences in their accounting treatment are illustrated.

Chapter 12 deals with issues relating to both short-term and long-term bond and share investments. Chapter 13 focuses on business combinations and ways in which an investor acquires a controlling interest in another entity. Such an investor is actually able to control the entity, which is then referred to as a subsidiary. Although there are some exceptions, the individual financial statements of the parent and subsidiary are combined for reporting purposes, as if they were one economic entity and not two separate corporations.

The Investment Cycle

One corporation often invests in the bonds or shares of another corporation. These investments can be either temporary or long-term. Temporarily idle cash is often invested in securities that can be readily reconverted into cash as financing needs require. Relevant questions of interest to investors include:

1. Are bonds or shares a more secure form of investment?
2. What are the advantages of investing in shares of a corporation?
3. Is it true that investors have little chance of making a substantial profit on the stock market as is claimed by the efficient market hypothesis?
4. What are the alternative methods of disclosure of investments in the balance sheet?
5. What are the differences in accounting for investments in shares and bonds?
6. How are marketable securities valued for balance sheet purposes?
7. How are bond premiums and bond discounts amortized?

A.   The Investment Decision

Every corporate entity is financed by capital transferred to it by both shareholders and creditors. The preceding chapters have viewed shares and bonds from the point of view of the issuing corporations. This chapter views shares and bonds from the viewpoint of the *purchasing entity* — the investor who transfers capital into a corporation. Investments in a corporation can take various forms, as shown in Figure 12-1.

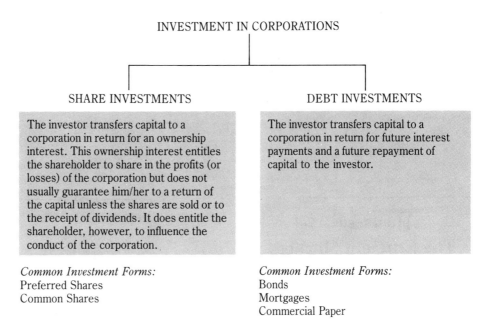

INVESTMENT IN CORPORATIONS

SHARE INVESTMENTS

The investor transfers capital to a corporation in return for an ownership interest. This ownership interest entitles the shareholder to share in the profits (or losses) of the corporation but does not usually guarantee him/her to a return of the capital unless the shares are sold or to the receipt of dividends. It does entitle the shareholder, however, to influence the conduct of the corporation.

Common Investment Forms:
Preferred Shares
Common Shares

DEBT INVESTMENTS

The investor transfers capital to a corporation in return for future interest payments and a future repayment of capital to the investor.

Common Investment Forms:
Bonds
Mortgages
Commercial Paper

Figure 12-1   Forms of investment in corporations

No investor is guaranteed against a loss of invested capital if the business entity is unsuccessful. In fact, both share and debt investments can be lost if a corporation becomes bankrupt and there remain insufficient assets to be distributed to investors. Alternatively, there may be insufficient cash to pay interest to debt investors even when a corporation is not bankrupt. This, in fact, has occurred — for instance in the cases of Massey-Ferguson Ltd. and the Chrysler Corporation.

In normal circumstances, bondholders are more secure than shareholders and are able to institute legal action to obtain at least partial repayment of their capital and the interest owed them, even if this would result in the liquidation of the corporation.

Shareholders are unable to force the repayment of their investments, unless the privileges and rights attaching to the shares include a redeemable or conversion privilege; usually shareholders are also unable to force a corporation to pay dividends. Why, then, would someone wish to invest in shares of a corporation? There are many reasons:

1. While it is true that an investor does risk capital, he/she also expects rewards in return. If the corporation is successful, the investor in common shares will increase the value of the investment substantially. This is *capital appreciation.*
2. The investor in common shares has a vote in the running of the corporation. The investor has an opportunity to participate in setting the goals of the corporation.

3. Dividends may be declared by the corporation and may become substantial in relation to the amount of the investor's original investment. If dividends are not declared but are re-invested within the corporation, the value of the investment in common shares should increase.

Stock Market Prices

Efficient markets hypothesis
The theory that securities are typically in equilibrium and that they are fairly priced in the sense that the price reflects all publicly available information on the security.

The **efficient market hypothesis** claims that investors have little chance of consistently making substantial profits on the stock market because prices reflect all publicly available information almost instantaneously. Thus, the price of shares always reflects real worth. This theory suggests that when stocks are undervalued so that investors could gain high yields, the market prices quickly adjust as soon as there is an awareness of these undervalued stocks. The applicability of this theory in real life is discussed in Conceptual Issue 12-1.

Conceptual Issue 12-1
The Efficient Markets Hypothesis

There is a passage in Lewis Carroll's *Through the Looking Glass* that sums up the stock market view of most finance professors at the University of Chicago Business School. "Here, you see," the Red Queen tells Alice, "it takes all the running you can do, to keep in the same place."

Translated into financial theory at Chicago, this means that no matter how carefully you pick your stocks, you cannot, on average, beat the market. In theory, therefore, the best plan is simply to buy all the stocks in the market. This idea is known as the random walk theory, or efficient markets hypothesis, and it rests on the assumption that all important information about the real value of a stock is already incorporated in the stock's price. It is also the theory for which the Chicago Business School's finance department is famous — if the stock market presents an overly advantageous investment opportunity, the market is efficient enough to spot it quickly and bid up prices almost immediately. In other words, the market sees everything.

The efficient markets theory has inspired an almost religious frenzy among generations of doctoral candidates. For years, computer tapes have spun day and night in Chicago, as scores of researchers have tried to discover the extent to which the efficient markets hypothesis fits the real world. And almost always, the theory works.

But from time to time a researcher discovers something that the Chicago theory of efficient markets does not explain and even contradicts. Rolf Banz was such a researcher. As a Chicago graduate student in the mid-1970s, he discovered that if publicly traded companies were ranked in order of total market value, the smallest 20 percent earned abnormally high investor returns, even after adjusting for risk.

The Banz anomaly, now known as the "small-firm effect," continues to puzzle scholars of finance, especially those who adhere strongly to the efficient markets theory. But this puzzlement has not stopped some from making money on the anomaly. Thus, in 1981, a group of Chicago graduates, with the help of their professors, founded Dimensional Fund Advisors, an investment company designed to take advantage of the contradictory small-firm effect. DFA began offering a mutual fund that invested in the common stocks of some 650 companies with market values below $69 million, weighted in proportion to each company's size.

An obvious question about the fund's success is how is it affecting the Ivory Tower thinking at the famed Chicago school? According to Professor Miller, some day either the small-firm effect or the Banz theory itself will disappear. The enduring threat is that the theory is like a "barnacle" clinging to the efficient markets hypothesis. Over time, more barnacles will accumulate, until the efficient market hypothesis finally collapses and a new one takes its place. Though that may shake up the Chicago school, DFA officers will be scratching their heads all the way to the bank.

Source   Claudia Rosett, "Chicago School Bets on Inefficiency", Copyright 1983 by *The New York Times Company*. Reprinted by permission.

Valuation of Investments

There are three different methods for the disclosure of investments on the balance sheet.

Alternative 1: Original Cost

Investments are reported at their acquisition costs, which include the original amount paid, brokerage fees, and any other acquisition costs. Under this method, the market value is disclosed on the balance sheet in parenthesis, even if market value declines below cost, provided that the decline is not expected to be permanent. This is the accepted Canadian method. In this method the temporary decline does not appear on the income statement. The *CICA Handbook* recommends that the cost of investments sold should be calculated on the basis of **average carrying value**.

Average carrying value
The average of the historical costs of an entity's investments.

Alternative 2: Lower of Cost and Market

Under this method, cost is compared with market value of the securities at each balance sheet date, and the lower of the two appears on the balance sheet. Where a substantial decline in market value has occurred, accepted practice is to value the securities at the lower of cost and market (LOCAM). However, if the market value of the securities subsequently increases, the increase is not recorded, even though the new market value is still lower than original cost.

Alternative 3: Current Market Value

The market value at balance sheet date is taken as the value of investments, regardless of what cost is. This is not a generally accepted method of valuing these securities and is seldom used in actual practice.

Accounting for Corporate Investments

Temporary investments
Investments of temporarily idle cash, usually in marketable securities, made for a period not exceeding one year from the balance sheet date.

Long-term investments
Investments in stocks and bonds that are not of a short-term nature.

Portfolio investments
Long-term investments in companies not owned or significantly influenced by the reporting enterprise.

Investments may be either **temporary** or **long-term**. The investor makes the decision. This decision affects the subsequent accounting treatment of the investment account. Although investments are always recorded at cost when the investment is made, special problems arise in the accounting for these investments after their acquisition dates. Temporary and long-term investments are also classified differently on the balance sheet of the investor.

Temporarily idle cash usually earns no income unless it is invested. If the investor's objective is to invest in securities on a temporary basis and if these securities are readily convertible into cash, then these investments are referred to as *marketable securities* and are classified on the balance sheet as current assets immediately under cash and before accounts receivable.

Investors may decide to invest in the bonds of a corporation, or in voting or non-voting shares of a corporation, as long-term *investments*. These investments are classified on the balance sheet as long-term assets.

The *CICA Handbook* (section 3050.03) defined **portfolio investments** as "long-term investments that are not investments in subsidiaries, joint ventures, or partnerships of the reporting enterprise, nor investments in companies that are subject to significant influence by the reporting enterprise". Both shares and bonds are included in this definition of portfolio investments.

Differences in Share and Bond Investment Accounting

The accounting for investments is influenced by a number of other considerations. The purchase of shares is always recorded at cost. However, because share purchases result in an ownership interest in the corporation, the subsequent accounting for the investment is affected by the influence that the investor is able to exert over the corporation. This matter is discussed further in Chapter 13.

When the investment in bonds is of a temporary nature, note that no amortization of bond premium or discount is recorded in the books of the investor. This is because the bonds are not expected to be held until maturity. The practice is further justified by the fact that the amounts involved would not be material. However, the premium or discount on bonds purchased as long-term investments is amortized. The amortization of an investor's bond premium or discount, if any, is discussed in section C of this chapter.

B.   Investments in Marketable Securities

Excess cash can be kept in a non-interest-bearing bank account or it can be invested in dividend-producing or interest-earning securities. A corporation's investment in such securities is considered temporary when its intention is to hold them for the short term and then reconvert them to cash. These securities are referred to as *marketable* when they are readily convertible to cash. **Marketable securities** usually consist of securities from government and publicly traded corporations; they may also include treasury bills, investment certificates, and call loans.

Marketable securities Investments in stock and bonds that are readily marketable; also includes investments in treasury bills, investment securities, and call loans.

The purchase of securities is always recorded at the purchase cost, including brokerage charges and any other acquisition costs. Assume the following are initial temporary investments in Bluebeard Computer Corporation in 19X1:

Share Purchase:
100 shares of BCC stock are purchased on the stock exchange for $45. Brokerage charges of $100 are paid. The purchase is recorded at cost as follows:

| Marketable Securities | 4,600 | |
| Cash | | 4,600 |

To record the purchase of 100 shares at $45 per share, plus $100 brokerage charges (cost per share is $46).

Bond Purchase:
A $1,000 bond of BCC is purchased on the stock exchange at 106. Brokerage charges of $15 are paid. The purchase is recorded at cost as follows:

| Marketable Securities | 1,075 | |
| Cash | | 1,075 |

To record the purchase of a $1,000 bond at 106, plus brokerage charges.

Often the purchase price of shares includes dividends that have been declared but not yet paid at the time of the purchase of shares; bonds often include interest accrued but not yet paid at the purchase date. In such cases, the entry to record the purchase separates the dividend or interest component of the purchase price.

Assume the following additional purchase of temporary investments in the Bluebeard Computer Corporation is made during 19X1. (Note: this example assumes that reversing entries are not used by the corporation.)

Share Purchase:

50 shares of BCC stock are purchased at $46 per share. Included in the purchase price is a $2 per-share dividend that has been declared but not yet paid. Brokerage charges of $50 are paid. The purchase is recorded as follows:

Marketable Securities	2,250	
Dividends Receivable	100	
Cash		2,350

To record the purchase of 50 shares at $46, including a $2 per share dividend (cost per share is $45), and $50 brokerage fee.

When the dividend is received, it is recorded as follows:

Cash	100	
Dividends Receivable		100

To record dividend received on shares.

Bond Purchase:

$5,000-worth of BCC bonds are purchased at 105 plus $200 of accrued interest. The purchase is recorded as follows:

Marketable Securities	5,250	
Bond Interest Receivable	200	
Cash		5,450

To record the purchase of $5,000-worth of bonds at 105, plus $200 accrued interest.

Note: the cost of the bonds does not include the accrued interest; the accrued interest is recorded as a separate asset.

When the semi-annual interest of $300 is received, it is recorded as follows:

Cash	300	
Bond Interest Receivable		200
Bond Interest Earned		100

To record receipt of semi-annual interest on bond.

All purchases are recorded at cost. Interest is earned on the bonds with the passage of time and is recorded as income when received or when an adjustment entry is prepared. Although dividends do not accrue with the passing of time, corporations often declare a quarterly dividend per share and it is at the date of declaration that the dividend is legally payable. The following journal entries illustrate the recording for dividend declaration and interest accrual.

Dividend Declaration:

When dividends are declared, the following entry is made:

Dividends Receivable	375	
Dividends Earned		375

To record the declaration of a $2.50 per-share dividend on 150 shares (150 shares × $2.50 = $375).

The subsequent receipt of the dividend is recorded as follows:

Cash	375	
Dividends Receivable		375

To record receipt of dividends on 150 shares.

Interest Accrual:

The accrual of interest is recorded as follows:

Bond Interest Receivable	360	
Bond Interest Earned		360

To record the accrual of interest earned on bonds

$$(\$6{,}000 \times 12\% \times \frac{6}{12} = \$360).$$

The subsequent receipt of interest is recorded as follows:

Cash	360	
Bond Interest Receivable		360

To record receipt of interest on $6,000-worth of bonds.

Temporary investments in bonds are not expected to be held until maturity; therefore, no amortization of any bond premium or discount is recorded. Rather, a gain or loss is recognized when the bonds are sold.

Stock Dividends

As illustrated in Chapter 10, a stock dividend consists of shares instead of cash. The stock dividend is expressed as a percentage of shares owned; for example, an investor owning 1000 shares receives 100 new shares when a 10 percent stock dividend is issued. No journal entry is made by the investor on receipt of a stock dividend, since there is no dividend income. The investor simply increases the number of shares owned in the declaring corporation and, of course, has 100 additional share certificates. The investor's total cost of shares remains the amount that was originally paid for the 1000 shares.

Investment in Shares

	Before Stock Dividend		After Stock Dividend	
	Cost	Shares Owned	Cost	Shares Owned
	$5,000	1000 shares	$5,000	1100 shares

Cost per Share:
$5,000 ÷ 1000 Shares $5
$5,000 ÷ 1100 Shares $4.55 (rounded)

As seen in these calculations, the $5,000 cost of this investor's shares is allocated over 1000 shares before the stock dividend, and over 1100 shares after the stock dividend. The cost of the shares continues to be $5,000 in total; only the cost per share changes.

Theoretically, the per-share market value of the common shares should fall somewhat to compensate for the increased number of shares. For example, the market price of the share should decrease as follows:

	Before Stock Dividend	After Stock Dividend (theoretically)
Market Price of Common Share	$4	A New, Lower Market Value
Total Market Value of Shares:		
1000 Shares × $4	$4,000	$4,000
1100 Shares × New Market Price		$3.64 (rounded)

In reality, the market price rarely decreases proportionately to the percentage of the stock dividend. Usually, if the stock dividend is not large in relation to the total of outstanding shares, no change occurs in the per-share market value of the shares. Therefore, the investor would see the market value of these shares increase as follows:

	Market Value of Investment	
	Before Stock Dividend	After Stock Dividend
Common Shares:		
1000 × $4	$4,000	
1100 × $4		$4,400

That is, the investor sees the total market value of common shares increase by $400. No journal entry is made by the investor to reflect this *unrealized* increase. If a gain (or loss) on the investment is realized, it is recorded when the shares have actually been sold.

Sale of Marketable Securities

The *CICA Handbook* recommends that the cost of investments sold should be calculated on the basis of average carrying value. In this way, the difficulties of identifying the specific cost of the investments, or the calculation of a FIFO or LIFO cost, are avoided. A gain or loss results from the difference between cost and the proceeds of sale. When bonds are sold, any accrued interest is included in the entry to record the sale with a credit to the Bond Interest Earned account.

Assume that the temporary investment in shares is subsequently reconverted to cash; the 150 shares are sold for $48 per share. The following entry records this transaction.

Cash	7,200	
Marketable Securities (4,600 + 2,250)		6,850
Gain on Sale of Marketable Securities		350
To record the sale of 150 shares.		

The gain on a disposal of marketable securities is classified on the income statement as *other income*. The gain calculated above must be considered along with the dividends received in evaluating the investment in shares.

Valuation of Marketable Securities

Canadian practice favours the valuation of marketable securities at cost and the disclosure of market values of these securities in parentheses on the balance sheet. Where a substantial decline in market value has occurred, accepted practice is to value both debt and equity securities at the lower of cost and market. In this situation, an unrealized loss from market fluctuations is recognized; an unrealized gain, however, is never recognized before the sale of the investment.

Issues in Ethics 12-1

Du Pont Changes Policy on CFCs

On March 4, Richard Heckert, chairman of E. I. du Pont de Nemours & Co., wrote the kind of combative letter du Pont executives have been writing for years. Answering three senators who had sharply criticized the company, he said there was no reason for du Pont to stop making chlorofluorocarbons, the compound that critics says destroys the Earth's protective layer of ozone.

Last week, just 20 days after he had dismissed the concerns of the latest critics, Mr. Heckert announced a dramatic turnaround. Du Pont, he said, will get out of the chlorofluorocarbon business entirely. Du Pont executives promptly began to call for new worldwide controls on the substance, of which their company is the world's leading producer, with about 25 per cent of the market.

Du Pont executives said the change of heart did not arise from the years of battling the company had done with environmentalists about the ozone layer. It was a result of pure, hard, cold science making its points in a company where, they said, science has always mattered as much as business.

For years, du Pont had said that it was as concerned about the ozone layer as anyone, but that it did not see any proved connection between CFCs and the thinning of the ozone layer. In the 1970s, the company took out full-page newspaper ads to assure the public that it would end CFC production if the chemical posed a threat to public health.

The rethinking at du Pont began on Tuesday, March 15. A panel of scientists assembled by the National Aeronautics and Space Administration issued new findings that day on the chlorofluorocarbons, known as CFCs. The panel said that it had detected a significant reduction in the thickness of the ozone layer that might be linked to CFCs. It also said that whatever caused a previously detected "hole" in the ozone layer over the Antarctic seemed to be thinning the layer in other parts of the atmosphere.

Within hours of the panel's news conference in Washington, the huge company began to change course. By the turn of the century, CFC production would no longer be a du Pont business, and the company wanted to announce that to the world now.

The task was a complex one. For 10 days, scientists, senior managers and communications specialists worked virtually around the clock to communicate the company's policy change clearly and quickly. The company wanted to notify customers, competitors and regulators before it went public. It did not want its 2,000 CFC workers all over the world — or its 145,000 other workers — to hear the news from press reports.

Although CFC production has been symbolically important to du Pont as a leader in chemicals, it accounts for only about 2 per cent of profit, or about $35-million (U.S.) last year.

Source William Glaberson, "Behind du Pont's Shift on Loss of Ozone Layer", Copyright 1988 by *The New York Times Company*. Reprinted by permission.

C. Long-Term Intercorporate Bond Investments

The accounting for long-term investments in bonds is essentially the reverse of the accounting required by the bond issues described in Chapter 11. The accounting for the long-term investments in bonds is similar to the accounting for short-term investments in bonds and the receipt of interest; the only exception is the accounting for the amortization of premiums and discounts.

Purchase Cost of Bonds

Investments in bonds are always recorded at cost; cost includes brokerage charges and any other applicable acquisition costs. The purchase price is affected by such factors as risk and the rate of inflation, but is largely determined by how investors view the bond contract interest rate in relation to the prevailing market interest rate.

1. If the bond contract interest rate is the same as that required in the market, then the bonds are usually purchased at par.
2. If the bond contract interest rate is greater than that required in the market, then the bonds are usually purchased at a premium (more than face value) to yield the investor a lower market rate.
3. If the bond contract interest rate is less than that required in the market, then the bonds are usually purchased at discount (less than face value) to yield the investor a higher market rate.

The sale of bonds by Bluebeard Computer Corporation is illustrated in section C of Chapter 11. The same data are used here as an example of an investor's purchase of these 12-percent, 3-year, $100,000 bonds paying interest semi-annually on June 30 and December 31 of each year. Their purchase at a premium and discount is shown below:

Purchased at a Premium		*Purchased at a Discount*	
Investment in Bonds 110,485.00		Investment in Bonds 90,754.00	
Cash	110,485.00	Cash	90,754.00

Note that the cost of the purchase is recorded at cost; no separate discount or premium account is required.

Amortizing Premiums and Discounts

In actual practice, the amount of premium or discount is amortized in equal amounts over the life of the bond remaining from the purchase date. It is also accepted practice to record amortization each time a journal entry is made to record interest earned. Therefore, where bond interest earned is recorded, an appropriate amount of amortization is also recorded. The periodically recorded amortization will change the carrying value of the investment (see Figure 12-2).

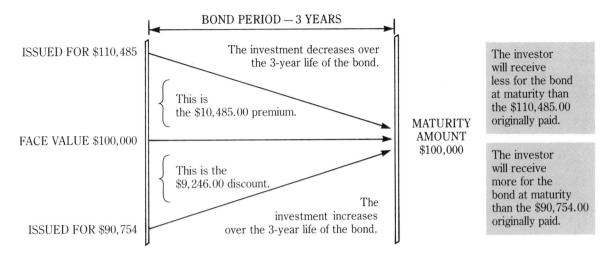

Figure 12-2   Change in carrying value over the life of the bond investment

The straight-line method of amortization is commonly used; an equal amount of amortization is allocated to each semi-annual period. The simplicity of calculation is this method's main advantage. The amortization is calculated as follows:

Amortization of a Premium		*Amortization of a Discount*	
Premium is	$10,485.00 (a)	Discount is	$9,246.00 (a)
Number of 6-month		Months left are	6 (b)
interest periods	6 (b)		
Calculation:		*Calculation:*	
(a ÷ b)		(a ÷ b)	
($10,485.00 ÷ 6) =	$1,747.50	($9,246 ÷ 6) =	$1,541.00

The straight-line method of amortization is used in the examples here. This method is easier to use, even though the effective interest method of amortization is preferable from a theoretical point of view. Canadian GAAP permits use of either method.

When the bond is redeemed at maturity, the following journal entry is recorded:

```
      19X4
      Jan. 4   Cash                                     100,000
                   Investment in Bonds                            100,000
                   To record retirement of
                   Bluebeard Computer Corporation bond.
```

The balance in the Investment in Bonds account has been reduced to face value at maturity; this entry reduces the balance in that account to zero.

How Is the Amortization of Premium Recorded in the Investor's Books?

In actual practice, the bond premium is commonly amortized using the straight-line method over the life of the bonds, until no premium remains at maturity. It is accepted practice to record amortization each time a journal entry is made to record interest. Therefore, when bond interest earned is recorded, an appropriate amount of premium amortization is also recorded. The amount of amortization applicable to each interest receipt period is calculated as follows:

$$\$10,485.00 \text{ Premium} \div 3 \text{ Years} \div 2 \text{ Interest Payments per year} = \$1,747.50 \text{ Amortization per Interest Period.}$$

The journal entries to record the receipt of interest and the appropriate amortization are as follows:

Receipt of Interest			*Amortization of Premium*		
Cash	6,000		Bond Interest Earned	1,747.50	
Bond Interest Earned		6,000	Investment in Bonds		1,747.50

> This entry decreases the investment account and also the bond interest earned. The interest rate is therefore lower than the 12 percent bond interest rate.

Similar entries are made each June 30 and December 31 until the BCC bonds mature in three years. Bond interest earned is usually recorded in a separate general ledger account. Note that premium amortization reduces the bond interest earned; the yield to the investor is less than the bond contract interest rate, in this case. Consequently, the discount amortization increases the bond interest earned, thereby increasing, in excess of the bond contract interest rate, the yield to the investor.

In these examples, the December 31 interest date coincides with the investor corporation's year-end. Therefore, no adjustment for bond interest earned is required at year-end. When the interest payment date does not coincide with the fiscal year-end, an adjusting journal entry is required at December 31 for the interest earned until that date and for the appropriate amount of amortization. The adjusting entry accruing interest to December 31 requires a debit to Bond Interest Receivable.

The amortization recorded during the three-year life of the bond will reduce the Investment in Bonds account to face value, $100,000. At maturity, the Investment in Bonds account appears as is shown in Figure 12-3.

Investment in Bonds

Date		Description	F	Debit	Credit	DR. or CR.	Balance
19X1							
Jan.	1	Purchase $100,000 Bonds		110 485 –			110 485 –
Jun.	30	Amortization of Premium			1 747 50		108 737 50
Dec.	31	Amortization of Premium			1 747 50		106 990 –
19X2							
Jun.	30	Amortization of Premium			1 747 50		105 242 50
Dec.	31	Amortization of Premium			1 747 50		103 495 –
19X3							
Jun.	30	Amortization of Premium			1 747 50		101 747 50
Dec.	31	Amortization of Premium			1 747 50		100 000 –

Figure 12-3   The Investment in Bonds account

The amount of premium has been amortized from the date of purchase to the date of maturity. If no amortization has been recorded, the amount of premium would be recognized as a loss in the accounting period during which the bonds mature. Such a loss would reflect only the failure to adjust the Bond Interest Earned account in earlier accounting periods.

How Is the Bond Discount Amortized in the Investor's Books?

The discount is amortized by periodic debits to the Investment in Bonds account and credits to Bond Interest Earned. Since interest is paid every six months, the periodic amortization is recorded as follows:

$9,246.00 ÷ 3 Years ÷ 2 Interest Payments per Year = $1,541.00 Amortization per Period.

Amortization is recorded every time bond interest expense is entered in the books:

Receipt of Interest:			*Amortization of Discount:*	
Cash	6,000		Investments in Bonds	1,541.00	
Bond Interest Earned		6,000	Bond Interest Earned		1,541.00

The debit to the investment account increases the amount of the investment recorded in the books; the credit to Bond Interest Earned represents additional interest earned over the 12 percent bond interest rate.

The recording of amortization during the three-year life of the bond is shown below. Study the effect of the discount amortization on both the Investment in Bonds and the Bond Interest Earned account.

		Investment in Bonds	Cash Interest Received	Actual Annual Bond Interest Earned
19X1				
Jan. 1	Purchase of Bonds	+$90,754		
Jun. 30	Interest Received		+$6,000	
	Discount Amortization	+1,541		
Dec. 31	Interest Received		+6,000	$15,082
	Discount Amortization	+1,541		
	Balance	$93,836	$12,000	$15,082
19X2				
Jun. 30	Interest Received		+$6,000	
	Discount Amortization	+1,541		
Dec. 31	Interest Received		+6,000	$15,082
	Discount Amortization	+1,541		
	Balance	$96,918	$12,000	$15,082
19X3				
Jun. 30	Interest Received		+$6,000	
	Discount Amortization	+1,541		
Dec. 31	Interest Received		+6,000	$15,082
	Discount Amortization	+1,541		
	Balance	$100,000	$12,000	$15,082
19X1				
Jan. 1		−100,000		
		-0-		

Interest received by the terms of the bond contract amounted to $12,000 per year; however, the interest earned was actually $15,082 per year. This additional interest usually compensates for the unfavourable bond interest rate in relation to the rate required in the securities market for this type of bond.

Study the following ledger accounts, which illustrate this increase over the first year of the bonds' term:

The investment account is increased each interest period by amortization.

Investment in Bonds		Bond Interest Earned	
90,754.00			6,000.00
1,541.00			1,541.00
1,541.00			6,000.00
			1,541.00
93,836.00			15,082.00

In the case of bonds purchased at a discount, bond interest earned consists of the 12 percent bond rate plus the amortized discount. Whenever an investor purchases bonds for less than face value, the investor's total interest earned is increased because of the discount amortization.

Comparison of Recording by the Bond Investor and the Investee

The following comparison of entries on the books of the investor and the investee illustrates the accounting for bonds. The comparison stresses the fact that the accounting for the investor is virtually the mirror image of the accounting for the investee.

19X1	*Transaction:*	*Recorded by the Investor*			*Recorded by the Investee (BCC)*		
Jan. 1	Investor purchases BCC's $100,000-worth of bonds	Investment in Bonds	90,754.00		Cash	90,754.00	
		Cash		90,754.00	Discount on Bonds		9,246.00
					Bonds Payable		100,000.00
Jun. 30	BCC pays semi-annual interest on bond. The bond premium is amortized for 6 months.	Cash	6,000.00		Bond Interest Expense	6,000.00	
		Bond Interest Earned		6,000.00	Cash		6,000.00
		Investment in Bonds	1,541.00		Bond Interest Expense	1,541.00	
		Bond Interest Earned		1,541.00	Discount on Bonds		1,541.00
Dec. 31	BCC pays semi-annual interest on bond. The bond premium is amortized for 6 months.	Cash	6,000.00		Bond Interest Expense	6,000.00	
		Bond Interest Earned		6,000.00	Cash		6,000.00
		Investment in Bonds	1,541.00		Bond Interest Expense	1,541.00	
		Bond Interest Earned		1,541.00	Discount on Bonds		1,541.00

Valuation of Long-Term Investments

Canadian practice favours the balance sheet valuation of long-term investments at cost. The market value is disclosed on the balance sheet in parentheses, even if the market value of these investments declines below cost, provided that the decline is not expected to be permanent. When a permanent loss in the value of the investment has occurred, the *CICA Handbook* recommends that the investment be written down to recognize the loss. In the case of shares, a write-down of the investment would be recorded by the following entry.

Loss in Value of Long-Term Investment	X	
Investment in Shares		X

The loss account would appear in the income statement as *Other Losses*. The written down cost of the investment is subsequently used in accounting for the investment. If there is a subsequent increase in the market value of the investment, the *CICA Handbook* recommends that the write-down of the investment should *not* be reversed.

A loss in the value of a long-term investment can arise not only in the case of a bankruptcy or an agreement to sell, but also in such situations as
• a prolonged period during which the quoted market value of the investment is less than its carrying value
• severe losses by the investee in the current year or current and earlier years
• continued losses by the investee for a period of years
• suspension of trading in the securities
• liquidity or going concern problems of the investee
• the current fair value of the investment (an appraisal) is less than its carrying value.

The CICA research study, "Accounting for Portfolio Investments", reviewed Canadian practice with the aim of identifying a common method of accounting suitable for most circumstances. One of the study's conclusions was that long-term portfolio investments in both shares and bonds should be carried at market value. This recommendation resulted from the fact that current market value represents the actual resources of the investor committed to the investment and, therefore, it provides the most realistic basis against which a return on investment can be calculated.

Although the use of current market prices would result in unrealized gains and losses being reported, there would be other advantages in valuing long-term portfolio investments and temporary investments at market value:

1. Current market values are readily available from stock exchanges and are objectively determined in the marketplace.
2. The amount of corporate resources available at the balance sheet date to pay debts would be indicated to the financial statement reader.
3. An evaluation of the effectiveness of management's investment decisions would be communicated to readers of financial statements, and the success of strategies by different corporations could be compared.

Although current market value is used in some industries, its general use is not at present in accordance with Canadian GAAP.

A S S I G N M E N T   M A T E R I A L S

Discussion Questions

1. Is an investor guaranteed against the loss of an investment? Explain.
2. How can bondholders obtain repayment of their investments? Are shareholders more secure than bondholders? Explain.
3. Why would someone prefer to invest in the shares of a corporation rather than in bonds?
4. What are three different alternative methods for investment disclosure on the balance sheet? Which is the accepted Canadian practice?
5. What are marketable securities? How are they classified on the balance sheet?
6. What are long-term investments? How are they classified on the balance sheet?
7. Is amortization of any bond premium or discount recorded for temporary investments in bonds? Why or why not?
8. If the purchase price of shares includes dividends that have been declared but not yet paid at the time of share purchase, how is the subsequent receipt of the dividend recorded? Do dividends accrue?
9. Does the price of bonds include accrued interest? How is accrued interest recorded by the investor?
10. How is the gain or loss on disposal of marketable securities classified on the income statement?
11. What is the Canadian practice in the valuation of marketable securities when there has been a substantial decrease in their market value? when there has been a substantial increase?
12. Explain how the price of an investment is influenced by the bond contract interest rate and the prevailing market interest rate.
13. How does Canadian practice favour the long-term valuation of long-term investments when a permanent market value decline has occurred?
14. What factors can result in a permanent market value decline in a long-term investment?
15. Refer to Conceptual Issue 12-1. How would dividends and stock splits affect the efficient markets hypothesis? Discuss.

Discussion Cases

Discussion Case 12-1: Compound Interest

Why is growth essential?

Unless your investments beat inflation, there is no "real" growth. High growth enables the magic of compounding to work best — to generate large sums of money over time. Every additional percent makes a big difference.

ANNUAL INVEST-MENT	% RETURN	GROWS TO AMOUNT INDICATED WITHIN:				
		10 YEARS	15 YEARS	20 YEARS	25 YEARS	30 YEARS
$1,000	8	$ 15,645	$ 29,324	$ 49,423	$ 78,954	$ 122,346
	10	17,531	34,950	63,002	108,182	180,943
	12	19,655	41,753	80,699	149,334	270,293
	14	22,045	49,980	103,768	207,333	406,737
	16	24,733	59,925	133,841	289,088	615,162
	18	27,755	71,939	173,021	404,272	933,319
	20	31,150	86,442	224,026	566,377	1,418,258
TOTAL INVESTED		$ 10,000	$ 15,000	$ 20,000	$ 25,000	$ 30,000
$3,500	8	$ 54,759	$102,635	$ 172,980	$ 276,340	$ 428,211
	10	61,359	122,324	220,509	378,636	633,302
	12	68,791	146,136	282,446	522,669	946,024
	14	77,156	174,931	363,189	725,665	1,423,580
	16	86,565	209,738	468,442	1,011,809	2,153,066
	18	97,143	251,787	605,574	1,414,952	3,266,615
	20	109,026	302,547	784,090	1,982,321	4,963,903
TOTAL INVESTED		$ 35,000	$ 52,500	$ 70,000	$ 87,500	$ 105,000
$5,500	8	$ 86,050	$161,284	$ 271,826	$ 434,249	$ 672,902
	10	96,421	192,224	346,514	595,000	995,189
	12	108,100	229,643	443,843	821,337	1,486,609
	14	121,245	274,892	570,726	1,140,330	2,237,054
	16	136,031	329,558	736,123	1,589,985	3,383,389
	18	152,653	395,665	951,616	2,223,497	5,133,252
	20	171,327	475,432	1,232,141	3,115,075	7,800,418
TOTAL INVESTED		$ 55,000	$ 82,500	$ 110,000	$ 137,500	$ 165,000

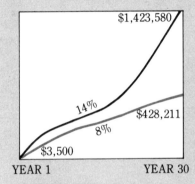

$1,423,580

14%

8%

$428,211

$3,500

YEAR 1 — YEAR 30

Extra growth does pay off in a big way through the effects of compounding. For example, $3,500 invested at 14% grows to $1,423.580 over 30 years versus just $428.211 for an investment yielding 8% over the same period. The trick, clearly, is to achieve high rates of growth without sacrificing security.

For Discussion

1. Comment on the usefulness of this type of analysis.
2. Consider setting up an RRSP for yourself so that in 25 years you would have a balance of $1.5 million. What are the advantages of saving money in an RRSP? What are the disadvantages?
3. What do you think the purchasing power of the dollar will be in 25 years? Would you be better off purchasing real estate with a large mortgage to be paid off over 25 years?

Discussion Case 12-2:   Black Monday

While the world mourned Black Monday on Wall Street, it was the next day that nearly washed away the foundations of the U.S. stock trading system, the *Wall Street Journal* reported yesterday.

Trading all but stopped and bank credit to securities firms dried up in the hours following the market collapse of Oct. 19, the *Journal* said in an investigative report.

"Tuesday was the most dangerous day we had in 50 years," Felix Rohatyn of the investment firm Lazard Freres and Co. told the financial newspaper.

Rohatyn said the market may have come "within an hour" of disintegrating as the panic climaxed at midday on Oct. 20.

As described by the *Journal*, the frightening events of Tuesday threatened to inflict more damage than the $500-billion collapse in U.S. stock prices the previous day.

Trading became so lopsided, buyers so scarce and cash so short that the New York Stock Exchange appeared close to meltdown.

The situation appeared so dire, the newspaper said, that a decision to close the NYSE, North America's biggest exchange, appeared imminent.

What saved the financial system, according to the *Journal's* account, was a combination of good fortune and cool-headed decision-making — and possibly some adroit market manipulation.

The *Journal* says that trading ground to a halt late Tuesday morning in stocks — even blue chips like IBM — as well as options and futures. The simplest transaction became impossible.

Investors couldn't sell, and the specialist firms that maintain markets in key share issues were swamped with sell orders while their capital bases were being rapidly eroded.

Banks appeared so spooked by Black Monday that they refused sorely needed credit to securities dealers. Some banks relented after being strong-armed by the Federal Reserve, which issued an extraordinary statement affirming its "readiness to serve as a source of liquidity to support the economic and financial system."

Two events near midday Tuesday appeared to pull the financial system out of its tailspin.

In what appeared to some as a miracle, a major stock index futures contract, based on the Major Market Index (MMI) of blue-chip stocks, staged a mysterious rally, raising the value of the underlying stocks.

At the same time, major corporations began announcing stock buybacks, bolstering the value of the depressed blue chips.

The source of the surge in the MMI futures contract is unclear, the *Journal* said, but some experts suspect the contract — then trading very thinly — was manipulated by a few major securities firms desperate to turn the market around.

Had it not been for the Fed's action to loosen credit and the surprising rise in the MMI contract, the pressure on the NYSE to close might have been too great to ignore, the *Journal* said.

NYSE chairman John Phelan, in constant consultation with the White House and financial officials worldwide, held off, arguing that if he closed the exchange, "we would never open it."

His patience served the market well, as the rally in the MMI contract drew buyers back into the market for blue-chip stocks.

These shares gathered enough momentum to push the Dow Jones industrial average of 30 industrials, which had lost 508 points on Black Monday, up 102.27 points. This then-record advance set the stage for an even bigger rally Oct. 21, when the Dow shot up 186.84 points and the broader market also rose strongly.

Regulators, meanwhile, are moving ahead with investigations that could lead to future market safeguards.

Source   Associated Press, "NYSE Almost Collapsed Oct. 20, Paper Says", *The (Montreal) Gazette*, November 21, 1987, p. D-2.

Where is the stock market headed? That question has been topmost in many minds since the Dow Jones industrial average plunged 22 percent to 1,738.74 on Oct. 19.

As 1987 draws to a close, the market is in a rally of sorts. Yet the Dow is still below the level, 2,027.85, that it regained two days after the plunge. And many investors, both individuals and professionals, fear that the Dow has yet to bottom — and may still fall below the Oct. 19 close.

One place investors have looked for possible clues to the market's future course is the 1929 stock market. As they did in 1987, stocks took a sharp dive in October 1929; the Dow fell 23 percent in two days. Both plunges were followed by two-day recoveries: in 1929 the Dow regained 63 percent of its loss; in 1987 it regained 57 percent.

But the 1929 crash was just a prelude. After a five-month climb, the market started falling in earnest. Market partici-

pants would later recall that while the October 1929 crash got the headlines, causing severe distress to the average investor, it was the rally in the spring of 1930 that hurt many Wall Street professionals.

Before the 1929 crash, many market professionals had pared back their exposure in stocks. The 1924-1929 bull market was then 63 months old, one of the longest on record. And the increasing public participation, particularly by new and inexperienced speculators, scared many brokers out of stocks before the crash.

But by the spring of 1930, when the Dow had very nearly recovered to its pre-crash level, many Wall Street professionals thought that the market had merely had a shakeout and that it was safe to own stocks again.

They were wrong. By July 8, 1932, the Dow had plummeted to this century's low point — 41.22 — for a loss of 86 percent from the post-crash high reached in April, 1930, and a loss of 89 percent from the Dow's record of 381.17 on Sept. 3, 1929.

But there are important differences between 1929 and today. For one thing, the government has introduced many more safeguards. For another, there is the opportunity to learn from past mistakes, including the Federal Reserve System's ill-timed tightening of credit in the early 1930's.

Another key difference is the strength of the economy. In 1929, the economy had already turned down — in August 1929 — before the market embarked on its prolonged crash. Today, if there is to be a recession, mild or otherwise, there is still no sign of it.

To be sure, economists, chastened by the market's October plunge, hastily began revising their projections downward, almost before the stock ticker finished chronicling the Dow's 508-point fall. But by December, some of these same economists were in the process of rebuilding their recently reduced estimates of economic activity. For the moment, the outlook for 1988 is good, but not great. In the aftermath of the plunge, many investors would be happy to settle for similar performance from the stock market.

Source William M. LeFevre, "Seeking Clues to the Market's Failure". Copyright © 1987 by *The New York Times Company.* Reprinted by permission.

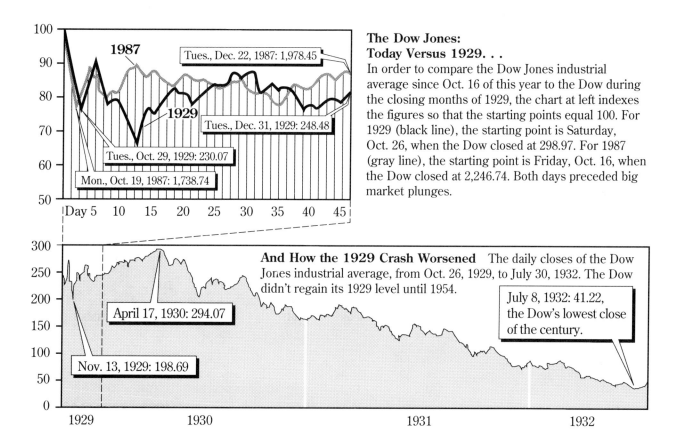

The Dow Jones: Today Versus 1929. . .

In order to compare the Dow Jones industrial average since Oct. 16 of this year to the Dow during the closing months of 1929, the chart at left indexes the figures so that the starting points equal 100. For 1929 (black line), the starting point is Saturday, Oct. 26, when the Dow closed at 298.97. For 1987 (gray line), the starting point is Friday, Oct. 16, when the Dow closed at 2,246.74. Both days preceded big market plunges.

And How the 1929 Crash Worsened The daily closes of the Dow Jones industrial average, from Oct. 26, 1929, to July 30, 1932. The Dow didn't regain its 1929 level until 1954.

A Week of History

The week of October 19, 1987 marked a period of change unprecedented in world financial markets. Each day our Canadian Action Wire, which contains up-to-the-minute analysis of events affecting investment decisions, is flashed electronically to the Merrill Lynch Canada offices across the country. Each Monday, this information wire has a front page summary of the previous week's activities. The front page of the Canadian Action Wire of October 26, 1987, reproduced below, graphically summarized a never-to-be-forgotten week in investing history.

	Week Ending October 23, 1987	Previous Week's Close
TSE 300	3079.39	3598.58
DJIA	1950.76	2246.74
S & P 500	248.22	282.70
London FT-SE 100	1795.00	2301.90
Tokyo	23201.22	26366.14
Bank Prime:		
Canada	9.50–9.75%	10.50%
U.S.	9.00–9.25%	9.25–9.75%
Short-term:		
Cda 91 Day T-Bills	7.85%	9.60%
U.S. Fed Funds	7.00%	7.38%
Mid-term:		
Cda 8.75% Jun 1996	9.75%	11.08%
Long-term:		
Cda 9.50% Oct 2001	9.68%	10.97%
Cda 9.00% Mar 2011	9.79%	11.00%
Gold/per ounce	US $473.40	$471.00
Oil/Dlr:		
W. Tex. Intermed/per barrel	US $ 20.15	$ 20.20
Fuel Oil No. 2/per gallon	US $0.5710	$0.5745
Canadian Dollar	US $0.7627	$0.7712

	TSE 300			DJIA		
Date	Close	Change	Vol (MM)	Close	Change	Vol (MM)
Monday, Oct. 19	3191.38	− 407.20	63.9	1738.41	− 508.33	604.3
Tuesday, Oct. 20	2977.31	− 214.07	77.2	1841.01	102.60	608.1
Wednesday, Oct. 21	3246.18	268.87	66.9	2027.85	186.84	449.4
Thursday, Oct. 22	3107.59	− 138.59	58.8	1950.43	− 77.42	392.2
Friday, Oct. 23	3079.39	− 28.20	37.9	1950.76	0.33	245.5
Weekly		− 519.19	304.7		− 295.98	2,299.5

Source   "A Week of History", Merrill Lynch Canada Ltd., *Spotlight*, November 87, p. 2.

For Discussion

1. On October 19, 1987, Black Monday, the Dow Jones industrial average lost 508 points, which translates into a $500-billion collapse. The Toronto stock exchange 300 lost 407 points. If your corporation's year-end was October 31, 1987, how would you disclose the cost and market value of its investments in shares assuming
   a. The investments were short term
   b. The investments were long term.
2. On October 20, 1987, the DJIA gained 102 points. How could the market collapse when the DJIA was increasing? Explain using the information in the article.
3. Review the graphs. Compare stock market behaviour in 1987 and 1929.
4. Could the situation on October 19, 1987 have become a repeat of the stock market crash in 1929? What might have been the implications for Canadians?
5. "A Week of History" lists financial data for the TSE 300 and DJIA for the week ending October 23, 1987. Explain how this information relates to the graphs.

Comprehension Problems

Comprehension Problem 12-1

On January 1, 19X1, Pep-Co Ltd. acquired $50,000-worth of 3-year, 12-percent face value bonds of Sarasota at 94. Semi-annual interest is payable every June 30 and December 31.

Required:
1. Record the following transactions:
   a. The purchase of these bonds as a long-term investment
   b. The receipt of interest on December 31, 19X1
   c. The amortization of the discount at December 31, 19X1 (use the straight-line method).
2. Calculate the amount of interest received in cash during 19X6 and the amount of bond interest that will appear in the 19X1 income statement.
3. Prepare a partial balance sheet at December 31, 19X1 showing this bond investment.
4. Prepare the journal entry to record the redemption of the bonds at maturity.
5. Prepare the journal entry on January 1, 19X2, when the bonds were called at 102.

Comprehension Problem 12-2

On January 1, 19X3, Pilot Inc. purchased $100,000-worth of face value, 3-year, 12-percent bonds at 112 as a long-term investment. Semi-annual interest is payable on June 30 and December 31.

Required:
1. Record the following transactions:
   a. The purchase of these bonds on January 1, 19X3
   b. The receipt of interest on June 30, 19X3
   c. The amortization of the premium at June 30, 19X3 (use the straight-line method).
2. Calculate the amount of interest received during 19X3 and the amount of bond interest earned that will appear in the 19X3 income statement. Why are these amounts different?
3. Prepare a partial balance sheet at December 31, 19X3 showing this bond investment.
4. Prepare the journal entry on January 1, 19X5, when the bonds were called at 106.

Comprehension Problem 12-3

On January 1, 19X4, the date of bond authorization, Grimly Ltd. purchased 3-year, 12-percent bonds of Hawley Inc. Semi-annual interest is payable on June 30 and December 31. The company uses the straight-line method of amortization. The journal entry that records the receipt of interest on June 30, 19X4 follows:

June 30	Investment in Bonds	250	
	Cash	8,250	
	Bond Interest Earned		8,500

Required: Reconstruct the entry made to record the purchase of these bonds on January 1, 19X4.

Comprehension Problem 12-4

Hilroy Inc. purchased 3-year, 12-percent bonds of Bryan Inc. on January 1, 19X6, the date of bond authorization. Semi-annual interest is payable on June 30 and December 31. The company uses the straight-line method of amortization. The journal entry that records the receipt of interest on Dec. 31, 19X6 follows:

Dec. 31	Cash	9,750	
	Investment in Bonds		350
	Bond Interest Earned		9,400

Required: Reconstruct the entry made to record the purchase of these bonds on January 1, 19X1.

Comprehension Problem 12-5

On January 1, 19X5, Jason Ltd. issued 3-year, 12-percent bonds with a face value of $100,000 at a price to yield 8 percent (4 percent each 6 months). Semi-annual interest is payable on June 30 and December 31.

Required:
1. Calculate the issuance price of the bonds
2. Prepare the journal entry to record the issuance of the bonds on January 1, 19X5.
3. Prepare the journal entries at December 31, 19X5 to record the payment of interest and amortization using the effective interest method. What is the difference between the effective interest and straight-line methods of recording amortization?

Comprehension Problem 12-6

On January 1, 19X2, the date of authorization, Kent Corp. issued 3-year, 12-percent bonds with a face value of $100,000 at a price to yield 14 percent (7 percent each 6 months). Semi-annual interest is payable on June 30 and December 31.

Required:
1. Calculate the issuance price of the bonds
2. Prepare the journal entry to record the issuance of the bonds on January 1, 19X2.

Comprehension Problem 12-7

Hot Springs Inc. had the following short-term investment transactions in marketable securities during 19X8.

Jan.	1	Purchased $50,000 face value, 12-percent bonds of Jay Restaurants Ltd. at 102, plus $1,000 brokerage fees (semi-annual interest is payable on June 30 and December 31)
Apr.	15	Purchased 1000 shares of Whip Court Inc. for $14.75 per share, plus $250 brokerage fees
May	25	Received a 10-percent stock dividend from Whip Court Inc. (recorded a memo entry in the Investment account noting the new number of shares held)
Jun.	7	Received a $0.10 per-share cash dividend for the shares in Whip
	30	Received the semi-annual interest on the Jay bonds
Oct.	4	Sold the bonds of Jay Restaurants Inc. at 99, less brokerage fees of $1,000 (recorded accrued interest at this date amounting to $1,578)
Dec.	31	The market value of a Whip share was $10 on this date.

Required:
1. Prepare journal entries to record the 19X8 transactions.
2. How should the market value of Whip shares be disclosed in the December 31, 19X8 balance sheet of Hot Springs Inc. according to the LOCAM method?

Comprehension Problem 12-8

Funk City Inc. paid $147,000 for $150,000 face value bonds of Tarsal Corporation. The bonds, which were acquired on January 1, 19X1 as a long-term investment, had the following features.

Date of Authorization	Term	Bond Contract Interest Rate	Interest Payment Dates
January 1, 19X1	3 Years	12%	Semi-annually on June 30 and December 31

Required:
1. Calculate
   a. The amount of interest received every interest payment date
   b. The amount of amortization to be recorded at each interest payment date (use the straight-line method of amortization).

2. Prepare the ledger entries for the Investment in Bonds account of Funk City Inc. to show the purchase of the bonds and the semi-annual amortization amounts until redemption. (Note that amortization is recorded each time bond interest income is recorded.)

Investment in Bonds

Date	Description	F	Debit	Credit	DR. or CR.	Balance
19X1						
Jan. 1	Purchase of Tarsal Corporation Bonds					
June 30	Amortization of Discount					
Dec. 31	Amortization of Discount					
19X2						
June 30	Amortization of Discount					
Dec. 31	Amortization of Discount					
19X3						
June 30	Amortization of Discount					
Dec. 31	Amortization of Discount					
19X4						
Jan. 1	Bonds Redeemed					

Comprehension Problem 12-9

Lapin Inc., the year-end for which is January 31, acquired $50,000-worth of face value bonds of Nada Corporation at 103. The bonds, acquired on January 1, 19X3 as a long-term investment, had the following features.

Date of Authorization	Term	Bond Contract Interest Rate	Interest Payment Dates
January 1, 19X3	2 Years	12%	Semi-annually on July 2 and January 2

Required:
1. Prepare a schedule (like the one in section C) for the two-year life of the bonds to show a running balance for the Investment in Bonds account. Calculate the cash interest received and the annual interest earned by Lapin.

	Investment in Bonds	Cash Interest Received	Annual Interest Income
19X3			
Jan. 1 Purchase of Bonds			
April 30 Interest Accrued and Amortization			
Balance	_____	_____	_____
July 1 Interest Received and Amortization			
19X4			
Jan. 1 Interest Received and Amortization			
April 30 Interest Accrued and Amortization			
Balance	_____	_____	_____
July 1 Interest Received and Amortization			
19X5			
Jan. 1 Interest Received and Amortization			
Balance	_____	_____	_____
Jan. 1 Bond Repaid			
	-0-		

The interest income of the corporation is reduce by the premium amortization.

2. Prepare journal entries to record the 19X3-19X5 transactions.
3. If the market rate of interest was 16 percent at December 31, 19X3, for how much could Lapin Inc. sell its investment in bonds?

Problems

Problem 12-1

Closius Services Inc. had the following short-term investment transactions in marketable securities during 19X7:

Jan. 1 Purchased $25,000-worth of face value 12-percent bonds of Côte St-Luc Farms Inc. at 95, plus $250 brokerage fee
Feb. 28 Purchased 200 shares of Côte Vertu Centres Ltée for $20 each, plus $600 brokerage fee
Jun. 30 Received the semi-annual interest on Côte St-Luc bonds
Oct. 4 Received a $0.50 per-share cash dividend from Côte Vertu
Dec. 31 Received the semi-annual interest on Côte St-Luc bonds
     31 The market value of Côte St-Luc bonds was 90 at this date; shares of Côte Vertu were trading at $15 per share.

Required:
1. Prepare journal entries to record the 19X7 transactions.
2. The shares of Côte Vertu were sold for $25 each on April 11, 19X8. Prepare journal entries to record the sale.

Problem 12-2

Monadnock Inc., the year-end for which is December 31, acquired $75,000-worth of face value bonds of Guelph Collegiate Inc. at 98. The bonds, which were acquired on January 1, 19X3 as a long-term investment, had the following features:

Date of Authorization	Term	Bond Contract Interest Rate	Interest Payment Dates
January 1, 19X3	3 Years	12%	Semi-annually on June 30 and December 31

Required:
1. Calculate
   a. The amount of interest applicable to each six-month period
   b. The amount of amortization to be recorded at each interest date (use the straight-line method of amortization).
2. Prepare the ledger for the Investment in Bonds account of Monadnock, recording the purchase and the amortization of discount amounts until redemption of the bonds.
3. Using a format similar to that at the end of section C, prepare all journal entries required on the books of both Monadnock and Guelph in 19X3. The year-end for Guelph is December 31.

Problem 12-3

Netele Inc. paid $110,000 for $100,000-worth of face value bonds of Zoe Limited. Both corporations have December 31 as their year-ends. The bonds, which were acquired as a long-term investment on January 1, 19X1, had the following features.

Date of Authorization	Term	Bond Contract Interest Rate	Interest Payment Dates
January 1, 19X1	2 Years	12%	Semi-annually on July 1 and January 1

Required:
1. Calculate
   a. The amount of interest applicable to each six-month period
   b. The amount of amortization to be recorded at each interest date (use the straight-line method of amortization).
2. Using a format similar to that at the end of section C, prepare journal entries on the following dates for both Netele (investor) and Zoe (issuer):
   a. January 1, 19X1
   b. July 1, 19X1 for interest and amortization
   c. December 31, 19X1 accrual for interest and to record amortization
   d. January 1, 19X2 for interest
   e. July 1, 19X2 for interest and amortization
   f. December 31, 19X2 accrual for interest and to record amortization
   g. January 1, 19X3 for interest
   h. January 1, 19X3 for bond redemption.

Problem 12-4

Kepi Investment Inc. purchased $100,000-worth of face value bonds on January 1, 19X1. On the date of bond authorization, Rorqual Corporation issued $100,000-worth of face value bonds.

Date of Authorization	Term	Bond Contract Interest Rate	Interest Payment Dates
January 1, 19X1	3 Years	12%	Semi-annually on June 30 and December 31

Required: Answer the questions for each of these cases.
Case A: the bonds were acquired at face value.
Case B: the bonds were acquired for $103,000.
Case C: the bonds were acquired for $94,000.

1. Calculate
   a. The amount of interest received every interest payment date
   b. The amount of amortization to be recorded at each interest payment date, if applicable (use the straight-line method of amortization).
2. Prepare journal entries to record
   a. The acquisition of bonds on January 1, 19X1
   b. The receipt of interest on June 30, 19X1
   c. The amortization on June 30, 19X1
   d. The receipt of interest on December 31, 19X1
   e. The amortization on December 31, 19X1
   f. The receipt of interest on December 31, 19X3
   g. The amortization on December 31, 19X3
   h. The redemption of the bonds at maturity, January 1, 19X4.
3. Calculate the amount of bond interest income shown in the income statement at December 31, 19X1. Is this amount the same as cash interest received by Kepi? Why or why not?

Problem 12-5

On July 1, 19X1, Rose Corporation purchased as a temporary investment 10-percent bonds of Pringle Limited with a face value of $50,000 at 103 plus accrued interest. Interest is paid on May 1 and November 1. The brokerage fee was $90. On August 1, 19X1, Rose Corporation purchased as a temporary investment 400 shares of Junius Corporation common stock at $65 per share. The shares are readily marketable, and brokerage fees amounted to $80.

Required:
1. Record the purchase of the above investments.
2. Record the receipt of the first interest payment on the Pringle bonds.
3. Record the receipt of a $1 per share dividend on the Junius Corporation stock received on November 15, 19X1.
4. Prepare all entries related to the investments on December 31, 19X1, assuming the Junius Corporation stock had a market value of $67 per share and was expected to be sold in March of 19X2.
5. On March 1, 19X2, the Junius Corporation stock was sold at $66 per share. Prepare the required entries on Rose Corporation's books.

Problem 12-6

On July 1, the Westminster Corporation purchased 8-percent first mortgage bonds of the Goode Limited with a face value of $100,000 at 100 plus $68 brokerage fees. Interest is payable on July 1 and January 1.

Required:
1. If these bonds were purchased as a temporary investment, what account title(s) would be debited and for what amount(s)?
2. If these bonds were purchased as a long-term investment, what account title(s) would be debited and for what amount(s)?
3. Explain briefly the difference in accounting for the purchase of the bonds and the subsequent treatment of the investment as a temporary investment as compared to a long-term investment.

Alternate Problems

Alternate Problem 12-1

Clarus Estates Inc. had the following short-term investment transactions in marketable securities during 19X6 and 19X7:

19X6
Jan. 1   Purchased $100,000-worth of face value, 12-percent bonds of Moro Corp. at 97, plus $1,000 brokerage fees; semi-annual interest is payable on June 30 and December 31
Apr. 1   Purchased 5000 shares of Homin Stores Inc. for $5 per share, plus $250 brokerage fees
May 1   Received a $0.25 per-share cash dividend from Homin
Jun. 30   Received the semi-annual interest from Moro; sold the Moro bonds at 102, less brokerage fees of $1,000
Dec. 31   The market value of Homin shares was $4 per share.
19X7
Apr. 15   Sold the Homin shares for $1.50 per share, less brokerage fees of $100.

Required:
  1. Prepare journal entries to record the 19X6 transactions.
  2. Prepare a journal entry to record the 19X7 sale of Homin shares.

Alternate Problem 12-2

Sparks Limited had the following transactions involving temporary investment during the year:

Jan. 1   Purchased 7-percent bonds of Good-deal Limited with a face value of $150,000 at 101 plus accrued interest. Interest is paid each March 1 and September 1; brokerage fees and other costs related to the purchase were $140. The bonds mature in 116 months from the purchase date
Mar. 1   Received semi-annual interest on bonds of Good-deal Limited
      15   Purchased 500 shares of $4 no par-value, 8-percent preferred stock of Riggsbee Limited at $60 a share; dividends are paid semi-annually on February 15 and August 15; brokerage fees and other costs related to the purchase were $104
Aug. 15   Sold 100 shares of preferred stock of Riggsbee Limited at $65 a share
      25   Received the dividend on the remaining preferred stock of Riggsbee Limited
Sept. 1   Received semi-annual interest on the bonds of Good-deal Limited
Oct. 1   Sold the bonds of Good-deal Limited at 102 plus accrued interest.

Required: Prepare journal entries to record the above transactions.

Alternate Problem 12-3

Liber Corporation paid $212,000 for $200,000-worth of face value bonds of Pottle Software Inc. The bonds, which were acquired on January 1, 19X1 as a long-term investment, had the following features.

Date of Authorization	Term	Bond Contract Interest Rate	Interest Payment Dates
January 1, 19X1	3 Years	12%	Semi-annually on June 30 and December 31

Required:
1. Calculate
   a. The amount of interest received every interest payment date
   b. The amount of amortization to be recorded at each interest date (use the straight-line method of amortization).
2. Prepare the ledger for the Investment in Bonds account to record the purchase of, amortization regarding, and redemption of the bonds. Note that amortization is recorded each time bond interest income is recorded.
3. Prepare journal entries to record the interest and amortization at June 30, 19X1.

Alternate Problem 12-4

Lignum Fertilizer Corporation paid $207,200 for $200,000-worth of face value bonds of Izzard Inc. The bonds, which were acquired as a long-term investment, had the following features.

Date of Authorization	Term	Bond Contract Interest Rate	Interest Payment Dates
January 1, 19X7	3 Years	12%	Semi-annually on June 30 and December 31

Required: Answer the questions for each of these cases.
Case A: the bonds were acquired on January 1, 19X7.
Case B: the bonds were acquired on April 1, 19X7 and the acquisition price included accrued interest.
Case C: the bonds were acquired on July 1, 19X7.

1. Calculate
   a. The amount of interest received every interest payment date
   b. The amount of amortization, if any, applicable to each month remaining in the life of the bonds subsequent to the issue date; calculate separately the amortization to be recorded at each interest payment date (use the straight-line method of amortization).
2. Prepare journal entries to record
   a. The acquisition of the bonds
   b. The receipt of interest and recording of amortization, if any, on June 30, 19X7
   c. The receipt of interest and recording of amortization, if any, on December 31, 19X7.
3. Calculate the amount of bond interest income shown in the income statement at December 31, 19X7. Is this amount the same as cash received as interest in 19X7? Why or why not?

Alternate Problem 12-5

On May 1, the Hobson Corporation purchased as a long-term investment 8-percent bonds of Potter Limited. Interest is paid semi-annually on May 1 and November 1. The bonds mature in 12 years. On November 1, the accountant for Hobson prepared the following entry to record the receipt of bond interest and the straight-line amortization of the premium:

Nov. 1	Cash	6,000	
	Investment in Bonds		375
	Bond Interest Earned		5,625
	To record the receipt of bond interest and		
	to amortize the premium for six months.		

Required: From the above information, complete the following, showing all your calculations on a separate page.
1. The amount of interest earned for each 6-month period is $_____.
2. The amount of interest earned for 12 months would be $_____.
3. If interest for the year is 8 percent, the face value of the bonds must be $_____.
4. The amount of amortization for each 6-month period is $_____.
5. The amount of amortization for 12 months would be $_____.
6. The total amount that will be amortized over 12 years will be $_____.
7. The total amount of cash paid on May 1 by Hobson Corporation must have been $_____.
8. On a separate sheet, reconstruct the journal entry that was made to record the issuance of the bonds.

Supplementary Problems

Supplementary Problem 12-1

Frons Products Corporation engaged in the following temporary investment transactions during 19X6 and 19X7:

19X6
Jan. 1 Purchased $100,000-worth of CPB's 12-percent, 3-year bonds on the interest date for 95, plus $500 brokerage fees
Feb. 1 Purchased 500 shares of Blue Sea Lake Corporation, paying $25 per share, plus $200 brokerage fees
May 1 Received a $1 per-share cash dividend on the investment in Blue Sea Lake Corporation shares
Jun. 30 Received the semi-annual interest on CPB bonds
Oct. 4 Received a 10-percent stock dividend from Blue Sea Lake Corporation (recorded a memo entry in the investment account to note the new number of shares held).
Dec. 31 Received the semi-annual interest on CPB bonds
31 The market value of CPB bonds on this date was 90; Blue Sea Lake Corporation shares were being traded at $20 per share.

19X7
Mar. 15 Sold $100,000-worth of CPB bonds at 92, less brokerage fees of $500, plus the accrued interest on these bonds at the time of sale
May 25 Blue Sea Lake Corporation shares were split 2 for 1; received the additional shares on this date (recorded a memo entry in the investment account to note the new number of shares).
Oct. 4 Received a $0.50 per-share cash dividend on the investment in Blue Sea Lake Corporation shares
Dec. 31 Blue Sea Lake Corporation shares were being traded for $27 at this date.

Required:
1. Prepare journal entries to record the 19X6 transactions.
2. Prepare journal entries required for 19X7 transactions.
3. Does the receipt of a stock dividend represent income to Frons Products Corporation? Why or why not?

Supplementary Problem 12-2

Part A

Firth Inc. paid $100,000 for $100,000-worth of face value bonds of Vezina Computer Corporation on January 1, 19X1. The bonds, which were acquired as a long-term investment, had the following features.

Date of Authorization	Term	Bond Contract Interest Rate	Interest Payment Dates
January 1, 19X1	3 Years	12%	Semi-annually on June 30 and December 31

Required:
1. Calculate the amount of interest received every six months.
2. Prepare journal entries to record
   a. The acquisition of the bonds on January 1, 19X1
   b. The receipt of interest on June 30, 19X1
   c. The receipt of interest on December 31, 19X1.

Part B

An additional $50,000-worth of face value bonds were acquired on January 1, 19X2 for $48,000.

Required:
3. Calculate
   a. The amount of interest income received on the $150,000-worth of face value bonds every interest payment date
   b. The amount of amortization to be recorded at each interest payment date (use the straight-line method of amortization).
4. Prepare journal entries to record
   a. Acquisition of the bonds on January 1, 19X2
   b. Receipt of interest on June 30, 19X2 on the $150,000-worth of face value issued bonds
   c. Amortization of bond discount on June 30, 19X2
   d. Receipt of interest on December 31, 19X2
   e. Amortization of bond discount on December 31, 19X2.
5. Prepare the ledger entries for the Investment in Bonds account of Firth Inc. from purchase to redemption.
6. Prepare a journal entry to record the redemption of the bonds at maturity, January 1, 19X4.

Supplementary Problem 12-3

On January 1, 19X3, Dashiki Inc. purchased $500,000-worth of face value bonds of Lotus P.C. Corporation as a long-term investment. The bonds had these features.

Date of Authorization	Term	Bond Contract Interest Rate	Interest Payment Dates
January 1, 19X3	3 Years	12%	Semi-annually on June 30 and December 31

The following information appears in the published balance sheet of Dashiki Inc. at December 31, 19X3, its fiscal year-end: "Long-Term Investments — $496,000". Dashiki uses the straight-line method of amortization.

Required:
1. Calculate
   a. The acquisition price of the bonds on January 1, 19X3
   b. The amount of cash interest paid in 19X3
   c. The amount of amortization recorded during 19X3
   d. The total amount of amortization to be recorded during the life of the bonds
   e. The amount of bond interest income appearing in the 19X3 income statement.
2. Prepare journal entries to record
   a. The acquisition of the bonds on January 1, 19X3
   b. The receipt of interest and recording of bond discount amortization on June 30, 19X3
   c. The receipt of interest and recording of bond discount amortization on December 31, 19X3.

Decision Problem

Decision Problem 12-1

You have been provided with the following financial information to aid in assessing the investment worthiness of two firms.

	(in millions)	
	Abbott, Co.	Costello, Inc.
Total assets		
December 31, 19X9	$50	$200
Total liabilities	30	120
Shareholders' equity	20	80
Net income, year 19X9	5	20
Income tax rate	40%	40%

Other information:
a. Abbott uses the LIFO inventory cost flow assumption and accelerated depreciation for plant and equipment for both book and tax purposes. Costello uses FIFO inventory costing and straight-line depreciation for book and tax purposes. If Abbott had been using FIFO and straight-line depreciation, then Abbott's pretax operating income for 19X9 would have been higher by $4 million. In addition, the book values of Abbott's inventory and plant and equipment at December 31, 19X9 would have been higher by $12 million.

b. Abbott's liabilities consist primarily of bonds issued at par in 19X6 when the market rate of interest was 10 percent; the bonds have 20 years to maturity and a market value of $25 million. Costello's liabilities consist of bonds issued at par in 19X1 when the market rate of interest was 20 percent; the bonds have 20 years to maturity and a market value of $180 million.

c. Abbott has 1 million common shares outstanding, with a market value of $50 per share on December 31, 19X9. Costello has 2 million common shares outstanding, with a market value of $90 per share on December 31, 19X9.

Required:
1. Determine the ratio of debt to equity (the financial leverage ratio) for both firms at December 31, 19X9, using the balance sheet information reported above.
2. Determine the financial leverage ratios for both firms at December 31, 19X9, using the relative market values for debt and equity. Is book value or market value more suitable in measuring financial leverage?
3. Discuss likely reasons for the differences between the book values and the carrying values of the debt and equity of both firms.
4. Determine the relationship between net income and total assets (the return on assets ratio) and between net income and shareholders' equity (the return on equity ratio) for both firms. How do the differences in inventory costing and depreciation methods affect your calculations of total assets, shareholders' equity, and net income?

The Investment Cycle: Business Combinations

Numerous publicly owned corporations prepare consolidated financial statements to indicate that all or a controlling interest is owned by one corporation in other corporations.

1. What two methods are used to record the acquisition of controlling interest in a corporation?
2. What criterion is used to establish existence of a corporation's interest?
3. What is the distinction in a business combination between a purchase and a pooling of interests?
4. What is the generally accepted method of recording the purchase of a subsidiary's shares?
5. When consolidated financial statements are prepared, does each corporation continue to have its own legal existence as a separate entity?
6. What are the steps used in preparing consolidated financial statements?
7. What are reciprocal amounts? Why are they eliminated in the combination process?
8. Are any entries recorded in the books of either parent corporation or its subsidiary in the preparation of consolidated financial statements?
9. How is goodwill created in the consolidation process?
10. What is minority interest, and how is it accounted for?
11. How is the acquisition of a subsidiary under a pooling of interests accomplished?

A.   Long-Term Intercorporate Share Investments

Intercorporate investments
Investments made by one corporation in voting common shares of another corporation, usually done to gain a voting influence over the other corporation; can also include investments in non-voting shares and bonds of the other corporation.

It is not uncommon for one corporation to invest in another corporation; such investments are commonly called **intercorporate investments**. Figure 13-1 compares the different types of intercorporate investments and the influence carried by each.

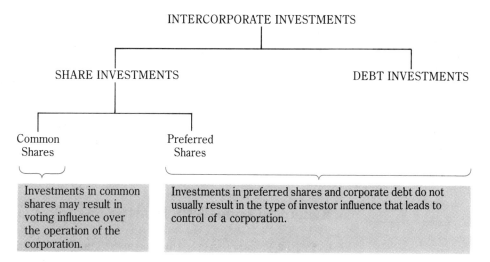

Figure 13-1   Forms of intercorporate investment

The accounting for intercorporate share investments is influenced by whether such investments provide a voting influence over another corporation or whether they are simply portfolio equity investments.

Investor Control of a Corporation

Intercorporate investments in common shares of a corporation may result in voting influence of one corporation over the operations of the other corporation (called the *investee*). Three levels of possible influence have been identified; these three levels of control, how they differ, and how they are accounted for are explained briefly here.

Level 1:   The under 20 Percent Level
The investor is usually seen as having little influence or control over the corporation when it has less than 20 percent ownership. The investment is reported on the financial statements of the investor at cost.

Level 2:   The 20 to 50 Percent Level
In this range of ownership, it is assumed that the investor has a significant influence and control over the corporation, unless circumstances make this assumption unrealistic. The investment is reported on the financial statements of the investor under the equity method.

Level 3:   The over 50 Percent Level

In excess of 50 percent ownership, the investor is actually able to control the corporation — which is then referred to as a **subsidiary** of the investing **parent**. The financial statements of the parent and subsidiary are combined as if they were for one legal entity, not two separate corporations. The combined financial statements are then referred to as **consolidated financial statements**.

Note that the accounting treatment of a long-term investment in common stock (usually the voting shares) differs, depending on the level of ownership by the investor. It should be remembered that these levels are merely intended to be guidelines. In some cases, it may be possible for a corporation with less than 20 percent ownership to exert a significant influence and, in other cases, an investor with a 20-50 percent ownership may not have a significant influence. The specific circumstances must be reviewed when selecting the most appropriate accounting treatment of a corporation's long-term investment in common, or voting, shares of another corporation.

Recording Long-Term Investments in Shares

Cost is the generally accepted method of recording an investment in shares. Regardless of the ownership level that results from the share purchase, the investment is recorded at cost by the investor. After acquisition, either the cost method or the equity method can be used to record these investments. The following paragraphs explain and contrast these two methods in the case of level 1 and level 2 investor control.

Recording Method 1:   Cost

After acquisition, the investment is kept in the records of the investor at cost. The investment is reported on the balance sheet at cost. The income or losses of the issuer are ignored by the investor. Dividends are recorded as income by the investor and included in the investor's income statement.

Recording Method 2:   Equity

After acquisition, the investment is kept in the records of the investor by the cost method or, alternatively, may be kept in the records by the equity method (as explained below). However, the investment is reported on the balance sheet only by the equity method. The cost of the investment is increased by the investor's share of the annual income of the issuer (or decreased by losses). This share of income is included in the income statement of the investor. The cost of the investment is reduced by the amount of dividends received by the investor. No dividend income appears on the income statement of the investor.

The important similarity to be noted between these two methods is that the investment is initially recorded at cost and may continue to be recorded on a cost basis in the day-to-day records of the investor.

Under the equity method, regardless of how the investment account is kept in the books of the investor, the investment is reported in the financial statements on an equity basis.

Following are the journal entries that would be required under the cost and equity methods. Assume that the investment for a 100 percent ownership was $100,000, the income of the investee for the relevant year is $25,000, and dividends paid by the investee during the same period were $4,000. Note the differences.

Transaction	The Cost Method		The Equity Method	
Investment in Shares of Investee	Investment in Shares 100,000 Cash	100,000	Investment in Shares 100,000 Cash	100,000
Income of Investee for the Year	(No entry is required.)		Investment in Shares 25,000 Income from Investee	25,000
Receipt of Dividend from Investee	Cash 4,000 Dividend Income	4,000	Cash 4,000 Investment in Shares	4,000

The effect of the cost and equity methods on the amounts reported in the financial statements of the investor is illustrated below:

	The Cost Method		The Equity Method	
	Balance Sheet	Income Statement	Balance Sheet	Income Statement
Original Investment	$100,000		$100,000	
Investment Income during the Year Reported by Investee			+ 25,000	+ $25,000
Dividend Received from Investee during the Year		+ $4,000	− 4,000	
Amounts Reported by Investor	$100,000	$4,000	$121,000	$25,000

B.   Business Combinations

Business combination
The acquisition of one corporation by another, also referred to as a *consolidation*.

Purchase
A business combination in which a subsidiary's shares are acquired through the payment of cash or other assets, or an exchange of shares.

Pooling of interests
A business combination in which the subsidiary's shares are acquired only through an exchange of shares, and in which voting control is shared equally.

Often a corporation acquires a controlling interest in another corporation; usually, this control is accomplished through the purchase of voting shares. As mentioned earlier, when the share purchase results in more than 50 percent ownership, the investor controls the voting shares of the other corporation, which is then referred to as a subsidiary of the investing parent. Although there are some exceptions, the individual financial statements of the parent and its subsidiary are combined for the parent's reporting purposes, as if the two were one economic entity, as in accordance with GAAP.

Business combinations can be identified as either a purchase or a pooling of interests. In a **purchase**, the new owners buy enough of the subsidiary's shares that they own more than 50 percent; the previous owners of the subsidiary no longer continue to have an ownership interest in the subsidiary, but may have an interest in the parent if the purchase was made by an issue of the parent's shares. In a **pooling of interests**, the parent acquires the subsidiary through an exchange of shares; in this situation, the subsidiary's shareholders exchange their shares in the subsidiary for shares of the parent. The original shareholders of the subsidiary then become shareholders in the parent and, thereby, share equally in voting control for the board of directors. The distinction between a purchase and pooling of interests is contrasted in Figure 13-2.

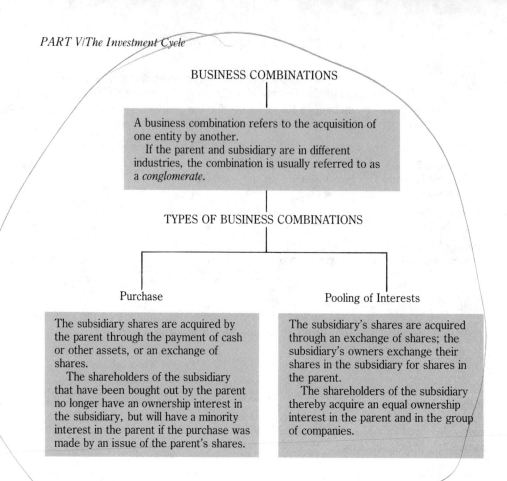

Figure 13-2   The distinctions between a purchase and a pooling of interests

The combination processes for purchases and poolings of interest are different. Sections B and C of this chapter discuss how financial statements are combined when a purchase occurs. Section D introduces how to combine financial statements when a pooling of interest occurs.

The Accounting Equation Reviewed

Since net assets are the focus of both a purchase and a pooling of interests, it is useful to review the accounting equation at this point. Simply stated, the accounting equation indicates that total assets belonging to an entity must always equal the total claims against those assets. Both creditors and owners contribute these assets and the accounting equation recognizes these contributions.

Assets	=	Liabilities	+	Equity
(Resources owned by the entity)		(Creditors' claims to assets)		(Owners' claims to assets)

In addition to recognizing the contribution of both creditors and owners to the assets of the entity, the equation also expresses the equality between assets and total claims by both creditors and owners to these assets.

Business combinations focus on the owners' claim to the net assets of a subsidiary; that is, the amount of net assets left for the owners after all other claims have been taken care of. The accounting equation can therefore be restated in the following manner to emphasize owners' claims to net assets:

$$\underset{\substack{\text{(Resources owned}\\\text{by the entity)}}}{\text{Assets}} \quad - \quad \underset{\substack{\text{(Creditors' claims}\\\text{to assets)}}}{\text{Liabilities}} \quad = \quad \underset{\substack{\text{(Owners' claims to}\\\text{remaining assets)}}}{\text{Equity}}$$

Since assets less liabilities is also referred to as net assets, the term *net assets* can be said to be synonymous with owners' equity; that is, the owners' claims to the assets of the entity. The difference between assets and liabilities can therefore be labelled as net assets or as equity. The discussion in business combinations focuses on the net assets of a subsidiary.

Purchase of a Controlling Interest

Controlling interest
The acquisition of more than 50 percent of another corporation's voting shares.

The acquisition of a **controlling interest**, or more than 50 percent of the voting shares of another corporation, was extensively reviewed in an analysis prepared for Bluebeard's management. The parent purchases the controlling interest in voting shares of the subsidiary by a cash payment; this payment is made to the subsidiary's shareholders in exchange for their shares in the subsidiary. In effect, the subsidiary's shareholders are bought out; these previous owners of the subsidiary therefore no longer continue to have any ownership interest in the subsidiary. The purchase results in the parent acquiring ownership claims to the net assets of the subsidiary.

The data used throughout the chapter are taken from the analysis prepared for executives of Bluebeard Computer Corporation. Intrigued by acquisitions occurring within the computer industry, particularly the acquisition of Rolm Corporation by IBM, the analysis was prepared as a working document for understanding business combinations and their financial reporting implications. First, this analysis reviewed the acquisition of a controlling interest in the shares of a subsidiary. This step included both a wholly owned subsidiary and a partially owned subsidiary; the three alternatives that can surface in the acquisition of a subsidiary were considered. Then, the acquisition of a subsidiary through a pooling of interests was evaluated. A different view of the nature of acquisitions is discussed in Real Life Example 13-1. The chapter itself presents BCC's analysis.

For convenience, the investor corporation is referred to as P, the parent, and the investee corporation as S, the subsidiary. The assignment material for this chapter continues this approach to facilitate the distinction between a parent and its subsidiary.

Recording the Acquisition at Cost

Cost is the generally accepted method of recording the purchase of any asset — in this case, the purchase of the subsidiary's shares. Therefore, the share purchase is recorded at acquisition cost. The acquisition cost includes not only the amount paid for the shares, but also brokerage fees and any other costs associated with the purchase. The purchase price is supposed to reflect the fair market value of the subsidiary's net assets.

The analysis prepared for Bluebeard's executives considered the three different alternatives possible in the parent's purchase of its ownership claims to the net assets of the subsidiary. These alternatives are applicable in every situation in which one company buys a controlling interest in another company.

Alternative 1
The purchase cost was the same amount as the book value of the subsidiary's net assets now owned by the parent.

Alternative 2
The purchase cost was greater than the amount of the book value of the subsidiary's net assets now owned by the parent.

The difference can result from the existence of unrecorded goodwill applicable to the subsidiary and/or to an undervaluation of the subsidiary's assets.

Alternative 3
The purchase cost was less than the amount of the book value of the subsidiary's net assets now owned by the parent.

The difference can result from the existence of so-called negative goodwill and/or to an overevaluation of the subsidiary's assets.

C. Wholly Owned Subsidiary

This section of the Bluebeard business combinations analysis deals with the purchase of all voting shares in a subsidiary; in this situation, the parent has in effect acquired ownership claims to 100 percent of the subsidiary's net assets. It is assumed that the acquisition is made on December 31, 19X8.

Recording the Acquisition

The acquisition cost for each alternative discussed in section B is recorded in the journal entries below. In each case, the parent has acquired a 100-percent ownership interest in the subsidiary. Note that the amount paid differs in each case.

Acquisition of 100-Percent Ownership Interest

	Alternative 1	Alternative 2	Alternative 3
Investment in Subsidiary	20,000	25,000	16,000
Cash	20,000	25,000	16,000

Although this purchase is effected in cash, the acquisition can also be made through a payment of other assets or an exchange of shares. Regardless, the parent purchases a 100-percent ownership interest in the subsidiary's net assets; none of the subsidiary's previous owners then has an ownership interest in the subsidiary.

Real Life Example 13-1
Acquisitions and Takeovers

Acquisition of companies, takeover bids, and defensive tactics by boards of takeover targets have increased dramatically in recent years. Acquisition attempts by corporations or individuals may occur for many different reasons. For example, the takeover of Rolm Corporation by IBM was fuelled because IBM was lagging behind its competitors in a vital technological area. Rather than develop this technology from within the corporation, IBM decided that the acquisition of Rolm would be less expensive and would produce this technology immediately. The management of the Rolm Corporation welcomed this takeover. Their "independence" within IBM was guaranteed and the employees and management were retained.

In other instances, acquisitions or takeover attempts are not welcomed by the target companies' managements. Many recent controversial takeover attempts have been viewed as unfriendly; among them is the attempt by Ted Turner, owner of TBS, and Senator Jesse Helms, of North Carolina, to take over CBS. Their actions were prompted by their view that CBS news reporting was politically biased; they wished to control the giant broadcasting company in order to impose their own bias over this medium. The CBS board of directors acted quickly in denouncing the takeover bid and advised shareholders not to accept the Turner proposal. At present, the takeover bid is at a standstill and industry analysts predict that it will never occur.

In Canada, too, the managements of some companies have undertaken defensive tactics in warding off unfriendly takeover attempts. For instance, Yellowknife Bear Resources Inc. of Toronto declared a special dividend of $7.00 per share, a total payout of over $31 million dollars, deliberately making the company less attractive to its suitors. The two acquisitors subsequently withdrew their offers.

Fleet Aerospace Corporation of St. Catharines, Ontario at its annual shareholders meetings, adopted by-laws protecting its board of directors in the event of a takeover. Under its new by-law, if one individual or group acquired 25 percent of the company's common shares and then attempted to change the composition of the board of directors, over 70 percent of the shares outstanding would have to be represented at the meeting called to vote on such changes. This move, in effect, protects the board of directors from being replaced after a takeover. The adoption of these by-laws was challenged by the Ontario Securities Commission.

The rumours of an imminent acquisition can cause a company's share price to rise quickly. A recent rumour of a takeover bid for the shares of Gulf Canada Ltd. sparked a flurry of trading, as over 350 000 shares changed hands. The area of acquisitions and takeovers is one of the most interesting and complicated accounting issues. Many issues occurring during an acquisition must be resolved, involving financing, legal regulations, and restrictions on information that is to be supplied to investors.

Preparation of Consolidated Financial Statements

Although there are some exceptions, the individual financial statements of the parent and its subsidiary are combined for reporting purposes, as if the two were one economic entity and not two separate corporations; this reporting process is in accordance with GAAP. Although accountants prepare this single composite financial report, both parent and subsidiary are, and continue to be, two separate legal entities.

The procedure was explained to the executives of Bluebeard Computer Corporation. At their year-end, December 31, each corporation prepares its own financial statements as usual. These separate statements are then combined to show a financial picture of the whole operation, as if the two were one economic entity. These combined financial statements are the consolidated financial statements.

The combination of statements consists of two steps. First, the changes that occurred as a result of the acquisition are indicated in the parent's balance sheet; the balances immediately before the purchase and immediately after are shown. Next the balances of both parent and subsidiary are combined and disclosed. Note that liabilities are not listed in the subsidiary's trial balance in the analysis example. This exclusion emphasizes both that the parent is actually purchasing the net assets of the subsidiary and that the assets are the focus of the consolidation. Another example incorporates liabilities; it appears in the illustrative problem later in this section.

Alternative 1

In this alternative, the purchase cost is $20,000; the subsidiary's net assets, recorded in the books, are valued at $20,000. Since the purchase is made on December 31, 19X8 (after closing entries have been posted), it is easy to compare the change to the parent's financial position immediately after the purchase. Next, the balances of both parent and subsidiary are combined. Note that the combination process involves the elimination of reciprocal amounts (indicated with arrows).

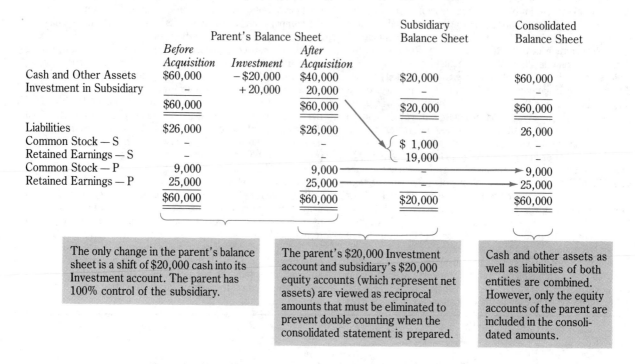

	Parent's Balance Sheet			Subsidiary Balance Sheet	Consolidated Balance Sheet
	Before Acquisition	*Investment*	*After Acquisition*		
Cash and Other Assets	$60,000	– $20,000	$40,000	$20,000	$60,000
Investment in Subsidiary	–	+ 20,000	20,000	–	–
	$60,000		$60,000	$20,000	$60,000
Liabilities	$26,000		$26,000	–	26,000
Common Stock — S	–		–	$ 1,000	–
Retained Earnings — S	–		–	19,000	–
Common Stock — P	9,000		9,000	–	9,000
Retained Earnings — P	25,000		25,000	–	25,000
	$60,000		$60,000	$20,000	$60,000

The only change in the parent's balance sheet is a shift of $20,000 cash into its Investment account. The parent has 100% control of the subsidiary.

The parent's $20,000 Investment account and subsidiary's $20,000 equity accounts (which represent net assets) are viewed as reciprocal amounts that must be eliminated to prevent double counting when the consolidated statement is prepared.

Cash and other assets as well as liabilities of both entities are combined. However, only the equity accounts of the parent are included in the consolidated amounts.

Note that the consolidated column is identical to the parent's column before its investment in the subsidiary. This correlation results because the combined group has the same resources before and after the acquisition in this example.

The important point to note is that the combination process combines only certain amounts. Other amounts, usually referred to as **reciprocal amounts**, are not combined; reciprocal amounts are eliminated in the combination process. The parent Investment in Subsidiary account and the subsidiary equity accounts comprise one example of reciprocal amounts that are eliminated for the following reasons:

- The combined entity cannot have an investment in itself, from a consolidation point of view
- The inclusion of the parent's Investment in Subsidiary account and the subsidiary's equity accounts would show more assets and equity than actually exist in the combined financial entity. In other words, the inclusion of these reciprocal amounts would result in a double counting of assets and equity in the combined financial statements.

The combination, therefore, eliminates the parent's Investment account and the subsidiary's reciprocal equity accounts. Intercompany transactions, if any, would also be

Reciprocal amounts
Amounts appearing in financial statements of both parent and subsidiary that are not combined in preparing consolidated financial statements; these amounts are eliminated in the consolidation process to prevent double counting.

eliminated. Since there have been no intercompany transactions at the acquisition date, no other elimination is required in this example.

Although reciprocal amounts are eliminated in the combination process, it is important to note that no journal entries are actually recorded in the books of either parent or subsidiary. Worksheet entries are prepared and used only toward preparation of consolidated financial statements. (See the illustrative problem in this section.)

Alternative 2

In this alternative, the purchase cost is $25,000; the subsidiary's net assets recorded in its books remain at $20,000 as in Alternative 1. A balance sheet is prepared to show the changes occurring in the parent's balance sheet immediately after the purchase; the balances of both parent and subsidiary are then combined. Note that, this time, the combination process involves not only the elimination of reciprocal amounts but also the creation of **goodwill from consolidation** (discussed briefly in Chapter 8); this goodwill arises because the parent has paid $5,000 in excess of the subsidiary's $20,000 net assets. (It is assumed for this example that the $5,000 payment is for goodwill in the subsidiary. In other examples, the $5,000 excess would counteract an undervaluation of assets in addition to the existence of goodwill.)

Note that the total of the consolidated column ($60,000) is identical to the parent's column total ($60,000) before its investment in the subsidiary. The combined group has the same resources before and after the acquisition in this alternative. However, the individual components within the asset amounts differ because of the existence of goodwill.

Goodwill (from consolidation)
The amount paid in excess of the fair market value of the net assets of a subsidiary.

	Parent's Balance Sheet			Subsidiary Balance Sheet	Consolidated Balance Sheet
	Before Acquisition	*Investment*	*After Acquisition*		
Cash and Other Assets	$60,000	− $25,000	$35,000	$20,000	$55,000
Investment in Subsidiary	–	+ 25,000	25,000	–	–
Goodwill from Consolidation	–		–	–	5,000
	$60,000		$60,000	$20,000	$60,000
Liabilities	$26,000		$26,000	–	$26,000
Common Stock — S	–		–	$ 1,000	–
Retained Earnings — S	–		–	19,000	–
Common Stock — P	9,000		9,000	–	9,000
Retained Earnings — P	25,000		25,000	–	25,000
	$60,000		$60,000	$20,000	$60,000

The only change in the parent's balance sheet is a shift of $25,000 cash into the Investment account. The parent has 100% ownership of the subsidiary.

The combination process excludes the reciprocal amounts to prevent double counting when the combination is prepared. Note that the combination process also results in the recognition of $5,000 of goodwill arising from the combination in this example.

Assets and liabilities (which exclude intercompany transactions) of both entities are combined.
The $5,000 excess is recognized as goodwill from consolidation. Only the equity accounts of the parent are included in the consolidated amounts.

In this alternative, the parent paid $25,000 to purchase ownership claims to $20,000 of net assets in the subsidiary. The $5,000 excess was paid for goodwill in the subsidiary. Although goodwill is an asset, it is never recorded in the accounts of an entity unless it has been purchased. In this example, the $5,000 excess payment is considered to be recognition of the existence of goodwill in the subsidiary. (If the excess amount was attributable to an undervaluation of the subsidiary's assets, in addition to the existence of goodwill, this situation would be disclosed as in the illustrative problem in this section.)

Alternative 3

In this third alternative, the purchase cost is $16,000; the subsidiary's net assets recorded in its books remain at $20,000, as in the preceding examples. The accounting for this acquisition at a purchase cost that is $4,000 less than the subsidiary's book value is more complex, is seldom seen in Canada, and is more fully explained in an advanced accounting course.[1]

Illustrative Problem — Wholly Owned Subsidiary

This illustrative problem demonstrates the use of a consolidation worksheet to prepare a consolidated balance sheet at the date of acquisition. The same problem used in the preceding discussions is used, with the following changes:

1. The amount of the investment is changed to $26,500 to incorporate an example of an amount paid in recognition of an undervaluation of assets in the subsidiary.
2. The assets and liabilities of the subsidiary are altered to include liabilities in the subsidiary's balance sheet. Net assets (assets − liabilities) remain at $20,000.
3. In addition to the previous data, P made a $15,000 loan to S at December 31, 19X8 after the acquisition, as agreed in the acquisition negotiations. P recorded the loan as a receivable; S recorded the amount as a payable. These are reciprocal amounts that must be eliminated on consolidation.

Here are the individual balance sheets of P and S immediately before and after acquisition.

	Parent's Balance Sheet				Subsidiary's Balance Sheet		
	Before Acquisition	*Investment*	*Loan*	*After Acquisition*	*Before Acquisition*	*Loan*	*After Acquisition*
Cash and Other Assets	$60,000	− $26,500	− $15,000	$18,500	$22,000	+ $15,000	$37,000
Loan Receivable — S			+ 15,000	15,000			
Investment in Subsidiary		+ 26,500		26,500			
	$60,000			$60,000	$22,000		$37,000
Liabilities	$26,000			$26,000	$ 2,000		2,000
Loan Payable — P						+ 15,000	15,000
Common Stock — S					1,000		1,000
Retained Earnings — S					19,000		19,000
Common Stock — P	9,000			9,000			
Retained Earnings — P	25,000			25,000			
	$60,000			$60,000	$22,000		$37,000

There are two changes in the parent's balance sheet: (a) $26,500 of cash is used for the investment and (b) $15,000 of cash is used for the loan. Note that the total assets have not changed.

The only change in the subsidiary's balance sheet is the receipt of $15,000 cash and the creation of loans payable of the same amount. Note that the total assets and total equity have changed, although net assets have not.

These comparisons are included to show the changes resulting from the investment and the loan. The preparation of consolidated financial statements requires the elimination of reciprocal amounts; the elimination of the Investment in Subsidiary account and the subsidiary's equity accounts was considered already. The Loan Receivable and Loan Payable accounts are also reciprocal amounts, since total assets and total liabilities of the combined economic entity did not increase.

Assume that, on December 31, 19X8, P Corporation purchased a 100-percent ownership interest in S Limited by paying $26,500 to the shareholders of S for their shares. Included in the purchase price was an amount in recognition of unrecorded goodwill in S and an undervaluation of an asset of S of $1,500.

On this date, as agreed in the acquisition, P also lent $15,000 to S. Here are the balance sheets prepared immediately after the purchase and recording of the loan.

	P Book Value	S Book Value	S Market Value
Cash and Other Assets	$18,500	$37,000	$38,500
Loan Receivable — S	15,000	–	
Investment in Subsidiary	26,500	–	
	$60,000	$37,000	
Liabilities	$26,000	$ 2,000	2,000
Loan Payable — P	–	15,000	15,000
Common Stock — S	–	1,000	
Retained Earnings — S	–	19,000	
Common Stock — P	9,000	–	
Retained Earnings — P	25,000	–	
	$60,000	$37,000	

How much was included in the purchase price in recognition of undervalued assets in S?

Market Value of S Assets	(a)	$38,500
Book Value of S Assets	(b)	37,000
S Assets Undervalued	(a – b)	$ 1,500 (c)

How much was included in the purchase price in recognition of unrecorded goodwill in S?

Purchase Payment	$26,500
P Purchased 100% of S	20,000
Excess	$ 6,500
Excess Resulting from Asset Undervaluation	1,500 (c)
Balance Is Goodwill	$ 5,000

Next, the worksheet elimination entries needed to consolidate the individual balance sheets must be prepared.

Worksheet entry (i):   To eliminate intercompany loan.

Loans Payable — P	15,000	
Loans Receivable — S		15,000

Worksheet entry (ii):   To eliminate the Investment in Subsidiary and subsidiary equity accounts and set up undervaluation of S's assets and unrecorded goodwill.

Common Stock — S	1,000	
Retained Earnings — S	19,000	
Assets — S	1,500	
Goodwill from Consolidation	5,000	
Investment in Subsidiary		26,500

A consolidation worksheet is prepared at December 31, 19X8 immediately following the purchase of S's shares and loan of $15,000.

Consolidation Worksheet

	Book Balances		Eliminations		Consolidated
	P	S	Debit	Credit	
Debits					
Cash and Other Assets	$18,500	$37,000	(b) $1,500		$57,000
Loan Receivable — S	15,000	–		(a) $15,000	–
Investment in Subsidiary	26,500	–		(b) 26,500	–
Goodwill from Consolidation	–	–	(b) 5,000		5,000
	$60,000	$37,000			$62,000
Credits					
Liabilities	$26,000	$ 2,000			$28,000
Loan Payable — P	–	15,000	(a) 15,000		–
Common Stock — S	–	1,000	(b) 1,000		–
Retained Earnings — S	–	19,000	(b) 19,000		–
Common Stock — P	9,000	–			9,000
Retained Earnings — P	25,000	–			25,000
	$60,000	$37,000	$41,500	$41,500	$62,000

A consolidated balance sheet is prepared at December 31, 19X8 immediately following the acquisition of S.

P Corporation and S Limited
Consolidated Balance Sheet
At December 31, 19X8

Assets		Liabilities and Equity		
Cash and Other Assets	$57,000	Liabilities		$28,000
Goodwill from Consolidation	5,000	Common Stock	$ 9,000	
		Retained Earnings	25,000	34,000
	$62,000			$62,000

Real Life Example 13-2

Shareholders Approve Comterm-Bytec Deal

Shareholders of Comterm Inc. yesterday pinned their hopes on market acceptance of the Hyperion, an IBM-compatible portable personal computer developed by Bytec Management Corp. of Ottawa.

Shareholders at the meeting voted 99.85 percent in favour of an amalgamation between Comterm and Bytec.

Bytec shareholders had accepted the deal — which gives them a 60.5-percent interest in the combined entity on a fully diluted basis — at a morning meeting in Ottawa.

The new company will be known as Bytec-Comterm Inc. and will operate from Comterm's head office in Pointe Claire. A prospectus for a new issue of common shares will be issued within a few weeks, Laurent Nadeau, Comterm's chairman and president, said after the meeting. Terms and conditions of the offering have not yet been revealed.

Nadeau denied an assertion by one shareholder, who later identified himself as Carl Evoniak, that the deal was "a sell-out" of Comterm's shareholders. Nadeau responded by calling the deal "really an amalgamation, a pooling of interests".

Evoniak was nearly alone in his opposition. Only 2993 shares or 0.15 percent of those represented were voted against the deal. The combined entity will rack up sales of more than $100 million in the fiscal year beginning Feb. 1, predicted Micheal Cowpland, a founder of Mitel Corp.

Bytec reported a loss of $14.6 million for the year ended July 31, on sales of $9.2 million.

But the company shipped about 1500 Hyperions in September and showed an unaudited profit during both August and September, Cowpland told reporters after the meeting. The Hyperion is priced between 10 and 15 percent below a comparably equipped IBM Personal Computer, Cowpland said. He said the company expects to be shipping between 3000 and 4000 Hyperions monthly by January.

Source Ian Ravensbergen, "Shareholders Approve Comterm-Bytee Deal", *The* (Montreal) *Gazette*, October 25, 1983, p. 1.

D. Pooling of Interests

The preceding section reviewed the purchase of a controlling interest in the shares of a subsidiary; in this situation, the parent has bought out all or some of the subsidiary's shareholders. The analysis prepared for Bluebeard management also evaluated the method of acquiring a subsidiary commonly referred to as a pooling of interests. The acquisition of the subsidiary under a pooling of interests is accomplished through an exchange of shares; specifically, shareholders of the subsidiary exchange their ownership in the subsidiary for an ownership interest in the parent. These original shareholders of the subsidiary therefore become shareholders in the parent and the group of corporations now controlled by the parent. The effective result of pooling is a shared control of the voting power within the parent company. Therefore, neither shareholder group can dominate the voting for the board of directors. For an example of a pooling of interests, see Real Life Example 13-2.

Preparation of Consolidated Financial Statements

The combination of individual financial statements of the parent and its subsidiary for a pooling of interests differs from that for the acquisition through a purchase of shares. The different combination process is reflected in the way the acquisition is recorded in the books of the parent. This difference is shown in Figure 13-3.

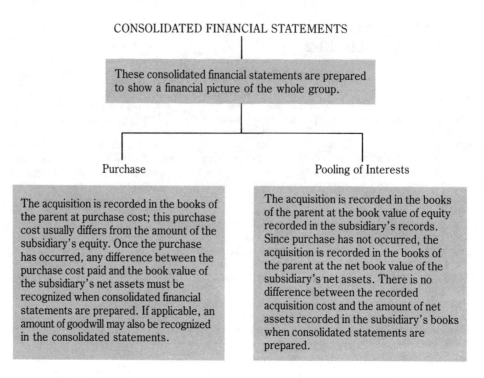

CONSOLIDATED FINANCIAL STATEMENTS

These consolidated financial statements are prepared to show a financial picture of the whole group.

Purchase

The acquisition is recorded in the books of the parent at purchase cost; this purchase cost usually differs from the amount of the subsidiary's equity. Once the purchase has occurred, any difference between the purchase cost paid and the book value of the subsidiary's net assets must be recognized when consolidated financial statements are prepared. If applicable, an amount of goodwill may also be recognized in the consolidated statements.

Pooling of Interests

The acquisition is recorded in the books of the parent at the book value of equity recorded in the subsidiary's records. Since purchase has not occurred, the acquisition is recorded in the books of the parent at the net book value of the subsidiary's net assets. There is no difference between the recorded acquisition cost and the amount of net assets recorded in the subsidiary's books when consolidated statements are prepared.

Figure 13-3 Contrast between a purchase and a pooling of interests as recorded in the consolidated financial statements

The accounting profession has made recommendations for the accounting treatment of business combinations, particularly in the distinction between a purchase and a pooling of interests, even if the acquisition has been made through the exchange of shares. The distinction centres on whether a dominant group emerges from the acquisition. These distinctions are complex and are usually dealt with in advanced accounting courses.

APPENDIX: Partially Owned Subsidiary

This section of the analysis prepared for Bluebeard's executives considers the possibility of a partially owned subsidiary; the purchase of any amount more than 50 percent of outstanding voting shares of another corporation results in a parent-subsidiary relationship. A 75-percent ownership interest is used in this example, which means that 75 percent of the subsidiary's shares were bought. In effect, the 75-percent share purchase results in the parent acquiring a 75-percent ownership claim to the net assets of the subsidiary.

Although the parent is then in a position to control the subsidiary's operations, 25 percent of the subsidiary is still owned by other shareholders. This one-quarter outside ownership is collectively referred to as the **minority interest**; it has a 25-percent ownership claim to the net assets of the subsidiary. This claim must be taken into consideration in the preparation of consolidated financial statements.

Minority interest
The ownership of a subsidiary's shares not owned by the parent corporation.

Recording the Purchase

The acquisition cost for the alternatives discussed in section B is recorded below. The difference in each case this time is that the parent has acquired a 75-percent ownership interest in the subsidiary. Note that the amount paid differs in each case.

Acquisition of 75-Percent Ownership Interest

	Alternative 1		Alternative 2		Alternative 3	
Investment in Subsidiary	15,000		18,000		13,000	
Cash		15,000		18,000		13,000

Although the purchase involves the payment of cash, the acquisition can also be made through a payment of other assets. Regardless, the parent in effect purchases a 75-percent ownership interest in the subsidiary's net assets; 75 percent of the subsidiary's previous owners no longer have any ownership interest in the subsidiary.

Preparation of Consolidated Financial Statements

The combination of individual parent and subsidiary financial statements is next prepared for the partially owned subsidiary. As before, accountants prepare consolidated financial statements to show a financial picture of the whole operation, as if they were one economic entity; this consolidation is done even though a minority interest exists in the subsidiary.

Alternative 1

In this alternative, the purchase cost is $15,000—75 percent of the subsidiary's net assets as recorded in the books ($20,000 × 75% = $15,000). This December 31,

	Parent's Balance Sheet			Subsidiary Balance Sheet	Consolidated Balance Sheet
	Before Acquisition	*Investment*	*After Acquisition*		
Cash and Other Assets	$60,000	− $15,000	$45,000	$20,000	$65,000
Investment in Subsidiary	–	+ 15,000	15,000	–	–
	$60,000		$60,000	$20,000	$65,000
Liabilities	$26,000		$26,000	–	$26,000
Common Stock — S	–		–	$ 1,000	–
Retained Earnings — S	–		–	19,000	–
Minority Interest	–		–	–	5,000
Common Stock — P	9,000		9,000		9,000
Retained Earnings — P	25,000		25,000		25,000
	$60,000		$60,000	$20,000	$65,000

The only change in the parent's balance sheet is a shift of $15,000 of cash into its Investment account. The parent has 75% ownership of the subsidiary.

The combination process excludes the reciprocal amount up to the $15,000 (75%) purchase. This $15,000 reciprocal amount is eliminated in the consolidation process.

Assets and liabilities of both entities are combined. Only the equity accounts of the parent are shown as equity. However, the $5,000 (25%) of the subsidiary not purchased is shown as a minority interest.

19X8 purchase changes the parent's balances immediately after the purchase, as shown next. Then, the amounts of both parent and subsidiary are combined. Note that the combination process results in the recognition of the 25-percent minority interest.

Note that the consolidated column total ($65,000) is $5,000 larger than the parent's column total ($60,000) before its investment in the subsidiary. The consolidated statements include the interests of both the parent and minority interests; therefore, the consolidated statements are increased when minority interests exist in a controlled subsidiary.

In this case, the combination of both entities eliminates the parent's Investment in Subsidiary account and 75 percent of the subsidiary's equity accounts; the ownership interest of the subsidiary's remaining shareholders (25 percent) is recognized as a minority interest. The consolidated column, therefore, indicates that both the parent and the minority shareholders of the subsidiary have an ownership interest in the consolidated net assets of the combined group. An important difference between the parent and the minority interest, however, is that the parent is in the position of control of the subsidiary's operations.

Alternative 2

In this second alternative, the purchase cost is $18,000; this amount is $3,000 greater than the 75-percent ownership interest in the subsidiary's net assets ($20,000 × 75% = $15,000). The changes occurring in the parent's balances immediately before and after the purchase are prepared; then, the balances of both parent and subsidiary are combined. Note that the combination process results in the recognition of goodwill

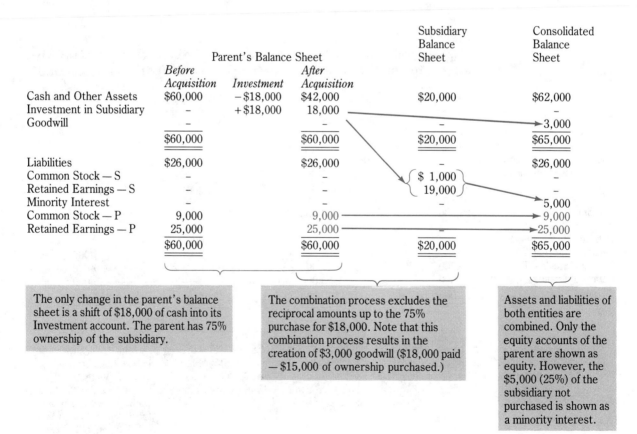

	Parent's Balance Sheet			Subsidiary Balance Sheet	Consolidated Balance Sheet
	Before Acquisition	*Investment*	*After Acquisition*		
Cash and Other Assets	$60,000	− $18,000	$42,000	$20,000	$62,000
Investment in Subsidiary	–	+ $18,000	18,000		–
Goodwill	–		–	–	3,000
	$60,000		$60,000	$20,000	$65,000
Liabilities	$26,000		$26,000	–	$26,000
Common Stock — S	–		–	$ 1,000	–
Retained Earnings — S	–		–	19,000	–
Minority Interest	–		–	–	5,000
Common Stock — P	9,000		9,000		9,000
Retained Earnings — P	25,000		25,000	–	25,000
	$60,000		$60,000	$20,000	$65,000

The only change in the parent's balance sheet is a shift of $18,000 of cash into its Investment account. The parent has 75% ownership of the subsidiary.

The combination process excludes the reciprocal amounts up to the 75% purchase for $18,000. Note that this combination process results in the creation of $3,000 goodwill ($18,000 paid − $15,000 of ownership purchased.)

Assets and liabilities of both entities are combined. Only the equity accounts of the parent are shown as equity. However, the $5,000 (25%) of the subsidiary not purchased is shown as a minority interest.

from consolidation, as well as the recognition of the 25-percent minority interest. The goodwill arises because the parent has paid $3,000 in excess of its 75 percent ownership of the subsidiary's $20,000 net assets (75% × $20,000 = $15,000). In other situations, this $3,000 excess could result from an undervaluation of assets in addition to the existence of goodwill, if any exists in the subsidiary. An example incorporating an asset undervaluation appears in the illustrative problem for Alternative 3.

Note that the consolidated column ($65,000) is also $5,000 greater than the parent's column ($60,000) before its investment in the subsidiary. This difference is due to the fact that the consolidated statements include both the parent and minority interests; therefore, the consolidated statements are increased when minority interests exist in a controlled subsidiary.

Alternative 3

In this third alternative, the purchase cost is $13,000; the subsidiary's net assets recorded in its books remain at $20,000, as in the preceding examples. The accounting for this acquisition of 75 percent of the shares at a purchase cost that is $2,000 less than their value is more complex, is seldom seen in Canada, and is more fully explained in advanced accounting courses.[2]

Illustrative Problem — Partially Owned Subsidiary

This illustrative problem is identical to the earlier one, with one exception: the parent has purchased only 75 percent of the subsidiary, paying $19,500 cash. Here are the individual balance sheets of P and S immediately before and after acquisition.

	Parent's Balance Sheet				Subsidiary's Balance Sheet		
	Before Acquisition	Investment	Loan	After Acquisition	Before Acquisition	Loan	After Acquisition
Cash and Other Assets	$60,000	−$19,500	−$15,000	$25,500	$22,000	+$15,000	$37,000
Loan Receivable — S			+15,000	15,000			
Investment in Subsidiary		+19,500		19,500			
	$60,000			$60,000	$22,000		$37,000
Liabilities	$26,000			$26,000	$ 2,000		$ 2,000
Loan Payable — P						+15,000	15,000
Common Stock — S					1,000		1,000
Retained Earnings — S					19,000		19,000
Common Stock — P	9,000			9,000			
Retained Earnings — P	25,000			25,000			
	$60,000			$60,000	$22,000		$37,000

On December 31, 19X8, P Corporation purchased a 75-percent ownership interest in S Limited by paying $19,500 to 75 percent of the shareholders of S for their shares. Included in the purchase price was an amount in recognition of unrecorded goodwill in

S and an undervaluation of an asset. On this date, P also lent $15,000 to S. The balance sheets prepared immediately after the purchase and recording of the loan appeared as follows:

	P	S	
	Book Value	*Book Value*	*Market Value*
Cash and Other Assets	$25,500	$37,000	$38,500
Loan Receivable — S	15,000	–	
Investment in Subsidiary	19,500	–	
	$60,000	$37,000	
Liabilities	$26,000	$ 2,000	$ 2,000
Loan Payable — P	–	15,000	
Common Stock — S	–	1,000	
Retained Earnings — S	–	19,000	
Common Stock — P	9,000	–	
Retained Earnings — P	25,000	–	
	$60,000	$37,000	

How much is included in the purchase price in recognition of undervalued assets in S?

		100%		*75%*
Market Value of S Assets	(a)	$38,500	× 75% purchased =	$28,875
Book Value of S Assets	(b)	37,000	× 75% purchased =	27,750
S Assets Undervalued	(a − b)	$ 1,500		$ 1,125 (c)

How much is included in the purchase price in recognition of unrecorded goodwill is S?

Purchase Payment	$19,500
P Purchased 75% of S	15,000
Excess	$4,500
Excess Resulting from Asset Undervaluation	1,125 (c)
Balance Is Goodwill	$ 3,375

The amount of minority interest is calculated.

Net Assets of S	$20,000
P Purchased 75% of S	15,000
($20,000 × 75%)	
Minority Interest	$ 5,000

The worksheet elimination entries needed to consolidate the individual balance sheets are prepared.

Worksheet entry (i): To eliminate intercompany loan.

Loans Payable — P	15,000	
Loans Receivable — S		15,000

Worksheet Entry (ii):   To eliminate the Investment in Subsidiary and subsidiary equity accounts and set up the undervaluation of S's assets, the unrecorded goodwill, and the minority interest.

Common Stock — S	1,000	
Retained Earnings — S	19,000	
Assets — S	1,125	
Goodwill from Consolidation	3,375	
Minority Interest		5,000
Investment in Subsidiary		19,500

A consolidation worksheet is prepared for December 31, 19X8 immediately following the purchase of S's shares and the loan of $15,000.

	Book Balances		Eliminations				Consolidated
	P	*S*		*Debit*		*Credit*	
Debits							
Cash and Other Assets	$25,500	$37,000	(b)	$ 1,125			$63,625
Loan Receivable — S	15,000	–			(a)	$15,000	–
Investment in Subsidiary	19,500	–			(b)	19,500	–
Goodwill from Consolidation	–	–	(b)	3,375			3,375
	$60,000	$37,000					$67,000
Credits							
Liabilities	$26,000	$ 2,000					$28,000
Loan Payable — P	–	15,000	(a)	15,000			–
Common Stock — S	–	1,000	(b)	1,000			–
Retained Earnings — S	–	19,000	(b)	19,000	(b)	5,000	5,000
Common Stock — P	9,000	–					9,000
Retained Earnings — P	25,000	–					25,000
	$60,000	$37,000		$39,500		$39,500	$67,000

A consolidated balance sheet is prepared for December 31, 19X8 immediately following the acquisition of S.

Assets		*Liabilities and Equity*		
Cash and Other Assets	$63,625	Liabilities		$28,000
Goodwill from Consolidation	3,375	Minority Interest		5,000
		Common Stock	$ 9,000	
		Retained Earnings	25,000	34,000
	$67,000			$67,000

A S S I G N M E N T   M A T E R I A L S

Discussion Questions

1. Contrast the accounting period required for income earned by an investee under the cost method and under the equity method. Is there any effect on the balance sheet or the income statement under either method?
2. How do corporate investments in common shares differ from investments in preferred shares as far as investor control of a corporation is concerned?
3. Identify and discuss three levels of voting influence by an investor corporation over the investee corporation.
4. Distinguish between the cost method and the equity method of accounting for long-term equity investments. What is one important similarity between these two methods?
5. What is a business combination?
6. What is the distinction between a parent and a subsidiary?
7. Distinguish between a purchase and a pooling of interests.
8. Does a parent corporation acquire the net assets or the equity of a subsidiary? Explain.
9. Why does a subsidiary maintain its own accounting records?
10. Why would the purchase cost of a subsidiary exceed the subsidiary's net assets?
11. Why are reciprocal amounts eliminated in the preparation of consolidated financial statements?
12. How are intercompany transactions handled in a combination? Why?
13. Describe the procedure used in the preparation of consolidated financial statements.
14. How does goodwill arise on consolidation?
15. How does the preparation of consolidated financial statements differ for a pooling of interests and a purchase?
16. How does partial ownership of a subsidiary result in a minority interest?

Discussion Cases

Discussion Case 13-1:   Fibonacci

Market prices tend to follow underlying natural laws, some observers say, and thus can be predicted. In fact, everything seems to hinge on the number 61.8.

Corrine Chaim is a mathematician who is also a broker at Dean Witter Reynolds (Canada) Inc. She contends that the behavior of stock prices during a bear market — where the over-all trend is downward — will follow a simple rule: sagging prices will reverse their decline and retrace 61.8 per cent of their initial drop before they head south again.

This is called a "Fibonacci retracement."

The direction of least resistance for stock values is always the same as in their last sharp move and the basic slumping trend of a bear market continues after the emotional period during which this retracement occurs.

The ratio 61.8 to 100 is found throughout nature and can also be derived from a series of numbers called the Fibonacci sequence. (The series is named after a 13th-century Italian mathematician who played a big role in popularizing the use of Arabic numerals.)

Fibonacci posed this problem: how many sets of rabbits will be produced in a year, beginning with a single pair, if each couple turns out a new pair monthly that becomes productive from its second month on? This celebrated puzzle gives rise to the so-called "Fibonacci sequence" — 1, 1, 2, 3, 5, 8 and so on — where each series member after the first pair of figures in the sum of the two numbers that immediately precede it (and is the total of new rabbit pairs in each successive month).

Except for the very early figures, the ratio of any Fibonacci number to the one that follows it is 61.8 to 100. The ratio of a number to the one that precedes it is 161.8 to 100.

The Fibonacci sequence is also observed in living organisms — for example, in the spiralling of leaves on a plant stem.

The proportion is the same as the Golden Section of classical art. This ratio, discovered by the ancient Greeks, was popularized by Euclid and worshipped by the Pythagoreans. As well, in the Great Pyramid of Gizeh, the ratio between the height of this Egyptian tomb to its base is roughly 61.8 per cent.

The Fibonacci ratio and its relatives, such as 161.8 or 261.8, underpin the Elliott Wave Theory, which tries to account for changes in investor psychology. R. N. Elliott, who developed the concept, is considered the giant among technical analysts. One of his followers, Robert Prechter, gained special prominence after last year's stock market crash because he had told his clients to get into cash shortly before prices tumbled.

Mr. Elliott's theory is based on a study of the ebbs and flows of emotion — as, indeed, is all technical analysis of markets. Technicians' views are opposed to those of "fundamental" analysts, who study such basics as the demand for a company's product, to determine what a reasonable price for its shares might be.

There is a basic rhythm to movements in stocks, Mr. Elliott contended, and the market has observable — and predictable — wave patterns. (He believed universal relationships underlie many things in life, such as the pattern of a daisy's petals, a mathematical series, the relationships between the sides of a triangle and the frequencies of musical notes.)

He contended that the stock market moves upward in five waves and then downward in three. The five-wave climb consists of three "up" waves interspersed with two declines. A major down wave consists of a down-up-down sequence.

These patterns can be seen in daily, monthly and even hourly price changes. "It is totally recursive" said Dean Witter's Ms Chaim, referring to the repetition involved. She added that when anticipated wave patterns exceed certain set limits, then data must be re-examined for the emergence of a new pattern that had not been discernible before. In such cases, there is either a new wave forming in the market or there has been some outside shock, such as a nuclear power-plant explosion.

Using wave theory, Ms Chaim predicts oil prices will drop to between $5 and $8 (U.S.). She said the cycles point to a decline until the end of November.

The long-term trend for the British pound is downward, she added. The currency dropped in value from 1981 until 1985. Then it underwent a three-year retracement from 1985 to 1988. It has now started to decline again after its Fibonacci correction. Thus, Ms Chaim said, it's time to consider shorting the pound.

Source   Alexander Eadie, "Forget 666, 61.8 Is Key Number for Markets", *The Globe and Mail*, Toronto, November 24, 1988, p. B-1, B-2.

For Discussion

1. Do you believe that the behaviour of stock prices during a bear market follows a Fibonacci retracement pattern? If so, wouldn't everyone use it to make a fortune on the stock market?

2. Assuming that the Fibonacci theory is valid, what information do you need before applying it successfully to the purchase and sale of stocks?

3. Is it possible for accountants preparing financial statements to predict the market value of shares at year-end?

Discussion Case 13-2:   The Seagram Company Ltd.

During the months from August 1980 through August 1981, The Seagram Company Ltd. completed one of the largest corporate asset redeployments in North American business history. Boiled down to the bare essentials, the company sold, for $2.3 billion, the United States properties of its Texas Pacific Oil Company subsidiary. After a period of economic analysis and interim investment of the proceeds, Seagram obtained ownership, at a cost of $2.6 billion, of a 20 percent equity interest in E.I. du Pont de Nemours and Company, one of the most distinguished of all North American corporate entities, which itself had been enhanced by its acquisition of Conoco Inc., ninth largest oil company in the United States and the parent of giant Consolidation Coal Company.

The combined Du Pont and Conoco now ranks as North America's seventh largest industrial corporation, a company with combined revenues of $32 billion and assets of $22 billion.

Shortly after completion of the Du Pont-Conoco merger, Seagram and Du Pont signed an agreement drawn to define the future relationship between the two companies. As a general matter Seagram has the right to increase its ownership of Du Pont voting securities up to a limit of 25 percent, and Du Pont has a right of first refusal should Seagram decide to sell its Du Pont holding during the term of the agreement. Seagram has representation on Du Pont's Board of Directors and, in evidence of the growing spirit of co-operation between the two companies, Du Pont now has representation on Seagram's. The agreement's term is for 10 years, but unless Seagram gives notice of its desire to terminate, it will be automatically extended for another five.

The first six months operating results following the acquisition of Du Pont shares, extracted from the second quarter report of the Seagram Company Ltd. are reproduced below:

An evaluation of these six month figures is also provided.

When liquor billionaires Charles and Edgar Bronfman signed a non-aggression pact with Du Pont's blue-blooded corporate chieftains last fall and were admitted to the chemical company's exclusive boardroom in Wilmington, Del., it was seen as a glittering consolation prize for their failure to win one of 1981's toughest takeover struggles.

The prize is not quite so helpful, though, to the corporate performance of the Bronfman-controlled Seagram Co. and to its non-Bronfman shareholders. The wheeling and dealing that finally put the brothers among the Du Pont directors is still costing the Montreal-based company plenty.

This fact is not immediately obvious from Seagram's latest profit report, published this week and covering the six months that ended January 31. But a closer look at the situation, and a check with financial industry sources, show that so far the American venture is not earning its keep.

The Bronfmans did not set out last year to acquire a 20-percent holding in Du Pont, although that's what they got. What they really wanted was control of the ninth-biggest oil company in the United States: Conoco. Oil and liquor could mix, they figured, and they were prepared to put more than $4 billion of their own and their bankers' money on the line to prove it. (Because this is an American story, all the money is counted in U.S. dollars, which are worth 20 percent more than Canadian bucks, in case you hadn't noticed.)

A gigantic corporate rumble followed. In the end Du Pont carried the day, through a $7.4-billion merger deal with Conoco. As part of that deal, Seagram turned over to Du Pont the Conoco shares it had acquired.

Those Conoco shares cost Seagram $2.6 billion, a lot of it borrowed money. In exchange for them, the company wound

	Six Months Ended January 31 (US $000s)	
	1982	*1981*
Sales and Other Income	$1,609,225	$1,555,756
Operating Income	174,000	161,010
Interest Expense	57,935	54,596
Income from Operations before Income Taxes	116,065	106,414
Provisions for Taxes	44,569	52,186
	71,496	54,228
Interest Expense, after Taxes, Relating to Share Repurchase	(4,661)	–
Income from Dividends and Interim Investments, after Taxes	56,947	72,400
	123,782	126,628
Equity in Unremitted Earnings of E.I. du Pont de Nemours and Company	42,131	–
Discontinued Operations (after taxes)	165,913	126,628
	–	6,802
Income before Extraordinary Gain	165,913	133,430
Extraordinary Gain on Sale of Oil and Gas Properties, after Taxes	–	1,222,481
Net Income	$ 165,913	$1,355,911

up with 20 percent of Du Pont. That's the largest single block, and it should be enough to lay down the law in Wilmington. The Du Pont family owns more shares in total, but they're scattered around in smaller parcels and it would be difficult to concentrate their power effectively.

But it didn't turn out that way. The Bronfmans took just their two seats on the 31-member board of directors, a mere 6 percent, and Edgar Bronfman became one of the 10 members of the influential finance committee (10 percent). They also promised not to increase the Seagram holding to more than 25 percent, and Du Pont has the first refusal on the shares if Seagram wants to sell them.

These are not exactly the kind of terms dictated by a conqueror to the conquered.

Meanwhile, the bills are coming in. On the face of it, the six-month report looks pretty good. Profit was up a gratifying 24 percent from the comparable six-month period a year earlier.

But all of that increase came from the inclusion in the tally for the most recent period of something called "equity in unremitted earnings" of Du Pont, amounting to $42 million. This is not your ordinary person's idea of a profit. It's a peculiar device dreamed up by the accountants to show, on the books, what Seagram's share of Du Pont's profit would amount to *if it could get at it.* Showing it on the financial statements is quite legitimiate, but it's strictly a paper amount. You can't spend it, or pay off your bank loans with it.

What Seagram actually gets from Du Pont in cash is a much smaller amount in the form of dividends paid on the shares it owns. It's not easy to tell from the published numbers how much this was in the latest six-month accounting period. But it's possible to make a good guess about the probable dividend income for the full year that will end next January.

Seagram owns roughly 47 million Du Pont shares. Most American analysts figure the chemical company's profit will be equivalent to about $6 a share this year, and the dividend paid to shareholders will be about $2.60. So that means about $122 million in cash for Seagram.

But the Bronfman company has to pay interest on the money it borrowed to buy the shares, or give up interest it could earn on any of its own cash that it used for the deal. There are taxes to take into account, but a conservative estimate of the effective cost puts it not far short of $200 million — a net cash drain of close to $80 million.

There's another thing for Seagram shareholders to think about. Their company is the proud possessor of 47 million shares that cost $54 apiece less than a year ago, and are selling at about $32 now.

That's a billion-dollar drop in the value of their investment. True, everybody's suffered from the collapse of the stock market. But the fact that Seagram bought into an oil company at the height of the industry's popularity among investors didn't help.

Just possibly, the investment may turn out well in the end. But on present form it would have been more profitable, if less glamorous, for Seagram to have stayed away from U.S. adventures — and put its money in the bank instead of borrowing more.

Sources The Seagram Company Ltd., *Annual Report 1981*, pp. 6 and 9; The Seagram Company Ltd., *Second Quarter Report, Six Months Ended January 31, 1982*, n.p.; Hugh Anderson, "Bronfman Prize Has Big Pricetag", *The* (Montreal) *Gazette*, March 13, 1982.

The Seagram Building is one of the jewels of Park Avenue — a sleek Mies Van de Rohe skyscraper of bronze and glass. At its epicenter is Edgar M. Bronfman, chief executive of the Seagram Company and son of its founder. But Seagram, the world's largest distiller, is finding liquor demand plummeting in the face of health concerns. And Bronfman, corporate scion of one of the world's wealthiest families, must now scramble to keep the business growing for the next generation and beyond.

Ironically, Seagram, a name synonymous with liquor in 175 countries, earns more from its investments than from distilled spirits. Thanks to Bronfman's abortive 1981 raid on Conoco, Seagram has gained a 22.5 percent stake — the biggest minority position — in Du Pont, the ultimate victor in the battle for Conoco. This stake provides nearly 75 percent of Seagram's earnings and, more importantly, is seen as the key to its future. Indeed, when asked what Seagram was doing to offset the drop in liquor consumption, Bronfman answered with one word: "Du Pont."

"The Bronfmans feel that distilled spirits is not going to make them terribly wealthy from here on and they are trying to locate the thing that will," said Arthur Kirsch, an analyst with Drexel Burnham Lambert. First Boston analyst Martin Romm is more blunt: "The liquor business has dried up."

The fortunes of Seagram rise and fall on the fate of E.I. du Pont de Nemours & Company, a cyclical company whose own business is weak right now. For the record, both sides proclaim fidelity. But, in private, there is intrigue between a liquor company that wants a bigger say in its investment and a chemical giant that resists any meddling. And, the big unanswered question is whether Seagram, at some point in the future, will vastly increase its Du Pont holding — and to what end. Not surprisingly, each company eyes the other, like two feudal tribes girding for a battle that may — or may not — erupt.

"It's been a four-year state of seige," said one observer familiar with both sides. Added Drexel's Kirsch: "I can't see the Bronfmans having $3 billion parked in one investment where all they get is three seats on the board. At some point, something is going to change."

Heading the Seagram side is Edgar Bronfman, 56, the tanned and lean guardian of the Bronfman dynasty, who surrounds himself with expensive art and well-paid management talent. The Bronfman family, immigrants from Czarist Russia, began their $2.8 billion business by making Canadian whiskey that found its way to America during Prohibition. Mr. Bronfman's view of Du Pont is simple: "Our intent is clearly to have an important voice."

Where Seagram's Earnings Come From

Seagram's earnings excluding extraordinary items, in millions of dollars

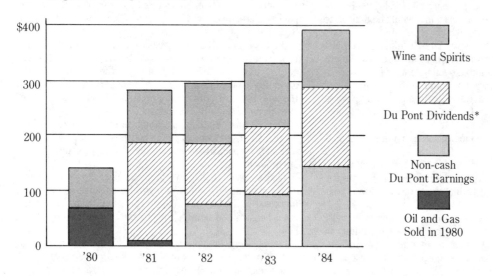

*1980 data are for gain on investments

Slower Growth for U.S. Wine and Spirits Market

Total U.S. consumption of wine and spirits, in billions of gallons

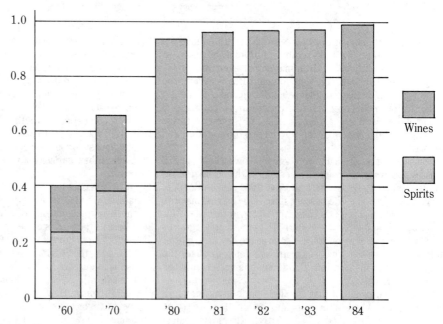

Source: Impact Review and Forecast of Beverage Trends in America

Du Pont, a $35 billion company that traces its origins to the original du Ponts who made gunpowder for the War of 1812, has long been viewed as the model of the modern corporation. Family control passed many decades ago to outside managers who oversee the making of everything from nylon to film to explosives. Du Pont, the nation's largest chemical company, is far more silent than Seagram. "There is little to be gained by getting into it," explained John R. Malloy, Du Pont's vice president for public affairs. "Our relations with Seagram are outstanding and constructive and there is not much more we can say than that."

Ties between the two companies are both formal and informal. Three Seagram representatives sit on the Du Pont board and two from Du Pont are members of the Seagram board. Edgar's brother, Charles, who is Seagram's deputy chairman, has become a close social friend of Edward G. Jefferson, Du Pont's chief executive — although some wonder whether the relationship is fueled by genuine friendship or an attempt to keep an eye on one another. Seagram receives Du Pont dividends — some $141.3 million last year — and has dedicated this cash stream to solely buying even more Du Pont shares. This money has enabled Seagram to increase its Du Pont shares from 20 percent of the company in 1981 to 22.5 percent today, and more purchases are on the way.

More than money, however, is influence. The Bronfmans say they are already involved in major decisions at Du Pont, and even though they are happy with the way Du Pont is managed, they want a bigger voice. "We see ourselves in the role of an active limited partner," said Bronfman. "We're allies of management at Du Pont to help them do a better job. We're involved in long-term decisions at Du Pont. We see eye-to-eye on the future of the company. It is superbly managed."

Others at Seagram are even more blunt. "We'd like to have a larger say in the policy direction of Du Pont," said David G. Sacks, executive vice president for administration and finance. "We are reasonable people and not a Boone Pickens or a Carl Icahn. We're Seagram Company and we operate with a certain style. We're not corporate takeovers artists. We've increased our stake to have meaningful impact on Du Pont policy."

Some within Du Pont say that the Bronfmans — despite what they say and the size of their position — play no greater a role than any other outside director. Seagram's three members — Edgar, his brother Charles and Seagram president Philip E. Beekman — have no more impact on long-term Du Pont policy than anyone else on Du Pont's 29-member board. They are not involved in the management of Du Pont and, in fact, there is little that the Bronfmans could do, since the two

AT A GLANCE

Seagram Company

All dollar amounts in thousands, except per share data

Three months ended April 30

	1985	1984
Revenues	$604,761	$625,620
Net Income	24,400	89,285
Earnings per share	$0.26	$0.99
Year ended Jan. 31	1985	1984
Revenues	$2,821,245	$2,647,552
Net Income	383,618	317,546
Earnings per share	$4.22	$3.53

Total assets, Jan. 31, 1985	$5,595,872
Current assets	1,535,084
Current liabilities	740,556
Long-term debt	780,760
Book value per share, Jan. 31, 1985	$33.50
Stock price, Aug. 9, 1985	
N.Y.S.E. consolidated close	40¾
Stock Price, 52-week range	44⅝–35⅜
Employees, Jan. 31, 1985	15,000
Headquarters	Montreal

AT A GLANCE

Du Pont

All dollar amounts in thousands, except per share data

Three months ended June 30

	1985	1984
Revenues	$8,614,000	$9,198,000
Net Income	268,000	437,000
Earnings per share	$1.10	$1.81
Year ended Dec. 31	1984	1983
Revenues	$36,218,000	$35,769,000
Net Income	1,431,000	1,127,000
Earnings per share	$5.93	$4.70

Main Lines of Business
Contribution to 1984 revenues

Oil, gas, coal	56%
Polymers, fibers	23%
Agricultural, industrial chemicals	10%
Industrial, consumer products	8%
Biomedical products	3%

Total assets, Dec. 31, 1984	$24,098,000
Current assets	8,651,000
Current liabilities	5,177,000
Long-term debt	3,421,000
Book value per share, Dec. 31, 1984	$50.06
Stock price, Aug. 9, 1985	
N.Y.S.E. consolidated close	58
Stock price, Aug. 9, 1985	61⅞–46⅛
Employees, Dec. 31, 1984	157,783
Headquarters	Wilmington, Del.

companies are in such dissimilar businesses and differ so much in size.

"The Bronfmans play no more or no less a role than any other outside director," said Andrew F. Brimmer, a board member and economic consultant. "I'm not conscious of the Bronfmans being any more active in questioning or probing than any other director. Neither they, nor any other outside director, have any management or initiating role."

Seagram stumbled into Du Pont more by accident than design. After stubbing its toes on acquisition passes at St. Joe Minerals and Conoco, Seagram ended up as the biggest shareholder of Du Pont — some 53.8 million shares valued at more than $3 billion. It got this in exchange for its Conoco stake. The Du Pont shares represent more than half of Seagram's corporate assets. Yet it is an investment that has performed well, but not spectacularly.

"It's an acquisition the Bronfmans chanced into," said Rex McCafferty, an analyst with Dominion Securities Pitfield in Toronto. "They are fighting what amounts to an environment of being in a sunset business and Du Pont gives them a stable cash flow. It hasn't been a bad investment, but it's not where I'd put my money. Liquor is in secular decline and Du Pont is large and cyclical. It's like buying a part of the U.S. economy."

On the positive side, the Du Pont contribution helps fatten a bottom line threatened by weakening liquor sales. Yet it comes at a price. Until 1984, Du Pont shares, which are now trading at about $60 a share, were selling below Seagram's average acquisition cost of $52 a share — creating hundreds of millions of dollars in paper losses. And, Seagram is in the unenviable position of having the bulk of its assets tied up in an investment that it does not actively manage.

Nor have the Du Pont returns been remarkable — except for their cyclicality. For instance, Du Pont's fiscal year 1985 earnings are expected to be weak due to a strong dollar and a sluggish economy. And Seagram's its earnings in its first quarter, ended April 30, fell to 26 cents a share from 99 cents a share in the 1984 first quarter, due largely to big write-offs taken by Du Pont. Even by Seagram's own admission, the 8 to 12 percent annual after-tax return on its Du Pont holding is "satisfactory, not spectacular", said Seagram's Sacks.

Seagram, however, dismisses each naysaying. "There's no question we could put $3 billion in something and make more money than Du Pont," said Sacks. "Maybe gold. Maybe casinos in Atlantic City. But that ignores the appreciation in the stock and right now the market price is higher than our carrying cost. We're delighted with our relationship."

All eyes, however, are where Seagram goes from here — especially now that key deadlines approach in a precisely worded standstill agreement between the two companies. The agreement was drafted after Bronfman elected to take a minority position in Du Pont rather than cash in his Conoco shares and, under its terms, Bronfman has promised not to buy more than 25 percent of Du Pont for a certain time period in exchange for three seats on the Du Pont board.

The agreement provided something for everyone. Du Pont got assurances that its biggest shareholder's appetite would be curbed for at least 10 years, until 1991. Seagram got Du Pont board representation and, under accounting rules, the vast size of its stock holdings and its board seats mean that Seagram is clearly able to claim up to 25 percent of Du Pont's earnings as its own.

For instance, in the fiscal year 1984, in addition to the cash Du Pont dividends, Seagram claimed about $141.4 million of Du Pont's earnings as its own — a percentage equal to Seagram's percentage ownership of Du Pont. This is a non-cash accounting entry that is added to Seagram's bottom line and makes the distiller look even more attractive to investors. Last year, Seagram earned $383.6 million, which included $282 million in cash and non-cash contributions from Du Pont.

The key date in the immediate future is October 1987, when Seagram must notify Du Pont whether it wants to extend the agreement for five years beyond the 1991 expiration date. If the agreement is not extended, Seagram immediately loses its Du Pont board seats and, perhaps, even its ability to claim Du Pont earnings as its own. But Seagram would be free to accumulate shares beyond the 25 percent limit starting in 1991 — perhaps as a prelude to a raid or an attempt to get an even larger bloc of Du Pont to gain an even higher premium price if sold as a single unit.

Conversely, extension of the agreement would be a signal of a continuation of the present situation. Seagram's hands as a raider would be tied, but its ability to draw upon Du Pont's earnings would be guaranteed. And, since Seagram would be barred from buying more than 25 percent of Du Pont, the enormous dividend stream that Seagram currently dedicates to buying more Du Pont could be used for other goals, perhaps other acquisitions or investments.

Right now, Bronfman is giving no hints of his intention. "What our plans are now and in 1987 are not fixed," he said. "Whether we renew the agreement or not has not been decided."

Ironically, one of the few other standstill agreements in effect at a major American company is between the Scott Paper Company, which is just down the road in Philadelphia from Wilmington-based Du Pont, and Brascan Ltd., a Toronto-based investment concern owned largely by Edgar Bronfman's cousins, Peter and Edward, generally known as the Canadian Bronfmans to distinguish them from the American branch that runs Seagram. That agreement halted Brascan's advances and limited its ownership of Scott to 25 percent in return for four board seats. Following adoption of this 1981 agreement, the Pennsylvania legislature enacted a measure to make takeovers in that state more difficult and greenmail impossible by banning the payment of premiums for large blocks of shares.

Bronfman, son of the legendary "Mr. Sam" who built Seagram, presides over a company that moved to the top of the liquor business during Prohibition and stayed there. But liquor, particularly the "brown goods" that Seagram is known for — its most famous brands are 7 Crown, V.O. Canadian and Chivas Regal — are being shunned by consumers concerned about diet and health.

Industry-wide shipments of distilled spirits fell in 1984 to a pre-1975 level of 440 million gallons a year, according to the trade publication Impact. Seagram brands have not been immune. Sales of 7 Crown and V.O. Canadian, two of its top brands, fell 4 percent last year, following even bigger declines in previous years. And no one, not even those at Seagram, believes that a turn-around is in sight.

"There's still a lot of liquor consumed, but it is declining in the long run," said First Boston's Romm. "The question is what do they do to restructure the company to lessen its dependence on liquor." Added Roy D. Burry, an analyst with Kidder, Peabody: "Seagram has a tremendous amount of product in the aging process and demand is contracting. Over time, this will generate large amounts of money. If demand goes down forever, production disappears and the company turns into a pile of cash. But I don't think that is what the Bronfmans want."

Mr. Bronfman sees his task to expand the company for his sons and for generations of Bronfmans yet to come. The Bronfman family owns about 38 percent of Seagram and Bronfman makes it clear that he wants Seagram to be the family treasure well into the next century. "And it is exactly how the next generation feels too," said Bronfman, while seated in an office decorated with a Miro tapestry and Rodin sculptures. And when Bronfman steps down as chief executive in the next four to six years, he will hand over the office to one of his sons, most likely Edgar Jr., age 30, or Sam, age 31, who already work for the company.

Yet as Bronfman looks to the future, he does not envision the day when Seagram or the Bronfmans will be out of the distilled spirits business. "The core business has its problems, but it's not all on the black side," said Bronfman.

Seagram has already begun moves to spur growth. Its overseas operations, which represent slightly under half of sales, are being expanded by products, acquisitions and forays into new markets. Under the aegis of Edgar Bronfman Jr., the domestic distilled spirits operation has been streamlined, resulting in the laying off of as many as 200 of 750 marketing and sales employees. Margins in distilled operations remain comfortable as the company sells off old products and spends less in production costs. Still, no one knows the impact of a $2-a-gallon Federal excise tax increase scheduled to go into effect on Sept. 30.

Seagram spent $237 million to buy the Wine Spectrum, makers of Sterling and Taylor California Wines, from Coca-Cola in 1984. This, combined with Seagram's existing Paul Masson wines, makes it the nation's second-largest wine producer and gives it a bigger stake in the domestic wine business, which has been reeling of late from the twin effects of a strong dollar and an oversupply of grapes. Analysts, however, say that in the long run, this investment should pay off, and, even in the short run, Seagram appears to be doing well with new products like Seagram Coolers, a wine and citrus mix.

And Bronfman talks about making a $1 billion to $2 billion acquisition of a consumer products or leisure time company, although he has no specific plans in mind. "We're not actively looking for acquisitions, but an acquisition is not beyond the scope of our imagination if the right acquisition came along and the timing was right."

With nearly 40 percent of the company in family hands and another 10 percent or so in the hands of corporate officers, Seagram is in the enviable position of being fairly impervious to an unfriendly takeover. Nonetheless, the company attempted last May to restructure Seagram's by proposing to increase its control to nearly 87 percent. The proposal sought to give the Bronfmans increased votes in exchange for a high dividend to non-Bronfman shareholders. That proposal, however, was withdrawn after opposition from non-Bronfman shareholders.

Indeed, the only threat could come from within — if members of the Bronfman family decided, over time, to sell their Seagram shares. Already, a trust representing Edgar's sister, Minda, sold more than 900 000 shares on the open market last March and some 4.9 million of her shares are now in the hands of her heirs following her death last July. As the generations continue, there will be more Bronfmans splitting the family holdings and more people with individual needs for cash that might result in a diminution of the family stake. For now, Bronfman said that he or his brother Edgar will buy the shares of any Bronfman heir who wants to sell his or her Seagram holdings.

And family ownership, he feels, is in the best interest of Seagram. "There's been a lot of criticism of American corporations where people are in their jobs a short time and don't have a long view," said Bronfman. "It's a great advantage to have a family tradition now and into the 21st century. That doesn't always justify family control, but I view it that way and it's even a good benefit to the Seagram shareholders."

Source Lesley Wayne, "The House of Seagram Puts its Faith in Chemicals," *The New York Times*, August 11, 1985, pp. F-1 and F-6.

For Discussion

1. It is assumed that the investor corporation has a significant influence and control over an investee corporation when the investor has between 20 and 50 percent ownership of the investee. From your reading of the preceding information, do you believe that Seagram has a significant influence and control over Du Pont? Why or why not?

2. Seagram reports its investment in Du Pont on the equity method. What are the journal entries that Seagram prepares to report under the equity method? Prepare sample journal entries.

3. Evaluate from a shareholder's view the fact that the Du Pont dividends received by Seagram appear to be considerably less than the cost to borrow money to purchase Du Pont shares or interest that Seagram could otherwise earn on its money. Consider both the short-term and long-term prospects.

4. Would the fact that 25 percent of Du Pont's earnings are recorded as revenue for Seagram prompt you to invest (or prevent you from investing) in the Seagram Company?

5. Suggest reasons why — from the perspective of Canadian GAAP — 20 percent stock ownership is used as the benchmark for significant influence.

6. Would you suggest that the Bronfmans divert their investment in liquor — owing to the apparently bleak future for such products? Why or why not?

Discussion Case 13-3: Seagram Profits

Despite a steady decline in liquor consumption, Seagram Co. Ltd. of Montreal has posted record profit and sales in its latest fiscal year.

The Montreal-based distiller reported profit of $589.5-million (U.S.) for the year ended Jan. 31, 1989, compared with $521.8-million a year earlier. Sales ballooned to $5.1-billion from $3.8-billion.

Seagram attributed the strong performance to its growing non-alcoholic beverage business and to its share in the results of E. I. du Pont de Nemours & Co. of Wilmington, Del. Seagram holds a 22.9 per cent interest in the U.S. chemical giant and has an option to acquire up to 25 per cent by 1999.

Du Pont dividends paid to Seagram rose to $202.5-million from $179.5-million and unremitted du Pont profit reached $284.4-million. The total contribution from du Pont of $486.9-million exceeded Seagram's operating income of $425.4-million.

The spirits market was more stable than predicted, noted Neil Wickham, a Toronto-based analyst for Canarim Investment Corp. Ltd. He also said newly acquired Tropicana Products Inc. added more to the bottom line than anticipated. Early last year, Seagram bought Tropicana from Beatrice Cos. Inc. of Chicago at a cost of $1.2-billion. It also purchased Martell & Co. SA, a leading French cognac producer for $924-million.

The acquisitions raised Seagram's debt to about $2-billion and interest expenses swelled last year to $238.5-million from $80.4-million a year earlier. The company still carries 60 cents of debt for every $1 of equity, but the considerable cash flow from the new businesses should help whittle down debt quickly, Mr. Wickham said.

Mr. Wickham figures Seagram could achieve a 10 per cent profit gain in the current fiscal year. Last year, profit rose 13.1 per cent. Some of this year's improvement may come from the company's moves to drop unprofitable lines, streamline operations and cut staff.

The consumption of distilled spirits is falling by 2 to 3 per cent a year, according to industry sources. That trend prompted Seagram's $1-billion entry into the wine cooler market — where it holds a 36 per cent share — and its move to take a leading position in the juice business through Tropicana. In fact, company executives are calling Seagram "an adult beverage company" without reference to the word alcohol.

At the same time, Seagram is capitalizing on a move toward premium brands that offer high margins. "Seagram has a long-standing emphasis on premium brands," a spokesman said. One of Seagram's advertisements for Chivas Regal scotch sums up the corporate strategy: "If you're drinking less, drink better."

The company is also preparing itself for a change in command July 1 when Edgar Bronfman Jr. becomes president and chief operating officer. His father, Edgar Bronfman, remains chairman. As part of the corporate shuffle, William Pietersen was appointed yesterday as president of a new division, Seagram USA, which will oversee U.S. distilling operations, the wine cooler business and Tropicana. Mr. Pietersen will also be an executive vice-president of both Seagram and New York-based Joseph E. Seagram & Sons Inc., its U.S. subsidiary.

Source   Harvey Enchin, "Du Pont, Non-liquor Concoction Brings Record Seagram Profit", *The Globe and Mail*, Toronto, March 17, 1989, p. B-7.

For Discussion

1. Evaluate the following aspects of Seagram's business:
   a. Its operations in distilled spirits
   b. Its other operations
   c. Its investment in Du Pont.
2. Seagram's 22.9-percent ownership interest in Du Pont doesn't give it control of Du Pont. Would it control Du Pont if it had a 25-percent ownership interest?
3. With declining sales and profits in its traditional business, Seagram must plan carefully for the future. What do you think Seagram should do?
4. If Seagram owned 50 percent of Du Pont, what would the impact be on Seagram's income statement? Make some calculations based on the information in this case.

Discussion Case 13-4: Seagram Debts

The recent large debts piled up by Seagram Co. Ltd. are making bond raters nervous.

Dominion Bond Rating Service of Toronto has cut the giant distiller's rating on all senior debt to single-A (high) from double-A.

The move follows a downgrade of Montreal-based Seagram by Standard & Poor's Corp. of New York last month to single-A from single-A plus.

Both agencies had placed Seagram on a rating alert after it borrowed heavily to make two major acquisitions.

The rating cut could add a few basis points to the cost of obtaining long-term financing.

The ratings on short-term commercial paper, which is much more sensitive to such changes, were not altered.

Seagram paid $1.2-billion (U.S.) to obtain Tropicana Products Inc. from Beatrice Cos. Inc. of Chicago and $924-million for Martell & Co. SA, a large French cognac maker.

The Tropicana purchase appears a high-risk venture, Dominion Bond said in its report on the company.

Besides paying a hefty price, Seagram has acquired a company that "operates in a highly competitive industry, is particularly sensitive to the price of oranges . . . and has little in (the way of) synergies with Seagram."

Martell also was costly, but the rating agency is happier with this purchase, which fits in well with Seagram's primary liquor business.

But the combined acquisitions have more than doubled the debt relative to equity — a key bond-rating criterion. The proportion of debt is now more than 40 per cent, compared with under 20 before the deals.

However, Seagram does have a bit of a cushion provided from the unrealized capital gains in its 22.7 per cent stake in E. I. du Pont de Nemours & Co. of Wilmington, Del.

But although a large chunk of the distiller's profits have been coming from du Pont, it cannot tap into that company's profit to help pay interest charges, because it lacks control.

Source Brian Milner, "Bond Raters Getting Jitters over Huge Seagram Debts", *The Globe and Mail*, Toronto, April 20, 1988, p. B-3.

For Discussion

1. How do you view Seagram's increasing debt? Could it lead to problems?
2. Tropicana "operates in a highly competitive industry, is particularly sensitive to the price of oranges . . . and has little in (the way of) synergies with Seagram". What problems might this acquisition create for Seagram?
3. Would Seagram have to sell Du Pont shares if its high equity-to-debt ratio became a problem? If it did sell, what would be the effect on its income statement?

Comprehension Problems

Comprehension Problem 13-1

On January 1, 19X2, Staedtler Inc. purchased 50 000 shares, representing a 20-percent interest in Sunna Ltd., for $150,000. The following transactions occurred subsequently:

May 10   Sunna paid $25,000 in dividends to its shareholders
Dec. 31   Sunna reported a net loss of $75,000 for 19X2.

Required: Prepare journal entries to record the above transactions, assuming that
1. Sunna uses the equity method
2. Sunna uses the cost method.

Comprehension Problem 13-2

On January 1, 19X6, Cancorp Inc. purchased 100 000 shares, representing a 100-percent interest in U-Corp., for $1,000,000. The following transactions occurred subsequently:

19X6
Dec. 31   U-Corp. reported a loss of $500,000.

19X7
Jun. 12   U-Corp. paid a dividend of $30,000
Dec. 31   U-Corp. reported a gain of $100,000.

Required: Prepare journal entries to record the above transactions.

Comprehension Problem 13-3

On December 31, 19X3, P Corporation purchased a 100-percent interest in S Corporation for $60,000. The purchase price included an amount in recognition of an undervaluation in the net assets of S. Assume there is no amount for goodwill.

	P Book Value	S Book Value
Net Assets	$200,000	$45,000
Common Stock	50,000	15,000
Retained Earnings	150,000	30,000

Required:

1. Calculate the amount of undervaluation in assets in S.
2. Prepare the elimination entry needed to consolidate the individual balance sheets.
3. What amounts would be recorded on the consolidated balance sheet for Net Assets, Common Stocks, and Retained Earnings?

Comprehension Problem 13-4

Use the same data given in Comprehension Problem 13-3, except that P Corporation purchased the shares of S Corporation at book value.

Required:

1. Prepare the elimination entry to consolidate the individual balance sheets.
2. What amounts would be recorded on the consolidated balance sheet for Net Assets, Common Stock, and Retained Earnings?

Comprehension Problem 13-5

Duncan Corporation purchased 20 000 shares, representing a 20-percent interest in Stacko Corporation, for $10 per share on January 1, 19X8. The following transactions occurred during the year:

Apr. 15	Stacko paid a $0.25 per-share dividend
Jun. 7	Stacko distributed a 10 percent stock dividend
Oct. 4	Stacko paid a $0.15 per-share dividend
Dec. 31	Stacko reported net income of $50,000; Duncan exercises a significant control over Stacko.

Required:

1. Prepare journal entries to record
   a. The purchase of the 20 000 shares as a long-term investment
   b. Receipt of its share of dividends paid by Stacko
   c. Duncan's share of net income reported by Stacko.
2. Prepare an investment schedule to show the amounts reported on the balance sheet and on the income statement under the equity method.

Comprehension Problem 13-6

On January 1, 19X2, P Corporation purchased 100 percent of S Limited's shares by paying $300,000 cash to the shareholders of S for their shares. The purchase price included an amount in recognition of an undervaluation in the asset Land and also an amount in recognition of goodwill in S. The balance sheet balances of both corporations immediately after the purchase are recorded in this partial consolidation worksheet.

Book Balances

	P	S		
Cash and Other Assets	$350,000	$150,000	300,000	500,000
Investment in Subsidiary	300,000	–		225,000
Land — S	–	200,000	25,000	25,000
Goodwill	–	–	75,000	750,000
	$650,000	$350,000		
Liabilities	$225,000	$100,000		325
Common Stock — P	250,000	–		250
Retained Earnings — P	175,000	–		175
Common Stock — S	–	200,000	200,000	750
Retained Earnings — S	–	50,000	50,000	
	$650,000	$350,000		

225
200
25,000

Required:
1. Calculate the amount by which land is undervalued. Assume that the current market value of land is $225,000. $25,000
2. Calculate the amount of goodwill included in the purchase price. 75,000
3. Prepare the worksheet elimination entry needed to consolidate the individual balance sheets.
4. Complete the consolidation worksheet, using the form in the illustrative problems in the chapter.

Comprehension Problem 13-7

On December 31, 19X7, P Corporation purchased an interest in S Limited by paying $250,000 cash to the shareholders of S for their shares. The balance sheets and consolidated balance sheet prepared immediately after the purchase are as follows:

	P	S	Consolidated
Assets			
Cash	$ 20,000	$ 10,000	$ 30,000
Notes Receivable	5,000	–	–
Accounts Receivable	100,000	65,000	150,000
Merchandise Inventory	175,000	160,000	335,000
Investment in Subsidiary	250,000	–	–
Land	150,000	75,000	249,000
Goodwill	–	–	26,000
	$700,000	$310,000	$790,000
Liabilities and Equities			
Accounts Payable	$190,000	$ 55,000	$230,000
Notes Payable	–	5,000	–
Minority Interest	–	–	50,000
Common Stock — P	210,000	–	210,000
Retained Earnings — P	300,000	–	300,000
Common Stock — S	–	200,000	–
Retained Earnings — S	–	50,000	–
	$700,000	$310,000	$790,000

Required:
1. What percentage of S's shares was purchased by P? (*Hint:* Start by calculating the percentage of S owned by minority shareholders.)
2. Was the purchase of S shares made at book value? Explain.
3. Prepare the worksheet elimination entries that were made on the consolidation worksheet to consolidate the balance sheets of P and S.

Problems

Problem 13-1

Reynold's Corporation (RC) purchased 20 000 shares, representing a 20-percent interest in Fedor Inc., for $100,000 on January 1, 19X7. The following transactions occurred subsequently:

19X7
Jun. 30   Fedor paid $5,000 in dividends to its shareholders
Dec. 31   Fedor reported net income of $20,000 for 19X7.

19X8
Jun. 30   Fedor paid $50,000 in dividends to its shareholders
Dec. 31   Fedor reported net loss of $75,000 for 19X8.

Required: Answer the questions for each of these cases.
Case A: RC has a significant influence over Fedor.
Case B: RC does not have a significant influence over Fedor.

1. Prepare journal entries to record
   a. The purchase of the 20 000 shares by RC
   b. Receipt of its share of dividends paid by Fedor
   c. RC's share of Fedor's net income or loss, if applicable.
2. Prepare a schedule to compare the amounts reported on the balance sheet and on the income statement of RC for 19X7 under both the cost method and the equity method.

Problem 13-2

Solomon Corporation purchased 60 000 shares, representing a 60-percent interest in Geldart Limited, for $360,000 on January 1, 19X7. Solomon is assumed to have a significant influence over Geldart. The following data are applicable to 19X7.

	Solomon		Geldart	
	Dividends Paid	*Net Income*	*Dividends Paid*	*Net Income*
	$40,000	$170,000	$20,000	$80,000

Required:
1. Indicate the method of accounting that can be used in the records of Solomon to account for its investment in Geldart. Under which method would the investment be reported in the financial statements of Solomon?
2. Assuming that the investment in shares of Geldart is maintained on the equity basis in the records of Solomon, prepare journal entries to record
   a. The purchase of the 60 000 shares as a long-term investment
   b. The receipt of Solomon's share of dividends paid by Geldart in 19X7
   c. Solomon's share of Geldart's 19X7 income.
3. How would Solomon's investment in Geldart be accounted for if 10 000 shares had been purchased instead of 60 000? Why?

Problem 13-3 (CGA adapted)

On December 31, 19X8, P Corporation purchased a 100-percent interest in S Limited by paying $120,000 cash to the shareholders of S for their shares. Included in this purchase price was an amount in recognition of an undervaluation of the net assets of S. Assume there is no goodwill. Here are some summarized financial data from the balance sheets of both corporations immediately after the purchase.

	P	S
	Book Value	Book Value
Net Assets	$400,000	$90,000
Common Stock	100,000	30,000
Retained Earnings	300,000	60,000

Required:
1. Calculate the amount of the undervaluation of S's net assets. $30,000
2. Prepare the worksheet elimination entry needed to consolidate the individual balance sheets. (The preparation of a consolidation worksheet is not required in this problem.)
3. What amounts would be reported on the consolidated balance sheet for
   a. Net Assets?
   b. Common Stock?
   c. Retained Earnings?

Problem 13-4

On December 31, 19X1, P Corporation purchased a 100-percent interest in S Limited by paying $175,000 cash to the shareholders of S for their shares. S is a newly formed developer of computer microchips that was about to begin manufacturing operations. Included in the purchase price was an amount in recognition of the existence of goodwill in S. Immediately before this purchase, the balance sheets of the corporations appeared as follows:

	P	S	
	Book Value	Book Value	Market Value
Cash and Other Assets	$450,000	$150,000	$150,000
Liabilities	$ 75,000	$ –	
Common Stock	175,000	$150,000	
Retained Earnings	200,000	–	
	$450,000	$150,000	

Required:
1. Calculate the amount of goodwill included in the purchase.
2. Prepare the entry to record in P's books the purchase of S's shares.
3. Prepare the worksheet elimination entry needed to consolidate the individual balance sheets. (The preparation of a consolidation worksheet is not required in this problem.)
4. Prepare a consolidated balance sheet at December 31, 19X1 immediately following the purchase of S's shares.

Problem 13-5

On January 2, 19X3, P purchased 100 percent of S shares by paying $210,000 to shareholders of S. Included in the purchase price was an amount in recognition of unrecorded goodwill in S. The following condensed financial statements of S and P were prepared immediately before the purchase:

	P	S	
	Book Value	*Book Value*	*Market Value*
Assets	$150,000	$190,000	
Liabilities	$ 10,000	$ 10,000	
Equity	140,000	?	
	$150,000		

Required:
1. Prepare the entry to record on P's books the purchase of S's shares.
2. Calculate the amount of goodwill to be shown on the consolidated balance sheet immediately after the purchase of S's shares.
3. Prepare the worksheet elimination entry needed to remove the Investment in Subsidiary account on P's books and S's equity immediately after the purchase of S's shares. You are not required to prepare a consolidation worksheet.

Problem 13-6

P is an investment company that has assets consisting of cash and investments. On December 31, 19X7, P purchased 70 percent of S's shares by paying $185,000 to shareholders of S. The balance sheet and other financial information of S immediately before the purchase are as follows:

	S				S	
	Book Value	*Market Value*		*Book Value*	*Market Value*
Cash	$ 75,000	$ 75,000	Accounts Payable	$ 55,000	$ 55,000
Land	40,000	85,000	Bonds Payable	80,000	80,000
Building (net)	110,000	190,000	Common Stock	120,000	
Equipment (net)	60,000	20,000	Retained Earnings (Jan. 2, 19X7)	140,000	
Goodwill	50,000	—	Net Loss for the Year	(60,000)	
	$ 335,000			$335,000	

Required:
1. Included in the purchase price was an amount in recognition of the undervaluation and overvaluation of various balance sheet items. Calculate the amount of the net undervaluation or overvaluation.
2. Was any amount included in the purchase price in recognition of unrecorded goodwill for S? Explain.
3. What amount of assets and liabilities of S would appear on the consolidated balance sheet immediately after the purchase of S's shares by P?
4. Calculate the amount of minority interest that would appear on the consolidated balance sheet immediately after purchase of S's shares by P.

Problem 13-7

Ur Homes Limited (UHL) has 100 000 common shares outstanding. The following data are applicable to its operations for 19X3, 19X4, and 19X5.

	Dividends Paid	Net Income (Loss)
19X3	$200,000	$ 300,000
19X4	100,000	(400,000)
19X5	100,000	600,000

Ux Farms Inc. (UFI) purchased 51 000 shares, representing a 51-percent interest in Ur Homes Limited, for $300,000 on January 1, 19X3.

Part A

Required:
1. Identify the relationship of UHL and UFI during 19X3, 19X4, and 19X5.
2. Indicate what method of accounting can be used in the records of UFI for its investment in UHL. Under what method would the investment be reported in financial statements of UFI?
3. Assuming UFI uses the cost method, prepare journal entries to record
   a. The purchase of the 51 000 shares as a long-term investment
   b. In 19X3, the receipt of UFI's share of dividends paid by UHL
   c. In 19X3, UFI's share of UHL's income.
4. Assuming that the market value of UFI's shares in UHL has increased by $50,000 over book value at December 31, 19X3, indicate how the CICA recommendations would require the increased market value to be disclosed in UFI's financial statements.

Part B

Assume use of the cost method.

Required:
5. Prepare journal entries to record
   a. In 19X4, the receipt of UFI's share of dividends paid by UHL
   b. In 19X4, UFI's share of UHL's loss.
6. Assuming that the market value of UFI's shares in UHL has decreased by $100,000 compared to book value (ignore the increase in market value in 19X3) at December 31, 19X4 and that this decline in market value is not expected to be permanent, indicate the CICA recommended way of handling this loss in the financial statements.

Part C

Assume use of the cost method.

Required:
7. Prepare journal entries to record
   a. In 19X5, the receipt of UFI's share of dividends paid by UHL
   b. In 19X5, UFI's share of UHL's income.
8. Assuming that the market value of UHL's shares had improved over that of 19X4 and that $25,000 of the 19X4 decline had been recovered at December 31, 19X5, indicate the CICA recommended method of handling this recovery in the financial statements.

Alternate Problems

Alternate Problem 13-1

P Corporation purchased 20 000 shares, representing a 20-percent interest in S Limited, for $500,000 on January 1, 19X4. The following financial data are applicable to S Limited.

	Dividends Paid	Net Income (Loss)
19X4	$200,000	$ 400,000
19X5	10,000	(300,000)

Part A

P Corporation does not have a significant influence over S Limited.

Required:
1. Prepare journal entries to record
   a. The purchase of the 20 000 shares as a long-term investment
   b. The receipt of P Corporation's share of dividends paid in 19X4 and 19X5.

Part B

P Corporation has a significant influence over S Limited.

Required:
2. Prepare journal entries to record
   a. The purchase of 20 000 shares as a long-term investment
   b. The receipt of P Corporation's share of dividends paid in 19X4 and 19X5
   c. P Corporation's share of S Limited's income.
3. Prepare a schedule to compare the amount reported on the balance sheet and on the income statement of P Corporation in 19X4 and 19X5, under both the cost method and the equity method.

Alternate Problem 13-2

Oread Corporation has 100 000 shares outstanding. The following data are applicable to 19X6 and 19X7.

	Dividends Paid	Net Income (Loss)
19X6	$100,000	$(300,000)
19X7	200,000	400,000

Part A

E. Tonne Inc. purchased 55 000 shares of Oread for $220,000 on January 1, 19X6.

Required:
1. Identify the relationship between these two corporations.
2. Indicate what method of accounting can be used in the records of E. Tonne Inc. for this long-term investment.
3. Assuming the cost method is used, prepare journal entries for 19X6 to record
   a. The purchase of the 55 000 shares
   b. The receipt of its share of 19X6 dividends paid by Oread
   c. E. Tonne's share of Oread's 19X6 income.

   4. Assuming the cost method is used, prepare journal entries for 19X7 to record
      a. The receipt of E. Tonne's share of 19X7 dividends paid by Oread
      b. E. Tonne's share of Oread's 19X7 income
      c. An unrealized recovery of $10,000 of the decline in market value of Oread shares held by E. Tonne; the market value of the shares had improved during the year.

Part B

Sim and Sons Ltd. purchased 35 000 shares, representing a 35-percent interest in Oread Corporation, for $160,000 on January 1, 19X7. Sim and Sons Ltd. is a fierce competitor of E. Tonne Inc. The purchase of these shares was viewed with concern by E. Tonne Inc.

Required:
   5. Identify the relationship between Oread Corporation and Sim and Sons Ltd.
   6. Indicate what method of accounting would be used in the records of Sim and Sons Ltd. for this long-term investment.
   7. Assuming Sim and Sons Ltd. uses the equity method, prepare journal entries to record
      a. The purchase of 35 000 shares
      b. The receipt of its share of 19X7 dividends paid by Oread
      c. Sim and Sons Ltd.'s share of Oread's income
      d. The sale of the 35 000 shares on January 1, 19X8 to E. Tonne Inc. at $6 per share, a price considerably above the stock market price of these shares. Why would E. Tonne Inc. pay more than market value for these shares?

Alternate Problem 13-3

P Corporation purchased 100 percent of S Limited's shares at December 31, 19X6, by paying $150,000 to shareholders of S. The following are financial statements and other financial information of P and S at December 31, 19X6.

	P	S	
	Book Value	Book Value	Market Value
Cash and Other Assets	$160,000	$ 30,000	$ 30,000
Patent	–	75,000	150,000
	$160,000	$105,000	
Liabilities	$ 50,000	$ 45,000	$ 45,000
Common Stock	10,000	15,000	
Retained Earnings	100,000	45,000	
	$160,000	$105,000	

Required:
   1. Prepare the entry to record in P's books the purchase of S's shares.
   2. Included in the purchase price was an amount in recognition of an undervaluation (or overvaluation) in the asset patent. Calculate the amount of this undervaluation (or overvaluation).
   3. Was any amount included in the purchase price in recognition of unrecorded goodwill in S? If so, calculate the amount of such goodwill.
   4. Prepare the worksheet elimination entry needed to consolidate the individual balance sheets. (The preparation of a consolidation worksheet is not required in this problem.)
   5. Prepare a consolidated balance sheet at December 31, 19X6, immediately after the purchase of S's shares.

Alternate Problem 13-4

On January 2, 19X2, P Corporation purchased a 60-percent interest in S Limited by paying $120,000 cash to the shareholders of S for their shares. The financial statements and other financial information of both corporations immediately before the purchase are as follows:

	P	S	
	Book Value	*Book Value*	*Market Value*
Cash and Other Assets	$205,000	$ 90,000	$90,000
Inventory	95,000	60,000	70,000
Fixed Assets	165,000	50,000	65,000
	$465,000	$200,000	
Liabilities	$ 55,000	$ 45,000	$45,000
Common Stock	260,000	95,000	
Retained Earnings	150,000	60,000	
	$465,000	$200,000	

Required:
1. Prepare the entry to record in P's books the purchase of S's shares.
2. Calculate the amount of the minority interest.
3. Was any amount included in the purchase price in recognition of unrecorded goodwill in S? If so, calculate the amount of such goodwill.
4. Calculate the consolidated balances for inventory and goodwill at January 2, 19X2 immediately after the purchase.
5. Prepare the worksheet elimination entry needed to consolidate the individual balance sheets. (The preparation of a consolidation worksheet is not required in this problem.)
6. Prepare a consolidated balance sheet at January 2, 19X2 immediately after the purchase of S's shares.

Alternate Problem 13-5

On January 2, 19X6, P Corporation purchased a 90-percent interest in S Limited by paying $120,000 cash to the shareholders of S for their shares. Included in this purchase price was an amount in recognition of the existence of goodwill in S. Here is selected financial information from the balance sheets of both corporations immediately before the purchase.

	P	S
Common Stock	$120,000	$75,000
Retained Earnings	70,000	25,000

Required: At January 2, 19X6,
1. Prepare the entry to record in P's books the purchase of S's shares.
2. Prepare the worksheet elimination entry needed to consolidate the individual balance sheets immediately after the purchase. (Assume that there are no other reciprocal amounts.)
3. Calculate the amount of equity (common stock and retained earnings) that would appear on the consolidated balance sheet.

Alternate Problem 13-6

On December 31, 19X2, P Corporation purchased a 70-percent interest in S Limited by paying $200,000 cash to the shareholders of S for their shares. The purchase price included an amount of an undervaluation of Fixed Assets and Bonds Payable and also an amount in recognition of goodwill in S. Here are the balance sheets of both corporations immediately after the purchase.

	P Book Value	S Book Value	S Market Value
Assets			
Current Assets	$ 65,000	$160,000	$160,000
Investment in Subsidiary	200,000	–	
Fixed Assets (net)	585,000	225,000	270,000
Goodwill	110,000	–	
	$960,000	$385,000	
Liabilities and Equities			
Current Liabilities	$ 50,000	$ 60,000	$ 60,000
Bonds Payable (5-year life)	200,000	100,000	115,000
Common Stock	250,000	75,000	
Retained Earnings	460,000	150,000	
	$960,000	$385,000	

Required: At the date of acquisition,
1. Calculate the undervaluation of Fixed Assets and Bonds Payable
2. Calculate the amount of goodwill included in the purchase price
3. Calculate the amount of minority interest
4. Prepare the worksheet elimination entry needed to consolidate the individual balance sheets
5. Prepare a consolidation worksheet at December 31, 19X2.

Alternate Problem 13-7

On December 31, 19X6, P Corporation purchased a 60-percent interest in S Limited by paying $150,000 cash to shareholders of S for their shares. Included in this purchase price was an excess of cost over book value. At that date, P owed $15,000 to S; the amount is included as an accounts payable in P's books and as an accounts receivable in S's books. Immediately after the purchase, the balance sheets of both corporations appeared as follows:

	P Book Value	S Book Value	S Market Value
Cash and Other Assets	$ 90,000	$105,000	$109,000
Accounts Receivable	160,000	95,000	95,000
Investment in Subsidiary	150,000	–	
	$400,000	$200,000	
Accounts Payable	$ 60,000	$ 25,000	$ 25,000
Common Stock	225,000	100,000	
Retained Earnings	115,000	75,000	
	$400,000	$200,000	

Required:
1. Calculate the excess of cost over book value of the investment in S.
2. Prepare the worksheet elimination entries needed to consolidate the individual balance sheets.
3. Prepare a consolidation worksheet.
4. Prepare a consolidated balance sheet at December 31, 19X6, immediately after the purchase of S's share.

Disclosure and Financial Reporting

Financial statements report information for analysis to shareholders and other interested parties at regular intervals. Although shareholders actually own the entity, they alone do not finance it; creditors finance some of its activities and, together with shareholders, form the entity's financial structure. This financial structure is carefully evaluated by readers of financial statements to ascertain whether shareholders' equity is inadequate or excessive.

In previous discussions of an entity's financing cycle, equity and debt were viewed as alternative forms of financing operations. Management must decide the proportion of equity to debt financing. Analysis of financial statements evaluates such decisions.

Financial reporting and disclosure of information is intended to help users of financial statements to make investment decisions. Accordingly, this information is expected to be timely and useful; statement users should be able to depend on the information and employ it in evaluating investment alternatives. The information must also be comparable to information of previous accounting time periods of the entity and to the statements of other entities in the same industry.

As discussed earlier, financial ratios constitute one way to evaluate an entity's short-term solvency. Ratio calculation is illustrated in Chapter 14. An evaluation of an entity's efficiency in earning net income can also be made through the calculation and study of relevant ratios.

The income statement and balance sheet are the focus of preceding chapters. The third financial statement, the statement of cash flow, is designed to show the increase or decrease in cash that has occurred during a particular accounting period. Chapter 15 illustrates its preparation using transactions analysis and T-accounts.

Financial Statements Analysis

Financial statements can be analyzed to evaluate a corporation's financial structure, solvency, and operations efficiency, as well as the impact of changing price levels on it. Ratios are used to answer such questions as the following:

1. What is the amount of shareholder claims against its assets compared to the amount of creditor claims?
2. Is the corporation underfinanced or overfinanced?
3. Under what circumstances is creditor financing more financially attractive than shareholder financing?

This chapter will help you answer such questions as

4. What are the relative advantages of short-term and long-term debt?
5. What is meant by *solvency*?
6. What are some ratios commonly used to evaluate solvency? What are some of their merits and weaknesses?
7. How long does it take a corporation to complete its revenue operating cycle?
8. How can the efficiency with which the corporation uses its assets to earn income be evaluated?
9. What is *trading on the equity*?
10. What is required for an accurate comparative analysis of corporations in different industries?
11. How can corporations that have a considerable amount of their assets tied up in fixed assets be evaluated?
12. What is a *horizontal analysis*? How does it differ from a *vertical analysis*?
13. What is the Consumer Price Index, and how does it measure a decrease in the dollar's purchasing power?
14. Why do some accountants propose that historical cost dollar amounts in financial statements be converted into constant dollars?
15. How does current cost accounting differ from constant dollar accounting?
16. What financial statement disclosure of changing prices is required by the AcSC?

A. Financial Structure: The Example of Bluebeard Computer Corporation

The accounting equation expresses a relationship between assets owned by an entity and the claims against those assets. Although shareholders own a corporation, they alone do not finance the corporation; creditors also finance some of its activities. Together, creditor and shareholder capital are said to form the *financial structure* of a corporation.

Bluebeard Computer Corporation's Financial Structure
ASSETS = LIABILITIES + SHAREHOLDERS' EQUITY
$2,486 = $1,255   + $1,231

Financial analysts and would-be investors look very carefully at the financial structure of a corporation, that is, at the amount of shareholder claims against the assets of a corporation compared to the creditor claims. BCC has a high reliance on debt in its financial structure; creditors have a substantial claim against the assets of Bluebeard.

The long-term financial strength of a corporation depends on its financial structure. In any given situation, a company is said to be *underfinanced* if there is inadequate shareholders' equity; it is considered to be *overfinanced* if shareholders' equity is excessive.

Equity to Debt

The proportion of shareholder-to-creditor claims is calculated by dividing shareholders' equity by total liabilities, BCC's situation is outlined below:

		(000s)		
		19X5	19X4	19X3
Shareholders' Equity	(a)	$1,231	$1,195	$1,148
Total Liabilities	(b)	1,255	917	269
Equity to Debt	(a ÷ b)	0.98	1.30	4.27

These calculations tell us that BCC has 98 cents of shareholders' equity for each dollar of liabilities in its current year, 19X5, and that the proportion of equity financing has been decreasing since 19X3, when there was $4.27 of equity for each $1 of liabilities. In 19X5, creditors are financing a greater proportion of BCC than are shareholders. This **equity-to-debt ratio** and the trend of the financing over the three years is a cause for concern.

Equity-to-debt ratio
A ratio indicating the shareholder and creditor claims to the assets of an entity.

On the one hand, management's reliance on creditor financing is good. Additional issues of shares would require existing shareholders to share their control of BCC with new shareholders, thereby making less available to existing shareholders. Creditor financing may also be more financially attractive to existing shareholders, if it enables BCC to earn more than the interest paid on the debt.

On the other hand, management's reliance on creditor financing is troublesome. If there is too much debt, creditors may not be willing to extend additional financing should it be necessary. This potential is one risk of excessive creditor financing. Another risk derives from the fact that interest has to be paid on this debt and repayment of the debt is required. The terms and timing of these payments are agreed to when the debt is incurred. Total earnings of BCC could be reduced if heavy interest payments have to be paid. Each of these risks could threaten the survival of the company.

The proportion of shareholder-to-creditor financing is decided by management. A reasonable balance has to be maintained. Although no specific figures can be stated as the most appropriate equity-to-debt ratio, there are techniques for discovering the optimum balance. They involve the weighing of leverage (the proportion of debt) against the risk involved; such material forms the subject matter of finance studies and cannot be covered in an accounting course. What can be attempted, however, is an evaluation of an existing financial structure.

Short-Term versus Long-Term Debt

Both short-term and long-term financing strategies have their advantages. The advantage of some short-term debt is that it does not require interest payments to creditors; for example, accounts payable do not usually require payment of interest if they are paid within credit terms. A further advantage of short-term debt is that income is not reduced by the debt. Short-term debt also has its disadvantages: payment is required in a short period of time and an increase in the proportion of short-term debt is more risky because it has to be renewed more frequently.

Long-term debt's advantages are that payment may be made over an extended period of time and that risk is reduced by this longer repayment period governed by a contractual agreement. The disadvantages of long-term debt are that interest payments are required to be made at specified times and that these interest payments reduce income. As a general rule, long-term financing should be used to finance long-term assets.

The Structure of Bluebeard's Creditor Financing

An analysis of the company's balance sheet reveals the following liabilities:

	(000s)		
	19X5	19X4	19X3
Current Liabilities	$1,255	$917	$269
Long-Term Liabilities	–	–	–

Issues in Ethics 14-1
Having Money Can Be Divine

Stanton Powers says his $2 bank account grew in just two weeks to more than $4 million through the grace of God, but the bank president doubts it.

Reese Davis, president of the County Bank of Santa Cruz, said that he wants an investigation into Powers's sudden wealth. And Powers's withdrawals have been stopped.

Powers said his windfall happened this way:

Friends told him to meditate on his financial problems. He did. After several days Powers walked up to the bank's automated teller. It said he had $21 in his account. A few minutes later he tried it again, and it said he had $281, and a third try gave him a balance of $600.

He went home to meditate some more, and, when he returned to the automated teller, he had $4 million in his account.

On Sept. 10, Powers said, he decided to ask Attorney Marchello DiMauro to help him withdraw the millions. DiMauro, with his client in tow, made several withdrawals from automated tellers throughout the county. And each time, he said, the balance increased. Finally one of the machines confiscated Powers's card and instructed him to see a bank manager.

Automated tellers do not allow customers to withdraw more than $500 in a 24-hour period.

DiMauro said he told bank investigators Sept. 14 the money belonged to his client because the growing balance was an act of God. Instead of meditating, DiMauro, said Powers was actually praying to God for the money — and God answered his prayers.

This is where the bank president rebelled, and Powers is unable to withdraw any more money. But Powers is holding on to the approximately $2,000 he withdrew, and DiMauro is threatening to sue the bank for the millions.

Source Reprinted with permission of United Press International. Copyright 1982.

This information indicates that BCC management relies solely on short-term creditor financing, part of which is $300,000-worth of accounts payable that bears no interest. The risk they have assumed is the need to replace existing liabilities, as they come due and are paid, with new liabilities. If creditors become unwilling to extend this short-term debt, the ability of Bluebeard to pay its other liabilities may be compromised. In fact, this is happening to BCC. Existing creditors have become less willing to extend new credit, and the bank is asking for the repayment of its loan. At this point, the company may have reached the end of its short-term financing rope.

Is Bluebeard Insolvent?

You may remember the implications of being insolvent listed in section E of Chapter 4:

Current Liabilities:
Creditors can refuse to provide any further goods or services on account.
Creditors can sue for payment.
Creditors can put the company into receivership or bankruptcy.

Long-Term Liabilities:
Creditors can refuse to lend additional cash.
Creditors can demand repayment of their long-term debts under some circumstances.

Shareholders' Equity:
Shareholders may be unwilling to invest in additional share capital of the company.
Shareholders risk the loss of their investments if the company is placed in bankruptcy.

At the present time, BCC is unable to pay its creditors. Although sales are rapidly increasing and an acceptable gross profit is being earned, the company is, technically, insolvent.

A company normally keeps a reasonable balance in its current assets among cash, receivables, and inventory. Unfortunately, there is no one indicator of what a "reasonable" balance really is. The balance is acceptable when debts are being paid. And, when current liabilities are not being paid, as is the case for Bluebeard Computer Corporation, a reasonable balance does not exist.

Study the following components of Bluebeard's 19X5 current assets:

	(000s)	
Current Assets in 19X5		*% Composition*
Cash	$ 19	1.33
Marketable Securities	37	2.58
Accounts Receivable — Trade	544	37.96
Inventory	833	58.13
Total Current Assets	$1,433	100.00

Given this financial balance, BCC appears to have an overinvestment both in receivables and in inventory — together they amount to approximately 96 percent of its current assets — although a final evaluation must relate investment to sales and cost of goods sold. Consider the current debts of the company in 19X5.

Current Liabilities in 19X5	(000s)
Bank Loan	$ 825
Accounts Payable — Trade	300
Accrued Liabilities	82
Income Tax Payable	48
Total Current Liabilities	$1,255

These are the short-term creditors of BCC. Short-term solvency analysis emphasizes factors that are important to these creditors.

The short-term creditors would be particularly concerned about these factors:

1. Trade accounts payable are due within the next 60 days. Will BCC be able to pay them?

2. Bluebeard has asked its bankers for additional loans. The bankers are unwilling to provide new loans and are asking for repayment of existing bank loans.

3. How will BCC cope with accrued liabilities and income taxes payable?

Obviously, Bluebeard is in trouble!

BCC has $19,000 cash on hand and $37,000 in marketable securities (which can be converted immediately into cash) to pay current liabilities. One alternative at this time appears to be to collect receivables as quickly as it can and sell inventory at whatever price it can get. This desperate action would undoubtedly result in losses that would jeopardize the company's existence. Another alternative might be to renegotiate its short-term bank loan into a long-term bank loan.

B. Short-Term Solvency Analysis

In Chapter 4, you saw that ratios are one way of evaluating any company's solvency. We will use information from the following comparative Bluebeard financial statements for 19X5, 19X4, and 19X3 for a detailed analysis of Bluebeard's financial position.

Bluebeard Computer Corporation
Balance Sheets
At December 31

(000s)

Assets

	19X5	19X4	19X3
CURRENT ASSETS:			
Cash	$ 19	$ 24	$ 50
Marketable Securities	37	37	37
Accounts Receivable — Trade	544	420	257
Inventory	833	503	361
Total Current Assets	$1,433	$ 984	$ 705
FIXED ASSETS:			
Land	$ 200	$ 200	$ 100
Buildings	350	350	200
Equipment	950	950	700
	$1,500	$1,500	$1,000
Less: Accumulated Depreciation —			
Buildings and Equipment	(447)	(372)	(288)
Net Fixed Assets	$1,053	$1,128	$ 712
Total Assets	$2,486	$2,112	$1,417

Liabilities and Shareholders' Equity

	19X5	19X4	19X3
CURRENT LIABILITIES:			
Bank Loan	$ 825	$ 570	–
Accounts Payable — Trade	300	215	$ 144
Other Liabilities	82	80	75
Income Tax Payable	48	52	50
Total Current Liabilities	$1,255	$ 917	$ 269
SHAREHOLDERS' EQUITY:			
Common Stock	$1,000	$1,000	$1,000
Retained Earnings	231	195	148
Total Shareholders' Equity	$1,231	$1,195	$1,148
Total Liabilities and Shareholders' Equity	$2,486	$2,112	$1,417

Bluebeard Computer Corporation
Combined Statements of Income and Retained Earnings
For the Years Ended December 31

| | (000s) | | |
	19X5	19X4	19X3
Sales	$3,200	$2,800	$2,340
Cost of Goods Sold	2,500	2,150	1,800
Gross Profit	$ 700	$ 650	$ 540
Expenses	584	533	428
Net Income	$ 116	$ 117	$ 112
Opening Retained Earnings	195	148	96
	$ 311	$ 265	$ 208
Less: Dividends	80	70	60
Closing Retained Earnings	$ 231	$ 195	$ 148

Other related information included in total expenses:

Interest Expense	$ 89	$ 61	–
Income Tax Expense	95	102	$ 97

Short-Term Solvency Analysis:	*Indicates:*
1. The Current Ratio	How many current asset dollars exist to pay current liabilities. (This ratio is only a crude measure of solvency.)
2. The Acid-Test Ratio	Whether the company is able to meet the immediate demands of creditors. (This ratio is a more severe measure of solvency. Inventory and pre-paid items are excluded from the calculation.)
3. Management Decisions Relating to Receivables:	
a. Accounts Receivable Collection Period	The average time needed to collect receivables.
b. Accounts Receivable Turnover	How often during the year accounts receivable have been converted into cash.
4. Management Decisions Relating to Inventory:	
a. Number of Days of Sales in Inventory	How many days of sales can be made with existing inventory.
b. Inventory Turnover	How many times during the year inventory has been sold and replaced.
5. The Revenue Operating Cycle	How long it is between the purchase of inventory and the subsequent collection of cash.

The following financial information of BCC is used in the analysis of its short-term solvency.

		(000s)	
CURRENT ASSETS:	19X5	19X4	19X3
Cash	$ 19	$ 24	$ 50
Marketable Securities	37	37	37
Accounts Receivable — Trade	544	420	257
Inventory	833	503	361
Total Current Assets	$1,433	$984	$705
CURRENT LIABILITIES:			
Bank Loan	$ 825	$570	–
Accounts Payable — Trade	300	215	$144
Other Liabilities	82	80	75
Income Tax Payable	48	52	50
Total Current Liabilities	$1,255	$917	$269
Net Working Capital	$ 178	$ 67	$436

Working Capital

Working capital
The excess of current assets over current liabilities; also referred to as net working capital.

The calculation of working capital is a starting point in short-term solvency analysis. For accountants, **working capital** refers to the mathematical difference between current assets and current liabilities at a particular point in time. The calculation is most useful to the reader when it is compared with the working capital of previous years. For example, an increase in working capital informs the reader about the entity's increased ability to pay its debts.

In the above schedule, working capital is calculated at $178,000 in 19X5 and represents the amount of current assets in excess of current liabilities. This working capital indicates short-term solvency in a dollar amount; notice the dollar difference in working capital between 19X5 and 19X3.

The current ratio discussed under the next heading calculates this same short-term solvency in terms of a ratio; a ratio is usually easier to interpret than the calculation of an absolute dollar amount.

The Current Ratio

Is the firm able to repay short-term creditors? The current ratio answers this question by expressing the working capital as a ratio of current assets to current liabilities — current assets are divided by current liabilities. The relevant BCC financial data required to calculate this ratio follows:

		(000s)		
		19X5	19X4	19X3
Current Assets	(a)	$1,433	$984	$705
Current Liabilities	(b)	1,255	917	269
Current Ratio	(a ÷ b)	1.14	1.07	2.62

The results of this calculation are an indication of how many current asset dollars exist to pay current liabilities. In 19X5, $1.14 of current assets exists to pay each $1 of current liabilities. Is $1.14 adequate? Unfortunately, no one current ratio can be identified as adequate in all situations. Figure 14-1 illustrates the possibilities.

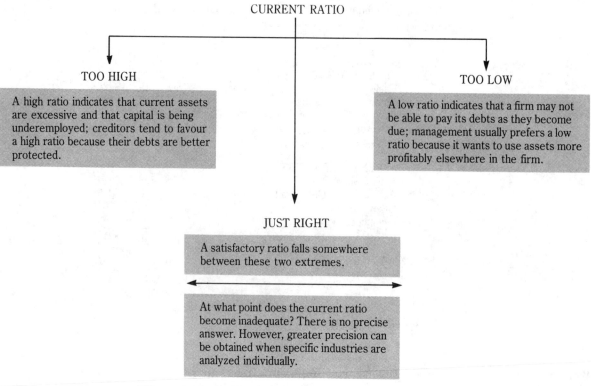

Figure 14-1   Current ratios

Bluebeard is suffering from cash shortages and is unable to pay its debts as they become due. Therefore, its current ratio of 1.14 is clearly inadequate and should be regarded unfavourably; the 19X4 ratio of 1.07 is also inadequate. Without other information, one cannot conclude whether 2.62, the 19X3 ratio, is just right or too high. Some analysts, as noted in an earlier chapter, consider that a corporation should maintain a 2 : 1 current ratio, depending on the industry in which the firm operates. For example, if there were $2 of current assets to pay each $1 of current liabilities, these current assets could shrink considerably in worth and the firm likely would still be able to pay its debts. However, it is recognized that no one current ratio is applicable to all entities; other factors — such as the composition of current assets and the credit terms extended by suppliers — must also be considered to arrive at an acceptable ratio.

Dun and Bradstreet, as well as trade publications, provide a range of current ratios that may be applicable to companies in a particular industry at a given time. Note that the adequacy of a current ratio depends on other developments within a company and that, while a given ratio may be satisfactory one year, it may not be the next year.

Composition of Specific Items in Current Assets

In the following example, each company has a 2 : 1 current ratio. Are the companies equally able to repay their short-term creditors?

	A Corp.	B Corp.
CURRENT ASSETS:		
Cash	$ 1,000	$10,000
Accounts Receivable	2,000	20,000
Inventory	37,000	10,000
Total Current Assets	$40,000	$40,000
Current Liabilities:	$20,000	$20,000
Current Ratio	2 : 1	2 : 1

The companies have equal dollar amounts of current assets and current liabilities, but they have different debt paying abilities. A Corp. could first sell some inventory and collect the resulting receivables; or, it can immediately sell its inventory as a single lot for cash, probably for less than it cost. (This type of shrinkage is provided for in the 2 : 1 current ratio discussed previously.) Clearly, B Corp. is in a better position to repay short-term creditors.

Since the current ratio doesn't consider the components of current assets, it is only a rough indicator of how able a firm is to pay its debts as they become due. This weakness is partly remedied by another ratio, called the *acid-test ratio*.

The Acid-Test Ratio

A more severe test of solvency is provided by the so-called acid-test ratio; often called the *quick ratio*, it provides an indication of instant solvency — the ability to meet the immediate demands of creditors. To calculate this ratio, current assets have to be broken down into quick current assets and non-quick current assets.

Quick Current Assets	*Non-Quick Current Assets*
Cash	Inventory
Marketable Securities	Prepaid Items
Accounts Receivable — Trade	
These current assets are considered to be readily convertible into cash.	Cash could not be obtained immediately from these current assets.

Inventory and prepaid items cannot usually be converted into cash in a short period of time. They are, therefore, excluded from quick assets in the calculation of this ratio. Their exclusion facilitates comparison of different entities since the acid-test ratio is not influenced by the use of a particular inventory method. The acid-test ratio is derived by dividing the total of quick current assets by current liabilities. The relevant BCC financial data required to calculate this ratio follows:

		(000s)		
		19X5	19X4	19X3
Quick Current Assets	(a)	$ 600	$ 481	$ 344
Current Liabilities	(b)	1,255	917	269
Acid-Test Ratio	(a ÷ b)	0.478	0.525	1.28

This ratio indicates how many quick asset dollars (cash, marketable securities, and trade accounts receivable) exist to pay each dollar of current liabilities. As can be seen, only 47.8 cents of quick assets are available to pay each $1 of current liabilities in 19X5.

This amount is clearly inadequate; 52.5 cents in 19X4 is also inadequate. The 19X3 ratio may be a reasonable guide for the adequacy of quick current assets. Of particular concern to financial analysts would be the trend of the acid-test ratio over the three years.

What is an adequate acid-test ratio? It is generally considered that a 1 : 1 acid test ratio is adequate to ensure that a firm will be able to pay its current obligations. However, this is a fairly arbitrary guideline and is not reliable in all situations. A lower ratio than 1 : 1 can often be found in successful companies.

When taken together, the current and acid-test ratios give the financial statement reader a better understanding of a company's financial health. While the current ratio may be favourable, the acid-test ratio may alert the reader to a preponderance of non-quick assets in the company.

Management Decisions Relating to Receivables

Short-term solvency is affected by management decisions related to trade accounts receivable. Lax collection of receivables can result in a shortage of cash to pay current obligations. The effectiveness of management decisions relating to receivables is analyzed by calculating the accounts receivable collection period and the accounts receivable turnover.

Accounts Receivable Collection Period

Accounts receivable collection period ratio
Average accounts receivable is divided by net credit sales and the result is multiplied by 365 days. This ratio indicates the average time needed to collect receivables.

The acid-test ratio is a more severe test of solvency than the current ratio, since it calculates how many quick current asset dollars exist to pay current liabilities. But the acid-test ratio can also be misleading, if accounts receivable are high because of slow receivables collection. The calculation of the **accounts receivable collection period ratio** establishes the average time needed to collect an amount. This figure indicates the efficiency of collection procedures when the collection period is compared with the firm's sales terms (in BCC's case, net 30). To calculate this ratio, average annual accounts receivable are divided by the net credit sales and the result is multiplied by 365 days. The BCC financial data required to make the calculation appear next.

		(000s)	
		19X5	19X4
Net Credit Sales	(a)	$3,200	$2,800
Average Accounts Receivable [(Opening Balance + Closing Balance) ÷ 2]	(b)	482	338
Total Days in the Year	(c)	365	365
Average Collection Period [b ÷ a) × (c)]		55 days	44 days

When Bluebeard's 30-day sales terms are compared to the 55-day collection period, it is obvious that an average 25 days sales (55 days − 30 days) have gone uncollected beyond the regular credit period in 19X5. Moreover, the trend is toward an increase in this collection period over that of the previous year. Therefore, some overextension of credit and possibly ineffective collection procedures are indicated by this ratio. Quicker collection would improve BCC's cash position.

Whether the increase in collection period is good or bad depends on other factors, such as increasing sales or increasing profits. Therefore, the average collection period is subject to further interpretation before a conclusion can be made. The ratio does provide, however, an indication of the effectiveness of credit and collection procedures in 19X5.

Accounts Receivable Turnover

Accounts receivable turnover ratio
Net credit sales is divided by average accounts receivable. This ratio indicates how often during the year accounts receivable have been converted into cash.

A further insight into the quality of trade accounts receivable is provided through the calculation of the **accounts receivable turnover ratio**. This ratio indicates how often accounts receivable have been converted into cash during the year. The higher the turnover, the less investment exists in accounts receivable.

Higher Turnover Indicates:	*Lower Turnover Indicates:*
1. Accounts receivable are more liquid.	1. Accounts receivable are less liquid.
2. Accounts receivable have decreased in relation to sales.	2. Accounts receivable have increased in relation to sales.
3. Investment in accounts receivable has decreased in relation to sales.	3. Investment in accounts receivable has increased in relation to sales.

The accounts receivable turnover ratio is calculated by dividing net credit sales during the year by average accounts receivable. The relevant BCC financial data required to calculate this ratio follow.

		(000s)	
		19X5	19X4
Net Credit Sales	(a)	$3,200	$2,800
Average Accounts Receivable [(Opening Balance + Closing Balance) ÷ 2]	(b)	482	338
Accounts Receivable Turnover	(a ÷ b)	6.64 times	8.28 times

As can be seen, the accounts receivable turnover has decreased during 19X5; that is, accounts receivable were converted into cash fewer times during the year than in the previous year. This simply means that trade receivables are less liquid in 19X5. The danger exists that they were less collectible in 19X5, because older receivables may be buried in the total amount of receivables.

Management Decisions Relating to Inventory

The acid-test ratio showed how short-term solvency is affected by management decisions involving inventory, since an overinvestment in inventory can reduce the amount of cash available to pay current liabilities. The effectiveness of management decisions relating to inventory can be analyzed by the number of days of sales in inventory and the inventory turnover.

Number of Days of Sales in Inventory

If current assets are tied up in inventory, then accounts payable cannot be paid within the discount period — a situation that would not be beneficial for the company. One method of analyzing whether there is an overinvestment in inventory is to calculate

Number of days of sales in inventory ratio
The average inventory is divided by cost of goods sold and the result is multiplied by 365 days. This ratio indicates how many days of sales can be made with existing inventory.

how many days of sales can be made with the existing inventory. The **number of days of sales in inventory ratio** is calculated by dividing average inventory by the cost of goods sold and multiplying the result by 365 days. The relevant BCC financial data required to calculate this ratio are reproduced below:

		(000s)	
		19X5	19X4
Cost of Goods Sold	(a)	$2,500	$2,150
Average Inventory [(Opening Balance + Closing Balance) ÷ 2]	(b)	668	432
Days in the Year	(c)	365	365
Number of Days of Sales in Inventory	[(b ÷ a) × (c)]	97.5 days	73.3 days

There are more days of sales in 19X5 inventory, which means that Bluebeard is increasing its investment in inventory. In 19X5, 97.5 days of sales in inventory indicates that BCC can handle approximately 3 months of sales with its existing inventory.

Inventory Turnover

Inventory turnover ratio
Cost of goods sold is divided by average inventory. This ratio indicates how many times during the year inventory has been sold and replaced.

An **inventory turnover ratio** can also be calculated for Bluebeard to measure how many times inventory has been sold and replaced during the year. This analysis is important because a gross profit is earned each time inventory is turned over. The ratio is calculated by dividing cost of goods sold by average inventory. The relevant BCC financial data required to calculate this ratio are reproduced below:

		(000s)	
		19X5	19X4
Cost of Goods Sold	(a)	$2,500	$2,150
Average Inventory [(Opening Balance + Closing Balance) ÷ 2]	(b)	668	432
Inventory Turnover	(a ÷ b)	3.74 times	4.98 times

Inventory has turned over fewer times in 19X5 than in 19X4. In other words, inventory was sold and replaced less often in 19X5. Usually a high turnover is considered favourable, and a low turnover is considered troublesome. However, the situation is more complex.

A high turnover is usually a sign of good inventory management, because the amount of assets tied up in inventory is lower and an optimum amount of inventory is being purchased. A high turnover is also important for controlling inventory losses owing to obsolescence or deterioration. A high turnover tends to indicate that these problems will be avoided. With a high turnover, inventory-related expenses such as insurance and taxes are lower because less storage space is being used for inventory. It should be noted, however, that high turnover can have negative consequences if turnover becomes so rapid that, at any one point in time, items are out of stock that customers want to purchase.

A low turnover is usually a sign of poor inventory management, because an excessive investment in inventory ties up assets that could be used for other purposes, and an excessive amount of inventory is being purchased. Furthermore, a low turnover tends to indicate that problems will be encountered in obsolescence (consider styling in women's shoes) or deterioration (consider groceries). Such inventories may become unsaleable. However, the positive aspect of low turnover is that there can be shorter delivery time to customers, and customers can always count on items being in stock. Customers remain satisfied and loyal.

Whether Bluebeard's reduced turnover is positive or negative depends on management's objectives. Is management increasing inventory to provide for increased sales in 19X6, or is inventory being poorly managed?

Inadequate information precludes a precise answer. Consider, however, the following factors:

Analyst's Questions:	*Facts:*
1. Is inventory turnover decreasing because of inadequate sales volume?	Sales volume is rapidly increasing.
2. Is an excessive inventory being purchased?	Sales are expected to increase in 19X6. Therefore, the 19X5 inventory should be considered in relation to anticipated 19X6 sales.
3. Are slow-moving items responsible for the decreasing turnover?	Bluebeard sells computer hardware and software, which are much in demand.

Based on this analysis, it would appear that the increased days of sales inventory and the decreased inventory turnover can be explained in relation to Bluebeard's anticipated 19X6 sales. The problem appears to be not so much an overinvestment in inventory in relation to sales, but an overinvestment in inventory in relation to the financial strength of the corporation. In the final analysis, a reasonable balance between inventory, sales, and the company's financial strength has to be maintained. Management must decide how to strike this balance. The calculation of inventory ratios can only give an insight into the quality of these management decisions.

What Is an Adequate Inventory Turnover?

Since no management aims to tie up assets in inventory, it is important for managers to uncover the underlying circumstances when turnover is low. Is the company "stuck" with its inventory (as automobile manufacturers were at one time with their big cars)? Or has the company stockpiled inventory (such as oil) because of anticipated shortages or price increases?

Turnovers vary from industry to industry and a firm's performance should be compared with industry averages. However, a problem with industry averages occurs when information in published financial statements is incomplete — for example, cost of goods sold is not often shown separately. Accordingly, sales, rather than cost of goods sold, is often used in actual practice to make calculations and comparisons. The resulting ratio, however, does not give the actual inventory; it gives the sales dollars from average inventory. Such a figure may not be entirely useful for judging performance.

The Revenue Operating Cycle

Every business repeats a **revenue operating cycle** over and over again. Inventory is purchased, an accounts receivable occurs when a sale is made, and cash is generated when the receivable is collected. This cycle is illustrated in Figure 14-2, page 634.

Real Life Example 14-1
Calculating the Z Score

Someone once said that if you have one clock, you always know what time it is, but if you have several clocks, you are never quite sure. I often get that feeling when I calculate financial ratios. This is because the dozens of financial ratios I use seem to provide different answers to the same simple question. "How'd we do?"

So I've been on the lookout recently for financial models that summarize one general aspect of overall company performance. One example is the Z score, which, though developed to measure the likelihood of bankruptcy, can be used as a handy measure of overall financial performance.

The original Z score was created by Edward I. Altman in the mid-1960s. It is the most widely used of the many bankruptcy classifications that exist, and it has stood the test of time.

Figure 1				
The Z Score Bankruptcy Classification Model				
Ratio Names	Description	Coefficient	Mean Ratio Values Altman's Sample Cos.	
			Bankrupt	Nonbankrupt
$X1 =$	$\frac{\text{Working Capital}}{\text{Total Assets}}$	6.56	(0.061)	0.414
$X2 =$	$\frac{\text{Retained Earnings}}{\text{Total Assets}}$	3.26	(0.626)	0.355
$X3 =$	$\frac{\text{EBIT}}{\text{Total Assets}}$	6.72	(0.318)	0.154
$X4 =$	$\frac{\text{Net Worth}}{\text{Total Liabilities}}$	1.05	0.494	2.684

Cutoff Values		Mean Scores	
Safe if greater than	2.60	Nonbankrupt	7.70
Bankrupt if less than	1.10	Bankrupt	(4.06)

Source   *Corporate Financial Distress* by Edward I. Altman, John Wiley & Sons, 1983

To get the Z score, you simply take the figures for the four ratios, which Altman calls X1, X2, etc., from your financial statements. Multiply their values by coefficients Altman has derived, and add up the results. The formula, explained in detail below, looks like this:

$$6.56(X1) + 3.26(X2) + 6.72(X3) + 1.05(X4).$$

If a company's total score is greater than 2.60, things are looking good. If it is less than 1.10, bankruptcy may well be in sight. Figure 2 shows the financial statements and Z-score calculations for a hypothetical company, The BC Corp., which, at 5.206, has scored well above the danger point.

The interesting thing about the Z score is that it is a good analytic tool no matter what shape your company is in. To find your company's Z score, first calculate the four ratios.

$$X1 = \frac{\text{Working Capital}}{\text{Total Assets}}$$

This measure of liquidity compares net liquid assets to total assets. The net liquid assets, or working capital, are defined as current total assets minus current total liabilities. Generally, when a company experiences financial difficulties, working capital will fall more quickly than total assets, causing this ratio to fall.

$$X2 = \frac{\text{Retained Earnings}}{\text{Total Assets}}$$

This ratio is a measure of the cumulative profitability of your company. To some degree, the ratio also reflects the age of your company, because the younger it is, the less time it has had to build up cumulative profits. This bias in favor of older firms is not surprising, given the high failure rate of young companies.

When a company begins to lose money, of course, the value of total retained earnings begins to fall. For many companies, this value — and the X2 ratio — will become negative.

$$X3 = \frac{\text{EBIT}}{\text{Total Assets}}$$

This is a measure of profitability, or return on assets, calculated by dividing your firm's EBIT (earnings before interest and taxes) for one year by its total assets balance at the end of the year.

Figure 2	
BC Corp. **Balance Sheet,** **December 1986** (All values in $1,000)	**BC Corp.** **Income Statement** **1986** (All values in $1,000)

Assets			Sales	845
Current Assets			Cost of Goods Sold	
Cash	13		Materials	250
Receivables	109		Direct Labor	245
Inventory	272		Utilities	32
Prepaid Expenses	9		Indirect Labor	28
Total Current Assets	403		Depreciation	31
Net Fixed Assets	169		Total Cost of Goods Sold	586
Total Assets	572		Gross Profit	259
			Operating Expense	
Liabilities			Selling Expense	99
Current Liabilities			General and Administrative Expenses	110
Accounts Payable	82		Total Operating Expense	209
Notes Payable	50		Earnings before Interest and Taxes	50
Other Current Liabilities	35		Interest Expense	14
Total Current Liabilities	167		Earnings before Taxes	36
Long-Term Debt	130		Taxes	8
Total Liabilities	297		Net Income	28

Shareholders' Equity		**Stock Data, December 31, 1986**	
Common Stock	110	Stock Price (in dollars)	3
Retained Earnings	165	Shares Outstanding	100
Net Worth	275	Market Value of Equity	300
Total Liabilities and Equity	572		

Z Score Calculations

Ratio	Description	Formula	Result	Coefficient	Z Score
X1	$\frac{\text{Working Capital}}{\text{Total Assets}}$	$\frac{403-167}{572}$ =	0.413	6.560 =	2.707
X2	$\frac{\text{Retained Earnings}}{\text{Total Assets}}$	$\frac{165}{572}$ =	0.288	3.260 =	0.940
X3	$\frac{\text{EBIT}}{\text{Total Assets}}$	$\frac{50}{572}$ =	0.087	6.720 =	0.587
X4	$\frac{\text{Net Worth}}{\text{Total Liabilities}}$	$\frac{275}{297}$ =	0.926	1.050 =	0.972
Z Score:					5.206

You can also use it as a measure of how productively you are using borrowed funds. If the ratio exceeds the average interest rate you're paying on loans, you are making more money on your loans than you are paying in interest.

To calculate this ratio in the middle of a fiscal year, use your month-end balance sheet and the EBIT from an income statement showing the most recent 12 months of activity.

$$X4 = \frac{\text{Net Worth}}{\text{Total Liabilities}}$$

This ratio is the inverse of the more familiar debt-to-equity ratio. It is found by dividing your firm's net worth (also known as stockholders' equity) by its total liabilities.

After you've calculated these four ratios, simply multiply the X1 ratio by its coefficient, shown in Figure 1, the X2 by its coefficient, and so on; add the results; and then compare the total with Altman's cutoff values, also shown in Figure 1.

The purpose of calculating your own Z score is to warn you of financial problems that may need serious attention and to provide a guide for action. If your Z score is lower than you would like, you should examine your financial statements to determine the reason why.

Start by calculating the scores from previous periods, comparing them with your current score. (Graph them if possible.) If the trend is down, try to understand what has changed to create ratios that are dragging your scores down. Monitoring the trend in your Z scores can also help you evaluate your turnaround efforts.

Another way to analyze your score is to compare your results with those of other companies. You could refer to Robert Morris Associates (RMA) *Annual Statement Studies*, which provides detailed financial ratios by Standard Industrial Classification code. (Ratio X2 cannot be calculated from RMA data, however, because retained earnings aren't included.) Compare your own calculations with industry ratios, and find the ones that are out of line.

When you use bankruptcy classification models, including the Z score, keep this reservation in mind: they are by no means infallible. They can complement the other reports and analyses that you use within your company. Seldom, however, should you use any of the models as your only means of financial analysis.

Source Reprinted with permission, *Inc. magazine* (February, 1987). Copyright © 1987 by Goldhirsh Group, Inc.

**Revenue
operating cycle**
The recurrent process
from the acquisition of
inventory to the sale of
inventory and the receipt
of cash. To calculate the
length of the cycle,
average number of days
to turn over inventory is
added to the average
number of days to collect
receivables.

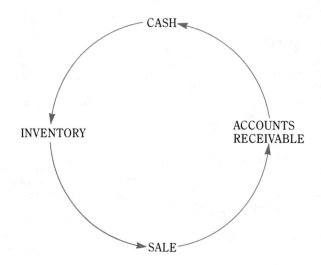

Figure 14-2   The revenue operating cycle

How much time elapses at Bluebeard between the purchase of inventory and the subsequent collection of cash? That is, how long does it take BCC to complete one revenue operating cycle? The amount of time required to complete a single cycle can be calculated using the number of days it takes to turn over inventory and the number of days it takes to collect receivables that result from sales. The relevant BCC financial data required for this calculation follows.

	19X5	19X4
Average Number of Days To Turn Over Inventory	97 days	73 days
Average Number of Days To Collect Receivables	55 days	44 days
Number of Days to Complete Cycle	152 days	117 days

In 19X5, 152 days were required to complete this cycle, compared to 117 days in 19X4. If accounts payable are due within 60 days, it is obvious that BCC will not be able to pay these liabilities with cash from the revenue operating cycle. Moreover, the situation in 19X5 is worse than it was in 19X4.

What Is Causing Bluebeard's Financial Problems?

The company is faced with financing its sales to customers and maintaining an adequate inventory in relation to sales, without having the financial strength to do so. Although inventory turnover could be improved, it is doubtful that accounts receivable could be collected much more rapidly. BCC is experiencing rapid growth and is not able to cope with its solvency requirements.

The company has relied too much on short-term financing for its expansion and its increased receivable and inventory requirements. BCC is no longer able to rely on this short-term financing and must reconsider its short-term and long-term financing objectives and requirements.

The preceding analysis used the financial data of Bluebeard Computer Corporation to introduce the calculation of solvency ratios and to discuss the merits and weaknesses of these ratios. The ratios that can be used to analyze the operations efficiency of a company are discussed next.

Real Life Example 14-1 introduces another way to measure an entity's performance — the Z score.

C.   Analysis of Operations Efficiency

As you saw in Chapter 4, ratios can reveal the current financial status of a company, show the trend in its performance over a number of years, and compare its performance with others in the same industry. However, the calculation of ratios does not indicate the state of such factors as labour relations, product quality, and the impact of the company's operations in its business environment.

The net income earned is the starting point for this analysis. The efficient use of assets can be judged by calculating net income as a return on assets, a return on shareholders' equity, earnings per share, and a return on sales. The reasonableness of a company's investment in fixed assets is also important. The following is a summary of the ratios used to analyze operating efficiency.

Analysis of Operating Efficiency:	*Indicates:*
1. Return on Total Assets	How efficiently a company uses its assets as resources to earn net income.
2. Return on Shareholders' Equity	The adequacy of net income as a return on shareholders' equity.
a. Trading on the Equity	The use of borrowed money to generate a higher return in the business than the rate being paid on the borrowed money.
b. Bondholder Protection: Times Interest Earned Ratio	The ability of a company to pay interest to long-term creditors.
3. Management Decisions Relating to Fixed Assets	
a. Sales to Fixed Assets Ratio	The adequacy of sales in relation to the investment in fixed assets.
b. Fixed Asset to Shareholders' Equity Ratio	The amount of shareholders' equity tied up in fixed assets.
4. Return on Sales	The percentage of sales revenue left in the business after payment of expenses, creditor interest, and government income taxes.
5. Earnings per Share	The amount of net income that has been earned on each share of common stock.
6. Market Ratios	
a. Price-Earnings Ratio	The reasonableness of market price in relation to per-share earnings.
b. Dividend Yield	The return that can be expected from an investment in a company's shares.

Return on Total Assets Ratio

The return on total assets ratio is designed to measure the efficiency with which assets are used. The ratio is calculated by the following formula:

$$\frac{\text{Income from Operations}}{\text{Average Total Assets}}$$

Income from operations is the amount earned by the company from the use of company assets. Expenses not applicable to operations of the company are excluded, such as expenses to finance the company (interest) and expenses on income due to government (income taxes). Average total assets are used in the calculation because the amount of assets used varies during the year.

Return on Shareholders' Equity Ratio

This return on shareholders' equity ratio is calculated by using the following formula:

$$\frac{\text{Net Income for the Year}}{\text{Average Shareholders' Equity}}$$

Net income after interest and income taxes is used in this calculation because only the balance remains to shareholders. Average equity is used because the amount of equity can vary during the year.

Trading on the Equity

Trading on the equity
A calculation made to indicate the ability of borrowed money to generate a higher return in the business than the rate being paid on the borrowed money.

Trading on the equity is not, strictly speaking, a ratio, but it is closely related to the return on shareholders' equity, which in turn is influenced by the use of long-term credit or financing. This use of borrowed funds can generate a higher return than the rate used to borrow the funds. Consider the following example, involving Companies H and D:

	Company H	Company D
Total Assets	$400,000	$400,000
Long-Term Liabilities (12%)	–	200,000
Equity	400,000	200,000

Although both H and D have the same amount of assets, Company H has no long-term liabilities, while Company D has $200,000-worth of 12-percent long-term liabilities. If both companies have $100,000 net income from operations, do they have a similar return on shareholders' equity?

	Company H	Company D
Income from Operations	$100,000	$100,000
Interest Expense ($200,000 × 12%)	–	24,000
	$100,000	$ 76,000
Income Tax (50% assumed)	50,000	38,000
Net Income for the Year	$ 50,000	$ 38,000

Notice that the use of long-term creditor financing resulted in a lower income figure for Company D, because of the interest expense. Now consider the implications of this lower income as a return on shareholders' equity:

		Company H	Company D
Income from Operations	(a)	$100,000	$100,000
Net Income for the Year	(b)	50,000	38,000
Total Assets	(c)	400,000	400,000
Shareholders' Equity	(d)	400,000	200,000
Return on Total Assets	(a ÷ c)	25%	25%
Return on Shareholders' Equity	(b ÷ d)	12.5%	19%

The return on total assets is 25 percent for both companies; however the return on shareholders' equity is considerably greater (19%) for Company D. This means that Company D borrowed funds at 12 percent to earn 25 percent in its business and this resulted in a 6.5 percent gain to shareholders. That is, trading on the equity magnified the return on shareholders' equity by 6.5 percent.

There is, however, risk involved in trading on the equity. While it magnifies the return on equity when the return on borrowed funds exceeds the cost of borrowing those funds, the opposite occurs when the cost of the borrowed funds exceeds the return on those borrowed funds. In general, companies with stable earnings can carry more debt in their financial structures than companies with fluctuating earnings.

Bondholder Protection: Times Interest Earned Ratio

Times interest earned ratio
Income from operations is divided by interest expense. This ratio indicates the ability of an entity to pay interest to long-term creditors.

Bondholders and other long-term creditors are aware that their funds are used for leverage and that there is a risk that the cost of borrowed funds may exceed the return made by the borrowing company on those borrowed funds. Therefore, they are interested in the **times interest earned ratio**, which is designed to measure the ability of a company to pay interest. It indicates the amount by which income from operations could decline before a default on interest would result. The ratio is calculated by the following formula:

$$\frac{\text{Income from Operations}}{\text{Interest Expense}}$$

Income tax is excluded in the calculation of this ratio because taxes are paid after interest. Income from operations is presumed to be income *before* the deduction of interest on debts. For 19X5, then, Bluebeard's income from operations is $300,000, composed of net income of $116,000, interest expense of $89,000, and income tax expense of $95,000.

Management Decisions Relating to Fixed Assets

Corporations usually have a considerable amount of their assets tied up in fixed assets that are used to produce products to be sold. The financial strength and success of these corporations depends on the reasonableness of their investments in these assets.

An analysis of these investment decisions can be made by calculating the ratio of sales to fixed assets and the ratio of fixed assets to shareholders' equity.

Sales to Fixed Assets Ratio

Ratio of sales to fixed assets
Net sales is divided by average fixed assets. This ratio indicates the adequacy of sales in relation to the investment in fixed assets.

Are sales adequate in relation to the investment in fixed assets? The calculation of the **ratio of sales to fixed assets** provides one answer to this question by establishing the number of sales dollars earned for each dollar invested in fixed assets. The ratio is calculated by the following formula:

$$\frac{\text{Net Sales}}{\text{Average Net Fixed Assets}}$$

From the comparative balance sheet of Bluebeard Computer Corporation, the average net fixed assets for 19X4 would be calculated as $712,000 + $1,128,000 \div 2 = $920,000$. The sales to fixed assets ratio would be the 19X4 sales, $2,800,000, divided by $920,000, or 3.04.

A low ratio in relation to other companies in the same industry may indicate their overinvestment in these assets or inefficiency in their use. The financial position of the company can be jeopardized by such errors in judgement; they are difficult to correct in the short run. It is important to recognize that results obtained by this ratio may be affected by one or both of the following factors:

1. Fixed assets are recorded at historic cost, while sales are made at current (inflation-increased) prices.
2. The age of the fixed assets can distort a comparison of companies. Two companies with the same investment can show entirely different results because the different ages of their assets result in differing net amounts for fixed assets in their financial statements.

Fixed Assets to Shareholders' Equity Ratio

Ratio of fixed assets to shareholders' equity
Average net fixed assets is divided by average shareholders' equity. This ratio indicates the amount of shareholders' equity tied up in fixed assets.

How much of shareholders' equity is tied up in fixed assets? The **ratio of fixed assets to shareholders' equity** calculates the amount of equity tied up in these assets and thus indicates what amount of equity is left over for working capital purposes. The ratio is calculated by the following formula:

$$\frac{\text{Average Net Fixed Assets}}{\text{Average Shareholders' Equity}}$$

There is no magic formula to indicate the proper amount of working capital to be provided by shareholders' equity. It is expected, however, that some part of working capital should be provided by shareholders' equity.

Return on Sales Ratio

This percentage of sales revenue retained by the company — after payment of operating expenses, creditor interest expenses, and government income taxes — is an index of performance that can be used to compare the company to others in the same industry. This ratio is calculated by the following formula:

$$\frac{\text{Net Income for the Year}}{\text{Net Sales}}$$

Note that each industry has different acceptable returns on sales. Consider these returns on sales.

	Food			Steel	
		Return			*Return*
	Company	*on Sales*		*Company*	*on Sales*
	Oshawa Group Limited	1.02		Stelco Inc.	7.5
	Steinberg Inc.	1.24		Algoma Steel Corp. Ltd.	10.3
	Loblaw Companies Limited	0.48		Dofasco Inc.	9.54

The comparison of return on sales between different industries is meaningless if other characteristics of each industry are not considered. Sales volume, accounts receivable turnover, and inventory turnover vary from industry to industry.

Industry		Ratios	
	Sales Volume	*Receivables Turnover*	*Inventory Turnover*
Food	high	not applicable	high
Steel	high	low	low

Any comparison of companies in different industries has to take distinctive industry characteristics into consideration for an accurate analysis. It is particularly difficult to evaluate the financial performance of so-called conglomerates, such as Canadian Pacific Limited and Genstar Corp. In the financial statements of such conglomerates, products in different industries are combined and one return on sales is calculated. This ratio is virtually meaningless and an informative comparison with other companies cannot easily be made.

Publicly owned corporations falling within the jurisdiction of the Securities and Exchange Commission (SEC) in the United States are required to report separately the financial status of each different type of business. The CICA also has requirements for the reporting of segmented information. From this information, a more useful analysis can be made through the calculation of an individual return on sales for each component of the conglomerate. Canadian corporations falling within SEC jurisdiction include Brascan Limited, Nu-West Inc., Alcan Aluminum Limited, and Massey-Ferguson, Ltd.

Earnings-per-Share Ratio

The return to shareholders calculated above indicates the overall return on assets financed by shareholders. This return to shareholders can also be expressed on a per-share basis. That is, the amount of net income can be divided by the number of common shares outstanding to establish how much net income has been earned for each share of stock. This ratio is calculated by the following formula:

$$\frac{\text{Net Income for the Year}}{\text{Number of Common Shares Outstanding}}$$

This expression of net income as a per-share amount is widely quoted in financial circles and is commonly referred to as earnings per share (EPS). Because of widespread interest in EPS, the AcSC of the CICA has recommended its inclusion in financial statements and has also issued guidelines for its preparation in certain complex situations. These guidelines cover the treatment of extraordinary items in the income statement and the convertibility of bonds and preferred shares into common stock. A full explanation of the CICA guidelines in such cases is the subject matter of more advanced studies in accounting and is not attempted in this text. You should be aware, however, that, if there are preferred shareholders, their claims on net income are deducted to calculate the amount available for common shareholders. The ratio formula would then be used in the following modified form:

$$\frac{\text{Net Income for the Year } - \text{ Preferred Dividends}}{\text{Number of Common Shares Outstanding}}$$

Market Ratios

Earnings per share is of particular interest to investors because of its importance in influencing share market value. Additional measurements used in the stock market to evaluate the selling price of shares are the price-to-earnings ratio and the dividend yield.

Price-to-Earnings Ratio

The price-to-earnings ratio is calculated by dividing the market value of a share by earnings per share:

$$\frac{\text{Market Price per Share}}{\text{Earnings per Share}}$$

This ratio indicates the market price in relation to earnings per share. In fact, it only indicates investors' beliefs as to whether a particular share is overvalued or undervalued.

Dividend Yield

Dividend yield ratio
Dividends per share is divided by market price per share. This ratio indicates the return that can be expected from an investment in a company's shares.

The **dividend yield ratio** is calculated by dividing annual dividends per share by a share's current market price.

$$\frac{\text{Dividends per Share}}{\text{Market Price per Share}}$$

This ratio indicates how large a return can be expected from an investment in the company's shares.

D. Bluebeard Computer Corporation's Performance

The following financial information from Bluebeard Computer Corporation is used in the calculation of ratios in this section. The ratios help to establish how efficiently the company uses its assets as resources to earn net income.

		19X5	19X4	19X3
Income from Operations	(a)	$300	$280	$209
Financing Charges — Interest		(89)	(61)	–
Income Tax		(95)	(102)	(97)
	(b)	$116	$117	$112
Average Fixed Assets — Net				
[(Opening and Closing Balances) ÷ 2]	(c)	$1,091	$ 920	–*
Total Assets				
[(Opening and Closing Balances) ÷ 2]	(d)	$2,299	$1,765	–*
Shareholders' Equity				
[(Opening and Closing Balances) ÷ 2]	(e)	1,213	1,172	–*
Sales	(f)	3,200	2,800	2,340
Common Shares Outstanding	(g)	100	100	100

Calculation of Selected Ratios:

1. Return on Total Assets	(a ÷ d)	13%	15.9%	–*
2. Return on Shareholders' Equity	(b ÷ e)	9.6%	9.98%	–*
3. a. Sales to Fixed Assets Ratio	(f ÷ c)	2.93	3.04	–*
b. Fixed Assets to Shareholders' Equity Ratio	(c ÷ e)	0.90	0.78	–*
4. Return on Sales	(b ÷ f)	3.6%	4.2%	4.8%
5. Earnings per Share	(b ÷ g)	$1.16	$1.17	$1.12

*The figure for 19X2 is not available for calculation of an average for 19X3.

Return on Total Assets

Bluebeard's net income was 13 percent of average total assets in 19X5, a decrease from 15.9 percent in 19X4. This decrease is disappointing not only because it seems to indicate a less efficient use of company assets, but also because the decrease has occurred during a period of rapidly expanding sales. Although total average assets have increased almost 30 percent (from $1,765,000 to $2,299,000 in 19X5), its net income has remained virtually unchanged. It may be that the investment in fixed assets during this period has not yet begun to pay off. In all probability, however, there are other efficiency factors affecting this disappointingly decreased return on total assets.

Return on Shareholders' Equity

In 19X5, Bluebeard earned a 9.6 percent return on shareholders' equity (represented by common stock and retained earnings) compared to 9.98 percent in 19X4. Is a 9 to 10 percent return adequate? It is consistent with previous years. A comparison with other companies in the same industries and the industry average would give an indication of Bluebeard's relative performance. Such averages are published by Dun and Bradstreet and in other trade publications.

Earnings per Share

Bluebeard's EPS has remained relatively constant over the three-year period because its expansion was financed by debt.

Return on Sales

Bluebeard has a lower return on sales in 19X5 than 19X4; this decline should be viewed with some concern. Comparison has to be made with other firms in the same industry to evaluate BCC's performance. The return on total assets and on equity should also be examined when appraising the efficiency of asset use.

A low return on sales is not necessarily unfavourable, if it is accompanied by a high return on shareholders' equity. What is unsettling in BCC's case is that both return on sales and return on shareholders' equity are declining. It is important to isolate the reasons for this decline in Bluebeard's performance. A **gross profit percentage** is widely used to establish whether additional sales are being made as a result of lower sales prices. A study of BCC's gross profit shows the following:

Gross profit percentage

Gross profit is divided by sales. This ratio indicates the percentage of sales revenue that is left to pay operating expenses, creditor interest, and government income taxes.

		(000s)		
		19X5	19X4	19X3
Sales	(a)	$3,200	$2,800	$2,340
Cost of Goods Sold		2,500	2,150	1,800
Gross Profit	(b)	$ 700	$ 650	$ 540
Gross Profit (%)	(b ÷ a)	21.9%	23.2%	23.1%

Bluebeard's gross profit percentage has remained fairly constant over the three-year period. Therefore, the decrease in the return on sales must be occurring within the operating expense category.

Management Decisions Relating to Fixed Assets

It is important to analyze the reasonableness of Bluebeard's increased investment in fixed assets in the current circumstances.

Sales to Fixed Assets Ratio

In 19X5, BCC made $2.93 of sales for each dollar invested in fixed assets, a little less than the $3.04 it earned in 19X4. Much will depend on the results of 19X6. Sales have been rapidly expanding and market acceptance of any computer-related innovation is assured; this growth is more important than the ratios. The fixed asset expansion does not appear unwise in the circumstances.

Fixed Assets to Shareholders' Equity Ratio

What does appear unwise is Bluebeard's method of financing its expansion. Consider the amount of shareholders' equity tied up in this expansion, calculated as follows:

		(000s)	
		19X5	19X4
Average Net Fixed Assets	(a)	$1,091	$ 920
Average Shareholders' Equity	(b)	1,213	1,172
Fixed Assets to Shareholder's Equity	(a ÷ b)	0.90	0.78

A significant change has occurred between 19X4 and 19X5. The amount of shareholders' equity tied up in fixed assets has increased from $0.78 for each dollar invested in plant and equipment to $0.90; therefore less working capital is being provided by shareholders' equity. The proportion of $0.90 to each dollar in fixed assets is not necessarily troublesome in itself. What is dangerous is the shortage of working capital.

E. Trends

Trend analysis
The comparison of the data for several years when analyzing financial statements.

In evaluating the various ratios used in this chapter, attention is frequently focused on **trend analysis**. Most public companies provide comparative ratios with their financial statements. The period of comparison usually is not less than 5 years and often covers 10 years or more. Such comparisons permit a better evaluation of a company's financial strength and profitability. They also aid comparisons with other companies in the same industry, with the industry average, and with companies in other industries. Each July, Dun and Bradstreet publishes *Key Business Ratios* for various Canadian corporations. Moody's and Standard and Poor's reporting services also provide for financial information covering extended periods of time.

Horizontal analysis
The analysis of financial statements through the calculation of percentage changes in statement components over two or more years.

Percentages can be used to analyze amounts appearing in financial statements using **horizontal** and **vertical analysis**.

Vertical analysis
The analysis of the composition of a financial statement through the restating of all items in the statement as percentages; comparison of the percentage between two or more years shows the change in composition of the statement components, such restated statements are often called common size statements.

Horizontal Analysis:
The balance for 19X5 can be compared with the balance for 19X4. The difference, or chnage, is shown as a dollar amount and also as a percentage. The percentage is calculated by dividing the dollar amount of change by the older of the two months being compared.

Vertical Analysis:
Each amount on a financial statement can be expressed as a percentage of a base. Net sales is the base in the income statement, total assets is the base for assets, and total equities is the base for equities in the balance sheet. Financial statements prepared in this manner are referred to as *common size statements*.

Horizontal and vertical analyses of the balance sheets and statements of income of Bluebeard Computer Corporation follow.

Horizontal Analysis: Balance Sheets

	19X5	19X4	Change Amount	Change Percent
Current Assets	$1,433	$ 984	+$449	+45.63
Fixed Assets	1,053	1,128	−75	−6.65
Total	$2,486	$2,112	+$374	+17.71
Current Liabilities	$1,255	$ 917	+$338	+36.86
Shareholders' Equity	1,231	1,195	+36	+3.01
Total	$2,486	$2,112	+$374	+17.71

Notice the special columns introduced here. Analysis of the changes indicates a large increase in current assets together with a large increase in current liabilities. There was a small decline in fixed assets and a small increase in shareholders' equity. The percentage change must always be interpreted together with the dollar amount of change to avoid incorrect conclusions; percentages can sometimes be misleading.

Vertical Analysis: Balance Sheets
Common Size Percentages

	19X5	19X4
Current Assets	57.64	46.59
Fixed Assets	42.36	53.41
Total	100.00	100.00
Current Liabilities	50.48	43.42
Shareholders' Equity	49.52	56.58
Total	100.00	100.00

In the common size balance sheets, it is clear that the composition of the assets has changed with an overall shift to current assets in 19X5. It is also shown that an increase in current liabilities has occurred. Vertical analysis places the balance sheet components in comparable terms through the conversion of all dollar amounts into percentages.

Horizontal Analysis: Income Statements

	19X5	19X4	Change Amount	Percent
Sales	$3,200	$2,800	+400	+14.29
Cost of Goods Sold	2,500	2,150	+350	+16.28
Gross Profit	$ 700	$ 650	+50	+7.69
Expenses	584	533	+51	+9.57
Net Income	$ 116	$ 117	−1	−0.85

Vertical Analysis: Income Statements
Common Size Percentages

	19X5	19X4
Sales	100.00	100.00
Cost of Goods Sold	78.12	76.79
Gross Profit	21.88	23.21
Expenses	18.25	19.04
Net Income	3.63	4.17

Consider the income statement and note that, although sales and gross profit increased, net income decreased. This decrease in net income resulted from an increase in cost of goods sold and expenses. The increased sales were insufficient to offset the increased cost of merchandise and increased expenses.

Looking at the income statement, note the relative change in the components of the statement. For example, cost of goods sold increased in 19X5 relative to sales, while expenses in 19X5 relative to sales decreased. The decrease in expenses, however, was insufficient to offset a decrease in net income.

The percentages calculated become more informative when compared to earlier years. Further analysis is usually undertaken in order to establish answers to the following questions:

Horizontal Analysis:
1. What caused this change?

2. Is the change favourable or negative?

These and other similar questions call attention to weak areas and help to spot trends in financial strength and profitability.

Vertical Analysis:
1. How do the percentages of this company compare with other companies in the same industry? in other industries?

2. Why is there such a large portion of assets tied up in current assets?

These and other similar questions call attention to areas that may require further study.

In fact, the published financial statements of actual companies tend to reduce the amount of information that can be used for analysis so that competitors will be left in the dark as much as possible. Accordingly, gross profits are often not shown separately and cost of goods sold is combined with operating expenses to prevent its calculation by the reader. The lack of individual breakdowns of salaries, audit fees, promotion expenses, and so on also prevent the statement reader from obtaining a detailed picture of a corporation's activities. Therefore, shareholders, analysts, and others are left in the dark. The calculation of all of the percentages and ratios that are possible from the figures provided will shed at least some light on the situation.

F. Review of Ratios

The ratios covered in this chapter are summarized here.

Reliance on Debt:	**Calculation of Ratio:**	**Indicates:**
1. Equity-to-Debt Ratio	$\dfrac{\text{Shareholders' Equity}}{\text{Total Liabilities}}$	What the proportion of shareholder to creditor financing is.
Short-Term Solvency Analysis:		
1. The Current Ratio	$\dfrac{\text{Current Assets}}{\text{Current Liabilities}}$	How many current asset dollars exist to pay current liabilities. (This is only a crude measure of solvency.)
2. The Acid-Test Ratio	$\dfrac{\text{Quick Current Assets}}{\text{Current Liabilities}}$	Whether the company is able to meet the immediate demands of creditors. (This is a more severe measure of solvency. Inventory and prepaid items are excluded from the calculation.)
3. Management Decisions Relating to Receivables:		
a. Accounts Receivable Collection Period	$\dfrac{\text{Average Accounts Receivable}}{\text{Net Credit Sales}} \times 365$	What the average time needed to collect receivables is.
b. Accounts Receivable Turnover	$\dfrac{\text{Net Credit Sales}}{\text{Average Accounts Receivable}}$	How often during the year accounts receivable have been converted into cash.
4. Management Decisions Relating to Inventory:		
a. Number of Days of Sales in Inventory	$\dfrac{\text{Average Inventory}}{\text{Cost of Goods Sold}} \times 365$	How many days of sales can be made with existing inventory.
b. Inventory Turnover	$\dfrac{\text{Cost of Goods Sold}}{\text{Average Inventory}}$	How many times during the year inventory has been sold and replaced.
5. The Revenue Operating Cycle	Average Number of Days To Turn Over Inventory + Average Number of Days To Collect Receivables.	How long it is between the purchase of inventory and the subsequent collection of cash.

Analysis of Operations Efficiency:

1. Return on Total Assets

$$\frac{\text{Income from Operations}}{\text{Average Total Assets}}$$

How efficiently a company uses its assets as resources to earn net income.

2. Return on Shareholders' Equity

$$\frac{\text{Net Income for the Year}}{\text{Average Shareholders' Equity}}$$

The adequacy of net income as a return on shareholders' equity.

  a. Trading on the Equity (This is not a ratio as such but is related to the return on shareholders' equity, which in turn is influenced by the use of long-term financing.)

[See example in section C.]

The use of borrowed money to generate a higher return in the business than the rate being paid on the borrowed money.

  b. Bondholder Protection: Times Interest Earned Ratio

$$\frac{\text{Income from Operations}}{\text{Interest Expense}}$$

The ability of a company to pay interest to long-term creditors.

3. Management Decisions Relating to Fixed Assets:

  a. Sales to Fixed Assets Ratio

$$\frac{\text{Net Sales}}{\text{Average Net Fixed Assets}}$$

The adequacy of sales in relation to the investment in fixed assets.

  b. Fixed Assets to Shareholders' Equity Ratio

$$\frac{\text{Average Net Fixed Assets}}{\text{Average Shareholders' Equity}}$$

The amount of shareholders' equity tied up in fixed assets.

4. Return on Sales

$$\frac{\text{Net Income for the Year}}{\text{Net Sales}}$$

The percentage of sales revenue left in the business after payment of expenses, creditor interest, and government income taxes.

5. Earnings per Share

$$\frac{\text{Net Income for the Year} - \text{Preferred Dividends}}{\text{Number of Common Shares Outstanding}}$$

The amount of net income that has been earned on each share of common stock.

6. Market Ratios:

  a. Price-to-Earnings Ratio

$$\frac{\text{Market Price per Share}}{\text{Earnings per Share}}$$

The reasonableness of market price in relation to earnings per share.

  b. Dividend Yield

$$\frac{\text{Dividends per Share}}{\text{Market Price per Share}}$$

The return that can be expected from an investment in a company's shares.

APPENDIX: The Impact of Changing Prices

The preceding historical cost financial statements of Bluebeard Computer Corporation were prepared according to the stable dollar assumption. Under this concept, the value of the dollar is assumed to be constant over time. In fact, the Canadian dollar has been unstable recently as a result of inflation, which has, over time, devalued the dollar's purchasing power. The magnitude of this drop is indicated by the Consumer Price Index (CPI), a general measure of retail prices prepared each month by Statistics Canada; Figure 14-3 shows the annual percentage change in the CPI during the 1970s and into the 1980s.

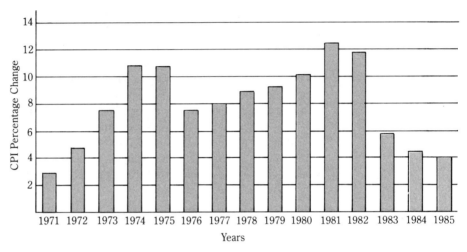

Figure 14-3   Percentage change in CPI

As can be seen, CPI-measured inflation amounted to 2.9 percent in 1971, peaked at 12.5 percent in 1981, and then declined. This annual change accumulates over time with the result that the dollar money unit is effectively devalued. Therefore, as inflation continues, it takes an increasing amount of dollars to make purchases; or, in other words, the dollar loses purchasing power during periods of inflation. This loss in purchasing power is actually hidden in financial statements, which mingle dollars of different purchasing powers. For example, the 1981 12.5-percent change means that, on the average $112.50 was required to buy what could have been purchased for $100 in 1980, the 4.4-percent 1984 change means that $104.40 was required to purchase what could have been purchased for $100 in 1983. Financial statements prepared at the end of 1985 would therefore include dollars of different purchasing powers.

Constant Dollar Accounting

Constant dollar accounting
The conversion of historical costs into a stable unit of measurement over time.

Some accountants propose that all historical cost dollars in financial statements be converted to end-of-the-current-year dollars; this conversion procedure is referred to as **constant dollar accounting**. It includes the construction of a general price index that is used to restate financial statement items from previous years to current year common dollars.

The CPI is a general price index that is available; it can be used to convert previous years' dollars into end-of-the-current year dollars. The following table prepared by

Statistics Canada lists the CPI from 1971 to 1985 and the annual percentage changes in the index.

Year	CPI	Percentage Change	Year	CPI	Percentage Change	Year	CPI	Percentage Change
1971	42.2	2.9	1976	62.9	7.5	1981	100.0	12.5
1972	44.2	4.8	1977	67.9	8.0	1982	110.8	10.8
1973	47.6	7.6	1978	73.9	8.0	1983	117.2	5.8
1974	52.8	10.9	1979	80.7	9.2	1984	122.3	4.4
1975	58.5	10.8	1980	88.9	10.1	1985	127.2	4.0

These CPI numbers are based on a survey of price changes in a fixed shopping basket of hundreds of goods and services. Since the index is a weighted average of prices for a number of different commodities, it is important to note that, while some commodity prices are increasing, others may actually be decreasing. Therefore, while it can be stated that on the average $301 (rounded) ($100 × 127.2 ÷ 42.2) was required to buy what could have been purchased for $100 in 1971, it cannot be claimed that this proportion could be accurately applied to individual assets or services. A specific price index would be required for this purpose. It is, therefore, important to distinguish between general and specific changes because the price of a particular commodity cannot be assumed to increase in the same proportion as a general price increase.

Keeping this in mind, the CPI can be used to illustrate the adjustment of historical cost financial statements. For example, a building purchased in 1971 for $100,000 would be converted into 1985 dollars by multiplying the $100,000 cost by its 1985 CPI divided by the 1971 CPI as follows:

$$\$100,000 \times \frac{127.2}{42.2} = \$301,422 \text{ (rounded)}.$$

Thus, the constant dollar value of the building is $301,422 in 1985. In actual fact, the building might be worth more or less. The $301,422 simply means that the dollar measurement of the asset is $201,422 more in 1985 than in 1971 as a result of a decrease in the purchasing power of the dollar.

The objective of constant dollar accounting is the preparation of financial statements using a stable measuring unit, a constant dollar in terms of purchasing power. This requires the conversion of previous years' dollars with differing purchasing power into end-of-the-current-year purchasing power dollars. A simple balance sheet conversion illustrates the techniques involved. An income statement conversion would also be prepared.

Balance Sheet Conversion

Constant dollar accounting can be illustrated using the following simple example. Assume that A Corporation was incorporated on January 2, 19X1 when the general price index amounted to 100. On this date, the corporation issued $100,000-worth of common shares for the following assets: Cash, $20,000; Land, $30,000; Building, $50,000. Its balance sheet prepared on this date would appear as follows:

A Corporation
Balance Sheet
At January 2, 19X1

Assets		Equity	
Cash	$ 20,000	Common Stock	$100,000
Land	30,000		
Building	50,000		
	$100,000		$100,000

Assume that the corporation was not involved in any other transactions during the year and that the general price index to convert these amounts was 120. A Corporation's balance sheet would be converted into constant dollars as follows:

A Corporation
Balance Sheet
At December 31, 19X1

Assets	*Historical Cost*	*Conversion Factor*	*Constant Dollars*
Cash	$ 20,000	(not converted)	$ 20,000
Land	30,000	120/100	36,000
Building	50,000	120/100	60,000
	$100,000		$116,000
Equity			
Common Stock	$100,000	120/100	$120,000
Purchasing Power Loss	–	$20,000 × 120/100	(4,000)
	$100,000		$116,000

As can be seen, A Corporation suffered a $4,000 purchasing power loss in 19X1, because cash is not converted to constant dollars; it represents $20,000 regardless of changes in the price index. The $4,000 purchasing power loss is converted as follows:

$$\$20,000 \times \frac{120}{100} \text{ (or: } \$20,000 \times 20\%) = \$4,000$$

Monetary Assets

The cash was not converted at December 31, 19X1. This is also true of other monetary assets, such as accounts receivable and long-term investments in bonds. They are referred to as *monetary assets* because their amount of dollars is fixed. Regardless of changes in the price index, only a certain number of dollars will be received. During inflationary periods, holding monetary assets results in purchasing power losses. Monetary liabilities include bank loans, accounts payable, and most liabilities. Because the amount to be paid is also fixed, holding monetary liabilities during inflationary periods results in purchasing power gains, since the purchasing power of the dollars used to repay these debts has been decreasing.

Non-monetary Assets

Assets that are converted for price index changes are referred to as *non-monetary assets*. These include inventory, fixed assets, and long-term investments in common stock. Note that this conversion of non-monetary assets into constant dollar amounts is not intended to indicate the current value of any converted items; it simply results in their being reported in dollars with the same purchasing power. In all probability, the land and building of A Corporation could not be sold or purchased for $36,000 and $60,000, respectively.

Therefore, during periods of inflation, monetary assets will result in a purchasing power loss, while monetary liabilities will produce a purchasing power gain. Non-monetary assets will tend to be understated during periods of rising prices, unless they are converted to constant dollars.

Income Statement Conversion

The income statement can also be converted to constant dollars. If it is assumed that sales are made and expenses are incurred evenly during the year, they can be converted into common dollars using the average price index for the year. Only inventory and depreciation of fixed assets that appeared in the preceding year's balance sheet are converted using the index of the year in which they were purchased.

Assume that Bluebeard Computer Corporation's income statement at December 31, 19X5 included in Cost of Goods Sold $536 of inventory that had been purchased on December 31, 19X4. Assume also that depreciation was calculated on fixed assets that had been purchased on December 31, 19X3. The price index at these different dates was the following:

		Index
19X3	Building purchased	100
19X4	Inventory purchased	120
19X4	December 31, 19X4	120
19X5	Average for 19X5	130
19X5	December 31, 19X5	140

Sales, purchases, and expenses other than depreciation are assumed to have been made evenly throughout the year. They are, therefore, converted to December 31, 1985 purchasing power dollars as follows: $3,200 × 140/130. Since opening inventory is assumed to have been purchased at December 31, 19X4, it is converted to December 31, 19X5 purchasing power dollars by the following calculation: $536 × 140/120. Depreciation expense is converted using the price index existing at the date the fixed asset was purchased; the calculation $75 × 140/100 makes the conversion of these 19X3 dollars into 19X5 purchasing power dollars.

	Historical Cost	*Conversion Factor*	*Constant Dollar*
Sales	$3,200	140/130	$3,446*
Cost of Goods Sold	$2,500	(see below)	$2,740
Depreciation	75	140/100	105
Selling & Administrative Expenses	325	140/130	350
Interest	89	140/130	96*
	$2,989		$3,291
Income before Income Tax	$ 211		$ 155
Income Tax	95	140/130	102*
Net Income for the Year	$ 116		$ 53
Cost of Goods Sold:			
Opening Inventory	$ 536	140/120	$ 625*
Purchases	2,764	140/130	2,977*
	$3,300		$3,602
Less: Ending Inventory	800	140/130	862
Total Cost of Goods Sold	$2,500		$2,740

*Rounded to nearest dollar.

As can be seen, net income for 19X5 has been reduced from $116 to $53 as a result of changes in the purchasing power of the dollar. Therefore, during periods of inflation, net income calculated using historical costs will tend to be overstated.

Current Cost Accounting

Current cost accounting focuses on the current cost of replacing assets. It emphasizes the maintenance of operating capability; that is, the entity's capability at the end of an accounting time period should be as great as it was at the beginning of that period. Although the example of constant dollar accounting converts dollars into end-of-the-current-year constant dollars, it does not incorporate into these numbers the current replacement cost of assets. This distinction can be made using the assets of A Corporation. The following balance sheet illustrates the difference between historical cost of assets, constant dollar inflation adjusted amounts, and the current cost of these assets.

A Corporation
Partial Balance Sheet
At December 31, 19X1

Assets	Historical Cost	Constant Dollar	Current Costs
Land	$30,000	$36,000	$50,000
Building	50,000	60,000	75,000

As can be seen, the current cost of acquiring similar land and a similar building exceeds both historical cost and historical cost adjusted for a decrease in purchasing power of the dollar. Therefore, only a part of the above increase results from inflation; that is, land has increased $6,000 owing to inflation ($36,000 − $30,000) and the building $10,000 ($60,000 − $50,000). In addition to this, the cost to replace these assets has also increased in excess of inflation; land would cost an additional $14,000 ($50,000 − $36,000) to be replaced, and building an additional $15,000 ($75,000 − $60,000). Therefore, in order to maintain its operating capability, A Corporation is faced not only with an increase resulting from inflation, but also with an additional increase in the current cost of the assets themselves. These amounts are summarized in the following schedule.

	Total Change	Change in Asset Value Because of Inflation	Because of Increase in Asset Cost
Land	$20,000	$ 6,000	$14,000
Building	25,000	10,000	15,000

The *CICA Handbook* does not require the separate disclosure of these two sets of figures. Rather, the information comparing changes that result from inflation and changes that result from asset cost increases are contained in the current cost supplementary disclosure included with financial statements.

In the United States, FASB Statement No. 33 recommends that large public corporations disclose both sets of figures: one to indicate the impact of inflation on historical costs, the other to indicate its impact on current cost changes.

Inventory Replacement

Inventory purchased in a preceding year has to be replaced when sold in a subsequent year. The calculation of current cost data is designed to indicate the impact on the entity of replacing this inventory when current costs have increased.

Impact on the Balance Sheet

The balance sheet impact of inventory replacement, discussed in Chapter 5, includes an analysis prepared for executives of Bluebeard Computer Corporation. This analysis uses current costs to replace year-end inventory; the current cost of ending inventory is $7,000 at the balance sheet date. A comparison of balance sheet amounts shows the following:

	FIFO	
	Historical Cost	Current Cost
Ending Inventory	$5,000	$7,000

This comparison illustrates that Bluebeard's ability to maintain its operating capability could be in jeopardy if this difference continues into the future.

Impact on the Income Statement

The analysis also illustrates the impact of current costs on the income statement.

	FIFO	
	Historical Cost	Current Cost
Sales	$20,000	$20,000
Cost of Goods Sold:		
Purchases	$15,000	
Ending Inventory	5,000	
Total Cost of Goods Sold	$10,000	$18,000
Gross Profit	$10,000	$ 2,000
Operating Expenses	6,000	6,000
Net Income (Loss) for the Period	$ 4,000	$ (4,000)

These current cost calculations indicate that Bluebeard is losing its operating capability and would eventually be unable to replace inventory without increasing borrowing. In this illustration, the current cost to replace ending inventory is used; this current cost is calculated as $18,000 as shown above.

Fixed Asset Replacement

Fixed assets usually represent a large amount of assets that have to be replaced eventually. The calculation of current cost data is intended to show the effects of increased costs and to draw attention to the entity's ability to maintain its future operating capability.

Impact on the Balance Sheet

The impact of current costs on the balance sheet, introduced in Chapters 5 and 8, includes an analysis prepared for executives of Bluebeard Computer Corporation. This analysis illustrated the impact of current cost accounting on fixed assets. Assuming that fixed assets originally cost $20,000, have an estimated useful life of 5 years, and have a salvage value of $2,000, straight-line depreciation is calculated as $3,600 ($20,000 − $2,000 = $18,000 ÷ 5 years = $3,600 per year).

	Historical Cost	Current Cost
Fixed Assets	$20,000	$28,000
Less: Accumulated Depreciation	3,600(18%)	5,040(18%)
Carrying Value	$16,400	$22,960

As can be seen, use of current costs results in different amounts. The current cost of fixed assets amounts to $28,000. The accumulated depreciation is calculated as 18 percent of this $28,000 current cost; this is the same proportion of accumulated depreciation as calculated under historical cost accounting.

A number of different measurement techniques has been suggested to calculate current cost. These techniques include the use of price indices, appraisals, and engineering estimates of the impact of technological change, as well as other factors. Because the calculation of current costs is currently in an experimental stage, further refinements are expected, as experience in their calculation and use develops. For illustrative purposes, the same estimated useful life and depreciation method (straight-line) was used for current cost as for historical cost calculations.

It should be noted that calculation of current costs is essentially a subjective process; here it was based on management's estimates and assumptions regarding replacement costs, impact of technological changes, and so on.

Impact on the Income Statement

The analysis used to show the impact of current cost calculations on inventory are further developed to illustrate the impact of current cost depreciation expense. The following historical cost and current cost income statements were prepared for executives of Bluebeard Computer Corporation.

	Historical Cost	Current Cost
Sales	$20,000	$ 20,000
Cost of Goods Sold	10,000	18,000
Gross Profit	$10,000	$ 2,000
Operating Expenses:		
Depreciation	$ 3,600	$ 5,040
Other Expenses	2,400	2,400
	$ 6,000	$ 7,440
Operating Income (Loss)	$ 4,000	$ (5,440)
Income Tax (50%)	2,000	2,000
Net Income (Loss)	$ 2,000	$ (7,440)

Conceptual Issue 14-1

A Case Study on Current Cost Reporting

Under the CICA's standards, financial data show the effect of specific price changes and the impact of general inflation.

Following are some sample — and simplified — current cost financial statements for a typical manufacturing concern.

First, the income statement:

For the year ended December 31, 1984
(000s)

Historical cost basis 1984		Current cost basis 1984
$169,000	Sales	$169,000
$116,000	Cost of Goods Sold	$121,190
8,000	Depreciation	13,750
21,900	Selling, General, and Administrative Expenses	21,900
3,900	Interest	3,900
(800)	Gain on Sale of Property, Plant, and Equipment	–
$149,000		$160,740
$ 20,000	Income before Income Taxes	$ 8,260
$ 6,000	Income Taxes — Current	$ 6,000
2,000	— Deferred	2,000
$ 8,000		$ 8,000
$ 12,000	Income	$ 260

As you can see, there are two main differences between the historical cost and current cost figures. First, cost of goods sold is increased from $116 million to $121.9 million because inventory replacement costs at the date of sale were higher than historically recorded. Second, the provision for depreciation is increased from $8 million to $13.75 million because the historical cost provisions do not take into account the increased cost of replacing the company's fixed assets at current prices. As a result, current cost operating income is significantly below the recorded historical cost income.

Current cost profits are lower than the historical cost profits because current cost profits are not reported until provision is made to maintain operating capability by necessary replacement of assets and inventories at today's, not yesterday's, costs. Historical cost profits make provision to replace assets at yesterday's costs.

The common shareholders may also be interested in knowing how their equity in the company has performed. Has common shareholders' equity grown at a rate sufficient to keep pace with inflation? Has it grown at a rate equal to or greater than the specific price changes experienced by the company?

The new accounting standards address these questions by showing three figures:
• the increase in the current costs of assets
• the gain or loss in general purchasing power from holding non-monetary items, and
• a financing adjustment.

The information is disclosed in the following format:

Other supplementary information	1984
Increase in the current cost amounts of inventory and property, plant, and equipment	(000s) $14,740
Effect of general inflation	9,471
Excess of increase in current cost over the effect of general inflation	$ 5,269
Gain in general purchasing power from having net monetary liabilities	$ 2,275
Financing adjustment	$ 3,685

The first three lines of the "Other supplementary information" tell us that the current cost of the inventory and fixed assets owned by the company increased at a rate greater than general inflation. Shareholders' equity increased in real terms by $5,269,000.

This company financed part of its operations with debt. The second item shows that because of inflation the amount of that debt declined in real terms. This resulted in a further "real" increase in shareholders' equity of $2,275,000, that is, the gain in general purchasing power having net monetary liabilities.

The third item is the financing adjustment of $3,685,000. The company has financed its operations through a combination of shareholders' funds and borrowed funds. If this situation continues, shareholders will not be called on to provide the whole of the increase in capital needed to support the higher current costs of inventory and fixed assets. The $3,685,000 financing adjustment is the increase in the current cost amounts of the portion of inventory and fixed assets financed through debt. It is calculated by multiplying the increase in current cost amounts — $14,740,000 — by the company's debt-to-equity ratio, in this case 1 : 4.

Overall, shareholders' equity has grown by $7,804,000 ($260,000 + $5,269,000 + $2,275,000) more than the amount needed simply to keep pace with inflation and by $3,945,000 ($260,000 + $3,685,000) more than the amount needed to keep pace with the rate of specific price changes experienced by the company.

The three items are not necessarily amounts available for distribution to the shareholders. They are a measure of how price changes have affected the company's financial position and the shareholders' stake in the company.

It is helpful to note that this supplementary information is based on two different ways of looking at what has been happening to the company's assets and liabilities. In each case, the information presents the impact of both general inflation and of specific price changes:
• The amount recorded as the current cost increases of inventory and fixed assets is a specific price change. The financing adjustment is also based on the specific price changes experienced by this company.

• The impact of inflation, $9,471,000, is, of course, a general figure arrived at by measuring the amount of the increase in inventory and fixed asset costs that would have to take place to keep pace with the Consumer Price Index. Similarly, the gain on net monetary liabilities is a general figure, the result of multiplying the company's net debt by the rate of inflation as measured by the CPI.

Although the income statement had certainly suffered from the rise in the cost of inventories and fixed assets, the news isn't all bad. As the following schedule of assets shows, the balance sheet of the company has been strengthened by the rise in value of the assets.

Schedule of Assets on a Current Cost Basis
At December 31, 1984
(000s)

Historical cost basis 1984		*Current cost basis 1984*
$34,000	Inventory	$36,000
$36,700	Property, Plant, and Equipment — Net	$56,200
$45,600	Net Assets (Common Shareholders' Equity)	$67,100

The Management Report

Particularly in the early years, perhaps the most important part of the supplementary current cost disclosures will be management's report on where the numbers came from and what they mean. Changing prices affect enterprises in different ways according to their particular circumstances, and annual report readers may not have detailed information about these circumstances. An enterprise's management is in the best position to understand and explain the impact of price changes on its operations. The final test of current cost information will be its usefulness.

The bottom line in current cost accounting is much more informative than the historical cost income figure. Different people who have contributed toward an enterprise have, for their own purposes, different ideas about what current cost income really is and about what the capital invested is supposed to do.

Source CICA, "Current Cost Reporting", (1983), pp. 10-15.

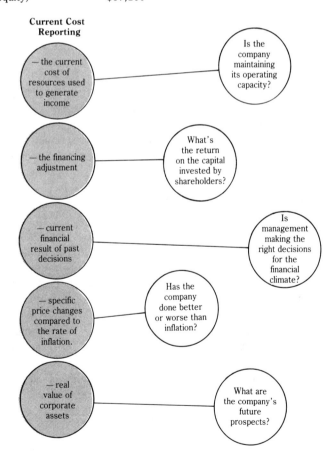

Figure 14-4 Current cost reporting (CICA case study)

This calculation disclosed a large loss when current costs were used. Under current cost accounting, depreciation expense is viewed as that part of the asset used during the year that has to be replaced eventually to maintain operating capability. On the basis of these calculations, Bluebeard would be unable to replace its fixed assets without additional borrowing; it is losing its ability to operate at the same level in the future.

Even worse, income tax estimated at 50 percent is paid on the historical cost calculation of operating income, while, in fact, an operating loss exists under the current cost net income calculation.

The current cost model, therefore, shows that Bluebeard is losing its operating capacity and will eventually be unable to replace its fixed assets without increased borrowing.

Use of the Historical Cost Concept

A dilemma for the accounting profession centres on its use of historical costs in the preparation of financial statements. Historical costs are used because they are objectively determined, even though the measure used, the stable dollar assumption, is invalid during periods of rapid inflation. Although current cost data are more relevant, their incorporation into financial statements is questioned because the determination of current costs is generally a subjective process, based, in some cases, on management's estimates and assumptions.

Financial Statement Disclosure

Although more relevant, the use of current costs in record-keeping or the incorporation of current costs into the body of financial statements, is not included among *CICA Handbook* recommendations. The AcSC released standards on current cost accounting in December 1982 effective for financial years beginning on or after January 2, 1983; the application of the standards is to be reviewed before 1987. These standards emphasize not only the effects of inflation on historical costs, but also additional increases in the current cost of the assets themselves. The standards recommend use of either the Consumer Price Index or the Gross National Expenditure Implicit Price Deflator to measure the effects of inflation.

The AcSC standards do not require current cost information for all items appearing in financial statements. Rather, this information is required only for the following: (a) inventory and cost of goods sold and (b) fixed assets and related depreciation expense. Further, it is recommended that current cost data be included with financial statements as supplementary information, rather than be incorporated into financial statements.

In addition to current cost supplementary information, the AcSC standards also require the calculation of a financing adjustment. The financing adjustment may alleviate, at least in part, the operating capability lost by an entity during the year.

A more complete discussion of these topics is beyond the scope of this book; they are usually the subject of advanced accounting courses. It should be noted that the AcSC standards are applicable only to large publicly traded corporations having inventory and fixed assets (before accumulated depreciation) of $50 million and whose total assets exceed $350 million. Financial institutions, however, are exempted from the standards.

A S S I G N M E N T   M A T E R I A L S

Discussion Questions

1. Why are analysts and investors concerned with the financial structure of a particular corporation? How is it possible that the corporation is overfinanced or underfinanced?
2. Is the reliance on creditor financing advisable or inadvisable? Explain its impact on net income.
3. Discuss the advantages and disadvantages of short-term debt financing compared to long-term debt financing.
4. Explain what *solvency* means. When a corporation is insolvent, what are the implications to shareholders? to creditors?
5. How is it possible that a corporation, which is making an acceptable gross profit on operations, can actually be insolvent?
6. What ratios can be calculated to evaluate solvency? Explain what each one indicates.
7. a. Define *working capital*. Distinguish between the current ratio and the acid-test ratio.
   b. "The current ratio is, by itself, inadequate to measure short-term solvency." Discuss this statement.
8. Two firms have the same working capital. Explain how it is possible that one is able to provide its short-term creditors with a guarantee from its current assets, while the other firm cannot.
9. Management decisions relating to accounts receivable and inventory can affect solvency. Explain. What is an acceptable accounts receivable turnover? an acceptable inventory turnover?
10. Discuss the advantages and disadvantages of increasing inventory turnover.
11. Financial analysts compute inventory turnover by dividing cost of goods sold by average inventory. Why is it not theoretically correct to estimate the turnover of inventories by dividing net sales by the average inventory?
12. What is the revenue operating cycle? How is its calculation useful in evaluating solvency?
13. Identify and explain four ratios (and any associated calculations) that evaluate a corporation's efficiency. What does each ratio specify?
14. How is trading on the equity related to the overfinancing or underfinancing of a corporation? Provide an example.
15. "Leverage is useful but only if you can pay the interest." Discuss this statement.
16. The ratio of sales to fixed assets is used to determine adequacy of sales revenue in relation to investment in fixed assets. Discuss what factors may affect the usefulness of this ratio.
17. Comparisons need to be made to determine what is an acceptable or unacceptable ratio. On what basis can comparison be made?
18. Distinguish between a horizontal and a vertical analysis of financial statements.
19. How is the dollar's purchasing power devalued during periods of continuing inflation?
20. What is the CPI and how is it used to convert previous years' dollars into end-of-the-current-year dollars?
21. What are monetary accounts, and why are they not converted?
22. What are non-monetary accounts? Why are they converted into constant dollars?
23. How does current cost accounting emphasize the maintenance of a corporation's operating capability?
24. In what way do changes resulting from inflation differ from changes resulting from asset cost increases?
25. What financial statement disclosure for the impact of changing prices is required by the AcSC?
26. Some accountants have stated that "the inflation accounting problem will go away as soon as inflation has been brought under control." Do you agree or disagree with this statement? Should changing price models only be used during periods of changing prices and then put away when no longer needed? Discuss.

Discussion Cases

Discussion Case 14-1:   Ben and Jerry's Homemade Inc.

If you have to work 60-hour weeks for a living, this small central Vermont town is the place to do it. Working here for Ben and Jerry's, the No. 2 super-premium ice cream producer in the United States, means taking home three free pints of Cherry Garcia or Dastardly Mash every day.

It also means working in a valley of lush green mountains for a company in which no one earns more than five times the lowest salary.

There really *are* a Ben and Jerry: Ben Cohen and Jerry Greenfield, both 36, are long-time best friends who met as pudgy seventh-graders in a Long Island gym class. Today, 10 years after starting an ice cream store in a Burlington, Vt., gas station, they run a company with $31.8-million (U.S.) in sales, 240 full-time employees and a growth record that has seen sales double every year since 1982. Last year, sales increased by 59.6 per cent.

In April, the first Ben and Jerry's opened its doors in downtown Montreal. Company president Michael Dorfman had predicted sales of $400,000 (Canadian) for the first year; he now says they will hit that mark by the end of the summer. A second store in the residential Montreal neighborhood of Nôtre Dame de Grace opened last week.

By summer's end, Ben and Jerry's Canada will open its first Toronto store, in the new North York City Centre. Mr. Dorfman is forecasting $350,000 in annual sales from the 800-square-foot ice cream parlor.

New in Canada, Ben and Jerry's is a household name in New England. It is *the* dessert of choice for people who like their ice cream creamy (15.5 per cent butterfat), chunky (smashed-up candy bars and chocolate-coated nuts are a specialty) and funky. The founders pride themselves on being "weird" and naming their ice creams accordingly. Cherry Garcia (vanilla with bing cherries and chocolate chunks) was named by a customer-fan of the 1960s rock group, the Grateful Dead, in honor of its leader, Jerry Garcia.

The newest flavor, Chunky Monkey (banana ice cream with walnuts and chocolate chunks) was named by a cafeteria worker; it's what college students call the heaps that they make of uneaten food.

The Ben and Jerry's trademark, a laid-back, we're-really-not-businessmen attitude, also reigns at the Waterbury plant. Ask spokesman Maureen Martin to name Mr. Greenfield's position and she turns to ask the receptionist: "What's Jerry's job title this week?" (It is "mobile promotions co-ordinator.")

But working for Ben and Jerry's is anything but laid back: Ms Martin and others routinely put in 12-hour days. Staff turnover, especially among $6.50-an-hour production workers, is high. A cover story last month in Inc. magazine, written after reporter Erik Larson had spent a week in

and around the 40,000-square-foot plant, raised the serious question: is Ben and Jerry's spinning out of control?

According to Mr. Larson, "a pervasive sense of crisis has always lingered within the company." That, says Mr. Cohen, the company president, is true. "The article is a pretty accurate snapshot of where we are right now," he says. As the company continues to grow at breakneck speed, new managers and consultants are taking over, diluting the long-haired company culture that includes a "joy committee," chaired by Jerry, designed to keep work fun.

Ben and Jerry's is on the verge of being consumed by its own success. The Waterbury plant, operating six days a week 17 hours a day, produces 979,200 pints a week, barely enough to keep up with demand. The ice cream is sold in more than 60 franchise locations on both coasts of the United States, but to keep control of quality, every pint is manufactured in Vermont and shipped by truck.

Montreal customers are eating ice cream imported (with a 15.5 per cent duty) from Waterbury, but not for long. Officials from the Dairy Bureau and the U.S. Department of Agriculture insist the ice cream be made locally, Mr. Dorfman says. The Canadian company, a licencee, is testing ice cream manufacturers in Ontario and Quebec and expects to be selling a locally made product within several months.

The Canadian version of Ben and Jerry's is identical to the parent company in some ways: the ice cream parlors have wainscotted walls, hanging lamps and huge wall murals of cows and green fields, the same as those in Burlington and Boston. You can buy T-shirts and hats, brownies and banana splits. Even the hand-drawn posters are the same, although in French. However, unlike the U.S. operation, Ben and Jerry's Canada will not be donating money to charity or giving 1 per cent of profit to promoting peace.

The parent company is well known for its social conscience: 7.5 per cent of pretax profits go to a company foundation, a policy that has made Ben and Jerry's a favorite of socially aware investors and financial advisers. Last year, the foundation distributed $280,000 (U.S.) to 90 organizations, including a Vermont child-abuse prevention program and a black leadership program in Charlotte, N.C.

"It's really important to define 'success,'" says Mr. Cohen. "It means maintaining a company that maximizes its contribution to the community and its employees and remains profitable. We serve three constituencies: our employees, the shareholders and the community. No one is worth more than any other one."

The company went public in 1980, initially offering shares only to Vermont residents.

"We wanted to help redistribute wealth," he adds. "We wanted people from all economic classes to get some equity and move up the economic ladder." (Due to several stock splits, an initial investment of $1,000 in the company is now worth $8,000.)

A recent move was to join an organization called One Per Cent for Peace, in which that fraction of company profits is used to promote pacifism. To help promote the idea, Ben and Jerry's recently opened a new plant in Springfield, Vt., where they will make "peace pops." Each chocolate-covered ice cream bar will carry a wrapper explaining the program and urging consumers to lobby politicians to reduce military spending.

For Mr. Cohen, still struggling conceptually with success — despite the company having been named Small Business of the Year by President Ronald Reagan in May — it's the only way.

"When I started, I didn't realize there was a different way to be a business person. When I realized I *was* a businessman, I was this thing I didn't like. That was a real hard thing to say."

The Ben and Jerry's Foundation and Peace Pops — and a new venture to sell ice cream in Moscow and use the money to bring Soviets to Vermont and vice versa — is changing his attitude.

"Now my business is using its credibility and power to make our world a better place to hang out in."

Source Caitlin Kelly, "Laid-Back Firm Comes North", *The Globe and Mail*, Toronto, May, 1988.

Ben & Jerry's Homemade, Inc.
Five Year Financial Highlights
(In thousands except per share data)

Summary of Operations:

	1983	1984	1985	1986	1987
Net sales	$1,849	$4,115	$9,858	$19,954	$31,838
Cost of sales	1,239	2,949	7,321	14,144	22,486
Gross profit	610	1,166	2,537	5,810	9,352
Selling, delivery and administrative expenses	518	822	1,812	4,101	6,961
Operating income	92	344	725	1,709	2,391
Other income (expense) — net	(21)	(13)	(31)	208	305
Income before income taxes	71	331	694	1,917	2,696
Income taxes	14	118	143	901	1,251
Net income	57	213	551	1,016	1,445
Net income per common share (1)	$ .04	$ .12	$ .28	$ .40	$ .56
Average common shares outstanding (1)	1,611	1,724	1,991	2,565	2,572

Year Ended December 31

Balance Sheet Data:

	1983	1984	1985	1986	1987
Working capital	$ 57	$ 676	$ 4,955	$ 3,678	$ 3,832
Total assets	509	3,894	11,076	12,805	20,090
Long-term debt	157	2,102	2,582	2,442	8,330
Stockholders' equity (2)	154	1,068	6,683	7,758	9,231

Year Ended December 31

(1) The per share amounts and average shares outstanding have been adjusted for the effects of all stock splits, including stock splits in the form of stock dividends.
(2) No cash dividends have been declared or paid by the Company on its capital stock since the Company's organization and none are presently contemplated.

Results of Operations

The following table shows certain items as a percentage of net sales which are included in the Company's statement of income.

| | Year Ended December 31 | | |
	1985	1986	1987
Net sales	100.0%	100.0%	100.0%
Cost of sales	74.3	70.9	70.6
Gross profit	25.7	29.1	29.4
Selling, delivery and administrative expenses	18.4	20.5	21.9
Operating income	7.3	8.6	7.5
Other income (expense)	(0.3)	1.0	1.0
Income before income taxes	7.0	9.6	8.5
Federal and state income taxes	1.4	4.5	3.9
Net income	5.6%	5.1%	4.6%

For Discussion

1. One of Ben and Jerry's aims is "to help redistribute wealth". How will they try to accomplish this goal?
2. Comment on the company's joy committee. Do the employees working 12-hour days have time for joy?
3. Why might the company not practice its One Per Cent for Peace program in Canada?
4. Mr. Cohen is quoted as saying, "I didn't realize there was a different way to be a business person." Is there a conflict developing between profits (business) and ethics?
5. Review the Five Year Financial Highlights and Results of Operations. What can you deduce about the financial strength of Ben and Jerry's from this information? Calculate and interpret appropriate ratios as part of your answer to this question.

Discussion Case 14-2: Murphy Inc.

The following are condensed comparative financial statements of Murphy Inc. for the three years ended December 31, 19X5, 19X4, and 19X3.

Balance Sheets
At December 31

	19X5	19X4	19X3
CURRENT ASSETS:			
Cash	$ 21	$ 8	$ 17
Accounts Receivable — Trade	38	30	20
Merchandise Inventory	60	40	30
Prepaid Expenses	1	2	3
Total Current Assets	$120	$ 80	$ 70
Fixed Assets (net)	260	150	76
Total Assets	$380	$230	$146
CURRENT LIABILITIES:			
Accounts Payable	$ 98	$ 78	$ 48
Income Tax Payable	2	2	2
Total Current Liabilities	$100	$ 80	$ 50
Bonds Payable	50	50	–
Common Stock	200	80	80
Retained Earnings	30	20	16
Total Liabilities and Equity	$380	$230	$146

Income Statements
For the Years Ended December 31

	19X5	19X4	19X3
Sales	$210	$120	$100
Cost of Goods Sold	158	80	55
Gross Profit	$ 52	$ 40	$ 45
Operating Expenses	42	36	37
Net Income for the Year	$ 10	$ 4	$ 8

Additional information:
a. The company's accounts receivable at December 31, 19X2 totalled $20.
b. The company's merchandise inventory as at December 31, 19X2 was $20.
c. Credit terms are net 60 days from date of invoice.

For Discussion

1. What is your evaluation of
   a. The financial structure of the corporation?
   b. The proportion of shareholder and creditor claims to its assets?
   c. The structure of its short-term and long-term credit financing?

2. Evaluate the short-term solvency of the corporation.
   a. Calculate appropriate ratios for the three years.
   b. Comment on the significant features in the corporation's balance sheet and income statement that are apparent from the ratios calculated and from the financial statements themselves.

Discussion Case 14-3:   Fitz Inc. and Roy Corp.

The following are comparative financial statements of Fitz Inc. and Roy Corp for the last four years.

Balance Sheets
At December 31
(0,000s)

	Fitz Inc.				Roy Corp.			
	19X5	*19X4*	*19X3*	*19X2*	*19X5*	*19X4*	*19X3*	*19X2*
Current Assets	$185	$165	$155	$140	$480	$450	$410	$381
Current Liabilities	160	135	130	110	272	251	170	180
	$ 25	$ 30	$ 25	$ 30	$208	$199	$240	$201
Fixed Assets (net)	535	397	392	378	599	603	572	601
	$560	$427	$417	$408	$807	$802	$812	$802
Bonds Outstanding								
12% Due in 10 Years	$120	–	–	–				
15% Due in 7 Years					$400	$400	$400	$400
Share Capital								
5% Cumulative Preferred —								
200 Shares	200	$200	$200	$200	200	200	200	200
Common — 100 Shares	100	100	100	100	50	50	50	50
Retained Earnings	140	127	117	108	157	152	162	152
	$560	$427	$417	$408	$807	$802	$812	$802

Income Statements
For the Years Ended December 31
(0,000s)

	19X5	*19X4*	*19X3*	*19X2*	*19X5*	*19X4*	*19X3*	*19X2*
Sales	$600	$540	$528	$516	$330	$220	$320	$270
Cost of Sales	460	430	420	410	105	75	100	90
Gross Profit	$140	$110	$108	$106	$225	$145	$220	$180
Operating Expenses	70	50	50	50	155	155	160	156
Income (Loss) from Operations	$ 70	$ 60	$ 58	$ 56	$ 70	$(10)	$ 60	$ 24
Income Tax	35	30	29	28	30	–	30	12
Net Income (Loss) for the Year	$ 35	$ 30	$ 29	$ 28	$ 40	$(10)	$ 30	$ 12
Dividends Paid —								
Preferred	$ 10	$ 10	$ 10	$ 10	$ 20	–	$ 10	$ 10
Common	12	10	10	10	15	–	10	–

The current stock market quotations for common shares of these corporations are as follows: Fitz Inc. — $2.60; Roy Cor. — $5.00.

For Discussion

1. What is your evaluation of
   a. The financial structure of each corporation?
   b. The proportion of shareholder and creditor claims to their assets?
   c. The structure of their short-term and long-term creditor financing?
2. Evaluate the success with which each corporation is using its assets to earn net income.
   a. Calculate appropriate ratios for each corporation.

  b. Comment on the significant features in each corporation's balance sheet and income statement as are apparent from the ratios calculated and from the financial statements themselves.
3. Which corporation would be a better investment if you were planning to purchase common shares in either Fitz or Roy? Support your decision with such calculations as are necessary.

Comprehension Problems

Comprehension Problem 14-1

The following information is taken from the records of Pleasant Productions Corp.:

	19X2	19X1
CURRENT ASSETS:		
Cash	$ 10	$ 15
Temporary Investments	35	35
Accounts Receivable	200	150
Inventory	600	400
Current Liabilities	745	580

Required:
1. Calculate the current ratio for each year.
2. Calculate the acid-test ratio for both years.
3. What observations can you make from a comparison of the two ratios?

Comprehension Problem 14-2

The following information is taken from the records of Blue Co. Ltd.:

	19X3	19X2	19X1
Sales	$252	$141	$120
Gross Profit	63	48	54
Net Income	12	5	15

Required: Analyze the above data and comment on any trends you observe.

Comprehension Problem 14-3

The following information relates to three companies in the same industry:

Company	Latest Market Price	Earnings per Share	Dividends per Share
A	$35	$11	None
B	40	5	$4
C	80	10	6

Required: On the basis of only the foregoing information, which company represents the most attractive investment opportunity? Explain.

Note: Solve problems involving changing prices only if the Appendix was studied in your course.

Comprehension Problem 14-4

The following data are taken from the records of Walter Corp.:

	19X2	19X1
Sales	$2,520	$1,440
Cost of Goods Sold	1,890	960
Gross Profit	630	480
Operating Expense	510	430
Net Income	$ 120	$ 50

Required: Prepare a horizontal analysis of the above data.

Comprehension Problem 14-5

In the left-hand column, a series of transactions is listed; in the right-hand column, a series of ratios is listed.

		Effect on Ratio		
Transaction	*Ratio*	*Inc.*	*Dcr.*	*No Change*
Declaration of a cash dividend	Current Ratio			
Write-off of an uncollectible account receivable	Accounts Receivable Turnover			
Purchase of inventory on open account	Acid-Test Ratio			
Issuance of 10-year mortgage bonds	Return on Total Assets			
Issuance of additional shares of stock for cash	Equity-to-Debt Ratio			
Issue of stock dividend on common stock	Earnings per Share			
Appropriation of retained earnings	Return on Shareholders' Equity			
Purchase of supplies on open account	Current Ratio			
Payment to short-term creditor in full	Acid-Test Ratio			
Payment of accounts payable, taking the cash discount	Inventory Turnover			

For the current ratio, receivables turnover, acid-test ratio, and inventory turnover, assume that the ratio was greater than 1:1 before each transaction occurred.

Required: For each transaction indicate whether the ratio will increase, decrease, or remain unchanged.

Comprehension Problem 14-6

Consider the following financial statement data.

Balance Sheet Data

Cash	$ 20	Current Liabilities	$ 20
Accounts Receivable (net)	20	Bonds Payable (10%)	60
Merchandise Inventory	40	Common Stock (8 shares)	80
Plant (net)	140	Retained Earnings	60
	$220		$220

Income Statement Data

Sales	$100
Cost of Goods Sold	50
Gross Profit	$ 50
Operating Expenses (incl. interest)	20
Net Income before Income Tax	$ 30
Income Tax	10
Net Income	$ 20

Assume that the average of all balance sheet items is equal to the year-end figure and that all sales are on credit.

Required:
1. Calculate the following ratios:
   a. Return on total assets (assume interest has been paid)
   b. Return on shareholders' equity
   c. Times interest earned ratio
   d. Earnings per share
   e. Inventory turnover
   f. Accounts receivable collection period
   g. Sales to fixed assets ratio
   h. Current ratio
   i. Acid-test ratio
   j. Equity-to-debt ratio.
2. Which of these ratios measure short-term solvency?

Comprehension Problem 14-7

Here are the balance sheet and income statement of Riczu Limited.

Riczu Limited
Balance Sheet
At December 31, 19X2

Assets		Liabilities and Shareholders' Equity	
Cash	$ 72	Accounts Payable	$ 60
Accounts Receivable (net)	88	Bonds Payable	80
Merchandise Inventory	100	Mortgage Payable	70
Prepaid Expenses	40	Preferred Stock (10%)	60
Land	220	Common Stock	250
Building (net)	100	Retained Earnings	100
Total Assets	$620	Total Liabilities and Shareholders' Equity	$620

Riczu Limited
Income Statement
For the Year Ended December 31, 19X2

Sales		$240
Cost of Goods Sold		144
Gross Profit		$ 96
Operating Expenses:		
Salaries	$44	
Depreciation	6	
Interest	8	58
Income before Income Tax		38
Income Tax		18
Net Income		$ 20

Assume that the average of all balance sheet items is equal to the year-end figure and that all preferred dividends have been paid currently. Number of shares outstanding is 10.

1. The current ratio is (approximately)
   a. 4.33
   b. 2.66
   c. 5
   d. 2.14
   e. None of the above.

2. The return on total assets is (approximately)
   a. 6.1%
   b. 7.4%
   c. 4.8%
   d. 15.4%
   e. None of the above.

3. The inventory turnover is (approximately)
   a. 0.96
   b. 1.44
   c. 2.40
   d. 1.50
   e. None of the above.

4. The acid-test ratio is (approximately)
   a. 4.2
   b. 5
   c. 3.33
   d. 2.66
   e. None of the above.

5. The times interest earned ratio is (approximately)
   a. 5.75
   b. 4.75
   c. 2.5
   d. 7.25
   e. None of the above.

6. The earnings per share of common stock is
   a. $1.40
   b. $2.00
   c. 3.80
   d. 4.60
   e. None of the above.

7. Eighty percent of sales are on account. The accounts receivable collection period is
   a. Under 108 days
   b. Over 170 days
   c. Between 150 and 165 days
   d. Between 109 and 148 days
   e. None of the above

8. The return on shareholders' equity is (approximately)
   a. 8%
   b. 9.3%
   c. 6.4%
   d. 4.9%
   e. None of the above.

Comprehension Problem 14-8

Shareholders' equity is $140; total liabilities are $40; non-current assets are $90. The current ratio is 2.5; the acid-test ratio is 1. Total sales are $420; total credit sales are $300.

Required:
1. The current liabilities are
   a. 40
   b. 36
   c. 20
   d. 16
   e. None of the above.
2. Prepaid expenses are zero. The inventory is
   a. 70
   b. 54
   c. 90
   d. 50
   e. 74.
3. Cash and marketable securities are $6. The accounts receivable turnover is (approximately)
   a. 15
   b. 10.5
   c. 13.33
   d. 10
   e. 7.5.
4. The gross profit is 30 percent of sales. The inventory turnover is (approximately)
   a. 5.44
   b. 2.33
   c. 5.55
   d. 6
   e. 8.4.

Comprehension Problem 14-9

Required: Match the following ratios with the appropriate formula.

Ratio or Rate	Formula
_____ Acid-test ratio	a. $\dfrac{\text{Income from Operations}}{\text{Interest Expense}}$
_____ Current ratio	b. $\dfrac{\text{Shareholder's Equity}}{\text{Total Liabilities}}$
_____ Return on shareholders' equity	c. $\dfrac{\text{Net Income for the Year } - \text{ Preferred Dividend}}{\text{Number of Common Shares Outstanding}}$
_____ Times interest earned	d. $\dfrac{\text{Net Sales}}{\text{Average Net Fixed Assets}}$
_____ Earnings per share	e. $\dfrac{\text{Market Price per Share}}{\text{Earnings per Share}}$
_____ Accounts receivable turnover	f. $\dfrac{\text{Current Assets}}{\text{Current Liabilities}}$
_____ Sales to fixed assets	g. $\dfrac{\text{Average Inventory}}{\text{Cost of Goods Sold}} \times 365$
_____ Dividend yield	h. $\dfrac{\text{Net Income for the Year}}{\text{Net Sales}}$
_____ Price-to-earnings ratio	i. $\dfrac{\text{Income from Operations}}{\text{Average Total Assets}}$
_____ Inventory turnover	j. $\dfrac{\text{Net Credit Sales}}{\text{Average Accounts Receivable}}$

_____ Number of days of sales in inventory

_____ Equity-to-debt ratio

_____ Return on sales

_____ Accounts receivable collection period

_____ Return on total assets

k. $\dfrac{\text{Dividends per Share}}{\text{Market Price per Share}}$

l. $\dfrac{\text{Net Income for the Year}}{\text{Average Shareholders' Equity}}$

m. $\dfrac{\text{Quick Current Assets}}{\text{Current Liabilities}}$

n. $\dfrac{\text{Cost of Goods Sold}}{\text{Average Inventory}}$

o. $\dfrac{\text{Average Accounts Receivable}}{\text{Net Credit Sales}} \times 365$

Comprehension Problem 14-10

A company began the month of May with $200,000 of current assets, a 2.5 to 1 current ratio, and a 1.25 to 1 acid-test (quick) ratio. During the month, it completed the following transactions:

	Current Ratio		
	Increase	*Decrease*	*No Change*
Bought $20,000 of merchandise on account (the company uses a perpetual inventory system)			
Sold for $10,000 merchandise that cost $5,000			
Collected a $2,500 account receivable			
Paid a $10,000 account payable			
Wrote off a $1,500 bad debt against the allowance for doubtful accounts			
Declared a $1 per-share cash dividend on the 10 000 shares of outstanding common stock			
Paid the dividend declared above			
Borrowed $10,000 by giving the bank a 60-day, 10-percent note			
Borrowed $25,000 by placing a 10-year mortgage on the plant			
Used the $25,000 proceeds of the mortgage to buy additional machinery.			

Required:
1. Indicate the effect on current ratio.
2. At the end of May, what was
   a. The current ratio?
   b. The acid-test ratio?
   c. The working capital?

Problems

Problem 14-1

The following is the balance sheet of the Universal Corporation.

Universal Corporation
Balance Sheet
At December 31, 19X0

Assets		*Liabilities and Shareholders' Equity*	
CURRENT ASSETS:		CURRENT LIABILITIES:	
Cash	$ 100	Accounts Payable	$ 300
Accounts Receivable	200	Wages Payable	50
Merchandise Inventory	500	Dividends Payable	50
Prepaid Expenses	50	Total Current Liabilities	$ 400
Total Current Assets	$ 850	Bonds Payable	800
Fixed Assets	1,000	Total Liabilities	$1,200
		Common Stock	500
		Retained Earnings	150
		Total Liabilities and	
Total Assets	$1,850	Shareholders' Equity	$1,850

Required:
1. Based on this information, calculate the
    a. Current ratio
    b. Acid-test ratio
    c. Equity-to-debt ratio.
2. What do these ratios tell you about Universal Corporation?
3. What other financial statements are necessary to complete the analysis of Universal Corporation?

Problem 14-2

The following information for 19X2 was gathered from the financial statements of the Manticore Corporation.

Balance Sheet		**Income Statement**	
Cash	$ 60	Net Credit Sales	$800
Accounts Receivable (net)	140	Cost of Sales	600
Merchandise Inventory	250	Gross Profit	$200
Prepaid Expenses	10	Selling & Administrative Expenses	100
Fixed Assets (net)	330	Income from Operations	$100
Total Assets	$790	Interest Expense	20
		Income before Income Tax	$ 80
Accounts Payable	$100	Income Tax	30
Notes Payable (6 months)	20	Net Income	$ 50
Current Portion of Bonds Payable	60		
Bonds Payable	140		
Preferred Stock, 10% (8 shares)	120		
Common Stock (50 shares)	250		
Retained Earnings	100		
Total Liabilities and Shareholders' Equity	$790		

Additional information from the December 31, 19X1 statements:

Accounts Receivable	$180
Merchandise Inventory	200
Fixed Assets (net)	250
Retained Earnings	80

Required:
1. Compute the following ratios for 19X2:
   - a. Equity-to-debt ratio
   - b. Current ratio
   - c. Acid-test ratio
   - d. Accounts receivable collection period
   - e. Inventory turnover
   - f. Return on shareholders' equity
   - g. Earnings per share.
2. Compute dividends per share (common stock) for 19X2.
3. What do these ratios tell you about Manticore Corporation?

Problem 14-3

Goulet Corporation's books were destroyed in a fire. The comptroller of the corporation can only remember a few odd pieces of information (given below) to reconstruct the financial statements:

a. The current ratio was 3.75 to 1.
b. Sales for the year were $73,000.
c. Inventories were $20,000 and were equal to fixed assets and equal to bonds payable.
d. The accounts receivable collection period was 40 days.
e. The bonds payable was 10 times cash.
f. Total current assets were twice common stock.

Required: Using this information, prepare Goulet Corporation's balance sheet at April 30, 19X1.

Problem 14-4

You are an accountant analyzing Jupiter Corporation's income statements. The Jupiter Corporation has expanded its production facilities by 200 percent since 19X0.

Jupiter Corporation
Comparative Income Statements
For the Years Ending December 31

	19X2	19X1	19X0
Sales	$250	$150	$120
Cost of Goods Sold	190	100	60
Gross Profit	$ 60	$ 50	$ 60
Selling and Administrative Expenses	35	34	35
Net Income	$ 25	$ 16	$ 25

Required:
1. Prepare a vertical analysis of Jupiter Corporation's income statement for the three years.
2. What important inferences can be drawn from this analysis?

Problem 14-5

The incomplete balance sheet of Pan Limited is given below.

Pan Limited
Balance Sheet
At December 31, 19X1
Assets

CURRENT ASSETS:		
Cash	$ 30,000	
Accounts Receivable	?	
Merchandise Inventory	?	
Total Current Assets		$?
FIXED ASSETS:	$?	
Less: Accumulated Depreciation	100,000	?
Total Assets		$?

Liabilities and Shareholders' Equity

CURRENT LIABILITIES:		
Accounts Payable	$ 50,000	
Accrued Liabilities	?	
Total Current Liabilities		$120,000
LONG-TERM LIABILITIES:		
8% Bonds Payable		?
SHAREHOLDERS' EQUITY:		
Common Stock		?
Retained Earnings		?
Total Liabilities and Shareholders' Equity		$?

Additional information:
  a. The amount of working capital is $150,000.
  b. The par value of the stock is $10 per share.
  c. Market price per share is $15.
  d. Price-to-earnings ratio is 3.
  e. Income before payment of interest and income tax is $80,000.
  f. The ratio of shareholder's equity to total assets is 0.60 to 1.
  g. Income tax equals $30,000.
  h. The acid-test ratio is 1.5 to 1.
  i. Times interest earned is 8.

Required: Complete Pan Limited's balance sheet.

Alternate Problems

Alternate Problem 14-1

The Regina Corporation reported the following information:

Net Income	$61,200
Interest Expense	5,000
Income Tax	20,000

The Regina Corporation's balance sheet, in the shareholders' equity section, yields the following information: preferred stock ($0.12 cumulative, 10 000 shares issued and outstanding) — $20; and common stock (15 000 shares issued and outstanding) — $25. The Regina Corporation has prided itself on never missing a dividend payment. During 19X1, $5 per-share cash dividends were declared and paid to the common shareholders. Dividend yield was 27.5 percent.

Required: Determine the
1. Earnings per share
2. Dividends per share
3. Price-to-earnings ratio.

Alternate Problem 14-2

The following financial statements belong to Alamo Corporation.

Alamo Corporation
Balance Sheet
At December 31, 19X0

Assets		*Liabilities and Shareholders' Equity*	
Cash	$ 20	Accounts Payable	$ 30
Accounts Receivable	60	Wages Payable	10
Merchandise Inventory	90	Total Current Liabilities	40
Total Current Assets	$170	Bonds Payable (8%)	100
		Total Liabilities	$140
Fixed Assets (net)	110		
		Common Stock	100
		Retained Earnings	40
		Total Liabilities and	
Total Assets	$280	Shareholders' Equity	$280

Alamo Corporation
Income Statement
For the Year ended December 31, 19X0

Sales	$300
Cost of Sales	180
Gross Profit	120
Selling and Administrative Expenses	80
Net Income	$ 40

The following additional information is available:
a. Income tax was 50 percent of net income; it is included in selling and administrative expenses.
b. Beginning balances of balance sheet accounts were the same as ending balances.
c. All sales are on credit.

Required: The significance of certain ratios or tests is given below. Give the name of the corresponding ratio or test, and calculate the ratios for the Alamo Corporation.

1. Primary test for solvency
2. A more severe test of immediate solvency
3. Test of efficiency of collection
4. Indication of liquidity of inventory
5. Reflection of financial strength and cushion for creditors
6. Indication of the net productivity of each sales dollar
7. Indication of management's ability to use efficiently the resources provided.

Alternate Problem 14-3

The following financial information is available for Esquire Enterprises Limited:

a. The acid-test ratio is 1.5 to 1.
b. Accounts receivable are $3,000 and are half of the quick assets, one-third of the current assets, and twice the fixed assets.
c. Notes payable are long-term liabilities; thus are four times the dollar amount of the marketable securities.
d. Total shareholders' equity is equal to the working capital, and common stock is 150 percent of the dollar amount of the retained earnings.

Required: Using this information, prepare the balance sheet at December 31, 19X8

Alternate Problem 14-4

The following information is taken from the records of Superior Corp.

	19X3	19X2
Sales	$1,397	$1,122
Cost of Goods Sold	935	814
Selling Expenses	154	121
General Expenses	88	77
Other Revenue	4	7
Other Expenses	2	9
Income Tax	134	66

Required:
1. Prepare a vertical analysis of the income statement.
2. Indicate the favourable and unfavourable changes.

Alternate Problem 14-5

The following ratios and other data are taken from the financial statements of Mohawk Company for the year ended December 31, 19X0.

Current Ratio	1.80 to 1
Acid-Test Ratio	1.3 to 1
Net Working Capital	$40,000
Inventory Turnover	5 times
Gross Profit as a Percentage on Sales	50%
Earnings per Share	$0.25
Accounts Receivable Collection Period	73 days
Common Stock Outstanding	50 000 shares
Fixed Assets to Shareholders' Equity Ratio	0.75 to 1
Par-Value on Common Stock	$2.25

The following additional information is available: beginning balance sheet account balances equal ending balance sheet balances.

Required: Using the information given, prepare the balance sheet and income statement.

Supplementary Problems

Supplementary Problem 14-1

Selected financial information of the Huss Corporation is given below.

Huss Corporation
Balance Sheet
At December 31

Assets	19X1	19X0
Cash	$ 60	$ 10
Marketable Securities	10	20
Accounts Receivable (net)	60	40
Merchandise Inventories	108	120
Prepaid Expenses	12	10
Total Current Assets	$250	$200
Fixed Assets (net)	100	120
Land	70	60
Total Assets	$420	$380
Liabilities and Shareholders' Equity		
Accounts Payable	$100	$ 80
Accrued Liabilities	20	10
Total Current Liabilties	$120	$ 90
Bonds Payable	50	30
Total Liabilities	$170	$120
Common Stock (10 Shares)	150	150
Retained Earnings	100	110
Total Liabilities and Shareholders' Equity	$420	$380

Required:
1. Prepare a horizontal analysis of Huss Corporation, showing each individual item.
2. What are readily apparent results of 19X1 operations? Did Huss make a profit in 19X1?

Supplementary Problem 14-2

Part A

The balance sheet and income statement of Kells Inc. are given below.

Balance Sheet
At December 31, 19X8

Assets		Liabilities and Shareholders' Equity	
Cash	$ 60	Accounts Payable	$ 26
Accounts Receivable (net)	120	Notes Payable	66
Merchandise Inventory	240	Accrued Liabilities	10
Prepaid Insurance	6	Common Stock (no par-value)	300
Land	40	Retained Earnings	384
Equipment (net)	320		
Total Assets	$786	Total Liabilities and Shareholders' Equity	$786

Income Statement
For the Year Ended December 31, 19X8

Sales			$1,000
Cost of Goods Sold:			
Opening Inventory (Jan. 1)		$200	
Purchases		770	
Cost of Goods Available for Sale		$970	
Ending Inventory (Dec. 31)		240	
Total Cost of Goods Sold			730
Gross Profit			$ 270
Operating Expenses			180
Net Income for the Year			$ 90

Additional Information: No shares were issued during the year, and no dividends were paid during the year.

Required: Calculate
1. The current ratio
2. The inventory turnover ratio
3. The earnings per share
4. The return on shareholders' equity ratio.

Part B

Assume that the following unrelated transactions occurred in Kells Inc. in 19X9.

Required: Indicate the effect of each transaction on the current ratio.

	Current Ratio		
	Increase	*Decrease*	*No Change*
Additional common stock was sold for cash			
Paid $20,000 of accounts payable			
Purchased $15,000 of inventory on account			
Wrote off $2,000 of accounts receivable as uncollectible.			

Supplementary Problem 14-3

The following are condensed comparative financial statements of Achilles Corporation for the three years ended December 31, 19X2, 19X1, and 19X0.

Achilles Corporation
Comparative Balance Sheets
As at December 31

	19X2		19X1		19X0	
Current Assets						
Cash		$24		$ 9		$ 20
Accounts Receivable	$46		$37		$24	
Less: Allowance for Doubtful Accounts	1	45	1	36	—	24
Inventory		72		48		36
Prepaid Expenses		3		3		4
Total Current Assets		$144		$ 96		$ 84
Fixed Assets	$405		$234		$118	
Less: Accumulated Depreciation	93	312	54	180	27	91
Total Assets		$456		$276		$175
Current Liabilities						
Accounts Payable		$ 90		$ 72		$ 40
Accrued Liabilities		30		24		20
Total Current Liabilities		$120		$ 96		$ 60
Bonds Payable		60		60		—
Total Liabilities		$180		$156		$ 60
Shareholders' Equity						
Common Stock (no par value)		240		96		96
Retained Earnings		36		24		19
Total Liabilities and Shareholders' Equity		$456		$276		$175

Achilles Corporation
Comparative Income Statements
For the Year Ended December 31

	19X2		19X1		19X0	
Sales		$252		$144		$120
Cost of Goods Sold:						
Opening Inventory	$ 48		$ 36		$ 24	
Add: Purchases	213		108		78	
	$261		$144		$102	
Less: Ending Inventory	72		48		36	
Cost of Goods Sold		189		96		66
Gross Profit		$ 63		$ 48		$ 54
Less: Selling and Administrative Expenses		37		34		30
Net Income from Operations		$ 26		$ 14		$ 24
Interest Expense		6		6		—
Income before Income Tax		$ 20		$ 8		$ 24
Income Tax		8		3		9
Net Income		$ 12		$ 5		$ 15

Achilles Corporation
Comparative Statements of Retained Earnings
For the Year Ended December 31

	19X2	19X1	19X0
Balance, January 1	$24	$19	$12
Add: Net Income for the Year	12	5	15
	$36	$24	$27
Less: Dividend	—	—	8
Balance, December 31	$36	$24	$19

The following additional information is available:
a. All sales are on credit; credit terms are net 60 days after invoice date.
b. Twenty shares of common stock were outstanding in years 19X0 and 19X1. On January 1, 19X2, an additional 30 shares of common stock were sold for $144.
c. Opening balance of accounts receivable on January 1, 19X0 was $19.
d. Net fixed assets for January 1, 19X0 were $91.
e. Total assets on January 1, 19X0 were $165.
f. Total shareholders' equity on January 1, 19X0 was $101.

Required:
1. From the above information, calculate the following for each of the three years:
    a. Short-term solvency:
        Current ratio
        Acid-test ratio
        Accounts receivable collection period
        Number of days of sales in inventory
        Revenue operating cycle.
    b. Long-term solvency:
        Return on total assets
        Return on shareholders' equity
        Times interest earned
        Earnings per share
        Return on sales
        Equity-to-debt ratio
        Sales to fixed assets ratio.
2. Perform a short-term solvency analysis of Achilles Corporation. What conclusion can be drawn from each of the financial ratios calculated in question 1a?
3. Perform a long-term solvency analysis of Achilles Corporation. What conclusion can be drawn from each of the financial ratios calculated in question 1b? Was Achilles Corporation wise to expand operations?

Decision Problems

Decision Problem 14-1

You are the bank manager of the Royal Bank. Two companies, A and B, are seeking bank loans. You are given the following financial statements.

Assume that a fair comparison between companies A and B can be made with these data. Ignore income tax.

Balance Sheets
At December 31, 19X1

Assets	Company A	Company B	Liabilities and Shareholders' Equity	Company A	Company B
Cash	$ 80	$ 165			
Accounts Receivable (net)	125	235	Current Liabilities	$ 240	$ 300
Merchandise Inventory	480	660	Long-Term Liabilities	600	500
Total Current Assets	$ 685	$1,060	Common Stock	250	640
			Retained Earnings	100	160
Fixed Assets (net)	505	540	Total Liabilities and		
Total Assets	$1,190	$1,600	Shareholders' Equity	$1,190	$1,600

Note: Receivables and inventories are not significantly different from the balances we have at December 31, 19X0.

Income Statements
For the Year Ended December 31, 19X1

	Company A	Company B
Sales (credit)	$1,500	$900
Cost of Goods Sold	1,050	540
Gross Profit	$ 450	$360
Selling and Administrative Expenses	150	200
Income from Operations	$ 300	$160
Interest Expense	60	50
Net Income	$ 240	$110

Required:
1. From this information, calculate for each company
   a. Short-term solvency ratios:
      Current ratio
      Acid-test ratio
      Accounts receivable collection period
      Accounts receivable turnover
      Number of days of sales in inventory
      Inventory turnover.
   b. Long-term solvency ratios:
      Return on total assets
      Times interest earned
      Equity-to-debt ratio.
2. From these ratios, determine to which company you would grant a 6-month, 12-percent loan of $150 without security, and give reasons for your choice. You must choose one company.

Decision Problem 14-2

As comptroller of ICV Corporation, you have calculated the following ratios, turnovers, and percentages to enable you to answer questions the directors are likely to ask at their next meeting.

	19X2	19X1	19X0
Current Ratio	3.1 : 1	2.6 : 1	2.0 : 1
Acid-Test Ratio	0.8 : 1	1.2 : 1	1.5 : 1
Inventory Turnover	9.5 times	10.0 times	11.2 times
Accounts Receivable Turnover	7.1 times	7.5 times	7.6 times
Return on Shareholders' Equity	12.0%	13.3%	14.1%
Return on Total Assets	12.6%	12.8%	13.3%
Sales Percentage Trend	123.0	118.0	100.0
Selling Expenses to Net Sales Ratio	13.9%	13.9%	14.2%

Required:
Using these statistics, answer each question with a brief explanation to support each answer.
1. Is it becoming easier than in previous years for the company to take advantage of cash discounts?
2. Is the company collecting its accounts receivable more rapidly than before?
3. Is the company's investment in accounts receivable decreasing?
4. Is the company's investment in inventory increasing?
5. Is the shareholders' investment becoming more profitable?
6. Did the dollar amount of selling expenses decrease during the three-year period?

Decision Problem 14-3

Price-to-earnings ratios differ from firm to firm for various reasons, including differences in risk, expected rates of growth, and accounting methods used in measuring income. Selected financial information is provided below for firms A, B, and C. Assume that the firms are in the same industry, have the same expected rates of growth, and are considered to have the same investment risk.

Selected Financial Information, Firms A, B, and C

	Firm A	Firm B	Firm C
Net income applicable to common stock	$120 million	$360 million	$240 million
Shares outstanding (unchanged during the year)	30 million	90 million	60 million

Tax rate, all firms: 40%

Additional information:
1. Firm A has outstanding bonds that are convertible into 5 million common shares. If the bonds are converted, interest expense (before tax) will decline by $25 million.
2. Firm B has outstanding options that enable the holders to purchase 20 million common shares at an average price of $30 per share. B's stock is currently valued at $50 per share.
3. Firm C has convertible cumulative preferred stock with a total annual dividend requirement of $80 million. The preferred stock is convertible into 10 million shares of common stock.

Required:
1. Assume that the average firm in the industry presently has a price-to-earnings ratio of 10. What would you expect to be the appropriate market value per share of common stock for firms A, B, and C?
2. On further inquiry you learn that firm C uses LIFO inventory costing and accelerated depreciation of plant and equipment costs. Firms A and B use FIFO costing and straight-line depreciation. If C had used FIFO and straight-line depreciation, the current year's after-tax operating income would be higher by $130 million. How (if at all) does this information affect your answer to question 1?

Statement of Cash Flow

The amount of cash received and paid out during an accounting period is not shown on the balance sheet, income statement, or statement of retained earnings. This task is performed by the statement of cash flow. This chapter will answer a number of questions about statements of cash flow.

1. What information does the statement of cash flow communicate?
2. How are funds defined?
3. What kinds of transactions affect cash flow?
4. How do accountants analyze transactions when preparing a statement of cash flow?
5. How is a statement of cash flow prepared?
6. What information does the balance sheet provide for the statement of cash flow?
7. What information does the income statement provide for the statement of cash flow?
8. What advantages are there to using the T-account method?

A. Financial Statement Reporting

Cash flow is an important factor in determining the success or failure of an entity. It is quite possible for a profitable business to be short of cash. Conversely, an unprofitable business might have sufficient cash to pay its bills. Being aware of its cash flow is important for an entity when making financing decisions (should cash be borrowed?), dividend payment decisions (should dividends be paid?), and investing decisions (should machinery be purchased?). An analysis is also useful to explain why cash may have decreased, even though net income has been earned. This chapter discusses the statement of cash flow in more detail than did Chapter 1.

The financial activities of an entity are reported through four financial statements: a balance sheet, an income statement, a statement of retained earnings, and a statement of cash flow (SCF).

The balance sheet reports the financial position of a company at a particular point in time. Just as a camera takes your snapshot and records for posterity how you look today, a balance sheet records a company's asset, liability, and equity accounts as they are at the date it is prepared. The balance sheet shows the financial results of a company's activities.

The income statement reports the results of a company's operations over a particular time period — for example, a year. This statement can be compared to a movie camera, which records what takes place over a period of time. The income statement provides details of revenues (an inflow of assets or reduction in liabilities) and expenses made to earn these revenues (an outflow of assets or incurrence of liabilities). Those activities of the entity that result in a net income or net loss are reported in the income statement.

Together with the income statement, a statement of retained earnings shows the changes in retained earnings. This statement reconciles the beginning and ending balances of the Retained Earnings account. It includes the results of operations as well as dividends paid during the accounting period.

Only the statement of cash flow, also referred to as the *statement of changes in financial position* (SCFP), reveals the financing and investing activities of the entity. It is important to consider these activities when evaluating the financial position and the results of operations of a particular entity. Cash flow information is useful to management when making decisions concerning the impact of renovating fixed assets, expansion, the retirement of long-term debt, or the declaration of dividends. It is useful to other readers of financial statements when evaluating the decisions of management.

Funds (defined as cash)
Cash plus cash equivalents less short-term bank loans.

Cash equivalents
Assets that are easily converted to cash, such as marketable securities.

The statement of cash flow reveals operating, financing, and investing activities by showing the amount of **funds** an entity has. Primarily, funds consist of cash — anything the bank will accept for deposit. However, funds also include **cash equivalents** — assets that can be quickly converted into cash, such as marketable securities, treasury bills, and money market funds. Conversely, short-term bank loans are deducted from cash, since they represent an outflow of cash in the near future. Cash flow, in actuality, refers to the flow of funds, not simply of cash.

In the past, funds were defined as working capital, which is current assets less current liabilities. However, in 1986 the CICA changed to the more useful definition of funds as cash. The importance of cash flow and the contrast between the concepts of cash and working capital are discussed in Real Life Example 15-1.

Cash flow results from the operating, financing, and investing activities of an entity as funds are received and disbursed over a period of time. Because accrual accounting matches expenses with revenues, it does not reflect cash receipts and disbursements

Real Life Example 15-1

Focus on Cash

"Focus on cash, not working capital, in funds statements." . . . How are accountants to react to this advice? Is a cash-based statement of changes right for your company? Is a funds statement based on working capital wrong? How companies deal with this issue depends on professional accountants' approach to this financial reporting problem. What are the options?

You can treat the cash vs. working capital dispute as a technical accounting question, but you will be hard pressed to choose between the two fund definitions. The reasons for changing to a cash-based funds statement are not in the *CICA Handbook*. Accounting theory will not settle this controversy. . . . A statement of changes that hides serious cash-flow problems behind a mask of working capital growth does not benefit business executives or their organizations.

One doesn't have to look far to realize that the funds statement based on working capital has been judged and found wanting. "There are two kinds of funds," quips one critic, "cash and all the rest. Pay me in cash every time." Working capital flows are poor proxies for cash flows; investors want cash-flow information that is not a working capital funds statement.

Some experts believe that a cash definition of funds will restore the statement of changes. Although they are on the right track, a new funds definition is not the whole story. If you really want to improve the funds statement, you also have to upgrade the format used to present cash-flow information.

The Writing on the Wall

. . . The history of the cash vs working capital controversy can be traced back to 1975. The problem is perspective. Busy accountants are aware of the many incidents that created support for a cash-based funds statement; they just have not had the time to put the whole picture together.

The W. T. Grant Controversy

It took a major business failure to trigger serious interest in the cash-based funds statement. The 1975 W. T. Grant bankruptcy shocked investors everywhere. "With all the facts and figures churned out by Grant," declared one bitter shareholder, "where was the truth? Why couldn't we see this coming?" Analysts point an accusing finger at the working-capital-based funds statement.

Figure 1 shows that W. T. Grant's operations were users, not providers, of cash from 1966 to 1975. In the decade preceding the bankruptcy, cash provided by operations was in the black for only two years. Until collapse was imminent, however, Grant's working capital from operations remained positive and fairly stable. Grant's funds statement hid a major liquidity problem.

W. T. Grant finally choked to death on its own inventory. Its failure served notice that there is an important difference between cash flows and working capital flows.

Source Reprinted, with permission, from the (February, 1983) issue of *CAmagazine*, published by the Canadian Institute of Chartered Accountants, Toronto, Canada.

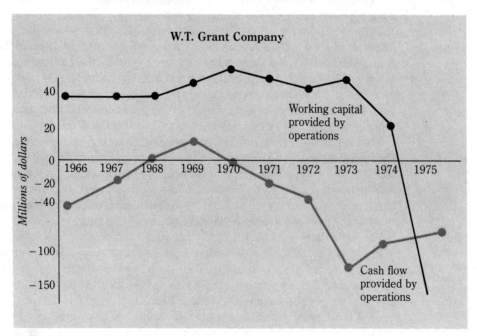

Figure 1

during the time period they were made. The statement of cash flow converts net income, the product of accrual accounting, to an increase or decrease in cash. Other titles for the statement of cash flow suggested by the *CICA Handbook* (section 1540.01) include *statement of changes in financial position, statement of operating, financing, and investing activities,* and *statement of cash resources.*

B. The Statement of Cash Flow

The statement of cash flow is classified into three sections: operations, financing activities, and investing activities. The effects of operations on cash flow are shown in detail on the statement of cash flow from operations, which is explained in Step 2 of the next section.

According to the *CICA Handbook*, cash flows from financing activities result in the change and composition of the debt and equity capital structure of the entity. This category is limited to increases and decreases in long-term liability and equity accounts. These include cash flows from the issue, assumption, redemption, and repayment of debt, and the issue, redemption, and acquisition of share capital (section 1540.15). Although there are different views concerning the disclosure of dividends, dividend outlays are considered as a financing activity for purposes of this chapter.

Cash flows from investing activities involve increases and decreases in long-term asset accounts. These include outlays for the acquisition of assets, as well as proceeds from their disposal (section 1540.16).

The analysis of cash inflows and cash outflows focuses on the Cash account and on any transactions that involve both Cash and any other balance sheet account. The following balance sheet format can be used to visualize this analysis. The bold black line separates the Cash account from all other accounts.

Balance Sheet Format

Assets	*Liabilities and Equity*
Cash	
Non-cash Current Assets	Current Liabilities
Non-current Assets	Non-current Liabilities
	Equity
	Share Capital
	Retained Earnings
	+ Revenue
	− Expenses

Any transaction that "crosses the black line" results in either a cash inflow or a cash outflow. Such transactions cause changes within the so-called *cash pool.*

Conceptual Issue 15-1

Another Look at Cash Flow

By Cornelius J. Casey, Dartmouth College
and Norman J. Bartczak, Harvard Business School

In recent years, financial analysts and investment advisory services have trumpeted the value of cash flow data in making investment decisions. It is argued that cash flow information is more objective and has greater intuitive appeal than accounting-based earnings as a measure of corporate performance.

Numerous articles in the financial press, as well as statements by the Financial Accounting Standards Board and the CICA, have touted cash flow from operations as an accurate barometer of a company's ability to withstand financial adversity.

Moreover, many analysts believe earnings data have been severely distorted by inflation during the last decade and by the creative accounting practices of some managements. A securities analyst who pierced the earnings veil of the Baldwin-United Corporation and forecast its financial collapse was praised for his studied application of its labyrinthine cash flow problems.

But perhaps surprisingly, investors who rely on cash flow data may find them more of a bane than a boon for their investment performance. A study we recently completed indicates that cash flow data do not predict a company's financial health more accurately than traditional earnings-based numbers. To the contrary, the earnings-based data significantly outperformed the cash flow information.

Our findings should jar advocates of cash flow analysis. We found that cash flow data did not predict bankruptcy as accurately as a combination of profitability, liquidity, leverage and asset turnover indexes. The sad truth is that the cash flow data did not possess even marginal value; predictive accuracy was not improved by combining cash flow with the earnings-based information.

We had expected the study results would favourably reflect the information value of the cash flow numbers. We had been seduced by an armchair theory advanced by proponents of cash flow analysis. This theory — perhaps myth is a better word — holds that businesses that generate lesser amounts of operating cash flow will find it more difficult to satisfy outstanding liabilities and, consequently, face a greater risk of failure. Our instincts proved wrong.

Analysts who accent cash flows are likely to overestimate the chances that financially sound companies will experience economic distress. As it turns out, some of these companies have relatively little debt in their capital structures and/or large reserves of cash and marketable securities. There are many such firms. ''Deep pockets'' allowed K Mart and Colgate-Palmolive, for example, to stave off financial difficulty during periods when operations were consuming more cash than they were generating.

Consider, too, high-growth companies that have difficulty generating cash flow as they build receivables and invest cash in inventories. This cash-consuming process, however, need not be the kiss of death. Companies such as Digital Equipment and Baxter-Travenol have not only survived but have prospered because of their access to the debt and equity markets. What would early investors in these companies have to show today if they had swallowed the cash flow myth?

Consider, also, companies having ''antiques in the barn'' that can be sold to cover operating cash flow shortages. For example, Pan American World Airways raised $1 billion in cash from the sale of its Pan Am Building in central Manhattan and its Intercontinental Hotel subsidiary. Another example is Kaiser Steel, which raised nearly $650 million pretax in 1980 by selling its interests in various investments. This strategy allowed Kaiser to survive long enough to be acquired. Contrast these two companies with Braniff and McLouth Steel; lacking sufficient salable capital assets, they were unable to avoid bankruptcy.

Our findings indicate that those who are surfing the cash flow wave are over-rating its value. Needless to say, we do not suggest that careful study of corporate cash flows is a useless exercise. We believe that cash flow data may provide insight in predicting not only bankruptcy but also other events, such as dividend payouts and corporate acquisitions — but only under certain conditions. Until these conditions are identified, however, cash flow analysis is best viewed as a slippery rock on which to gain a foothold for assessing company prospects, and thus its value in these other uses remains an interesting but untested hypothesis.

One such condition for establishing the value of cash flow data is suggested by a provocative study on the bankruptcy of W. T. Grant, the giant retailer that failed in 1975. That study demonstrated how careful analysis of Grant's sizeable and negative operating cash flows gave a clearer and more timely signal than either Grant's earnings-based financial data or its stock price behaviour. Grant was a mature company in the decade prior to its collapse, but had embarked on a program involving a record number of new stores. To finance this expansion, it should have been generating substantial operating cash flows. As its creditors discovered, this was not the case, and the company eventually went under.

We draw two implications, among others, from our study. First, if there is an alpha and omega for evaluating a company's future prospects, it is not to be found in cash flow data. This is especially important when current developments are enticing financial report users to weigh cash flow data even more heavily. Expanded disclosure requirements for financial reporting and the increased accessibility of computerized financial data bases might encourage analysts to simplify their information search and analysis. Also, financial reports by non–United States companies are becoming an important source of information for a growing number of American investors. Because the quality of earnings data reported by these companies frequently falls short of the standard set by American companies, we expect increased importance to be attached to the foreign concerns' cash flows.

Second, there is a major need for careful research to replace the armchair theories on the relative merits of cash flow analysis. A recent monograph by the FASB notes that surprisingly little research has been done in evaluating the usefulness of historical cash flow data for forecasting business performance.

Financial analysts and academicians owe more than intuitively appealing rules of thumb to their constituencies who engage daily in multi-billion-dollar trading activity. The time has come to devote greater research attention to exploring the value of existing financial measures than to searching for a new "bottom line". We should be able to provide investors with the steak as well as the sizzle.

Given the known limitations of earnings data, the findings of our study beg a more fundamental question. Can the serious investor/ analyst find value in pouring over companies' historical financial reports?

Source   Cornelius J. Casey and Norman J. Bartczak, "Another Look at Cash Flow". Copyright © 1984 by The New York Times Company. Reprinted by permission.

The following balance sheet and income statement of Bluebeard Computer Corporation are used in this chapter to illustrate the preparation of an SCF.

Bluebeard Computer Corporation
Comparative Balance Sheets
At December 19X8 and 19X7
(000s)

	19X8	19X7	Debit Changes	Credit Changes
Assets				
CURRENT ASSETS:				
Cash	$ 27	$ 150		$123
Marketable Securities	25	50		25
Accounts Receivable	350	400		50
Merchandise Inventory	900	450	$450	
Prepaid Expenses	20	10	10	
Total Current Assets	$1,322	$1,060		
Investments	$ 140	$ 220		80
FIXED ASSETS:				
Land	$ 70	$ 70		
Buildings	1,200	400	800	
Machinery[1]	1,000	700	300	
Accumulated Depreciation[2]	(550)	(300)		250
Total Fixed Assets	$1,720	$ 879		
Total Assets	$3,182	$2,150		
Liabilities and Shareholders' Equity				
CURRENT LIABILITIES:				
Accounts Payable	$ 235	$ 145		90
Accrued Liabilities	25	30	5	
Income Tax Payable	40	25		15
Total Current Liabilities	$ 300	$ 200		
LONG-TERM LIABILITIES:				
Mortgage Payable	$1,000	$ 500		500
SHAREHOLDERS' EQUITY:				
Common Stock	$1,210	$ 800		410
Retained Earnings[3]	672	650		22
Total Shareholders' Equity	$1,882	$1,450		
Total Liabilities and Shareholders' Equity	$3,182	$2,150		

Notes to the Balance Sheet:
1. Machinery costing $50,000 with accumulated depreciation of $10,000 was sold for $30,000 cash.
2. This item represents an increase in an asset contra account, which in turn represents a decrease in an asset account.
3. Dividends of $58,000 were declared and paid during 19X8.

Bluebeard Computer Corporation
Income Statement
For the Year Ended December 31, 19X8
(000s)

Sales		$1,200
Cost of Goods Sold		674
Gross Profit		$ 526
Operating Expenses:		
Depreciation — Buildings & Machinery	$260	
Other Expenses	200	460
		$ 66
Income from Operations:		
Gain on Sale of Long-Term Investment	$ 24	
Loss on Sale of Machinery	(10)	14
Net Income		$ 80

An SCF can be prepared from an analysis of transactions recorded in the Cash account. Rarely, however, does the reader of financial statements have access to the entity's accounting records. Therefore, accountants must show in a financial statement what inflows and outflows of cash have occurred. The following summarized transactions from the records of Bluebeard Computer Corporation form the basis of subsequent cash flow discussions in this chapter.

Transaction Number	(000s) Description of the Transaction
1	Investments costing $80 were sold for $104.
2	A building was purchased for $800 cash.
3	Machinery costing $350 was purchased for cash.
3	Machinery costing $50 and, having accumulated depreciation of $10, was sold for $30 cash.
4	Depreciation expense of $260 was recorded during the year.
5	BCC borrowed $500 cash as a mortgage payable during the year.
6	Common shares with no par-value were sold for $410 cash.
7	Retained Earnings was reduced by $58-worth of dividends declared and paid during the year.
7	Retained Earnings was increased by $80 net income for the year.

Analysis of Cash Flow

The following five steps are used in the preparation of a statement of cash flow.

Step 1   Calculate the increase or decrease in the Cash account.
Step 2   Calculate cash flow from operations; prepare a classified statement.
Step 3   Analyze the changes in Non-current Asset, Liability, and Equity accounts, and identify transactions that resulted in cash inflows and outflows.
Step 4   Analyze any current accounts not used in the measurement of income.
Step 5   Prepare a classified statement of cash flow in good form. The net increase or decrease in cash shown in the statement of cash flow must equal the amount calculated in Step 1.

Step 1   Calculation of the Increase or Decrease in Cash

The change in the Cash account for Bluebeard Computer Corporation is calculated by comparing the end-of-year balance with the beginning-of-year balance.

			Change in Cash (000s)	
			Debit Change	*Credit Change*
	19X8	19X7		
Cash	$27	$150	—	$123

Cash has decreased by $123,000 during the year. Rather than cash having been generated during the year, it has been deployed in this case, because it has decreased.

The amount of available cash is important to financial statement readers. An increase in cash is usually required for growth, since additional sales result in more receivables being financed and in a larger amount of liabilities incurred as a result of increased purchases. Excess cash is unproductive; however, inadequate cash can affect the entity's liquidity, that is, its ability to pay its debts as they become due. Cash management deals with the optimal amount of cash to be kept on hand.

In the case of BCC, the reader is faced with the following question. Is the decrease in cash a result of good cash management? Or, does it signal a liquidity problem? Also, what are the cash inflows and outflows that resulted in the $123,000 cash decrease?

Step 2   Calculation of Cash Flow from Operations

Calculating cash flow from operations is the next step in preparing a statement of cash flow. The net income of $80,000 reported on the income statement has been calculated on the basis of accrual accounting and GAAP. Accordingly, net income includes three categories of items that must be adjusted in calculating cash flow from operations: expenses and revenues not involving cash, losses and gains not due to the normal operations of the entity, and net debit and credit changes in current assets and current liability accounts.

Expenses and Revenue Not Involving Cash

Expenses and revenue not involving cash consist of non-cash amounts that were included as net income:

Debits (which reduced net income	*Credits* (which increased net income)
Depreciation Expense	
Amortization of Bond Discount	Amortization of Bond Premium

To eliminate debits, add them to net income. To eliminate credits, deduct them from net income.

Losses and Gains Not Due to Normal Operations

Losses and gains not due to normal operations do not affect cash flow. Since a loss is deducted when calculating net income, it is added back when calculating cash flow from operations. Conversely, a gain, which is added when calculating net income, is deducted from net income when calculating cash flow from operations.

Analysis of the Income Statement

Before we look at the third category of items from net income that must be adjusted when calculating cash flow, we will look at the first two categories in more detail.

On the following income statements, Basis 1, the accrual basis, shows the normal net income, which includes non-cash expense and revenue items, as well as losses and gains not due to normal operations. Basis 2 excludes these categories. Although Basis 1 reports a net income of $80,000 for the year, the amount increases to $326,000 when these items not affecting cash are eliminated.

Income Statements
(000s)

	Basis 1 (Including items that do not affect Cash)		Basis 2 (Excluding items that do not affect Cash)	
Sales		+$1,200		+$1,200
Cost of Goods Sold		− 674		− 674
Gross Profit		+$ 526		+$ 526
Operating Expenses:				
Depreciation	− $260		-0-	
Other Expenses	− 200	− 460	− $200	− 200
		+$ 66		+$ 326
Net Income from Operations:				
Gain on Sale of Investment	+ $ 24		-0-	
Loss on Sale of Machinery	− (10)	14	-0-	-0-
Net Income		+$ 80		+$ 326

The same result can be achieved by using the following calculation.

Wasting asset
A natural resource with a limited useful life.

Net Income
{
Plus
1. Depreciation of Fixed Assets
2. Depletion of **Wasting Assets**
3. Amortization of Intangible Assets (eg. patents)
4. Amortization of Bond Discount
5. Losses on Sales of Non-current Assets

Minus
1. Amortization of Bond Premium
2. Gains on Sale of Non-current Assets
}
= Partial Cash Flow from Operations

Regardless of the method used to analyze the income statement, the following partial calculation of cash flow from operations is prepared:

Partial Calculation of
Cash Flow from Operations
(000s)

Net Income		$ 80
Add: Expenses Not Reducing Cash		
Depreciation Expense	$260	
Add: Loss Not Due to Normal Operations		
Loss on Sale of Machinery	10	270
Total		$350
Less: Gain Not Due to Normal Operations		
Gain on Sale of Investment		24
Total		$326

This statement is not the final calculation of cash flow from operations. One additional category of items must be adjusted: net debit and net credit changes in current asset and current liability accounts.

Analysis of Current Accounts that Affect the Income Statement

A third category of adjustments involves the following balance sheet accounts that are used in accrual accounting:

Current Assets	Current Liabilities
Accounts Receivable (net)	Accounts Payable
Merchandise Inventory	Accrued Liabilities
Prepaid Expense	Income Tax Payable
Supplies	

These current asset and current liability accounts have off-setting expense and revenue items in the income statement that affect net income. Examples of off-setting items are sales on account and purchases on account. If cash has not yet been received or paid, the offsetting account must be omitted when calculating cash flow from operations. This is done by calculating the net debit or net credit change in the following income statement related current asset and current liability accounts as follows:

	(000s)			
Current Assets	19X8	19X7	*Debit*	*Credit*
Accounts Receivable	$350	$400		$50
Inventory	900	450	$450	
Prepaid Expenses	20	10	10	
Current Liabilities				
Accounts Payable	235	145		90
Accrued Liabilities	25	30	5	
Income Tax Payable	40	25		15

Debits are deducted from net income.	Credits are added to net income.

Add credits
subt. debits

Alternative Method of Analysis

Another way to calculate cash flow from operations is to add net credit changes and subtract net debit changes as follows:

Bluebeard Computer Corporation
Cash Flow from Operations
For the year ended December 31, 19X8
(000s)

Net Income			$ 80
Add:	Expenses Not Reducing Cash		
	Depreciation Expense	$260	
Add:	Loss Not Due to Normal Operations		
	Loss on Sale of Machinery	10	
Add:	Net Credit Change in Current Accounts		
	Decrease in Accounts Receivable	50	
	Increase in Accounts Payable	90	
	Increase in Income Tax	15	425
	Total		$505
Less:	Gain Not Due to Normal Operations		
	Gain on Sale of Investment	$ 24	
	Net Debit Changes in Current Accounts		
	Increase in Inventory	450	
	Increase in Prepaid Expenses	10	
	Decrease in Accrued Liabilities	5	489
Cash Flow from Operations			$ 16

(handwritten annotation: "added if decreased")

Step 3 Analysis of Changes in Non-current Accounts

Step 3 is to analyze the cash inflows and outflows included in non-current account transactions. The transactions involving these accounts were introduced earlier in the chapter; they are reproduced here for your convenience.

Transaction Number	(000s) Description of the Transaction
1	Investments costing $80 were sold for $104.
2	A building was purchased for $800 cash.
3	Machinery costing $350 was purchased for cash.
3	Machinery costing $50, having accumulated depreciation of $10, was sold for $30 cash.
4	Depreciation expense of $260 was recorded during the year.
5	BCC borrowed $500 cash as a mortgage payable during the year.
6	Common shares with no par-value were sold for $410 cash.
7	Retained Earnings was reduced by $58-worth of dividends declared and paid during the year.
7	Retained Earnings was increased by $80 net income for the year.

The impact of these transactions on cash is calculated by reconstructing the journal entry for each transaction. Note that the effects on net income (covered in Step 2) is also indicated. Although these changes have already been identified from the income statement analysis, their recalculation double checks that they have all been identified. Note also that the type of activity — operating, financing, or investing — is also indicated.

(000s)	Original Journal Entry			Effect on Cash		Effect on Net Income		Type of Activity
				Debit	Credit	Debit	Credit	
Transaction 1								
Investments costing $80 were sold for $104.	Cash	104,000		104,000				
	Investments		80,000					
	Gain on Sale		24,000					Investing
							24,000	Operating
Transaction 2								
A building was purchased for $800 cash.	Building	800,000						
	Cash		800,000		800,000			Investing
Transaction 3								
Machinery costing $350 was purchased for cash.	Machinery	350,000						Investing
	Cash		350,000		350,000			
Transaction 3								
Machinery costing $50, having accumulated depreciation of $10, was sold for $30 cash.	Cash	30,000		30,000				Investing (net)
	Accumulated Depreciation	10,000						
	Loss on Disposal	10,000				10,000		Operating
	Machinery		50,000					
Transaction 4								
Depreciation expense of $260 was recorded during the year.	Depreciation Expense	260,000		—		260,000		Operating
	Accumulated Depreciation		260,000		—			Not a cash item (see operating)
Transaction 5								
BCC borrowed $500 cash as a mortgage payable during the year.	Cash	500,000		500,000				Financing
	Mortgage Payable		500,000					
Transaction 6								
Common shares with no par-value were sold for $410 cash.	Cash	410,000		410,000				Financing
	Common Shares		410,000					
Transaction 7a								
Retained Earnings was reduced by $58-worth of dividends declared and paid during the year.	Dividends	58,000				58,000		Financing
	Cash		58,000					
Transaction 7b								
Retained Earnings was increased by $80 net income for the year.	Income Summary	80,000		Refer to Cash Flow from Operations on page 691				Operating
	Retained Earnings		80,000					

Step 4 Analysis of Current Accounts Not Used in the Measurement of Income

The analysis of current accounts in Step 2 focused only on those current accounts that affected the income statement. Current accounts that do not affect the income statement include the current asset, Marketable Securities, and the current liabilities, Dividends Payable and the current portion of long-term debt. These current accounts must be analyzed before the statement of cash flow is complete.

(000s)

	Current Assets				Current Liabilities		
	19X8	19X7	↑or↓		19X8	19X7	↑or↓
Marketable Securities	$25	$50	↓$25	Dividends Payable	–	–	–
				Current Portion of Long-Term Debt	–	–	–

Here, cash flows were increased by the decrease in Marketable Securities so that they are included in the SCF. Since dividends declared during the year were paid, Cash was decreased by the amount of these dividends. There is no change to cash flows resulting from dividends declared but unpaid. Dividends declared but unpaid would be excluded from the SCF.

The decrease of $25,000 in Marketable Securities is reported under the investing classification in the SCF.

Step 5 Preparation of the Formal Statement of Cash Flow

On the basis of the analysis of balance sheet accounts (including the cash flow from operations), the formal statement of cash flow can now be prepared.

Note that this is a classified statement of cash flow. The data is organized according to the following categories:

1. **Operations of the entity**
The details of this amount are found in the statement of cash flow from operations.

2. **Financing activities of the entity**
This category is limited to changes in long-term liability and equity accounts. Both increases and decreases in these accounts are listed.

3. **Investing activities of the entity**
This category contains information applicable to long-term asset accounts. Both increases and decreases in these accounts are identified.

Bluebeard Computer Corporation
Statement of Cash Flow
For the Year Ended December 31, 19X8

(000s)

CASH FLOW GENERATED (deployed):			
From Operations			$ 16
Financing:			
Increase in Mortgage		$ 500	
Issue of Common Stock		410	
Total		$ 910	
Payment of Dividends		(58)	852
			$ 868
Investing:			
Disposal of Marketable Securities		$ 25	
Sale of Investments		104	
Sale of Machinery		30	
Total		$ 159	
Purchase of Building	$(800)		
Purchase of Machinery	(350)	(1,150)	
			(991)
Net Cash Generated (Deployed)			$(123)

Non-cash Financing and Investing Activities

Significant financing and investing activities that do not affect cash are also included in the statement of cash flow. For example, assume that in addition to the transactions described earlier, BCC had also purchased additional land (an investing activity) through the issue of common stock (a financing activity). Although no cash was involved and common stock was issued directly to the owners of the land, the transaction would have to be disclosed as both an investing and financing activity on the statement of cash flow.

C.   The T-Account Method

Although in simple situations, the statement of cash flow can be prepared as shown in section B, the numerous transactions involved in actual practice necessitate a systematic approach. The T-account method is suitable for preparing more complex statements of cash flow. This method requires that a T-account indicating the net change be set up for each asset, liability, and equity account. In this section, the T-account method is explained, using the financial statements of Bluebeard Computer Corporation that were introduced earlier in the chapter.

The preparation of a statement of cash flow using T-accounts is similar to that discussed previously, although we identify seven individual steps instead of five:

Step 1   Calculate the net debit and net credit change for every account on the balance sheet.

Step 2   Set up T-accounts for each account on the balance sheet that has a change. Record the net debit or net credit change in each T-account, drawing a line under the amount, across both sides of the T-account. Set up a special T-account called Cash Flow from Operations.

Step 3   Analyze the change in each current asset and liability account that affects the income statement (i.e., that is used in the measurement of income under accrual accounting).

Step 4   Analyze the change in each current asset and liability account that does not affect the income statement (i.e., that is not used in the measurement of income under accrual accounting).

Step 5   Analyze each non-current account, reconstructing the debit or credit change during the year.

Step 6   Prepare a statement of cash flow from operations.

Step 7   Prepare a formal statement of cash flow.

Step 1   Calculation of Changes

Calculate the net debit and net credit changes for every account on the balance sheet. This step has already been done for you on the comparative balance sheets for Bluebeard Computer Corporation on page 686. Recalculate the amounts to assure yourself that they are accurate. Notice that the change in Cash is $123,000.

Step 2 Set Up T-Accounts

Set up T-accounts for each account reported in the balance sheet, and record the net debit change or credit change in each T-account. The T-accounts are only used to prepare the statement of cash flow; they are not part of the general ledger. Under the amount, draw a line, as illustrated below. The T-account for Cash follows:

Cash
| | Credit |
| | Change   123,000 |

Note that the $123,000 net credit change is recorded in the credit side of the account. In the next step, we will analyze the balance sheet accounts and record the appropriate reconstructed amounts below this line.

Set up a special T-account called Cash Flow from Operations. No entry is made in this account at this time, and no line is required.

Cash Flow from Operations

Step 3 Analysis of Changes in Current Accounts

Analyze the change in each current asset and current liability account that affects the income statement. The following accounts are used in accrual accounting to measure income, and they have a net debit or net credit change at the end of 19X8.

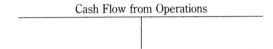

Accounts Receivable
| | Credit |
| | Change   50,000 |

Accounts Payable
| | Credit |
| | Change   90,000 |

Merchandise Inventory
| Debit | |
| Change 450,000 | |

Accrued Liabilities
| Debit | |
| Change   5,000 | |

Prepaid Expenses
| Debit | |
| Change   10,000 | |

Income Tax Payable
| | Credit |
| | Change   15,000 |

We must account for these net debit and net credit changes as they affect cash flow. This analysis is facilitated because these accounts show net changes, rather than listing each transaction posted during the year.

Since these accounts affect the income statement, they go into the calculation of Cash Flow from Operations. For example, Accounts Receivable shows a net credit change of $50,000, which is offset by a debit of $50,000 to the Cash Flow from

Operations T-account. Although we do not have access to all the journal entries posted to the Accounts Receivable account during the year, we can reconstruct a journal entry using the net balance:

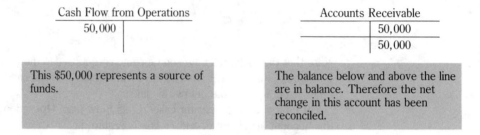

a. Cash Flow from Operations	50,000
    Accounts Receivable	50,000

This T-account journal entry is then posted to the T-accounts below:

Cash Flow from Operations		Accounts Receivable	
50,000			50,000
			50,000

This $50,000 represents a source of funds.

The balance below and above the line are in balance. Therefore the net change in this account has been reconciled.

In a similar fashion, T-account journal entries for the remaining accounts are prepared and posted to the T-accounts:

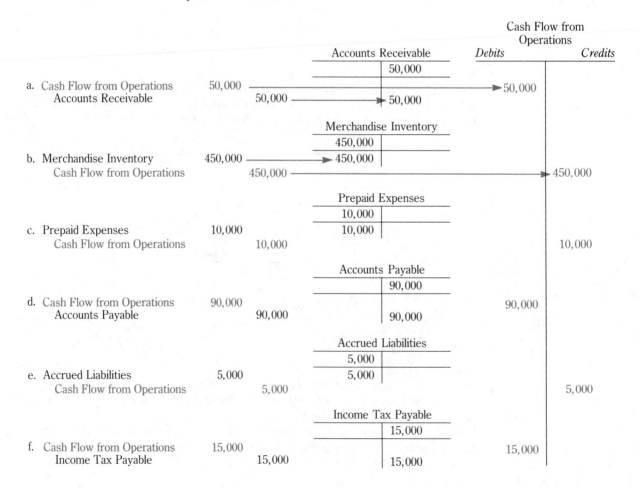

			Accounts Receivable		Cash Flow from Operations	
					Debits	Credits
				50,000		
a.	Cash Flow from Operations	50,000			50,000	
	Accounts Receivable		50,000	50,000		
			Merchandise Inventory			
			450,000			
b.	Merchandise Inventory	450,000	450,000			
	Cash Flow from Operations		450,000			450,000
			Prepaid Expenses			
			10,000			
c.	Prepaid Expenses	10,000	10,000			
	Cash Flow from Operations		10,000			10,000
			Accounts Payable			
				90,000		
d.	Cash Flow from Operations	90,000			90,000	
	Accounts Payable		90,000	90,000		
			Accrued Liabilities			
				5,000		
e.	Accrued Liabilities	5,000		5,000		
	Cash Flow from Operations		5,000			5,000
			Income Tax Payable			
				15,000		
f.	Cash Flow from Operations	15,000			15,000	
	Income Tax Payable		15,000	15,000		

The Cash Flow from Operations account now appears as follows:

Cash Flow from Operations (000s)			
(a) Decrease in Accounts Receivable	50,000	(b) Increase in Merchandise Inventory	450,000
(d) Increase in Accounts Payable	90,000	(c) Increase in Prepaid Expenses	10,000
(f) Decrease in Income Tax Payable	15,000	(e) Decrease in Accrued Liabilities	5,000
	155,000		465,000

Step 4 Analysis of Changes in Current Accounts that Do Not Affect the Income Statement

The analysis so far has focused only on those current accounts that affect the income statement. There are, however, other current accounts that do not interact with the income statement. These include Marketable Securities (a current asset), and Dividends Payable (a current liability), and the current portion of long-term debt. These current accounts must be analyzed before the statement of cash flow can be prepared.

Bluebeard Computer Corporation's Marketable Securities account showed a credit change during the year:

	19X8	19X7	Credit Change
Marketable Securities	$25,000	$50,000	$25,000

This credit change resulted from the disbursement of marketable securities during the year. The original journal entry, the T-account entry, and the T-accounts for these transactions are shown below:

Original Journal Entry:

Cash   25,000
    Marketable Securities   25,000

T-Account Entry:

Cash   25,000
    Marketable Securities   25,000

Cash	
	123,000
(g) 25,000	

Marketable Securities	
	25,000
	(g) 25,000

The increase in cash amounted to $25,000.

Since the balance below the line is the same as above, we know that an increase in cash resulted from the sale of marketable securities.

Note 3 to the balance sheet indicates that dividends of $58,000 were declared and paid during the year. This transaction resulted in a cash decrease. It will be further discussed as part of transaction 7a. Note that cash flow does not change when dividends have been declared but are not yet paid; these unpaid dividends are excluded from the SCF.

Step 5   Analysis of Non-current Accounts

Analyze each non-current account to reconstruct its net debit or credit change during the year. First, make a T-account for each account:

Non-current Assets	**Non-current Liabilities**	**Non-current Equities**

Investments

	Credit Change 80,000

Land

-0-	-0-

Buildings

Debit Change 800,000	

Machinery

Debit Change 300,000	

Accumulated Depreciation

	Credit Change 250,000

Mortgage Payable

	Credit Change 500,000

Common Stock

	Credit Change 410,000

Retained Earnings

	Credit Change 22,000

A T-account has been prepared for Land even though there has been no net change because two offsetting changes may have occurred during the year. Usually a T-account is not made for accounts that show no net change during the year.

Next, the T-account entries are made and each account is analyzed. Changes are posted to the Cash Flow from Operations T-account.

Transaction 1:

The asset account, Investments, is the first non-current account on the balance sheet.

	19X8	19X7	*Credit Change*
Investments	$140,000	$220,000	$80,000

This $80,000 decrease resulted from the sale of investments during the year. The original journal entry is shown again below to help you understand the T-account entry. This transaction provided cash for the company and, therefore, the Cash account is debited (*a debit to this account records an increase, or source, of cash*). This accounts for part of the increase in Cash in 19X8.

The Investments account is credited because the asset was decreased by the sale and Cash Flow from Operations is credited because the gain appears on the income statement.

	Original Journal Entry:			*T-Account Entry:*	
Cash	104,000		Cash	104,000	
Investments		80,000	Investments		80,000
Gain on Sale		24,000	Cash Flow from Operations		24,000

Cash			Investments			Cash Flow from Operations	
	123,000			80,000			
(1) 104,000			(1) 80,000				(1) 24,000

The increase in cash from the sale of investments amounted to $104,000.	Since the balance below the line is the same as above the line, it is known that the increase in cash resulted from this sale of investments.	The effect on cash flow from operations is recorded in this account.

Transaction 2:

The asset account, Land, is the next non-current account on the balance sheet requiring analysis.

	19X8	19X7	*No Change*
Land	$70,000	$70,000	—

As can be seen, there is no change in the amount between 19X7 and 19X8. This does not necessarily mean that no transactions took place during the year, but it can be assumed that none did. Therefore, the non-current Building account is the next to be considered.

	19X8	19X7	*Debit Change*
Building	$1,200,000	$400,000	$800,000

This $800,000 increase resulted from a purchase made during the year. The purchase represented a use of cash. The T-account entry for the building purchase is posted:

	Original Journal Entry:			*T-Account Entry:*	
Building	800,000		Building	800,000	
Cash		800,000	Cash		800,000

Building			Cash	
800,000				123,000
(2) 800,000				(2) 800,000

Since the balance below the line is the same as that above the line it is known that a decrease in cash resulted from this purchase of a building.	The decrease in cash from the purchase of a building amounted to $800,000.

Transactions 3a and 3b:
Machinery is the next non-current account to be analyzed.

	19X8	19X7	Debit Change
Machinery	$1,000,000	$700,000	$300,000

a. Note 2 to the balance sheets indicated that machinery costing $50,000 and having accumulated depreciation of $10,000 was sold for $30,000 cash. The original recording of this transaction and its reconstruction are shown below.

Original Journal Entry:			*T-Account Entry:*	
Cash	30,000		Cash	30,000
Accumulated Depreciation	10,000		Accumulated Depreciation	10,000
Loss on Sale	10,000		Cash Flow from Operations	10,000
Machinery		50,000	Machinery	50,000

This sale provided a $30,000 source of funds and, therefore, the Cash account is debited. Accumulated Depreciation is also debited, because the accumulated depreciation applicable to the sold machinery has to be removed. Machinery is credited to remove the cost of machinery from the accounts; the loss on sale is debited to Cash Flow from Operations because the loss appears on the income statement.

Cash		Accumulated Depreciation		Cash Flow from Operations		Machinery	
	123,000		250,000			300,000	
(3) 30,000		(3) 10,000		(3) 10,000			(3) 50,000

An increase in cash is recorded as a debit.

The balance in this account is considered in the next transaction (4).

The effect on cash provided by operations is recorded in this account.

The balance below the line is not the same as above the line; an additional transaction for $350,000 was recorded.

b. Machinery costing $350,000 was purchased for cash. The original recording of this transaction and its reconstruction are shown below. This $350,000 purchase of machinery represents a use of cash. Therefore Cash is credited.

Original Journal Entry:			*T-Account Entry:*	
Machinery	350,000		Machinery	350,000
Cash		350,000	Cash	350,000

Machinery		Cash	
300,000			123,000
	(3) 50,000	(3) 30,000	
(3) 350,000			(3) 350,000
300,000			

The balance above and below are now the same.

A decrease in cash is recorded as a credit.

Transaction 4:
Accumulated Depreciation is the next non-current account to be analyzed.

	19X8	19X7	Credit Change
Accumulated Depreciation	$(550,000)	$(300,000)	$(250,000)

According to the income statement, depreciation expense amounting to $260,000 was recorded during the year. The original journal entry and its reconstruction are shown below.

Original Journal Entry:			*T-Account Entry:*	
Depreciation Expense	260,000		Cash Flow from Operations	260,000
Accumulated Depreciation		260,000	Accumulated Depreciation	260,000

Depreciation expense is an item that appears on the income statement and, therefore, the Cash Flow from Operations account is debited.

Cash Flow from Operations	
(4) 260,000	

The effect on cash provided by operations is recorded in this account.

Accumulated Depreciation	
	250,000
(3) 10,000	
	(4) 260,000
	250,000

Since the balance below the line agrees with the balance above the line, all transactions in this account have been analyzed.

Transaction 5:
Mortgage Payable, a non-current liability account, is analyzed next.

	19X8	19X7	Credit Change
Mortgage Payable	$1,000,000	$500,000	$500,000

A $500,000 mortgage payment was made during the year. The original journal entry and its reconstruction are shown below. The mortgage increase is a source of cash; therefore, Cash is debited. Mortgage Payable is credited to record the liability in the company's records. The T-account entry is posted.

Original Journal Entry:			*T-Account Entry:*	
Cash	500,000		Cash	500,000
Mortgage Payable		500,000	Mortgage Payable	500,000

Cash	
	123,000
(5) 500,000	

An increase in cash is recorded by a debit.

Mortgage Payable	
	500,000
	(5) 500,000

Since the balances below and above the line are the same, all transactions in this account have been analyzed.

Transaction 6:

Common Stock is analyzed next.

	19X8	19X7	Credit Change
Common Stock	$1,210,000	$800,000	$410,000

Common shares with no par-value were sold for $410,000. The original journal entry and its reconstruction are shown below. The sale of common shares provided a source of cash and, therefore, Cash is debited. Common Stock is credited to record the sale. The T-account is posted.

Original Journal Entry:			T-Account Entry:	
Cash	410,000		Cash	410,000
Common Stock		410,000	Common Stock	410,000

Cash	
	123,000
(6) 410,000	

Common Stock	
	410,000
	(6) 410,000

An increase in cash is recorded by a debit.

The balances below and above the line are the same; therefore all transactions in these accounts have been analyzed.

Transaction 7a and 7b:

Retained Earnings is the last non-current account on the balance sheet to be analyzed.

	19X8	19X7	Credit Change
Retained Earnings	$672,000	$650,000	$22,000

a. Note 3 of the balance sheets indicated that dividends of $58,000 were declared and paid at the end of the year. The original journal entry to record this dividend declaration and payment and its reconstruction are reproduced below. The declaration and payment of dividends decreases cash and therefore is a use of cash. The Dividends account is closed to Retained Earnings at year-end, thereby decreasing this non-current equity account. The T-account entry is posted.

Original Journal Entry:			T-Account Entry:	
Dividends	58,000		Dividends	58,000
Cash		58,000	Cash	58,000

Retained Earnings	
	22,000
(7) 58,000	

Cash	
	123,000
	(7) 58,000

The balance below the line is not the same as the balance above the line; an additional transaction remains to be analyzed.

A decrease in cash is recorded as a credit.

b. Net Income for the year is $80,000. The original entry recording Net Income in Retained Earnings was made by means of a closing entry. The original closing entry and its reconstruction are shown below. Net income is recorded in Cash Flow from Operations because it comes from the income statement; Retained Earnings is credited because net income increases this account.

Original Journal Entry:

Income Summary	80,000	
Retained Earnings		80,000

T-Account Entry:

Cash Flow from Operations	80,000	
Retained Earnings		80,000

Cash Flow from Operations

(7) 80,000	

Retained Earnings

	22,000
(7) 58,000	
	(7) 80,000
	22,000

The effect on cash flow from operations is recorded in this account.	The balances below and above the line are now the same; therefore all transactions affecting this account have been analyzed.

Step 6   Preparation of a Statement of Cash Flow from Operations

The data recorded in the following T-account shows the following:

Sources of Cash	$505,000
Uses of Cash	489,000
Increase in Cash	$ 16,000

Cash Flow from Operations

(a) Decrease in Accounts Receivable	50,000	(b) Increase in Merchandise Inventory	450,000
(d) Increase in Accounts Payable	90,000	(c) Increase in Prepaid Expenses	10,000
(f) Increase in Income Tax Payable	15,000	(e) Decrease in Accrued Liabilities	5,000
	155,000		465,000
(3) Loss on sale of machinery	10,000	(1) Gain on sale of investments	24,000
(4) Depreciation expense	260,000		
(7) Net income	80,000		24,000
	350,000		489,000
		(8) Cash flow from operations	16,000
	505,000		505,000

Note that entry (8), an adjustment similar to a closing entry, is made to transfer the $16,000 increase in cash to the Cash account.

(8) Cash	16,000	
Cash Flow from Operations		16,000

The following statement of cash flow from operations is now prepared from the data in the preceding account.

Bluebeard Computer Corporation
Statement of Cash Flow from Operations
For the Year Ended December 31, 19X8
(000s)

CASH FLOW FROM OPERATIONS:		
Net Income		$ 80
Add: Deductions Not Decreasing Cash during the Year		
Depreciation Expense	$260	
Decrease in Accounts Receivable	50	
Increase in Accounts Payable	90	
Increase in Income Tax Payable	15	
	$415	
Add: Loss Not Due to Normal Operations		
Loss on Sale of Machinery	10	
Total		425
		$505
Less: Additions Not Increasing Cash during the Year		
Increase in Merchandise Inventory	$450	
Increase in Prepaid Expenses	10	
Decrease in Accrued Liabilities	5	
	$465	
Less: Gain Not Due to Normal Operations		
Gain on Sale of Investment	24	
Total		489
Cash Flow from Operations		$ 16

Step 7   Preparation of a Statement of Cash Flow

After adjustment (8) has been recorded, the Cash balance is calculated to make sure that the cash decrease of $123,000 has been reconciled. Note that the credit change of $123,000 balances with the $123,000 change during the year.

Cash

		Credit change		123,000
(g) Disposal of marketable securities	25,000			
(1) Sale of investments	104,000	(2) Purchase of building		800,000
(3) Sale of machinery	30,000	(3) Purchase of machinery		350,000
(5) Increase in mortgage	500,000	(7) Payment of dividends		58,000
(6) Issue of common stock	410,000			
(8) Cash flow from operations	16,000			
	1,085,000			1,208,000
		Balance		123,000

The Cash T-account now contains all the information needed to prepare the statement of cash flow:

Bluebeard Computer Corporation
Statement of Cash Flow
For the Year Ended December 31, 19X8

(000s)

CASH FLOW GENERATED (deployed):			
From Operations			$ 16
Financing:			
Increase in Mortgage		$ 500	
Issue of Common Stock		410	
Total		$ 910	
Payment of Dividends		(58)	852
			$ 868
Investing:			
Disposal of Marketable Securities		$ 25	
Sale of Investments		104	
Sale of Machinery		30	
Total		$ 159	
Purchase of Building	$(800)		
Purchase of Machinery	(350)	(1,150)	
			(991)
Net Cash Generated (Deployed)			$(123)

┌─ A S S I G N M E N T   M A T E R I A L S ─┐

Discussion Questions

1. Using an example, explain in your own words the function of a statement of cash flow. Why is it prepared? What does it communicate to the reader of financial statements? What is its advantage over a balance sheet?

2. Why are financing and investing activities of a corporation important to financial statement readers?

3. Explain in your own words how an increase in accounts receivable during the year affects the cash flow from operations? a decrease in accounts receivable?

4. Is a statement of cash flow really only a summary of cash receipts and disbursements recorded in the corporation's Cash account?

5. What effect does the declaration of a cash dividend have on cash flow? the payment of a dividend declared and paid during the current year? the payment of a dividend declared in the preceding year?

6. Why does an increase or a decrease in the Marketable Securities account not affect the amount of cash provided by operations?

7. Why is it possible that cash may have decreased during the year, even though there has been a substantial net income during the same period?

8. Why does the net income for the year usually differ from the increase (decrease) in cash flow for the same year? What causes the difference?

9. What causes cash to be depleted? Give actual examples of items that cause an outflow of cash.

10. Indicate the main items that use cash. Explain how balance sheet items are analyzed to identify the uses that have occurred during the year.

11. The T-account method is often used for instructional purposes in illustrating the preparation of an SCF. How does the T-account method work?

12. What is the basic format of an SCF? Prepare a model format.

Discussion Cases

Discussion Case 15-1:   Ben & Jerry's SCFP

Ben & Jerry's Homemade, Inc.
Statement of Changes in Financial Position

	Years Ended December 31,		
	1987	**1986**	**1985**
Cash provided by operations:			
Net income	$1,444,538	$1,016,375	$ 550,625
Add charges not affecting working capital:			
Depreciation	751,248	566,227	251,006
Deferred income taxes	108,000	97,000	48,000
Amortization and reduction of unearned compensation	62,020	58,118	
Loss on disposition of assets	23,341		72,442
	2,389,147	1,737,720	922,073
Cash provided (used) by working capital:			
Accounts receivable	(1,271,447)	(817,039)	(430,684)
Income taxes	(730,091)	744,746	(154,749)
Inventories	(403,701)	(628,890)	(372,653)
Prepaid expenses	14,484	(5,824)	(16,958)
Accrued royalties		(33,820)	(18,180)
Accounts payable	25,586	(462,574)	1,010,393
Accrued payroll and related costs	42,947	159,546	18,336
Accrued expenses	25,940	196,360	23,264
Deferred revenue	120,000		
Franchise deposits	298,750	156,850	31,100
	(1,877,532)	(690,645)	89,869
Cash provided by operations	511,615	1,047,075	1,011,942
Cash provided (used) by investing activities:			
Additions to property, plant and equipment	(2,917,442)	(2,876,768)	(3,504,865)
(Increase) decrease in other assets	(703,422)	2,324	(3,548)
Proceeds from sale of assets	11,000		19,417
Construction funds	(4,600,000)		1,322,759
	(8,209,864)	(2,874,444)	(2,166,237)
Cash provided (used) by financing activities:			
Repayment of long-term debt	(138,994)	(134,113)	(74,212)
Increase in long-term debt	6,036,525		613,475
Proceeds from issuance of preferred stock			9,000
Proceeds from issuance of common stock		161,438	5,850,000
Issuance costs of common stock including underwriter discounts			(794,393)
Purchase of treasury stock	(24,342)		
Unearned compensation		(161,438)	
Purchase of fractional shares	(8,779)		
	5,864,410	(134,113)	5,603,870
Increase (decrease) in cash and cash equivalents and certificates of deposit	(1,833,839)	(1,961,482)	4,449,575
Cash and cash equivalents and certificates of deposit at beginning of period	3,399,921	5,361,403	911,828
Cash and cash equivalents and certificates of deposit at end of period	$1,566,082	$3,399,921	$5,361,403

Source   From the Annual Report for the Year Ended
December 31, 1987, Reprinted with permission.

For Discussion

1. In 1986 and 1987, cash, cash equivalents, and certificates of deposit decreased. Does Ben & Jerry's have a problem with cash flow?
2. How is Ben & Jerry's using most of its cash?
3. Review the cash provided by operations section of the SCFP. (Prepare a separate statement of cash from operations similar to that shown on p. 704.)
4. Evaluate the company in terms of operations, investing activities, and financing activities.

Discussion Case 15-2:   Majestic Contractors Limited

Majestic Contractors Limited
Consolidated Statement of Changes in Cash Resources
For The Three Months Ended March 31, 1987
(with the three months ended March 31, 1986 for comparison)
(unaudited)

	1987	1986
Operating Activities:		
Net income (loss)	$ 663,000	$ (394,000)
Add (deduct) items not involving cash:		
Depreciation and amortization	245,000	533,000
Deferred income taxes	(486,000)	(209,000)
Loss (gain) on sale of equipment	(1,901,000)	(3,000)
	(1,479,000)	(73,000)
Net change in non-cash working capital balances related to operating activities	1,398,000	1,583,000
Cash used for operating activities	(81,000)	1,510,000
Financing Activities:		
Purchase of shares	(37,000)	—
Other	—	7,000
Cash provided by (used for) financing activities	(37,000)	7,000
Investing Activities:		
Additions to property and equipment	(4,000)	(7,000)
Proceeds from sale of equipment	1,198,000	4,000
Reclassification of assets held for resale	2,931,000	—
Cash provided by (used for) investing activities	4,125,000	(3,000)
Increase in cash	4,007,000	1,514,000
Cash, beginning of period	14,733,000	14,878,000
Cash, end of period	$18,740,000	$16,392,000

Source   From the Quarterly Report dated March 31, 1987.
Reprinted with permission.

For Discussion

1. How much did Cash increase over 1986 and 1987? What is the Cash balance at the end of each year?
2. Evaluate operations, financing activities, and investing activities separately. What information can you gather from the statement to give an assessment of this entity's activities? Where is Majestic's cash coming from? Where is it going? Is the company in a good or a bad situation?

Discussion Case 15-3: Varity Corporation

Varity Corporation
Consolidated Statements of Changes in Financial Position
(Millions of U.S. dollars)
Years Ended December 31,

	1989	1988	1987
Cash provided by operations:			
Net income (loss)	$ 81.7	$ 4.5	$(23.3)
Add (deduct) items not affecting working capital:			
Extraordinary items	(28.5)	46.1	
Deferred income taxes	34.9	16.8	
Depreciation and amortization	75.2	68.0	33.9
Gain on sale of assets	(25.8)	(64.4)	(13.3)
Excess (deficiency) of dividends received over equity in earnings			
of finance subsidiaries	21.8	(4.1)	(8.4)
Exchange adjustments and other	(3.8)	9.8	10.5
Working capital provided by (used in) operations	155.5	76.7	(0.6)
Net change in non-cash working capital balances:			
Decrease (increase) in receivables	(1.1)	(9.8)	12.8
Increase in inventories	(27.3)	(4.7)	(10.5)
Decrease (increase) in prepaid expenses	(3.6)	(6.0)	5.3
Increase in accounts payable and accruals	73.5	90.4	35.6
Foreign currency translation adjustment to net current assets	12.8	9.9	9.4
Cash provided by operations	209.8	156.5	52.0
Cash provided by (used for) investment activities:			
Additions to fixed assets	(45.3)	(46.4)	(64.4)
Proceeds from sale of fixed assets	36.3	78.9	19.6
Additions to investments	(2.2)	(7.5)	(5.3)
Proceeds from disposal of investments		12.0	9.9
Disposition of businesses	35.8		
Acquisition of subsidiary:			
Net non-cash assets acquired (27.0)			
Acquisition financing 22.0	(5.0)		(3.1)
Additions to other assets and deferred charges	(14.7)	(4.5)	(11.8)
	4.9	32.5	(55.1)
Cash provided by (used for) financing activities:			
Increase (decrease) in bank borrowings	3.5	(14.8)	11.5
Increase in long-term debt	7.5	84.6	44.3
Reduction in long-term debt	(151.3)	(204.8)	(64.1)
Issue of Class I Preferred Shares, net		69.7	
Dividends paid on Class I Preferred Shares	(15.9)	(13.6)	(10.0)
Other	(0.3)	(5.9)	(7.1)
	(156.5)	(84.8)	(25.4)
Increase (decrease) in cash during the year	58.2	104.2	(28.5)
Cash and bank term deposits at beginning of year	160.4	56.2	84.7
Cash and bank term deposits at end of year	$218.6	$160.4	$ 56.2

Source From the Annual Report, 1989. Reprinted with permission.

For Discussion

1. Using the data from this statement, prepare a statement of cash flow from operations.
2. Evaluate operations, financing activities, and investing activities separately. Where is Varity's cash coming from? Where is it going to?
3. Prepare a statement of cash flow showing only sources of cash and uses of cash. Use the total of cash from operations but reclassify the financing and investing items. Calculate the net change in cash.
4. Which statement is easier to understand: the one prepared by Varity or the one you prepared in question 3, above?

Discussion Case 15-4:   Mux Lab

Mux Lab
Consolidated Changes in Cash Resources
Year Ended July 31, 1988

	1988	1987
OPERATIONS		
Earnings (loss) before extraordinary items	$ 781,271	$(5,228,874)
Non-cash items		
Depreciation	319,753	265,803
Amortization of development costs	61,479	137,905
Current income taxes	853,678	
Deferred income taxes	(412,004)	(236,172)
Extraordinary items		(122,067)
Changes in non-cash working capital items (Note 7)	(921,851)	2,075,075
Source (use) of cash	682,326	(3,108,330)
FINANCING		
Financial reorganization	(1,199,871)	
Long-term debt	104,421	203,689
Instalments on long-term debt	(147,140)	(440,863)
Deferred income	255,125	
Issue of shares	429,435	4,810,212
Investment tax credit		
Fixed assets		10,259
Scientific research	198,180	63,126
Increase in investment tax credit receivable	(198,180)	(69,572)
Source (use) of cash	(558,030)	4,576,851
INVESTMENT		
Note receivable	(45,000)	
Additions to fixed assets	(79,304)	(1,770,249)
Disposal of fixed assets	155,947	
Development costs	(556,467)	(940,577)
Foreign private corporation		(274,755)
Use of cash	(524,824)	(2,985,581)
Decrease in cash	(400,528)	(1,517,060)
Overdraft and bank loan, beginning of year	(1,735,217)	(218,157)
Overdraft and bank loan, end of year	$(2,135,745)	$(1,735,217)

Changes in Non-cash Working Capital Items:	1988	1987
Accounts receivable	$ 429,705	$ (182,905)
Investment tax credit receivable	(107,380)	140,263
Inventories	(241,691)	(1,509,510)
Prepaid expenses	(64,937)	111,254
Accounts payable and accrued liabilities	(937,548)	3,652,414
Deferred credit		(136,441)
	$ (921,851)	$ 2,075,075

Source   From the Annual Report for the year ended July 31, 1988. Reprinted with permission.

For Discussion

1. Is there a cash decrease or increase over 1987 and 1988? Why?
2. Prepare a statement of cash flow showing only sources of cash and uses of cash. Use the total of cash from operations, but reclassify the financing and investing activities according to their sources or uses. Calculate the net change in cash.
3. Prepare a statement of cash flow from operations.
4. Which is more useful: the consolidated changes in cash resources prepared by Mux Lab or the statements you prepared in questions 2 and 3 above? Why?

Comprehension Problems

Comprehension Problem 15-1

The following transactions were carried out by Crozier Manufacturing Limited.

Required: Indicate into which category each transaction is placed in the statement of cash flow: operations, financing activities, or investing activities.

A disbursement of $5,000 was made in payment of the current portion of a long-term loan.

Depreciation expense for equipment was $1,000.

$10,000-worth of common stock was issued for cash.

Cash dividends of $2,500 were declared and paid to shareholders.

Bonds were given in exchange for equipment costing $7,000.

Land was purchased for $25,000 cash.

$750 of accrued salaries were paid.

$5,000 was borrowed by issuing a 60-day note.

$10,000 of accounts receivable were collected.

A building was purchased for $80,000: $30,000 was paid in cash and the rest was in mortgage.

Investment in subsidiary company was sold for $50,000 cash.

Equipment was sold for $6,000. The accumulation depreciation for it was $3,000 with an original cost of $10,000.

$1,200 was paid for a 12-month insurance policy in effect next year.

Patent was amortized for $500.

Bonds were issued for $50,000 cash.

Comprehension Problem 15-2

The following table includes transactions carried out by the Tetu and Horne Specialist Corporation and columns for each of the three categories found in the statement of cash flow: operations, financing activities, and investing activities.

Required: For each event shown, indicate whether there is an increase or decrease in each of the following categories, and indicate the amount of the increase or decrease. If the event does not appear on the statement of cash flow, do not enter any amount:

	Operations	Financing Activities	Investing Activities
1. Issued $100-worth of bonds for cash		100	
2. Purchased a building for $90; $60 was on mortgage and the rest was paid in cash		60	(90)
3. Declared and paid dividends of $12 during the year		(12)	
4. Purchased equipment for $20-worth of common stock		20	(20)
5. Paid long-term debt of $50 in cash		(50)	
6. Sold land for $30 in cash			30
7. Earned net income of $75	75		
8. Purchased equipment costing $15; of this, $5 was paid in cash and the rest with a 90-day note payable		10	(15)
9. Amortized patent by $2	2		
10. Redeemed $100-worth of bonds for common stock		100 (100)	

	Operations	Financing Activities	Investing Activities
11. Purchased marketable securities for $5 cash			(5)
12. Sold a machine that cost $20 for $7 cash; the accumulated depreciation on it was $10	3		7
13. Depreciation expense for building and equipment amounted to $8	8		
14. Paid in cash the note mentioned in transaction 8 above		(10)	
15. Issued $20-worth of preferred shares for cash		20	
16. Purchased a patent for $25 cash			(25)
17. Paid $1 for the next 2 months of advertising; recorded as prepaid expense	(2)		
18. Purchased $60-worth of ABC Ltd. common stock for cash.			(60)

Comprehension Problem 15-3

Required: For each of the following items indicate whether it increases, decreases or has no effect on cash flow:

Cash Flow

↑	↓	N.E.	
✓			1. Net income for the year
	✓		2. Payment of bonds payable
	✓		3. Increase in inventory
		✓	4. Issue of common stock for equipment
✓			5. Issue of bonds payable for cash
			6. Declaration of a cash dividend for this year
			7. Increase in accounts receivable
			8. Increase in accounts payable
			9. Purchase of land for cash
			10. Issue of common stock for cash
			11. Reclassification from long-term liabilities of current portion of bonds payable due next year
			12. Payment of cash dividend declared last year
			13. Decrease in marketable securities
			14. Increase in income tax payable.

Problems

Problem 15-1

The following transactions occurred in the Hubris Corporation during the year ended December 31, 19X8.

a.	Net income for the year (accrual basis)	$800
b.	Depreciation expense	120
c.	Increase in wages payable	20
d.	Increase in accounts receivable	40
e.	Decrease in merchandise inventory	50
f.	Amortization of patents	5
g.	Payment of long-term liabilities	250
h.	Issuance of common stock for cash	500
i.	Amortization of bond premium	6
j.	Declaration of dividends	30

Handwritten annotations:
Net Income 800
Add: Dep'n exp. 20
add: ↑ in wages pay (20)
less ↑ in A/R (20)
add: ↓ merch inv. 50
amort. of patents 5
payment of long term liab 250
amort of bond premiums 6

Required:
1. Calculate the cash flow from operations.
2. Prepare in proper form the statement of cash flow, showing the detailed calculation of cash flow from operations on a separate schedule.
3. Does the declaration of dividends affect cash flow? Why or why not?

Problem 15-2

During the year ended December 31, 19X3, the Kern Co. Ltd. reported $95,000 of revenues, $70,000 of expenses, and $5,000 of income tax. Following is a list of transactions that occurred during the year:

a. Depreciation expense, $3,000
b. Increase in wages payable, $500
c. Increase in accounts receivable, $900
d. Decrease in merchandise inventory, $1,200
e. Amortization of patent, $100
f. Long-term liabilities paid in cash, $5,000
g. Issue of common stock for cash, $12,500
h. Amortization of bond discount, $150
i. Fixed assets, cost $10,000, acquired through issuing 1000 shares of stock
j. Just prior to end of the fiscal year, $5,000 cash dividend was declared, payable one month later
k. Old machinery sold for $6,000 cash; it originally cost $15,000 (one-half depreciated). Loss reported on income statement as ordinary item and included in the $70,000 of expenses.
l. Decrease in accounts payable, $1,000.

Required:
1. Calculate the statement of cash flow from operations.
2. Prepare a statement of cash flow.
3. Explain what this statement of cash flow tells you about the Kern Co. Ltd.

Note: Use the T-account method only if instructed to do so.

Problem 15-3

The comparative balance sheets of Loess Corporation showed the following at December 31, 19X2 and 19X1.

[handwritten notes in left margin: IN NET WORKING CAPITAL, INVESTMENT]

	19X2	19X1	
Debits			
Cash	$ 10	$ 8	2
Accounts Receivable (net)	18	10	8
Merchandise Inventory	24	20	4
Long-Term Investments	10	24	(14)
Fixed Assets	94	60	34
	$156	$122	
Credits			
Accumulated Depreciation	$ 14	$ 10	4
Accounts Payable	16	12	4
Notes Payable — Long Term	40	32	8
Common Stock	60	50	10
Retained Earnings	26	18	8
	$156	$ 122	

[handwritten notes beside Credits: OPER (Accumulated Depreciation), L.T. DEBT (Notes Payable), FINANCING (Common Stock), OPER (Retained Earnings)]

The income statement for 19X2 appears below:

Loess Corporation
Income Statement
For the Year Ended December 31, 19X2

Sales		$ 300
Cost of Sales		200
Gross Profit		$ 100
Operating Expenses		
Expenses, including Income Tax	$ 78	
Depreciation	6	84
Income from Operations		$ 16
Other Gains (Losses)		
Gain on Disposal of Fixed Assets		2
Loss on Disposal of Investments		(4)
Net Income		$ 14

[handwritten note in left margin: ADDITIONAL DATA: CASH DIVIDEND 6 FIN, ISSUE OF SHARES FOR CASH 10 FIN, FIXED ASSETS DISPOSED - COST 6 INV, IGNORE INCOME TAXES]

Additional data concerning changes in the non-current accounts during 19X2:
a. Cash dividends paid, $6
b. Issue of shares for cash, $10
c. Fixed assets disposed during the year cost $6
d. Ignore income taxes.

Required:
1. Prepare a statement of cash flow from operations for the year ended December 31, 19X2.
2. Prepare a statement of cash flow in good form for the year ended December 31, 19X2.
3. Comment on the operations, financing activities, and investing activities of Loess Corporation at December 31, 19X2.

Problem 15-4

The following trial balance has been prepared from the ledger of Obsius Corporation at December 31, 19X3, following its first year of operations.

	Account Balances	
	Debit	Credit
Cash	$ 50	
Accounts Receivable — net	100	
Merchandise Inventory, December 31, 19X3	60	
Prepaid Rent	10	
Equipment	160	
Accumulated Depreciation — Equipment		$ 44
Land	0	
Accounts Payable		50
Dividends Payable		5
Salaries Payable		8
Bonds Payable — due 19X8		80
Premium on Bonds		3
Common Stock, no par-value		140
Retained Earnings		—
Dividends	10	
Sales		225
Cost of Goods Sold	136	
Selling and Administrative Expenses	42	
Interest Expense	7	
Gain on Sale of Land		20
	$575	$575

Additional information:
a. The company paid $15 cash dividends during the year.
b. Actual interest paid during the year amounted to $8. Amortization of bond premium amounting to $1 was credited to interest expense during the year.
c. Bonds were redeemed during the year for $21 cash (par-value, $20, and bond premium $1). The bond premium had been amortized prior to the redemption.
d. Obsius issued common stock for equipment, $40.
e. Land costing $30 was purchased and sold during the year for $50.
f. Obsius issued bonds during the year for $105 cash (par-value $100 and bond premium $5).
g. The cost of goods sold amounting to $136 includes depreciation expense of $44.

Required:
1. Calculate the cash flow from operations during the year on a separate schedule. (Hint: Prepare an income statement before making this calculation.)
2. Prepare in proper form a statement of cash flow.
3. Explain what this statement of cash flow tells you about Obsius Corporation at December 31, 19X3.

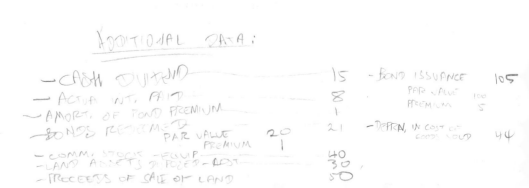

Problem 15-5

The balance sheet data of Orestes Limited at December 31 appear below.

Orestes Limited
Comparative Balance Sheets
At December 31, 19X2 and 19X1
(000s)

	19X2	19X1
Debits		
Cash	$ 40	$ 30
Accounts Receivable (net)	38	28
Merchandise Inventory	102	106
Prepaid Expenses	8	6
Long-Term Investment	—	20
Buildings	240	180
Machinery	134	80
Patents	8	10
	$570	$460
Credits		
Accounts Payable	$ 18	$ 26
Notes Payable — Short Term	26	18
Wages Payable	4	6
Accumulated Depreciation	76	80
Notes Payable — Long Term	70	60
Common Stock, No par*	310	240
Retained Earnings	66	30
	$570	$460

*Shares outstanding December 31, 19X1 — 15; December 31, 19X2 — 22

The following additional information is available:
a. Net income for the year was $56,000.
b. Depreciation recorded on fixed assets was $14,000.
c. Amortization of patents amounted to $2,000.
d. Machinery costing $30,000 was purchased; one-third was paid in cash and a 5-year interest-bearing note was given for the balance.
e. Machinery costing $60,000 was purchased, and was paid for by issuing 6,000 common shares.
f. Machinery was sold for $14,000 that originally cost $36,000 (one-half depreciated); loss or gain reported on the income statement.
g. Addition to building was made costing $60,000; paid cash.
h. A $10,000 long-term note was paid by issuing 1,000 common shares.
j. Cash dividends were paid.
k. Sales of $240,000 were made on account.
l. Accounts receivable, $230,000, were collected.

Required:
1. Using the T-account method, prepare a statement of cash flow from operations at December 31, 19X2.
2. Prepare a statement of cash flow at December 31, 19X2.
3. What observations about Orestes can you make from these statements?

Alternate Problems

Alternate Problem 15-1

The comparative balance sheets of Riffle Corporation showed the following information at December 31.

Debits	19X8	19X7
Cash	$ 22	$ 20
Accounts Receivable (net)	48	38
Merchandise Inventory	100	104
Prepaid Expenses	8	6
Land	—	20
Buildings	240	180
Machinery	124	80
Patents	8	10
	$550	$458

Credits	19X8	19X7
Accounts Payable	$ 16	$ 24
Notes Payable	26	18
Wages Payable	4	6
Accumulated Depreciation	78	80
Notes Payable — Long Term	70	60
Common Stock	300	240
Retained Earnings	56	30
	$550	$458

[handwritten: AP = B + P − Payments]

[handwritten: Use − 48·26 = 22. new dividends]

[handwritten: 26−48 = −22. 26 48]

Additional data for 19X8:
a. Net income for the year amounted to $48. *[handwritten arrow]*
b. Amortization of patents amounted to $2.
c. Purchased machinery for $30, paying $10 in cash, and gave a 5-year note for the balance.
d. Purchased $50 of machinery through the issue of common stock.
e. Paid $60 cash for an addition to the building.
f. Paid a $10 long-term note through the issue of common stock.
g. Sold land for $24 (gain or loss is included in the income statement).
h. Paid cash dividends.
i. Depreciation expense for the year amounted to $16.
j. Sold machinery for $14 that had originally cost $36; it was one-half depreciated at the time of sale (gain or loss is included in the income statement).

Required:
1. Calculate the cash flow from operations in a separate schedule.
2. Prepare in proper form a statement of cash flow.
3. Explain what the statement of cash flow tells you about Riffle Corporation.
4. Explain why you handled any non-cash investing and financing activities as you did.

Alternate Problem 15-2

The records of Permian Corporation showed the following information in the balance sheet accounts at December 31, 19X2 and 19X1.

Debits	19X2	19X1	
Cash	$ 11	$ 10	)
Accounts Receivable (net)	24	19	5
Merchandise Inventory	50	52	(2)
Prepaid Expenses	4	3	1
Long-Term Investments	—	10	(10)
Fixed Assets (net)	147	95	52.
	$236	$189	

Credits	19X2	19X1	
Accounts Payable	$ 8	$ 12	(4)
Wages Payable	2	3	(1)
Notes Payable — Long Term	48	39	9
Common Stock	150	120	30
Retained Earnings	28	15	13.
	$236	$189	

Additional information for 19X2:
a. Net income was $24.
b. Cash dividends of $11 were paid.
c. Depreciation expense was $3.
d. Common stock was given in exchange for fixed assets costing $30.
e. Fixed assets were purchased for $25; $16 was paid in cash and a long-term note was issued for the difference.

Required:
1. Calculate the cash flow from operations.
2. Prepare in proper form a statement of cash flow; show the detailed calculation of cash flow from operations on a separate schedule.
3. Explain what the statement of cash flow tells you about the Permian Corporation.
4. Explain why you handled the non-cash acquisition of fixed assets as you did.

Alternate Problem 15-3

The comparative balance sheets for Sors Limited, as at December 31, were as follows:

Sors Limited
Comparative Balance Sheets
At December 31, 19X5 and 19X4

	19X5	19X4
Assets		
Cash	$ 6,000	$ 7,000
Accounts Receivable	4,000	5,000
Allowance for Doubtful Accounts	(1,000)	(500)
Merchandise Inventory	12,000	11,000
Long-Term Investment	13,000	10,000
Land	10,000	—
Equipment	40,000	30,000
Accumulated Depreciation	(10,000)	(8,000)
	$ 74,000	$ 54,500

Liabilities and Shareholders' Equity

Accounts Payable	$ 5,000	$ 7,000
Current Portion — Bonds Payable	6,000	6,000
Bonds Payable	10,000	16,000
Common Shares — No par	8,000	3,000
Retained Earnings — Unrestricted	26,250	22,500
— Restricted	8,750	–
Donated Capital	10,000	–
	$ 74,000	$ 54,500

The 19X5 ledger accounts for non-current items are reproduced below in the format of T-accounts.

Investment

Bal X4	10,000	
X5 Purchase	3,000	
Bal X5	13,000	

Land

X5 Addition	10,000	

Equipment

Bal. X4	30,000		
X5 Acquisition	5,000	X5 Disposal	10,000
X5 Purchase	15,000		
	50,000		10,000
Bal X5	40,000		

Accumulated Depreciation

		Bal. X4	8,000
X5 Disposal	1,000	X5 Deprec.	3,000
	1,000		11,000
		Bal X5	10,000

Bonds Payable

X5 Transferred to current	6,000	Bal. X4	16,000
		Bal X5	10,000

Common Stock

		Bal. X4	3,000
		X5 Issued for Equipment	5,000
		Bal X5	8,000

Retained Earnings

		Bal. X4	22,500
X5 Restriction	8,750	X5 Net Income	17,500
X5 Dividends	5,000		
	13,750		40,000
		Bal X5	26,250

Retained Earnings (Restricted)

		X5 Addition	8,750

Donated Capital

		X5 Donation of Land	10,000

Additional data: There was a $2,000 loss on disposal of equipment.

Required:
1. Prepare a statement of cash flow from operations.
2. Prepare a statement of cash flow.
3. What observations about Sors Limited can you make from these statements?

Alternate Problem 15-4

The president of the Costa Company Ltd. is concerned about the company's cash position at the end of December 31, 19X2. The following data summarized the financial situation of the company for 19X2 and 19X1:

	(000s)	
Debits	19X2	19X1
Accounts Receivable	$ 180	$ 220
Building	610	500
Cash	—	50
Merchandise Inventory	110	125
Land	175	90
Long-Term Investment	40	100
Machinery	300	170
Prepaid Expenses	5	4
Unamortized Bond Discount	4	5
	$1,424	$1,264

Credits		
Accounts Payable	$ 70	$ 50
Accumulated Depreciation	241	218
Allowance for Doubtful Accounts	10	12
Bank Overdraft	50	—
Bonds Payable	100	50
Common Stock	500	450
Notes Payable — Trade	25	—
Retained Earnings	423	480
Wages Payable	5	4
	$1,424	$1,264

The following additional information is available:
a. A dividend of 15 cents per share was declared and paid on the 500,000 outstanding shares.
b. Shares have been issued during the year at $1.
c. Some shares in the long-term investment account were sold during the year to finance a portion of the new building. These shares were carried at a cost of $60,000 in the books of the company. The selling price was $40,000.
d. Old machinery that cost $10,000 was sold for $2,000. Depreciation on this equipment was $6,000. The loss was included in operating expenses for the year.
e. The income statement for the current year is as follows:

Sales	$1,350,000
Cost of Sales	720,000
Gross Profit	$ 630,000
Operating Expenses	577,000
Operating Income	$ 53,000
Other Gains (Losses)	
Loss on Sale of Investment	(20,000)
Income before Income Tax	$ 33,000
Income Tax	15,000
Net Income	$ 18,000

Required:
1. Using the T-account method, prepare a statement of cash flow from operations at December 31, 19X2.
2. Prepare a statement of cash flow at December 31, 19X2.
3. Explain what these statements tell you about Costa Company Ltd.

Decision Problems

Decision Problem 15-1

The year-end of Campion Inc. is December 31, 19X6. The following summarized data are taken from its records.

	(000s)
Cash sales	$492
Sales on account	168
Cash purchases of merchandise	340
Credit purchases of merchandise	80
Miscellaneous Expenses paid in cash	142
Accounts Receivable:	
Balance January 1, 19X6	46
Balance December 31, 19X6	60
Accounts Payable:	
Balance January 1, 19X6	28
Balance December 31, 19X6	32
Merchandise Inventory:	
Inventory, January 1, 19X6	100
Inventory, December 31, 19X6	120
Wages Payable at December 31, 19X6 (none at January 1, 19X6)	4
Prepaid Rent at December 31, 19X6 (none at January 1, 19X6)	6
Fixed Assets — Equipment:	
Cost	200
Annual Depreciation	20

Required:

1. Using the above information, complete the following income statements on both accrual and cash bases.

Accrual Basis			*Cash Basis*		
Sales		$	Sales		$
Cost of Goods Sold		_____	Cost of Goods Sold		_____
Gross Profit		$	Gross Profit		$
Operating Expenses			Operating Expenses		
Depreciation	$		Depreciation	$	
Miscellaneous			Miscellaneous		
Rent			Rent		
Wages	_____	_____	Wages	_____	_____
Net Income for the Year		$	Net Income for the Year		$

2. Beginning with the net income calculated according to the accrual basis,
   a. Prepare a statement of cash flow from operations at December 31, 19X6.
   b. Prepare a partial statement of cash flow at December 31, 19X6.

Decision Problem 15-2

Bight Incorporated
Comparative Balance Sheets
At December 31, 19X2 and 19X1

	19X1		19X2
Assets			
Cash		$ 25,000	$48,000
Accounts Receivable (net)		25,000	?
Merchandise Inventory		70,000	?
Marketable Securities		35,000	?
Prepaid Expenses		—	?
Long-Term Investment		40,000	?
Unamortized Discount on Bonds		1,200	?
Machinery	$40,000		$?
Less: Accumulated Depreciation	10,000	30,000	? ?
Building		$?	
Less: Accumulated Depreciation		—	2,000 ?
Land		—	?
Other Assets		15,000	?
		$241,200	$?
Liabilities and Shareholders' Equity			
Accounts Payable		$ 20,000	$?
Dividends Payable		—	?
Bonds Payable		50,000	?
Common Stock		100,000	?
Retained Earnings			
— Unrestricted		61,200	?
— Restricted		10,000	20,000
		$241,200	$?

The following additional information is available:
a. $3,000 of marketable securities were sold for cash.
b. Long-term investments were sold for $60,000 cash ($10,000 of expenses related to the disposal were incurred).
c. Land and building were acquired in exchange for $100,000 of par-value bonds. The building is to be depreciated on a 40-year straight-line basis.
d. $10,000 of common stock was issued as a stock dividend.
e. A new piece of machinery was acquired in exchange for an old piece of machinery and $24,000 cash. The old machinery had cost $8,000 and was half depreciated. No loss or gain was incurred.
f. The depreciation charge for machinery in 19X2 was $4,000.
g. The discount on bonds is being amortized on a straight-line basis. The discount will be completely amortized by December 31, 19X7.
h. On March 1, 19X2 the company paid $6,000 of insurance premiums for a period of one year.
i. The net purchases of merchandise for 19X2 were $515,000.
j. Sales for the period amounted to $700,000. The gross profit is 30 percent of sales.
k. Accounts payable increased by 40 percent.
l. Accounts receivable (net) have increased by 52 percent.
m. During 19X2, $10,000 of cash dividends have been declared. Half of these have been paid, the rest will be paid in January of 19X3.
n. Net income for 19X2 is $28,800.
o. Other assets were purchased for $5,000 cash.

Required:
1. Complete the balance sheet for 19X2 based on the above information.
2. Using the T-account method, prepare a statement of cash flow from operations at December 31, 19X2.
3. Prepare a statement of cash flow at December 31, 19X2.
4. What observations about Bight can you make from these statements?

Decision Problem 15-3

Sal Vage is a successful realtor who owns and operates three hotels on Prince Edward Island. In September, 19X8, she told her auditor, "Claude Hopper bought the White Sands Hotel in Rustico five years ago. It hasn't yet shown a profit, and he's approached me with an offer to sell the assets at net book value of $1.5 million, even though the property has been appraised at $2 million.

Claude had no previous experience in the hotel business. I believe that with proper management the White Sands would be a very good investment. From mid-May to mid-September, customers are being turned away. During December and January, the hotel is closed. In my judgement, the room rates are too low at White Sands compared with similar hotels.

As you know, my primary interest is in cash flow. Because it is not a cash flow item, I consider depreciation to be an irrelevant expense. In order to raise the $1.5 million purchase price, I would have to sell some relatively secure bonds, which are now earning 10 percent interest. I am interested in investing in the White Sands only if I can obtain a cash flow of at least double the interest I would be losing.

Mr. Hopper has agreed to let you review his hotel's books."

An income statement for the year ended September 30, 19X8 prepared by Claude Hopper and his staff is presented on the following page. After reviewing this income statement, Ms Vage made the following assumptions for 19X9:

a. Room Rentals:

Room rates from June 1 to September 30 would be raised $15 per day, but the occupancy rate would drop 10 percent.

Room rates and occupancy rates from February 1 to May 31 and from October 1 to November 30 would not change.

The hotel would remain open during December and January, with 50 daily rentals at a reduced rate of $40 per room per day.

Revenues from room rentals would thus amount to $1,222,750 for 19X9.

b. Fixed Expenses:

Advertising expenses would be increased by $20,000.

Fixed salaries would be reduced by $10,000.

Sal Vage would not assume the existing loan from the Bank of Nova Scotia: she would sell bonds if she decided to purchase the hotel.

c. Variable Expenses:

Variable expenses would increase to $615,400.

d. Income Tax Expense:

The income tax rate is 40 percent.

White Sands Hotel
Income Statement
For the Year Ended September 30, 19X8

Revenues	$1,050,000
Less: Operating Expenses	
Fixed Expenses*	
Depreciation — Hotel	$ 60,000
Depreciation — Equipment, Furniture, and Fixtures	60,000
Depreciation — Outdoor Facilities	30,000
Fixed Portion of Utility Expenses	20,000
Property Taxes	40,000
Tennis and Pool Attendants	30,000
Building Maintenance and Security	40,000
Bookkeeping and Front Desk	50,000
Advertising	60,000
Hotel and Room Management	60,000
Legal and Auditing	25,000
Payroll Taxes	10,000
Interest on Loans from Bank of Nova Scotia	90,000
Miscellaneous	25,000
Total	$ 600,000
Variable Expenses**	510,000
Total Expenses	1,110,000
Net Loss	$ (60,000)

*Fixed expenses remain constant during the time period regardless of occupancy rates.
**Variable expenses change during the time period in response to occupancy rates.

Required:
1. Calculate the expected 19X9 income before income tax based on the preceding information. You are not required to prepare an income statement.
2. Calculate the estimated income tax expense for 19X9 and the resulting amount of net income.
3. Calculate the amount of cash flow in 19X9. Assume that revenues are collected in cash and that expenses are paid in cash.
4. On the basis of her investment criterion, should Ms Vage purchase the White Sands Hotel?
5. Evaluate the investment criterion used by Ms Vage.

Accounting for Manufacturing Operations

The nature of a manufacturing business is different from that of a merchandiser. Some cost concepts are unique to a manufacturer. The classified statement of cost of goods manufactured and income statement facilitate the communication of information necessary for decision making.

1. How does the income statement of a manufacturer differ from that of a merchandiser?
2. What accounts are used only by a manufacturer?
3. What is *factory overhead,* and what does it include?
4. What type of inventory accounts are used by a manufacturer?
5. How do product and period costs differ?
6. At what point do product costs become period costs?
7. How does the worksheet for a manufacturer differ from that of a merchandiser?
8. How are opening and ending inventories recorded on a manufacturer's worksheet?
9. What is a Manufacturing Summary account, and why is one used?
10. What is the impact of the perpetual inventory method on manufacturing operations?

A. Manufacturing Cost Concepts

The income statement for a merchandising firm differs from that prepared for an entity involved in manufacturing operations. Merchandising involves the purchase and subsequent resale of goods, while a manufacturer's income statement emphasizes the production of these goods. This difference is indicated in the calculation of cost of goods sold.

Merchandising Operations			*Manufacturing Operations*		
Cost of Goods Sold:			Cost of Goods Sold:		
Opening Inventory	$ 4,000		Opening Finished Goods Inventory	$ 4,000	
Cost of Goods Purchased	12,000		Cost of Goods Manufactured	12,000	
Cost of Goods Available	$16,000		Cost of Goods Available	$16,000	
Less: Ending Inventory	6,000		*Less:* Ending Finished Goods Inventory	6,000	
Total Cost of Goods Sold	$10,000		Total Cost of Goods Sold	$10,000	

Real Life Example 16-1

The Case of the Disappearing Inventory

To hear some auditors talk, inventory has been disappearing from companies at a record pace recently. The reason, they say, is a dramatic increase in employee theft related to drugs. The fact is that inventory shrinkage is a perennial problem in manufacturing companies, and its causes have less to do with dope fiends than with poorly trained employees and inadequate accounting systems.

This is not to diminish the seriousness of the problem. Inaccurate inventory figures can literally drive a company out of business. A chief executive officer depends on a controller's inventory reports to guide his or her actions. If controller's reports show inventory to be more (almost always the case) or less than it actually is, a CEO can be misled into making some bad, even company-threatening, decisions.

Moreover, inaccurate inventory reports make bankers and investors nervous.

Sometimes inventory variances can be traced to a single, easy-to-fix cause. More likely, though, inventory accumulates on the books from several sources at every step of the process, from purchasing to manufacturing to shipping finished goods. Identification of the trouble spots is a major step toward their elimination.

The Purchasing Phase

• *Maintain an accurate bill of materials.*
Inventory problems often start with the bill of materials — the list that purchasing, manufacturing, and accounting use to buy, assemble, and cost the parts that go into a product. Parts may be missing from the bill; part numbers, quantities, or units of measure may be wrong. Since manufacturing generally knows what parts are required, it goes ahead and uses what it needs to build and ship the product. But unless somebody there lets accounting know about the errors, there is a good chance that the costs — and, in turn, the book value of the inventory — will be wrong.

• *Check vendor invoices against parts received.*
Vendors sometimes make mistakes in arithmetic. The only way you will discover if a vendor bills you for 100 parts, but ships just 95, is to count the parts when they arrive.

• *Keep close tabs on purchased parts.*
When inventory is stored in the open, parts are there for the taking. Outright theft is one possibility, but not the most likely. More often, the parts are lifted for legitimate work, but nobody keeps track. Finished goods are cannibalized; parts reserved for one product are taken to replace damaged parts on another; parts are lost and damaged in storage; and incoming parts are used before they're counted — with accounting none the wiser. From the time parts arrive to the time finished goods are shipped, they should be kept under tight control. And when inventory is withdrawn, always insist on proper documentation.

• *Watch out for different prices and numbers on identical parts.*
A purchased part that costs $2 on one invoice but $2.15 on the next increases the value of your inventory, unless your accounting system takes note of the 15¢ price difference by classifying it as an expense at the time of purchase. If you don't note the difference, it won't show up until you take a physical inventory, at which time it becomes part of your shrinkage problem. Similarly, you should be careful about giving identical parts different part numbers and different costs, perhaps because one is purchased and the other made

The cost of goods purchased calculation for a merchandiser is comparable to the manufacturer's cost of goods manufactured. The merchandiser purchases finished goods for resale, while the manufacturer produces finished goods to be sold.

Manufacturing Costs

The manufacturing process requires several accounts to accumulate the specific costs incurred by manufacturers. These costs are grouped into three categories: (a) raw materials, (b) direct labour, and (c) factory overhead. Errors in any of these areas can be devastating if they lead management to make bad decisions. Real Life Example 16-1 explains how this miscommunication can happen.

in-house. The practice virtually guarantees inventory variances, by making it nearly impossible to match a part with its cost.

• *Bill to inventory only what belongs there.*
Poorly trained accounts-payable clerks can add a lot of inappropriate items to the book inventory. All of this shows up as shrinkage when the physical inventory is taken.

• *Install procedures to thwart embezzlement.*
Auditors have lists of internal control procedures that reduce the potential for employee embezzlement. Generally, these procedures require that several employees be involved in the process of receiving goods and spending cash. For example, the person who orders parts should not be the person who confirms that the parts have been received. And at the other end of the production process, the person who handles cash sales should never be responsible for processing the supporting paperwork.

The Manufacturing Phase

• *Don't ignore scrap.*
Scrap, when not reported accurately, stays in inventory, hiking the book value.

• *Beware of producing phantom parts.*
When your workers' wages are based on their productivity, they might tend to overstate their output, and the nonexistent parts stay on the books until your next physical inventory.

• *Note unusual labor rates.*
At times, supervisors with higher than average pay get directly involved in production, and your books will show a higher inventory value unless adjustments are made for the difference in labor rates.

• *Monitor overhead charges.*
When a company accountant makes a mistake in booking the overhead at the end of the month, the book value of inventory can swell significantly. And since the general subject of manufacturing overhead is a mystery to most non-accountants this can be a particularly difficult problem to recognize. If you have an accounting system that breaks out the costs of labor, raw materials, and overhead each month, keep close tabs on the figures to see that the balances are reasonable over time.

• *Keep finished goods separate from returns for repairs.*
If products returned for repair are stored with finished goods, mix-ups can occur. An accounting clerk can mistakenly book repairs into inventory, for example, or a manufacturing supervisor can mistakenly count them during a physical inventory.

The Shipping Phase

• *Coordinate billing and shipping.*
When products are shipped but not billed, inventory will be overstated. This is such an obvious problem, and one that has such a significant effect on cash, that most companies set up systems to deal with it.

• *Beware of computer errors.*
Many computer programs can generate their own errors. Several years ago, for example, a widely used program went awry whenever the system showed a negative quantity of a product on hand.

When all is said and done, the best way to keep abreast of a shrinkage problem is to take physical inventories frequently — quarterly, or even monthly. A physical inventory is about as accurate a measure as you'll ever get. And it provides a benchmark against which you can judge the adequacy of your cost-accounting system.

Source   Reprinted with permission, *Inc. magazine.* Copyright by Goldhirsh Group, Inc., 38 Commercial Wharf, Boston, MA 02110.

Raw Materials

Direct raw materials
The materials used in production that are identifiable in the final product.

Raw materials consist of the goods used in manufacturing the finished product. Usually, more raw materials are purchased than are actually used during a given time period; the unused amount is the raw materials inventory. Bluebeard Computer Company's manufacturing operations assemble computer terminals from parts purchased from highly specialized manufacturers. Examples of raw materials for BCC's manufacturing include the computer monitor, keyboard, micro chips, cabinet, and wiring. These are referred to as **direct raw materials** because they can be easily identified in the final product. Certain raw materials are not easily identified; these are referred to as **indirect raw materials** and are usually accounted for as overhead. Examples of indirect materials for BCC include supplies required for the assembly work, such as screws, nuts, bolts, glue, and rivets.

Indirect raw materials
The materials used in production that cannot be easily identified in the final product; included as part of factory overhead.

Direct Labour

Direct labour
Wages paid to employees who are directly involved in manufacturing the product.

Direct labour consists of wage payments for employees directly involved in manufacturing the product. Employees who actually assemble computers are included in direct labour. The wages of employees who are not directly involved in manufacturing the product — such as accountants, supervisors, payroll clerks, cleaners, executive assistants — are referred to as **indirect labour**; their wages are usually accounted for as overhead.

Indirect labour
Wages paid to employees who are not directly involved in manufacturing the product; included as part of factory overhead.

Factory Overhead

Factory overhead
Manufacturing costs, other than direct raw materials and direct labour.

Factory overhead includes indirect materials, indirect labour, and all other costs incurred in the manufacturing process other than direct materials and direct labour. Factory overhead includes

Plant depreciation and insurance	Municipal taxes assessed on the factory
Heating and other utilities expense	Cost of small tools
Repairs and maintenance of the factory	Employer's shares of payroll taxes.

These and similar overhead expenses are only affected by relatively large changes in the level of production; reduced levels of output do not usually have the proportional effect on these expenses as they would on direct materials and direct labour. In other words, reduced output requires fewer direct materials and labour; factory overhead is not as immediately affected by changes in the level of output.

Product and Period Costs

Period costs
Costs identified with the time period in which they are incurred; not included in the cost of the product manufactured.

The manufacturer's income statement distinguishes between period and product costs. **Period costs** include non-manufacturing general and administrative expenses, in addition to selling expenses; these are payments that do not become part of product costs. They are identified with the time period in which they are incurred and are treated as expenses because the resources they represent are assumed to have been used up during the period. Period costs are disclosed on the income statement below the calculation of gross profit.

Product costs
Costs identified with the manufactured item; included in the calculation of the cost of work in process and finished goods inventory.

Product costs include payments for direct raw materials, direct labour, and factory overhead; they become part of the product manufactured, the asset produced by the manufacturing process. Product costs represent an inventory asset until the manufactured goods are sold; accordingly, the costs of ending inventory are deducted from cost of goods manufactured in the calculation of gross profit. Ending inventory also appears as an asset in the balance sheet.

B. Manufacturing Income Statement

Production is often a continuous process and three different types of inventory usually exist at any given point in time: (a) raw materials, (b) work in process, and (c) finished goods.

Raw Materials Inventory

Raw materials inventory
The balance of raw materials purchased but not yet used in the production process.

Not all raw materials purchased are used immediately in the production process; the unused amount is the **raw materials inventory**. Any materials spoiled or lost during the manufacturing process are automatically included in the cost of materials used, since they do not appear in the ending inventory calculation. The cost of raw materials used during the accounting period is calculated as follows:

Opening Raw Materials Inventory		$20,000
Purchases	$75,000	
Less: Purchases Returns and Allowances $3,500		
Purchases Discounts 1,500	5,000	
Net Purchases	$70,000	
Add: Transportation In	5,000	
Cost of Goods Purchased		75,000
Cost of Goods Available		$95,000
Less: Ending Raw Materials Inventory		35,000
Total Cost of Raw Materials Used		$60,000

Work in Process Inventory

Work in process inventory
The accumulated production costs during the manufacturing process.

Partially completed products are identified as **work in process inventory** at the end of an accounting period. Work in process inventory includes the amount of direct materials, labour, and factory overhead associated with the stage of completion for the partially completed units. The cost of work in process inventory at the end of the accounting period is calculated as follows:

Raw Materials Used	$ 60,000
Direct Labour	130,000
Factory Overhead	41,720
Total Manufacturing Costs	$231,720
Add: Opening Work in Process Inventory	15,000
Total Goods in Process	$246,720
Less: Ending Work in Process Inventory	25,000
Total Cost of Goods Manufactured	$221,720

Finished Goods Inventory

Finished goods inventory
An accumulation of goods manufactured but not yet sold.

All costs incurred in the manufacture of products completed but not yet sold are included in the **finished goods inventory**. The cost of finished goods inventory at the end of the accounting period is calculated as follows:

Opening Finished Goods Inventory	$ 45,000
Add: Cost of Goods Manufactured	221,720
Goods Available for Sale	$266,720
Less: Ending Finished Goods Inventory	60,000
Total Cost of Goods Sold	$206,720

A physical count of each of the three manufacturing inventories is taken at the end of every accounting time period. This physical count is used to calculate the amount of ending inventory. The periodic inventory system is used when the manufacturer has many different items in stock and when maintenance of detailed records would be expensive. Under the perpetual inventory system, a continuous balance of inventory on hand is calculated in terms of units and, often, also in terms of cost. A physical count of inventory at the end of an accounting period verifies the quantities actually on hand.

The Flow of Production Costs

The flow of production costs through work in process and finished goods inventories is illustrated in Figure 16-1.

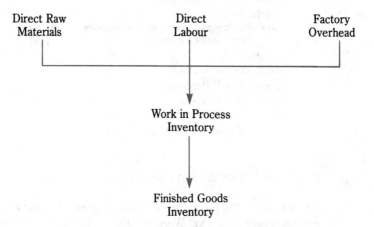

Figure 16-1   The flow of production costs

Calculation of Cost of Goods Manufactured

Cost of goods manufactured
A calculation of the cost of goods manufactured during the accounting time period.

The calculation of **cost of goods manufactured** and the balance sheet disclosure of ending inventories is illustrated below:

Bluebeard Computer Corporation
Cost of Goods Manufactured Statement
For the Year Ended December 31, 19X3

Raw Materials Used:

Opening Raw Materials Inventory	$20,000	
Cost of Goods Purchased (net)	75,000	
Cost of Goods Available	$95,000	
Less: Ending Raw Materials Inventory	35,000	
Total Cost of Raw Materials Used		$ 60,000
Direct Labour		$130,000

Factory Overhead:

Depreciation Expense — Machinery	$ 1,600	
Factory Supplies Expense	6,000	
Indirect Labour	25,000	
Maintenance Expense	4,000	
Rent Expense	3,600	
Utilities Expense	1,520	
Total Factory Overhead		41,720
Total Manufacturing Costs		$231,720
Add: Opening Work in Process Inventory		15,000
Total Goods in Process		$246,720
Less: Ending Work in Process Inventory		25,000
Total Cost of Goods Manufactured		$221,720

Partial Balance Sheet
At December 31, 19X3

Assets

Cash		$ 10,800
Accounts Receivable		26,000
Inventories:		
Raw Materials	$35,000	
Work in Process	25,000	
Finished Goods	60,000	120,000

The cost of goods manufactured is added to the amount of opening finished goods inventory in the calculation of goods available for sale. The income statement then appears as shown on the following page.

Bluebeard Computer Corporation
Income Statement
For the Year Ended December 31, 19X3

Sales (net)		$300,000
Cost of Goods Sold:		
Opening Finished Goods Inventory	$ 45,000	
Cost of Goods Manufactured	221,720	
Goods Available for Sale	$266,720	
Less: Ending Finished Goods Inventory	60,000	
Total Cost of Goods Sold		206,720
Gross Profit		$ 93,280
OPERATING EXPENSES:		
Selling Expenses:		
Advertising Expense	$10,000	
Commissions Expense	15,000	
Delivery Expense	6,000	
Total Selling Expenses	$ 31,000	
General and Administrative Expenses:		
Insurance Expense	$ 1,200	
Salaries Expense	20,000	
Telephone Expense	1,080	
Total General and Administrative Expenses	22,280	
Total Operating Expenses		53,280
Income from Operations		$ 40,000
Financing Costs:		
Interest Expense		10,000
Income before Income Tax		$ 30,000
Income Tax		15,000
Net Income for the Year		$ 15,000

Note that period costs, consisting of selling and general and administrative expenses, are classified separately from the product costs included in the cost of goods manufactured and cost of goods sold. Most product costs are readily identified as such and are included in these latter categories; however, some period costs require allocation between product cost and period expense categories. For example, insurance may be allocated to both factory overhead for the factory space and to general and administrative expenses for office space.

In actual practice, estimates are often used in allocating period costs. Sometimes the classification is made on the basis of expediency, particularly if the amounts involved are not material; insurance expenses, for example, which apply to both product cost and period cost categories, have not been allocated by Bluebeard because the amounts are immaterial.

In addition to these categories of period costs, it should be noted that product costs become period costs as finished goods inventory is sold. That is, cost of goods sold represent a period cost that is matched with sales revenue in the calculation of a gross profit amount.

C.   The Transactions Worksheet for a Manufacturer

A manufacturer's worksheet differs from that prepared for a merchandiser in several respects. First, an additional pair of columns labelled "Cost of Goods Manufactured" is used to gather all costs subsequently reported in the cost of goods manufactured statement. All manufacturing costs are extended to these columns. Second, the opening inventory balances for raw materials and work in process are extended to the cost of goods manufactured columns; the opening finished goods inventory is extended to the income statement columns, as is the case for a merchandiser.

The worksheet procedure for raw materials, work in process, and finished goods inventories is as follows:

1. Opening raw materials inventory appears in the trial balance as the opening work in process inventory. These amounts have not changed during the year because Bluebeard follows the periodic inventory system to record the purchase of merchandise for resale.

2. These opening inventory amounts are transferred to the cost of goods manufactured debit columns, because they are used in the calculation of the cost of goods manufactured amount on the income statement.

3. The amounts of ending raw materials and work in process inventories are recorded directly on the worksheet
   a. As credits in the cost of goods manufactured columns, because they are later used in the calculation of cost of goods manufactured
   b. As debits in the balance sheet columns, because they represent the amount of raw materials and work in process inventories at year-end; assets that appear in the balance sheet require a worksheet debit balance.

4. The beginning finished goods inventory is carried from the adjusted trial balance to the debit income statement column. The ending finished goods inventory is recorded in the income statement credit column and the balance sheet debit column.

The recording of the ending raw materials, work in process, and finished goods inventories amounts into the records is discussed later in this chapter.

Bluebeard Computer Corporation
Manufacturing Worksheet
For the Year Ended December 31, 19X3

Account Title	Trial Balance Dr.	Trial Balance Cr.	Adjustments Dr.	Adjustments Cr.	Cost of Goods Manufactured Dr.	Cost of Goods Manufactured Cr.	Income Statement Dr.	Income Statement Cr.	Balance Sheet Dr.	Balance Sheet Cr.
Cash	10,800								10,800	
Accounts Receivable	26,000								26,000	
Raw Materials Inventory	20,000				20,000	35,000			35,000	
Work in Process										
Inventory	15,000				15,000	25,000			25,000	
Finished Goods										
Inventory	45,000						45,000	60,000	60,000	
Prepaid Insurance	2,400			(a) 1,200					1,200	
Equipment	13,600								13,600	
Accumulated										
Depreciation				(d) 1,600						1,600
Bank Loan—Current		39,000								39,000
Accounts Payable		25,000								25,000
Income Tax Payable				(c)15,000						15,000
Bank Loan—Long Term		48,500								48,500
Common Stock		10,000								10,000
Retained Earnings		21,750								21,750
Dividends	4,250								4,250	
Sales		308,500						308,500		
Sales Returns and										
Allowances	6,000						6,000			
Sales Discounts	2,500						2,500			
Raw Materials Purchases	75,000				75,000					
Raw Materials Purchases										
Returns and Allowances		3,500				3,500				
Raw Materials Purchases										
Discounts		1,500				1,500				
Transportation In	5,000				5,000					
Direct Labour Expense	130,000				130,000					
Indirect Labour Expense	25,000				25,000					
Factory Supplies Expense	6,000				6,000					
Maintenance Expense	4,000				4,000					
Rent Expense	3,600				3,600					
Utilities Expense	1,520				1,520					
Advertising Expense	10,000						10,000			
Commissions Expense	15,000						15,000			
Delivery Expense	6,000						6,000			
Interest Expense	10,000						10,000			
Salaries Expense	20,000						20,000			
Telephone Expense	1,080						1,080			
Totals	457,750	457,750								
Insurance Expenses			(a) 1,200				1,200			
Depreciaton Expense			(b) 1,600		1,600					
Income Tax Expense			(c)15,000				15,000			
Totals			17,800	17,800	286,720	65,000				
Cost of Goods										
Manufactured						221,720	221,720			
					286,720	286,720	353,500	368,500	175,850	160,850
Net Income for the Year							15,000			15,000
Totals							368,500	368,500	175,850	175,850

Closing Entries

The preparation of year-end closing entries for a manufacturer requires an additional intermediate account called Manufacturing Summary. The debit and credit balances in the cost of goods manufactured columns are closed to the Manufacturing Summary account.

Entry 1: Closing the Debit Balance Accounts

The opening Raw Materials Inventory and Work in Process Inventory balances, in addition to other cost of goods manufactured accounts with a debit balance, are closed to Manufacturing Summary.

Entry 2: Closing the Credit Balance Accounts

The ending Raw Materials Inventory and ending Work in Process Inventory balances, in addition to other cost of goods manufactured accounts with a credit balance, are next closed to Manufacturing Summary.

The data from the transactions worksheet of BCC's manufacturing operations are used to illustrate preparation of these closing entries.

19X3	*Closing Entries*		
Dec. 31	Manufacturing Summary	286,720	
	Raw Materials Inventory (opening)		20,000
	Work in Process Inventory (opening)		15,000
	Raw Materials Purchases		75,000
	Transportation In		5,000
	Direct Labour		130,000
	Indirect Labour		25,000
	Depreciation Expense — Equipment		1,600
	Factory Supplies Expense		6,000
	Maintenance Expense		4,000
	Rent Expense		3,600
	Utilities Expense		1,520
	To close opening inventories and cost of goods manufactured accounts with a debit balance.		
31	Raw Materials Inventory (ending)	35,000	
	Work in Process Inventory (ending)	25,000	
	Raw Materials Purchases Returns and Allowances	3,500	
	Raw Materials Purchases Discounts	1,500	
	Manufacturing Summary		65,000
	To record ending inventories and to close manufacturing accounts with a credit balance.		

The income statement columns of the worksheet are next closed. The preparation of closing entries follows the format discussed in Chapter 3.

Entry 3: Closing the Expense Accounts

The opening Finished Goods Inventory balance, other accounts with a debit balance, and the Manufacturing Summary account are then closed to Income Summary.

Dec. 31	Income Summary	353,500	
	Finished Goods Inventory (opening)		45,000
	Sales Returns and Allowances		6,000
	Sales Discounts		2,500
	Advertising Expense		10,000
	Commissions Expense		15,000
	Delivery Expense		6,000
	Insurance Expense		1,200
	Interest Expense		10,000
	Salaries Expense — Office		20,000
	Salaries Expense — Sales		1,080
	Income Tax Expense		15,000
	Manufacturing Summary		221,720

To close opening inventory and to close income statement accounts with a debit balance.

Entry 4:   Closing the Revenue Accounts

The ending Finished Goods Inventory balance and other accounts with a credit balance are closed to Income Summary.

Finished Goods Inventory (ending)	60,000	
Sales	308,500	
Income Summary		368,500

To record ending inventory and to close income statement accounts with a credit balance.

Entry 5:   Closing the Income Summary Account

The Income Summary account is then closed to Retained Earnings.

Income Summary	15,000	
Retained Earnings		15,000

To close Income Summary account.

Entry 6:   Closing the Dividend Account

The Dividend account is closed to Retained Earnings.

Retained Earnings	4,250	
Dividends		4,250

To close Dividends account.

Once all six closing entries have been posted, all manufacturing, revenue, expense, and dividends accounts have a zero balance. The accounts with a remaining balance are the opening balances of asset, liability, and equity accounts in the new fiscal year.

D. Cost Accounting Systems and Inventory Valuation

The periodic inventory method is used in this chapter to illustrate accounting for manufacturing operations. This method is useful for small single-product manufacturers, particularly when the cost of maintaining more detailed records would be expensive. Inventories are physically counted whenever financial statements are prepared; a cost of goods sold is then calculated. This method is less useful for large manufacturers that require frequent financial statements in addition to continuous information about production costs for decision making and control. In actual practice, perpetual inventory systems are used to facilitate both inventory costing and financial statement preparation. Cost accounting systems, therefore, incorporate the use of perpetual inventory.

Costing Manufacturers' Inventories

The preceding sections of this chapter introduced the different types of manufacturing inventories, including raw materials, work in process, and finished goods. The cost of raw materials can be easily determined by reference to purchases documents. Calculating the cost of work in process and finished goods is more complex, however, since it includes all or part of each of raw materials, direct labour, and factory overhead components. The amount and cost of raw materials and direct labour in work in process for example, are often estimated as an average quantity, which is then multiplied by an individually calculated cost amount applicable to both raw materials and direct labour. These costs are directly related to the units being manufactured. Factory overhead, however, is indirectly related to production units. For this reason; a **factory overhead rate** is established; this rate is used to allocate total factory overhead not only to units still in process at year-end but also to units completed during the year. A relationship is often established between direct labour costs and factory overhead costs. For example, in 19X3 for Bluebeard Computer Corporation, direct labour is $130,000 and factory overhead amounts to $41,720. As calculated, Bluebeard incurred approximately $0.32 of factory overhead for each direct labour dollar. Using these amounts, an overhead rate of 32 percent of the amount of direct labour incurred would be used for overhead cost allocation. The total cost of work in process and finished goods inventories includes an allocated overhead amount, as well as the cost of raw materials and direct labour appropriate to the completion stage of the work in process.

Factory overhead rate
A predetermined rate used to allocate total factory overhead to work in process and finished goods.

Issues in Ethics 16-1

The Right To Blow the Whistle

Few people know that there is a right to refuse to pollute. The Environmental Protection Act was amended in 1983 to protect workers who care about the environment. Section 134b makes it an offence for an employer to dismiss, discipline, penalize or attempt to coerce or intimidate an employee for doing any of the following:

- Complying with the five key environmental statutes, the Environmental Protection Act, the Ontario Water Resources Act, the Pesticides Act, the Fisheries Act or the Environmental Assessment Act. This includes refusing work that will pollute or that is lacking a necessary ministry approval.
- Complying with a ministry order, permit or approval.
- "Whistleblowing" — reporting pollution by an employer to the Ministry of the Environment.
- Seeking enforcement by the ministry of an environmental statute.

An employee can, therefore, without loss of pay, refuse to put dangerous wastes into the garbage, or refuse to allow an unlicenced hauler to take it away. An employee can refuse to operate a machine that is spewing smoke into the sky, or a pump that is putting toxic chemicals into a stream. An employee can even refuse to operate equipment that requires a ministry permit, if the permit has not been obtained.

Employees have a growing personal interest in avoiding pollution. As the number of environmental prosecutions grows each year, from 54 in 1984 to more than 200 in 1987, employees are coming under the gun, too. Incidents of pollution are being traced to particular employees, and they and their employers face prosecution.

Several employees have been convicted, including a Toronto truck driver who emptied barrels of an unknown chemical into the back of his truck, creating a cloud of toxic gas, a pilot who sprayed pesticides improperly and a Nanticoke technician who opened a valve to fill a tank of caustic soda and then forgot to close it. He was personally fined $1,500 and ordered to perform 200 hours of community service.

Front-line employees are not the only ones affected. A pollution offence is committed by everyone in a position of influence and control who could have prevented the discharge, including supervisors and management.

After the City of Sault Ste. Marie hired an independent contractor who put garbage in an unsuitable place, causing pollution, both the contractor and the city were convicted.

In 1986, the Environmental Protection Act (EPA) was amended to expand the responsibility of corporate directors and officers. They are personally liable to prosecution unless they take all reasonable care to prevent their corporation from causing or permitting pollution.

The EPA goes to considerable lengths to protect employees who refuse to pollute. Any employee punished for refusing to pollute, or for whistleblowing, may write to the Ontario Labor Relations Board. After an inquiry, the board can order the employer to do whatever the board considers just.

This can include ordering the employer to cease harassing the employee, to rectify the harassment, compensate the employee and reinstate a dismissed employee with full back pay and seniority. These board orders can be enforced as though they were orders of the Supreme Court of Ontario.

It is no defence for the employer that the acts complained of may have been performed by a supervisor; the employer is liable for the actions of its supervisory staff. If there is any doubt, it will be resolved in favor of the employee; the burden of proof is upon the employer.

In addition, the employer can be prosecuted by the environment ministry. The penalties for harassing an employee for refusing to pollute can be as high as $25,000 for each day that the employee was harassed or kept off the job, and the labor relations board can demand complete compensation and back pay for the employee.

Employers have something to gain, too, by informing employees of their right not to pollute. Many enterprises have the potential to pollute, and may someday find themselves at the wrong end of a prosecution.

The most important defence available to a company that has polluted is "due diligence" — in other words, did the company do everything reasonably possible to prevent the pollution before it happened? One that has instructed its employees to refuse any work that pollutes will have taken a major step toward establishing this defence.

As the Worldwatch Institute has said, "The world has come a long way from the mid-seventies, when environmental concerns were considered something only the rich could afford to worry about. Today, they are concerns no one can afford to ignore."

Source Excerpts from Dianne Saxe, "The Right To Blow the Whistle", *The Globe and Mail*, Toronto, January 3, 1989, p. A-7.

A S S I G N M E N T   M A T E R I A L S

Discussion Questions

1. How do the financial statements of a manufacturing firm and a merchandising firm differ?
2. What accounts are used for a manufacturing firm that are not used for a merchandising or a service firm?
3. What is *factory overhead*, and what does it include?
4. Why are several inventory accounts used by manufacturers?
5. What is the difference between period and product costs?
6. When do product costs become period costs?
7. Explain how the transactions worksheet for a manufacturing firm differs from that for a merchandising firm.
8. How are opening and ending inventories recorded on a manufacturer's worksheet?
9. What is a Manufacturing Summary account, and how is one used?
10. How does a perpetual inventory system affect a manufacturing firm?

Discussion Cases

Discussion Case 16-1:   The Case of the Disappearing Inventory

Read Real Life Example 16-1, then discuss the following questions.

For Discussion

1. Does the article discuss entities that use periodic or perpetual inventory systems? Explain how you know.
2. What kind of bad decisions can a CEO make when accounting reports show inventory to be more than it actually is?
3. In small entities, the author suggests that the bookkeeper's work should be reviewed periodically and that a professional accountant should make a review annually. What is it in the bookkeeper's work that should be reviewed?
4. Most entities, both large and small, require continuous information about production costs for decision making. If a formal cost-accounting system is too costly for a small entity, what information can and should be prepared periodically?

Discussion Case 16-2:   Software Costing

Quite a few items go into producing a software package: the diskette itself, the labels, and the envelope or sleeve to cover it. Other elements include printed documentation, reference or registration cards, the packaging (such as the vinyl folders in which PC software is often sold), and possibly colour-printed wrap-around or shrink-wrap.

Acceptable quality single-sided diskettes cost $1.30 to $1.70 each. The advertisements in *P.C. Magazine* and other computer magazines are a good place to shop for volume diskette suppliers. You'll find that prices are much lower than you'd pay at retail computer stores—after all, we're talking wholesale here.

To label your diskettes, you could have custom die-cut labels made. If you don't want to get fancy, you can buy standard ones at a paper supply house or stationery store, for instance, Avery labels number 5523, which cost about $0.01 each. You can have them printed at a neighbourhood quick-printing store for a cost of about $0.01 for each colour print. Let's price labels at $0.03 each.

Envelopes may come free with the diskettes, although bulk-price diskettes without envelopes are often cheaper. If you want customized printed envelopes, a supplier can make them up for you. Expect to pay $0.05 to $0.20 for each envelope.

Copying the diskettes is another element. You may do it yourself at no cost. When you're starting out, in low volume, that can be reasonable.

Another option is to employ a diskette copying service. Copying runs about $0.30 to $0.50 per diskette. That may seem steep, but it can save you time and trouble and give you a technically much higher-quality copy. For the cost estimate we're building, let's take a range of zero (do-it-yourself) to $0.40.

Next let's consider the documentation. The price varies greatly by the size, number of copies, and number of colors printed. Games usually do nicely with just a few pages of documentation. . . . You might expect a range of costs from $0.20 to $1 each, and that's what we'll work with here. You should be able to find local printers that can handle the full job for you—printing, collating, and stapling. Many printers also can arrange typography and layout work for you; or you can use a graphics arts service to produce the camera-ready art that a printer needs. Many services are prepared to set type from files on a PC diskette, which can save you the cost of having a typesetter keyboard your documentation and also avoid the typos that usually come with re-keying.

Packaging is the next major item. Thanks to IBM's lead, two kinds of program packaging have become standards for the PC. One is the slip-case three-ring binder such as ones that encase the DOS and BASIC manuals; the other is a small vinyl folder that holds a diskette and a pamphlet.

We're not really discussing big-league programs here, so the vinyl folder is the sort that we're likely to want. These folders have to be custom-made to your specifications, and most large cities have several companies that specialize in this sort of work. Prices seem to range from $0.80 to $1.20 each. We'll take $1 as a typical price.

To complete your packaging, you may want an eye-catching four-colour, paper cover on one side of the package, similar to the wrapper IBM uses on many of the games it publishes. I'll guess that this small extravagance (which, by the way, makes good marketing sense) will cost $0.10 each. If you shrink-wrap your package in clear plastic, add another $0.10 or $0.20. (A consideration against shrink-wrap is that it prevents potential buyers from being able to browse through the documentation booklet.)

The total production cost of a small software package is about $3.85 per copy.

$1.30 Diskette
0.30 Copying
0.15 Envelopes
0.10 Labels, cards
0.50 Documentation
1.00 Vinyl folder
0.25 Colour card, shrink-wrap
0.25 Your labour

The figures used to produce this total are based on a reasonably high volume of program sets.

Source   Peter Norton, "The Kitchen Table Software Handbook". Reprinted from *P.C. Magazine*, June 12, 1984, pp. 119-225. Copyright © 1984 Ziff-Communications Company.

For Discussion

1. What other issues should you explore before undertaking to manufacture your own software program diskettes?
2. How does the size of a manufacturing operation influence the overhead costs? What are the advantages and disadvantages of a small manufacturer, as opposed to a larger company?

Discussion Case 16-3:   How the U.S. Navy Paid $436 for a $7 Hammer

How did the United States Navy end up paying $436 ($562 in 1984 Canadian dollars) for a hammer that costs $7 (Cdn $9) in a neighbourhood hardware store?

The admirals have given congress the following breakdown of their contract with a defence contractor, identified as Gould Inc., headquartered in suburban Maryland, for: "hammer, hand, sledge—quantity one each". Cost of the basic hammer is $7. Then add, for each hammer, the following costs (in US$):

— $41 to pay general overhead cost of Gould's engineering staff involved in mapping out the hammer problem. This figure also includes 12 minutes in secretarial time preparing the hammer purchase order, 26 minutes of management time spent on the hammer purchase and 2 hours and 36 minutes the engineers spent mulling over the proper design of the hammer.
— $93 for the 18 minutes it took for "mechanical sub-assembly" of the hammer, 4 hours for engineers to map out the hammer assembly process, 90 minutes spent by managers overseeing the hammer manufacturing process, 60 minutes for a project engineer to ensure the hammer was properly assembled, 54 minutes spent by quality control engineers examining the hammer to ensure it didn't have any defects, and 7 hours and 48 minutes devoted to other support activities involved in assembling the hammer.

— $102 went toward "manufacturing overhead".
— $37 for 60 minutes Gould's "spares/repair department" spent gearing up for either repairing or finding parts, should the hammer ever break.
— $2 for "material handling overhead" representing the payroll costs for the people to wrap the hammer and send it out.
— $1 for wrapping paper and a box.

This brought the sub-total of costs for the hammer to $283. This figure was multiplied by a factor of 31.8 percent, representing general administrative costs for Gould, and another $56 was added in a finders' fee given Gould for locating the sort of specific hammer that fitted the navy's needs.

Another $7 was given Gould for the "capital cost of money" Gould expended in the hammer purchase.

"How do we explain a system that allows this to happen to our taxpayers?" protested Rep. Berkley Bedell (Democrat—Iowa), who obtained the navy's explanation for the costly hammer.

A navy official explained that large defence contractors, such as Gould, are permitted to charge off general costs against all contracted items and that, in the case of relatively inexpensive items, these costs may appear disproportionately large.

Source Scripps-Howard News Service, "How U.S. Navy Paid $562 for a $9 hammer", *The* (Montreal) *Gazette*, May 19, 1984, p. G-8.

For Discussion

1. Calculate the overhead rate for Gould Inc., using data from this article. Do you think Gould uses this rate for all its products? for all its customers? Why?
2. Comment on Congressman Bedell's question.
3. Should the navy purchase a hammer at a neighbourhood hardware store? How can it control the cost of such relatively inexpensive items?

Comprehension Problems

Comprehension Problem 16-1

The Polywog Toy Corporation of Port Hope, Ontario manufactures and distributes to retailers its best-selling toy, "The Polywog". This toy is aimed at the young adult market and is similar to Rubik's Cube. The manufacture and assembly of The Polywog requires plastic, springs, paint, as well as skilled workers. Once assembled, The Polywog is placed in a cardboard box and sealed.

Required: Classify each of the following costs as Materials, Direct Labour, Factory Overhead, Selling Costs, or Administrative Costs. State whether each is a period or a product cost.
1. Freight out
2. Sales commissions
3. Accounting fees paid to Clarkson Gordon
4. Port Hope municipal taxes assessed to the factory
5. Lubricants for the machines
6. Plastic to be injected into the moulds
7. Cardboard to make the boxes
8. Overtime paid to workers
9. A wrench to fix the conveyor belt
10. An executive training program.

Comprehension Problem 16-2

Following are manufacturing costs for the Sandbanks Boat Works Ltd. of Souris, PEI. Sandbanks Boat Works manufactures small fishing and lobster boats. Consider the following data for 19X0.

Grease (used for tools and construction)	$ 2,500	Finished Goods — Beginning (1 boat)	$ 24,100
Rent — Manufacturing Shed	15,000	Finished Goods — Ending (1 boat)	25,200
Direct Labour	110,000	Work in Process — Beginning	28,200
Indirect Materials	1,500	Work in Process — Ending	50,400
Factory Utilities	4,600	General Administrative Expenses	50,000
Insurance — Shed	1,200	Raw Materials — Beginning	21,000
Purchases of Raw Materials	110,000	Raw Materials — Ending	7,400

Required:
1. Prepare a statement of the cost of goods manufactured.
2. Why did the boat built at the beginning of the year cost less than the one being built at the close of the year?

Comprehension Problem 16-3

Lynne Missen works as an assembler in the Ford plant in Oakville, Ontario. Last week, she worked 52 hours; during the week, she was idle for 2 hours while there was a back-up in the installation of the rack-and-pinion steering to the main chassis assembly. In the remaining 50 hours, Lynne spent 49 directly on the manufacture of a new Ford "Taurus". The other hour Lynne spent in a meeting of the Management-Employee Safety Committee. Lynne is paid $12.00 per hour for 40 hours a week; she is paid time and a half for work in excess of 40 hours and double time for work in excess of 50 hours per week.

Required: Allocate Lynne Missen's wages between direct labour costs and factory overhead.

Comprehension Problem 16-4

The Cook Copier Corporation manufactures its photocopiers for specific orders, which are then sold by several retailers of office equipment under its own brand name. The following information is available about a job that is being prepared under company job number 1067-GHB-376.

Direct Materials issued:
   1000 circuits for assembly: 109.55 per circuit
   1000 photo lens attachments: $153.95 each
   Plastic casing fluid: 10 000 kL at $0.13/kL
   Electric wire: 10 000m at $0.02/m
   Direct labour: 2200 hours at $8/h
   The overhead rate for the factory is $3/h per each direct labour hour.
   Unused material returned: 2000kL of plastic fluid
   Photocopiers started: 1000
   Photocopiers completed: 880
   Photocopiers sold: 240

Required:
   1. Calculate the unit cost of production.
   2. Prepare journal entries to record these transactions.

Problems

Problem 16-1

The following compound closing entry is taken from the records of Nadrofsky Manufacturing Ltd. at December 31, 19X8 its fiscal year-end.

Dec. 31	Raw Materials Inventory	12,000	
	Work in Process Inventory	9,000	
	Raw Materials Purchases Returns and Allowances	5,000	
	Raw Materials Purchases Discounts	1,000	
	Manufacturing Summary	601,000	
	Raw Materials Inventory		10,000
	Work in Process Inventory		15,000
	Raw Materials Purchases		100,000
	Transportation In		3,000
	Direct Labour		300,000
	Indirect Labour		75,000
	Depreciation Expense — Machinery		40,000
	Factory Supplies Expense		4,000
	Rent Expense		36,000
	Maintenance Expense		25,000
	Utilities Expense		20,000
	To close manufacturing accounts		
	and set up Manufacturing Summary.		

Required:
1. Calculate the net cost of materials purchased during 19X8. (Use the form in section B of the chapter.)
2. Prepare a statement of cost of goods manufactured for 19X8 in proper form. Include the net cost of goods purchased amount calculated in 1, above.
3. How much factory overhead was incurred in 19X8 for each dollar of direct labour?

Problem 16-2

The following information is extracted from the worksheet of Kaufman Corporation at December 31, 19X8, its fiscal year-end.

	Cost of Goods Manufactured		Income Statement	
	Dr.	*Cr.*	*Dr.*	*Cr.*
Raw Materials Inventory	36,000	40,000		
Work in Process Inventory	66,000	90,000		
Finished Goods Inventory			60,000	75,000
Sales				1,171,800
Net Cost of Goods Purchased	300,000			
Direct Labour Expense	360,000			
Indirect Labour Expense	100,000			
Depreciation Expense — Machinery	40,000			
Factory Supplies Expense	15,000			
Maintenance Expense	7,000			
Rent Expense	48,000			
Small Tools Expense	10,000			
Advertising Expense			48,820	
Commissions Expense			117,180	
Delivery Expense			10,640	
Insurance Expense (office)			8,600	
Salaries Expense (office)			39,000	
Telephone Expense			3,600	
Interest Expense			40,000	
Income Tax Expense			33,480	
Totals	982,000	130,000		
Cost of Goods Manufactured		852,000	852,000	
	982,000	982,000	1,213,320	1,246,800
Net Income for the Year			33,480	
			1,246,800	1,246,800

Required:

1. Prepare a statement of cost of goods manufactured in proper form for the year ended December 31, 19X8.
2. Prepare a classified income statement for the year ended December 31, 19X8.
3. Prepare all necessary closing entries at December 31, 19X8.

Problem 16-3

The trial balance and adjustments columns of Earl Corporation worksheet at December 31, 19X6, its fiscal year-end, are reproduced below.

	Trial Balance		Adjustments	
Account Title	Dr.	Cr.	Dr.	Cr.
Cash	12,000			
Raw Materials Inventory	58,300			
Work in Process Inventory	31,725			
Finished Goods Inventory	25,000			
Prepaid Insurance	2,100			(b) 800
Equipment (factory)	16,000			
Accumulated Depreciation		4,000		(a) 2,500
Accounts Payable		27,000		
Common Stock		125,000		
Retained Earnings		24,000		
Dividends	10,000			
Sales		308,625		
Raw Materials Purchases (net)	91,000			
Transportation In	1,000			
Direct Labour Expense	98,000			
Indirect Labour Expense	27,000			
Maintenance Expense	7,000			
Rent Expense (factory)	12,000			
Small Tools Expense	2,000			
Advertising Expense	6,000			
Commission Expense	50,000			
Delivery Expense	2,000			
Rent Expense (office)	4,000			
Salaries Expense (office)	29,500			
Telephone Expense (office)	4,000			
Totals	488,625	488,625		
Depreciation Expense			(a) 2,500	
Insurance Expense (factory)			(b) 800	
Income Tax Expense			(c) 4,800	
Income Tax Payable				(c) 4,800
Totals			8,100	8,100

Ending Inventories, December 31, 19X8:

Raw Materials	$69,000
Work in Process	52,000
Finished Goods	50,000

Required:
1. Complete the manufacturing worksheet from the data given.
2. Prepare a cost of goods manufactured statement.
3. Prepare a classified income statement.

Problem 16-4

The following account balances are taken from the records of Fizzell Freezing Ltd. at December 31, 19X6, the corporation's fiscal year-end.

	January 1	December 31
Raw Materials Inventory	65,000	52,000
Work in Process Inventory	50,000	120,000
Finished Goods Inventory	120,000	140,000
Raw Materials Purchases (net)		970,000
Transportation In		12,500
Direct Labour		80,000
Indirect Labour		40,000
Depreciation Expense — Factory Machinery		65,500
Factory Supplies Expense		60,900
Rent Expense — Factory		120,000
Small Tools Expense		16,560
Advertising Expense		20,150
Commissions Expense		185,460
Delivery Expense		46,500
Rent Expense — Office		12,900
Salaries Expense — Office		60,350

Required:
1. Prepare a statement of cost of goods manufactured in proper form for the year ended December 31, 19X6.
2. Prepare the cost of goods sold section of the income statement.
3. Assuming that a relationship between direct labour and factory overhead exists in this corporation, calculate how much factory overhead was incurred for each direct labour dollar.
4. Prepare all necessary closing entries at December 31, 19X6.

Alternate Problems

Alternate Problem 16-1

The following compound closing entry is taken from the records of Yosemite Manufacturing Corp. at December 31, 19X5, the corporation's fiscal year-end.

Dec. 31	Raw Materials Inventory	48,000	
	Work in Process Inventory	36,000	
	Raw Materials Purchases Returns and Allowances	20,000	
	Raw Materials Purchases Discounts	3,200	
	Manufacturing Summary	1,604,800	
	Raw Materials Inventory		40,000
	Work in Process Inventory		60,000
	Raw Materials Purchases		400,000
	Transportation In		12,000
	Direct Labour		800,000
	Indirect Labour		75,000
	Depreciation Expense — Machinery		160,000
	Factory Heating		44,000
	Factory Insurance		50,000
	Factory Supplies Expense		46,000
	Maintenance Expense		25,000
	To close manufacturing accounts and set up Manufacturing Summary.		

Required:
1. Calculate the net cost of materials purchased during 19X4.
2. Prepare a statement of cost of goods manufactured for 19X4 in proper form. Include the net cost of materials purchased calculated in 1, above.
3. How much factory overhead was incurred in 19X4 for each dollar of direct labour?

Alternate Problem 16-2

The following information is extracted from the worksheet of Munro Corporation at December 31, 19X8, its fiscal year-end.

	Cost of Goods Manufactured		Income Statement	
	Dr.	Cr.	Dr.	Cr.
Raw Materials Inventory	52,000	65,000		
Work in Process Inventory	110,000	84,000		
Finished Goods Inventory			65,000	67,000
Sales				1,285,600
Raw Materials Purchases (net)	290,000			
Transportation In	6,500			
Direct Labour Expense	450,000			
Indirect Labour Expense	123,000			
Depreciation — Machinery	45,000			
Insurance Expense	5,000			
Maintenance Expense	6,700			
Rent Expense	12,000			
Utilities Expense	8,000			
Advertising Expense			3,000	
Commissions Expense			82,000	
Depreciation Expense — Truck			12,000	
Insurance Expense (truck)			3,000	
Office Supplies Expense			9,000	
Salaries Expense (office)			49,000	
Telephone Expense			5,000	
Income Tax Expense			24,870	
Totals	1,108,200	149,000		
Cost of Goods Manufactured		959,200	959,200	
	1,108,200	1,108,200	1,212,070	1,352,600
Net Income for the year			140,530	
			1,352,600	1,352,600

Required:
1. Prepare a statement of cost of goods manufactured in proper format for the year ended December 31, 19X8.
2. Prepare a classified income statement for the year ended December 31, 19X8.
3. Prepare all necessary closing entries at December 31, 19X8.

Alternate Problem 16-3

The trial balance and adjustments columns of Hirst Corporation's worksheet at December 31, 19X9, its fiscal year-end, are reproduced below.

Account Title	Trial Balance		Adjustments		
	Dr.	Cr.		Dr.	Cr.
Cash	15,800				
Raw Materials Inventory	20,000				
Work in Process Inventory	25,000				
Finished Goods Inventory	85,000				
Prepaid Rent	6,000		(b)		6,000
Equipment (factory)	13,000				
Accumulated Depreciation			(a)		4,000
Accounts Payable		26,000			
Common Stock		35,000			
Retained Earnings		21,000			
Dividends	4,200				
Sales		408,000			
Raw Materials Purchases	83,200				
Transportation	6,000				
Direct Labour	120,000				
Indirect Labour	15,000				
Maintenance Expense	6,000				
Advertising Expense	10,000				
Commissions Expense	36,000				
Delivery Expense	7,000				
Insurance Expense (office)	3,000				
Salaries Expense (office)	27,000				
Telephone Expense (office)	1,800				
Utilities Expense (office)	6,000				
Totals	490,000	490,000			
Depreciation Expense			(a)	4,000	
Rent Expense (factory)			(b)	6,000	
Income Tax Expense			(c)	15,000	
Income Tax Payable			(c)		15,000
Totals				25,000	25,000

Ending Inventories, December 31, 19X8	
Raw Material	$25,000
Work in Process	27,000
Finished Goods	80,000

Required:
1. Complete the manufacturing worksheet.
2. Prepare a cost of goods manufactured statement.
3. Prepare a classified income statement.

Use of the Worksheet

A.   The Worksheet

Worksheet
A multi-column schedule used to organize the many details that are brought together when financial statements are being prepared; facilitates the preparation of financial statements.

Accountants usually use a columnar schedule to aid in preparing financial statements. This columnar schedule is called a **worksheet**. In Chapter 3, a trial balance for Bluebeard Computer Corporation was prepared as a separate schedule, following the recording and posting of the corporation's February transactions. As an alternative practice, the trial balance could be recorded directly on the worksheet. The arrangement of a typical worksheet consists of a series of debit and credit columns, as shown in Figure A-1.

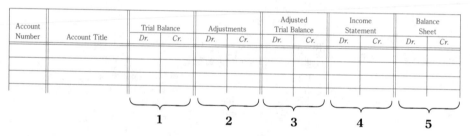

Figure A-1   The worksheet

The columns on the worksheet are explained below.

1. The debit and credit account balances are entered in these columns directly from the general ledger.
2. The adjusting entries for the period are recorded on the worksheet in the second pair of debit and credit columns.
3. The amounts in the preliminary trial balance and adjustment columns are combined, and the new balances are recorded in this third pair of debit and credit columns; these totals are referred to as an adjusted trial balance.
4. The revenue and expense account balances listed in the adjusted trial balance columns are transferred to the income statement debit and credit columns. The income statement will later be prepared from the amounts listed in these columns.
5. The asset, liability, and equity account balances listed in the adjusted trial balance columns are transferred to the balance sheet debit and credit columns. The statement of retained earnings and the balance sheet will later be prepared from the amounts listed in these columns.

The worksheet is not a formal accounting record, as are the journal and ledger. Rather, it is an intermediate step that bridges the gap between the accounting records and the financial statements.

The worksheet organizes the many details that are brought together when statements are being prepared. It also provides an opportunity to check financial data, since its debit and credit column totals prove the equality of the account balances. An error is indicated whenever total debits do not equal total credits in any pair of columns. The worksheet is also a convenient place to calculate the net income or net loss for the period. The worksheet gives the accountant a preview of the final financial statements before these statements are prepared.

A worksheet is unnecessary in actual practice if there are only a few accounts in the trial balance and if only a few adjusting entries are required. The worksheet is very useful, however, when numerous accounts and adjustments must be organized before financial statements are prepared. In the case of the Bluebeard Computer Corporation, the February 28 worksheet might not be used by an experienced accountant, although its use may be convenient.

In the next few pages, a worksheet for BCC at February 28 is prepared to demonstrate the methodology. The use of the worksheet in the preparation of the corporation's year-end financial statements is also examined.

Recording a Trial Balance in the Worksheet

When all February transactions are journalized and posted, a trial balance is prepared on the worksheet to prove the equality of debit and credit balances in the ledger. The trial balance is recorded directly on the worksheet, to reduce the duplication that would otherwise result from preparing the trial balance elsewhere and then transferring the identical information to the worksheet. Figure A-2 illustrates the four steps required in worksheet preparation, which are discussed next.

Worksheet
For the Period Ended February 28, 19X1

Account Number	Account Title	Trial Balance Dr.	Trial Balance Cr.	Adjustments Dr.	Adjustments Cr.	Adjusted Trial Balance Dr.	Adjusted Trial Balance Cr.	Income Statement Dr.	Income Statement Cr.	Balance Sheet Dr.	Balance Sheet Cr.
101	Cash	11,595				11,595				11,595	
110	Accounts Receivable	3,500				3,500				3,500	
120	Notes Receivable	5,000				5,000				5,000	
161	Prepaid Insurance	1,200			(a) 200	1,000				1,000	
183	Equipment	3,000				3,000				3,000	
184	Truck	8,000				8,000				8,000	
201	Bank Loan		5,000				5,000				5,000
210	Accounts Payable		1,900				1,900				1,900
248	Unearned Rent		500	(b) 300			200				200
320	Common Stock		11,000				11,000				11,000
340	Retained Earnings		0								
450	Repair Revenue		23,895	(e) 2,000			21,895		21,895		
654	Rent Expense	1,200				1,200		1,200			
656	Salaries Expense	5,000		(h) 150		5,150		5,150			
668	Supplies Expense	2,100			(f) 495	1,605		1,605			
670	Truck Expense	1,400				1,400		1,400			
676	Utilities Expense	300				300		300			
	Totals	42,295	42,295								
631	Insurance Expense			(a) 200		200		200			
440	Rent Earned				(b) 300		300		300		
623	Deprec. Exp.–Eqpmt.			(c) 45		45		45			
193	Accum. Deprec.–Eqpmt.				(c) 45		45				45
624	Depre. Exp.–Truck			(d) 240		240		240			
194	Accum. Deprec.–Truck				(d) 240		240				240
247	Unearned Repair Rev.				(e) 2,000		2,000				2,000
173	Supplies			(f) 495		495				495	
116	Interest Receivable			(g) 25		25				25	
430	Interest Earned				(g) 25		25		25		
226	Salaries Payable				(h) 150		150				150
632	Interest Expense			(i) 92		92		92			
222	Interest Payable				(i) 92		92				92
830	Income Tax Expense			(j) 5,994		5,994		5,994			
260	Income Tax Payable				(j) 5,994		5,994				5,994
	Totals			9,541	9,541	48,841	48,841	16,226	22,220	32,615	26,621
	Net Income							5,994			5,994
	Totals							22,220	22,220	32,615	32,615

Total Debit Balances = Total Credit Balances

The equality of these columns is proved to help insure that no errors have been made.

Figure A-2   The worksheet illustrated

Step 1: The Trial Balance Is Recorded Directly in the Worksheet
Accountants often refer to this trial balance as the *unadjusted trial balance*, because the adjusting entries required to match revenues with expenses are not yet included in the account balances. The preparation of financial statements from an unadjusted trial balance would cause misleading information to be communicated.

Following the recording of the unadjusted trial balance in the worksheet, the adjusting entries are entered in the second pair of columns (as in Figure A-2).

Step 2: The Adjustments Are Recorded in the Appropriate Columns of the Worksheet
The adjustments recorded on the worksheet are identified by the following key letters:
(a) The February expense portion of prepaid insurance
(b) The February revenue portion of unearned rent
(c) Depreciation of the equipment during February
(d) Depreciation of the truck during February
(e) The amount of unearned revenue in February
(f) Repair supplies not used in February
(g) Interest earned on note during February
(h) Salaries accrued at February 28
(i) Interest expense on bank loans
(j) Estimated income taxes at February 28.
These are the adjustments that were prepared in Chapter 3.

Step 3: The Trial Balance Columns Amounts Are Combined with the Adjustments Columns Amounts
The accountant uses the worksheet to organize the many details that have to be brought together from the ledger and the schedule of adjustments before the financial statements can be prepared. Following the recording of adjusting entries on the worksheet, an adjusted trial balance is calculated in the third pair of columns.

Step 4: The Amounts in the Adjustments Columns Are Transferred to the Income Statement and Balance Sheet Columns
The adjusted trial balance columns amounts are transferred either to the income statement columns or to the balance sheet columns in this way:

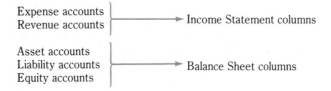

Balancing the Worksheet

The income statement and balance sheet debit and credit columns are now totalled. The difference between the totals of the income statement columns is the net income of $5,994 at February 28; a net income exists because the total of the credit column exceeds the total of the debit expenses column. The $5,994 difference is entered in the income statement debit column and in the balance sheet credit column, as shown below.

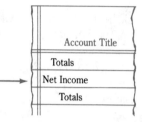

Entering Net Income on this line brings the columns into balance. This is the self-balancing feature of the accounting equation.

Account Title	Adjusted Trial Balance		Income Statement		Balance Sheet	
	Dr.	Cr.	Dr.	Cr.	Dr.	Cr.
Totals	48,841	48,841	16,226	22,220	32,615	26,621
Net Income			5,994			5,994
Totals						

The next step in the completion of the worksheet is the addition of the income statement and balance sheet columns.

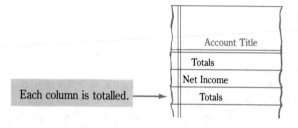

Each column is totalled.

Account Title	Adjusted Trial Balance		Income Statement		Balance Sheet	
	Dr.	Cr.	Dr.	Cr.	Dr.	Cr.
Totals	48,841	48,841	16,226	22,220	32,615	26,621
Net Income			5,994			5,994
Totals			22,220	22,220	32,615	32,615

Note that the totals in the two income statement columns are equal, and that the totals in the two balance sheet columns are also equal. These balances indicate the equality of debits and credits that has been maintained in recording the trial balance and adjustments in the worksheet. The fact that debits equal credits indicates that all calculations in the worksheet are mathematically correct.

If the worksheet reveals that expenses exceed revenues during a period (that is, when there is a net loss), the procedure to be followed is as follows:

Account Title	Adjusted Trial Balance		Income Statement		Balance Sheet	
	Dr.	Cr.	Dr.	Cr.	Dr.	Cr.
Totals	50,000	50,000	8,000	5,000	42,000	45,000
Net Loss				3,000◄──► 3,000		
Totals			8,000	8,000	45,000	45,000

In this case, a $3,000 net loss exists, since the total of the income statement debit column exceeds that of the income statement credit column. The $3,000 difference is recorded in the income statement credit column and in the balance sheet debit column.

Completion of the Worksheet for a Merchandising Firm

As in the case of a service business, the completion of a worksheet for a merchandising firm organizes the many details that must be brought together when financial statements are being prepared. As well, the worksheet gives the accountant a preview of the final statements before they are actually prepared.

The adjacent completed worksheet is for Bluebeard Computer Corporation for 19X3. Note that the opening inventory is extended to the income statement debit column. Ending inventory is recorded directly on the worksheet as a credit in the income statement columns and as a debit in the balance sheet columns.

Note that the worksheet for a merchandising firm differs in one respect from that of the service business: the treatment of inventory.

1. Opening inventory appears in the trial balance as $80,000. This amount has not changed during the year because Bluebeard follows the periodic inventory system in recording the purchase of merchandise for resale in the Purchases account. The Merchandise Inventory account remains unchanged until the closing entries are recorded.
2. The opening inventory amount is transferred to the income statement debit column because it is later used in the calculation of the cost of goods sold sub-total, which appears in the income statement.
3. The amount of ending inventory is recorded directly on the worksheet
   a. as a credit in the income statement columns because it is later used in the calculation of cost of goods sold; in this calculation, it is deducted from the cost of goods available for sale, and
   b. as a debit in the balance sheet columns because it represents the amount of inventory at year-end; an asset appearing in the balance sheet requires a debit balance.

The recording of the ending inventory amount into the records is discussed later in this chapter.

After the recording of ending inventory in the worksheet, the columns are added and balanced, as explained in Chapter 3. Note that there are no adjusted trial balance columns; this set of columns is simply an intermediate step between the recording of adjustments and the transfer of adjusted balances to the income statement and balance sheet columns. Omission of the adjusted trial balance columns reduces the time required to complete the worksheet without any corresponding loss of accuracy.

Bluebeard Computer Corporation
Worksheet
For the Year Ended December 31, 19X3

Account Number	Account Title	Trial Balance Dr.	Trial Balance Cr.	Adjustments Dr.	Adjustments Cr.	Adjusted Trial Balance Dr.	Adjusted Trial Balance Cr.	Income Statement Dr.	Income Statement Cr.	Balance Sheet Dr.	Balance Sheet Cr.
101	Cash	10,800								10,800	
110	Accounts Receivable	26,000								26,000	
150	Merchandise Inventory	80,000						80,000	120,000	120,000	
161	Prepaid Insurance	2,400			(a) 1,200					1,200	
183	Equipment	13,600								13,600	
193	Accum. Deprec.-Eqpmt.		–		(b) 1,600						1,600
201	Bank Loan — Current		39,000								39,000
210	Accounts Payable		25,000								25,000
260	Income Tax Payable		–		(c) 15,000						15,000
271	Bank Loan—Long-Term		48,500								48,500
320	Common Stock		10,000								10,000
340	Retained Earnings		21,750								21,750
350	Dividends	4,250								4,250	
500	Sales		308,500						308,500		
508	Sales Returns and										
	Allowances	6,000						6,000			
509	Sales Discounts	2,500						2,500			
550	Purchases	240,000						240,000			
558	Purchases Returns and										
	Allowances		12,600						12,600		
559	Purchases Discounts		2,400						2,400		
560	Transportation In	15,000						15,000			
610	Advertising Expense	10,000						10,000			
615	Commissions Expense	15,000						15,000			
620	Delivery Expense	6,000						6,000			
632	Interest Expense	10,000						10,000			
654	Rent Expense	3,600						3,600			
656	Salaries Expense	20,000						20,000			
669	Telephone Expense	1,080						1,080			
676	Utilities Expense	1,520						1,520			
	Totals	467,750	467,750								
623	Deprec. Expense-Eqpmt.			(a) 1,200				1,200			
631	Insurance Expense			(b) 1,600				1,600			
830	Income Tax Expense			(c) 15,000				15,000			
	Totals			17,800	17,800			428,500	443,500	175,850	160,850
	Net Income for the Year							15,000			15,000
	Totals							443,500	443,500	175,850	175,850

B. Preparation of Financial Statements from the Worksheet

The data listed in the income statement and balance sheet columns of the worksheet are used to prepare the financial statements of Bluebeard Computer Corporation at the end of February. In the following pages, extracts from the worksheet are used to demonstrate the tie-in between the worksheet and end-of-period financial statement preparation.

Income Statement Preparation

The income statement is prepared from the amounts in the income statement columns of the worksheet. Notice in Figure A-3 that all the amounts contained in the income statement columns are rearranged and repeated in the formal statement.

Partial Worksheet

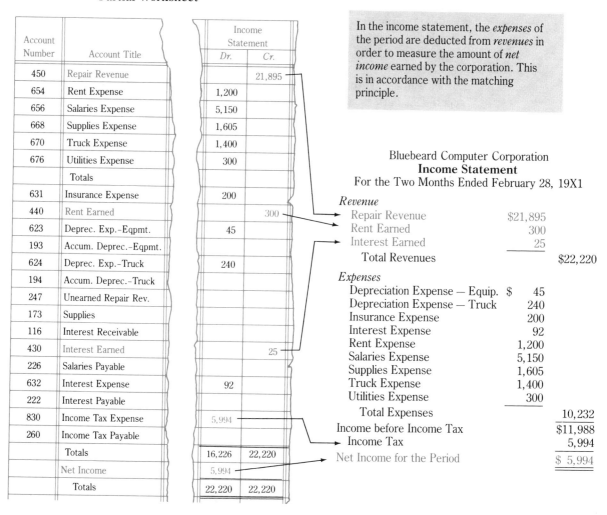

In the income statement, the *expenses* of the period are deducted from *revenues* in order to measure the amount of *net income* earned by the corporation. This is in accordance with the matching principle.

Bluebeard Computer Corporation
Income Statement
For the Two Months Ended February 28, 19X1

Revenue
Repair Revenue	$21,895	
Rent Earned	300	
Interest Earned	25	
Total Revenues		$22,220

Expenses
Depreciation Expense — Equip.	$ 45	
Depreciation Expense — Truck	240	
Insurance Expense	200	
Interest Expense	92	
Rent Expense	1,200	
Salaries Expense	5,150	
Supplies Expense	1,605	
Truck Expense	1,400	
Utilities Expense	300	
Total Expenses		10,232
Income before Income Tax		$11,988
Income Tax		5,994
Net Income for the Period		$ 5,994

Figure A-3   Income statement preparation

A sole proprietor pays personal income tax on business income; a partner pays personal income tax on his/her share of a partnership's income. Accordingly, the income statement of a proprietorship or partnership does not include an income tax calculation. A corporation, however, pays income tax as a percentage of income from operations; Bluebeard Computer Corporation has estimated that the amount of tax due will be $5,994. Shareholders do not pay income tax on the corporation's income; rather, they are subject to tax only on the amount of cash dividends received by them.

Statement of Retained Earnings and Balance Sheet Preparation

Retained earnings represent the net income of a corporation that has been retained in the business; this amounts to $5,994 for Bluebeard Computer Corporation at February 28, 19X1. The statement of retained earnings is the financial statement that, in effect, links the income statement with the balance sheet. Net income (or net loss) reported in the income statement is added (or deducted, if a loss) to any opening Retained Earnings account balance (less any dividends paid) in calculating the ending Retained Earnings amount reported on the balance sheet. In this way, the statement of retained earnings reconciles the opening Retained Earnings amount with the ending Retained Earnings amount appearing in the balance sheet. There is no opening retained earnings in the case of Bluebeard Computer Corporation, since it only began operations during the year. The $5,994 Retained Earnings balance at February 28, 19X1 becomes the opening Retained Earnings amount on March 1.

The statement of retained earnings and the balance sheet are prepared from amounts in the balance sheet columns of the worksheet. Preparation of these financial statements is facilitated by using these worksheet columns, since all necessary financial information is already listed there. (See Figure A-4.)

Care must be taken in the preparation of financial statements from a worksheet. The debit/credit relationship shown on the worksheet is not emphasized by these statements, although it is obviously present. In the balance sheet for example, Accumulated Depreciation — Truck, with a credit balance of $240, is deducted from Truck, which has a debit balance. Care must also be taken to use each amount just once and in its proper debit/credit relation.

Partial Worksheet

Account Number	Account Title	Balance Sheet Dr.	Balance Sheet Cr.
101	Cash	11,595	
110	Accounts Receivable	3,500	
120	Notes Receivable	5,000	
161	Prepaid Insurance	1,000	
183	Equipment	3,000	
184	Truck	8,000	
201	Bank Loan		5,000
210	Accounts Payable		1,900
248	Unearned Rent		200
320	Common Stock		11,000
340	Retained Earnings		
450	Repair Revenue		
654	Rent Expense		
656	Salaries Expense		
668	Supplies Expense		
670	Truck Expense		
676	Utilities Expense		
	Totals		
631	Insurance Expense		
440	Rent Earned		
623	Deprec. Exp.-Eqpmt.		
193	Accum. Deprec.-Eqpmt.		45
624	Deprec. Exp.-Truck		
194	Accum. Deprec.-Truck		240
247	Unearned Repair Rev.		2,000
173	Supplies	495	
116	Interest Receivable	25	
430	Interest Earned		
226	Salaries Payable		150
632	Interest Expense		
222	Interest Payable		92
830	Income Tax Expense		
260	Income Tax Payable		5,994
	Totals	32,615	26,621
	Net Income		5,994
	Totals	32,615	32,615

This is the date at which the assets, liabilities, and equity of the corporation are taken.

The statement of retained earnings shows the changes that occurred from January 1 to February 28, which is the end of the time period.

Bluebeard Computer Corporation
Statement of Retained Earnings
For the Two Months Ended February 28, 19X1

Balance, Nov. 1		$ -0-
Add: Net Income		5,994
Balance, Dec. 31		$5,994

Bluebeard Computer Corporation
Balance Sheet
At February 28, 19X1

Assets

Cash		$11,595
Accounts Receivable		3,500
Interest Receivable		25
Notes Receivable		5,000
Prepaid Insurance		1,000
Supplies		495
		$21,615
Equipment	$ 3,000	
Less: Accumulated Depreciation	45	2,955
Truck	$ 8,000	
Less: Accumulated Depreciation	240	7,760
		$32,330

Liabilities

Bank Loan		$ 5,000
Accounts Payable		1,900
Interest Payable		92
Salaries Payable		150
Income Tax Payable		5,994
Unearned Repair Revenue		2,000
Unearned Rent		200
		$15,336

Shareholders' Equity

Common Stock	$11,000	
Retained Earnings	$5,994	16,994
		$32,330

Figure A-4   Statement of retained earnings and balance sheet preparation

A S S I G N M E N T   M A T E R I A L S

Problems

Problem A-1

The adjusted trial balance of Ichor Services Inc. follows.

Partial Worksheet
For the Year Ended December 31, 19X1

Account Title	Adjusted Trial Balance	
	Dr.	Cr.
Cash	500	
Accounts Receivable	10,000	
Truck	11,000	
Accumulated Deprec.		2,500
Bank Loan		10,000
Accounts Payable		6,000
Common Stock		1,000
Revenue		27,000
Advertising Expense	1,500	
Commissions Expense	5,000	
Depreciation Expense	2,500	
Insurance Expense	1,200	
Interest Expense	750	
Rent Expense	3,600	
Salaries Expense	10,000	
Supplies Expense	250	
Telephone Expense	200	
Totals		
Net Income for Year		
Totals		

Required:
1. Calculate the totals of the adjusted trial balance debit and credit columns.
2. Complete the income statement and balance sheet columns of the worksheet.
3. Prepare the formal year-end income statement of the corporation.
4. Prepare all closing entries.

Problem A-2

The following partial worksheet and additional information are taken from the records of Maxilla Inc. at the end of its first year of operations.

Partial Worksheet
For the Year Ended December 31, 19X1

Account Title	Trial Balance Dr.	Trial Balance Cr.
Cash	3,300	
Accounts Receivable	4,000	
Prepaid Insurance	1,200	
Supplies	500	
Truck	8,500	
Accounts Payable		5,000
Unearned Rent		2,400
Common Stock		6,000
Revenue		16,600
Advertising Expense	200	
Commissions Expense	1,000	
Interest Expense	400	
Rent Expense	3,600	
Salaries Expense	7,000	
Telephone Expense	300	
Totals		
Insurance Expense		
Supplies Expense		
Depreciation Expense		
Accumulated Deprec.		
Salaries Payable		
Rent Earned		
Totals		
Net Income for Year		
Totals		

The following additional data are available:
a. Prepaid insurance at December 31 amounts to $600.
b. A physical count indicates that $300-worth of supplies are still on hand at December 31.
c. The truck was purchased on July 1 and has a useful life of 4 years with an estimated salvage value of $500.
d. One day of salaries for December 31 is unpaid; the unpaid amount of $200 will be included in the first Friday payment in January.
e. The unearned rent represents 6 months rental of some warehouse space, effective October 1.
f. A $100 bill for December telephone charges has not yet been received or recorded (record in Accounts Payable).

Required:
1. Prepare all necessary adjusting entries.
2. Complete the worksheet.
3. Prepare all necessary reversing entries.

Problem A-3

The following columns are taken from the worksheet of Nootka Service Corporation:

Partial Worksheet
For the Year Ended December 31, 19X1

Account Title	Income Statement Dr.	Income Statement Cr.	Balance Sheet Dr.	Balance Sheet Cr.
Cash			650	
Prepaid Insurance			1,100	
Supplies			700	
Equipment			3,000	
Accumulated Deprec.				250
Accounts Payable				2,000
Unearned Revenue				750
Income Tax Payable				725
Common Stock				1,000
Revenue		11,750		
Advertising Expense	400			
Commissions Expense	1,500			
Depreciation Expense	250			
Insurance Expense	100			
Rent Expense	2,400			
Salaries Expense	5,000			
Supplies Expense	300			
Telephone Expense	350			
Income Tax Expense	725			
Totals				
Net Income for Year				
Totals				

Required:
1. Complete the worksheet income statement and balance sheet columns.
2. Prepare all closing entries.
3. Prepare a post-closing trial balance.

Problem A-4

The adjusted trial balance of Enta Services Ltd. follows.

Partial Worksheet
For the Year Ended Decemer 31, 19X1

Account Title	Adjusted Trial Balance		Income Statement		Balance Sheet	
	Dr.	Cr.	Dr.	Cr.	Dr.	Cr.
Cash	2,500					
Accounts Receivable	9,000					
Equipment	5,500					
Accumulated Deprec.		600				
Bank Loan		5,000				
Accounts Payable		6,000				
Common Stock		3,000				
Revenue		17,300				
Advertising Expense	200					
Commissions Expense	3,000					
Depreciation Expense	600					
Interest Expense	500					
Rent Expense	2,400					
Salaries Expense	7,500					
Supplies Expense	400					
Telephone Expense	300					
Totals						
Net Income for the Year						
Totals						

Required:
1. Calculate the totals of the adjusted trial balance debit and credit columns.
2. Complete the income statement and balance sheet columns of the worksheet.
3. Prepare the formal year-end income statement of the corporation.
4. Prepare all closing entries.

Problem A-5

The following partial worksheet is taken from Pean Movers Corp. at the end of its first year of operations.

Partial Worksheet
For the Year Ended December 31, 19X1

Account Title	Trial Balance Dr.	Trial Balance Cr.
Cash	1,500	
Accounts Receivable	7,000	
Prepaid Rent	1,200	
Supplies	100	
Equipment	3,500	
Accounts Payable		6,000
Unearned Commissions		3,000
Common Stock		1,000
Revenue		20,000
Advertising Expense	850	
Commissions Expense	3,600	
Interest Expense	550	
Rent Expense	4,400	
Supplies Used	700	
Wages Expense	6,600	
Totals		
Depreciation Expense		
Accumulated Deprec.		
Wages Payable		
Unearned Revenue		
Interest Payable		
Totals		
Net Income for the Year		
Totals		

The following additional data are available:
a. Prepaid rent represents rent for the months of December 19X1 and January and February 19X2.
b. A physical count indicates that $200-worth of supplies are on hand at December 31.
c. The equipment was purchased on July 1 and has a useful life of 3 years with an estimated salvage value of $500.
d. Wages for December 30 and 31 are unpaid; the unpaid amount of $300 will be included in the first Friday payment in January.
e. Revenue includes $2,500 received for work to be started in January 19X2.
f. Unrecorded interest expense amounts to $150.

Required:
1. Prepare all necessary adjusting entries.
2. Complete the entire worksheet.
3. Prepare all reversing entries.

Problem A-6

The following columns are taken from the worksheet of Reis Polish Inc.

Partial Worksheet
For the Year Ended December 31, 19X1

Account Title	Income Statement Dr.	Income Statement Cr.	Balance Sheet Dr.	Balance Sheet Cr.
Cash			2,700	
Prepaid Rent			900	
Supplies			600	
Equipment			5,000	
Accum. Depreciation				500
Accounts Payable				4,500
Unearned Revenue				1,500
Income Tax Payable				850
Common Stock				1,000
Revenue		14,500		
Advertising Expense	300			
Depreciation Expense	500			
Interest Expense	100			
Rent Expense	2,400			
Supplies Expense	400			
Truck Expense	2,500			
Utilities Expense	600			
Wages Expense	6,000			
Income Tax Expense	850			
Totals				
Net Income for Year				
Totals				

Required:
1. Complete the worksheet income statement and balance sheet columns.
2. Prepare all closing entries.
3. Prepare a post-closing trial balance.

Special Journals

A. Special Journals

The general journal was introduced and used to record each financial transaction of Bluebeard Computer Corporation. This procedure was useful for explaining the fundamentals of the accounting process, but it is practical only when a business has a small number of transactions.

The volume of transactions facing most entities makes it impractical to record each transaction in a general journal. It is not inconceivable for even a small business to have 200 to 300 customers and perhaps 50 to 100 suppliers of goods and services. Consider the number of journal entries that would be required to record sales and purchases on account, cash sales and cash purchases, cash receipts and cash disbursements, and payroll transactions. Recording these transactions in a general journal would be time consuming; the additional labour of posting entries to the general ledger would become overwhelming, increasing the possibility of posting errors so that the ledger does not balance.

In actual practice, transactions are grouped into a number of classifications common to most business entities and recorded in various **special journals** as indicated below:

Special journals
Multi-column journals specially designed not only to record similar transactions chronologically but also to reduce the writing of repetitious information. They are collectively referred to as *books of original entry*; the general journal is used to record transactions that cannot be recorded in any special journal.

Transaction:	*Recorded in:*
Sales or services on account	Sales Journal
Collection of cash	Cash Receipts Journal
Purchases on account	Purchases Journal
Payment of cash	Cash Disbursements Journal
Payroll	Payroll Journal

Most entities maintain a separate journal in each of these categories, often collectively referred to as *books of original entry*. The frequency with which certain types of transactions occur determines how many and what types of journals the entity will use.

The common feature in the actual design of all special journals is the use of multiple columns for debit and credit entries and for the recording of related information. In addition to reducing the time required for posting transactions, the use of multiple columns reduces the need to repeat information. Although the actual layout of the columns differs among entities and is also influenced by the availability of mechanical devices or electronic data processing, the types of columns listed on the facing page are always present.

Columns for Information:	Columns for Recording Debits and Credits:
Date of transaction	Accounts to be debited or
Name of other party involved	credited
Other details relevant to the transaction	Amount actually debited or credited for each transaction
Other details relevant to the posting information	

Although the arrangement of columns may differ from one entity to another, the column sequence used in this chapter is designed to emphasize the information to be recorded for each transaction and the equality of debits and credits. Once the methodology of special journals is understood, any variation in format can be easily accommodated by any accountant.

The use of special journals permits an efficient division of duties among employees. For example, while one employee is recording transactions in one journal, another can be recording other transactions in another journal. In this way, the recording process is expedited.

The accounting system of each entity is organized to achieve certain objectives, which include the accurate recording of accounting information in the appropriate special journal. An additional objective is the accumulation of amounts in the appropriate general ledger and any **subsidiary ledgers** used by the entity. Internal control systems are designed to ensure this accuracy; they are also designed to maximize efficiency and to control the entity's assets. The control of cash is one area of particular concern for obvious reasons; internal controls are designed to protect it and also to ensure its accurate recording. Control of inventory is another area of concern. To help maintain bookkeeping accuracy, a **control account** that accumulates balances of particular accounts in a subsidiary ledger is maintained. In these ways, management can keep an eye on operating efficiency through its accounting system.

Special journals can be grouped within a number of operating cycles continuously occurring within the entity. These cycles comprise major areas of the entity's activities; the preceding discussion has identified major categories of financial transactions and the applicable special journals.

The cycles focused on in this appendix are the sales and collection cycle and the purchase and payment cycle. The discussion in section A begins with the inception of transactions in each of these cycles. Section B focuses on the flow of data through the entity's accounts. Both are a part of the accounting process and lead to the reporting of information useful to users of financial statements; the preparation of these statements was the emphasis of the preceding chapters.

GAAP have an impact on each of these cycles because accountants are concerned with whether the information produced by each cycle is in accordance with generally accepted accounting principles.

The Sales and Collection Cycle

This cycle focuses on sales, accounts receivable, and the subsequent collection of cash. Transactions in this cycle begin with the preparation of a sales invoice, which is a source document. The collection of cash occurs to end this cycle; the source documents

Subsidiary ledger
A group of homogenous accounts kept in a separate ledger, which correspond to related ledger control accounts in the general ledger; examples include an accounts receivable subsidiary ledger and an accounts payable subsidiary ledger.

Control account
A general ledger account, a balance in which equals the total of many account balances in a related subsidiary ledger.

here is the deposit slip stamped by the bank as evidence of the deposit of cash and cheques received. This information is recorded in the appropriate special journals, which are posted to the general ledger and a subsidiary customer ledger. (The interrelationship of the general and subsidiary ledgers is discussed in section B.) The accounting process applicable to this cycle is illustrated in Figure B-1.

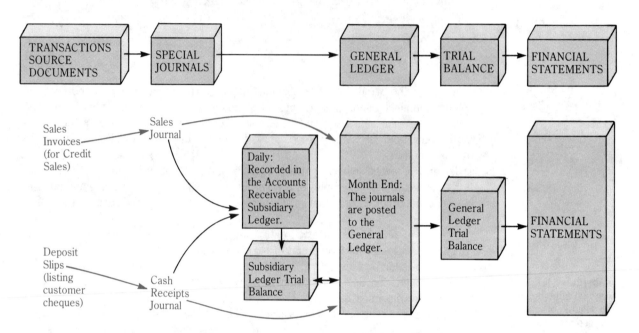

Figure B-1   The accounting process of the sales and collection cycle

The Sales Journal

Sales journal
A special journal used to record all sales on account.

All sales on account are recorded in the **sales journal**. (Cash sales are recorded in the cash receipts journal.) Figure B-2 shows an extract from the sales journal of Bluebeard Computer Corporation, in which January sales have been recorded and the columns totalled. The single column in this sales journal is designed for recording the debit to the Accounts Receivable account for each sale and the credit to the Sales account.

			Sold To	Invoice Number	Terms	F	Accts Rec — Dr. Sales — Cr.
	Date						
19X3							
Jan.	5		Devco Marketing Ltd.	301	net 30		1,000
	9		Perry Co. Ltd.	302	2/10, net 30		200
	10		Horngren Corp.	303	2/10, net 30		650
	19		Bendix Inc.	304	1/10, net 45		100
			Totals				1,950

SALES JOURNAL   Page 1

A   B   C   D   E   F

Figure B-2   Sales journal illustrated

Every entry in the sales journal includes a debit to Accounts Receivable and a credit to Sales. Recall that a sale would have been recorded in BCC's general journal as follows:

Jan. 5	Accounts Receivable	1,000	
	Sales		1,000
	To record a sale on account		

Note that, in the sales journal, this transaction would be recorded on a single line, with a single entry recording debit and credit. Since such a sale can be recorded in a special journal, it need not be recorded in the general journal.

The columns in the sales journal shown in Figure B-2 are explained below:

Columns for Information:

A The date of the sales invoice is recorded in the Date column.

B The name of the customer is recorded in the Sold To column. (This column is also often called the Account Debited column.)

C The sales invoice number is recorded in the Invoice Number column. Sales invoices are recorded in numerical sequence and all sales invoice numbers, including cancelled sales invoices, must be recorded.

D The terms of the sale are listed in the Terms column. If the same terms are extended to all customers this column can be left out.

E The use of this column is explained in section B of this appendix.

Column for Recording of Sales on Account:

F The amount in this column is debited to Accounts Receivable and credited to Sales.

Other columns, if needed, could be added to the sales journal that appears here. For example, there could be a credit column for Sales Tax or columns for crediting sales by department or by product. In such cases, there would be a debit column for Accounts Receivable.

The Cash Receipts Journal

Cash receipts journal
A special journal used to record all receipts of cash.

All *receipts of cash* are recorded in the **cash receipts journal**. Figure B-3 is a page from the cash receipts journal of Bluebeard Computer Corporation, after January cash receipts have been recorded and the columns totalled. The columns used in this journal are designed to record the debits to the Cash and Sales Discounts accounts and the credits to Accounts Receivable, as well as to other accounts that might be affected.

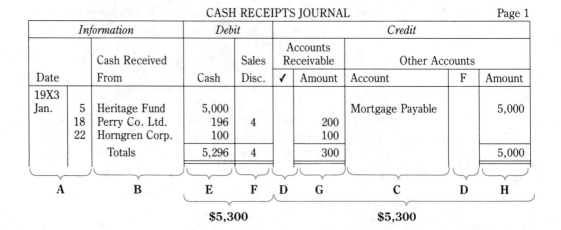

Figure B-3   Cash receipts journal illustrated

The columns in the cash receipts journal shown in Figure B-3 are explained below:

Columns for Information:

A The date of the receipt is recorded in the date column.

B The source of the cash receipt is written in the Cash Received From column. Cash receipts in payment of customers' accounts are shown individually, while cash sales are recorded as a daily total or weekly total amount, depending on the frequency and the dollar value of the transactions.

C The Other Accounts Credit column is used to record the name of general ledger accounts for which no special column has been provided. When applicable, cash sales are recorded here.

D The use of this column is explained in section B of this appendix.

Columns for Recording Receipts of Cash:
Columns for Debits

E The amount of cash actually received is recorded in the Cash columns.

F Any cash discount granted a customer is recorded in the Sales Discount column.

Columns for Credits

G The amount of accounts receivable paid by the customer is recorded in this column; the amount recorded is the total of cash received plus any sales discounts granted to the customer.

H This column is for credits to general ledger accounts for which no special column has been provided in the cash receipts journal.

Every entry in the cash receipts journal includes a debit to Cash; any other debit or credit entry depends on the transaction involved. For example, the receipt of a $5,000 mortgage would have been recorded in BCC's general journal as follows:

```
Jan. 5    Cash                          5,000
              Mortgage Payable                    5,000
              To record payment of mortgage.
```

Note that this transaction is recorded on a single line in the cash receipts journal, and that the equality of the debit and credit is still maintained through the use of the journal columns. The receipt of cash is recorded in the Debit Cash column; since there is no special column for mortgage payable, the account name and amount are entered in Other Accounts. Since the cash receipt is now recorded in a special journal, it is not recorded in the general journal.

The receipt of cash within the discount period would have been recorded in BCC's general journal as follows:

```
Jan. 18   Cash                          196
          Sales Discounts                 4
              Accounts Receivable                  200
```

In this case, Perry Co. Ltd. paid its account within 10 days and, accordingly, BCC deducted 2 percent from the $200 amount of the sale ($200 \times 0.02 = $4). Since this cash receipt is now recorded on a single line in a special journal, it is not recorded in the general journal.

Other columns could be added to the cash receipts journal to meet the specific needs of another entity. For example, a Cash Sales column could be added for an entity that has frequent cash sales.

Since special journals are designed to facilitate not only the recording but also the posting process, the sequence of the Debit and Credit columns is often reversed in actual practice; that is, the Credit columns are placed before the Debit columns, as illustrated in Figure B-4.

CASH RECEIPTS JOURNAL								Page 1	
		Credit						*Debit*	
Date		Accounts Receivable		Other Accounts					Sales
		F	Amount	Account	F	Amount	Cash	Disc.

Figure B-4   Alternative cash receipts journal

The posting process and the subsidiary accounts receivable ledger are explained in section B of this appendix.

The Purchase and Payment Cycle

This cycle focuses on purchases, accounts payable, and cash payments. Transactions in this cycle begin with the preparation of a purchase requisition and purchase order within the entity. The recording begins with an invoice from the supplier involved, which is the source document. The payment of cash completes this cycle; the source document here is the cheque prepared by the entity. These source documents are recorded in the appropriate special journals, the transaction then being posted to the general ledger and a subsidiary suppliers ledger. (The interrelationship of the general and subsidiary ledgers is discussed in section B.) The accounting process applicable to this cycle is illustrated in Figure B-5.

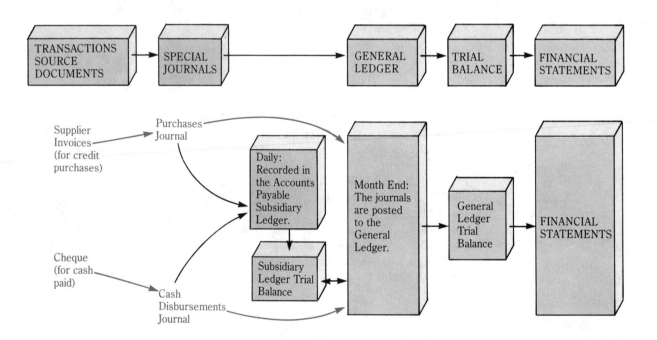

Figure B-5   The accounting process of the purchase and payment cycle

During the month, purchases on account and payments on account are posted from the purchases journal and the cash disbursement journal to an accounts payable subsidiary ledger. The total debit and credit column balances in both the purchases and the cash disbursement journals are posted to the general ledger at the end of each month.

The Purchases Journal

Purchases journal
A special journal used to record all purchases for resale that are made on account.

All purchases on account of merchandise for resale by the entity are recorded in the **purchases journal**. (Cash purchases are recorded in the cash disbursements journal.) Figure B-6 is a page from the purchases journal of Bluebeard Computer Corporation in which January purchases have been recorded and the column totalled.

PURCHASES JOURNAL   Page 1

Date		Purchased From	Terms	F	Purchases — Debit Accts Pay. — Credit
19X3 Jan.	3	Pemberton Ltd.	2/10, net 30		600
	4	Kensington Ltd.	net 30		350
	11	Canark Co. Ltd.	net 30		500
	26	Jaycor Ltd.	2/10, net 30		250
					1,700
A		B	C	D	E

Figure B-6   Purchases journal illustrated

The columns in the purchases journal shown in Figure B-6 are explained below:

Columns for Information:
A The date of the supplier's invoice is recorded in the Date column.
B The name of the supplier is recorded in the Purchased From column. (This column is also often called the Account Credit column.)
C The terms of purchase are listed in the Terms column.
D The use of this column is explained in section B of this appendix.

Columns for Recording Purchases on Account:
E The amount of the purchase is recorded in the column as a debit to Purchases and a credit to Accounts Payable.

Every entry in the purchases journal includes a debit to the Purchases account and a credit to Accounts Payable. The purchase from Pemberton Ltd. would have been recorded in BCC's general journal as follows:

Jan. 3	Purchases	600	
	Accounts Payable		600
	To record purchase on account from Pemberton Ltd.		

Note that this transaction is recorded on a single line in the purchases journal, with debit and credit recorded by a single entry.

Other columns could be added to meet specific needs. For example, a debit column for each department might be added, or for classes of products.

Separate columns are frequently used for debits and credits. Since special journals are designed to facilitate not only the recording but also the posting process, the sequence of the debit and credit columns is often reversed in actual practice; that is, the Credit columns are placed before Debit columns, as illustrated in Figure B-7.

PURCHASES JOURNAL   Page 1

Date		F	Credit	Debit		
			Accounts Payable	Purchases		
				A	B	C

Figure B-7   Alternative purchases journal

The posting procedure and the subsidiary accounts payable ledger are explained in section B of this appendix.

The Cash Disbursements Journal

Cash disbursements journal
A special journal used to record all payments made by cheque. Payments of cash are usually handled as part of a petty cash fund.

All payments of cash made by cheque are recorded in the **cash disbursements journal**. Payments made in bills and coins are usually handled as part of a petty cash fund. Figure B-8 is a page from the cash disbursements journal of Bluebeard Computer Corporation, in which January cash disbursements have been recorded and the columns totalled. The columns in this cash disbursements journal are designed for recording debits to accounts applicable in a particular transaction and the credit to Cash.

CASH DISBURSEMENTS JOURNAL   Page 1

Information		Debit						Credit		
		Accounts Payable		Other Accounts						
Date	Cash Paid To	✓	Amount	Account	F	Amount	Purchases Discount	Cash	Cheque Number
19X3 Jan. 2	Kybo Properties Ltd.			Rent Expense		900		900	101
8	Speedy Freight			Transportation In		50		50	102
12	Pemberton Ltd.		600				12	588	103
25	Glenco Ltd.			Supplies Expense		35		35	104
	Totals		600			985	12	1,573	

A   B   D   F   C   D   G   H   I   E

$1,585 $1,585

Figure B-8   Cash disbursements journal illustrated

The columns in the cash disbursements journal shown in Figure B-8 are explained below:

Columns for Information:
A The date recorded on the cheque is recorded in the Date column.
B The name of the payee is recorded in the Cash Paid To column.
C The Other Accounts Debit column is used to record the name of the general ledger accounts for which no special column has been provided.
D The use of this column is explained in section B of this appendix.
E The cheque number is recorded in the Cheque Number column.

Columns for Recording Payments of Cash:
Columns for Debits
F The amount of the accounts payable paid to the supplier is recorded in this column; the amount recorded is the total of the actual cheque amount plus any purchase discount taken.
G This column is for debits to general ledger accounts for which no special column has been provided in the cash disbursements journal.

Columns for Credits
H Any cash discount taken is recorded in the Purchases Discount column.
I The actual amount of the cheque is recorded in the Cash column.

Every entry in the disbursements journal consists of a debit to some account and a credit to Cash. The payment to Pemberton Ltd. on January 12 would have been recorded in BCC's general journal as follows:

Jan. 12	Accounts Payable	600	
	Purchases Discounts		12
	Cash		588
	To record payment, less discount		
	of amount due Pemberton Ltd.		

In this case, Bluebeard paid Pemberton within 10 days and accordingly deducted $12 from the $600 amount of the purchase made on January 3 ($600 $\times$ 0.02 = $12). Since this cash receipt is now recorded on a single line in a special journal, it is not recorded in the general journal.

Other columns could be added to the cash disbursements journal to meet the specific needs of another entity, based on the frequency with which certain cash disbursements occur.

The General Journal

When special journals are used, the general journal is still used to record all other transactions that cannot be recorded in any of the special journals. For example, sales returns, purchases returns, and adjusting and closing entries continue to be recorded in the general journal.

The three January entries in the general journal of Bluebeard Computer Corporation (in Figure B-9) illustrate its use for transactions that cannot be recorded in a special journal.

GENERAL JOURNAL   Page 10

Date		Description	F	*Debit*	*Credit*
19X3					
Jan.	12	Sales Returns and Allowances	508	100	
		Accounts Receivable	110✓		100
		To record return from Horngren Corp.			
	27	Accounts Payable	210✓	50	
		Purchases Returns and Allowances	558		50
		To record goods returned to Jaycor Ltd.			
	31	Depreciation Expense — Trucks	624	200	
		Accumulated Depreciation — Truck	194		200
		To record depreciation for January.			

Note that a (✓) is entered into the Folio column (F) to indicate that the posting has also been made to the account of the customer and the supplier. This procedure is necessary whenever a control account is used.

Figure B-9   General journal illustrated

Other Special Journals

Additional special journals can also be designed as required by an entity. In the sales and collection cycle, for example, a sales returns and allowances journal may be a labour-saving journal; in the purchase and payment cycle, a purchases returns and allowances journal may improve efficiency. The frequency with which these transactions occur determines the need for such additional special journals; the volume of other types of transactions would determine the need for other special journals.

B.   The General Ledger and Subsidiary Ledgers

An entity often has a large number of customers; a department store, for example, may have in excess of 50 000 credit customers for whom detailed financial information has to be maintained. If each customer had an account in the general ledger, the general ledger would become unwieldy. For this reason, a subsidiary accounts receivable ledger is designed to include each customer's account; only one Accounts Receivable account — in this case, the control account — is kept in the general ledger. After all transactions for the month have been recorded, the total of the accounts receivable subsidiary ledger should be equal to the balance in the control account:

GENERAL LEDGER	ACCOUNTS RECEIVABLE SUBSIDIARY LEDGER		
Accounts Receivable	Bendix Inc.	Devco Marketing Inc.	Horngren Corp.
1,650	100	1,000	550

CONTROL TOTAL	=	SUBSIDIARY TOTAL
$1,650		$1,650

Other subsidiary ledgers, such as a subsidiary fixed assets ledger, can also be created to control volume.

A trial balance of the accounts receivable subsidiary ledger (also called a schedule of accounts receivable) is prepared at the end of the month to check that the subsidiary ledger total agrees with the Accounts Receivable control account in the general ledger.

Bluebeard Computer Corporation
Schedule of Accounts Receivable
January 31, 19X3

Bendix Inc.	$ 100
Devco Marketing Inc.	1,000
Horngren Corp.	550
Total	$1,650

The Flow of Accounting Information through the Accounts

Accounting information is initially recorded in special journals, as illustrated in section A. This information is next accumulated in both subsidiary and control accounts; this procedure is referred to as a flow of accounting information through the accounts of an entity. This flow for each cycle can be illustrated by looking at the posting process, that is, how the information flows through both control and subsidiary accounts.

Flow through the Sales and Collection Cycle Accounts

Flow through the Accounts Receivable Control Account

Each amount in the Accounts Receivable columns of the sales journal and the cash receipts journal is posted to the accounts receivable subsidiary ledger — usually daily. This posting updates the balance of each customer's account and makes the information readily available. (The "S1" refers to page 1 of the sales journal.)

Accounts Receivable			*No. 110*	Sales			*No. 500*
19X3				19X3			
Jan. 31	S1	1,950		Jan. 31	S1	1,950	

At the end of each month, each debit and credit total appearing in the cash receipts journal is also posted to the appropriate general ledger account. The general ledger account number is placed in parentheses below each total in the cash receipts journal to indicate that the posting has been done. (See Figure B-10.)

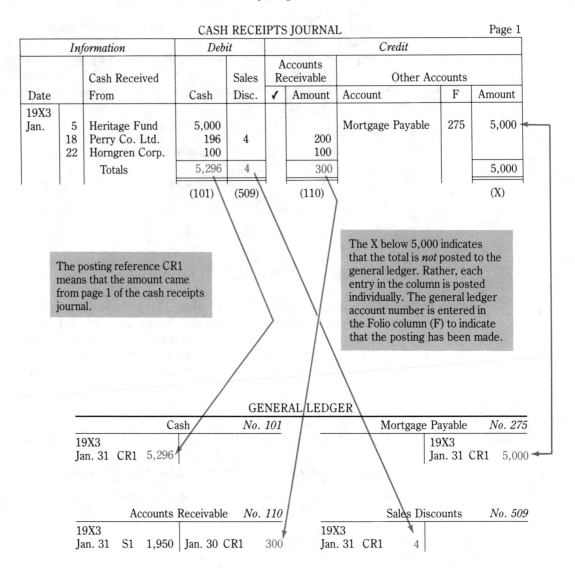

Figure B-10   Cash receipts journal transactions posted to the general ledger

Flow through the Subsidiary Accounts

Each amount in the Accounts Receivable columns of the sales journal and the cash receipts journal is posted to the accounts receivable subsidiary ledger — usually daily. This posting updates the balance of each customer's account and makes the information readily available for trial balance preparation.

Note that the Folio column (F) is used to indicate postings to the accounts receivable subsidiary ledger. A check (✓) is entered to indicate that the posting has been done.

Note that the abbreviation S is used as a posting reference from the sales journal; CR stands for the cash receipts journal.

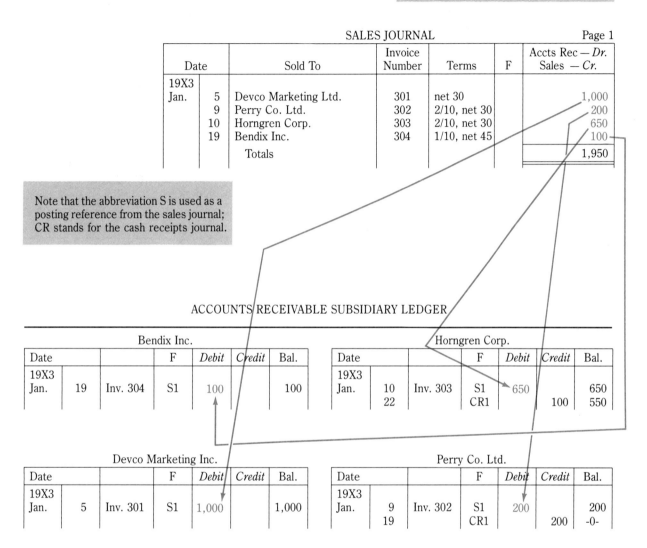

SALES JOURNAL   Page 1

Date	Sold To	Invoice Number	Terms	F	Accts Rec — Dr. Sales — Cr.
19X3					
Jan. 5	Devco Marketing Ltd.	301	net 30		1,000
9	Perry Co. Ltd.	302	2/10, net 30		200
10	Horngren Corp.	303	2/10, net 30		650
19	Bendix Inc.	304	1/10, net 45		100
	Totals				1,950

ACCOUNTS RECEIVABLE SUBSIDIARY LEDGER

Bendix Inc.

Date			F	Debit	Credit	Bal.
19X3						
Jan.	19	Inv. 304	S1	100		100

Horngren Corp.

Date			F	Debit	Credit	Bal.
19X3						
Jan.	10	Inv. 303	S1	650		650
	22		CR1		100	550

Devco Marketing Inc.

Date			F	Debit	Credit	Bal.
19X3						
Jan.	5	Inv. 301	S1	1,000		1,000

Perry Co. Ltd.

Date			F	Debit	Credit	Bal.
19X3						
Jan.	9	Inv. 302	S1	200		200
	19		CR1		200	-0-

Figure B-11   **Posting of sales journal entries to accounts receivable subsidiary ledger**

Flow through the Purchase and Payment Cycle Accounts

Flow through the Accounts Payable Control Account

At the end of each month, each debit and credit total appearing in the purchases journal is posted to the appropriate general ledger account. The general ledger account number is placed in parentheses below each total in the purchases journal to indicate that the posting has been done. (The "P1" refers to page 1 of the purchases journal.)

	Purchases			*No. 550*		Accounts Payable			*No. 210*
19X3						19X3			
Jan. 31	P1	1,700				Jan. 31	P1	1,700	

At the end of each month, each debit and credit total appearing in the cash disbursements journal is also posted to the appropriate general ledger account. The general ledger account number is placed in parentheses below each total in the cash disbursements journal to indicate that the posting has been done.

CASH DISBURSEMENTS JOURNAL   Page 1

Information			Debit					Credit			
			Accounts Payable		Other Accounts						
Date	Cash Paid To		✓	Amount	Account	F	Amount	Purchases Discount	Cash	Cheque Number
19X3										
Jan.	2	Kybo Properties Ltd.			Rent Expense	654	900		900	101
	8	Speedy Freight			Transportation In	560	50		50	102
	12	Pemberton Ltd.	✓	600				12	588	103
	25	Glenco Ltd.			Supplies Used	668	35		35	104
		Totals		600			985	12	1,573	
				(210)			(X)	(559)	(101)	

The posting reference CD1 means that the amount came from page 1 of the cash disbursements journal.

The X below the 985 total indicates that this total is *not* posted to the general ledger. Rather, each entry is posted individually. The general ledger account number is entered in the Folio column (F) to indicate that the posating has been made.

GENERAL LEDGER

	Cash		*No. 101*			Transportation In		*No. 560*			Accounts Payable		*No. 210*
19X3			19X3		19X3					19X3		19X3	
Jan. 31	CR1	5,296	Jan. 31 CD1 1,573		Jan. 31	CD1	50			Jan. 31	CD1 600	Jan. 31 P1	1,700

	Supplies Used		*No. 668*			Rent Expense		*No. 654*			Purchases Discounts		*No. 559*
19X3					19X3							19X3	
Jan. 31	CD1	35			Jan. 31	CD1	900					Jan. 31 CD1	12

Figure B-12   Posting of cash disbursement journal entries to general ledger

Flow through the Subsidiary Accounts

Each amount in the Accounts Payable columns of the purchase journal and the cash disbursements journal is posted to the accounts payable subsidiary ledger — usually daily. This posting updates the balance of each creditor's account and makes the information readily available. The date of the entry in the subsidiary ledger account is the invoice date, which is needed if a discount is to be taken.

PURCHASES JOURNAL   Page 1

Date		Purchased From	Terms	F	Purchases — Dr. Accts Pay. — Cr.
19X3 Jan.	3	Pemberton Ltd.	2/10, net 30	✓	600
	4	Kensington Ltd.	net 30	✓	350
	11	Canark Co. Ltd.	net 30	✓	500
	26	Jaycor Ltd.	2/10, net 30	✓	250
		Totals			1,700

Note that the abbreviation P is used as a posting reference from the purchases journal; CD stands for the cash disbursement journal.

Note that the Folio column (F) is used to indicate postings to the accounts payable subsidiary ledger. A check (✓) is entered to indicate that the posting has been made.

ACCOUNTS PAYABLE SUBSIDIARY LEDGER

Canark Co. Ltd.

			F	Debit	Credit	Bal.
19X3 Jan.	11		P1		500	500

Kensington Ltd.

			F	Debit	Credit	Bal.
19X3 Jan.	4		P1		350	350

Jaycor Ltd.

			F	Debit	Credit	Bal.
19X3 Jan.	26		P1		250	250

Pemberton Ltd.

			F	Debit	Credit	Bal.
19X3 Jan.	3		P1		600	600
	12		CD1	600		-0-

Figure B-13   Posting of purchases journal entries to accounts payable subsidiary ledger

A trial balance of the accounts payable subsidiary ledger (also called a schedule of accounts payable) is prepared at the end of the month to check that the subsidiary ledger total agrees with the Accounts Payable control account in the general ledger.

Bluebeard Computer Corporation
Schedule of Accounts Payable
January 31, 19X3

Canark Co. Ltd.	$ 500
Jaycor Ltd.	250
Kensington Ltd.	350
Total	$1,100

C.   Computerized Accounting Systems

A typical Canadian entity processes numerous routine accounting jobs, most of which involve some sort of record-keeping. In small companies, all records may be kept manually, while a large corporation, such as General Motors or Seagram, may have a totally computerized system. Bookkeepers may take care of the payroll, sales orders, inventory control, accounts receivable and payable, and the general ledger either manually or through automated processing. Computerized accounting may involve numerous systems with specific programs tailored to the entity's particular needs.

Payroll System

Payroll system
A computer system that assists in the preparation of salary cheques, maintains payment records, and provides reports related to payroll activities.

A **payroll system** accumulates data for individual employees in order to compute deductions for provincial and federal taxes, unemployment insurance, pension, and health insurance. The system, on the pay day, produces a paycheque for each employee, like the computer-printed statement of earnings and deductions illustrated in Figure B-14. Notice that this statement notifies the employee that his/her paycheque has been automatically deposited in his/her bank account. Each employee's deductions are accumulated by the payroll system, so that reports for managerial purposes and for reporting taxes withheld for Revenue Canada and other government agencies can be prepared through the system. In addition, the payroll system can communicate with the general ledger system so that it can incorporate the payroll data and summarize the financial status of the organization.

```
                    Bluebeard Computer Corporation
                  STATEMENT OF EARNINGS AND DEDUCTIONS

 NAME: R. River              S.I.N.: 244-897-153         EMPLOYEE NO.: 05225

 ┌───────────┬───────────┬──────────┬─────────────────┬──────────────┐
 │ EARNINGS  │ HRS/UNITS │  AMOUNT  │    DEDUCTIONS   │ YEAR TO DATE │
 ├───────────┼───────────┼──────────┼─────────────────┼──────────────┤
 │ Regular   │    40     │   $250   │ * Fed. Tax $18 *│ Gross $250   │
 │ Txb Benefit│   -0-    │    .00   │ * Prov. Tax $24 *│  UIC   $4    │
 │ Overtime  │    0      │    .00   │ *UIC Contr. $4 *│ F. Tax $18   │
 │           │           │          │  * Pension $4  *│ P. Tax $24   │
 └───────────┴───────────┴──────────┴─────────────────┴──────────────┘

 TOTAL EARNINGS: $250.00          TOTAL DEDUCTIONS: $50.00
 WEEK ENDING: X3/01/05      NET PAY: $200.00

 NOTE: Deposited at Queen and University Royal Bank Branch.
```

Figures B-14   A computerized statement of earnings for individual paycheques

Sales Order Entry System

Sales order entry system
A computer system that initiates shipping orders, keeps track of back orders, and produces various reports.

All merchandisers have some sort of organized procedure for processing customers' orders as they are received either in person, by telephone, or by mail. This procedure is called the **sales order entry system**. Many merchandisers have computerized their sales order entry systems. Each order contains the customer's name, as well as a description of and the quantity of items to be sold. A good system can be designed to permit fast processing of orders, to update the inventory on hand, and to flag bad credit risks.

Inventory Control System

Inventory control system
A computer system used to monitor inventories and minimize inventory costs.

As mentioned, one routine job that can be handled through computer procedures is inventory control. A computerized **inventory control system** can accumulate the number of units of each product purchased for inventory, deduct each item sold or used, and ensure that proper quantities of products are kept in stock. Automatic updates reduce the number of time-consuming manual counts needed to control inventory.

When a customer requests a product, the order is entered by a clerk into the sales order entry system; if there is a sufficient number to fill the order, the goods are made available for shipment. The appropriate data are relayed to the accounts receivable system, which produces an invoice for the customer. If the goods are not in stock, the customer's order may be placed on back-order and the inventory control system will produce a notice to this effect indicating when the customer can expect the goods to be delivered.

A good inventory control system should be designed to maintain an economical inventory level; it should have a warning procedure to notify managers when stock levels are too low. Most inventory control systems contain a variety of mathematical routines to help managers calculate an economical inventory level for each product.

Accounts Receivable System

Accounts receivable system
A computer system that bills customers, maintains records of amounts due from customers, and generates reports on overdue amounts.

The accounts receivable for a large merchandiser must be tracked efficiently. The high volume of transactions can be handled by an **accounts receivable system** to control customers' purchases, payments, unpaid accounts, and account balances. The system can be designed to calculate and print customers' purchases, payments, unpaid accounts, and account balances. The system can be designed to calculate and print customers' bills and management reports. Other output can include sales analyses that describe changing sales pattern and reports of current and past due accounts.

Accounts Payable System

Accounts payable system
A computer system that provides control over payments to suppliers, issues cheques to suppliers, and provides information necessary for effective cash management.

The accounts payable a merchandiser owes to its suppliers can also be handled by a computerized system designed for the individual entity. An **accounts payable system** can control bills and invoices received and generate cheques to pay the bills in much the same way that the payroll system operates.

General Ledger System

General ledger system
A computer system that keeps track of all financial summaries, produces ledger balances, and financial statements.

The **general ledger system** in a computerized merchandising operation can determine whether the books balance and produce general ledger balances and financial statements.

Once a company has decided to computerize one or more of its routine activities, it must decide whether to develop its own software or buy a software package from a vendor. A computerized system developed by the company can have the advantage of being designed precisely for the company's particular needs. Vendor-supplied software, on the other hand, is quite inexpensive; for example, a general ledger package may retail for as little as $200. Regardless of which way a company decides to go, it must be sure that the general ledger system will be compatible with other systems that the entity's computer already runs. Figure B-15 illustrates the interrelationships of the various systems discussed in this section; the importance of the general ledger system is clear.

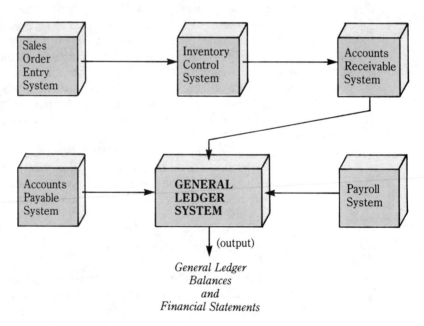

Figure B-15   Relationships among accounting systems

Management Uses of Computerized Accounting Systems

Management information system (MIS)
An information system designed to aid in the performance of management functions.

Decision support system (DSS)
An information system that managers can use easily that provides highly refined information to help make non-routine decisions.

Spreadsheet
A program that allows the user to create a large two-dimensional table and manipulate data in many different ways.

While the automation of routine data-processing tasks undoubtedly reduces accounting and other clerical expenses, the computer can do much more than perform these programs. The computer's efficient organization of information can assist many levels of management in their decision-making roles. Again, programs can be designed to suit a particular entity's needs. For instance, based on trends in the historical sales results accumulated by the sales order entry system, forecasts for future sales can be calculated. A system that both reports routine data processing and generates information is called a **management information system** (MIS). Lately, **decision support systems** have also been introduced; unlike MIS, these systems permit the user to pose questions while the user is online. One of the most popular microcomputer applications of decision support systems is spreadsheet analysis.

Spreadsheet

A **spreadsheet** is a table of columns and rows. Various commercial spreadsheets, such as VisiCalc, SuperCalc, and Lotus 1-2-3, perform many of the same functions and operate using similar logic; however, some spreadsheet software packages may have additional features that others are lacking. A spreadsheet program prepares the computer to accept tables, values, or mathematical formulas into the pre-established spreadsheet cells.

For example, the payroll information for BCC could be entered into the spreadsheet program. The real advantage of a spreadsheet program is that, if a single datum changes, the entire spreadsheet is recalculated by the program. For instance, if the hourly wage of R. River is increased to $9.00 per hour, the user enters the new rate and the program automatically recalculates any amounts in the spreadsheet that are affected by the change. This is a simple example. A spreadsheet, such as Lotus 1-2-3 with 2043 rows and 254 columns, can perform calculations that would take hours with a calculator.

A S S I G N M E N T   M A T E R I A L S

Problems

Problem B-1

The following accounts payable subsidiary ledger accounts have been posted during March 19X2 from two books of original entry.

ACCOUNTS PAYABLE SUBSIDIARY LEDGER
Avon Stores Inc.

Date			F	Debit	Credit	Bal.
19X2						
Bal.		(purchase made Feb. 2, 19X2, terms n/30)				1,000
Mar.	15		P.3		500	
	17		P.3		750	
	20		CD.7	1,000		

Clanranald Novelties Ltd.

Date			F	Debit	Credit	Bal.
19X2						
Mar.	3		P.3		1,500	
	12		CD.7	1,500		
	26		P.3		1,250	

Fulton Place Products Inc.

Date			F	Debit	Credit	Bal.
19X2						
Mar.	25		P.3		3,000	
Mar.	31		CD.7	1,500		

Otterburn College Inc.

Date			F	Debit	Credit	Bal.
19X2						
Bal.		(purchase made Feb. 10, 19X2, terms n/30)				2,000
Mar.	20		P.3		400	
	31		CD.7	1,600		

Richmond Renovators Corp.

Date			F	Debit	Credit	Bal.
19X2						
Mar.	10		P.3		900	
	24		CD.7	900		

Required:
1. Calculate and record the balance in each of the above accounts.
2. Using the information in these accounts, complete the purchases journal and calculate the column total.

PURCHASES JOURNAL   Page 3

Date		Purchased From	Terms	F	Purchases — Dr. Accts Pay. — Cr.
19X2 Mar.	3		2/10, n/30		
	10		2/15, n/30		
	15		n/30		
	17		n/30		
	20		n/30		
	25		2/10, n/30		
	26		2/10, n/30		
					(550) (210)

3. Using the information in the subsidiary ledger accounts, complete the cash disbursements journal and calculate all column totals. Assume that all cash disbursements in March were for the payment of accounts payable.

CASH DISBURSEMENTS JOURNAL   Page 7

Information			Debit					Credit		
		Accounts Payable		Other Accounts						
Date	Cash Paid To	✓	Amount	Account	F	Amount	Purchases Discount	Cash	Cheque number
19X2										
	Totals									
			(210)			(X)	(559)	(101)	

4. Open general ledger accounts for Cash, Accounts Payable, Purchases, and Purchases Discounts. Post the column totals of the purchases journal and cash disbursements journal.
5. Prepare a schedule of accounts payable at March 31, 19X2. The total should agree with the balance in the general ledger Accounts Payable account. The February 28, 19X2 balance in this control account amounted to $3,000.

Problem B-2

The following accounts receivable subsidiary ledger accounts have been posted during January, 19X3 from two books of original entry.

ACCOUNTS RECEIVABLE SUBSIDIARY LEDGER

Atwater Marketers Corp.

Date			F	Debit	Credit	Bal.
19X3						
Bal.						5,250
Jan.	15		S.6	1,000		

Coolbrooke Distributors Ltd.

Date			F	Debit	Credit	Bal.
19X3						
Jan.	6		S.6	500		
	9		S.6	250		
	15		CR.9		500	

Hymus Sales Corp.

Date			F	Debit	Credit	Bal.
19X3						
Bal.						1,500
Jan.	2		S.6	1,200		
	11		CR.6		2,700	

Mackay Products Inc.

Date			F	Debit	Credit	Bal.
19X3						
Bal.						200
Jan.	7		S.6	800		
	10		CR.9		200	

Park Extension Ltd.

Date			F	Debit	Credit	Bal.
19X3						
Bal.						900
Jan.	18		CR.9		900	
	25		S.6	600		

TransCanada Sales Inc.

Date			F	Debit	Credit	Bal.
19X3						
Jan.	10		S.6	400		
	14		S.6	300		
	19		CR.9		400	

Required:
1. Calculate and record the balance in each of the accounts.
2. Using the information in the accounts, complete the sales journal and calculate the column total.

SALES JOURNAL   Page 6

Date			Sold To	Invoice Number	Terms	F	Accts Rec. — Dr. Sales — Cr.
19X3 Jan.	2			31	2/10, n/30		
					2/10, n/30		
					2/10, n/30		
					2/10, n/30		
					2/10, n/30		
					2/10, n/30		
					2/10, n/30		
					2/10, n/30		
					2/10, n/30		
							(110) (500)

3. Using the information in the subsidiary ledger accounts, complete the cash receipts journal and calculate all column totals. Assume that all cash receipts in January were from the collection of accounts receivable. Note that all eligible customers took discounts.

CASH RECEIPTS JOURNAL   Page 9

Information			Debit		Credit				
					Accounts Receivable		Other Accounts		
Date		Cash Received From	Cash	Sales Disc.	✓	Amount	Account	F	Amount
19X3 Jan.	10								
		Totals							
			(101)	(509)		(110)			(X)

4. Open general ledger accounts for Cash, Accounts Receivable, Sales, and Sales Discounts. Post the column totals of the sales journal and cash receipts journal.
5. Prepare a schedule of accounts receivable at January 31, 19X3; the total should agree with the balance in the general ledger Accounts Receivable account. The January 1, 19X3 balance in this control account amounted to $7,850.

Problem B-3

Convex Hill Corp. was incorporated on July 2, 19X1 to operate a merchandising business. Its sales and purchases during July are recorded below.

SALES JOURNAL   Page 1

Date		Sold To	Invoice Number	Terms	F	Accts Rec. — Dr. Sales — Cr.
19X1						
Jul.	2	Hampstead Tool Rentals. Inc.	1	2/10, n/30		2,000
	15	Condor Products Corp.	2	2/10, n/30		2,000
	20	Pine Promotions Corp.	3	2/10, n/30		3,500
	26	Daytona Sales Ltd.	4	2/10, n/30		600
	31	Argyle Inc.	5	2/10, n/30		1,900
						10,000
						(110) (500)

PURCHASES JOURNAL   Page 1

Date		Purchased From	Terms	F	Purchases — Dr. Accts Pay — Cr.
19X1					
Jul.	2	Westmount Pencils Ltd.	2/10, n/30		3,500
	8	MacDonald Distributors Inc.	2/15, n/30		2,000
	10	Peel Products Inc.	n/30		200
	15	Draper Door Inc.	2/10, n/30		1,500
	26	Gold & Silver Co.	2/10, n/30		800
					8,000
					(550) (210)

Other transactions during the month were as follows:

Jul. 2 Issued common shares for $5,000 cash to George Hill, the incorporator and sole shareholder of the corporation

3 Issued cheque no. 1 to Concordia Rentals Corp. for $500 in payment of July rent

5 Issued cheque no. 2 to Westwood Furniture Ltd. for $1,000 in payment for equipment

8 Collected $200 for a cash sale made today to Byron Peel

9 Received the amount due from Hampstead Tool Rentals Inc. for the July 2 sale (less discount)

10 Issued cheque no. 3 to Westmount Pencils Ltd. in payment for the July 2 purchase (less discount)

15 Received a credit note memo from MacDonald Distributors Inc. for $100-worth of defective merchandise included in the July 9 purchase.

16 Condor Products Corp. returned $200-worth of merchandise (issued a credit memo)

20 Issued cheque no. 4 to MacDonald Distributors Inc. in payment of half the purchase made July 8 (less credit note, less discount on payment)

24 Received half the amount due from Condor Products Corp. in partial payment for the July 15 sale (less discount on payment)

24 Issued cheque no. 5 to Draper Door Inc. in payment of the purchase made July 15 (less discount)

31 Issued cheque no. 6 to Real Quick Transport Co. for $350 in payment for transportation to our warehouse during the month (all purchases are fob shipping point).

Required:

1. Record the July transactions in the following journals:
   a. Cash receipts journal
   b. Cash disbursements journal
   c. General journal.
2. Calculate the total of each column in the cash receipts and cash disbursements journals. For each journal, ascertain whether total debits equal total credits.
3. Open subsidiary ledger accounts for each of the customers listed in the sales journal and post the sales transactions and appropriate cash receipts transactions to these accounts.
4. Open subsidiary ledger accounts for each of the suppliers recorded in the purchases journal and post the purchase transactions to these accounts.
5. Post the appropriate entries from the general journal to the subsidiary accounts receivable and subsidiary accounts payable accounts.
6. Open the following general ledger control accounts:
   a. Accounts Receivable
   b. Accounts Payable.
   Post all appropriate balances from the cash receipts and cash disbursements journals and the appropriate amounts from the general journal.
7. Prepare a schedule of accounts receivable; the total should agree with the Accounts Receivable control account.
8. Prepare a schedule of accounts payable; the total should agree with the Accounts Payable control account.

Problem B-4

Draco Sales Corp. was incorporated on May 1, 19X1 to operate a merchandising business. Its sales and purchases journals for May are reproduced below.

SALES JOURNAL   Page 1

Date		Sold To	Invoice Number	Terms	F	Accts Rec. — Dr. Sales — Cr.
19X1						
May	1	Montreal West Distributors	1	2/10, n/30		2,500
	2	Terrebonne Sales Inc.	2	2/10, n/30		2,000
	5	Brock Stores Corporation	3	2/10, n/30		1,000
	10	Western Warehouse	4	2/10, n/30		2,400
	15	Roxboro Outlets Inc.	5	2/10, n/30		1,500
	25	Kirkland Centres Ltd.	6	2/10, n/30		700
	28	Lachine Wharf Corp.	7	2/10, n/30		900
						11,000
						(110) (500)

PURCHASES JOURNAL   Page 1

Date		Sold To	Terms	F	Purchases — Dr. Accts Pay. — Cr.
19X1					
May	1	St Luc Wholesalers Corp.	2/10, n/30		2,000
	2	Rosedale Products Ltd.	n/30		1,800
	8	Elmhurst Novelties Inc.	2/15, n/30		2,800
	15	Hudson Distributors Inc.	2/10, n/30		1,500
	19	Mid-Island Stores Corp.	1/10, n/30		1,200
	22	Quick Sales Co.	n/30		600
	29	Sidekicks Inc.	2/15, n/30		100
					10,000
					(550) (210)

Other transactions during the month were as follows:

May 1 Issued common shares for $2,000 cash to Harry Jones, the incorporator and sole shareholder of the corporation

  1 Received $10,000 from the Royal Bank of Canada as a demand bank loan

  1 Issued cheque no. 1 to Cadillac Corp. for $1,500 in payment for 3 months rent in advance — May, June, and July (recorded as a asset)

  1 Issued cheque no. 2 to Avanti Equipment Ltd. for $5,000 in payment for equipment

  3 Collected $500 for a cash sale made today to Irwin Peabody

  5 Issued cheque no. 3 to All Province Insurance Inc. for $1,200 in payment for a 1-year insurance policy, effective May 1 (recorded as an asset)

  6 Terrebonne Sales Inc. returned $500-worth of merchandise (issued a credit memo)

  8 Received a credit memo from St Luc Wholesalers Corp. for $300-worth of defective merchandise included in the May 1 purchase and returned subsequently to St Luc

  9 Received the amount due from Montreal West Distributors from the May 1 sale (less discount)

  9 Issued cheque no. 4 to St Luc Wholesalers Corp. in payment of the May 1 purchase (less discount)

May 11 Received the amount due from Terrebonne Sales Inc. (less the May 6 credit memo and discount)

13 Issued cheque no. 5 to Express Corporation for $100 in payment for transportation in

15 Issued cheque no. 6 for $500 commissions to Harry Jones, *re* sales invoices nos. 1, 2, and 3

19 Issued cheque no. 7 to Rosedale Products Ltd. in payment for the May 2 purchase

22 Issued cheque no. 8 to Elmhurst Novelties Inc. in payment for the May 8 purchase (less discount)

24 Issued cheque no. 9 to Express Corporation for $150 in payment for transportation in

26 Received the amount due from Brock Stores Corporation

27 Issued cheque no. 10 for $200 to Yale Deliveries Ltd. for deliveries made to customers

28 Collected $300 for a cash sale made today to Joe Montclair

28 Make a $200 cash purchase from Ballantyne Sales Inc. today (issued cheque no. 11; debited purchases)

29 Issued the following cheques:
no. 12 to Speedy Ltd. for $300 in payment for deliveries (debited account 620)
no. 13 to Impetus Advertising Agency for $400 in payment for advertising materials used during May
no. 14 to Hydro-Bec for $100 in payment for electricity
no. 15 to Harry Jones for $350 commissions, *re:* sales invoices nos. 4, 5, 6, and 7

30 Collected $1,000 on account from Roxboro Outlets Inc.

31 Issued cheque no. 16 to Mid-Island Stores Corp. for $700 on account

31 Issued cheque no. 17 to Harry Jones for $100 in payment of dividends declared today.

Required:

1. Record the May transactions in the following journals:
   a. Cash receipts journal
   b. Cash disbursements journal
   c. General journal.
2. Calculate the total of each column in the cash receipts and cash disbursements journals. For each journal, ascertain whether total debits equal total credits.
3. Open subsidiary accounts receivable accounts for each of the seven customers recorded in the sales journal, and post the sales transactions and appropriate cash receipts transactions to these accounts.
4. Open subsidiary accounts payable accounts for each supplier listed in the purchases journal, and post the purchases transactions and appropriate cash disbursements transactions to these accounts.
5. Post all appropriate entries from the general journal to the subsidiary accounts receivable and subsidiary accounts payable accounts.
6. Open the following general ledger control accounts:
   a. Accounts Receivable   b. Accounts Payable.
   Post all appropriate balances from the cash receipts and disbursements journals, and post appropriate amounts from the general journal.
7. Prepare a schedule of accounts receivable accounts; the total should agree with the Accounts Receivable control account.
8. Prepare a schedule of accounts payable accounts; the total should agree with the Accounts Payable control account.

Chapter 1
[1] Ray G. Harris, "A Message from the President", *CA Magazine*, June 1981, p. 5.

Chapter 2
[1] From an *amicus curiae* brief submitted by the American Institute of Certified Public Accountants in a 1968 legal case. Quoted by Howard Ross, *Financial Statements: A Crusade for Current Values* (Toronto, 1969), p. 50.

Chapter 3
[1] FASB, Statement of Financial Accounting Concept No. 3, *Elements of Financial Statements of Business Enterprises* (December 1980), para. 19, 28, 63, 65, 67, 68.

Chapter 4
[1] Miriam Medom, "News and Notes for the Computing Community", *P.C. World*, May 1984, p. 39.

Chapter 5
[1] Henry Rand Hatfield, *Accounting: Its Principles and Problems* (New York, 1927), p. 256.

Chapter 8
[1] Henry Rand Hatfield, *Accounting: Its Principles and Problems* (New York, 1927), p. 130.

Chapter 10
[1] C. A. Barker, "Evaluation of Stock Dividends", *Harvard Business Review*, vol. 36 (July-August 1958), 99–114. Barker's study has been replicated several times in recent years, and his results are still valid — they have withstood the test of time. Another excellent study, using an entirely different methodology yet reaching similar conclusions, is that of E. Fama, L. Fisher, M. C. Jensen, and R. Roll, "The Adjustment of Stock Prices to New Information", *International Economic Review*, February 1969, 1–21.

A follow-up study to Fama, *et al.* that further refines their method is S. Bar-Yosef and L. D. Brown, "A Re-examination of Stock Splits Using Moving Betas", *Journal of Finance*, September 1977, 1069–1080.

Chapter 13
[1] For a full treatment, refer to: Thomas H. Beechy, *Canadian Advanced Financial Accounting* (Toronto: Holt, Rinehart and Winston of Canada, Limited, 1985), ch. 6–12.
[2] Beechy, p. 196.

I N D E X

Page references appearing in boldface indicate where the marginal glossary definitions will be found.

INDEX OF CASES, CONCEPTUAL ISSUES, ISSUES IN ETHICS, AND REAL LIFE EXAMPLES BY TITLE

To the Owner of this Book

We are interested in your reaction to Henry Dauderis' *Financial Accounting: An Introduction to Decision Making,* second edition. Through feedback from you, we may be able to improve this book in future editions.

1. What was your reason for using this book?

_____ college course

___✓___ university course

_____ continuing education

_____ other (please specify)

2. If you used this text for a program, what was the name of that program?

3. Which chapters or sections were omitted from your course?

4. Have you any suggestions for improving this text?

Fold here

Chapter 11

Problem	11-1	Earnings per Common Share, 12% Bonds	$ 9.50
Problem	11-2	Annual Interest Expense, Dec. 31, 19X3	$ 19,000
Problem	11-3	No Check Figure	
Problem	11-4	No Check Figure	
Problem	11-5	Bond Carrying Value, 6-Month Period 6	$ 295,378
Problem	11-6	Original Issue Price	$ 523,800
Problem	11-7	Issue Price, Case C	$ 581,107
Problem	11-8	No Check Figure	
Problem	11-9	Bond Carrying Value, 6-Month Period 6	$ 294,445
Problem	11-10	Bond Carrying Value, Straight-Line Method, 6-Month Period 2	$ 106,949
Alt. Prob.	11-1	Earnings per Common Share, 12% Bonds	$ 0.64
Alt. Prob.	11-2	No Check Figure	
Alt. Prob.	11-3	Issue Price, Case C	$ 105,076
Alt. Prob.	11-4	No Check Figure	
Alt. Prob.	11-5	No Check Figure	
Alt. Prob.	11-6	Bonds Payable Authorized and Issued, Dec. 31, 19X2	$ 200,000
Alt. Prob.	11-7	No Check Figure	
Alt. Prob.	11-8	Original Issue Price	$ 714,300
Alt. Prob.	11-9	Bond Carrying Value, 6-Month Period 6	$ 201,692
Alt. Prob.	11-10	Bond Carrying Value, 6-Month Period 6	$ 238,383
Alt. Prob.	11-11	Bond Carrying Value, 6-Month Period 2, Straight-Line Method	$ 219,804

Chapter 12

Problem	12-1	Gain on Sale of Marketable Securities, Dec. 31, 19X8	$ 400
Problem	12-2	Ledger Balance, Dec. 31	$ 75,000
Problem	12-3	No Check Figure	
Problem	12-4	Cash Interest Received, Dec. 31, 19X1	$ 12,000
Problem	12-5	No Check Figure	
Problem	12-6	No Check Figure	
Alt. Prob.	12-1	No Check Figure	
Alt. Prob.	12-2	No Check Figure	
Alt. Prob.	12-3	Ledger Balance, Dec. 31, 19X3	$ 200,000
Alt. Prob.	12-4	No Check Figure	
Alt. Prob.	12-5	Cash Paid, May 1 by Hobson	$ 159,000

Chapter 13

Problem	13-1	No Check Figure	
Problem	13-2	No Check Figure	
Problem	13-3	Retained Earnings (P)	$ 300,000
Problem	13-4	Total Assets, Dec. 31, 19X1	$ 450,000
Problem	13-5	Goodwill from Subsidiary	$ 30,000
Problem	13-6	Minority Interest	$ 60,000
Problem	13-7	No Check Figure	
Alt. Prob.	13-1	No Check Figure	
Alt. Prob.	13-2	No Check Figure	
Alt. Prob.	13-3	Minority Interest	$ 62,000
Alt. Prob.	13-4	Total Assets	$ 205,000
Alt. Prob.	13-5	Retained Earnings	$ 70,000
Alt. Prob.	13-6	Total Assets, Consolidated	$ 1,198,000
Alt. Prob.	13-7	Total Assets, Consolidated	$ 480,000

Chapter 14

Problem	14-1	No Check Figure	
Problem	14-2	No Check Figure	
Problem	14-3	Retained Earnings	$ 7,000
Problem	14-4	Net Income, 19X0	20.8
Problem	14-5	Total Assets	$ 612,500
Alt. Prob.	14-1	No Check Figure	
Alt. Prob.	14-2	No Check Figure	
Alt. Prob.	14-3	Total Assets	$ 10,500
Alt. Prob.	14-4	Net Income, 19X3	$ 88
Alt. Prob.	14-5	Net Income	$ 12,500

Chapter 15

Problem	15-1	Net Cash Generated	$ 1,199
Problem	15-2	Net Cash Generated	$ 38,050
Problem	15-3	Net Cash Generated	$ 2
Problem	15-4	Net Cash Generated	$ 50
Problem	15-5	Net Cash Generated	$ 10
Alt. Prob.	15-1	Net Cash Generated	$ 2
Alt. Prob.	15-2	Net Cash Generated	$ 1
Alt. Prob.	15-3	Net Cash Generated	$ (1,000)
Alt. Prob.	15-4	Net Cash Generated	$ (100)

Chapter 16

Problem	16-1	Cost of Goods Manufactured	$ 601,000
Problem	16-2	Cost of Goods Manufactured	$ 852,000
Problem	16-3	Net Income, 19X6	$ 23,000
Problem	16-4	Cost of Goods Sold, 19X6	$ 1,288,460
Alt. Prob.	16-1	Cost of Goods Manufactured	$ 1,604,800
Alt. Prob.	16-2	Net Income	$ 140,530
Alt. Prob.	16-3	Net Income	$ 64,000